International Handbook of Suicide Prevention

International Handbook of Suicide Prevention

Research, Policy and Practice

Edited by

**Rory C. O'Connor, Stephen Platt,
Jacki Gordon**

WILEY-BLACKWELL

A John Wiley & Sons, Ltd., Publication

This edition first published 2011
© 2011 John Wiley & Sons, Ltd.

Wiley-Blackwell is an imprint of John Wiley & Sons, formed by the merger of Wiley's global Scientific, Technical and Medical business with Blackwell Publishing.

Registered Office
John Wiley & Sons Ltd, The Atrium, Southern Gate, Chichester, West Sussex, PO19 8SQ, United Kingdom

Editorial Offices
350 Main Street, Malden, MA 02148-5020, USA
9600 Garsington Road, Oxford, OX4 2DQ, UK
The Atrium, Southern Gate, Chichester, West Sussex, PO19 8SQ, UK

For details of our global editorial offices, for customer services, and for information about how to apply for permission to reuse the copyright material in this book please see our website at www.wiley.com/wiley-blackwell.

The right of Rory C. O'Connor, Stephen Platt, Jacki Gordon to be identified as the authors of the editorial material in this work has been asserted in accordance with the UK Copyright, Designs and Patents Act 1988.

Wiley also publishes its books in a variety of electronic formats. Some content that appears in print may not be available in electronic books.

Designations used by companies to distinguish their products are often claimed as trademarks. All brand names and product names used in this book are trade names, service marks, trademarks or registered trademarks of their respective owners. The publisher is not associated with any product or vendor mentioned in this book. This publication is designed to provide accurate and authoritative information in regard to the subject matter covered. It is sold on the understanding that the publisher is not engaged in rendering professional services. If professional advice or other expert assistance is required, the services of a competent professional should be sought.

Library of Congress Cataloging-in-Publication Data

International handbook of suicide prevention : research, policy and practice/edited by Rory C. O'Connor, Stephen Platt, Jacki Gordon.
  p. cm.
  Includes index.
  ISBN 978-0-470-68384-2 (cloth)
1. Suicide–Prevention–Research. 2. Suicidal behavior–Research. I. O'Connor, Rory C.
II. Platt, Stephen, 1948– III. Gordon, Jacki.
  HV6545.I594 2011
  616.85′8445–dc22

                                    2011002519

A catalogue record for this book is available from the British Library.

This book is published in the following electronic formats: ePDFs 9781119998563; Wiley Online Library 9781119998556; ePub 9781119996149

Set in 10.5/12.5pt AGaramond by SPi Publisher Services, Pondicherry, India
Printed and bound in Malaysia by Vivar Printing Sdn Bhd

1 2011

Contents

List of Editors ix
List of Contributors xi
Dedication xvii
Acknowledgements xviii

Introduction 1
Rory C. O'Connor, Stephen Platt, and Jacki Gordon

Part I Suicidal Determinants and Frameworks 7

1 Challenges to Classifying Suicidal Ideations, Communications, and Behaviours 9
Morton M. Silverman

2 International Perspectives on the Epidemiology and Aetiology of Suicide and Self-Harm 27
Kirsten Windfuhr and Navneet Kapur

3 Depression and Suicidal Behaviour 59
Zoltán Rihmer

4 Schizophrenia, Other Psychotic Disorders, and Suicidal Behaviour 75
Alexander McGirr and Gustavo Turecki

5 Substance Use Disorders and Suicidal Behaviour 93
Kenneth R. Conner and Mark A. Ilgen

6 Personality Disorders and Suicidal Behaviour 109
Joel Paris

7 Deliberate Self-Harm: Extent of the Problem and Prediction of Repetition 119
Ella Arensman, Paul Corcoran, and Anthony P. Fitzgerald

8 Relationships of Genes and Early-life Experience to the Neurobiology
of Suicidal Behaviour 133
J. John Mann and Dianne Currier

9 Understanding the Suicidal Brain: A Review of Neuropsychological Studies
of Suicidal Ideation and Behaviour 151
Kees van Heeringen, Karen Godfrin, and Stijn Bijttebier

10 Present Status and Future Prospects take up the Interpersonal–Psychological
Theory of Suicidal Behaviour 169
Jessica D. Ribeiro and Thomas E. Joiner

11 Towards an Integrated Motivational–Volitional Model
of Suicidal Behaviour 181
Rory C. O'Connor

12 Worrying and Rumination as Proximal Risk Factors for Suicidal Behaviour 199
Ad Kerkhof and Bregje van Spijker

13 Inequalities and Suicidal Behaviour 211
Stephen Platt

14 Religion and Suicide: Integrating Four Theories Cross-nationally 235
Steven Stack and Augustine J. Kposowa

15 Rurality and Suicide 253
Cameron Stark and Vincent Riordan

16 Body Weight, Obesity, and Suicide across the Life Course 275
David Gunnell and Kyla Thomas

Part II   Intervention, Treatment, and Care **289**

17 Evidence-based Prevention and Treatment of Suicidality in Children
and Adolescents 291
Cendrine Bursztein Lipsicas and Alan Apter

18 Prevention and Treatment of Suicidality in Old Age 309
Diego De Leo and Urška Arnautovska

19 Clinical Care of Deliberate Self-Harm Patients:
An Evidence-based Approach   329
Keith Hawton, Tatiana L. Taylor, Kate E. A. Saunders, and Su Mahadevan

20 After the Suicide Attempt: The Need for Continuity and Quality of Care   353
Lars Mehlum and Erlend Mork

21 Treating the Suicidal Patient: Cognitive Therapy and Dialectical
Behaviour Therapy   369
*Nadine A. Chang, Barbara Stanley, Gregory K. Brown,
and Amy Cunningham*

22 Clinical Trial Feasibility Studies of the Collaborative Assessment
and Management of Suicidality   383
*David A. Jobes, Katherine Anne Comtois, Lisa A. Brenner,
and Peter M. Gutierrez*

23 Modes of Mind and Suicidal Processes: The Potential Role of Mindfulness
in Changing Minds   401
*J. Mark G. Williams, Danielle S. Duggan, Catherine Crane,
and Silvia Hepburn*

24 The Role of the Therapist in the Treatment of the Suicidal Patient   419
Konrad Michel

25 Recognition of Suicide Risk, Crisis Helplines, and Psychosocial
Interventions: A Selective Review   435
Rory C. O'Connor, Susan Rasmussen, and Annette Beautrais

26 Antidepressants and Suicide Prevention   457
Robert D. Goldney

**Part III   Suicide Prevention: Bringing Together Evidence,
Policy, and Practice**   **473**

27 Suicide Prevention Strategies: Case Studies from across the Globe   475
*Gergö Hadlaczky, Danuta Wasserman, Christina W. Hoven,
Donald J. Mandell, and Camilla Wasserman*

28 Suicide in Asia: Epidemiology, Risk Factors, and Prevention   487
Murad M. Khan and Ehsan Ullah Syed

29 School-based Strategies for Youth Suicide Prevention   507
Alison M. Lake and Madelyn S. Gould

30   Media Influences on Suicide and Attempted Suicide   531
     Jane Pirkis and Merete Nordentoft

31   Suicide Prevention through Restricting Access to Suicide
     Means and Hotspots   545
     Ying-Yeh Chen, Kevin Chien-Chang Wu, and Paul S. F. Yip

32   The Sequelae of Suicide: Survivors   561
     Onja Grad

33   Challenges in US Suicide Prevention Public Awareness Programmes   577
     Jane L. Pearson

34   What Kind of Research Do We Need in Suicidology Today?   591
     Heidi Hjelmeland and Birthe Loa Knizek

35   Understanding the Relationship between Mental Illness and Suicide
     and the Implications for Suicide Prevention   609
     Brian L. Mishara and François Chagnon

36   Achievements and Challenges in Suicidology: Conclusions
     and Future Directions   625
     Rory C. O'Connor, Stephen Platt, and Jacki Gordon

Name Index   643
Subject Index   663

List of Editors

Rory C. O'Connor,
Suicidal Behaviour Research Group,
Centre for Health and Behaviour Change,
School of Natural Sciences,
University of Stirling,
Scotland

Stephen Platt,
Centre for Population Health Sciences,
School of Clinical Sciences and Community Health,
University of Edinburgh,
Scotland

Jacki Gordon,
Jacki Gordon + Associates,
Glasgow,
Scotland

List of Contributors

Alan Apter, Feinberg Child Study Center and the Department of Child and Adolescent Psychiatry, Schneider Children Medical Center, Petah-Tikva, Israel; Sackler School of Medicine University of Tel Aviv, Tel Aviv, Israel

Ella Arensman, National Suicide Research Foundation, Department of Epidemiology and Public Health, University College Cork, Cork, Ireland

Urška Arnautovska, Australian Institute for Suicide Research and Prevention, WHO Collaborating Centre on Research and Training in Suicide Prevention and Life Promotion Clinic, Griffith University, Queensland, Australia

Annette Beautrais, Department of Emergency Medicine, Yale University School of Medicine, New Haven, Connecticut, USA

Stijn Bijttebier, Unit for Suicide Research, Ghent University, Ghent, Belgium

Lisa A. Brenner, Post-Doctoral Training Veteran Integrated Service Network 19 – Mental Illness Research, Education, and Clinical Center, USA

Gregory K. Brown, Department of Psychiatry, University of Pennsylvania, Philadelphia, USA

François Chagnon, Chair in Knowledge Application on Youth and Families in Difficulty, Centre for Research and Intervention on Suicide and Euthanasia and Psychology Department, Université du Québec à Montréal, Montréal, Canada

Nadine A. Chang, Psychopathology Research Unit, Department of Psychiatry, University of Pennsylvania, Philadelphia, USA

Ying-Yeh Chen, Taipei City Psychiatric Center, Taipei, Taiwan; Associate Professor, National Yang-Ming University, Taipei, Taiwan

Katherine Anne Comtois, Department of Psychiatry and Behavioral Sciences; Department of Psychology Harborview Medical Center, University of Washington, Seattle, Washington, USA

Kenneth R. Conner, University of Rochester Medical Center, Rochester, New York; VA VISN 2 Center of Excellence, Canandaigua, New York, USA

Paul Corcoran, National Suicide Research Foundation, Cork, Ireland

Catherine Crane, Department of Psychiatry, University of Oxford, Oxford, England

Amy Cunningham, Psychopathology Research Unit, Department of Psychiatry, University of Pennsylvania, Philadelphia, USA

Dianne Currier, Division of Molecular Imaging and Neuropathology Department of Psychiatry, College of Physicians and Surgeons, Columbia University, New York, USA

Diego De Leo, Australian Institute for Suicide Research and Prevention, WHO Collaborating Centre on Research and Training in Suicide Prevention and Life Promotion Clinic, Griffith University, Queensland, Australia

Danielle S. Duggan, Department of Psychiatry, University of Oxford, Oxford, England

Anthony P. Fitzgerald, Department of Epidemiology and Public Health and School of Mathematical Sciences, University College Cork, Ireland

Karen Godfrin, Patient and Resident Care Department, Brothers of Charity, Ghent, Belgium

Robert D. Goldney, Discipline of Psychiatry, University of Adelaide, Royal Adelaide Hospital, Adelaide, Australia

Jacki Gordon, Jacki Gordon + Associates, Glasgow, Scotland

Madelyn S. Gould, Division of Child and Adolescent Psychiatry (College of Physicians and Surgeons) and Department of Epidemiology (School of Public Health), Columbia University and the New York State Psychiatric Institute, New York, USA

Onja Grad, Suicide Prevention Service, University Psychiatric Hospital – Center for Mental Health, Ljubljana, Slovenia

David Gunnell, School of Social and Community Medicine, University of Bristol, Bristol, England

Peter M. Gutierrez, VA VISN 19 Mental Illness Research, Education and Clinical Center Denver, Colorado, USA

Gergö Hadlaczky, National Swedish Prevention of Suicide and Mental Ill-Health (NASP), Karolinska Institutet, Stockholm, Sweden

Keith Hawton, Centre for Suicide Research, University of Oxford, Oxford, England

Kees van Heeringen, Unit for Suicide Research, Ghent University, Ghent, Belgium

Silvia Hepburn, Department of Clinical Health Psychology, St Mary's Hospital, London, England

Heidi Hjelmeland, Department of Social Work and Health Science, Norwegian University of Science and Technology, Trondheim, Norway; Department of Suicide Research and Prevention, Norwegian Institute of Public Health, Oslo, Norway

Christina W. Hoven, Department of Epidemiology and Division of Child Psychiatry; Child Psychiatric Epidemiology Group, College of Physicians and Surgeons and Mailman School of Public Health, Columbia University; New York State Psychiatric Institute, New York, USA

Mark A. Ilgen, VA Serious Mental Illness Treatment Research and Evaluation Center, Ann Arbor, Michigan; University of Michigan Department of Psychiatry, Ann Arbor, Michigan, USA

David A. Jobes, The Catholic University of America, Department of Psychology, Washington, DC, USA

Thomas E. Joiner, Department of Psychology, Florida State University, USA

Navneet Kapur, Centre for Suicide Prevention, University of Manchester, Manchester, England

Ad Kerkhof, Department of Clinical Psychology and the EMGO Institute for Health and Care Research, Faculty of Psychology and Education, VU University, Amsterdam, the Netherlands

Murad M. Khan, Department of Psychiatry, Aga Khan University, Karachi, Pakistan

Birthe Loa Knizek, Department of Psychology, Norwegian University of Science and Technology, Trondheim, Norway

Augustine J. Kposowa, Department of Sociology, University of California, Riverside, California, USA

Alison M. Lake, New York State Psychiatric Institute, New York, USA

Cendrine Bursztein Lipsicas, National Prevention of Suicide and Mental Ill-Health (NASP) at Karolinska Institute; Stockholm County Council's Centre for Suicide Research and Prevention, Sweden; Feinberg Child Study Center; Department of Child and Adolescent Psychiatry, Schneider Children Medical Center, Petah-Tikva, Israel

Su Mahadevan, Centre for Suicide Research, University of Oxford, Oxford, England

Donald J. Mandell, International Center for Child Mental Health, National Center for Disaster Preparedness, Mailman School of Public Health, Columbia University; New York State Psychiatric Institute, New York, USA

J. John Mann, Division of Molecular Imaging and Neuropathology Department of Psychiatry, College of Physicians and Surgeons, Columbia University, New York State Psychiatric Institute, New York, USA

Alexander McGirr, McGill Group for Suicide Studies, Douglas Mental Health University Institute, McGill University, Montreal, Canada

Lars Mehlum, National Centre for Suicide Research and Prevention, Institute of Clinical Medicine, University of Oslo, Oslo, Norway

Konrad Michel, Outpatient Department, University Psychiatric Hospital, Berne, Switzerland

Brian L. Mishara, Centre for Research and Intervention on Suicide and Euthanasia and Psychology Department, Université du Québec à Montréal, Montréal, Canada

Erlend Mork, National Centre for Suicide Research and Prevention, Institute of Clinical Medicine, University of Oslo, Oslo; Oslo University Hospital, Aker, Norway

Merete Nordentoft, Psychiatric Center Copenhagen, University of Copenhagen, Copenhagen, Denmark

Rory C. O'Connor, Suicidal Behaviour Research Group, Centre for Health and Behaviour Change, School of Natural Sciences, University of Stirling, Scotland

Joel Paris, McGill University, Institute of Community and Family Psychiatry, Montreal, Quebec, Canada

Jane L. Pearson, National Institute of Mental Health Suicide Research Consortium, National Institutes of Health, Bethesda, Maryland, USA

Jane Pirkis, Centre for Health Policy, Programs and Economics, Melbourne School of Population Health, University of Melbourne, Melbourne, Australia

Stephen Platt, Centre for Population Health Sciences, School of Clinical Sciences and Community Health, University of Edinburgh, Edinburgh, Scotland

Susan Rasmussen, School of Psychological Sciences and Health, University of Strathclyde, Glasgow, Scotland

Jessica D. Ribeiro, Department of Psychology, Florida State University, USA

Zoltán Rihmer, Department of Psychiatry and Psychotherapy, Semmerlweis University, Faculty of Medicine, Budapest; Department of Clinical and Theoretical Mental Health, Semmerlweis University, Faculty of Medicine, Budapest, Hungary

Vincent Riordan, West Cork Mental Health Services, Ireland

Kate E. A. Saunders, Department of Psychiatry, University of Oxford, Oxford, England

Morton M. Silverman, Department of Psychiatry, School of Medicine, University of Colorado, Denver, Colorado, USA

Bregje van Spijker, Department of Clinical Psychology and the EMGO Institute for Health and Care Research, Faculty of Psychology and Education, VU University Amsterdam, the Netherlands

Steven Stack, Departments of Criminology, and Psychiatry and Behavioral Neuroscience, Wayne State University, Detroit, USA

Cameron Stark, Department of Public Health, NHS Highland, Inverness; Centre for Rural Health, University of Aberdeen, Scotland

Barbara Stanley, Department of Psychiatry, Columbia University College of Physicians and Surgeons; Molecular Imagining and Neuropathology Division, New York State Psychiatric Institute, USA

Ehsan Ullah Syed, Department of Psychiatry, Penn State Milton S. Hershey Medical Center, Penn State College of Medicine, Harrisburg, Pennsylvania, USA

Tatiana L. Taylor, Research Department of Mental Health Sciences, UCL Medical School, London, England

Kyla Thomas, School of Social and Community Medicine, University of Bristol, Bristol, England

Gustavo Turecki, McGill Group for Suicide Studies, Douglas Mental Health University Institute, McGill University, Montreal, Canada

Camilla Wasserman, Child Psychiatric Epidemiology, Department of Child and Adolescent Psychiatry, Columbia University; New York State Psychiatric Institute, New York, USA

Danuta Wasserman, National Swedish Prevention of Suicide and Mental Ill-Health (NASP), Karolinska Institute; Karolinska University Hospital, Stockholm, Sweden; WHO Lead Collaborating Centre on Suicide Prevention

J. Mark G. Williams, Department of Psychiatry, University of Oxford, Oxford, England

Kirsten Windfuhr, Centre for Suicide Prevention, University of Manchester, Manchester, England

Kevin Chien-Chang Wu, Department of Social Medicine, National Taiwan University College of Medicine; Department of Psychiatry, National Taiwan University Hospital, Taiwan

Paul S. F. Yip, Centre for Suicide Research and Prevention; Department of Social Work and Social Administration, University of Hong Kong, Hong Kong

Dedication

Dr Clare Cassidy (1968–2008)

But then with autumn upon us, so breezy and cruel,
Clare left us in Paris, heartbroken and cool.
But we remember Clare's grace, her beauty, her light;
her kindness, her smile and sadness, its might.

(RO'C, 2008)

Acknowledgements

Suzy, Poppy, and Oisin for their incredible forbearance of my late-night working. (RO'C)

Norman Kreitman for his sensitive mentorship and exemplary scholarship. (SP)

L – for showing me the way through the woods. (JG)

Introduction

Rory C. O'Connor, Stephen Platt, and Jacki Gordon

Suicidology is the science of suicide and suicide prevention (Maris, 1993). As the scale of suicide has become more widely recognized, so has the discipline and so have national and international efforts to tackle this tragic phenomenon. Although the growth in suicidology is welcome, our understanding of suicide is still fragmented and incomplete. Suicide is now a major public health concern across the globe, accounting for approximately one million deaths per annum (World Health Organization, 2010). Indeed, it is the tenth leading cause of death worldwide (Hawton & van Heeringen, 2009), the third leading cause of death among 15–44 years olds, and the second leading cause of death among 10–24 year olds in some countries (World Health Organization, 2010). Although the international data on non-fatal suicide attempts are limited, as they are not consistently recorded across countries and are often limited to hospital-treated suicide attempts, it is estimated that suicide attempts are 20 to 30 times more common than completed suicides (Wasserman, 2001).

In this Handbook, we try to understand why people attempt suicide and what can be done to make death by suicide less likely by harnessing the expertise of some 80 suicidologists from across the world. This Handbook offers kaleidoscopic views on the multitude of suicidal determinants and the multifaceted nature of suicide prevention. It should appeal to anyone with an interest in the comprehension and prevention of suicide. To this end, one of the guiding principles of this volume is to improve our understanding of the relationship between attempted suicide and completed suicide. A more comprehensive understanding of this relationship is important not only for theoretical and conceptual reasons, but also because secondary prevention interventions are frequently directed at those who attempt suicide. Any national or international suicide prevention strategy, to be effective, must be able to engage those who have attempted suicide. Although this may

International Handbook of Suicide Prevention: Research, Policy and Practice, First Edition.
Edited by Rory C. O'Connor, Stephen Platt, Jacki Gordon.
© 2011 John Wiley & Sons, Ltd. Published 2011 by John Wiley & Sons, Ltd.

seem self-evident, it is crucial, given the universal recognition that maintaining suicide attempt patients in treatment is fraught with difficulties (see Chapter 25). Further, it is sobering to note that the best predictor of *future* suicidal behaviour (and completed suicide) is *past* suicidal behaviour. Therefore, if we can intervene with those who have tried previously, we should be able to prevent at least some of the future deaths by suicide. Consequently, non-fatal suicidal behaviour and completed suicide receive equal attention in this Handbook. As suicide attempt and self-harm are often used interchangeably in the research literature (see below also), for this Introduction where we use the term 'suicide attempt'/'behaviour', we are referring to self-injurious behaviour with evidence of suicidal intent. 'Self-harm' is used to describe all other self-harming behaviours where suicidal intent is not explicitly ascertained.

The overarching aim of this Handbook is to bring together the different exponents of suicidology irrespective of professional background or country of origin, because only through learning and working together internationally and *across disciplines* will we rise to the challenge of reducing suicidal behaviour in every country. Suicidology is little over 50 years old, and embraces researchers, practitioners, and policy planners whose disciplinary backgrounds include psychology, psychiatry, epidemiology, sociology, social work, nursing, emergency medicine, ethics, law, and public health. This heterogeneity is a major strength, as the whole (i.e., the discipline of suicidology) is much greater than the sum of its constituent disciplines. We continue to learn from each others' difficulties and successes and to exchange a broad range of theoretical and methodological perspectives. However, one of the challenges of interdisciplinary working is that there are inevitable differences in emphasis, which can lead to difficulties in how we communicate about self-injurious behaviour across professions and countries. Although there have been several efforts to reach consensus about definitions and nomenclature (O'Carroll, Berman, Maris, Moscicki, Silverman, & Tanney, 1996; Silverman, Berman, Sanddal, O'Carroll, & Joiner, 2007a, 2007b), as a discipline we have yet to agree on a common definition of suicidal behaviour. This renders the comparison of studies difficult. One study may include a heterogeneous sample of patients, some of whom are reporting suicidal intent and others who are not, while another may include only individuals who have engaged in potentially lethal suicide attempts, with explicit and high suicidal intent. Despite our best efforts, we are unlikely to achieve an agreed definition of suicidal behaviour for some considerable time. Indeed, an inspection of the international literature yields a myriad of different terms to describe the broad spectrum of self-injurious thoughts and behaviours (e.g., self-harm, parasuicide, attempted suicide, suicidal behaviour, non-suicidal self-injury; see Chapter 1). Consequently, we asked each contributing author to make explicit early in their chapter how they operationalized and defined suicidal behaviour therein.

Additional aims of the book are to showcase the state of the science in terms of research, policy, and practice, to share insights and expertise, and to enhance mutual learning. In this Handbook we present the latest research on suicidal determinants and the most promising interventions, treatments, and care of those at risk, as well as the challenges of translating research, policy, and practice into saving lives. The extent to which we meet this latter challenge will determine, in large part, how successful we will be in attaining the universal goal of reducing suicide rates across the globe. In short, this Handbook addresses the key questions of why people attempt suicide, what are the best (known) interventions and care for those at risk, and what are the key international challenges in our pursuit of suicide prevention. In addressing these questions, it is important to recognize that the evidence base is, by and large, limited and that it must be understood in terms of the specific characteristics of a study population or the context of a specific intervention.

This Handbook is organized into three parts. Part I is concerned with the determinants and frameworks that inform our understanding of suicide and attempted suicide. Part II focuses on treatment, intervention, and care, while Part III reviews a range of suicide prevention issues that span research, policy, and practice. The first two chapters of Part I provide important contextual information about the epidemiology and aetiology of suicide and self-harm and how the international research community defines, classifies, and communicates about self-injury with and without suicidal intent. These are followed by four chapters (Chapters 3–6) which summarize the research and clinical literature on the relationship between suicidal behaviour and psychiatric illness (depression (Chapter 3), schizophrenia (Chapter 4), personality disorders (Chapter 6), and other psychotic disorders (Chapter 4)). The authors also consider the extent to which the treatment of these disorders can reduce suicide and attempted suicide. In the substance use disorders chapter (Chapter 5), the available research evidence is integrated into a conceptual framework which models risk of future suicidal behaviour. Chapter 7 focuses on self-harm as a public health concern in its own right, as well as a correlate of suicide, specifically looking at those factors which predict repetition in different populations. The neurobiological and neuropsychological substrates that underpin suicidal behaviour are considered in Chapters 8 and 9. In Chapter 8, the role of the serotonergic and noradrenergic neurotransmitter systems and the hypothalamic–pituitary–adrenal axis are reviewed. This highlights the importance of studying the interaction between genetic vulnerability and environmental adversity in early life as a means of understanding how the effects of developmental changes in neurobiological systems can persist into adulthood and affect suicide risk. Chapter 9 investigates how changes in brain function are mediated via neuropsychological factors to increase the risk of suicide in response to stressors.

The role of psychology in suicide risk is further amplified in Chapters 10, 11, and 12. For example, the interpersonal–psychological theory of suicidal behaviour is described in Chapter 10, together with its history, its current status, as well as suggestions for further directions. The integrated motivational–volitional model (IMV) of suicidal behaviour, a new, tripartite model that maps the relationship between background factors and trigger events and the development of suicidal ideation/intent into suicidal behaviour is elaborated in Chapter 11. Chapter 12 theorizes that worrying and rumination, both characterized by repetitive and uncontrollable thinking, are proximal risk factors for suicidal behaviour.

The focus of the Handbook shifts to the relationship between the social environment and suicidal behaviour in Chapters 13, 14, and 15. The topics addressed in these chapters, namely, social inequality (Chapter 13), religion (Chapter 14), and rurality (Chapter 15), speak to Durkheim's idea 'that the individual is dominated by a moral reality greater than himself: namely, collective reality' (Durkheim 1952 [1897], p. 38). Indeed, this issue is tackled head-on in Chapter 14, which reviews theories of religious integration, commitment, and networks and outlines a new moral community perspective. The impact of socio-economic inequalities on suicidal behaviour is considered in Chapter 13. Lower socio-economic status (at an individual level) and socio-economic deprivation (at an area level) are both risk factors, although the evidence suggests that the 'area effect' is compositional (rather than contextual). In Chapter 15, drawing on evidence from across the globe, the relationship between the nature of rurality and suicide is disentangled, following a critical dissection of the potential influence of other recognized suicide risk factors in the rural context. The final chapter of Part I considers the growing evidence that low birth weight and low body mass index are associated with increased risk of suicide (Chapter 16).

Part II begins with two chapters that review the evidence-based treatment and care of suicidality in children and adolescents (Chapter 17) and in older adults (Chapter 18). In the former, the interplay between biological, genetic, environmental, social, and psychological factors in the aetiology and course of suicidal behaviour is considered alongside the effectiveness of prevention and treatment among children and young people. Chapter 18 highlights the age-specific and gender-specific risk and protective factors in old age, as well as reviewing the efficacy of existing treatment and preventative strategies. The next three chapters (Chapters 19, 20, and 21) address the clinical issues concerning treatment of patients who have attempted suicide, are actively suicidal or who have presented to hospital following self-harm. Recent systematic reviews of studies of attitudes of self-harm patients towards clinical services and staff attitudes towards self-harm patients are included in Chapter 19, as well as a study of service provision with recommendations for the clinical management of self-harm patients. Results of a systematic review of aftercare interventions are also summarized in Chapter 19. Following a review of the literature, including a particular focus on clinical practice in Norway, Chapter 20 suggests a set of requirements to ensure the continuity of care of suicide attempters, together with recommendations for policy and clinical practice.

Chapters 21–23 focus on key psychological processes in suicidality and how a better understanding of such processes is integral to a range of psychotherapeutic treatments. Cognitive Therapy, Dialectical Behaviour Therapy, and the Collaborative Assessment and Management of Suicidality are reviewed in Chapters 21 and 22. Chapter 23, which explores the conditions under which suicidal ideas may persist and escalate, describes mindfulness training, a promising intervention that changes the way people respond to distressing situations, thereby reducing suicide risk. A comprehensive evaluation of psychotherapy in suicide prevention would not be complete without explicit consideration of the therapeutic alliance. To this end, in Chapter 24 patients' life-oriented goals and the patient's suicide-related narrative are identified as integral to the development of a good quality therapeutic alliance.

Chapter 25 highlights some of the challenges of recognizing suicide risk, reviews the role and function of crisis helplines, and describes recent developments in a selection of psychosocial interventions including postcard interventions. Chapter 26 reviews the evidence for and against antidepressants in suicide prevention and raises important issues which clinicians ought to consider as part of any treatment plan.

Part III of the Handbook comprises 10 chapters directed at a selection of hot topics in suicide prevention. These topics bring together the different domains of research evidence, policy, and practice, and highlight many of the challenges and successes in suicide prevention internationally. Chapter 27 compares the widely used primary, secondary, and tertiary model of suicide prevention with the US Institute of Medicine model oriented towards universal, selective, and indicated approaches. In Chapter 28, attention shifts to Asia, the world's largest continent, which accounts for approximately 60% of the globe's total deaths by suicide. Research gaps are identified and consideration is given to the establishment of culturally relevant suicide prevention programmes.

The next three chapters evaluate the extent to which preventative strategies, either implemented institutionally (e.g., schools; Chapter 29) or at a wider community (local or national) level (e.g., media reporting strategies (Chapter 30) or restricting access to lethal means (Chapter 31)), are effective in reducing suicide. A comprehensive review of screening for at-risk young people, adult and peer gatekeeper training, skills training, and whole-school programmes forms the basis for Chapter 29. Chapter 30 reviews the evidence for and against the 'Werther effect', the presumed impact of media reporting on completed suicide, derived from the suicide of the protagonist in Goethe's (1774) novel *The Sorrows of Young Werther*, following an ill-fated love affair and subsequent so-called 'copycat' suicides following its publication. The ubiquity of restricting access to lethal means of suicide as a component of national suicide prevention strategies is described in Chapter 31, as well as a critique of the most up-to-date research evidence about their effectiveness. Mindful of the number of people who are affected by an individual suicide (estimates vary from four to 10 people per death), Chapter 32 describes the complexity of the bereavement process and how it impacts on family, friends, and professionals.

Chapter 33 extends discussion of suicide prevention initiatives from research and theory to the challenges of implementation. Similar to the restriction of access to means interventions, public awareness programmes are an integral part of suicide prevention the world over. Taking the United States as a case example, the goals and outcomes of public awareness programmes as well as the research opportunities they present are described in Chapter 33. In Chapter 34, mainstream suicidological research is critiqued, and consideration is given to the extent to which suicidology has disproportionately focused on *explaining* suicidality to the detriment of *understanding* it. This chapter also reviews the posited (im)balance between quantitative and qualitative methods used in international suicide research. The penultimate chapter of the Handbook (Chapter 35) returns to the relationship between mental illness and suicide, proposing potential mechanisms that may explain why mental disorder is so closely associated with suicide. It is argued that a better understanding of such mechanisms will improve our understanding of why only a minority of people with mental health problems die by suicide.

The Handbook ends with a chapter summarizing the key recent achievements in suicidology and presents an appraisal of the key challenges which face the discipline in the future (Chapter 36). We acknowledge with gratitude the input from many of the contributors to this Handbook, who generously responded to our request to identify what they thought to be the major achievements of the past 25 years and the key challenges for the next 25 years. In this final part, it is recognized that suicide prevention efforts should build on the judicious use of the best available evidence (across disciplines), but crucially in ways that are context appropriate. Thus, suicide prevention is not only a science but an art, and this final part grapples with these challenges. We hope these observations, from leading international experts, are insightful, inform existing thinking, and stimulate the next generation of suicidologists to work together in research, policy, and practice to prevent suicide across the globe.

References

Durkheim, E. (1952 [1897]). *Suicide: A study in sociology*. London: Routledge.

Goethe, J. (1774). *The Sorrows of Young Werther*. London: Penguin.

Hawton, K. & van Heeringen, K. (2009). Suicide. *The Lancet, 373*, 1372–1381.

Maris, R. W. (1993). The evolution of suicidology. In A. A. Leenaars (Ed.), *Suicidology: Essays in Honor of Edwin Shneidman*. Northvale, NJ: Jason Aronson.

O'Carroll, P. W., Berman, A. L., Maris, R. M., Moscicki, E., Silverman, M., & Tanney, B. (1996). Beyond the Tower of Babel: A nomenclature for suicidology. *Suicide and Life-Threatening Behavior, 26*, 237–252.

Silverman, M. M., Berman, A. L., Sanddal, N. D., O'Carroll, P. W., & Joiner, T. E. (2007a). Rebuilding the Tower of Babel: A revised nomenclature for the study of suicide and suicidal behaviors. Part 1: Background, rationale, and methodology. *Suicide and Life-Threatening Behavior, 37*, 248–263.

Silverman, M. M., Berman, A. L., Sanddal, N. D., O'Carroll, P. W., & Joiner, T. E. (2007b). Rebuilding the Tower of Babel: A revised nomenclature for the study of suicide and suicidal behaviours. Part 2: Suicide-related ideations, communications and behaviors. *Suicide and Life-Threatening Behavior, 37*, 264–277.

Wasserman, D. (2001). *Suicide: An unnecessary death*. London: Martin Dunitz.

World Health Organization (2010). http://www.who.int/mental_health/prevention/suicide/suicide prevent/en, accessed 14 June 2010.

PART I

Suicidal Determinants and Frameworks

CHAPTER ONE

Challenges to Classifying Suicidal Ideations, Communications, and Behaviours

Morton M. Silverman

Abstract

There is no uniform set of terms, definitions, and classifications for the range of thoughts, communications, and behaviours that are related to self-injurious behaviours, with or without the intent to die. Nor is there an agreed taxonomy that encompasses the full spectrum of what is clinically defined as suicide-related behaviours. As a result, researchers cannot easily compare their study populations or results, and clinicians have difficulty in translating research findings into practical applications when working with patients at risk for suicidal behaviours. This chapter will briefly review this issue from a historical perspective, and present some of the current efforts to improve our ability to communicate clearly, consistently, and confidently about suicidal individuals. Recommendations are made as to the next steps in the process of developing and implementing a standardized nomenclature and classification system for the field of suicidology.

Introduction

After a century of serious attention to the public health problem of suicide and suicidal behaviours, there have been many significant advances in suicidology; yet many challenges remain. We now know a great deal about the epidemiology of suicide and suicidal behaviours. We are beginning to develop a body of knowledge about the biological underpinnings to suicidal behaviour through research on the neurobiology and genetics of risk.

International Handbook of Suicide Prevention: Research, Policy and Practice, First Edition.
Edited by Rory C. O'Connor, Stephen Platt, Jacki Gordon.
© 2011 John Wiley & Sons, Ltd. Published 2011 by John Wiley & Sons, Ltd.

However, we still know little about protective factors and what places an individual at acute risk for suicidal behaviour. We need to bridge the gap between our expanding knowledge base about the aetiology and transmission of suicidal behaviour and the development of effective clinical and population-based interventions, protocols, practices, procedures, and policies.

In order to achieve this goal we need to translate what we have learned from epidemiological surveillance and research studies into practical applications. Similarly what is learned in clinical settings needs to be communicated to researchers and theoreticians so they can better investigate and understand these behaviours. One major stumbling block is that the suicide literature remains replete with confusing terms, definitions, and classifications that make it difficult, if not impossible, to compare and contrast research, epidemiological or clinical studies. Advances in suicidology are hindered by a lack of a standardized nomenclature and classification system. This remains a challenge.

Most individuals who die by suicide are reported to have communicated their intent to others (usually next of kin or friends), and the majority have also visited or been treated by psychiatrists, psychologists, clinical social workers, other mental health professionals, general practitioners or other physicians during the weeks or months preceding their death by suicide (Luoma, Martin, & Pearson, 2002). Why is this so? A compelling answer is that suicidal behaviour is often undiagnosed, under-treated, or mistreated in clinical settings because it is misunderstood and associated with stigma, denial, guilt, anger, and shame (Malone, Szanto, Corbitt, & Mann, 1995; Mann, Apter, Bertolote, Beautrais, Currier, *et al.*, 2005).

One of the major difficulties in communicating about suicidal phenomena with our patients and within our discipline (as well as across disciplines) is that we do not speak the same scientific language. We also do not share the same conceptualizations of what constitutes self-harm and the suicidal process. The terminology we use is often based on our training; theoretical, political, social, psychological, biological, and religious perspectives; and the professional needs to identify and count these behaviours in the first place (clinical, epidemiological, public health, research, etc.). Conceptual, methodological, and clinical problems result from widely varying definitions and classification schemes for such terms as suicide attempt (Nock & Kessler, 2006). As a result, researchers cannot easily compare their study populations, and clinicians have difficulty in translating research findings into practical applications when working with an individual at risk for suicidal behaviours.

It is a known fact that there is inaccuracy in the reporting of suicidal deaths (Jobes & Berman, 1985; Shneidman, 1980). Estimates of under-reporting have ranged from 10% to 50% (Jobes, Berman, & Josselson, 1987; Litman, 1980). Some have noted substantial under-reporting and misclassification of children and adolescent suicides (Wekstein, 1979). Jobes and Berman (1985) reported that the majority (58%) of medical examiners they surveyed in the United States either agreed or strongly agreed that 'the actual suicide rate is probably two times the reported rate'. It appears that there may be variations in both the death certification process and the manner of death determination.

Jobes and colleagues (1987) have identified over 20 possible sources of variability in the official reporting of suicide data. They suggest that perhaps the single most important source of variability and error in suicide statistics arises from the virtual absence of any standardized classification criteria that coroners and medical examiners might use more uniformly to evaluate cases of equivocal suicide. Although relatively small in number, the category of 'undetermined manner of death' may represent a significant number of true suicides (O'Carroll, 1989).

If we cannot even agree upon what defines a suicide, how, then, are we to determine what is an attempt at suicide? There is considerable debate about the differential attributes of those who die by suicide and those who attempt suicide. The resolution of this controversy is hampered because studies have used descriptive methods and dissimilar definitions for suicide attempts (Linehan, 1986; Maris, 1992). When the suicide attempts are medically serious (e.g., admission to an intensive care unit, requiring surgery under general anaesthesia, needing extensive, specialized medical care, etc.) these two populations overlap considerably. However, because most epidemiological studies are based on self-report of prior suicidal behaviour without defining these terms for the population being surveyed, the profile of those engaging in non-medically serious suicide attempts remains inconsistent and unreliable.

The suicide literature remains replete with confusing (and sometimes derogatory or pejorative) terms, definitions, descriptors, and classifications that make it difficult, if not impossible, to compare and contrast different research studies, clinical reports or epidemiological surveys (Jenkins & Singh, 2000; Rudd & Joiner, 1998; Shneidman, 1985; Silverman, 2006), or to make comparisons, generalizations, or extrapolations (Linehan, 1997; Westefeld, Range, Rogers, Maples, Bromley, *et al.*, 2000). There is no national or international surveillance system for the primary purpose of estimating annual national rates of suicide attempts (Silverman, Berman, Sanddal, O'Carroll, & Joiner, 2007a).

Challenges to developing and implementing a standardized nomenclature and classification system

The ongoing debate concerning nomenclature has perpetuated the use of multiple terms to refer to the same behaviour (Bille-Brahe, Kerkhof, De Leo, & Schmidtke, 2004; O'Carroll, Berman, Maris, Moscicki, Tanney, *et al.*, 1996; Silverman, 2006). Such variability in terminology not only contributes to imprecise communication, but also limits comparison of epidemiological prevalence rates nationally and internationally, and hampers clinical and preventive interventions.

There are currently several nomenclatures and/or classification systems that are being developed and tested in the United States (Posner, Oquendo, Gould, Stanley, & Davies, 2007; Silverman, Berman, Sanddal, O'Carroll, & Joiner, 2007b), as well as internationally (De Leo, Burgis, Bertolote, Kerkhof, & Bille-Brahe, 2006). I argue elsewhere that not only must we use the same terminology and definitions, but that these terms must be easily understood, easily applied, and internally consistent, and should relate to each other in a way that has utility, meaning, and relevance to the real world of at-risk individuals (Silverman, 2006). We must develop an accurate suicide mortality database in order to do meaningful research, develop and implement prevention efforts, and advance general public health (Jobes, Berman, & Josselson, 1987; O'Carroll, 1989).

Clarifying Terminology

Before I review some of the current attempts to develop and implement nomenclature and classification systems, it is pertinent to provide some definitions for these constructs. The following terms and definitions illustrate the degree of overlap or 'fuzziness' when discussing the development of a uniform classification system.

Nomenclature: a set or system of names or terms, as those used in a particular science or art; a system of words used technically to name things in a particular discipline.

Classification: the act of distributing things into classes or categories of the same type; the act or method of distributing into a class or category according to characteristics.

Taxonomy: the practice and science of classification as well as the laws or principles underlying such a classification; the science dealing with the description, identification, naming, and classification of organisms.

Almost anything (e.g., behaviours, concepts, events) may be classified according to some taxonomic scheme. Hence, a nomenclature is simply establishing the words (and definitions) chosen for use in the development of a classification, using taxonomic principles.

Terminology in Suicide Classification Systems

Although one can argue about the degree of specificity for describing suicidal behaviours, there is a set of commonly used terms that generally describes the universe of suicidal thoughts and behaviours. These suicide-related generic terms are: ideation (with or without a plan); communication (verbal or non-verbal); intent; motivation; preparatory acts (towards imminent self-harm); self-harm or self-injurious behaviours (with or without injury, or fatal); undetermined suicide-related or self-injurious behaviours (with or without injury, or fatal); suicide attempt (with or without injury); and suicide.

The definitions of terms such as 'suicide attempt' or 'self-harm' are predicated on the definition of 'suicide'. After all, a suicide attempt is an action whose goal is to die by suicide. However, as noted elsewhere (Silverman, 2006), there are 15 definitions of suicide in our scientific literature. Until we establish a standardized nomenclature we will continue to have differences between and among official reporting sources (e.g., police, coroner, medical examiner death certificates), research studies, clinical population reports (e.g., hospital discharge summaries, emergency department reports, first-responder reports), and epidemiological surveys (self-report).

A brief list of the challenges to resolving these conundrums are:

1. Agreeing on which terms should be used and defining them as mutually exclusive. There remains confusion about when to apply and what exactly constitutes terms such as suicidality, deliberate or intentional self-harm (DSH), suicide-related behaviour, parasuicide, and non-suicidal self-injury (NSSI).

2. Developing a nomenclature that is free of bias – philosophical, theoretical, biological, sociological, political, religious, cultural, etc. Furthermore, a nomenclature must be sensitive to different needs, depending upon the constituency. For example, the epidemiologist, public health officer, first-responder, researcher, clinician, and emergency room physician often focus on different aspects of the suicidal continuum, and use different measures in order to record their findings and observations, and in order to do their own work. Furthermore, they require different standards of evidence, different levels of certainty for such evidence, and place different emphases on different aspects of evidence.

3. Remaining internally consistent. Agreeing a clear definition of the term 'suicide' has remained elusive, and, as a result, has implications for defining those terms which are related to the act of 'death by suicide', such as 'suicide ideation', 'suicide intent', and 'suicide attempt'. The nomenclature must be internally consistent and all the terms must be based on, and relate to, the clear definition of *suicide*.

4. Resolving disagreements about the meaning, connotations, and appropriateness of terms such as *committed suicide*, *attempted suicide*, *completed suicide*, *suicide gesture*, *failed attempt*, *suicide victim*, *cry for help*, and *non-fatal suicide* or *non-fatal suicide attempt* (Silverman, 2006).

5. Remaining consistent with the terminologies and approaches used by scientific fields that study other forms of violence (e.g., homicides and sexual assault) and unintentional injuries (e.g., motor vehicle crashes).

6. Deciding which terms are pejorative or have a negative bias and should be eliminated from the lexicon. For example, suicide gesture, suicide threat, failed attempt, etc. (Silverman, 2006).

7. Resolving the distinctions between what we label as a suicide attempt and deliberate (intentional or instrumental), self-harm (DSH), or non-suicidal self-injury (NSSI).

8. Developing a standardized nomenclature that is sufficiently adaptable to allow some alterations for specific uses within certain specialties or professions. However, there must be a clear *cross-over table* to demonstrate equivalencies between and among terms currently used in existing nomenclatures, so that clinical, research and epidemiological studies can be compared.

We are dependent upon other scientific fields of inquiry to help us understand how aspects of cognition, brain development (acquisition of reasoning, cognitive skills, executive functioning), social behaviour, and risk-taking behaviours impact on the development of suicidal thinking and the unfolding of suicidal actions. For example, when does ideation become clinically significant? Under what conditions? What are the elements that go into an individual's risk appraisal? At what age and under what conditions can an individual develop and access executive functioning, such as understanding the consequences of certain actions?

Another challenge is to overcome the factors that might affect the reliable self-reporting of self-destructive behaviours, for example, fear of reprisal (involuntary hospitalization), being judged by the researcher, care provider, or first-responder as 'crazy' or 'mentally ill'. Until we destigmatize suicide, and redefine it as a self-inflicted injury that is mediated by biology or other external factors, we will never be able to accurately count or acquire the data we need to improve understanding of the suicidal process and the suicidal patient, develop interventions to address these components, and ultimately develop preventive interventions.

We must get beyond our almost total reliance on self-report for understanding and recording such important components of the suicidal process as suicidal thoughts, intent, motivation, planning, accurately remembering and reporting prior life events, assigning significance to life events, appraisal of current stressors, history of prior self-destructive behaviours, etc.

Examples of Definitional Obfuscation

There remains confusion about what exactly constitutes suicidal behaviour, deliberate self-harm, suicidality or suicide-related behaviour, and how to define suicide and suicide attempt (Silverman, 2006; Silverman *et al.*, 2007a). In this section I will briefly highlight some of the issues that still exist.

Suicidality

There is no definition of 'suicidality' other than that it is the state of being suicidal. But what does that mean? Does that mean having suicidal ideations, intent, motivations, and plans? Does it mean that you have had a suicide attempt, been exposed to others who have been suicidal, or rehearsed a suicidal act? Is it the equivalent of being in a 'suicidal condition' or 'suicidal, state of mind'? The term suicidality has been used to cover a broad range of suicide-related cognitions, emotions, and behaviours (Silverman, 2006). For the most part it has been used to categorize individuals who have expressed a combination or permutation of cognitions (ideation, intent, motivation, and planning), as well as behaviour (threats, gestures, rehearsals, and attempts). It has also been used to categorize mentally-ill patients who are so depressed that they feel suicidal (emotions). Hence, it becomes nearly impossible to compare populations who are deemed to be expressing *suicidality*. I would argue strongly that such a term be removed from the lexicon because it has no real utility other than to identify a situation or state where an individual is possessed by, or expresses some form of, suicide-related cognition, emotion, or behaviour.

Two lines of evidence suggest that suicidal behaviours are repetitive: many of those who die by suicide have made a previous suicide attempt; and many of those who make a non-fatal suicide attempt will make subsequent attempts (Beautrais, 2004; Conner, Langley, Tomaszewski, & Conwell, 2003). In a five-year follow-up study of a consecutive series of 302 individuals admitted for medically serious suicide attempts, Beautrais (2004) found that 37% made at least one further attempt and 6.7% died by suicide. In a larger study of all patients admitted for any degree of attempted suicide during the 10-year period, 1993–2002, Gibb, Beautrais, and Fergusson (2005) found that within 10 years, 28.1% of those who had been admitted for an index suicide attempt were readmitted for a further non-fatal suicide attempt, and 4.6% died by suicide. A prior suicide attempt is statistically the best predictor of future suicide attempts and death by suicide, and a history of repeated attempts further increases the risk of death by suicide.

It follows that concerted efforts need to be made to identify those at most risk of an index suicide attempt, as well as providing services to those who have engaged in an index suicide attempt, irrespective of its level of lethality. To that end, it is imperative that clinicians, researchers, and epidemiologists have a clear and consistent definition of what is a *suicide attempt*. Such a standardized definition does not presently exist.

Deliberate Self-Harm (DSH) and Non-Suicidal Self-Injury (NSSI)

The development of the concept of deliberate self-harm arose out of Kreitman's term 'parasuicide' to label all non-accidental hospital-treated self-poisoning and self-injury that did not result in death, regardless of the intention of the act (Kreitman, 1977). As a result, the term gained much favour in Europe broadly, but not so in the United States. In fact, the WHO used the term to describe a number of large-scale epidemiological studies that were undertaken in multiple sites in Europe (Schmidtke, Bille-Brahe, De Leo, Kerkhof, Bjerke, *et al.*, 1996; Schmidtke, Bille-Brahe, De Leo, Kerkhof, & Wasserman, 2001).

Over time the term 'deliberate self-harm' replaced 'parasuicide', but this term has a potentially pejorative connotation. Hence, the current term being used in Europe to describe self-injury that does not lead to death is self-harm (with or without intent). In the United States, the term 'non-suicidal self-harm' is gathering momentum to describe similar behaviours. A further complication is that the term 'suicide gesture' has not left the lexicon in the United States. In fact, it was used in the National Comorbidity Study (NCS) to describe 'self-injury in which there is no intent to die, but instead an intent to give the appearance of a suicide attempt in order to communicate with others' (Nock & Kessler, 2006, p. 616).

The original definition of deliberate self-harm included all self-injurious behaviours whether or not the individual had intended to die. DSH has been identified as a behaviour that carries considerable risk of subsequent self-harm, including death by suicide. An early study by Hawton and Fagg (1988) found that at least 1% of patients referred to general hospitals in the United Kingdom for DSH die by suicide within a year of an episode of DSH, and 3–5% within 5–10 years. Another study found that 1%–2% of patients die by suicide in the year following being seen in a hospital emergency department or admitted for treatment (Owens, Horrocks, & House, 2002), with an estimated 7%–10% of individuals eventually dying by suicide (Nordentoft, Breum, Munck, Nordestgaard, Hunding, *et al.*, 1993). Of note is that, until recently, researchers have almost totally ignored studying non-hospital-treated self-harm. As a result, we know very little about the incidence and prevalence of deliberate self-harm that occurs in the community.

The DSH literature, as well as the suicide attempt literature, rarely distinguishes the populations by method (self-poisoning, cutting, etc.), location of the injury (wrists, arms, legs, head, etc.), physical location at the time of self-injury, time of day, day of week, etc. Without such a classification system it is more difficult to differentiate between non-suicidal deliberate self-harm and suicide-attempt behaviours. Thus, we are describing a deliberately initiated act of self-harm with a non-fatal outcome, including both self-poisoning and self-injury. This self-injurious behaviour has been labelled attempted suicide, parasuicide, intentional self-harm, deliberate self-harm, and non-suicidal self-injury.

DSH is more common among females (upwards of two-thirds of patients in some studies). Similarly in the United States, suicide attempts occur at a ratio of about 3–4:1 for females versus males. In both populations, the largest percentage of cases are among adolescents and young adults. In the hospital-treated DSH literature, the large majority of the patients are self-poisoning (Hawton, 1997).

Recent studies suggest that DSH differs from suicide attempts in clinically important ways (Brown, Henriques, Sosdjan, & Beck, 2004; Chapman & Dixon-Gordon, 2007; Chapman, Gratz, & Brown, 2006). Reasons for suicide attempts are more likely to involve 'making others better off' (reducing burdensomeness), while reasons for DSH included 'anger expression' and 'distraction' (Brown *et al.*, 2004). Other studies highlight the differing emotional experiences associated with these behaviours, although emotional relief is a key motivation for both DSH and suicide attempts (Brown *et al.*, 2004). Individuals who engage in DSH report that the behaviour relieves unendurable anxiety or tension; temporarily reduces anger, anxiety, sadness, depression, and shame; or as a form of self-punishment, relieves anger directed inward, self-blame and self-loathing for perceived social transgressions (Chapman & Dixon-Gordon, 2007; Krasser, Rossman, & Zapotoczky, 2003; Kemperman, Russ, & Shearin, 1997).

Chapman and Dixon-Gordon (2007) found that relief was the most common consequence of DSH, whereas anger was the most common consequence of a suicide attempt. They suggest that DSH serves an emotion regulatory function. However, a significant proportion of individuals reported that their predominant emotional experience following DSH was negative, most notably including sadness. How these characteristics differ from those who engage in suicide attempts is yet to be delineated. Linehan (2000) has suggested that the presence or absence of the intent to die during self-harm is a critical factor that can differentiate the two behaviours. However, it is important to note that multiple motives often underpin both suicide attempts and DSH.

Determining intent to die

The presence or absence of intent to die is a key factor in differentiating non-suicidal from suicidal self-harm behaviours (Beck, Beck, & Kovacs, 1975; Hjelmeland & Knizek, 1999; Silverman, 2006; Silverman *et al.*, 2007a). Many patients who self-harm, when asked by clinicians at the time of the injury, will deny that they had an intent to die, despite the evidence to the contrary (e.g., high lethality of the act, prior history of near-lethal suicide attempts, corroborating information from family, friends, or support network). Difficulties in diagnosis can arise when the assessment of the intent to die is denied by the patient yet some ambivalence is present. As Rosenberg, Davidson, Smith, Berman, Buzbee, *et al.* (1988) stated, 'with respect to intent, absence of evidence is not evidence of absence' (p. 1446).

The Need for Sensitivity

Measures of suicide and non-fatal suicidal behaviour continue to be hindered by the lack of a standard nomenclature and classification system (De Leo *et al.*, 2006; Silverman *et al.*, 2007a, 2007b), clear operational definitions (Garrison, McKeown, Valois, & Vincent, 1993; Silverman & Maris, 1995) and standardized lethality measures (Berman, Shepherd, & Silverman, 2003).

Current difficulties in communicating between and among professionals, as well as their patients, include: limitations of hindsight bias and informant bias regarding the reporting of suicidal thoughts, intent, and behaviours (Duberstein & Conwell, 1997); difficulty in comparing and contrasting epidemiological surveys or clinical research studies; inconsistency of scale development and validation when most measures assume that the respondent already possesses a definition and understanding of the suicidal behaviours being measured; and lack of specificity and consistency of definition for such terms as suicide attempt, self-injurious behaviour, and self-harm (Silverman, 2006). Furthermore, each clinical specialty, research group, or surveillance team has developed their own reporting forms and systems to gather similar information.

Not only must we use the same terminology, but these terms must be easily understood, 'user-friendly', easily applied, and internally consistent. The terms must relate to each other in a way that has utility, meaning, and relevance to the real world of at-risk individuals.

The measurement needs of epidemiologists differ from those of clinicians or researchers. Epidemiologists are interested in counting discrete outcomes (e.g., deaths). Primary care physicians do not need to know sub-types of self-destructive behaviours or the nuances of suicidal intentions or plans. They do need to know the few screening questions to ask that will elicit an answer that broadly identifies the patient as requiring a referral to a mental health professional. The emergency department physician needs to know the criteria to determine whether the behaviour being assessed is life-threatening. The clinical researcher needs to differentiate accurately within the population of persons who are engaged in self-destructive behaviours, and to be able to compare populations across research sites. Given the multidimensional aspects of suicidal thoughts and behaviours, the researcher needs to have valid and reliable criteria for allocating the study samples into discrete groups or categories. The mental health clinician needs to know the specifics of the current ideation, intent, plans, and actions, as well as the history of prior self-destructive behaviours (who, where, when, why, how much, how often) in order to determine which treatment approach has the best likelihood of succeeding. The mental health clinician also needs to determine what contribution a mental disorder may add to the expression of self-destructive behaviours.

Recent Efforts to Clarify Suicidal Behaviours

The intent of this overview is not to present an exhaustive review of all the attempts to develop nomenclatures and classification systems for the study of suicide and suicide-related thoughts and behaviours, but to highlight some notable examples.

Beck et al., *classification of suicidal behaviours (1973)*

The first modern attempt to systematically develop a 'classification and nomenclature scheme' was put forth by Beck, Davis, Frederick, Perlin, Pokorny, *et al.* (1973). This classification system is entirely based on three key terms: suicidal ideas; suicide attempts; and completed suicide. These three terms then encompass the entire range of suicidal phenomena. Each of these three types is further specified by: (a) certainty of the rater (0%–100%); (b) lethality (zero, low, medium, or high); (c) intent to die (zero, low, medium, or high); (d) mitigating circumstances (zero, low, medium, or high); and (e) method (list actual method used). Beck and colleagues argued that a key variable in the three forms of suicidal behaviour was the intent to die, especially when the behaviour was non-lethal in nature. However, they acknowledged that intention is difficult to measure, as evidenced by allowing for four categories (zero, low, medium, high). Intent 'includes consideration of subject's statements, the likelihood of rescue, past history, and other evidence; requires inference and judgment on part of the rater' (p. 9).

In their classification schema, suicidal ideas 'includes all overt suicidal behavior and communications except for overt acts classifiable under suicide attempt or completed suicide. Includes suicide threats, suicide preoccupation, expressions of wish to die, and indirect indicators of suicide planning, etc.' (p. 11). Beck *et al.* went on to develop many psychometric scales, including the Beck Suicide Intent Scale, Beck Hopelessness Scale, and the Beck Suicide Ideation Scale (Beck, Herman, & Schuyler, 1974; Beck, Weissman, & Lester, 1974).

Operational Classification for Determination of Suicide (OCDS)

In the mid-1980s, the US Centers for Disease Control and Prevention (CDC) convened a working group representing coroners, medical examiners, statisticians, and public health agencies to develop operational criteria to assist in the determination of suicide. These criteria are based on a definition of suicide as 'death arising from an act inflicted upon oneself with the intent to kill oneself' (Rosenberg *et al.*, 1988). This definition highlights two clear components: that the lethal outcome is self-inflicted (the agent); and that it is intentionally inflicted (awareness of outcome).

The criteria were intended to improve the validity and reliability of suicide statistics by: (1) promoting consistent and uniform classifications; (2) making explicit the criteria for decision-making in death certification; (3) increasing the amount of information used in decision-making; (4) aiding certifiers in exercising their professional judgement; and (5) establishing common standards of practice for the determination of suicide.

Rosenberg *et al.* (1988) placed great importance on establishing the evidence of intent to die. They introduced the concept of explicit (verbal or non-verbal) and implicit (or indirect) evidence of intent and provided 11 examples of the latter. They acknowledge that some of the examples of indirect evidence include many commonly identified risk factors (e.g., previous suicide attempt), while recognizing that a risk factor is not necessarily a causal factor. For Rosenberg *et al.* (1988), 'intent' requires that the decedent knew or had in mind that a specific act would probably result in death. They acknowledge that intent is often difficult to determine when: death is delayed or when it is the unanticipated consequence of a potentially self-destructive act; a body is never found; drownings, leaps, or falls are unwitnessed; or the death is of a child too young to realize the consequences of jumping from a window, swallowing a lethal number of pills, or running in front of a car. Nonetheless, they agree that the establishment of intent may require judgement and that 'absolute certainty is not the goal in certifying deaths' (p. 1451). Instead, the basis for the determination should correspond to the legal notion of 'preponderance of the evidence'; otherwise stated, it is an opinion based on 'reasonable probability' (p. 1451).

Despite its name, this is not a classification system because the working group only defines the term suicide and it is not operationalized. What they accomplished, through a consensus of experts was to establish the evidence needed to define a suicidal death to assist the decision-maker in answering two fundamental questions: (1) whether or not the injury was self-inflicted; and (2) whether or not the decedent intended to kill himself or herself. This tool has both relatively high content and face validity.

O'Carroll et al., 'Tower of Babel' nomenclature

In 1996, O'Carroll *et al.* published their 'Tower of Babel' nomenclature, which distinguished suicidal behaviours by three characteristic features: intent to die; evidence of self-inflicted injury; and outcome (injury, no injury, or death). They attempted to build on the Beck *et al.* classification system and to provide definitions for commonly used terms in suicide research. Although a number of investigators and professional organizations adopted the nomenclature (American Psychiatric Association, 2003; Daigle & Cote, 2006; Rudd & Joiner, 1998), the nomenclature was not widely used in the research and clinical communities, partially due to its introduction of unfamiliar terms and definitions.

WHO/EURO definitions (De Leo et al., 2006 revision)

In the 1980s the World Health Organization (WHO) embarked on the EURO/WHO Parasuicide Multi-Centre Study, which required a nomenclature to differentiate various suicidal behaviours (with a specific emphasis on the identification of parasuicidal behaviours) (Schmidtke *et al.*, 1996). The use of the term 'parasuicide' was based on Kreitman's definition of parasuicide as a non-fatal act in which an individual deliberately causes self-injury or ingests a substance in excess of any prescribed or generally recognized therapeutic dosage. As is evident, Kreitman's term avoids any reference to intent or motivation (Kreitman, 1977).

Subsequently, after the study ended, members of the multi-centre study (De Leo *et al.*, 2004) revised the initial WHO nomenclature based on some of their observations from the study. They established the key components of fatal and non-fatal suicidal behaviours: self-initiated; with or without intent to die; and outcome. One criticism is that although they collapsed 'parasuicide', 'deliberate self-harm', and 'attempted suicide' under one term, 'non-fatal suicidal behaviour', this term can be applied with or without the presence of intent to die.

Columbia University suicidality classification

Suicidologists at Columbia University were approached by the US Food and Drug Administration (FDA) to assist them in reviewing all the adverse event reporting associated with antidepressant drug trials involving children and adolescents. The FDA was concerned about whether some of the adverse events being reported were appropriately being labelled as 'suicidality'. Under contract to the FDA, the Columbia team developed a 'Classification Scheme' – which is a nomenclature of terms and definitions. These researchers reviewed all the adverse events reports to determine how many actually were related to suicidal behaviours. The 'Classification Scheme' was also used for the review of adverse event reporting for drug trials with adults (Posner *et al.*, 2007). It is hoped that this classification scheme will ideally lead to a more systematic assessment of suicidality and improved identification of high-risk groups for research protocols (clinical registries).

Subsequent to conducting the FDA analysis, the Columbia group developed the 'Columbia Suicidality Severity Rating Scale' (C-SSRS). Specifically, it measures the degree of suicidal ideation and the level of lethality. Suicidal ideation is measured on a 1–5 point scale (from 'wish to die', 'active suicidal ideation', 'method', 'intent' to 'plan'). Hence, the assessment of intent, motivation, and plans are part of the measurement of suicidal ideation. Suicidal behaviour is measured on five levels: (1) actual attempt; (2) interrupted attempt; (3) aborted attempt; (4) preparatory act or behaviour; and (5) non-suicidal self-injury. Lethality is measured on a 0–4 scale with the level of severity defined as the frequency, duration, controllability, deterrents, and reasons for ideation.

CDC self-directed violence surveillance system

In the spring of 2003, the CDC began to develop surveillance definitions for self-directed violence, based on their prior work in developing surveillance definitions for other forms of violence. Over the ensuing years, this process included two major meetings of national experts in the field of suicidology and injury surveillance, as well as international external (national and international) and internal review. As of this writing, the current iteration is being reviewed for approval by officials within CDC.

Silverman et al., revised nomenclature

In 2006, with the support of the Department of Veterans Affairs' Mental Illness, Research, Education, and Clinical Center (VA VISN 19 MIRECC) located in Denver, Colorado, critical input from the medical and psychiatric staff at the Denver VA Medical Center, and representatives from the Department of Defense, Silverman *et al.* (2007a, 2007b) published a revised nomenclature based on the O'Carroll *et al.* 'Tower of Babel' nomenclature (O'Carroll *et al.*, 1996). This revision of the 1996 O'Carroll nomenclature also benefited from numerous recommendations and contributions from the international suicidology community. One improvement was to include a category of 'undetermined', which includes 'undetermined suicide attempt', 'undetermined suicide-related behaviour', 'undetermined suicide-related death', and 'self-inflicted death with undetermined intent'. The goal was to simplify the nomenclature and definitions in a manner that would increase communication between and among clinicians, researchers, administrators, policy-makers, and the public. It was hoped that a standardized nomenclature would lead to a standardized set of questions for determining the presence or absence of suicidal cognitions, motivations, emotions, and behaviours. As with the initial O'Carroll *et al.* (1996) effort, the authors struggled with the concepts of intent, motivation, risk, threat, gesture and non-suicidal self-harm.

Denver VA VISN 19 MIRECC self-directed violence classification system

Using the Silverman *et al.* (2007b) nomenclature as a template, researchers at the Denver MIRECC developed a nomenclature and classification system that has clinical utility and can be used across the US Department of Defense and the Veterans Administration Hospital system. The system has been 'mapped' onto developing surveillance systems, such as that of the CDC Self-Directed Violence Surveillance system. This system is currently undergoing clinical trials.

Conclusions

Unless and until the field of suicidology (comprising epidemiologists, sociologists, psychologists, physicians, neurobiologists, researchers, clinicians, first-responders, survivors, community leaders, etc.) speaks the same language and approaches the classification of suicidal behaviours in a clear, concise, and consistent manner, communications between and among all those who work for the goal of suicide prevention will remain clouded.

Consensus is required with regard to the development, implementation, and evaluation of clinical and preventive interventions (Silverman, 2006). All the components of the suicidal process then must be identified, labelled, and classified if we are ever to reach the point where we all can share information and observations to help identify and treat truly suicidal individuals and develop interventions to prevent the onset, maintenance, duration, intensity, frequency, and recurrence of suicidal thoughts and behaviours. Classifying individuals on the basis of the intent of their self-injury is a useful scientific and clinical endeavour (Nock & Kessler, 2006). Carefully defining key constructs, such as suicide attempts, will reduce variation in reporting and will enhance interpretation and communication of study results (Linehan, 1997; Meehan, Lamb, Saltzman, & O'Carroll, 1992).

Even if we are able to differentiate a range of self-destructive thoughts and behaviours into broad categories (such as suicide-related ideations, communications, and behaviours) and sub-categories (such as suicide ideation, suicide attempt, and suicide), not all suicide ideations are identical across domains (e.g., time, duration, frequency, context, degree of lethality, degree of planning, etc). It is our goal to have as few categories and sub-categories as needed to accurately label someone, so that finer differentiations can be made between and among individuals in each 'cell'.

Within each sub-category (sub-classification) we need to provide more levels of detail and depth to fully describe the presentation in as many domains as possible. To differentiate further within each sub-category, we need to recognize and establish criteria for finer differentiation that are believed to be critical to understanding and classifying suicidal behaviours: levels of lethality; time frames; levels of intent; types of methods used; degree of planning; etc.

An ideal goal is to develop, for example, a classification system similar to that used in oncology, where first a tumour is classified by type of cancer, and then by staging (e.g., based on size, location, degree of invasiveness, extent of metastasis, etc.), which not only informs diagnosis, but also treatment, management, monitoring, and prognosis. In a similar fashion, 'staging' criteria for suicidal behaviours might be degree of intent, lethality of method used, likelihood of rescue, degree of planning (impulsivity), and presence and status of psychiatric or medical illness. Scales or ranking systems can be developed to measure these elements and provide clinicians and researchers with a richly nuanced approach to classifying the full range of suicidal thoughts, communications, and behaviours.

Although progress is being made on a number of different fronts, there remains a need for the establishment of an international working group to resolve differences between and among the existing nomenclatures, definitions and classification systems. This would be an important step towards improving our efforts to prevent suicide and suicidal behaviours.

References

American Psychiatric Association (2003). Practice guidelines for the assessment and treatment of patients with suicidal behaviors. *American Journal of Psychiatry, 160* (Suppl.), 1–60.

Beautrais, A. L. (2004). Further suicidal behavior amongst medically serious suicide attempters. *Suicide and Life-Threatening Behavior, 34,* 1–11.

Beck, A. T., Herman, I., & Schuyler, D. (1974). Development of suicidal intent scales. In A. T. Beck, H. L. P. Resnick & D. Lettieri (Eds.), *The Prediction of Suicide* (pp. 45–56). Bowie, MD: Charles Press.

Beck, A. T., Weissman, A., Lester, D., & Trexler, D. (1974). The measurement of pessimism: The hopelessness scale. *Journal of Consulting and Clinical Psychology, 42,* 861–865.

Beck, A. T., Davis, J. H., Frederick, C. J., Perlin, S., Pokorny, A. D., Schulman, R. E., Seiden, R. H., & Wittlin, B. J. (1973). Classification and nomenclature. In H. L. P. Resnik & B. C. Hathorne (Eds.), *Suicide Prevention in the Seventies* (pp. 7–12). Washington, DC: US Government Printing Office.

Beck, A. T., Beck, R., & Kovacs, M. (1975). Classification of suicidal behaviors: 1. Quantifying intent and medical lethality. *American Journal of Psychiatry, 132,* 285–287.

Berman, A. L., Shepherd, G., & Silverman, M. M. (2003). The LSARS-II: Lethality of suicide attempt rating scale – Updated. *Suicide and Life-Threatening Behavior, 33,* 261–276.

Bille-Brahe, U., Kerkhof, A., De Leo, D. & Schmidtke, A. (2004). Definitions and terminology used in the World Health Organization/EURO Multicentre Study. In A. Schmidtke, U. Bille-Brahe, D. De Leo & A. Kerkhof (Eds.), *Suicidal Behaviour in Europe* (pp. 11–14). Gottingen: Hogrefe & Huber.

Brown, G. K., Henriques, G. R., Sosdjan, D., & Beck, A. T. (2004). Suicide intent and accurate expectations of lethality: Predictors of medical lethality of suicide attempts. *Journal of Consulting and Clinical Psychology, 72,* 1170–1174.

Chapman, A. L., Gratz, K. L., & Brown, M. (2006). Solving the puzzle of deliberate self-injury: The experiential avoidance model. *Behaviour Research & Therapy, 44,* 371–394.

Chapman, A. L. & Dixon-Gordon, K. L. (2007). Emotional antecedents and consequences of deliberate self-harm and suicide attempts. *Suicide & Life-Threatening Behavior, 37*, 543–552.

Conner, K. R., Langley, J., Tomaszewski, M. S., & Conwell, Y. (2003). Injury hospitalization and risks for subsequent self-injury and suicide: A national study in New Zealand. *American Journal of Public Health, 93*, 1128–1131.

Daigle, M. S. & Cote, G. (2006). Nonfatal suicide-related behavior among inmates: Testing for gender and type differences. *Suicide and Life-Threatening Behavior, 36*, 670–681.

De Leo, D., Burgis, S., Bertolote, J., Kerkhof, A. D. M., & Bille-Brahe, U. (2004). Definitions of suicidal behavior. In D. De Leo, U. Bille-Brahe, A. D. M., Kerkhof, & A. Schmidtke (Eds.), *Suicidal Behavior: Theories and Research Findings* (pp. 17–39). Washington, DC: Hogrefe & Huber.

De Leo, D., Burgis, S., Bertolote, J. M., Kerkhof, A. D. M., & Bille-Brahe, U. (2006). Definitions of suicidal behaviour: Lessons learned from the WHO/EURO multicentre study. *Crisis, 27*, 4–15.

Duberstein, P. R. & Conwell, Y. (1977). Personality disorders and completed suicides: A methodological and conceptual review. *Clinical Psychology: Science and Practice, 4*, 359–376.

Garrison, C. Z., McKeown, R. E., Valois, R. F., & Vincent, M. L. (1993). Aggression, substance abuse, and suicidal behaviors in high school students. *American Journal of Public Health, 83*, 179–184.

Gibb, S. J., Beautrais, A. L., & Fergusson, D. M. (2005). Mortality and further suicidal behaviour after an index suicide attempt: A 10-year study. *Australian and New Zealand Journal of Psychiatry, 39*, 95–100.

Hawton, K. (1997). Attempted suicide. In D. M. Clarke & C. G. Fairburn (Eds.), *Science and Practice of Cognitive Behaviour Therapy* (pp. 285–312). Oxford: Oxford University Press.

Hawton, K. & Fagg J. (1988). Suicide, and other causes of death, following attempted suicide. *British Journal of Psychiatry, 152*, 359–366.

Hjelmeland, H. & Knizek, B. L. (1999). Conceptual confusion about intentions and motives of nonfatal suicidal behaviour: A discussion of terms employed in the literature of suicidology. *Archives of Suicide Research, 5*, 275–281.

Jenkins, R. & Singh, B. (2000). General population strategies of suicide prevention. In K. Hawton & K. van Heeringen (Eds.), *The International Handbook of Suicide and Attempted Suicide* (pp. 597–615). Chichester, England: John Wiley & Sons, Ltd.

Jobes, D. A. & Berman, A. L. (1985). The numbers game: A critique of mortality stats. Paper presented at the 18th annual meeting of the American Association of Suicidology, Toronto.

Jobes, D. A. Berman, A. L., & Josselson, A. R. (1987). Improving the validity and reliability of medical-legal certifications of suicide. *Suicide and Life-Threatening Behavior, 17*, 310–325.

Kemperman, I., Russ, M. J., & Shearin, E. (1997). Self-injurious behaviour and mood regulation in borderline patients. *Journal of Personality Disorders, 11*, 146–157.

Krasser, G., Rossmann, P., & Zapotoczky, H. G. (2003). Suicide and auto-aggression, depression, hopelessness, self-communication: A prospective study. *Archives of Suicide Research, 7*, 237–246.

Kreitman, N. (1977). *Parasuicide*. London: Wiley.

Linehan, M. M. (1986). Suicidal people: One population or two? *Annals of the New York Academy of Science, 487(1)*, 16–33.

Linehan, M. M. (1997). Behavioral treatments of suicidal behavior: Definitional obfuscation and treatment outcomes. *Annals of the New York Academy of Sciences, 836*, 302–328.

Linehan, M. M. (2000). Behavioral treatment of suicidal behavior: Definitional obfuscation and treatment outcomes. In R. W. Maris, S. S. Canetto, J. L. McIntosh, & M. M. Silverman (Eds.), *Review of Suicidology 2000* (pp. 84–111). New York: Guilford Press.

Litman, R. E. (1980). Psychological aspects of suicide. In W. J. Curran, A. L. McGarry, & C. S. Petty (Eds.), *Modern Legal Medicine: Psychiatry and forensic science*. Philadelphia: F. A. Davis.

Luoma, J. B., Martin, C. E., & Pearson, J. L. (2002). Contact with mental health and primary care providers before suicide: Review of the evidence. *American Journal of Psychiatry, 159*, 909–916.

Malone, K. M., Szanto, K., Corbitt, E., & Mann, J. J. (1995). Clinical assessment versus research methods in the assessment of suicidal behavior. *American Journal of Psychiatry, 152(11)*, 1601–1607.

Mann, J. J., Apter, A., Bertolote, J., Beautrais, A., Currier, D., Haas, A., Hegerl, U., Lonnqvist, J., Malone, K., Marusic, A., Mehlum, L., Patton, G., Phillips, M., Rutz, W., Rihmer, Z., Schmidtke, A., Shaffer, D., Silverman, M., Takahashi, Y., Varnik, A., Wasserman, D., Yip, P., & Hendin, H. (2005). Suicide prevention strategies: A systematic review. *Journal of the American Medical Association, 294*, 2064–2074.

Maris, R. W. (1992). The relationship of nonfatal suicide attempts to completed suicides. In R. W. Maris, A. L. Berman, J. T. Maltsberger, & R. I. Yufit (Eds.), *Assessment and Prediction of Suicide*. New York: Guilford Press.

Meehan, P. J., Lamb, J. A., Saltzman, L. E., & O'Carroll, P. W. (1992). Attempted suicide among young adults: Progress toward a meaningful estimate of prevalence. *American Journal of Psychiatry, 149*, 41–44.

Nock, M. K. & Kessler, R. C. (2006). Prevalence of and risk factors for suicide attempts versus suicide gestures: Analysis of the national comorbidity survey. *Journal of Abnormal Psychology, 115*, 616–623.

Nordentoft, M., Breum, L., Munck, L., Nordestgaard, A., Hunding, A., & Bjaedager, P. (1993). High mortality by natural and unnatural causes: A 10-year follow-up study of patients admitted to a poisoning treatment centre after suicide attempts. *British Medical Journal, 306*, 1637–1641.

O'Carroll, P. W. (1989). A consideration of the validity and reliability of suicide mortality data. *Suicide and Life-Threatening Behavior, 19*, 1–16.

O'Carroll, P. W., Berman, A. L., Maris, R. W., Moscicki, E. K., Tanney, B. L., & Silverman, M. M. (1996). Beyond the Tower of Babel: A nomenclature for suicidology. *Suicide and Life-Threatening Behavior, 26*, 237–252.

Owens, D., Horrocks, J., & House, A. (2002). Fatal and non-fatal repetition of self-harm. Systematic review. *British Journal of Psychiatry, 181*, 193–199.

Posner, K., Oquendo, M. A., Gould, M., Stanley, B., & Davies. M. (2007). Columbia classification algorithm of suicide assessment (C-CASA): Classification of suicidal events in the FDA pediatric suicidal risk analysis of antidepressants. *American Journal of Psychiatry, 164*, 1035–1043.

Rosenberg, M. L., Davidson, L. E., Smith, J. C., Berman, A. L., Buzbee, H., Gantner, G., Gay, G. A., Moore-Lewis, B., Mills, D. H., Murray, D., O'Carroll, P. W., & Jobes, D. (1988). Operational criteria for the determination of suicide. *Journal of Forensic Sciences, 32*, 1445–1455.

Rudd, M. D. & Joiner, T. E., Jr. (1998). The assessment, management and treatment of suicidality: Towards clinically informed and balanced standards of care. *Clinical Psychology: Science and Practice, 5*, 135–150.

Schmidtke, A., Bille-Brahe, U., De Leo, D., Kerkhof, A. D. M., Bjerke, T., Crepet P., Haring, C., Hawton, K., Lonnqvist, J., Pommereau, X., Querejeta, I., Phillipe, I., Salander-Renberg, E., Temesvary, B., Wasserman, D., Fricke, S., Weinacker, B., & Sampaio-Faria, J. G. (1996). Attempted suicide in Europe: Rates, trends and sociodemographic characteristics of suicide attempters during the period 1989–1992. Results of the WHO/Euro Multicentre Study on Parasuicide. *Acta Psychiatrica Scandinavia, 93*, 327–338.

Schmidtke, A., Bille-Brahe, U., De Leo, D., Kerkhof, A. D. M., & Wasserman, D. (Eds.) (2001). *Suicidal Behavior in Europe: Results from the WHO/Euro Multicentre Study on Suicidal Behaviour*. Gottingen: Hogrefe & Huber.

Shneidman, E. S. (1980). The reliability of suicide statistics: A bomb burst. *Suicide and Life-Threatening Behavior, 10*, 67–69.

Shneidman, E. S. (1985). *Definition of Suicide*. Northvale, NJ: Jason Aronson.

Silverman, M. M. (2006) The language of suicidology. *Suicide and Life-Threatening Behaviour, 36*, 519–532.

Silverman, M. M. & Maris, R. W. (1995) The prevention of suicidal behaviors: An overview. *Suicide and Life-Threatening Behavior, 25*, 10–21.

Silverman, M. M., Berman, A. L., Sanddal, N. D., O'Carroll, P. W., & Joiner, T. E. (2007a). Rebuilding the Tower of Babel: A revised nomenclature for the study of suicide and suicidal behaviors. Part I: Background, rationale, and methodology. *Suicide and Life-Threatening Behavior, 37*, 248–263.

Silverman, M. M., Berman, A. L., Sanddal, N. D., O'Carroll, P. W., & Joiner, T. E. (2007b). Rebuilding the Tower of Babel: A revised nomenclature for the study of suicide and suicidal behaviors. Part II: Suicide-related ideations, communications and behaviours. *Suicide and Life-Threatening Behavior, 37*, 264–277.

Wekstein, L. (1979). *Handbook of Suicidology*. New York: Brunner/Mazel.

Westefeld, J. S., Range, L., Rogers, J. R., Maples, M. R., Bromley, J. L., & Alcorn, J. (2000). Suicide: An overview. *The Counselling Psychologist, 28*, 445–510.

CHAPTER TWO

International Perspectives on the Epidemiology and Aetiology of Suicide and Self-Harm

Kirsten Windfuhr and Navneet Kapur

Abstract

Suicide and self-harm are major public health issues worldwide. Suicide is the tenth leading cause of death worldwide and self-harm is strongly associated with suicide risk. Although the literature on the epidemiology and aetiology of suicide consistently report mental illness to be a key contributory factor to suicide risk, it is also recognized that mental illness alone does not account for all the risk associated with suicidal behaviour. As such, this chapter brings together the international literature on the factors associated with suicide and self-harm from different disciplines, including psychology, sociology, biology, and psychiatry. We describe the rates, characteristics, and indicators of risk for suicide and self-harm, including demographic factors (e.g., sex, age), socio-economic and cultural factors (e.g., marital status, ethnicity, religion, migration, unemployment, political regime), temporal factors (e.g., seasonality, significant dates), psychological factors (e.g., personality traits), biological factors (e.g., genetics), and psychiatric factors (e.g., mental illness). Further, we discuss the relationship between suicide and self-harm, in addition to current perspectives on the management of self-harm. Although there is a large literature on suicide and self-harm, there are still considerable gaps in our knowledge about the factors associated with suicidal behaviour. First, there is substantial variation in the depth of understanding of factors associated with suicidal behaviour. Second, the literature is not truly international, with comparatively little research from developing, low-income and non-Western countries. Future work should contextualize the rates and risk factors associated with suicide and suicidal behaviour in different countries.

International Handbook of Suicide Prevention: Research, Policy and Practice, First Edition.
Edited by Rory C. O'Connor, Stephen Platt, Jacki Gordon.
© 2011 John Wiley & Sons, Ltd. Published 2011 by John Wiley & Sons, Ltd.

Introduction

The global disease burden of suicide is considerable. It is the tenth leading cause of death worldwide and accounts for 1.5% of all deaths (Hawton & van Heeringen, 2009). One key risk factor for suicide is previous self-harm.

This chapter is intended to provide a broad overview of the current international literature on the rates and risk factors for suicide and self-harm, and how services manage the risk of suicide and self-harm. International perspectives on suicidal behaviour are essential to improve understanding of the characteristics specific to different population sub-groups. These insights will help to more effectively inform the development of suicide prevention strategies. Cross-national epidemiological differences may also provide clues to the aetiology and course of suicidal behaviour. However, there is a paucity of truly international research on many aspects of suicidal behaviour.

In this chapter the literatures on suicide and self-harm are discussed separately. We begin each section with a discussion of terminology, before moving on to a discussion of rates. We then provide a broad overview of some of the key sociological, psychological, biological, and psychiatric aspects of suicidal behaviour from an international perspective. The chapter ends with a brief summary and discussion of possible future directions for suicidal behaviour research.

Suicide

Definitions and case ascertainment

Suicide can be described as an intentional self-inflicted act which results in death (Maris, 2002). Although there is a general consensus on the broad concept of suicide, there are in excess of a dozen different definitions. There is even less agreement about how a suicide death is ascertained (see also Chapter 1, above).

The determination of death is made by the medical examiner or coroner in many countries, but this is not always the case. In some countries (e.g., Finland), the police take a leading role, in others (e.g., China) physicians are involved (Hawton & van Heeringen, 2009). The criteria used to determine a suicide death also varies between and within countries, as does the standard of proof required before a suicide verdict can be recorded (e.g., presence of a suicide note, intent of self-inflicted injury) (Hawton & van Heeringen, 2009).

Cross-national differences in ascertainment may occur for a variety of reasons. Stigma resulting from socio-cultural norms or religious beliefs may lead to under-reporting or mis-classification of suicide deaths (Lester, 2006). This may be a particular problem in countries where suicidal behaviour is still illegal (e.g., India) or has been decriminalized relatively recently (e.g., Ireland in 1993) (Corcoran, Arensman, & O'Mahony, 2006). Suicide is prohibited in Islam and some Islamic countries have very low reported rates of suicide. This may be because of actual differences in rates or may reflect bias in case ascertainment (Lester, 2006). Mis-classification of deaths may occur to a greater degree in children and the elderly (Grøholt & Ekeberg, 2003; Schmidtke, Sell, & Loehr, 2008; Windfuhr, While,

Hunt, Turnbull, Lowe, *et al.*, 2008). The extent of mis-classification is also likely to vary by method of suicide. For example, death by firearms is less likely to be mis-classified than suicide by other methods, such as drowning (Salib & Agnew, 2005).

Cross-national rates and trends in suicide

Rates   As of 2009, 104 countries within six World Health Organization (WHO) regions (African: $n = 4$; Americas: $n = 33$; Eastern Mediterranean: $n = 6$; European: $n = 48$; Southeast Asia: $n = 4$; Western Pacific: $n = 8$) have reported suicide data. Based on this sample, the worldwide suicide rate is estimated to be approximately 14.5/100,000 persons per year.

In general, eastern European countries have the highest rates, Central–South American and eastern Mediterranean countries have the lowest rates, with suicide rates in the United States, Western Europe, Asia, and Africa somewhere in between (Nock, Borges, Bromet, Cha, Kessler, *et al.*, 2008) (Figure 2.1). However, data are not collected across countries as part of a cross-national epidemiological study, and there may be variations in how the data reported to the WHO are compiled within individual countries. It is also worth noting that there is great variation across countries within each region that report suicide rates. Further, there are large parts of the world for which robust suicide data are not available (e.g., western Pacific region, Middle Eastern countries). Consequently, current data on the rates and characteristics of suicide in these parts of the world are derived from individual research studies (De Leo, Milner, & Xiangdong, 2009; Lester, 2006). The overall picture of regions of the world with high and low suicide rates may therefore be misleading.

Trends   Given the inconsistencies and variability in available suicide data, definitive cross-national trends are difficult to ascertain. In a recent study, Liu (2009) reported global suicide trends from 1950 to 2004 (Figure 2.2(a) and Figure 2.2(b)). Of the 71 countries included in the study, 20 had an increase of 30% or more in their national suicide rates, with five countries showing more than a 100% increase over this period, while nine countries showed a decrease of between 30% and 80%.

Interpreting rates of suicide   There are several difficulties in interpreting cross-national suicide rates. First, differences between countries may reflect different procedures for case ascertainment or differences in the priority assigned to recording suicide (see above). Second, crude rates are often reported, which do not take into account the age structures of individual countries (Kapur & Appleby, 2008). Third, rates are sometimes reported for one site within a country and may not be representative of the country as a whole (although data reported to WHO do reflect national suicide rates). Fourth, there is substantial variation in the most recent year of suicide data reported to the WHO, varying from 1978 (Honduras) to 2007 (e.g., Finland). Finally, there are many countries (perhaps 40%–60% of countries worldwide) for which data are not available or easily accessible (De Leo, Milner, & Xiangdong, 2009; Lester, 2006; Wasserman, Cheng, & Jian, 2005).

It is likely that there are genuine (non-artefactual) differences in suicide rates cross-nationally (Andriessen, 2006), although these should be interpreted with caution. Variation

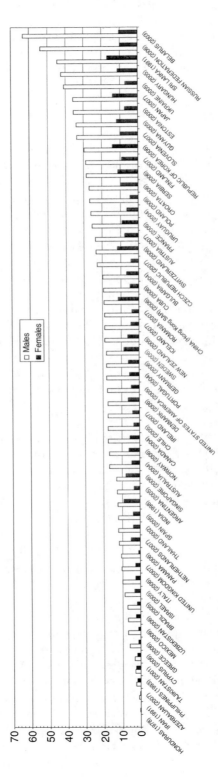

Figure 2.1 Suicide rates for selected countries based on most recent data from the WHO (accessed 21 April 2009).

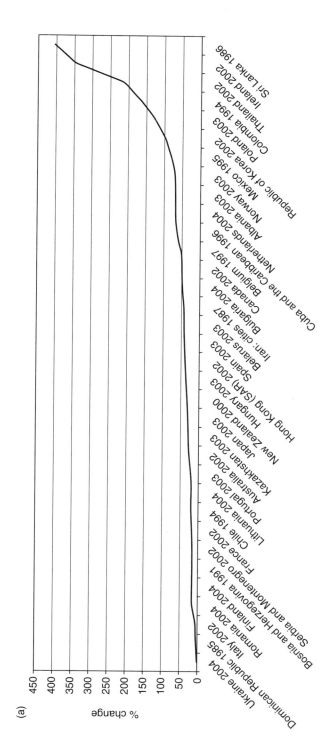

Figure 2.2 (a) Increase (percentage change) in suicide rates in selected countries (data based on figures from WHO reported in Liu (2008)). (b) Decrease (percentage change) in suicide rates in selected countries (data based on figures from WHO reported in Liu (2008)).

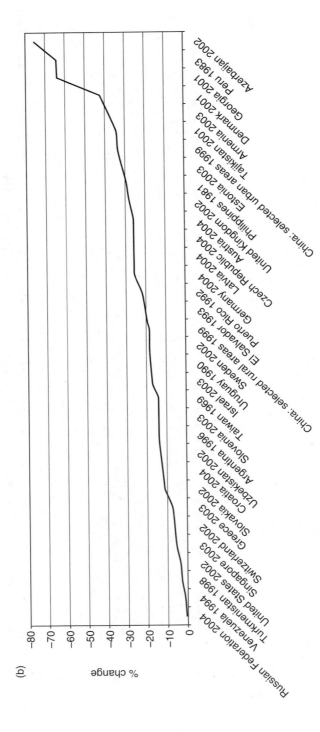

Figure 2.2 (cont'd)

in national rates could reflect differences in the prevalence of known risk factors for suicide, including mental illness, self-harm, and alcohol misuse. National rates might also be influenced by broader societal factors, including mental health service provision, social deprivation and fragmentation, religious beliefs, and political change.

Methods of suicide

Common methods of suicide include hanging, self-poisoning, and jumping from a height, although the preferred methods of choice vary substantially by sex and country (Ajdacic-Gross, Weiss, Ring, Hepp, Bopp, *et al.*, 2008). For example, WHO data reported by Ajdacic-Gross, Weiss and colleagues (2008) showed that, across nations, hanging is the most common method among men compared with self-poisoning among women (Figure 2.3(a) and Figure 2.3(b)). However, there was more variability in method selection by country than by gender, suggesting that availability of method is an important determining factor for both male and female suicides. Further, there were international differences in the type of substances used to self-poison: pesticide poisoning was more common among women from Latin American and Asian countries, while women from Nordic countries, Canada, and the United Kingdom most often used drugs (Ajdacic-Gross, Weiss, *et al.*, 2008).

In the United States, firearms are the most common method, accounting for approximately 60% of all suicide deaths (Mościcki, 1995). In contrast, deliberate ingestion of pesticides is the most common method of death in many Asian countries, in particular Sri Lanka and rural China (Eddleston & Phillips, 2004), while suicide by charcoal burning has emerged as a common method of suicide in Hong Kong (Ajdacic-Gross, Weiss, *et al.*, 2008).

Availability is an important factor in both the choice of method and the lethality of the suicide attempt (Eddleston & Phillips, 2004), and there is evidence to suggest that reducing the availability of some methods of suicide may be beneficial (Mann, Apter, Bertolote, Beautrais, Currier, *et al.*, 2005). For example, there was a 30% reduction in UK suicide rates in the 1960s and 1970s, corresponding to changes in the lethality of domestic gas (Kreitman, 1976). However, substitution of method may occur when availability of a particular suicide method is restricted. For example, Largey, Kelly, and Stevenson (2009) showed an increase in the use of hanging from 1984 to 2002 in Northern Ireland, at a time when deaths by carbon monoxide poisoning decreased with the introduction of catalytic converters. In an international study of suicide methods, Ajdacic-Gross, Weiss, and colleagues (2008) showed that hanging deaths generally decreased as poisoning and firearms suicides increased.

The availability of new means of suicide can also have a dramatic effect on suicide rates. Charcoal burning became one of the predominant methods of suicide within a very short period of time in Hong Kong (De Leo, Milner, & Xiangdong, 2009), possibly as a result of media portrayal of these suicide deaths (Liu, Beautrais, Caine, Chan, Chao, *et al.*, 2007). Liu and colleagues (2007) found that substitution of method did not occur with increasing use of charcoal burning. Rather, the increasing use of this new method contributed to a rise in the overall suicide rate.

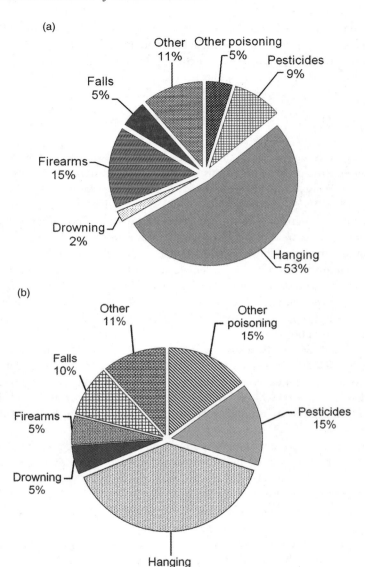

Figure 2.3 (a) Average % method of suicide for males across 56 countries (WHO data reported by Ajdacic-Gross, Weiss, *et al.*, 2008). (b) Average % method of suicide for females across 56 countries (WHO data reported by Ajdacic-Gross, Weiss, *et al.*, 2008).

Ethno-cultural factors also affect method of suicide. In the United Kingdom, South Asian women are over-represented among cases of self-immolation (Khan & Waheed, 2009). One study found variation in substances ingested by ethnic group, with White women being more likely to ingest drugs, whereas South Asian women more commonly ingested non-medicinal agents (Cooper, Husain, Webb, Waheed, Kapur, *et al.*, 2006).

Demographic factors

Sex   Suicide rates are generally higher among males than females, but there are wide variations in the male:female ratio across countries. An exception to this general gender difference is China (excluding Hong Kong), where the male:female ratio is 0.9:1 (WHO, 2009). The male:female ratios in India and Hong Kong are also less pronounced than in other countries, with male:female ratios of 1.3:1 and 2.0:1, respectively (Nock, Borges, Bromet, Cha, Kessler, *et al.*, 2008). Possible explanations include the availability of more lethal methods (e.g., agro-chemical poisoning) (Eddleston & Phillips, 2004) or political upheaval, gender, or religious beliefs (Phillips, Yang, Zhang, Wang, Ji, *et al.*, 2002; Sharma, Gupta, Sharma, Sharma, Gupta, *et al.*, 2007).

Age   There have been significant changes in age-specific suicide rates over the past several decades. From the 1960s to the 1980s there was an increase in suicide among young adults. Since the 1990s there has been a decline in suicide rates among 15–24-year-olds (especially males) in many countries (Värnik, Kõlves, Allik, Arensman, Aromaa, *et al.*, 2009), including England (Biddle, Brock, Brookes, & Gunnell, 2008), Scotland (Stark, Stockton, & Henderson, 2008), and Canada (Steele & Doey, 2007). A recent cross-national study of older adult suicide in 54 countries by Shah, Bhat, MacKenzie, and Koen (2008) showed a decline in many countries over ten consecutive years, based on data reported to the WHO. As a result of these age-related changes, the age profile of suicide has been altered considerably (Gould, Greenberg, & Velting, 2003; Sharma *et al.*, 2007). Broadly speaking, suicide rates increase with advancing age in most countries (Bertolote & Fleischmann, 2002), although the gradient is less steep than used to be the case and, in some countries, there are greater absolute numbers of suicide among young adults. For example, in the United Kingdom, suicide numbers and rates are now highest among males aged 25–44 years (Kapur & Appleby, 2008).

Socio-economic and cultural factors

In three review articles, Stack provides a comprehensive overview of demographic, socio-economic, and cultural factors associated with suicide (Stack, 1982, 2000a, 2000b). While a detailed review of sociological issues is beyond the scope of this chapter, some issues merit further discussion in a cross-national context: marital status and children; ethnicity, culture and religion; migration and social integration; and socio-economic and wider societal factors. Each of these is discussed below.

Marital status and children   Since the seminal work of Durkheim (1951 [1897]), the association between marital status and suicide has been explored in several countries (Heikkinen, Isometsa, Marttunen, Aro, & Lonnqvist, 1995; Mohanty, Sahu, Mohanty, & Patnaik, 2007; Wyder, Ward, & De Leo, 2009). Suicide is generally more common among those who are single, divorced or widowed (Heikkinen *et al.*, 1995). Typically, marriage confers a protective effect (O'Reilly, Rosato, Connolly, & Cardwell, 2008), particularly for women, with widowhood increasing the risk in older individuals. Risk of suicide has also been shown to be even greater for separated individuals compared with those who are divorced, particularly for young males (Wyder, Ward, & De Leo, 2009). However, there are international variations in the pattern of association between suicide and marital status. These differences may, in part, be accounted for by differences in socio-cultural norms (Yeh, Xirasagar, Liu, Li, & Lin, 2008). For example, in contrast to the international literature, Yeh and colleagues found that young married women in Taiwan had an elevated risk of suicide, while older widowed women had a decreased risk. The authors suggest that the increased risk among young married women may, in part, be explained by the changing roles of women in Taiwanese society. The deceased risk for older widowed women may have been indicative of the greater familial ties and social networks in Taiwan compared with some Western cultures.

Children have also been found to confer a protective effect on their parents, and this effect is more pronounced for women than for men (Høyer & Lund, 1993; Qin, Agerbo, & Mortensen, 2003). However, there are few cross-national studies on the association between children and suicide risk in parents, and it is likely that socio-cultural norms will also affect the association between children and parental risk of suicide.

Ethnicity, culture and religion   The rate of suicide among African Americans has historically been lower than that of White Americans of European origin, although a rise in the suicide rate of African Americans in the 1980s and 1990s has resulted in an increasing convergence of rates between these two populations (Utsey, Hook, & Stanard, 2007). Indigenous populations (i.e., Alaska, Native, Pacific Islanders, American Indian communities), however, have higher rates of suicide than non-indigenous populations (Alcántara & Gone, 2007; Else, Anrade, & Nahulu, 2007). Young Hispanic Americans and other ethnic groups (Duarté-Vélez & Bernal, 2007; Leong & Leach, 2007) also have comparatively high rates of suicidal behaviour. In England and Wales, age-standardized suicide rates are lower for South Asian men compared with White males, while women of South Asian origin show slightly elevated rates of suicide compared with their White peers (McKenzie, Bui, Nanchahal, & Blizard, 2008).

Religion, spirituality, greater familial and social ties, as well as the collectivist and communitarian ideals promoted by many religious belief systems, have been proposed as contributory factors to lower suicide rates in African American and other ethnic groups (Leong & Leach, 2007; Utsey, Hook, & Stanard, 2007). However, factors associated with risk of suicide, such as the stigma of mental health problems and less contact with mental health services, as well as substance misuse, are thought to disproportionately affect some ethnic groups (Alcántara & Gone, 2007; Utsey, Hook, & Stanard, 2007) and may contribute to higher suicide rates.

One limitation of the research on ethnic minority groups and suicide is the selective focus on a small number of ethnic groups (e.g., African American, South Asians in the United Kingdom), with comparatively little research on other ethnic groups (e.g., Hispanic Americans, Asian Americans, indigenous populations). Further, the heterogeneity of ethnic minority groups has been largely overlooked in the research literature. For example, the term Asian American encompasses approximately 50 ethnic sub-groups, speaking approximately 30 languages (Leong *et al.*, 2007). Similarly, the term South Asian, when used in the United Kingdom, encompasses people from several ethnically diverse nations (e.g., India, Pakistan, Sri Lanka), speaking a variety of languages (e.g., Hindi, Bengali, Urdu).

Migration and social integration   There is evidence to suggest that the suicide rate among immigrants reflects that of their country of origin (Burvill, 1998; Ferrada-Noli, 1997; Soni Raleigh & Balarajan, 1992). However, assimilation (decline or disappearance of distinct ethnic features), acculturation (the transference of attitudes or behaviour between cultures), immigration status (relocation of an individual from their country of birth to a new country), and social integration also play an important role in determining the risk of suicide among immigrants (Wadsworth & Kubrin, 2007). Indeed, a recent study by Westman, Martelin, Härkänen, Koskinen, and Sundquist (2008) showed that, while the suicide rates of migrants to Sweden broadly reflected the rates of suicide in their country of origin, the rates of Finnish immigrants were higher than in their country of origin (even after adjustment for socio-economic status and psychiatric hospitalization).

Consequently, factors associated with the process of migration, such as the threat to family ties and social networks, may confer additional risk (Stack, 2000b). Alternatively, migrants may be less physically and mentally well prior to migration, although this is in contrast to research evidence suggesting that they typically have a *better* health status prior to migration (the so-called healthy migrant hypothesis) (Lu, 2008). It is likely that a combination of factors affects suicide rates among migrants (Westman *et al.*, 2008). Interestingly, there may also be an elevated risk of suicide in second-generation migrants (Hjern & Allebeck, 2002). It is possible that culturally specific factors that affect the risk of suicide (e.g., religious beliefs, attitudes towards alcohol or attitudes towards help seeking/disclosing suicidal thoughts) are transferred from the first to the second generation.

Socio-economic and wider societal factors   To date, fluctuations in the rate of suicide have been associated with fluctuations in macro-economic indices (Berk, Dodd, & Henry, 2006), including measures of financial loss (Turvey, Stromquist, Kelly, Zwerling, & Merchant, 2002) and social fragmentation (Middleton, Whitley, Frankel, Dorling, Sterne, *et al.*, 2004). In particular, unemployment has generally been strongly associated with suicide (Platt & Hawton, 2000).

Cross-national research in 10 European countries has shown that there are associations between macro-economic indices and suicide in most of the countries studied, although there was some variation in the magnitude of the association (Lorant, Kunst, Huisman, Costa, & Mackenback, 2005). Differences could be accounted for by the prevalence of different social problems (e.g., drug use) and different mental healthcare systems between countries, as well as the specific socio-economic indicators used in any particular study (e.g., housing tenure, educational status).

Recently, Stuckler, Basu, Suhrcke, Coutts, and McKee (2009) examined the association between economic recession (in particular unemployment) and mortality rates in a large cross-national study of 26 European nations over a 37-year period (1970–2007). Rapid rises in unemployment experienced during a recession were associated with short-term rises in suicide among both males and females, although there were differences in the magnitude of the association across countries. However, the negative effect of unemployment appeared to be mitigated by increased government expenditure on active labour market programmes. A commitment to increased expenditure to counter negative recessionary effects (e.g., expenditure on active labour markets) may have accounted for the finding that economic crises in Finland and Sweden were not associated with increases in suicide rates.

Political regime has also been associated with suicide. For example, some studies have shown higher suicide rates when Conservative governments are in power compared with Labour (i.e., social democratic) governments (Page, Morrell, & Taylor, 2002). However, it is unclear what factors underpin this association. The inclusion of other social factors (e.g., unemployment) in an analysis of political regime and suicide is important and may indicate a more complex picture than has been presented previously (Stack, 2002).

Related to the work on political regime is the literature on the relationship between war and suicide. Evidence on the latter is mixed, with some studies showing lower suicide rates during times of war and others showing increased rates of suicide (van Tubergen & Ultee, 2006). Lester (2002) reported that suicide rates were higher in Northern Ireland when deaths from civil unrest were lower, which suggests that 'the Troubles' were associated with reduced suicide rates. The literature reporting a decrease in suicide during wartime attributes this to Durkheim's theory of social integration, namely, that war fosters greater social cohesion and individuals therefore feel more integrated into society. A more recent study by van Tubergen and Ultee (2006) looked at suicide in the Netherlands during the Second World War and found that there was an increase in certain sub-groups of the population during this period, in contrast to Durkheim's proposed social integration theory. Van Tubergen and Utlee propose that the relationship between war and suicide can be explained with a refined version of Durkheim's theory to include people's expectations about their level of social integration during wartime. In their study, high rates of suicide were found among the Jewish community and those who were politically outspoken against the war. These people experienced persecution not social integration as a result of the war. Of course, it may also be that war time decreases unemployment, which fosters greater social cohesion (Marshall, 1981). However, the Netherlands did not prosper economically during the Second World War and so this explanation of the war–suicide relationship seems less likely (van Tubergen & Utlee, 2006). People may also not prosper during civil wars. In line with van Turbergen and Utlee (2006), Selakovic-Bursic, Haramic, & Leenaars (2006) found that suicide rates increased during the Balkan civil war, a likely reflection of the unpopularity of the war and a decrease in social cohesion.

Temporal factors

Temporal factors that have been associated with suicide include seasonality, personally significant dates (e.g., birthday, anniversary) and public holidays (e.g., Christmas, New Year). A seasonal peak in spring/summer time has been reported in the literature since Durkheim (1951 [1897]), both in studies of individual countries (Ajdacic-Gross, Wang, Bopp, Eich, Rossler, *et al.*, 2003; Reutfors, Ösby, Ekbom, Nordström, Jokinen, *et al.*,

2009) and in a cross-national study of 28 countries (Chew & McCleary, 1995). However, a critical review of 46 studies on seasonality and suicide published in major psychiatric journals from 1970 to 1997 (Hakko, Räsänen, Tiihonen, & Nieminen, 2002) concluded that the effects of seasonality were largely uninterpretable given the lack of consistent methods, as well as serious statistical shortcomings. The impact of seasonality on suicide is, therefore, unclear.

Suicide has been shown to occur in the days around a birthday, rather than on the day itself (Jessen & Jensen, 1999). It has also been found to decrease in and around public holidays (Ajdacic-Gross, Lauber, Bopp, Eich, Gostynki, *et al.*, 2008; Carley & Hamilton, 2004). However, the impact of temporal factors on suicide cross-nationally has not yet been conclusively demonstrated (Skala & Friedland, 2004).

Psychological factors

The literature on the psychology of suicidal behaviour and completed suicide has focused on the identification of personality traits and associated cognitive features (see Chapters 9–12 for detailed discussion of the psychological variables).

Personality traits　The personality traits associated with suicidal behaviour and completed suicide include neuroticism, psychoticism, introversion, sensitivity, dependency, and cynicism. Two of the most widely studied personality traits are impulsivity and perfectionism.

Evidence suggests that impulsive individuals are more vulnerable to suicide when faced with triggers such as substance misuse, stress, and depression (Dumais, Lesage, Alda, Rouleau, Dumont, *et al.*, 2005). However, the contribution of impulsivity to suicidal behaviour and completed suicide remains unclear (Zouk, Tousignant, Seguin, Lesage, & Turecki, 2006). Impulsivity remains poorly defined. Research to date has investigated the role of cognitive, trait, and motor impulsivity (Leshem & Glicksohn, 2007). Indeed, there is a lack of consensus that impulsivity is even a construct in its own right. Enticott & Ogloff (2006) posit that impulsivity refers to 'characteristically similar behaviours that are determined by one of a number of underlying constructs' (p. 12), and that it is these which should be the focus of future research.

It is broadly agreed that perfectionism is a multidimensional construct. In a systematic review, O'Connor (2007) identified 29 studies that investigated the association between perfectionism and suicidality. There is some evidence that there is an association between self-critical evaluative concerns perfectionism (i.e., being excessively self-critical and concerned about other people's expectations) and suicidality. However, interpretation of the results is hampered due to methodological problems (e.g., lack of consistency in the measures of perfectionism, weak study designs and statistical analysis). Further, studies have been carried out in predominately Western or European countries: 16 studies in the United States, seven in Canada, and two in the United Kingdom, with only one other study in Europe (Germany) and three other studies in non-European countries (Australia, China, and Japan). Given the paucity of international research, the generalizability of the findings is limited.

Cognitive variables   There are several cognitive variables that have been associated with suicidal behaviour, including hopelessness (Beck, Emery, & Greenberg, 1985), autobiographical memory (Williams, Barnhofer, Crane, & Duggan, 2006), burdensomeness (Joiner, Pettit, Walker, Voelz, Cruz, *et al.*, 2002), rumination (Crane, Barnhofer, & Williams, 2007; Morrison & O'Connor, 2008), dichotomous thinking and cognitive rigidity (see Ellis & Rutherford, 2008 for a review), and problem-solving skills (Reinecke, 2006). Variables such as future thinking and optimism–pessimism have received less attention, although more recent studies have started to draw together the literature from different areas of cognitive psychology to clarify the relationship between hopelessness and related concepts (O'Connor & Cassidy, 2007; O'Connor, Rasmussen, Mile, & Hawton, 2009). However, once again the generalizability of the findings is limited because most studies have been carried out in Western or European countries (Morrison & O'Connor, 2008).

Biological factors

There is growing evidence to suggest that a predisposition to suicide is at least partly heritable (see Chapter 8, this volume). Although the international literature on twin studies has mainly developed in Europe or North America, the findings from existing studies converge in support of a genetic component to suicidality (Voracek & Loibl, 2007). Data from adoption studies show that rates are higher in the biological relatives of adopted children who end their life compared with the biological relatives of adopted children who do not do so (Mann, 2002); although again, there is a dearth of international research. Molecular genetic studies have focused on the serotonergic system (Baldessarini & Hennen, 2004). In particular, such studies have indicated that candidate genes may include tryptophan hydroxylase (TPH), which is involved in the biosynthesis of serotonin (Roy, Rylander, Forslund, Asberg, Mazzanti, *et al.*, 2001), and serotonin 5-HT2a receptor gene (Mann, 2002).

Migrant studies offer an alternative method of investigating the genetic component to suicide. Indeed, there is some consistency in the finding that the rate of suicide among immigrants mirrors that of their country of origin, including studies of immigrants to the United States, Australia, Canada, Sweden, and the United Kingdom (Voracek & Loibl, 2008). In a meta-analysis of 33 immigration studies involving 55 nationalities in seven host countries, Voracek and Loibl (2008) found a strong correlation between the suicide rates of the country of origin and that of the country of immigration, for both sexes and for all host countries.

Suicide and mental illness

Mental illness is consistently cited as one of the key contributory factors to suicide risk (Barraclough, Bunch, Nelson, & Sainsbury, 1974; Cavanagh, Carson, Sharpe, & Lawrie, 2003; Gould, Greenberg, & Velting, 2003; Harris & Barraclough, 1997; Mann *et al.*, 2005). However, there is variation in the prevalence of mental illness internationally, with higher rates found in Western countries and lower rates in Asian countries. Studies from Western countries show that approximately 90%–95% of suicide cases have a mental disorder (Cavanagh *et al.*, 2003), whereas the prevalence of mental illness in Asia is approximately 60%–90% (Vijayakumar, 2004) and sometimes less (Phillips *et al.*, 2002). The type of mental disorder also differs among suicide cases in developed and developing countries. For example, in developed countries, more than two-thirds of suicide cases were reported to have a diagnosis of depressive disorder (Mann, 2002), compared with only 35%–40% in developing countries (Vijayakumar, 2004).

Suicide among people in recent contact with mental health services   The UK National Confidential Inquiry into Suicide and Homicide by People with Mental Illness (NCI) is a unique national database of all suicide cases in contact with mental health services in the 12 months preceding suicide. Much of what we know about suicide in the mental health patient population in the United Kingdom is derived from the NCI (Kapur & Appleby, 2008).

Between one-quarter and one-third of individuals who complete suicide have been in contact with mental health services in the United Kingdom, equating to about 1,200–1,300 suicide cases annually. The rates of contact with mental health services in the year prior to death are broadly similar between nations within the United Kingdom (Scotland: 28%; England/Wales: 23%). These rates of contact are consistent with the international literature (Luoma, Martin, & Pearson, 2002). However, studies investigating contact with mental health services prior to suicide have been carried out mainly in the United States, Nordic countries and the United Kingdom. Contact with mental health services is likely to be different in developing countries (Vijayakumar, 2004).

Rates and characteristics of suicide among patient suicide cases vary by demographic (e.g., age, sex) and clinical (e.g., patient group, diagnosis) characteristics. For example, psychiatric in-patients are a particularly vulnerable patient group. Fourteen per cent of suicide cases were in-patients (*n* = 1,851) in England and Wales (Appleby, Shaw, Kapur, Windfur, Ashton, *et al.*, 2006); in-patients represented a smaller group in Scotland (9%). However, in both nations in-patient suicides appear to be falling (Appleby *et al.*, 2006; Appleby, Shaw, Kapur, Windfuhr, Ashton, *et al.*, 2008). Guidance on the removal of specific ligature points (Department of Health, 2002) and continued vigilance regarding ward safety may have contributed to the reduction of hanging/strangulation deaths on psychiatric in-patient wards. Comparison of UK in-patient suicide rates and trends with other countries is difficult given the paucity of robust international research in this patient population (Tishler & Reiss, 2009).

Self-Harm

Definitions and terminology

Self-harm is a multifaceted and complex behaviour varying in both severity and intent (Nada-Raja, Skegg, Langley, Morrison, & Sowerby, 2004). Defining this heterogeneous set of behaviours has posed a challenge for researchers for several decades (O'Carroll, Berman,

Maris, Moscicki, Tanney, *et al.*, 1996; Skegg, 2005) and continues to do so today (see Chapter 1, above). In the remainder of this chapter, the broad term 'self-harm' will be used to describe intentional acts irrespective of intent, including self-poisoning and self-injury (Kapur, 2009).

The relationship between suicide and self-harm

Self-harm (and repeated self-harm) is one of the strongest risk factors for subsequent suicide. Based on hospital admitted or treated populations, individuals who have self-harmed have a 30- to 200-fold increased risk of suicide in the year following an episode compared with individuals who have not self-harmed (Cooper, Kapur, Webb, Lawlor, Guthrie, *et al.*, 2005; Owens, Horrocks, & House, 2002). Individuals who repeat self-harm are at even greater risk of subsequent suicide compared with individuals who have only one self-harm episode (Zahl & Hawton, 2004). Cross-national risk factors for self-harm are reasonably consistent and include female gender, younger age, fewer years of education, and mental disorder (Nock, Borges, Bromet, Alonso, Angermeyer, *et al.*, 2008). Some risk factors for self-harm overlap with risk factors for suicide (e.g., mental disorder), suggesting that the two behaviours are related, although their relationship is complex.

Rates and trends of self-harm

Rates   For a comprehensive overview of the international literature on the epidemiology of suicidal behaviour over the period 1970–2007, see Welch (2001) and recent papers by Nock and colleagues (Nock, Borges, Bromet, Alonso, *et al.*, 2008; Nock, Borges, Bromet, Cha, *et al.*, 2008). A summary of key studies is presented below.

Two international register-based studies of suicidal behaviour were carried out as part of the WHO/EURO Multicentre Study of Parasuicide (Bille-Brahe, Schmidtke, Kerkhof, De Leo, Lönnqvist, *et al.*, 1995). Schmidtke and colleagues (Schmidtke, Bille-Brahe, De Leo, Kerkhof, Bjerke, *et al.*, 1996; Schmidtke, Weinacker, Loehr, Bille-Brahe, De Leo, *et al.*, 2004) reported that self-harm was more common among females than males, and higher rates were generally found among younger adults. In particular, young women aged 15–24 years and young men aged 25–29 years had the highest rates of self-harm. There was also substantial variation, even among countries within one WHO region (i.e., European region). For example, between 1995 and 1999 the highest male rate was found for Helsinki, Finland (327/100,000) and the lowest for Ankara, Turkey (35/100,000), representing a nine-fold difference between centres. The highest average female rate was found for Rennes, France (504/100,000), while the lowest was again found for Ankara, Turkey (81/100,000), representing a six-fold difference between centres.

Registration-based studies such as the WHO/EURO study on suicidal behaviour provide data on the incidence of self-harm behaviours that are treated within the healthcare system, usually hospital emergency departments. However, studies that focus on medically treated self-harm underestimate the extent of the problem, as not all episodes of self-harm require or result in medical intervention (Kapur & Appleby, 2008).

Weissman, Bland, Canino, Greenwald, Hwu, and colleagues (1999) were among the first to carry out a large-scale, cross-national, population-based epidemiological study, involving nine countries (United States, Canada, Puerto Rico, France, West Germany, Lebanon, Taiwan, Korea, New Zealand) to determine the rates of suicidal ideation and attempts. Data were collected as part of a community household survey using similar diagnostic tools across all participating countries. The lifetime prevalence of suicidal ideation varied from 2% in Beirut, Lebanon to 18% in Christchurch, New Zealand. Lifetime prevalence of reported suicide attempts ranged from 0.7% in Beirut, Lebanon to 5.9% in Puerto Rico. In the majority of countries, 10–18% of individuals had suicidal thoughts at some point in their lifetime, and between 3% and 5% had attempted suicide.

Extending Weissman and colleagues' study (1999), Bertolote, Fleischmann, De Leo, Bolhari, Botega, *et al.* (2005) reported the findings from the WHO SUPRE-MISS study of suicidal behaviour, which was initiated to gain a better understanding of suicidal behaviour in culturally diverse locations. As part of this study, a community survey was conducted between 2002 and 2004 at eight sites across each of the six WHO regions (Americas: Brazil; Southeast region: India, Sri Lanka; African region: South Africa; Western Pacific region: Viet Nam; Eastern Mediterranean region: Islamic Republic of Iran; European region: Estonia). China, Australia, and Sweden were also included in the study, although these sites were able to complete only part of the survey.

The study yielded a lifetime prevalence of suicidal ideation ranging from 2.6% in Chennai, India to 25.4% in Durban, South Africa. Lifetime prevalence of suicide attempts ranged from 0.4% in Hanoi, Vietnam, to 4.2% in both Brisbane (Australia) and Karaj (Islamic Republic of Iran).

Most recently, Nock, Borges, Bromet, Alonso, and colleagues (2008) reported the prevalence of suicidal behaviours (including suicidal ideation, planning, and attempts) from the WHO World Mental Health Survey initiative. Lifetime prevalence of suicide attempt was 2.7%, with a prevalence of 9.2% for ideation and 3.1% for suicide planning. There was substantial cross-national variability, less so in respect of planned suicide attempts compared with other suicidal thoughts and behaviours (e.g., suicidal ideation, suicide planning). Cross-nationally, the presence of a mental disorder was consistently associated with suicidal behaviour, although the type of mental disorder varied by income level (e.g., low-, medium-, high-income level countries).

Geographically, patterns of suicidal behaviour differed from those for completed suicide (Nock, Borges, Bromet, Cha, *et al.*, 2008). For example, countries in regions of the world with typically high suicide rates (e.g., Eastern Europe) did not necessarily have high rates of suicidal behaviour. There were also no systematic differences in suicidal behaviour between developed and developing countries (Nock, Borges, Bromet, Cha, *et al.*, 2008).

School-based studies of self-harm   In a recent international school-based survey of self-harm in adolescents (Child and Adolescent Self-Harm in Europe study; CASE), Madge, Hewitt, Hawton, De Wilde, Corcoran, and colleagues (2008) reported prevalence rates (for self-harm in the previous year) of 8.9% for females and 2.6% for males, with lifetime prevalence rates of 13.5% for females and 4.3% for females and males, respectively. Many countries show similar prevalence rates of self-harm in their adolescent populations (e.g., De Leo & Heller, 2004; Hawton, Rodham, Evans, & Weatherall, 2002; O'Connor *et al.*, 2009), although there is some variation between countries (Madge *et al.*, 2008), sometimes even between neighbouring countries (Portzky, De Wilde, & van Heeringen, 2008), but not between UK nations (O'Connor *et al.*, 2009). In the first study looking at the prevalence of adolescent self-harm in Scotland using a similar methodology, O'Connor, *et al.* (2009) found that the prevalence of self-harm in adolescents was 13.8% (i.e., those who answered yes to the following question: 'Have you ever deliberately taken an overdose (e.g., pills or other medication) or tried to harm yourself in some other way (e.g., such as cut yourself)?'). This compares with a lifetime prevalence of adolescent self-harm in England of 13.2% (Hawton *et al.*, 2002). The similar rates of prevalence in self-harm among young people among UK nations is not consistent with the data on those who complete suicide (O'Connor *et al.*, 2009). Suicide rates are twice as high in Scotland as they are in England; rates among children and adolescents under 18 years of age are more than three times as high in Scotland (Appleby *et al.*, 2008, Lessons for Mental Health Care in Scotland). Further data from the international CASE study and other similar school-based studies will help to elucidate the similarities and differences in the rates and characteristics of adolescent self-harm and help to inform interventions for vulnerable adolescents.

Trends   There was a substantial increase in the rates of self-harm during the 1960s and 1970s (Kapur & Gask, 2009). However, in their comprehensive review of suicide and suicidal behaviour, Nock and colleagues report that, internationally, the prevalence of suicidal behaviour appears to have remained relatively stable across time, with the most recent prevalence estimates similar to those reported in earlier studies (Nock, Borges, Bromet, Cha, *et al.*, 2008).

Interpreting rates of self-harm   Rates of self-harm are difficult to ascertain, largely because the relevant data are not comprehensively and systematically collected within individual countries or cross-nationally (Bille-Brahe *et al.*, 1995; Kapur & Appleby, 2008). Furthermore, where the data are collected comparison between locations is difficult for several reasons. First, there are often methodological differences in how (e.g., inclusion criteria), and where the data are collected (e.g., hospital-based studies, general population surveys/interviews). Second, there are cultural differences in how self-harming behaviour is viewed by the medical profession that affect how data are recorded. Third, register-based studies underestimate the prevalence of self-harming behaviour in the wider population, as not all episodes of self-harm require medical intervention or present to health services (Kapur & Appleby, 2008). Fourth, in population-based studies, surveys can elicit different information as a result of differences in data collection approaches (e.g., interview, self-reported) and question wording; response rates can also differ. However, both register- and population-based studies generate important data, which can inform clinical services and public health initiatives to reduce the prevalence of self-harm. In short, further cross-national studies, as well as those involving multiple sites within countries, are needed to give a comprehensive national and international view of the incidence and prevalence of self-harming behaviour.

Methods of self-harm

Self-harm comprises a variety of self-directed harmful behaviours. In the United Kingdom, the majority of hospital-treated self-harm presentations are accounted for by self-poisoning, with self-injury – mainly self-laceration– representing a minority (Duffy, 2009; Kapur & Gask, 2009). However, self-injury is the most common method of self-harm recorded in community studies of adolescent self-harm (Hawton & Rodham, 2006). Indeed, as outlined in the following section, it is possible that self-injury is a distinct behaviour, separate from self-harm and other suicidal behaviours (Duffy, 2009). The following section discusses these two behaviours separately.

Self-poisoning   Self-poisoning can be described as 'the self-exposure of an individual … to an amount of substance associated with the significant potential to cause harm' (Camidge, Wood, & Bateman, 2003, p. 56). Self-poisoning is one of the most common methods of self-harming behaviour: upwards of 80% of all hospital self-harm presentations are self-poisoning episodes (Hawton, Bergen, Casey, Simkin, Palmer, *et al.*, 2007). Previous research showed that there were in excess of 170,000 self-harm presentations to hospitals annually (Kapur, House, Creed, Feldman, Friedman, *et al.*, 1998). More recently, the rate of presentations to hospital following self-harm in England have been shown to vary between 285,000 and 460/100,000 population for males and 342,000 and 587/100,000 population for females (Hawton *et al.*, 2007). One of the most common means of self-poisoning in the United Kingdom is paracetamol ingestion, accounting for approximately 40% of all self-poisoning episodes (Kapur & Gask, 2009). Generally, the substances used in self-poisoning reflect ease of access or prescription patterns (Kapur & Gask, 2009; Prescott, Stratton, Freyer, Hall, & Le Jeune, 2009; Shahid, Khan, Khan, Jamal, Badshah, *et al.*, 2009). Agro-chemicals are most commonly used in developing countries and in rural areas, with organophosphates accounting for the majority of fatalities (e.g., Sri Lanka, Thailand, Taiwan) (Eddleston, 2000). In more urban areas of developing countries, medicines, particularly drugs acting on the central nervous system, are common (Eddleston, 2000).

Self-injury   Self-injury can be described as 'the intentional destruction of body tissue without suicidal intent and for purposes not socially sanctioned' (Klonsky & Muehlenkamp, 2007, p. 1045). The majority of self-injury episodes are lacerations, estimated to account for over 70% of self-injury episodes (Duffy, 2009; Prescott *et al.*, 2009). Less common methods of self-injury include burning, stabbing, and self-hitting (Duffy, 2009; Klonsky & Muehlenkamp, 2007). Cutting is a common method of self-injury in the United Kingdom (Lilley, Owens, Horrocks, House, Noble, *et al.*, 2008), although methods of self-injury differ cross-nationally.

Prevalence estimates of self-injurious behaviour are difficult to ascertain due to the secret nature of the behaviour (Duffy, 2009). However, studies have noted that 4% of adults report a history of self-injury (Klonsky & Muehlenkamp, 2007). Madge and colleagues (2008) found that the prevalence of self-injurious behaviour was higher among an international community sample of young people (Europe and Australia) when compared with the prevalence rates of hospital samples (Hawton, Fagg, Simkin, Bales, & Bond, 2000). Of all self-harm episodes in the previous year, 56% were self-lacerations, compared with 22% overdoses (Madge *et al.*, 2008).

Outcomes

Two outcomes following self-harm are of particular interest: non-fatal repetition and suicide.

Non-fatal repetition   Repetition of self-harm is not uncommon (Kapur, Cooper, King-Hele, Webb, Lawlor, *et al.*, 2006). Based on hospital-treated samples, the rate of repetition within one year of an episode is approximately 15%–16%, rising to between 20%–25% in the years thereafter (Owens, Horrocks, & House, 2002). Repetition often occurs within a short period of time. Much of the literature on the repetition of hospital-treated self-harm comes from the United Kingdom and Ireland, Nordic countries and the rest of Europe, with fewer studies from North America, Australia, and New Zealand (Owens, Horrocks, & House, 2002).

Factors associated with repetition of self-harm are numerous, including: demographic (e.g., female sex, younger age, non-married civil state); socio-economic (e.g., unemployment, low level of education/skill); substance misuse; psychological factors (e.g., hopelessness, hostility, impulsivity); previous suicide attempts; and psychiatric symptoms and history (Kapur *et al.*, 2006; Scoliers, Portzky, van Heeringen, & Audenaert, 2009). In a cross-national, school-based survey Madge and colleagues (2008) found there were no gender differences in repetition rates between adolescent males (53%) and adolescent females (55%). Generally, risk factors for repetition have poor predictive value and are, therefore, of limited usefulness (Kapur & Gask, 2009).

Fatal repetition of self-harm   In an international review of the literature on repetition of individuals who self-harmed and presented to hospital, Owens, Horrocks, and House (2002) found that approximately 2% of those who had self-harmed completed suicide at one-year follow-up. In follow-up studies of approximately nine years or more, the proportion who ended their own life increased to approximately 7%. The median one-year suicide rate was substantially lower in the United Kingdom than in other countries reviewed, suggesting geographical differences in outcome for self-harm, or differences in ascertainment rates of self-harm or suicide between countries (Owens, Horrocks, & House, 2002).

The risk of subsequent suicide appears to be elevated in those who self-injure compared with those who self-poison (Cooper *et al.*, 2005). Kapur *et al.* (2006) found that self-injurers were more likely to repeat than individuals using other methods of self-harm. Both studies included only episodes of self-injury which presented to hospital. Madge and colleagues (2008) found that previous self-harm (lifetime occurrence of self-harm) varied according to the method of self-harm used in the most recent episode. Self-cutting in the current episode was more likely to be associated with a past history of self-harm compared with self-poisoning.

Socio-demographic features of self-harm

Consistent with previous research, in a recent cross-national study of adults from 17 countries Nock, Borges, Bromet, Alonso, and colleagues (2008) reported that non-fatal suicidal behaviour was associated with female sex and low educational achievement. Furthermore, risk of suicide decreased substantially with increasing age. Recent findings from the CASE survey (Europe and Australia) also showed higher prevalence rates among females adolescents (Madge *et al.*, 2008) compared with males. With the exception of gender distributions for suicide and self-harm (i.e., suicidal behaviour more common among females; completed suicide more common among males), the socio-demographic characteristics of self-harm are consistent cross-nationally, and are broadly similar to those reported for suicide (see earlier sections in this chapter).

Cultural features of self-harm

As with suicide, the prevalence of self-harm varies by ethnic group. Bhui, McKenzie, and Rasul (2007) carried out a systematic literature review of studies investigating self-harm in UK ethnic minority groups. Important findings of that review included the higher rates of self-harm among young Asian women and apparently increasing rates of self-harm among young people of Caribbean origin. However, the prevalence of repetition was generally reported to be lower among adults from Caribbean and Asian origins compared with non-ethnic groups. Given the paucity of available evidence regarding the risk of self-harm in adolescents from different ethnic minority backgrounds, definitive conclusions cannot be drawn. In addition, those studies that have been published are not representative of all ethnic groups in the United Kingdom. Consequently, more research is required to elucidate further the specific features of self-harm in different ethnic minority groups internationally.

Temporal features

Self-harm presentations may vary by season, time of week, and time of day, but the research literature is less extensive than that on suicide, thereby curbing our ability to draw firm conclusions. Nonetheless, the WHO/EURO Multicentre Study on Parasuicide found broadly consistent temporal fluctuations across 13 European countries (Jessen, Jensen, Arensman, Bille-Brahe, Crepet, *et al.*, 1999). An examination of suicide attempts across public holidays (religious and non-religious) generally revealed a decrease in suicide attempts prior to and during holidays, with an increase following holidays. However, it is unclear how well these findings generalize to non-Christian holidays and national holidays in non-Western and developing countries. The majority of self-harm presentations to hospital generally occur outside normal working hours, with females more likely to present at the weekend (Gunnell, Bennewith, Peters, House, & Hawton, 2005).

Clinical features

Many of the clinical features of hospital-treated self-harm are similar to those of suicide. A psychiatric diagnosis may be common among self-harm patients, with some studies citing that as many as 90% of individuals who self-harm have an Axis 1 psychiatric disorder (Kapur & Appleby, 2008). In a recent systematic review of the self-harm literature, Fliege, Lee, Grimm, and Klapp (2009) reported that individuals who self-harm are heterogeneous diagnostically, presenting with personality disorders, affective disorders, substance abuse disorders, eating disorders, and schizophrenia. In a recent multinational study of the prevalence and risk factors for suicidal behaviour, Nock, Hwang, Sampson, Kessler, Angermeyer, and colleagues (2009) found a strong and consistent relationship between mental disorder and increased risk of suicidal behaviour, after controlling for socio-demographic and country variables. The strongest associations were found between suicide attempts and mood disorders and suicide attempts and impulse-control disorders. There were international variations in the association between suicidal behaviour and mental illness. Mood disorders were a stronger predictor of suicidal behaviour in high-income countries, whereas impulse-control disorders were a stronger predictor in low–middle-income countries.

Psychological traits associated with self-harming behaviour include poor coping and problem-solving skills, high levels of anxiety, impulsivity, aggression, and depression. The number of negative life events (e.g., sexual abuse) has been shown to be associated with self-harm, particularly in younger people (Fliege *et al.*, 2009).

Management of hospital-treated self-harm

Although there are national guidelines on the clinical management of general hospital self-harm in some countries (e.g., Australia, the United Kingdom), this is not the norm internationally. Nonetheless, there is some consensus both in the existing guidance and in individual studies that a robust assessment, particularly including a psychosocial component, is a prerequisite to effective management (Kapur, 2005; Olfson, Gameroff, Marcus, Greenberg, & Shaffer, 2005; Shahid *et al.*, 2009). It has been suggested that psychosocial assessments should include a review of both risk and needs (National Collaborating Centre for Mental Health, 2004). Given the poor predictive value of risk assessment (Kapur, 2005; Kapur & Appleby, 2008) there has been an increasing emphasis in the United Kingdom on the assessment of patient need in order to inform an individualized management plan. It is, however, unclear whether this change in emphasis is happening internationally. There appears to be substantial variation in the management of self-harm patients even within individual countries (Bennewith, Gunnell, Peters, Hawton, & House, 2004). A better understanding of the reasons underpinning variations in the management of self-harm nationally and internationally would be clinically useful. There is also a need for more evidence on the most effective ways of managing self-harm patients in different countries.

Conclusion

Despite variations in international rates and risk factors, it is clear that suicide and self-harm are major public health issues contributing to substantial morbidity and mortality worldwide. Perhaps one of the most consistent findings in the work to date is the association of mental illness with suicide and self-harm suicidal behaviour. However, despite the extensive epidemiological and clinical literature, there are still major gaps in our knowledge, as well as a relatively poor depth of understanding of the factors associated with suicidal behaviour. Better and more timely reporting of the rates of suicide and suicidal behaviour can only improve our understanding of these complex phenomena. More international research using robust methodologies to investigate suicidal behaviour in different populations is required. In particular, there is a dearth of research in, and published findings from, developing, low-income, and non-Western countries. Truly international research will help to inform local, national, and international approaches to suicide prevention.

Note

1   Countries were included if the final year of available data fell between 1998 and 2003. Different years of data were therefore examined for each country.

References

Ajdacic-Gross, V., Lauber, C., Bopp, M., Eich, D., Gostynki, M., Gutzwiller, F., Burns, T., & Rössler, W. (2008). Reduction in the suicide rate during Advent – A time series analysis. *Psychiatry Research, 157*, 139–146.

Ajdacic-Gross, V., Wang, J., Bopp, M., Eich, D., Rossler, W., & Gutzwiller, F. (2003). Are seasonalities in suicide dependent on suicide methods? A reappraisal. *Social Science and Medicine, 57*, 1173–1181.

Ajdacic-Gross, V., Weiss, M. G., Ring, M., Hepp, U., Bopp, M., Gutzwiller, F., & Rössler, W. (2008). Methods of suicide: International suicide patterns derived from the WHO mortality database. *Bulletin of the World Health Organization, 86*, 726–732.

Alcántara, C. & Gone, J. P. (2007). Reviewing suicide in Native American communities: Situating risk and protective factors within a transactional-ecological framework. *Death Studies, 31*, 457–477.

Andriessen, K. (2006). Do we need to be cautious in evaluating suicide statistics? *European Journal of Public Health, 16*, 445–447.

Appleby, L., Shaw, J., Kapur, N., Windfuhr, K., Ashton, A., Swinson, N., While, D., Lowe, R., Bickley, H., Flynn, S., Hunt, I. M., McDonnell, S., Pearson, A., Da Cruz, D., Rodway, C., Roscoe, A., Saini, P., Turnbull, P., Burns, J., Hadfield, K., & Stones, P. (2006). *Avoidable Deaths: Five-year report of the National Confidential Inquiry into Suicide and Homicide by People with Mental Illness*, available at www.manchester.ac.uk/nci, accessed 14 June 2010.

Appleby, L., Shaw, J., Kapur, N., Windfuhr, K., Ashton, A., Swinson, N., While, D., Lowe, R., Bickley, H., Flynn, S., Hunt, I. M., Pearson, A., Turnbull, P., Da Cruz, D., Rodway, C.,

Roscoe, A., Saini, P., Burns, J., Hadfield, K., & Stones, P. (2008). *Lessons for Mental Health Care in Scotland,* available at www.manchester.ac.uk/nci, accessed 14 June 2010.

Baldessarini, R. & Hennen, J. (2004). Genetics of suicide: An overview. *Harvard Review of Psychiatry, 12,* 1–13.

Barraclough, B., Bunch, J., Nelson, B., & Sainsbury, P. (1974). One hundred cases of suicide: clinical aspects. *British Journal of Psychiatry, 125,* 355–373.

Beck, A. T., Emery, G., & Greenberg, R. L. (1985). *Anxiety Disorders and Phobias: A cognitive perspective.* New York: Basic Books.

Bennewith, O., Gunnell, D., Peters, T. J., Hawton, K., & House, A. (2004). Variations in the hospital management of self-harm in adults in England: An observational study. *British Medical Journal, 328,* 1108–1109.

Berk, M., Dodd, S., & Henry, M. (2006). The effect of macroeconomic variables in suicide. *Psychological Medicine, 36,* 181–189.

Bertolote, J. M., & Fleischmann, A. (2002). Suicide and psychiatric diagnosis: A worldwide perspective. *World Psychiatry, 1,* 181–185.

Bertolote, J. M., Fleischmann, A., De Leo, D., Bolhari, J., Botega, N., De Silva, D., Huong, H. T. T., Phillips, M., Schlebusch, L., Värnik, L., Vijayakumar, L., & Wasserman, D. (2005). Suicide attempts, plans, and ideation in culturally diverse sites: the WHO SUPRE-MISS community survey. *Psychological Medicine, 35,* 1457–1465.

Bhui, K. S. & McKenzie, K. (2008). Rates and risk factors by ethnic group for suicides within a year of contact with mental health services in England and Wales. *Psychiatric Services, 59,* 414–420.

Biddle, L., Brock, A., Brookes, S. T., & Gunnell, D. (2008). Suicide rates in young men in England and Wales in the 21st century: time trend study. *British Medical Journal, 336,* 539–542.

Bille-Brahe, U., Schmidtke, A., Kerkhof, A. J. F. M., De Leo, D., Lönnqvist, J., Platt, S., & Sampaio Faria, J. (1995). Background and introduction to the WHO/EURO Multicentre Study on Parasuicide. *Crisis, 16,* 72–84.

Burvill, P. W. (1998). Migrant suicide rates in Australia and in country of birth. *Psychological Medicine, 28,* 201–208.

Camidge, D. R., Wood, R. J., & Bateman, D. N. (2003). The epidemiology of self-poisoning. *British Journal of Clinical Pharmacology, 56,* 613–619.

Carley, S. & Hamilton, M. (2004). Suicide at Christmas. *Emergency Medicine Journal, 21,* 716–717.

Cavanagh, J. T. O., Carson, A. J., Sharpe, M., & Lawrie S. M. (2003). Psychological autopsy studies of suicide: A systematic review, *Psychological Medicine, 33,* 395–405.

Chew, K. S. Y. & McCleary, R. (1995). The spring peak in suicide: A cross-national analysis. *Social Science and Medicine, 40,* 223–230.

Cooper, J., Husain, N., Webb, R., Waheed, W., Kapur, N., Guthrie, E., & Appleby, L. (2006). Self-harm in the UK. *Social Psychiatry and Psychiatric Epidemiology, 41,* 782–788.

Cooper, J., Kapur, N., Webb, R., Lawlor, M., Guthrie, E., Mackway-Jones, K., & Appleby, L. (2005). Suicide after deliberate self-harm: A 4-year cohort study. *American Journal of Psychiatry, 162,* 297–303.

Corcoran, P., Arensman, E., & O'Mahony, D. (2006). Suicide and other external-cause mortality statistics in Ireland. *Crisis, 27,* 130–134.

Crane, C., Barnhofer, T., & Williams, J. M. G. (2007). Reflection, brooding, and suicidality: A preliminary study of different types of rumination individuals with a history of major depression. *British Journal of Clinical Psychology, 46,* 497–504.

De Leo, D. & Heller, T. S. (2004). Who are the kids who self-harm? An Australian self-report school survey. *Medical Journal of Australia, 181*, 140–144.

De Leo, D., Milner, A., & Xiangdong, W. (2009). Suicidal behavior in the Western Pacific region: Characteristics and trends. *Suicide and Life-Threatening Behavior, 39*, 72–81.

Department of Health (2002). available at http://www.dh.gov.uk/en/Publicationsandstatistics/ Lettersandcirculars/Estatesalerts/DH_4122863, accessed 15 September 2009.

Duarté-Vélez, Y. M. & Bernal, G. (2007). Suicide behavior among Latino and Latina adolescents: Conceptual and methodological issues. *Death Studies, 31*, 435–455.

Duffy, D. F. (2009). Self-injury. *Psychiatry, 5*, 263–265.

Dumais, A., Lesage, A. D., Alda, M., Rouleau, G., Dumont, M., Chawky, N., Roy, M., Mann, J. J., Benkelfat, C., & Turecki, G. (2005). Risk factors for suicide completion in major depression: A case-control study of impulsive and aggressive behaviours in men. *American Journal of Psychiatry, 162*, 2116–2124.

Durkheim E. (1951 [1897]). *Suicide: study in sociology*. New York: Free Press.

Eddleston, M. (2000). Patterns and problems of deliberate self-poisoning in the developing world. *Quarterly Journal of Medicine, 93*, 715–731.

Eddleston, M. & Phillips, M. R. (2004). Self poisoning with pesticides. *British Medical Journal, 328*, 42–44.

Ellis, T. E. & Rutherford, B. (2008). Cognition and suicide: Two decades of progress. *International Journal of Cognitive Therapy, 1*, 47–68.

Else, I. R. N., Andrade, N. N., & Nahulu, L. B. (2007). Suicide and suicidal-related behaviors among Indigenous Pacific Islanders in the United States. *Death Studies, 31*, 479–501.

Enticott, P. G. & Ogloff, J. R. P. (2006). Elucidation of impulsivity. *Australian Psychologist, 41*, 3–14.

Ferrada-Noli, M. (1997). A cross-cultural breakdown of Swedish suicide. *Acta Psychiatrica Scandinavica, 96*, 108–116.

Fliege, H., Lee, J. R., Grimm, A., & Klapp, B. F. (2009). Risk factors and correlates of deliberate self-harm behaviour: A systematic review. *Journal of Psychosomatic Research, 66*, 477–493.

Gould, M. S., Greenberg, T., & Velting, D. (2003). Youth suicide risk and preventive interventions: A review of the past 10 years. *Journal of the American Academy of Child and Adolescent Psychiatry, 42*, 386–405.

Grøholt, B., & Ekeberg, Ø. (2003). Suicide in young people under 15 years: Problems of classification. *Nordic Journal of Psychiatry, 57*, 411–417.

Gunnell, D., Bennewith, O., Peters, T. J., House, A., & Hawton, K. (2005). The epidemiology and management of self-harm amongst adults in England. *Journal of Public Health, 27*, 67–73.

Hakko, H., Räsänen, P., Tiihonen, J., & Nieminen, P. (2002). Use of statistical techniques in studies of suicide seasonality, 1970–1997. *Suicide and Life Threatening Behavior, 32*, 191–208.

Harris, E. C. & Barraclough, B. (1997). Suicide as an outcome for mental disorders. A meta-analysis. *British Journal of Psychiatry, 170*, 205–228.

Hawton, K., Bergen, H., Casey, D., Simkin, S., Palmer, B., Cooper, J., Kapur, N., Horrocks, J., House, A., Lilley, R., Noble, R., & Owens, D. (2007). Self-harm in England: A tale of three cities. *Social Psychiatry and Psychiatric Epidemiology, 42*, 513–521.

Hawton, K., Fagg, J., Simkin, S., Bales, E., & Bond, A. (2000). Deliberate self-harm in adolescents in Oxford, 1985–1995. *Journal of Adolescence, 23*, 47–55.

Hawton, K. & Rodham, K. (2006). *By Their Own Young Hand: Deliberate self-harm and suicidal ideas in adolescents*. London: Jessica Kingsley.

Hawton, K., Rodham, K., Evans, E., & Weatherall, R. (2002). Deliberate self-harm in adolescents: Self-report survey in schools in England. *British Medical Journal, 325*, 1207–1211.

Hawton, K. & van Heeringen, K. (2009). Suicide. *The Lancet, 373*, 1372–1381.

Heikkinen, M. E., Isometsa, E. T., Marttunen, M. J., Aro, H. M., & Lönqvist, J. K. (1995). Social factors in suicide. *British Journal of Psychiatry, 167*, 747–753.

Hjern, A. & Allebeck, P. (2002). Suicide in first- and second-generation immigrants in Sweden. A comparative study. *Social Psychiatry and Psychiatric Epidemiology, 37*, 423–429.

Høyer, G. & Lund, E. (1993). Suicide among women related to number of children in marriage. *Archives of General Psychiatry, 50*, 134–137.

Jessen, G. & Jenson, B.F. (1999). Postponed suicide death? Suicides around birthdays and major public holidays. *Suicide and Life Threatening Behavior, 29*, 272–283.

Jessen, G., Jensen, B. F., Arensman, E., Bille-Brahe, U., Crepet, P., DeLe, D., Hawton, K., Haring, C., Hjelmeland, H., Ostamo, M. K., Salander-Renberg, E., Schmidtke, A., Temesvary, B., & Wasserman, D. (1999). Attempted suicide and major public holidays in Europe: Findings from the WHO/EURO Multicentre Study on Parasuicide. *Acta Psychiatrica Scandinavica, 99*, 412–418.

Joiner, T. E., Pettit, J. W., Walker, R. L., Voelz, Z. R., Cruz, J., Rudd, M. D., & Lester, D. (2002). Perceived burdensomeness and suicidality: Two studies on the suicide notes of those attempting and those completing suicide. *Journal of Social and Clinical Psychology, 21*, 531–545.

Kapur, N. (2005). Management of self-harm in adults: Which way now? British *Journal of Psychiatry, 187*, 497–499.

Kapur, N. (2009). Suicide in the mentally ill. *Psychiatry, 8*, 257–260.

Kapur, N. & Appleby, L. (2008). Suicide and self-harm. In R. Murray, K. Kendelr, P. McGuffin, S. Wessely, & D. Castle (Eds.), *Essential Psychiatry*, 4th ed. (pp. 451–475). Cambridge: Cambridge University Press.

Kapur, N., Cooper, J., King-Hele, S., Webb, R., Lawlor, M., Rodway, C., & Appleby, L. (2006). The repetition of suicidal behaviour: A multicentre cohort study. *Journal of Clinical Psychiatry, 67*, 1599–1609.

Kapur, N. & Gask, L. (2009). Introduction to suicide and self-harm. *Psychiatry, 8*, 233–236.

Kapur, N., House, A., Creed, F., Feldman, E., Friedman, T., & Guthrie, E. (1998). Management of deliberate self-poisoning in adults in four teaching hospitals: Descriptive study. *British Medical Journal, 316*, 831–832.

Khan, F. & Waheed, W. (2009). Suicide and self-harm in South Asian immigrants. *Psychiatry, 8*, 261–264.

Klonsky, E. D. & Muehlenkamp, J. J. (2007). Self-injury: A research review for the practitioner. *Journal of Clinical Psychology, 63*, 1045–1056.

Kreitman, N. (1976). Coal-gas story – United Kingdom suicide rates, 1960–71. *British Journal of Preventive & Social Medicine, 30*, 86–93.

Largey, M., Kelly, B., & Stevenson, M. (2009). A study of suicide rates in Northern Ireland 1984–2002. *Ulster Medical Journal, 78*(1), 16–20.

Leong, F. T. L., Leach, M. M., Yeh, C., & Chou, E. (2007). Suicide among Asian Americans: What do we know? What do we need to know? *Death Studies, 31*, 417–434.

Leshem, R. & Glicksohn, J. (2007). The construct of impulsivity revisited. *Personality and Individual Differences, 43*, 681–691.

Lester, D. (2002). The 'Troubles' in Northern Ireland and suicide. *Psychological Reports, 90*, 722.

Lester, D. (2006). Suicide and Islam. *Archives of Suicide Research, 10*, 77–97.

Lilley, R., Owens, D., Horrocks, J., House, A., Noble, R., Bergen, H., Hawton, K., Casey, D., Simkin, S., Murphy, E., Cooper, J., & Kapur, N. (2008). Hospital care and repetition following self-harm: Multicentre comparison of self-poisoning and self-injury. *British Journal of Psychiatry, 192*, 440–445.

Liu, K. Y. (2009). Suicide rates in the world: 1950–2004. *Suicide and Life Threatening Behavior, 39*, 204–213.

Liu, K. Y., Beautrais, A., Caine, E., Chan, K., Chao, A., Conwell, Y., Law, C., Lee, D., Li, P. C., & Yip, P. (2007). Charcoal-burning suicides in Hong Kong and urban Taiwan: An illustration of the impact of a novel suicide method on overall regional rates. *Journal of Epidemiology and Community Health, 61*, 248–253.

Lorant, V., Kunst, A. E., Huisman, M., Costa, G., & Mackenbach, J. (2005). Socio-economic inequalities in suicide: A European comparative study. *British Journal of Psychiatry, 187*, 49–54.

Lu, Y. (2008). A test of the 'healthy migrant hypothesis': A longitudinal analysis of health selectivity of internal migration in Indonesia. *Social Science and Medicine, 67*, 1331–1339.

Luoma, J. B., Martin, C. E., & Pearson, J. L. (2002). Contact with mental health and primary care providers before suicide: A review of the evidence. *American Journal of Psychiatry, 159*, 909–916.

Madge, N., Hewitt, A., Hawton, K., De Wilde, E. J., Corcoran, P., Fekete, S., van Heeringen, K., De Leo, D., & Ystgaard, M. (2008). Deliberate self-harm within an international community sample of young people: Comparative findings from the Child and Adolescent Self-harm in Europe (CASE) Study. *Journal of Child Psychology and Psychiatry, 49*, 667–677.

Mann, J. J. (2002). A current perspective of suicide and attempted suicide. *Annals of Internal Medicine, 136*, 302–311.

Mann, J. J., Apter, A., Bertolote, J., Beautrais, A., Currier, D., Haas, A., Hegerl, U., Lonnqvist, J., Malone, K., Marusic, A., Mehlum, L., Patton, G., Phillips, M., Rutz, W., Rihmer, Z., Schmidtke, A., Shaffer, D., Silverman, M., Yoshitomo, T., Varnik, A., Wasserman, D., Yip, P., & Hendin, H. (2005). Suicide prevention strategies: A systematic review. *Journal of the American Medical Association, 294*, 2064–2074.

Maris, R. W. (2002). Suicide. *The Lancet, 360*, 319–326.

Marshall, J. R. (1981). Political-integration and the effect of war on suicide – United States, 1933–76. *Social Forces, 59*, 771–785.

McKenzie, K., Bui, K., Nanchahal, K., & Blizard, B. (2008). Suicide rates in people of South Asian origin in England and Wales: 1993–2003. *British Journal of Psychiatry, 193*, 406–409.

Middleton, N., Whitley, E., Frankel, S., Dorling, D., Sterne, J., & Gunnell, D. (2004). Suicide risk in small areas in England and Wales, 1991–1993. *Social Psychiatry and Psychiatric Epidemiology, 39*, 45–52.

Mohanty, S., Sahu, G., Mohanty, M. K., & Patnaik, M. (2007). Suicide in India – A four year retrospective study. *Journal of Forensic and Legal Medicine, 14*, 185–189.

Morrison, R. & O'Connor, R. C. (2008). A systematic review of the relationship between rumination and suicidality. *Suicide and Life Threatening Behavior, 38*, 523–538.

Mościcki, E. K. (1995). Epidemiology of suicide. *International Psychogeriatics, 7*, 137–148.

Nada-Raja, S., Skegg, K., Langley, J., Morrison, D., & Sowerby, P. (2004). Self-harmful behaviors in a population-based sample of young adults. *Suicide and Life Threatening Behavior, 34*, 177–186.

National Collaborating Centre for Mental Health (2004). Self-harm: The short-term physical and psychological management and secondary prevention of self-harm in primary and secondary care. Clinical Guideline 16. London: Gaskell & British Psychological Society.

Nock, M. K., Borges, G., Bromet, E. J., Alonso, J., Angermeyer, M., Beautrais, A., Bruffaerts, R., Chiu, W. T., de Girolamo, G., Gluzman, S., de Graaf, R., Gureje, O., Haro, J. M., Huang, Y., Karam, E., Kessler, R. C., Lepine, J. P., Levinson, D., Medina-Mora, M. E., Ono, Y., Posada-Villa, J., & William, D. (2008). Cross-national prevalence and risk factors for suicidal ideation, plans and attempts. *British Journal of Psychiatry, 192*, 98–105.

Nock, M. K., Borges, G., Bromet, E. J., Cha, C. B., Kessler, R. C., & Lee, S. (2008). Suicide and suicidal behaviour. *Epidemiologic Reviews, 30*, 133–154.

Nock, M. K., Hwang, I., Sampson, N., Kessler, R. C., Angermeyer, M., Beautrais, A., Borges, G., Bromet, E., Bruffaerts, R., de Girolamo, G., de Graaf, R., Florescu, S., Gureje, O., Haro, J. M., Hu, C., Huang, Y., Karam, E. G., Kawakami, N., Kovess, V., Levinson, D., Posada-Villa, J., Sagar, R., Tomor, T., Viana, M. C., & Williams, D. R. (2009). Cross-national analysis of the associations among mental disorders and suicidal behaviour: Findings from the WHO World Mental Health Surveys. *Public library of Science Medicine, 6*, 1–17.

O'Carroll, W., Berman, A. L., Maris, R. W., Moscicki, E. K., Tanney, B. L., & Silverman, M. M. (1996). Beyond the Tower of Babel: A nomenclature for suicidology. *Suicide and Life Threatening Behavior, 26*, 237–252.

O'Connor, R. C. (2007). The relations between perfectionism and suicidality: A systematic review. *Suicide and Life-Threatening Behavior, 37*, 698–714.

O'Connor, R. C. & Cassidy, C. (2007). Predicting hopelessness: The interaction between optimism/ pessimism and specific future expectancies. *Cognition and Emotion, 21*, 596–613.

O'Connor, R. C., Rasmussen, S., Mile, J., & Hawton, K. (2009). Self-harm in adolescents: Self-report survey in schools in Scotland. *British Journal of Psychiatry, 194*, 68–72.

Olfson, M., Gameroff, M., Marcus, S. C., Greenberg, T., & Shaffer, D. (2005). Emergency treatment of young people following deliberate self-harm. *Archives of General Psychiatry, 62*, 1122–1128.

O'Reilly, D., Rosato, M., Connolly, S., & Cardwell, C. (2008). Area factors and suicide: 5-year follow-up of the Northern Ireland population. *British Journal of Psychiatry, 192*, 106–111.

Owens, D., Horrocks, J., & House, A. (2002). Fatal and non-fatal repetition of self-harm: Systematic review. *British Journal of Psychiatry, 181*, 193–199.

Page, A., Morrell, S., & Taylor, R. (2002). Suicide and political regime in New South Wales and Australia during the 20th century. *Journal of Epidemiology and Community Health, 56*, 766–772.

Phillips, M. R., Yang, G., Zhang, Y., Wang, L., Ji, H., & Zhou, M. (2002). Risk factors for suicide in China: A national case-control psychological autopsy study. *The Lancet, 360*, 1728–1736.

Platt, S. & Hawton, K. (2000). Suicidal behaviour and the labour market. In K. Hawton & K. van Heeringen (Eds.), *The International Handbook of Suicide and Attempted Suicide* (pp. 309–384). Chichester: John Wiley & Sons, Ltd.

Portzky, G., De Wilde, E. J., & van Heeringen, K. (2008). Deliberate self-harm in young people: Differences in prevalence and risk factors between the Netherlands and Belgium. *European Child and Adolescent Psychiatry, 17*, 179–186.

Prescott, K., Stratton, R., Freyer, A., Hall, I., & Le Jeune, I. (2009). Detailed analysis of self-poisoning episodes presenting to a large regional teaching hospital in the UK. *British Journal of Clinical Pharmacology, 68*, 260–266.

Qin, P., Agerbo, E., & Mortensen, P. B. (2003). Suicide risk in relation to socioeconomic, demographic, psychiatric, and familial factors: A national register-based study of all suicides in Denmark, 1981–1997. *American Journal of Psychiatry, 160*, 765–772.

Reinecke, M. A. (2006). Problem solving: A conceptual approach to suicidability and psychotherapy. In T. Ellis (Ed.), *Cognition and Suicide: Theory, research, and therapy* (pp. 173–192). Washington, DC: American Psychological Association.

Reutfors, J., Ösby, U., Ekbom, A., Nordström, P., Jokinen, J., & Papadopoulos, F. C. (2009). Seasonality of suicide in Sweden: Relationship with psychiatric disorder. *Journal of Affective Disorders, 119*, 59–65.

Roy, A., Rylander, G., Forslund, K., Asberg, M., Mazzanti, C. M., Goldman, D., & Nielsen, D. A. (2001). Excess tryptophan hydroxylase 17 779C allele in surviving cotwins of monozygotic twin suicide victims. *Neuropsychobiology, 43*, 233–236.

Salib, E. & Agnew, N. (2005). Suicide and undetermined death by drowning. *International Journal of Psychiatry in Clinical Practice, 9*, 107–115.

Schmidtke, A., Bille-Brahe, U., De Leo, D., Kerkhof, A., Bjerke, T., Crepet, P., Haring, C., Hawton, K., Lonnqvist, J., Michel, K., Pommereau, X., Querejeta, I., Phillipe, I., Salander-Renberg, E., Temesvary, B., Wasserman, D., Fricke, S., Weinacker, B., & Sampaio Faria, J. G. (1996). Attempted suicide in Europe: Rates, trends and sociodemographic characteristics of suicide attempters during the period 1989–1992. Results of the WHO/EURO multicentre study on parasuicide. *Acta Psychiatrica Scandinavica, 93*, 327–338.

Schmidtke, A., Sell, R., & Loehr, C. (2008). Epidemiology of suicide in older persons. *Zeitschrift für Gerontologie and Geriatrie, 4*, 3–13.

Schmidtke, A., Weinacker, B., Loehr, C., Bille-Brahe, U., De Leo, D., Kerkhof, A., Apter, A., Batt, A., Crepet, P., Fekete, S., Grad, O., Haring, C., Hawton, K., van Heeringen, K., Hjelmeland, H., Kelleher, M., Loennquist, J., Michel, K., Pommereau, X., Querejeta, I., Philippe, A., Salander-Renberg, E., Sayil, I., Temesvary, B., Vaernik, A., Wasserman, D., & Rutz, W. (2004). Suicide and suicide attempts in Europe: An overview. In A. Schmidtke, U. Bille-Brahe, D. De Leo, & A. Kerkof (Eds.), *Suicidal Behaviour in Europe: Results from the WHO/EURO Multicentre Study on Suicidal Behaviour* (pp. 15–28). Gottingen: Hogrefe & Huber.

Scoliers, G., Portzky, G., van Heeringen, K., & Audenaert, K. (2009). Sociodemographic and psychopathological risk factors for repetition of attempted suicide: A 5-year follow-up study. *Archives of Suicide Research, 13*, 201–213.

Selakovic-Bursic, S., Haramic, E., & Leenaars, A. A. (2006). The Balkan Piedmont: Male suicide rates pre-war, wartime, and post-war in Serbia and Montenegro. *Archives of Suicide Research, 10*, 225–238.

Shah, A., Bhat, R., MacKenzie, S., & Koen, C. (2008). Elderly suicide rates: Cross-national comparisons of trends over a 10-year period. *International Psychogeriatrics 20*, 673–686.

Shahid, M., Khan, M. M., Khan, S., Jamal, Y., Badshah, A., & Rehmani, R. (2009). Deliberate self-harm in the emergency department: Experience from Karachi, Pakistan. *Crisis, 31*, 85–89.

Sharma, B. R., Gupta, M., Sharma, A. K., Sharma, S., Gupta, H., Relhan, N., & Singh, H. (2007). Suicide in Northern India: Comparison of trends and review of literature. *Journal of Forensic and Legal Medicine, 14*, 318–326.

Skala, J. A. & Freedland, K. E. (2004). Death takes a raincheck. *Psychosomatic Medicine, 66*, 382–386.

Skegg, K. (2005). Self-harm. *The Lancet, 366*, 1471–1483.

Soni Raleigh, V. & Balarajan, R. (1992). Suicide levels and trends among immigrants in England and Wales. *Health Trends, 24*, 91–94.

Stack, S. (1982). Suicide: A decade review of the sociological literature. *Deviant Behavior, 4*, 41–66.

Stack, S. (2000a). Suicide: A 15-year review of the sociological literature. Part 1: Cultural and economic factors. *Suicide and Life Threatening Behavior, 30*, 145–162.

Stack, S. (2000b). Suicide: A 15-year review of the sociological literature. Part II: Modernization and social integration perspectives. *Suicide and Life Threatening Behavior, 30*, 163–172.

Stack, S. (2002). Political regime and suicide: Some relevant variables to be considered. *Journal of Epidemiology and Community Health, 56*, 727.

Stark, C., Stockton, D., & Henderson, R. (2008). Reduction in young male suicide in Scotland. *BMC Public Health, 8*, 80.

Steele, M. M. & Doey, T. (2007). Suicidal behaviour in children and adolescents. Part 1: Etiology and risk factors. *Canadian Journal of Psychiatry, 52*, 21S–33S.

Stuckler, D., Basu, S., Suhrcke, M., Coutts, A., & McKee, M. (2009). The public health effect of economic crisis and alternative policy responses in Europe: An empirical analysis. *The Lancet, 374*, 315–323.

Tishler, C. L. & Reiss, N. S. (2009). Inpatient suicide: Preventing a common sentinel event. *General Hospital Psychiatry, 31*, 103–109.

Turvey, C., Stromquist, A., Kelly, K., Zwerling, C., & Merchant, J. (2002). Financial loss and suicidal ideation in a rural community sample. *Acta Scandinavica Psychiatrica, 106*, 373–380.

Utsey, S. O., Hook, J. N., & Stanard, P. (2007). A re-examination of cultural factors that mitigate risk and promote resilience in relation to African American Suicide: A review of the literature and recommendations for future research. *Death Studies, 31*, 399–416.

van Tubergen, F. & Ultee, W. (2006). Political integration, war and suicide. *International Sociology, 21*, 221–236.

Värnik, A., Kõlves, K., Allik, J., Arensman, E., Aromaa, E., van Audenhove, C., Bouleau, J. H., van der Feltz-Corenlis, C. M., Giupponi, G., Gusmão, R., Kopp, M., Marusic, A., Maxwell, M., Óskarsson, H., Palmer, A., Pull, C., Realo, A., Eisch, T., Schmidtke, A., Sola, V. P., Wittenburg, L., & Hegerl, U. (2009). Gender issues in suicide rates, trends and methods among youths aged 15–24 in 15 European countries. *Journal of Affective Disorders, 113*, 216–226.

Vijayakumar, L. (2004). Suicide prevention: The urgent need in developing countries. *World Psychiatry, 3*, 158–159.

Voracek, M. & Loibl, L. M. (2007). Genetics of suicide: A systematic review of twin studies. *Wiener Klinische Wochenschrift, 119*, 463–475.

Voracek, M. & Loibl, L. M. (2008). Consistency of immigrant and country-of-birth suicide rates: A meta-analysis. *Acta Psychiatrica Scandinavica, 118*, 259–271.

Wadsworth, T. & Kubrin, C.E. (2007). Hispanic suicide in US metropolitan areas: Examining the effects of immigration, assimilation, affluence, and disadvantage. *American Journal of Sociology, 112*, 1848–1885.

Wasserman, D., Cheng, Q., & Jian, G. X. (2005). Global suicide rates among young people aged 15–19. *World Psychiatry, 4*, 114–120.

Weissman, M. M., Bland, R. C., Canino, G. J., Greenwald, S., Hwu, H. G., Joyce, P. R., Karam, E. G., Lee, C. K., Lellouch, J., Lepine, J. P., Newman, S. C., Rubio-Stipec, M., Wells, J. E., Wickramaratne, P. J., Wittchen, H. U., & Yeh, E. K. (1999). Prevalence of suicide ideation and suicide attempts in nine countries. *Psychological Medicine, 29*, 9–17.

Welch, S. S. (2001). A review of the literature on the epidemiology of parasuicide in the general population. *Psychiatric Services, 52*, 368–375.

Westman, J., Martelin, T., Härkänen, T., Koskinen, S., & Sundquist, K. (2008). Migration and self-rates health: A comparison between Finns living in Sweden and Finns living in Finland. *Scandinavian Journal of Public Health, 36*, 698–705.

Williams, J. M. G., Barnhofer, T., Crane, C., & Duggan, D. S. (2006). The role of overgeneral memory in suicidality. In T. Ellis (Ed.), *Cognition and Suicide: Theory, research, and therapy* (pp. 173–192). Washington, DC: American Psychological Association.

Windfuhr, K., While, D., Hunt, I., Turnbull, P., Lowe, R., Burns, J., Swinson, N., Shaw, J., Appleby, L., Kapur, N., & the National Confidential Inquiry into Suicide and Homicide by People with Mental Illness (2008). Suicide in juveniles and adolescents in the United Kingdom. *Journal of Child Psychology and Psychiatry, 49*, 1155–1165.

World Health Organisation (WHO). available at http://www.who.int/mental_health/prevention/suicide_rates/en/index.html, accessed 21 April 2009.

Wyder, M., Ward, P., & De Leo, D. (2009). Separation as a suicide risk factor. *Journal of Affective Disorders, 116*, 208–213.

Yeh, J. Y., Xirasagar, S., Liu, T. C., Li, C. Y., & Lin, H. C. (2008). Does marital status predict the odds of suicidal death in Taiwan? A seven-year population based study. *Suicide and Life Threatening Behavior, 38*, 302–310.

Zahl, D. L. & Hawton, K. (2004). Repetition of deliberate self-harm and subsequent suicide risk: Long-term follow-up study of 11,583 patients. *British Journal of Psychiatry, 185*, 70–75.

Zouk, H., Tousignant, M. Seguin, M., Lesage, A., & Turecki, G. (2006). Characterization of impulsivity in suicide completers: Clinical, behavioural and psychosocial dimensions. *Journal of Affective Disorders, 92*, 195–204.

CHAPTER THREE

Depression and Suicidal Behaviour

Zoltán Rihmer

Abstract

Although suicidal behaviour (suicide and suicide attempt) is a complex, multi-causal human behaviour, associated with several risk and protective factors, an untreated major depressive episode is its most important risk factor. Up to 15% of patients with major mood disorders die by suicide and about half of them make at least one suicide attempt during their lifetime. Suicidal behaviour in mood disorder patients occurs almost exclusively during an acute, severe, major depressive episode, less frequently during a mixed affective episode or in dysphoric mania, and very rarely during euphoric mania, hypomania, and euthymia. This suggests that suicidal behaviour in patients with major mood disorders is a state- and severity-dependent phenomenon. However, since the majority of mood disorder patients never take their own lives (and up to 50% of them never attempt to), other risk factors should also play a significant contributory role. This chapter summarizes the clinically detectable suicide risk and protective factors in patients with major mood disorders and highlights effective suicide prevention strategies. Illness- and personality-related suicide risk factors, as well as specific data on family and personal history, can help clinicians in the identification of mood disorder patients at high suicidal risk. Appropriate acute and long-term treatment of depressive disorders, including both pharmacological and non-pharmacological methods, markedly reduces the risk of completed and attempted suicide, even in this high-risk population.

International Handbook of Suicide Prevention: Research, Policy and Practice, First Edition.
Edited by Rory C. O'Connor, Stephen Platt, Jacki Gordon.
© 2011 John Wiley & Sons, Ltd. Published 2011 by John Wiley & Sons, Ltd.

Introduction

Major mood disorders (both unipolar major depression and bipolar disorder) are associated with a substantial burden of illness-related health and economic problems. Given the 12%–17% lifetime prevalence of unipolar major depressive episode and 1.3%–5% lifetime prevalence of bipolar I and bipolar II disorders (Rihmer & Angst, 2005), they are among the most frequent and also the potentially most life-threatening psychiatric illnesses (Angst, Angst, Gerber-Werder, & Gamma, 2005; Goodwin & Jamison, 2007; Hawton, Sutton, Haw, Sinclair, & Harris, 2005; Rihmer, 2005). In spite of the great clinical and public health significance of major mood disorders, they are still under-referred, under-diagnosed, and under-treated (Dunner, 2003; Rihmer & Angst, 2005). This is particularly true for those who die by suicide and attempters: more than 90% of them have at least one Axis I (mostly untreated) major mental disorder, most frequently major depressive episode (56%–87%), substance use disorders (26%–55%) and schizophrenia (6%–13%). Comorbid anxiety and personality disorders are also frequently present, but they are rare as principal (or sole) diagnoses (Balázs, Lecrubier, Csiszér, Koszták, & Bitter, 2003; Goodwin & Jamison, 2007; Hawton *et al.*, 2005; Rihmer, 2007; Rihmer, Benazzi, & Gonda, 2007; Rihmer, Rózsa, Rihmer, Gonda, Akiskal, *et al.*, 2009; Tondo, Isacsson, & Baldessarini, 2003). Although suicidal behaviour (completed suicide and suicide attempt) is very rare in the absence of current major mental disorders, it is not the linear/direct consequence of them. It is a very complex and multi-causal human behaviour, involving some personality characteristics, as well as several psychosocial and cultural components that play an important role, not only in the development of suicidal processes but also in the recognition and management of suicidal risk.

Although the ratio of attempted to completed suicide in the general population is about 20:1, it is much lower (5–10:1) among patients with major mood disorders, indicating that these patients use more lethal (or more violent) suicide methods (Goodwin & Jamison, 2007; Tondo, Isacsson, & Baldessarini, 2003; Tondo, Lepri, & Baldessarini, 2007). Completed suicide and suicide attempt are two different, but greatly overlapping, phenomena: more than one-third of those who complete suicide have attempted suicide at least once previously, and the first attempt (even if the method used is non-violent or non-lethal) significantly increases the risk of future completed suicide. This is partly due to the fact that repeat suicide attempters frequently switch their method from non-violent to violent or from non-lethal to lethal (Goodwin & Jamison, 2007; Rihmer, 2007; Rihmer *et al.*, 2007).

As the risk factors for attempted and completed suicide in mood disorder patients show only a few differences and prior suicide attempt is the most powerful predictor of completed suicide in this patient population (Goodwin & Jamison, 2007; Hawton *et al.*, 2005; Rihmer 2007; Simon, Hunkeler, Fireman, Lee, & Savarino, 2007), the risk factors for attempted and completed suicide are not discussed separately in this chapter. For the present purposes, this chapter summarizes the most relevant and clinically modifiable suicide risk and protective factors in depressive disorders and highlights the most effective preventive strategies. It will focus on completed suicide (an act of deliberately taking one's life) and suicide attempt (a self-injurious act with intent to end one's life), both of which are commonly referred to as 'suicidal behaviour', but it will not cover deliberate self-harm (defined as an intentional injuring of one's body without apparent suicidal intent).

Suicidal Behaviour in Depressive Patients

Harris and Barraclough (1997) analysed separately the risk of completed suicide in patients with an index diagnosis of unipolar major depression or bipolar disorder (37 reports and more than 11,000 patients). Based on long-term cohort studies (with some patients followed for many decades) they report standardized mortality ratios (SMRs) for completed suicide of about 20-fold for patients with index diagnoses of unipolar major depression and 15-fold for patients with bipolar disorders.

A recent meta-analysis of 28 reports, published between 1945 and 2001 (including only patients with an index diagnosis of bipolar disorder without long-term lithium treatment) by Tondo, Isacsson, and Baldessarini (2003) found that during an average 10 years of follow-up the SMR for completed suicide in bipolar patients was as high as 22 (15 for males and 21 for females). These authors also calculated that suicide rates in bipolar disorder patients average 0.4% a year, which is more than 25 times higher than the same rate in the general population.

In a 40–44-year prospective follow-up study of 406 formerly hospitalized (186 unipolar and 220 bipolar) major mood disorder patients, in which the unipolar–bipolar conversion was carefully considered during the follow-up, Angst *et al.* (2005) found that 14.5% of unipolar and 8.2% of bipolar (I + II) patients completed suicide; the SMRs for suicide in unipolar and bipolar patients were 26 and 12, respectively. On the other hand, in their very recent long-term prospective follow-up study (average 11 years) of 1983 unipolar major depressives and 843 bipolar (I + II) patients, Tondo, Lepri, and Baldessarini (2007) found a five times higher rate of completed suicide in bipolar (I + II) than in unipolar patients (0.25% of patients/year versus 0.05% of patients/year). This study also found that the ratio of attempted to completed suicide in bipolar II, bipolar I, and unipolar depression was 5, 11, and 10, respectively, indicating that the lethality of suicide attempts was highest in bipolar II patients. In contrast to a major depressive episode, minor depression and pure dysthymic disorder (dysthymia without 'comorbid' major depression) do not markedly increase the risk of suicide (Goodwin & Jamison, 2007; Rihmer, 2007).

In patients with major mood disorders, previous suicide attempt is the most powerful predictor of future completed suicide (Harris & Barraclough, 1997; Hawton *et al.*, 2005; Goodwin & Jamison, 2007; Rihmer, 2007). Based only on the 10 clinical studies (including more than 3,100 patients) in which unipolar and bipolar (I + II) patients were analysed separately, the lifetime rate of prior suicide attempt(s) was much higher in bipolar (I + II) patients (mean: 28%, range: 10%–61%) than in unipolar depressives (mean: 13%, range: 9%–30%) (Rihmer, 2005). A recent long-term prospective study also found that the rate of suicide attempts during follow-up was more than double in bipolar (I + II) than in unipolar patients (Tondo, Lepri, & Baldessarini, 2007). Community-based epidemiological studies (Chen & Dilsaver, 1996; Kessler, Borges, & Walters, 1999; Szádóczky, Vitrai, Rihmer, & Füredi, 2000) showed that the lifetime rate of prior suicide attempts was 1.5 to 2.5 times higher in bipolar (types I and II combined) than in unipolar patients. The higher risk of suicidality in bipolar than in unipolar depression has been supported by a recent epidemiological survey showing that current suicidal ideation was significantly more common in bipolar I depression (72%, $n = 1,154$) than in unipolar depression (39%, $n = 11,904$) (Weinstock, Strong, Ueblacker, & Miller, 2009).

Clinically Detectable Suicide Risk Factors in Depressive Disorders

Retrospective and prospective follow-up clinical studies consistently show that suicidal behaviour (completed suicide and suicide attempt) and suicidal ideation in patients with mood disorders occur almost exclusively during a severe major depressive episode, less frequently in mixed affective episode and dysphoric mania, and very rarely during euphoric mania, hypomania, and euthymia (Hawton *et al.*, 2005; Rihmer, 2007; Sokero, Eerola, Rytsala, Melartin, Leskala, *et al.*, 2006; Tondo, Lepri, & Baldessarini, 2008; Valtonen, Suominen, Mantere, Leppamaki, Avrilommi, *et al.*, 2005; Valtonen, Suominen, Haukka, Mantere, Leppamaki, *et al.*, 2008). This indicates that suicidal behaviour in unipolar and bipolar major depressed patients is a state- and severity-dependent phenomenon. However, since the majority of unipolar and bipolar depressed patients never end their lives (and up to 50% of them never attempt to do so) (Goodwin & Jamison, 2007; Rihmer, 2007; Sokero *et al.*, 2006; Tondo, Isacsson, & Baldessarini, 2003), other risk factors, in addition to an acute major mood episode such as special clinical characteristics as well as some personality, familial, and psychosocial factors, should also play a significant contributory role (Balázs, Benazzi, Rihmer, Rihmer, Akiskal, *et al.*, 2006; Hawton *et al.*, 2005; Mann, Waternaux, Haas, & Malone, 1999; Rihmer, 2007; Tondo, Isacsson, & Baldessarini, 2003). Most of the suicide risk factors in patients with mood disorders are related to acute (mostly major) depressive episodes, but there are several personality characteristics and historical data that can help clinicians identify highly suicidal patients.

Suicide risk factors during acute mood episodes

The clinical condition which is the most alarming for suicidal behaviour in mood disorder patients is a recent suicide attempt and severe (melancholic) major depressive episode, frequently accompanied by hopelessness, guilt, few reasons for living, and suicidal ideation, as well as with agitation, insomnia, appetite and weight loss, and psychotic features (Akiskal, Benazzi, Perugi, & Rihmer, 2005; Angst *et al.*, 2005; Goodwin & Jamison, 2007; Hawton *et al.*, 2005; McGirr, Renaud, Seguin, Alda, Benkelfat, *et al.*, 2007; Oquendo, Galfaly, Russo, Ellis, Grunebaum, *et al.*, 2004; Rihmer, 2005, 2007; Valtonen *et al.*, 2005). Recent results also suggest that atypical depressive features (Sánchez-Gistau,

Colom, Mané, Romero, Sugranyes, *et al.*, 2009) and mixed depressive episodes (major depression plus three or more co-occurring intra-depressive hypomanic symptoms, which corresponds highly to the category of 'agitated depression'), that are present in between 30% and 60% of major unipolar and bipolar depressives (Akiskal *et al.*, 2005; Benazzi, 2006; Goldberg, Perlis, Bowden, Thase, Miklowitz, *et al.*, 2009), substantially increase the risk of both attempted and completed suicide (Akiskal *et al.*, 2005; Balázs *et al.*, 2006; Benazzi, 2005; Goldberg *et al.*, 2009; Rihmer *et al.*, 2007; Sato, Bottlender, Kleindienst, & Möller, 2005; Valtonen *et al.*, 2008). These results can explain, at least in part, rare 'anti-depressant-induced' suicidal behaviour: antidepressant monotherapy, unprotected by mood stabilizers or atypical antipsychotics, particularly in bipolar and bipolar spectrum disorder (including 'unipolar' depressive mixed state), can lead not only to hypomanic/manic switches and rapid cycling, but can also worsen the pre-existing mixed state or generate *de novo* mixed conditions, making the clinical picture more serious and ultimately leading to self-destructive behaviour (Akiskal, 2007; Benazzi, 2005; Rihmer & Akiskal, 2006; Rihmer, 2007).

Suicidal behaviour in patients with bipolar disorder, however, is not exclusively restricted to depressive episodes. In contrast to classical (euphoric) mania, where suicidal tendencies are extremely rare, suicidal thoughts and attempts are relatively common in patients with mixed affective episode and dysphoric mania. This supports the common clinical sense that suicidal behaviour in bipolar patients is linked to depressive symptomatology (Angst *et al.*, 2005; Goodwin & Jamison, 2007; Valtonen *et al.*, 2005, 2008).

Comorbid anxiety/anxiety disorders, substance-use disorders, personality disorders (mainly borderline personality disorders), and serious medical illnesses, particularly in the case of multiple comorbidities, increase the risk of all forms of suicidal behaviour (Balázs *et al.*, 2003; Goodwin & Jamison, 2007; Hawton *et al.*, 2005; Leverich, Altshuler Frye, Suppes, Keck, *et al.*, 2003; Rihmer, 2005; 2007; Simon *et al.*, 2007; Valtonen *et al.*, 2005). Acute alcohol use is also an important risk factor for attempted and completed suicide even in non-alcoholic depressives, since it increases both the risk and the lethality of suicide acts (Sher, Oquendo, Richardson-Vejlgaard, Makhija, Posner, *et al.*, 2009; see also Chapter 5, below). As successful acute and long-term treatment of unipolar depression and bipolar disorders substantially reduces the risk of both completed and attempted suicide (Baldessarini, Tondo, Davis, Pompili, Goodwin, *et al.*, 2006; Guzzetta, Tondo, Centorrino, & Baldessarini, 2007; Tondo, Isacsson, & Baldessarini, 2003), lack of medical and family support and the first few days of the therapy, when antidepressants usually do not work (Akiskal, 2007; Rihmer & Akiskal, 2006; Valenstein, Kim, Ganoczy, McCarthy, Zivin, *et al.*, 2009), should also be considered as suicide risk factors.

Suicide risk factors related to prior course of the depressive illness

For suicide risk factors related to prior course of mood disorders, previous suicide attempt(s), particularly in the case of violent or more lethal methods, is the most powerful single predictor of future attempts and fatal suicide in patients with depressive disorders (Goodwin & Jamison, 2007; Hawton *et al.*, 2005; Rihmer, 2007; Tondo, Isacsson, & Baldessarini, 2003). Other historical variables, like early onset of the illness and early stage of the mood disorder

(Angst *et al.*, 2005; Goodwin & Jamison, 2007; Rihmer, 2007; Simon *et al.*, 2007; Tondo, Lepri, & Baldessarini, 2007), rapid cycling course, predominant depressive or mixed polarity, and more prior hospitalizations for depression (Azorin, Kaladjian, Adida, Hantouche, Hameg, *et al.*, 2009; Hawton *et al.*, 2005; Leverich *et al.*, 2003; Tondo, Isacsson, & Baldessarini, 2003; Valtonen *et al.*, 2005, 2008), as well as recent hospital discharge (Oquendo *et al.*, 2004; Valenstein *et al.*, 2009), have also been shown to markedly increase the chance of both attempted and completed suicide in this patient population.

Suicide risk factors related to personality features

Several recent studies show that some personality features also play a significant role in suicidal behaviour: aggressive/impulsive personality traits appear to be especially potent in combination with current hopelessness and pessimism (MacKinnon, Potash, McMahon, Simpson, dePaulo, Jr., *et al.*, 2005; Mann *et al.*, 1999; Oquendo *et al.*, 2004; Sarchiapone, Jaussent, Roy, Carli, Guillaume, *et al.*, 2009; Swann, Moeller, Steinberg, Schneider, Barratt, *et al.*, 2007; Zalsman, Braun, Arendt, Grunebaum, Sher, *et al.*, 2006), markedly increasing the risk of suicidal behaviour in patients with mood disorder. The interaction between personality features and illness characteristics in the suicidal process is best formulated by Mann *et al.* (1999) in their 'stress–diathesis model', which proposes that suicidal behaviour is determined not only by the stressor (acute major psychiatric illness), but also by a diathesis or predisposition (impulsive, aggressive, pessimistic personality traits). Most recent studies have demonstrated a strong relationship between some specific types of affective temperament and suicidal behaviour. In patients with major depression, cyclothymia/cyclothymic temperament (a chronic condition characterized by numerous hypomanic episodes and many periods of depressive symptoms) was significantly related to lifetime and current suicidal behaviour (attempts) and ideation both in adult and paediatric samples (Akiskal, Hantouche, & Allilare, 2003; Kochman, Hantouche, Ferrari, Lancrenon, Bayart, *et al.*, 2005). Depressive, anxious, cyclothymic, and irritable affective temperaments were markedly over-represented and hyperthymic temperament was under-represented among (non-violent) suicide attempters, the majority of whom have experienced a current major depressive episode (Pompili, Rihmer, Akiskal, Innamorati, Iliceto, *et al.*, 2008; Rihmer *et al.*, 2009).

Although the vast majority of suicide cases in the general population are males and the opposite is true for suicide attempters (Goodwin & Jamison, 2007; Harris & Barraclough, 1997; Rihmer & Akiskal, 2006), this gender difference is much smaller among suicidal patients with mood disorder (Angst *et al.*, 2005; Hawton *et al.*, 2005; Simon *et al.*, 2007; Tondo, Isacsson, & Baldessarini, 2003). This suggests that gender is not a significant, clinically useful predictor for completed and attempted suicide in this otherwise high-risk population.

Suicide risk factors related to personal and family history

Early negative life-events (e.g., parental loss, isolation, emotional, physical and, particularly, sexual abuse) (Hawton *et al.*, 2005; Leverich *et al.*, 2003; Mann *et al.*, 1999; Sarchiapone *et al.*, 2009), permanent adverse life situations (e.g., unemployment, isolation, separation), and acute psychosocial stressors (e.g., loss events, financial disasters) (Hawton *et al.*, 2005; Isometsä, Heikkinen, Henriksson, Aro, & Lönqvist, 1995; Leverich *et al.*, 2003; Rihmer, 2005, 2007) are the most important and clinically useful indicators of possible suicidality in patients with depressive disorders, primarily if other known risk factors are also present. However, acute psychosocial stressors are commonly dependent on the individual's own behaviour, particularly in the case of bipolar I disorder (Isometsä *et al.*, 1995). Hypomanic and, particularly, manic episodes can easily lead to aggressive–impulsive behaviour, financial extravagance or episodic promiscuity, thus generating several interpersonal conflicts, marital breakdown, and new negative life events, all of which have a deleterious impact on the further course of the illness.

Family history of suicidal behaviour and/or major mood disorders in first- and second-degree relatives is also a strong risk factor for both attempted and completed suicide (Hawton *et al.*, 2005; Leverich *et al.*, 2003; MacKinnon *et al.*, 2005; Mann *et al.*, 1999; Rihmer, 2007; Sánchez-Gistau *et al.*, 2009). However, the familial component of suicidality seems to be independent, at least in part, of psychiatric disorders: suicidal persons are over 10 times more likely than relatives of comparison subjects to attempt or complete suicide after controlling for psychopathology (Kim, Seguin, Therrien, Riopel, Chawkay, *et al.*, 2005). There is a complex relationship between the three main groups of suicide risk factors (illness-related, personality-related, and historical data) that are, in general, additive in their nature: the more risk factors that are present, the higher the risk of suicidal behaviour. The clinically detectable suicide risk factors in mood disorders are listed in Box 3.1.

Suicide Protective Factors in Depressive Disorders

In contrast to the myriad of research studies on suicide risk factors, much less is known about what protects against suicidal behaviour. Good family and social support, pregnancy and the postpartum period, having a large number of children, holding strong religious beliefs, and restricting lethal suicide methods (e.g., to reduce domestic and car exhaust gas toxicity and to introduce stricter laws on gun control), whenever possible, seem to have some protective effect (Dervic, Oquendo, Grunebaum, Ellis, Burke, *et al.*, 2004; Driver & Abed, 2004; Godwin & Jamison, 2007; Marzuk, Tardiff, Leon, Hirsch, Portera, *et al.*, 1997; Rihmer, 2005, 2007). As for the specific symptoms of depression, only appetite, weight gain, and hypersomnia seem to be associated with decreased risk of completed suicide in patients with current major depressive disorder (McGirr *et al.*, 2007). One of the most extensively studied suicide protective factors in major mood disorders is acute and long-term pharmacological treatment that results in a marked decline in all forms of suicidal behaviour in this high-risk patient population (Angst *et al.*, 2005; Baldessarini *et al.*, 2006; Guzzetta *et al.*, 2007; Rihmer, 2005, 2007; Tondo, Isacsson, & Baldessarini, 2003, 2008).

Although suicide is a statistically rare event in the community, it is more common among patients with mood disorder, most of whom have had different levels of healthcare contact in the weeks before their death (Goodwin & Jamison, 2007; Rihmer, 2005, 2007; Tondo, Isacsson, & Baldessarini, 2003). This underlines the potentially key role of healthcare

---

Box 3.1　Clinically detectable suicide risk factors in depressive disorders

(1) Risk factors related to current mood episodes:
   (a) Severe major depressive episode:
      ○ current suicide attempt, plan, ideation,
      ○ hopelessness, guilt, pessimism, few reasons for living,
      ○ agitation, depressive mixed state, insomnia, appetite and/or weight loss,
      ○ atypical and psychotic features,
      ○ past mania or hypomania (bipolar I or II diagnosis),
      ○ comorbid Axis I (substance use and anxiety) disorders, acute alcohol use,
      ○ comorbid Axis II and disabling Axis III disorders,
      ○ lacking medical care and family/social support,
      ○ first few days of the treatment (particularly if appropriate care and co-medication is lacking);
   (b) Mixed affective episode (simultaneously occurring manic and major depressive episode).
   (c) Dysphoric mania (mania and three or more intramanic depressive symptoms).
(2) Risk factors related to prior course of the depressive disorder:
      ○ previous suicide attempt/ideation (particularly in the case of violent/highly lethal methods);
      ○ early onset/early stage of the illness/predominantly depressive course;
      ○ rapid cycling course.
(3) Risk factors related to personality features:
      ○ aggressive/impulsive/pessimistic personality traits;
      ○ cyclothymic, depressive, irritable temperament.
(4) Risk factors related to personal history and/or family history:
      ○ early childhood traumas (separation, emotional, physical and sexual abuse);
      ○ permanent adverse life situations (unemployment, financial problems, isolation, chronic/disabling medical disorders);
      ○ acute psycho-social stressors (loss events, acute financial catastrophe);
      ○ family history of depressive or bipolar disorders (first- and second-degree relatives);
      ○ family history of suicide and/or suicide attempt (first- and second-degree relatives).

---

workers in suicide prevention. Indeed, GP-based depression training programmes show promising results. Following the pioneering Swedish Gotland Study, several studies (the Nuremberg Alliance Against Depression, the Swedish Jamtland Study, and the recent Hungarian Kiskunhalas GP-Suicide Prevention Study) have demonstrated that the education of GPs in the diagnosis and treatment of depression, particularly in combination with public education, improves the identification and treatment of depressive disorders and, consequently, there are fewer suicide attempts and completed suicides in the areas served by trained GPs (Hegerl, Althaus, Schmidtke, & Niklewski, 2006; Henriksson & Isacsson, 2006; Rutz, Walinder, von Knorring, Rihmer, & Pihlgren, 1997; Szántó, Kalmár, Hendin, Rihmer, & Mann, 2007). However, as health and social care workers can only help those who contact them, public education media campaigns on symptoms, dangers, treatability, and referral pathways are vitally important. In short, careful consideration of all suicide risk factors should improve the early detection of risk and facilitate more timely intervention prior to the patient making the first suicide act (see Box 3.1).

Prevention of Suicide in Patients with Depressive Disorders

Prevention of suicide in patients with depressive disorder is a great challenge for everyone who cares for, or has contact with, psychiatric patients. The role of the healthcare system in suicide prevention varies as a function of the setting (e.g., psychiatric settings versus primary care practice), with specialized suicide prevention centres (where they exist) playing a most important role. As suicidal behaviour in patients with depressive disorders is strongly related to severe major depressive episode and initially suicidal depressives become non-suicidal with antidepressant treatment (Rihmer, 2007; Sokero *et al.*, 2006; Tondo, Lepri, & Baldessarini, 2008), it is logical to assume that successful acute and long-term pharmacotherapy of depression markedly reduces the risk of suicidal behaviour.

Indeed, large-scale, long-term, observational (retrospective and prospective) clinical studies, which included severely ill, frequently suicidal depressed patients (usually inpatients), have shown that, compared with no treatment, the risk of completed and attempted suicide among unipolar and bipolar patients on long-term pharmacotherapy (antidepressants and/or mood stabilizers) is reduced by 56%–93% (Angst *et al.*, 2005; Baldessarini *et al.*, 2006; Guzzetta *et al.*, 2007; Leon, Keller, Warshaw, Mueller, Solomon, *et al.*, 1999; Yerevanian, Koek, Feusner, Hwang, & Mintz, 2004). The marked anti-suicidal effect of lithium in bipolar and unipolar major mood disorder patients has also been supported recently from an epidemiological perspective: investigating the lithium levels in tap water in 18 municipalities in Japan in relation to the suicide mortality in each municipality, the authors found that lithium levels were significantly and negatively associated with suicide rate averages for 2002–2006 (Ohgami, Tearao, Shiotsuke, Ishii, & Iwata, 2009).

Register-based observational cohort studies also show that former in-patients with unipolar major depression who continued treatment with antidepressants (Sondergard, Lopez, Andersen, & Kessin, 2007), and former in-patients with bipolar disorder who continuously took mood stabilizers (Sondergard, Lopez, Andersen, & Kessin, 2008) had a markedly decreased rate of completed suicide compared with those who stopped taking antidepressants and mood stabilizers. The evidence that suicide rates of depressed patients have progressively and significantly lowered through the 'pretreatment era' (1900–1939), 'ECT era' (1940–1959), and 'antidepressant era' (1960–1992) (6.3, 5.7, and 3.3 per 1000 patients per year, respectively) also supports the suicide preventive effect of antidepressants in depressed patients (O'Leary, Paykel, Todd, & Vardulaki, 2001; see also Chapter 26, below).

The significant role of more widespread pharmacotherapy of depression in reducing suicide mortality has been supported by the findings from the United States and the Netherlands (Gibbons, Brown, Hur, Marcus, Bhaumik, *et al.*, 2007), as well as from Canada (Katz, Kozyrskyj, Prior, Enns, Cox, *et al.*, 2008). A recent marked decline in the use of antidepressants in children and adolescents has been accompanied by a sharp increase in suicide mortality in that age group, while there has been a further decrease in the suicide rate among older people where the utilization of antidepressants increased or declined only slightly. The marked decline of national suicide rates in countries where antidepressant utilization has increased three- to eight-fold in the last two decades also suggests that the beneficial effect of better and more widespread treatment of depression can be detected at the general population level (Rihmer & Akiskal, 2006; Ludwig, Marcotte, & Norberg, 2009). However, the increase in antidepressant usage, at the level of the general population, is only a proxy marker of greater access of patients to appropriate care; and the decrease of national or regional suicide rates could reflect a general improvement in mental healthcare rather than being caused by increasing antidepressant sales alone (Kapusta, Niederkrotenthaler, Etzersdorfer, Voracek, Dervic, *et al.*, 2009; Pirkola, Sund, Sailas, & Wahlbeck, 2009; Rihmer, Rutz, & Barsi, 1993).

On the other hand, the slightly elevated (but, in an absolute sense, quite low) risk of suicidal behaviour among (primarily young) patients taking antidepressants compared with those taking placebo in phase II/III randomized controlled antidepressant trials of unipolar major depression might be the consequence of the rarely occurring, depression-worsening potential of antidepressant monotherapy (unprotected by mood stabilizers) in sub-threshold and mixed bipolar depressed patients. It may be that these latter patients were included in these trials, but were falsely diagnosed as suffering from unipolar depression (Akiskal, 2007; Rihmer & Akiskal, 2006; Rihmer, 2007; Rihmer *et al.*, 2007). In other words, antidepressant pharmacotherapy (as one component of appropriate treatment of depression) decreases and extinguishes suicidal behaviour in the vast majority of depressed patients, but can exacerbate depression (and consequently can 'induce' suicidality) in a small but vulnerable sub-population. The concomitant use of mood stabilizers and/or atypical antipsychotics, as well as anxiolytics in overt or covert bipolar depressives, might prevent or minimize the chance of this unwanted 'iatrogenesis' (Akiskal, 2007; Rihmer & Akiskal, 2006).

It should also be noted that in the only clinical psychotherapy trial (Bridge, Barbe, Birmaher, Kolko, & Brent, 2005) that enrolled adolescent outpatients with major depression similar to those enrolled in antidepressant clinical trials (Whittington, Kendall, Fonagy, Cottrell, Cotgrove, *et al.*, 2004), the rate of newly emerging suicidality in patients receiving psychotherapy only was much higher (12.5%, Bridge *et al.*, 2005) than among those receiving antidepressants (4.7%, Whittington *et al.*, 2004).

Pharmacotherapy, however, is a necessary but not a sufficient method of reducing suicidal behaviour in depressed patients. There is some recent evidence that concurrent depression-focused psychotherapies also improve the compliance of patients and increase the effectiveness of pharmacotherapy, and may therefore contribute to suicide prevention for patients with severe recurrent unipolar or bipolar disorders (Fountoulakis, Gonda, Siamouli, & Rihmer, 2009; Michalak, Yatham, & Lam, 2004; Rucci, Frank, Kostelnik, Fagiolini, Malinger, *et al.*, 2002). The role of psychosocial interventions in suicide prevention is also supported by a recent World Health Organization (WHO) organized study of 1,867 suicide attempters (many of whom have current major depression) seen at emergency care departments. A brief individual intervention before discharge and regular contact thereafter (eight contacts during the 18-month follow-up) resulted in significantly fewer completed suicides (0.2%) in the intervention group ($n = 872$) than in the treatment as usual (TAU) group ($n = 827$, 2.2%) (Fleischmann, Bertolote, Wasserman, Bolhari, Botega, *et al.*, 2008).

Conclusions

Unrecognized/untreated unipolar and bipolar major depressive episodes are the major causes of attempted and completed suicide in this patient population. However, suicidal behaviour in these patients has a good chance of being predicted and healthcare workers play a key role in recognizing and managing suicidal risk. Doctors must always be vigilant of the risk of suicidality when prescribing antidepressants or implementing psychotherapy for patients with depressive disorders where the risk of suicidality is inherently very high. Successful acute and long-term care of depressed patients, using both pharmacological and non-pharmacological methods, substantially improves patients' quality of life and reduces the risk of suicidal behaviour even in this high-risk population.

Although our recognition and management of depressive disorders, including the detection of suicide risk, has improved substantially in recent decades, the main problem in everyday clinical practice remains the same: the under-diagnosis and under-treatment of mood disorders both with pharmacotherapy and with psychotherapeutical interventions. The misdiagnosis of a depressive episode of bipolar disorder as unipolar depression, leading to inadequate acute and long-term treatment, is still quite common. The accurate identification of the unipolar or bipolar nature of a depressive episode is crucial because antidepressant monotherapy (unprotected by mood stabilizers) can exacerbate the short-term and long-term course of the illness, including increasing the risk of suicidal behaviour. In addition, more research focused on community-based educational programmes is required to determine whether these complex and resource-consuming community interventions work and, if so, to what extent. However, it should also be noted that early recognition and effective treatment of mental illnesses, including depressive disorders, would be an ideal target, irrespective of their relationship with suicide.

References

Akiskal, H. S. (2007). Targeting suicide prevention to modifiable risk factors: Has bipolar II been overlooked? *Acta Psychiatrica Scandinavica, 116*, 395–402.

Akiskal, H. S., Benazzi, F., Perugi, G., & Rihmer Z. (2005). Agitated 'unipolar' depression reconceptualized as a depressive mixed state: Implications for the antidepressant–suicide controversy. *Journal of Affective Disorders, 85*, 245–258.

Akiskal, H. S., Hantouche, E. G., & Allilare, J. F. (2003). Bipolar II with and without cyclothymic temperament: 'Dark' and 'sunny' expressions of soft bipolarity. *Journal of Affective Disorders, 73*, 49–57.

Angst, J., Angst, F., Gerber-Werder, R., & Gamma, A. (2005). Suicide in 406 mood-disorder patients with and without long-term medication: A 40 to 44 years' follow-up. *Archives of Suicide Research, 9*, 279–300.

Azorin, J-M., Kaladjian, A., Adida, M., Hantouche, E., Hameg, A., Lancrenon, S., & Akiskal, H. S. (2009). Risk factors associated with lifetime suicide attempts in bipolar I patients: Findings from a French national cohort. *Comprehensive Psychiatry, 50*, 115–120.

Balázs, J., Benazzi, F., Rihmer, Z., Rihmer, A., Akiskal, K. K., & Akiskal, H. S. (2006). The close link between suicide attempts and mixed (bipolar) depression: Implications for suicide prevention. *Journal of Affective Disorders, 91*, 133–138.

Balázs, J., Lecrubier, Y., Csiszér, N., Koszták, J., & Bitter, I. (2003). Prevalence and comorbidity of affective disorders in persons making suicide attempts in Hungary: Importance of the first episode and of bipolar II diagnosis. *Journal of Affective Disorders, 76*, 113–119.

Baldessarini, R. J., Tondo, L., Davis, P., Pompili, M., Goodwin, F. K., & Hennen, J. (2006). Decreased risk of suicides and attempts during long-term lithium treatment: A meta-analytic review. *Bipolar Disorder, 8*, 625–639.

Benazzi, F. (2005). Suicidal ideation and depressive mixed states. *Psychotherapy and Psychosomatics, 74*, 107–108.

Benazzi, F. (2006). Mood patterns and classification in bipolar disorder. *Current Opinion in Psychiatry, 19*, 1–8.

Bridge, J. A., Barbe, R. P., Birmaher, B., Kolko, D. J., & Brent, D. A. (2005). Emergent suicidality in a clinical psychotherapy trial for adolescent depression. *American Journal of Psychiatry, 162*, 2173–2175.

Chen, Y. W. & Dilsaver, S. C. (1996). Lifetime rates of suicide attempts among subjects with bipolar and unipolar disorders relative to subjects with other Axis I disorders. *Biological Psychiatry, 39*, 896–899.

Dervic, K., Oquendo, M. A., Grunebaum, M. F., Ellis, S., Burke, A. K., & Mann, J. J. (2004). Religious affiliation and suicide attempt. *American Journal of Psychiatry, 161*, 2303–2308.

Driver, K. & Abed, R (2004). Does having offspring reduce the risk of suicide in women? *International Journal of Psychiatry in Clinical Practice, 8*, 25–29.

Dunner, D. L. (2003). Clinical consequences of under-recognized bipolar spectrum disorder. *Bipolar Disorder, 5*, 456–463.

Fleischmann, M., Bertolote, J. M., Wasserman, D., Bolhari, D. J., Botega, N. J., de Silva, D., Philipps, D., Vijaykumar, L., Varnik, A., Schleibusch, L., & Thann, H. T. T. (2008). Effectiveness of a brief intervention and contact for suicide attempters: A randomized controlled trial in five countries. *Bulletin of the WHO, 86*, 703–709.

Fountoulakis, K. N., Gonda, X., Siamouli, M., & Rihmer, Z. (2009). Psychotherapeutic intervention and suicide risk reduction: A review of the evidence. *Journal of Affective Disorders, 113*, 21–29.

Gibbons, R. D., Brown, C. H., Hur, K., Marcus, S. M., Bhaumik, D. K., Erkens, J. A., Herings, R. M., & Mann, J. J. (2007). Early evidence on the effects of regulators' suicidality warnings on SSRI prescription and suicide in children and adolescents. *American Journal of Psychiatry, 164*, 1356–1363.

Goldberg, J., Perlis, R. H., Bowden, C. L., Thase, M. E., Miklowitz, D. J., Marangell, L. B., Calabrese, J. R., Nierenberg, A. A., & Sachs, G. (2009). Manic symptoms during depressive episodes in 1380 patients with bipolar disorder: Findings from the STEP-BD. *American Journal of Psychiatry, 166*, 173–181.

Goodwin, F. K. & Jamison, K. R. (2007). *Manic-Depressive Illness: Bipolar disorders and recurrent depression*. New York: Oxford University Press.

Guzzetta, F., Tondo, L., Centorrino, F., & Baldessarini, R. J. (2007). Lithium treatment reduces suicide risk in recurrent major depressive disorder. *Journal of Clinical Psychiatry*, 68, 380–383.

Harris, E. C. & Barraclough, B. (1997). Suicide as an outcome for mental disorders: A meta-analysis. *British Journal of Psychiatry*, 170, 205–228.

Hawton, K., Sutton, L., Haw, C., Sinclair, J., & Harris, L. (2005). Suicide and attempted suicide in bipolar disorder: A systematic review of risk factors. *Journal of Clinical Psychiatry*, 66, 693–704.

Hegerl, U., Althaus, D., Schmidtke, A., & Niklewski, G. (2006). The Alliance Against Depression: 2-year evaluation of a community-based intervention to reduce suicidality. *Psychological Medicine*, 36, 1225–1233.

Henriksson, S. & Isacsson, G. (2006). Increased antidepressant use and fewer suicides in Jamtland county, Sweden, after a primary care educational programme on the treatment of depression. *Acta Psychiatrica Scandinavica*, 114, 159–167.

Isometsä, E., Heikkinen, M., Henriksson, M., Aro, H., & Lönqvist, J. (1995). Recent life events and completed suicide in bipolar affective disorder: A comparison with major depressive disorder in Finland. *Journal of Affective Disorders*, 33, 99–106.

Kapusta, N. D., Niederkrotenthaler, T., Etzersdorfer, E., Voracek, M., Dervic, K., Jandl-Jager, E., & Sonneck, G. (2009). Influence of psychotherapist density and antidepressant sales on suicide rates. *Acta Psychiatrica Scandinavica*, 119, 236–242.

Katz, L. Y., Kozyrskyj, A. L., Prior, H. J., Enns, M. W., Cox, B. J., & Sareen, J. (2008). Effect of regulatory warnings on antidepressant prescription rates, use of health services and outcomes among children, adolescents and young adults. *Canadian Medical Association Journal*, 178, 1005–1011.

Kessler, R. C., Borges, G., & Walters, E. E. (1999). Prevalence and risk factors for lifetime suicide attempts in the National Comorbidity Survey. *Archives of General Psychiatry*, 56, 617–626.

Kim, C. D., Seguin, M., Therrien, N., Riopel, G., Chawkay, N., Lesege, A. D., & Turecki, G. (2005). Familial aggregation of suicidal behavior: A family study of male suicide completers from the general population. *American Journal of Psychiatry*, 162, 1017–1019.

Kochman, F. J., Hantouche, E. G., Ferrari, P., Lancrenon, S., Bayart, D., & Akiskal, H. S. (2005). Cyclothymic temperament as a prospective predictor of bipolarity and suicidality in children and adolescents with major depressive disorder. *Journal of Affective Disorders*, 85, 181–189.

Leon, A. C., Keller, M. B., Warshaw, M. G., Mueller, T. I., Solomon, D. A., Coryell, W., & Endicott, J. (1999). Prospective study of fluoxetine treatment and suicidal behavior in affectively ill subjects. *American Journal of Psychiatry*, 156, 195–201.

Leverich, G. S., Altshuler Frye, M. A., Suppes, T., Keck, P. E., McElroy, S. L., Denicoff, K. D., Obrocea, G., Nolen, W. A., Kupka, R., Walden, J., Grunze, H., Perez, S., Luckenbaugh, D. A., & Post, R. M. (2003). Factors associated with suicide attempts in 684 patients with bipolar disorder in the Stanley Foundation Bipolar Network. *Journal of Clinical Psychiatry*, 64, 506–515.

Ludwig, J., Marcotte, D. E., & Norberg, K. (2009). Anti-depressants and suicide. *Journal of Health Economics*, 28, 659–676.

MacKinnon, D. F., Potash, J. B., McMahon, F. J., Simpson, S. G., dePaulo, Jr., J. R., The National Institutes of Mental Health Bipolar Disorder Genetics Initiative, & Zandi, P. P. (2005). Rapid mood switching and suicidality in familial bipolar disorder. *Bipolar Disorder*, 7, 441–448.

Mann, J. J., Waternaux, C., Haas, G. L., & Malone, K. M. (1999). Toward a clinical model of suicidal behavior in psychiatric patients. *American Journal of Psychiatry*, 156, 181–189.

Marzuk, P. M., Tardiff, K., Leon, A. C., Hirsch, C. S., Portera, L., Hartwell, N., & Iqbal, M.I. (1997). Lower risk of suicide during pregnancy. *American Journal of Psychiatry*, 154, 122–123.

McGirr, A., Renaud, J., Seguin, M., Alda, M., Benkelfat, C., Lesage, A., & Turecki, G. (2007). An examination of DSM-IV depressive symptoms and risk for suicide completion in major depressive disorder: A psychological autopsy study. *Journal of Affective Disorders*, 97, 203–209.

Michalak, E. E., Yatham, L. N., & Lam, R. W. (2004). The role of psychoeducation in the treatment of bipolar disorder: A clinical perspective. *Clinical Approaches to Bipolar Disorder, 3,* 5–11.

Ohgami, H., Tearao, T., Shiotsuki, I., Ishii, N., & Iwata, N. (2009). Lithium in drinking water and risk of suicide. *British Journal of Psychiatry, 194,* 464–465.

O'Leary, D., Paykel, E., Todd, C., & Vardulaki, K. (2001), Suicide in primary affective disorders revisited: A systematic review by treatment era. *Journal of Clinical Psychiatry, 62,* 804–811.

Oquendo, M, A., Galfalvy, H., Russo, S., Ellis, S. P., Grunebaum, M. F., Burke, A., & Mann, J. J. (2004). Prospective study of clinical predictors of suicidal acts after a major depressive episode in patients with major depressive disorder and bipolar disorder. *American Journal of Psychiatry, 161,* 1433–1441.

Pirkola, S., Sund, R., Sailas, E., & Wahlbeck, K. (2009). Community mental-health services and suicide rate in Finland: A nationwide small-area study. *The Lancet, 373,* 147–153.

Pompili, M., Rihmer, Z., Akiskal, H. S., Innamorati, M., Iliceto, P., Akiskal, K. K., Lester, D., Narciso, V., Ferracuti, S., Tatarelli, R., De Pisa, E., & Girardi, P. (2008). Temperament and personality dimensions in suicidal and non-suicidal psychiatric inpatients. *Psychopathology, 41,* 313–321.

Rihmer, A., Rózsa, S., Rihmer, Z., Gonda, X., Akiskal, K. K., & Akiskal, H. S. (2009). Affective temperaments, as measured by TEMPS-A, among non-violent suicide attempters. *Journal of Affective Disorders, 116,* 18–22.

Rihmer, Z. (2005). Prediction and prevention of suicide in bipolar disorder. Clinical *Neuropsychiatry, 2,* 48–54.

Rihmer Z. (2007). Suicide risk in mood disorders. *Current Opinion in Psychiatry, 20,* 17–22.

Rihmer, Z. & Akiskal, H. S. (2006). Do antidepressants t(h)reat(en) depressives? Toward a clinically judicious formulation of the antidepressant–suicidality FDA advisory in light of declining national suicide statistics from many countries. *Journal of Affective Disorders, 94,* 3–13.

Rihmer, Z. & Angst, J. (2005). Epidemiology of bipolar disorder. In S. Kasper & R. M. A. Hirschfeld (Eds), *Handbook of Bipolar Disorder* (pp. 21–35). New York: Taylor & Francis.

Rihmer, Z., Benazzi, F., & Gonda, X. (2007). Suicidal behavior in unipolar depression: Focus on mixed states. In R. Tatarelli, M. Pompili & P. Girardi (Eds.), *Suicide in Psychiatric Disorders* (pp. 223–235). New York: Nova Science Publishers.

Rihmer, Z., Rutz, W., & Barsi, J. (1993). Suicide rate, prevalence of diagnosed depression and prevalence of working doctors in Hungary. *Acta Psychiatrica Scandinavica, 88,* 391–394.

Rucci, P., Frank, E., Kostelnik, B., Fagiolini, A., Malinger, A. G., Swartz, H. A., Thase, M. E., Siegel, L., Wilson, D., & Kupfer, D. J. (2002). Suicide attempts in patients with bipolar I disorder during acute and maintenance phases of intensive treatment with pharmacotherapy and adjunctive psychotherapy. *American Journal of Psychiatry, 159,* 1160–1164.

Rutz, W., Walinder, J., von Knorring, L., Rihmer, Z., & Pihlgren, H. (1997). Prevention of depression and suicide by education and medication: Impact on male suicidality. An update from the Gotland study. *International Journal of Psychiatry in Clinical Practice, 1,* 39–46.

Sánchez-Gistau, V., Colom, F., Mané, A., Romero, S., Sugranyes, G., & Vieta, E. (2009). Atypical depression is associated with suicide attempt in bipolar disorder. *Acta Psychiatrica Scandinavica, 120,* 30–36.

Sarchiapone, M., Jaussent, I., Roy, A., Carli, V., Guillaume, S., Jollant, F., Malafosse, A., & Courtet, P. (2009). Childhood trauma as a correlative factor of suicidal behaviour – via aggression traits. Similar results in an Italian and in a French sample. *European Psychiatry, 24,* 57–62.

Sato, T., Bottlender, R., Kleindienst, N., & Möller, H-J. (2005). Irritable psychomotor elation in depressed inpatients: A factor validation of mixed depression. *Journal of Affective Disorders, 84,* 187–196.

Sher, L., Oquendo, M. A., Richardson-Vejlgaard, R., Makhija, N. M., Posner, K., Mann, J. J., & Stanley, B. H. (2009). Effect of acute alcohol use on the lethality of suicide attempts in patients with mood disorders. *Journal of Psychiatric Research, 43*, 901–905.

Simon, G. E., Hunkeler, E., Fireman, B., Lee, J. Y., & Savarino, J. (2007). Risk of suicide attempt and suicide death in patients treated for bipolar disorder. *Bipolar Disorder, 9*, 526–530.

Sokero, P., Eerola, M., Rytsala, H., Melartin, T., Leskela, U., Lestela-Mielonen, P., & Isometsä, E. (2006). Decline in suicidal ideation among patients with MDD is preceded by decline in depression and hopelessness. *Journal of Affective Disorders, 95*, 95–102.

Sondergard, L., Lopez, A. G., Andersen, P. K., & Kessing, L. V. (2007). Continued antidepressant treatment and suicide in patients with depressive disorder. *Archives of Suicide Research, 11*, 163–175.

Sondergard, L., Lopez, A. G., Andersen, P. K., & Kessing, L. V. (2008). Mood stabilizing pharmacological treatment in bipolar disorders and the risk of suicide. *Bipolar Disorder, 10*, 87–94.

Swann, A. C., Moeller, F. G., Steinberg, J. L., Schneider, L., Barratt, E. S., & Dougherty, D. M. (2007). Manic symptoms and impulsivity during bipolar depressive episode. *Bipolar Disorder, 9*, 206–212.

Szádóczky, E., Vitrai, J., Rihmer, Z., & Füredi, J. (2000). Suicide attempts in the Hungarian adult population. Their relation with DIS/DSM-III-R affective and anxiety disorders. *European Psychiatry, 15*, 610–617.

Szántó, K., Kalmár, S., Hendin, H., Rihmer, Z., & Mann, J. J. (2007). A suicide prevention program in a region with very high suicide rate. *Archives of General Psychiatry, 64*, 914–920.

Tondo, L., Isacsson, G., & Baldessarini, R. J. (2003). Suicidal behavior in bipolar disorder. *CNS Drugs, 17*, 491–511.

Tondo, L., Lepri, B., & Baldessarini, R. (2007). Suicidal risk among 2826 Sardinian major affective disorder patients. *Acta Psychiatrica Scandinavica, 116*, 419–428.

Tondo, L., Lepri, B., & Baldessarini, R. J. (2008). Suicidal status during antidepressant treatment in 789 Sardinian patients with major affective disorder. *Acta Psychiatrica Scandinavica, 118*, 106–115.

Valenstein, M., Kim, H. M., Ganoczy, D., McCarthy, J. F., Zivin, K., Austin, K. L., Hoggatt, K., Eisenberg, D., Piette, J. D., Blow, F. C., & Olfson, M. (2009). Higher-risk for suicide among VA patients receiving depression treatment: Prioritizing suicide prevention efforts. *Journal of Affective Disorders, 112*, 50–58.

Valtonen, H. M., Suominen, K., Haukka, J., Mantere, O., Leppamaki, S., Arvilommi, P., & Isometsä, E. T. (2008). Differences in incidence of suicide attempts during phases of bipolar I and bipolar II disorders. *Bipolar Disorder, 10*, 588–596.

Valtonen, H., Suominen, K., Mantere, O., Leppamaki, S., Arvilommi, P., & Isometsä, E. (2005). Suicidal ideation and attempts in bipolar I and bipolar II disorders. *Journal of Clinical Psychiatry, 66*, 1456–1462.

Weinstock, L. M., Strong, D., Uebelacker, L. A., & Miller, I. W. (2009). Differential item functioning of DSM-IV depressive symptoms in individuals with a history of mania versus without: An item response theory analysis. *Bipolar Disorder, 11*, 289–297.

Whittington, C. J., Kendall, T., Fonagy, P., Cottrell, D., Cotgrove, A., & Boddington, E. (2004). Selective serotonin reuptake inhibitors in childhood depression: Systematic review of published and unpublished data. *The Lancet, 363*, 1341–1345.

Yerevanian, B. I., Koek, R. J., Feusner, J. D., Hwang, S., & Mintz, J. (2004). Antidepressants and suicidal behaviour in unipolar depression. *Acta Psychiatrica Scandinavica, 110*, 452–458.

Zalsman, G., Braun, M., Arendt, M., Grunebaum, M. F., Sher, L., Burke, A. K., Brent, D., Chaudhury, S. R., Mann, J. J., & Oquendo, M. A. (2006). A comparison of the medical lethality of suicide attempts in bipolar and major depressive disorder. *Bipolar Disorder, 8*, 558–565.

CHAPTER FOUR

Schizophrenia, Other Psychotic Disorders, and Suicidal Behaviour

Alexander McGirr and Gustavo Turecki

Abstract

Chronic psychotic disorders are relatively common and are found in all societies and all geographic regions of the world. In addition to the toll taken on the individual and their family, these disorders are associated with a significant risk for death by suicide. The specific symptoms manifested as part of the disorder can aid in the detection of suicide risk, yet the greatest indicator of suicide risk remains active psychotic illness and concurrent depressive symptoms. Insight into psychotic illness, the need for treatment, and the consequences of the disorder is strongly related to suicide risk, yet this appears to be contingent on the individual's pre-morbid expectations. Newer, non-pharmacological therapies, such as cognitive enhancement therapy, may have great potential for improving the individual's social and occupational functioning, and therefore improve the burden of 'lost potential' with consequent improvement in suicide outcomes. Among pharmacological treatments, only clozapine has evidence from placebo-controlled trials supporting an effective reduction of suicide risk, and therefore, additional basic and translational research is required to improve the clinician's armamentarium in the psychotic patient at risk for suicide.

Introduction

Schizophrenia is a severe disorder characterized by disturbances in perception, thought, language, social function, and volition. With the absence of pathognomonic features, that is, features distinctively and characteristically associated with the disorder, a diagnosis of

International Handbook of Suicide Prevention: Research, Policy and Practice, First Edition.
Edited by Rory C. O'Connor, Stephen Platt, Jacki Gordon.
© 2011 John Wiley & Sons, Ltd. Published 2011 by John Wiley & Sons, Ltd.

schizophrenia is considered after ruling out relevant medical conditions, as well as sub-stance abuse or medication-induced symptoms (APA, 1994).

The signs and symptoms of schizophrenia are categorized as 'positive' and 'negative'. The distinction between positive and negative relates to what is normally observed in the general population. A positive symptom refers to a symptom that is not normally observed in the general population, or the manifestation of a new behaviour or system or thought, whereas negative symptoms refer to the absence or attenuation of normal behaviour and cognition. In other words, positive symptoms reflect aberrant thought processes in which behavioural and thought disturbances represent a gain, or the novel appearance of symp-toms, and are classically thought of as delusions, hallucinations, and disorganized or unu-sual thinking. Conversely, negative symptoms reflect a deterioration of normal behaviour and include phenomena such as anhedonia (the loss of pleasure), flat affect, decreased emotional expression, concentration difficulties, and a progressive withdrawal from social activities.

For a diagnosis of schizophrenia, two symptoms of 'active' psychosis must be present for a one-month period and evidence of symptomatology for a continuous period of six months. This period includes the prodrome, or the period characterized by deterioration and/or insidious onset of symptomatology preceding the clear onset of psychotic symp-toms. While a sub-population of individuals with schizophrenia experience acute onset, insidious onset is the more common presentation (Buchanan & Carpenter, 2005). This typically begins in late adolescence, and first episodes of psychosis typically peak between 18 to 25 years of age in males and 20 to 35 years of age in females (Buchanan & Carpenter, 2005). Schizophrenia is a chronic psychotic disorder, with the overwhelming majority experiencing multiple exacerbations of psychotic symptoms, known as psychotic decom-pensations, during their lifetime. There is some evidence to suggest that positive symp-toms decrease in intensity with age, yet negative symptoms are more stable and are associated with poor response to pharmacological therapy as well as poorer long-term functional outcomes (Kirkpatrick & Tek, 2005).

Chronic psychotic disorders are remarkably evenly distributed throughout the world, with schizophrenia affecting approximately 1% of individuals in most societies (Buchanan & Carpenter, 2005). In terms of prevalence, the disorder appears to affect men slightly more than women (Buchanan & Carpenter, 2005).

There are several main sub-types of chronic psychotic disorder. Schizophrenia itself is divided into four main subtypes: catatonic; paranoid; disorganized; and residual. Catatonic-type describes a clinical presentation with drastic changes in motor activity and, commonly, echolalia or echopraxia, referring to the tendency to repetitively imitate the speech or movements of others, respectively. The catatonic presentation can also often result in the sustained absence of motion or maintenance of bizarre postures. Paranoid-type describes a clinical presentation characterized primarily by positive symp-toms, such as bizarre delusional thoughts and hallucinations. Disorganized-type refers to a clinical presentation characterized by disorganized speech in the form of disturbed flow of speech, as well as incoherent or loosely connected sentences. This is also often accompanied by incongruent or superficial affect. The final sub-type, residual-type, is characterized by significant negative symptomatology but with limited or no positive symptomatology.

In the event that the six-month duration for a full diagnosis of schizophrenia is not met, the psychotic syndrome is termed a brief psychotic episode or schizophreniform disorder. Other important diagnoses among chronic psychotic disorders are schizoaffective disorders, which are characterized by criteria warranting a diagnosis of schizophrenia in addition to independent periods of mood disorder, as well as delusional disorders, which refer to non-bizarre delusions in the absence of prominent hallucinations and with no marked impairment on function.

The pathophysiology of chronic psychotic disorders is not yet fully understood. It is clear, however, that the disorder is the result of an interaction between biological and psychosocial factors, with an important role for prenatal, perinatal, and early life environment. The classical neurobiological view involves dysregulation of the mesolimbic pathway and the dopamine system. As additional research continues on the pathophysiology of schizophrenia, it is becoming increasingly clear that the disorder is developmental, with alterations in additional neurotransmitter systems, including GABA, glutamate, as well as indirect effects on the adrenergic and serotonergic systems.

The economic burden of chronic psychotic disorders on society is tremendous, a 1990 estimate placed the direct and indirect costs at US$33 billion annually in the United States alone (Buchanan & Carpenter, 2005). The burden derives from the cost of treatments (including pharmacotherapy regimens), as well as the lost productivity of the affected individual and, often, loved ones charged with their care. The greatest and most distressing social burden of chronic psychotic disorders, however, is the loss of life associated with suicide in this population.

Suicide in Psychotic Disorders

Psychological autopsy studies examining consecutive, and therefore representative, deaths by suicide have revealed several major psychiatric diagnostic categories associated with elevated risk of suicide. In the context of the present chapter, such studies have revealed the importance of chronic psychotic disorders, with approximately 7% of suicides meeting criteria for schizophrenia (Heila, Isometsa, Henriksson, Heikkinen, Marttunen, *et al.*, 1997; Lesage, Boyer, Grunberg, Vanier, Morissette, *et al.*, 1994) and an additional 5% meeting criteria for schizoaffective disorder (Henriksson, Aro, Marttunen, Heikkinen, Isometsa, *et al.*, 1993; Lesage *et al.*, 1994). Death by suicide in individuals with schizophrenia usually occurs early in the course of the disorder (Palmer, Pankratz, & Bostwick, 2005), and suicide is the leading cause of premature death in this population (Fenton, 2000). The loss of life in this young population and the potential years of life lost are a clear impetus for a better understanding.

In this chapter, we discuss recent progress in clinical research examining suicide in populations affected by chronic psychotic disorders, such as schizophrenia. Clear definitions and a specific classification system are critical to studying the aetiology and underlying neurobiology of suicide. Standardized criteria, however, have been an obstacle despite the clear consensus on their importance. In this chapter, we use the term 'suicidality' to refer to a spectrum of self-harming behaviours, cognitions, and aggregate variables of related concepts. We use the terms 'suicide' or 'completed suicide' as the most concrete and valid concept in suicide studies, defining a phenotype characterized by (1) death as the result of some form of injury, which is both (2) self-inflicted, and (3) intentional. Finally, we use the term 'attempted suicide' as 'a potentially self-injurious behaviour with a non-fatal outcome for which there is some evidence that the person intended to kill himself/herself'. Our discussion prioritizes those studies examining death by suicide and suicidal attempts above studies examining suicidal ideation or suicide risk.

The Risk of Suicide and Other Psychotic Disorders

It is often cited in psychiatric textbooks and the broader scientific literature that 10% of schizophrenic patients die by suicide (Miles, 1977; Tsuang, 1978). However, closer inspection of these seminal studies reveals that the authors were reporting the proportionate mortality attributable to suicide in this population. When examining proportionate mortality, only the deceased individuals in a population or sample are considered and the causes of death for these individuals are defined. Applied to suicide, proportionate mortality refers to the proportion of deceased individuals who had died by suicide. By doing so, the proportion of deaths accounted for by the outcome of interest (suicide) can be determined, yet this approach comes with the clear caveat that the proportionate mortality of causes of death occurring early in life will be over-represented if all deaths have not yet been recorded (i.e., some of the sample is still alive). It is not surprising, therefore, that suicide is likely to proportionally represent a greater number of deaths early in life and decrease as other causes of death, including chronic medical conditions, exert their influence later in life.

More recently, the lifetime risk for suicide in schizophrenia has been re-evaluated, estimating this risk to be 4.9% (Palmer, Pankratz, & Bostwick, 2005). This, interestingly, is similar to other major psychiatric illnesses associated with death by suicide (Inskip, Harris, & Barraclough, 1998), such as major depressive disorder (4.2%) (Coryell & Young, 2005) and borderline personality disorder (4%) (Zanarini, Frankenburg, Hennen, Reich, & Silk, 2005). Suicidal behaviour, however, is estimated to occur in approximately 20%–40% of schizophrenic patients (Meltzer, 1998). The apparent 'gender paradox' observed in suicide more generally, where approximately twice as many women attempt suicide as males, while males represent approximately 80% of deaths by suicide, appears to apply to suicide in this diagnostic category as well (Alaraisanen, Miettunen, Rasanen, Fenton, Koivumaa-Honkanen, *et al.*, 2009; Hawton, Sutton, Haw, Sinclair, & Deeks, 2005; McGirr, Seguin, Renaud, Benkelfat, Alda, *et al.*, 2006).

Several lines of evidence suggest that the period of greatest risk for suicide in schizophrenia is early on in the course of the disorder. It has often been reported that suicide usually occurs within the first 10 years of illness onset (Brown, 1997; Caldwell & Gottesman, 1990). In their re-evaluation of the lifetime risk of suicide in schizophrenia, Palmer and colleagues provide strong evidence that the rate of suicide observed in samples composed of patients with first episode psychosis was considerably higher than in samples composed of patients at various stages in the course of the disorder (Palmer,

Pankratz, & Bostwick, 2005). This is consistent with the notion that those surviving the initial period of heightened risk go on to have lesser, although still considerable, risk of death by suicide (Palmer, Pankratz, & Bostwick, 2005). Similarly, a recent birth cohort study has reported that over 70% of suicides in this population occurred within the first three years of illness onset, and all suicides occurred within the first seven years after onset (Alaraisanen *et al.*, 2009).

The decreasing temporal risk after onset begs the question: is suicide even more strongly associated with psychotic symptoms of insufficient duration to meet criteria for a diagnosis of schizophrenia (six months)? The evidence as a whole suggests that the relationship between suicide risk and onset of psychosis does not respect a simple function that decreases with time. Although perhaps limited in their ability to detect such disturbances, psychological autopsy studies suggest that brief psychotic disorders are not common among representative suicide completers (Lesage *et al.*, 1994). In fact, among representative suicides selected for the presence of a psychotic spectrum disorder, less than 3% did not meet the full criteria for schizophrenia or schizoaffective disorder (McGirr, Tousignant, *et al.*, 2006). On the whole the evidence suggests that we should focus our research efforts on chronic psychotic disorders, such as schizophrenia and schizoaffective disorder.

Relationship with Other Suicide and Socio-Demographic Characteristics

Suicide in the context of schizophrenia is different from suicide more generally in a number of respects. Consistent with previously discussed data, individuals with chronic psychotic disorders who take their own lives tend to be younger (McGirr & Turecki, 2008) and are less likely to be married when compared with other suicides (McGirr & Turecki, 2008). Yet, consistent with the toll taken by the disorder on social functioning, being single is not a significant risk factor for suicide when psychotic suicides are compared with psychotic controls. This is contrary to what is observed in suicides more generally and suggests a uniformly high prevalence of this civil status in this population, irrespective of suicide status. As such, unlike in suicides more generally, being single is of limited use as an indicator of risk for suicide in populations affected by chronic psychotic disorders (Hawton *et al.*, 2005). Similarly, unemployment is a significant risk factor for suicide (Qin, Agerbo, & Mortensen, 2003), yet in chronic psychotic disorders it does not appear to be associated with an increased risk of suicide (Hawton *et al.*, 2005). This is also likely to be related to the extremely high prevalence of unemployment in this population (Bell, Lysaker, & Milstein, 1996), and therefore its limited ability to aid in the detection of suicide risk. Another point of departure relates to education. While there are conflicting reports (Agerbo, 2007), the most consistent finding in psychiatric populations has been an association between increased risk for suicide and lower levels of education (Qin, Agerbo, & Mortensen, 2003). In schizophrenia, however, there is a significant association with higher levels of education and suicide (Hawton *et al.*, 2005; McGirr, Tousignant, *et al.*, 2006).

As many of these differences can be attributed to the toll taken by the disorder, it is clear that trends from diagnostically unrestricted studies of suicide are of limited use in detecting, predicting, and preventing suicide in psychotic disorders. As such, researchers have highlighted the need to move beyond generalizing findings from suicides in general to this population and also progress beyond conducting studies in which psychotic suicides are compared with non-psychotic psychiatric out-patients. One way of doing this is to improve research design by examining psychotic patients who go on to die by suicide and those who do not to determine important indicators of risk specifically within this population.

Characteristics of Psychotic Illness in Suicide

With the increased risk associated with chronic psychotic disorders, many researchers have investigated the characteristics specific to these disorders. Recently, Hawton and colleagues (Hawton *et al.*, 2005) used a meta-analytical approach to systematically examine the risk factors for suicide in schizophrenia. In the following section, we summarize these characteristics and risk factors drawing from a range of studies including Hawton *et al.*'s (2005) review.

In the systematic review, negative symptoms (e.g., anhedonia, flat affect, decreased emotional expression, concentration difficulties, and a progressive withdrawal from social activities) were associated with a decreased risk of suicide in schizophrenia (Hawton *et al.*, 2005), and we have also replicated this association in a consecutive sample of suicides with chronic psychotic disorders (McGirr, Tousignant, *et al.*, 2006). Intuitively, this is consistent with data suggesting poorer long-term functional (i.e., not suicidal) outcomes in schizophrenia associated with negative symptoms: implicit in the concept of long-term functional outcome is surviving the early years of chronic psychotic illness during which there is the greatest suicide risk. Yet the process underlying the lower risk associated with negative symptoms has not been well elucidated, and it is unclear whether this represents a protective factor or more simply deficits in planning and inertia.

Positive symptoms (e.g., delusions, hallucinations, and disorganized or unusual thinking), interestingly, have been associated with inconsistent and conflicting results. Indeed, in the meta-analysis by Hawton and colleagues, when hallucinations and delusions were examined separately, delusions were associated with an increased risk for suicide, while hallucinations were associated with a decreased risk for suicide (Hawton *et al.*, 2005). However, these relationships held true only when studies employing a psychotic comparison group were examined.

While a selection of both positive and negative symptoms are associated with a decreased risk for suicide, the literature also highlights that suicide occurs in the context of active psychotic illness. In their national cohort of suicides from Finland, Heila and colleagues (1997) report an elevated frequency of active psychotic illness among individuals with schizophrenia. Similarly, compared with controls with psychotic disorders, schizophrenic suicides were more likely to exhibit psychotic symptoms in the month preceding their deaths (Hu, Sun, Lee, Peng, Lin, *et al.*, 1991). Prospective studies report that suicidal behaviour occurs predominantly among patients with schizophrenia who have experienced psychotic recurrences during the follow-up period (Kaplan & Harrow, 1996). Further, in a sample of representative suicides, the severity, as opposed to mere presence, of psychotic symptoms is associated with an increased risk for suicide in this population (McGirr, Tousignant, *et al.*, 2006).

To resolve the apparent inconsistency between a protective relationship with positive symptoms yet an increased risk during active psychosis, some have appealed to the clinical phenomenon of command hallucinations, or voices explicitly instructing the patient to engage in certain behaviours, including suicide. Yet the evidence in general does not support the association between suicidal behaviour and command hallucinations (Hellerstein, Frosch, & Koenigsberg, 1987; Zisook, Byrd, Kuck, & Jeste, 1995). Moreover, studies that have tended to yield positive results have, for the most part, been retrospective in design, examining patients' past history of suicidal behaviour as a function of the presence or absence of command hallucinations. In addition, while some support has been obtained for an association between command hallucinations and increased risk of suicide, neither a systematic review (Rudnick, 1999) nor a meta-analysis (Hawton *et al.*, 2005) have concluded that an association between command hallucinations and suicide is robust.

Conceptually, cortical disinhibition (decreased inhibitory inputs to key cortical regions) leading to thought disturbances is consistent with changes in decision-making that could result in suicide. For this reason, many researchers have attempted to discriminate suicide risk in chronic psychotic disorders as a function of clinical presentation. As just reviewed, the research into the association between characteristics of psychotic disorders and suicide, however, suggests that such characteristics do not provide vital information where suicide is concerned. While further research going beyond the broad clinical indicators is required, active illness appears to be the most useful indicator of risk for clinicians. Psychotic decompensation (exacerbation of the psychotic illness) comes with a plethora of priorities and treatment decisions, among which suicide risk should feature prominently.

Insight into Psychotic Illness

It has been well recognized for 20 years or more that there is a relationship between the degree of insight that an individual has into their illness and their risk of suicide. In short, greater insight into psychotic illness is associated with increased suicide risk. Insight into illness consists of three components: awareness of the presence of illness; awareness of the need for treatment; and awareness of the consequences of the disorder (Amador, 2004). A recent, large, multi-centre study confirmed this relationship: greater insight into illness was associated with a shorter latency to future suicide attempts (Bourgeois, Swendsen, Young, Amador, Pini, *et al.*, 2004). In terms of potential mechanisms of effect, this relationship may be as a consequence of increased depressive symptoms that remain consistently elevated in the sub-group of patients with greater insight. Moreover, the Bourgeois *et al.* study suggested a difference in risk between those who had pre-existing insight and those patients in whom insight evolved as a result of treatment. The latter was associated with decreased risk of future suicide attempts.

Clinically and conceptually, it is reasonable (and intuitive) to expect an association between a realistic and accurate evaluation of the difficulties associated with chronic psychotic disorder, the resulting 'lost potential', and an increase in the range of thoughts and feelings associated with suicide risk. The relationship between insight into psychotic illness and increased risk of suicide may relate to the previously discussed socio-demographic differences from suicide more generally, namely, the increased risk associated with higher levels of education and higher socio-economic status. Our previous discussion also suggested that unemployment is not associated with an increased risk for suicide among those with chronic psychotic disorders. This is not surprising given the low specificity with respect to the prediction of suicide of a characteristic shared by more than 80% of patients with chronic psychotic disorders at any given time (Bell, Lysaker, & Milstein, 1996).

Indeed, a recent small-scale study explored the interrelatedness of social class, an individual's evaluation of their lost potential, and feelings of depression and hopelessness (Lewine, 2005). Lewine reasoned astutely that it is not the dichotomous view of one's ability or inability to secure and maintain employment that is related to risk in this population, but rather it is the influence of their pre-morbid professional expectations which is crucial. This study found increased depressive symptoms and hopelessness to be associated with the degree of disparity between patients' current employment prospects and their professional expectations prior to the onset of psychotic illness. Most importantly, however, this association appeared to mediate (explain) the relationship between social class and increases in depressive symptoms and hopelessness. This study is also noteworthy as it provides a potential mechanism to explain why the socio-demographic profile of suicide deaths among those with psychotic illness differs from that of the wider population of completed suicides. Moreover, the relationship between familial social class and increased risk of suicide can also be observed in unaffected relatives of individuals with schizophrenia (Silverton, Mednick, Holst, & John, 2008).

Although meta-analyses have not yet confirmed the association between degree of insight and an increased risk of suicide (Hawton *et al.*, 2005), this is likely to be related to the inconsistent use of definitions of insight. In the context of Lewine's previously discussed findings, however, the relationship between suicide and insight may be contingent on the individual's pre-morbid expectations. Consistent with this prediction, a demoralization syndrome has been described in schizophrenia where functional deterioration compared with pre-morbid abilities and non-delusional awareness of the toll of the illness leads to feelings of hopelessness, depression, and ultimately suicide (Drake, Gates, Whitaker, & Cotton, 1985). A recent test of this demoralization hypothesis suggested that depressive symptoms mediated the association between insight, greater pre-morbid adjustment, and history of suicidal behaviour among patients with schizophrenia (Restifo, Harkavy-Friedman, & Shrout, 2009).

What has been confirmed by meta-analysis is a direct association between fear of mental disintegration and increased risk of death by suicide (Hawton *et al.*, 2005). Thus, not only are the immediate consequences of the disorder important risk factors for suicide, but a person's uncertainty regarding their future ability to function is also pertinent.

Psychopathology, Personality Traits, and Family History of Suicidal Behaviour

Comorbid psychopathology

Studies on suicide have consistently demonstrated the importance of psychopathology. Such studies suggest that upwards of 90% of suicide completers meet diagnostic criteria for a psychiatric disorder at the time of death (Arsenault-Lapierre, Kim, & Turecki, 2004). As previously discussed, chronic psychotic disorders are one of the diagnostic categories strongly associated with suicide. Other important diagnostic categories include depressive disorders (see Chapter 3), personality disorders (see Chapter 6), and substance abuse disorders (see Chapter 5).

An important question in determining risk for suicide in chronic psychotic disorders has been the importance of concomitant psychopathology. This is a natural extension of the consistent finding from studies of suicide more generally that have highlighted the importance of comorbid disorders (Beautrais, Joyce, Mulder, Fergusson, Deavoll, *et al.*, 1996; Hawton, Houston, Haw, Townsend, & Harriss, 2003; Henriksson *et al.*, 1993; Lesage *et al.*, 1994; Marttunen, Aro, Henriksson, & Lonqvist, 1991; Muller, Barkow, Kovalenko, Ohlraun, Fangerau, *et al.*, 2005; Rudd, Dahm, & Rajab, 1993), particularly mood disorders and psychopathology related to impulse dyscontrol such as substance abuse. However, when schizophrenia and other chronic psychotic disorders are compared with other suicides, the prevalence of comorbid psychopathology is considerably lower (McGirr & Turecki, 2008). The exception is drug abuse, where the prevalence is comparable in cases of chronic psychotic suicides and non-psychotic suicides. Indeed, latent class analysis (an analytical technique that eschews hypothesis-driven analyses to identify clusters of similar individuals) has been applied to a representative sample of suicides and it points to a decreased likelihood for psychotic suicides to meet criteria for comorbid psychopathology compared with other suicides (Kim, Lesage, Seguin, Chawky, Vanier, *et al.*, 2003). This latter study suggested that the cluster characterized by the lack of comorbidity was largely comprised of suicides meeting criteria for chronic psychotic disorders.

Nevertheless, the individual with chronic psychotic disorders who also meets criteria for certain concomitant psychopathologies is at an increased risk for suicide. Indeed, meta-analyses have confirmed the increased risk of suicidal behaviour when schizophrenia is comorbid with depressive disorders (Hawton *et al.*, 2005), and they have also confirmed that a range of depressive symptomatology including hopelessness, worthlessness, low self-esteem, and sleep disturbances are associated with suicidal behaviour (Hawton *et al.*, 2005). While some studies since the publication of the meta-analysis have failed to find an association between depressive disorders and suicide (Pompili, Lester, Grispini, Innamorati, *et al.*, 2009), almost all have replicated this association using a variety of designs, including psychological autopsies (McGirr, Tousignant, *et al.*, 2006) and chart reviews (Kuo, Tsai, Lo, Wang, & Chen, 2005; Sinclair, Mullee, King, & Baldwin, 2004). Moreover, comorbid depressive symptoms are strongly related to the latency between date of discharge and date of suicide in patients with schizophrenia, particularly among men (Karvonen, Sammela,

Rahikkala, Hakko, Sarkioja, *et al.*, 2007). Yet it is important to consider that, while depression is associated with an increased risk for suicide in the population affected by chronic psychotic disorders, the prevalence of this comorbidity among psychotic suicides is significantly less elevated than suicides more generally.

Psychopathology related to impulse dyscontrol, specifically cluster B personality disorders and substance abuse disorders, are also consistent risk factors in suicide more generally. Interestingly, the association between alcohol abuse and suicide has not typically emerged in studies comparing psychotic suicides with psychotic controls in meta-analyses (Hawton *et al.*, 2005) or in more recent studies (Kuo *et al.*, 2005; McGirr, Tousignant, *et al.*, 2006; Pompili *et al.*, 2009). The association between alcohol abuse has, however, been reported in studies examining non-lethal suicidal behaviour (Baca-Garcia, Perez-Rodriguez, Diaz Sastre, Saiz-Ruiz, & de Leon, 2005; Gut-Fayand, Dervaux, Olie, Loo, Poirier, *et al.*, 2001).

As mentioned earlier, suicides with chronic psychotic disorders are as likely as other suicides to meet criteria for drug abuse in the period preceding death, and meta-analysis suggests this factor is associated with an increased risk of suicide in this population (Hawton *et al.*, 2005). Nevertheless, it is clear that the association between drug abuse and suicide in this population is weaker than in other diagnostic categories; indeed, the relationship was not observed in the individual studies examined, but rather it emerged after pooling effects across studies (Hawton *et al.*, 2005). Moreover, more recent studies which have compared suicides with controls with chronic psychotic disorders have also failed to find this association (Kuo *et al.*, 2005; McGirr, Tousignant, *et al.*, 2006; Pompili *et al.*, 2009).

Cluster B psychopathology includes borderline personality disorder, the only diagnosis for which suicidal behaviour figures in the definition. There is a paucity of studies examining the role of personality psychopathology in chronic psychotic disorders, and those that have been conducted are severely limited by the early onset of psychotic disease, and therefore, the inherent difficulty in disentangling manifestations of psychosis from pre-existing personality. Nevertheless, one study has examined this issue and found no difference in cluster B symptomatology (McGirr, Tousignant, *et al.*, 2006). Similarly, impulsive aggression, a personality predisposition to suicide strongly associated with cluster B disorders (Turecki, 2005), has not been found to be elevated among suicides with chronic psychotic disorders than among similarly affected living controls (McGirr, Tousignant, *et al.*, 2006).

Overall, the evidence relating to comorbid psychopathology in the context of suicide occurring in chronic psychotic disorders suggests that depressive symptoms represent the greatest risk factor for suicide in this population. At the same time, drug abuse does appear to be associated with a marginal increase in risk for suicide in this population. Important psychopathological categories, such as substance abuse and other psychopathology related to impulse dyscontrol, appear to have limited predictive value as comorbid conditions in the context of chronic psychotic disorder.

Family history

In the suicide literature more broadly, there is support for a genetic contribution to suicide using a variety of methodologies. Family studies are one such methodology, where the occurrence of suicidal behaviour among the relatives of individuals who have attempted or died by suicide is compared with the occurrence of suicidal behaviour in the relatives of comparison subjects. Higher levels among the relatives of individuals who have engaged in suicidal behaviour is evidence of familial aggregation and suggestive of heritability. Such studies in suicide have confirmed familial aggregation and suggested that it operates independent of psychopathology (Brent, Bridge, Johnson, & Connolly, 1996; McGirr, Alda, Séguin, Cabot, Lesage, *et al.*, 2009). It is undoubtedly the case that suicide is the result of genetic and environmental interactions, yet both twin and adoption studies support a role for the genetic contribution to suicide risk beyond shared and unshared environment (Roy, Segal, Centerwall, & Robinette, 1991; Statham, Heath, Madden, Bucholz, Bierut, *et al.*, 1998). This is also supported by adoption studies, which also confirm a genetic contribution to suicide (Wender, Kety, Rosenthal, Schulsinger, Ortmann, *et al.*, 1986).

While the increased risk for suicide and independence of familial liability from psychopathology has been reported in chronic psychotic disorders (McGirr, Tousignant, *et al.*, 2006), the majority of studies do not support familial aggregation of suicide in the context of chronic psychotic disorders (Hawton *et al.*, 2005; Kuo *et al.*, 2005; Reutfors, Brandt, Jonsson, Ekbom, Sparen, *et al.*, 2009; Roy, 1982). It is, thus, important for the clinician to consider family history of suicide on a case-by-case basis, although the weight of evidence does not support incorporating this information into treatment decisions.

Treatment of Chronic Psychotic Disorders: Implications for Suicide Risk

An important concept in the treatment of chronic psychotic disorders is the inverse relationship between the duration of untreated psychosis and patient outcomes. Studies have demonstrated that poorer outcomes (on numerous indicators) are associated with the length of time an individual experiences a first psychotic episode without receiving medical attention (Kirkpatrick & Tek, 2005), the so-called 'duration of untreated psychosis'. Recently, a large Scandinavian programme for the early detection of schizophrenia demonstrated a reduction in suicidal behaviour among psychotic individuals in the detection programme's catchment area compared with neighbouring areas (Melle, Johannesen, Friis, Haahr, Joa, *et al.*, 2006). Consequently, this study illustrates the importance of early treatment and the considerable potential of reducing suicide risk in this population. Similarly, once detected, meta-analyses have emphasized the importance of treatment adherence and the increased risk for suicide associated with non-adherence to treatment (Hawton *et al.*, 2005).

Pharmacotherapy

It has been more than a decade since initial reports suggested that pharmacological treatment with clozapine (an atypical antipsychotic) is associated with decreased suicidality in schizophrenia (Meltzer & Okayli, 1995). This initial study reported on a sample of neuroleptic-resistant patients who then went on a course of clozapine, and found a reduction in suicide attempts compared with pre-clozapine treatment periods. This study's suicide attempt results were reinforced by large decreases in a number of other indicators of suicide risk, including depressive symptoms, helplessness, and suicidal ideation.

A retrospective chart review study has since replicated this finding in a naturalistic setting by comparing the prevalence of suicide attempts prior to treatment with clozapine to the incidence of suicide attempts while on clozapine and the incidence after discontinuation of clozapine (Modestin, Dal Pian, & Agarwalla, 2005). Rates of suicidal behaviour while following a treatment course of clozapine were compared with suicidal behaviour prior to this therapeutic approach, and also following this approach. This study reported that 28% of the patients with schizophrenia reported having engaged in suicidal behaviour prior to clozapine therapy, but only 3% of patients reported engaging in suicidal behaviour during a mean treatment time of 15 months. Moreover, while the data after termination of clozapine therapy were only available for approximately one-fifth of the sample, the rate of suicidal behaviour returned to a rate of 18% in this sub-sample. While acknowledging that this study did not yield the level of evidence of a double-blind randomized placebo-controlled trial, these findings nevertheless suggest that clozapine therapy may be directly and causally associated with a reduction in suicide risk.

Additional evidence supporting the efficacy of clozapine in reducing suicidal behaviour comes from a large multinational, prospective clinical trial in schizophrenic and schizoaffective patients at high risk of suicide. The InterSePT trial (Meltzer, Alphs, Green, Altamura, *et al.*, 2003), investigated a total of 980 patients who were followed up for 2 years and found evidence that clozapine reduced suicide attempts, hospitalizations due to attempts and overall depressive symptomatology. Further, the role of clozapine as a suicide risk reducing agent in schizophrenia has been confirmed using a meta-analytical approach (Hennen & Baldessarini, 2005). This meta-analysis reported a greater than three-fold reduction in the risk of suicidal behaviour and, importantly, just under a three-fold reduction in the rates of death by suicide when patients with schizophrenia are treated with clozapine.

Unfortunately, the benefits of pharmacological management of suicidality in schizophrenia do not appear to extend beyond clozapine. In a study examining the effectiveness of many conventional and atypical antipsychotics in reducing rates of suicidal behaviour compared with placebo, no other drug demonstrated benefits compared with placebo (Khan, Khan, Leventhal, & Brown, 2001). This is unfortunate, for clozapine is associated with numerous and significant side-effects in addition to five black box warnings ((1) agranulocytosis, (2) seizures, (3) myocarditis, (4) increased mortality in geriatric patients – notably from cardiac-related events, (5) other cardiovascular and respiratory effects – notably orthostatic hypotension resulting in collapse, respiratory, and/or cardiac arrest), and is consequently only indicated for the treatment of resistant schizophrenia.

From a pharmacodynamic (the physiological effects of a drug) standpoint, however, the success of clozapine in reducing suicidal behaviour suggests potential for isolating some of the therapeutic aspects of clozapine and perhaps developing new treatment options for the chronic psychotic patient at high risk of suicide. This avenue, however, has not yet yielded beneficial outcomes. In a randomized treatment trial comparing clozapine and olanzapine, a structural analogue of clozapine, olanzapine did not reduce suicidal behaviour (Meltzer, Alphs, Green, Altamura, Anand, *et al.*, 2003). Nevertheless, additional research may reveal the mechanism underlying the suicide-reducing benefits of clozapine and lead to the development of alternative pharmacological agents with more tolerable side-effect profiles.

Taken together, there is some evidence to suggest that early identification and treatment reduces suicidal behaviour in chronic psychotic disorders. Yet studies examining the role of specific medications have revealed benefits only for clozapine, a medication indicated only for treatment-resistant schizophrenia and, therefore, a minority of patients. Thus, the limited benefits of pharmacological management on suicidal behaviour over placebo are difficult to reconcile with the clear benefits of psychiatric intervention on suicide outcomes, suggesting a strong role for the therapeutic relationship between healthcare provider and the patient with a chronic psychotic disorder over the specific actions of certain medications. More importantly, it suggests that support and vigilance on the part of clinicians and service providers can play an important role in curbing the significant loss of life in this population.

Non-pharmacological therapy

Non-pharmacological therapy is an integral component of the treatment for schizophrenia. Supportive therapies, family-based therapies, and conflict training (aimed at educating the patient in the appropriate management of cognition and behaviour in situations of conflict) are important in contributing to successful outcomes. Moreover, psychotherapy offers patients a forum facilitated by a trained therapist for discussing any difficulties, concerns regarding their illness or medication, stigma, or social isolation. Unfortunately, the opportunity to provide guidance and support is of limited value during the active phases of psychotic illness, yet guidance and support are of great value between such phases.

Research on non-pharmacological therapy in reducing suicidal behaviour among individuals with chronic psychotic disorders has not received the same attention in recent years as pharmacological treatments. However, several older studies suggest benefits in respect of the recurrence of psychotic decompensations and overall outcomes (Mueser & Berenbaum, 1990), particularly when individuals benefit from the additional support of living with family (Hogarty, Greenwald, Ulrich, Kornblith, DiBarry, *et al.*, 1997; Hogarty, Kornblith, Greenwald, DiBarry, Cooley, *et al.*, 1997). Yet, there is a dearth of information on the effects of psychotherapy specifically on suicidal behaviour in this population.

One promising form of non-pharmacological therapy, cognitive behavioural therapy (CBT), was shown in a recent meta-analysis to reduce positive symptoms, not suicide, in schizophrenia (Zimmermann, Favrod, Trieu, & Pomini, 2005). This meta-analysis indicated that CBT is most effective at reducing positive symptoms early in the course of the disorder.

To directly investigate the effectiveness of CBT in relation to suicidal behaviour in chronic psychotic disorders, a multi-centre controlled trial was conducted. This trial had two arms: treatment as usual combined with either supportive therapy or CBT. In the first reports, the previously shown benefits on positive symptoms were replicated (Lewis, Tarrier, Haddock, Bentall, Kinderman, *et al.*, 2002; Tarrier, Lewis, Haddock, Bentall, Drake, *et al.*, 2004). In the report focusing on suicidal behaviour, however, the authors report that their CBT programme did not have an effect on suicidal behaviour (Tarrier, Haddock, Lewis, Drake, & Gregg, 2006). It is important to specify, however, that the form of CBT applied in this study was designed to reduce positive symptoms and no modification was made to make it suitable for reducing suicidal behaviour. From the standpoint of CBT, the authors argue that reducing suicide risk in this population may be achieved by incorporating additional components targeting depression and hopelessness.

An additional and exciting avenue in the treatment of schizophrenia that has shown considerable promise is cognitive enhancement therapy (CET) (Hogarty & Flesher, 1999), whereby training is used to improve attention, memory, problem-solving, and social cognition. The underlying theory of this therapeutic approach is that deficits in social cognition and neurocognition are key components of chronic psychotic disorders. By providing multidimensional approaches that integrate computer-assisted training with group-based social cognition exercises, significant and sustained recovery of these deficits have been observed in chronic psychotic disorders (Hogarty, Flesher, Ulrich, Carter, Greenwald, et al., 2004). Similarly, studies that have incorporated neurocognitive training into vocational services for individuals with chronic psychotic disorders have demonstrated sustained improvements in cognitive ability (Greig, Zito, Wexler, Fiszdon, & Bell, 2007), but most importantly, they have demonstrated increases in participants' ability to secure employment and increased productivity (Bell, Zito, Greig, & Wexler, 2008). While systematic research is required to test whether these improvements extend to suicide and suicidal behaviour, the improvements demonstrated with respect to social and occupational functioning should spur on those interested in improving suicide outcomes in this population to incorporate neurocognitive and social training. This may prove to be an invaluable approach to addressing the previously discussed expectation gap between pre-morbid abilities and functional deterioration as a consequence of psychotic illness.

Conclusion

Suicide in chronic psychotic disorders is unacceptably high and poses a major public health problem. Studies suggest that suicide is the leading cause of premature death in this population, occurring early in the course of the disorder, particularly among males. Acute psychotic illness and concomitant depressive disorders greatly increase the risk for suicide. Early recognition of these risk factors and swift intervention are clinically important for reducing suicide in this population.

Similarly, programmes targeted at the early detection of first episode psychosis and clinical treatment are associated with a decreased risk for suicide. Yet, with the exception of clozapine, pharmacological therapy does not reduce rates of suicidal behaviour significantly more than placebo. In addition, treatment non-adherence is strongly associated with suicide and is likely to be as a result of increased acute psychotic decompensation.

The degree of insight that an individual has into the disorder is associated with increased risk of suicide and suicidal behaviour, particularly among individuals from a background characterized by higher socio-economic status, and who are confronted with a large disparity between their pre-morbid expectations and their current prospects. Newer treatment strategies, including social and neurocognitive training offer promise in this respect, as they are associated with sustained improvements in social and neurocognitive deficits and additionally they improve patients' ability to seek and maintain gainful employment.

Finally, additional basic and applied research is required into the pharmacotherapeutic and non-pharmacotherapeutic treatments for suicide in schizophrenia and other chronic psychotic disorders.

References

Agerbo, E. (2007). High income, employment, postgraduate education, and marriage: A suicidal cocktail among psychiatric patients. *Archives of General Psychiatry, 64*, 1377–1384.

Alaraisanen, A., Miettunen, J., Rasanen, P., Fenton, W., Koivumaa-Honkanen, H. T., & Isohanni, M. (2009). Suicide rate in schizophrenia in the Northern Finland 1966 Birth Cohort. *Social Psychiatry & Psychiatric Epidemiology, 25*, 25.

Amador, X. (2004). Understand and assessing insight. In X. Amador & A. David (Eds.), *Insight and Psychosis*, 2nd ed. New York: Oxford University Press.

APA. (1994). *DSM-IV: Diagnostic and statistical manual of mental disorders*, 4th. ed. American Psychiatric Press.

Arsenault-Lapierre, G., Kim, C., & Turecki, G. (2004). Psychiatric diagnoses in 3275 suicides: A meta-analysis. *BMC Psychiatry, 4*, 37.

Baca-Garcia, E., Perez-Rodriguez, M. M., Diaz Sastre, C., Saiz-Ruiz, J., & de Leon, J. (2005). Suicidal behaviour in schizophrenia and depression: A comparison. *Schizophrenia Research, 75*, 77–81.

Beautrais, A. L., Joyce, P. R., Mulder, R. T., Fergusson, D. M., Deavoll, B. J., & Nightingale, S. K. (1996). Prevalence and comorbidity of mental disorders in persons making serious suicide attempts: A case-control study. *American Journal of Psychiatry, 153*, 1009–1014.

Bell, M. D., Lysaker, P., & Milstein, R. (1996). Clinical benefits of paid work activity in schizophrenia. *Schizophrenia Bulletin, 22*, 51–67.

Bell, M. D., Zito, W., Greig, T., & Wexler, B. E. (2008). Neurocognitive enhancement therapy with vocational services: Work outcomes at two-year follow-up. *Schizophrenia Research, 105*, 18–29.

Bourgeois, M., Swendsen, J., Young, F., Amador, X., Pini, S., Cassano, G. B., *et al.* (2004). Awareness of disorder and suicide risk in the treatment of schizophrenia: Results of the international suicide prevention trial. *American Journal of Psychiatry, 161*, 1494–1496.

Brent, D. A., Bridge, J., Johnson, B. A., & Connolly, J. (1996). Suicidal behavior runs in families: A controlled family study of adolescent suicide victims. *Archives of General Psychiatry, 53*, 1145–1152.

Brown, S. (1997). Excess mortality of schizophrenia. A meta-analysis. *British Journal of Psychiatry, 171*, 502–508.

Buchanan, R. W., & Carpenter, W. T. (2005). Concept of schizophrenia. In B. J. Sadock & V. A. Sadock (Eds.), *Kaplan & Sadock's Comprehensive Textbook of Psychiatry*, 8th ed. (vol. I). Philadelphia: Lippincott Williams & Wilkins.

Caldwell, C. B., & Gottesman, II. (1990). Schizophrenics kill themselves too: A review of risk factors for suicide. *Schizophrenia Bulletin, 16*, 571–589.

Coryell, W., & Young, E. A. (2005). Clinical predictors of suicide in primary major depressive disorder. *Journal of Clinical Psychiatry, 66*, 412–417.

Drake, R. E., Gates, C., Whitaker, A., & Cotton, P. G. (1985). Suicide among schizophrenics: A review. *Comprehensive Psychiatry, 26*, 90–100.

Fenton, W. S. (2000). Depression, suicide, and suicide prevention in schizophrenia. *Suicide & Life Threatening Behavior, 30*, 34–49.

Greig, T. C., Zito, W., Wexler, B. E., Fiszdon, J., & Bell, M. D. (2007). Improved cognitive function in schizophrenia after one year of cognitive training and vocational services. *Schizophrenia Research, 96*, 156–161.

Gut-Fayand, A., Dervaux, A., Olie, J. P., Loo, H., Poirier, M. F., & Krebs, M. O. (2001). Substance abuse and suicidality in schizophrenia: A common risk factor linked to impulsivity. *Psychiatry Research, 102*, 65–72.

Hawton, K., Houston, K., Haw, C., Townsend, E., & Harriss, L. (2003). Comorbidity of Axis I and Axis II disorders in patients who attempted suicide. *American Journal of Psychiatry*, 160, 1494–1500.

Hawton, K., Sutton, L., Haw, C., Sinclair, J., & Deeks, J. J. (2005). Schizophrenia and suicide: Systematic review of risk factors. *British Journal of Psychiatry*, 187, 9–20.

Heila, H., Isometsa, E. T., Henriksson, M. M., Heikkinen, M. E., Marttunen, M. J., & Lonqvist, J. K. (1997). Suicide and schizophrenia: A nationwide psychological autopsy study on age- and sex-specific clinical characteristics of 92 suicide victims with schizophrenia. *American Journal of Psychiatry*, 154, 1235–1242.

Hellerstein, D., Frosch, W., & Koenigsberg, H. W. (1987). The clinical significance of command hallucinations. *American Journal of Psychiatry*, 144, 219–221.

Hennen, J., & Baldessarini, R. J. (2005). Suicidal risk during treatment with clozapine: A meta-analysis. *Schizophrenia Research*, 73, 139–145.

Henriksson, M. M., Aro, H. M., Marttunen, M. J., Heikkinen, M. E., Isometsa, E. T., Kuoppasalmi, K. I., et al. (1993). Mental disorders and comorbidity in suicide. *American Journal of Psychiatry*, 150, 935–940.

Hogarty, G. E. & Flesher, S. (1999). Practice principles of cognitive enhancement therapy for schizophrenia. *Schizophrenia Bulletin*, 25, 693–708.

Hogarty, G. E., Flesher, S., Ulrich, R., Carter, M., Greenwald, D., Pogue-Geile, M., et al. (2004). Cognitive enhancement therapy for schizophrenia: effects of a 2-year randomized trial on cognition and behavior. *Archives of General Psychiatry*, 61, 866–876.

Hogarty, G. E., Greenwald, D., Ulrich, R. F., Kornblith, S. J., DiBarry, A. L., Cooley, S., et al. (1997). Three-year trials of personal therapy among schizophrenic patients living with or independent of family, II: Effects on adjustment of patients. *American Journal of Psychiatry*, 154, 1514–1524.

Hogarty, G. E., Kornblith, S. J., Greenwald, D., DiBarry, A. L., Cooley, S., Ulrich, R. F., et al. (1997). Three-year trials of personal therapy among schizophrenic patients living with or independent of family, I: Description of study and effects on relapse rates. *American Journal of Psychiatry*, 154, 1504–1513.

Hu, W. H., Sun, C. M., Lee, C. T., Peng, S. L., Lin, S. K., & Shen, W. W. (1991). A clinical study of schizophrenic suicides. 42 cases in Taiwan. *Schizophrenia Research*, 5, 43–50.

Inskip, H. M., Harris, E. C., & Barraclough, B. (1998). Lifetime risk of suicide for affective disorder, alcoholism and schizophrenia. *British Journal of Psychiatry*, 172, 35–37.

Kaplan, K. J. & Harrow, M. (1996). Positive and negative symptoms as risk factors for later suicidal activity in schizophrenics versus depressives. *Suicide & Life Threatening Behavior*, 26, 105–121.

Karvonen, K., Sammela, H. L., Rahikkala, H., Hakko, H., Sarkioja, T., Meyer-Rochow, V. B., et al. (2007). Sex, timing, and depression among suicide victims with schizophrenia. *Comprehensive Psychiatry*, 48, 319–322.

Khan, A., Khan, S. R., Leventhal, R. M., & Brown, W. A. (2001). Symptom reduction and suicide risk among patients treated with placebo in antipsychotic clinical trials: An analysis of the food and drug administration database. *American Journal of Psychiatry*, 158, 1449–1454.

Kim, C., Lesage, A., Seguin, M., Chawky, N., Vanier, C., Lipp, O., et al. (2003). Patterns of co-morbidity in male suicide completers. *Psychological Medicine*, 33, 1299–1309.

Kirkpatrick, B., & Tek, C. (2005). Schizophrenia: Clinical features and psychopathology concepts. In B. J. Sadock & V. A. Sadock (Eds.), *Kaplan & Sadock's Comprehensive Textbook of Psychiatry*, 8th ed. (vol. I). Philadelphia: Lippincott Williams & Wilkins.

Kuo, C. J., Tsai, S. Y., Lo, C. H., Wang, Y. P., & Chen, C. C. (2005). Risk factors for completed suicide in schizophrenia. *Journal of Clinical Psychiatry*, 66, 579–585.

Lesage, A. D., Boyer, R., Grunberg, F., Vanier, C., Morissette, R., Menard-Buteau, C., et al. (1994). Suicide and mental disorders: A case-control study of young men. *American Journal of Psychiatry*, 151, 1063–1068.

Lewine, R. R. (2005). Social class of origin, lost potential, and hopelessness in schizophrenia. *Schizophrenia Research, 76,* 329–335.

Lewis, S., Tarrier, N., Haddock, G., Bentall, R., Kinderman, P., Kingdon, D., *et al.* (2002). Randomised controlled trial of cognitive-behavioural therapy in early schizophrenia: Acute-phase outcomes. *British Journal of Psychiatry Suppl., 43,* s91–s97.

Marttunen, M. J., Aro, H. M., Henriksson, M. M., & Lonqvist, J. K. (1991). Mental disorders in adolescent suicide. DSM-III-R Axes I and II diagnoses in suicides among 13- to 19-year-olds in Finland. *Archives of General Psychiatry, 48,* 834–839.

McGirr, A., Alda, M., Séguin, M., Cabot, S., Lesage, A., & Turecki, G. (2009). Familial aggregation of suicide explained by cluster B traits: A three-group family study of suicide controlling for major depressive disorder. *American Journal of Psychiatry, 166,* 1124–1134.

McGirr, A., Seguin, M., Renaud, J., Benkelfat, C., Alda, M., & Turecki, G. (2006). Gender and risk factors for suicide: Evidence for heterogeneity in predisposing mechanisms. *Journal of Clinical Psychiatry, 67,* 1612–1617.

McGirr, A., Tousignant, M., Routhier, D., Pouliot, L., Chawky, N., Margolese, H. C., *et al.* (2006). Risk factors for completed suicide in schizophrenia and other chronic psychotic disorders: A case-control study. *Schizophrenia Research, 84,* 132–143.

McGirr, A., & Turecki, G. (2008). What is specific to suicide in schizophrenia? Behavioural, clinical and sociodemographic dimensions. *Schizophrenia Research, 98,* 217–224.

Melle, I., Johannesen, J. O., Friis, S., Haahr, U., Joa, I., Larsen, T. K., *et al.* (2006). Early detection of the first episode of schizophrenia and suicidal behavior. *American Journal of Psychiatry, 163,* 800–804.

Meltzer, H. Y. (1998). Suicide in schizophrenia: Risk factors and clozapine treatment. *Journal of Clinical Psychiatry, 59* (Suppl. 3), 15–20.

Meltzer, H. Y., Alphs, L., Green, A. I., Altamura, A. C., Anand, R., Bertoldi, A., *et al.* (2003). Clozapine treatment for suicidality in schizophrenia: International Suicide Prevention Trial (InterSePT). *Archives of General Psychiatry, 60,* 82–91.

Meltzer, H. Y., & Okayli, G. (1995). Reduction of suicidality during clozapine treatment of neuroleptic-resistant schizophrenia: Impact on risk-benefit assessment. *American Journal of Psychiatry, 152,* 183–190.

Miles, C. P. (1977). Conditions predisposing to suicide: a review. *Journal of Nervous & Mental Disorder, 164,* 231–246.

Modestin, J., Dal Pian, D., & Agarwalla, P. (2005). Clozapine diminishes suicidal behavior: A retrospective evaluation of clinical records. *Journal of Clinical Psychiatry, 66,* 534–538.

Mueser, K. T. & Berenbaum, H. (1990). Psychodynamic treatment of schizophrenia: Is there a future? *Psychological Medicine, 20,* 253–262.

Muller, D. J., Barkow, K., Kovalenko, S., Ohlraun, S., Fangerau, H., Kolsch, H., *et al.* (2005). Suicide attempts in schizophrenia and affective disorders with relation to some specific demographical and clinical characteristics. *European Psychiatry, 20,* 65–69.

Palmer, B. A., Pankratz, V. S., & Bostwick, J. M. (2005). The lifetime risk of suicide in schizophrenia: A re-examination. *Archives of General Psychiatry, 62,* 247–253.

Pompili, M., Lester, D., Grispini, A., Innamorati, M., Calandro, F., Iliceto, P., *et al.* (2009). Completed suicide in schizophrenia: Evidence from a case-control study. *Psychiatry Research, 167,* 251–257.

Qin, P., Agerbo, E., & Mortensen, P. B. (2003). Suicide risk in relation to socioeconomic, demographic, psychiatric, and familial factors: A national register-based study of all suicides in Denmark, 1981–1997. *American Journal of Psychiatry, 160,* 765–772.

Restifo, K., Harkavy-Friedman, J. M., & Shrout, P. E. (2009). Suicidal behavior in schizophrenia: A test of the demoralization hypothesis. *Journal of Nervous & Mental Diseases, 197,* 147–153.

Reutfors, J., Brandt, L., Jonsson, E. G., Ekbom, A., Sparen, P., & Osby, U. (2009). Risk factors for suicide in schizophrenia: Findings from a Swedish population-based case-control study. *Schizophrenia Research, 108,* 231–237.

Roy, A. (1982). Suicide in chronic schizophrenia. *British Journal of Psychiatry, 141,* 171–177.

Roy, A., Segal, N. L., Centerwall, B. S., & Robinette, C. D. (1991). Suicide in twins. *Archives of General Psychiatry, 48,* 29–32.

Rudd, M. D., Dahm, P. F., & Rajab, M. H. (1993). Diagnostic comorbidity in persons with suicidal ideation and behavior. *American Journal of Psychiatry, 150,* 928–934.

Rudnick, A. (1999). Relation between command hallucinations and dangerous behavior. *Journal of American Academy of Psychiatry Law, 27,* 253–257.

Silverton, L., Mednick, S. A., Holst, C., & John, R. (2008). High social class and suicide in persons at risk for schizophrenia. *Acta Psychiatrica Scandinavica, 117,* 192–197.

Sinclair, J. M., Mullee, M. A., King, E. A., & Baldwin, D. S. (2004). Suicide in schizophrenia: A retrospective case-control study of 51 suicides. *Schizophrenia Bulletin, 30,* 803–811.

Statham, D. J., Heath, A. C., Madden, P. A., Bucholz, K. K., Bierut, L., Dinwiddie, S. H., *et al.* (1998). Suicidal behavior: An epidemiological and genetic study. *Psychological Medicine, 28,* 839–855.

Tarrier, N., Haddock, G., Lewis, S., Drake, R., & Gregg, L. (2006). Suicide behavior over 18 months in recent onset schizophrenic patients: The effects of CBT. *Schizophrenia Research, 83,* 15–27.

Tarrier, N., Lewis, S., Haddock, G., Bentall, R., Drake, R., Kinderman, P., *et al.* (2004). Cognitive-behavioural therapy in first-episode and early schizophrenia: 18-month follow-up of a randomized controlled trial. *British Journal of Psychiatry, 184,* 231–239.

Tsuang, M. T. (1978). Suicide in schizophrenics, manics, depressives, and surgical controls. A comparison with general population suicide mortality. *Archives of General Psychiatry, 35,* 153–155.

Turecki, G. (2005). Dissecting the suicide phenotype: the role of impulsive-aggressive behaviors. *Journal of Psychiatry & Neuroscience, 30,* 398–408.

Wender, P. H., Kety, S. S., Rosenthal, D., Schulsinger, F., Ortmann, J., & Lunde, I. (1986). Psychiatric disorders in the biological and adoptive families of adopted individuals with affective disorders. *Archives of General Psychiatry, 43,* 923–929.

Zanarini, M. C., Frankenburg, F. R., Hennen, J., Reich, D. B., & Silk, K. R. (2005). The McLean Study of Adult Development (MSAD): Overview and implications of the first six years of prospective follow-up. *Journal of Personality Disorders, 19,* 505–523.

Zimmermann, G., Favrod, J., Trieu, V. H., & Pomini, V. (2005). The effect of cognitive behavioural treatment on the positive symptoms of schizophrenia spectrum disorders: A meta-analysis. *Schizophrenia Research, 77,* 1–9.

Zisook, S., Byrd, D., Kuck, J., & Jeste, D. V. (1995). Command hallucinations in outpatients with schizophrenia. *Journal of Clinical Psychiatry, 56,* 462–465.

CHAPTER FIVE

Substance Use Disorders and Suicidal Behaviour

Kenneth R. Conner and Mark A. Ilgen

Abstract

Individuals with substance use disorders (SUDs), including those with alcohol use disorders (AUDs) and several specific drug use disorders (DUDs), are at elevated risk for suicidal behaviour. Although many SUDs confer risk, most individuals with an SUD do not attempt suicide or die by suicide. This fact has stimulated research on risk factors for suicidal behaviour among SUD populations. This chapter focuses on risk for suicidal behaviour in those with SUDs and discusses distal risk factors, defined as variables that create a long-term diathesis (or susceptibility) for suicidal behaviour among individuals with SUDs, as well as proximal risk factors, defined as variables that are in evidence near the time of suicidal behaviour that exert a causal influence. Research findings support the role of three key distal risk factors in suicidal behaviour: (1) severity of the SUD; (2) aggression/impulsivity; and (3) negative affectivity. Evidence is also presented for three key proximal risk factors: (1) active substance use and symptoms; (2) interpersonal stress; and (3) major depressive symptoms. Available research is integrated into a conceptual model that jointly considers these distal and proximal risk factors. The model posits that the distal factors promote the occurrence and intensification of the proximal factors, which in turn increase the short-term risk for suicidal behaviour. The chapter closes with a discussion of strategies to test the model. Throughout, research specific to AUDs is distinguished from findings on other SUDs.

International Handbook of Suicide Prevention: Research, Policy and Practice, First Edition.
Edited by Rory C. O'Connor, Stephen Platt, Jacki Gordon.
© 2011 John Wiley & Sons, Ltd. Published 2011 by John Wiley & Sons, Ltd.

Introduction

The discussion begins with a review of evidence to show that individuals with substance use disorders (SUDs), including those with alcohol use disorders (AUDs) and some other drug use disorders (DUDs), are at elevated risk for suicidal behaviour. Next, the chapter focuses on key distal risk factors (SUD severity, aggression/impulsivity, negative affectivity) and proximal risk factors (active substance use and symptoms, interpersonal stress, depressive symptoms) for suicidal behaviour within substance use disorder populations. Distal and proximal risk factors are integrated into a parsimonious theoretical model that posits that the distal risk factors (e.g., negative affectivity) increase the probability for the proximal risk factors (e.g., depressive symptoms), which in turn increase the likelihood of suicidal behaviour. In this scenario, the proximal risk factors are conceptualized as factors that partially or fully explain the relationship between the distal risk factors and suicidal behaviour. Key decisions in developing the model along with limitations and caveats are explained. The chapter concludes with a discussion of possible ways to test the conceptual framework.

Evidence that Individuals with SUDS are at Elevated Risk

Suicidal behaviour is an acute, self-injurious act with at least some intent to die including acts that are non-fatal (i.e., suicide attempt) and fatal (i.e., suicide). Much of the research on SUDs and suicidal behaviour is based on studies of individuals with AUDs. Individuals with AUDs are at elevated risk for suicide with a meta-analysis showing that those identified through treatment venues are at approximately 9.8 (9.0–10.7) times greater risk for eventual suicide compared with the general population (Wilcox, Conner, & Caine, 2004). AUDs and other SUDs are the second most prevalent mental disorder among suicide decedents, behind only mood disorders (Cavanagh, Carson, Sharpe, & Lawrie, 2003). Moreover, psychological autopsy studies of adults using a controlled research design have consistently shown that an AUD confers risk after adjusting for other risk factors (Cheng, 1995; Foster, Gillespie, McClelland, & Patterson, 1999; Kolves, Varnik, Tooding, & Wasserman, 2006; Lesage, Boyer, Grundberg, Vanier, Morisette, *et al.*, 1994). An exception comes from a report from China that did not show that an AUD confers risk for suicide (Phillips, Yang, Zhang, Wang, Ji, *et al.*, 2002). However, the increased rates of drinking and AUDs among men in China over the past several years (Zhou, Conner, Phillips, Caine, Xiao, *et al.*, 2009) suggest that AUDs may now play an increasing role in suicidal behaviour in China. Data also support that AUDs confer risk for suicide attempts (Kessler, Borges, & Walters, 1999) and, indeed, may be an especially potent risk factor for an attempt (Rossow, Romelsjo, & Leifman, 1999). Individuals enrolled in alcoholism treatment are especially likely to have a history of attempt (Roy, Lamparski, DeJong, Moore, & Linnoila, 1990; Roy & Janal, 2007; Wojnar, Ilgen, Czyz, Strobbe, Klimkiewicz, *et al.*, 2009).

We refer to DUDs to describe abuse or dependence on (non-alcohol) substances including cocaine, opiates, etc., excluding tobacco dependence. Drawing firm conclusions about the relationship between many specific DUDs and suicide is difficult due to limited data.

A recent meta-analysis was not able to estimate risk for most specific categories of DUDs (Wilcox, Conner, & Caine, 2004). However, there were sufficient data to estimate that individuals obtaining treatment for an opioid use disorder were at 13.5 (10.5–17.2) times greater risk for eventual suicide compared with individuals of comparable age and sex residing in the community. Similar results were obtained when intravenous drug use disorders were examined. Although lacking a control group and limited to those tested for specific substances (less than 50% who died by suicide), results of coroners' reports from 13 states in the United States indicate that cocaine was present in 9% to 17% of suicide decedents and opiates present in 8% to 18% depending on the racial/ethnic group (Karch, Barker, & Strine, 2006). An Australian study found that approximately 16% of amphetamine-related deaths and 11% of opiate-related deaths were due to suicide (Degenhardt, Roxburgh, & Barker, 2005). Overall, the available evidence consistently links stimulants (cocaine and amphetamines) and opiates (both licit and illicit) to suicide mortality. In terms of research on suicide attempts, national survey data in the United States indicate that risk of lifetime attempt is 5.9 (3.4–10.2) times greater in those with a diagnosis of drug abuse and 5.8 (3.3–10.1) times greater for those with a diagnosis of drug dependence. Data from SUD treatment settings also indicates that individuals treated for cocaine dependence (Roy, 2001), opiate dependence (Darke, Ross, Lynskey, & Teesson, 2004), and a mixture of SUDs (Conner, Swogger, & Houston, 2009; Ilgen, Jain, Lucas, & Moos, 2007; Wines, Saitz, Horton, Lloyd-Travaglini, & Samet, 2004) have high lifetime prevalence rates of attempt.

Distal Risk Factors for Suicidal Behaviour among Individuals with SUDS

Severe substance use disorder as a distal risk factor

A risk factor is a variable that divides a population into individuals at higher- and lower-risk for suicidal behaviour. *Distal* risk factors are those that create a long-term diathesis (propensity) for suicidal behaviour. AUD severity has been measured in a variety of ways including earlier onset of problem drinking or alcoholism, greater number of lifetime AUD symptoms, alcohol dependence versus abuse only, binge drinking pattern, comorbid drug use disorder, and comorbid medical disorders (Penick, Nickel, Powell, Liskow, Campbell, *et al.*, 1999). Studies of individuals with AUDs consistently show that such indicators of AUD severity serve as distal risk factors for suicide attempts (Hasin, Grant, & Endicott, 1988; Preuss, Schuckit, Smith, Danko, Buckman, *et al.*, 2002; Roy *et al.*, 1990; Roy & Janal, 2007). Limited prospective data also support that alcoholism severity predicts subsequent suicide attempts (Preuss, Schuckit, Smith, Danko, Bucholz, *et al.*, 2003). Co-occurring drug use and drug use disorders stand out as the indicators of AUD severity that has been most consistently demonstrated to represent a distal risk factor for suicidal behaviour among individuals with AUDs (Dick, Agrawal, Wang, Hinrichs, Bertelsen, *et al.*, 2007; Gomberg, 1989; Hesselbrock, Hesselbrock, Syzmanski, & Weidenman, 1988; Preuss *et al.*, 2002; Roy *et al.*, 1990).

Severity is assessed in similar ways among individuals with other SUDs as it is with those with AUDs (e.g., earlier onset of SUD, polysubstance dependence, etc.). Findings support that individuals with more severe SUDs are at greater risk for suicide attempts compared with those with less severe SUDs, with cross-sectional analyses indicating that individuals treated for SUDs who make suicide attempts have greater sedative use, more polysubstance use, and more severe drinking patterns and course of alcoholism compared with non-attempters (Conner, Swogger, & Houston, 2009; Ilgen, Harris, Moos, & Tiet, 2007; Landheim, Bakken, & Vaglum, 2006; Wines *et al.*, 2004). These findings are consistent with data from samples of individuals in treatment for specific DUDs. Among those treated for cocaine use disorders, greater severity of alcohol or opiate use prior to treatment is associated with greater likelihood of a history of suicide attempt (Roy, 2001). Among individuals with opiate use disorders, lifetime suicide attempts are more common in those with co-occurring alcohol, marijuana, cocaine, and sedative use disorders (Maloney, Degenhardt, Darke, Mattick, & Nelson, 2007), benzodiazepine use (Darke *et al.*, 2004), and more extensive polysubstance use (Darke *et al.*, 2004; Maloney *et al.*, 2007). A few studies have examined the longitudinal predictors of suicide attempt following SUD treatment and have found that sedative use (Wines *et al.*, 2004) and longer duration of lifetime cocaine use and greater severity of baseline alcohol problems (Ilgen, Harris, *et al.*, 2007) predict post-treatment suicide attempts. Additionally, in a study of opiate users, greater polysubstance misuse was associated with greater likelihood of subsequent suicide attempt even after accounting for baseline suicidal thoughts and prior attempts (Darke, Ross, Williamson, Mills, Havard, *et al.*, 2007). Collectively, these findings indicate that individuals with more severe SUDs are at elevated long-term risk for suicidal behaviour compared with individuals with less severe SUDs.

Negative affectivity as a distal risk factor

Vulnerability to experiencing negative affect, commonly referred to as neuroticism or negative affectivity, is associated with most psychiatric conditions including major depressive disorder (Ormel, Oldehinkel, & Vollebergh, 2004; Widiger & Trull, 1992). There is a wealth of evidence that negative affectivity is strongly associated with depression, including as a predictor of major depression (Kendler, Neale, Kessler, Heath, & Eaves, 1993), and the recurrence and persistence of depressive symptoms (Surtees & Wainwright, 1996). Similarly, studies of SUDs also show that negative affectivity distinguishes those with higher levels of depressive symptoms (Ball & Schottenfeld, 1997; McCormick, Dowd, Quirk, & Zegarra, 1998; Piedmont & Ciarrochi, 1999). Negative affectivity may play a role in suicidal behaviour among individuals with SUDs by promoting depressive disorders and symptoms. Substance use may also develop or continue as an effort to cope with high levels of negative affect (Cooper, Frone, Russell, & Mudar, 1995; Khantzian, 1985), suggesting another mechanism in which negative affectivity may increase long-term risk. Individuals with AUDs as opposed to other SUDs may be especially vulnerable to this cycle (McGue, Slutske, & Iacono, 1999). Although data are limited, studies that have examined negative affectivity consistently show that it differentiates individuals with AUD (Roy, 2003) and SUD (Darke *et al.*, 2004; Landheim, Bakken, & Vaglum, 2006; Roy,

2003; Wines *et al.*, 2004) with a history of suicide attempts, consistent with the idea that it serves as a distal risk factor.

Aggression/impulsivity as a distal risk factor

A comprehensive review identified numerous reports showing that measures of aggression distinguish individuals making suicide attempts and dying by suicide (Brezo, Paris, & Turecki, 2006). Studies using AUD samples of veterans (Windle, 1994) and with comorbid depression (Sher, Oquendo, Galfalvy, Grunebaum, Burke, *et al.*, 2005) as well as those in treatment (Koller, Preuss, Bottlender, Wenzel, & Soyka, 2002) showed that measures of aggression or diagnoses associated with aggression/impulsivity differentiated those with and without a history of suicide attempts. Borderline personality disorder but no other personality disorder conferred lifetime risk for a suicide attempt after rigorous adjustment for other risk factors and personality disorders in a study using a large clinical sample of individuals with AUDs (Preuss, Koller, Barnow, Eikmeier, & Soyka, 2006). Although a diagnosis of borderline personality disorder is not the same as an assessment of aggression/ impulsivity or negative affectivity, nonetheless, individuals with this disorder show elevated levels of aggression/impulsivity and negative affectivity (Widiger & Costa, 1994) that help to explain why the disorder confers elevated risk.

The findings among individuals with SUDs are similar to studies of AUDs, for example, those seeking SUD treatment who have a lifetime suicide attempt report more difficulty controlling violent behaviour than those without a lifetime attempt (Tiet, Ilgen, Byrnes, & Moos, 2006). Additionally, a recent study examined the association between self-reports of prior aggression and suicidal ideation in patients seeking SUD treatment (Ilgen, Chermack, Murray, Walton, Barry, *et al.*, 2009). The results of this study indicate that aggression towards a partner is more strongly associated with risk of suicidal ideation than aggression towards a non-partner. Opiate-dependent patients with borderline personality disorder are also more likely to report a lifetime suicide attempt than those without (Darke *et al.*, 2004).

There are fewer reports showing that measures that are specifically designed to assess impulsivity confer risk for suicide attempts or suicide compared with abundant evidence using measures of aggression or those that tap both aggression and impulsivity (Brezo, Paris, & Turecki, 2006). Also, the lone study of an SUD sample that specifically examined a measure designed to assess impulsive aggression (also known as reactive aggression) failed to show that this type of aggression was more strongly implicated in suicide attempts than a measure of premeditated (proactive) aggression (Conner, Swogger, & Houston, 2009). Such data suggest that it may be premature to conclude that impulsivity *per se* confers risk for suicidal behaviour among individuals with AUDs or other SUDs. On the other hand, there is compelling evidence that altered brain serotonin-mediated neurotransmission implicated in impulsive aggression confers risk for suicide attempts and suicide, along with some reports showing that measures specifically designed to assess impulsivity confer added risk (Turecki, 2005). Moreover, studies of impulsivity and suicidal behaviour have generally used limited self-report measures of impulsivity, while the use of superior laboratory measures of impulsivity (i.e., go–no go task, a computerized test designed to detect signs of cognitive and motor impulsivity) may show stronger associations (Dougherty, Mathias, Marsh, Papageorgiou, Swann, *et al.*, 2004). Along these lines, a recent study found that individuals with AUDs who make impulsive suicide attempts (those with 30 minutes or less of pre-planning) also have deficits in behavioural measures of impulsivity (i.e., greater stop–go task latency) (Wojnar *et al.*, 2009). Overall, while evidence pertaining to impulsivity and suicidal behaviour is leaner compared with data on aggression, most experts agree that impulsivity increases risk for suicidal behaviours, perhaps by acting in combination with aggression consistent with the notion of impulsive (reactive) aggression.

Proximal Risk Factors among Individuals with SUDS

Active substance use and impairment as a proximal risk factor

A proximal risk factor is a variable that is in evidence near the time of suicidal behaviour and exerts a causal influence. Psychological autopsy investigations that focus on proximal risk factors indicate that most individuals with AUDs who die by suicide meet criteria for alcohol dependence, not alcohol abuse, a less severe syndrome (Cheng, 1995; Foster *et al.*, 1999; Henriksson, Aro, Marttunen, Heikkinen, Isometsä, *et al.*, 1993; Lesage *et al.*, 1994). Moreover, although there is a clear relationship between current alcohol *dependence* and suicide risk some controlled psychological autopsy studies have failed to show alcohol *abuse* to be associated with suicide (Cheng, 1995; Lesage *et al.*, 1994). Available data suggest that *recent* drinking patterns are more severe among those with AUDs attempting suicide (Cornelius, Salloum, Day, Thase, & Mann, 1996) or dying by suicide (Murphy, Wetzel, Robins, & McEvory, 1992) compared with non-suicidal individuals with AUDs. Similarly, in a large national sample of veterans seeking SUD treatment, use of cocaine and use of alcohol to the point of intoxication in the prior 30 days was related to a greater likelihood of making a suicide attempt during the same time period (Ilgen, Harris, *et al.*, 2007). Collectively, these reports of individuals with AUDs, as well as more general samples, support the common-sense conclusion that active and severe alcohol use serves as a proximal risk factor for suicidal behaviour. Despite consistent evidence that risk is heightened during periods of active drinking and alcohol-related problems, remission is not fully protective, as borne out by a psychological autopsy report that 45% of suicide decedents with a history of AUD had *remitted* alcoholism at the time of death, with most of these individuals dying during a major depressive episode (Conner, Duberstein, Conwell, Herrmann, Cox, *et al.*, 2000).

Depressive disorders and symptoms as a proximal risk factor

Psychological autopsy studies that have contained control groups of living individuals with AUDs (or SUDs) have shown increased rates of depression immediately preceding suicide among those with AUDs (Conner, Beautrais, & Conwell, 2003; Murphy *et al.*, 1992) and SUDs (Cheng, 1995; Schneider, Georgi, Weber, Schnabel, Ackermann, *et al.*,

2006), substantiating the role of depression in proximal risk. Indeed, an empirical review of psychological autopsy studies concluded that SUD (most often AUD) and major depression is the most frequent pattern of comorbidity reported in studies worldwide (Cavanagh *et al.*, 2003). Presumably, a similar relationship exists between depression and proximal risk for suicide in those with other DUDs (in addition to alcohol), however, little data exist on this topic because psychological autopsies have typically either reported data on AUDs or combined data on AUDs and DUDs into the category of SUDs, although the majority of these diagnoses are AUDs.

Concerning suicide attempts, numerous secondary analyses have shown that co-occurring depression confers risk for an attempt among individuals with SUDs (Darke *et al.*, 2007; Preuss *et al.*, 2002; Roy & Janal, 2007; Wines *et al.*, 2004). With few exceptions (Conner, Beautrais, & Conwell, 2003; Cornelius *et al.*, 1996), studies of SUD populations have not gathered data on depression proximal to the time of the attempt, yet there is no reason to suspect that depression would not confer proximal risk for an attempt just as it does with suicide. Indeed, the results of a case-control study comparing suicides and suicide attempts with non-suicidal controls, all with AUDs, suggests that depression confers a similar magnitude of risk for suicide attempt and suicide (Conner, Beautrais, & Conwell, 2003). Finally, available data show that substance-induced episodes of depression as well as depressive episodes that occur independent of substance use confer risk for suicide attempts among individuals with AUDs (Conner, Hesselbrock, Meldrum, Schuckit, Bucholz, *et al.*, 2007; Preuss *et al.*, 2002). Comparable findings on the role of substance-induced versus independent depression in suicidal behaviour among individuals with SUDs are not available.

Interpersonal stress as a proximal risk factor

Knowledge of stressful events as proximal risk factors overwhelmingly comes from psychological autopsy studies. The literature on this topic is almost exclusively derived from studies of individuals with AUDs or SUDs broadly defined. Interpersonal life events, most commonly a partner relationship disruption, were the most common stressful event preceding suicide in several psychological autopsy case series of adults with AUDs (Duberstein, Conwell, & Caine, 1993; Heikkinen, Aro, Henriksson, Isometsä, Sarna, *et al.*, 1994; Murphy, 1992; Rich, Fowler, Fogarty, & Young, 1988). A study of this type which included a control group of non-suicidal individuals with AUDs (Conner, Beautrais, & Conwell, 2003) showed that, after controlling for depressive episodes and other risk factors, those who experienced a partner relationship event were at elevated risk for suicide, OR (95% CI) = 4.60 (1.46, 14.57). The analysis also showed that those who experienced an interpersonal event involving another important person in the individual's life were at similar risk, OR (95% CI) = 4.85 (1.50, 15.66).

Along with acute disruptions in interpersonal relationships, findings also show that more chronic interpersonal stress, particularly aloneness, confer risk among SUD populations. In a study of 92 patients admitted for drug detoxification (Johnsson & Fridell, 1997), the most common reasons for a prior suicide attempt were interpersonal loss and loneliness. Individuals with AUDs who die by suicide or attempt suicide are more commonly living alone than non-AUD suicides/attempters (Haw, Houston, Townsend, & Hawton, 2001; Heikkinen *et al.*, 1994), and this situation is not merely attributable to impoverished interpersonal relations in alcoholism as borne out by a psychological autopsy study showing that AUD suicides were more likely to live alone than two groups of non-suicide AUD comparison subjects (Murphy *et al.*, 1992). Findings indicating that the death of a family member or confidant (Kingree, Thompson, & Kaslow, 1999) are associated with suicidal behaviour among individuals with SUDs may also be interpreted to indicate that aloneness confers risk, acknowledging that there are other explanations for this finding (i.e., bereavement). Although what it is about aloneness that confers risk is unclear, an investigation of patients in treatment for opiate dependence showed that low perceived belonging, but not loneliness, was associated with suicide attempts after adjustment for other interpersonal variables (Conner, Britton, Sworts, & Joiner, 2007), suggesting that thwarted belonging is key, as has been theorized in Joiner's interpersonal–psychological model of suicidal behaviour (Joiner, 2005; Chapter 10, below). Overall, the research evidence supports the view that interpersonal stress may be manifested through conflicted relations that lead to an acute disruption, most commonly a partner relationship break-up, as well as among individuals with impoverished interpersonal relationships who presumably experience chronic aloneness.

Integration: Model of Suicidal Behaviour

Conceptual model

Consistent with the ideas presented above, we provide a figure of distal and proximal risk factors for suicidal behaviour among individuals with SUDs (Figure 5.1). Among individuals with an SUD, we posit that greater substance-related severity and personality features of aggression/impulsivity and negative affectivity distinguish those at greater long-term risk. Proximal variables that confer risk in the short term include active substance use and impairment, interpersonal stress, and depressive episodes and symptoms. Integrating distal and proximal risk factors, we further hypothesize that distal risk factors promote proximal variables that in turn lead to acts of suicide, consistent with the idea that proximal risk factors partially or fully explain the association of distal risk factors and suicidal behaviour. That is, individuals with an SUD who have a severe substance use disorder, a propensity for aggressive/impulsive behaviour, and/or who are prone to experience negative affect are judged to be more likely at any given time to show active substance use and symptoms, to experience current depressive symptoms, and/or to experience interpersonal stress. Supporting these ideas, a pattern of aggression and severe substance use disorder may be expected to increase the likelihood of chronic substance use and symptoms, relapse to substance use, and interpersonal conflicts and disruptions. The role of negative affectivity in the development of depressive episodes is also clear as discussed previously. Although we have emphasized the distinction between distal and proximal risk factors and discussed their interrelationship, variables within a category may also influence one another. For example, within the proximal risk domain active substance use

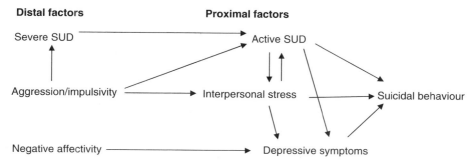

Figure 5.1   Model of distal and proximal risk for suicidal behaviour among individuals with SUDs.

and interpersonal stress influence one another (e.g., interpersonal stress is a common precursor of substance use relapse and substance abuse contributes to interpersonal conflict) and each in turn is a potent predictor of major depressive episodes. Finally, in the figure we have used arrows to depict associations for which there is the best evidence for a causal relationship, acknowledging that other paths are plausible (e.g., from depression to active SUD) in a given SUD population.

Key decisions in developing the model along with limitations and caveats

The model was developed with the goal of synthesizing the available literature on risk for suicidal behaviour in those with SUDs; all proposed relationships are intended to be testable so that the model can be refined through future research. The model is intended to be applicable to both suicide attempts and suicide, outcomes that are largely distinguished by age, sex, and method (Beautrais, 2001; Friedmann & Kohn, 2008). A focus on active substance use and impairment is straightforward given a focus on individuals with SUDs. A focus on depression and interpersonal stress in proximal risk is also indicated because these are prevalent difficulties among individuals with SUDs as well as potent risk factors for suicidal behaviour. As these attributes (prevalence, degree of risk) determine the extent to which an outcome is attributable to a given predictor (Afifi, Enns, Cox, Asmundson, Stein, *et al.*, 2008), strategies that effectively lessen depression and interpersonal stress among SUDs may be hypothesized to lead to a pronounced reduction in suicidal behaviour. Because the study of proximal risk among individuals with an SUD is a nascent research area, particularly among individuals with specific DUDs, further study of other stressors and other disorders may show the need to expand the model. Special populations may also require a focus on additional factors, for example, soldiers exposed to combat may require the targeting of post-traumatic stress disorder or other conditions.

Much of the basis for the model comes from studies of individuals with AUD and so its relevance to other SUD populations requires further study. The model begins with distal risk factors but does not seek to explain the causes (genetic, developmental, etc.) of these factors. The model is a general framework and does not address nuances of risk associated with specific SUDs (e.g., cocaine use disorder). Other distal risk factors may also contribute to risk after accounting for other predictors in the model; in particular a prior history of suicidal behaviour (Joiner, Conwell, Fitzpatrick, Witte, Schmidt, *et al.*, 2003) and child sexual abuse (Afifi *et al.*, 2008) are potent distal risk factors that are likely to be predictive of suicidal behaviour even after accounting for the other variables in the model. The terms distal and proximal are useful heuristics though the boundaries between categories are permeable, for example, between negative affectivity and major depression. The model considers who is at risk and when, but does not focus on warning signs for suicidal behaviour (Rudd, Berman, Joiner, Nock, Mandrusiak, *et al.*, 2006), acute substance intoxication effects (National Center for Injury Prevention and Control, 2009), or the availability of a method (Miller & Hemenway, 2008) that concern the probability of suicidal behaviour within a short window of time.

Conclusions and Future Directions

The model predicts that among individuals with SUDs, severity of substance use disorder, negative affectivity, and/or aggression/impulsivity create a diathesis for suicidal behaviour that will be most likely to occur during a period of active substance use, while depressed, and/or following an interpersonal stressor. The tenets of the model are testable. We anticipate that individuals with more than one distal risk factor (e.g., severe AUD plus high negative affectivity) will be at greater long-term risk than individuals with a single distal risk factor, other things being equal. Similarly, rarely do we anticipate that suicide attempts or suicides will occur during periods of remission from SUD, while non-depressed, and in the absence of marked interpersonal stress. We also presume that suicidal behaviour will be most likely to occur when more than one proximal risk factor is in evidence (e.g., active substance use disorder and major depressive episode) and that risk will be especially high when all three proximal factors are present.

We posit that at any given time, individuals with severe SUD, those prone to aggression/impulsivity, and/or those vulnerable to negative affect are especially likely to experience the aforementioned proximal risk factors (interpersonal stress, etc.). In other words, distal risk variables are purported to promote the occurrence of proximal risk factors that in turn mark periods of increased risk among vulnerable SUDs. In this scenario, proximal risk factors are hypothesized to explain or mediate the association between distal risk factors and suicidal behaviour. Moreover, formal statistical procedures can be used to determine whether or not the proximal variables in the model fully mediate (i.e., fully explain) or, more likely, partially mediate (i.e., partially explain) the role of the distal variables in promoting suicidal behaviour (Cole & Maxwell, 2003). Finally, specific predictions concerning the interrelationships among predictors (i.e., active SUD and interpersonal stress promote depressive symptoms) are testable using formal statistical techniques (Cole & Maxwell, 2003).

Another strategy to examine the model is to design and test interventions that target the risk factors in the model. Consistent with the call for the study of mechanisms of change in intervention research (Nock, 2007), we predict that the incidence or recurrence of suicidal behaviour will be reduced to the extent to which the distal and proximal risk factors are successfully addressed in treatment, with proximal factors being most amenable to short-term change. Given the low rate of suicidal behaviour, proxy outcomes (e.g., suicidal ideation), and/or the use of high-risk clinical sub-populations (e.g., recent suicide attempters) will be needed to provide practical tests of these ideas. Recent studies suggesting that interventions targeting suicidal behaviour are efficacious in reducing substance use disorder symptoms (Harned, Chapman, Dexter-Mazza, Murray, Comtois, *et al.*, 2008) and that SUD treatment may reduce the risk for suicidal behaviour (Ilgen, Harris, *et al.*, 2007; Ilgen, Jain, *et al.*, 2007) provide reasons for optimism that individuals with SUDs at elevated risk stand to benefit from clinical interventions.

References

Afifi, T. O., Enns, M. W., Cox, B. J., Asmundson, G. J., Stein, M. B., & Sareen, J. (2008). Population attributable fractions of psychiatric disorders and suicide ideation and attempts associated with adverse childhood experiences. *American Journal of Public Health, 98*, 946–952.

Ball, S. A. & Schottenfeld, R. S. (1997). A five-factor model of personality and addiction, psychiatric, and AIDS risk severity in pregnant and postpartum cocaine misusers. *Substance Use and Misuse, 32*, 25–41.

Beautrais, A. L. (2001). Suicides and serious suicide attempts: Two populations or one? *Psychological Medicine, 31*, 837–845.

Brezo, J., Paris, J., & Turecki, G. (2006). Personality traits as correlates of suicidal ideation, suicide attempts, and suicide completion: a systematic review. *Acta Pscyhiatrica Scandinavica, 113*, 180–206.

Cavanagh, J. T. O., Carson, A. J., Sharpe, M., & Lawrie, S. M. (2003). Psychological autopsy studies of suicide: A systematic review. *Psychological Medicine, 33*, 395–405.

Cheng, A. T. A. (1995). Mental illness and suicide. *British Journal of Psychiatry, 170*, 441–446.

Cole, D. A. & Maxwell, S. E. (2003). Testing mediational models with longitudinal data: Questions and tips in the use of Structural Equation Modelling. *Journal of Abnormal Psychology, 4*, 558–577.

Conner, K. R., Beautrais, A. L., & Conwell, Y. (2003). Risk factors for suicide and medically serious suicide attempts among alcoholics: Analyses of Canterbury Suicide Project Data. *Journal of Studies on Alcohol, 64*, 551–554.

Conner, K. R., Britton, P. C., Sworts, L. M., & Joiner, T. (2007). Suicide attempts among individuals with opiate dependence: The role of belonging. *Addictive Behaviors, 32*, 1395–1404.

Conner, K. R., Duberstein, P. R., Conwell, Y., Herrmann, J. H., Cox, C., Barrington, D. S., & Caine, E. D. (2000). After the drinking stops: Completed suicide in individuals with remitted alcohol use disorders. *Journal of Psychoactive Drugs, 32*, 333–337.

Conner, K. R., Hesselbrock, V. M., Meldrum, S. C., Schuckit, M. A., Bucholz, K. K., Gamble, S. A., Wines, J. T., & Kramer, J. (2007). Transitions to, and correlates of, suicidal ideation, plans, and unplanned and planned suicide attempts among 3729 men and women with alcohol dependence. *Journal of Studies on Alcohol and Drugs, 68*, 654–662.

Conner, K. R., Swogger, M. A., & Houston, R. J. (2009). A test of the reactive aggression–suicidal behaviour hypothesis: Is there a case for proactive aggression? *Journal of Abnormal Psychology, 118*, 235–240.

Cooper, L. M., Frone, M. R., Russell, M., & Mudar, P. (1995). Drinking to regulate positive and negative emotions: A motivational model of alcohol use. *Journal of Personality and Social Psychology, 69*, 990–1005.

Cornelius, J. R., Salloum, I. M., Day, N. L., Thase, M. E., & Mann, J. J. (1996). Patterns of suicidality and alcohol use in alcoholics with major depression. *Alcoholism: Clinical and Experimental Research, 20*, 1451–1455.

Darke, S., Ross, J., Lynskey, M., & Teesson, M. (2004). Attempted suicide among entrants to three treatment modalities for heroin dependence in the Australian Treatment Outcome Study (ATOS): Prevalence and risk factors. *Drug and Alcohol Dependence, 73*, 1–10.

Darke, S., Ross, J., Williamson, A., Mills, K. L., Havard, A., & Teesson, M. (2007). Patterns and correlates of attempted suicide by heroin users over a 3-year period: Findings from the Australian treatment outcome study. *Drug and Alcohol Dependence, 87*, 146–152.

Degenhardt, L., Roxburgh, A., & Barker, B. (2005). Underlying causes of cocaine, amphetamine and opioid related deaths in Australia. *Journal of Clinical Forensic Medicine, 12*, 187–195.

Dick, D. M., Agrawal, A., Wang, J. C., Hinrichs, A., Bertelsen, S., Bucholz, K. K., Schuckit, M., Kramer, J., Nurnberger, J., Tischfield, J. Edenberg, H. J., Goate, A., & Bierut, L. J. (2007). Alcohol dependence with comorbid drug dependence: Genetic and phenotypic associations suggest a more severe form of the disorder with stronger genetic contribution to risk. *Addiction, 102*, 1131–1139.

Dougherty, D. M., Mathias, C. W., Marsh, D. M., Papageorgiou, T. D., Swann, A. C., & Moeller, F. G. (2004). Laboratory measured behavioral impulsivity relates to suicide attempt history. *Suicide and Life-Threatening Behavior, 34*, 374–385.

Duberstein, P. R., Conwell, Y., & Caine, E. D. (1993). Interpersonal stressors, substance abuse, and suicide. *Journal of Nervous and Mental Disease, 181*, 80–85.

Foster, T., Gillespie, K., McClelland, R., & Patterson, R. (1999). Risk factors for suicide independent of DSM-III-R Axis I disorder. *British Journal of Psychiatry, 175*, 175–179.

Friedmann, H. & Kohn, R. (2008). Mortality, or probability of death, from a suicidal act in the United States. *Suicide and Life-Threatening Behavior, 38*, 287–301.

Gomberg, E. S. L. (1989). Suicide risk among women with alcohol problems. *American Journal of Public Health, 79*, 1363–1365.

Harned, M. S., Chapman, A. L., Dexter-Mazza, E. T., Murray, A., Comtois, K. A., & Linehan, M. M. (2008). Treating co-occurring Axis I disorders in recurrently suicidal women with borderline personality disorder: A 2-year randomized trial of Dialectical Behaviour Therapy versus Community Treatment by Experts. *Journal of Consulting and Clinical Psychology, 76*, 1068–1075.

Hasin, D., Grant, B. F., & Endicott, J. (1988). Treated and untreated suicide attempts in substance abuse patients. *Journal of Nervous and Mental Disease, 176*, 289–294.

Haw, C., Houston, K., Townsend, E., & Hawton, K. (2001). Deliberate self-harm patients with alcohol use disorders: Characteristics, treatment, and outcome. *Crisis, 22*, 93–101.

Heikkinen, M. E., Aro, H. M., Henriksson, M. M., Isometsä, E. T., Sarna, S. J., Kuoppasalmi, K. I., & Lönqvist, J. K. (1994). Differences in recent life events between alcoholic and depressive nonalcoholic suicides. *Alcoholism: Clinical and Experimental Research, 18*, 1143–1149.

Henriksson, M. M., Aro, H. M., Marttunen, M. J., Heikkinen, M. E., Isometsä, E. T., Kuoppasalmi, K. I., & Lönqvist, J. (1993). Mental disorders and comorbidity in suicide. *American Journal of Psychiatry, 150*, 935–940.

Hesselbrock, M., Hesselbrock, V. M., Syzmanski, K., & Weidenman, M. (1988). Suicide attempts and alcoholism. *Journal of Studies on Alcohol, 49*, 436–442.

Ilgen, M. A., Chermack, S. T., Murray, R., Walton, M. A., Barry, K. L., Wojnar, M., & Blow, F. C. (2009). The association between partner and non-partner aggression and suicidal ideation in patients seeking substance use disorder treatment. *Addictive Behaviors, 34*, 180–186.

Ilgen, M. A., Harris, A. H. S., Moos, R. H., & Tiet, Q. Q. (2007). Predictors of suicide attempt one year after entry into substance use disorder treatment. *Alcoholism: Clinical and Experimental Research*, *31*, 635–642.

Ilgen, M. A., Jain, A., Lucas, E., & Moos, R. H. (2007). Substance use–disorder treatment and a decline in attempted suicide during and after treatment. *Journal of Studies on Alcohol*, *68*, 503–509.

Johnsson, E. & Fridell, M. (1997). Suicide attempts in a cohort of drug abusers: A 5-year follow-up study. *Acta Pscyhiatrica Scandinavica*, *96*, 362–366.

Joiner, T. E. (2005). *Why People Die by Suicide*. Cambridge, MA: Harvard University Press.

Joiner, T. E., Conwell, Y., Fitzpatrick, K. K., Witte, T. K., Schmidt, N. B., Berlim, M. T., Fleck, M.P., & Rudd, M. D. (2003). Four studies on how past and current suicidality relate even when 'everything but the kitchen sink' is covaried. *Journal of Abnormal Psychology*, *114*, 291–303.

Karch, D. L., Barker, L., & Strine, T. W. (2006). Race/ethnicity, substance abuse, and mental illness among suicide victims in 13 US states: 2004 data from the National Violent Death Reporting System. *Injury Prevention*, *12*(Suppl.), ii22–ii27.

Kendler, K. S., Neale, M. C., Kessler, R. C., Heath, A. C., & Eaves, L. J. (1993). A longitudinal twin study of personality and major depression in women. *Archives of General Psychiatry*, *50*, 853–862.

Kessler, R. C., Borges, G., & Walters, E. E. (1999). Prevalence of and risk factors for lifetime suicide attempts in the National Comorbidity Survey. *Archives of General Psychiatry*, *56*, 617–625.

Khantzian, E. J. (1985). The self-medication hypothesis of addictive disorders: Focus on heroin and cocaine dependence. *American Journal of Psychiatry*, *142*, 1259–1264.

Kingree, J. B., Thompson, M. P., & Kaslow, N. J. (1999). Risk factors for suicide attempts among low-income women with a history of alcohol problems. *Addictive Behaviors*, *24*, 583–587.

Koller, G., Preuss, U. W., Bottlender, M., Wenzel, K., & Soyka, M. (2002). Impulsivity and aggression as predictors of suicide attempts in alcoholics. *European Archives of Psychiatry and Clinical Neuroscience*, *252*, 155–160.

Kolves, K., Varnik, A., Tooding, L. M., & Wasserman, D. (2006). The role of alcohol in suicide: A case-control psychological autopsy study. *Psychological Medicine*, *36*, 923–930.

Landheim, A. S., Bakken, K., & Vaglum, P. (2006). What characterizes substance abusers who commit suicide attempts? Factors related to Axis I disorders and patterns of substance use disorders. A study of treatment-seeking substance abusers in Norway. *European Addiction Research*, *12*, 102–108.

Lesage, A. D., Boyer, R., Grunberg, F., Vanier, C., Morisette, R., Ménard-Buteau, C., & Loyer, M. (1994). Suicide and mental disorders: A case-control study of young men. *American Journal of Psychiatry*, *151*, 1063–1068.

Maloney, E., Degenhardt, L., Darke, S., Mattick, R. P., & Nelson, E. (2007). Suicidal behaviour and associated risk factors among opioid-dependent individuals: A case-control study. *Addiction*, *102*, 1933–1941.

McCormick, R. A., Dowd, E. T., Quirk, S., & Zegarra, J. H. (1998). The relationship of NEO-PI performance to coping styles, patterns of use, and triggers for use among substance abusers. *Addictive Behaviors*, *23*, 497–507.

McGue, M., Slutske, W., & Iacono, W. G. (1999). Personality and substance use disorders: II. Alcoholism versus drug use disorders. *Journal of Consulting and Clinical Psychology*, *67*, 394–404.

Miller, M., & Hemenway, D. (2008). Guns and suicide in the United States. *New England Journal of Medicine*, *359*, 989–991.

Murphy, G. E. (1992). *Suicide in Alcoholism*. New York: Oxford.

Murphy, G. E., Wetzel, R. D., Robins, E., & McEvory, L. (1992). Multiple risk factors predict suicide in alcoholism. *Archives of General Psychiatry*, *49*, 459–463.

National Center for Injury Prevention and Control (2009). Alcohol and suicide among racial/ethnic populations – 17 States, 2005–2006. *Morbidity and Mortality Weekly Report, 58,* 637–641.

Nock, M. K. (2007). Conceptual and design essentials for evaluating mechanisms of change. *Alcoholism: Clinical and Experimental Research, 31*(Suppl.), S3–S12.

Ormel, J., Oldehinkel, A. J., & Vollebergh, W. (2004). Vulnerability before, during, and after a major depressive episode: A 3-wave population based study. *Archives of General Psychiatry, 61,* 990–996.

Penick, E. C., Nickel, E. J., Powell, B. J., Liskow, B. I., Campbell, J., Dale, T. M., Hassanein, R. E., & Noble, E. (1999). The comparative validity of eleven alcoholism typologies. *Journal of Studies on Alcohol, 60,* 188–202.

Phillips, M. R., Yang, G., Zhang, Y., Wang, L., Ji, H., & Zhou, M. (2002). Risk factors for suicide in China: A national case-control psychological autopsy study. *The Lancet, 360,* 1728–1736.

Piedmont, R. L., & Ciarrochi, J. W. (1999). The utility of the Revised NEO Personality Inventory in an outpatient, drug rehabilitation context. *Psychology of Addictive Behaviors, 13,* 213–226.

Preuss, U. W., Schuckit, M. A., Smith, T. L., Danko, G. P., Buckman, K., Bierut, L., Bucholz, K. K., Hesselbrock, M. N., Hesselbrock, V. M., & Reich, T. (2002). Comparison of 3190 alcohol-dependent individuals with and without suicide attempts. *Alcoholism: Clinical and Experimental Research, 26,* 471–477.

Preuss, U. W., Schuckit, M. A., Smith, T. L., Danko, G. P., Bucholz, K. K., Hesselbrock, M. N., Hesselbrock, V. M., & Kramer, J. (2003). Predictors and correlates of suicide attempts over 5 years in 1237 alcohol-dependent men and women. *American Journal of Psychiatry, 160,* 56–63.

Preuss, U. W., Koller, G., Barnow, S., Eikmeier, M., & Soyka, M. (2006). Suicidal behaviour in alcohol-dependent subjects: The role of personality disorders. *Alcoholism: Clinical and Experimental Research, 30,* 866–877.

Rich, C. L., Fowler, R. C., Fogarty, L. A., & Young, D. (1988). San Diego suicide study III. Relationships between diagnoses and stressors. *Archives of General Psychiatry, 45,* 589–592.

Rossow, I., Romelsjo, A., & Leifman, H. (1999). Alcohol abuse and suicidal behaviour in young and middle aged men: Differentiating between attempted and completed suicide. *Addiction, 94,* 1199–1207.

Roy, A. (2001). Characteristics of cocaine-dependent patients who attempt suicide. *American Journal of Psychiatry, 158,* 1215–1219.

Roy, A. (2003). Distal risk factors for suicidal behaviour in alcoholics. *Journal of Affective Disorders, 77,* 267–271.

Roy, A. & Janal, M. N. (2007). Risk factors for suicide attempts among alcohol dependent patients. *Archives of Suicide Research, 11,* 211–217.

Roy, A., Lamparski, D., DeJong, J., Moore, V., & Linnoila, M. (1990). Characteristics of alcoholics who attempt suicide. *American Journal of Psychiatry, 147,* 761–765.

Rudd, M. D., Berman, A. L., Joiner, T. E., Nock, M. K., Mandrusiak, M., Van Orden, K. A., & Witte, T. (2006). Warning signs for suicide: Theory, research, and clinical applications. *Suicide and Life-Threatening Behavior, 36,* 255–262.

Schneider, B., Georgi, K., Weber, B., Schnabel, A., Ackermann, H., & Wetterling, T. (2006). Risk factors for suicide in substance-related disorders. *Psychiatrische Praxis, 33,* 81–87.

Sher, L., Oquendo, M. A., Galfalvy, H. C., Grunebaum, M. F., Burke, A. K., Zalsman, G., & Mann, J. J. (2005). The relationship of aggression to suicidal behavior in depressed patients with a history of alcoholism. *Addictive Behaviors, 30,* 1144–1153.

Surtees, P. G., & Wainwright, N. W. (1996). Fragile states of mind: Neuroticism, vulnerability and the long-term outcome of depression. *British Journal of Psychiatry, 169,* 338–347.

Tiet, Q. Q., Ilgen, M. A., Byrnes, F. H., & Moos, R. H. (2006). Suicide attempts among substance use disorder patients: An initial step toward a decision tree for suicide management. *Alcoholism: Clinical and Experimental Research, 30*, 998–1005.

Turecki, G. (2005). Dissecting the suicide phenotype: The role of impulsive–aggressive behaviours. *Journal of Psychiatry and Neuroscience, 30*, 398–408.

Widiger, T. A. & Costa Jr., P. T. (1994). Personality and personality disorders. *Journal of Abnormal Psychology, 103*, 78–91.

Widiger, T. A. & Trull, T. J. (1992). Personality and psychopathology: An application of the Five-Factor Model. *Journal of Personality, 60*, 363–394.

Wilcox, H. C., Conner, K. R., & Caine, E. D. (2004). Association of alcohol and drug use disorders and completed suicide: An empirical review of cohort studies. *Drug and Alcohol Dependence, 76* (Suppl.), S11–S19.

Windle, M. (1994). Characteristics of alcoholics who attempted suicide: Co-occurring disorders and personality differences with a sample of male Vietnam era veterans. *Journal of Studies on Alcohol, 55*, 571–577.

Wines, J. D., Saitz, R., Horton, N. J., Lloyd-Travaglini, C., & Samet, J. H. (2004). Suicidal behaviour, drug use and depressive symptoms after detoxification: A 2-year prospective study. *Drug and Alcohol Dependence, 76* (Suppl. 7), S21–S29.

Wojnar, M., Ilgen, M. A., Czyz, E., Strobbe, S., Klimkiewicz, A., Jakubczyk, A., Glass, J., & Brower, K. (2009). Impulsive and non-impulsive suicide attempts in patients treated for alcohol dependence. *Journal of Affective Disorders, 115*, 131–139.

Zhou, L., Conner, K. R., Phillips, M. R., Caine, E. D., Xiao, S., Zhang, R., & Gong, Y. (2009). Epidemiology of alcohol abuse and dependence in rural Chinese men. *Alcoholism: Clinical and Experimental Research, 33*, 1770–1776.

CHAPTER SIX

Personality Disorders and Suicidal Behaviour

Joel Paris

Abstract

Personality disorders can be associated with suicide and attempted suicide. Overdoses and cutting are particularly common in patients with borderline personality disorder (BPD), a group in which up to 10% can die by suicide. The most evidence-based treatment methods for this population are specifically designed psychotherapies. No research data have supported suicide prevention in personality disorders, and hospitalization has not been shown to be effective.

Introduction

As defined by DSM-IV-TR (American Psychiatric Association (APA), 2000), personality disorders (PDs) are characterized by abnormal patterns of inner experience and behaviour that affect cognition, emotion, interpersonal functioning, and impulse control; are inflexible and pervasive; lead to clinically significant distress or impairment; are stable and of long duration; and have an onset in adolescence or early adulthood.

Personality disorders are common in practice, and were found to be present in about 45% of all patients in one large clinical sample (Zimmerman, Rothschild, & Chelminski, 2005). While there is some evidence that about 5% of patients with antisocial personality

International Handbook of Suicide Prevention: Research, Policy and Practice, First Edition.
Edited by Rory C. O'Connor, Stephen Platt, Jacki Gordon.
© 2011 John Wiley & Sons, Ltd. Published 2011 by John Wiley & Sons, Ltd.

will complete suicide (Links, Gould, & Ratnayake, 2003; Martin, Cloninger, Guze, & Clayton, 1985; Robins, 1966), these patients are more likely to be seen in forensic settings rather than clinics.

BPD has been the object of greatest concern. The reason is that this category is associated with a wide range of severe psychopathology, including unstable mood, a wide range of impulsive behaviours, and unstable interpersonal relationships (Paris, 2008a). Suicidal behaviour, that is, actions that have a suicidal intent, as well as chronic suicidal ideation, are among the defining features of the disorder; Soloff, Lynch, Kelly, Malone, and Mann (2000) reported that BPD patients have a mean of three lifetime attempts. This disorder has therefore been the subject of a large body of research.

In BPD, self-harm behaviours, usually involving superficial cuts to the wrists and arms, are also common, but this behaviour is not suicidal in intent. Patients cut to relieve emotional tension, not to die (Brown, Comtois, & Linehan, 2002). BPD patients have serious problems with emotion regulation, and can cut themselves addictively to reduce painful inner states (Linehan, 1993).

While overdoses of pills can be suicidal in intent, and can sometimes be life-threatening, these behaviours vary greatly in nature and intent (Soloff *et al.*, 2000). Overdoses usually occur following stressful life events, and patients describe their motivation as a wish to escape (Brown, Comtois, & Linehan, 2002). Most incidents are marked by ambivalent motivation, using small quantities of medication and/or calling significant others for help. Even when potentially fatal overdoses are taken, patients may contact people who are in a position to intervene (Gunderson & Links, 2008).

It is well established that attempters and completers are separate but overlapping populations (Beautrais, 2001). Hawton, Zahl, and Weatherall (2003), in a large-scale follow-up of attempters seen in an emergency room (ER), found that only about 3% eventually died by suicide. Most repetitive attempts in young women occur in their twenties and decrease with time (Maris, 1981), and overdoses are most common in younger BPD patients (Soloff *et al.*, 2000).

Even so, some patients with BPD do kill themselves. Psychological autopsy methods have examined the frequency of this diagnosis in completed suicide (Hunt, Kapur, Robinson, Shaw, Flynn, *et al.*, 2006; Lesage, Boyer, Grunberg, Morisette, Vanier, *et al.*, 1994; Lesage, Seguin, Guy, Daigle, Bayle, *et al.*, 2008; Tidemalm, Elofsson, Stefansson, Waern, & Runeson, 2005). In these studies, PDs were present in about half of cases under the age of 35 years, with BPD being the most common category.

Follow-back research (i.e., examination of outcome in cohorts in which baseline data are available) has examined how often BPD patients kill themselves. Two major studies found that suicide occurs in about 10% of cases (Paris & Zweig-Frank, 2001; Stone, 1990). Lower rates (3%–4%) were reported in another study (McGlashan, 1986), as well as in one prospectively followed cohort (Zanarini, Frankenburg, Hennen, & Silk, 2003). However, the higher rate could be more accurate. One of the studies with a higher rate included more patients from lower socio-economic groups (Paris & Zweig-Frank, 2001). Additionally, patients who agree to be followed prospectively may be less likely to complete suicide.

By and large, suicides in BPD occur late in the course of illness and follow long courses of unsuccessful treatment (Paris, 2003). In one study, the mean age at suicide was 30 years

(Stone, 1990), while another, longer follow-up reported a mean age of 37 years, with a standard deviation of 10 years (Paris & Zweig-Frank, 2001). Thus, patients are not at highest risk when they are young and are most likely to be frequent visitors to ER. Thus, while the great majority of BPD patients improve over time (Paris, 2003), those who complete suicide are most likely to do so if they fail to recover.

While most clinical cases of BPD are female and treatment-seeking (Zimmerman, Rothschild, & Chelminski, 2005), epidemiological studies suggest that males in the community may have the disorder in equal numbers, even if they do not often present clinically (Coid, Yang, Tyrer, Roberts, & Ullrich, 2006; Lenzenweger, Lane, Loranger, & Kessler, 2007). Males with BPD have a different pattern of suicidality: nearly a third of youth suicides (most being male) can be diagnosed by psychological autopsy (Lesage *et al.*, 1994). Autopsy studies of BPD patients who died by suicide also show a preponderance of males (McGirr, Paris, Lesage, Renaud, & Turecki, 2007). Few of these cases were in treatment at the time of their death.

The Treatment of Suicidality in BPD

The research literature on the management of suicidality in BPD is surprisingly thin. A search of Medline from 1950 to 2008 with the key words {personality disorder} and {suicide or suicidality} yields 2,642 references, but the vast majority are clinical reports or studies in which personality disorder was assessed incidentally. A Medline search over the same period using the keywords {personality disorder and suicide prevention} yielded only 18 references, none of which actually assessed prevention. Another problem is that, while clinical trials are essential, they may not be generalizable to populations seen in clinical practice (Westen & Morrison, 2001).

Patients with BPD have complex courses of treatment, with many failed suicide attempts. Multiple periods of psychotherapy, repeated emergency room visits and hospitalizations, and multiple prescriptions in a polypharmacy 'cocktail' are all common (Zanarini, Frankenburg, Khera, & Bleichmar, 2001).

Much effort goes into trying to prevent BPD patients from ending their lives. One of the most frequent interventions is hospitalization (Hull, Yeomans, Clarkin, Li, & Goodman, 1996). Admission for suicidal threats is recommended by the APA guidelines for the treatment of BPD (Oldham, Gabbard, Goin, Gunderson, Soloff, *et al.*, 2001). However, there are no data showing that hospital admissions have any preventive effect against suicide in this population (Paris, 2008a).

Moreover, repeated hospitalization tends to be counter-productive, since it can interfere with out-patient treatment and make it impossible for patients to stay in the workplace (Gunderson & Links, 2008; Paris, 2008a). It also sometimes leads to 'regression', with an increase of symptoms based on behavioural reinforcement of suicidal behaviour (Linehan, 1993).

There is much stronger evidence for well-structured ambulatory treatment. The last few years have been marked by new data on the effectiveness of psychotherapies specifically designed for patients with BPD (Paris, 2008b). It is now clear that, while psychological treatments of a generic nature are often ineffective, well-structured methods that have been tested in clinical trials are often effective.

The most extensively investigated method is dialectical behaviour therapy (DBT) (Linehan, 1993), whose efficacy has been confirmed in two RCTs by its originators (Linehan, Armstrong, Suarez, Allmon, & Heard, 1991; Linehan, Comtois, Murray, Brown, Gallop, *et al.*, 2006), bolstered by several replications (Paris, 2008b).

The main outcomes of DBT are reductions in overdoses, in ER visits for suicidality, reduced frequency of self-harm, and reduced hospital admissions (Linehan *et al.*, 1991; Linehan *et al.*, 2006). There was only one death by suicide in the first trial (Linehan *et al.*, 1991) and none in the second (Linehan *et al.*, 2006), although patients likely to die by suicide may be less likely to enter clinical trials (Paris, 2008a).

Several other methods of psychotherapy have been tested in clinical trials. Mentalization-based therapy (Bateman & Fonagy, 1999) has some resemblance to DBT in that it teaches patients to observe emotions in interpersonal settings, and its efficacy has recently been replicated in a larger trial (Bateman & Fonagy, 2009). Other methods are supported by single clinical trials. Transference-focused psychotherapy (Clarkin, Levy, Lenzenweger, & Kernberg, 2007) attempts to correct distortions in the relationship to a therapist. Schema therapy (Giesen-Bloo, van Dyck, Spinhoven, van Tilburg, Dirksen, *et al.*, 2006) focuses on maladaptive schema and their relationship to childhood experiences. Standard cognitive therapy (Davidson, Norrie, Tyrer, Gumley, Tata, *et al.*, 2006) works to modify maladaptive schema in the patient's current life.

All of these methods share common features, and have some evidence for efficacy. As shown by a recent comparative trial (McMain, Links, Gnam, Guimond, Cardish, *et al.*, 2009), the results of a well-established treatment such as DBT can be duplicated using other well-structured methods. Moreover psychological treatments specifically designed for BPD patients are consistently superior to standard clinical management (Paris, 2008a).

We do not know whether findings from clinical trials are fully generalizable to practice. We also do not know which patients are most likely to benefit from which kind of treatment. A Cochrane report (Binks, Fenton, McCarthy, Lee, Adams, *et al.*, 2006a) reached the conservative conclusion that cognitive therapy for BPD has 'promise', although an updated report from this source, taking into account more recent research is forthcoming.

One can also understand the management of suicidality by considering the personality traits that underlie BPD (Siever & Davis, 1991). Suicidal thoughts and actions are responses to painful emotions, and BPD patients suffer from severe affective instability (AI), also called emotion dysregulation (ED): rapid changes in mood related to environmental stressors (Russell, Moskowitz, Zuroff, Sookman, & Paris, 2007). This is the least likely aspect of the disorder to remit on long-term follow-up (Paris, 2003).

Most effective therapies target AI. DBT specifically aims to modify the regulation of emotion (Linehan, 1993). All methods involve teaching patients how to regulate negative emotions in ways other than cutting or overdoses.

The second trait that characterizes BPD is impulsivity (Crowell, Beauchaine, & Linehan, 2009; Links, Heslegrave, & van Reekum, 1999). A lack of control over impulses makes patients more likely to turn to suicidal actions when emotionally dysregulated, and the frequency of suicide attempts is strongly related to this trait (Soloff *et al.*, 2000). Again, all methods of psychotherapy attempt to reduce impulsivity by teaching patients to stand outside their emotions and hold off action pending reflection.

The efficacy of pharmacological agents in BPD is not firmly established. No clinical trials have documented remission with drug treatment. Even so, most BPD patients are on multiple medications, including antidepressants, mood stabilizers, and/or neuroleptics (Zanarini *et al.*, 2001). These practices are generally supported only by single trials in small samples. A Cochrane report (Binks, Fenton, McCarthy, Lee, Adams, *et al.*, 2006b) found insufficient evidence to prescribe *any* drug for patients with BPD, and a recent update (Lieb, Vollm, Rucker, Timmer, & Stoffers, 2010) found that current pharmacological agents have only marginal effects. My own review of all clinical trials concluded that the effects of the drugs that have been tested are, at best, modest and that all these agents can have troubling side-effects (Paris, 2008b). Moreover, the use of multiple drugs to treat BPD leads to an even greater side-effect burden. Unfortunately, polypharmacy was encouraged by the APA guidelines (Oldham *et al.*, 2001). This document clearly needs revision and the evolving guidelines from the National Institute for Health and Clinical Excellence (NICE, 2009) seem likely to be more evidence-based.

Another problem in planning treatment is that BPD may not be diagnosed at all. Its clinical picture has sometimes been seen as a bipolar variant (Akiskal, Chen, Davis, & Puzantian, 2001). Those who take that point of view will prescribe mood-stabilizing drugs, even though these agents have, at best, unclear effects on suicidal behaviour (Paris, Gunderson, & Weinberg, 2007; Paris, 2008b). In contrast, psychotherapies have clearly been shown to reduce self-harm and suicide attempts.

Conclusions and Implications for Practice

One of the most unique aspects of BPD is the chronicity of suicidal ideation in this population (Paris, 2008a). Patients with mood disorders are suicidal when depressed, but put these ideas aside when they go into remission. In contrast, BPD patients may consider suicide on a daily basis for months to years, and only go into remission much later. Suicidal ideas will vary in intensity over time, waxing when life events are stressful, and waning when they are not (Paris, 2006).

By themselves, suicidal thoughts are too common to be useful in predicting suicidal actions. But while patients with suicidal behaviours are at a statistically higher risk of completion, one cannot predict who are most likely to die by suicide. Completions are rare events relative to attempts and large-scale follow-up studies have found it impossible to determine who will complete suicide (Goldstein, Black, Nasrallah, & Winokur, 1991; Pokorny, 1982). The problem is false positives (patients who fit the profile but never kill themselves).

In spite of having suicidal thoughts for long periods of time and multiple suicide attempts, most patients with BPD never kill themselves. Thus, the level of alarm created by young women with BPD who present in clinics and ERs with suicidal ideas is not justified, even if threats can sometimes be dramatic and blood-curdling. By and large, clinicians should not be distracted from their tasks by chronic suicidality.

Needless to say, chronic suicidality can be draining and no one wants to lose a patient (Maltsberger & Buie, 1974). But in BPD, suicidality 'goes with the territory' (Schwartz, Flinn, & Slawson, 1974). Most patients cannot be treated without accepting a calculated risk (Maltsberger, 1994). Moreover, recommending ER visits and hospitalization reinforces the very behaviours they are designed to treat (Linehan, 1993; Paris *et al.*, 2007).

Hospitalization has never been supported by evidence, and, when suicidality is chronic, admission to hospital provides only temporary relief; most patients continue to have suicidal ideas after discharge. To avoid the harm of repetitive admissions, one might prefer day treatment, which has an evidence base and offers the advantages of admission (intensive treatment by an experienced team) without its disadvantages, such as worsening of symptoms in hospital and isolation of patients from their interpersonal environment (Paris, 2008a). Unfortunately, day programmes usually have waiting lists and are not available in a crisis.

In practice, BPD patients continue to be held over in ERs or admitted to wards when they threaten suicide, cut themselves, or take overdoses. These options are determined to some extent by a fear of litigation. However, to minimize the risk of lawsuits one can ensure careful record-keeping, frequently consult with colleagues, and get families involved early (Gutheil, 1992; Gutheil & Brodsky, 2008).

Based on current evidence, it is clear that we should treat suicidal patients with BPD on an out-patient basis. Psychopharmacology is adjunctive and optional. Hospital admission can be justified only by either a near-fatal attempt or a micropsychotic episode (Paris, 2008a). While some patients may take their own lives, we have no evidence that this outcome can be prevented. We should, therefore, focus on providing evidence-based psychological treatments designed for this challenging population.

References

Akiskal, H., Chen, S., Davis, G., & Puzantian, V. (2001). Do patients with borderline personality disorder belong to the bipolar spectrum? *Journal of Affective Disorders, 67*, 221–228.

American Psychiatric Association (APA) (2000). *Diagnostic and Statistical Manual of Mental Disorders*, 4th ed, Text Revision, Washington, DC: American Psychiatric Press.

Bateman, A. & Fonagy, P. (1999). Effectiveness of partial hospitalization in the treatment of borderline personality disorder: a randomized controlled trial. *American Journal of Psychiatry, 156*, 1563–1569.

Bateman, A. & Fonagy, P. (2009). Randomized controlled trial of outpatient mentalization-based treatment versus structured clinical management for borderline personality disorder. *American Journal of Psychiatry, 166*, 1355–1364.

Beautrais, A. L. (2001). Suicides and serious suicide attempts: two populations or one? *Psychological Medicine, 31*, 837–845.

Binks, C.A., Fenton, M., McCarthy, L., Lee, T., Adams, C. E., & Duggan, C. (2006a). Psychological therapies for people with borderline personality disorder. *Cochrane Database of Systematic Reviews*. (1):CD005652.

Binks, C.A., Fenton, M., McCarthy, L., Lee, T., Adams, C. E., & Duggan, C. (2006b). Pharmacological interventions for people with borderline personality disorder. *Cochrane Database of Systematic Reviews*. (1):CD005653.

Brown, M. Z., Comtois, K. A., & Linehan, M. M. (2002). Reasons for suicide attempts and non-suicidal self-injury in women with borderline personality disorder. *Journal of Abnormal Psychology*, *111*, 198–202.

Clarkin, J. F., Levy, K. N., Lenzenweger, M. F., & Kernberg, O. F. (2007). Evaluating three treatments for borderline personality disorder: a multiwave study. *American Journal of Psychiatry*, *164*, 922–928.

Coid, J., Yang, M., Tyrer, P., Roberts, A., & Ullrich, S. (2006). Prevalence and correlates of personality disorder in Great Britain. *British Journal of Psychiatry*, *188*, 423–431.

Crowell, S. E., Beauchaine, T. P., & Linehan, M. M. (2009). A biosocial developmental model of borderline personality: Elaborating and extending Linehan's theory. *Psychological Bulletin*, *135*, 495–510.

Davidson, K., Norrie, J., Tyrer, P., Gumley, A., Tata, P., Murray, H., & Palmer, S. (2006). The effectiveness of cognitive behaviour therapy for borderline personality disorder: Results from the borderline personality disorder study of cognitive therapy (BOSCOT) trial. *Journal of Personality Disorders*, *20*, 450–465.

Giesen-Bloo, J., van Dyck, R., Spinhoven, P., van Tilburg, W., Dirksen, C., van Asselt, T., Kremers, I., Nadort, M., & Arntz, A. (2006). Outpatient psychotherapy for borderline personality disorder: Randomized trial of schema-focused therapy vs transference-focused psychotherapy. *Archives of General Psychiatry*, *63*, 649–658.

Goldstein, R.B., Black, D.W., Nasrallah, A., & Winokur, G. (1991). The prediction of suicide. *Archives of General Psychiatry*, *48*, 418–422.

Gunderson, J. G. & Links, P. S. (2008). *Borderline Personality Disorder: A clinical guide*, 2nd ed. Washington, DC: American Psychiatric Press.

Gutheil, T. G. (1992). Suicide and suit: liability after self-destruction. In D. Jacobs (Ed.), *Suicide and Clinical Practice* (pp. 147–167). Washington, DC: American Psychiatric Press.

Gutheil, T.A. & Brodsky, A. (2008). *Preventing Boundary Violations in Clinical Practice*. New York: Guilford Press.

Hawton, K., Zahl, D., & Weatherall, R. (2003). Suicide following deliberate self-harm: Long-term follow-up of patients who presented to a general hospital. *British Journal of Psychiatry*, *182*, 537–542.

Hull, J.W., Yeomans, F., Clarkin, J., Li, C., & Goodman, G. (1996). Factors associated with multiple hospitalizations of patients with borderline personality disorder, *Psychiatric Services*, *47*, 638–641.

Hunt, I.M., Kapur, N., Robinson, J., Shaw, J., Flynn, S., Bailey, H., Meehan, J., Bickley, H., Burns, J., Appleby, L., & Parsons, R. (2006). Suicide within 12 months of mental health service contact in different age and diagnostic groups: National clinical survey. *British Journal of Psychiatry*, *188*, 135–142.

Lenzenweger, M. F., Lane, M. C., Loranger, A. W., & Kessler, R. C. (2007). DSM-IV Personality Disorders in the National Comorbidity Survey Replication. *Biological Psychiatry*, *62*, 553–556.

Lesage, A. D., Boyer, R., Grunberg, F., Morisette, R., Vanier, C., Morisette, R., Ménard-Buteau, C., & Loyer, M. (1994). Suicide and mental disorders: a case control study of young men. *American Journal of Psychiatry*, *151*, 1063–1068.

Lesage, A.L., Seguin, M., Guy, A., Daigle, F., Bayle, M. N., Chawky, N., Tremblay, N., & Turecki, G. (2008). Systematic services audit of consecutive suicides in New Brunswick: The case for coordinating specialist mental health and addiction services. *Canadian Journal of Psychiatry*, *53*, 671–678.

Lieb, K., Vollm, B., Rucker, G., Timmer, A., & Stoffers, J. M. (2010). Pharmacotherapy for borderline personality disorder: Cochrane systematic review of randomized trials. *British Journal of Psychiatry, 196*, 4–12.

Linehan, M. M. (1993). *Cognitive Behavioral Therapy of Borderline Personality Disorder*. New York: Guilford Press.

Linehan, M. M., Armstrong, H. E., Suarez, A., Allmon, D., & Heard, H. (1991). Cognitive behavioral treatment of chronically parasuicidal borderline patients. *Archives of General Psychiatry, 48*, 1060–1064.

Linehan, M. M., Comtois, K. A., Murray, A. M., Brown, M. Z., Gallop, R. J., Heard, H. L., Korslund, K. E., Tutek, D. A., Reynolds, S. K., & Lindenboim, N. (2006). Two-year randomized controlled trial and follow-up of dialectical behaviour therapy vs therapy by experts for suicidal behaviors and borderline personality disorder. *Archives of General Psychiatry, 63*, 757–766.

Links, P. S., Heslegrave, R., & van Reekum, R. (1999). Impulsivity: Core aspect of borderline personality disorder. *Journal of Personality Disorders, 13*, 1–9.

Links, P. S., Gould, B., & Ratnayake, R. (2003). Assessing suicidal youth with antisocial, borderline, or narcissistic personality disorder. *Canadian Journal of Psychiatry, 48*, 301–310.

Maltsberger, J. T. (1994). Calculated risk taking in the treatment of suicidal patients: Ethical and legal problems. *Death Studies, 18*, 439–452.

Maltsberger, J. T., & Buie, D. H. (1974). Countertransference hate in the treatment of suicidal patients. *Archives of General Psychiatry, 30*, 625–633.

Maris, R. (1981). *Pathways to Suicide*. Baltimore, MD: Johns Hopkins University Press.

Martin R. L., Cloninger, C. R., Guze, S. B., & Clayton, P. J. (1985). Mortality in a follow-up of 500 psychiatric outpatients. II. Cause-specific mortality. *Archives of General Psychiatry, 42*, 58–66.

McGirr, A., Paris, J., Lesage, A., Renaud, J., & Turecki, G. (2007). Risk factors for suicide completion in borderline personality disorder: A case-control study of cluster B comorbidity and impulsive aggression. *Journal of Clinical Psychiatry, 68*, 721–729.

McGlashan, T. H. (1986). The Chestnut Lodge follow-up study III: Long-term outcome of borderline personalities. *Archives of General Psychiatry, 43*, 2–30.

McMain, S. F., Links, P. S., Gnam, W. H., Guimond, T., Cardish, R. J., Korman, L., & Streiner, D. L. (2009). A randomized trial of dialectical behaviour therapy versus general psychiatric management for borderline personality disorder. *American Journal of Psychiatry, 166*, 1365–1374.

National Institute for Health and Clinical Excellence (NICE) (2009). Guidelines for the treatment of borderline personality disorder, available at http://www.nice.org.uk/guidance/index.jsp?action=byID&o=11651, accessed 10 May 2009.

Oldham, J. M., Gabbard, G. O., Goin, M. K., Gunderson, J., Soloff, P., Spiegel, D., Stone, M., & Phillips, K. A. (2001). Practice guideline for the treatment of Borderline Personality Disorder. *American Journal of Psychiatry, 158* (Suppl.), 1–52.

Paris, J. (2003). *Personality Disorders Over Time*. Washington, DC: American Psychiatric Press.

Paris, J. (2006). *Half in Love with Easeful Death: The meaning of chronic suicidality*. Hillsdale, NJ: Lawrence Erlbaum.

Paris, J. (2008a). *Treatment of Borderline Personality Disorder: A guide to evidence-based practice*. New York: Guilford Press.

Paris, J. (2008b). Clinical trials in personality disorders. *Psychiatric Clinics of North America, 31*, 517–26.

Paris, J., Gunderson, J. G., & Weinberg, I. (2007). The interface between borderline personality disorder and bipolar spectrum disorder. *Comprehensive Psychiatry, 48*, 145–154.

Paris, J. & Zweig-Frank, H. (2001). A twenty-seven year follow-up of borderline patients. *Comprehensive Psychiatry, 42*, 482–487.

Pokorny, A. D. (1982). Prediction of suicide in psychiatric patients: Report of a prospective study. *Archives of General Psychiatry, 40*, 249–257.

Robins, L. (1966). *Deviant Children Grown Up*. Baltimore, MD: Williams & Wilkins.

Russell, J. J., Moskowitz, D. S., Zuroff, D. C., Sookman, D., & Paris J. (2007). Stability and variability of affective experience and interpersonal behavior in borderline personality disorder. *Journal of Abnormal Psychology, 116*, 578–588.

Schwartz, D. A., Flinn, D. E., & Slawson, P. F. (1974). Treatment of the suicidal character. *American Journal of Psychotherapy, 28*, 194–207.

Siever, L. J. & Davis, K. L. (1991). A psychobiological perspective on the personality disorders. *American Journal of Psychiatry, 148*, 1647–1658.

Soloff, P. H., Lynch, K. G., Kelly, T. M., Malone, K. M., & Mann, J. J. (2000). Characteristics of suicide attempts of patients with major depressive episode and borderline personality disorder: A comparative study. *American Journal of Psychiatry, 157*, 601–608.

Stone, M. H. (1990). *The Fate of Borderline Patients*. New York: Guilford Press.

Tidemalm, D., Elofsson, S., Stefansson, C. G., Waern, M., & Runeson, B. (2005). Predictors of suicide in a community-based cohort of individuals with severe mental disorder. *Social Psychiatry and Psychiatric Epidemiology, 40*, 595–600.

Westen, D. & Morrison, K. (2001). A multidimensional meta-analysis of treatments for depression, panic, and generalized anxiety disorder: an empirical examination of the status of empirically supported therapies. *Journal of Consulting and Clinical Psychology, 69*, 875–899.

Zanarini, M. C., Frankenburg, F. R., Hennen, J., & Silk, K. R. (2003). The longitudinal course of borderline psychopathology: 6-year prospective follow-up of the phenomenology of Borderline Personality Disorder. *American Journal of Psychiatry, 160*, 274–283.

Zanarini, M. C., Frankenburg, F. R., Khera, G. S., & Bleichmar, J. (2001). Treatment histories of borderline inpatients. *Comprehensive Psychiatry, 42*, 144–150.

Zimmerman, M., Rothschild, L., & Chelminski, I. (2005). The prevalence of DSM-IV personality disorders in psychiatric outpatients. *American Journal of Psychiatry, 162*, 1911–1918.

CHAPTER SEVEN

Deliberate Self-Harm: Extent of the Problem and Prediction of Repetition

Ella Arensman, Paul Corcoran, and Anthony P. Fitzgerald

Abstract

Deliberate self-harm (DSH) is a major public health problem in many countries and varies by age group, gender, and ethnicity. Having engaged in an act of DSH is the strongest predictor of future suicidal behaviour, both non-fatal and fatal. Development and implementation of effective assessment procedures for DSH patients are required in order to assess risk of repetition and prevent repeated suicidal behaviour. In this chapter we present the outcomes of a review of studies addressing the extent of the problem of DSH and repetition, prediction of factors associated with repeated DSH including age, gender, ethnicity, and assessment procedures for DSH patients presenting to hospital emergency departments.

The extent of the problem of DSH varies across countries, with relatively high rates in the United Kingdom and Belgium and low rates in Scandinavia. DSH rates are consistently higher in females compared to males. However, recent studies in Ireland indicate that rates of repeated DSH are similar for men and women. Factors predicting repeated DSH vary by age (young, adults, older adults) with some overlap. A history of previous DSH is a predictor for repetition in both young people and adults. Even though most national suicide prevention programmes prioritize the implementation of uniform guidelines for the assessment of DSH patients, there is still considerable variation within and across countries with regard to the types of assessment and aftercare offered to DSH patients. A four-question tool (Manchester Self-Harm Rule) is an example of an

International Handbook of Suicide Prevention: Research, Policy and Practice, First Edition.
Edited by Rory C. O'Connor, Stephen Platt, Jacki Gordon.
© 2011 John Wiley & Sons, Ltd. Published 2011 by John Wiley & Sons, Ltd.

evidence-based screening tool for identifying risk of repeated suicidal behaviour (non-fatal and fatal) and is recommended for wider implementation.

Introduction

Engaging in deliberate self-harm (DSH) is the strongest predictor of future suicidal behaviour, both non-fatal and fatal (Gilbody, House, & Owens, 1997; Gunnell, Hawton, Ho, Evans, O'Connor, et al., 2009; Kerkhof & Arensman, 2001; Zahl & Hawton, 2004). Deliberate self-harm frequently leads to non-fatal repetition, with an estimated median risk of repetition of 16% within one year and 23% over four years of follow-up, based on the findings of a systematic review (Owens, Horrocks, & House, 2002). However, more recent estimates from a UK multicentre study suggest even higher rates of repeat DSH (33%) in the 12 months following an index case (Lilley, Owens, Horrocks, House, Noble, et al., 2008). Subsequent repeated self-harm often occurs within days of an index DSH act (Cedereke & Ojehagen, 2005; Kapur, Turnbull, Hawton, Simkin, Mackway-Jones, et al., 2006).

Worldwide, few countries have reliable data on deliberate self-harm. There is a broad spectrum of self-harming behaviours, ranging from deliberate recklessness to highly lethal attempts at suicide, and only a minority of persons who self-harm present to hospital (Skegg, 2005). However, hospital presentations with deliberate self-harm provide a potentially important indicator of the burden of psychiatric and psychological morbidity in the population. They also provide an important opportunity for the health and social care system to provide targeted interventions to reduce the risk of suicide in a well-delineated group of patients at high risk of suicide.

An internationally agreed definition of deliberate self-harm has been endorsed by the World Health Organization (WHO) and will be used to define deliberate self-harm in this chapter: 'an act with non-fatal outcome in which an individual deliberately initiates a non-habitual behaviour, that without intervention from others will cause self harm, or deliberately ingests a substance in excess of the prescribed or generally recognized therapeutic dosage, and which is aimed at realizing changes that the person desires via the actual or expected physical consequences' (Platt, Bille-Brahe, Kerkhof, Schmidtke, Bjerke, et al., 1992). This definition facilitated international comparisons of deliberate self-harm incidence and trends in a European multicentre study (Schmidtke, Bille-Brahe, Kerkhof, & De Leo, 2004), which demonstrated a more than 10-fold variation in DSH rates across more than 20 regions. These rates were based on single centres as reliable estimates of national rates are not available.

A National Registry of Deliberate Self-harm (NRDSH) has been operating in the Republic of Ireland since 2002. The NRDSH is a national system of population monitoring for the occurrence of deliberate self-harm presenting to all hospital emergency departments in the country. The NRDSH had near complete coverage of the country's hospitals for the period 2002–2005. From 2006 onwards, all general hospital and paediatric hospital emergency departments have contributed data to the registry (NSRF, 2009).

The present chapter includes an overview of outcomes of the Irish self-harm registry in terms of the incidence of DSH and repetition. In addition, a review of the international literature has been conducted on deliberate self-harm, prediction of repetition, and assessment procedures to identify self-harm patients at risk of future repetition.

Extent of the Problem of Deliberate Self-Harm and Repetition

Extent of the problem of deliberate self-harm

In Ireland, the NRDSH records all DSH presentations made to hospital emergency departments. Over the period 2003–2008, 63,154 DSH presentations to hospital were made involving 41,205 individuals. The average annual total, male and female rates of persons presenting with DSH were 202, 172, and 234 per 100,000, respectively. There was evidence of a downward trend over the period 2003–2006 (11.5%), followed by increases in 2007 (4%) (NSRF, 2008) and 2008 (6%) (NSRF, 2009).

Hawton, Bergen, Casey, Simkin, Palmer, and colleagues (2007) conducted a multicentre study of self-harm in the United Kingdom in which a similar methodology was used to obtain data on hospital presentations of DSH in Oxford, Manchester, and Leeds over an 18-month period (March 2000–August 2001). DSH rates for males ranged from 285 per 100,000 in Oxford to 460 in Manchester and for females the rates ranged from 342 per 100,000 in Oxford to 587 in Manchester. These rates are higher than those found in Ireland.

The Network for International Collaboration on Evidence in Suicide Prevention (NICE-SP) conducted an international comparative study to examine the variation in DSH rates by gender in eight European regions between 1989 and 2003 (Arensman, Fitzgerald, Bjerke, Cooper, Corcoran, *et al.*, 2008). Trends in DSH rates over time vary considerably across the different European regions and by gender. DSH rates were consistently higher among women than among men, with the highest rates in Manchester (United Kingdom) (580), Oxford (United Kingdom) (416), and Ghent (Belgium) (319), and the lowest rates in Sor-Trondelag (Norway) (148), Umea (Sweden) (128), and Ljubljana (Slovenia) (72). The low DSH rates in Ljubljana are remarkable considering the high suicide rates at national level. With the exception of Oxford, similar trends over time were found for female and male DSH rates. After 1995, an increasing trend for DSH was found in females in Oxford, whereas the rates for males remained stable. In Manchester, rates of DSH for both males and females were fairly stable. In the two Irish regions, Cork and Limerick, an increase in DSH was observed in both males and females after 1999. In the two Scandinavian regions, Sor-Trondelag and Umea, a decreasing trend for both males and females was observed over the period 1989–1995 followed by a stable pattern in the following years. In Ghent, both male and female DSH rates showed a steep decline after 1995.

Schmidtke *et al.* (2004) compared trends in DSH rates in 11 European regions over a maximum period of 10 years (1989–1999). In females, a decrease in DSH rates was observed in most regions from the mid-1990s. In males, the DSH rates showed a less consistent pattern over time. The decreasing trend of DSH in women may be associated with the wider implementation of national suicide prevention programmes and specific treatment programmes such as Cognitive Behavioural Therapy or Dialectical Behaviour Therapy aimed at reducing the risk of repeated self-harm, which occurred during the same period.

Repetition of deliberate self-harm

Hospital-based studies   Based on the Irish NRDSH data over the period 2003–2008, 8,755 patients (21.2%) presented to the hospital Emergency Department on at least two occasions (at least one repetition), 3,811 (9.2%) presented at least three times (at least two repetitions), and 366 (0.9%) presented at least 10 times (NSRF, 2009; Perry *et al.*, in progress).

The risk of repetition was highest immediately after a DSH presentation, with half (50%) of all repeat events occurring in the first three months and almost two-thirds (64%) within the first six months. There was a clear association between repetition and the method of DSH: the highest rates were found among individuals who engaged in self-cutting (either as the sole method or in combination with drug overdose). The risk of repetition within the first 12 months following the study index episode was 39.1% and 37.6% in individuals whose methods were cutting alone or cutting and overdose, respectively. The 12-month risk of repetition was 26.0% for the overdose alone group. Among those who used highly lethal methods of DSH, such as attempted hanging, drowning, and poisoning by chemical substances, lower rates of repetition were found. The risk of repetition within the first 12 months increased from 16.5% among those under 15 years to 35.3% in those aged 35 to 40 years and then fell to 13.1% in those over 65 years. Repetition rates were similar in men and women (28.7% versus 29.0%, respectively).

The UK multicentre study reported a slightly lower overall repetition rate of 33% at 12 months following the study index DSH episode, but a higher repetition rate after self-cutting (47%), and a lower repetition rate for the overdose alone group (15%) (Lilley *et al.*, 2008). Based on the NICE-SP study covering the period 1989–2003, the overall repetition rates at 12-month follow-up were lower, ranging from 10% in Limerick to 20% in Oxford, among men, and from 7% in Limerick to 19% in Oxford among women (Arensman *et al.*, 2008).

Community-based studies   A limited number of studies have addressed repetition of DSH in community-based populations, with most studies focusing on young people and do not include follow-up measurements limiting the possibility to determine prospective repetition. An international comparative school-based cross-sectional study, known as the Child and Adolescent Self-Harm in Europe (CASE) study, revealed relatively high levels of repeated self-harm retrospectively (Madge, Hewitt, Hawton, de Wilde, Corcoran, *et al.*, 2008). Over 30,000 mainly 15- and 16-year-olds completed anonymous self-report questionnaires at school in six European countries and Australia. Just over half of school-going adolescents who reported an act of DSH in the year prior to the study, reported more than one DSH episode over their lifetime. Repetition rates ranged from 44.4% in Hungary to 62.4% in Norway. Repetition was more strongly associated with DSH acts involving multiple methods (63.0%) and self-cutting only (58.8%) than drug overdose (44.9%) or other single methods (46.6%) (Madge *et al.*, 2008). Using the CASE study methodology,

O'Connor, Rasmussen, and Hawton (2009) conducted a six-month follow-up study among 500 school-going adolescents, 6.2% reporting an act of DSH during the follow-up period. Factors associated with repeated DSH included worries about sexual orientation, history of sexual abuse, DSH by family members, anxiety, and low self-esteem (O'Connor, Rasmussen and Hawton, 2009).

Chen, Tan, Cheng, Chen, Liao, *et al.* (2010) conducted a population-based prospective cohort study in Taiwan using a community-based suicidal behaviour registry. Of the 970 individuals who had engaged in an act of DSH, 5.7% repeated at one-year follow-up, 7.8% after two years, and 9.5% after four years. Independent risk factors included female gender, self-cutting, and self-poisoning (Chen *et al.*, 2010).

Prediction of Repeated Deliberate Self-Harm Across the Lifespan

We reviewed prospective studies including self-harm patients in different age groups who presented to Emergency Departments and who were followed up over different time periods.

Prediction of repeated deliberate self-harm in young people

Taking into account different follow-up periods, repetition of deliberate self-harm in adolescents aged 13–19 years varies from 15% at six-month follow-up (Chitsabesan, Harrington, Harrington, & Tomenson, 2003) to 17.2% at two-year follow-up (Hultén, Jiang, Wasserman, Hawton, Hjelmeland, *et al.*, 2001), and 42% at nine-year follow-up (Groholt, Ekeberg, & Haldorsen, 2006). These findings indicate that repeated self-harm in young people is most likely to occur in the first months following presentation to hospital.

Across the different studies, several factors were found to be consistently associated with increased risk of repeat self-harm. These included previous DSH, alcohol or drug misuse, depression, chronic psychosocial problems and behaviour disturbance, developmental or personality disturbance, social isolation, disturbed family relationships, alcohol dependence in the family, and poor school record (Hawton & James, 2005; Portzky & van Heeringen, 2007).

Other, less frequently reported factors associated with DSH repetition were hopelessness (Goldston, Reboussin, & Daniel, 2006; Groholt, Ekeberg, & Haldorsen, 2006), treatment history for mental or behaviour problems (Groholt, Ekeberg, & Haldorsen, 2006), recent DSH by a friend (Lewinsohn, Rohde, & Seeley, 1994), and limited problem-solving and effectiveness of problem-solving (Hawton, Kingsbury, Steinhardt, James, & Fagg, 1999).

Consequently, it is important to collect information on risk factors as part of screening procedures to assess the risk of repeat DSH in young people (Mann, Apter, Bertelote, Beautrais, Currier, *et al.*, 2005). Research in this area has focused mainly on school-based screening programmes in order to identify young people at risk of suicidal behaviour

(Scott, 2009; Shaffer, Scott, Wilcox, Maslow, Hicks, *et al.*, 2004). An example is the Columbia Suicide Screen (CSS), a brief self-administered screening questionnaire intended to identify high school students at risk for suicidal behaviour (suicidal ideation or suicide attempt) (Shaffer *et al.*, 2004). A study including over 1,700 students revealed good sensitivity (0.75) and reasonable specificity (0.83), and a positive predictive value (16%). However, further research is required into the cost-effectiveness of screening general populations versus at-risk populations, as well as the appropriateness of screening instruments across different cultures.

Prediction of repeated deliberate self-harm in adults

Various studies have addressed the prediction of repeated DSH in adults. For example, based on a European multicentre study in which 836 adult DSH patients were followed up over a 12-month period, McAuliffe, Corcoran, Keeley, Arensman, Bille-Brahe, *et al.* (2006) found that the problem-solving dimension 'passive avoidance' was significantly associated with repeated DSH. Passive avoidance is characterized by preoccupation with problems, feeling unable to do anything, worrying about the past, and trying to avoid problems, and was attenuated by self-esteem. In an Irish study by McAuliffe, Corcoran, Hickey, and McLeavey (2008) including 152 DSH patients who presented to an Emergency Department, a history of previous DSH was found to be predictive of prospective repetition. Poor optional thinking (poor optional thinking ability on interpersonal problems based on the Optional Thinking Test by Platt & Spivak (1977)) was significantly associated with increased risk of repetition among DSH patients who had engaged in a first ever DSH act at the time of the index episode.

Sinclair, Hawton, and Gray (2010) conducted a six-year follow-up study including 150 patients who had presented to hospital following an act of DSH. A relatively high proportion (57.4%) had engaged in repeated DSH acts. The presence of a psychiatric disorder and harmful use of alcohol were significantly associated with prospective repetition. In a seven-year follow-up study by Sinclair, Caren, Hawton, and Williams (2007) among 68 DSH patients, evidence was found for a mediating effect of low autobiographical memory specificity between childhood sexual abuse and recent DSH and a partial mediating effect between affective disorders and recent DSH. These findings suggest that one of the mechanisms through which abuse history and presence of an affective disorder increase an individual's risk of further deliberate self-harm is via low autobiographical memory specificity.

Prediction of repeated deliberate self-harm in older adults

A review of research into DSH in older adults by Chan, Draper, and Banerjee (2007) found that four out of 24 studies had addressed repetition prospectively. The one-year repetition rate ranged from 3.6% in a Chinese study by Chiu, Lam, Pang, Leung, and Wong (1996) to 11.1% in a European study by De Leo, Padoani, Lönnqvist, Kerkhof, Bille-Brahe, *et al.* (2002). According to Chiu *et al.*, the relatively low repetition rate among

Chinese older adults (age 65+) may reflect under-reporting due to the strong stigma surrounding mental illness and suicidal behaviour in Chinese societies.

The research evidence for risk factors associated with repeated DSH in older adults is inconsistent across studies, which is largely due to differences in study design, variable, and instrument selection. De Leo *et al.* (2002) conducted a 12-month prospective study among older adults (aged 60+) who had presented to a general hospital following an act of DSH. Individuals who made a repeated DSH act at follow-up had a lower score on the Beck Suicide Intent Scale compared with non-repeaters, reflecting a lower level of suicidal intent associated with repeat DSH. Repeaters had also more often reported loss of their father during childhood. However, considering the relatively low number of repeaters (seven out of 55), these outcomes should be interpreted with caution. Hepple and Quinton (1997) followed 100 patients aged 65 years and over who were referred to a liaison psychiatric service following DSH. At 3.5 years (average) follow-up, 19% of the sample (all female) had engaged in further DSH acts. Compared with non-repeaters, repeaters were significantly more likely (1) to have received a diagnosis of depression at the time of the index DSH act, (2) to have suffered from persistent psychiatric disorder during follow-up, and (3) to be receiving psychiatric treatment.

Gender Differences

For many years, studies addressing gender differences in relation to DSH and repetition reported consistently higher rates of DSH and repetition rates among females. However, recent findings from the NRDSH in Ireland show that males are now over-represented among those who repeat DSH following an index episode at a hospital emergency department (NSRF, 2009; Perry *et al.*, in progress). In a European multicentre study using a prospective design, including 1,264 DSH patients, no significant gender differences were found with regard to 12-month repetition rates (Hultén *et al.*, 2001). This was also true when comparing prospective repetition rates among DSH patients with a history of previous DSH and those without at the time of the index DSH episode. Based on a 23-year follow-up study among 11,583 DSH patients, Zahl and Hawton (2004) found that repetition of DSH was associated with an increased risk of suicide in both males and females. However, repetition of DSH was found to be a better predictor of suicide in females than males.

Ethnicity

Research into the role of ethnicity in relation to repeated self-harm is limited. Cooper, Husain, Webb, Waheed, Kapur, *et al.* (2006) conducted a four-year prospective cohort study of 7,158 DSH patients presenting to hospital emergency departments in Manchester and Salford. Young South Asian women (aged 16–24 years) were more likely to engage in DSH compared with White women in the same age group (1010.9 versus 754 per 100,000). South Asian men had lower DSH rates than White men and South Asian women across all age groups. In terms of risk of repeated DSH, South Asian men and women showed a lower risk compared with White men and women. These findings were confirmed by Johnston, Cooper, Webb, and Kapur (2006), who conducted a study among 4,743 DSH patients to identify individual- and area-level predictors of self-harm repetition. The study showed that individual factors were more strongly associated with DSH repetition than area-level factors. Previous self-harm, previous psychiatric treatment, employment status, marital status and White ethnicity were independently associated with repetition.

Assessment of Risk of Repeated Deliberate Self-Harm

Assessing the risk of repeated DSH as well as the broader psychosocial needs of deliberate self-harm patients attending emergency departments is an important task (Tidemalm, Waern, Stefansson, Elofsson, & Runeson, 2008). Most suicide and self-harm prevention strategies (e.g., Reach Out, 2005; Protect Life, 2006) recognize the need for all deliberate self-harm patients attending emergency departments to be given a comprehensive assessment by a suitably trained health professional, followed by appropriate referral and follow-up, as recommended by the Self-Harm Guideline of the National Institute for Health and Clinical Excellence in the United Kingdom (NICE, 2004). However, the assessment procedures for deliberate self-harm patients presenting to emergency departments is inconsistent and patchy within and between countries (Arensman, Corcoran, Reulbach, Fitzgerald, Daly, *et al.*, 2010; Bennewith, Peeters, Hawton, House, & Gunnell, 2005).

Indeed, a study in England found that almost half (45%) of self-harm patients left the emergency department without being comprehensively assessed by a suitably qualified health professional. That this percentage ranged from 18% to 64% across the 32 hospitals under study was a clear indication of a lack of standardized protocols (Bennewith, Gunnell, Peters, Hawton, & House, 2004). A similar study in Wales (Barr, Leitner, & Thomas, 2005) found that 45% of self-harm patients left without a specialist psychosocial assessment. However, they found that this percentage had fallen from 52% to 42% over the five-year study period. There were indications for more frequently conducted specialist assessments among high-risk patient groups.

Based on data from the Irish NRDSH, there appeared to be widespread variation between Hospital Groups in the care of self-harm patients following treatment at the emergency department (Arensman *et al.*, 2010). The percentage admitted to a general ward ranged from 13% to 67%, psychiatric admission direct from emergency departments ranged from 6% to 26%, while the total percentage of patients who either refused to allow themselves to be admitted, left against medical advice, or were discharged from the emergency departments was 47% nationally and ranged from 25% to 72% by Hospital Group. It is likely that the vast majority of this group of self-harm patients was not adequately assessed. While those who used lethal methods, such as hanging and drowning, were more often referred for inpatient psychiatric treatment, a relatively high percentage of those who tried to hang (31%) or drown themselves (27%) were not admitted at all.

The consequences of non-standardized procedures for the assessment and aftercare of deliberate self-harm patients include increased risk of repeated deliberate self-harm (non-fatal and fatal), undiagnosed problems such as alcohol dependence and depression, inadequate treatment plans, and poor compliance with treatment (Hickey, Hawton, Fagg, & Weitzel, 2001; Kapur, Cooper, Hiroeh, May, Appleby, *et al.*, 2004). Different sets of guidelines have been produced in recent years (Australasian College for Emergency Medicine, 2000; NICE, 2004). According to Kapur (2005) these guidelines include elements of accepted good practice, but they are generally not evidence-based.

Cooper, Kapur, Dunning, Guthrie, Appleby, *et al.* (2006) developed a four-question tool, known as the Manchester Self-Harm (MASH) rule, in order to improve assessment of repeat self-harm, both non-fatal and fatal, by emergency department clinical staff. The four questions address (1) history of self-harm, (2) previous psychiatric treatment, (3) benzodiazepine use in current DSH act, and (4) any current psychiatric treatment. Based on a study including over 9,000 patients who presented with self-harm at emergency departments in Manchester and Salford, the MASH rule successfully predicted 94% of all DSH patients who engaged in a repeated DSH act within six months of their hospital index DSH act, reflecting high sensitivity. The MASH rule also successfully identified all 22 suicides that occurred during the study period. The specificity was lower at 25%, indicating that a quarter of all DSH patients were identified as non-repeaters. The MASH rule performed slightly better for women than men (sensitivity: 96% versus 93%), and for patients aged 35 years and older versus those younger than 35 years (sensitivity: 96% versus 93%). A slightly higher sensitivity for the MASH rule was found when comparing DSH episodes assessed by emergency department staff (97%) versus those assessed by psychiatric staff (94%).

Taking into account the objectives of the MASH rule and the target group involved, high sensitivity is more important than specificity, since a highly sensitive tool has few false negatives. Considering the absence of accurate screening tools in identifying risk of repeated self-harm and suicide, the evidence obtained in the study by Cooper *et al.* (2006) supports wider implementation of the MASH rule in emergency departments. Previously developed methods to predict repetition have shown similar levels of sensitivity (Corcoran, Kelleher, Keeley, Byrne, Burke, *et al.*, 1997; Kreitman & Foster, 1991). The Edinburgh Risk of Repetition Scale was designed by Kreitman and Foster for both clinical and research use and includes 11 items covering socio-demographic and clinical information. The scale aimed to identify self-harm patients with high, medium, and low risk of repetition in a calendar year. On average, 50% of self-harm patients in the high-risk group were identified as repeaters. This implies that a similar proportion did not engage in a repeat self-harm act, but were considered high risk and treated accordingly. Since the main focus was on the high-risk group, repeaters in the medium- and low-risk group were likely to go untreated.

Corcoran *et al.* (1997) presented a preliminary statistical repetition prediction model based on 11 socio-demographic and clinical items that were slightly different from the Kreitman and Foster scale, and that involved information that could be collected by non-clinical hospital personnel. The aim was to predict risk of repetition at six months and to distinguish repeaters from non-repeaters. Both the sensitivity and specificity levels were higher than reported by Kreitman and Foster. However, the repetition prediction model has not been further validated among large samples of DSH patients.

Comparing the different assessment protocols, the MASH rule would be recommended for wider implementation since this has been validated among a large sample of DSH patients, it has shown to be effective in predicting both non-fatal and fatal repeated self-harm, and it can be conducted efficiently by both clinical and non-clinical hospital personnel.

Conclusions

Deliberate self-harm and repetition are still major challenges for professionals in healthcare and community-based services, both in terms of the extent of the problem and the heterogeneity in terms of risk factors associated with repetition. There is increasing evidence supporting the need to address age- and gender-specific factors in predicting repetition. The research clearly underlines the need to develop and implement uniform guidelines for the assessment of DSH patients in order to prevent repeated suicidal behaviour (non-fatal and fatal). A recommendation is made for wider implementation of an evidence-based screening tool identifying risk of suicidal behaviour.

Acknowledgement

The National Suicide Research Foundation is funded by the Irish Health Service Executive's National Office for Suicide Prevention.

References

Arensman, E., Fitzgerald, T., Bjerke, T., Cooper, J., Corcoran, P., Grad, O., Hawton, K., Hjelmeland, H., Kapur, N, Perry, I. J., Salander-Renberg, E., & Van Heeringen, K. (2008). Deliberate self-harm and suicide: gender-specific trend in eight European regions – preliminary findings. Abstract. *Journal of Epidemiology & Community Health, 62* (Suppl. 1).

Arensman, E. Corcoran, P., Reulbach, U., Fitzgerald, T., Daly, C., & Perry, I. J. (2010). *Deliberate Self Harm in Ireland 2003–2008: Incidence, repetition and aftercare.* National Suicide Research Foundation.

Australasian College for Emergency Medicine (2000). Guidelines for the management of deliberate self harm in young people, available at http://www.acem.org.au/media/publications/youthsuicide.pdf.

Barr, W., Leitner, M., & Thomas, J. (2005). Psychosocial assessment of patients who attend an accident and emergency department with self-harm. *Journal of Psychiatric and Mental Health Nursing, 12,* 130–138.

Bennewith, O., Peeters, T. J., Hawton, K., House, A., & Gunnell, D. (2005). Factors associated with the non-assessment of self-harm patients attending an Accident and Emergency Department: results of a national study. *Journal of Affective Disorders, 89,* 91–97.

Bennewith, O., Gunnell, D., Peters, T., Hawton, K., & House, A. (2004). Variations in the hospital management of self harm in adults in England: observational study. *British Medical Journal, 328,* 1108–1109.

Cedereke, M. & Ojehagen, A. (2005). Prediction of repeated parasuicide after 1–12 months. *European Psychiatry, 20,* 101–109.

Chan, J., Draper, B., & Banerjee, S. (2007). Deliberate self-harm in older adults: A review of the literature from 1995 to 2004. *International Journal of Geriatric Psychiatry, 22,* 720–732.

Chen, V. C., Tan, H. K., Cheng, A. T., Chen, C. Y., Liao, L. R., & Stewart, R. (2010). Non-fatal repetition of self-harm: population based prospective cohort study in Taiwan. *British Journal of Psychiatry, 196,* 31–35.

Chitsabesan, P., Harrington, R., Harrington, V., & Tomenson, B. (2003). Predicting repeat self-harm in children – how accurate can we expect to be? *European Child and Adolescent Psychiatry, 12,* 23–29.

Chiu, H. F., Lam, L. C., Pang, A. H., Leung, C. M., & Wong, C. K. (1996). Attempted suicide by Chinese elderly in Hong Kong. *General Hospital Psychiatry, 18,* 444–447.

Cooper, J., Kapur, N., Dunning, J., Guthrie, E., Appleby, L., & Mackway-Jones, K. (2006). A clinical tool for assessing risk after self-harm. *Annals of Emergency Medicine, 48,* 459–466.

Cooper, J., Husain, N., Webb, R., Waheed, W, Kapur, N, Guthrie, E., & Appleby, L. (2006). Self-harm in the UK: Differences between South Asians and Whites in rates, characteristics, provision of service and repetition. *Social Psychiatry and Psychiatric Epidemiology, 41,* 782–788.

Corcoran, P., Kelleher, M. J., Keeley, H. S., Byrne, S., Burke, U., & Williamson, E. (1997). A preliminary statistical model for identifying repeaters of parasuicide. *Archives of Suicide Research, 3,* 65–74.

De Leo, D., Padoani, W., Lönnqvist, J., Kerkhof, A. J., Bille-Brahe, U., Michel, K., Salander-Renberg, E., Schmidtke, A., Wasserman, D., Caon, F., & Scocco, P. (2002). Repetition of suicidal behaviour in elderly Europeans: a prospective longitudinal study. *Journal of Affective Disorders, 72,* 291–295.

Department of Health, Social Services and Public Safety (2006). *Protect Life: A shared vision.* Belfast: HMSO.

Gilbody, S., House, A., & Owens, D. (1997). The early repetition of deliberate self-harm. *Journal of the Royal College of Physicians in London, 31,* 171–172.

Goldston, D. B., Reboussin, B. A., & Daniel, S. S. (2006). Predictors of suicide attempts: State and trait components. *Journal of Abnormal Psychology, 115,* 842–849.

Groholt, B., Ekeberg, Ø., & Haldorsen, T. (2006). Adolescent suicide attempters: What predicts future suicidal acts? *Suicide & Life-Threatening Behaviour, 36,* 638–650.

Gunnell, D., Hawton, K., Ho, D., Evans, J., O'Connor, S., Potokar, J., Donovan, J., & Kapur, N. (2008). Hospital admissions for self-harm after discharge from psychiatric inpatient care: Cohort study. *British Medical Journal, 337,* a2278.

Hawton, K., Kingsbury, S., Steinhardt, K., James, A., & Fagg, J. (1999). Repetition of deliberate self-harm by adolescents: The role of psychological factors. *Journal of Adolescence, 22,* 369–378.

Hawton, K. & James, A. (2005). Suicide and deliberate self harm in young people. *British Medical Journal, 330,* 891–894.

Hawton, K., Bergen, H., Casey, D., Simkin, S., Palmer, B., Cooper, J., Kapur, N., Horrocks, J., House, A., Lilley, R., Noble, R., & Owens, D. (2007). Self-harm in England: A tale of three cities. Multicentre study of self-harm. *Social Psychiatry and Psychiatric Epidemiology, 42,* 513–521.

Hepple, J. & Quinton, C. (1997). One hundred cases of attempted suicide in the elderly. *British Journal of Psychiatry, 171,* 42–46.

Hickey, L., Hawton, K., Fagg, J., & Weitzel, H. (2001). Deliberate self-harm patients who leave the accident and emergency department without a psychiatric assessment: A neglected population at risk of suicide. *Journal of Psychosomatic Research, 50,* 87–93.

Hultén, A., Jiang, G. X., Wasserman, D., Hawton, K., Hjelmeland, H., De Leo, D., Ostamo, A., Salander-Renberg, E., & Schmidtke, A. (2001). Repetition of attempted suicide among teenagers in Europe: Frequency, timing and risk factors. *European Child and Adolescent Psychiatry, 10,* 161–169.

Johnston, A., Cooper, J., Webb, R., & Kapur, N. (2006). Individual- and area-level predictors of self-harm repetition. *British Journal of Psychiatry, 189*, 416–421.

Kapur, N., Turnbull, P., Hawton, K., Simkin, S., Mackway-Jones, K., & Gunnell, D. (2006). The hospital management of fatal self-poisoning in industrialized countries: An opportunity for suicide prevention? *Suicide and Life-Threatening Behavior, 36*, 302–312.

Kapur, N., Cooper, J., Hiroeh, U., May, C., Appleby, L., & House, A. (2004). Emergency department management and outcome for self-poisoning: A cohort study. *General Hospital Psychiatry, 26*, 36–41.

Kapur, N. (2005). Management of self-harm in adults: Which way now? *British Journal of Psychiatry, 187*, 497–499.

Kerkhof, A. J. & Arensman, E. (2001). Pathways to suicide. In K. van Heeringen (Ed.), *Understanding Suicidal Behaviour: The suicidal process approach to research, treatment and prevention* (pp. 15–39). Chichester: John Wiley & Sons, Ltd.

Kreitman, N. & Foster, J. (1991). The construction and selection of predictive scales, with special reference to parasuicide. *British Journal of Psychiatry, 159*, 185–192.

Lewinsohn, P. M., Rohde, P., & Seeley, J. R. (2004). Psychosocial risk factors for future adolescent suicide attempts. *Journal of Consulting and Clinical Psychology, 62*, 297–305.

Lilley, R., Owens, D., Horrocks, J., House, A., Noble, R., Bergen, H., Hawton, K., Casey, D., Simkin, S., Murphy, E., Cooper, J., & Kapur, N. (2008). Hospital care and repetition following self-harm: Multicentre comparison of self-poisoning and self-injury. *British Journal of Psychiatry, 192*, 440–445.

Madge, N., Hewitt, A., Hawton, K., de Wilde, E. J., Corcoran, P., Fekete, S., van Heeringen, K., De Leo, D., & Ystgaard, M. (2008). Deliberate self-harm within an international community sample of young people: Comparative findings from the Child & Adolescent Self-harm in Europe (CASE) Study. *Journal of Child Psychology & Psychiatry, 49*, 667–677.

Mann, J., Apter, A., Bertolote, J., Beautrais, A., Currier, D., Haas, A., Hegerl, U., Lönqvist, J., Malone, K., Marusic, A., Mehlum, L., Patton, G., Phillips, M., Rutz, W., Rihmer, Z., Schmidtke, A., Shaffer, D., Silverman, M., Takahashi, Y., Varnik, A., Wasserman, D., Yip, P., & Hendin, H. (2005). Suicide prevention strategies: A systematic review. *Journal of the American Medical Association, 294*, 2064–2074.

McAuliffe, C., Corcoran, P., Hickey, P., & McLeavey, B. C. (2008). Optional thinking ability among hospital-treated deliberate self-harm patients: A 1-year follow-up study. *British Journal of Clinical Psychology, 47*, 43–58.

McAuliffe, C., Corcoran, P., Keeley, H. S., Arensman, E., Bille-Brahe, U, De Leo, D., Fekete, S., Hawton, K., Hjelmeland, H., Kelleher, M., Kerkhof, A. J., Lönqvist, J., Michel, K., Salander-Renberg, E., Schmidtke, A., van Heeringen, K., & Wasserman, D. (2006). Problem-solving ability and repetition of deliberate self-harm: A multicentre study. *Psychological Medicine, 36*, 45–55.

National Institute for Health and Clinical Excellence (NICE) (2004). Self-harm: The short-term physical and psychological management and secondary prevention of self-harm in primary and secondary care, available at http://www.nice.org.uk/nicemedia/pdf/CG016NICEguideline.pdf.

National Suicide Research Foundation (NSRF) (2008). National registry of deliberate self-harm Ireland-Annual report 2006/07, available at http://www.nsrf.ie/reports/RegistryReport2006_07/NSRF_06_07_NRDSH.pdf.

National Suicide Research Foundation (NSRF) (2009). National registry of deliberate self-harm Ireland-Annual report 2008, available at http://www.nsrf.ie/reports/2008AnnualReportNRDSH_Final.pdf.

O'Connor, R.C., Rasmussen, S., & Hawton, K. (2009). Predicting deliberate self-harm in adolescents: A six month prospective study. *Suicide and Life-Threatening Behavior, 39*, 364–375.

Owens, D., Horrocks, J., & House, A. (2002). Fatal and non-fatal repetition of self-harm. Systematic review. *British Journal of Psychiatry*, *181*, 193–199.

Perry, I. J. *et al.* (paper in progress). The incidence and repetition of hospital-treated deliberate self-harm in Ireland 2003–2008.

Platt, S., Bille-Brahe U., Kerkhof A., Schmidtke A., Bjerke T., Crepet P., De Leo, D., Haring, C., Lönqvist, J., Michel, K., Philippe, A., Pommereau, X., Querejeta, I., Salander-Renberg, E., Temesvary, B., Wasserman, D., & Sampaio Faria, J. (1992). Parasuicide in Europe: The WHO/EURO multicentre study on parasuicide. I. Introduction and preliminary analysis for 1989. *Acta Psychiatrica Scandinavica*, *85*, 97–104.

Platt, J. & Spivak, G. (1977). *Measures of Interpersonal Cognitive Problem Solving for Adults and Adolescents*. Philadelphia, PA: Hahnemann Medical College and Hospital.

Reach Out, Irish National Strategy for Action on Suicide Prevention 2005–2014 (2005). Health Service Executive.

Portzky, G. & van Heeringen, K. (2007). Deliberate self-harm in adolescents. *Current Opinion in Psychiatry*, *20*, 337–342.

Schmidtke, A., Bille-Brahe, U., Kerkhof, A. J. F. M., & De Leo, D. (2004). *Suicidal Behaviour in Europe – Results from the WHO/EURO Multicentre Study on Suicidal Behaviour*. Göttingen: Hogrefe & Huber.

Scott, A. (2009). Cognitive behavioural therapy and young people: An introduction. *Journal of Family Health Care*, *19*, 80–82.

Shaffer, D., Scott, M., Wilcox, H., Maslow, C., Hicks, R., Lucas, C. P., Garfinkel, R., & Greenwald, S. (2004). The Columbia Suicide Screen: Validity and reliability of a screen for youth suicide and depression. *Journal of the American Academy of Child and Adolescent Psychiatry*, *43*, 71–79.

Sinclair, J. M., Caren, C., Hawton, K., & Williams, J. M. (2007). The role of autobiographical memory specificity in deliberate self-harm: Correlates and consequences. *Journal of Affective Disorders*, *102*, 11–18.

Sinclair, J. M., Hawton, K., & Gray, A. (2010). Six-year follow-up of a clinical sample of self-harm patients. *Journal of Affective Disorders*, *121*, 247–252.

Skegg K. (2005). Self-harm. *The Lancet*, *366*, 1471–1483.

Tidemalm, D., Waern, M., Stefansson, C. G., Elofsson, S., & Runeson, B. (2008). Excess mortality in persons with severe mental disorder in Sweden: A cohort study of 12,103 individuals with and without contact with psychiatric services. *Clinical Practice & Epidemiology in Mental Health*, *14*, 23–32.

Zahl, D. L. & Hawton, K. (2004). Repetition of deliberate self-harm and subsequent suicide risk: Long-term follow-up study of 11,583 patients. *British Journal of Psychiatry*, *185*, 70–75.

CHAPTER EIGHT

Relationships of Genes and Early-life Experience to the Neurobiology of Suicidal Behaviour

J. John Mann and Dianne Currier

Abstract

Alterations in a number of neurobiological systems have been associated with suicidal behaviour. The serotonergic and noradrenergic neurotransmitter systems and the hypothalamic–pituitary–adrenal axis have been most studied. Alteration in functioning of these systems is associated with increased risk of suicidal behaviour. The origins of altered neurobiological function may be both genetic and developmental. Moreover, the interaction between genetic vulnerability and environmental adversity in early life has been shown in animal studies to result in developmental alterations in neurobiological systems. These alterations in function persist into adulthood. This chapter will review current knowledge of putative aetiologic effects of genes, early-life experiences, and the interaction between the two, upon neurobiological systems associated with suicidal behaviour.

Introduction

Suicidal behaviour (suicide, non-fatal suicide attempt, and suicidal ideation) occurs in the context of a diathesis or predisposition that is characterized by traits in multiple domains: behavioural, clinical, personality, biological, and cognitive (Mann & Currier, 2008). These traits have their origins in combinations of genetic effects and early-life experiences during

International Handbook of Suicide Prevention: Research, Policy and Practice, First Edition.
Edited by Rory C. O'Connor, Stephen Platt, Jacki Gordon.

critical formative periods of development. Thirty years of research have yielded considerable insight into neurobiological dysfunction associated with suicidal behaviour as a phenotype, and with a number of traits belonging to the diathesis, such as impulsive aggression, deficits in executive function, negative or rigid cognitive processes, and recurrent mood disorders. The major systems where abnormalities have been observed in suicide and non-fatal suicide attempt are the serotonergic system and the stress-response systems of the noradrenergic system and hypothalamic–pituitary–adrenal (HPA) axis. In this chapter we outline the main alterations in neurobiological function that have been documented in suicide attempters and suicide, and then review current knowledge of putative aetiological pathways from genes, early-life experiences, and the interaction between the two, to those functional alterations.

Biological Alterations in Suicidal Behaviour

Serotonergic system

The most consistent finding associated with suicidal behaviour is dysfunction in the serotonergic system (Mann, 2003). Altered serotonergic function indices include the serotonin metabolite 5-hydroxyindoleacetic acid in cerebrospinal fluid (CSF 5HIAA), serotonin receptors and transporters in postmortem brain, gene variants, and *in vivo* brain imaging (Mann, Brent, & Arango, 2001; Nordstrom, Samuelsson, Asberg, Traskman-Bendz, Aberg-Wistedt, *et al.*, 1994; Oquendo, Placidi, Malone, Campbell, Keilp, *et al.*, 2003; Pandey, Dwivedi, Rizavi, Ren, Pandey, *et al.*, 2002). Postmortem studies of the brain in suicide show a localized lower serotonin transporter (SERT) binding in the ventro-medial prefrontal cortex and anterior cingulate, which might reflect reduced serotonin input to these brain areas which are known to be involved in behavioural inhibition and/or decision-making (Arango, Underwood, Gubbi, & Mann, 1995; Mann, Huang, Underwood, Kassir, Oppenheim, *et al.*, 2000). Findings of more serotonin neurons, greater tryptophan hydroxylase 2 gene expression and protein, and lower SERT expression and protein, in suicide favour enhancement of serotonin transmission and are mitigated by lower levels of serotonin and/or 5-HIAA and more 5-HT_{1A} inhibitory autoreceptors in the brainstem of suicides and lower 5-HIAA in CSF of serious suicide attempters (Arango, Underwood, & Mann, 2003). Therefore, the former set of changes may be homeostatic mechanisms that arise secondary to primary serotonergic deficit (Arango, Underwood, & Mann, 2003). In a meta-analysis of prospective studies individuals with major depression who had below median levels of CSF 5-HIAA were 4.5 times more likely to die by suicide than those in the above median group (Mann, Currier, Stanley, Oquendo, Amsel, *et al.*, 2006). Lower concentration of CSF 5-HIAA has also been reported in patients who use violent methods to complete suicide or make non-fatal attempts of higher lethality (Cooper, Kelly, & King, 1992; Jones, Stanley, Mann, Frances, Guido, *et al.*, 1990; Mann & Malone, 1997).

In vivo imaging studies provide further evidence supporting a role for altered serotonergic function in suicidal behaviour. Lower C-α-methyl-L-tryptophan trapping in the orbital and ventromedial prefrontal cortex was found in suicide attempters who made high-intent attempts (Leyton, Paquette, Gravell, Rosa-Neto, Weston, *et al.*, 2006), and 5-HT$_{2A}$ binding negatively correlated with levels of hopelessness, a correlate of suicide and suicide attempt (van Heeringen, Audenaert, van Laere, Dumont, Slegers, *et al.*, 2003). Postmortem studies report higher expression, binding and protein for the 5-HT$_{2A}$ receptor in suicides, although some studies find this only in youth suicides (Arango, Ernsberger, Marzuk, Chen, Tierney, *et al.*, 1990; Pandey *et al.*, 2002; Stanley & Mann, 1983). Oquendo and colleagues, in a PET study, reported that, in response to the administration of the serotonin agonist fenfluramine, depressed high-lethality suicide attempters had lower fluorodeoxyglucose (^{18}F) regional cerebral metabolism of glucose (rCMRGlu) in anterior cingulate and superior frontal gyri, compared with depressed low-lethality attempters (Oquendo *et al.*, 2003). In that study, lethality of the most serious lifetime suicide attempt correlated negatively with rCMRGlu in the anterior cingulate, right superior frontal, and right medial frontal gyri, consistent with prefrontal cortex hypofunction in high-lethality depressed suicide attempters.

There is substantial evidence that altered serotonergic function is related to clinical and behavioural traits and to recurrent major depressive disorder. All are part of the diathesis for suicidal behaviour. A role for serotonergic dysfunction in aggressive and, to a lesser extent, impulsive behaviour is well documented (Congdon & Canli, 2008; Ryding, Lindstrom, & Traskman-Bendz, 2008), consistent with observations that low SERT binding associated with suicide appears to be concentrated in the ventromedial PFC and anterior cingulate regions known to mediate inhibition and restraint (Arango *et al.*, 1995; Mann *et al.*, 2000). Moreover, the observed association between prefrontal hypofunction and impaired serotonergic responsivity and lethality of non-fatal suicide attempts, and the linkage in familial transmission of suicide attempts and aggressive traits (Brent, Oquendo, Birmaher, Greenhill, Kolko, *et al.*, 2002), suggest that aggressive traits may be an intermediate clinical phenotype linking serotonergic dysfunction and suicidal behaviour (Oquendo *et al.*, 2003). Further support for this hypothesis comes from brain imaging studies reporting lower serotonin transporter binding in the frontal and midbrain regions in impulsive violent subjects (Tiihonen, Kuikka, Bergstrom, Karhu, Viinamaki, *et al.*, 1997), altered ventral PFC white matter structure in schizophrenia associated with aggression, and an inverse correlation between 5-HT$_{1A}$ binding in the orbital frontal cortex and aggression scale scores (Parsey, Oquendo, Simpson, Ogden, van Heertum, *et al.*, 2002). Other clinical and cognitive traits associated with suicidal behaviour have also been linked to altered serotonin function, including pessimism and dysfunctional attitudes (Carballo, Hatkavy-Friedman, Burke, Sher, Baca-Garcia, *et al.*, 2008; Meyer, 2007) and hopelessness (Bhagwagar, Hinz, Taylor, Fancy, Cowen, *et al.*, 2006; van Heeringen *et al.*, 2003).

Stress-response systems

The stress-diathesis model of suicidal behaviour proposes that stressful events can be precipitants for suicidal behaviour in individuals with a diathesis or predisposition for suicidal behaviour. Accordingly, the stress-response system function is a key neurobiological candidate in the search for the biological aetiology of suicidal behaviour. There are two main systems involved in the regulation of stress-response: the neuroendocrine hypotha-lamic–pituitary–adrenal axis and the noradrenergic system.

Abnormalities in the noradrenergic system in suicide attempts include fewer norepine-phrine (NE) neurons in the *locus ceruleus* in depressed suicides (Arango, Underwood, & Mann, 1996), greater β-adrenergic cortical receptor binding in suicides (Mann, Stanley, McBride, & McEwen, 1986), and lower alpha$_2$ α-adrenergic binding (Ordway, Widdowson, Smith, & Halaris, 1994). We have proposed that these changes suggest a pattern of cortical noradrenergic over-activity that may be the outcome of excessive NE release, with stress leading to depletion due to the smaller population of NE neurons found in suicide victims (Mann, 2003; Arango, Ernsberger, Sved, & Mann, 1993). The excessive norepinephrine release when stressed in adulthood can result from sensitization of the system as a result of childhood adversity (Heim & Nemeroff, 2001). In living subjects lower cerebrospinal fluid 3-methoxy-4-hydroxphenylglycol (CSF MHPG), a metabolite of norepinephrine, is reported in some studies of suicide attempters compared with non-attempters with major depression (Agren & Niklasson, 1986) and criminal offenders (Virkkunenm de Jong, Bartko, & Linnoila, 1989); however, most studies observe no differences (Lester, 1995). Prospective studies, which are better suited to examining potential trait and state-dependent markers such as noradrenergic stress-response, also provide varying results, with one report that individuals engaging in repeat suicidal behaviour in the year following hospitalization for a suicide attempt are more likely to have above median CSF MHPG levels (Traskman-Bendz, Alling, Blennow, Regnell, Vinge, *et al.*, 1992), and others finding no association with future suicidal behaviour (Cooper *et al.*, 1992; Engstrom, Alling, Blennow, Regnell, & Traskman-Benz, 1999; Nordstrom *et al.*, 1994; Sher, Carballo, Grunebaum, Burke, Zalsman, *et al.*, 2006; Sunnqvist, Westrin, & Traskman-Bendz, 2008). A recent prospective study using survival analysis found lower baseline CSF MHPG was associated with increased risk of suicidal behaviour (fatal or non-fatal) in the 12 months following a presentation with major depressive episode; and the lower the CSF MHPG, the more lethal the suicide attempt at follow-up (Galfalvy, Currier, Oquendo, Sullivan, Huang, *et al.*, 2009).

Several potential intermediate clinical phenotypes between noradrenergic system dysfunction and suicidal behaviour have been uncovered. For example, higher NE con-centrations have been associated with higher levels of aggression (Mann, 2003) and higher CSF MHPG with greater hostility (Prochazka & Agren, 2003). In remitted depressed individuals treated with norepinephrine reuptake inhibitors, acute catecho-lamine depletion resulted in an increase in hopelessness or depression (Miller, Delgado, Salomon, Berman, Krystal, *et al.*, 1996), consistent with preclinical studies suggesting that NE is involved in the development of pessimism and hopelessness or depression (Henn & Vollmayr, 2005).

The HPA axis is the other major stress-response system. Failure to suppress cortisol secretion following the administration of dexamethasone (DST) and higher levels of plasma and urinary cortisol and loss of diurnal variation due to less afternoon decline in cortisol levels indicate hyperactivity of the HPA axis and have been associated with suicide (Coryell & Schlesser, 2001). There is a more than four-fold risk of dying by suicide in depressed individuals who are cortisol non-suppressors in DST challenge

(Mann *et al.*, 2006). There is less corticotrophin releasing hormone (CRH) receptor binding in the frontal cortex in suicides (Nemeroff, 1988) and higher CSF CRH (Arato, Banki, Bissette, & Nemeroff, 1989). DST non-suppression is not clearly related to future non-fatal suicide attempt, although some studies report an association with serious or violent attempts (reviewed in Mann & Currier, 2007). In other indices of HPA axis function suicide attempt is associated with lower CSF CRH, but no difference in plasma CRH or plasma cortisol (Brunner, Nelen, Breakefield, Robers, & van Oost, 2001), higher urinary cortisol in violent attempters (van Heeringen, Audenaert, van de Wiele, & Verstraete, 2000), and higher serum cortisol after 5-hydroxytryptophan challenge (Meltzer, Perline, Tricou, Lowy, & Robertson, 1984).

The HPA axis is complexly interrelated with the serotonergic and noradrenergic systems. The HPA axis and serotonergic system have a bidirectional relationship (Meijer & De Kloet, 1998). CRH neurons project to the serotonin *raphe nuclei*, and projections from the *raphe nuclei* extend to various brain regions that contain CRH and participate in stress-response (Owens & Nemeroff, 1991). Hyperactivity of the HPA axis observed in suicidal patients may mediate or moderate some of the serotonin abnormalities seen in these patients (Lopez, Vazquez, Chalmers, & Watson, 1997); modulation of serotonin receptors by corticosteroids in response to stress may have important implications for the pathophysiology of suicide (Lopez *et al.*, 1997; Stoff & Mann, 1997). There is also a bidirectional relationship between the HPA axis and the NE system. Stress activates both the HPA axis and *locus coeruleus* (LC), the major source of NE neurons in the brain (Aston-Jones, Shipley, Chouvet, Ennis, van Bockstaele, *et al.*, 1991), leading to increased NE release during stress. LC neurons influence the neuroendocrine stress-response system through their broad innervation of the paraventricular nucleus (PVN) projection pathways (Dunn, Swiergiel, & Palamarchouk, 2004). Severe anxiety in response to stress may be related to NE over-activity and hyperactivity of the HPA axis, contributing to suicide risk (Brown, Stoll, Stokes, Frances, Sweeney, *et al.*, 1988). Thus, there are multiple potential pathways through which stress may be involved in the biological anomalies observed in suicidal behaviour: directly through dysfunction of the HPA axis and the noradrenergic system and interactions between those two systems, as well as indirectly through downstream effects on serotonergic system function.

Developmental Factors Related to the Neurobiology of Suicide

Early-life environment

Reported childhood adversity, including sexual or physical abuse, neglect, parental loss, or severe family discord, has been associated with suicidal behaviour (Brodsky & Stanley, 2008). Sexual and physical abuse are independently associated with repeated suicide attempts after controlling for other childhood adversities (Ystgaard, Hestetun, Loeb, & Mehlum, 2004). One of the pathways through which early-life adversity contributes to suicidal behaviour later in life is via developmental effects on neurobiological systems that have functional consequences in adulthood. With respect to serotonergic system function, studies of adult rodents exposed to maternal separation in early life show alterations in multiple markers of serotonergic function, including: increased 5-HT and 5-HIAA in the dorsal raphe nucleus, and elevated 5-HIAA in the *nucleus accumbens* (Arborelius & Eklund, 2007), decreased 5-HT cell firing in the *raphe nuclei* in response to increased doses of the SSRI citalopram suggestive of alterations in 5-HT transporter and/or 5-HT1A autoreceptors (Arborelius, Hawks, Owens, Plotsky, & Nemeroff, 2004), altered 5-HT_{2C} mRNA editing (Bhansali, Dunning, Singer & Schmauss, 2007), reduced 5-HT level in the dorsal hippocampus, and lower 5-HT in the mPFC in males (Matthews, Dalley, Matthews, Tsai, & Robbins, 2001), and a decrease in the sensitivity of $alpha_1$-adrenergic receptors mediating excitation of 5-HT neurons in the DRN and of 5-HT_{1A} receptors regulating 5-HT release in the frontal cortex (Gartside, Johnson, Leitch, Troakes, & Ingram, 2003). 5-HT_{1A} knockout mice display an increased anxiety phenotype (Olivier, Pattij, Wood, Oosting, Sarnyai, *et al.*, 2001). Selective reinstatement of 5-HT_{1A} expression in the hippocampus and cortex reverses the anxiety behaviours, but only when implemented during early postnatal development and not in adulthood (Gross, Zhuang, Stark, Ramboz, Oosting, *et al.*, 2002), suggesting that interrupted postnatal 5-HT_{1A} receptor developmental processes contribute to anxiety behaviour in adulthood. In adult rhesus macaques, those that had experienced adversity in infancy had lower levels of CSF 5-HIAA (Higley, Suomi, & Linnoila, 1992; Maestripieri, McCormack, Lindell, Higley, & Sanchez, 2006), and lower serotonin transporter binding on PET scanning (Ichise, Vines, Gura, Anderson, Suomi, *et al.*, 2006). Lower transporter binding has also been found using PET scanning in adults with major depression who report childhood abuse (Miller, Kinnally, Ogden, Oquendo, Mann, *et al.*, 2009). In humans, abnormal response to serotonergic challenge has likewise been shown in individuals who experience adversity in childhood, with the effect appearing to persist into adulthood. In studies of children and adolescents, depressed children who experienced abuse had increased prolactin, but normal cortisol responses, to L-5-hydroytrptophan, a precursor of 5-HT, compared with non-abused depressed children and controls (Kaufmann, Birmaher, Perel, Dahl, Stull, *et al.*, 1998), and increased prolactin response to fenfluramine challenge was seen in boys in juvenile detention who had experienced adverse rearing environments (Pine, Coplan, Wasserman, Miller, Fried, *et al.*, 1997). In adults, borderline personality disorder women with a history of severe childhood abuse had a blunted prolactin response to the serotonergic agonist meta-chlorophenylpiperazine (Rinne, Westerberg, Den Boer, & van den Brink, 2000).

Alterations in stress-response function have also been reported in animal and human studies of the effects of early-life environment. In preclinical studies, rhesus monkeys exposed to maternal separation in infancy have elevated CSF norepinephrine in adulthood (Kraemer, Ebert, Schmidt, & McKinney, 1989) and rats exposed to early-life stress had altered noradrenergic response to stress in adulthood, showing evidence of over-activity and subsequent depletion. Higher PVN levels of norepinephrine were observed during restraint stress in adult rats which had been exposed in early-life to maternal separation than in control animals (Liu, Caldji, Sharma, Plotsky, & Meaney, 2000). Another report is suggestive of depletion: following restraint stress, norepinephrine level in adult rats was significantly lower in the hypothalamus and hippocampus and MHPG levels significantly lower in the frontal cortex in the maternal separation group compared with control animals (Daniels, Pietersen, Carstens, & Stein, 2004). There have been few studies in humans; however, one study found that suicide attempters who reported sexual abuse during childhood and adolescence had significantly higher levels of CSF MHPG and urinary norepinephrine/epinephrine compared with those with no history of abuse, a possible stress response to a lumbar puncture (Sunnqvist *et al.*, 2008).

Early-life stress leads to lasting alterations in HPA axis stress-response, perhaps through mechanisms involving enduring alteration of CRH expression in limbic regions involved in the regulation of the HPA axis (Brunson, Avishai-Eliner, Hatalski, & Baram, 2001). In animal models, maternal separation in infancy altered glucocorticoid receptor gene expression in hippocampus and frontal cortex, two brain regions implicated in the negative-feedback regulation of CRH (Liu *et al.*, 2000; Meaney, Diorio, Francis, Widdowson, LaPlante, *et al.*, 1996), which results in excessive corticosterone and ACTH release under stress in adulthood. Thus, stress in early life can alter gene expression within the brain leading to permanent modifications in HPA axis function which later in life result in abnormal molecular and hormonal responses to further stressful stimuli (Avishai-Eliner, Eghbal-Ahmadi, Tabachnik, Brunson, & Baram, 2001; Plotsky & Meaney, 1993). Increased DNA methylation in suicides with a history of childhood abuse is also linked with greater methylation of CpG islands in the glucocorticoid receptor gene, implicating epigenetic mechanisms (McGowan, Saski, D'Alessio, Dymov, Labonte, *et al.*, 2009). Similarly, in humans, early adversity or abuse has been associated with abnormal HPA axis function in adulthood. Women with varied psychiatric diagnoses and a history of childhood abuse showed hypersuppression of salivary cortisol concentrations in response to dexamethasone, indicating supersensitivity of the corticosteroid feedback inhibitory mechanisms (Stein, Yehuda, Koverola, & Hanna, 1997). Lower basal plasma cortisol concentration has also been reported in women with a history of childhood abuse (Heim, Newport, Bonsall, Miller, & Nemeroff, 2001), and abused women with or without current depression showed markedly increased plasma ACTH and increased cortisol responses in response to laboratory stress compared with controls and depressed women without early-life stress (Heim, Newport, Heit, Graham, Wilcox, *et al.*, 2000). This exaggerated sympathetic response to stress exhibited by individuals with a history of childhood trauma (Heim & Nemeroff, 2001) might also further deplete NE function (Weiss, Ratner, Voltura, Savage, Lucero, *et al.*, 1994).

Genes and suicidal behaviour

Evidence of a role for genetics in suicidal behaviour, independent of psychiatric disorder, is found in twin, adoption and family studies (Brent & Mann, 2005; Brent & Melhem, 2008). Population-based estimates of the contribution of additive genetic factors is between 30% and 50% for a broad phenotype of suicidal behaviour (ideation, plans, and/or attempts) (Voracek & Loibl, 2007). Concordance rates for suicide are higher in monozygotic (24.1%) compared with dizygotic twins (2.8%) (Voracek & Loibl, 2007), and adoption studies reveal higher suicide rates in the biological parents of adoptees who died by suicide (Schulsinger, Kety, Rosenthal, & Wender, 1979; Wender, Kety, Rosenthal,

Schulsinger, Ortmann, *et al.*, 1986), compared with biological parents of adoptees who did not. Offspring of depressed suicide attempters are more likely to become suicide attempters themselves compared with offspring of depressed non-attempters (Brent & Melhem, 2008).

Candidate genes have been sought largely based on evidence from neurobiological studies of suicide. The serotonergic system has been most extensively investigated; there are fewer but increasing numbers of studies of genes related to the HPA axis, and growing interest in neurotrophic factors such as BDNF. Given the likelihood of a polygenic mode of inheritance, more recent studies employ functional genomic methodologies such as microarray technologies for profiling expression of thousands of genes simultaneously (Sequeira & Turecki, 2006), and genome wide arrays for hundreds of thousands of SNPs (Hodgkinson, Yuan, Xu, Shen, Heinz, *et al.*, 2008).

Serotonergic system genes   The 5-HT$_{2A}$ receptor gene is not clearly associated with suicide attempt in mood disorder patients (Brezo, Klempan, & Turecki, 2008). One of the most studied polymorphisms is a relatively common functional polymorphism of the serotonin transporter gene 5″ upstream regulatory region (5-HTTLPR) where the low expressing S allele may be associated with suicidal behaviour (Anguelova, Benkelfat, & Turecki, 2003; Lesch, Bengel, Heils, Sabol, Greenberg, *et al.*, 1996). There is no agreement that there is an association between 5-HTTLPR genotype and serotonin transporter density in post-mortem brains of individuals who died by suicide (Arango, Underwood, & Mann, 2002; Du, Faludi, Palkovits, Demeter, Balkish, *et al.*, 1999; Mann, Huang, Underwood, *et al.*, 2000) or *in vivo* (Bah, Lindstrom, Westberg, Manneras, Ryding, *et al.*, 2008; Parsey, Hastings, Oquendo, Xianzhang, Goldman, *et al.*, 2006). Healthy adults with the lower expressing SS genotype show increased amygdala activity when exposed to angry or fearful faces, negative words, or aversive pictures (Brown & Hariri, 2006). The amygdala is densely innervated by serotonergic neurons and 5-HT receptors are abundant; such an association is therefore plausible (Azmitia & Gannon, 1986; Sadikot & Parent, 1990; Smith, Daunais, Nader, & Porrino, 1999).

Other genes related to serotonergic function that have been investigated include the two variants of tryptophan hydroxylase (TPH1 and TPH2), the rate-limiting enzyme in the synthesis of serotonin. Some, but not all, studies reported TPH1 SNP associations with suicidal behaviour (Bellivier, Chaste, & Malafosse, 2004), and aggression (Baldessarini & Hennen, 2004; Rujescu, Giegling, Bondy, Gietl, Zill, *et al.*, 2002). For TPH2, haplotype association has been reported with suicide (Zill, Buttner, Eisenmenger, Moller, Bondy, *et al.*, 2004) and suicide attempt (Lopez, Detera-Wadleigh, Cardona, Kassem, & McMahon, 2007; Zhou, Roy, Lispky, Kuchipudi, Zhu, *et al.*, 2005) in psychiatric samples, and single SNP associations between TPH2 genotype and suicidal behaviour in Chinese (Ke, Qi, Ping, & Ren, 2006) and German Caucasian (Zill, Baghai, Zwanger, Schule, Eser, *et al.*, 2004) psychiatric samples, although others fail to observe any associations (Brezo *et al.*, 2008). TPH2 genotype association has been found with altered amygdala response (Furmark, Appel, Henningsson, Ahs, Faria, *et al.*, 2008) and, in an fMRI study with altered function in prefrontal and parietal brain regions (Reuter, Esslinger, Montag, Lis, Gallhofer, *et al.*, 2008). Monoamine oxidase A (MAOA) variants have been associated with aggression (Brunner *et al.*, 1993), an element in the diathesis for suicidal behaviour, and the MAOA-uVNTR lower expressing polymorphisms are been associated with greater impulsivity in males (Huang, Cate, Battistuzzi, Oquendo, Brent, *et al.*, 2004). Because the gene for MAOA is sex linked, it is hypothesized that the higher prevalence of suicide in males may be, in part, due to greater impulsivity and aggression secondary to specific MAOA polymorphisms (Du, Faludi, Palkovits, Sotonyi, Bakish, *et al.*, 2002). An fMRI study found and association between the low expressing alleles of the u-VNTR and increased risk of violent behaviour, as well as with alterations in the corticolimbic circuitry involved in affect regulation, emotional memory, and impulsivity (Meyer-Lindeberg, Buckholtz, Kolachana, Hariri, Pezawas, *et al.*, 2006). Two other fMRI studies showed MAOA genotype affected performance on response tasks indicative of impulsivity (Fan, Fossella, Sommer, Wu, & Posner, 2003; Passamonti, Fera, Magariello, Cerasa, Gioia, *et al.*, 2006).

Stress-response related genes   Stress-response systems have been less studied to date with respect to candidate genes; no consistent results in the noradrenergic system or HPA axis related genes (Currier & Mann, 2008) have been found. In the HPA axis, a promising candidate is the CRH receptor 1 gene, reported in a recent study to be associated with cortisol response to dexamethasone challenge (Tyrka, Price, Gelernter, Schepker, Anderson, *et al.*, 2009). One study found an association between CRHR1 genotype and suicidality in depressed males exposed to low levels of life stressors (Wasserman, Sokolowski, Rozanov & Wasserman, 2007).

Genes and early-life environment interaction

The disparate findings in genetic association studies may in part be attributable to differences in environmental characteristics of study samples. Pre-clinical studies demonstrate that early-life adversity interacts with genotype to produce biological and behavioural alterations that endure into adulthood (Barr, Newman, Shannon, Parker, Dvoskin, *et al.*, 2004; Bennett, Lesch, Heils, Long, Lorenz, *et al.*, 2002). In humans, there have been multiple studies of early-life environment–5-HTTLPR interaction and vulnerability for psychiatric disorder, with most, but not all, reporting an effect (Uher & McGuffin, 2008). For suicidal behaviour specifically, reported childhood maltreatment only in those with the low expressing 5-HTTLPR S allele increased risk for suicide attempt (Caspi, Sudgen, Moffitt, Taylor, Craig, *et al.*, 2003). Other studies of the 5-HTTLPR polymorphism report childhood adversity–genotype interactions and suicidal behaviour in mixed diagnosis inpatients (Gibb, McGeary, Beevers, & Miller, 2006) and among abstinent African American substance-dependent patients (Roy, Hu, Janal, & Goldman, 2007). Adverse child-rearing, in combination with a lower expressing variant of the MAO A gene, was also found to contribute, in males only, to the development of antisocial behaviour and more impulsivity, both of which may contribute to suicidal behaviour (Caspi *et al.*, 2002; Huang *et al.*, 2004).

It is likely that such effects occur with genes related to the other neurobiological systems involved in suicidal behaviour. For example, a recent study found an interaction effect between CRH Receptor 1 haplotype and early-life stress on the severity of depression (Bradley, Binder, Epstein, Tang, Nair, *et al.*, 2008). Although that study did not examine suicide-related outcomes, it is suggestive of another potential pathway whereby genes and environment contribute to vulnerability for suicidal behaviour.

Epigenetics   Epigenetic effects involve a modulation of gene expression through mechanisms superimposed on those conferred by primary DNA sequence and can result in different patterns of expression for different copies of the same gene in a given cell nucleus. For example, the same allele on different chromosomes may show different expression levels due to epigenetic effects. Thus, the familial transmission of suicidality may not just be a case of direct intergenerational transmission of a vulnerability gene; it may also occur in the context of early-life environment effects on epigenetic mechanisms that in turn result in altered neurobiological function. Adverse experiences, such as physical or sexual abuse, which have been shown to be transmitted intergenerationally (Brosdky, Mann, Stanley, Tin, Oquendo, *et al.*, 2008), may alter gene expression and behaviour through methylation of key genes. Methylation is an epigenetic modification that alters gene expression and involves methyl groups attaching to DNA and blocking transcriptional factors from gaining access to the gene and thus effectively silencing or altering expression of the gene. Microarray technologies permit whole genome DNA methylation profiling in human tissues, including the brain, and can provide data on total and allele-specific methylation which can then be examined for suicide-related alterations. There is evidence from rodent studies that early-life environment affects HPA axis gene expression (Liu, Diorio, Tannenbaum, Caldji, Francis, *et al.*, 1997), and DNA methylation is one mechanism through which this may occur. In rats the GR receptor promotor region 1_7 in hippocampal tissues taken from adult offspring born to low maternal care mothers indicates elevated levels of DNA methylation compared with adult offspring of high maternal care mothers. This would explain the decreased level of glucocorticoid receptor expression observed in low maternal care offspring (Weaver, Cervoni, Champagne, *et al.*, 2004). This methylation process can be modified later in life, whereby silenced GR promotor DNA treated with trichostatin-A (allowing expression and reversal of HPA reactivity). An unmethylated GR promotor DNA can be silenced with methionine treatment with consequences for HPA reactivity and behaviour (Weaver, Cervoni, Champagne, D'Alessio, Sharma, *et al.*, 2004; Weaver, Champagne, Brown, Dymov, Sharma, *et al.*, 2005). Thus, early-life environment can affect behavioural and biological responses to stress in adulthood via epigenetic mechanisms, which are potential targets for intervention.

Conclusion

Genes and early-life environment contribute, both independently and in combination, to the development of dysfunction in neurobiological systems observed in adult suicide attempters and suicides. Identifying the responsible genes and epigenetic mechanisms and environmental contexts which result in those abnormalities may reveal new targets for interventions to prevent suicidal behaviour.

Acknowledgements

This work was supported by PHS grants MH059710, MH062185, and MH056390.

References

Agren, H. & Niklasson, F. (1986). Suicidal potential in depression: focus on CSF monoamine and purine metabolites. *Psychopharmacology Bulletin, 22,* 656–660.

Anguelova, M., Benkelfat, C., & Turecki, G. (2003). A systematic review of association studies investigating genes coding for serotonin receptors and the serotonin transporter: II. Suicidal behavior. *Molecular Psychiatry, 8,* 646–653.

Arango, V., Ernsberger, P., Marzuk, P. M., Chen, J.S., Tierney, H., Stanley, M., Reis, D. J., & Mann, J. J. (1990). Autoradiographic demonstration of increased serotonin 5-HT2 and beta-adrenergic receptor binding sites in the brain of suicide victims. *Archives of General Psychiatry, 47,* 1038–1047.

Arango, V., Ernsberger, P., Sved, A. F., & Mann, J. J. (1993). Quantitative autoradiography of α_1- and α_2-adrenergic receptors in the cerebral cortex of controls and suicide victims. *Brain Research, 630,* 271–282.

Arango, V., Underwood, M. D., Gubbi, A. V., & Mann, J. J. (1995). Localized alterations in pre- and postsynaptic serotonin binding sites in the ventrolateral prefrontal cortex of suicide victims. *Brain Research, 688,* 121–133.

Arango, V., Underwood, M. D., & Mann, J. J. (1996). Fewer pigmented locus coeruleus neurons in suicide victims: Preliminary results. *Biological Psychiatry, 39,* 112–120.

Arango, V., Underwood, M. D., & Mann, J. J. (2002). Serotonin brain circuits involved in major depression and suicide. *Progressive Brain Research, 136,* 443–453.

Arango, V., Underwood, M. D., & Mann, J. J. (2003). Serotonin and neuropeptide circuitry in depression and suicide. Abstract. ACNP 42nd Annual Meeting.

Arato, M., Banki, C. M., Bissette, G., & Nemeroff, C. B. (1989). Elevated CSF CRF in suicide victims. *Biological Psychiatry, 25,* 355–359.

Arborelius, L. & Eklund, M. B. (2007). Both long and brief maternal separation produces persistent changes in tissue levels of brain monoamines in middle-aged female rats. *Neuroscience, 145,* 738–750.

Arborelius, L., Hawks, B. W., Owens, M. J., Plotsky, P. M., & Nemeroff, C. B. (2004). Increased responsiveness of presumed 5-HT cells to citalopram in adult rats subjected to prolonged maternal separation relative to brief separation. *Psychopharmacology (Berlin), 176,* 248–255.

Aston-Jones, G., Shipley, M. T., Chouvet, G., Ennis, M., van Bockstaele, E., Pieribone, V., Shiekhattar, R., Akaoka, H., Drolet, G., Astier, B., Charlety, P., Valentino, R. J., & Williams, J. T. (1991). Afferent regulation of locus coeruleus neurons: Anatomy, physiology and pharmacology. *Progress in Brain Research, 88,* 47–75.

Avishai-Eliner, S., Eghbal-Ahmadi, M., Tabachnik, E., Brunson, K. L., & Baram, T. Z. (2001). Down-regulation of hypothalamic corticotropin-releasing hormone messenger ribonucleic acid (mRNA) precedes early-life experience-induced changes in hippocampal glucocorticoid receptor mRNA. *Endocrinology, 142,* 89–97.

Azmitia, E. C. & Gannon, P. J. (1986). The primate serotonergic system: a review of human and animal studies and a report on Macaca fascicularis. *Advances in Neurology, 43,* 407–468.

Bah, J., Lindstrom, M., Westberg, L., Manneras, L., Ryding, E., Henningsson, S., Melke, J., Rosen, I., Traskman-Bendz, L., & Eriksson, E. (2008). Serotonin transporter gene polymorphisms: effect on serotonin transporter availability in the brain of suicide attempters. *Psychiatry Research, 162,* 221–229.

Baldessarini, R. J. & Hennen, J. (2004). Genetics of suicide: An overview. *Harvard Review of Psychiatry, 12,* 1–13.

Barr, C. S., Newman, T. K., Shannon, C., Parker, C., Dvoskin, R. L., Becker, M. L., Schwandt, M., Champoux, M., Lesch, K. P., Goldman, D., Suomi, S. J., & Higley, J. D. (2004). Rearing condition and rh5-HTTLPR interact to influence limbic-hypothalamic-pituitary-adrenal axis response to stress in infant macaques. *Biological Psychiatry, 55*, 733–738.

Bellivier, F., Chaste, P., & Malafosse, A. (2004). Association between the TPH gene A218C polymorphism and suicidal behavior: a meta-analysis. *American Journal of Medical Genetics, 124B*, 87–91.

Bennett, A. J., Lesch, K. P., Heils, A., Long, J. C., Lorenz, J. G., Shoaf, S. E., Champoux, M., Suomi, S. J., Linnoila, M. V., & Higley, J. D. (2002). Early experience and serotonin transporter gene variation interact to influence primate CNS function. *Molecular Psychiatry, 7*, 118–122.

Bhagwagar, Z., Hinz, R., Taylor, M., Fancy, S., Cowen, P., & Grasby, P. (2006). Increased 5-HT(2A) receptor binding in euthymic, medication-free patients recovered from depression: A positron emission study with [(11)C]MDL 100,907. *American Journal of Psychiatry, 163*, 1580–1587.

Bhansali, P., Dunning, J., Singer, S. E., David, L., & Schmauss, C. (2007). Early life stress alters adult serotonin 2C receptor pre-mRNA editing and expression of the alpha subunit of the heterotrimeric G-protein Gq. *Journal of Neuroscience, 27*, 1467–1473.

Bradley, R. G., Binder, E. B., Epstein, M. P., Tang, Y., Nair, H. P., Liu, W., Gillespie, C. F., Berg, T., Evces, M., Newport, D. J., Stowe, Z. N., Heim, C. M., Nemeroff, C. B., Schwartz, A., Cubells, J. F., & Ressler, K. J. (2008). Influence of child abuse on adult depression: Moderation by the corticotropin-releasing hormone receptor gene. *Archives of General Psychiatry, 65*, 190–200.

Brent, D. A., & Mann, J. J. (2005). Family genetic studies, suicide, and suicidal behavior. *American Journal of Medical Genetics Part C: Seminars in Medical Genetics, 133*, 13–24.

Brent, D. A. & Melhem, N. (2008). Familial transmission of suicidal behavior. *Psychiatric Clinics of North America, 31*, 157–177.

Brent, D. A., Oquendo, M. A., Birmaher, B., Greenhill, L., Kolko, D., Stanley, B., Zelazney, J., Brodsky, B., Bridge, J., Ellis, S., Salazar, O., & Mann, J. J. (2002). Familial pathways to early-onset suicide attempt: risk for suicidal behavior in offspring of mood-disordered suicide attempters. *Archives of General Psychiatry, 59*, 801–807.

Brezo, J., Klempan, T., & Turecki, G. (2008). The genetics of suicide: a critical review of molecular studies. *Psychiatric Clinics of North America, 31*, 179–203.

Brodsky, B. S., Mann, J. J., Stanley, B., Tin, A., Oquendo, M., Birmaher, B., Greenhill, L., Kolko, D., Zelazny, B., Burke, A. K., Melhem, N. M., & Brent, D. (2008). Familial transmission of suicidal behavior: Factors mediating the relationship between childhood abuse and offspring suicide attempts. *Journal of Clinical Psychiatry, 69*, 584–596.

Brodsky, B. S. & Stanley, B. (2008). Adverse childhood experiences and suicidal behavior. *Psychiatry Clinics of North America, 31*, 223–235.

Brown, S. M. & Hariri, A. R. (2006). Neuroimaging studies of serotonin gene polymorphisms: Exploring the interplay of genes, brain, and behavior. *Cognitive, Affective and Behavioral Neuroscience, 6*, 44–52.

Brown, R. P., Stoll, P. M., Stokes, P. E., Frances, A., Sweeney, J., Kocsis, J. H., & Mann, J. J. (1988). Adrenocortical hyperactivity in depression: Effects of agitation, delusions, melancholia, and other illness variables. *Psychiatry Research, 23*, 167–178.

Brunner, J., Stalla, G. K., Stalla, J., Uhr, M., Grabner, A., Wetter, T. C., & Bronsich, T. (2001). Decreased corticotropin-releasing hormone (CRH) concentrations in the cerebrospinal fluid of eucortisolemic suicide attempters. *Journal of Psychiatric Research, 35*, 1–9.

Brunner, H. G., Nelen, M., Breakefield, X. O., Ropers, H. H., & van Oost, B. A. (1993). Abnormal behavior associated with a point mutation in the structural gene for monoamine oxidase A. *Science, 262*, 578–580.

Brunson, K. L., Avishai-Eliner, S., Hatalski, C. G., & Baram, T.Z. (2001). Neurobiology of the stress response early in life: evolution of a concept and the role of corticotropin releasing hormone. *Molecular Psychiatry, 6*, 647–656.

Carballo, J. J., Harkavy-Friedman, J., Burke, A. K., Sher, L., Baca-Garcia, E., Sullivan, G. M., Grunebaum, M. F., Parsey, R. V., Mann, J. J., & Oquendo, M. A. (2008). Family history of suicidal behavior and early traumatic experiences: Additive effect on suicidality and course of bipolar illness? *Journal of Affective Disorders, 109*, 57–63.

Caspi, A., McClay, J., Moffitt, T. E., Mill, J., Martin, J., Craig, I. W., Taylor, A., & Poulton, R. (2002). Role of genotype in the cycle of violence in maltreated children. *Science, i297*, 851–854.

Caspi, A., Sugden, K., Moffitt, T. E., Taylor, A., Craig, I. W., Harrington, H., McLay, J., Mill, J., Martin, J., Braithwaite, A., & Poulton, R. (2003). Influence of life stress on depression: Moderation by a polymorphism in the 5-HTT gene. *Science, 301*, 386–389.

Cooper, S. J., Kelly, C. B., & King, D.J. (1992). 5-Hydroxyindoleacetic acid in cerebrospinal fluid and prediction of suicidal behaviour in schizophrenia. *The Lancet, 340*, 940–941.

Congdon, E. & Canli, T. (2008). A neurogenetic approach to impulsivity. *Journal of Personality, 76*, 1447–1483.

Coryell, W. & Schlesser, M. (2001). The dexamethasone suppression test and suicide prediction. *American Journal of Psychiatry, 158*, 748–753.

Currier, D. & Mann, J. J. (2008). Stress, genes and the biology of suicidal behavior. *Psychiatric Clinics of North America, 31*, 247–269.

Daniels, W. M., Pietersen, C. Y., Carstens, M. E., & Stein, D. J. (2004). Maternal separation in rats leads to anxiety-like behavior and a blunted ACTH response and altered neurotransmitter levels in response to a subsequent stressor. *Metabolic Brain Disorders, 19*, 3–14.

Du, L., Faludi, G., Palkovits, M. Demeter, E., Bakish, D., Lapierre, Y. D., Sotonyi, P., & Hrdina, P. D. (1999). Frequency of long allele in serotonin transporter gene is increased in depressed suicide victims. *Biological Psychiatry, 46*, 196–201.

Du, L., Faludi, G., Palkovits, M., Sotonyi, P., Bakish, D., & Hrdina, P. D. (2002). High activity-related allele of MAO-A gene associated with depressed suicide in males. *Neuroreport, 13*, 1195–1198.

Dunn, A. J., Swiergiel, A. H., & Palamarchouk, V. (2004). Brain circuits involved in corticotropin-releasing factor-norepinephrine interactions during stress. *Annals of the New York Academy of Science, 1018*, 25–34.

Engstrom, G., Alling, C., Blennow, K., Regnell, G., & Traskman-Bendz, L. (1999). Reduced cerebrospinal HVA concentrations and HVA/5-HIAA ratios in suicide attempters. Monoamine metabolites in 120 suicide attempters and 47 controls. *European Neuropsychopharmacology, 9*, 399–405.

Fan, J., Fossella, J., Sommer, T., Wu, Y., & Posner, M. I. (2003). Mapping the genetic variation of executive attention onto brain activity. *Proceedings of the National Academy of Sciences of the United States of America, 100*, 7406–7411.

Furmark, T., Appel, L., Henningsson, S., Ahs, F., Faria, V., Linnman, C., Pissiota, A., Frans, O., Bani, M., Bettica, P., Pich, E. M., Jacobsson, E., Wahlstedt, E., Oreland, L., Lanstrom, B., Eriksson, E., & Fredrikson, M. (2008). A link between serotonin-related gene polymorphisms, amygdala activity, and placebo-induced relief from social anxiety. *Journal of Neuroscience, 28*, 13066–13074.

Galfalvy, H., Currier, D., Oquendo, M. A., Sullivan, G., Huang, Y. Y., & Mann, J. J. (2009). Lower CSF MHPG predicts short-term risk for suicide attempt. *International Journal of Neuropsychopharmacology, 12*, 1327–1335.

Gartside, S. E., Johnson, D. A., Leitch, M. M., Troakes, C., & Ingram, C. D. (2003). Early life adversity programs changes in central 5-HT neuronal function in adulthood. *European Journal of Neuroscience, 17*, 2401–2408.

Gibb, B. E., McGeary, J. E., Beevers, C. G., & Miller, I. W. (2006). Serotonin transporter (5-HTTLPR) genotype, childhood abuse, and suicide attempts in adult psychiatric inpatients. *Suicide and Life Threatening Behavior, 36*, 687–693.

Gross, C., Zhuang, X., Stark, K., Ramboz, S., Oosting, R., Kirby, L., Santarelli, L., Beck, S., & Hen, R., (2002). Serotonin 1A receptor acts during development to establish normal anxiety-like behaviour in the adult. *Nature, 416*, 396–400.

Heim, C. & Nemeroff, C. B. (2001). The role of childhood trauma in the neurobiology of mood and anxiety disorders: Preclinical and clinical studies. *Biological Psychiatry, 49*, 1023–1039.

Heim, C., Newport, D. J., Bonsall, R., Miller, A. H., & Nemeroff, C. B. (2001). Altered pituitary–adrenal axis responses to provocative challenge tests in adult survivors of childhood abuse. *American Journal of Psychiatry, 158*, 575–581.

Heim, C., Newport, D. J., Heit, S., Graham, Y. P., Wilcox, M., Bonsall, R., Miller, A. H., & Nemeroff, C. B. (2000). Pituitary–adrenal and autonomic responses to stress in women after sexual and physical abuse in childhood. *Journal of American Medical Association, 284*, 592–597.

Henn, F. A. & Vollmayr, B. (2005). Stress models of depression: Forming genetically vulnerable strains. *Neuroscience and Biobehavior Review, 29*, 799–804.

Higley, J. D., Suomi, S. J., & Linnoila, M. (1992). A longitudinal assessment of CSF monoamine metabolite and plasma cortisol concentrations in young rhesus monkeys. *Biological Psychiatry, 32*, 127–145.

Hodgkinson, C. A., Yuan, Q., Xu, K., Shen, P., Heinz, E., Lobos, E. A., Binder, E. B., Cubells, J., Ehlers, C. L., Gelernter, J., Mann, J. J., Riley, B., Roy, A., Tabakoff, N., Todd, R. D., Zhou, Z., & Goldman, D. (2008). Addictions biology: Haplotype-based analysis for 130 candidate genes on a single array. *Alcohol and Alcoholism, 43*, 505–515.

Huang, Y. Y., Cate, S. P., Battistuzzi, C., Oquendo, M. A., Brent, D., & Mann, J.J. (2004). An association between a functional polymorphism in the monoamine oxidase A gene promoter, impulsive traits and early abuse experiences. *Neuropsychopharmacology, 29*, 1498–1505.

Ichise, M., Vines, D. C., Gura, T., Anderson, G. M., Suomi, S. J., Higley, J. D., & Innis, R. B. (2006). Effects of early life stress on [11C]DASB positron emission tomography imaging of serotonin transporters in adolescent peer- and mother-reared rhesus monkeys. *Journal of Neuroscience, 26*, 4638–4643.

Jones, J. S., Stanley, B., Mann, J. J., Frances, A. J., Guido, J. R., Traskman-Bendz, L., Winchel, R., Brown, R. P., & Stanley, M. (1990). CSF 5-HIAA and HVA concentrations in elderly depressed patients who attempted suicide. *American Journal of Psychiatry, 147*, 1225–1227.

Kaufman, J., Birmaher, B., Perel, J., Dahl, R. E., Stull, S., Brent, D., Trubnick, L., Al-Shabbout, M., & Ryan. N. D. (1998). Serotonergic functioning in depressed abused children: Clinical and familial correlates. *Biological Psychiatry, 44*, 973–981.

Ke, L., Qi, Z. Y., Ping, Y., & Ren, C. Y. (2006). Effect of SNP at position 40237 in exon 7 of the TPH2 gene on susceptibility to suicide. *Brain Research, 1122*, 24–26.

Kraemer, G. W., Ebert, M. H., Schmidt, D. E., & McKinney, W. T. (1989). A longitudinal study of the effect of different social rearing conditions on cerebrospinal fluid norepinephrine and biogenic amine metabolites in rhesus monkeys. *Neuropsychopharmacology, 2*, 175–189.

Lesch, K. P., Bengel, D., Heils, A., Sabol, S. Z., Greenberg, B. D., Petri, S., Benjamin, J., Muller, C. R., Hamer, D. H., & Murphy, D. L. (1996). Association of anxiety-related traits with a polymorphism in the serotonin transporter gene regulatory region. *Science, 274*, 1527–1531.

Lester, D. (1995). The concentration of neurotransmitter metabolites in the cerebrospinal fluid of suicidal individuals: a meta-analysis. *Pharmacopsychiatry, 28*, 45–50.

Leyton, M., Paquette, V., Gravel, P., Rosa-Neto, P., Weston, F., Diksic, M., & Benkelfat, C. (2006). Alpha-[11C]Methyl-L-tryptophan trapping in the orbital and ventral medial prefrontal cortex of suicide attempters. *European Neuropsychopharmacology, 16*, 220–223.

Liu, D., Caldji, C., Sharma, S., Plotsky, P. M., & Meaney, M. J. (2000). Influence of neonatal rearing conditions on stress-induced adrenocorticotropin responses and norepinepherine release in the hypothalamic paraventricular nucleus. *Journal of Neuroendocrinology, 12*, 5–12.

Liu, D., Diorio, J., Tannenbaum, B., Caldji, C., Francis, D., Freedman, A., Sharma, S., Pearson, D., Plotsky, P. M., & Meaney, M. J. (1997). Maternal care, hippocampal glucocorticoid receptors, and hypothalamic–pituitary–adrenal responses to stress. *Science, 277,* 1659–1662.

Lopez, V. A., Detera-Wadleigh, S., Cardona, I., Kassem, L., & McMahon, F. J. (2007). Nested association between genetic variation in tryptophan hydroxylase II, bipolar affective disorder, and suicide attempts. *Biological Psychiatry, 61,* 181–186.

Lopez, J. F., Vazquez, D. M., Chalmers, D. T., & Watson, S. J. (1997). Regulation of 5-HT receptors and the hypothalamic–pituitary–adrenal axis. Implications for the neurobiology of suicide. *Annals of the New York Academy of Science, 29,* 106–134.

Maestripieri, D., McCormack, K., Lindell, S. G., Higley, J. D., & Sanchez, M. M. (2006). Influence of parenting style on the offspring's behaviour and CSF monoamine metabolite levels in cross-fostered and non-cross-fostered female rhesus macaques. *Behavioral Brain Research, 175,* 90–95.

Mann, J. J. (2003). Neurobiology of suicidal behaviour. *National Review of Neuroscience, 4,* 819–828.

Mann, J. J., Brent, D. A., & Arango, V. (2001). The neurobiology and genetics of suicide and attempted suicide: a focus on the serotonergic system. *Neuropsychopharmacology, 24,* 467–477.

Mann, J. J. & Currier, D. (2007). A review of prospective studies of biologic predictors of suicidal behavior in mood disorders. *Archives of Suicide Research, 11,* 3–16.

Mann, J. J. & Currier, D. (2008). Suicide and attempted suicide. In S. H. Fatemi & P. J. Clayton (Eds.), *The Medical Basis of Psychiatry,* 3rd ed. (pp. 561–576). Philadelphia, PA: Humana Press.

Mann, J. J., Currier, D., Stanley, B., Oquendo, M. A., Amsel, L. V., & Ellis, S. P. (2006). Can biological tests assist prediction of suicide in mood disorders? *International Journal of Neuropsychopharmacology, 9,* 465–474.

Mann, J. J., Huang, Y. Y., Underwood, M. D., Kassir, S. A., Oppenhem, S., Kelly, T. M., Dwork, A. J., & Arango, V. (2000). A serotonin transporter gene promoter polymorphism (5-HTTLPR) and prefrontal cortical binding in major depression and suicide. *Archives of General Psychiatry, 57,* 729–738.

Mann, J. J. & Malone, K. M. (1997). Cerebrospinal fluid amines and higher-lethality suicide attempts in depressed inpatients. *Biological Psychiatry, 41,* 162–171.

Mann, J. J., Stanley, M., McBride, P. A., & McEwen, B. S. (1986). Increased serotonin$_2$ and β-adrenergic receptor binding in the frontal cortices of suicide victims. *Archives of General Psychiatry, 43,* 954–959.

Matthews, K., Dalley, J. W., Matthews, C., Tsai, T. H., & Robbins, T. W. (2001). Periodic maternal separation of neonatal rats produces region- and gender-specific effects on biogenic amine content in postmortem adult brain. *Synapse, 40,* 1–10.

McGowan, P. O., Sasaki, A., D'Alessio, A. C., Dymov, S., Labonte, B., Szyf, M., Turecki, G., & Meaney, M. J. (2009). Epigenetic regulation of the glucocorticoid receptor in human brain associates with childhood abuse. *Natural Neuroscience, 12,* 342–348.

Meaney, M. J., Diorio, J., Francis, D., Widdowson, J., LaPlante, P., Caldji, C., Sharma, S., Secki, J., & Plotsky, P. M. (1996). Early environmental regulation of forebrain glucocorticoid receptor gene expression: implications for adrenocortical responses to stress. *Developmental Neuroscience, 18,* 49–72.

Meijer, O. C. & De Kloet, E. R. (1998). Corticosterone and serotonergic neurotransmission in the hippocampus: Functional implications of central corticosteriod receptor diversity. *Critical Reviews in Neurobiology, 12,* 1–20.

Meltzer, H. Y., Perline, R., Tricou, B. J., Lowy, M., & Robertson, A. (1984). Effect of 5-hydroxytryptophan on serum cortisol levels in major affective disorders. II. Relation to suicide, psychosis, and depressive symptoms. *Archives of General Psychiatry, 41,* 379–387.

Meyer, J. H. (2007). Imaging the serotonin transporter during major depressive disorder and anti-depressant treatment. *Journal of Psychiatry and Neuroscience, 32*, 86–102.

Meyer-Lindenberg, A., Buckholtz, J. W., Kolachana, B., Hariri, A. R., Pezawas, L., Blasi, G., Wabnitz, A., Honea, R., Verchinski, B., Callicott, J. H., Egan, M., Mattay, V., & Weinberger, D. R. (2006). Neural mechanisms of genetic risk for impulsivity and violence in humans. *Proceedings of the National Academy of Sciences of the United States of America, 103*, 6269–6274.

Miller, H. L., Delgado, P. L., Salomon, R. M., Berman, R., Krystal, J. H., Heninger, G. R., & Charney, D. S. (1996). Clinical and biochemical effects of catecholamine depletion on antidepressant-induced remission of depression. *Archives of General Psychiatry, 53*, 117–128.

Miller, J. M., Kinnally, E. L., Ogden, R. T., Oquendo, M. A., Mann, J. J., & Parsey, R. V. (2009). Reported childhood abuse is associated with low serotonin transporter binding in vivo in major depressive disorder. *Synapse, 63*, 565–573.

Nemeroff, C. B. (1988). The neurobiology of aging and the neurobiology of depression: Is there a relationship? *Neurobiology and Aging, 9*, 120–122.

Nordström, P., Samuelsson, M., Åsberg, M., Traskman-Bendz, L., Aberg-Wistedt, A., Nordin, C., & Bertilsson, L. (1994). CSF 5-HIAA predicts suicide risk after attempted suicide. *Suicide and Life Threatening Behavior, 24*, 1–9.

Olivier, B., Pattij, T., Wood, S. J., Oosting, R., Sarnyai, Z., & Toth, M. (2001). The 5-HT(1A) receptor knockout mouse and anxiety. *Behavioral Pharmacology, 12*, 439–450.

Oquendo, M. A., Placidi, G. P., Malone, K. M., Campbell, C., Keilp, J., Brodsky, B., Kegeles, L. S., Cooper, T. B., Parsey, R. V., van Heertum, R. L., & Mann, J. J. (2003). Positron emission tomography of regional brain metabolic responses to a serotonergic challenge and lethality of suicide attempts in major depression. *Archives of General Psychiatry, 60*, 14–22.

Ordway, G. A., Widdowson, P. S., Smith, K. S., & Halaris, A. (1994). Agonist binding to α_2-adrenoceptors is elevated in the locus coeruleus from victims of suicide. *Journal of Neurochemistry, 63*, 617–624.

Owens, M. J. & Nemeroff, C. B. (1991). Physiology and pharmacology of corticotropin-releasing factor. *Pharmacology Review, 43*, 425–473.

Pandey, G. N., Dwivedi, Y., Rizavi, H. S., Ren, X., Pandey, S. R., Pesold, C., Roberts, R. C., Conley, R. R., & Tamminga, C. A. (2002). Higher expression of serotonin 5-HT(2A) receptors in the postmortem brains of teenage suicide victims. *American Journal of Psychiatry, 159*, 419–429.

Parsey, R. V., Hastings, R. S., Oquendo, M. A., Xianzhang, H., Goldman, D., Huang, Y., Simpson, N., Arcement, J., Huang, Y., Ogden, T., van Heertum, R. L., Arango, V., & Mann, J. J. (2006). Effect of a triallelic functional polymorphism of the serotonin-transporter-linked promoter region on expression of serotonin transporter in the human brain. *American Journal of Psychiatry, 163*, 48–51.

Parsey, R. V., Oquendo, M. A., Simpson, N. R., Ogden, R. T., van Heertum, R., Arango, V., & Mann, J. J. (2002). Effects of sex, age, and aggressive traits in man on brain serotonin 5-HT(1A) receptor binding potential measured by PET using [C-11]WAY-100635. *Brain Research, 954*, 173–182.

Passamonti, L., Fera, F., Magariello, A., Cerasa, A., Gioia, M. C., Muglia, M., Nicoletti, G., Gallo, O., Provinciali, L., & Quattrone, A. (2006). Monoamine oxidase – a genetic variations influence brain activity associated with inhibitory control: New insight into the neural correlates of impulsivity. *Biological Psychiatry, 59*, 334–340.

Pine, D. S., Coplan, J. D., Wasserman, G. A., Miller, L. S., Fried, J. E., Davies, M., Cooper, T. B., Greenhill, L., Shaffer, D., & Parsons, B. (1997). Neuroendocrine response to fenfluramine challenge in boys: Associations with aggressive behavior and adverse rearing. *Archives of General Psychiatry, 54*, 839–846.

Plotsky, P. M. & Meaney, M. J. (1993). Early, postnatal experience alters hypothalamic corticotropin-releasing factor (CRF) mRNA, median eminence CRF content and stress-induced release in adult rats. *Brain Research and Molecular Brain Research, 18*, 195–200.

Prochazka, H. & Agren, H. (2003). Self-rated aggression and cerebral monoaminergic turnover. Sex differences in patients with persistent depressive disorder. *European Archives of Psychiatry and Clinical Neuroscience, 253*, 185–92.

Reuter, M., Esslinger, C., Montag, C., Lis, S., Gallhofer, B., & Kirsch, P. (2008). A functional variant of the tryptophan hydroxylase 2 gene impacts working memory: a genetic imaging study. *Biological Psychology, 79*, 111–117.

Rinne, T., Westenberg, H. G., Den Boer, J. A., & van den Brink, W. (2000). Serotonergic blunting to meta-chlorophenylpiperazine (m-CPP) highly correlates with sustained childhood abuse in impulsive and autoaggressive female borderline patients. *Biological Psychiatry, 47*, 548–556.

Roy, A., Hu, X.Z., Janal, M. N., & Goldman, D. (2007). Interaction between childhood trauma and serotonin transporter gene variation in suicide. *Neuropsychopharmacology, 32*, 2046–2052.

Rujescu, D., Giegling, I., Bondy, B., Gietl, A., Zill, P., & Moller H. J. (2002). Association of anger-related traits with SNPs in the TPH gene. *Molecular Psychiatry, 7*, 1023–1029.

Ryding, E., Lindstrom, M., & Traskman-Bendz, L. (2008). The role of dopamine and serotonin in suicidal behaviour and aggression. *Progress in Brain Research, 172*, 307–315.

Sadikot, A. F. & Parent, A. (1990). The monoaminergic innervation of the amygdala in the squirrel monkey: an immunohistochemical study. *Neuroscience, 36*, 431–447.

Schulsinger, F., Kety, S. S., Rosenthal, D., & Wender, P. H. (1979). A family study of suicide. In M. Schou, & E. Stromgren (Eds.), *Origin, Prevention and Treatment of Affective Disorders.* New York: Academic Press.

Sequeira, A. & Turecki, G. (2006). Genome wide gene expression studies in mood disorders. *OMICS, 10*, 444–454.

Sher, L., Carballo, J. J., Grunebaum, M. F., Burke, M. F., Zalsman, A. K., Huang, G., & Mann, J. J. (2006). A prospective study of the association of cerebrospinal fluid monoamine metabolite levels with lethality of suicide attempts in patients with bipolar disorder. *Bipolar Disorders, 8*, 543–550.

Smith, H. R., Daunais, J. B., Nader, M. A., & Porrino, L. J. (1999). Distribution of [3H]citalopram binding sites in the nonhuman primate brain. *Annals of the New York Academy of Science, 877*, 700–702.

Stanley, M. & Mann, J. J. (1983). Increased serotonin-2 binding sites in frontal cortex of suicide victims. *The Lancet*, i:214–216.

Stein, M. B., Yehuda, R., Koverola, C., & Hanna, C. (1997). Enhanced dexamethasone suppression of plasma cortisol in adult women traumatized by childhood sexual abuse. *Biological Psychiatry, 42*, 680–686.

Stoff, D. M. & Mann, J. J. (1997). Suicide research. Overview and introduction. *Annals of the New York Academy of Science, 836*, 1–11.

Sunnqvist, C., Westrin, A., & Traskman-Bendz, L. (2008). Suicide attempters: Biological stress-markers and adverse life events. *European Archives of Psychiatry and Clinical Neuroscience, 258*, 456–462.

Tiihonen, J., Kuikka, J. T., Bergström, K. A., Karhu, J., Viinamaki, H., Lehtonen, J., Hallikainen, T., Yang, J., & Haloka, P. (1997). Single-photon emission tomography imaging of monoamine transporters in impulsive violent behaviour. *European Journal of Nuclear Medicine, 24*, 1253–1260.

Traskman-Bendz, L., Alling, C., Oreland, L., Regnell, G., Vinge, E., & Ohman, R. (1992). Prediction of suicidal behavior from biologic tests. *Journal of Clinical Psychopharmacology, 12*, 21S–26S.

Tyrka, A. R., Price, L. H., Gelernter, J., Schepker, C., Anderson, G. M., & Carpenter, L. L. (2009). Interaction of childhood maltreatment with the corticotropin-releasing hormone receptor gene: effects on hypothalamic–pituitary–adrenal axis reactivity. *Biological Psychiatry*, *66*, 681–685.

Uher, R. & McGuffin, P. (2008). The moderation by the serotonin transporter gene of environmental adversity in the aetiology of mental illness: review and methodological analysis. *Molecular Psychiatry*, *13*, 131–146.

van Heeringen, K., Audenaert, K., Van de Wiele, L., & Verstraete, A. (2000). Cortisol in violent suicidal behaviour: association with personality and monoaminergic activity. *Journal of Affective Disorders*, *60*, 181–189.

van Heeringen, C., Audenaert, K., Van Laere, K., Dumont, F., Slegers, G., Mertens, J., & Dierckx, R. A. (2003). Prefrontal 5-HT2a receptor binding index, hopelessness and personality characteristics in attempted suicide. *Journal of Affective Disorders*, *74*, 149–158.

Virkkunen, M., De Jong, J., Bartko, J., & Linnoila, M. (1989). Psychobiological concomitants of history of suicide attempts among violent offenders and impulsive fire setters. *Archives of General Psychiatry*, *46*, 604–606.

Voracek, M. & Loibl, L. M. (2007). Genetics of suicide: a systematic review of twin studies. *Wiener Klinische Wochenschrift*, *119*, 463–475.

Wasserman, D., Sokolowski, M., Rozanov, V., & Wasserman, J. (2007). The CRHR1 gene: A marker for suicidality in depressed males exposed to low stress. *Genes, Brain and Behavior*, *7*, 14–19.

Weaver, I. C., Cervoni, N., Champagne, F. A., D'Alessio, A. C., Sharma, S., Seckl, J. R., Dymov, S., Szyf, M., & Meaney, M. J. (2004). Epigenetic programming by maternal behavior. *Nature Neuroscience*, *7*, 847–854.

Weaver, I. C., Champagne, F. A., Brown, S. E., Dymov, S., Sharma, S., Meaney, M. J., & Szyf, M. (2005). Reversal of maternal programming of stress responses in adult offspring through methyl supplementation: altering epigenetic marking later in life. *Journal of Neuroscience*, *25*, 11045–11054.

Weiss, G. K., Ratner, A., Voltura, A., Savage, D., Lucero, K., & Castillo, N. (1994). The effect of two different types of stress on locus coeruleus alpha-2 receptor binding. *Brain Research Bulletin*, *33*, 219–221.

Wender, P. H., Kety, S. S., Rosenthal, D., Schulsinger, F., Ortmann, J., & Lunde, I. (1986). Psychiatric disorders in the biological and adoptive families of adopted individuals with affective disorders. *Archives of General Psychiatry*, *43*, 923–929.

Ystgaard, M., Hestetun, I., Loeb, M., & Mehlum, L. (2004). Is there a specific relationship between childhood sexual and physical abuse and repeated suicidal behavior? *Child Abuse and Neglect*, *28*, 863–875.

Zhou, Z., Roy, A., Lipsky, R., Kuchipudi, K., Zhu, G., Taubman, J., Enoch, M., Virkkunen, M., & Goldman, D. (2005). Haplotype-based linkage of tryptophan hydroxylase 2 to suicide attempt, major depression, and cerebrospinal fluid 5-hydroxyindoleacetic acid in 4 populations. *Archives of General Psychiatry*, *62*, 1109–1118.

Zill, P., Baghai, T. C., Zwanzger, P., Schule, C., Eser, D., Rupprecht, R., Moller, H. J., Bondy, B., & Ackenheil, M. (2004). SNP and haplotype analysis of a novel tryptophan hydroxylase isoform (TPH2) gene provide evidence for association with major depression. *Molecular Psychiatry*, *9*, 1030–1036.

Zill, P., Buttner, A., Eisenmenger, W., Moller, H. J., Bondy, B., & Ackenheil, M. (2004). Single nucleotide polymorphism and haplotype analysis of a novel tryptophan hydroxylase isoform (TPH2) gene in suicide victims. *Biological Psychiatry*, *56*, 581–586.

CHAPTER NINE

Understanding the Suicidal Brain:
A Review of Neuropsychological Studies
of Suicidal Ideation and Behaviour

Kees van Heeringen, Karen Godfrin, and Stijn Bijttebier

Abstract

In order to understand the neural mechanisms underlying suicidal behaviour following exposure to psychosocial stressors, neuropsychological studies are used to investigate changes in brain functions, which mediate the behavioural reaction to such stressors. Neuropsychological studies have identified the role of disturbances in attention, memory, fluency, mental flexibility, problem-solving, and decision-making in the development of suicidal behaviour. Substantial methodological issues hamper the interpretation of the association between these disturbances and the occurrence of suicidal behaviour. For example, it is not possible to dismiss the possibility that demonstrated neuropsychological impairments related to suicidal ideation and/or behaviour are, at least in part, due to a more general effect of depression. However, there appears to be a causal effect on the occurrence of suicidal behaviour of at least some of the identified neuropsychological impairments. Impairments on conflict tasks such as the Stroop task suggest a difficulty in shifting attention from compelling but inappropriate stimuli. Taken together with memory-related deficits in problem-solving, these impairments may predispose suicidal individuals to attend to prepotent emotional states, such as intense feelings of hopelessness, and to formulate actions based on a narrow view of their condition. Neuropsychological impairments may thereby interact with mood disturbances, whereby small changes in

International Handbook of Suicide Prevention: Research, Policy and Practice, First Edition.
Edited by Rory C. O'Connor, Stephen Platt, Jacki Gordon.
© 2011 John Wiley & Sons, Ltd. Published 2011 by John Wiley & Sons, Ltd.

mood lead to a simultaneous increase in hopelessness and decrease in problem-solving ability. Neuropsychological impairments may thus fuel a suicidal crisis. It remains to be demonstrated whether, and to what extent, these impairments are amenable to treatment, and whether adequate treatment is a prerequisite for the successful prevention of suicidal behaviour. There is, however, increasing evidence of a beneficial effect of interventions targeting neuropsychological deficits on suicidal behaviour and its risk factors.

Introduction

The core question in suicide prevention is: why does a person in a particular condition complete suicide, while another person in the same situation reacts in a different way?

There is no doubt that environmental and social characteristics exert a strong influence on the occurrence of suicidal behaviour. Comparative postmortem studies have clearly shown changes in the brains of those who have died by suicide (Mann, 2003), suggesting that changes in the characteristics of the brain play an intermediate role between such environmental influences and the occurrence of suicidal behaviour. Successful prevention of suicidal behaviour may thus depend on our ability to modify certain characteristics of the brain. Knowledge of such characteristics or brain functions may thus be a prerequisite for successful prevention.

From a neuroscientific point of view the core question in suicide prevention can thus be rephrased as: which differences exist between suicidal and non-suicidal individuals in brain functions that are involved in the processing of information between sensory input and decision making, leading individuals to attempt or complete suicide? There are two ways to study these differences and their effects on the occurrence of suicidal behaviour *in vivo*: by means of functional imaging studies or by means of neuropsychological studies of the brain.

Williams and Pollock (2001) have provided evidence for the role such differences play in the development of suicidal behaviour. They have argued convincingly that a predisposition to suicidal behaviour is associated with biases in attention, memory, and fluency. More particularly, such a predisposition may become manifest through a trait-dependent tendency, when confronted with psychosocial adversity, to perceive the situation as characterized by a combination of:

(a) a sensitivity to particular life events, reflecting signals of defeat, based on biases in *attention* leading to involuntary hypersensitivity to stimuli, signalling 'loser' status;
(b) the sense of being trapped, which is related to an insufficient capacity to solve problems, which in turn appears to depend upon deficits in a particular component of *memory*; and
(c) the absence of rescue factors, mediated by deficient *fluency* and prospective cognitive processes and leading to feelings of hopelessness.

This chapter will investigate to what extent the comparative neuropsychological study of suicidal ideation and behaviour can contribute to our understanding of suicidal behaviour. In order to achieve this goal, the literature on neuropsychological studies of suicidal ideation and behaviour will be systematically reviewed and discussed. Taking into account the heterogeneous nature of definitions of suicidal behaviour in the reviewed literature, characteristics of the studied populations in terms of suicidal intent or lethality of attempts will be described in as much detail as possible.

Neuropsychological Studies of Suicidal Ideation and Behaviour

Perception/attention

Gibbs, Dombrovski, Morse, Siegle, Houck, *et al.* (2009) showed that depressed elderly suicide attempters (with strong suicidal intent) perceive life problems to be more threatening and insoluble than non-suicidal depressed elderly.

A modified Stroop task was used in studies of attentional biases in suicide attempters. Williams and Broadbent (1986) used a Stroop task containing suicide-related words, negatively valenced words, neutral words, and '0's. There were two control groups: hospital patients with physical complaints and controls from a panel. The main finding was that suicide attempters took longer to name the colour of suicide-related words than the control groups. However, the same was true for negatively valenced words, suggesting an attentional bias for negatively toned words in general instead of a specific suicidal schema.

Becker, Strohbach, and Rinck (1999) also used a modified Stroop task and showed that suicide attempters (not defined in more detail) took significantly longer than patients who suffered from depression or anxiety without suicidal ideation/behaviour to name the colours of suicide-related words compared with other words, whereas the colour-naming times of the control participants did not differ for suicide-related, neutral, positive, or negative words. This specific attentional bias for suicide-related material exhibited by suicide attempters was independent of anxiety, depression or hopelessness. While controlling for the effects of depression, anxiety, and hopelessness, the attentional bias correlated significantly with suicidal ideation.

King, Conwell, Cox, Henderson, Denning, *et al.* (2000) found no differences on attentional measures using the Wechsler Memory Scale (WMS) between older in-patients with major depression who were admitted following a suicide attempt and older depressed in-patients who had never attempted suicide.

Keilp, Sackeim, Brodsky, Oquendo, Malone, *et al.* (2001) compared neuropsychological performance, including attention, among depressed patients with at least one prior high-lethality suicide attempt, depressed patients with prior low-lethality attempts, depressed controls without prior suicide attempts, and healthy controls. Attentional characteristics were assessed using the WMS-R Attention/Concentration sub-test, Continuous Performance Test (CPT), and Stroop interference task. High-lethality suicide attempters scored significantly worse than controls on these measures, with depressed non-attempters and low-lethality attempters intermediate between these two groups. In a further study of a similar, though larger, sample no group differences were found on the CPT examining attentional characteristics (Keilp, Gorlyn, Oquendo, Burke, & Mann, 2008). However, Stroop interference was significantly poorer in all depressed subjects when compared with controls, and poorer still in high-lethality suicide attempters relative to all other groups.

Comparing depressed individuals with suicidal ideation to those without such ideation, Marzuk, Hartwell, Leon, and Portera (2005) found no differences in Stroop performance.

Depressed bipolar (type II) suicide attempters performed significantly more poorly than either controls or type I bipolar depressed attempters on the Stroop test (Harkavy-Friedman, Keilp, Grunebaum, Sher, et al., 2006). Raust, Slama, Mathieu, Roy, Chenu, et al. (2007) showed impaired performance on the Stroop test in suicide attempters when compared with healthy controls. Stroop performance was normal in adolescent girls with self-injurious behaviour (Ohmann, Schuch, König, Blaas, Fliri, et al., 2008).

No significant differences in Stroop performance were found between schizophrenic out-patients with and without a lifetime history of one or more suicide attempts (Rüsch, Spoletini, Wilke, Martinotti, Bria, et al., 2008).

Depressed elderly with suicidal ideation and attempts showed poorer performance on the attention sub-scale of the Dementia Rating Scale, compared with depressed controls without suicidal behaviour (Dombrovski, Butters, Reynolds, Houck, Clark, et al., 2008).

Using the d2 task, a standardized and computerized test of attention and concentration, Westheide and colleagues (2008) showed that attentional characteristics were not significantly different between depressed suicide attempters with or without current suicidal ideation (Westheide, Quednow, Kuhn, Hoppe, Copper-Mahkorn, et al., 2008).

Using the Stroop task and the CPT, Malloy-Diniz, Neves, Abrantes, Fuentes, and Corrêa (2009) studied attentional characteristics in type I bipolar patients. They could not demonstrate an effect of a lifetime history of attempted suicide. However, there was a significant positive correlation between the number of suicide attempts and the amount of errors in the Stroop test.

Memory

Different aspects of memory have been studied in the context of suicidal behaviour. The results of the 15 studies identified for this review appear to depend on the tasks that were applied. Using the Auditory Verbal Learning Test (AVLT), no changes in memory functions were found in association with suicidal behaviour (Malloy-Diniz et al., 2009; Rüsch et al., 2008; Westheide et al., 2008). Using the Wechsler Memory Scale, Keilp et al. (2001) found lower scores on verbal and visual memory in high-lethality suicide attempters than controls. A group of older suicide attempters scored worse on the memory sub-scale of the Dementia Rating Scale than non-suicidal depressed elderly (Dombrovski et al., 2008).

Most studies of the association between memory and suicidal behaviour have focused on the involvement of a particular aspect of memory, that is, autobiographical memory, in suicidal behaviour. The term autobiographical memory refers to the recollection of personally experienced past events. In their seminal study, Williams and Broadbent (1986) identified a delayed retrieval of positive memories due to the recollection of general memories rather than specific memories in attempted suicide patients when compared with non-suicidal control groups. Williams and Dritschel (1988) showed that, compared with controls, suicide attempters tend to recall less specific memories to positive than to negative cues. The studies of Evans, Williams, O'Loughlin, and Howells (1992) and Sidley,

Whitaker, Calam, and Wells (1997) provided further evidence of an association between attempted suicide and over-general autobiographical memory.

In a sample of depressed individuals, Kaviani, Rahimi, Rahimi-Darabad, Kamyar, and Naghavi (2003) showed that the presence of suicidal ideation was associated with more over-general memories, particularly in response to negative cue-words. Depressed individuals without suicidal ideation retrieved more specific memories in response to positive cue-words, compared with the neutral condition. In a subsequent study, it was shown that suicide attempters with major depressive disorder produced more over-general memories and responded more slowly to positive cue-words than to negative cue-words when compared with matched healthy controls (Kaviani, Rahimi, & Naghavi, 2004; Kaviani, Rahimi-Darabad, & Naghavi, 2005).

Repeating suicide attempters were significantly more over-general in their recall of positive memories, but not negative memories, than first-time attempters (Rasmussen, O'Connor, & Brodie, 2008).

Leibetseder, Rohrer, Mackinger, and Fartacek (2006) showed reduced specific autobiographical memory in patients with major depression, independent of a lifetime history of attempted suicide (defined as a self-destructive act requiring medical attention). Suicide attempters showed reduced specific autobiographical memory, whether they were affected by depression or not.

Thus, some, though not all, studies have identified reduced specificity of autobiographical memory in depressed attempted suicide patients. It is not clear which clinical variables are associated with low memory specificity in this group, or whether low specificity is particularly associated with recent suicidal behaviour. Sinclair, Crane, Hawton, and Williams (2007) confirmed that a history of attempted suicide is associated with low memory specificity. Their findings suggest that low specificity is one of the mechanisms through which affective disorder increases an individual's vulnerability to suicidal behaviour. This finding was confirmed by Arie, Apter, Orbach, Yefet, and Zalsman (2008), who showed a clear association between suicidal behaviour and the impaired ability to produce specific autobiographical memories in a sample of adolescents and young adults.

Fluency

Bartfai, Winborg, Nordström, and Asberg (1990) assessed aspects of fluency in male psychiatric patients, hospitalized after a suicide attempt, compared with non-attempters. Suicidal patients had significantly lower scores in verbal and design fluency.

Using an adapted verbal fluency paradigm, MacLeod, Rose, and Williams (1993) and MacLeod, Pankhania, Lee, and Mitchell (1997) examined the ease with which hospitalized suicide attempters, hospital controls, and non-hospital controls were able to think about future positive and negative events. The suicide attempters showed a deficit in being able to think of future positive events, both for the immediate and the longer-term future. There were no differences between the groups on being able to think of future negative events. Suicide attempters showed an overall reduced anticipation of positive experiences and no overall increased anticipation of negative experiences. However, they did show evidence of increased negative anticipation for the immediate future. The results for depressed and non-depressed suicide attempters were essentially the same.

King *et al.* (2000) were not able to show any differences between older depressed suicide attempters and non-attempters using tests of verbal and figural fluency.

A group of depressed high-lethality suicide attempters performed significantly worse than control groups (depressed patients with prior low-lethality attempts, depressed controls without prior suicide attempts, and healthy controls) on measures of letter and category fluency (Keilp *et al.*, 2001).

Performance on the Verbal Fluency Test (word production for letter and category fluency) was reduced in depressed patients who had recently attempted suicide compared with healthy controls. Depressed suicide attempters and healthy controls produced significantly fewer words in the letter fluency test compared with the category fluency test (Audenaert, Goethals, van Laere, Lahorte, Brans, *et al.*, 2002).

Older depressed suicide attempters showed decreased positive future thinking, but no increase in negative future thinking in comparison with a healthy control group (Conaghan & Davidson, 2002). Using the Future-Thinking Task, Hunter and O'Connor (2003) found further support for a central role of impaired positive future thinking in relation to attempted suicide. A discriminant function analysis revealed that social perfectionism and reduced positive future thinking did indeed discriminate attempted suicides from controls beyond the effects of hopelessness, depression, and anxiety.

Comparing depressed individuals with suicidal ideation to those without such ideation Marzuk *et al.* (2005) found no differences in verbal or figural fluency.

Harkavy-Friedman *et al.* (2006) showed that participants with type II bipolar disorder performed significantly worse than controls on a test of verbal fluency. Performance of type I bipolar patients was not significantly different from that in type II bipolar patients.

Mental flexibility

The Wisconsin Card Sorting Test (WCST) is the most commonly used neuropsychological test of mental flexibility. This test assesses 'set-shifting', that is, the ability to display flexibility in the face of changing schedules of reinforcement. The WCST allows the assessment of strategic planning, organized searching, utilizing environmental feedback to shift cognitive sets, directing behaviour towards achieving a goal, and modulating impulsive responding. The Trail-Making Test (TMT) is another commonly used test of mental flexibility.

King *et al.* (2000) showed that, with increasing age, depressed suicide attempters when compared with depressed non-attempters performed worse on the TMT but not on the WCST.

Depressed high-lethality suicide attempters performed significantly worse than depressed non-attempters, depressed low-lethality attempters, and healthy controls on the WCST. There was no effect of depression on this deficit (Keilp *et al.*, 2001). Marzuk *et al.* (2005) found reduced mental flexibility in depressed individuals with suicidal ideation when compared with depressed patients without suicidal ideation using the WCST and TMT. Ohmann *et al.* (2008) found no association between WCST performance and self-injurious behaviour in adolescent girls.

Problem-solving

Several studies have examined problem-solving abilities in association with suicidal behaviour using the Means-Ends Problem-Solving procedure (MEPS). Depressed patients reporting suicidal ideation generated significantly less effective problem-solving strategies than depressed patients without suicidal ideation (Kaviani *et al.*, 2003). Further study showed that suicide attempters with major depressive disorder showed less effective problem-solving strategies and took longer to respond to the task, compared with healthy controls (Kaviani, Rahimi, & Naghavi, 2004; Kaviani, Rahimi-Darabad, & Naghavi, 2005).

Pollock and Williams (2004) showed that suicide attempters display a poorer problem-solving ability than non-suicidal psychiatric controls, dependent on specific autobiographical recall (Pollock & Williams, 2001). This difference did not change with improving mood. Passivity in problem-solving was not unique to suicide attempters, but its combination with a smaller number and less effective alternatives may increase vulnerability to suicidal behaviour.

A recent study comparing formerly depressed patients with and without a history of suicidal ideation during past episodes of depression (Williams, Barnhofer, Crane, & Beck, 2005) found that previously suicidal participants showed significant decreases in interpersonal problem-solving ability following induction of sad mood. By contrast, problem-solving performance in those without a history of suicidal ideation remained relatively unchanged.

Using the MEPS, Arie *et al.* (2008) showed an association between difficulties with interpersonal problem-solving and attempted suicide (with an intent to die) in adolescents. Oldershaw, Grima, Jollant, Richards, Simic, *et al.* (2009) studied problem-solving abilities in association with self-harming behaviours (regardless of intent) in adolescents. They found that performance on the MEPS is affected by depression but not by self-harming status.

Nock and Mendes (2008) used a novel measure for problem-solving, the Social Problem-Solving Skills Test (SPST), in a sample of adolescents and young adults with a history of non-suicidal self-injury and a matched non-injurious control group. Self-injurers and non-injurers did not differ in the average number of self-critical attributions, in the average number of solutions generated in response to the challenging social situations, or in the average quality of solutions generated. However, self-injurers chose significantly more negative solutions across the scenarios and rated their self-efficacy for performing adaptive solutions as significantly lower than that of non-injurers.

Gibbs *et al.* (2009) used the Social Problem-Solving Inventory to measure perceived social problem-solving in elderly depressed suicide attempters (with suicidal intent), depressed non-attempters, and non-depressed controls. In particular, adaptive problem-solving dimensions (positive problem orientation and rational problem-solving) and dysfunctional dimensions (negative problem orientation, impulsivity/carelessness, and avoidance) were assessed. The suicide attempters perceived their problems more negatively and their problem-solving as deficient compared with the control groups.

Decision-making

Jollant, Bellivier, Leboyer, Astruc, Torres, *et al.* (2005) showed that patients with a history of suicidal behaviour (with at least some intent to die) scored significantly worse than healthy controls on the Iowa Gambling Task (IGT). Violent suicide attempters scored significantly worse than affective comparison subjects without a history of suicidal behaviour. There were no significant differences between violent and non-violent suicide attempters, between the affective and healthy comparison groups, and between non-violent attempters and affective controls. IGT performance correlated positively with affective lability and anger expression, but not with impulsivity. The association between impaired IGT performance and suicidal behaviour, independent of mood disorder, was confirmed in a large comorbid psychiatric population (Jollant, Guillaume, Jaussent, Bellivier, *et al.*, 2007). There was no difference in performance between violent and non-violent suicide attempters. No association was found between decision-making skills and specific suicidal characteristics such as the intent or lethality of suicidal acts. Malloy-Diniz *et al.* (2009) found an impaired performance on the IGT in bipolar suicide attempters (not further defined) when compared with bipolar non-attempters. There was a significant negative correlation between the number of suicide attempts and IGT performance. Within a group of (violent and non-violent) suicide attempters, patients with current suicidal ideation performed worse on the IGT than those without suicidal ideation even after controlling for depressive symptoms (Westheide *et al.*, 2008).

Dombrovski, Clark, Siegle, Butters, *et al.* (2010) further studied decision-making processes in association with attempted suicide (with strong suicidal intent) using a probabilistic reversal learning task in individuals aged 60 and older. Suicide attempters showed impaired reward/punishment learning, discounting previous history, to a higher degree than controls. This finding suggests that suicide attempters make overly present-focused decisions and ignore past experiences. Memory, reflecting the effect of prior reinforcement history on choices, was significantly poorer in suicide attempters than in controls. Using the Rolls task, Raust *et al.* (2007) were not able to show differences in reversal learning and reward sensitivity between suicide attempters (with intent to die) and healthy controls.

Discussion

This chapter seeks to contribute to our understanding of suicidal brains by providing an overview of neuropsychological studies in patients with suicidal ideation and/or behaviour. The major findings from this review can be summarized as follows, according to studied neuropsychological domains.

Attention/perception

One study shows that suicide attempters (with strong suicidal intent) perceive life problems to be more threatening and insoluble than non-suicidal depressed elderly. Ten studies of attentional characteristics were found. CPT and the Stroop tasks were the most commonly used measures of attention. While performance on the CPT does not appear to be related to suicidal behaviour, the overall picture emerging from these studies is that performance on the Stroop task is poor in depressed individuals, but even worse in those with a history of suicidal behaviour. Moreover, deficits become evident without any type of explicit emotional provocation or emotionally biased stimuli, suggesting that cognitive control mechanisms themselves are dysfunctional, and not simply susceptible to specific types of emotional arousal, as was suggested by Williams and Pollock (2001). It thus appears that depression-related impairments of attention, especially susceptibility to interference, are accentuated in those with a history of suicidal behaviour (Keilp *et al.*, 2008).

Memory

As was the case with attention, this review shows that involvement of memory in suicidal behaviour can be demonstrated with some but not all applied tests. It appears that visual and verbal memory deficits are implicated. An association between autobiographical memory impairment and suicidal behaviour is consistently demonstrated. This impairment is, however, not specific to suicidal behaviour, as it has also been consistently demonstrated in depression and trauma-related disorders (Williams, Barnhofer, Crane, Hermans, Raes, *et al.*, 2007). On the basis of currently available data, it is difficult to conclude whether, or to what extent, depression is responsible for the impairment in autobiographical memory in attempted suicide patients. Sinclair, Crane, Hawton, and Williams (2007) suggest that impaired autobiographical memory is one of the mechanisms through which affective disorder increases an individual's vulnerability to suicidal behaviour. On the other hand, Leibetseder *et al.* (2006) specifically studied suicide attempters without a current or lifetime diagnosis of depression, and reported that these patients showed an impaired autobiographical memory equal to that of control patients with depression with or without a (lifetime) history of suicide attempts. However, as suicide attempters without depression in this study showed a significantly increased severity of depressive symptoms when compared with healthy controls, a contribution of elevated depression scores cannot be ruled out. The authors nevertheless conclude that reduced specific autobiographical memory is a common vulnerability factor for depression and attempted suicide.

Fluency

Of the nine studies that focused on the effect of disturbed fluency and suicidal behaviour, some showed decreased word production using tests of verbal fluency in attempted suicide patients. The findings are considerably more consistent when the anticipation of future events was studied: suicide attempters show a reduced anticipation of positive events. Thus, impaired positive future thinking appears to be associated with attempted suicide.

Mental flexibility

Findings regarding mental flexibility, as assessed with the WCST, are mixed in the four studies identified in relation to suicidal ideation and/or behaviour. In general, WCST performance appears to be associated with suicidal ideation and behaviour (in particular, high-lethality attempts and not self-injurious behaviour) in depressed individuals.

Problem-solving

Seven studies addressed problem-solving abilities. In general, the study findings suggest that the vulnerability to suicidal ideation and behaviour is associated with the production of a smaller number and less effective problem-solving strategies. Psychiatric disorders such as depression appear to increase this vulnerability by adding a component of passivity to impaired problem-solving.

Decision-making

Characteristics of decision-making in relation to suicidal behaviour were studied in six recent studies. In general, suicide attempters showed impaired performance on the IGT, used in four studies, compared with non-attempters. Among individuals with a suicide attempt those with current suicidal ideation performed worse on the IGT than those without such ideation. Investigating the extent to which individuals use past experiences to make decisions, a recent study shows that depressed suicide attempters make overly present-focused decisions, thereby ignoring past experiences, when compared with depressed non-attempters. The latter finding suggests a role of 'myopia for the past' in the development of suicidal behaviour.

Methodological issues

Before discussing these findings and their implications for prevention and further research, several methodological issues need to be addressed. First, heterogeneity of study populations constitutes a major problem in comparing the findings of studies. While some studies in this review do not provide definitions of 'suicidal behaviour' or 'attempted suicide', self-harming behaviours in included patient populations in other studies range from 'non-suicidal self-injury' to 'high-lethality suicide attempts'. The implications of this heterogeneity for the interpretation of the association between neuropsychological impairments and suicidal behaviour is discussed below.

Sample sizes are relatively small in many studies and, in fact, may have been too small to detect differences between study groups. A comparison of the findings from Keilp *et al.* in 2001 and Keilp *et al.* in 2008 illustrates the importance of sample size. A first analysis on a relatively small sample showed that Stroop performance is poor in past suicide attempters, but only distinguished them from non-patients. An increase in sample size enabled the authors to demonstrate that the impairment in attention is worse in those with a past history of more severe suicidal behaviour, relative to other depressed patients.

Most studies did not provide adequate control for patient characteristics that may have confounded the findings. Such characteristics include general intellectual functioning and educational level. The potential importance of such characteristics is underlined by findings of lower educational levels in psychological autopsy studies of suicide victims (Pompili, Innamorati, Masotti, Personnè, Lester, et al., 2008).

Brain damage as a consequence of suicidal behaviour can be responsible for neuropsychological deficits. The finding that the use of more lethal methods in suicidal behaviour is associated with more severe neuropsychological impairment may support this interpretation of reverse causality. However, as pointed out by many authors, according to this line of reasoning one would expect a more global neuropsychological deficit instead of particular impairments. In addition, suicide attempters do not show deficits in neuropsychological functions that are typically most sensitive to diffuse brain dysfunction, such as motor speed and psychomotor functioning (Keilp *et al.*, 2001). Although an effect of brain damage cannot be ruled out completely, reverse causality therefore is an unlikely interpretation of the findings from this review.

Neuropsychological functions such as memory, decision-making, and problem-solving are complex constructs. For example, as noted by Wenzel and Beck (2008), problem-solving is a broad category that has many distinct operational definitions, and there is some evidence that problem-solving is associated differently, with the broad spectrum of suicidal ideation and behaviours depending on the manner in which it is conceptualized. When problem-solving is defined as the ability to generate multiple solutions to problems, it is associated with suicide ideation, but not hopelessness, and interacts with stress to predict suicide ideation over time. However, when problem-solving is defined as confidence in one's ability to solve problems, it is strongly associated with hopelessness and moderately associated with suicide ideation.

The cross-sectional nature of reviewed studies precludes causal inferences. The convergent nature of the findings in many studies using different populations, however, supports such a causal inference. The association between suicidal behaviour and a number of neuropsychological deficits can be explained by a common third factor, such as depression. However, in a substantial number of studies of neuropsychological functions depressed individuals without a history of suicidal behaviour were included as control groups, so that it is unlikely that such a common third factor accounts for the findings of this review. The findings nevertheless underline the complexity of the association between depression and suicidal behaviour. It is not possible to dismiss the possibility that demonstrated neuropsychological impairments related to suicidal ideation and/or behaviour are, at least in part, indeed due to a more general effect of depression. In particular, with regard to attentional biases, it appears that depression-related impairments are accentuated in individuals with a history of suicidal behaviour (Keilp *et al.*, 2008). With regard to autobiographical memory, impairment may be one of the mechanisms through which depression increases an individual's vulnerability to suicidal behaviour (Sinclair *et al.*, 2007). With regard to problem-solving and future fluency, findings suggest that small changes in mood may reinstate deficits (Williams *et al.*, 2005; Williams, van der Does, Barnhofer, Crane, & Segal, 2008). An important clinical implication is that a small change in mood may thus lead to a simultaneous increase in hopelessness and decrease in problem-solving ability, thus fuelling a suicidal crisis (Hepburn, Barnhofer, & Williams, 2006). Other neuropsychological impairments appear to be related directly to suicidal behaviour, independent of depression. This may be the case for decision-making deficits and decreased problem-solving abilities. However, regarding the latter, depression appears to add a component of passivity and may be responsible for a lower rating of self-efficacy in problem-solving as demonstrated in association with suicidal behaviour. Thus, not only actual, but also perceived, aspects of problem-solving may be important in understanding the role of problem-solving in the development of suicidal behaviour (Gibbs *et al.*, 2009). In other words, having a positive attitude towards problem-solving may buffer a person from the depression and hopelessness that would in turn prompt suicide ideation (Wenzel & Beck, 2008).

This review demonstrates an association between neuropsychological deficits and suicidal behaviour. It is, however, unclear to what extent dysfunctions in basic neuropsychological functions (such as attention or memory) contribute to, or are responsible for, impairments in more complex neuropsychological functions (such as decision-making and problem-solving). Indeed, decision processes may be corrupted by a failure to adequately focus attention and control the information on which they are based (Keilp *et al.*, 2008). At least one study found that poor decision-making task performance using the IGT was associated with impairments of selective attention and memory (Hardy, Hinkin, Levine, Castellon, & Lam, 2006). Impaired selective attention performance may underlie the 'cognitive rigidity' that is a common clinical feature of suicide attempters (Pollock & Williams, 1998). Furthermore, there is evidence of a correlation between (over-general) autobiographical memory and (less effective) problem-solving strategies (Arie *et al.*, 2008; Kaviani *et al.*, 2003; Kaviani, Rahimi, & Naghavi, 2004; Kaviani, Rahimi-Darabad, & Naghavi, 2005; Pollock and Williams, 2001). Indications for a correlation between autobiographical memory and future thinking are also found. Williams (1996) examined whether the specificity with which suicidal patients and healthy controls retrieve episodes from their past determines the specificity with which they imagine the future. Suicidal subjects' memory and future responses were more generic, and specificity level for the past and the future was correlated for both groups. A recent neuroimaging study showed that evocation of past and future events involves highly similar patterns of brain activation (Botzung, Denkova, & Manning, 2008). Thus, a number of neuropsychological (dys-) functions may tend to cluster, which suggests that they are manifestations of a common underlying substrate of suicidal behaviour.

Causality

These methodological considerations do not undermine a causal interpretation of the association between particular neuropsychological deficits and suicidal behaviour. Such a causal interpretation is supported by, among others, the convergent nature of the findings using different study populations, or by the apparent existence of a biological gradient (Hill, 1965). Indeed, the findings from this review suggest a correlation between impairment in neuropsychological functions and suicidal intent or lethality of suicide attempts. Attentional biases are apparently absent in self-injurious behaviour without suicidal intent, and are more outspoken in high-lethality attempters than in low-lethality attempters. Deficits in memory, fluency, and mental flexibility are also more marked in high-lethality than in low-lethality attempters. Neuropsychological dysfunction may thus play a particular role in determining risk of highly lethal suicidal behaviour (Keilp *et al.*, 2001).

Experimental proof is another argument supporting a causal interpretation (Hill, 1965). Such proof is provided when manipulation of the cause has a predictable effect. In the current context of this chapter, this would mean that treatment of the neuropsychological deficit would lead to a decrease in suicidal behaviour. Such an effect has not yet been studied, but indirect support is available. Mindfulness training reduces over-general memories, increases autobiographical memory specificity, and improves cognitive flexibility (Heeren, van Broeck, & Philippot, 2009; Williams, Teasdale, Segal, & Soulsby, 2000). A recent large randomized controlled trial shows that mindfulness-based cognitive therapy (MBCT) leads to a decrease in suicidal ideation and levels of hopelessness (van Heeringen, Godfrin, Williams, Raes, & Dewulf, submitted). Memory-specificity training (MEST) (Raes, Williams, & Hermans, 2009) increases specificity of autobiographical memory retrieval, but its effects on the risk of suicidal behaviour are yet to be demonstrated. A study of the effects of training of future thinking on suicidal ideation is under way (van Beek, Kerkhof, & Beekman, 2009). Thus, support for experimental proof is becoming available.

If neuropsychological deficits do, indeed, play a causal role in the development of suicidal behaviour, pathogenetic mechanisms remain to be elucidated. As pointed out by Keilp *et al.* (2008) with regard to the role of attention, defects in emotion regulation networks, which are most severe when risk of suicidal behaviour is high, will be manifested in persistent impairments of attentional control. At a phenomenological level, impairments on conflict tasks, such as the Stroop task, suggest a difficulty in shifting attention from compelling but inappropriate stimuli. Taken together with memory-related deficits in problem-solving, these impairments may predispose suicidal individuals to attend to prepotent emotional states, such as intense feelings of hopelessness, and to formulate actions based on a narrow view of their condition.

However, the question about the causes of such underlying neuropsychological deficits remains to be answered. Genetic effects, developmental problems, and functional suppression, among others, may play a role. Studies have, indeed, shown a considerable heritability in performance on neuropsychological tasks. For example, the heritability of Stroop Interference Test performance is up to 50% and the effects of (dopaminergic) genes have been identified. Neuropsychological deficits may thus meet the criteria for endophenotypes (Mann, Arango, Avenevoli, Brent, Champagne, *et al.*, 2009). Restricted fetal growth is a documented risk factor for suicidal behaviour that may be associated with disturbed development of the brain and thus constitute an intrauterine determinant of the diathesis for suicide (Hawton & van Heeringen, 2009). Prenatal maternal stress is associated with attention deficits in offspring (Weinstock, 2008).

Neuropsychological functions may be suppressed following exposure to stress. Johnson, Tarrier, and Gooding (2008) recently demonstrated in healthy volunteers that perceived defeat, a common stressor which precipitates suicidal behaviour, impairs memory functions. Studies on how acute stress affects learning and memory have yielded inconsistent findings, but Tops, van der Pompe, Wijers, Den Boer, Meijman, *et al.* (2004) showed that the administration of cortisol, that is, the stress hormone the concentration of which is commonly increased in depressed suicidal individuals, is associated with impaired recall of pleasant words, while recall of unpleasant words is not affected. Neuropsychological deficits in association with suicidal behaviour may thus be functional and state-dependent or trait-dependent.

Conclusion

It thus appears to be important that treatment of suicide risk does not focus only on state-dependent characteristics. Hopelessness and risk of suicide may disappear when patients are euthymic, but remain ready to be reactivated when depression returns and underlying neuropsychological disturbances persist. As pointed out by Williams *et al.* (2008), focusing on reducing hopelessness itself is not sufficient, nor does a lower level of hopelessness or suicidal ideation at the end of treatment provide reassurance that the underlying vulnerability has been treated. There is the danger that clinicians will see a patient's reduction in hopelessness as indicating treatment success, but fail to see that the underlying neuropsychological impairments resulting in, for example, cognitive reactivity has not changed. The introduction of a relapse prevention task near the end of treatment is therefore a promising approach (Brown, Ten Have, Henriques, Xie, Hollander, *et al.*, 2005). The objective is to prime thoughts and feelings associated with prior suicide attempts and to determine whether patients are able to respond to their problems in an adaptive way. Successful completion of the task is justification of the completion of treatment, while additional sessions are provided in case patients fail to respond adaptively. It remains to be demonstrated whether or to what extent the elimination of underlying neuropsychological deficits is a prerequisite for treatment to be successful in preventing suicide.

References

Arie, M., Apter, A., Orbach, I., Yefet, Y., & Zalsman, G. (2008). Autobiographical memory, interpersonal problem-solving, and suicidal behavior in adolescent inpatients. *Comprehensive Psychiatry*, *49*, 22–29.

Audenaert, K., Goethals, I., van Laere, K., Lahorte, P., Brans, B., Versijpt, J., Vervaet, M., Beelaert, L., van Heeringen, K., & Dierckx, R. (2002). SPECT neuropsychological activation procedure with the Verbal Fluency Test in attempted suicide patients. *Nuclear Medicine Communications*, *23*, 907–916.

Bartfai, A., Winborg, I. M., Nordström, P., & Asberg, M. (1990). Suicidal behavior and cognitive flexibility: Design and verbal fluency after attempted suicide. *Suicide and Life-Threatening Behavior*, *20*, 254–266.

Becker, E. S., Strohbach, D., & Rinck, M. (1999). A specific attentional bias in suicide attempters. *Journal of Nervous and Mental Disease*, *187*, 730–735.

Botzung, A., Denkova, E., & Manning, L. (2008). Experiencing past and future events: Functional neuroimaging evidence on the neural bases of mental time travel. *Brain and Cognition*, *66*, 202–212.

Brown, G. K., Ten Have, T., Henriques, G. R., Xie, S. X., Hollander, J. E., & Beck, A. T. (2005). Cognitive therapy for the prevention of suicide attempts: A randomized controlled trial. *Journal of the American Medical Association*, *294*, 563–570.

Conaghan, S. & Davidson, K. M. (2002). Hopelessness and the anticipation of positive and negative future experiences in older parasuicidal adults. *British Journal of Clinical Psychology*, *41*, 233–242.

Dombrovski, A. Y., Butters, M. A., Reynolds, C. F., Houck, P. R., Clark, L., Mazumdar, S., & Szanto, K. (2008). Cognitive performance in suicidal depressed elderly: Preliminary report. *American Journal of Geriatric Psychiatry*, *16*, 109–115.

Dombrovski, A. Y., Clark, L., Siegle, G. J., Butters, M. A., Ichikawa, N., Sahakian, B., & Szanto, K. (2010). Reward/punishment learning in older suicide attempters. *American Journal of Psychiatry, 167*, 699–707.

Evans, J., Williams, J. M. G., O'Loughlin, S., & Howells, K. (1992). Autobiographical memory and problem-solving strategies of parasuicide patients. *Psychological Medicine, 22*, 399–405.

Gibbs, L. M., Dombrovski, A. Y., Morse, J., Siegle, G. J., Houck, P. R., & Szanto, K. (2009). When the solution is part of the problem: Problem-solving in elderly suicide attempters. *International Journal of Geriatric Psychiatry, 24*, 1396–1404.

Hardy, D. J., Hinkin, C. H., Levine, A. J., Castellon, S. A., & Lam, M. N. (2006). Risky decision making assessed with the gambling task in adults with HIV. *Neuropsychology, 20*, 355–360.

Harkavy-Friedman, J. M., Keilp, J. G., Grunebaum, M. F., Sher, L., Printz, D., Burke, A. K., Mann, J. J., & Oquendo, M. (2006). Are BPI and BPII suicide attempters distinct neuropsychologically? *Journal of Affective Disorders, 94*, 255–259.

Hawton, K. & van Heeringen, K. (2009). Suicide. *The Lancet, 373*, 1372–1381.

Heeren, A., van Broeck, N., & Philippot, P. (2009). The effects of mindfulness on executive processes and autobiographical memory specificity. *Behaviour Research and Therapy, 47*, 403–409.

Hepburn, S. R., Barnhofer, T., & Williams, J. M. G. (2006). Effects of mood on how future events are generated and perceived. *Personality and Individual Differences, 41*, 801–811.

Hill, A. B. (1965). The environment and disease: Association or causation? *Proceedings of the Royal Society of Medicine, 58*, 295–300.

Hunter, E. C. & O'Connor, R. C. (2003). Hopelessness and future thinking in parasuicide: The role of perfectionism. *British Journal of Clinical Psychology, 42*, 355–365.

Johnson, J., Tarrier, N., & Gooding, P. (2008). An investigation of aspects of the cry of pain model of suicide risk: The role of defeat in impairing memory. *Behaviour Research and Therapy, 46*, 968–975.

Jollant, F., Bellivier, F., Leboyer, M., Astruc, B., Torres, S., Verdier, R., Castelnau, D., Malafosse, A., & Courtet, P. (2005). Impaired decision-making in suicide attempters. *American Journal of Psychiatry, 162*, 304–310.

Jollant, F., Guillaume, S., Jaussent, I., Bellivier, F., Leboyer, M., Castelnau, D., Malafosse, A., & Courtet, P. (2007). Psychiatric diagnoses and personality traits associated with disadvantageous decision-making. *European Psychiatry, 22*, 455–461.

Kaviani, H., Rahimi, M., Rahimi-Darabad, P., Kamyar, K., & Naghavi, H. (2003). How autobiographical memory deficits affect problem-solving in depressed patients. *Acta Medica Iranica, 41*, 194–198.

Kaviani, H., Rahimi, P., & Naghavi, H. R. (2004). Iranian depressed patients attempting suicide showed impaired memory and problem-solving. *Archives of Iranian Medicine, 7*, 113–117.

Kaviani, H., Rahimi-Darabad, P., & Naghavi, H. R. (2005). Autobiographical memory retrieval and problem-solving deficits of Iranian depressed patients attempting suicide. *Journal of Psychopathology and Behavioral Assessment, 27*, 39–44.

Keilp, J. G., Sackeim, H. A., Brodsky, B. S., Oquendo, M. A., Malone, K. M., & Mann, J. J. (2001). Neuropsychological dysfunction in depressed suicide attempters. *American Journal of Psychiatry, 158*, 735–741.

Keilp, J. G., Gorlyn, M., Oquendo, M. A., Burke, A. K., & Mann, J. J. (2008). Attention deficit in depressed suicide attempters. *Psychiatry Research, 159*, 7–17.

King, D. A., Conwell, Y., Cox, C., Henderson, R. E., Denning, D. G., & Caine, E. D. (2000). A neuropsychological comparison of depressed suicide attempters and non-attempters. *The Journal of Neuropsychiatry and Clinical Neurosciences, 12*, 64–70.

Leibetseder, M. M., Rohrer, R. R., Mackinger, H. F., & Fartacek, R. R. (2006). Suicide attempts: Patients with and without affective disorder show impaired autobiographical memory specificity. *Cognition and Emotion, 20*, 516–526.

MacLeod, A. K., Pankhania, B., Lee, M., & Mitchell, D. (1997). Parasuicide, depression and the anticipation of positive and negative future experiences. *Psychological Medicine, 27*, 973–977.

MacLeod, A. K., Rose, G. S., & Williams, J. M. G. (1993). Components of hopelessness about the future in parasuicide. *Cognitive Therapy and Research, 17*, 441–455.

Malloy-Diniz, L. F., Neves, F. S., Abrantes, S. S. C., Fuentes, D., & Corrêa, H. (2009). Suicide behavior and neuropsychological assessment of type I bipolar patients. *Journal of Affective Disorders, 112*, 231–236.

Mann, J. J. (2003). Neurobiology of suicidal behaviour. *Nature Reviews Neuroscience, 4*, 819–828.

Mann, J. J., Arango, V. A., Avenevoli, S., Brent, D. A., Champagne, F. A., Clayton, P., Currier, D., Dougherty, D. M., Haghighi, F., Hodge, S. E., Kleinman, J., Lehner, T., McMahon, F., Moscicki, E. K., Oquendo, M. A., Pandey, G. N., Pearson, J., Stanley, B., Terwilliger, J., & Wenzel, A. (2009). Candidate endophenotypes for genetic studies of suicidal behavior. *Biological Psychiatry, 65*, 556–563.

Marzuk, P. M., Hartwell, N., Leon, A. C., & Portera, L. (2005). Executive functioning in depressed patients with suicidal ideation. *Acta Psychiatrica Scandinavica, 112*, 294–301.

Nock, M. K. & Mendes, W. B. (2008). Physiological arousal, distress tolerance, and social problem-solving deficits among adolescent self-injurers. *Journal of Consulting and Clinical Psychology, 76*, 28–38.

Ohmann, S., Schuch, B., König, M., Blaas, S., Fliri, C., & Popow, C. (2008). Self-injurious behavior in adolescent girls. *Psychopathology, 41*, 226–235.

Oldershaw, A., Grima, E., Jollant, F., Richards, C., Simic, M., Taylor, L., & Schmidt, U. (2009). Decision-making and problem-solving in adolescents who deliberately self-harm. *Psychological Medicine, 39*, 95–104.

Pollock, L. R. & Williams, J. M. G. (1998). Problem-solving and suicidal behavior. *Suicide and Life-Threatening Behavior, 28*, 375–387.

Pollock, L. R. & Williams, J. M. G. (2001). Effective problem-solving in suicide attempters depends on specific autobiographic recall. *Suicide and Life-Threatening Behavior, 31*, 386–396.

Pollock, L. R. & Williams, J. M. G. (2004). Problem-solving in suicide attempters. *Psychological Medicine, 34*, 163–167.

Pompili, M., Innamorati, M., Masotti, V., Personnè, F., Lester, D., Di Vittorio, C., Tatarelli, R., Girardi, P., & Amore, M. (2008). Suicide in the elderly: A psychological autopsy study in a North Italy area (1994–2004). *American Journal of Geriatric Psychiatry, 16*, 727–735.

Raes, F., Williams, J. M. G., & Hermans, D. (2009). Reducing cognitive vulnerability to depression: A preliminary investigation of Memory Specificity Training (MEST) in inpatients with depressive symptomatology. *Journal of Behavior Therapy and Experimental Psychiatry, 40*, 24–38.

Rasmussen, S. A., O'Connor, R. C., & Brodie, D. (2008). The role of perfectionism and autobiographical memory in a sample of parasuicide patients – An exploratory study. *Crisis, 29*, 64–72.

Raust, A., Slama, F., Mathieu, F., Roy, I., Chenu, A., Koncke, D., Fouques, D., Jollant, F., Jouvent, E., Courtet, P., Leboyer, M., & Bellivier, F. (2007). Prefrontal cortex dysfunction in patients with suicidal behaviour. *Psychological Medicine, 37*, 411–419.

Rüsch, N., Spoletini, I., Wilke, M., Martinotti, G., Bria, P., Trequattrini, A., Bonaviri, G., Caltagirone, C., & Spalletta, G. (2008). Inferior frontal white matter volume and suicidality in schizophrenia. *Psychiatry Research, 164*, 206–214.

Sidley, G. L., Whitaker, K., Calam, R. M., & Wells, A. (1997). The relationship between problem-solving and autobiographical memory in parasuicide patients. *Behavioural and Cognitive Psychotherapy, 25*, 195–202.

Sinclair, J. M. A., Crane, C., Hawton, K., & Williams, J. M. G. (2007). The role of autobiographical memory specificity in deliberate self-harm: Correlates and consequences. *Journal of Affective Disorders, 102*, 11–18.

Tops, M., van der Pompe, G., Wijers, A. A., Den Boer, J. A., Meijman, T. F., & Korf, J. (2004). Free recall of pleasant words from recency positions is especially sensitive to acute administration of cortisol. *Psychoneuroendocrinology, 29*, 327–338.

van Beek, W., Kerkhof, A., & Beekman, A. (2009). Future oriented group training for suicidal patients: A randomized clinical trial. *BMC Psychiatry, 9*, 65.

van Heeringen, C., Godfrin, K., Williams, J. M. G., Raes, F., Dewulf, D. (submitted). The effects of Mindfulness-based cognitive therapy (MBCT) on suicide risk factors.

Weinstock, M. (2008). The long-term behavioural consequences of prenatal stress. *Neuroscience and Biobehavioral Reviews, 32*, 1073–1086.

Wenzel, A. & Beck, A. T. (2008). A cognitive model of suicidal behavior: Theory and treatment. *Applied & Preventive Psychology, 12*, 189–201.

Westheide, J., Quednow, B. B., Kuhn, K. U., Hoppe, C., Cooper-Mahkorn, D., Hawellek, B., Eichler, P., Maier, W., & Wagner, M. (2008). Executive performance of depressed suicide attempters: The role of suicidal ideation. *European Archives of Psychiatry and Clinical Neuroscience, 258*, 414–421.

Williams, J. M. G. (1996). Depression and the specificity of autobiographical memory. In D. C. Rubin (Ed.), *Remembering Our Past: Studies in autobiographical memory* (pp. 244–267). Cambridge: Cambridge University Press.

Williams, J. M. G., Barnhofer, T., Crane, C., & Beck, A. T. (2005). Problem-solving deteriorates following mood challenge in formerly depressed patients with a history of suicidal ideation. *Journal of Abnormal Psychology, 114*, 421–431.

Williams, J. M. G., Barnhofer, T., Crane, C., Hermans, D., Raes, F., Watkins, E., & Dalgleish, T. (2007). Autobiographical memory specificity and emotional disorder. *Psychological Bulletin, 133*, 122–148.

Williams, J. M. G. & Broadbent, K. (1986). Autobiographical memory in suicide attempters. *Journal of Abnormal Psychology, 95*, 144–149.

Williams, J. M. G., & Dritschel, B. H. (1988). Emotional disturbance and the specificity of autobiographical memory. *Cognition and Emotion, 2*, 221–234.

Williams, J. M. G. & Pollock, L. (2001). Psychological aspects of the suicidal process. In K. van Heeringen (Ed.), *Understanding Suicidal Behaviour: The suicidal process approach to research, treatment and prevention* (pp. 76–94). Chichester: John Wiley & Sons, Ltd.

Williams, J. M. G., Teasdale, J. D., Segal, Z. V., & Soulsby, J. (2000). Mindfulness-based cognitive therapy reduces over-general autobiographical memory in formerly depressed patients. *Journal of Abnormal Psychology, 109*, 150–155.

Williams, J. M. G., van der Does, A. J. W., Barnhofer, T., Crane, C., & Segal, Z. S. (2008). Cognitive reactivity, suicidal ideation and future fluency: Preliminary investigation of a differential activation theory of hopelessness/suicidality. *Cognitive Therapy and Research, 32*, 83–104.

CHAPTER TEN

Present Status and Future Prospects
take up the Interpersonal–Psychological
Theory of Suicidal Behaviour

Jessica D. Ribeiro and Thomas E. Joiner

Abstract

Broadly described, the interpersonal–psychological theory of suicidal behaviour (Joiner, 2005) proposes that individuals who die by suicide must have both the desire to die and the ability to act on that desire. More specifically, the model holds that the desire for death by suicide results from the interaction of two perceived psychological states: namely, thwarted belongingness and perceived burdensomeness. Further, the model holds that an individual will act on that desire only if he or she has acquired the capability to do so. Thus, it is the interaction of all three factors that produces the greatest risk of death by suicide. The intention of the present chapter is to discuss the current status, emerging developments, and future directions of the theory.

Introduction

Over the past 50 years, suicide rates have increased by approximately 60% (WHO, 2005). As the tenth leading cause of death worldwide, suicide claims the lives of approximately one million individuals each year around the world, which equates to roughly one death every 40 seconds (WHO, 2005). Based on the current trends, by

International Handbook of Suicide Prevention: Research, Policy and Practice, First Edition.
Edited by Rory C. O'Connor, Stephen Platt, Jacki Gordon.
© 2011 John Wiley & Sons, Ltd. Published 2011 by John Wiley & Sons, Ltd.

the year 2020 the number of deaths due to suicide is expected to reach nearly 1.53 million around the world. The seriousness and scope of the issue has prompted suicide prevention efforts worldwide. Despite its increased recognition, however, suicide has persisted as a significant public health concern over the past several decades (WHO, 2005).

Prevention depends largely on the accuracy of prediction. Unfortunately, death by suicide is extremely difficult to predict. This is not surprising, given the relative rarity of the phenomenon: most individuals who have thoughts of suicide or even have a history of suicide attempts,[1] which is one of the strongest risk factors for suicide, will not die by suicide. According to a national study conducted by the Substance Abuse and Mental Health Services Administration (2009), in a 12-month period approximately 8.3 million (3.7%) adults in the United States report having serious thoughts of suicide, 2.3 million (2.3%) report having developed a plan, and 1.1 million adults attempt suicide. Fewer still actually lose their lives to suicide. Based on past trends, it is estimated that approximately 33,000 individuals (0.01%) actually die by suicide each year in the United States (McIntosh, 2002). Therefore, although many individuals may have thoughts about suicide, the majority of individuals will not act on those thoughts.

A number of noteworthy theories examining the underlying processes of suicidal behaviour have been proposed (e.g., theories proposed by Shneidman, Baumeister, Beck, and Linehan). Many of the theories are limited, however, by their failure to address the important difference between suicidal ideation and suicidal behaviour. As noted above, theories focused on predicting suicidal behaviour may increase our ability to target those individuals at greatest risk of dying by suicide. One such theory is Joiner's Interpersonal–Psychological Theory of Suicidal Behaviour (2005). The Interpersonal–Psychological Theory of Suicidal Behaviour holds that an individual will die by suicide only if he or she has both the desire to die by suicide and the capability to act on that desire. This proposition – straightforward and simple – underscores the crucial difference between suicidal ideation and suicidal behaviour.

The present chapter is intended as a review of the current status of the Interpersonal–Psychological Theory of Suicidal Behaviour, as well as a discussion of viable future directions to advance the theory (Joiner, 2005). To that end, we first provide a brief overview of the theory's principal concepts. Subsequently, we examine the theory's four main predictions and empirical evidence collected to date to substantiate those predictions. In the last section, we turn our attention to several viable areas for future research that we feel would prove to be timely and important advances to further the theory and, by consequence, the field of suicide research.

Key Concepts

As described above, Joiner's Interpersonal–Psychological Theory of Suicidal Behaviour (henceforth referred to as the 'interpersonal–psychological theory') proposes that an individual will be able to die by suicide only if he or she has developed both the desire to die and the ability to act on that desire. Within the framework of the theory, the desire for death by suicide develops in the presence of two interpersonal states: thwarted belongingness and perceived burdensomeness. The former refers to feelings of social isolation, alienation, or disconnection from valued social networks. Joiner (2005) posits that the need for connection and belonging is so strong that thwarting that basic human desire can increase the likelihood of having thoughts of suicide. This proposition draws from research on basic interpersonal needs, which clearly demonstrates the negative effects of not fulfilling the need-to-belong (Van Orden, Witte, James, Castro, Gordon, *et al.*, 2008a). Relatedly, believing that the self is so incompetent that one's existence is a liability for or a burden on others – perceived burdensomeness – is also believed to increase the risk of developing the desire for suicide, since holding on to that belief may lead to the potentially dangerous thought that one's death is worth more than one's life. Although each state may independently contribute to the desire for suicide, Joiner (2005) argues that experiencing both states concurrently is particularly pernicious.

In addition to holding the desire for suicide, an individual must also have developed the ability to engage in lethal self-injury. Joiner (2005) argues that inherent self-preservation instincts are extremely difficult to overcome. The ability to engage in behaviours that oppose those instincts must be developed over time. According to the theory, repeated exposure to painful and provocative events acts to increase the tolerance of pain and decrease the fear of death. Primarily, this proposition draws from opponent–process theory, which suggests that repeated exposure to an affective stimulus leads to a shift in the response to that stimulus, such that the original response to the stimulus is weakened and the opposing response is strengthened over time (Solomon, 1980). Therefore, the acquired capability to engage in lethal self-injury is conceptualized as a continuous construct that becomes stronger over time with repeated exposure to salient experiences. According to the theory, it is influenced by the nature of those experiences, such that the more painful and provocative stimuli confer greater capability for death by suicide.

Main Predictions

Four main predictions can be derived from the interpersonal–psychological theory. First, two interpersonal states – thwarted belongingness and perceived burdensomeness – act as proximal, causal risk factors for developing the desire for suicide. Second, the likelihood of developing the desire for death by suicide is highest when both states are experienced concurrently. Third, the ability to engage in suicidal behaviour is acquired through repeated exposure to painful and provocative experiences. Fourth, serious suicidal behaviour will occur only in the presence of all three constructs – thwarted belongingness, perceived burdensomeness, and the acquired capability for lethal self-injury. Below, we examine the empirical evidence for each in turn.

A series of studies has directly examined the proposition that thwarted belongingness and perceived burdensomeness each act as proximal, causal risk factors for suicidal ideation. Results have generally been supportive: significant positive correlations have been found between suicidal ideation and feelings of thwarted belongingness and perceived burdensomeness independently. The correlation between perceived burdensomeness and suicidal ideation has been examined and supported in a range of samples, including undergraduates, methadone outpatients, suicide attempters, and suicide decedents (Conner, Britton, Sworts, & Joiner, 2007; Joiner, Pettit, Walker, Voelz, Cruz, et al., 2002; van Orden, Lynam, Hollar, & Joiner, 2006; Van Orden, Witte, Gordon, Bender, & Joiner, 2008b). Alternatively, experiences that foster kinship and connectedness have been found to be associated with lower suicide rates. For instance, Joiner, Hollar, and van Orden (2006) reported that suicide rates were significantly lower during positive collective events like sporting events.

The theory also predicts that suicidal ideation is most probable if both interpersonal states are experienced in conjunction. It would follow that the statistical interaction between levels of perceived burdensomeness and thwarted belongingness should be predictive of suicide ideation severity and able to account for level of suicidal ideation even after controlling for the two independent effects of either construct alone. In support of this prediction, Van Orden et al. (2008b) reported that the statistical interaction between levels of perceived burdensomeness and thwarted belongingness was predictive of current suicidal ideation in a diverse sample of undergraduates. Joiner, Van Orden, Witte, Selby, Ribeiro, et al. (2009) further substantiated this prediction by examining the relation between levels of family support, feelings of mattering, and suicidal ideation. In the study conducted by Joiner et al. (2009), the respondent's perceived level of family support was used as a proxy variable for the belongingness construct and self-reported feelings of mattering, which refers to the individual's perceptions of how others feel toward him or her, was used as a proxy for burdensomeness. Consistent with the theory's predictions, individuals who experienced both feelings of low family support and low feelings of mattering reported the highest levels of suicidal ideation. The relationship held even after accounting for six-month depression and lifetime history of depression, which are both strong predictors of current suicidal ideation.

The theory's third main prediction is that the ability to engage in potentially lethal self-injury is strengthened over time through repeated exposure to painful and provocative experiences. The nature of those experiences will also influence the process of acquiring the capability to engage in lethal self-injury, such that the more painful and provocative an experience, the greater risk it will confer. Given that, it would follow that the most direct means of acquiring the capability to engage in lethal self-injury is through past suicide attempts. In a direct test of this proposition using an instrument designed directly to tap the acquired capability construct, Van Orden and colleagues (2008b) found past attempt history to be predictive of the level of acquired capability in a sample of clinical outpatients. Furthermore, the literature examining the relationship between suicide attempt history and death by suicide is consistent with the theory's proposition: this relationship is indeed strong (Brown, Beck, Steer, & Grisham, 2000). Research has also found that the most severe suicidal plan in an individual's history is more predictive of completed suicide (as well as number of past attempts) than current plans (Joiner et al., 2003). In addition, Beck, Brown, Steer, Dahlsgaard, and Grisham (1999) reported that suicidality severity during the most severe suicidal period is predictive of eventual death by suicide, finding death by suicide approximately 14 times more likely for those individuals with the most severe worst-point plans than individuals who endorsed less severe worst-point plans.

This is not to suggest that the only means of acquiring the capability to engage in serious suicidal behaviour is via past attempts. Nock, Joiner, Gordon, Lloyd-Richardson, and Prinstein (2006) provide evidence for other paths that increase the likelihood of engaging in lethal self-injury. In the study conducted by these researchers, adolescents who endorsed having a longer history of non-suicidal self-injury (NSSI) and reported less pain during self-injury were twice as likely to have a history of suicide attempts. Additionally, the individuals who endorsed in a variety of methods of NSSI, as well as longer histories of NSSI use, were found to have a significantly higher rate of suicide attempts.

Integrating the three main components of the model, the final prediction derived from the theory suggests that, although each factor is necessary, none alone is sufficient to result in death by suicide. Rather, only the confluence of all three factors is sufficient for individuals to engage in serious suicidal behaviour. In a test of the three-way interaction proposed by the theory, Joiner and colleagues (2009) reported that suicide attempts were significantly more likely for individuals with a history of suicide attempts who endorsed the highest levels of feelings of burdensomeness and lowest levels of belongingness. This relationship held even after controlling for the effects of levels of depression, borderline personality disorder traits, and hopelessness – all potent risk factors for suicide.

Future Directions

Thus far, we have presented an overview of the key concepts and main predictions of the interpersonal–psychological theory. With evidence generally falling in line with the model, in the final section of this chapter we turn to viable avenues for future research. We focus our discussion on two areas of prime importance: further theory-relevant research that would enhance our understanding of the mechanisms of suicidal behaviour; and future research guided by the theory that would enhance the likelihood of accurate prediction of suicidal behaviour.

Mechanisms of suicidal behaviour

Research focused on further exploring the mechanisms that lead to suicidal behaviour is crucial. Joiner's (2005) interpersonal–psychological theory suggests that the mechanism underlying suicidal behaviour involves facilitating feelings of thwarted belongingness, perceptions of burdensomeness, and the acquisition of the ability to engage in lethal self-injury. As discussed earlier in this chapter, evidence to date has generally supported Joiner's (2005) proposition. Future research focused on further specifying the proposed process would likely enhance the predictive power of the theory.

One means of further specifying the theory would be to describe the exact conditions that would result in suicidal behaviour. One viable future direction would be to determine whether there are specific thresholds for each element of the theory that must be met in order to result in death by suicide. To that end, research should focus on exploring parameters of each construct – such as the duration, frequency, and intensity – that confer the greatest risk. Beyond simply examining the parameters for each element, it would also be interesting to consider whether the model might fit a kind of 'titration model' whereby lower levels of one factor would require higher levels of the other factors in order to result in expected result. For instance, for individuals with very high levels of acquired capability (e.g., individuals with a history of suicide attempts) the necessary thresholds for feelings of thwarted belongingness or perceived burdensomeness may be lower as compared with individuals with lower levels of acquired capability. Conceptualizing the theory as such would allow for the thresholds of each construct to vary, that is, the thresholds necessary for each component of the theory would not be absolute. What would be crucial would be whether the interaction of the three elements confers sufficient risk.

Another means of further qualifying the nature of the relationships proposed by the interpersonal–psychological theory is to examine whether key constructs from other models should also be included as a means of increasing its predictive utility. For instance, there is an extensive literature base supporting the strong relationship between hopelessness and suicidal ideation, as well as death by suicide (Beck, Brown, Berchick, Stewart, & Steer, 2006). Incorporating hopelessness-related parameters into the model, such that thwarted belongingness and perceived burdensomeness confer the greatest risk for suicidal ideation when perceived to be permanent and irremediable, for instance, may increase the specificity of the predictions made by the model. Should the inclusion of concepts related to hopelessness increase the predictive utility of the model, it would be interesting to consider whether it is necessary for both states to be permanent. If only one factor is perceived as irremediable, is it sufficient to produce suicidal ideation in the presence of the other factor or can the other construct serve as a protective factor?

Similarly, another salient construct to consider is emotion dysregulation proposed by Linehan (1993). Linehan suggests that emotion regulation deficits, such as poor distress tolerance, may contribute to engaging in self-injurious behaviours. It would, therefore, be worth investigating whether poor distress tolerance intensifies the emotional experience of situations that may threaten belongingness or prompt feelings of burdensomeness. Poor distress tolerance has also been linked to the use of dysregulated behaviours, including self-injurious behaviour (Chapman, Gratz, & Brown, 2006; Favazza, 1996; Klonsky, 2007). Therefore, poor distress tolerance may enhance the likelihood of engaging in dysregulated behaviours, which may be painful and provocative in nature, and, as a result, increase an individual's acquired capability for serious suicidal behaviour.

Relatedly, future research examining the factors that might contribute to, or facilitate, the acquisition of the acquired capability would be useful. Based on the theory, the ability to engage in serious suicidal behaviour is acquired with repeated exposure to painful and provocative events. Determining which painful and provocative experiences confer the greatest risk would be useful. Moreover, future research examining whether self-inflicted injury is necessary in terms of developing the ability to engage in serious suicidal behaviour or whether elevated pain tolerance levels are sufficient, regardless of the nature of those experiences, would also be informative. It may also be possible that certain individuals are inherently predisposed to engage in behaviours that increase the ability to engage in lethal self-injury. Research focused on identifying vulnerability factors that make individuals more susceptible to facing painful and provocative experiences might be used to inform preventative efforts.

Another promising avenue of research would be further examination of the complexity of the interactions proposed by the model. For instance, future work exploring the possible interplay between the three main constructs of the theory would likely be informative. As it stands, the theory does not make any specific predictions with respect to the possible effects of perceived burdensomeness and thwarted belongingness on the acquired capability component of the theory. Prior research, however, suggests a potentially meaningful interplay between the three factors that extends beyond the theory's main predictions. More specifically, there is some evidence – albeit indirect and preliminary – that suggests that the two interpersonal states contributing to the desire for suicide may also have an effect on the acquired capability to engage in serious suicidal behaviour. For instance, in a study conducted by Joiner and colleagues (2002), perceived burdensomeness was found to be a significant predictor of death by suicide as well as the lethality of the method used, such that higher levels of perceived burdensomeness predicted more violent means.

Particularly relevant to Joiner's (2005) model, social exclusion has been found to be associated with increased pain tolerance and threshold level (DeWall & Baumeister, 2006). Since pain tolerance is a key component of acquired capability and there is evidence to suggest that experiencing emotional pain is compatible with experiencing physical pain, it would be interesting to examine whether experiencing emotional pain can increase acquired capability levels. Relatedly, there is also evidence to suggest that social support is associated with attenuated physical pain during pain-inducing tasks. Several experimental studies have shown that social support during a pain-inducing task (e.g., cold pressor task, which involves immersing the hand or forearm into ice water as a means of producing steadily increasing pain of moderate intensity) to be predictive of lower pain ratings (Brown, Sheffield, Leary, & Robinson, 2003; Master, Eisenberger, Taylor, Naliboff, Shirinyan, *et al.*, 2009; McClelland & McCubbin, 2008). One question that arises is whether social support reduces the pain felt during painful and provocative experiences and, by consequence, buffers the degree to which those experiences strengthen acquired capability levels.

Prediction and prevention of suicidal behaviour

Many existing theories of suicide address the phenomenon of suicidality more broadly, failing to account for the critical distinction between suicidal ideation and behaviour. In that respect, the interpersonal–psychological theory extends beyond current theories as it increases the specificity with which predictions can be made. Enhancing the specificity of predictions has important implications for improving our risk assessment, intervention, and prevention procedures.

The main prediction of the interpersonal–psychological theory holds that the greatest risk of death by suicide results from the interaction of perceived burdensomeness, thwarted belongingness, and the acquired capability to engage in lethal self-injury. Empirically, there is evidence supporting this proposition (cf. Joiner *et al.*, 2009). Stellrecht, Gordon, Van Orden, Witte, Wingate, *et al.* (2006) recommend assessing the presence of the three factors highlighted in Joiner's model in order to inform risk assessment and crisis intervention in clinical settings. Further research is necessary to quantify the advantages of an approach drawing on the interpersonal–psychological theory.

In addition to improving risk assessment at the level of the individual, the theory can also be useful in understanding the environmental stressors and negative life events that are associated with increased suicide risk. Having information on which events are most likely to heighten suicide risk would be particularly informative for intervention and assessment. To this end, the interpersonal–psychological theory offers some direction on which events might be most salient. In particular, the theory predicts that events that promote feelings of belongingness and community would be associated with lower suicide rates, while, conversely, events that decrease one's sense of connectedness and belonging would be predictive of heightened suicide rates. Supporting this proposition, findings from Joiner *et al.* (2006) speak to the positive effects on suicide rates of 'pulling together' after sports-related events. The authors found that local suicide rates were correlated with final national rankings of college football teams. In addition, the authors reported that suicide rates are lower during Super Bowl Sundays as compared with Sundays not airing the Super Bowl. Further, the authors also reported that the number of deaths by suicide in the United States on the day of the 'Miracle on Ice' (which refers to the United States' unexpected win over the Soviet Union in men's hockey during the 1980s Winter Olympic Games) were significantly lower than any other 22 February. The authors argue that the mechanism accounting for the findings (at least in part) is the increased connectedness associated with the positive sporting events. Importantly, the protective effects of 'pulling together' are not limited to positive events. There is also evidence to suggest that bolstering connectedness in times of national crises is also predictive of lower suicide rates. Conversely, national tragedies that do not increase belongingness and are instead associated with displacement would not be predictive of lower suicide rates, according to the theory.

Beyond prediction of suicidal behaviour, the interpersonal–psychological theory can also inform intervention research. Preliminary work conducted by Stellrecht and colleagues (2006) discusses implications of the theory for practice. In particular, the authors emphasize the utility of Situational Analysis, which is a primary technique used in the Cognitive-Behavioural System of Psychotherapy (CBASP; McCullough, 2003), which provides clients with a useful framework for evaluating the thoughts and behaviours associated with discrete interpersonal interactions. Targeting stable, global beliefs about social isolation or burdensomeness may prove useful in decreasing strong suicidal desire. In terms of addressing suicidal behaviour, situational analysis may also help individuals to recognize and reduce impulsive behaviour patterns that contribute to levels of the acquired capability for suicide. Furthermore, the interpersonal–psychological theory can also inform primary prevention efforts. In particular, based on the theory, preventative efforts should be designed to increase public awareness of the importance of social connectedness and social contribution, since bolstering these factors may act as a buffer against suicidal ideation.

Conclusion

The interpersonal–psychological theory (Joiner, 2005) proposes that an individual will die by suicide only if he or she has both the desire and capability to do so. More specifically, desire is a result of the joint experience of two interpersonal states: thwarted belongingness and perceived burdensomeness. The capability to engage in serious suicidal behaviour, according to the theory, is acquired, mainly, through repeated exposure to painful and provocative experiences. It is the interaction of all three components that confers the greatest risk for death by suicide. With evidence generally in line with theory's main predictions, Joiner's (2005) interpersonal–psychological theory of suicidal behaviour stands as a promising model of the process underlying death by suicide. In this chapter, we have focused our discussion on viable areas for future research, which we believe would be promising additions to the literature base on the interpersonal–psychological theory in particular and suicidal behaviour more generally.

Note

1   We acknowledge that there is considerable variability in the definitions and nomenclature used in the field of suicide study. As such, we would like to briefly define the suicide-related terminology used in this chapter, which is largely consistent with the recommendations outlined by Silverman, Berman, Sanddal, O'Carroll, and Joiner (2007a, 2007b). Specifically, we use the term *suicide* to refer to self-inflicted death with evidence of intent to die. The term *suicide attempt* refers to a self-inflicted, potentially injurious behaviour with a non-fatal outcome with evidence of intent to die. We also mention *non-suicidal self-injury*, which is defined as intentional damage to one's body in the absence of suicidal intent (Nock & Prinstein, 2004) and is differentiable from suicidal behaviours on the basis of the intent and function of the behaviours.

References

Beck, A. Brown, G. Berchick, R. Stewart, B., & Steer, R. (2006). Relationship between hopelessness and eventual suicide: A replication with psychiatric outpatients. *Focus, 4*, 291–296.

Beck, A. T., Brown, G. K., Steer, R. A., Dahlsgaard, K. K., & Grisham, J. R. (1999). Suicide ideation at its worst point: A predictor of eventual suicide in psychiatric outpatients. *Suicide and Life-Threatening Behavior, 29*, 1–9.

Brown, G. K., Beck, A. T., Steer, R. A., & Grisham, J. R. (2000). Risk factors for suicide in psychiatric outpatients: A 20-year prospective study. *Journal of Consulting and Clinical Psychology, 68*, 371–377.

Brown, J. L., Sheffield, D., Leary, M. R., & Robinson, M. E. (2003). Social support and experimental pain. *Psychosomatic Medicine, 65*, 276–283.

Chapman, A. L., Gratz, K. L., & Brown, M. Z. (2006). Solving the puzzle of deliberate self-harm: The experiential avoidance model. *Behaviour Research and Therapy, 44*, 371–394.

Conner, K., Britton, P., Sworts, L., & Joiner, T. (2007). Suicide attempts among individuals with opiate dependence: The critical role of felt belonging. *Addictive Behaviors, 32*, 1395–1404.

DeWall, N. & Baumeister, R. (2006). Alone but feeling no pain: Effects of social exclusion on physical pain tolerance and pain threshold, affective forecasting, and interpersonal empathy. *Journal of Personality and Social Psychology*, 9, 1–15.

Favazza, A. R. (1996). *Bodies under Siege: Self-mutilation and body modification in culture and psychiatry*, 2nd ed. Baltimore, MD: Johns Hopkins University Press.

Joiner, T. E., Jr. (2005). *Why People Die by Suicide*. Cambridge, MA: Harvard University Press.

Joiner, T. E., Jr., Hollar, D., & Van Orden, K. A. (2006). On Buckeyes, Gators, Super Bowl Sunday, and the Miracle on Ice: 'Pulling Together' is associated with lower suicide rates. *Journal of Social and Clinical Psychology*, 25, 179–195.

Joiner, T., Pettit, J. W., Walker, R. L., Voelz, Z. R., Cruz, J., Rudd, M. D., & Lester, D. (2002). Perceived burdensomeness and suicidality: Two studies on the suicide notes of those attempting and those completing suicide. *Journal of Social & Clinical Psychology*, 21, 531–545.

Joiner, T., Steer, R., Brown, G., Beck, A., Pettit, J., & Rudd. D. (2003). Worst point suicidal plans: A dimension of suicidality predictive of past suicide attempts and eventual death by suicide. *Behaviour Research and Therapy*, 41(12), 1469–1480.

Joiner, T., Van Orden, K., Witte, T., Selby, E., Ribeiro, J., Lewis, R., & Rudd, D. (2009). Main predictions of the interpersonal–psychological theory of suicidal behavior: Empirical tests in two samples of young adults. *Journal of Abnormal Psychology*, 118, 634–646.

Klonsky, E. D. (2007). The functions of deliberate self-injury: A review of the evidence. *Clinical Psychology Review*, 27, 226–239.

Kung, H., Hoyert, D., Xu, J., & Murphy, S. (2009). Deaths: Final data for 2005. National Vital Statistics Reports, 56(10), available at http://www.cdc.gov/nchs/data/nvsr/nvsnvsr56_10.pdf, accessed April 2009.

Linehan, M. M. (1993). *Cognitive Behavioral Treatment of Borderline Personality Disorder*. New York: Guilford Press.

Master, S., Eisenberger, N., Taylor, B., Naliboff, B., Shirinyan, D., & Lieberman M. (2009). A picture's worth: Partner photographs reduce experimentally induced pain. *Psychological Science*, 22, 1316–1318.

McClelland, L. E. & McCubbin, J. A. (2008). Social influence and pain response in women and men. *Journal of Behavioral Medicine*, 31, 413–420.

McCullough, J. P. (2003). Treatment for chronic depression using Cognitive Behavioural Analysis System of Psychotherapy (CBASP). *Journal of Clinical Psychology*, 59, 833–846.

McIntosh, J. L. (2002). *USA Statistics for the Year 1999: Overheads and a presentation guide*. Washington, DC: American Association of Suicidology.

Nock, M. K., Joiner, T. E., Gordon, K. H., Lloyd-Richardson, E., & Prinstein, M. J. (2006). Non-suicidal self-injury among adolescents: Diagnostic correlates and relation to suicide attempts. *Psychiatry Research*, 144, 65–72.

Nock, M. K. & Prinstein, M. J. (2004). A functional approach to the assessment of self-mutilative behavior in adolescents. *Journal of Consulting and Clinical Psychology*, 72, 885–890.

Silverman, M., Berman, A., Sanddal, N., O'Carroll, P., and Joiner, T. (2007a). Rebuilding the Tower of Babel: A revised nomenclature for the study of suicide and suicidal behaviors. Part 1: Background, rationale, and methodology. *Suicide and Life Threatening Behavior*, 37, 248–263.

Silverman, M., Berman, A., Sanddal, N., O'Carroll, P., and Joiner, T. (2007b). Rebuilding the Tower of Babel: A revised nomenclature for the study of suicide and suicidal behaviors. Part 2: Suicide-related ideations, communications, and behavior. *Suicide and Life Threatening Behavior*, 37, 264–277.

Solomon, R. L. (1980). The opponent–process theory of acquired motivation: The costs of pleasure and benefits of pain. *American Psychologist*, 35, 691–712.

Stellrecht, N. E., Gordon, K. H., van Orden, K., Witte, T. K., Wingate, L. R., Cukrowicz, K. C., Butler, M., Schmidt, N. B., Fitzpatrick, K. K., & Joiner, T. E. (2006). Clinical applications of the interpersonal–psychological theory of attempted and completed suicide. *Journal of Clinical Psychology, 62,* 211–222.

Substance Abuse and Mental Health Services Administration (2009). *Suicidal Thoughts and Behaviors among Adults. National Survey on Drug Use and Health Report,* available at http://oas.samhsa.gov/2k9/165/SuicideHTML.pdf, accessed November 2009.

Van Orden, K. A., Lynam, M. E., Hollar, D., & Joiner, T. E., Jr. (2006). Perceived burdensomeness as an indicator of suicidal symptoms. *Cognitive Therapy and Research, 30,* 457–467.

Van Orden, K. A., Witte, T. K., James, L. M., Castro, Y., Gordon, K. H., Braithwaite, S. R., Hollar, D. L., & Joiner, T. E., Jr. (2008a). Suicidal ideation in college students varies across semesters: The mediating role of belongingness. *Suicide and Life Threatening Behavior, 38,* 427–436.

Van Orden, K., Witte, T., Gordon, K., Bender, T., & Joiner, T., Jr. (2008b). Suicidal desire and the capability for suicide: Tests of the Interpersonal–Psychological Theory of Suicidal Behavior among adults. *Journal of Consulting and Clinical Psychology, 76,* 72–83.

World Health Organisation (2005). *Figures and Facts about Suicide: Introduction,* available at http://www.who.int/mental_health/media/en/382.pdf, accessed 5 May 2005.

CHAPTER ELEVEN

Towards an Integrated Motivational–Volitional Model of Suicidal Behaviour

Rory C. O'Connor

Abstract

The aetiology of suicide is complex, encompassing a multifaceted array of risk and protective factors. Although a comprehensive understanding of suicidality requires an appreciation of biological, psychological, and social perspectives, the focus in this chapter is primarily on the psychological determinants of suicidal behaviour. Herein I explore the research literature with a view to identifying those psychological factors that increase the likelihood that someone chooses death rather than life. However, as these psychological factors do not operate in isolation, they are presented as components within a new model, the Integrated Motivational–Volitional (IMV) Model of Suicidal Behaviour. This tripartite model maps the relationship between background factors and trigger events, and the development of suicidal ideation/intent through to suicidal behaviour. Before proceeding to the IMV model, I set the scene by outlining a number of the predominant models of suicide. This is followed by a description of the IMV model and a discussion of how theoretical constructs from other models fit within the IMV model. The chapter ends with a brief discussion of potential next steps in the development, refinement, and testing of the model.

International Handbook of Suicide Prevention: Research, Policy and Practice, First Edition.
Edited by Rory C. O'Connor, Stephen Platt, Jacki Gordon.
© 2011 John Wiley & Sons, Ltd. Published 2011 by John Wiley & Sons, Ltd.

Introduction

Historical perspective

Psychological approaches to understanding the suicidal mind have grown considerably since the turn of the twentieth century, with early psychological investigations into suicide beginning with Freud (see Litman, 1967). Indeed, Freud has been credited with championing a change of perspective on suicide, from a moral, legal, philosophical, or spiritual phenomenon to a clinical concern for which one should receive help rather than moral judgement (Ellis, 2001). However, systematic psychological research is little over 50 years old, pioneered by Edwin Shneidman, the founder of the American Association of Suicidology in the 1950s (e.g., Shneidman & Farberow, 1957). More recent developments have been driven forward by exponents of social learning theory and cognitive and behavioural models (Beck, Steer, Kovacs, & Garrison, 1985; O'Connor & Sheehy, 2000; Weishaar, 2000; Williams & Pollock, 2001).

Towards an Integrated Perspective: The Integrated Motivational–Volitional Model of Suicidal Behaviour

In the past 25 years, numerous models of suicidal behaviour have been put forward which have led to important developments in our understanding of the aetiology and course of suicidal behaviour (see Table 11.1). As a consequence, there is growing recognition that we need to move beyond the classic psychiatric diagnostic categories if we are to further understand the causes of suicidal behaviour (van Heeringen, 2001). Some models, such as suicide as escape from self (Baumeister, 1990), have focused on a single driving motivation (i.e., escape); others, for example, the cognitive model of suicidal behaviour (Wenzel & Beck, 2008), have attended to a specific domain of risk, that is, cognition. Others still, including Schotte's and Clum's (1987) diathesis–stress model, have highlighted cognitive vulnerabilities which become pernicious when activated by stress. As a result of the emergence of these theoretical models, a plethora of personality factors (e.g., impulsivity) and cognitive factors (e.g., social problem-solving) have been identified and shown to increase risk of repeat self-harm and completed suicide (e.g., Brezo, Paris, & Turecki, 2006; Ellis & Rutherford, 2008; O'Connor, 2010). Despite these developments, many of the predictive models have adopted a narrow focus or have failed to build on the growing empirical evidence base. Therefore, the central aim of developing a new integrated model was an attempt to synthesize the evidence that has already been garnered from the predominant models. Moreover, with only a few exceptions, these models have not been particularly successful in differentiating those who develop suicidal ideation (but do not attempt suicide) from those who go on to engage in suicidal behaviour (Ribeiro & Joiner, Chapter 10, above). Indeed, as the majority of suicide ideators do not go on to attempt suicide (Kessler, Borges, & Walters, 1999), any model has to be both specific and sensitive to be useful. As suicide attempt

Table 11.1   Selected predominant models of suicidal behaviour from past 25 years

Author	Model	Basic premise
Shneidman (1985)	Cubic model of suicide	Press (stress) + pain (psychache) + perturbation = suicide risk.
Schotte & Clum (1987)	Diathesis–stress–hopelessness model of suicidal behaviour	Cognitive vulnerability (e.g., social problem-solving) accounts for the relationship between stress and suicide risk.
Baumeister (1990)	Suicide as escape from self	Primary motivation of suicide is to escape from painful self-awareness.
Mann *et al.* (1999)	Clinical model of suicidal behaviour	Stress–diathesis model wherein suicide risk is determined not only by psychiatric disorder (stressor) but by a diathesis (including tendency to experience more suicidal ideation, impulsivity).
Rudd *et al.* (2001)	Suicidal mode as cognitive behavioural model of suicidality	Based on 10 CBT requirements and has four system characteristics of the suicidal mode (cognitive, affective, behavioural, physiological).
Williams (2001)	Arrested flight model	Suicide risk is elevated when defeat and entrapment are high and the potential for rescue (e.g., social support) is low.
Joiner (2005)	Interpersonal–psychological model	Suicidal desire is determined by high levels of burdensomeness and thwarted belongingness. Desire is likely translated into suicidal behaviour when acquired capability is high.
Johnson *et al.* (2008)	Schematic Appraisal Model of Suicide	An appraisal model which proposes risk is determined by the interplay between information processing biases, schema, and appraisal systems.
Wenzel & Beck (2008)	A cognitive model of suicidal behaviour	Diathesis–stress model with three main constructs: dispositional vulnerability factors; cognitive processes associated with psychiatric disturbance; and cognitive processes associated with suicidal acts.
Williams *et al.* (2008)	Differential activation theory of suicidality	Associative network model. The experience of suicidal ideation/behaviour during a depressive episode increases the likelihood that it will re-emerge during subsequent episodes.
O'Connor (2011)	Integrated Motivational–Volitional Model (IMV) of suicidal behaviour	The IMV model is a diathesis–stress model which specifies the components of the pre-motivational, motivational (ideation/intent formation), and volitional (behavioural enaction) phases of suicidality

and self-harm are often used interchangeably, for the present purposes where I use the term 'suicide attempt'/'behaviour', I am referring to self-injurious behaviour with evidence of suicidal intent. 'Self-harm' is used to describe all other self-harming behaviours where suicidal intent was not explicitly ascertained.

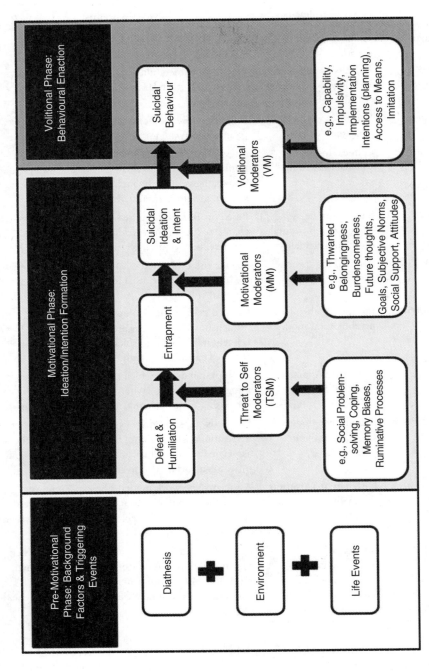

Figure 11.1 Integrated Motivational–Volitional (IMV) Model of Suicidal Behaviour.

Brief overview of integrated motivational–volitional model
of suicidal behaviour

I have attempted to incorporate the major components from the predominant models of suicidal behaviour (outlined in Table 11.1) into an integrated three-phase model of suicidal behaviour, the Integrated Motivational–Volitional (IMV) Model of Suicidal Behaviour, which is intended to discriminate between suicide ideators and suicide attempters. In brief, the IMV proposes that suicidal behaviour results from a complex interplay of factors, the proximal predictor of which is one's *intention* to engage in suicidal behaviour (behavioural intention). Behavioural intention, in turn, is determined by feelings of entrapment where suicidality is seen as the salient solution to life circumstances and entrapment is triggered by defeat/humiliation appraisals (see Figure 11.1). Crucially, the transitions from the defeat/humiliation stage to entrapment, from entrapment to suicidal ideation/intent, and from ideation/intent to suicidal behaviour are determined by state-specific moderators (i.e., factors which facilitate/obstruct movement between states), entitled threat to self, motivational, and volitional moderators, respectively. In addition, background factors (e.g., deprivation, vulnerabilities) and life events (e.g., relationship crises), which collectively comprise the pre-motivational phase (i.e., before the commencement of ideation formation), provide the broader biosocial context for suicide.

Conceptual and empirical rationale for IMV

In addition to integrating the major constructs from existing models and building on the existing evidence base, the IMV model borrows from the Theory of Planned Behaviour (TPB) (Ajzen, 1991), a social cognitive model of behaviour, to provide a unifying theoretical framework. The TPB posits that the proximal predictor of any behaviour is one's behavioural intention (i.e., one's motivation to engage in the behaviour). In turn, attitudes, subjective norms, and perceived behavioural control are thought to determine intention. Attitudes are positive or negative evaluations of the behaviour and subjective norms are indices of the social pressure to engage (or not) in a behaviour. According to Ajzen (1991), perceived behavioural control is akin to self-efficacy (i.e., confidence in one's own ability; Bandura, 1997) and can directly relate to behavioural enaction when perceived control is high.

As an overarching framework, the TPB is a particularly attractive candidate to describe suicidal behaviour as it makes the distinction between the formation of behavioural intention (i.e., development of suicidal ideation and intent), on the one hand, and acting on that intention (i.e., suicide attempt), on the other. Those factors that inform ideation/intention formation comprise the *motivational* phase of the model and those concerned with the translation of intention into suicidal behaviour encompass the *volitional* phase of behavioural enaction. In short, therefore, as suicide is a behaviour or an action, it should be conceptualized as such. This sentiment is described eloquently by Konrad Michel: 'both suicide and attempted suicide are actions that are planned and carried out by individuals, involving conscious processes, and they are thus not mere signs of illness and pathology' (Michel & Valach, 2001, p. 230).

In contrast to the traditional view of suicidal behaviour as a symptom associated with a mental disorder, the health professional's task being the treatment of the patient's underlying pathology (Michel & Valach, 2001), I posit that a focus on the behaviour itself, rather than merely seeing it as an epiphenomenon of mental disorder, opens up a number of theoretical and prevention possibilities which may yield considerable fruit.

To this end, the development of the IMV model had five guiding principles: the model (1) despite being grounded within the psychological literature, should be interdisciplinary; (2) should build upon other theoretical models which have existing empirical support; (3) should be able to differentially predict suicidal ideation and behaviour; (4) should yield testable hypotheses; and (5) should point to avenues for potential intervention and prevention. Although the development of the IMV model was influenced by a number of different models, the main drivers were the Theory of Planned Behaviour (Ajzen, 1991), the diathesis–stress hypothesis (Schotte & Clum, 1987), and the arrested flight model of suicidal behaviour (Williams, 2001). I address each of these influences in turn, including exemplars, where appropriate, from studies with direct or indirect support for the new model. To this end, I have drawn in large part from the work conducted within my research group.

In addition to specifying four constructs (i.e., attitudes, subjective norms, perceived control, and intention) as predictors of behaviour, as noted above, the Theory of Planned Behaviour (TPB) (Ajzen, 1991) posits that the process of behavioural enaction comprises (1) a motivational phase (ideation/intention formation) and (2) a volitional phase (behavioural enaction). The motivational phase is concerned with the formation of the intention to engage in a behaviour, so for the present purposes this refers to the development of suicidal ideation and suicidal intent.

As most people who experience suicidal ideation and intent do not engage in suicidal behaviour, the focus of the second phase of the model, the volitional phase, is on defining those factors that determine when suicidal ideation/intent is translated into suicidal behaviour. The important point here is that the factors associated with ideation formation are distinct from those factors concerned with behavioural enaction. In short, the TPB serves as an overarching framework which conceptualizes the pathway from ideation/intention formation to behavioural enaction. Not only is the TPB conceptually useful, but there is empirical evidence in support of its utility in the context of hospital-treated self-harm (O'Connor, Armitage, & Gray, 2006).

A biopsychosocial perspective and the pre-motivational phase   The proposed motivational and volitional phases of the model do not operate in a biosocial vacuum. Rather, they are influenced by the interactive diathesis–environment–life events triad, which comprises the pre-motivational phase of the model, that is, background factors and triggering events. In essence, the diathesis–stress model posits that suicidal behaviour occurs as a result of the interaction between nature and nurture. Specifically, the diathesis, which may be biological or genetic, confers vulnerability and it is this vulnerability that becomes activated or exacerbated in the presence of stress. Stress may take the form of environmental factors (e.g., deprivation) or negative life events (e.g., relationship break-up), and the diathesis–stress hypothesis posits that the impact of environment and events is more marked among those who are, by definition, vulnerable. The experience of psychiatric illness is characterized as a stressor in Mann's clinical model of suicidal behaviour (Mann, Waternaux, Haas, & Malone, 1999; Mann, Apter, Bertolote, Beautrais, Currier, *et al.*, 2005). Vulnerability may also develop in the context of adverse environmental circumstances. For example, the development of perfectionism may be associated with inconsistent, absent, or conditional parental approval (Barrow & Moore, 1983).

Personality and individual differences variables which confer personal vulnerability (e.g., perfectionism) are included in the pre-motivational phase, but may also impact on risk during the motivational phase when triggered by defeat and humiliation. This apparent double counting acknowledges the fact that many of the individual differences variables implicated in suicidality are state-like as well as being trait-like (Williams, Crane, Barnhofer, & Duggan, 2005). Moreover, in a recent study of adolescents, we found that, although socially prescribed perfectionism (a recognized vulnerability factor, see below) is a relatively stable personality construct, minor short-term fluctuations in perfectionism were accounted for by changes in depression and anxiety (O'Connor & Rasmussen, 2011). This suggests that the underlying vulnerability is present irrespective of mood, but that it becomes particularly activated in the context of depression/anxiety.

The differential activation model of suicidal behaviour (Williams, Barnhofer, Crane, & Beck, 2005; Williams, Crane, *et al.*, 2005) accounts for these trait and state components. This model posits that associations made when an individual is in a low mood are reactivated when the same mood is encountered again. Within the context of suicidal risk, there is an important consequence of such network associations: if suicidal ideation or behaviour is experienced in one depressive episode it is more likely to be triggered and experienced in subsequent episodes. Although mood may return to normal, the associations remain but they are latent, becoming more and more easily activated following each episode of low mood. Consequently, it is this differential activation that accounts, in part, for the increased repetition of suicidal ideation/behaviour once initially experienced. The extent to which differential activation acts as a motivational and/or volitional moderator varies as a function of whether suicidal ideation and/or behaviour are experienced during a depressive mood or triggered by defeat or entrapment.

Motivational and volitional phases   As noted earlier, the arrested flight model of suicidal behaviour (Williams, 2001) was a key driver for the IMV model. Consequently, the core pathway to suicidal behaviour which traverses both the motivational and volitional phases is adapted from Williams and colleagues' model (Williams, 2001; Williams, Barnhofer, *et al.*, 2005; Williams, Crane, *et al.*, 2005). Taking the motivational phase first, Williams posits in his model that the development of suicidal ideation is predicated on feelings of entrapment which have been triggered by the experience of defeat and/or humiliation. The central roles of defeat and entrapment in the aetiology and course of psychological health arose out of the work by Gilbert and colleagues on the origins of depression (e.g., Gilbert & Allan, 1998). Williams extended Gilbert and Allen's work to encompass suicidal behaviour by arguing that, when the desire to escape from a defeating and/or humiliating situation is thwarted, feelings of entrapment ensue and the likelihood of suicidal ideation is increased if there is little hope of rescue, for example, when positive future thinking is absent (Williams, Crane, *et al.*, 2005).

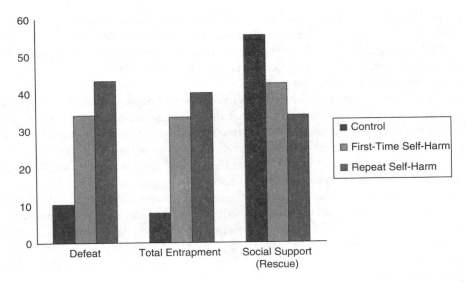

Figure 11.2   Perceptions of the arrested flight variables (defeat, entrapment, and social support) as a function of patient group (from Rasmussen *et al.* (2010). *British Journal of Clinical Psychology, 49,* 15–30).

There is growing empirical evidence for the central tenets of the arrested flight model of suicidal behaviour (O'Connor, 2003; Rasmussen, Fraser, Gotz, MacHale, Mackie, *et al.*, 2010; Williams, Barnhofer, *et al.*, 2005; Williams, Crane, *et al.*, 2005). In a case-control study, O'Connor (2003) found that the arrested flight variables (high inescapability, high defeat, and low social support) significantly discriminated between self-harm patients and controls. Moreover, in the multivariate analyses none of the clinical variables (anxiety, depression, hopelessness) was a statistically significant predictor when considered alongside the arrested flight variables. In a more recent case-control study, Rasmussen *et al.* (2010) compared three groups of patients (first-time self-harm patients versus repeat self-harm patients versus hospital controls) on the arrested flight variables and found that the three groups differed along each of these constructs in the predicted directions (see Figure 11.2). Thus, repeat self-harm patients reported significantly higher levels of entrapment than first-time self-harm patients and hospital controls.

Defeat and humiliation   Within the IMV model, it is hypothesized that sensitivity to signals of defeat and humiliation are determined by background factors (pre-motivational phase). As an example, this sensitivity to signals of defeat may be increased by what we believe others expect of us. In suicidal individuals such expectations are often excessive and unrealistic, with the suicidal individual believing that they will be considered a failure if they do not achieve certain standards (Hewitt, Flett, Sherry, & Caelian, 2006; O'Connor, Whyte, Fraser, Masterton, Miles, *et al.*, 2007). Individuals with such beliefs are thought to score highly on the personality dimension called socially prescribed perfectionism (Hewitt & Flett, 1991; Hewitt *et al.*, 2006; O'Connor *et al.*, 2007; O'Connor & O'Connor,

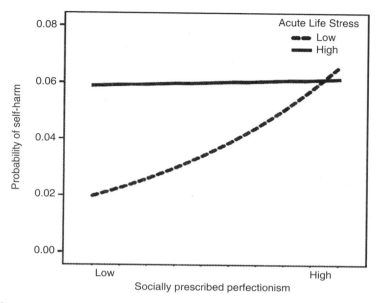

Figure 11.3   The probability of self-harm between Time 1 and Time 2 as a function of acute life stress and socially prescribed perfectionism (from O'Connor *et al.*, 2010. *Behaviour Research and Therapy, 48*, 52–59).

2003). Socially prescribed perfectionism assesses the degree of personal belief that others hold unrealistically high expectations of one's behaviour and that they would be satisfied only with these standards (Hewitt & Flett, 1991).

In a recent study (O'Connor, Rasmussen, & Hawton, 2010), we yielded evidence that points to one mechanism through which socially prescribed perfectionism may increase the risk of self-harm. We tracked 500 adolescents over a period of six months and recorded the number of acute life stressors that they had experienced over this period, as well as recording their socially prescribed perfectionism levels when they entered the study (using the Child and Adolescent Perfectionism Scale (CAPS-14) (O'Connor, Dixon, & Rasmussen, 2009; Flett, Hewitt, Boucher, Davidson, & Munro, 1997)). Therefore, we were able to determine the extent to which the personal experience of acute life stress and socially prescribed perfectionism predicted self-harm.

As expected, those adolescents who had encountered high levels of acute life stress (including bullying, sexual abuse, concerns about sexual orientation, etc.) were more likely to report self-harm than those who reported low levels of stress (31 out of the 500 adolescents reported self-harm during the six months of the study). In addition, we found evidence of a perfectionism–diathesis interaction, although the moderating effect was not quite as we had anticipated. Our data suggest that socially prescribed perfectionism lowers stress tolerance. In other words, it seems to have a 'stress-threshold lowering effect' (O'Connor *et al.*, 2010): among social perfectionists, relatively low levels of acute stress were associated with a self-harm episode (see Figure 11.3). This latter finding is consistent with the differential activation theory of suicidal behaviour (Williams, Crane, *et al.*, 2005), but needs to be investigated in more detail within an experimental paradigm, to determine whether experiences and appraisals of stressors vary as a function of socially prescribed perfectionism.

From defeat and humiliation to entrapment: threat to self moderators   Although entrapment can be triggered by defeat/humiliation, it is not inevitable that the experience of defeat/humiliation will lead to entrapment: *threat to self moderators* (*TSM*) have the potential to increase the likelihood that the former leads to feelings of entrapment. TSMs are defined as any variable that attenuates or strengthens the relationship between threat to self-appraisals, that is, defeat/humiliation, and entrapment. Components within the TSM are activated in response to a defeating or humiliating appraisal (usually following the experience of negative life stress or a change in severity of existing chronic stress). Social problem-solving is a likely candidate as a moderator of the defeat–entrapment relationship, since it is activated in an attempt to resolve the defeating/humiliating situation. Over-general autobiographical memory biases are also included here as they are known to be associated with impaired social problem-solving (e.g., Evans, Williams, O'Loughlin, & Howells, 1992; Pollock & Williams, 2001). The evidence implicating social problem-solving and autobiographical memory in the suicidal process is well established (Speckens & Hawton, 2005; Williams, Barnhofer, Crane, Hermans, Raes, *et al.*, 2007). Over-general memories are incomplete, lacking in specific detail, and often referring to activities/objects without specifying a time period or covering a time period which is greater than a day (Evans *et al.*, 1992). Given that we rely heavily on memories to solve interpersonal problems, it is easy to see how this over-general memory bias impairs problem-solving and is implicated in emotional distress more generally (Pollock & Williams, 2001; Williams *et al.*, 2007).

Rumination, defined as enduring and repetitive, self-focused thinking in response to depressed mood (Rippere, 1977), is another TSM. Despite its well-established and persistent relationship with depression, its relationship with suicidality has only recently been established (Morrison & O'Connor, 2008). For example, Smith, Alloy, and Abramson (2006) found that rumination predicted the presence and duration of suicidal ideation over 2.5 years. Recent research also suggests that a particular type of rumination, known as brooding rumination, is especially deleterious in the suicidal process. According to Treynor, Gonzalez, and Nolen-Hoeksema (2003) brooding is the 'passive comparison of one's current situation with some unachieved standard' (p. 256). It is easy to see how this type of thinking could be problematic: although the individual is thinking about the cause(s) of their distress, they are not actively seeking to solve the problem; rather, they are dwelling on their distress, comparing their situation unfavourably with the outcome that they desire, but they are not actively pursuing the desired outcome. This type of thinking can escalate and explains, in part, the sometimes apparent time lag between the experience of defeat and entrapment and subsequent suicidality (Williams, Crane, *et al.*, 2005). Rumination is also known to interfere with autobiographical memory and social problem-solving (Watkins & Baracaia, 2002; Watkins, Teasdale, & Williams, 2000), thereby highlighting further mechanisms that account for the former's relationship with suicidality. There is also some observational evidence that rumination is elevated among individuals who score highly on measures of self-criticism (O'Connor & Noyce, 2008).

From entrapment to suicidal ideation/intent: motivational moderators   The IMV model suggests that the presence/absence of *motivational moderators* (*MM*) increases/decreases the likelihood that entrapment is translated into suicidal ideation and intent. A motivational moderator is broadly defined as any factor (moderator) that changes the likelihood that entrapment will lead to suicidal ideation and intent. Absence of positive future thinking, lack of goal re-engagement, and low levels of social support would be typical of motivational moderators – as they increase the likelihood that suicidal ideation will develop following entrapment. They would include what Williams (2001) describes as rescue factors in his arrested flight model. In the following section, I consider some of the evidence for positive future thinking and goal re-engagement.

There is now a robust body of evidence confirming that a pattern of future thinking characterized by a dearth of positive thinking is particularly implicated in the aetiology of suicide risk independent of depression (Hunter & O'Connor, 2003; MacLeod, Pankhania, Lee, & Mitchell, 1997; MacLeod, Tata, Evans, Tyrer, Schmidt, *et al.*, 1998; O'Connor, 2010). Conversely, suicidal individuals are not preoccupied by impending doom or overwhelmed by negative future expectations (MacLeod *et al.*, 1997, 1998; O'Connor *et al.*, 2007). In clinical studies, positive future thinking is usually assessed with the Future Thinking Task (FTT) (MacLeod *et al.*, 1997). The FTT asks respondents to think of as many things as possible that they are looking forward to (positive future thinking) or worried about (negative future thinking) across different future time frames (e.g., the next week, the next year, the next 5–10 years). These things, events, or future experiences can be anything (e.g., playing in the park with my son); the only constraint is that there must be a realistic possibility of their occurrence. In terms of the IMV and the motivational moderator construct, following defeat/humiliation and entrapment, the development of suicide ideation/intent should be significantly more likely when there is a concomitant paucity in positive future thinking. I have found that this is, indeed, the case. In a recent clinical study (largely consisting of patients admitted to hospital following an overdose), impaired positive future thinking moderated the relationship between entrapment and suicidal ideation (Rasmussen *et al.*, 2010). In other words, patients who felt trapped (i.e., high entrapment) were significantly more suicidal if they also had impaired positive future thinking, compared with those with high levels of positive future thinking.

Nor does positive future thinking appear to be an artefact of mood, as the impairment in positive future thinking is not accounted for by severity of depressive symptoms (Hunter & O'Connor, 2003; MacLeod *et al.*, 1997; O'Connor, Connery, & Cheyne, 2000). Moreover, these expectancies are powerful predictors of suicidal ideation, in the short term, at least. For example, I compared the relative strength of the widely used Beck Hopelessness Scale (BHS) (Beck, Schuyler, & Herman, 1974), an established index of generalized hopelessness for the future, with positive future thinking, as assessed via the FTT (O'Connor, Fraser, Whyte, MacHale, & Masterton, 2008). After controlling for baseline depression, anxiety, and suicidal ideation in a sample of repeat self-harm patients ($n = 144$), impaired positive future thinking but not generalized hopelessness predicted residual suicidal ideation 2.5 months after admission to hospital. In short, there is reasonable evidence that positive future thinking is a motivational moderator of the entrapment–suicidal ideation relationship. However, the extent to which it predicts repeat self-harm and completed suicide has yet to be established.

Psychological science studies focusing on self-regulation have grown markedly in recent years (e.g., Baumeister & Vohs, 2004; Carver & Scheier, 1998). Self-regulation is defined as 'the many processes by which the psyche exercises control over its functions, states and inner processes' (Vohs & Baumeister, 2004, p. 1). Indeed, one of the processes implicit in adaptive self-regulation is the successful identification, pursuit, and attainment of goals. Moreover, the self-regulation literature has recently been extended to include dysfunctional regulation, characterized by a failure to relinquish a goal that is not attainable and the subsequent re-engagement in new goals when existing goal pursuit is thwarted (Wrosch, Scheier, Carver, & Schulz, 2003a; Wrosch, Scheier, Miller, Schulz, & Carver, 2003a). To investigate these dual processes, Wrosch and colleagues developed a new psychological measure (Wrosch *et al.*, 2003b), the Goal Adjustment Scale, to assess goal disengagement (i.e., disengaging from an unattainable goal) and goal re-engagement (i.e., redirecting attention to a new attainable goal).

For the present purposes, I reasoned that goals would be akin to positive future thoughts. Therefore, in a study of suicide attempters (O'Connor *et al.*, 2009), I posited that suicidality would be associated with low levels of goal re-engagement. In addition, I also thought that the absence of goal re-engagement would be exacerbated if an individual had also disengaged from existing goals. I wondered what would motivate an individual to continue living if they are not engaged in goal pursuit, especially if one considers that goals give meaning to people's lives (Carver, 2004). Consistent with this view, Carver and Scheier (1998) suggested that the concept of complete disengagement (i.e., high goal disengagement and low goal re-engagement) may be central to the suicidal impulse. This self-regulatory approach has merit: I found levels of suicidal ideation a few months following a suicide attempt to be significantly higher among those who had reported high levels of disengagement and low levels of goal re-engagement in the 24 hours following their suicide attempt (O'Connor *et al.*, 2009). In sum, these findings suggest that goal adjustment is another potential motivational moderator that could be targeted therapeutically to reduce the likelihood that entrapment triggers suicidal ideation/intent. It would also be useful to improve understanding as to how and why disengagement happens and what prevents goal re-engagement. For example, to what extent are trait personality factors, such as perfectionism and pessimism, implicated?

From suicidal ideation/intent to suicidal behaviour: volitional moderators   This section addresses the transition of suicidal intent to suicidal behaviour. As noted above, the majority of models of suicide risk fail to make predictions about those factors which are specifically associated with ideation/intention versus those which are associated with translating ideation/intention into action. The IMV model is explicit in this regard as it proposes that a group of factors, the *volitional moderators* (*VM*), determines the conditions and situations in which an individual is at increased risk of suicidal behaviour. A volitional moderator is defined as any factor which bridges the suicidal intention–behaviour gap (i.e., any factor that renders it more or less likely that an individual will act on their suicidal intentions). This behavioural enaction phase is derived from the TPB and is consistent with Williams' arrested flight model and Joiner's interpersonal–psychological model of suicidal behaviour (Joiner, 2005). Having access to the means of suicide, having the capability to attempt suicide, knowing others who have engaged in suicidal behaviour, and impulsivity are examples of volitional moderators.

The concepts of behavioural enaction and bridging the intention–behaviour gap are well established within health psychology. Their use has expanded markedly in recent decades because behavioural scientists were frustrated by their relative failure in predicting behaviour from intention (in other words, they were quite good at predicting intention and much less effective at predicting behaviour) (Orbell & Sheeran, 1998; Sheeran, 2002). Whereas behavioural scientists are often keen to identify the barriers to behavioural enaction (i.e., why there is a gap between intention and behaviour), suicidologists wish to obviate the bridging of the intention–behaviour gap. Therefore, a better understanding of those factors which bridge the intention–behaviour gap will inform the development of interventions to reduce the likelihood of behavioural enaction. To this end, a key development within the intention–behaviour gap field was proffered by Gollwitzer (1999), who described implementation intentions, which are defined as plans which link critical situations to goal-directed responses. In short, these are plans which include thinking about the when, the where, and the how of behavioural enaction (i.e., action and coping planning).

In the traditional health behaviour context, it is thought that the mere formation of these simple plans passes control of the goal-directed behaviour over to the environment, such that when the environmental cues are subsequently encountered, the target behaviour is elicited (and perhaps automatically (Gollwitzer, 1999)). For present purposes, the when, the where, and the how relate to planning when an individual will attempt suicide, where will that be, and what method will they choose. The attraction of implementation intentions in understanding suicide risk is three-fold: first, they are akin to developing a suicidal plan, which is a well-established indicator of elevated risk of completed suicide (Jobes, 2006); second, in a meta-analysis of 94 independent tests, they had a medium–large effect on behavioural enaction/goal attainment (Gollwitzer & Sheeran, 2006); and, third, they provide opportunities for intervention. Indeed, O'Connor, Armitage, and Smyth (2011) have developed a brief psychosocial intervention based on the implementation intentions literature to reduce self-harm. This pilot trial (still in progress) aims to investigate whether administering a volitional help sheet (which encourages respondents to link critical situations when they are tempted to self-harm with solutions other than self-harm) to patients in hospital following an episode of self-harm will reduce repetition and suicidal ideation.

Finally, Joiner's acquired capability concept is also a volitional moderator. Acquired capability describes one's ability to act upon suicidal desires or to enact lethal self-injury, and is thought to increase via exposure and habituation to self-injury (Joiner, 2005; Van Orden, Witte, Gordon, Bender, & Joiner, 2008). In short, higher levels of capability increase the likelihood that suicidal intent is translated into behaviour. Full details of the interpersonal–psychological model are described in Chapter 10.

Conclusions

I have presented a new integrated model of suicidal behaviour which accounts for the complex interplay between biology, psychology, and social factors in the aetiology and course of suicidal behaviour. The IMV model builds on the empirical and conceptual evidence from other models and perspectives and is able to make differential predictions in respect of suicidal ideation/intent and behaviour. However, the presentation of the model is only the first step. The model needs to be further tested and refined, to determine the extent to which factors associated with, for example, the motivational phase are phase-specific. It should be noted that I have included only a selection of likely moderators to illustrate the model; there are others which require further empirical attention. In addition, although I believe that factors like social problem-solving are primarily modera-tors of the defeat–entrapment–suicidality pathway, there may be occasions when they act as mediators being causally related to a preceding factor. There has also been a recent sug-gestion that defeat and entrapment are better represented as a single construct (Taylor, Wood, Gooding, Johnson, & Tarrier, 2009). My sense is that they are distinct but overlap-ping constructs, in the same way that depression and hopelessness are correlated but have considerable discriminant validity. However, further investigation is required to disentan-gle the operationalization of a construct (i.e., how it is measured) from its conceptualiza-tion (i.e., what characterizes the construct).

We need to test each of the mediating and moderating pathways in turn to establish which factors are necessary and sufficient to lead to suicidal behaviour. As suicidology has been dominated by the search for risk factors since its inception, greater emphasis should also be given to the further identification and promotion of protective factors. Indeed, the IMV model identifies three stages along the motivational–volitional pathway for potential intervention, not to mention numerous opportunities to ameliorate risk in the pre-motivational phase. For example, we could bolster social problem-solving, thereby attenu-ating the defeat/humiliation–entrapment path, or we could increase positive future thinking in order to reduce the likelihood of developing suicidal ideation/intent following entrapment. In conclusion, the IMV model details an integrated theoretical framework which should stimulate further research questions, as well as pointing to a range of poten-tial opportunities to reduce the risk that the experience of emotional distress manifests itself as suicidal ideation and behaviour.

References

Ajzen, I. (1991). The theory of planned behavior. *Organizational Behavior and Human Decision Processes, 50*, 179–211.

Bandura, A. (1997). *Self-efficacy: The exercise of control.* New York: Freeman.

Barrow, J. C. & Moore, C. A. (1983). Group interventions with perfectionistic thinking. *Personnel and Guidance Journal, 61*, 612–615.

Baumeister, R. F. (1990). Suicide as escape from self. *Psychological Review, 97*, 90–113.

Baumeister, R. F. & Vohs, K. D. (Eds.) (2004). *Handbook of Self-regulation: Research, theory, and applications* (pp. 13–39). New York: Guilford Press.

Beck, A. T., Schuyler, D., & Herman, I. (1974). Development of suicidal intent scales. In A. T. Beck, H. L. P. Resnik, & D. J. Lettieri (Eds.), *The Prediction of Suicide* (pp. 45–56). Philadelphia, PA: Charles Press.

Beck, A. T., Steer, R. A., Kovacs, M., & Garrison, B. (1985). Hopelessness and eventual suicide: A 10-year prospective study of patients hospitalized with suicidal ideation. *American Journal of Psychiatry, 142*, 559–563.

Brezo, J., Paris, J., & Turecki, G. (2006). Personality traits as correlates of suicidal ideation, suicide attempts, and suicide completions: A systematic review. *Acta Psychiatrica Scandinavica, 113*, 180–206.

Carver, C. S. (2004). Self-regulation of action and affect. In R. F. Baumeister & K. D. Vohs (Eds.), *Handbook of Self-regulation: Research, theory, and applications* (pp. 13–39). New York: Guilford Press.

Carver, C. S., & Scheier, M. F. (1998). *On the Self-regulation of Behavior*. New York: Cambridge University Press.

Ellis, T. (2001). Psychotherapy with suicidal patients. In D. Lester (Ed.), *Suicide Prevention: Resources for the millennium*. (pp. 129–151). Philadelphia, PA: Brunner-Routledge.

Ellis, T. E. & Rutherford, B. (2008). Cognition and suicide: Two decades of progress. *International Journal of Cognitive Therapy, 1*, 47–68.

Evans, J., Williams, J. M. G., O'Loughlin, S., & Howells, K. (1992). Autobiographical memory and problem-solving strategies of parasuicide patients. *Psychological Medicine, 22*, 399–405.

Flett, G. L., Hewitt, P. L., Boucher, D. J., Davidson, L. A., & Munro, Y. (1997). *The child–adolescent perfectionism scale: Development, validation, and association with adjustment*. Unpublished manuscript.

Gilbert, P. & Allan, S. (1998). The role of defeat and entrapment (arrested flight) in depression: An exploration of an evolutionary view. *Psychological Medicine, 22*, 399–405.

Gollwitzer, P. M. (1999). Implementation intentions: Strong effects of simple plans. *American Psychologist, 54*, 493–503.

Gollwitzer, P. M. & Sheeran, P. (2006). Implementation intentions and goal achievement: A meta-analysis of effects and processes. *Advances in Experimental Social Psychology, 38*, 69–119.

Hewitt, P. L. & Flett, G. L. (1991). Perfectionism in the self and social contexts: conceptualization, assessment, and association with psychopathology. *Journal of Personality and Social Psychology, 60*, 456–470.

Hewitt, P. L., Flett, G. L., Sherry, S. B., & Caelian, C. (2006). Trait perfectionism and suicide behavior. In T. Ellis (Ed.), *Cognition and Suicide: Theory, research, and practice* (pp. 215–235). Washington, DC: APA.

Hunter, E. C. & O'Connor, R. C. (2003). Hopelessness and future thinking in parasuicide: The role of perfectionism. *British Journal of Clinical Psychology, 42*, 355–365.

Jobes, D. A. (2006). *Managing Suicidal Risk. A collaborative approach*. New York: Guilford Press.

Johnson, J., Gooding, P., & Tarrier, N. (2008). Suicide risk in schizophrenia: Explanatory models and clinical implications, The Schematic Appraisal Model of Suicide (SAMS). *Psychology and Psychotherapy, 81*, 55–77.

Joiner, T. (2005). *Why People Die by Suicide*. Boston, MA: Harvard University Press.

Kessler, R. C., Borges, G., & Walters, E. E. (1999). Prevalence of and risk factors for suicide attempts in the national comorbidity survey. *Archives of General Psychiatry, 56*, 617–626.

MacLeod, A. K., Pankhania, B., Lee, M., & Mitchell, D. (1997). Parasuicide, depression and anticipation of positive and negative future experiences. *Psychological Medicine, 27*, 973–977.

MacLeod, A. K., Tata, P., Evans, K., Tyrer, P., Schmidt, U., Davidson, K., Thornton, S., & Catalan, J. (1998). Recovery of positive future thinking within a high-risk parasuicide group: Results from a pilot randomized controlled trial. *British Journal of Clinical Psychology, 37*, 371–379.

Mann, J. J., Apter, A., Bertolote, J., Beautrais, A., Currier, D., Haas, A., Hegerl, U., Lönqvist, J., Malone, K., Marusic, A., Mehlum, L., Patton, G., Phillips, M., Rutz, W., Rihmer, Z.,

Schmidtke, A., Shaffer, D., Silverman, M., Takahashi, Y., Varnik, A., Wasserman, D., Yip, P., & Hendin, H. (2005). Suicide prevention strategies: A systematic review. *Journal of American Medical Association, 294*, 2064–2074.

Mann, J. J., Waternaux, C., Haas, G. L., & Malone, K. M. (1999). Towards a clinical model of suicidal behavior in psychiatric patients. *American Journal of Psychiatry, 156*, 181–189.

Michel, K. & Valach, L. (2001). Suicide as goal-directed action. In K. van Heeringen (Ed.), *Understanding Suicidal Behaviour. The suicidal process approach to research, treatment and prevention* (pp. 230–254). Chichester: John Wiley & Sons, Ltd.

Morrison, R. & O'Connor, R. C. (2008). Rumination and suicidality: A systematic review. *Suicide and Life-Threatening Behavior, 37*, 698–714.

O'Connor, R. C. (2003). Suicidal behaviour as a cry of pain: Test of a psychological model. *Archives of Suicide Research, 7*, 297–308.

O'Connor, R. C. (2010). Psychological perspectives on suicidal behaviour. In U. Kumar & M. K. Mandal (Eds.), *Suicidal Behaviour: Assessment of people at risk.* (pp. 1–19). India: Sage Publications.

O'Connor, R. C., Armitage, C. J., & Gray, L. (2006). The role of clinical and social cognitive variables in parasuicide. *British Journal of Clinical Psychology, 45*, 465–481.

O'Connor, R. C., Armitage, C. J., & Smyth, R. (2011). A Pilot Volitional Helpsheet to Reduce Self-harm: Study protocol, unpublisher paper.

O'Connor, R. C., Connery, H., & Cheyne, W. (2000). Hopelessness: The role of depression, future directed thinking and cognitive vulnerability. *Psychology, Health & Medicine, 5*, 155–161.

O'Connor, R. C., Dixon, D., & Rasmussen, S. (2009). The structure and temporal stability of the Child and Adolescent Perfectionism Scale. *Psychological Assessment, 21*, 437–443.

O'Connor, R. C., Fraser, L., Whyte, M.C., MacHale, S., & Masterton, G. (2008). A comparison of specific positive future expectancies and global hopelessness as predictors of suicidal ideation in a prospective study of repeat self-harmers. *Journal of Affective Disorders, 110*, 207–214.

O'Connor, R. C., Fraser, L., Whyte, M. C., MacHale, S., & Masterton, G. (2009). Self-regulation of unattainable goals in suicide attempters: The relationship between goal disengagement, goal re-engagement and suicidal ideation. *Behaviour Research and Therapy, 47*, 164–169.

O'Connor, R. C. & Noyce, R. (2008). Personality and cognitive processes: Self-criticism and different types of rumination as predictors of suicidal ideation. *Behaviour Research and Therapy, 46*, 392–401.

O'Connor, R. C. & O'Connor, D. B. (2003). Predicting hopelessness and psychological distress: The role of perfectionism and coping. *Journal of Counseling Psychology, 50*, 362–372.

O'Connor, R. C. & Rasmussen, S. (2011). The stability of perfectionism over time as a function of mood. Unpublished data, University of Stirling.

O'Connor, R. C., Rasmussen, S., & Hawton, K. (2010). Predicting depression, anxiety and self-harm in adolescents: The role of perfectionism and acute life stress. *Behaviour Research and Therapy, 48*, 52–59.

O'Connor, R., & Sheehy, N. (2000). *Understanding Suicidal Behaviour.* Chichester: John Wiley & Sons, Ltd.

O'Connor, R. C., Whyte, M. C., Fraser, L., Masterton, G., Miles, J., & MacHale, S. (2007). Predicting short-term outcome in well-being following suicidal behaviour: The conjoint effects of social perfectionism and positive future thinking. *Behaviour Research and Therapy, 45*, 1543–1555.

Orbell, S. & Sheeran, P. (1998). 'Inclined abstainers': A problem for predicting health-related behaviour. *British Journal of Social Psychology, 37*, 151–165.

Pollock, L. R. & Williams, J. M. G. (2001). Effective problem-solving in suicide attempters depends on specific autobiographical recall. *Suicide and Life-Threatening Behavior, 31*, 386–396.

Rasmussen, S., Fraser, L., Gotz, M., MacHale, S., Mackie, R., Masterton, G., McConachie, S., & O'Connor, R. C. (2010). Elaborating the Cry of Pain model of suicidality: Testing a psychological model in a sample of first-time and repeat self-harm patients. *British Journal of Clinical Psychology, 49,* 15–30.

Rasmussen, S., O'Connor, R. C., & Brodie, D. (2008). The role of perfectionism and autobiographical memory in a sample of parasuicide patients. *Crisis, 9,* 64–72.

Rippere, V. (1977). 'What's the thing to do when you're feeling depressed?' A pilot study. *Behaviour Research and Therapy, 15,* 185–191.

Rudd, M. D., Joiner, T., & Rajab, M. H. (2001). *Treating Suicidal Behavior. An effective, time-limited approach.* New York: Guilford Press.

Schotte, D. E. & Clum, G. A. (1987). Problem-solving skills in psychiatric patients. *Journal of Consulting and Clinical Psychology, 55,* 49–54.

Sheeran, P. (2002). Intention–behaviour relations: A conceptual and empirical review. In W. Stroebe & M. Hewstone (Eds.), *European Review of Social Psychology,* Volume 12 (pp. 1–30). New York: John Wiley & Sons, Inc.

Shneidman, E. S. (1985). *Definition of Suicide.* Chichester: John Wiley & Sons, Ltd.

Shneidman, E. S. & Farberow, N. L. (Eds.) (1957). *Clues to Suicide.* New York: Blakiston Division, McGraw-Hill.

Smith, J. M., Alloy, L. B., & Abramson, L. Y. (2006). Cognitive vulnerability to depression, rumination, hopelessness and suicidal ideation: Multiple pathways to self-injurious thinking. *Suicide and Life-Threatening Behavior, 36,* 443–454.

Speckens, A. E. M. & Hawton, K. (2005). Social problem-solving in adolescents with suicidal behavior: A systematic review. *Suicide and Life-Threatening Behavior, 35,* 365–387.

Taylor, P. J., Wood, A. M., Gooding, P., Johnson, J., & Tarrier, N. (2009). Are defeat and entrapment best defined as a single construct? *Personality and Individual Differences, 47,* 795–797.

Treynor, W., Gonzalez, R., & Nolen-Hoeksema, S. (2003). Rumination reconsidered: A psychometric analysis. *Cognitive Therapy and Research, 27,* 247–259.

Van Heeringen, K. (2001). Towards a psychobiological model of the suicidal process. In K. van Heeringen (Ed.), *Understanding Suicidal Behaviour.* Chichester: John Wiley & Sons, Ltd.

Van Orden, K. A., Witte, T. K., Gordon, K. H., Bender, T. W., & Joiner, T. E. (2008). Suicidal desire and the capability for suicide: Tests of the Interpersonal–Psychological Theory of Suicidal Behavior among adults. *Journal of Consulting and Clinical Psychology, 76,* 72–83.

Vohs, K. D. & Baumeister, R. F. (2004). Understanding self-regulation: An Introduction. In R. F. Baumeister & K. D. Vohs (Eds.), *Handbook of Self-Regulation: Research, theory and its applications* (pp. 1–12). New York: Guilford Press.

Watkins, E. & Baracia, S. (2002). Rumination and social problem-solving in depression. *Behaviour Research and Therapy, 40,* 1179–1189.

Watkins, E., Teasdale, J. D., & Williams, J. M. G. (2000). Decentring and distraction reduce over-general autobiographical memory in depression. *Psychological Medicine, 30,* 911–920.

Weishaar, M. E. (2000). Cognitive risk factors in suicide (pp. 113–139). In R. W. Maris, S. S. Canetto, J. L., McIntosh & M. M. Silverman (Eds.), *Review of Suicidology 2000.* New York: Guilford Press.

Wenzel, A. & Beck, A. T. (2008). A cognitive model of suicidal behavior: Theory and treatment. *Applied and Preventive Psychology, 12,* 189–201.

Wenzlaff, R. & Wegner, D. (2000). Thought suppression. *Annual Review of Psychology, 51,* 59–91.

Williams, J. M. G. (2001). *Suicide and Attempted Suicide: Understanding the cry of pain.* London: Penguin.

Williams, J. M. G., Barnhofer, T., Crane, C., & Beck, A. T. (2005). Problem-solving deteriorates following mood challenge in formerly depressed patients with a history of suicidal ideation. *Journal of Abnormal Psychology*, *114*, 421–431.

Williams, J. M. G., Barnhofer, T., Crane, C., Hermans, D., Raes, F., Watkins, E., & Dalgleish, T. (2007). Autobiographical memory specificity and emotional disorder. *Psychological Bulletin*, *133*, 122–148.

Williams, J. M. G., Crane, C., Barnhofer, T., & Duggan, D. (2005). Psychology and suicidal behaviour: Elaborating the entrapment model. In K. Hawton (Ed.), *Prevention and Treatment of Suicidal Behaviour: From science to practice* (pp. 71–89). Oxford: Oxford University Press.

Williams, J. M. G. & Pollock, L. (2000). Psychology of suicide behaviour. In K. Hawton & K. van Heeringen (Eds.), *The International Handbook of Suicide and Suicidal Behaviour* (pp. 79–93). Chichester: John Wiley & Sons, Ltd.

Williams, J. M. G. & Pollock, L. (2001). Psychological aspects of the suicidal process. In K. van Heeringen (Ed.), *Understanding Suicidal Behaviour: The suicidal process approach to research, treatment and prevention* (pp. 76–94). Chichester: John Wiley & Sons, Ltd.

Williams, J. M. G., van der Does, A. J. W., Barnhofer, T., Crane, C., & Segal, Z. S. (2008). Cognitive reactivity, suicidal ideation and future fluency: Preliminary investigation of a differential activation theory of hopelessness/suicidality. *Cognitive Therapy and Research*, *32*, 83–104.

Wrosch, C., Scheier, M. F., Carver, C. S., & Schulz, R. (2003a). The importance of goal disengagement in adaptive self-regulation: When giving up is beneficial. *Self and Identity*, *2*, 1–20.

Wrosch, C., Scheier, M., F., Miller, G. E., Schulz, R., & Carver, C. S. (2003b). Adaptive self-regulation of unattainable goals: Goal disengagement, goal re-engagement and subjective well-being. *Personality and Social Psychology Bulletin*, *29*, 1494–1508.

CHAPTER TWELVE

Worrying and Rumination as Proximal Risk Factors for Suicidal Behaviour

Ad Kerkhof and Bregje van Spijker

Abstract

Suicidal individuals are often tormented by ruminative, repetitive thoughts. These thoughts, which are commonly heard by clinicians, include: '*I wanted to stop my terrible thoughts*', '*Nobody loves me*', '*I am unlovable*', '*I cannot live alone*', '*I have no future*'. They can be torturing when rehearsed mentally many times a day for many hours. The wish to end consciousness can itself also become a repetitive, compulsive thought that is rehearsed up to 24 hours a day: '*I have to stop thinking*'. We hypothesize that the wish to end these repetitive thoughts is one of the driving forces behind the suicidal act. In the end, the continuous repetition of these statements becomes a compulsion that cannot be controlled. In that sense, repetitive thinking about dying, about stopping consciousness, and associated motives show similarities with characteristics of worrying and rumination. In this chapter, drawing from theory as well as empirical findings, we summarize the similarities between worrying/rumination and suicidal thinking. Theoretically, the chapter explores the notion of *Constructive and Unconstructive Repetitive Thinking* posited by Watkins (2008). The scant empirical findings are summarized. We conclude that, in many instances, suicidal thinking can be usefully conceptualized as a special type of extensive and prolonged worrying or rumination. Further research should endeavour to incorporate worrying or rumination as proximal risk factors in the suicidal process. Finally, we believe that the notion of suicidal worrying or suicidal rumination can be helpful, both in research and in clinical care for suicidal patients.

International Handbook of Suicide Prevention: Research, Policy and Practice, First Edition.
Edited by Rory C. O'Connor, Stephen Platt, Jacki Gordon.
© 2011 John Wiley & Sons, Ltd. Published 2011 by John Wiley & Sons, Ltd.

Introduction

'*My thoughts were so unbearable that I could not endure them any longer*' is one of the most frequently cited motives for attempted suicide (as defined by De Leo, Burgis, Bertolote, Kerkhof, & Bille-Brahe, 2006) in empirical studies and in clinical practice (Hjelmeland, Hawton, Nordvik, Bille-Brahe, De Leo, *et al.*, 2002; Hjelmeland & Hawton, 2004). The unbearability of such thoughts may lie in both the content and the frequency with which they are repeated mentally. The contents of these terrible thoughts have been studied extensively, resulting in the identification of typical suicidal cognitions such as: '*Nobody loves me*'; '*I am unlovable*'; '*I have no future*'; '*My life has no meaning*'; '*I am better off dead*'; '*I can't stand my depression*'; '*When does this stop?*' and '*When will there be an end to my misery?*' These thoughts frequently centre on hopelessness, helplessness, and distress tolerance (Rudd, Joiner, & Rajab, 2001).

The other aspect of the unbearability of these distressing cognitions, their frequency, has not received much attention. The importance of frequency became clear to us when we tried to measure the number of times suicidal cognitions were being rehearsed mentally during a day or the total amount of time spent each day by patients repeating their suicidal cognitions. We discovered that many suicidal clients were repeating their suicidal thoughts several hundred times a day, and that the total amount of time that these suicidal thoughts occupied their minds amounted to 10 to 15 hours per day. In times of crisis they became obsessive intrusions that kept clients awake for several days. The suicidal patients themselves attributed their sleeplessness and vital exhaustion to the impossibility of stopping these thoughts. Some even stated that this irrepressible repetition of suicidal thoughts was decisive in their suicide attempt. A typical example consisted of the endless repetition of a particular thought such as: '*I have to stop thinking*', '*I have to stop thinking*', '*I have to …*'. For those who suffer from these obsessive thoughts, attempting suicide is often perceived as the only way out; suicide seems the logical means of stopping oneself thinking. We concentrate on this relatively neglected part of the suicidal process in this chapter. We recognize that within the psychological domain there are many studies on similar cognitive processes, such as obsessive intrusions, worrying, rumination, or repetitive thinking (see Watkins, 2008). However, these processes are seldom linked to suicidal behaviour. Nevertheless, many similarities can be observed.

Similarities between Suicidal Thinking and Worrying or Rumination

Worrying can be defined as: 'A chain of thoughts and images negatively affect-laden and relatively uncontrollable, as an attempt to engage in mental problem-solving on an issue whose outcome is uncertain but contains the possibility of one or more negative outcomes' (Borkovec, DePree, Pruzinsky, & Robinson, 1983, p. 10). Rumination is defined as: 'Behaviors and thoughts that focus one's attention on one's depressive symptoms and on the implications of these symptoms … repetitively focusing on the fact that one is depressed, on one's symptoms of depression, and on the causes, meanings, and consequences of depressive symptoms' (Nolen-Hoeksema, 1991, p. 569). Typical ruminative thoughts include: '*Why did this happen to me*' and '*Why do I feel so depressed*?' Both definitions emphasize the repetitive character of these processes and the uncontrollability experienced when worrying or ruminating. Worry and rumination are very similar to one another, so much so that they may share the same cognitive processes but involve different content (Watkins, 2008). In general, rumination has been aligned to depression, while worry has been associated with anxiety, but to complicate matters, worrying is evident in depression and rumination is common in anxiety (Covin, Ouimet, Seeds, & Dozois, 2008; Simon, Pollack, Ostacher, Zalta, Chow, *et al.*, 2007). There are numerous other terms that overlap or relate to worry and rumination, including perseverating cognition, stagnating deliberation, anticipatory stress, habitual negative self-thinking, cognitive and emotional processing, and mind-wandering (see Watkins, 2008). However, the most global and neutral term for all of these processes is *repetitive thinking*, proposed by Watkins (2008). Worry, rumination, and repetitive suicidal thinking have similar characteristics and similar consequences. They each characterize a phenomenon that is repetitive (often occurring hundreds of times a day), uncontrollable (people say they cannot control these thoughts from occurring; they often occur without an obvious trigger), unstoppable (they cannot be stopped or postponed), future-oriented ('*My future has no meaning*'; '*I'll never be normal again*'; '*I will always remain a psychiatric patient*'; '*When will this stop?*'), threatening to major personal concerns (a future that threatens the self and threatens relations with close family and friends), and offers neither solution nor relief. Moreover, meta-processing is possible: people can worry about their worries (Wells, 1995), ruminate about their ruminations, and become more suicidal because of their repetitive suicidal thoughts.

These different types of repetitive thinking also have similar consequences: worry, rumination, and repetitive suicidal ideation each produce obsessive attention to particular thoughts and, in respect of the thoughts one wishes to stop, they produce stress, sleeplessness, vital exhaustion, hopelessness, and helplessness. For the most part, they do not contribute to effective problem-solving, sometimes resulting in a desire to end consciousness.

It is not surprising that worry and rumination are related to suicidal ideation: worry and rumination are associated with anxiety and depression, which are, in turn, associated with suicidal ideation. There are other commonalities: worry and rumination are related to neuroticism, probably reflecting a long-term vulnerability that occurs at times of stress; they also obstruct remission in depressed patients and contribute to relapse (Watkins, 2008).

Within the rumination literature, a recent re-evaluation of one of the most commonly used scales to measure rumination identified two different ruminative dimensions, namely, *reflection* and *brooding* (Treynor, Gonzales, & Nolen-Hoeksema, 2003). These two dimensions emerged following factor analysis of the Ruminative Response Scale (Nolen-Hoeksema & Morrow, 1991; Raes, Hermans, & Eelen, 2003). Reflection is concerned with overcoming problems and difficulties and refers to self-focus, which is aimed at problem-solving in response to depressed mood. Brooding is characterized by thinking anxiously and/or gloomily about events, and refers to cognitions which compare one's present situation with another, unachieved benchmark (Morrison & O'Connor, 2008). In a series of recent studies, brooding seems to be particularly relevant in suicidality. However, there is some evidence that reflection may, in some circumstances be protective (see below).

Repetitive Thinking

Repetitive thinking has been defined as: 'A process of thinking attentively, repetitively, or frequently about oneself and one's world, which is at the core of many different models of adjustment and maladjustment' (Segerstrom, Stanton, Alden, & Shortridge, 2003, p. 909). Watkins (2008) argues that repetitive thinking is engaged in whenever there is a reason to do so, mostly in the context of perceived problems or threats. Repetitive thinking can have constructive or unconstructive consequences depending upon certain characteristics of the repetitive thinking process. Repetitive thinking can be adaptive, functional, and beneficial across a range of scenarios, including in successful cognitive processing and recovery from upsetting and traumatic events, adaptive preparation and planning for the future, recovery from depression, and the uptake of health-promoting behaviours. In his review, Watkins suggests that unconstructive repetitive thinking is involved in the onset and maintenance of depression, that it predicts future depression, and increases negative affect when experimentally induced (see Watkins, 2008, p. 177). Questionnaires measuring worry and rumination have also been found to correlate highly with other measures of perseverative thinking, anxiety, and depression (Fresco, Frankel, Mennin, Turk, & Heimberg, 2002; Harrington & Blankenship, 2002; Papageorgiou, 2006; Segerstrom, Tsao, Alden, & Craske, 2000).

   What characterizes constructive and unconstructive repetitive thinking? According to Watkins (2008), there are several properties which are important: the valence of thought content (attention to positive or negative aspects of the self, optimism versus pessimism, etc.), the context (in a negatively valenced intrapersonal or situational context, repetitive thinking would amplify the effect of that context on mood and cognition, e.g.. mood-congruent memory), and the level of construal (the way in which people perceive, comprehend. and interpret actions of others towards him- or herself; higher-level construals are abstract, such as being unlovable, lower-level construals are concrete, such as being afraid of failing your driving test tomorrow). In experimental studies, construals that cause participants most worry are those that tend to be more abstract and less concrete. In respect of suicidal ideation, worrying in general seems to be very abstract. Thoughts about the future, future competency, hopelessness, and helplessness seem to be very abstract global construals which contribute to prolonged worrying.

Worry Components

Research into pathological worry has revealed four major psychological components (Koerner & Dugas, 2006): intolerance of uncertainty (the most important); positive beliefs about worry; negative problem orientation/poor problem-solving; and cognitive avoidance. Koerner and Dugas describe individuals intolerant of uncertainty as people who 'believe that uncertainty is stressful and upsetting, that being uncertain about the future is unfair, that unexpected events are negative and should be avoided, and that uncertainty interferes with one's ability to function' (Koerner & Dugas, 2006, pp. 202–203). When faced with a problem, intolerant individuals prefer a negative outcome to an uncertain one. Intolerance of uncertainty is thought to be a dispositional characteristic. This conceptualization of intolerance of uncertainty has an immediate appeal as it may explain, in part, why suicidal persons worry so much. Facing an uncertain future, people who are high on intolerance will be upset and try to use cognitive avoidance to manage the anxious arousal associated with their anticipation of uncertainty. However, cognitive avoidance inevitably activates suppressed emotions and increases the anxious anticipation of the future. Consequently, we hypothesize that suicidal persons have higher levels of intolerance of uncertainty than non-suicidal persons.

Differential Activation Hypothesis

Many scholars have observed between-episode consistency in the recurrence of suicidal ideation (e.g., Williams, Crane, Barnhofer, van der Does, & Segal, 2006). The differential activation hypothesis posits that during episodes of depression associations are reactivated between sad mood and negative dysfunctional beliefs and cognitive biases. Several key factors determine whether one's initial depression becomes more severe or persistent, including the degree of activation and the content of negative thinking patterns that become accessible in the depressed state (Lau, Segal, & Williams, 2004). Once established, these depressed cognitions are repeated over and over again. Consequently, a small setback or disappointment that leads to a mild mood fluctuation can trigger the chain of negative cognitions that have come to be associated with depression. This is also referred to as cognitive reactivity. If suicidal ideation becomes part of the pattern of thinking, it is more likely to re-emerge the next time the person is depressed. Worrying can trigger this chain of cognitions, and, when operating, this repetitive rehearsal of reactivated cognitions may show characteristics of worrying and rumination.

The differential activation hypothesis arose out of the 'scar hypothesis', which suggests that each successive period of depression leaves a scar on the mind of the patient rendering him or her more vulnerable the next time disappointment or failure is encountered (Lewinsohn, Steinmetz, Larson, & Franklin, 1981). Interestingly, the scar hypothesis in the case of rumination can be considered to be similar to the concept of a long-term vulnerability. In a seven-year longitudinal study by Beevers, Rohde, Stice, and Nolen-Hoeksema (2007), out of a sample of 496 female adolescents who were followed up, 49 experienced a first episode of major depression and then recovered. Subsequent analyses identified 13 'scarring' variables that were elevated during and after the major depressive episode, but all of these were already elevated before the first episode. Negative emotionality, rumination, and social adjustment were elevated prior to the major depressive episode, but they became more pronounced during the episode and then, on recovery, returned to their baseline level (which already was elevated).

Empirical Studies

Morrison and O'Connor (2008) reported that, in 10 out of the 11 studies in their systematic review, higher levels of rumination were associated with increased suicidality. This finding is even more impressive when account is taken of the heterogeneity of methods, samples, and measures of suicidal ideation or behaviour found in the studies. Five studies were cross-sectional, one was a case-control study, and five studies employed a prospective design. In some of the studies, rumination was split into reflection and brooding. In one prospective study by O'Connor, O'Connor, and Marshall (2007), brooding rumination was significantly positively correlated with suicidal ideation. In addition, in another prospective study (O'Connor & Noyce, 2008) brooding, but not reflection, significantly predicted suicidal ideation over a three-month period. However, both studies were conducted among college students, thereby limiting their generalizability. In a one-year prospective study, Miranda and Nolen-Hoeksema (2007) followed a community sample of adults and found that brooding and reflection predicted suicide ideation. Given the paucity of such studies, clearly there is a need for replication of these rumination effects in clinical samples.

One of the few studies to have employed a clinical population was a large-scale cross-sectional study of depressed ($n = 2,383$) and schizophrenic ($n = 1,920$) patients admitted to in-patient psychiatric care (Ahrens & Linden, 1996). In both groups the same set of factors was predictive of suicidality: hopelessness, social withdrawal, lack of activity, and ruminative thinking. Ahrens and Linden (1996) concluded that these factors constitute a suicidality syndrome that is independent of specific major psychiatric disorder: 'These symptoms merely appear to be the expression of an underlying predilection ... which in latent form would exhibit no symptoms. This syndrome only becomes clinically important if it is triggered by negative life situations, of which major psychiatric disorders are clearly prime examples' (Ahrens & Linden, 1996, p. 85).

In a more recent study, which appeared after the Morrison and O'Connor (2008) review, Surrence, Miranda, Marroquin, and Chan (2009) compared 37 young adults with a history of attempted suicide with 59 controls without such a history. They found that brooding was associated with higher self-reported suicidal ideation, whereas reflection was not. However, reflection, and not brooding, interacted with suicide attempt history to predict suicidal ideation. Consequently, the authors concluded that 'among vulnerable individuals, in particular those with a history of a suicide attempt, a higher degree of reflective rumination is associated with increased suicidal ideation' (Surrence et al., 2009, p. 803). These data suggest that the relationship between the components of rumination and suicidal risk vary as a function of suicidal history. In another college student sample studied by the same research group (Chan, Miranda, & Surrence, 2009), depressive symptoms partially mediated the relationship between the impact of life events and suicidal ideation and between brooding and suicidal ideation. This led Chan and colleagues (2009) to conclude that: 'People who brood in response to negative life events may be vulnerable to thinking about suicide, partly due to symptoms of depression, but also as a result of brooding itself' (Chan, Miranda, & Surrence, 2009, p. 123).

A Dutch cross-sectional study (Antypa, van der Does, & Penninx, 2010) examined the association between reactivity of suicidal cognitions during recovery and the presence of suicidal ideation and behaviour during the previous depressive episode. In a hierarchical logistic regression analysis hopelessness, rather than rumination, predicted previous suicidal behaviour. Despite being limited by its retrospective study design, this is an important finding as it suggests that cognitive suicidal reactivity may be mediated largely by hopelessness. The findings of this study need to be replicated using a prospective design in order to determine the relative importance of rumination and hopelessness in the suicidal process.

In a seven-year follow-up study of the Dutch component of the WHO/EURO Multicentre Study on Suicidal Behaviour, a group of 40 suicide attempters showed elevated worry scores on the Penn State Worry Questionnaire (PSWQ; Meyer, Miller, Metzger, & Borkovec, 1990) (mean score 51 compared with 34 in community samples) (Kerkhof, Hermans, Figee, Laeremans, Peters, *et al.*, 2000). PSWQ scores were significantly correlated with depression ($r = 0.49$) and hopelessness ($r = 0.37$).

In a Dutch study by Verwey, Bozdag, van Waarde, van Rooij, De Beurs, *et al.* (2007), attempted suicide patients assessed in hospital showed PSWQ scores well above normal (mean score of 59). When reassessed at home a few days later, they showed PSWQ scores of 62 (compared with 34 in community samples).

Discussion

Although much more sophisticated research designs are required in this domain, especially utilizing clinical samples, there is a preliminary consensus that rumination and worrying are related to suicidal ideation and to depression and hopelessness. Therefore, we conclude that worrying and rumination and associated recurrent hopelessness reflect dispositional characteristics that explain cross-episode consistency in suicidal behaviour. The studies summarized here fit with the literature on hopelessness, depression, and suicidality (e.g., Beck, Brown, Berchick, Stewart, & Steer, 1990).

The results are also concordant with research in the field of self-focused attention (Ingram, 1990), emphasizing the role of self-referent internally generated information in various clinical disorders. Worrying and rumination can be understood as high levels of repetitive self-focused attention.

The results of this review are in line with work on explicit and automatic self-associations related to suicidal ideation. Automatic and explicit anxious and depressed self-associations are related to suicidal ideation and past suicide attempt (Glashouwer, De Jong, Penninx, Kerkhof, *et al.*, 2009). These automatic self-associations may explain why suicidal patients report difficulties in preventing and managing suicidal thoughts.

Clinical Implications

Awareness of worrying and ruminative self-talk by suicidal patients may provide new clues for the treatment of suicidal ideation. Indeed, cognitive behavioural treatment approaches, such as Wells' (2006) meta-cognitive therapy for worry, applied relaxation and cognitive therapy for pathological worry (Borkovec, 2006), and cognitive behavioural treatment targeting intolerance of uncertainty (Robichaud & Dugas, 2006), have led to good progress in the treatment of pathological worry and rumination. These approaches could usefully be modified for the more depressed (and anxious) suicidal patients. Although rumination in depression is now better recognized and addressed as part of the treatment of depression, more work is required to determine which treatments are most effective. Moreover, exercises fostering worry postponement, positive worrying, distraction, mindfulness, and so on can be helpful in psychological and psychiatric treatment. It would also be helpful to harness the Internet by developing and evaluating web-based self-help interventions for suicidal ideation which incorporate components focusing on rumination and worrying. In the Netherlands such a web-based intervention is now being tested (van Spijker, van Straten, & Kerkhof, 2010). This intervention is based mainly on CBT, but also makes use of techniques derived from Dialectical Behaviour Therapy, Mindfulness Based Cognitive Therapy, and Problem-Solving Treatment. It consists of six modules, each of which contains theory and several exercises. The repetitive style of thinking is addressed in the first module. Accompanying exercises aimed at reducing worry, for example, by confining (suicidal) worrying to 2×15 minute sessions per day, are also included in the first module. The second module targets improving one's toleration and regulation of intense emotions. In the third module, the ABC model is explained (A = Activating event, B = Belief about the event, C = Consequence, i.e., a feeling is a consequence of the belief about the event and not a direct consequence of the event itself), followed by a focus on common distortions in thinking in the fourth module. The fifth module concerns challenging one's negative thoughts. In the sixth and final module, attention is directed at relapse prevention. The results of this ongoing study are not yet available and the efficacy of such an intervention has yet to be determined. In clinical practice, the notion of suicidal worrying has been welcomed by chronic suicidal patients and this has been helpful in individual cases (Kerkhof & van Luyn, 2010). Indeed, clinicians who treat suicidal patients have been trained in the application of worry techniques and they report finding such techniques easy to apply.

Conclusion

In conclusion, there is some empirical evidence that worrying and rumination may be proximal risk factors for suicidal behaviour. This is a new and additional way of explaining the development of suicidal phenomena, in terms that appear helpful in understanding and treating suicidal individuals, especially those that think about suicide repetitively for many hours per day.

References

Ahrens, B. & Linden, M. (1996). Is there a suicidality syndrome independent of specific major psychiatric disorder? Results of a split-half multiple regression analysis. *Acta Psychiatrica Scandinavica, 94*, 79–86.

Antypa, N., van der Does, A. J. W., & Penninx, B. W. J. H. (2010). Cognitive reactivity: Investigation of a potentially treatable marker of suicide risk in depression. *Journal of Affective Disorders, 122,* 46–52.

Beck, A. T., Brown, G., Berchick, R. J., Stewart, B. I., & Steer, R. A. (1990). Relationship between hopelessness and ultimate suicide. A replication with psychiatric outpatients. *American Journal of Psychiatry, 1472,* 190–195.

Beevers, C. G., Rohde, P., Stice, E., & Nolen-Hoeksema, S. (2007). Recovery from major depressive disorder among female adolescents: A prospective test of the scar hypothesis. *Journal of Consulting and Clinical Psychology, 75,* 888–900.

Borkovec, T. D., DePree, J. A., Pruzinsky, T., & Robinson, E. (1983). Preliminary exploration of worry: some characteristics and processes. *Behaviour Research and Therapy, 21,* 9–16.

Borkovec, T. D. (2006). Applied relaxation and cognitive therapy for pathological worry and generalized anxiety disorder. In G. C. L. Davey & A. Wells (Eds.), *Worry and its Psychological Disorders.* (pp. 273–288). Chichester: John Wiley & Sons, Ltd.

Chan, S., Miranda, R., & Surrence, K (2009). Subtypes of rumination in the relationship between negative life events and suicidal ideation. *Archives of Suicide Research, 13,* 123–125.

Covin, R., Ouimet, A. J., Seeds, P. M., & Dozois, D. J. A. (2008). A meta-analysis of CBT for pathological worry among clients with GAD. *Journal of Anxiety Disorders, 22,* 108–116.

De Leo, D., Burgis, S., Bertolote, J. M., Kerkhof, A. J. M., & Bille-Brahe, U. (2006). Definitions of suicidal behaviour. Lesson learned from the WHO/EURO Multicentre Study on Suicidal Behaviour, *Crisis, 27,* 4–15.

Fresco, D. M., Frankel, A. N. Mennin, D. S., Turk, C. L., & Heimberg, R. G. (2002). Distinct and overlapping features of rumination and worry: The relationship of cognitive production to negative affective states. *Cognitive Therapy and Research, 26,* 179–188.

Glashouwer, K. A., De Jong, P. J., Penninx, B. W. J. H., Kerkhof, A. J. F. M., van Dyck, R., & Ormel, J. (2009). Do automatic self-associations relate to suicidal ideation? *Journal of Psychopathology and Behavioral Assessment,* doi 10.1007/s10862-009-9156-y.

Harrington, J. & Blankenship, V. (2002). Ruminative thoughts and their relation to depression and anxiety. *Journal of Applied Social Psychology, 32,* 465–485.

Hjelmeland, H., Hawton, K., Nordvik, H., Bille-Brahe, U., De Leo, D., Fekete, S., Grad, O., Haring, C., Kerkhof, A. J. F. M., Lönqvist, J., Michel, K., Salander Renberg, E., Schmidtke, A., van Heeringen, K., & Wasserman, D. (2002). Why people engage in parasuicide: A cross-cultural study of intentions. *Suicide and Life-Threatening Behavior, 32,* 380–393.

Hjelmeland, H. & Hawton, K. (2004). Intentional aspects of non-fatal suicidal behaviour. In D. De Leo, U. Bille Brahe, A. Kerkhof, & A. Schmidtke (Eds.), *Suicidal Behaviour: Theories and research findings* (pp. 67–78). Göttingen: Hogrefe & Huber.

Ingram, R. E. (1990). Self-focused attention in clinical disorders: Review and a conceptual model. *Psychological Bulletin, 107,* 156–176.

Kerkhof, A. J. F. M. & van Luyn, J. B. (2010). *Suïcidepreventie in de Praktijk (The Prevention of Suicide in Clinical Practice).* Houten: Bohn Stafleu van Loghum.

Kerkhof, A. J. F. M., Hermans, D., Figee, A., Laeremans, I. Pieters, G., & Aardema, A. (2000). De Penn State Worry Questionnaire en de Worry Domains Questionnaire: eerste resultaten bij Nederlandse en Vlaamse klinische en poliklinische populaties. *Gedragstherapie, 33,* 135–146.

Koerner, N. & Dugas, M. J. (2006). A cognitive model of generalized anxiety disorder: The role of intolerance of uncertainty. In G. C. L. Davey & A. Wells (Eds.), *Worry and its Psychological Disorders* (pp. 201–216). Chichester: John Wiley & Sons, Ltd.

Lau, M. A., Segal, Z. V., & Williams, J. M. G. (2004). Teasdale's differential activation hypothesis: Implications for mechanisms of depressive relapse and suicidal behaviour. *Behaviour Research and Therapy, 42,* 1001–1017.

Lewinsohn, P. M., Steinmetz, J. L., Larson, D. W., & Franklin, J. (1981). Depression-related cognitions: Antecedent or consequence? *Journal of Abnormal Psychology, 90*, 213–219.

Miranda, R. & Nolen-Hoeksema, S. (2007). Brooding and reflection: Rumination predicts suicidal ideation at 1-year follow-up in a community sample. *Behaviour Research and Therapy, 45*, 3088–3095.

Morrison, R. & O'Connor, R. (2008). A systematic review of the relationship between rumination and suicidality. *Suicide and Life-Threatening Behavior, 38*, 523–538.

Nolen-Hoeksema, S. (1991). Responses to depression and their effects on the duration of depressive episodes. *Journal of Abnormal Psychology, 100*, 569–582.

Nolen-Hoeksema, S. & Morrow, J. (1991). A prospective study of depression and posttraumatic stress symptoms after a natural disaster: The 1989 Loma Prieta earthquake. *Journal of Personality and Social Psychology, 61*, 115–121.

O'Connor, D. B., O'Connor, R. C., & Marshall, R. (2007). Perfectionism and psychological distress: Evidence of the mediating effects of rumination. *European Journal of Personality, 21*, 429–452.

O'Connor, R. C. & Noyce, R. (2008). Personality and cognitive processes: Self-criticism and different types of rumination as predictors of suicidal ideation. *Behaviour Research and Therapy, 46*, 392–401.

Papageorgiou, C. (2006). Worry and rumination: Styles of persistent negative thinking in anxiety and depression. In G. C. L. Davey & A. Wells (Eds.), *Worry and its Psychological Disorders: Theory, assessment and treatment.* (pp. 21–40). Chichester: John Wiley & Sons, Ltd.

Raes, F., Hermans, D., & Eelen, P. (2003). The Dutch version of the Ruminative Response Scale (RRS-NL) and the Rumination on Sadness Scale (RSS-NL). *Gedragstherapie, 36*, 97–104.

Robichaud, M. & Dugas, M. J. (2006). A cognitive behavioral treatment targeting intolerance of uncertainty. In G. C. L. Davey & A. Wells (Eds.), *Worry and its Psychological Disorders* (pp. 289–304). Chichester: John Wiley & Sons, Ltd.

Rudd, M. D., Joiner, T., & Rajab, M. H. (2001). *Treating Suicidal Behavior.* New York: Guilford Press.

Segerstrom, S. C., Stanton, A. L., Alden, L. E., & Shortridge, B. E. (2003). A multidimensional structure for repetitive thought: What's on your mind, and how, and how much? *Journal of Personality and Social Psychology, 85*, 909–921.

Segerstrom, S. C., Tsao, J. C. I., Alden, L. E., & Craske, M. G. (2000). Worry and rumination: Repetitive thought as a concomitant and predictor of negative mood. *Cognitive Therapy and Research, 24*, 671–688.

Simon, N. M., Pollack, M. H., Ostacher, M. J., Zalta, A. K., Chow, C. W., Fischmann, D., Demopulos, C. M., Nierenberg, A. A., & Otto, M. W. (2007). Understanding the link between anxiety symptoms and suicidal ideation and behaviors in outpatients with bipolar disorder. *Journal of Affective Disorders, 97*, 91–99.

Surrence, K., Miranda, R., Marroquin, B. M., & Chan, S. (2009). Brooding and reflective rumination among suicide attempters: Cognitive vulnerability to suicidal ideation. *Behaviour Research and Therapy, 47*, 803–808.

Treynor, W., Gonzalez, R., & Nolen Hoeksema, S. (2003). Rumination reconsidered: A psychometric analysis. *Cognitive Therapy and Research, 26*, 167–177.

van Spijker, B. A. J., van Straten, A. & Kerkhof, A. J. F. M. (2010). The effectiveness of a web-based self-help intervention to reduce suicidal thoughts: A randomized controlled trial. *Trials*, 11:25.

Verwey, B., Bozdag, M. A., van Waarde, J., van Rooij, I. A. L. M., De Beurs, E., & Zitman, F. (2007). Reassessment of suicide attempters at home shortly after admittance to a general hospital.

In B. Verwey, *Don't Forget*. Leiden: Leiden University, available at https://openaccess,leidenuniv. nl/bitstream/1887/9728/17/Don't+forget-bwcorr.pdf.

Watkins, E. R. (2008). Constructive and unconstructive repetitive thought. *Psychological Bulletin*, *134*, 163–206.

Wells, A. (1995). Metacognition and worry: A cognitive model of generalized anxiety disorder. *Behavioural and Cognitive Psychotherapy*, *23*, 301–320.

Wells, A. (2006). Metcognitive therapy for worry and generalized anxiety disorder. In G. C. L. Davey & A. Wells (Eds.), *Worry and its Psychological Disorders* (pp 259–272). Chichester: John Wiley & Sons, Ltd.

Williams, J. M. G., Crane, C., Barnhofer, T., van der Does, A. J. W., & Segal, Z. V. (2006). Recurrence of suicidal ideation across depressive episodes. *Journal of Affective Disorders*, *91*, 189–194.

CHAPTER THIRTEEN

Inequalities and Suicidal Behaviour

Stephen Platt

Abstract

Despite increasing recognition in economically developed countries of the importance of addressing health inequalities, there has been a nearly universal failure to consider equality issues in both academic reviews of approaches to suicide prevention and the formulation of national suicide prevention strategies. This has occurred despite ample evidence of systematic inequalities in suicide risk associated with different indicators of social position, including labour market status, occupational social class, education, income, housing tenure, and labour market position, at the individual level, and socio-economic deprivation, at the aggregate level. This chapter reports an investigation of intentional self-harm and undetermined deaths occurring in Scotland, 1989–2002. The findings confirm evidence in the wider literature that low social class and socio-economic deprivation are associated with increased suicide risk; and that the influence of individual social class is far stronger than the influence of area-level socio-economic affluence–deprivation in accounting for suicide-related inequality. An exceptionally high relative risk of suicide was found among those in the lowest social class living in the most deprived areas (approximately 10 times higher than the risk of suicide among those in the highest social class in the most affluent areas). The cumulative research evidence suggests that national suicide prevention strategies need to apply an equity lens to suicide prevention strategy but many policy challenges need to be resolved, including the strategic approach to inequality reduction, whether people or places are to be targeted, and the identification of interventions that are likely to be effective in reducing socio-economic inequalities in suicide risk.

International Handbook of Suicide Prevention: Research, Policy and Practice, First Edition.
Edited by Rory C. O'Connor, Stephen Platt, Jacki Gordon.
© 2011 John Wiley & Sons, Ltd. Published 2011 by John Wiley & Sons, Ltd.

Introduction

Health inequality refers to the 'systematic and avoidable differences in health outcomes between social groups such that poorer and/or more disadvantaged people are more likely to have illnesses and disabilities and shorter lives than those who are more affluent' (Judge, Platt, Costongs, & Jurczak, 2006, p. 11). As Mackenbach (2006) has shown, the problem of health inequality is universal. Those lower down the socio-economic hierarchy, whether measured in terms of economic position (e.g., being unemployed or workless), occupational status (e.g., routine and manual occupations), income level (e.g., living in poverty), or educational attainment (e.g., without qualifications), are at greater risk of morbidity and premature mortality than those higher up the hierarchy. The persistence of large health inequalities, even in countries with long-standing social, healthcare, and other policies aimed at creating more equality in welfare, highlights their deep roots in the social stratification systems of modern societies.

As a result of growing international recognition of the importance of health inequalities and consensus about their unacceptability (inequality as inequity), the goals of public health policy, particularly in post-industrial Western countries, have widened:

> A narrow concern with promoting population health is giving way to a broader vision of the goals of policy. The broader vision combines a focus on health gain with a commitment to reducing inequalities in its social distribution. (Graham, 2004, p. 115)

Different types of national strategic approaches have been developed to address health inequalities, including legislative commitments (e.g., Greece, Germany), policy statements (e.g., Denmark, France), and quantitative targets (e.g., United Kingdom, Ireland). With respect to suicide prevention, however, there has been a nearly universal failure to consider equality issues in the formulation of national strategies. While the latter typically aim to reduce completed suicide (and sometimes non-fatal suicidal behaviour (NFSB)[1]), with or without quantitative targets, New Zealand is the only country to identify a reduction in inequalities in suicide and suicidal behaviour as a primary strategic purpose (Associate Minister of Health (New Zealand), 2006). *The Suicide Prevention Strategy for England* (Department of Health (England), 2002) includes a commitment to monitor suicides by social class, as well as by age and gender; these data, it is suggested, will help to identify 'who should be a target of prevention efforts and suggest ways in which prevention might be achieved' (p. 8). In Scotland a suicide inequalities target (reduce the suicide rate among 10–24 year olds for the most deprived communities by 15% between 2001–2003 and 2007–2009) was included in a previous governmental health improvement strategy (Scottish Executive, 2003). (However, the Scottish Government's suicide prevention strategy, 'Choose Life', made no mention of socio-economic inequalities and did not identify people living in deprivation as a priority group (Scottish Executive, 2002).[2]) In academic reviews of strategic approaches to suicide prevention (e.g., Mann, Apter, Bertolote, Beautrais, Currier, *et al.*, 2005) there is also a striking absence of concern with equality issues. A review of the evidence base on the effectiveness of interventions to prevent suicide, suicidal behaviour, and suicidal ideation, commissioned by the Scottish Government, concludes (Leitner, Barr, & Hobby, 2008):

> Weakest of all was the availability of evidence specifically addressing interventions to reduce the risk of suicidal behaviour or ideation in asylum seekers, people who are lesbian, gay, bisexual or transgender; the recently bereaved; socio-economically deprived; unemployed; homeless populations; and survivors of sexual abuse. The review team was unable to identify any intervention studies that had focused specifically on these groups and provided evidence of pertinent outcomes. (Summary report, p. 4)

Socio-Economic Inequalities in Suicide: The Evidence

How important is the relative failure to apply an equity lens to suicide prevention strategy and activity? In this section I consider the research evidence relating to socio-economic inequalities in suicide and non-fatal suicidal behaviour (NFSB), typically defined operationally as hospital-treated self-poisoning or self-injury. Inequalities will be considered at both individual and aggregate levels. Common indicators of socio-economic inequality that have been explored in empirical research include occupational social class, education, income, housing tenure, and labour market position (economic position/employment status), at the individual level, and socio-economic deprivation, at the aggregate level. (The impact of other sources of inequality, such as gender and age, are outside the scope of the chapter.)

Employment and unemployment

Two systematic reviews on the labour market and suicidal behaviour have been published (Platt, 1984; Platt & Hawton, 2000; see also, Platt, 1986; Platt, Micciolo, & Tansella, 1992). When reporting findings these reviews distinguish between four major types of research design, based on two orthogonal dimensions: individual versus aggregate measures; and cross-sectional versus longitudinal collection of measures. Individual-level studies measure the relationship between labour market status and suicidal behaviour of individuals, while aggregate-level studies consider the relationship between the unemployment rate and suicidal behaviour over time or over geographical areas. The temporal design of the research can be either cross-sectional, measuring the relationship between unemployment data and suicidal behaviour data (individual- or aggregate-level) at one point in time, or longitudinal, where unemployment in individuals or aggregates is associated with subsequent suicidal behaviour over two or more points in time. The intersection of these two dimensions results in four types of study: individual cross-sectional; aggregate cross-sectional; individual longitudinal; and aggregate longitudinal.

In the earlier review (Platt, 1984), evidence from cross-sectional individual studies conducted in a range of countries, including the United States, the United Kingdom, India, and Hong Kong, revealed that significantly more hospital-treated NFSB patients were unemployed than would be expected among general population samples. Likewise, rates of suicide or NFSB among the unemployed were always considerably higher than among the employed. Increasing duration of unemployment was associated with increasing risk of NFSB. Aggregate cross-sectional studies provided no evidence of a consistent relationship between unemployment and completed suicide, but a significant geographical association between unemployment and NFSB rates was found. Results from all but one of the individual longitudinal studies pointed to significantly more unemployment, job instability, and occupational problems among suicides compared with non-suicides. The England & Wales Longitudinal Study (Fox & Goldblatt, 1982) also found a high suicide rate among the unemployed in the general population. The aggregate longitudinal analyses pointed to a significant positive association between unemployment and suicide in the United States. The negative relationship in Great Britain in the 1960s has been shown to result from a unique decline in the suicide rate due to the unavailability of the most common method of suicide (Kreitman, 1976; Kreitman & Platt, 1984).

The later review (Platt & Hawton, 2000) updates and extends the earlier review by concentrating on publications during the period 1984–1999. The range of countries included in this review is extremely wide, including the United States, Canada, Australia, New Zealand, Japan, Taiwan, and several European nations. The strongest evidence about the relationship between suicide and unemployment is derived from individual-level longitudinal studies. Significantly higher odds ratios (ORs), relative risks (RRs), or standardized mortality ratios (SMRs) for suicide among the unemployed are consistently reported, even after the introduction of control variables (such as age, sex, civil state, social class, and education level). The most rigorous analyses are those based on the England and Wales Longitudinal Study. Lewis and Sloggett (1998), for example, calculate an OR of 2.6 for suicide over a 20-year follow-up period among those unemployed at baseline, after controls for a range of socio-demographic variables. Based on the findings reported in nine different studies, the OR or RR for suicide among the unemployed over the medium to long term appears to be in the region of 2–3. In other words, those who are unemployed are two to three times more likely to die prematurely by suicide than those who are in work. The interpretation of this finding is, however, not obvious. On the one hand, the experience of unemployment might have led, directly or indirectly (e.g., via increased psychological distress or even psychiatric illness), to an increased vulnerability to suicide. On the other hand, individuals who become unemployed (especially long-term) might also be more likely to be psychologically vulnerable (indeed, their unemployment may have come about as a result of their psychological ill-health) and, therefore, also at greater risk of suicidal behaviour. The weight of evidence supports the conclusion reached in earlier studies, based on a shorter follow-up period and controlling only for social class, but also demonstrating a significant effect on the wives of unemployed men, that there is indeed a direct causal effect of unemployment on suicide. However, it is not possible to exclude the possibility that personal characteristics increase the risk of both unemployment and suicidal behaviour.

At least 50 studies using an aggregate longitudinal design to explore the relationship between the suicide rate and the unemployment rate over time were published after the earlier review. The findings are inconsistent, with some studies reporting a significant positive association, some reporting a significant negative association, and some finding no significant association. Overall, the weight of evidence points to a positive association, more convincingly among men than among women. We should note, however, that many studies explore simple bivariate relationships and fail to use more sophisticated multivariate modelling with controls for potential confounders (particularly those measuring major socio-demographic change, e.g., divorce rate). In several studies, when appropriate controls are introduced, the association between suicide is attenuated or else disappears altogether (e.g., Leenaars & Lester, 1995).

With respect to unemployment and hospital-treated NFSB, findings from Great Britain point to instability in the temporal association, with a positive relationship in the 1970s followed by a negative or non-significant relationship in the 1980s. At the individual level Platt, Hawton, Kreitman, Fagg, and Foster (1988) reported relative risks (NFSB among the unemployed versus the employed) in excess of 12 (men) and nine (women) in two UK cities. Long-term unemployment carried the greatest risk, with RRs of between 19 and 36 among men. These risk estimates are high, suggesting a causal impact of unemployment. On the other hand, findings from several studies, including evidence of considerably higher levels of chronic psychopathology and personality disorder among unemployed NFSB patients, compared with their employed counterparts, suggest once again that it would be inadvisable to rule out the possibility of self-selection (i.e., non-causal) processes in the relationship between deliberate self-harm and unemployment.

Occupational status, occupation, and suicidal behaviour

Findings relating to the association between occupational social class and suicidal behaviour were also presented in the review by Platt and Hawton (2000). The strongest evidence can be found in research using an individual-level cross-sectional design. Two studies provide data on variation in suicide by social class in Great Britain (Drever, Bunting, & Harding, 1997; Kreitman, Carstairs, & Duffy, 1991). Both report lower suicide standardized mortality ratios (SMRs) among men in the non-manual social classes and among skilled manual workers and significantly elevated suicide SMRs in the semi- and (especially) unskilled manual classes. Kreitman and colleagues (1991) confirm the finding of higher SMRs for men in social classes IV and V in England and Wales around 1981, for Scotland at about the same time, and for all three countries around 1971. In a subsequent analysis, Drever and colleagues (1997) report the same inverse relationship between social class and suicide (including undetermined deaths) among men aged 20–64 years in England and Wales for the period 1991–1993. SMRs (England & Wales = 100) were 55 in social class (SC) I (professional), 63 in SCII (managerial and technical), 87 in SCIIINM (non-manual skilled), 96 in SCIIIM (manual skilled), 107 in SCIV (semi-skilled), and 215 in SCV (unskilled). Drever and Bunting (1997) note that the two-fold difference in suicide between social classes I and V in 1970–1972 had increased to a four-fold difference by 1991–1993. Uren, Fitzpatrick, Reid, and Goldblatt (2001) extended this analysis to explore differences in the social gradient of suicide in the United Kingdom as a whole and in each of its four constituent countries (England, Wales, Scotland, Northern Ireland). The evidence of a steep increase ('step change') in suicide risk in SCV is notable in all countries. Scotland had the worst level of suicide mortality, with higher rates in each social class than all other countries. One other important finding reported by Kreitman, Carstairs, and Duffy (1991) is that of a significant interaction between age and social class, with particularly high suicide rates among those aged 25–44 years in SCV.

In a study using the same research design Platt *et al.* (1988) demonstrated a marked social class gradient in the incidence of hospital-treated NFSB among men in two UK cities in the early 1980s: the higher the social class, the lower the rate of NFSB. In Edinburgh, for example, the mean annual incidence of NFSB (1980–1982) per 100,000 economically active males aged 16+ years was 72 in SCI+II, 236 in SCIII, 526 in CIV and 879 in SCV.

Analysis of variation in suicide risk by occupational group is reported in three publications relating to England and Wales (Charlton, Kelly, Dunnell, Evans, & Jenkins, 1992; Kelly, Charlton, & Jenkin, 1995; Kelly & Bunting, 1998). The statistic used in these studies is the proportional mortality ratio (PMR), which is the number of observed suicide deaths divided by the number of expected suicide deaths, expressed as a percentage. This statistic is used where the total number of individuals in an occupational group and their age distribution not known, so that the SMR cannot be computed. It should be noted, however, that the PMR for suicide in a particular group can be misleading since it depends not only on the number of deaths from suicide in the group but also on the number of deaths from other causes. Thus, an elevated suicide PMR may represent a true difference, but can also reflect a relative deficit of deaths from other causes.

Occupational groups in England and Wales which, on the basis of PMRs, appear to have had a high risk of suicide during the 1980s and 1990s were medical and allied occupations and farming among males, while among females additional groups with elevated PMRs were nurses, professionals in education, health and welfare, and those in personal service employment. Kelly and Bunting (1998) draw attention to the discrepancy between the *PMR-based* findings, with high suicide risk occupations coming predominantly from social classes I and II, and *SMR-based* findings, which show much lower suicide rates in the same social classes. They speculate that 'the high PMRs found for doctors, vets and dentists reflect the fact that their overall mortality is low and therefore the proportion of deaths from suicide is high relative to other causes'. Empirical support for this suggestion can be found in Charlton *et al.* (1992). Nevertheless, there is also evidence from other data (e.g., Stark, Belbin, Hopkins, Gibbs, Hay, *et al.*, 2006) and other countries that some occupational groups, particularly medical doctors, nurses, and farmers, are generally at increased risk of suicide.

Education and housing tenure

A study by Lorant, Kunst, Huisman, Costa, and Mackenbach (2005) explored socio-economic inequalities in suicide mortality among men and women. They used a prospective follow-up of censuses matched with vital statistics in 10 European populations (Austria, Belgium, Denmark, England & Wales, Finland, Italy (Torino), Norway,

Switzerland, Spain (Barcelona, Madrid)). Directly standardized rates of suicide were computed for each country. Inequalities were measured by educational level (low secondary versus upper secondary versus superior) and housing tenure (owner versus tenant). In most countries, the greater the socio-economic disadvantage, the higher the risk of suicide. Among men a low level of educational attainment was a risk factor for suicide in eight out of 10 countries. Among women, however, the pattern of educational inequalities was very different. Overall, lower educational attainment was protective against suicide, with only two countries showing the same association as found among men, while a reverse association was evident in three countries. In five out of six countries for which data were available, the risk of suicide was greater in tenants than in house owners, for both men and women. Housing tenure was a more important risk factor than education, and yielded more consistent results between men and women. The authors conclude: 'Socio-economic inequalities in suicide are a generalized phenomenon in western Europe' (p. 49).

Socio-economic characteristics of geographical areas

Rehkopf and Buka (2005) conducted a systematic review of the literature exploring the association between area socio-economic characteristics and area suicide rates. Search terms relating to socio-economic characteristics included 'socio-economic factors', 'socio-economic status', 'education', 'educational status', 'employment', 'income', 'occupation', 'poverty', 'social class', 'social conditions', 'deprivation' and 'disadvantaged'. Among the 221 analyses (covering North America, Europe, Australia, New Zealand, Australia, and Asia) reported in 86 retrieved papers, more than half (55%) found no significant association between the socio-economic characteristics of a region and suicide, while 32% reported a significant and inverse relationship (i.e., areas of lower socio-economic position tended to have higher suicide incidence) and 14% a significant and direct relationship (i.e., areas of lower socio-economic position tended to have lower suicide incidence). Among significant analyses, 70% showed an inverse relationship and 30% showed a direct relationship. The strength of association varied according to the size of the geographical unit (from city neighbourhoods, at one extreme, to countries, at the other) that was analysed: studies based on smaller geographical units were significantly more likely to report higher rates of suicide in lower socio-economic areas than studies based on larger areas of aggregation. Measures of area poverty and deprivation were most likely to be inversely associated, and median income least likely to be inversely associated, with suicide rates. Analyses using measures of unemployment, education, and occupation were equally likely to demonstrate inverse associations.

The authors draw attention to the well-known risk of committing the 'ecological fallacy', that is, making causal inferences about individuals from aggregate-level data (Greenland, 2001; Morgenstern, 1995; Robinson, 1950). They note that area-level effects comprise both compositional effects and contextual effects (see Box 13.1); given the nature of the studies included in the review, these components of area rates could not be unpacked. Nevertheless, they argue that area correlates should be examined in order

---

Box 13.1   Compositional versus contextual effects

Compositional: variation in (health) outcome (e.g., suicide) between areas can be explained in terms of the characteristics (e.g., social, psychological, genetic) of residents of those areas.

Contextual: variation in (health) outcome (e.g., suicide) between areas can be explained in terms of the characteristics (e.g., physical, cultural, economic, social) of the areas.

---

to avoid the 'atomistic fallacy' (Diez-Roux, 1998) of exclusively focusing on individual-level risk factors.

A relevant study whose publication postdates the review by Rehkopf and Buka (2005) was conducted by Exeter and Boyle (2007). Seeking to determine whether suicide deaths among those aged 15–44 years in Scotland were geographically clustered, the authors examined deaths from suicide and undetermined causes during three time periods – 1980–1982, 1990–1992, and 1999–2001 – across 10,058 small areas. In all three time periods a significant geographical cluster of suicide among young adults was identified in north and east Glasgow (centred in the Maryhill parliamentary constituency, but also including Govan, Strathkelvin, and Bearsden, and Rutherglen in 1999–2001). The authors reject contagion as a possible explanation for the cluster and hypothesize instead that the key explanation is the concentration of socio-economic deprivation in this area.

Relative importance of individual- and area-level inequalities on suicide risk

Using linked population registers, Agerbo, Sterne, and Gunnell (2007) investigated whether an individual's risk of suicide in relation to marital status, employment status, or income differs depending on levels of single-person households, employment, and income in their area of residence. Relevant data were obtained for all suicides in Denmark during 1982–1997 (n = 9,011) and age–sex matched controls (n = 180,220). Individual-level associations between suicide and the selected risk factors were as expected (e.g., higher rate of suicide among the unmarried, unemployed/non-employed, lowest income) and rate ratios were only marginally lower after adjusting for area-level factors. On the other hand, controlling for compositional effects markedly reduced ecological associations of increased risk for suicide with declining area levels of socio-economic disadvantage. Additionally, the association between area-level risk factors and suicide was much weaker than the association between individual-level risk factors and suicide. The authors conclude that ecological associations between indicators of socio-economic disadvantage and suicide can be attributed primarily to characteristics of residents (compositional effects) rather than to contextual effects *per se*.

New Empirical Investigation of Socio-Economic Inequalities in Suicide in Scotland

Together with colleagues at the University of St Andrews (Scotland), I have undertaken a new empirical investigation of the association between social class, socio-economic deprivation, and suicide in Scotland over the period 1989–2002. The study was intended to assess whether findings from Scotland complemented those reported for other countries, in particular the emerging evidence that individual-level social class has greater power in explaining suicide-related inequality than area-level socio-economic affluence/deprivation. (A full account of the findings of this study can be found in Platt, Boyle, Crombie, Feng, & Exeter, 2007.)

Study hypotheses

There were three study hypotheses, each supported by evidence from previous empirical studies (see above). The third hypothesis was also consistent with the findings of a systematic review of studies of the effect of local area social characteristics on individual health outcomes, controlling for individual socio-economic status, in developed countries (Pickett & Pearl, 2001). Although all but two of the 25 reviewed studies reported a statistically significant association between at least one measure of social environment and a health outcome (contextual effect), after adjusting for individual level socio-economic status (compositional effect), contextual effects were generally modest and much smaller than compositional effects.

H1: low(er) socio-economic status is a risk factor for suicide in Scotland;
H2: living in an area of socio-economic deprivation is a risk factor for suicide in Scotland;
H3: individual socio-economic status is a more important risk factor than area-level socio-economic deprivation (compositional rather than contextual effect).

Methods

Data

Deaths data   An anonymized dataset of intentional self-harm and undetermined deaths occurring during the period 1989–2002 was provided by the General Registrar Office for Scotland (GROS). For the purposes of this study, a *suicide death* is defined to comprise *both* those deaths which are officially classified as suicide/intentional self-harm (ICD9 E950–959; ICD10 X60–84) *and* also 'undetermined' deaths (ICD9 E980–989; ICD10 Y10–34). The inclusion of 'undetermined' deaths is consistent with accepted international research practice: 'undetermined' deaths are often considered to be *probable* suicides, whereas suicide/intentional self-harm deaths are labelled *definite* suicides. (Platt *et al.*

(2007, Appendix A1) includes a discussion of the possible impact of using two different ICD systems on the reliability of the classification of suicide.)

The dataset is confined to deaths among adults aged 15+ years. There were 13,185 deaths recorded over the period 1989–2004, of which 74% occurred in males ($n = 9759$) and 26% in females ($n = 3426$). Deaths among children under 15 years of age are omitted from the analysis because, first, suicide is only rarely recorded in this age group, and, second, some of the deaths labelled undetermined will result from uncertainty between accident and homicide (rather than between accident and suicide).

Data have been provided for each death on a range of socio-demographic variables, including social class (see below). With the exception of 189 deaths which did not have Output Area codes, each death record was assigned by the research team to a 2001 Census Output Area and also to a Consistent Area Through Time (CATT). The CATT enables small areas to be reliably compared using data from the 1981, 1991, and/or the 2001 Censuses (Exeter, Boyle, Feng, Flowerdew, & Scheirloh, 2005). On the basis of residential address (postcode sector), the research team assigned the Carstairs deprivation score to each death (see Platt *et al.* (2007, Appendix A3) for technical details). The original Carstairs index of deprivation was divided into seven disproportionate categories, based on a normal distribution curve, in order to make comparisons between the least and most deprived areas in Scotland. In this study, the continuous score was also divided into categories for comparative analyses. At national level population weighted quintiles (five categories) were used, each quintile comprising approximately 800,000 adults aged 15 years and older.

Population data   In order to conduct the epidemiological analysis, population (denominator) data, including for social class, were obtained from the mid-year population estimates (from GROS) and from the 1991 census (used for analyses relating to the period 1989–1995) and the 2001 census (used for analyses relating to the period 1996–2002).

Data analyses   The software package STATA was used for all data management and analysis. Graphs were prepared using Microsoft Excel.

Social class analysis   National suicide rates by social class (at death) and 95% confidence intervals (95% CI) were computed for males during two time periods (separately): 1989–1995 (based on 1991 census) and 1996–2002 (based on 2001 census). This analysis was not undertaken for women due to the high proportion of female suicide deaths that were not assigned a substantive social class category. The main reason appears to be non-involvement in the labour market.

The Registrar General's Social Class (SC) has been used as the measure of socio-economic classification in this study. There are five SC categories, with one divided into two sub-groups. These categories are:

     I: professional, etc. occupations;
    II: managerial and technical occupations;
 IIIN: skilled non-manual occupations;
 IIIM: skilled manual occupations;
   IV: partly-skilled occupations;
    V: unskilled occupations.

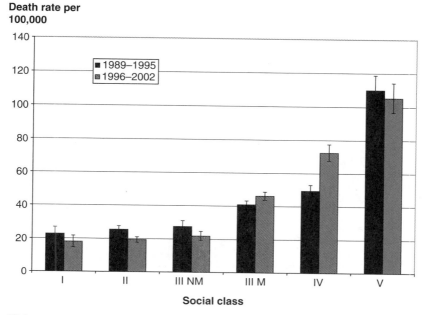

Figure 13.1 Suicide rates by social class, males, Scotland, 1989–1995 and 1996–2002.

Technical details relating to the use of the SC scheme can be found in Platt *et al.* (2007, Appendix A4).

Area deprivation analysis   We calculated suicide standardized mortality ratios (SMRs) and 95% confidence intervals (95% CI) for all persons aged 15+ years in 1989–1995 and 1996–2002, by population weighted deprivation quintile. If observed deaths were equal to expected deaths, the SMR would equal 100.

Social class × area deprivation analysis   Male suicide rates (and 95% CI) by social class were calculated within each deprivation quintile during 1989–1995 and 1996–2002. The relative risk of suicide over the whole period (1989–2002) was estimated for each social class × deprivation quintile category, with the reference value (1) assigned to social class I in the least socio-economically deprived area.

Findings

Suicide rates by social class   At the national level there was a marked variation in male suicide rates by social class in 1989–1995 and 1996–2002 (Figure 13.1). Differences between rates in the non-manual groups were not statistically significant. However, there were significant differences between rates in the non-manual groups and SCIIIM, between SCIIIM and SCIV and between SCIV and SCV. This suggests *both* a 'step-change' in risk between non-manual and manual social classes *and* a gradient

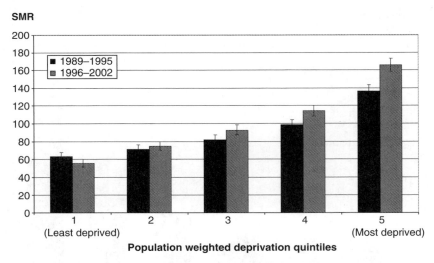

Figure 13.2   Standardized mortality ratios (SMRs) by population weighted deprivation quintile, all persons, Scotland, 1989–1995 and 1996–2002.

between non-manual social classes (considered as a whole) and each successively 'lower' manual social class.

Area deprivation analysis   There was a clear social gradient during both periods, whereby suicide increased with increasing levels of area deprivation (see Figure 13.2). This gradient was steeper in the later period, indicating that the association between suicide and deprivation became more pronounced over time. Differences between the two time periods in SMRs were not statistically significant in the three least deprived quintiles. However, the SMRs in the two most deprived quintiles were significantly higher in 1996–2002. The same pattern of linear trend and widening gap over time between SMRs of least deprived and most deprived areas was found among both males and females, and in persons aged 15–44 years and 45+ years (data not shown; see Platt *et al.* (2007, pp. 46–48) for charts).

Relationship between area deprivation and social class   The relationship between area-level socio-economic deprivation and individual-level social class position is depicted in Figure 13.3 (relating to 1989–1995) and Figure 13.4 (1996–2002). There was no significant difference in suicide rates between the non-manual classes in the different deprivation categories during either time period. There was a gradient, however, between the non-manual classes, on the one hand, and classes IIIM, IV and V, on the other, in each deprivation category. Thus, the suicide rate was significantly higher in SCV than in SCIV (and all the other social classes) in all areas, irrespective of the degree of socio-economic deprivation in the areas in which people live. In the earlier time period the patterning of social class differences did not differ markedly between categories of socio-economic deprivation. This suggests a strong compositional effect and a very weak or non-existent contextual effect: that is to say, the main influence on suicide rates was at the individual-, rather than area-, level. The situation changed somewhat in 1996–2002. Figure 13.4 gives some suggestion

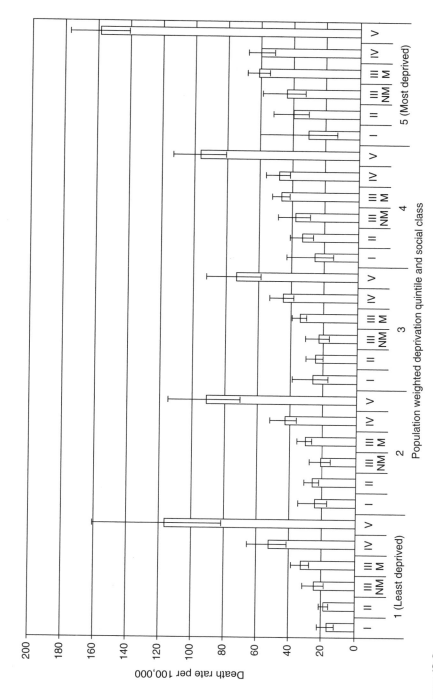

Figure 13.3 Male suicide rates by deprivation quintile and social class, 1989–1995, Scotland.

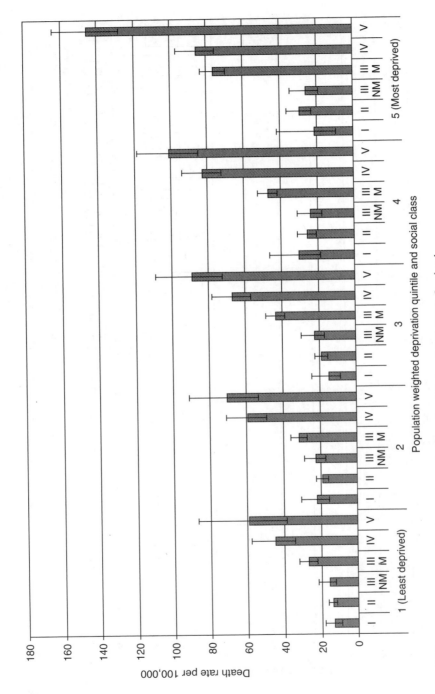

Figure 13.4 Male suicide rates by deprivation quintile and social class, 1996–2002, Scotland.

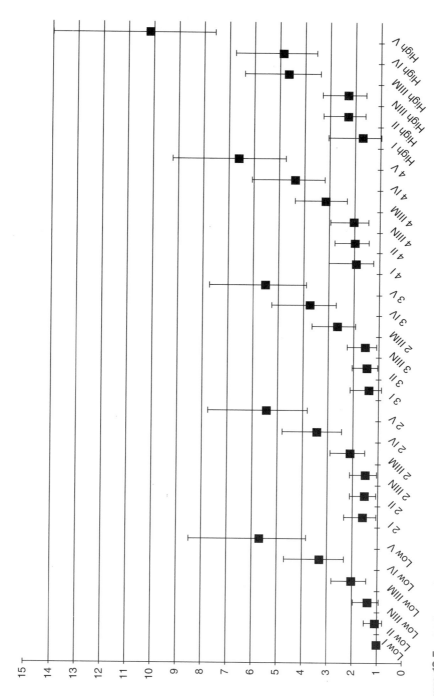

Figure 13.5 Male suicide rates by deprivation quintile and social class, 1989–2002, Scotland: relative risks (multi-level analysis).

of a contextual effect as well as a compositional effect, as evidenced by the trend towards an increase in the social class gradient as the level of socio-economic deprivation worsens. However, Figure 13.5, which presents risk ratios for the whole period (1989–2002 combined), demonstrates that the compositional effect (the influence of individual social class) was undoubtedly far stronger than the area effect (the influence of the level of socio-economic deprivation in the locality). An exceptionally high relative risk of suicide among those in the lowest social class living in the most deprived areas was also found: it was approximately 10 times higher than the risk of suicide among those in the highest social class in the most affluent areas. (This finding is suggestive rather than definitive because of the large confidence interval surrounding the central estimate. There is, in fact, an overlap in confidence intervals between risk ratios for all social class V groups across the deprivation quintiles.)

Summary of findings

The empirical evidence broadly supports all three study hypotheses:

- Low(er) socio-economic status is a risk factor for suicide. (There is evidence of *both* a 'step-change' in risk between non-manual and manual social classes *and* a gradient between non-manual social classes (considered as a whole) and each successively 'lower' manual social class.)
- Living in an area of socio-economic deprivation is a risk factor for suicide. (There is a clear social gradient: suicide risk increases with increasing levels of area deprivation.)
- Individual socio-economic status is a more important suicide risk factor than area-level socio-economic deprivation. (However, a possible interaction between (low) social class and area characteristics (greater deprivation) should be noted.)

Discussion

Tackling inequalities in suicide: what should be the national policy response?

Focus of intervention: two key dimensions   In considering the national policy response to evidence of inequalities, governments need to give consideration to two key issues: what broad strategic approach is being taken to reduce health inequalities; and whether action be directed at people or places or both people and places.

Strategic approach to tackling health inequalities   It is not simply the poorest who experience less than optimum health; there is a gradient of risk across the whole population. It is helpful, therefore, to keep in mind Graham's (2004, p. 118, p. 120, p. 123) typology of classifications of health inequality, which distinguishes between the poor health of socio-economically disadvantaged people, health gaps between different socio-economic groups and social gradients across whole populations. Governments need to be clear whether they are seeking to *improve the health of the most disadvantaged* in absolute terms, *reduce the health gap* between the most disadvantaged and the most advantaged/average, or *reduce the gradient* of health inequalities associated with the gradient of socio-economic inequalities. Each of these strategic approaches has strengths and weaknesses. Strengths of a focus on disadvantage or reducing the gap include a concentration of resources on the most needy (in both socio-economic and health terms) and an ambitious target and goal to galvanize action. Disadvantages include: directing attention away from those who are privileged; shifting focus from inequality-generating structures to assumed personal deficits of those at the bottom of the socio-economic hierarchy; and obscuring inequalities in life chances and health chances across the socio-economic hierarchy. The strengths of a focus on health inequalities as health gradients include: explicit recognition that narrowing the gap is not sufficient for reducing socio-economic inequalities in health; and turning the spotlight on social inequalities – in life chances, living standards, economic wealth, and political power – and the structures which maintain them. However, this latter strength is also a potential weakness, in that it requires a political ideology which is far too radical for most governments at the best of economic times (and virtually unthinkable in these, the worst of economic times). The approach to tackling inequalities in suicide risk will be largely dependent on the overarching philosophy of health inequality reduction that is adopted by government. Concentration on reducing the overall level of suicide in society or on reducing suicide risk only among the most disadvantaged (failure to address the socio-economic gradient) may result in little change in relative risk between the most and least privileged, and may even result in an increased relative risk (widening inequalities).

People or places?   Health inequality is most commonly discussed in the context of individual-level indicators of social position, such as class, education, and income. There is also increasing recognition of the fact that social groups with poor health outcomes are often clustered in particular regions, localities, and neighbourhoods. If governments wish to reduce inequalities in suicide risk, should they focus on people or places or both? Over recent decades the UK and other governments of developed Western countries have used urban policy as a means of improving economic opportunities and living standards, typically through large-scale programmes of urban regeneration or neighbourhood economic renewal. A recent review of these area-based initiatives concluded that 'the overwhelming epidemiological evidence supporting the hypothesis that alleviating socio-economic deprivation will generate health improvement suggests that healthy urban policy is still worth pursuing.' However, while '[a]rea-based approaches to tackling deprivation have their advantages', 'a mix of area and individual-level targeting is likely to be needed' (Thomson, 2008).

With respect to addressing suicide-related inequalities, Rehkopf and Buka (2005, p. 153, p. 154) argue that the findings of their systematic review of the literature on area socio-economic characteristics and area suicide rates (see above) provides empirical support for area-based targeting:

> We regard [to the … findings of an inverse association between area socio-economic position and area suicide rates] as supporting the theory that social processes operating at the contextual … level do impact on the likelihood of completed suicides within these groups.

> These ... findings are consistent with a contextual explanation where area suicide rates are driven by social and economic isolation of neighbourhoods with higher levels of deprivation ... Even without attribution of causality to this association this evidence implies that suicide prevention resources should focus more on communities of a relatively lower socio-economic level, in particular, those at high levels of concentrated disadvantage.

Likewise, on the basis of their demonstration of a suicide cluster in Glasgow city, Exeter and Boyle (2007, p. 736) highlight the importance of area-based targeting: 'We believe that our present study strengthens the argument for targeting deprived communities in suicide prevention strategies.'

It is hardly surprising that the studies by Rehkopf and Buka (2005) and Exeter and Boyle (2007), given their geographical focus, conclude by recommending redirection of suicide prevention efforts towards areas of socio-economic disadvantage. However, nowhere do they reject the targeting of inequality at an individual level. More consistent with findings from the wider literature would be a twin-track approach, mixing area- and individual-level approaches, proposed by Thomson (2008) with respect to tackling socio-economic deprivation and by Agerbo *et al.* (2007, p. 460) more specifically with respect to tackling inequalities in suicide risk:

> Our findings suggest health policy might best focus on people within places rather than places alone. Ecological studies are important in identification of high-risk areas for targeted interventions and ecological information in individual-based studies can be useful in identifying causal relationships.

Evidence from the present study supports this approach. We have seen that compositional effects are undoubtedly more important than contextual effects, with a particularly high suicide rate among those at the bottom of the socio-economic hierarchy. Nevertheless, there does appear to be an interaction between individual- and area-level risks, as shown in the very high risk associated with belonging to the lowest social class and living in the most deprived areas. This sub-group almost certainly includes suicides among those living in north and east Glasgow (Exeter & Boyle, 2007).

Implications for intervention   One of the reasons why area-based initiatives have appealed to politicians and policy-makers is the apparent opportunity to target intervention efforts very precisely.[3] However, the major drawback is that a focus on areas of deprivation will not necessarily result in successful reach of socio-economically deprived people: 'At the local authority scale, most deprived people are not in deprived areas and most people in deprived areas are not deprived' (Haynes & Gayle 2000).

On the other hand, targeting the most vulnerable individuals in a cost-effective way is extremely challenging. There is the problem of reaching and engaging those in SCV, when they are living virtually anywhere in the country and there is an absence of an appropriate sampling frame even to identify them. If they could be reached and engaged, the vast majority will be 'false positives', not at risk of suicide (or self-harm) now or in the future. The likelihood of intervening successfully to prevent a relatively infrequent event such as suicide even in this 'high-risk' group will be extremely low and will almost certainly be highly cost-ineffective, entailing an unacceptably high expenditure of resources and effort for very little (if any) return (Goldney, 2000; Rosen, 1954). Additionally, the emphasis on the highest risk group takes attention away from the fact that there is a gradient in suicide risk in the manual occupational groups (Figure 13.1). A more radical inequalities strategy would be looking at ways to minimize suicide risk in SCIIIM (which has a higher suicide risk that the non-manual social classes (SCI-IIINM)) and SCIV (which has a higher suicide risk than SCIIIM) as well as SCV.

Assuming that a strategic decision has been taken to intervene at both individual and area levels, policy-makers and practitioners face major challenges in identifying the actions that are likely to be effective in reducing inequalities in suicide risk. It is only minimally helpful to know that lower socio-economic status and living in a socio-economically deprived area are, to some degree, suicidogenic. This knowledge is far too non-specific to be of practical value, since the aspects or attributes of low social class or area deprivation that need to be targeted have not been identified. The suggestion in the *Suicide Prevention Strategy for England* (Department of Health (England), 2002) that monitoring social class data will help to identify 'who should be a target of prevention efforts and suggest ways in which prevention might be achieved' (p. 8) is therefore well wide of the mark because it disregards the key problem: what precisely is it about low social class (or any other low social status) that increases suicide risk? Unless this question is satisfactorily answered it is unlikely that interventions will be appropriately targeted or effective (and cost-effective). Boxes 13.2 and 13.3 set out some of the possible suicidogenic attributes of low socio-economic status and the local socio-economically deprived environment, respectively. All these attributes appear to have some plausibility as pathways or mechanisms which lead to suicidal behaviour, directly or via acting through a negative impact on mental health and well-being. Unfortunately, our current models of suicidal behaviour are general and heuristic, rather than precise and descriptive, with the result that we lack confidence about where to intervene and target our resources.

There is one final problem facing those who seek to intervene successfully to minimize or eliminate inequalities in suicide risk. Even if we were in a position to identify the (individual- and/or area-level) pathways from inequalities to suicide, we still face the challenge

---

Box 13.2   Low socio-economic status: possible pathways to increased individual suicide risk

- accumulated lifetime adverse experiences (e.g., health, employment, living conditions);
- powerlessness, stigma, and disrespect;
- experiencing other features of social exclusion (e.g., poverty, poor educational attainment);
- living in socio-economically deprived area;
- poor mental health;
- unhealthy lifestyles.

Box 13.3   Socio-economically deprived localities: possible pathways to increased contextual suicide risk

- physical (e.g., poor housing conditions);
- cultural (e.g., tolerant attitudes to suicide);
- political (e.g., adverse local public policy);
- economic (e.g., lack of job opportunities);
- social (e.g., weak social capital);
- history (e.g., high suicide incidence);
- infrastructure (e.g., poor quality, accessibility, acceptability of services);
- health and well-being (e.g., high prevalence of poor general and mental health).

---

of effectively intervening to prevent suicide. To take an example: people who are long-term unemployed (to be found in SCV) are likely to face stigma, feelings of powerlessness and helplessness, and mental distress. Randomized controlled trials of interventions for unemployed people (including cognitive behaviour therapy, workshops, and problem-solving) have demonstrated a positive effect on mental health and re-employment rates (Caplan, Vinokur, Price, & van Ryan, 1989; Proudfoot, Guest, Carson, Dunn, & Gray, 1997; Vinokur, Schul, Vuori, & Price, 2000; Vuori & Silvonen, 2005). However, there is no evidence of any intervention that is effective in reducing suicide risk in this group. In fact, as we have seen, the evidence base relating to effective interventions to prevent suicide is very limited indeed and non-existent in respect of tackling socially patterned differences in suicide risk, especially relating to socio-economic status.

Conclusion

This chapter has presented a considerable body of research, supported by the findings of a new study from Scotland, which demonstrates the pervasiveness and magnitude of socio-economic inequalities in suicide, at both area and individual levels. There is a gradient of risk, such that those in the lowest social classes or socio-economic groups and those living in areas of greatest deprivation have the highest risk of suicide, with risk tending to reduce at each successive step up the socio-economic ladder (here the evidence is stronger in respect of area effects). A test of the relative importance of compositional and contextual effects shows that the influence of individual social class is far stronger than the influence of area-level socio-economic affluence–deprivation in accounting for suicide-related inequality. However, an interaction effect between individual- and area-level effects is suggested by the exceptionally high relative risk of suicide among those in the lowest social class living in the most deprived areas (approximately 10 times higher than the risk of suicide among those in the highest social class in the most affluent areas). National suicide prevention strategies have tended to focus on the overall reduction of suicide incidence and, with only a few exceptions, have ignored the unequal distribution of risk (inequality). There is clearly a need to apply an equity lens to suicide prevention strategy but many policy challenges need to be resolved. Should the strategic target be the reduction of suicide among those living in the most disadvantaged circumstances, or the closing of the risk gap between the most disadvantaged and the most advantaged, or reducing the slope of the gradient of risk across the whole socio-economic hierarchy? Should interventions target people or places or a combination? What (mix of) interventions is likely to be effective in reducing socio-economic inequalities in suicide risk? It is high time that these questions were addressed in national suicide prevention strategies and action plans.

Notes

1   Self-poisoning or self-injury with suicidal intent (collectively referred to as 'self-harm', 'deliberate self-harm', or 'attempted suicide'), typically defined in operational terms as an admission to hospital following such behaviour.
2   The national evaluation of the first phase of 'Choose Life' (Platt, McLean, McCollam, Blamey, Mackenzie, *et al.*, 2006, p. 9) commented on the 'need to reinforce the equity focus of current priorities'. In response, the Scottish Government committed itself to 'an enhanced focus on equalities … for the next stages of work'.
3   Unfortunately, robust evaluations of the effects of these interventions on health inequalities are scarce. The evidence that is available is equivocal. A systematic review of 19 evaluations published between 1980 and 2004 of UK regeneration programmes was unable to draw conclusions about their impact on health and mortality due the paucity and conflicting nature of the empirical evidence (Thomson, Atkinson, Petticrew, & Kearns, 2006; Thomson 2008). Where changes were found these tended to be modest, and some adverse impacts were noted.

References

Agerbo, E., Sterne, J. A. C., & Gunnell, D. J. (2007). Combining individual and ecological data to determine compositional and contextual socio-economic risk factors for suicide. *Social Science & Medicine, 64*, 451–461.

Associate Minister of Health (New Zealand) (2006). *The New Zealand Suicide Prevention Strategy 2006–2016*. Wellington (NZ): Ministry of Health, available at http://www.moh.govt.nz/moh. nsf/pagesmh/4904/$File/suicide-prevention-strategy-2006-2016.pdf.

Caplan, R. D., Vinokur, A. D., Price, R. H., & van Ryan, M. (1989). Job seeking, reemployment, and mental health: A randomized field experiment in coping with job loss. *Journal of Applied Psychology, 74*, 759–769.

Charlton, J., Kelly, S., Dunnell, K., Evans, B., & Jenkins, R. (1992). Suicide deaths in England and Wales: Trends in factors associated with suicide deaths. *Population Trends, 71*, 34–42.

Department of Health (England) (2002). *National Suicide Prevention Strategy for England*. London: Department of Health, available at http://www.dh.gov.uk/prod_consum_dh/groups/dh_ digitalassets/@dh/@en/documents/digitalasset/dh_4019548.pdf.

Diez-Roux A. V. (1998). Bringing context back into epidemiology: Variables and fallacies in multilevel analysis. *American Journal of Public Health, 88*, 216–222.

Drever, F. & Bunting, J. (1997). Patterns and trends in male mortality. In F. Drever & M. Whitehead (Eds.), *Health Inequalities* (pp. 95–107). London: The Stationery Office.

Drever, F., Bunting, J., & Harding, D. (1997). Male mortality from major causes of death. In F. Drever & M. Whitehead (Eds.), *Health Inequalities* (pp. 122–142). London: The Stationery Office.

Exeter, D. & Boyle, P. (2007). Does young adult suicide cluster geographically in Scotland? *Journal of Epidemiology & Community Health, 61*, 731–736.

Exeter, D., Boyle, P., Feng, Z., Flowerdew, R., & Scheirloh, N. (2005). The creation of 'Consistent Areas Through Time' (CATTs) in Scotland, 1981–2001. *Population Trends, 119*, 28–36.

Fox, A. J. & Goldblatt, P. O. (1982). *Longitudinal Study: Socio-demographic and mortality differentials, 1971–1975*. London: HMSO.

Goldney, R. D. (2000). Prediction of suicide and attempted suicide. In K. Hawton & K. van Heeringen (Eds.), *International Handbook of Suicide and Attempted Suicide* (pp. 585–595). Chichester: John Wiley & Sons, Ltd.

Graham, H. (2004). Tackling inequalities in health in England: Remedying health disadvantages, narrowing health gaps or reducing health gradients? *Journal of Social Policy, 33*, 115–131.

Greenland, S. (2001). Ecologic versus individual-level sources of bias in ecologic estimates of contextual health effects. *International Journal of Epidemiology, 30*, 1343–1350.

Haynes, R. & Gayle, S. (2000). Deprivation and poor health in rural areas: Inequalities hidden by averages. *Health & Place, 6*, 275–285.

Judge, K., Platt, S., Costongs, C., & Jurczak, K. (2006). *Health Inequalities: A challenge for Europe*. Independent report commissioned by, and published under the auspices of, the UK Presidency of the EU. London: COI, available at http://www.dh.gov.uk/prod_consum_dh/groups/dh_digitalassets/@dh/@en/documents/digitalasset/dh_4121583.pdf.

Kelly, S. & Bunting, J. (1998). Trends in suicide in England and Wales, 1982–96. *Population Trends, 92*, 29–41.

Kelly, S., Charlton, J., & Jenkins, R. (1995). Suicide deaths in England and Wales, 1982–92: The contribution of occupation and geography. *Population Trends, 80*, 16–25.

Kreitman, N. (1976). The coal gas story: UK suicide rates, 1960–71. *British Journal of Preventive and Social Medicine, 30*, 86–93.

Kreitman, N., Carstairs, V., & Duffy, J. (1991). Association of age and social class with suicide among men in Great Britain. *Journal of Epidemiology & Community Health, 45*, 195–202.

Kreitman, N. & Platt, S. (1984). Suicide, unemployment and domestic gas detoxification in Great Britain. *Journal of Epidemiology & Community Health, 38*, 1–6.

Leenaars, A. A. & Lester, D. (1995). The changing suicide pattern in Canadian adolescents and youth compared to their American counterparts. *Adolescence, 30*, 539–547.

Leitner, M., Barr, W., & Hobby, L. (2008). *Effectiveness of Interventions to Prevent Suicide and Suicidal Behaviour: A systematic review*. Edinburgh: Scottish Government Social Research, available at http://www.scotland.gov.uk/Resource/Doc/209331/0055420.pdf (full report); http://www.scotland.gov.uk/Resource/Doc/208325/0055246.pdf (summary report).

Lewis, G. & Sloggett, A. (1998). Suicide, unemployment, and deprivation: Record linkage study. *British Medical Journal, 317*, 1283–1286.

Lorant., V., Kunst, A., Huisman, M., Costa, G., & Mackenbach, J. (2005). Socio-economic inequalities in suicide: a European comparative study. *British Journal of Psychiatry, 187*, 49–54.

Mackenbach, J. (2006). *Health Inequalities: Europe in profile*. Independent report commissioned by, and published under the auspices of, the UK Presidency of the EU. London: COI, available at http://www.dh.gov.uk/prod_consum_dh/groups/dh_digitalassets/@dh/@en/documents/digitalasset/dh_4121584.pdf.

Mann, J. J., Apter, A., Bertolote, J., Beautrais, A., Currier, D., Haas, A., *et al.* (2005). Suicide prevention strategies: A systematic review. *Journal of the American Medical Association, 294,* 2064–2074.

Morgenstern, H. (1995). Ecologic studies in epidemiology: Concepts, principles, and methods. *Annual Review of Public Health, 16,* 61–81.

Pickett, K. E. & Pearl, M. (2001). Multilevel analyses of neighbourhood socioeconomic context and health outcomes: A critical review. *Journal of Epidemiology & Community Health, 55,* 111–122.

Platt, S. (1984) Unemployment and suicidal behaviour: A review of the literature. *Social Science and Medicine, 19,* 93–115.

Platt, S. (1986). Parasuicide and unemployment. *British Journal of Psychiatry, 149,* 401–405.

Platt, S., Boyle, P., Crombie, I., Feng, Z., & Exeter, D. (2007). *The Epidemiology of Suicide in Scotland 1989–2004: An examination of temporal trends and risk factors at national and local levels.* Edinburgh: Scottish Executive Social Research,, available at http://www.scotland.gov.uk/Publications/2007/03/01145422/20; http://www.scotland.gov.uk/Publications/2007/03/01 145517/2.

Platt, S. & Hawton, K. (2000). Suicidal behaviour and the labour market. In K. Hawton & K. van Heeringen (Eds.), *International Handbook of Suicide and Attempted Suicide* (pp. 309–384). Chichester: John Wiley & Sons, Ltd.

Platt, S., Hawton, K., Kreitman, N., Fagg, J., & Foster, J. (1988). Recent clinical and epidemiological trends in parasuicide in Edinburgh and Oxford: A tale of two cities. *Psychological Medicine, 18,* 405–418.

Platt, S., McLean, J., McCollam, A., Blamey, A., Mackenzie, M., McDaid, D., Maxwell, M., Halliday, E., & Woodhouse, A. (2006). *Evaluation of the First Phase of Choose Life: The National Strategy and Action Plan to Prevent Suicide in Scotland.* Edinburgh: Scottish Executive Social Research, available at http://www.scotland.gov.uk/Publications/2006/09/06094657/22 (main report); http://www.scotland.gov.uk/Publications/2006/09/06094756/0 (summary).

Platt, S., Micciolo, R., & Tansella, M. (1992). Suicide and unemployment in Italy: Description, analysis and interpretation of recent trends. *Social Science and Medicine, 34,* 1191–1201.

Proudfoot, J., Guest, D., Carson, J., Dunn, G., & Gray, J. (1997). Effect of cognitive-behavioural training on job-finding among long-term unemployed people. *The Lancet, 350,* 96–100.

Rehkopf, D. H. & Buka, S. L. (2005). The association between suicide and the socio-economic characteristics of geographical areas: a systematic review. *Psychological Medicine, 36,* 145–157.

Robinson, W. S. (1950). Ecological correlations and the behavior of individuals. *American Sociological Review, 15,* 351–357.

Rosen, A. (1954). Detection of suicidal patients: An example of some limitations in the prediction of infrequent events. *Journal of Consulting Psychology, 18,* 397–403.

Scottish Executive (1999). *Social Justice … A Scotland Where* Everyone *Matters.* Edinburgh: The Scottish Executive, available at http://scotland.gov.uk/Resource/Doc/158142/0042789.pdf.

Scottish Executive (2002). *Choose Life. A national strategy and action plan to prevent suicide in Scotland.* Edinburgh: The Stationery Office.

Scottish Executive (2003). *Improving Health in Scotland: The challenge, 2003.* Edinburgh: The Stationery Office, available at http://www.scotland.gov.uk/Resource/Doc/47034/0013854.pdf.

Scottish Executive (2006). *Scottish Executive Response to Choose Life Evaluation,* available at http://www.chooselife.net/web/FILES/Research&Reviews/SE_Response_to_Choose_Life_Evaluation_-_Copy_for_Distribution.pdf.

Stark, C., Belbin, A., Hopkins, P., Gibbs, D., Hay, A., & Gunnell, D. (2006). Male suicide and occupation in Scotland. *Health Statistics Quarterly, 29,* 26–29.

Thomson, H. (2008). A dose of realism for healthy urban policy: Lessons from area based initiatives in the UK. *Journal of Epidemiology & Community Health, 62,* 932–936.

Thomson, H., Atkinson, R., Petticrew, M., & Kearns, A. (2006). Do urban regeneration programmes improve public health and reduce health inequalities? A synthesis of the evidence from UK policy and practice (1980–2004). *Journal of Epidemiology and Community Health, 60,* 108–115.

Uren, Z., Fitzpatrick, J., Reid, A., & Goldblatt, P. (2001). Geographic variation in mortality by social class and alternative social classifications. In C. Griffiths & J. Fitzpatrick (Eds.), *Geographic Variations in Health* (pp. 339–358). Norwich: HMSO.

Vinokur, A. D., Schul, Y., Vuori, J., & Price, R. H. (2000). Two years after a job loss: Long-term impact of the JOBS program on reemployment and mental health. *Journal of Occupational Psychology, 5,* 32–47.

Vuori, J. & Silvonen, J. (2005). The benefits of a preventative job search program on re-employment and mental health at 2-year follow-up. *Journal of Occupational and Organizational Psychology, 78,* 43–52.

CHAPTER FOURTEEN

Religion and Suicide: Integrating Four Theories Cross-nationally

Steven Stack and Augustine J. Kposowa

Abstract

The literature on religion and suicide has neglected cross-national analysis, an integration of the three principal sociological perspectives, and the moral community's perspective. The present study fills these gaps in the literature. It briefly reviews the traditional perspectives: religious integration, where the sheer number of shared religious beliefs and practices lowers suicide; religious commitment, where adherence to a few life-saving beliefs can lower suicide; and religious networks, where the social support derived from interaction with co-religionists lowers suicide. A new moral community perspective, where individual-level suicidality is shaped by the level of religiosity in the nation of residence, is delineated. In such a case, social interaction can lower suicide risk for both religious and non-religious persons. The analysis includes a bi-level test of an integrated model. Data are from the World Values Surveys and refer to 50,547 individuals nested in 56 nations. Individual-level suicide acceptability serves as the dependent variable. Results from a hierarchical linear model confirm all three traditional perspectives on religion and suicide. Protective factors include Islam, church attendance, and time spent with co-religionists. Indicators of all three perspectives are linked to reports that religion provides comfort and strength. Importantly, the moral community hypothesis was also supported. Controlling for a variety of socio-demographic variables, individuals nested in nations with high levels of religiosity are found to have lower suicide acceptability. Both the characteristics of nations and individuals predict individual suicidality. Clinicians can reinforce existing religiosity levels in clients to enhance effectiveness in suicide prevention.

International Handbook of Suicide Prevention: Research, Policy and Practice, First Edition.
Edited by Rory C. O'Connor, Stephen Platt, Jacki Gordon.
© 2011 John Wiley & Sons, Ltd. Published 2011 by John Wiley & Sons, Ltd.

Introduction

Religiosity has been discussed and debated as a major protective factor against suicidality in over a century of sociological work (Bankston, Allen, & Cunningham, 1983; Lester, 2000; Morselli, 1882; Pope & Danigelis, 1981; Stack, 2000). The empirical findings of this literature have been assessed through several narrative reviews (e.g., Colucci & Martin, 2008; Koenig, McCullough, & Larson, 2001; Lester, 2000; Stack, 1982, 2000). These findings are mixed, but tend to support the basic premise that religion provides protection against suicide risk.

There are, however, several recurrent limitations of the literature on suicidality and religion. First, there has been a neglect of multi-level models. These are models that suggest that contextual factors affect individual behaviour or outcomes. For example, in the multi-level framework, a person dies by suicide because of influences due to personal characteristics plus factors due to the parish, county, or even country of residence. The bulk of sociological work has been based on highly aggregated data (e.g., Breault, 1986, 1988; Cutright & Fernquist, 2000a, 2000b, 2005; Stack, 1980, 1985; for reviews see Colucci & Martin, 2008; Lester, 2000; Stack, 1982, 2000). It is unclear whether social processes at the macro-level operate at the individual-level of analysis (Breault, 1994; Stack, 2000). In the related fields of social psychiatry and social psychology there has been some individual-level analysis. However, this work neglects macro-level mediators (which are affected by risk factors, and in turn affect suicidality) and moderators (which, when combined with risk factors, multiply the risk of suicidality) of individual-level relationships (e.g., Dervic, Grunebaum, Burke, Mann, & Oquendo, 2006; Dervic, Oquendo, Currier, Grunebaum, Burke, *et al.*, 2006; Joe, Romer, & Jamieson, 2007; Kaslow, Thompson, Okun, Price, Young, *et al.*, 2002). Clearly, bi-level models are needed to fully understand the mix of individual social forces behind suicidality. Suicidality includes suicide ideation, suicide plans, suicide attempts, and suicide completions. Second, the literature is based mostly on single-nation studies of developed nations, with a focus on the United States (e.g., Bankston, Allen, & Cunningham, 1983; Cleary & Brannick, 2007; Dervic, Gruenebaum, *et al.*, 2006; Dervic, Oquendo, *et al.*, 2006; Joe *et al.*, 2007; Kaslow *et al.*, 2002; Maris, 1981; Pescosolido, 1990; Pescosolido & Georgiana, 1989; Stack, 1985; Stack & Wasserman, 1992; Trovato, 1986; 1992; van Tubergen, te Grotenhuis, & Ultee, 2005). Relatively little attention has been given to the less developed nations and to investigations based on large samples of countries (for exceptions, see Cutright, Stack, & Fernquist, 2007; Neeleman, Halpern, Leon, & Lewis, 1997; Stack & Kposowa, 2008). It is largely unclear to what extent the religion–suicidality relationship would apply to other nations, including those in the traditions of Eastern religious faiths. Third, the research has neglected an integrated model, which would combine indicators of the three principal sociological perspectives on religion as a protective factor against suicide into a coherent whole. These perspectives are religious integration, religious commitment, and religious networks and will be discussed in detail below. In no case have all three perspectives been tested in a single paper, and in many studies indicators of key theoretical constructs, such as the number of religious beliefs/integration and frequency of interaction with co-religionists, have been measured only indirectly as religious books produced and affiliation with a fundamentalist church (e.g., Cutright, Stack, & Fernquist, 2007; Pescosolido, 1990; Stack, 1983). Finally, while all perspectives on religion and suicide assume that religion promotes coping mechanisms that help the individual through stressful times, it is rare for direct measures of religious coping to be included in analyses of suicidality (for an exception see a study of African American high school students by Molock, Puri, Matlin, & Barksdale, 2006).

The present chapter starts by reviewing the existing research on religion and suicide. It then contributes to the empirical literature by performing a cross-national investigation which addresses three key limitations of that literature. Using cross-national data representing all major religions, a multi-level model of suicide acceptability is tested. The present study also synthesizes aspects of religious integration, religious commitment, and religious network theories into a coherent model. Finally, there is an analysis of the extent to which religion actually promotes religious coping (Stack, 1983, 2000). The investigation is the first rigorous, world-wide exploration of a multi-level analysis of an integrated theoretical model of religion and suicidality.

Religion and Suicidality: A Review of Research and Theory

An inspection of previous narrative reviews (e.g., Colucci & Martin, 2008; Lester, 2000; Stack, 1982, 2000) and a search through Sociological abstracts found a total of 162 relevant studies. These contained at least one empirical finding relating some aspect of religion to some dimension of suicidality (completion, attempt, ideation, or acceptability). These studies span 117 years, dating between 1882 and 2008. Most of the existing studies that report a relevant finding do so in passing as part of a much larger epidemiological investigation. Many such inquiries report a single metric, such as a rate, correlation coefficient, or pair of percentages (e.g., Danto & Danto, 1983; Comstock & Partridge, 1972; Lester, 1996, 1998; Middleton, Ashby, & Clark, 1961).

A total of 133 out of 162 studies (82.1%) report one or more finding suggesting that religion serves as a protective factor against suicide. In 63 studies (38.9%), all findings suggest this protective effect, while 29 studies (17.9%) find no evidence of a protective effect. However, 70 of the studies (43.2%) present both negative and positive effects, which suggest that the relationship is often conditional or mediated or moderated by other variables. The studies vary tremendously in their measurement of constructs and also differ substantially in their samples, which range from specialized sets of individuals, such as highly depressed patients seen in a single emergency room or a class of students in a university, to investigations based on national probability samples of the general population or studies of suicide rates in up to 71 nations (e.g., Joe *et al.*, 2007; Simpson & Conklin, 1989).

This large body of work is organized herein around how its findings relate to three sociological models: integration, commitment, and networks (Stack, 2000). Each theory is discussed briefly and a succinct assessment of its empirical validity is presented through a selection of the better designed investigations, including those employing a control group, a wide variety of control variables, and representative, community-based samples.

Investigations are grouped into two categories: those based on highly aggregate data, such as counties, cities, and nations; and those based on individual-level data, such as students, representative samples of non-institutionalized individuals, and samples of psychiatric patients.

Religious integration

The first analysis of religion and suicide documented a relationship between the religious affiliation of European states and their suicide rates. Catholic states had a rate of 5.8/100,000 compared with a rate of 19.0/100,000 in Protestant states (Morselli, 1882). Durkheim (1897) explained these social facts with a theory of religious integration. Integration involved subordination of the individual to the collectivity. In particular, the greater the sheer number of religious beliefs and practices of a religious system, the higher the integration and lower the suicide risk (Durkheim, 1897; Stack 1982, 2000). In the nineteenth-century European context, Catholicism represented a religious system with a high number of religious beliefs and practices (e.g., divorce and remarriage were prohibited, weekly church attendance was required, meatless Fridays, confession of sins, etc.).

Research on religion and suicide over the 100 years since Morselli (1882) was dominated by studies measuring religion in terms of Christian and Jewish religious affiliations (Durkheim, 1897; Halbwachs, 1930; Moreselli, 1882; for reviews see Colucci & Martin, 2008; Stack 1982, 2000). However, in the century after Morselli's and Durkheim's classic works, Catholic theology has been liberalized and shared religious practices, such as confession and church attendance, have declined. Hence, given a convergence between Christian faiths in modern times, indicators such as the percentage of the population that is Catholic are often found to be unrelated to aggregate-level suicide rates (for reviews, see Lester, 2000; Stack, 1982, 2000).

Aggregate-level research   Nearly all sociological work on denomination and suicide has been set at the ecological or aggregate-level (e.g., Kowalski, Faupel, & Starr, 1987; Lester, 1998; Pescosolido & Georgiana, 1989; Pescosolido, 1990; Stack, 1980). A limitation of this level of analysis is that it is not possible to make any definitive assertions on the exact religious affiliation of the people who complete suicide, if percentage Catholic is related to suicide rates in nations or other aggregates. Further, when percentage Catholic is related to suicide rates, much or all of the effect is often due to a mediator, most notably the vitality of family life, measured typically by the divorce rate (e.g., Burr, McCall, & Powell-Griner, 1994; Stack, 1980). To the extent that Catholicism still discourages divorce more than other religious denominations, we would expect that Catholicism would lower suicide rates indirectly through such normative controls (Stack, 2000).

Related aggregate-level work on suicidality has advanced new denominational measures, including Islam and Protestant fundamentalism (e.g., Pescosolido & Georgiana, 1989; Simpson & Conklin, 1989). Some denominational measures of religion still capture high levels of religious integration and reduce suicide risk. Islam in particular is well known for its strong condemnation of suicide in the Quran and its associated low suicide rates (e.g., Bertolote & Fleishman, 2002; Colucci & Martin, 2008; Koenig, McCullough, & Larson, 2001).

A related body of research has focused on church membership as an index of integration (e.g., Bainbridge, 1989; Breault, 1986, 1988; Burr, McCall, & Powell-Griner, 1994; Cutright & Fernquist, 2000a, 2000b; Ellison, Burr, & McCall, 1997; Girard, 1988; Stark, Doyle, & Rushing, 1983). Persons belonging to a church, as a group, are arguably higher in religious beliefs and practices than the unaffiliated. At the aggregate-level of analysis, while church membership rates tend to be associated with lower suicide rates of aggregates such as counties and states, a control for the covariates of church membership, such as divorce rates, often weakens or removes the association between church membership rates and suicide rates, especially in the case of city- and state-level data (Bainbridge, 1989; Breault, 1986, 1988; Burr, McCall, & Powell-Griner, 1994; Ellison, Burr, & McCall, 1997; Girard, 1988). In all analyses it remains unclear to what extent non-church members account for the actual suicides in counties and states.

Individual-level research   Studies based on community, non-psychiatric populations at the individual-level tend to suggest the persistence of denominational differences well into the twentieth century (e.g., Danto & Danto, 1983; Maris, 1981). For example, in Chicago male Catholics under 25 years had a suicide rate of 16/100,000 compared with 28/100,000 for Protestants under 25 years (Maris, 1981). However, in areas where Catholics are in a minority of the population, such as in the United Kingdom, research on psychiatric patients tends to find that Catholics do not have a suicide risk lower than that of Protestants (e.g., Middleton, Ashby, & Clark, 1961).

Research at the individual level that uses basic church membership versus non-affiliation as its measure of religiosity also tends to find an association between religion and suicide. For example, Dervic, Oquendo, Grunbaum, Ellis, Burke, *et al.* (2004) found that 66% of 371 highly depressed inpatients with no religious affiliation had attempted suicide compared with only 48% of the patients with a religious affiliation. Dervic *et al.* (2004) determined that having a religious affiliation was associated with lower risk of suicide ideation.

In the late 1960s researchers started to draw on religious measures other than religious affiliation (Kranitz, Abrahams, Spiegel, & Keith-Spiegel, 1968). Two new perspectives, derived from Durkheim, developed in the last quarter of a century. Each placed emphasis on one of his two principal dimensions of religious integration: shared beliefs or orthodoxy in the religious commitment perspective; and religious practices or interaction in the religious networks perspective (Stack, 2000).

Religious commitment

The religious commitment perspective argues that the sheer number of religious beliefs and practices, fundamental to the concept of religious integration, might not be as critical as the commitment to a few life-saving beliefs (Stack, 1983, 2000; Stark, Doyle, & Rushing, 1983). For example, a belief in an afterlife, where one who suffered through stressful life events such as widowhood, divorce, job loss, and physical disabilities, could experience bliss, would save more lives from suicide than a belief in the Virgin birth (Stack, 1983, 2000). Further, the degree of adherence to some central components of religious orthodoxy could save lives no matter what denomination one happened to belong to.

Aggregate-level research   These studies use suicide rates of populations, such as nations, and religious characteristics of these populations, such as religious book production, as indirect measures of exposure to, and internalization of, specific life-saving religious beliefs. Fourteen studies have used religious book production as an index of religious commitment/integration (e.g., Cutright & Fernquist, 2000a, 2000b, 2001a, 2001b, 2008; Cutright, Stack, & Fernquist, 2007; Fernquist, 2003, 2007; Fernquist & Cutright, 1998; Stack, 1983, 1989, 1991, 1992a, 1992b). While the findings are mixed, most of this work documents the expected protective effect of religious commitment on suicide rates and suicide risk.

Individual-level research   There is a limited literature from social psychology that tests the individual-level relationship between religious orthodoxy and suicidality. Investigations of completed suicide at the local level have found that the frequency of exposure to religious beliefs (church attendance) tends to reduce suicidality (e.g., Comstock & Partridge, 1972; Maris, 1981). For example, in a six-year study, frequent church attendees had a suicide rate of 7.5/100,000, approximately half that of the rate of infrequent attendees (15.8/100,000) (Comstock & Partridge, 1972). An investigation of 1,098 high school students' religious orthodoxy (adherence to a set of religious beliefs) and intrinsic or existential religiosity significantly reduced the perceived risk of suicide. In the authors' multivariate analysis only religious orthodoxy, depression, and race lowered suicide ideation. Religious orthodoxy significantly lowered both depression and hopelessness covariates of suicide ideation (Greening & Stoppelbein, 2002). Further, in a study of 499 college students, Walker and Bishop (2005) tied intrinsic religiosity to lower risk of suicide ideation. In the largest study to date ($n = 33,135$ high school students), the greater the church attendance, the lower the odds of suicide ideation (Kay & Francis, 2006). Unfortunately, this body of work is largely restricted to local student populations in the United States and the United Kingdom. Its generalizability to less developed nations, the adult population, and Eastern religions is largely unknown. Further, no study on the adult population has ever measured the extent of actual religious coping as it relates to suicidality.

Religious networks

Religious networks theory presents a third way of linking religiosity to suicidality (e.g., Pescosolido, 1990; Pescosolido & Georgiana, 1989; Stack, 2000). This perspective highlights the life-saving features of religion, including social ties to co-religionists. The social support derived from contact with religious persons of the same faith was a new point of emphasis. Certain religious structures promote friendship ties and generalized interaction among co-religionists. These structural components include non-ecumenicalism, non-hierarchical power relations, a conservative ideology, and a tension between religious and mainstream culture.

Aggregate-level research   Empirical investigations of this perspective have centred largely on highly aggregate data. For example, counties with a high proportion of fundamentalist Christians (which presumably also have strong social networks and high participation rates) tend to have lower overall suicide rates than their counterparts, especially in areas where they represent the dominant or traditional faith group (e.g., Pescosolido & Georgiana, 1989; Pescosolido, 1990).

Individual-level research   An analysis of American individual-level data found relation-ships between suicide acceptability, on the one hand, and denominational indicators of non-ecumenicalism, tension between religious and societal cultures, and Presbyterian gov-erning structures, on the other hand. This supported the structural elements of the net-work theory of suicide (Stack & Wasserman, 1992).

Of the 162 studies on religion and suicide, there is not one that measures interaction with co-religionists directly (e.g., number of times per month such interaction takes place). It still remains largely unclear if individuals who have extensive religious networks with co-religionists actually have a lower level of suicidality.

We view these three perspectives as complementary, rather than mutually exclusive. For example, persons high in religious orthodoxy may be more apt than others to seek out social relationships with co-religionists, who may, in turn, provide emotional support. However, none of the three leading perspectives on religion and suicide has tested a multi-level model, specifically the moral community perspective, to which we now turn.

Moral community perspective

According to the moral community perspective, the aggregate-level of religion in a group (e.g., neighbourhood, city, county, state or nation) will affect the attitudes and behaviours of individuals in that group (Baier & Wright, 2001; Stack & Kposowa, 2006; Stark, 1996). Religious teachings have more of an influence on lone individuals if these teachings are reinforced by those around them in everyday life. Further, a strong moral community can be expected to help to reduce the 'deviant' behaviours and attitudes (e.g., those concerning both criminal behaviour and behaviour that deviates from group norms) of non-believers, as religious persons interact with their counterparts (van Tubergen, te Grotenhuis, & Ultee, 2005). In such moral communities, there should be relatively less deviant behav-iours and attitudes, including a lower level of suicide acceptability.

In order to undertake a rigorous assessment of the moral community hypothesis, data on both individual-level and aggregate-level religiosity need to be collected in the same investigation. Of the 162 studies on religion and suicide, only two include refer-ence to multi-level results (Neeleman *et al.*, 1997; van Tubergen, te Grotenhuis, & Ultee, 2005). Van Tubergen and colleagues (2005) determined that an increase in the proportion of religious persons in a particular denomination in a municipality decreased the odds of death by suicide for individuals in each of the four religious categories studied. Hence, the protective influence of religious groups spreads out and affects the community as a whole, not just the members of a particular denomination. Neeleman *et al.* (1997) make a brief mention of some auxiliary findings from a multi-level model, where the religion–suicide acceptability relationship is stronger in nations with high levels of religiousness.

The recurrent limitations of the work on religion and suicide include a lack of research that tests an integrated model of the four explanatory schemes discussed above, neglect of cross-national analysis, and a relative lack of work using individual-level data and measures of key constructs from religious network theory. We now turn to a discussion of the present original analysis that addresses such limitations.

New Analysis of an Integrated Model

Data were obtained from the World Values Survey, Wave 4, conducted during 1999–2001 (Inglehart, 2004). The World Values surveys constitute the largest set of investigations ever conducted on the attitudes, beliefs, and values of scores of nations from around the world (Inglehart & Baker, 2000). The survey is based on nationally representative samples of the adult population. After taking into account missing information, data were available for 50,547 persons in 56 countries.

Variables and measurement

The dependent variable is suicide acceptability, which was measured as a single-item index. The item was: 'Please tell me whether or not you think that suicide can always be justified, never be justified or somewhere in between?' Respondents were given a set of possible answers, on a global scale ranging from 1 = low approval of suicide to 10 = high approval of suicide, where 1 and 10 are anchor points.

Suicide acceptability is significantly related to other categories of suicidal behaviour, including suicide ideation or thinking about ending one's life (e.g., Dervic, Grunebaum, *et al.*, 2006; Eskin, 2004; Eshun, 2003; Kocmur & Dernovsek, 2003; Stein, Witzum, Brom, DeNour, & Elizur, 1992), the presence of actual plans for carrying out suicide (Joe *et al.*, 2007), suicide attempts (e.g., Anglin, Kamien, & Kaslow, 2005; De Wilde, Kienhorst, Diekstra, & Wolters, 1993, Dervic, Grunebaum, *et al.*, 2006; Dervic, Oquendo, *et al.*, 2006; King, Hampton, Bernstein, & Schichor, 1996) and suicide completions measured at the aggregate level (e.g., Cutright & Fernquist 2000a, 2000b, 2001, 2005, 2008; Cutright, Stack, & Fernquist, 2007; Neeleman *et al.*, 1997; Stack, 1996; Stack & Kposowa, 2008). For example, an investigation of a large, nationally representative sample of young persons (*n* = 3,301) found that those who strongly believe that it is acceptable to end one's life are 12.7 times more likely than their counterparts to make a plan to kill themselves (Joe *et al.*, 2007). Given close associations between suicide acceptability and higher levels of suicidality, it is assumed that conditions found linked to suicide acceptability in the present analysis would be predictive of suicide attempts and completions. Past research has tended to establish such a connection.

Moral community

The macro-level predictor is the mean level of national attendance at religious services. Here the unit of analysis is the nation. Nations are divided into two groups using the grand mean: (a) low religiosity group, comprising those nations with mean religiosity levels from 1.42 (China) to 4.40 (Austria); and (b) high religiosity nations with a range from 4.49 (Morocco) to a high of 7.39 (Nigeria). Low religiosity countries comprised the reference group for comparison.

Measures of individual-level religiosity

The measures of individual-level religiosity were grouped into the three theoretical models on religion and suicidality.

Religious integration   Following Durkheim (1897), the religions of the world were divided into major denominations: Buddhist, Catholic, Hindu, Muslim, Orthodox, Protestant, and a residual category of all other religions. Persons with no religious affiliation constituted the reference category.

Religious commitment   The essence of religious coping is captured in the WVS item: 'Do you find that you get comfort and strength from religion or not?' We coded 1 = yes, and 0 all others (mainly no, with some don't knows and less than 1% no answers).

Religious orthodoxy   The World Values Survey contains complete data on three core life-saving beliefs: beliefs in God, Hell and Afterlife. Positive responses were summed. The index ranges from 0 to 3. Cronbach's alpha reliability coefficient for the index was 0.69.

Exposure to religious beliefs   The degree of exposure to life-saving beliefs was measured as the frequency of attendance at religious services. The item in the World Values Survey is: 'Apart from weddings, funerals, and christenings, how often do you attend religious services these days?' The responses were coded from 0 (never, practically never) through to 6 (more than once a week). This variable is treated as a quantitative variable and, as such, there is no reference category, although the baseline is zero.

Religious networks   The following item was used to measure interaction with co-religionists: 'How often do you spend time with people from your church, mosque, or synagogue?' Scores ranged from 0 (not at all) through to 3 (weekly, nearly every week).

Control variables

Social learning theory   From social learning theory (Akers, 1998; Stack & Kposowa, 2008), wherein persons' attitudes are learned through their interaction in social networks, approval of suicidality might be part of a broader commitment to a generalized ideology of liberalism (e.g., Stack & Kposowa, 2008). *Political liberalism*, a general index from social learning theory, was captured using a scale derived from the WVS that ranged from very conservative to very liberal. The range is 10 with a minimum of 1 and a maximum of 10. For the few missing cases, the mean was substituted.

Social control theory   Social control theory (e.g., Hirschi, 1969; Stack & Kposowa, 2008) posits that individuals with weak bonds to social institutions have less to lose from crime and deviant behaviours. In contrast, persons with strong bonds to family and other institutions are more controlled by such ties. This perspective anticipates that those with weak attachments to others have less of a stake in life, thus increasing the probability of deviant behaviour and attitudes, including those comprising suicidality. We employ three measures of stake in life. *Marital status* was measured using three dummy variables: divorced (0,1), widowed (0,1), and single (0,1). The married were the reference group. To measure *life satisfaction*, the survey asked respondents to rank order their global satisfaction with life on a scale ranging from 1 (very dissatisfied) to 10 (very satisfied). As for *social class* (social status), survey respondents were posed the following question: 'People sometimes describe themselves as belonging to the working class, the middle class, or the upper or lower class. Would you describe yourself as belonging to the (5) upper class, (4) upper middle class, (3) lower middle class, (2) working class, (1) lower class?'

Finally, age was coded in years. Older generations are often more conservative in their attitudes towards deviance (e.g., Stack, 1998a; Stack, Wasserman, & Kposowa, 1994). Gender was measured as 1 = male. Females were the reference group. Women are generally more conservative in their beliefs and attitudes regarding the acceptability of deviance, behaviours including crimes against organizations such as tax fraud and its acceptability, crimes without victims such as prostitution and its acceptability, and crimes involving aggression such as assault and its acceptability (e.g., Agnew, 1998; Stack, 1998a, 1998b).

Statistical estimation

Since the World Values Survey constitutes a hierarchical data structure with individual respondents located in their countries of residence, hierarchical linear and non-linear modelling techniques were used (Raudenbush & Bryk, 2002; SAS Institute, 2006, 2007; Singer, 1998). Level 1 comprises individual respondents, and the second level consists of countries. Parameters for the model were estimated using the SAS MIXED procedure, version 9.1 (SAS Institute, 2007).

Results

The results are summarized in Table 14.1. The findings provide evidence in support of the *moral community hypothesis, the notion that individual-level attitudes are conditioned by those of the group within which they reside.* High religiosity nations were significantly less likely to have accepting attitudes towards suicide ($\beta = -0.268$; $t = -4.67$).

Table 14.1 Hierarchical linear regression results of the effect of national religiosity on suicide acceptability, World Values surveys, 1999–2000

Variables	β	Std Error	*t*-value	*p*-value
Intercept (γ_{00})	0.922*	0.052	18.41	0.0001
Moral Community Theory				
National religious attendance				
Low attendance	Reference			
High attendance	−0.268*	0.058	−4.67	0.0001
Religious integration				
No denomination	Reference			
Catholic	0.002	0.013	0.19	0.8458
Orthodox	−0.007	0.018	−0.38	0.7063
Muslim	−0.101*	0.016	−6.41	0.0001
Hindu	−0.001	0.032	−0.02	0.9853
Buddhist	−0.060*	0.025	−2.40	0.0027
Protestant	−0.019	0.015	−1.21	0.2761
Other denomination	−0.024	0.015	−1.61	0.1065
Religious commitment				
Comfort and strength in religion	−0.076*	0.008	−9.18	0.0001
Religious orthodoxy	−0.049*	0.004	−13.09	0.0001
Exposure to religious beliefs				
Attendance at religious services	−0.009*	0.001+	−5.68	0.0001
Religious networks				
Time spent with co-religionists	−0.019*	0.004	−6.71	0.0001
Social learning theory				
Liberalism	0.005*	0.001	3.94	0.0001
Social control theory				
Marital status				
Married	Reference			
Divorced/separated	0.052*	0.013	4.06	0.0001
Widowed	0.003	0.012	0.27	0.7864
Single/never married	0.038*	0.007	5.12	0.0001
Life satisfaction	−0.009*	0.001	−7.41	0.0001
Social class	0.023*	0.003	6.75	0.0001
Control variables				
Sex				
Female	Reference			
Male	0.007	0.005	1.16	0.2459
Age	−0.003*	0.000	−14.65	0.0001
Variance components				
Intercept (τ_{00}) (between-country)	0.042*	0.008	5.19[†]	0.0001
Level 1 variance (σ^2) (within-country)	0.251*	0.002	158.89[†]	0.0001
Intra-class correlation	14.34			
−2 log likelihood	99707.000*			

Continued

Table 14.1   *(cont'd)*

Variables	β	Std Error	*t*-value	*p*-value
LRS (df)	1787 (21)			
Maximum obs. per subject	2926			
Number of individuals	50,547			
Number of countries	56			

LRS = likelihood ratio statistic.
* p < 0.05.
† Based on z-test.

Concerning *religious integration* variables, persons of the Muslim denomination (religion) were much less likely than those without denomination to favour suicide. Buddhists were also less likely to favour suicide than individuals without denomination. With regard to *religious commitment theory*, both indicators were strongly associated with suicide tolerance. First, the greater the strength and comfort taken in religion, the lower the level of support for suicide. Second, religious orthodoxy significantly reduced support for suicide. Similarly, *exposure to religious beliefs* was strongly tied to attitudes against suicide. Frequency of attendance at religious services had a negative effect on pro-suicide ideology.

Religious network theory also had significant support. Controlling for the other variables (which include national religious attendance, religious denomination measures, religious commitment measures, attendance at religious services, liberalism, marital status, life satisfaction, social class, and demographic measures), the more time people spent with co-religionists, that is, others who shared their religious faith, the less likely were they to approve of suicide.

Both *social learning theory* and *social control theory* were supported by the statistical analyses. Liberalism (the measure of social learning) increased attitudes favouring suicide. Divorced and separated individuals were significantly more likely to support suicide than their married counterparts. Similarly, respondents who were single (never married) were more likely to favour suicide than married respondents. Widowhood was unrelated to suicide tolerance. Finally, older respondents were more likely to disapprove of suicide than younger ones.

Strength and comfort in religion, an index of religious coping, was one of the main predictors of suicide acceptability. In an analysis not fully reported here (contact the authors for the details), the set of independent variables from Table 14.1 were used to predict strength of religious coping. Highly religious nations were over 86% as likely to exhibit comfort and strength in religion as low religiosity countries. The religious integration measures were all associated with comfort and strength in religion. For example, adherents to the Muslim religion were 4.8 times more likely to admit deriving comfort and strength from their religion than individuals without denomination. Findings also showed that individuals with higher commitment to their faith (in terms of religious orthodoxy) were 2.4 times more likely to find strength and comfort in religion than persons with less commitment. In support of network theory, respondents who spent more time with fellow religionists were 38% more likely to have comfort and strength in religion than their counterparts who spent less or no time with other religionists.

Discussion

Previous research on religion and suicide acceptability has not tested the moral community hypothesis. The present investigation found that, controlling for a variety of sociodemographic factors, persons who reside in nations with a high mean level of religiosity had a lower level of suicide acceptability than persons who resided in nations with a low level of religiosity. This suggests that the influence of religion in a nation affects a variety of persons, both religious and non-religious, and of various faith groups.

The findings at the individual-level provided qualified to strong support for all three perspectives on religion and suicide. The principal finding supporting a religious integration perspective was a very strong association between an under-studied Eastern religion, Islam, and low suicide acceptability. Given very high levels of religious rituals and shared religious beliefs among contemporary Muslims, we would anticipate this finding (Bertolote & Fleishman, 2002).

With respect to religious commitment theory, controlling for other variables, the index of adherence to key religious beliefs, including belief in an afterlife, was an important predictor of suicidality. Exposure to religious beliefs, with attendance at religious services serving as a marker, also lowered suicide acceptability net of controls. Further, the greater the reported strength and comfort received from religion, the lower the suicide acceptability. This particular finding provides the most direct support for the notion that commitment to religion assuages problems with living. The vast majority of previous research has used very indirect measures of commitment to religious doctrines, including 14 studies that use national rates of religious book production. The present study establishes a firmer empirical grounding for religious commitment theory by using direct measures of commitment.

The results also provide the first individual-level results that confirm the third sociological perspective, the relationship between religious networks and suicide. The greater the actual interaction with co-religionists, the less the suicide acceptability reported by individuals. Previous work on network theory has overwhelmingly used indirect measures of presumed interaction with co-religionists, such as membership in a fundamentalist church (e.g., Pescosolido, 1990; Pescosolido & Georgiana, 1989; Stack & Wasserman, 1992). In summary, future work on religion and suicide will be strengthened by adopting an integrative model with indicators from all three theories of religion and suicide.

While all perspectives on religion and suicide received strong support in the present investigation, the policy implications are limited. From a Durkheimian or sociological perspective on suicide, the characteristics of nations (e.g., level of economic development, degree of modernization in the cultural system (including religious systems) which conditions suicide acceptability, and major dysfunctions in the economic system such as depressions) are the principal predictors of suicidality. Levels of religiosity in societies tend to weaken with societal development and, consequently, if all else is equal, suicide rates tend to rise. Nevertheless, those interested in suicide prevention at the individual-level might determine if their patients or clients have religious ties. If so, these ties might be emphasized as part of an individual-centred treatment package.

Conclusion

Finally, while the literature on religion and suicide has generally assumed that religion helps to prevent suicide, in part, through providing a set of coping mechanisms, this core assumption has rarely been tested in any direct fashion. The present investigation provides the first comparative results documenting that indicators of all major sociological perspectives on religion reduce suicidality by promoting religious coping. However, the measure of suicidality in the present study is suicide acceptability. While previous research has found that suicide acceptability tends to predict other measures of suicidality (such as suicide ideation, suicide plans, suicide attempts, and suicide completions), due to the lack of appropriate data within the World Values surveys, we were unable to demonstrate these associations in the present investigation. Possibly in future waves of the World Values survey a question on another measure of suicidality will be asked. If so, this gap in the literature can be addressed cross-nationally.

Note: Requests for the data used in this study should be directed to the Inter-University-Consortium for Political and Social Research (ICPSR), University of Michigan, Ann Arbor; this organization provided the data to the authors under standard contractual arrangements with ICPSR member institutions.

References

Agnew, R. (1998). The approval of suicide: A social psychological model. *Suicide and Life-Threatening Behavior, 28,* 205–225.

Akers, R. (1998). *Social Learning and Social Structure: A general theory of crime and deviance.* Boston, MA: Northeastern University Press.

Anglin, D. M., Kamien, O. S. G., & Kaslow, N. J. (2005). Suicide acceptability and religious well-being: A comparative analysis in African American suicide attempters and non-attempters. *Journal of Psychology and Theology, 33,* 140–150.

Baier, C. & Wright, B. R. E. (2001). If you love me keep my commandments: A meta analysis of the effect of religion on crime. *Journal of Research on Crime and Delinquency, 38,* 3–21.

Bainbridge, W. S. (1989). The religious ecology of deviance. *American Sociological Review, 54,* 288–295.

Bankston, W. B., Allen, H. D., & Cunningham, D. S. (1983). Religion and suicide: A research note on sociology's one law. *Social Forces, 62,* 521–528.

Bertolote, J. M. & Fleishmann, A. (2002). A global perspective in the epidemiology of suicide. *Suicidologi, 7,* 6–8.

Breault, K. (1986). Suicide in America: A test of Durkheim's theory of religious and family integration, 1933–1980. *American Journal of Sociology, 92,* 628–656.

Breault, K. (1988). Beyond the quick and dirty: Problems associated with analyses based on small samples of large ecological aggregates: Reply to Girard. *American Journal of Sociology, 93,* 1479–1486.

Breault, K. (1994). Was Durkheim right? A critical survey of the empirical literature on *Le Suicide.* In L. David (Ed.), *Emile Durkheim Le Suicide, 100 Years Later* (pp. 11–29). Philadelphia, PA: Charles Press.

Burr, W., McCall, P., & Powell-Griner, E. (1994). Catholic religion and suicide: The mediating effect of divorce. *Social Science Quarterly, 75*, 300–318.

Cleary, A. & Brannick, T. (2007). Suicide and changing values and beliefs in Ireland. *Crisis, 28*, 82–88.

Colucci, E. & Martin, G. (2008). Religion and spirituality along the suicidal path. *Suicide and Life-Threatening Behavior, 38*, 229–244.

Comstock, G. W. & Partridge, K. B. (1972). Church attendance and health. *Journal of Chronic Diseases, 25*, 665–672.

Cutright, P. & Fernquist, R. M. (2000a). Effects of social integration, period, region, and culture of suicide on male age specific suicide rates: 20 developed countries, 1955–1989. *Social Science Research, 29*, 148–172.

Cutright, P. & Fernquist, R. M. (2000b). Social integration, culture and period: Their impact on female age specific suicide rates in 20 developed countries, 1955–1989, *Sociological Focus, 33*, 299–319.

Cutright, P. & Fernquist, R. M. (2001a). The relative gender gap in suicide: Social integration, the culture of suicide, and period effects in 20 developed countries, 1955–1994. *Social Science Research, 30*, 76–99.

Cutright, P. & Fernquist, R. M. (2001b). The age structure of male suicide rates. *Social Science Research, 30*, 627–640.

Cutright, P. & Fernquist, R. M. (2005). Marital status integration, psychological well-being, and suicide acceptability as predictors of marital status differentials in suicide rates. *Social Science Research, 34*, 570–590.

Cutright, P. & Fernquist, R. (2008). Three explanations of marital status differences in suicide rates: Social integration, marital status integration, and the culture of suicide, *Omega, 56*, 175–190.

Cutright, P., Stack, S., & Fernquist, R. (2007). Marital status integration, suicide disapproval, and social integration as explanations of marital status differences in female age specific suicide rates. *Suicide and Life-Threatening Behavior, 37*, 715–724.

Danto, B. & Danto, J. M. (1983). Jewish and non-Jewish suicide in Oakland county, Michigan. *Crisis, 4*, 33–60.

Dervic, K., Grunebaum, M. F, Burke, A., Mann, J. J., & Oquendo, M. A. (2006). Protective factors against suicidal behavior in depressed adults reporting childhood abuse. *Journal of Nervous and Mental Disease, 194*, 971–974.

Dervic, K., Oquendo, M. A., Currier, D, Grunebaum, M. F., Burke, A., & Mann, J. (2006). Moral objections to suicide: Can they counteract suicidality in patients with cluster B psychopathology? *Journal of Clinical Psychiatry, 67*, 620–625.

Dervic, K., Oquendo, M. A., Grunebaum, M. F., Ellis, S., Burke, A., & Mann, J. J. (2004). Religious affiliation and suicide attempt. *American Journal of Psychiatry, 161*, 2303–2308.

De Wilde, E. J., Kienhorst, I. C. W. M., Diekstra, R., & Wolters, W. H. G. (1993). The specificity of psychological characteristics of adolescent suicide attempters. *Journal of the American Academy of Child and Adolescent Psychiatry, 32*, 59.

Durkheim, E. (1897). *Suicide*. New York: Free Press.

Ellison, C. G., Burr, J., & McCall, P. (1997). Suicide homogeneity and metropolitan suicide rates. *Social Forces, 76*, 273–299.

Eshun, S. (2003). Sociocultural determinants of suicide ideation: A comparison between American and Ghanaian college samples. *Suicide and Life-Threatening Behavior, 33*, 165–171.

Eskin, M. (2004). The effects of religious versus secular education on suicide ideation and suicide attitudes in adolescents in Turkey. *Social Psychiatry and Psychiatric Epidemiology, 39*, 536–542.

Fernquist, R. (2003). Does the level of divorce or religiosity make a difference? Cross-national suicide rates in 21 developed countries, 1955–1994. *Archives of Suicide Research, 7*, 265–277.

Fernquist, R. (2007). How do Durkheimian variables impact variation in national suicide rates when proxies for depression and alcoholism are controlled? *Archives of Suicide Research, 11,* 361–374.

Fernquist, R. & Cutright, P. (1998). Social integration and age standardized suicide rates in 21 developed countries, 1955–1989. *Social Science Research, 27,* 109–127.

Girard, C. (1988). Church membership and suicide reconsidered, comment on Breault. *American Journal of Sociology, 93,* 1471–1486.

Greening, L. & Stoppelbein, L. (2002). Religiosity, attribution style, and social support as buffers for African American and white adolescents' perceived risk for suicide. *Suicide and Life-Threatening Behavior, 32,* 404–417.

Halbwachs, M. (1930). *The Causes of Suicide.* New York: Free Press.

Hirschi, T. (1969). *The Causes of Delinquency.* New York: Free Press.

Inglehart, R. (2004). *World Values Surveys and European Values Surveys, 1999–2001.* Ann Arbor, MI: Inter-University Consortium for Political and Social Research.

Inglehart, R. & Baker, W. (2000). Modernization, cultural change, and the persistence of traditional values. *American Sociological Research, 65,* 19–51.

Joe, S., Romer, D., & Jamieson, P. E. (2007). Suicide acceptability is related to suicide planning in U.S. adolescents and young adults. *Suicide and Life-Threatening Behavior, 37,* 165–178.

Kaslow, N. J., Thompson, M. P., Okun, A., Price, A., Young, S., Bender, M., Wyckoff, S., Twoney, H., Goldin, J., & Parker, R. (2002). Risk and protective factors for suicidal behavior in abused African American women. *Journal of Counselling and Clinical Psychology, 70,* 311–319.

Kay, W. K. & Francis, L. J. (2006). Suicide ideation among young people in the UK: Churchgoing as an inhibiting influence. *Mental Health, Religion, and Culture, 9,* 127–140.

King, S. R., Hampton, W. R., Bernstein, B., & Schichor, A. (1996). College students' views on suicide. *Journal of American College Health, 44,* 283–287.

Kocmur, M., & Dernovsek, M. Z. (2003). Attitudes toward suicide in Slovenia: A cross-sectional survey. *The International Journal of Social Psychiatry, 49,* 8–16.

Koenig, H. G., McCullough, M. E., & Larson, D. B. (2001). *Handbook of Religion and Health.* New York: Oxford University Press.

Kowalski, G. S., Faupel, C., & Starr, P. D. (1987). Urbanism and suicide: A study of American counties. *Social Forces, 66,* 85–101.

Kranitz, L., Abrahams, J., Spiegel, D., & Keith-Spigel, P. (1968). Religious beliefs of suicidal patients. *Psychological Reports, 22,* 936.

Lester, D. (1996). Suicide in Indian states and religion. *Psychological Reports, 79,* 342.

Lester, D. (1998). Ethnicity, religion and suicide in Swiss cantons. *Perceptual and Motor Skills, 86,* 1210.

Lester, D. (2000). *Why People Kill Themselves.* Springfield, IL: Charles C. Thomas.

Maris, R. (1981). *Pathways to Suicide.* Baltimore, MD: Johns Hopkins University Press.

Middleton, G. D., Ashby, D. W., & Clark, M. B. (1961). An analysis of attempted suicide in an industrial city. *The Practitioner, 187,* 776–782.

Molock, S. D., Puri, R., Matlin, S., & Barksdale, C. (2006). Relationship between religious coping and suicidal behaviours among African American adolescents. *Journal of Black Psychology, 32,* 366–389.

Morselli, H. (1882). *Suicide: An essay on comparative moral statistics.* New York: Appleton.

Neeleman, J., Halpern, D., Leon, D., & Lewis, G. (1997). Tolerance of suicide, religion, and suicide rates: An ecological and individual study in 19 Western countries. *Psychological Medicine, 27,* 1165–1171.

Pescosolido, B. (1990). The social context of religious integration and suicide: Pursuing the networks explanation. *Sociological Quarterly, 31,* 337–357.

Pescosolido, B. A. & Georgiana, S. (1989). Durkheim, suicide and religion: Toward a network theory of suicide. *American Sociological Review, 54,* 33–48.

Pope, W. & Danigelis, N. (1981). Sociology's one law. *Social Forces, 60,* 495–516.

Raudenbush, S. W. & Bryk, A. S. (2002). *Hierarchical Linear Models: Applications and data analysis methods.* 2nd edn. Thousand Oaks, CA: Sage.

SAS Institute (2007). *SAS/Stats: The MIXED Procedure,* Computer software, Cary, NC: SAS Institute, Inc.

Simpson, M. & Conklin, G. (1989). Socioeconomic development, suicide and religion: A test of Durkheim's theory of religion and suicide. *Social Forces, 67,* 945–964.

Singer, J. D. (1998). Using SAS PROC MIXED to fit multilevel models, hierarchical models, and individual growth models. *Journal of Educational and Behavioural Statistics, 24,* 323–355.

Stack, S. (1980). Religion and suicide: A re-analysis. *Social Psychiatry, 15,* 65–70.

Stack, S. (1982). Suicide: A decade review of the sociological literature. *Deviant Behavior, 4,* 41–66.

Stack, S. (1983). The effect of religious commitment on suicide: A cross-national analysis. *Journal of Health and Social Behavior, 24,* 362–374.

Stack, S. (1985). The effect of domestic–religious individualism on suicide, 1954–1978. *Journal of Marriage and the Family, 47,* 431–447.

Stack, S. (1989). The impact of divorce on suicide in Norway, 1951–1980. *Journal of Marriage and the Family, 5,* 229–237.

Stack, S. (1991). The effect of religiosity on suicide in Sweden: A time series analysis. *Journal for the Scientific Study of Religion, 30,* 462–468.

Stack, S. (1992a). The effect of divorce on suicide in Japan: A time series analysis, 1950–1980. *Journal of Marriage and the Family, 54,* 327–334.

Stack, S. (1992b). The effect of divorce on suicide in Finland: A time series analysis. *Journal of Marriage and the Family, 54,* 636–642.

Stack, S. (1996). Culture and suicide: An analysis of 36 nations. Paper presented at the annual meetings of the American Association of Suicidology, 15–17 April, St. Louis, MO.

Stack, S. (1998a). Gender, marriage and suicide acceptability. *Sex Roles, 38,* 501–20.

Stack, S. (1998b). The relationship between culture and suicide: An analysis of African Americans. *Transcultural Psychiatry, 35,* 253–269.

Stack, S. (2000). Suicide: A fifteen-year review of the sociological literature: Part II: Modernization and social integration perspectives. *Suicide and Life-Threatening Behavior, 30,* 163–176.

Stack, S. & Kposowa, A. J. (2006). The effect of religiosity on tax fraud acceptability: A cross-national analysis. *Journal for the Scientific Study of Religion, 45,* 325–351.

Stack, S. & Kposowa, A. J. (2008). The association of suicide rates with individual level suicide attitudes. *Social Science Quarterly, 89,* 39–59.

Stack, S. & Wasserman, I. (1992). The effect of religion on suicide ideology: An analysis of the networks perspective. *Journal for the Scientific Study of Religion, 31,* 457–466.

Stack, S, Wasserman, I., & Kposowa, A. (1994). The effects of religion and feminism on suicide ideology: An analysis of national survey data. *Journal for the Scientific Study of Religion, 33,* 110–121.

Stark, R. (1996). Religion as context: Hellfire and delinquency one more time. *Sociology and Religion, 57,* 163–173.

Stark, R., Doyle, D. P., & Rushing, J. L. (1983). Religion and Suicide. *Journal for the Scientific Study of Religion,* 120–131.

Stein, D., Witztum, E., Brom, D., DeNour, A. K., & Elizur, A. (1992). The association between adolescent's attitudes towards suicide and their psychosocial background and suicidal tendencies. *Adolescence, 27,* 108–959.

Trovato, F. (1986). The relationship between marital dissolution and suicide: The Canadian case. *Journal of Marriage and the Family, 48,* 341–348.

Trovato, F. (1992). A Durkheimian analysis of youth suicide in Canada, 1971 and 1981. *Suicide and Life-Threatening Behavior, 22*, 413–427.

van Tubergen, F., te Grotenhuis, M., & Ultee, W. (2005). Denomination, religious context, and suicide: Neo-Durkheimian multilevel explanations tested with individual and contextual data. *American Journal of Sociology, 111*, 797–823.

Walker, R. & Bishop, S. (2005). Examining a model of the relation between religiosity and suicidal ideation in a sample of African American and white college students. *Suicide and Life-Threatening Behavior, 35*, 630–639.

CHAPTER FIFTEEN

Rurality and Suicide

Cameron Stark and Vincent Riordan

Abstract

The nature of rurality varies considerably across the world, and there is no single pattern of suicide in rural areas. However, some common themes are evident from countries as diverse as India, the United States, Australia, the United Kingdom, and China. Suicide rates tend to be higher in rural populations compared with urban, with relatively higher female rates in some areas. North American and Australian data suggest that indigenous people may be at particularly high risk. Specific rural occupations, such as farming, often seem to be associated with higher risk. Although mental illness plays an important role in suicide in rural areas, as it does elsewhere, it is unclear whether higher rural suicide rates are linked to a correspondingly higher prevalence of mental illness in such populations. Instead, other factors may be important including: adverse socio-economic conditions; higher rates of alcohol or substance misuse; greater access to potentially lethal methods, such as pesticides or firearms; cultural attitudes which promote independence and discourage help-seeking behaviour; poor access to services providing help at times of psychological crisis; and cultural discontinuity in traditional societies. Not all factors apply in all areas, hence, the literature on rural suicide prevention initiatives varies considerably. Strategies have involved: the restriction of access to lethal methods; improving attitudes to, and knowledge of, mental illness in high-risk populations; improving the accessibility of conventional mental health services; making the use of such supports more culturally acceptable; and the development of context-specific supports, such as programmes addressing specific cultural issues.

International Handbook of Suicide Prevention: Research, Policy and Practice, First Edition.
Edited by Rory C. O'Connor, Stephen Platt, Jacki Gordon.
© 2011 John Wiley & Sons, Ltd. Published 2011 by John Wiley & Sons, Ltd.

Introduction

Any consideration of rural suicide first requires consideration of the nature of rurality. Intuitively, small populations and settlements, remoteness, and low population density are all features associated with rurality. As Hewitt (1989) points out, however, these characteristics change linearly, yet they are often categorized as dichotomous variables, that is, low versus high population density. She identifies four main dimensions which are routinely considered in US studies: population size; population density; adjacency to a metropolitan area; and urbanization (defined as the proportion of an area that is urban). Other authors have noted that sparsity may be misleading: while the overall population density may be low, people often live in small communities. Irving and Davidson (1973) suggested that social distance, the degree of contact between individuals, might be a useful way of considering distance.

Bibby and Shepherd (2004) describe an English classification system, which clusters areas by sparsity and then separates them by settlement type (small town and fringe, village, and hamlets or dispersed households). This allows areas to be both described geographically and set in a context.

There are enormous differences in the nature of rurality across the world. Distances between settlements in North America, Australia, Africa, and Asia dwarf distances in Europe. Communication infrastructure varies with level of economic development. Affluent European countries with centrally funded healthcare systems can use differential investment to partially overcome distance (Grytten, Rongen, & Sorensen, 1995), but such options are not open to less affluent countries. Better health and better availability of healthcare, however, does not always follow increased societal affluence (Hsiao, 1995; Liu, Hsiaoa, & Eggleston, 1999; Zhang & Kanbur, 2003), and rural areas may be disadvantaged by urban models of investment, which often see efficiency as a key goal. In rural areas, with long distances and sparse populations, unit costs are usually higher, and so services may appear less efficient than urban counterparts.

Suicide in Rural Areas

There is no single pattern of suicide deaths in rural areas and, as Khan points out, there are no data for about half of the countries in the world (Khan, 2005). Although Hirsch (2006) provides a review of the published epidemiology, rather than cover all areas in detail here, we selected regional examples to illustrate specific issues concerning incidence and epidemiological characteristics.

India and Sri Lanka

The suicide rate in India may be very much higher than suggested by government estimates (Gajalakshmi & Peto, 2007). Bose, Konradsen, John, Suganthy, Muliyil, *et al.* (2006) reported that, in the area around Vellore in south India, suicide accounted for just over 11% of all deaths. Across all age groups, hanging was the most common method of suicide, followed by poisoning, burning, and drowning. Poisoning with pesticides is particularly important in India, and was the suicide method most frequently reported in the largest verbal autopsy study (i.e., a process by which investigators obtain information from key informants who are able to provide details of a death) (Gajalakshmi & Peto, 2007). Eddleston and Konradsen (2007) note that the type of pesticide used varies as a function of region, and the choice of pesticide influences the likelihood of survival. In northern India, aluminium phosphide, a very toxic pesticide, is often used for self-harm, while organophosphorous pesticides are more commonly used in southern India. 70%–80% of hospital-treated patients survive organophosphate poisoning, compared with 20%–30% of those who have aluminium phosphate poisoning (Eddleston, 2000; Siwach & Gupta, 1995).

In India, information about causes of death is often obtained from police records. However, as suicide is illegal (Eddleston & Konradsen, 2007), it is possible that death by suicide is under-reported and under-recorded. Aaron, Joseph, Abraham, Muliyil, George, *et al.* (2004) also used verbal autopsy information, derived from a system of weekly collection of information on deaths, and consensus decision on cause, to examine rates in younger people in southern India. Suicide accounted for between 50% and 75% of deaths in women aged 10–19 years, and a quarter of deaths in young men. The rates were very much higher than those recorded in India using other recording mechanisms, such as police records. The authors note that commonly reported acute stressors included family conflicts, domestic violence, academic failures, disappointments in love, and mental illness. Pesticides were a common method in this age group and access to treatment facilities was limited.

Official estimates in India of suicide deaths are very much lower than extrapolations from research findings. Gajalakshmi and Peto (2007) estimate 686,626 deaths from suicide in India by extrapolating from their study of a rural community, compared with government estimates of around 100,000 deaths per year. Eddleston and Konradsen (2007) point out that the lower availability of pesticides in urban areas suggests that the true number of deaths in India will be lower than this extrapolation, but conclude that it is likely to be considerably higher than official estimates.

In a psychological postmortem study conducted in Sri Lanka (Abeyasinghe & Gunnell, 2008), about a third of those who died by suicide were thought to have moderate or severe depression at the time of their deaths. Two-thirds of the men were problem drinkers or alcohol dependent. Alcohol was also noted as a risk factor by van der Hoek and Konradsen (2005). The most common type of alcohol consumed in Abeyasinghe's cohort was kasippu, a local illegal spirit, followed by arack, a spirit made from palm trees or coconut. There was a family history in about a fifth of these deaths and the main method of suicide was pesticide poisoning, followed by yellow oleander seeds and hanging. There was evidence of planning in almost all of the cases, and of those who died from pesticide poisoning, approximately 50% had bought it specifically for the suicide attempt. Three-quarters of deaths occurred in hospital, suggesting possibilities for intervention if improved treatment methods were available. The overall rate of suicide was about three times higher than that recorded for the country, suggesting either under-recording or higher rates in rural areas.

The case fatality (the proportion of the people who harm themselves using a particular method who die as a result) for pesticide poisoning in van der Hoek and Konradsen's study was 18% overall, but it was as high as 64% for one pesticide (endosulfan) (van der Hoek & Konradsen, 2005). A family history of suicide was also often reported, as it was in Abeyasinghe's study.

North America

As Hirsch (2006) notes, some earlier studies found lower rates of suicide in rural areas than in urban areas; and by the 1990s a more consistent picture of higher suicide rates in rural compared with urban areas was emerging. In addition, Hempstead (2006) found that, even in a relatively populated US state such as New Jersey, there was an association between population density and suicide (i.e., low population density associated with high suicide incidence). Rates increased in rural men in the 1980s and 1990s, but reduced in urban areas, resulting in higher rates in rural areas (Singh & Siapush, 2002). In women, urban rates also decreased in the 1980s and 1990s. By the end of the period, unadjusted rates in rural and urban women were similar, but when divorce rates and ethnic composition were taken into account, rural suicide rates in young rural women were higher than their urban counterparts (Singh & Siahpush, 2002).

Suicide rates in indigenous populations are also particularly high (Olson & Wahab, 2006). While most Native Americans live in cities, the majority of recent research has focused on individuals living in traditional tribal areas (Goldston, Molock, Whitbeck, Murkami, Zayas, et al., 2008). For example, Kruger and Gray (2005) supply a discussion of factors affecting both tribal and non-tribal groups in North Dakota, and conclude that mental illness and barriers to care access; alcohol and other substance misuse; rural isolation and stigma; violence; and historical trauma against indigenous groups are all likely to be important. In Canada (Allard, Wilkins, & Berthelot, 2004), areas with high indigenous populations[1] have high rates of injury deaths, including suicide, with suicide rates being around twice as high as in areas with a low indigenous population (Statewide Suicide Prevention Council, 2004).

Deprivation, alcohol use, and cultural issues such as the use of reservations and associated social exclusion have all been implicated in the deaths of indigenous people in the United States (Alcantara & Gone, 2007; Wexler, Hill, Bertone-Johnson, & Fenaughty, 2008). It is also necessary to understand suicide from a social and cultural perspective in order to understand culturally-specific suicide pathways (Cutcliffe, 2005; Tester & McNicoll, 2004). Wexler, who worked in a suicide prevention project in northwest Alaska, provides a useful analysis of this in an analysis of Inupiat youth suicide (Wexler, 2006a).

Wexler notes that discussions on youth suicide in local communities were permeated by ideas of what had been lost. Traditional culture had been disrupted by having a generation educated away in English-speaking boarding schools, who could no longer talk to Inupiat grandparents. Traditional values were believed to have faded, with less family involvement and less guidance being provided to children. Wexler describes numerous community meetings dominated by the presentation of suicide statistics, and repeated analyses of problems, resulting in a feeling of a problem that was too big to change. This,

Wexler suggests, left the community mired in despondency, with young people seen as the problem, rather than as their future.

For their part, young people often felt they had failed because they had not managed to negotiate their way between Western and indigenous cultures, resulting in problems in schools, such as failure to graduate from high school. Wexler argues that making young people aware of the history of their culture, and the way it has been and continues to be affected by colonization, produces benefits by allowing people to locate the problems they experience as part of a wider social situation rather than a personal failure alone. To avoid perpetuating despair, she argues that younger generations of indigenous groups should work to reinterpret their history in a modern context, rather than eulogizing a lost past. Chandler and Lalonde (1998) have argued that cultural continuity may be an important protection against suicide, where people have a shared understanding of their past and interest in a shared future, and this has echoes in Wexler's construction of the Inupiat experience.

Thorslund (1992) reports that Inuit youth in Denmark felt suicide was an acceptable response to life problems and was not associated with mental illness, and suggests that this made it easier to move from suicidal thoughts to suicidal actions. However, cultural factors may also be protective (Goldston *et al.*, 2008). Indeed, American Indians who have strong associations with tribal spiritual culture have fewer suicide attempts than those with weak associations (Garroutte, Goldberg, Beals, Herrell, & Manson, 2003). Having a sense of belonging or connectedness also offers some protection against suicidal ideation (Hill, 2009). Similarly, Sami in Arctic Norway who are involved in reindeer herding have a lower suicide rate than Sami who do not have a family member involved in herding, again suggesting that strong cultural links are a protective factor in indigenous groups (Silviken, Haroldsen, & Kvernmo, 2006).

Australia

The ratio of rural to urban suicides has increased in Australia over the last 30 years (Kapusta, Zorman, Etzerdorfer, Ponocny-Seliger, Jandl-Jager, *et al.*, 2008), with hanging and firearms more common in less densely populated areas compared with more densely population areas. Comparable findings, though less marked, have been reported in New Zealand (Pearce, Barnett, & Jones, 2007).

Caldwell, Jorm, and Dear (2004) used previously collected national information to explore the relationships between suicide, mental ill-health, and service use. As with previous Australian studies, they found a higher suicide rate among men in non-metropolitan areas than in metropolitan areas. Although there was no evidence of higher rates of mental illness in rural areas, the young men with a mental disorder living in a rural area were significantly less likely to seek professional help than those living in a metropolitan area (11.4% compared with 25.2%).

This is broadly consistent with studies of Australian farmers (Judd, Jackson, Fraser, Murray, Robins, *et al.*, 2006; Miller & Burns, 2008). For example, in a recent study of qualitative interviews, Judd *et al.* (2006b) identified substantial unwillingness to acknowledge problems or to seek professional help. This study also found that farmers were no more likely than a comparison group of other rural dwellers to have a mental illness, but they showed higher levels of conscientiousness than those in the comparison group. Higher conscientiousness may be related to both likelihood of help-seeking and to greater feelings of failure when problems occur. On small family-run farms, taking time off imposed great demands on other family members, and farming respondents reported turning to family, friends, and neighbours for help. The National Rural Health Alliance suggests that current problems of drought, living at work, and stoic, masculine attitudes promoting a feeling that individuals should be able to cope, may all contribute to this problem (National Rural Health Alliance, 2009).

Taylor and colleagues (Taylor, Page, Morrell, Harrison, & Carter, 2005) attempted to disentangle the effects of poverty, rurality, migration, and service access using survey information and national suicide data. The higher rural rate compared with urban areas became non-significant after adjusting for socio-economic status and country of birth. After adjusting for service availability and survey results, they concluded that higher male suicide rates in rural Australia could be mediated by social and economic circumstances, prevalence of mental disorder, and availability and use of mental health services.

Consistent with other countries, suicide in indigenous people may be up to six times more frequent than the national average in some age groups (National Rural Health Alliance, 2009). Tatz (1999) suggests that Aboriginal suicide needs to be placed in a social context, and that poverty, powerlessness, and the disruption and disconnection produced by the historic removal of Aboriginal people from their families are all relevant issues to understanding suicide risk. He interprets this as producing a norm of high suicide rates, in the context of ennui (a state of boredom and lack of interest) and a lack of purpose that he believes produces self-harm, violence, and addiction. However, Goldney (2002) argues that, while these culture-specific factors may be correct, mental illness and traditional risk factors are still likely to be important.

United Kingdom

A recent summary of research in the United Kingdom identified a number of key themes (Stark, 2008). There is evidence of higher rates of suicide in some rural areas, particularly in men, and some occupations are at particularly high risk of suicide compared with others (Stark et al., 2006a). Many of the themes are similar to those discussed elsewhere in this chapter and are not considered here, but UK research usefully illustrates issues relating to rural occupations.

Across a series of studies, Hawton and colleagues conducted a detailed investigation of suicide in farmers in England and Wales (Hawton, Fagg, Simkin, Harriss, Malmberg, et al., 1999; Hawton, Simkin, & Malmberg, 1998; Malmberg, Simkin, & Hawton, 1999). They found that many farmers had financial problems, but that these problems were no more common in farmers who died by suicide than they were in the general farming population. By contrast, farmers who died by suicide were more likely to live alone and to lack a close confidant. Mental illness was common in the farmers who had died, with depression being the most common retrospective diagnosis. Farmers were also more likely to have used firearms than men in the population as a whole. Indeed, Stark et al. (2006b) reported similar findings on firearm use in Scotland and also noted that Scottish farming suicide rates were higher in areas where farming was a less common occupation, thereby lending support to Hawton's findings that social support is an important risk factor in this population.

China

The characteristics of suicide in China are distinctive from those found in many Western regions and countries. Consequently, China is an important country to include in this chapter. National statistics suggest that about a quarter of a million people in China kill themselves each year. However, this is thought to be an underestimate, as it is an extrapolation from the 10% of the population covered by vital events recording (Phillips, Li, & Zhang, 2002) and these tend to live in urban areas. Phillips *et al.* (2002) estimate that suicide rates in rural areas are around three times higher than in urban areas. In recent years, both urban and rural areas have shown an increase in middle-aged suicides, but this increase is much more marked in rural areas, with the result that they estimate that over 90% of all suicides in China occur in rural areas. Rates among rural women tend to be higher than those in rural men, but this is mainly related to younger age groups, where female suicide rates were estimated to be two-thirds higher than male rates. It is worth noting, however, that the data sources need careful interpretation. For example, in the 1990s most deaths of rural residents who died after moving to urban areas for work were registered as rural deaths due to the nature of their work permits (Phillips *et al.*, 2002).

In a recent case-control study of people dying by suicide in one area of China, Zhang, Conwell, Zhou, and Jiang (2004) concluded that just under 70% of those who took their own lives had a mental illness at the time of their death. Of those, 63% had used pesticides. The minority of people with no retrospective diagnosis of mental illness were more likely to have experienced a life event in the month prior to their death. Zhang *et al.* (2004) also found that people dying by suicide were more likely to be poor, unemployed, and less educated than controls. Life events were also frequently reported prior to a death by suicide, and Zhang commented on the possible importance of *diu mianzi*, or loss of face, in the aetiology of suicide. These authors go on to argue that cultural, and particularly religious, beliefs may be significant factors in the high rate of suicide in China.

China is also distinctive as the suicide rate is higher in females than in males, although Phillips *et al.* (2002) note that there are also lower male to female suicide rates reported in some other Asian countries. The male to female ratios for China, India, and Other Asia and Islands in an international study were 0.81, 1.10, and 1.48, respectively, while male to female ratios were considerably higher in other regions of the world (Murray & Lopez, 1996). The ratio has altered more recently in urban areas of China, with an increased male to female ratio, and a decrease in suicide in younger women in rural areas, possibly reflecting changing social circumstances (Yip, Liu, Hu, & Song, 2005).

Themes in Rural Suicide Epidemiology

These area-specific summaries identify some common themes which are present to greater or lesser extents in different areas.

Changes over time

Notwithstanding the commonalities outlined above, the characteristics of rural suicide differ between and within countries and over time. The recent finding of increasing rural suicide rates in many countries may reflect adverse socio-economic trends in these areas, which have experienced slower economic development than urban areas, thereby leading to wider inequalities. The association between deprivation and suicide is discussed elsewhere in this book (see Chapter 13, above). In short, in rural areas, poverty can be compounded by distance, difficulty in service access, and reduced educational opportunity, which can lead to a spiral of deprivation (Shaw, 1979).

Prevalence of mental illness

As discussed in other chapters, mental illness is an important risk factor for death by suicide. However, most studies find no persuasive evidence of higher rates of mental illness in rural areas compared with urban areas, once the effects of deprivation are taken into account (e.g., Caldwell, Jorm, & Dear, 2004; Judd *et al.*, 2006a; Paykel, Abbott, Jenkins, Brugha, & Meltzer, 2000). This is not to say that mental illness is not an important risk factor in rural communities; rather, that there is no compelling evidence that it alone accounts for observed differences in urban versus rural suicide rates.

Social and cultural context, including models of distress   Psychological distress is conceptualized in many different ways. The way in which distress is believed to be caused, and the responses that are regarded as being appropriate, affect the decisions made about help-seeking (Sheikh & Furnham, 2000). The Indian work discussed above found that interpersonal conflict was important in precipitating some suicide attempts.

There is some evidence of inter-country differences in prevalence of mental illness in people dying by suicide. For example, a Finnish study found that people dying by suicide in urban areas were more likely to have had a mental disorder, whereas those in rural areas were more likely to have lacked a close relationship or to have had a physical disorder (Isometsä, Heikkinen, Henriksson, Marttunen, Aro, *et al.*, 1997). This finding may represent a real qualitative difference between urban and rural suicide, although it is also possible that it reflects a tendency among rural dwellers to be less inclined to conceptualize psychological distress according to the medical/psychiatric model of illness.

Indeed, following a review, Tatz (1999) argued that mental illness was rarely present in Australian Aboriginal suicide deaths (although this is contested by Goldney (2002)), and he suggested that cultural issues, such as the loss of tradition and dislocation from much of Australian society were more important than mental illness. Tatz (1999) does, however, report the presence of other familiar risk factors, including substance misuse mainly involving cannabis, and poverty. One additional issue he raised was 'jealousing', where one person's success was seen as diminishing other, less successful, individuals, with resultant bullying of the successful person, although this appeared to be relevant in only a small number of cases. He also cited the Maori Suicide Review Group as reporting that cultural factors were important in New Zealand's indigenous population, including a perceived lack of *mana* (status) resulting in *whakama* (an illness with a spiritual dimension).

Method access

Choice of suicide method varies between urban and rural populations. However, method selection is likely to reflect access differences in the physical environment. Thus, the greater incidence of suicide by drowning in rural areas may result from easier access to rivers, while jumping from a height is more common in urban areas where there is easier access to tall buildings (Cullen & Connolly, 1997; Levin & Leyland, 2005). Other methods are likely to reflect social or cultural differences, two of the most common being self-poisoning with pesticides in the developing world, and the use firearms in the developed world.

The availability of particular means by which to harm oneself is also important. The number of deaths from suicide is a product of the number of suicide attempts and the number of people dying from these events. The rate of people dying when a particular method is used is known as the case fatality rate. Having access to particularly lethal means of self-harm, such as pesticides, can result in a higher suicide rate even without any increase in self-harming behaviour. Firearms are a good example of a self-harm method with a high case fatality rate (Sadowski & Munoz, 1996). Firearm ownership can be high in rural areas, because of their use in hunting and pest control (Hintikka, Lehtonen, & Viinamaki, 1997). Availability of guns in a home is associated with a higher suicide rate (Dudley, Canor & De Moore, 1996; Kellermann, Rivara, Somes, Reay, Francisco, *et al.*, 1992). Consequently, higher suicide rates in rural areas could be partly caused by greater availability of lethal means of self-harm. This is supported by information that occupational groups with high suicide rates in some countries, such as farmers, have a greater proportion of firearm suicide deaths than in the population a whole (Stark *et al.*, 2006b).

Help-seeking behaviours

The following quotation highlights a key issue in some rural communities, namely, the reluctance to seek help:

> Reluctance to expose their private lives to strangers or acquaintances from locally based services, or to undertake the journey to distant services where cultural or behavioural differences could be misunderstood, may impact on rural dwellers' wellbeing. (Penn, Simpson, Edie, Leggett, Wood *et al.*, 2005, p. 276)

In affluent countries, there is reasonable evidence that some rural dwellers, particularly men, are less willing to seek help for mental health problems than urban dwellers (Hirsch, 2006). There are a number of potential explanations including: a lack of awareness of the nature of mental health problems; concerns over anonymity; and feelings of stigma associated with the use of mental health services (Stark, 2008).

Service access

Residents of rural communities tend to face greater difficulties than their urban counterparts in accessing health and social care services (Betts & Thornicroft, 2001). The literature suggests that service access is a product of both the availability of services and the willingness of individuals to use these services. In less affluent countries, there may be markedly reduced service availability in rural areas (although this is also sometimes the case in more affluent countries). This lack of access is often linked to pressures for increased service efficiency: if population densities are low and distances are great, the unit cost of a home visit or clinic session can be markedly increased. Consequently, this can lead to a view that delivering services in rural areas is inefficient. The corollary is that productive efficiency, with the greatest economy of scale, is valued over any imperative to deliver a minimum level of service to those in need.

Rural services, where they do exist, tend to be smaller with less specialization and to have greater difficulties recruiting and maintaining appropriately qualified staff (Commission for Rural Communities, 2008; Lau, Kumar, & Thomas, 2002). In addition, crisis services, which require rapid availability, may be particularly limited and so less available to help those who are acutely suicidal.

Occupational risks

Some rural occupations have been reported to have higher than average rates of suicide. Where present, this appears to be due to a combination of financial pressures, reluctance to take time off work or to seek help, difficulty accessing services, and access to lethal means of suicide (Hawton *et al.*, 1998; Hirsch, 2006; Judd *et al.*, 2006b; Malmberg *et al.*, 1999; Stark, 2008). Occupational risk, therefore, appears to be a particular example of the factors affecting rural areas as a whole.

Areas for Intervention

The best intervention or combination of interventions to prevent rural suicide depends upon the precise mix of risk factors and cultural issues in a particular country or area. Nonetheless, it is possible to identify a range of options for interventions based on the available evidence (summarized earlier).

Population level

While the primary aim of national social policy is obviously not suicide prevention, many of the aims (and associated actions) common to most national plans are likely to contribute to: increased affluence; improved transport and communication; increased education opportunities; and decreases in social inequalities (Judd *et al.*, 2006a).

Improving mental health

Some of the issues affecting mental health are the macro-level issues noted above, such as poverty and access to education. Children and young people are often seen as an important group for mental health improvement work. Generic programmes may be appropriate in some countries, but in other areas specifically tailored programmes will be required. One US theory-driven example of a tailored programme is a skills-based course on well-being, coping skills, and knowledge of suicide and delivered in schools and targeted at the Zuni people of New Mexico, most of whom live in the Zuni Pueblo (LaFromboise & Howard-Pitney, 1995; LaFromboise & Lewis, 2008). Suicide is a difficult topic for the Zuni, as suicide is forbidden in their traditional culture, but the Zuni Pueblo reservation has experienced a high suicide rate in younger people. As a result, the Zuni collaborated with Stanford University to create a tailored prevention programme for young people. The programme, based on Social Learning Theory (Bandura, 1986), was designed to increase protective factors thought to be important in this setting, such as self-esteem, and to enhance social competence skills, such as problem-solving. The delivery of the programme, in school, took account of cultural restrictions, such as a taboo that prevented Zuni from playing the role of a suicidal person. The work included carefully structured sessions aimed at reinforcing a view that suicide was unnecessary and preventable. Learning on depression took account of cultural constructions of low mood and its antecedents, to ensure that the work was culturally congruent. The teaching was integrated into the standard curriculum.

Awareness of mental illness and management of stigma

Mental illness is a major risk factor for death by suicide in rural communities. Greater awareness of mental illness and the management of the associated stigma should be central to suicide prevention initiatives. Indeed, Suicide Prevention Australia argue for 'the development of mental health education and awareness campaigns to reduce the prevalence of social stigma in rural and remote communities' (Suicide Prevention Australia, 2008). A practical example of such a public awareness intervention is the Reach Out! Rural and Regional Tour which is organized by the Inspire Foundation and beyondblue (the Australian national depression initiative). This programme is targeted at young people and aims to increase the regard with which young people are held in rural communities, to encourage help-seeking behaviours and coping skills in young people, to help others to know how to support them, and to promote the use of Internet resources in suicide prevention (O'Brien, 2002).

Addressing the issue of stigma associated with mental health services in rural areas may also have potential, not only in the context of improving service utilization, but also because an approach which strives to preserve patients' social relationships may be more likely to improve outcome (Crawford & Brown, 2002).

Availability of services   Service availability is subject to political decision-making, national wealth, and infrastructure, as well as competition for scarce resources within health and social care organizations and local government. In rural areas, support methods, such as the provision of services by local volunteers, may be important, particularly in supporting people to seek help.

There are many challenges to delivering services in rural areas. Penn *et al.* (2005) list the following:

- professional isolation and limited contact with other mental health professionals;
- lack of continuing education and training opportunities;
- limited supervision;
- limited opportunities for networking;
- lack of support systems (e.g., to cover staff absences);
- demands to provide extra services with limited referral options;
- the need to be multi-skilled;
- inadequate access to resources and information;
- social and personal challenges around the client–counsellor relationship (the blurred differentiation between work and private life).

These are major challenges. In Queensland, Australia, ACROSSnet (Australians Creating Rural Online Support Systems) provides access to resources on suicide. The ACROSSnet website supports professionals, for example, with e-mail support groups and specialist chat rooms (Penn *et al.*, 2005). It has three tiers: a public tier which provides information to the community on resources, services, and organizations; a second tier aimed at community workers, including volunteers (e.g., ministers of religion, emergency workers, education and youth workers), where ideas and resources are discussed among the professionals; and a third tier, where specialist mental health professionals can submit case queries for specific advice and guidance.

The designers of ACROSSnet point out that their system has the unusual characteristic of combining research and experiential knowledge, with those who work in these areas contributing to the design and content of the website (Penn *et al.*, 2005). ACROSSnet could provide a useful template for other regions and countries with substantial rural communities.

Wexler describes a culturally sensitive approach to suicide prevention in a north Alaskan suicide prevention project, wherein suicide is re-framed in terms of Inuit values, such as responsibility to tribe, as illustrated by the following quotation: 'Responsibility to tribe means that you don't give up when times get hard. Fight for yourself, find support, and better times will follow' (Wexler, 2006b, p. 6).

Recognition of suicide risk and use of non-traditional support routes   It is likely that the accessibility of community-based services (other than health services) may be of importance to rural suicide prevention. Individuals who hold key positions in rural societies, such as employers, community leaders, or clergy, may have a gatekeeper role to play in identifying those at high risk and directing them to appropriate supports or services (Goldsmith, Pellmar, Kleinman, & Bunney, 2002). Other routes to support, such as electronic social networks, may be important.

In the United States, where most rural healthcare is provided in primary care, the Suicide Prevention Resource Center has produced information intended to help clinical staff to make judgements on risk. Their website includes a web-based resource library with information on education for clinicians, advice on developing mental health partnerships, and patient management and patient education tools (available at http://www. sprc.org). The patient management tools include a pocket-sized care with information on risk assessment and management (Western Interstate Commission for Higher Education, 2009), and guides on safety planning, including materials to use collaboratively with patients.

Many areas have used programmes such as Applied Suicide Intervention Skills Training (ASIST) (Livingworks, 2002) to train professionals and community groups. ASIST is intended to provide caregivers with the skills to reduce the immediate risk of suicide in an individual. An interesting example of local work aimed at farmers in Tasmania is the Rural Alive and Well (RAW) (Rural Alive and Well, 2009) project which was set up in response to the enormous drought problems experienced in the region. The programme includes work aimed at increasing community skills in order to identify and respond to suicide risk. An innovative part of this programme is the 'Keep a Mate Safe' initiative, which is intended to encourage men to respond to symptoms in friends (Southern Midlands Council, 2008). Similar ideas have been proposed by Suicide Prevention Australia, which suggests that groups such as sports coaches, financial counsellors, teachers, and small business people could be taught independently to refer clients in crisis to the most appropriate agency (Suicide Prevention Australia, 2008).

Tatz (1999) argues that responses should be culturally sensitive. He suggests that, for disenfranchized indigenous peoples in Australia, three roles may be key. He points to individuals who are seen as sources of wisdom, to mentors, and to those who can be what he terms 'enlightened witnesses': people who can bear witness to the experience of distressed people, and who can acknowledge its value and legitimacy (Tatz, 1999).

Restriction of method   Restricting access to methods can be considered using the Haddon matrix (Eddleston, Buckley, Gunnell, Dawson, & Konradsen, 2006), which is named after William Haddon, who developed harm reduction approaches to road traffic accidents in the United States in the 1960s. His matrix considers three factors – the host (i.e., the person involved), the agent, and the environment – across three time periods (pre-event, event, and post-event).

Taking pesticides as an example, host factors include the individual's mental health and tendency to be impulsive; environmental issues include psychosocial support and education, availability of alcohol, and, importantly, the availability of prompt medical treatment after the event. Several approaches can be employed to address the issue of the agent, for example, the pesticide (Mishara, 2007). From a social policy perspective, the relevant authorities can regulate the availability of the more toxic agents. Indeed, Gunnell, Eddleston, Phillips, and Konradsen (2007) reported encouraging findings in Sri Lanka suggesting that the regulation of toxic means availability was associated with a significant drop in suicide rates in recent years, a fall which would seem to be independent of any secular trends. Another option is for manufacturers to be required to add agents such as emetics (drugs which induce vomiting), or an unpalatable odour or taste to pesticides. This may well reduce the risk of impulsive ingestion, although the efficacy of such an approach has not yet been demonstrated.

Other initiatives have focused on secure storage of pesticides, with a number of schemes in Sri Lanka providing locked boxes to farmers. There have been concerns that this could result in farmers storing pesticides in their houses rather than in the fields, with a risk of increasing, rather than reducing availability. A recent study reported that lockers were well used, and that although their use decreased over time, they did result in safer storage of pesticides (Hawton, Ratneyeke, Simkin, Harriss, & Scott, 2009).

Firearms   The use of firearms as a method of suicide has been found to be more common in rural areas in Western countries such as the United States, Scotland, and Australia (Branas, Nance, Elliott, Richmond, & Schwab, 2004; Levin & Leyland, 2005; Stark, Matthewson, Oates, & Hay, 2002). Like pesticides, firearms are an agricultural tool, often readily available within the home. Between a quarter and a half of self-harm episodes are considered for periods as brief as five minutes, so rapid access to a lethal means of self-harm may markedly increase the likelihood of action, and resulting in death (Shenassa, Rogers, Spalding, & Roberts, 2004).

Efforts by the authorities to regulate the availability of firearms in the general population tend to be driven by wider political, cultural, and historical considerations. The risk of firearms deaths tends to be lower when the weapon is stored, locked, and unloaded, and the ammunition is stored and locked elsewhere (Grossman, Mueller, Riedy, Dowd, Villaveces, *et al.*, 2005). There is some evidence that parental education may also be helpful (Markus, Grossman, Pennington, Woodward, Duda, *et al.*, 1999). In one US study, the implementation of laws requiring firearms to be stored safely (thereby restricting children's access) were associated with a reduction in overall suicide rates, as well as in suicide deaths by firearms among children (Webster, Vernick, Zeoli, & Manganello, 2004). Encouraging findings were also reported in Canada. Although the Canadian legislation to restrict access was associated with lower gun death rates, the overall suicide rate did not decrease (Caron, 2004). An initiative in rural Alaska confirmed that firearm ownership was very common in native villages, and that it was possible to improve firearm storage practices by distributing gun safes and trigger locks, and by providing advice (Horn, Grossman, Jones, & Berger, 2003).

Integrated Programmes

There are examples of integrated programmes aimed at tackling specific elements of a local problem. In general, these are public health approaches which include an assessment of the problem, a review of the effectiveness of interventions, and subsequent design and monitoring of a programme to meet the local requirements. The underlying theory is not always stated in programme protocols, but in most cases the elements being addressed are apparent.

Older people

The Akita prefecture in the Tohoku region had, since 1997, the highest suicide rate in Japan. As a result, Motohashi and colleagues (Motohashi, Kaneko, Sasaki, & Yamaji, 2007) designed a suicide prevention programme aimed at middle-aged and older people in this rural area, as they were seen as the most vulnerable groups. The programme is based on the assumption that both social factors and mental illness need to be tackled in the fight against suicide. The programme consists of a number of interventions, including:

- a community survey of mental health and distribution of the results to local residents;
- community education on depression and suicide prevention;
- specialist training on suicide prevention for public health and welfare staff;
- community-driven initiatives, such as theatrical performances;
- distribution of information on access to mental health services;
- development of social networks for older people, and home visits to the housebound in the winter.

Evaluations of interventions on rural suicide have often had methodological problems, including lack of an underlying theory of change, limited clarity on the nature of the target population, and little description of the methods used in the intervention (Middlebrook, LeMaster, Beals, Novins, & Manson, 2001). The Akita Prefecture study, however, addressed many of these issues. It had a coherent theory of change, based on public and professional education, signposting to sources of intervention, and an attempt to decrease isolation in older people, which was hypothesized to be a risk factor for suicide. The programme was associated with a substantial fall in suicide rates in the intervention area compared with control areas. A similar programme in a different prefecture used health education and screening of older people for depression as its main intervention. There was a significant decrease in suicide deaths in women in the intervention area, but not in men (Oyama, Goto, Fujita, Shibuya, & Sakashita, 2006).

A well-defined community   May and colleagues (May, Serna, Hurt, & DeBruyn, 2005) reported on a long-running intervention in an American Indian tribal area. The work, lasting 15 years, had been initiated because of concerns about levels of suicidal behaviour in the late 1980s (Serna, May, & Sitaker, 1998). Consultation work with the local community identified a range of problems, such as alcohol misuse, unemployment, child abuse, and family violence, that were believed to underpin suicide, and these were tackled in a systematic manner. The programme included:

- surveillance;
- screening and clinical interventions in both traditional and non-traditional settings (such as tribal gatherings);
- school-based prevention programmes, including life-skills development;
- educational initiatives aimed at adults, for example, on parenting;
- identifying 'natural helpers', lay people who provided help and support in less formal settings.

The project acted as a catalyst for large-scale community activity and the development of a much expanded mental health and social care system. The programme has been associated with a reduction in suicidal gestures (defined in the study as behaviours that are not in themselves physically life-threatening but that require intervention because of their self-destructive intent) and suicide attempts. Indeed, completed suicide numbers have remained at a low level.

Culturally relevant work   An interesting example of a model which tries to reflect local culture was designed for use with American Indian college students (Muehlenkamp, Marrone, Gray, & Brown, 2009). It used the metaphor of a Lakota prayer wheel to bring together aspects of the programme. It works to promote the connectedness noted earlier as being important. The programme trained student helpers and staff in Question, Persuade, Refer (QPR) Gatekeeper training (Quinnett, 2007), and in Sources of Strength, a programme developed for Plains Indians and intended to help the person to identify and expand sources of support. Educational workshops on issues such as communication skills and problem-solving are offered annually. Cultural ceremonies are supported and promoted, as are links with students' home settings, allowing for two-way communication. Peer support workers are trained and supported. A trained counsellor with experience and knowledge of the cultural context of the students is available. Initial evaluation suggests that the programme is promising, and potentially transferable to other settings (Muehlenkamp *et al.*, 2009).

Conclusions

Suicide rates in rural areas differ between countries and change over time. They are not, therefore, fixed characteristics of an area, but rather the result of the processes acting upon people in an area at a particular time. Information on suicide in rural areas is partial, and there are many countries about which there is little or no information. Despite this, some broad themes can be identified in the literature.

Poverty and marginalization, substance misuse problems, ready access to lethal methods of self-harm, limited mental health service availability, and reluctance to seek help are frequently implicated in rural suicide. Not all of these factors apply in every area, and none should be assumed to be relevant to an area without further investigation. Particularly potent mixtures of these factors can affect indigenous groups.

As Middlebrook and colleagues note (2001), there is limited evaluation of many of the suicide prevention programmes in rural areas. The components of programmes are, however, familiar, including work on: precursors and coping skills; early identification of mental illness; recognition of suicide risk and signposting to services; method restriction; and methods of supporting people in rural areas.

Innovative programmes include careful consultation with local groups and involvement of communities in the design and monitoring of programmes. Work with American Indians and Alaskan Natives suggests that positive results can be obtained by this route.

Rural suicide is not a problem of rurality, but rather an interaction of time and circumstance. Building local solutions to rural deaths requires careful review of the nature of the problem, and of the solutions open and acceptable to local residents. The examples described here illustrate that practical help can be provided by integrating theory with local enthusiasm and practical knowledge of an area and its culture.

Note

1   Aboriginal in this study refers to people who defined themselves as belonging to an Aboriginal group: First Nations, Inuit, or Métis.

References

Aaron, R., Joseph, A., Abraham, S., Muliyil, J., George, K., Prasad, J., Minz, S., Abraham, V. J., & Bose, A. (2004). Suicides in young people in rural southern India. *The Lancet, 363*, 1117–1118.

Abeyasinghe, R. & Gunnell, D. (2008). Psychological autopsy study of suicide in three rural and semi-rural districts of Sri Lanka. *Social Psychiatry & Psychiatric Epidemiology, 43*, 280–285.

Alcantara, C. & Gone, J. P. (2007). Reviewing suicide in native American communities: Situating risk and protective factors within a transactional–ecological framework. *Death Studies, 31*, 457–477.

Allard, Y. E., Wilkins, R., & Berthelot, J. M. (2004). Premature mortality in health regions with high aboriginal populations. *Health Reports, 15*, 51–60.

Bandura, A. (1986). *Social Foundations of Thought and Action*. Englewood Cliffs, NJ: Prentice Hall.

Betts, V. T. & Thornicroft, G. (2001). *International Mid-term Review of the Second National Mental Health Plan for Australia: Mental Health and Special Programmes Branch*. Canberra: Australian Department of Health and Ageing.

Bibby, P. & Shepherd, J. (2004). *Developing a New Classification of Urban and Rural Areas for Policy Purposes: The methodology*. London: Defra.

Bose, A., Konradsen, F., John, J., Suganthy, P., Muliyil, J., & Abraham, S. (2006). Mortality rate and years of life lost from unintentional injury and suicide in south India. *Tropical Medicine and International Health, 11*, 1553–1556.

Branas, C. C., Nance, M. L., Elliott, M. R., Richmond, T. S., & Schwab, C. W. (2004). Urban–rural shifts in intentional firearm death: Different causes, same results. *American Journal of Public Health, 94*, 1750–1755.

Caldwell, T. M., Jorm, A. F., & Dear, K. B. (2004). Suicide and mental health in rural, remote and metropolitan areas in Australia. *Medical Journal of Australia, 181* (Suppl), S10–S14.

Caron, J. (2004). Gun control and suicide: Possible impact of Canadian legislation to ensure safe storage of firearms. *Archives of Suicide Research, 8*, 361–374.

Chandler, M. J. & Lalonde, C. E. (1998). Cultural continuity as a hedge against suicide in Canada's first nations. *Transcultural Psychiatry, 35*, 191–219.

Commission for Rural Communities (2008). *Health Care in Peripheral and Remote Rural Areas*. Cheltenham: Commission for Rural Communities.

Crawford, P. & Brown, B. (2002). 'Like a friend going around': Reducing the stigma attached to mental health care in rural communities. *Health and Social Care in the Community, 10*, 229–238.

Cullen, A. & Connolly, J. F. (1997). Aspects of suicide in rural Ireland 1978–1994. *Archives of Suicide Research, 3*, 43–52.

Cutcliffe, J. (2005). Toward an understanding of suicide in first-nation Canadians. *Crisis, 26*, 141–145.

Dudley, M., Cantor, C., & De Moore, G. (1996). Jumping the gun: Firearms and the mental health of Australians. *Australian and New Zealand Journal of Psychiatry, 30*, 370–381.

Eddleston, M. (2000). Patterns and problems of deliberate self-poisoning in the developing world. *Quarterly Journal of Medicine, 93*, 715–731.

Eddleston, M., Buckley, N. A., Gunnell, D., Dawson, A. H., & Konradsen, F. (2006). Identification of strategies to prevent death after pesticide self-poisoning using a Haddon matrix. *Injury Prevention, 12*, 333–337.

Eddleston, M. & Konradsen, F. (2007). Commentary: Time for a re-assessment of the incidence of intentional and unintentional injury in India and South East Asia. *International Journal of Epidemiology, 36*, 208–211.

Gajalakshmi, V. & Peto, R. (2007). Suicide rates in rural Tamil Nadu, south India: Verbal autopsy of 39 000 deaths in 1997–98. *International Journal of Epidemiology, 36,* 203–207.

Garroutte, E. M., Goldberg, J., Beals, J., Herrell, R., & Manson, S. M. (2003). Spirituality and attempted suicide among American indians. *Social Science and Medicine, 56,* 1571–1579.

Goldney, R. G. (2002). Is Aboriginal suicide different? A commentary on the work of Colin Tatz. *Psychiatry Psychology and Law, 92,* 257–259.

Goldsmith, S. K., Pellmar, T. C., Kleinman, A. M., & Bunney, W. E. (2002). *Reducing Suicide: A national imperative.* Washington, DC: National Academic Press.

Goldston, D. B., Molock, S. D., Whitbeck, L. B., Murakami, J. L., Zayas, L. H., & Nagayama Hall, G. C. (2008). Cultural considerations in adolescent suicide prevention and psychosocial treatment. *American Psychologist, 63,* 14–31.

Grossman, D. C., Mueller, B. A., Riedy, C., Dowd, M. D., Villaveces, A., Prodzinski, J., Nakagawara, J., Howard, J., Thiersch, N., & Harruff, R. (2005). Gun storage practices and risk of youth suicide and unintentional firearm injuries. *Journal of the American Medical Association, 293,* 707–714.

Grytten, J., Rongen, G., & Sorensen, R. (1995). Can a public health care system achieve equity? *Medical Care, 33,* 938–951.

Gunnell, D., Eddleston, M., Phillips, M. R., & Konradsen, F. (2007). The global distribution of fatal pesticide self-poisoning: Systematic review. *BMC Public Health, 7,* 357.

Hawton, K., Simkin, S., & Malmberg, A. (1998). *Suicide and Stress in Farmers.* London: The Stationery Office.

Hawton, K., Fagg, J., Simkin, S., Harriss, L., Malmberg, A., & Smith, D. (1999). The geographical distribution of suicides in farmers in England and Wales. *Social Psychiatry and Psychiatric Epidemiology, 34,* 122–127.

Hawton, K., Ratnayeke, L., Simkin, S., Harriss, L., & Scott, V. (2009). Evaluation of acceptability and use of lockable storage devices for pesticides in Sri Lanka that might assist in prevention of self-poisoning, *BMC Public Health, 9,* 6.

Hempstead, K. (2006). The geography of self-injury: Spatial patterns in attempted and completed suicide. *Social Science and Medicine, 62,* 3186–3196.

Hewitt, M. (1989). *Defining 'Rural' Areas: Impact on health care policy and research.* Washington, DC: Office of Technology Assessment.

Hill, D. L. (2009). Relationship between sense of belonging as connectedness and suicide in American Indians. *Archives of Psychiatric Nursing, 23,* 65–74.

Hintikka, J., Lehtonen, J., & Viinamaki, H. (1997). Hunting guns in homes and suicides in 15–24-year-old males in eastern Finland. *Australian and New Zealand Journal of Psychiatry, 31,* 858–861.

Hirsch, J. K. (2006). A review of the literature on rural suicide: Risk and protective factors, incidence, and prevention. *Crisis, 27,* 189–199.

Horn, A., Grossman, D. C., Jones, W., & Berger, L. R. (2003). Community-based program to improve firearm storage practices in rural Alaska. *Injury Prevention, 9,* 231–234.

Hsiao, W. C. (1995). The Chinese health care system: Lessons for other nations. *Social Science and Medicine, 41*(8), 1047–1055.

Irving, H. W. & Davidson, R. M. (1973). A working note on the measurement of social interaction. *Transactions of the Barnett Society, 9,* 19.

Isometsä, E., Heikkinen, M., Henriksson, M., Marttunen, M., Aro, H., & Lönqvist, J. (1997). Differences between urban and rural suicides. *Acta Psychiatrica Scandinavica, 95,* 297–305.

Judd, F., Cooper, A. M., Fraser, C., & Davis, J. (2006a). Rural suicide – People or place effects? *Australian and New Zealand Journal of Psychiatry, 40,* 208–216.

Judd, F., Jackson, H., Fraser, C., Murray, G., Robins, G., & Komiti, A. (2006b). Understanding suicide in Australian farmers. *Social Psychiatry and Psychiatric Epidemiology, 41*, 1–10.

Kapusta, N. D., Zorman, A., Etzersdorfer, E., Ponocny-Seliger, E., Jandl-Jager, E., & Sonneck, G. (2008). Rural–urban differences in Austrian suicides. *Social Psychiatry and Psychiatric Epidemiology, 43*, 311–318.

Kellermann, A. L., Rivara, F. P., Somes, G., Reay, D. T., Francisco, J., Banton, J. G., Prodzinski, J., Fligner, C., & Hackman, B. B. (1992). Suicide in the home in relation to gun ownership. *New England Journal of Medicine, 327*, 467–472.

Khan, M. M. (2005). Suicide prevention and developing countries. *Journal of the Royal Society of Medicine, 98*, 459–463.

Kruger, G. & Gray, J. (2005). *Suicide in North Dakota: A dialogue across state and tribal boundaries.* Grand Forks, ND: Center for Rural Health, University of North Dakota.

LaFromboise, T. D. & Howard-Pitney, B. (1995). The Zuni life skills development curriculum: Description and evaluation of a suicide prevention program. *Journal of Counseling Psychology, 42*, 479–486.

LaFromboise, T. D. & Lewis, H. A. (2008). The Zuni life skills development program: A school/community-based suicide prevention intervention. *Suicide and Life-Threatening Behavior, 38*, 343–353.

Lau, T., Kumar, S., & Thomas, D. (2002). Practising psychiatry in New Zealand's rural areas: Incentives, problems and solutions. *Australasian Psychiatry, 10*, 33–38.

Levin, K. A. & Leyland, A. H. (2005). Urban/rural inequalities in suicide in Scotland, 1981–1999. *Social Science and Medicine, 60*, 2877–2890.

Liu, Y., Hsiaoa, W. C., & Eggleston, K. (1999). Equity in health and health care: The Chinese experience. *Social Science and Medicine, 49*, 1349–1356.

LivingWorks (2002). *Does ASIST Work?* Calgary, Canada: LivingWorks.

Malmberg, A., Simkin, S., & Hawton, K. (1999). Suicide in farmers. *British Journal of Psychiatry, 175*, 103–105.

Markus, K., Grossman, J., Pennington, J., Woodward, P., Duda, D., & Hirsch, J. (1999). Suicide and violence prevention: Parent education in the emergency department. *Journal of the American Academy of Child and Adolescent Psychiatry, 38*, 250–255.

May, P. A., Serna, P., Hurt, L., & DeBruyn, L. M. (2005). Outcome evaluation of a public health approach to suicide prevention in an American Indian tribal nation. *Research and Practice, 95*, 1238–1244.

Middlebrook, D. L., LeMaster, P. L., Beals, J., Novins, D. K., & Manson, S. M. (2001). Suicide prevention in American Indian and Alaska native communities: A critical review of programs. *Suicide and Life-Threatening Behavior, 31* (Suppl), 132–149.

Miller, K., & Burns, C. (2008). Suicides on farms in South Australia, 1997–2001. *Australian Journal of Rural Health, 16*, 327–331.

Mishara, B. (2007). Prevention of deaths from intentional pesticide poisoning. *Crisis, 28*, 10–20.

Motohashi, Y., Kaneko, Y., Sasaki, H., & Yamaji, M. (2007). A decrease in suicide rates in Japanese rural towns after community-based intervention by the health promotion approach. *Suicide and Life-Threatening Behavior, 37*, 593–599.

Muehlenkamp, J. J., Marrone, S., Gray, J. S., & Brown, D. L. (2009). A college suicide prevention model for American Indian students. *Professional Psychology: Research and Practice, 40*, 134–140.

Murray, C. J. L. & Lopez, A. D. (1996). *Global Health Statistics: A compendium of incidence, prevalence and mortality estimates for over 200 conditions.* Cambridge, MA: Harvard University Press.

National Rural Health Alliance (2009). *Fact Sheet 14: Suicide in rural Australia.* Deakin West, Australia: National Rural Health Alliance.

O'Brien, M. (2002). *Evaluation of the Reach Out! Rural and Regional Tour of Victoria*. Balmain, New South Wales: Inspire Foundation.

Olson, L. M. & Wahab, S. (2006). American Indians and suicide. A neglected area of research. *Trauma, Violence, and Abuse, 7*, 19–33.

Oyama, H., Goto, M., Fujita, M., Shibuya, H., & Sakashita, T. (2006). Preventing elderly suicide through primary care by community-based screening for depression in rural Japan. *Crisis, 27*, 58–65.

Paykel, E., Abbott, R., Jenkins, R., Brugha, T. S., & Meltzer, H. (2000). Urban–rural mental health differences in Great Britain: Findings from the National Morbidity Survey. *Psychological Medicine, 30*, 269–280.

Pearce, J., Barnett, R., & Jones, I. (2007). Have urban/rural inequalities in suicide in New Zealand grown during the period 1980–2001? *Social Science and Medicine, 65*, 1807–1819.

Penn, D. L., Simpson, L., Edie, G., Leggett, S., Wood, L., Hawgood, J., Krysinska, K., Yellowlees, P., & De Leo, D. (2005). Development of ACROSSnet: An online support system for rural and remote community suicide prevention workers in Queensland, Australia. *Health Informatics Journal, 11*, 275–293.

Phillips, M. R., Li, X. Y., & Zhang, Y. P. (2002). Suicide rates in China, 1995–99. *The Lancet, 359*, 835–840.

Quinnett, P. (2007). *QPR Gatekeeper Training for Suicide Prevention: The model, rationale and theory*. Spokane, WA: QPR Institute.

Rural Alive and Well (2009). *Our Objectives*, available at http://rawtas.com.au, accessed 22 February 2010.

Sadowski, L. S. & Munoz, S. R. (2006). Nonfatal and fatal firearm injuries in a rural county. *Journal of the American Medical Association, 275*, 1762–1764.

Serna, P., May, P. A., & Sitaker, M. (1998). Suicide prevention evaluation in a Western Athabaskan American indian tribe – New Mexico, 1988–1997. *CDC, Morbidity and Mortality Weekly Report, 47*, 257–261.

Shaw, J. M. (1979). *Rural Deprivation and Planning*. Norwich: Geobooks.

Shenassa, E. D., Rogers, M. L., Spalding, K. L., & Roberts, M. B. (2004). Safer storage of firearms at home and risk of suicide: A study of protective factors in a nationally representative sample. *Journal of Epidemiology and Community Health, 58*, 841–848.

Silviken, A., Haldorsen, T., & Kvernmo S. (2006). Suicide among Indigenous Sami in Arctic Norway, 1970–1998. *European Journal of Epidemiology, 21*, 707–713.

Singh, G. K. & Siahpush, M. (2002). Increasing rural–urban gradients in US suicide mortality, 1970–1997. *American Journal of Public Health, 92*, 1161–1167.

Siwach, S. B. & Gupta, A. (1995). The profile of acute poisoning in Harayana–Rohtak Study. *Journal of Association of Physicians of India, 43*, 756–759.

Southern Midlands Council (2008). *Rural Alive and Well Program*, available at http://www.southernmidlands.tas.gov.au/site/page.cfm?u=283, accessed 21 April 2010.

Sheikh, S. & Furnham, A. (2000). A cross-cultural study of mental health beliefs and attitudes towards seeking professional help. *Social Psychiatry and Psychiatric Epidemiology, 35*, 36–334.

Stark, C., Matthewson, F., Oates, K., & Hay, A. (2002). Suicide in the Highlands of Scotland. *Health Bulletin, 60*, 27–32.

Stark, C., Belbin, A., Hopkins, P., Gibbs, D., Hay, A., & Gunnell, D. (2006a). Male suicide and occupation in Scotland. *Health Statistics Quarterly, 29*, 26–29.

Stark, C., Gibbs, D., Hopkins, P., Belbin, A., Hay, A., & Selvaraj, S. (2006b). Suicide in farmers in Scotland. *Rural and Remote Health, 6*, 509.

Stark, C. (2008). Suicide in rural areas. In S. Palmer (Ed.), *Suicide: Strategies and interventions for reduction and prevention* (pp. 48–68). London: Routledge.

Statewide Suicide Prevention Council (2004). *Alaska Suicide Prevention Plan*. Anchorage, AL: Commissioner's Office.

Suicide Prevention Australia (2008). *Position Statement – Responding to suicide in rural Australia*. Leichhardt, NSW: Suicide Prevention Australia.

Tatz, C. (1999). *Aboriginal Suicide is Different: Aboriginal youth suicide in New South Wales, the Australian Capital Territory and New Zealand: Towards a model of explanation and alleviation*. Macquarie University, Sydney: Centre for Comparative Genocide Studies.

Taylor, R., Page, A., Morrell, S., Harrison, J., & Carter, G. (2005). Social and psychiatric influences on urban–rural differentials in Australian suicide. *Suicide & Life-Threatening Behavior, 35*, 277–290.

Tester, F. J. & McNicoll, P. (2004). Isumagijaksaq: Mindful of the state: Social constructions of Inuit suicide. *Social Science and Medicine, 58*, 2625–2636.

Thorslund, J. (1992). Why do they do it? Proposals for a theory of Inuit suicide. Looking to the future. *Proceedings of the Seventy Inuit studies Conference*. Quebec, Canada: Inuit Studies Occasional Papers 4.

van der Hoek, W. & Konradsen, F. (2005). Risk factors for acute pesticide poisoning in Sri Lanka. *Tropical Medicine and International Health, 10*, 589–596.

Webster, D. W., Vernick, J. S., Zeoli, A. M., & Manganello, J. A. (2004). Association between youth-focused firearm laws and youth suicides. *Journal of the American Medical Association, 292*, 594–601.

Western Interstate Commission for Higher Education (2009). *Assessment and Interventions with Potentially Suicidal Patients: A pocket guide for primary care professionals*. Boulder, CO: Western Interstate Commission for Higher Education.

Wexler, L. M. (2006a). Inupiat youth suicide and culture loss: Changing community conversations for prevention. *Social Science and Medicine, 63*, 2938–2948.

Wexler, L. M. (2006b). Talking differently to prevent suicide. *Sivutmuuluta, 6*.

Wexler, L., Hill, R., Bertone-Johnson, E., & Fenaughty, A. (2008). Correlates of Alaska native fatal and nonfatal suicidal behaviors 1990–2001. *Suicide and Life-Threatening Behavior, 38*(3), 311–320.

Yip, P. S., Liu, K. Y., Hu, J., & Song, X. M. (2005). Suicide rates in China during a decade of rapid social changes. *Social Psychiatry and Psychiatric Epidemiology, 40*, 792–798.

Zhang, X. & Kanbur, R. (2003). *Spatial Inequality in Education and Health Care in China*. Ithaca, NY: Department of Applied Economics and Management, Cornell University.

Zhang, J., Conwell, Y., Zhou, L., & Jiang, C. (2004). Culture, risk factors and suicide in rural China: A psychological autopsy case control study. *Acta Psychiatrica Scandinavica, 110*, 430–437.

CHAPTER SIXTEEN

Body Weight, Obesity, and Suicide across the Life Course

David Gunnell and Kyla Thomas

Abstract

There is growing evidence that low birth weight and low body mass index (BMI) in adulthood are associated with an increased risk of suicide. Associations are seen in different settings, in both men and women, and risk appears to increase linearly with declining weight: the obese are at the lowest risk of suicide. Intriguingly, and in contrast to the direction of association with suicide, adults who are overweight appear to be at increased risk of depression. The proportions of suicides 'attributable' to low birth weight (1%) and low BMI in adulthood (1–3%) are relatively small, although estimates of attributable risk should be treated with caution until the causality of BMI–suicide associations is clarified. These associations require further investigation in more detailed studies, looking at a range of psychiatric outcomes and assessing possible causal pathways. If confirmed, biological mechanisms underlying them should be sought as these may shed light on novel interventions to detect and reduce suicide risk. Such interventions might include better identification of people at risk of suicide and drug development targeted at neurotransmitter pathways that affect weight and mood.

Introduction

At first glance the study of body weight as a risk factor for suicide appears unlikely to yield important insights into the aetiology and prevention of this complex and distressing cause of death. Nevertheless, a growing number of studies have found strong associations between

International Handbook of Suicide Prevention: Research, Policy and Practice, First Edition.
Edited by Rory C. O'Connor, Stephen Platt, Jacki Gordon.
© 2011 John Wiley & Sons, Ltd. Published 2011 by John Wiley & Sons, Ltd.

indicators of body size and suicide mortality (see, e.g., Bjerkeset, Romundstad, Evans, & Gunnell, 2008). Understanding the mechanisms that underlie these associations may provide clues concerning the aetiology of mental illness and its most serious adverse outcome – suicide.

The impact of being overweight or obese on overall health, particularly the risk of cardiovascular disease, is well recognized (Prospective Studies Collaboration, 2009) and there is considerable current health policy focus in many developing and developed nations on stemming the epidemic rise in obesity (Cross Government Obesity Unit, 2008).

The association of body weight with mental health is much less clearly understood, although studies dating back over 100 years have highlighted the relationship between an individual's physique and mental illness. Individuals with short, stocky builds ('pyknic'/'endomorphic' body types) were thought to be at increased risk of depression, whereas a lean (aesthenic/ectomorphic) physique was thought to predispose to schizophrenia (Burchard, 1936).

Recently, the long-term impact on adult health of low birth weight (which indicates foetal growth restriction) has become a focus of research interest. For example, low birth weight babies are at increased risk of cardiovascular disease, diabetes, and other adult chronic diseases (Barker, 1992). There is emerging evidence that low birth weight may also influence an individual's risk of psychiatric illness. The study of the accumulating and interacting influences on health of risk factors operating at different stages of pre- and post-natal life has become known as life course epidemiology (Kuh & Ben Shlomo, 1997).

This chapter focuses on the recent research evidence concerning the association of body weight and obesity with suicide. We begin by providing a brief overview of the associations of weight at various stages of the life course with mental illnesses, particularly depression and schizophrenia, as these two conditions confer risk in a high proportion of suicides in industrialized countries. We then go on to summarize evidence concerning the association of birth weight and adult body weight with suicide and discuss possible mechanisms underlying these associations. Throughout the chapter we have used the definitions of self-harm/suicide used by the authors of individual studies. Within this chapter these definitions are sufficiently similar to ensure the comparability of findings.

As background, the most commonly used measure of body fat/adiposity is body mass index (BMI). This is a pragmatic measure of body weight. It is calculated by dividing an individual's weight (in kg) by their height (in metres) squared; it is thus a measure of body weight that is relatively independent of height. The World Health Organization (WHO) defines obesity in adults as a BMI > $30 \, \text{kg/m}^2$, overweight: $25–30 \, \text{kg/m}^2$ and normal weight: $18.8–25 \, \text{kg/m}^2$. A small proportion of individuals have a high BMI because they are fit and muscular, but in most people their BMI is an indicator of their degree of fatness.

Birth Weight, BMI, and Mental Illness

Birth weight

A number of studies have reported that low birth weight is associated with an increased risk of depression (Thompson, Syddall, Rodin, Osmond, & Barker, 2001; Wiles, Peters, Leon, & Lewis, 2005). Similarly, low birth weight, short birth length, and other indicators of foetal growth restriction are associated with an increased risk of schizophrenia (Cannon, Jones, & Murray, 2002; Gunnell, Harrison, Whitley, Lewis, Tynelius, *et al.*, 2005). These findings are supported by studies of the effect of famine exposure *in utero* on risk of psychiatric illness. Such studies suggest that infants whose mothers were exposed to periods of extreme starvation during pregnancy are at an increased risk of developing depression and psychosis in later life (Brown, Susser, Lin, Neugebauer, & Gorman, 1995; Susser & Lin, 1992). Mechanisms underlying these associations are uncertain but it is possible that impaired brain development, resulting from growth restriction *in utero*, may increase an individual's later susceptibility to mental illness. Another possibility is that early life programming of the hypothalamo–pituitary–adrenal axis (HPA) or other metabolic systems linked to mental health may play a role.

Weight in childhood

Relatively few studies have investigated the association of BMI in childhood with adult mental health. Such studies are important to understanding associations of adult BMI with mental illness and suicide as childhood BMI is both strongly correlated with adult BMI and is unlikely to be influenced by any impact on appetite and weight on depression or the effect of psychotropic drugs on weight (Papakostas, 2008). Low BMI in childhood (age seven years) and early adulthood (ages 15 and 18 years) is strongly inversely associated with the risk of developing psychosis (Gunnell *et al.*, 2005; Wahlbeck, Forsen, Osmond, Barker, & Eriksson, 2001). Low weight children are at increased risk.

Weight in adolescence and adulthood

The Northern Finland 1966 Birth Cohort study investigated the association between obesity in adolescence and depression in young adulthood (Herva, Laitinen, Miettunen, Veijola, Karvonen, *et al.*, 2006). Obesity at 14 years was associated with depressive symptoms at 31 years. After adjustment for father's social class, family type, smoking, alcohol use, and chromatic somatic diseases at age 14 years, the odds ratio (OR) in males was 1.97, 95% CI 1.06–3.68 and in females the OR was 1.64, 95% CI 1.16–2.32.

An increasing number of studies has examined the relationship between obesity in adulthood and depression. While there is some evidence that depressed people are significantly more likely to be obese at follow-up compared with non-depressed people (Blaine, 2008), the evidence for the reciprocal relationship – the impact of obesity on later risk of depression – is unclear. A recent systematic review found that most of the available evidence is from cross-sectional studies, with inconsistent results (Atlantis & Baker, 2008). While some studies showed no association (Hallstrom & Noppa, 1981; Han, Tijhuis, Lean, & Seidell, 1998; Ross, 1994), others yielded an inverse association, that is, people with greater BMI have a reduced risk of depression (Crisp & McGuiness, 1976; Palinkas, Wingard, & Barrett-Connor, 1996), and others suggested an association in the opposite direction, that is, an increased risk of depression in people with greater BMI (Onyike, Crum, Lee, Lyketsos, & Eaton, 2003; Simon, von Korff, Saunders, Migliaretti, Crane, *et al.*, 2006). The authors also reported that cross-sectional studies that were performed outside the United States were less likely than US studies to find significant associations between depression and obesity. This was hypothesized to be the result of unique cultural differences between the United States and other populations. Many studies have simply compared the risk of depression among those who are obese with the non-obese, rather than investigating associations across the range of BMI. Since cross-sectional studies are limited by their inability to clarify the temporality of an association, it is more important to critique the findings of the relatively small number of available prospective studies (see below).

The Alameda County Study (*n* = 2,123 people aged 50 years and older) was one of the first prospective studies to examine the relationship between obesity and depression (Roberts, Kaplan, Shema, & Strawbridge, 2000). The authors reported a two-fold increased risk of depression among people who had been classified as obese in the previous year. In an updated analysis they reported that obesity at baseline was associated with increased risk of depression five years later, even after controlling for depression at baseline and other confounding factors (Roberts, Deleger, Strawbridge, & Kaplan, 2003). They found no evidence that depression at baseline increased the risk of obesity five years later.

In the HUNT study, a large Norwegian general population cohort (*n* =74,000), the association between adult ($\geq$ 20 years of age) BMI and anxiety and depression symptoms 11 years later was explored (Bjerkeset *et al.*, 2008). Higher BMI was associated with an increased risk of depression at follow-up; the OR for depression per standard deviation increase in BMI was 1.12 (95% CI 1.06–1.18) in males and 1.09 (95% CI 1.03–1.15) in females. In the same cohort there was an *inverse* association between BMI and suicide (see later).

The Renfrew/Paisley study investigated the association between BMI in Scottish participants aged 45–64 and future risk of hospital admission for psychoses or depression (Lawlor, Hart, Hole, Gunnell, & Smith, 2007). Paradoxically, the authors found that greater BMI and obesity were associated with a reduced risk of hospital admission for psychoses or depression/anxiety disorders in both genders. An important potential limitation of this study is the fact that cases would have excluded anyone with depression/anxiety which was not serious enough to result in hospital admission. However, it is unclear why this study's findings differ from the other prospective studies.

The balance of evidence indicates that those who are overweight are at increased risk of depression but reduced risk of psychosis. However, the relative lack of data on the temporal association between obesity and depression, particularly in young people, makes it difficult to understand the possible natural histories of these conditions as well as the biological mechanisms that may underlie these relationships.

Birth weight and suicide

Two recent record linkage studies, one from Scotland (of around 1,500 suicides; Riordan, Selvaraj, Stark, & Gilbert, 2006), the other from Sweden (*n* = 500 suicides) (Mittendorfer-Rutz, Rasmussen, & Wasserman, 2004) have reported inverse associations

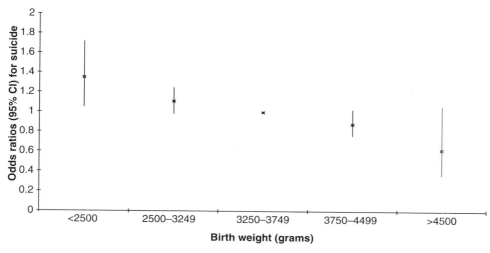

Figure 16.1   Association of birth weight with suicide.
n = 1.464 suicides. *Source*: Riordan *et al.* (2006).

between birth weight and suicide mortality. The authors of both studies found almost two-fold differences in suicide risk between high and low weight babies. The associations were not weakened in multivariable models which controlled for socio-economic position.

Figure 16.1 (based on data from Riordan *et al.*, 2006) illustrates how suicide risk changes as a function of birth weight: each black square represents the relative risk of suicide among people with a particular birth weight, compared with the risk in infants who weighed 3,250–3,749 g at birth; the vertical lines above and below the box show the upper and lower 95% confidence intervals associated with these risk estimates. In short, suicide risk increases as birth weight decreases.

In a small prospective study of suicides (*n*=43), although no association was found between birth weight and suicide, increased risk of the latter was related to poor growth in the first year of life (Barker, Osmond, Rodin, Fall, & Winter, 1995). The authors speculated that this may be due to neglect in early childhood and its possible impact on the HPA axis, which is known to be programmed in early life and may influence subsequent risk of mental illness.

The public health importance of these findings is relatively limited. Riordan and colleagues estimated that if the low birth weight–suicide associations were causal, the proportion of all suicides attributable to low birth weight would be 1%, at most (Riordan *et al.*, 2006). Nevertheless, they merit further investigation in datasets where a fuller range of intermediary variables and confounding factors (e.g., maternal mental illness, serious mental illness in adulthood, life course socio-economic position) can be controlled for, to understand better the underlying pathways and possible biological mechanisms.

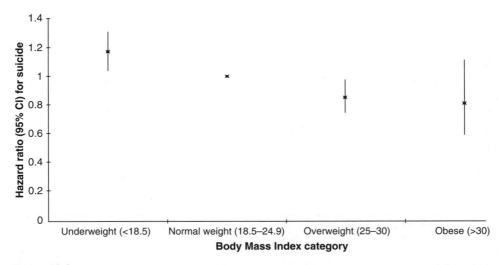

Figure 16.2   Association of BMI in early adulthood with suicide.
n = 3.075 suicides. *Source*: Magnusson *et al.* (2005).

BMI and Suicide

A growing number of prospective studies have reported that an individual's risk of suicide declines with increasing BMI. This association is seen across the range of adult BMI. The earliest investigation of this issue employed the records of 410,000 American university alumni; height adjusted weight measures were lower among the 225 suicides compared with non-suicides (Paffenbarger & Asnes, 1966). The authors speculated that 'the reduced weight characteristic of the suicide may be organic in origin or it may reflect dieting or over-scrupulous self-attention' (Paffenbarger & Asnes, 1966, p. 1029). In the last decade prospective and record linkage studies from Norway, Sweden, Denmark, the United Kingdom, and the United States have similarly reported inverse associations of suicide with body weight. In the UK's General Practice Research Database, suicide risk among people with high BMI (i.e., BMI > 25; overweight and obese) was two thirds lower than risk among those with normal or low BMI (Gasse, Derby, Vasilakis, & Jick, 2000).

The largest study, to date, is a Swedish record linkage study based on the records of over one million male conscripts followed for up to 31 years (Magnusson, Rasmussen, Lawlor, Tynelius, & Gunnell, 2006). During this period, there were 3,075 suicides. The risk of suicide declined by 15% (95% CI 9% to 21%) for each 5 kg/m^2 increase in BMI (see Figure 16.2). These associations were essentially unchanged when deaths occurring in the first five or 10 years of follow-up were excluded from the analysis. Furthermore, the relationship was unchanged after excluding conscripts with pre-existing mental disorder identified at conscription; within the sub-set of 67,000 conscripts with mental disorder at baseline a similar association was seen. Parental socio-economic position and birth weight also did not appear to confound the associations.

In the US Male Health Professionals study (Mukamal, Kawachi, Miller, & Rimm, 2007) inverse associations were reported between BMI at baseline and subsequent suicide; similarly, mental health-related quality of life was higher in people with greater BMI. Associations in this study were not confounded by medical illness, antidepressant medication, physical activity, diet, or social support. Similar associations were seen for firearm and non-firearm suicides. Other prospective studies from Denmark (Osler, Nybo Andersen, & Nordentoft, 2008) and the United States (Kaplan, McFarland, & Huguet, 2007) also report inverse associations of BMI with suicide.

Intriguingly, in an analysis of the Norwegian HUNT cohort data ($n = 74,000$), in which men and women were followed up for 17 years for suicide and 11 years for depression (see earlier), raised BMI was associated with reduced risk of suicide in both males and females. However, as already discussed, increasing BMI was associated with an increased risk of developing depression (Bjerkeset *et al.*, 2008). This finding indicates that depression-associated weight loss may not explain the inverse association between BMI and suicide.

In keeping with the findings from cohort studies where an individual's BMI is related to their risk of suicide, in a recent ecological analysis the prevalence of obesity in a number of US states correlated negatively with the rates of both fatal and non-fatal self-harm (Mukamal, Wee, & Miller, 2009). What is more, lower case fatality ratios for overdose (the proportion of people dying following an overdose) were seen in states with high levels of obesity, indicating a possible impact of obesity on drug overdose lethality. However, similar findings were seen for firearm suicides, a method where being overweight is unlikely to offer protection.

There are, however, inconsistencies in the research carried out in this field. In an analysis of the UK's Whitehall cohort ($n = 19,000$), obesity and unexplained weight loss were associated with an increased risk of suicide (hazard ratio 2.48 95% CI 1.04–5.92 and hazard ratio 5.58 95% CI 2.37–13.13 for obesity and unexplained weight loss, respectively). However, this study is likely to be under-powered as there were only six suicides among those who were obese at baseline (Elovainio, Shipley, Ferrie, Gimeno, Vahtera, *et al.*, 2009). Bridges and Tran (2008) failed to find an ecological association between BMI and suicide in the Caribbean islands.

Possible Explanations for BMI–Suicide Associations

Chance, bias, and confounding

When assessing the findings from observational studies such as those described above, it is important to consider the possibility of chance, bias, and confounding before considering causality (Box 16.1).

First, in view of the consistent findings across most of the cohort studies that have investigated BMI–suicide associations, chance is an unlikely explanation for the association. Second, as a wide range of different population groups have been studied and loss to follow-up is generally low in the studies described, selection bias is unlikely. In addition, cohort studies are less prone to bias than other epidemiological study designs. Furthermore,

---

Box 16.1   Possible explanations for BMI–suicide associations

Chance, bias, confounding:

- Associations are confounded by pre-existing mental illness.
- Associations are confounded by other risk factors for suicide, e.g., low socio-economic position, substance misuse, smoking.

Causal explanations:

- Low weight predisposes to and overweight protects versus the mental illnesses associated with suicide risk.
- Low weight is associated with impulsivity: low weight individuals may be more likely to act on suicidal impulses.
- High BMI is associated with higher levels of the hormone leptin and this hormone may have antidepressant properties.
- Body weight and influences on body weight in pre-adult life may programme/ have a permanent influence on the neuroendocrine systems influencing the risk of depression, such as the HPA axis.
- Genes associated with appetite, metabolism, and weight control are closely linked to those associated with mood, impulsivity, and suicide.
- Low weight increases the case fatality of suicide attempts, e.g., smaller amounts of medicines are required to cause death, nooses used for hanging are less likely to break.

---

weight was measured (rather than self-reported) in most of the studies, often many years before the study end-points occurred; therefore, observers will have been blind to the outcome (suicide) and it seems unlikely that suicide was more likely to be recorded for deaths amongst the underweight than the overweight, thereby minimizing the impact of information bias.

The impact of possible confounding is more difficult to rule out. Some studies have controlled for a range of possible confounding factors, including socio-economic position, smoking, antidepressant use, physical activity, and alcohol use; when controlled for, these variables have had little impact on the associations in fully adjusted models (Bjerkeset *et al.*, 2008; Magnusson *et al.*, 2006; Mukamal *et al.*, 2007; Osler *et al.*, 2008). Mukamal and Miller (2009) have investigated associations of BMI with a series of possible risk factors for suicide in a large cross-sectional survey and found little consistent evidence of associations.

Reverse causality/causal pathways

Many studies investigating associations of weight with mental illness, suicide, and suicidal behaviour use measurements taken in adulthood. A challenge with interpreting such studies is that mental illness and treatments for mental illness may themselves influence body weight.

An extreme example of weight reduction occurring in the context of mental illness is that seen with anorexia nervosa, a condition associated with extreme weight loss and mood alteration. People with anorexia are, in turn, at greatly increased risk of suicide (Harris & Barraclough, 1997). So, this raises the question of whether low weight *per se* is a risk factor for mental illness/suicide or is it that mental disorders increase risk of suicide themselves and also lead to weight loss? It is not straightforward to rule out the impact of pre-existing mental illness on weight and suicide risk, although among Swedish conscripts BMI–suicide associations were similar in those with and without mental illness at baseline (Magnusson *et al.*, 2006). In the Norwegian HUNT study the direction of the association between BMI and depression was opposite to that for BMI and suicide, indicating that depression is unlikely to underlie the association with suicide. Further longitudinal studies of this issue are required.

Studies in which weight has been measured long before the onset of mental illness, where weight is experimentally influenced or where Mendelian randomization is used will help resolve these issues (Mendelian randomization is an emerging genetic epidemiological approach in which the associations between genetic polymorphisms that affect levels of disease-specific risk factors, such as obesity, are related to health outcomes, to give unconfounded estimates of risk factor associations) (Davey Smith & Ebrahim, 2003).

A further challenge to interpretation is that many treatments for mental illness themselves are associated with weight gain (Correll & Carlson, 2006). Mechanisms underlying these associations are the subject of ongoing research (Kishi & Elmquist, 2005) but the fact that effective treatments for mental illness may lead to weight gain further highlights the important interrelationship between changes in weight and changes in mental health.

Causality

If low BMI truly affects an individual's risk of suicide, then what are the possible biological pathways underlying this association? Box 16.1 outlines some plausible causal explanations. First, it is possible that low weight may influence the risk of developing psychiatric disorders that, in turn, increase the risk of suicide. As described earlier, there is evidence that low BMI is associated with an increased risk of schizophrenia, though evidence concerning the association of BMI with depression is inconsistent. Second, low BMI may be associated with impulsivity, and so while the prevalence of suicidal thoughts may not be higher in people with low BMI, they may be more likely to act on such thoughts. People with low BMI tend to have lower cholesterol levels; it has been hypothesized that low circulating cholesterol levels may reduce cerebral serotonin (Engelberg, 1992), which in turn predisposes to suicidal behaviour (Mann, 1998).

Third, hormones and metabolic pathways associated with obesity may have beneficial effects on suicide risk. For example, leptin, a hormone secreted by adipose tissue and the product of the obesity (ob) gene, has been postulated as having antidepressant effects (Lu, Kim, Frazer, & Zhang, 2006). However, if this hormone contributes to the BMI–suicide association one would predict raised BMI to be associated with a reduced risk of depression as well as a reduced risk of suicide, and this does not seem to be the case.

A number of genes associated with suicide risk influence food intake and metabolism and it has been suggested that excessive food intake may offset suicide risk (Ogden, Rich, Schork, Paulus, Geyer, *et al.*, 2004). Further evidence for such biological mechanisms linking weight and suicide risk come from recent findings from randomized trials that new medicines designed to aid weight loss may increase the risk of suicidal behaviour. Regulatory bodies have highlighted possible links between the weight loss agent rimonabant and suicidal behaviour. In a large clinical trial of rimonabant there was evidence that it was effective in reducing BMI, but was also associated with an increased risk of depression and anxiety (Nissen, Nicholls, Wolski, Rodes-Cabau, Cannon, *et al.*, 2008).

Lastly, low weight may increase the lethality of suicide attempts or the likelihood that a suicide attempt ends in death. For example, among people who take an overdose, blood levels of the drug may be lower, on average, in overweight individuals as they have a greater blood/tissue volume in which the drug may be dispersed; although in a US prospective study inverse BMI–suicide associations were similar for firearm- and non-firearm-related suicides (Mukamal *et al.*, 2007). BMI seems unlikely to impact on the case fatality of suicide attempts using firearms.

Conclusion: Public Health Relevance

Studies ranging in size from large prospective investigations of over a million subjects to small-scale laboratory/genetic research have suggested a link between low body weight and suicide risk. Fewer studies have examined associations with birth weight, but they point to similar associations of low weight at birth with heightened risk.

Several plausible mechanisms may contribute to these associations. If real, these observations offer opportunities to better understand the aetiology of suicide and may open new avenues for therapeutic development or risk screening. In the meantime some areas warrant further investigation.

The extent to which low weight is a cause or a consequence of the mental disorders that frequently precede suicide should be clarified using appropriate study designs, as should the link between body weight and impulsiveness. The neurochemical pathways underlying these associations also need further elucidation.

Based on the findings from the larger studies of the association between BMI and suicide (Kaplan *et al.*, 2007; Magnusson *et al.*, 2006; Mukamal *et al.*, 2007), we crudely estimate that the population attributable fraction of suicide from being of low BMI as opposed to normal BMI is 1%–3%. In other words, if the association between BMI and suicide is causal, 1%–3% of suicides are 'caused' by low BMI. As the associations between BMI and suicide are linear across the whole range of BMI the population attributable fraction (PAF) is somewhat greater. Similarly, Riordan *et al.* (2006) estimated that 1% of suicides may be attributable to low birth weight. Such calculations make major assumptions concerning causality, but they do highlight the potential importance of achieving a better understanding of the mechanisms underlying body weight–suicide associations.

Importantly, it would be foolish to advocate a policy of weight increase to prevent suicide. The proportion of deaths due to suicide in most populations (1%–2%) is an order of magnitude lower than that for deaths from cardiovascular disease and cancer, both of which are strongly associated with high BMI.

References

Atlantis, E. & Baker, M. (2008). Obesity effects on depression: systematic review of epidemiological studies. *International Journal of Obesity, 32*, 881–891.

Barker, D. J. P. (1992). *Fetal and Infant Origins of Adult Disease*. London: BMJ Publishing.

Barker, D. J. P., Osmond, C., Rodin, I., Fall, C. H. D., & Winter, P. D. (1995). Low weight gain in infancy and suicide in adult life. *British Medical Journal, 311*, 1203–1203.

Bjerkeset, O., Romundstad, P., Evans, J., & Gunnell, D. (2008). The association of adult body mass index and height with anxiety, depression, and suicide in the general population: The HUNT study. *American Journal of Epidemiology, 167*, 193–202.

Blaine, B. (2008). Does depression cause obesity? A meta-analysis of longitudinal studies of depression and weight control. *Journal of Health Psychology, 13*, 1190–1197.

Bridges, F. S. & Tran, X. V. (2008). Body mass index suicide and homicide among inhabitants of the Caribbean islands. *Perceptual and Motor Skills, 106*, 650–652.

Brown, A. S., Susser, E. S., Lin, S. P., Neugebauer, R., & Gorman, J. M. (1995). Increased risk of affective disorders in males after second trimester prenatal exposure to the Dutch hunger winter of 1944–45. *British Journal of Psychiatry, 166*, 601–606.

Burchard, E. M. L. (1936). Physique and psychosis. *Comparative Psychology Monographs, 13*, 1–73.

Cannon, M., Jones, P. B., & Murray, R. M. (2002). Obstetric complications and schizophrenia: An historical and meta-analytic review. *American Journal of Psychiatry, 159*, 1080–1092.

Correll, C. U. & Carlson, H. E. (2006). Endocrine and metabolic adverse effects of psychotropic medications in children and adolescents. *Journal of the American Academy of Child & Adolescent Psychiatry, 45*, 771–791.

Crisp, A. & McGuiness, B. (1976). Jolly fat: Relation between obesity and pyschoneurosis in the general population. *British Medical Journal, 1*, 7–9.

Cross Government Obesity Unit. (2008). *Healthy Weight, Healthy Lives: A cross government strategy for England*. London: Department of Health.

Davey Smith, G. & Ebrahim, S. (2003). 'Mendelian randomization': Can genetic epidemiology contribute to understanding environmental determinants of disease? *International Journal of Epidemiology, 32*, 1–22.

Elovainio, M., Shipley, M. J., Ferrie, J. E., Gimeno, D., Vahtera, J., Marmot, M. G., & Kivimaki, M. (2009). Obesity, unexplained weight loss and suicide: The original Whitehall study. *Journal of Affective Disorders, 116*, 218–221.

Engelberg, H. (1992). Low serum cholesterol and suicide. *The Lancet, 339*, 727–729.

Gasse, C., Derby, L. E., Vasilakis, C., & Jick, H. (2000). Risk of suicide among users of calcium channel blockers: Population based, nested case-control study. *British Medical Journal, 320*, 1251–1251.

Gunnell, D., Harrison, G., Whitley, E., Lewis, G., Tynelius, P., & Rasmussen, F. (2005). The association of fetal and childhood growth with risk of schizophrenia. Cohort study of 720,000 Swedish men and women. *Schizophrenia Research, 79*, 315–322.

Hallstrom, T. & Noppa, H. (1981). Obesity in women in relation to mental illness, social factors and personality traits. *Journal of Psychosomatic Research, 25*, 75–82.

Han, T. S., Tijhuis, M. A., Lean, M. E., & Seidell, J. C. (1998). Quality of life in relation to over-weight and body fat distribution. *American Journal of Public Health, 88*, 1814–1820.

Harris, E. C. & Barraclough, B. (1997). Suicide as an outcome for mental disorders. A meta-analysis. *British Journal of Psychiatry, 170*, 205–228.

Herva, A., Laitinen, J., Miettunen, J., Veijola, J., Karvonen, J. T., Laksy, K., & Joukamaa, M. (2006). Obesity and depression: Results from the longitudinal Northern Finland 1966 Birth Cohort Study. *International Journal of Obesity, 30*, 520–527.

Kaplan, M. S., McFarland, B. H., & Huguet, N. (2007). The relationship of body weight to suicide risk among men and women: results from the US National Health Interview Survey Linked Mortality File. *Journal of Nervous and Mental Disease, 195*, 948–951.

Kishi, T. & Elmquist, J. K. (2005). Body weight is regulated by the brain: A link between feeding and emotion. *Molecular Psychiatry, 10*, 132–146.

Kuh, D. & Ben-Shlomo, Y. (Eds) (1997). *A Life Course Approach to Chronic Disease Epidemiology*. Oxford: Oxford University Press.

Lawlor, D., Hart, C., Hole, D., Gunnell, D., & Smith, G. D. (2007). Body mass index in middle life and future risk of hospital admission for psychoses or depression: Findings from the Renfrew/Paisley study. *Psychological Medicine, 37*, 1151–1161.

Lu, X. Y., Kim, C. S., Frazer, A., & Zhang, W. (2006). Leptin: A potential novel antidepressant. *Proceedings of the National Academy of Sciences of the US A, 103*, 1593–1598.

Magnusson, P., Rasmussen, F., Lawlor, D., Tynelius, P., & Gunnell, D. (2006). Association of body mass index with suicide mortality – A prospective cohort study of over 1 million men. *American Journal of Epidemiology, 163*, 1–8.

Mann, J. J. (1998). The neurobiology of suicide. *Nature Medicine, 4*, 25–30.

Mittendorfer-Rutz, E., Rasmussen, F., & Wasserman, D. (2004). Restricted fetal growth and adverse maternal psychosocial and socioeconomic conditions as risk factors for suicidal behaviour of offspring: A cohort study. *The Lancet, 364*, 1135–1140.

Mukamal, K. J., Kawachi, I., Miller, M., & Rimm, E. B. (2007). Body mass index and risk of suicide among men. *Archives of Internal Medicine, 167*, 468–475.

Mukamal, K. J. & Miller, M. (2009). BMI and risk factors for suicide: why is BMI inversely related to suicide? *Obesity, 17*, 532–538.

Mukamal, K. J., Wee, C. C., & Miller, M. (2009). BMI and rates of suicide in the United States: An ecological analysis. *Obesity, 17*, 1946–1950.

Nissen, S. E., Nicholls, S. J., Wolski, K., Rodes-Cabau, J., Cannon, C. P., Deanfield, J. E., Despres, J. P., Kastelein, J. J. P., Steinhubl, S. R., Kapadia, S., Yasin, M., Ruzyllo, W., Gaudin, C., Job, B., Hu, B., Bhatt, D. L., Lincoff, A. M., Tuzcu, E. M., & STRADIVARIUS Investigators (2008). Effect of rimonabant on progression of atherosclerosis in patients with abdominal obesity and coronary artery disease: the STRADIVARIUS randomized controlled trial. *Journal of the American Medical Association, 299*, 1547–1560.

Ogden, C. A., Rich, M. E., Schork, N. J., Paulus, M. P., Geyer, M. A., Lohr, J. B., Kuczenski, R., & Niculescu, A. B. (2004). Candidate genes, pathways and mechanisms for bipolar (manic-depressive) and related disorders: an expanded convergent functional genomics approach. *Molecular Psychiatry, 9*, 1007–1029.

Onyike, C., Crum, R., Lee, H., Lyketsos, C., & Eaton, W. (2003). Is obesity associated with major depression? Results from the Third National Health and Nutritional Examination Survey. American Journal of Epidemiology, *158*, 1139–1147.

Osler, M., Nybo Andersen, A. M., & Nordentoft, M. (2008). Impaired childhood development and suicidal behaviour in a cohort of Danish men born in 1953. *Journal of Epidemiology and Community Health, 62*, 23–28.

Paffenbarger, R. S. & Asnes, D. P. (1966). Chronic disease in former college students III. Precursors of suicide in early and middle life. *American Journal of Public Health, 56*, 1026–1036.

Palinkas, L., Wingard, D., & Barrett-Connor, E. (1996). Depressive symptoms in overweight and obese older adults: A test of the 'jolly fat' hypothesis. *Journal of Psychosomatic Research, 40*, 59–66.

Papakostas, G. I. (2008). Tolerability of modern antidepressants. *Journal of Clinical Psychiatry, 69*, 8–13.

Prospective Studies Collaboration (2009). Body mass index and cause specific mortality in 900 000 adults: collaborative analyses of 57 prospective studies. *The Lancet, 373*, 1083–1096.

Riordan, D. V., Selvaraj, S., Stark, C., & Gilbert, J. S. (2006). Perinatal circumstances and risk of offspring suicide. Birth cohort study. *British Journal of Psychiatry, 189*, 502–507.

Roberts, R., Deleger, S., Strawbridge, W., & Kaplan, G. (2003). Prospective association between obesity and depression: Evidence from the Alameda County Study. *International Journal of Obesity, 27*, 514–521.

Roberts, R., Kaplan, G., Shema, S., & Strawbridge, W. (2000). Are the obese at greater risk of depression? *American Journal of Epidemiology, 152*, 163–170.

Ross, C. (1994). Overweight and depression. *Journal of Health and Social Behaviour, 35*, 63–79.

Simon, G., von Korff, M., Saunders, K., Migliaretti, D. L., Crane, P. K., van Belle, G., & Kessler, R. (2006). Association between obesity and psychiatric disorders in the US adult population. *Archives of General Psychiatry, 63*, 824–830.

Susser, E. S. & Lin, S. P. (1992). Schizophrenia after prenatal exposure to the Dutch Hunger Winter of 1944–1945. *Archives of General Psychiatry, 49*, 983–988.

Thompson, C., Syddall, H., Rodin, I., Osmond, C., & Barker, D. J. (2001). Birth weight and the risk of depressive disorder in late life. *British Journal of Psychiatry, 179*, 450–455.

Wahlbeck, K., Forsen, T., Osmond, C., Barker, D. J., & Eriksson, J. G. (2001). Association of schizophrenia with low maternal body mass index, small size at birth, and thinness during childhood. *Archives of General Psychiatry, 58*, 48–52.

Wiles, N. J., Peters, T. J., Leon, D. A., & Lewis, G. (2005). Birth weight and psychological distress at age 45 to 51 years: Results from the Aberdeen 'Children of the 1950s' study. *British Journal of Psychiatry, 187*, 21–28.

PART II

Intervention, Treatment, and Care

CHAPTER SEVENTEEN

Evidence-based Prevention and Treatment of Suicidality in Children and Adolescents

Cendrine Bursztein Lipsicas and Alan Apter

Abstract

This chapter reviews the literature on evidence-based prevention and treatment of suicidality in children and adolescents. Initially, we explore the epidemiology and risk factors, since this knowledge is fundamental to successful prevention and treatment. The recent drop in adolescent suicide rates is reviewed in the light of theories relating to the increased use of SSRI medications for adolescent depression and the attempts to control pesticides in Eastern nations. The extent to which biological and genetic risk factors interact with environmental factors is considered, as well as the more recent evidence on social and psychological factors. There is still a paucity of assessment tools for evaluating suicide risk and effectiveness of prevention or treatment among children and adolescents. Primary and secondary prevention with a specific focus on school-based programmes is also reviewed, including screening, gatekeeper training, and suicide awareness educational curricula for students. These clearly need further systematic and longer-term evaluation. There are only two evidence-based therapies which are effective in the treatment of suicidal adolescents (tertiary prevention).

Introduction

In this chapter we review the literature on recent changes in epidemiology and biological, social, and psychological risk factors for suicide and their relation to prevention and treatment. We concentrate on the assessment of child and adolescent suicidality, and on

International Handbook of Suicide Prevention: Research, Policy and Practice, First Edition.
Edited by Rory C. O'Connor, Stephen Platt, Jacki Gordon.
© 2011 John Wiley & Sons, Ltd. Published 2011 by John Wiley & Sons, Ltd.

primary, secondary, and tertiary prevention (evidence-based treatment of suicidal children and adolescents). Most of the literature surveyed relates to children and adolescents up to the age of 20 years.

Definitions of suicidal ideation and behaviour

Definitions of suicidal ideation and behaviour remain vague and are often used imprecisely. This semantic uncertainty is problematic as preventative and treatment methods may vary as a function of the sub-types of suicidal behaviour in youth (Bursztein & Apter, 2009).

This chapter covers suicidal ideation (thoughts), non-habitual self-injurious behaviour with at least some intent to die ('attempted suicide'), and completed suicide.

Understanding Effective Prevention Through Changes in the Epidemiology of Youth Suicide

Epidemiological monitoring of suicidal behaviour plays an important role in assessing the effectiveness of preventative actions. From 1980 to 1992 the rate of suicide in the United States among pre-pubertal children and young adolescents (10–14 years old) increased by 120% (from 0.8/100,000 to 1.7/100,000), the fastest growing age-specific rate of suicide during that period. From 1992 to the present, the rate has decreased by 33% (Roche, Giner, & Zalsman, 2005). Recently, O'Leary, Frank, Grant-Knight, Beeghly, Augustyn, *et al.* (2006) reported the rate of completed suicide in children aged 5 to 14 years to be 0.9 per 100,000.

Since 1990, rates of suicide in young males have declined steadily, and by 2005 in Britain and 2003 in the United States they were at their lowest level for almost 30 years. According to Biddle, Brock, Brookes, and Gunnell (2008) this decline partly resulted from a reduction in poisoning from car exhaust gas due to an increase in the number of cars with catalytic converters. However, there have been declines in suicide from all methods, including hanging, suggesting a more pervasive effect.

One controversial explanation put forward to explain this reduction in suicide rates was the increased use of antidepressants, especially selective serotonin reuptake inhibitors (SSRIs) in the child and adolescent population (Olfson, Shaffer, Marcus, & Greenberg, 2003). Paradoxically, in 2003, the US Food and Drug Administration (FDA) raised concerns that children and adolescents being treated with antidepressant medication had increased suicidal adverse events. A meta-analysis commissioned by the FDA to assess this issue found that suicidal ideation may be increased in children on antidepressant medication (Hammad, 2004). Although it appears that there is an association between the use of antidepressants and the occurrence of suicidal adverse events, based on more extensive data, the association is not with deaths by suicide but rather with suicidal ideation (Brent, 2009).

The FDA warning resulted in decreased case finding of paediatric depression and, among new cases, decreased antidepressant prescribing with no compensatory increases in talking therapies or pharmaceutical alternatives (Libby, Orton, & Valuck, 2009). Indeed, Gibbons, Brown, Hur, Marcus, Bhaumik, *et al.* (2007) showed that between 2003 and 2005 youth suicide in the Netherlands increased by 49% and in the United States by 14%, while SSRI prescriptions for adolescents declined by approximately 22% in both the United States and the Netherlands. This controversy continues. Some propose that it was the reduction in use of SSRIs which led to the increase in youth suicide (Gibbons *et al.*, 2007; Katz, Kozyrskyj, Prior, Enns, Cox, *et al.*, 2008), while others do not find such an association (Wheeler, Gunnell, Metcalfe, Stephens, & Martin, 2008).

One other major epidemiological finding in recent years has been the difference in youth suicide in Asian versus Western countries. It appears that in China, southern India, and Singapore, the gender differences for suicide are reversed and that young females are more at risk for suicide than males. In these countries, young female suicide appears to be related to impulsive attempts using pesticides (Conner, Phillips, & Meldrum, 2007; Li, Phillips, Zhang, Xu, & Yang, 2008). The high fatality rate may also be related to the lack of emergency medical facilities (Conner *et al.*, 2007). Mental illness seems to be less of a factor in these suicides than has been reported in the West (Li *et al.*, 2008). Undoubtedly, the restriction on the use of pesticides is a very important preventative measure in these areas, as has been shown in Sri Lanka, where, following regulatory control on imports and sales of pesticides, completed suicide rates fell by half over a 10-year period (Gunnell, Fernando, Hewagama, Priyangika, Konradsen, *et al.*, 2007) (see also Chapters 28 and 31, below).

Risk Factors for Suicidal Behaviour as Targets of Prevention and Treatment

Understanding the risk factors for suicidal behaviour is a central element in the planning of prevention and treatment programmes. We highlight below some of the risk factors investigated in recent years (although this is not an exhaustive list).

Risk factors are largely unstudied in pre-pubertal children and have usually been inferred from adolescent studies. However, inferences should be made only with considerable caution, as supporting evidence is lacking (Kloos, Collins, Weller, & Weller, 2007).

Previous suicide attempts

A history of suicide attempt, especially having made multiple attempts, increases the likelihood of further attempts in adolescents (Miranda, Scott, Hicks, Wilcox, Harris Munfakh, *et al.*, 2008). Miranda *et al.* (2008) showed that multiple attempters present with a different diagnostic profile compared with single attempters and ideators. They more often wished to die, their attempts were timed so that intervention was less likely, and they more often regretted recovery. These findings suggest that assessment of psychiatric history, together with a definite or uncertain wish to die at the time of an attempt, must be assessed to estimate risk and prevent future attempts.

Familial transmission of suicidal behaviour

Suicidality in younger age groups must be considered in the context of the family, as family psychopathology is closely linked to suicidality in children and adolescents (Mann & Currier, 2007). Suicide attempt rates are elevated in families of suicide completers and suicide rates are elevated in family members of attempters (Brent & Mann, 2005). This holds even after adjusting for the presence of psychiatric disorder in the probands (the first affected family member who seeks medical attention) and family, indicating that youth suicide is inherited distinctively from the psychiatric illness (Brent & Mann, 2005). The biological mechanisms which may be involved in suicide risk are probably related to serotonin metabolism (impulsivity and aggression) and to a dysfunctional HPA axis (hyper-reactivity to stress) (Mann & Currier, 2007). Genetic factors exert their impact on suicidal behaviour via an interaction with a stressful environment (Brent & Melhem, 2008).

Other, non-genetic factors related to suicidal behaviour in the young include parent–child discord, which has been found to be the single most common precipitant for completed suicide in adolescents younger than 16 years (Brent, Baugher, Bridge, Chen, & Chiappetta, 1999). Child abuse increases the risk of and decreases the age of onset for suicidal behaviour (Molnar, Buka, & Kessler, 2001). Children of parents with a history of abuse are at higher risk of suicidal behaviour through both genetic and environmental trajectories (Melhem, Brent, Ziegler, Iyengar, Kolko, *et al.*, 2007).

Better understanding of the mechanisms of the familial transmission of suicidal behaviour can help to identify individuals at high risk of developing suicidal behaviour, as well as in the planning of early intervention and prevention (Brent & Melhem, 2008).

Social risk factors

Other risk factors for depression and suicidal behaviour in children and adolescents include bullying and peer victimization. A population-based birth-cohort study in Finland, in which participants were followed up to the age of 25, found that bullying behaviour at the age of eight years was associated with later suicide attempts and completed suicides (Klomek, Sourander, Niemelä, Kumpulainen, Piha, *et al.*, 2009).

The influence of media reporting on suicide in the young has been widely researched over the last few decades. There is evidence of increased risk of suicidal behaviour associated with media accounts of suicide that romanticize or dramatize the description of suicidal deaths (Sudak & Sudak, 2005). Specific guidelines for the media, devised in many countries, appear to be effective in altering ways of reporting (Pirkis, Dare, Blood, Rankin, Williamson, *et al.*, 2009) in some countries (such as Austria) and have been associated with a decrease in suicidal behaviour (Niederkrotenthaler & Sonneck, 2007).

Nevertheless, the existence of Internet sites that promote suicide is raising much concern (Biddle, Donovan, Hawton, Kapur & Gunnell, 2008; Recupero, Harms, & Noble, 2008), especially given the increasing importance of the Internet as a widespread source of information and social networking for the young. On the other hand, the Internet has also been used as a platform for suicide prevention activity, such as online support groups combined with personal chat and a telephone helplines (Gilat & Shahar, 2009). However, empirical research on this topic is still insufficient to reach a firm judgement about the overall influence of the Internet on suicidal behaviour.

Two recent studies have shown that binge drinking, a common behaviour among high school (Miller, Naimi, & Brewer, 2007) and college youths (Schaffer, Jeglic, & Stanley, 2008), is strongly associated with suicidal ideation and behaviour. Another study identified the use of alcohol while sad or depressed as a marker for suicidal behaviour in adolescents who did not report having suicidal thoughts prior to an attempt and, hence, might not be detected by current strategies for assessing suicide risk (Schilling, Aseltine, Glanovsky, James, & Jacobs, 2009). The association between binge drinking and suicidal behaviour is stronger among adolescents age 13 years and younger than among youths aged 18 years and older (Aseltine, Schilling, James, Glanovsky, & Jacobs, 2009).

Psychological risk factors

The vast majority of adolescents who are engaged in suicidal behaviour have a diagnosable psychiatric disorder, primarily some form of depression (Brunstein Klomek & Stanley, 2007).

An interesting finding in the Finnish longitudinal study (described above) was that male completed suicide or serious suicide attempt in adolescence or early adulthood was related to psychiatric problems at the age of eight, while female severe suicidality could not be predicted by psychopathologic disorders in childhood (Sourander, Klomek, Niemelä, Haavisto, Gyllenberg, *et al.*, 2009). This may be due to the fact that suicidality among girls is related to the sharp increase in affective disorders after the onset of puberty. Hence, early detection and treatment of psychiatric disorders seems especially crucial for males, but may be possible only at a later stage in the development of females.

There is a significant overlap between non-suicidal self-injury (NSSI) and suicide attempts in adolescents. Clinicians need to be aware of the demographic and diagnostic correlates of each of these behaviours and undertake prompt assessment of suicidal ideation and behaviour in NSSI (Nock, Joiner, Gordon, Lloyd-Richardson, & Prinstein, 2006).

Recent studies support previous findings in pointing to the importance of coping and problem-solving in adolescent suicidal behaviour (Speckens & Hawton, 2005). An interesting and relevant study for prevention found that poor decision-making is present in adolescents who currently self-harm, but not in those with a previous history of self-harm. Improvement in decision-making skills may therefore be linked to cessation of self-harm (Oldershaw, Grima, & Jollant, 2008).

As mentioned earlier, aggression and impulsivity seem to play an important role in the pathways to suicidality as precursors of suicidal behaviour and as possible mediators between other pathologies and suicidality. One hypothesis is that aggression may mark a dispositional tendency to act impulsively in states of negative affect, and it may, in some individuals, facilitate acting upon suicidal thoughts (Brent & Mann, 2005).

Attention-deficit hyperactivity disorder (ADHD) has been related indirectly to suicidality in adolescents via increasing severity of comorbid conditions, particularly conduct disorder and depression (James, Lai, & Dahl, 2004). However, some suggest that it is the associated impulsivity that may increase the risk of suicide in these youths (Roche, Giner, & Zalsman, 2005).

Eating disorders, which are widespread among adolescents (Pompili, Mancinelli, Girardi, Ruberto, & Tatarelli, 2004), are also related to high rates of suicidal behaviour. Again, it appears to be related primarily to depression and aggression, as well as with lack of control, including impulsivity (Bulik, Thornton, Pinheiro, Plotnicov, Klump, *et al.*, 2008).

Another important risk factor for suicidality is insight (awareness of illness, the need for treatment, and the consequences of the disorder), which has mostly been investigated in psychotic disorders, showing that increased awareness of the illness and its consequences raises the risk of suicide (Amador & Kronengold, 2004; Schwartz-Stav, Apter, & Zalsman, 2006). This subject is in urgent need of further research as it has not been investigated sufficiently in adolescent samples.

Assessment

Clinicians' ability to undertake accurate assessment of suicidality among adolescents has been compromised by a lack of well-defined terminology and understanding as to what constitutes suicidal behaviour (Posner, Oquendo, Gould, Stanley, & Davies, 2007; see also Chapter 1, above). Some behaviour that is not suicidal is labelled as such, while suicidal behaviour may be missed, leading to misinterpretation in research and clinical settings (Posner, Melvin, Stanley, Oquendo, & Gould, 2007) and failure to intervene appropriately. Although there are subjective self-report instruments assessing the presence of suicidality as well as risk factors for suicide, and the principles of clinical evaluation are well known and used by clinicians all over the world, an objective assessment scale using standardized terminology is desperately needed to enable reliable assessment of suicidal adolescents. The only recent publication to deal with this problem is a study by Posner, Oquendo, *et al.* (2007) describing the Columbia Classification Algorithm for Suicide Assessment (C-CASA), which is a standardized suicidal rating system providing data for the paediatric suicidal risk analysis of antidepressants conducted by the FDA.

Following the development of the C-CASA, a low-burden measure of the spectrum of suicidal ideation and behaviour, the Columbia-Suicide Severity Rating Scale (C-SSRS), was developed in the National Institute of Mental Health (NIMH) Treatment of Adolescent Suicide Attempters Study (TASA) to assess severity and track suicidal events through treatment. It is a clinical interview, focusing on both ideation and behaviour that can be administered during evaluation or risk assessment to identify the level and type of suicidality present. It can also be used during treatment to monitor clinical deterioration or improvement (Posner, Melvin, *et al.*, 2007). Although this tool needs further assessment, it is an important step in the development of much needed common terminology and assessment procedures.

Suicide Prevention in Youth

Although many prevention programmes are employed in various settings (community resources, schools, emergency departments, etc.), evidence of their effectiveness is limited (Rodgers, Sudak, Silverman, & Litts, 2007). Current efforts to establish better empirical evidence for suicide prevention include the National Registry of Evidence-Based Programmes and Practices (NREPP), a federal registry of effective prevention programmes in the United States (Rodgers *et al.*, 2007).

Primary prevention

Primary prevention aims to reduce suicidal behaviour by eliminating or attenuating risk factors and strengthening protective factors (Wasserman & Durkee, 2009). This is usually directed towards whole populations or specific settings, such as schools, and typically works through legislation, public policy interventions, and the mass media, rather than via mental health professionals. The most important programmes are those that use public campaigns to promote detection and treatment of depression, such as the European Alliance Against Depression (EAAD) (Hegerl, Wittmann, Arensman, Van Audenhove, Bouleau, *et al.*, 2008).

    Other examples of successful primary prevention strategies mentioned earlier in this chapter are involvement of the media in responsible reporting of suicides (Niederkrotenthaler & Sonneck, 2007; Pirkis *et al.*, 2009) and limiting the access to commonly used and potentially lethal methods of suicide, such as guns, pesticides, pills, etc. (Biddle, Brock, *et al.*, 2008; Gunnell *et al.*, 2007).

Secondary prevention

Secondary prevention strategies address individuals at risk, such as those with mental disorder, and aim to provide early treatment (Anderson & Jenkins, 2006). An example of secondary prevention in youth is gatekeeper training in schools, community or healthcare settings. The idea is to train school staff and healthcare professionals to recognize youths at risk and refer them to appropriate treatment facilities/services.

    Another strategy is screening of the general adolescent population for individuals with suicidal ideation and previous attempts, as well as depression and other suicide risk factors (Gould, Marrocco, Kleinman, Thomas, Mostkoff, *et al.*, 2005). The recent studies on the relation between bullying and suicidality (described earlier in the chapter) suggest that early school years suicide prevention and active screening strategies should also focus on those who are frequently bullied and victimized.

Primary and secondary prevention in schools

School-based prevention programmes are appropriate for addressing suicide risk in the young and have become a significant feature of most national suicide prevention strategies (Gould, Brunstein Klomek, & Batejan, 2009). In school, children and adolescents can easily be reached, although drop-outs comprise a definite risk group which is often missed.

    School-based programmes are based on the principles of primary and secondary prevention. Some are aimed at case-finding using suicide awareness educational curricula, gatekeeper training or screening, while others aim at risk reduction through skills training or a combination of skills training and suicide awareness educational curricula.

While there have been worries about possible detrimental consequences of suicide awareness educational curricula (Gould *et al.*, 2009), today there are some promising programmes avoiding past mistakes (such as minimizing the importance of mental illness in suicidal behaviour and describing suicide as an understandable response to stress).

Thus far, Signs of Suicide (SOS) is the best empirically supported school-based prevention programme and is listed as such in the NREPP (National Registry of Evidence-based Programs and Practices). SOS is a two-day programme for adolescents aged 13–18 years, combining a curriculum component (a video and teacher-led class discussion) aimed at raising awareness, with a screening component to identify students with depression and at-risk of suicide. An evaluation in more than 6,000 students in five high schools showed a 40% short-term decrease in self-reported suicide attempts and modest changes in knowledge and attitudes. Yet no changes were found in suicide ideation and help-seeking behaviours (Aseltine & DeMartino, 2004). The most recent replication study of SOS (Aseltine, James, Schilling, & Glanovsky, 2007) involved over 4,000 adolescents from diverse ethnic/racial background in nine different high schools across three states in the United States. Results confirmed earlier findings and showed significantly lower rates of suicide attempts, greater knowledge about, and more adaptive attitudes towards, depression, independent of race/ethnicity, grade, and gender. However, no effect was found for help-seeking behaviours. Both studies lack follow-up data beyond three months and baseline pre-test data.

Another school-based strategy is skills training, with a specific focus on improving problem-solving and coping skills, thereby aiming to 'immunize' youths against suicidal behaviour. These programmes also intend to reduce suicide risk factors, such as depression, hopelessness, and drug abuse. Assessing a group-based prevention programme in Israeli schools, Orbach and Bar-Joseph (1993) found that a gradual, controlled exploration of inner experiences and life difficulties related to suicidal behaviour, while teaching coping strategies, can immunize adolescents against self-destructive feelings.

Overall, the evaluation of skills training programmes has yielded positive results. Yet there may be iatrogenic effects, as found in a study by Cho, Hallfores, and Sanchez (2005) (e.g., students bonding with other at-risk youth, lower grade point average, and higher level of anger) in specific target groups (e.g., students at risk for drop-out) that need further evaluation (Gould *et al.*, 2009).

Limited research on gatekeeper training has shown significant improvement in knowledge, attitudes, intervention skills, and willingness to cope with a crisis, as well as referral practices among school personnel (King & Smith, 2000; Wyman, Brown, & Hendricks, 2008). Two gatekeeper programmes in particular have been widely used: Living Works' Applied Suicide Intervention Skills Training (ASIST) (www.livingworks.net) and Question Persuade and Refer (QPR) (www.qprinstitue.com). ASIST is a two-day workshop involving interactive skills training, including role playing, to enhance 'suicide intervention competencies'. The ASIST programme has been field-tested, but to date there has been no controlled study of the programme (Gould *et al.*, 2009). However, a non-experimental evaluation of ASIST in Scotland has been conducted. The findings are available at http://www.chooselife.net/web/FILES/Research&Reviews/ASISTEvaluationFullReport.pdf.

QPR targets all adults in contact with youths and is designed to enhance gatekeepers' ability to recognize at-risk youths, to approach and ask questions about suicide, and to refer for treatment. A cluster randomized study conducted in 32 schools involving 252 school staff in the United States yielded an increase in knowledge of suicide warning signs (Wyman *et al.*, 2008). The training also increased the perceived preparedness of staff to intervene. However, at (on average) one-year follow-up, only 14% of trained staff actually increased the number of queries about suicidal thoughts among students. These staff members tended to have been already communicating with students before the training. Hence, it seems that successful appraisal of risk and assistance to suicidal youths depends on pre-existing empathy and communication style. In addition, the study found that vulnerable youths were reluctant to share their distress with adults. In conclusion, the authors point to the need to add skills training to any gatekeeper training for staff, as well as implementing interventions that modify students' help-seeking behaviours.

Case-finding through screening is based on evidence that suicidal adolescents are under-identified, exhibit identifiable risk factors, and often suffer from a treatable mental illness (Gould, Greenberg, Velting, & Shaffer, 2003). Although screening appears to be a promising prevention strategy, there has been considerable public debate about possible stigmatization (Friedman, 2006).

Other problems with screening include the fluctuation of suicidal risk over time, resulting in the need for repeated screening in order to avoid missing at-risk youths (Gould *et al.*, 2003). It should also be remembered that identification and referral following screening does not guarantee adherence to treatment, which is a major issue in the treatment of suicidal adolescents.

The Teen Screen programme (the most well-known adolescent screening programme) (www.teenscreen.org) has been rated as promising by the NREPP. The screening includes completion of a self-administered screening instrument assessing past suicidal behaviour and risk factors for teen suicidality. Students who score 'positive' are interviewed by a mental health professional to determine if further evaluation is required. Those who are in need are offered assistance with referral to mental healthcare in the community. The Teen Screen is active in more than 400 communities in the United States and other countries. There is evidence that school-based screening can identify suicidal and emotionally troubled students who are not recognized as such by school professionals (Scott, Wilcox, Schonfeld, Davies, Hicks, *et al.*, 2009).

Prior to the implementation of any case-finding strategy in school or in the community, a well-prepared referral network and treatment resources need to be in place.

Tertiary prevention/treatment

The goal of tertiary prevention is to reduce the rate of relapse in adolescents with known suicidal ideation and attempts. This requires multidisciplinary services with easy access, continuity of care, and rehabilitation, as well as inclusion of the family in the process (Wasserman & Durkee, 2009). Included in this category are postvention programmes which aim to assist survivors in their grief process, in addition to identifying and referring those who may be at risk of developing morbidity and mortality related to pathological bereavement. However, although the value of suicide postvention is increasingly recognized, there is insufficient research on the efficacy of programmes targeting youths in general and school-based programmes specifically.

Psychosocial therapies

There have been major advances in the treatment of adolescent depression. Many studies have assessed the use of Cognitive Behaviour Therapy (CBT), interpersonal therapy (IPT) and medication in reducing symptoms (Brunstein Klomek, & Stanley, 2007; March, Silva, Petrycki, Curry, Wells, *et al.*, 2007; Rohde, Silva, Tonev, Kennard, Vitiello, *et al.*, 2008). On the other hand, little research is available on treatment targeting suicidal adolescents and, until recently, suicidal adolescents were excluded from clinical trials. Currently, there are only two psychotherapies that have been found to be effective in reducing suicide attempts among adults: CBT (Brown, Have, Henriques, Xie, Hollander, *et al.*, 2005) and Dialectical Behaviour Therapy (DBT) (Linehan, Armstrong, Suarez, Allmon, & Heard, 1991). These have been adapted to adolescents and appear to be promising, as described below.

DBT has been adapted for adolescents with borderline features (DBT-A) in a 16-week treatment that includes individual psychotherapy, multi-family skills training group (a didactic framework in which the patients and parent/family members are taught four sets of skills and practise with one another), and the therapist's consultation team. Parents are an integral part of DBT-A and participate in the skills training group and in the individual sessions, as needed, to address familial issues. DBT-A is based on a dialectical perspective and a mindfulness orientation (based on Eastern Zen Buddhist principles). The dialectic of the treatment is the emphasis on balancing change and acceptance. Identity problems, impulsivity, emotional instability, and interpersonal problems are targeted by teaching mindfulness, distress tolerance, emotion regulation, and interpersonal effectiveness. Behaviour change in DBT-A is facilitated by a combination of direct instruction about the skills to be learned, modelling of the behaviour, repeated practice by the patient, and positive reinforcements offered by the therapist (Brunstein Klomek, & Stanley, 2007).

Rathus and Miller (2002) conducted a quasi-experimental investigation of DBT with a group of 111 suicidal adolescents with borderline personality features. The DBT-A group received 12 weeks of twice weekly individual therapy and a multi-family training group. The treatment as usual (TAU) group received 12 weeks of twice-weekly supportive-psychodynamic individual therapy plus weekly family therapy. Although not statistically significant, fewer subjects made suicide attempts in the DBT condition (3.4% versus 8.6%). The DBT-A group also had significantly fewer psychiatric hospitalizations during treatment and a significantly higher rate of treatment completion than the TAU group. Moreover, within the DBT-A group there were significant reductions in suicidal ideation, general psychiatric symptoms and symptoms of borderline personality disorder. This study supports further work in the application of DBT to the treatment of suicidal adolescents.

Evaluating the feasibility of DBT-A in a general child and adolescent inpatient psychiatric unit, Katz, Cox, Gunasekara, and Miller (2004) reported that DBT-A significantly reduced behavioural incidents compared with TAU. Both groups demonstrated reductions in suicidal behaviour, depressive symptoms, and suicidal ideation at one-year follow-up. The study showed that DBT-A is feasible in an adolescent in-patient unit, but did not demonstrate its superiority to standard in-patient care. It should be stressed that this was a pilot study with a small sample size; hence, the findings should be viewed as preliminary.

A multi-site NIMH funded study, Treatment of Adolescent Suicide Attempters (TASA), has pilot tested an individual cognitive behavioural treatment for depressed adolescents who have attempted suicide. Data have been collected from 120 adolescents aged 12–18 years in five sites in the United States (Brunstein Klomek & Stanley, 2007). The primary goals of this treatment are to prevent re-attempts and suicide completion among adolescent suicide attempters. The study compared three treatment conditions: CBT combined with medication management; CBT alone; and medication management alone. The intervention included a 12-week acute phase and a six-month continuation phase.

The TASA therapy is a combination of cognitive behavioural techniques based on Beck's model (Brown *et al.*, 2005), skills enhancement based on DBT, and family therapy. The goals of family therapy are to encourage family support, improve the family's problem-solving skills, and modify the family's communication patterns (Brunstein Klomek & Stanley, 2007). Initial results have recently been published which show positive results for adolescents vigorously treated with a combination of medication and psychotherapy. Adolescents with depression who have recently attempted suicide showed rates of improvement and remission of depression that seem comparable with those observed in non-suicidal adolescents with depression (Vitiello, Brent, Greenhill, Emslie, Wells, *et al.*, 2009).

Results of other psychotherapies, usually family- or group-based, have been highly variable. These include Multisystemic Therapy (MST) (Huey, Henggler, Rowland, Halliday-Boykins, Cunningham, *et al.*, 2004), psychoeducation and cognitive-behavioural family therapy (Rotheram-Borus, Piacentini, van Rossem, Graae, Cantwell, *et al.*, 1996), home-based family therapy (Harrington, Kerfoot, Dyer, McNiven, Gill, *et al.*, 1998), developmental group therapy (Wood, Harrington, & Moore, 2001), and Youth-Nominated Support Team (YST-1) (King, Kramer, Preuss, Kerr, Weisse, *et al.*, 2006). A recent study in Australia failed to replicate the benefits of the developmental group therapy (Hazell, Martin, McGill, Kay, Wood, *et al.*, 2009). As far as we are aware, none of the other studies has been replicated, so these therapies remain unproven.

Open access to hospital (i.e., immediate, unconditional re-admission to hospital) may be protective for adolescents at low or moderate risk for suicide re-attempt (Cotgrove, Zirinsky, Black, & Weston, 1995), although more studies are needed to prove effectiveness. Written contact after discharge from the hospital was not found to reduce the number of re-attempts in adolescents, despite being effective for adults (Carter, Clover, Whyte, Dawson, & D'Este, 2005).

Pharmacotherapy

As mentioned above, there have been many studies on the use of antidepressant medication either alone or in combination with psychotherapy for depression. None has addressed suicidality as the main object of therapy, although there has been much discussion about the potentiating effects of these drugs on suicide. Only one medication, lithium, has been shown to have a potential anti-suicide effect (Cipriani, Pretty, Hawton, & Geddes, 2005). Apart from one report describing the preventive effects of lithium on suicidal thoughts and behaviours in adolescents (Masters, 2008), there have been no studies on the effects of this treatment on adolescent suicidal behaviour (Bursztein & Apter, 2009).

Conclusions

Adolescent suicide remains a major clinical problem and cause of death in young people. Non-fatal suicidal behaviour is also associated with a great deal of morbidity and suffering. The identification of more specific risk factors for suicide is a prerequisite for improving the prediction of suicidality and an enhanced assessment process, more effective treatment, and more targeted prevention programmes.

Major problems that remain to be solved include the improvement of definitions of different sub-types and phenotypes of suicidal behaviour and the development of objective assessment tools. There is also need for better understanding of the biological and genetic factors which interact with environmental factors, as well as social and psychological factors that put individuals at high risk of suicide, including the influence of bullying, Internet use, binge drinking, ADHD, insight into illness, and non-suicidal self-injury. Certainly, more research is required on specific risk factors of suicidal behaviour in children in order to plan prevention at an earlier stage. Most of all, there is urgent need for more systematic study of suicide prevention programmes for youth in different settings, as well as targeted psychotherapies. These must include long-term follow-up to assess the possibility of sustained effects of these interventions, as well as possible detrimental effects in some sub-groups.

References

Amador, X. F. & Kronengold, H. (2004). Understanding and assessing insight. In X. Amador & A. David (Eds.), *Insight and Psychosis: Awareness of illness in schizophrenia and related disorders* (pp. 3–30). New York: Oxford University Press.

Anderson, M. & Jenkins, R. (2006). The national suicide prevention strategy for England: The reality of a national strategy for the nursing profession. *Journal of Psychiatric and Mental Health Nursing, 13*, 641–650.

Aseltine, R. H. & DeMartino, R. (2004). An outcome evaluation of the SOS Suicide Prevention Program. *American Journal of Public Health, 94*, 446–451.

Aseltine, R., James, A., Schilling, E., & Glanovsky, J. (2007). Evaluating the SOS suicide prevention programme: A replication and extension. *BMC Public Health, 7*, 161.

Aseltine, R. H., Schilling, E. A., James, A., Glanovsky, J. L., & Jacobs, D. (2009). Age variability in the association between heavy episodic drinking and adolescent suicide attempts: Findings from a large-scale, school-based screening program. *Journal of the American Academy of Child and Adolescent Psychiatry, 48*, 262–270.

Biddle, L., Brock, A., Brookes, S. T., & Gunnell, D. (2008). Suicide rates in young men in England and Wales in the 21st century: Time trend study. *British Medical Journal, 336*, 539–542.

Biddle, L., Donovan, J., Hawton, K., Kapur, N., & Gunnell, D. (2008). Suicide and the internet. *British Medical Journal, 336*, 800–802.

Brent, D. A. (2009). Selective serotonin reuptake inhibitors and suicidality: A guide for the perplexed. *Canadian Journal of Psychiatry, 54*, 72–74.

Brent, D. A., Baugher, M., Bridge, J., Chen, T., & Chiappetta, L. (1999). Age- and sex-related risk factors for adolescent suicide. *Journal of the American Academy of Child and Adolescent Psychiatry, 38*, 1497–1505.

Brent, D. A. & Mann, J. J. (2005). Family genetic studies, suicide, and suicidal behavior. *American Journal of Medical Genetics, 133*, 13–24.

Brent, D. A. & Melhem, N. (2008). Familial transmission of suicidal behavior. *Psychiatric Clinics of North America, 31*, 157–177.

Brown, G. K., Have, T. T., Henriques, G. R., Xie, S. X., Hollander, J. E., & Beck, A. T. (2005). Cognitive therapy for the prevention of suicide attempts: A randomized controlled trial. *Journal of the American Medical Association, 294*, 563–570.

Brunstein Klomek, A. & Stanley, B. (2007). Psychosocial treatment of depression and suicidality in adolescents. *CNS Spectrums, 12*, 135–144.

Bulik, C. M., Thornton, L., Pinheiro, A. P., Plotnicov, K., Klump, K. L., Brandt, H., Crawford, S., Fichter, M. M., Halmi, K. A., Johnson, C., Kaplan, A. S., Mitchell, J., Nutzinger. D., Strober, M., Treasure, J., Woodside, D. B., Berrettini, W. H., & Kaye, W. H. (2008). Suicide attempts in anorexia nervosa. *Psychosomatic Medicine, 70*, 378–383.

Bursztein, C. & Apter, A. (2009). Adolescent suicide. *Current Opinion in Psychiatry, 22*, 1–6.

Carter, G. L., Clover, K., Whyte, I. M., Dawson, A. H., & D'Este, C. (2005). Postcards from the Edge project: Randomized controlled trial of an intervention using postcards to reduce repetition of hospital treated deliberate self-poisoning. *British Medical Journal, 331*, 805.

Cho, H., Hallfores, D. D., & Sanchez, V. (2005). Evaluation of a high school peer group intervention for at risk youth. *Journal of Abnormal Child Psychology, 33*, 363–374.

Cipriani, A., Pretty, H., Hawton, K., & Geddes, J. R. (2005). Lithium in the prevention of suicidal behavior and all-cause mortality in patients with mood disorders: A systematic review of randomized trials. *American Journal of Psychiatry, 162*, 1805–1819.

Conner, K. R., Phillips, M. R., & Meldrum, S. (2007). Predictors of low-intent and high-intent suicide attempts in rural China. *American Journal of Public Health, 97*, 1842–1846.

Cotgrove, A., Zirinsky, L., Black, D., & Weston, D. (1995). Secondary prevention of attempted suicide in adolescence. *Journal of Adolescence, 18*, 569–577.

Friedman, R. A. (2006). Uncovering an epidemic – Screening for mental illness in teens. *New England Journal of Medicine, 35*, 2717–2719.

Gibbons, R. D., Brown, C. H., Hur, K., Marcus, S. M., Bhaumik, D. K., Erkens, J. A., Herings, R. M., & Mann, J. J. (2007). Early evidence on the effects of regulators' suicidality warnings on SSRI prescriptions and suicide in children and adolescents. *American Journal of Psychiatry, 164*, 1356–1363.

Gilat, I. & Shahar, G. (2009). Suicide prevention by online support groups: An action theory-based model of emotional first aid. *Archives of Suicide Research, 13*, 52–63.

Gould, M., Brunstein Klomek, A., & Batejan, K. (2009). The role of schools, colleges and universities in suicide prevention. In D. Wasserman & C. Wasserman (Eds.), *The Oxford Textbook of Suicidology and Suicide Prevention – A global perspective* (pp. 551–560). New York: Oxford University Press.

Gould, M. S., Greenberg, T., Velting, D. M., & Shaffer, D. (2003). Youth suicide risk and preventive interventions: A review of the past 10 years. *Journal of the American Academy of Child and Adolescent Psychiatry, 42*, 386–405.

Gould, M. S., Marrocco, F. A., Kleinman, M., Thomas, J. G., Mostkoff, K., Cote, J., & Davies, M. (2005). Evaluating iatrogenic risk of youth suicide screening programs: A randomized controlled trial. *Journal of the American Medical Association, 293*, 1635–1643.

Gunnell, D., Fernando, R., Hewagama, M., Priyangika, W. D., Konradsen, F., & Eddleston, M. (2007). The impact of pesticide regulations on suicide in Sri Lanka. *International Journal of Epidemiology, 36*, 1235–1242.

Hammad, T. A. (2004). *Review and Evaluation of Clinical Data. Washington DC: Food and Drug Administration*, available at http://www.fda.gov/ohrms/dockets/ac/04/briefing/2004-4065b1-10-TAB08-Hammads-Review.pdf.

Harrington, R., Kerfoot, M., Dyer, E., McNiven, F., Gill, J., Harrington, V., Woodham, A., & Byford, S. (1998). Randomized trial of a home-based family intervention for children who have deliberately poisoned themselves. *Journal of the American Academy of Child and Adolescent Psychiatry, 37*, 512–518.

Hazell, P. L., Martin, G., McGill, K., Kay, T., Wood, A., Trainor, G., & Harrington, R. (2009). Group therapy for repeated deliberate self-harm in adolescents: Failure of replication of a randomized trial. *Journal of the American Academy of Child and Adolescent Psychiatry, 48*, 662–670.

Hegerl, U., Wittmann, M., Arensman, E., Van Audenhove, C., Bouleau, J. H., van der Feltz-Cornelis, C., Gusmao, R., Kopp, M., Löhr, C., Maxwell, M., Meise, U., Mirjanic, M., Oskarsson, H., Sola, V. P., Pull, C., Pycha, R., Ricka, R., Tuulari, J., Värnik, A., & Pfeiffer-Gerschel T. (2008). The 'European Alliance Against Depression (EAAD)': A multifaceted, community-based action programme against depression and suicidality. *World Journal of Biological Psychiatry, 9*, 51–58.

Huey, S. J., Henggeler, S. W., Rowland, M. D., Halliday-Boykins, C. A., Cunningham, P. B., Pickrel, S. G., & Edwards, J. (2004). Multisystemic therapy effects on attempted suicide by youths presenting psychiatric emergencies. *Journal of the American Academy of Child and Adolescent Psychiatry, 43*, 183–190.

James, A., Lai, F. H., & Dahl, C. (2004). Attention deficit hyperactivity disorder and suicide: A review of possible associations. *Acta Psychiatrica Scandinavica, 110*, 408–415.

Katz, L. Y., Cox, B. J., Gunasekara, S., & Miller, A. L. (2004). Feasibility of dialectical behavior therapy for suicidal adolescent inpatients. *Journal of the American Academy of Child and Adolescent Psychiatry, 43*, 276–282.

Katz, L. Y., Kozyrskyj, A. L., Prior, H. J., Enns, M. W., Cox, B. J., & Sareen J. (2008). Effect of regulatory warnings on antidepressant prescription rates, use of health services and outcomes among children, adolescents and young adults. *Canadian Medical Association Journal, 178*, 1005–1011.

King, C. A., Kramer, A., Preuss, L., Kerr, D. C., Weisse, L., & Venkataraman S. (2006). Youth-nominated support team for suicidal adolescents (Version 1): A randomized controlled trial. *Journal of Consulting and Clinical Psychology, 74*, 199–206.

King, K. A. & Smith, J. (2000). Project SOAR: A training program to increase school counselors' knowledge and confidence regarding suicide prevention and intervention. *Journal of School Health, 70*, 402–407.

Klomek, A. B., Sourander, A., Niemelä, S., Kumpulainen, K., Piha, J., Tamminen, T., Almqvist, F., & Gould, M. S. (2009). Childhood bullying behaviors as a risk for suicide attempts and completed suicides: A population-based birth cohort study. *Journal of the American Academy of Child and Adolescent Psychiatry, 48*, 254–261.

Kloos, A. L., Collins, R., Weller, R. A., & Weller, E. B. (2007). Suicide in pre-adolescents: Who is at risk? *Current Psychiatry Reports, 9*, 89–93.

Li, X. Y., Phillips, M. R., Zhang, Y. P., Xu, D., & Yang, G. H. (2008). Risk factors for suicide in China's youth: A case-control study. *Psychological Medicine, 38*, 397–406.

Libby, A. M., Orton, H. D., & Valuck, R. J. (2009). Persisting decline in depression treatment after FDA warnings. *Archives of General Psychiatry, 66*, 633–639.

Linehan, M. M., Armstrong, H. E., Suarez, A., Allmon, D., & Heard, H. L. (1991). Cognitive-behavioral treatment of chronically parasuicidal borderline patients. *Archives of General Psychiatry, 48,* 1060–1064.

Mann, J. J. & Currier, D. (2007). A review of prospective studies of biologic predictors of suicidal behavior in mood disorders. *Archives of Suicide Research, 11,* 3–16.

March, J. S., Silva, S., Petrycki, S., Curry, J., Wells, K., Fairbank, J., Burns, B., Domino, M., McNulty, S., Vitiello, B., & Severe J. (2007). The Treatment for Adolescents with Depression Study (TADS): Long-term effectiveness and safety outcomes. *Archives of General Psychiatry, 64,* 1132–1143.

Masters, K. J. (2008). Anti-suicidal and self-harm properties of lithium carbonate. *CNS Spectrums, 13,* 109–110.

Melhem, N. M., Brent, D. A., Ziegler, M., Iyengar, S., Kolko, D., Oquendo, M., Birmaher, B., Burke, A., Zelazny, J., Stanley, B., & Mann, J. J. (2007). Familial pathways to early-onset suicidal behavior: Familial and individual antecedents of suicidal behavior. *American Journal of Psychiatry, 164,* 1364–1370.

Miller, J. W., Naimi, T. S., & Brewer, R. D. (2007). Binge drinking and associated health risk behaviors among high school students. *Pediatrics, 119,* 76–85.

Miranda, R., Scott, M., Hicks, R., Wilcox, H. C., Harris Munfakh, J. L., & Shaffer, D. (2008). Suicide attempt characteristics, diagnoses, and future attempts: Comparing multiple attempters to single attempters and ideators. *Journal of the American Academy of Child and Adolescent Psychiatry, 47,* 32–40.

Molnar, B. E., Buka, S. L., & Kessler, R. C. (2001). Child sexual abuse and subsequent psychopathology: Results from the National Comorbidity Survey. *American Journal of Public Health, 91,* 753–760.

Niederkrotenthaler, T. & Sonneck, G. (2007). Assessing the impact of media guidelines for reporting on suicides in Austria: Interrupted time series analysis. *Australian and New Zealand Journal of Psychiatry, 41,* 419–428.

Nock, M. K., Joiner, T. E., Gordon, K. H., Lloyd-Richardson, E., & Prinstein, M. J. (2006). Non-suicidal self-injury among adolescents: Diagnostic correlates and relation to suicide attempts. *Psychiatry Research, 144,* 65–72.

Oldershaw, A., Grima, E., & Jollant, F. (2008). Decision making and problem solving in adolescents who deliberately self-harm. *Psychological Medicine, 23,* 1–10.

O'Leary, C. C., Frank, D. A., Grant-Knight, W., Beeghly, M., Augustyn, M., Rose-Jacobs, R., Cabral, H. J., & Gannon K. (2006). Suicidal ideation among urban nine and ten year olds. *Journal of Developmental and Behavioral Pediatrics, 27,* 33–39.

Olfson, M., Shaffer, D., Marcus, S. C., & Greenberg, T. (2003). Relationship between antidepressant medication treatment and suicide in adolescents. *Archives of General Psychiatry, 60,* 978–982.

Orbach, I. & Bar-Joseph, H. (1993). The impact of a suicide prevention program for adolescents on suicidal tendencies, hopelessness, ego identity, and coping. *Suicide and Life-Threatening Behavior, 23,* 120–129.

Pirkis, J., Dare, A., Blood, R.W., Rankin, B., Williamson, M., Burgess, P., & Jolley, D. (2009). Changes in media reporting of suicide in Australia between 2000/01 and 2006/07. *Crisis, 30,* 25–33.

Pompili, M., Mancinelli, I., Girardi, P., Ruberto, A., & Tatarelli, R. (2004). Suicide in anorexia nervosa: A meta-analysis. *International Journal of Eating Disorders, 36,* 99–103.

Posner, K., Melvin, G. A., Stanley, B., Oquendo, M. A., & Gould, M. (2007). Factors in the assessment of suicidality in youth. *CNS Spectrums, 12,* 156–162.

Posner, K., Oquendo, M. A., Gould, M., Stanley, B., & Davies, M. (2007). Columbia Classification Algorithm of Suicide Assessment (C-CASA): Classification of suicidal events in the FDA's pediatric suicidal risk analysis of antidepressants. *American Journal of Psychiatry, 164*, 1035–1043.

Rathus, J. H. & Miller, A. L. (2002). Dialectical behavior therapy adapted for suicidal adolescents. *Suicide and Life-Threatening Behavior, 32*, 146–157.

Recupero, P. R., Harms, S. E., & Noble, J. M. (2008). Googling suicide: Surfing for suicide information on the internet. *Journal of Clinical Psychiatry, 69*, 878–888.

Roche, A. M., Giner, L., & Zalsman, G. (2005). Suicide in early childhood: A brief review. *International Journal of Adolescent Medicine and Health, 17*, 221–224.

Rodgers, P. L., Sudak, H. S., Silverman, M. M., & Litts, D. A. (2007). Evidence-Based Practices Project for suicide prevention. *Suicide and Life-Threatening Behavior, 37*, 154–164.

Rohde, P., Silva, S. G., Tonev, S. T., Kennard, B. D., Vitiello, B., Kratochvil, C. J., Reinecke, M. A., Curry, J. F., Simons, A. D., & March, J. S. (2008). Achievement and maintenance of sustained response during the Treatment for Adolescents with Depression Study continuation and maintenance therapy. *Archives of General Psychiatry, 65*, 447–455.

Rotheram-Borus, M. J., Piacentini, J., van Rossem, R., Graae, F., Cantwell, C., Castro-Blanco, D., Miller, S., & Feldman, J. (1996). Enhancing treatment adherence with a specialized emergency room program for adolescent suicide attempters. *Journal of the American Academy of Child and Adolescent Psychiatry, 35*, 654–663.

Schaffer, M., Jeglic, E. L., & Stanley, B. (2008). The relationship between suicidal behavior, ideation, and binge drinking among college students. *Archives of Suicide Research, 12*, 124–132.

Schilling, E. A., Aseltine, R. H., Glanovsky, J. L., James, A., & Jacobs, D. (2009). Adolescent alcohol use, suicidal ideation, and suicide attempts. *Journal of Adolescent Health, 44*, 335–341.

Schwartz-Stav, O., Apter, A., & Zalsman, G. (2006). Depression, suicidal behaviour and insight in adolescents with schizophrenia. *European Child and Adolescent Psychiatry, 15*, 352–359.

Scott, M. A., Wilcox, H. C., Schonfeld, I. S., Davies, M., Hicks, R. C., Turner, J. B., & Shaffer, D. (2009). School-based screening to identify at-risk students not already known to school professionals: The Columbia suicide screen. *American Journal of Public Health, 99*, 334–339.

Sourander, A., Klomek, A. B., Niemelä, S., Haavisto, A., Gyllenberg, D., Helenius, H., Sillanmäki, L., Ristkari, T., Kumpulainen, K., Tamminen, T., Moilanen, I., Piha, J., Almqvist, F., & Gould, M. S. (2009). Childhood predictors of completed and severe suicide attempts: findings from the Finnish 1981 Birth Cohort Study. *Archives of General Psychiatry, 66*, 398–406.

Speckens, A. & Hawton, K. (2005). Social problem solving in adolescents with suicidal behavior: A systematic review. *Suicide and Life-Threat Behavior, 35*, 365–387.

Sudak, H. S. & Sudak, D. M. (2005). The media and suicide. *Academic Psychiatry, 29*, 495–459.

Vitiello, B., Brent, D., Greenhill, L. L., Emslie, G., Wells, K., Walkup, J. T., Stanley, B., Bukstein, O., Kennard, B. D., Compton, S., Coffey, B., Cwik, M. F., Posner, K., Wagner, A., March, J. S., Riddle, M., Goldstein, T., Curry, J., Capasso, L., Mayes, T., Shen, S., Gugga, S. S., Turner, B. J., Barnett, S., & Zelazny, J. (2009). Depressive symptoms and clinical status during the treatment of adolescent suicide attempters study. *Journal of the American Academy of Child and Adolescent Psychiatry, 48*, 997–1004.

Wasserman, D. & Durkee, T. (2009). Strategies in suicide prevention. In D. Wasserman and C. Wasserman (Eds.), *The Oxford Textbook of Suicidology and Suicide Prevention – A global perspective* (pp. 381–386). New York: Oxford University Press.

Wheeler, B. W., Gunnell, D., Metcalfe, C., Stephens, P., & Martin, R. M. (2008). The population impact on incidence of suicide and non-fatal self harm of regulatory action against the use of selective serotonin reuptake inhibitors in under 18s in the United Kingdom: Ecological study. *British Medical Journal, 336*, 542–545.

Wood, A., Harrington, R., & Moore, A. (1996). Controlled trial of a brief cognitive-behavioural intervention in adolescent patients with depressive disorders. *Journal of Child Psychology and Psychiatry, 37,* 737–746.

Wyman, P. A., Brown, C., & Hendricks, I. (2008). Randomized trial of a gatekeeper program for suicide prevention: 1-year impact on secondary school staff. *Journal of Consulting and Clinical Psychology, 76,* 104–115.

CHAPTER EIGHTEEN

Prevention and Treatment of Suicidality in Old Age

Diego De Leo and Urška Arnautovska

Abstract

In spite of frequently under-reported suicide data, suicide rates among the elderly remain globally the highest. In this particular age group, there are certain peculiarities, for example, age-specific risk and protective factors as well as gender differences, which need to be considered in the prevention and treatment of suicidality. This chapter provides an overview of existing practices, by examining the specific impact of most common conditions that may be present in late life, such as depression, physical illness, retirement, relocation to a nursing home, etc. Several different types of prevention approaches have been proposed for the elderly; however, only few of the derived programmes have been evaluated in the context of controlled studies. Furthermore, their outcomes may not be universally generalized. This calls for more evidence-based research and for investigations across different cultures, in order to establish a convincing level of efficacy of preventative interventions for elderly persons at risk for suicide.

Introduction

Old age is characterized by various physical, psychological, social, and behavioural changes, which have both negative and positive consequences. From a psychological perspective, as explained by Erikson in his psychosocial theory of human development (1982), older adults usually either resolve this last stage of their life by acquiring a feeling of integrity or

International Handbook of Suicide Prevention: Research, Policy and Practice, First Edition.
Edited by Rory C. O'Connor, Stephen Platt, Jacki Gordon.
© 2011 John Wiley & Sons, Ltd. Published 2011 by John Wiley & Sons, Ltd.

fail to resolve it, resulting in a sense of despair. If, when looking back, they cannot find enough positive achievements, they are likely to feel that their life has become meaningless and not worth living. This chapter focuses on older adults whose psychological state makes them particularly vulnerable to suicidal behaviour.

Peculiarities of Suicidal Behaviour in Late Life

Older adults differ from other age groups in a variety of biological, psychological, and social characteristics. Suicidal behaviour (here and subsequently used to include self-harm, attempted suicide, and suicide) among elderly persons also presents with certain peculiarities. For example, suicide in old age is often considered to be the result of a rational decision. This is especially the case in the suicide of a dependent and frail male closely following the death of a spouse. Suicide can also be seen as a 'legitimate exit' from life when loss of dignity, change in social role, and increased emotional isolation are experienced. In contrast, there is substantial evidence that suicidal behaviour among the elderly is particularly influenced by psychiatric disorder, especially if characterized by the presence of mood alterations (Conwell, Lyness, Duberstein, Cox, Seidlitz, et al., 2000; Fiske, Wetherell, & Gatz, 2009). Contrary to 'ageistic' perspectives, depression is not a normal feature of old age (Rabheru, 2004), nor is a natural response to deterioration of physical conditions or social or financial difficulties, which are common in the last phase of life. Confusing depression with 'obvious sadness' may dangerously lower the level of vigilance shown to patients and amplify the widespread problem of under-recognizing and under-treating depression in older adults (De Leo & Diekstra, 1990). Prevention, identification, and treatment of depression in old age may not only counteract suicidal ideation, but may also reduce general mortality risk (Capurso, Capurso, Solfrizzi, Colacicco, D'Introno, et al., 2007).

Another widely observed characteristic of elderly suicides is the increase in the male: female ratio. This becomes particularly evident at very advanced old age. Worldwide, the male:female suicide ratio for all ages is around 3:1 (De Leo, Krysinka, Bertolote, Fleischmann, & Wasserman, 2009a). However, among those aged 80+ years, the rate ratio can reach as high as 12:1, as reported in Italy (De Leo, 1999), or 9:1 in Australia (De Leo & Heller, 2004). In 2006, in the United States, the suicide rate in the 65–84 years age group was 28.5 per 100,000 for men, but only 3.9 per 100,000 for women. While the suicide rate of women aged 85+ years remained stable in comparison with the 65–84 years age group, the male rate increased to over 40 per 100,000 (McIntosh, 2009).

Epidemiological Trends

Suicide rates among the elderly, although declining in most parts of the world over the last three decades, are still globally the highest; death by suicide in old age is on average three times more common than among people aged less than 25 years of age (De Leo *et al.*,

2009a). As the number of elderly people continues to increase, the absolute number of elderly suicides is predicted to rise even further.

Elderly suicide rates are greatly affected by cultural and social changes within nations. The decrease in elderly suicide rates has been particularly remarkable in Anglo-Saxon countries (such as New Zealand, Australia, Canada, and the United States), possibly related to their investment in old-age socio-economic policies, such as comprehensive retirement cover and improved social security (De Leo & Spathonis, 2003). Conversely, elderly suicide rates in Latin countries (such as Spain, Italy, France, and some South American nations) appear to have been negatively affected by a number of structural changes in society, particularly in terms of the traditional family configuration (De Leo, 1999). There has been a move away from the patriarchal model (often with three generations living under the same roof), once perceived to provide feelings of safety and belonging, as well as economic and emotional security (De Leo & Scocco, 2000). A study in 54 countries over a 10-year period showed that suicide rates among 65–74 and 75+ year olds (both sexes) either declined (in several European countries) or remained unchanged (in several Central and South American countries, Eastern European countries, and nations previously part of the former Soviet Union) (Shah, Bhat, MacKenzie, & Koen, 2008).

The incidence of suicide and non-fatal suicidal behaviour exhibits opposite tendencies with respect to age. Suicide rates tend to peak in advanced old age (75+ years), while the rates for suicide attempts decline proportionately with increasing age (De Leo & Scocco, 2000). The WHO/EURO Multicentre Study on Suicidal Behaviour, including data from 13 European countries between 1989 and 1993, found that among 22,665 episodes of 'parasuicide' (hospital-treated non-fatal suicidal behaviour), only 9% were made by the elderly (65+) compared with 50% of the total number of episodes made by patients in the 15–34 year age group (De Leo et al., 2001). The ratio between non-fatal and fatal suicidal behaviours in the young is estimated to be approximately 200:1, while in older adults the ratio may range between 2:1 (De Leo et al., 2001) and 4:1 (McIntosh, Santos, Hubbard, & Overholser, 1994). Similar ratios were noted by Hawton and Harriss (2008) in their study of deliberate self-harm episodes across the life-cycle. While non-fatal behaviour is predominantly found in women of younger age groups, incidence is similar in both genders as age increases (Shah et al., 2008). Gender differences in suicide rates are often explained by the use of more violent methods (such as firearms or hanging) adopted by elderly men in comparison with elderly women, who predominantly use self-poisoning (Chan, Draper, & Banarjee, 2007; Conwell & Thomson, 2008).

The 'true' incidence of elderly suicide might not be fully captured by official statistics. Elderly suicide mortality data are frequently under-reported (see Box 18.1). Suicide deaths from falling or drowning may be incorrectly identified as 'accidents'. Suicide may also not be recognized in cases of passive suicidal behaviours, such as self-starvation or refusal to take life-sustaining medication (De Leo & Diekstra, 1990; Osgood & Eisenhandler, 1995). Further, 'ageistic' social attitudes related to elderly suicide, as well as a 'shared therapeutic nihilism' (passive attitudes towards clinical interventions) (Draper, 1995), might affect the objective reporting of elderly deaths as suicide. Apart from known cases of euthanasia or assisted suicide, the widespread liberalism currently seen in many Western hospital environments in the administration of opioids to hasten death (particularly where somatic pain is involved) could also affect the official count of suicide mortality, by hiding a certain number of assisted suicides.

> **Box 18.1   Ubiquitous causes of under-reporting of suicide mortality data in old age**
>
> - Unreported Death;
> - Remoteness of Reportable Death;
> - Missing Person;
> - Life-Sustaining Medication Not Assumed;
> - Self-Starvation;
> - Euthanasia/Assisted Suicide;
> - Particular Suicide Methods (e.g. MV Accidents, Opiate Overdose);
> - Dubious Circumstances of the Act (e.g. Falls, Drowning);
> - Social Conditions (Insurance Policy);
> - Social Position of Deceased;
> - Political Pressures;
> - Changes in Coding (e.g. from ICD-9 to ICD-10);
> - Lack of Standardized Certification Procedures.

Risk Factors for Suicide among the Elderly

There are strong justifications as to why elderly suicide prevention research has tended to focus on depression. Age-related physical processes (such as inflammatory and degenerative diseases, which compromise the integrity of prefrontal striatal pathways and amygdale) and environmental factors (such as impoverishment, isolation, relocation, intense care-giving, and bereavement) may increase susceptibility to depression in older adults (Capurso *et al.*, 2007). In addition, there are several other psychiatric, physical and psychosocial risk factors for suicidal behaviour in older people.

Psychiatric disorders

At least one major psychiatric diagnosis is found in 71%–95% of elderly suicide deaths, with an affective disorder being present in 54%–87% of these cases (Conwell & Thomson, 2008; Shah & De, 1998). Consequently, suicide among the elderly is most likely to happen in the context of a depressive episode. However, it should be noted that a depressive disorder in the general elderly population occurs in 8%–16% of cases (Blazer, 2003). Depression, presenting as either chronic depressive symptoms or a first episode in late life, has been identified as the most powerful independent risk factor for suicide in old age (Reynolds & Kupfer, 1999). In this context, depression often coexists with a medical, age-related condition, such as cardiovascular disease, stroke, or chronic pain (Montano, 1999). This sometimes makes the identification of depression difficult or very late, and its treatment considered as irrelevant or secondary to that of the somatic condition.

Furthermore, depression in the elderly is often accompanied by symptoms of anxiety or an anxiety disorder itself. Symptoms of severe anxiety and agitation, when comorbid with mood and other psychiatric disorders, have been identified as indicative of heightened suicide risk (De Leo, 1997; Diefenbach, Woolley, & Goethe, 2009; Fawcett, 2009; Hawgood & De Leo, 2008). Moreover, there is a growing body of literature underlining the independent role of anxiety on suicidality more generally (Diefenbach *et al.*, 2009; Fawcett, 2009); therefore, it is likely that its role in the aetiology of older adult suicide will be confirmed before long.

The second most common psychiatric condition associated with both suicide and attempted suicide is one of the substance use disorders, particularly alcohol abuse and/ or dependence (Blow, Brockman, & Lawton, 2004). Alcohol abuse usually heightens suicide risk through its interaction with other factors that are especially prevalent among the elderly, such as depressive symptoms, medical illness, negatively perceived health status, and poor control over the social environment. Although alcohol abuse is less frequently found in suicide deaths among the elderly than among younger adults (Krysinska, Heller, & De Leo, 2006), it remains an important risk factor for suicide in late life for both genders. This pattern of findings has been observed mostly in Slavic (Russia, Ukraine, and Byelorussia) and Baltic (Estonia, Latvia, Lithuania) republics of the former Soviet Union (Kolves, Varnik, Tooding, & Wasserman, 2006), being especially pronounced when associated with depressive disorders (De Leo, Draper, & Krysinka, 2009b).

In contrast to the younger population, schizophrenia and psychotic disorders among the elderly account for a lower proportion of suicides (up to 12%) (Harwood & Jacoby, 2000).

While only a few studies have thus far paid attention to the role of certain personality traits in old-age suicide, it has been estimated that personality disorders are less common in the suicidal elderly than in youth (Neulinger & De Leo, 2001). However, the intensity and rapidity of stressors and losses can seriously undermine the resources of individuals with personality disorders. Consequently, the lack of prompt identification and reaction may negatively influence the life of the individual and those close to them. In general, anancastic (obsessive compulsive) or anxious personality traits and cognitive rigidity (particularly lower openness to experiences) appear to be particularly common among elderly suicides (Duberstein, 1995; Harwood, Hawton, Hope, & Jacoby, 2001).

The diagnosis of dementia, which is especially frequent among elderly persons, does not increase the risk of suicide (Schneider, Maurer, & Frolich, 2001). When suicide, however, does occur in subjects diagnosed with dementia, putative risk factors include depression, hopelessness, mild cognitive impairment, preserved insight, younger age, and failure to respond to anti-dementia drugs (Haw, Harwood, & Hawton, 2009).

Physical illness

The role of physical illness in older adults' suicidal behaviour is equivocal. Somatic conditions and functional impairments significantly increase suicide risk across the whole life-span (Conwell, Dubenstein, & Caine, 2002). However, some case-control studies of people aged 55 years and older have not been able to find any differences in severity of illnesses, hospital admissions, and general practitioner visits between suicidal cases and controls (Beautrais, 2002). Conversely, studies comparing suicide decedents over the age of 65 years with living controls found that serious physical illnesses, especially visual impairment, neurological disease, and malignancies, were independently associated with suicide among males (Waern, Rubenowitz, Runeson, Skoog, Wilhelmson, & Allebeck, 2002). In a population-based study, Kaplan, McFarland, Huguet, and Newsom (2007) reached similar conclusions on physical impairments and illnesses.

A case-control study by Quan, Arboleda-Florez, Fick, Stuart, and Love (2002) compared 822 cases of completed suicide with 944 controls who died in a motor vehicle accident aged 55 years or older. They found a small, but statistically significant increase in the rates of several physical conditions (i.e., cancer, chronic lung disease, and non-malignant prostatic disease) in the suicide group. Using a retrospective case-control design, Conwell, Duberstein, Hirsch, Conner, Eberly, and colleagues (2009) compared 86 people over the age of 50 years who died by suicide with an equal number of matched living controls. The investigation found that suicide decedents had more DSM-IV Axis I diagnoses (including current mood and anxiety disorders), worse physical health status, and greater impairment in functional capacities than the controls. Suicide cases were also more likely to have required psychiatric treatment, and medical or surgical hospitalization in the last year, and needed a nurse visitation or home health aide services. In a multivariate model, the presence of any active Axis I disorder and any impairment to the instrumental activities of daily living (e.g., food preparation, shopping, ability to use telephone, etc.) made independent contributions to suicide risk.

Comorbidity of physical impairments with psychiatric disorders, in particular, seems to increase suicide risk in elderly individuals (Kaplan *et al.*, 2007). Two large, independent cohort studies showed that the combination of depression, poor physical health, and loneliness elevated suicide risk among older people (Ross, Bernstein, Trent, Henderson, & Paganini-Hill, 1990; Turvey, Conwell, Jones, Phillips, Simonsick, *et al.*, 2002). This demonstrates the importance of the recognition and treatment of depression in the elderly (Grek, 2007; Montano, 1999; Unützer, Tang, Oishi, Katon, Williams, *et al.*, 2006).

Psychosocial stressors

Social factors and age-related life events are consistently reported to increase suicide risk in old age. Men, particularly when single, widowed, or divorced, are frequently reported to be at increased risk of suicide (De Leo & Meneghel, 2001; Harwood *et al.*, 2000). Lack of supportive social networks and/or religious participation (Turvey *et al.*, 2002), family discord, financial troubles, low level of education, and feelings of loneliness (Rubenowitz, Waern, Wilhelmson, & Allebeck, 2001) can all increase the risk of suicide.

Loneliness can result from the loss of an important intimate relationship, or a social role, that previously maintained a person's self-esteem and feelings of worthiness. In general terms, bereavement represents a significant stressful event, especially if it involves the loss of a child or close relative (McIntosh, Santos, Hubbard, & Overholser, 1994). Consequently, widow(er)hood may increase the risk of suicide and suicide attempt in the elderly (De Leo *et al.*, 2001), particularly in males (Canetto, 1995). Loneliness is also reflected in the solitary nature of suicides among the elderly, which are most often carried out in a home environment (Harwood & Jacoby, 2000).

Retirement is another age-related event with potentially negative effects on an older person's mental health. The risk of suicide is particularly elevated in the first two to three years after termination of employment (De Leo & Diekstra, 1990). Of special relevance in this context are changes in income, social status, social interactions, and family roles. These changes may result in feelings of uselessness and loss of self-esteem and life purpose (De Leo *et al.*, 2009b).

Another age-related change considered to be a precipitating factor for suicide among the elderly is recent placement in a nursing home or the anticipation of this event (Loebel, Loebel, Dager, Centerwall, & Reay, 1991). While suicide is reported to be a relatively rare event in nursing homes (De Leo & Spathonis, 2004), non-fatal suicidal behaviours are common among residents and reported to be related to dementia processes (Draper, Brodaty, Low, Richards, Paton, *et al.*, 2002). In addition, suicide in nursing homes may be a response to the powerlessness and marginalization experienced by residents, particularly elderly women (Canetto, 1995).

Protective Factors

Protective factors include high levels of education and socio-economic status, engagement in valued activities, and religious or spiritual involvement (Fiske *et al.*, 2009). The importance of shared religious practices and beliefs, such as those associated with Catholicism, as protective factors against suicide have been recognized for over a century (Durkheim 1951 [1897]). Indeed, church attendance and a degree of commitment and involvement in religion may have a strong influence against suicidal behaviours (De Leo, 2002). Further, the availability of social support, expressed by either the number of friends and relatives acting as confidants, or being part of a community (as opposed to living alone), has also been recognized as an important protective factor in both genders (Conwell & Thomson, 2008). Additionally, marriage appears to be a protective factor, particularly for elderly males (Harwood *et al.*, 2000).

Treatment of Suicidality among the Elderly

When planning and implementing effective interventions targeting elderly people, awareness of the peculiarities of their suicidal behaviour is crucial. For example, elderly suicidal behaviour is usually characterized by high lethality and strong intent to die (McIntosh, 1994). Furthermore, interventions need to balance risk and protective factors, bearing in mind that these will differ in relevance depending on the cultural and social context (De Leo, 1999). For example, a risk factor such as depression might have a stronger association with suicidality in the United States than in countries such as China, Lebanon, or Puerto Rico (Weismann, Bland, Canino, Greenwald, Hwu, *et al.*, 1999). Additionally, marriage may be a protective factor in Australia, where the unmarried elderly of both sexes have higher suicide rates in comparison with married people; however, married elderly women in Hong Kong have higher suicide rates than the widowed or divorced women of the same age (Yip, 1998).

Suicidal risk is often not recognized in older patients (De Leo *et al.*, 2009a). In fact, the majority of older adults who take their lives have consulted their primary care physician shortly before their death. A review article by Montano (1999) indicates the following percentages: 75% within one month of completing suicide; 40% within one week; and 20% within 24 hours (Montano, 1999). A substantial level of contact with primary care services is consistently reported in Western countries, where 40%–80% of elderly persons presented in the 30 days prior to the suicide (Alexopoulos, Bruce, Hull, Sirey, & Kakuma, 1999; Cattell, 2000; Harwood *et al.*, 2000). In Hong-Kong, Chiu, Yip, Chi, Chan, Tsoh, and colleagues (2004) found that those who completed suicide had a significantly higher rate of medical consultation within one month of suicide than the control group (77% versus 39%, respectively). In addition, in the United States, primary care physicians are less willing to treat older suicidal subjects than younger patients, and they are more likely to believe that suicidal ideation in older patients is rational and normal (Uncapher & Arean, 2000).

Detection of suicidal ideas and assessment of suicide risk

Identifying suicidal ideas and tendencies is the first and central step in the treatment of an older adult at risk of suicide. Compared with younger adults, this essential task may present with particular challenges for health professionals (De Leo *et al.*, 2009a). In fact, communication of suicidal thoughts tends to be less frequent among men and elderly suicide victims than among women and younger victims (Conwell, Dubenstein, Cox, Herrman, Forbes, *et al.*, 1998).

Furthermore, older adults tend to minimize their psychological problems and consider them to be related to physical illness. For example, a study of 450 randomly selected residents in a rural area of Japan, aged between 40 and 75 years, showed that 10% considered it natural to have suicidal ideation (Sakamoto, Tanaka, Neichi, & Ono, 2006). Consequently, family and friends may be the first to note that an elderly person is at risk of suicide (Dombrovski & Szanto, 2005). Indeed, Waern, Beskow, Runeson, & Skoog (1999), comparing information gained from psychological autopsies and medical records, found that relatives detected suicidal feelings in 73% of cases, particularly in elderly female suicides, while doctors detected suicidal feelings in only 39% of cases.

An assessment of suicide risk in elderly people requires recognition of age-specific clinical characteristics, such as depression, somatic comorbidities, poor social support, and a history of suicide attempts (Alexopoulos *et al.*, 1999). Other clinical correlates of suicidal behaviour (particularly alcoholism) must also be recognized in elderly people (Murphy, 2002). In addition, it is critical to pay attention and predict possible suicide risk in people who show only indirect self-destructive behaviours (e.g., refusal of medication, eating, drinking, etc.). These behaviours may be particularly frequent in recently institutionalized elderly people (Draper *et al.*, 2002), and may also appear in people with 'low openness to experiences' personality traits, who have a limited capacity to adapt to environmental changes and the deteriorations imposed by the ageing process (De Leo *et al.*, 2009a).

Several psychosocial events are typically connected to the ageing process (Conwell & Thomson, 2008), including bereavement, financial stressors, retirement, family discord, loss of an intimate relationship, and adaptation and acceptance of physical (and chronic) illnesses. Any of these conditions can leave an elderly person more vulnerable to suicide, and their presence should alert family members and caregivers to the possible onset of suicidal ideation. A study using the psychological autopsy method showed that those older adults who completed suicide shortly after the death of a spouse had a higher rate of psychiatric treatment, experienced more early loss/separation, and were more likely to have seen a physician after the spouse's death (Duberstein, Conwell, & Cox, 1998). These findings clearly demonstrate the need for a more rigorous monitoring of suicide risk in the widowed population, particularly in those with previous psychiatric or developmental vulnerabilities.

However, in addition to considering acute stressors, assessment of suicidal risk in the elderly should not neglect the impact of chronic stressors, such as pain, loneliness, complicated grief, and severe disability. These might trigger suicidal tendencies, particularly in the absence of social support (De Leo *et al.*, 2009b).

As noted earlier, older adults may present a greater determination to die than their younger counterparts. Consequently, the investigation of previous suicidality acquires special importance, particularly when old age patients show symptoms of depression. In fact, previous suicide attempts in the elderly strongly indicate a risk of repeated suicide attempts and completed suicide (Hawton & Harris, 2006), as confirmed by the results of the WHO/EURO Multicentre Study on Suicidal Behaviour. Over a 12-month period following an index suicide attempt, 11% of subjects aged 65 years and more repeated their non-fatal behaviour, but 13% died by suicide (De Leo *et al.*, 2001).

Gender-sensitive treatment

Several recent studies (Vörös, Osvath, & Fekete, 2004; Liu, Chen, Cheung, & Yip, 2009) have illustrated the importance of taking gender differences into account when planning and implementing suicide prevention strategies targeted at older adults.

First, suicide rates throughout the life course vary with regard to gender. In most countries, males have higher rates of completed suicide (Bertolote & Fleischmann, 2009; McKeown, Cuff, & Schultz, 2006), while females have higher rates of non-fatal suicidal behaviour (Hawton & Harris, 2008).

Second, suicide prevention strategies with a focus on access to means need to consider the notable differences in the choice of suicide method between males and females (Chan *et al.*, 2007). Different methods of suicide necessitate different methods of prevention. In fact, men tend to be responsive to more systematic approaches, for example, restricting access to the means of suicide, such as restricting access to firearms or detoxification of domestic gas (Gunnell, Middleton, & Frankel, 2000; Ludwig & Cook, 2000; Oyama, Watanabe, Ono, Sakashita, Takenoshita, *et al.*, 2005). A decrease in female suicide rates is more often associated with community-based support programmes, such as telephone-based systems or group activities (De Leo, Carollo, & Dello Buono, 1995, 2002; Oyama *et al.*, 2005). A remarkable exception was the significant decrease in female rates which followed the control of barbiturate sales in Australia (De Leo, 2006; Oliver & Hetzel, 1972).

Finally, there are well-established gender differences in various psychiatric disorders (Sinha & Rounsaville, 2002). Depression is approximately twice as common in women as in men (Accortt, Freeman & Allen, 2008; Cohen, 2003). Given the prominent role of depression in suicidal behaviour, this should theoretically render women more exposed to suicide risk than men. However, despite this epidemiological difference, females appear to cope better with life stressors than their male counterparts and possess particularly resilient attitudes even at a very advanced age (Canetto, 1995). Compared with elderly women, elderly men, especially those older than 80 years, display more difficulties adapting to stressful life changes and losses, such as the death of a spouse (Apter, Krispin, & Bursztein, 2009). Disparities in resilience could be explained by different coping strategies employed by men and women during times of stress (Canetto, 1995). Men are less likely than women to seek treatment for psychological problems, such as depression, substance abuse, physical disabilities, and stressful life events (Cochran & Rabinowitz, 2003; Galdas, Cheater, & Marshall, 2005). In addition, male suicidal patients are less likely to comply with therapy than female subjects (Vörös *et al.*, 2004). Gender-specific differences are also well acknowledged in the clinical characteristics and treatment responses of depression (Sinha & Rounsaville, 2002; Cochran & Rabinowitz, 2003; Gatz & Fiske, 2003). Differences in coping mechanisms might also be explained in the context of masculine gender socialization. In patriarchal societies, masculinity has favoured suppression of emotions in men, discouraging them from showing sadness, grief, or tears, or seeking interpersonal support in times of distress (Cochran & Rabinowitz, 2003).

Treatment of depression

Compared with depressed younger adults, depressed older adults are less likely to show affective symptoms and more likely to display cognitive changes, somatic symptoms, and loss of interest (Fiske *et al.*, 2009). Major depressive disorder is frequently under-diagnosed and under-treated in older patients. Age-related comorbid conditions, with associated neurobiological changes, can have a significant impact on depression, and vice versa (Rabheru, 2004). Furthermore, the multiple medications prescribed to treat other illnesses may complicate the clinical presentation of affective symptoms in the elderly (Conwell & Thomson, 2008).

Despite the complex phenomenology of depression in old age, research suggests that geriatric patients respond readily to appropriate treatment (Khouzam, 2009; Reynolds & Kupfer, 1999). However, when given the choice, older adults tend to indicate an equal, if not greater, preference for psychological rather than pharmacological treatment and may even prefer a combination treatment (Scogin, Welsch, Hanson, Stump, & Coates, 2005). A meta-analysis on the effects of 122 psychosocial and psychotherapeutic interventions in late-life concluded that psychotherapeutic interventions improved self-rated depression and other measures of psychological well-being by about 0.5 STD and clinician-rated depression by more than 1 STD (Pinquart & Soerensen, 2001). Psychotherapy can not only reduce psychopathology but also physical complaints, pain, and disability (Klausner & Alexopoulos, 1999). It can also improve compliance with medical regimens and has been found to be effective in the treatment of depression related to bereavement and caregiver burden (Klausner & Alexopoulos, 1999). Evidence-based psychological treatments for geriatric depression identified as beneficial include behavioural therapy, cognitive-behavioural therapy (CBT), cognitive bibliotherapy, problem-solving therapy, brief psychodynamic therapy and life review/reminiscence therapy (Scogin *et al.*, 2005). The last example is of special interest, since it is one of the few treatments specifically designed for older adults. Other potentially useful preventative interventions comprise education for individuals with chronic illness, behavioural activation, cognitive restructuring, problem-solving skills training, group support, interpersonal counselling, and psychodynamic therapy (Scogin *et al.*, 2005).

Suicidal risk factors can complicate diagnosis and treatment planning of geriatric depression (Reynolds & Kupfer, 1999). In fact, suicidal older adults with depression have lower response rates to treatment and subsequently require increased and continuing therapeutic attention to address residual symptoms in follow-up assessments (Szanto, Mulsant, Houck, Miller, Mazadumer, *et al.*, 2003). For example, a trial in which patients with recurrent major depression received combined pharmacotherapy (nortriptyline) and interpersonal psychotherapy showed that the group of 30 elderly suicide ideators had higher relapse rates during continuation treatment than the group of 150 non-ideators (26% versus 13%, respectively) (Szanto *et al.*, 2001).

In the light of the evidence that the systematic treatment of depression in the elderly also reduces suicidal ideation (Bruce, Ten Havem, Reynolds, Katz, Schulberg, *et al.*, 2004; Grek, 2007; Unützer *et al.*, 2006), the majority of studies have approached elderly suicide prevention primarily in this way. A controlled trial, known as PROSPECT (Prevention of Suicide in Primary Care Elderly: Collaborative Trial), evaluated whether primary care intervention reduced major risk factors for suicide in late life (Bruce *et al.*, 2004). PROSPECT's intervention combined treatment guidelines, tailored for the elderly, with care management carried out by social workers, nurses, and psychologists. The intervention group consisted of 598 patients recruited from 20 primary care practices in New York City. They were assessed at baseline, four, eight, and 12 months for suicidal ideation and depression severity. Compared with the usual care patients, at four months the intervention patients showed a faster decline in suicidal ideation (3.0% versus 12.9%, respectively). Furthermore, the intervention patients had a more favourable course of depression both in terms of severity and speed of symptom reduction; group differences peaked at four months. However, the effects on depression were not significant among patients with minor depression, unless suicidal ideation was present. These findings are consistent with the results of the IMPACT trial (Improving Mood-Promoting Access to Collaborative Treatment) (Unützer *et al.*, 2006). This study included 1,801 adults, aged 60 years and over, who suffered from major depression or dysthymia. Randomized participants had access to a depression care manager who offered problem-solving treatment for 12 months in addition to antidepressants prescribed by primary care clinicians. The control group received care as usual. Participants were assessed at baseline, and at three, six, 12, 18, and 24 months. Intervention subjects had significantly lower rates of suicidal ideation than usual care subjects at all follow-ups.

Treatment of other mental disorders

Few studies have investigated the connection between older adult suicidal behaviour and mental disorders other than depression (De Leo *et al.*, 2009a). Treatment of anxiety symptoms and disorder in relation to elderly suicidality has thus far been studied predominantly in the context of depression comorbidity (De Leo *et al.*, 2009a). However, a study re-assessed the clinical charts of 15 in-patients, aged 60 years and over, who completed suicide in the general and geriatric hospitals of Padua, Italy. It was found that most of these patients had recent records of severe and persistent anxiety and insomnia (De Leo, 1997). Ten of the 15 suicides occurred between 6.00 am and midday, which is when anxiety symptoms are generally stronger (probably related to cortisol zenith peak) (De Leo, 1997). Research findings and clinical experience suggest that recognition and aggressive treatment of severe anxiety, panic attacks, and insomnia could reduce the likelihood of suicide in all subjects (Fawcett, 2009), and the elderly seem to make no exception.

Substance use disorders are a common correlate of suicide and suicidality in general. Among the elderly, the problem is especially pronounced in Eastern European, Scandinavian, and Anglo-Saxon countries, but much less evident in France and other Mediterranean countries (De Leo *et al.*, 2009a). It has been proposed that questions about alcohol misuse, in addition to depressive symptoms and suicidality, should be incorporated into standard health screening in old-age patients. This is especially relevant given the frequency of age-related events with potentially high emotional impact, such as retirement, major illness, and loss of family members (Blow, Brockman, & Lawton, 2004). Engagement of older adults in mental health/substance abuse treatment has been found to be more successful if it involves the collaborative management of physicians and social workers at the primary care level (Rinfrette, 2009).

Hopelessness has been identified as the most important psychological condition to be screened in different types of suicidal ideation and behaviour (plans and attempts). It has also been identified as a moderator between cognitive functioning in dementia and suicidal behaviour. In fact, the preservation of some level of insight may lead to depression and hopelessness, which in turn can lead to suicide ideation (Haw *et al.*, 2009). Detecting hopelessness can have particular relevance in primary care settings, where elderly patients might feel hopeless about their experience of chronic and/or life-threatening physical illnesses.

Cognitive, psychodynamic, or interpersonal therapy can be appropriate to treat an elderly person with a personality disorder. These types of approaches may be especially relevant when the patient is cognitively intact, well-educated, and motivated (De Leo *et al.*, 1999; Scocco, De Leo, & Frank, 2002). The use of Dialectical Behaviour Therapy, combining directive, problem-oriented techniques with supportive techniques, has also been proposed (Shearin & Linehan, 1994).

General prevention principles

Universal suicide prevention, targeted at the general population, aims to improve the emotional and social well-being of the elderly and should include social security programmes, improved healthcare availability, community-based suicide prevention programmes, and restricted access to lethal means of suicide. Selective suicide prevention strategies are aimed at populations identified as potentially at risk of suicide. Indicated suicide prevention is aimed at populations already showing signs of suicidal behaviour.

The few studies that have evaluated the effects of different welfare and social support programmes for older adults (universal prevention) have yielded promising results. A community-based suicide prevention programme, carried out from 1995 to 2002 in Yuri,

Japan, involving 6,819 elderly people (aged 65 years and over) suggested that a combination of group activity (including social, voluntary, and recreational activities), psycho-education (focusing on depression and suicide risk factors), and self-assessment of depression (but not screening for depression) was effective in reducing suicide in women (but not in men) (Oyama *et al.*, 2005).

A multidimensional suicide prevention programme in Korea also indicated the protective effect of social support on suicidal behaviour among the elderly. By utilizing a community network for elderly Koreans, the experimental group (*n* = 20) experienced a significant decrease in depression and suicidal ideation and an increase in life satisfaction compared with the control group who had no access to the intervention (*n* = 19) (Jo & Kim, 2008).

Restricting access to the means of suicide is one of the most effective universal strategies to reduce suicide rates throughout the world (Mann, Apter, Bertolote, Beautrais, Currier, *et al.*, 2005). Consequently, this could also be relevant in the prevention of elderly suicide. Indeed, there is evidence to suggest that the detoxification of domestic gas in the United Kingdom reduced the incidence of suicide in elderly men (Gunnell *et al.*, 2000). The same effect was observed following hand-gun control legislation in the United States (Ludwig & Cook, 2000).

There are various types of preventative approaches for elderly people at the selective/indicated levels, such as help-lines and community support programmes for special groups. However, there are only a limited number of studies evaluating their outcomes in controlled conditions.

The well-known Tele-Help/Tele-Check programme was established in the Veneto region of Italy. It used a phone-based approach to help approximately 20,000 elderly people enrolled in the service on the basis of standardized screening criteria, including presence of chronic somatic and/or mental problems, physical or emotional isolation, etc. (De Leo *et al.*, 1995). Each client was contacted at least twice per week. During these contacts, a trained staff member was able to offer emotional support and, at the same time, monitor the client's condition. This programme is considered to have made a significant contribution to the prevention of elderly suicide. Ten years after its introduction, the number of elderly suicide deaths in the region was much lower than expected, with the impact being particularly noteworthy among female users (De Leo *et al.*, 2002).

The identification of older adults at risk of suicide, and the possible ways of approaching them, remains a concern in the implementation of selective/indicated interventions. The elderly appear to be more likely to approach primary care settings for help rather than specialist mental health services, where older adults are usually under-represented (Conwell & Thomson, 2008). Social services (such as senior centres, public transportation companies, and peer-support groups) and wider community entities (such as banks, utility companies, pharmacists, and mailmen) may also constitute potential gatekeepers. In the United States, a community-based gatekeeper programme was able to approach socially and economically disadvantaged at-risk elderly people. These were identified through employees of community businesses, who were specifically trained to recognize people in need of help and refer them to geriatric and mental health services. In this project, community gatekeepers were responsible for 40% of all referrals to the local Elder Services (Florio, Hendryx, Jensen, Rockwood, Raschko, *et al.*, 1997).

Smaller sub-community settings may also prove to be effective in preventing elderly suicide. Membership and participation in religious and spiritual communities have long been perceived to be protective (Durkheim, 1951 [1897]). These environments may help to moderate social isolation and loneliness by providing a social support network and promoting feelings of belonging and worth (Krause, 2006).

National strategies and programmes

National programmes have recognized the importance of community and broader public involvement in suicide prevention efforts. Common elements in national prevention strategies include: raising awareness of suicide and its public health dimension; recognizing suicide risk factors and avenues of prevention; coordinating mental health and substance abuse programmes; developing and implementing strategies to reduce the stigma associated with mental illness and suicidal behaviour; and setting up programmes to improve help-seeking behaviour, particularly among males (National Strategy for Suicide Prevention, 2001).

In general, national suicide prevention strategies acknowledge the heightened risk of suicidal behaviour in those aged over 65 years (e.g., Commonwealth Department of Health and Aged Care, 2000; National Strategy for Suicide Prevention, 2001; National Suicide Prevention Strategy, 2002). Actions targeted at this age group usually aim to promote mental health, with particular emphasis on early recognition and treatment of depression. In order to achieve these aims, access to integrated mental health services and adequate treatment and support for the elderly and their carers are often provided. Studies on the effectiveness of old-age mental health services provide encouraging evidence, particularly for services such as community multidisciplinary teams (Draper & Low, 2004).

Furthermore, high-risk sub-populations of the elderly, namely, men and 'old-old' individuals (75+ years), have been recognized. Australia's 'Living is for Everyone' Framework (2007) identified elderly males living in rural and remote areas as a special at-risk population. Consequently, the Australian strategy pushes for the systematic screening of depression and other mental illnesses, and promotes men's help-seeking behaviour.

Conclusions

In the past two decades, suicide rates among the elderly have declined in most Western countries (De Leo *et al.*, 2009a). Nevertheless, when compared with rates in other age groups, they have remained the highest. Many of the characteristics of elderly suicidal behaviour are unique, and risk and protective factors tend not to be universally translatable. All these factors can inhibit preventative efforts. However, further research on gender differences in relation to suicidality, particularly evident at very advanced age, and risk factors specific to isolated males, matched by protective factors for females, may provide the grounds for more effective interventions.

There is evidence that improving social support and detecting and treating affective disorders in a timely manner are key interventions for reducing suicide risk in old age

(Kennedy, 1996; Pinquart & Soerensen, 2001). Therefore, routine screening for living conditions and presence of depression and suicidal ideation in primary care settings is essential. Additionally, community-based prevention programmes, collaborative care interventions, help-lines and gatekeeper training seem to be important in preventing late-life suicide. However, evaluations of such programmes in controlled settings and across different cultures are needed.

More research on the impact of physicians' education on geriatric depression and limiting access to means should also be encouraged. Very few controlled investigations on the treatment of suicidality in old age exist. However, supported by the present decline in suicide rates, the available data suggest that elderly people may respond positively to suicide prevention and health/life-improving initiatives.

Ageist social attitudes, deeply rooted among both lay people and professionals, need to be tackled in order to implement specific and vigorous national prevention strategies. Social changes that impact on the elderly, especially within the family, need to be counteracted by community programmes that promote a sense of usefulness and belonging and preserve social integration and social status. Policy-makers and governments should continue to pay attention to improving retirement programmes, facilitating access to mental health services, and developing support systems.

To paraphrase Erikson (1982), old people can successfully resolve the last stage of their lives. They can nourish feelings of integrity, happiness, and contentment. They can experience a general sense of meaningfulness in their lives. Actively promoting the ability to adapt to age-related conditions might constitute the essential part of a truly successful ageing process.

References

Accortt, E. E., Freeman, M. P., & Allen, J. J. (2008). Women and major depressive disorder: Clinical perspectives on causal pathways. *Journal of Women's Health, 17*, 1583–1590.

Alexopoulos, G., Bruce, M. L., Hull, J., Sirey, J. A., & Kakuma, T. (1999). Clinical determinants of suicidal ideation and behavior in geriatric depression. *Archives of General Psychiatry, 56*, 1048–1053.

Apter, A., Krispin, O., & Bursztein, C. (2009). Psychiatric disorders in suicide and suicide attempters. In D. Wasserman & C. Wasserman (Eds.), *Oxford Textbook of Suicidology and Suicide Prevention* (pp. 653–660). New York: Oxford University Press.

Beautrais A. L. (2002). A case control study of suicide and attempted suicide in older adults. *Suicide and Life-Threatening Behavior, 32*, 1–9.

Bertolote, J. & Fleischmann, A. (2009). A global perspective on the magnitude of suicide mortality. In D. Wasserman & C. Wasserman (Eds.), *Oxford Textbook of Suicidology and Suicide Prevention* (pp. 91–98). New York: Oxford University Press.

Blazer, D. G. (2003). Depression in late life: Review and commentary. *The Journals of Gerontology: Series A, 58*, 249–265.

Blow, F. C., Brockman, L. M., & Lawton, B. K. (2004). Role of alcohol in late-life suicide. *Alcoholism: Clinical and Experimental Research, 28*, 48–57.

Bruce, M. L., Ten Have, T. R., Reynolds III, C. F., Katz, I. I., Schulberg, H. C., Mulsant, B. H., Brown, G. K., McAvay, G. J., Pearson, J. L., & Alexopoulos, G. S. (2004). Reducing suicidal ideation and depressive symptoms in depressed older primary care patients: A randomized controlled trial. *Journal of the American Medical Association, 291*, 1081–1091.

Canetto, S. S. (1995). Elderly women and suicidal behavior. In S. S. Canetto & D. Lester (Eds.), *Women and Suicidal Behavior*. New York: Springer.

Capurso, A., Capurso, C., Solfrizzi, V., Colacicco, A. M., D'Introno, A., & Panza, F. (2007). Depression in old age: A diagnostic and therapeutic challenge. *Recenti progressi in medicina, 98*, 43–52.

Cattell, H. (2000). Suicide in the elderly. *Advances in Psychiatric Treatment, 6*, 102–108.

Chan, J., Draper, B., & Banerjee, S. (2007). Deliberate self-harm in older adults: A review of the literature from 1995 to 2004. *International Journal of Geriatric Psychiatry, 22*, 720–732.

Chiu, H. F., Yip, P. S., Chi, I., Chan, S., Tsoh, J., Kwan, C. W., Li, S. F., Conwell, Y., & Caine, E. (2004). Elderly suicide in Hong Kong – A case-controlled psychological autopsy study. *Acta Psychiatrica Scandinavica, 109*, 299–305.

Cochran, S. V. & Rabinowitz, F. E. (2003). Gender-sensitive recommendations for assessment and treatment of depression in men. *Professional Psychology, 2*, 132–140.

Cohen, L. S. (2003). Gender-specific considerations in the treatment of mood disorders in women across the life cycle. *Journal of Clinical Psychiatry, 64*, 15–18.

Commonwealth Department of Health and Aged Care 2000. *LIFE: A Framework for Prevention of Suicide and Self-harm in Australia*. Canberra, Australia.

Conwell, Y., Dubenstein, P. R., & Caine, E. D. (2002). Risk factors for suicide in later life. *Biological Psychiatry, 52*, 193–204.

Conwell, Y., Dubenstein, P. R., Cox, C., Herrmann, J., Forbes, N. & Caine, E. D. (1998). Age differences in behaviors leading to completed suicide. *American Journal of Geriatric Psychiatry, 6*, 122–126.

Conwell, Y., Duberstein, P. R, Hirsch, J. K., Conner, K. R., Eberly, S., & Caine, E. D. (2009). Health status and suicide in the second half of life. *International Journal of the Geriatrics Psychiatry, 6*, 147–148.

Conwell, Y., Lyness, J. M., Duberstein, P., Cox, C., Seidlitz, L., DiGiorgio, A., & Caine, E. D. (2000). Completed suicide among older patients in primary care practices: A controlled study. *Journal of the American Geriatrics Society, 48*, 23–29.

Conwell, Y. & Thomson, C. (2008). Suicidal behaviour in elders. *The Psychiatric Clinics of North America, 31*, 333–356.

De Leo, D. (1997). Suicide in a general hospital: The case of the elderly. *Crisis, 18*, 5–7.

De Leo, D. (1999). Cultural issues in suicide and old age. *Crisis, 20*, 53–55.

De Leo, D. (2002). Struggling against suicide. *Crisis, 23*, 23–31.

De Leo, D. (2006). Suicide in Australia: What we know and are seeking to discover. In D. De Leo, H. Herrman, S. Ueda, & T. Takeshima (Eds.), *An Australian–Japanese Perspective on Suicide Prevention: Culture, community, and care* (pp. 21–38). Selected symposium papers from the 24–26 November Conference, Melbourne, Australia. Commonwealth of Australia, Department of Health and Aging, Canberra.

De Leo, D., Carollo, G., & Dello Buono, M. (1995). Lower suicide rates associated with a Tele-Help/Tele-Check service for the elderly at home. *American Journal of Psychiatry, 152*, 632–634.

De Leo, D., Dello Buono, M., & Dwyer, J. (2002). Suicide among the elderly: The long-term impact of a telephone support and assessment intervention in northern Italy. *British Journal of Psychiatry, 181*, 226–229.

De Leo, D. & Diekstra, R. F. W. (1990). *Depression and Suicide in Late Life*. Goettingen: Hogrefe & Huber.

De Leo, D., Draper, B., & Krysinska, K. (2009b). Suicidal elderly people in clinical and community settings. In D. Wasserman & C. Wasserman (Eds.), *Oxford Textbook of Suicidology and Suicide Prevention* (pp. 703–719). New York: Oxford University Press.

De Leo, D. & Heller, T. (2004). *Suicide in Queensland, 1999–2004*. Brisbane: Australian Institute for Suicide Research and Prevention.

De Leo D., Hickey P., Meneghel, G., & Cantor, C. H. (1999a). Blindness, fear of sight loss, and suicide. *Psychosomatics, 40*, 339–344.

De Leo, D., Krysinska, K., Bertolote, J. M., Fleischmann, A., & Wasserman, D. (2009a). Suicidal behaviours on all the continents among the elderly. In D. Wasserman & C. Wasserman (Eds.), *Oxford Textbook of Suicidology and Suicide Prevention* (pp. 693–700). New York: Oxford University Press.

De Leo, D. & Meneghel, G. (2001). The elderly and suicide. In D. Wasserman (Ed.), *Suicide – Unnecessary death* (pp. 195–207). London: Martin Dunitz.

De Leo, D., Padoani, W., Scocco, P. Lie, D., Bille-Brahe, U., Arensman, E., Hjelmeland, H., Crepet, P., Haring, C., Hawton, K., Lönqvist, J., Michel, K., Pommereau, X., Querejeta, I., Phillipe, J., Salander-Renberg, E., Schmidtke, A., Fricke, S., Weinacker, B., Tamesvary, B., Wasserman, D., & Faria, S. (2001). Attempted and completed suicide in older subjects: Results from the WHO/EURO Multicentre Study of Suicidal Behaviour. *International Journal of Geriatric Psychiatry, 16*, 300–310.

De Leo, D., Scocco, P., & Meneghel, G. (1999b). Pharmacological and psychotherapeutic treatment of personality disorders in the elderly. *International Geriatrics, 11*, 191–206.

De Leo, D. & Scocco, P. (2000). Treatment and prevention of suicidal behaviour in the elderly. In K. Hawton & K. van Heeringen (Eds.), *The International Handbook of Suicide and Attempted Suicide* (pp. 555–570). Chichester: John Wiley & Sons, Ltd.

De Leo, D. & Spathonis, K. (2003). Culture and suicide in late life. *Psychiatric Times, 20*, 14–17.

De Leo, D. & Spathonis, K. (2004). Suicide and suicidal behaviour in late life. In D. De Leo, U. Bille-Brahe, A. Kerkhof, & A. Schmidtke (Eds.), *Suicidal Behaviour. Theories and research findings* (pp. 253–286). Göttingen: Hogrefe & Huber.

Diefenbach, G. J., Woolley S. B., & Goethe, J. V. (2009). The association between self-reported anxiety-symptoms and suicidality. *Journal of Nervous and Mental Disease, 197*, 92–99.

Dombrovski, A. Y. & Szanto, K. (2005). Prevention of suicide in the elderly. *Annals of Long-Term Care, 13*, 52–32.

Draper, B. M. (1995). Prevention of suicide in old age. *The Medical Journal of Australia, 162*, 533–534.

Draper, B., Brodaty, H., Low, L. F., Richards, V., Paton, H., & Lie, D. (2002). Self-destructive behaviors in nursing home residents. *Journal of the American Geriatrics Society, 50*(2), 354–362.

Draper, B. & Low, L. (2004). *What is the Effectiveness of Old-age Mental Health Services?* available at WHO Regional Office for Europe, http://www.euro.who.int/document/E83685.pdf, retrieved 5 September 2009,

Duberstein, P. R. (1995). Openness to experience and completed suicide across the second half of life. *Psychogeriatrics, 7*, 183–198.

Duberstein, P. R., Conwell, Y., & Cox, C. (1998). Suicide in widowed persons: A psychological autopsy comparison of recently and remotely bereaved older subjects. *The American Journal of Geriatric Psychiatry, 6*, 328–335.

Durkheim, E. (1951 [1897]). *Suicide: A study in sociology*. Chicago, IL: Free Press.

Erikson, E. H. (1982). *The Life Circle Completed*. New York: Norton.

Fawcett, J. (2009). Severe anxiety and agitation as treatment modifiable risk factors for suicide. In D. Wasserman & C. Wasserman (Eds.), *Oxford Textbook of Suicidology and Suicide Prevention* (pp. 407–411). New York: Oxford University Press.

Fiske, A., Wetherell, J. L., & Gatz, M. (2009). Depression in older adults. *Annual Review of Clinical Psychology, 5*, 369–389.

Florio, E. R., Hendryx, M., Jensen, J. E. Rockwood, T. H., Raschko, R., & Dyck, D. G. (1997). A comparison of suicidal and non-suicidal elders referred to a community mental health program. *Suicide and Life-Threatening Behavior, 27*, 182–193.

Galdas, P. M., Cheater, F., & Marshall, P. (2005). Men and help-seeking behaviour: Literature review. *Journal of Advanced Nursing*, *49*, 616–623.

Gatz, M. & Fiske, A. (2003). Aging women and depression. *Professional Psychology*, *34*, 3–9.

Grek, A. (2007). Clinical management of suicidality in the elderly: an opportunity for involvement in the lives of older patients. *The Canadian Journal of Psychiatry*, *52*, 47–57.

Gunnell, D., Middleton, N., & Frankel, S. (2000). Method availability and the prevention of suicide – A re-analysis of secular trends in England and Wales 1950–1975. *Social Psychiatry and Psychiatric Epidemiology*, *35*, 437–443.

Harwood, D. M. J., Hawton, K., Hope T., & Jacoby, R. (2000). Suicide in older people: Mode of death, demographic factors, and medical contact before death. *International Journal of Geriatric Psychiatry*, *15*, 736–743.

Harwood, D. M. J., Hawton, K., Hope, T., & Jacoby, R. (2001). Psychiatric disorder and personality factors associated with suicide in older people: A descriptive and case-control study. *International Journal of Geriatric Psychiatry*, *16*, 155–165.

Harwood, D. & Jacoby, R. (2000). Suicidal behaviour among the elderly. In K. Hawton & K. van Heeringen (Eds.), *The International Handbook of Suicide and Attempted Suicide* (pp. 275–292). Chichester: John Wiley & Sons, Ltd.

Haw, C., Harwood, D., & Hawton, K. (2009). Dementia and suicidal behaviour: A review of the literature. *International Psychogeriatrics*, *21*, 440–453.

Hawgood, J. & De Leo, D. (2008). Anxiety disorder and suicidal behaviour: An update. *Current Opinion on Psychiatry*, *1*, 51–64.

Hawton, K. & Harriss, L. (2006). Deliberate self-harm in people aged 60 and over: Characteristics and outcome of a 20-year cohort. *International Journal of Geriatric Psychiatry*, *21*, 572–581.

Hawton, K. & Harriss, L. (2008). The changing gender ratio in occurrence of deliberate self-harm across the lifecycle. *Crisis*, *29*, 4–10.

Jo, K. H. & Kim, Y. K. (2008). Development and application of a multidimensional suicide prevention program for Korean elders by utilizing a community network. *Taehan Kanho Hakhoe chi*, *38*, 372–382.

Kaplan, M. S., McFarland, B. H., Huguet, N., & Newsom, J. T. (2007). Physical illness, functional limitations, and suicide risk: A population-based study. *American Journal of Orthopsychiatry*, *77*, 56–60.

Khouzam, H. R. (2009). The diagnosis and treatment of depression in the geriatric population. *Comprehensive Therapy*, *35*, 103–114.

Kennedy, G. J. (1996). *Suicide and Depression in Late Life: Critical issues in treatment, research, and public policy*. New York: John Wiley & Sons, Inc.

Klausner, E. J. & Alexopoulos, G. S. (1999). The future of psychosocial treatments for elderly patients. *Psychiatric Services*, *50*, 1198–1204.

Kolves, K., Varnik, A., Tooding, L. M., & Wasserman, D. (2006). The role of alcohol in suicide: A case-control psychological autopsy study. *Psychological Medicine*, *36*, 923–930.

Krause, N. (2006). Church-based social support and mortality. *Journal of Gerontology*, *61B*, 140–146.

Krysinska, K., Heller, T. S., & De Leo, D. (2006). Suicide and deliberate self-harm in personality disorders. *Current Opinion in Psychiatry*, *18*, 95–101.

Liu, K. Y, Chen, E. Y., Cheung, A. S., & Yip, P. S. (2009). Psychiatric history modifies the gender ratio of suicide: An East and West comparison. *Social Psychiatry and Psychiatric Epidemiology*, *44*, 130–134.

Living is For Everyone Framework (2007). *Living is For Everyone (LIFE) Framework*. Canberra: The Australian Government Department of Health and Aging.

Loebel, J. P., Loebel, J. S., Dager, S. R., Centerwall, B. S., & Reay, D. T. (1991). Anticipation of nursing home placement may be a precipitant of suicide among the elderly. *Journal of the American Geriatrics Society, 91*, 407–415.

Ludwig, J. & Cook, P. J. (2000). Homicide and suicide rates associated with implementation of the Brady Handgun Violence Prevention Act. *The Journal of the American Medical Association, 284*, 585–591.

Mann, J. J., Apter, A., Bertolote, J., Beautrais, A., Currier, D., Haas, A., Hegerl, U., Lönqvist, J., Malone, K., Marusic, A., Mehlum, L., Patton, G., Phillips, M., Rutz, W., Rihmer, Z., Schmidtke, A., Shaffer, D., Silverman, M., Takahashi, Y., Varnik, A., Wasserman, D., Yip, P., & Hendin, H. (2005). Suicide prevention strategies: a systematic review. *Journal of the American medical Association, 294*, 2064–2074.

McIntosh, J. L. (2009). *Elderly Suicide: Slide Set* (PowerPoint slides). Indiana University South Bend, http://mypage.iusb.edu/~jmcintos, retrieved 18 August 2009.

McIntosh, J. L., Santos, J. F., Hubbard, R. W., & Overholser, J. C. (1994). *Elderly Suicide Research, Theory and Treatment*. Washington, DC: American Psychological Association.

McKeown, R. E., Cuffe, S. P., & Schultz, R. M. (2006). US suicide rates by age group, 1970–2002: An examination of recent trends. *American Journal of Public Health, 96*, 1744–1751.

Montano, C. B. (1999). Primary care issues related to the treatment of depression in elderly patients. *Journal of Clinical Psychiatry, 60*, 45–51.

Murphy, G. E. (2002). Alcoholism, drug abuse, and suicide in the elderly. In A. M. Gurnack, R. Atkins, & H. J. Osgood (Eds.), *Treating Alcohol and Drug Abuse in the Elderly* (pp. 72–82). New York: Springer.

National Strategy for Suicide Prevention (2001). *National Strategy for Suicide Prevention: Goals and objectives for action*. Washington, DC: US Department of Health and Human Services.

National Suicide Prevention Strategy (2002). *National Suicide Prevention Strategy for England*. London: Department of Health.

Neulinger, K. & De Leo, D. (2001). Suicide in elderly and youth populations – How do they differ? In D. De Leo (Ed.), *Suicide and Euthanasia in Older Adults. A transcultural journey*. Toronto: Hogrefe & Huber.

Oliver R. G. & Hetzel, B. S. (1972). Rise and fall of suicide rates in Australia: Relation to sedative availability. *Medical Journal of Australia, 2*, 919–923.

Osgood, N. J. & Eisenhandler, S. A. (1995). By her own hand: The acquiescent suicide of older women. In S. S. Canetto & D. Lester (Eds.), *Women and Suicidal Behavior*. New York: Springer.

Oyama, H., Watanabe, N., Ono, Y., Sakashita, T., Takenoshita, Y., Taguchi, M., Takizawa, T., Miura, R., & Kumagai, K. (2005). Community-based suicide prevention through group activity for the elderly successfully reduced the high suicide rate for females. *Psychiatry and Clinical Neurosciences, 59*, 337–344.

Pinquart, M. & Soerensen, S. (2001). How effective are psychotherapeutic and other psychosocial interventions with older adults? A meta analysis. *Journal of Mental Health and Aging, 7*, 207–243.

Quan, H., Arboleda-Flórez, J., Fick, G., Stuart, H. L., & Love, E. J. (2002). Association between physical illness and suicide among the elderly. *Social Psychiatry and Psychiatric Epidemiology, 37*, 190–197.

Rabheru, K. (2004). Special issues in the management of depression in older patients. *The Canadian Journal of Psychiatry, 49*, 41–50.

Reynolds III, C. F. & Kupfer, D. J. (1999). Depression and aging: A look to the future. *Psychiatric Services, 50*, 1167–1172.

Rinfrette, E. S. (2009). Treatment of anxiety, depression, and alcohol disorders in the elderly: social work collaboration in primary care. *Journal of Evidence-Based Social Work, 6*, 79–91.

Ross, R. K., Bernstein, L., Trent, L., Henderson, B. E., & Paganini-Hill, A. (1990). A prospective study of risk factors for traumatic deaths in a retirement community. *Preventive Medicine, 19*, 323–334.

Rubenowitz, E., Waern, M., Wilhelmson, K., & Allebeck, P. (2001). Life events and psychosocial factors in elderly suicides – A case-control study. *Psychological medicine, 31*, 1193–1202.

Sakamoto, S., Tanaka, E., Neichi, K., & Ono, Y. (2006). Sociopsychological factors relating to suicide prevention in a Japanese rural community: Coping behaviours and attitudes toward depression and suicidal ideation. *Psychiatry & Clinical Neurosciences, 60*(6), 676–686.

Schneider, B., Maurer, K., & Frölich, L. (2001). Dementia and suicide. *Fortschritte der Neurologie-Psychiatrie, 69*, 164–173.

Scocco P., De Leo D., & Frank E. (2002). Is interpersonal psychotherapy in group format a therapeutic option in late-life depression? *Clinical Psychology and Psychotherapy, 9*, 68–75.

Scogin, F., Welsch, D., Hanson, A., Stump, J., & Coates, A. (2005). Evidence-based psychotherapies for depression in older adults. *Clinical Psychology: Science and Practice, 12*, 222–237.

Shah, A., Bhat, R., MacKenzie, S., & Koen, C. (2008). Elderly suicide rates: Cross-national comparison of trends over a 10-year period. *International Psychogeriatrics, 20*, 673–686.

Shah, A. K. & De, T. (1998). Suicide and the elderly. *International Journal of Psychiatry in Clinical Practise, 2*, 3–17.

Shearin, E. N. & Linehan, M. M. (1994). Dialectical behaviour therapy for borderline personality disorder: Theoretical and empirical foundations. *Acta Psychiatrica Scandinavica, 89*, 61–68.

Sinha, R. & Rounsaville, B. J. (2002). Sex differences in depressed substance abusers. *Journal of Clinical Psychiatry, 63*, 616–627.

Szanto, K., Mulsant, B. H., Houck, P. R., Dew, M. A., & Reynolds, C. F., III (2003). Occurrence and course of suicidality during short-term treatment of late-life depression. *Archives of General Psychiatry, 60*, 610–617.

Szanto, K., Mulsant, B. H., Houck, P. R., Miller, M. D., Mazadumar, S., & Reynolds, C. F., III (2001). Treatment outcome in suicidal vs. non-suicidal elderly patients. *American Journal of Geriatric Psychiatry, 9*, 261–269.

Turvey, C. L., Conwell, Y., Jones, M. P., Phillips, C., Simonsick, E., Pearson, J. L., & Wallace, R. (2002). Risk factors for late-life suicide: A prospective, community-based study. *The American Journal of Geriatric Psychiatry, 10*, 398–407.

Uncapher, H. & Arean, P. A. (2000). Physicians are less willing to treat suicidal ideation in older patients. *Journal of the American Geriatrics Society, 48*, 188–192.

Unützer, J., Tang, L., Oishi, S., Katon, W., Williams, J. W. Jr., Hunkeler, E., Hendrie, H., Lin, E. H., Levine, S., Grypma, L., Steffens, D. C., Fields, J., & Langston, C. (2006). Reducing suicidal ideation in depressed older primary care patients. *The American Geriatrics Society, 54*, 1550–1556.

Vörös, V., Osváth, P., & Fekete, S. (2004). Gender differences in suicidal behaviour. *Neuropsychopharmacol Hung, 6*, 65–71.

Waern, M., Beskow, J., Runeson, B., & Skoog, I. (1999). Suicidal feelings in the last year of life in elderly people who commit suicide. *British Medical Journal, 354*, 917–918.

Waern, M., Rubenowitz, E., Runeson, B., Skoog, I., Wilhelmson, K., & Allebeck, P. (2002). Burden of illness and suicide in elderly people: Case-control study. *British Medical Journal, 324*, 1355.

Weissman, M. M., Bland, R. C., Canino, G. J., Greenwald, S., Hwu, H. G., Joyce, P. R., Karam, E. G., Lee, C. K., Lellouch, J., Lepine, J. P., Newman, S. C., Rubio-Stipec, M., Wells, J. E., Wickramaratne, P. J., Wittchen, H. U., & Yeh, E. K. (1999). Prevalence of suicide ideation and suicide attempts in nine countries. *Psychological Medicine, 29*, 9–17.

Yip, P. S. F. (1998). Age, sex, marital status and suicide: An empirical study of East and West. *Psychological Reports, 82*, 311–322.

CHAPTER NINETEEN

Clinical Care of Deliberate Self-Harm Patients: An Evidence-based Approach

Keith Hawton, Tatiana L. Taylor, Kate E. A. Saunders, and Su Mahadevan

Abstract

Deliberate self-harm (DSH) (intentional self-poisoning or self-injury) is a frequent reason for hospital presentation. It represents considerable morbidity in terms of interpersonal and social problems and psychiatric disorder and carries a significant risk of future suicide. Effective clinical management is therefore essential. In this chapter the results of systematic reviews of studies of attitudes of DSH patients towards hospital services, staff attitudes towards DSH patients, and the effectiveness of aftercare intervention for DSH patients, together with the results of a study of service provision, are summarized, with the aim of defining the essential elements of appropriate and effective services and clinical management for this patient population.

It is clear that patients who present to hospital following DSH often represent a relatively neglected patient group. Thus, patients often perceive negative attitudes of staff, especially in medical settings. Results of studies of staff attitudes largely confirm this view. Negative staff attitudes often appear to reflect lack of training and understanding regarding the problems and needs of DSH patients. Studies of provision of training programmes for general hospital staff appear to indicate that they are effective in improving staff knowledge and attitudes. Results of a systematic review of aftercare interventions indicate that short-term psychological treatment (e.g., Cognitive Behaviour Therapy/problem-solving therapy) can be effective in terms of preventing repetition of DSH, reducing depression, hopelessness and suicidal ideation, and helping improve patients' problems. Specialized

International Handbook of Suicide Prevention: Research, Policy and Practice, First Edition.
Edited by Rory C. O'Connor, Stephen Platt, Jacki Gordon.
© 2011 John Wiley & Sons, Ltd. Published 2011 by John Wiley & Sons, Ltd.

services for DSH patients should be available in all large general hospitals. There should be specific training and clear guidelines for all staff. Attention to the needs of DSH patients is rightly a key element in most national suicide prevention strategies. There is now considerable evidence on which to base the development of appropriate services for this important group of patients.

Introduction

Deliberate self-harm (DSH) is the term used in the United Kingdom, much of Europe, and several other parts of the world to describe intentional, non-fatal self-poisoning (e.g., overdoses of prescribed drugs, swallowing of non-ingestible substances such as pesticides), and self-injury (e.g., self-cutting, hanging, jumping from a height), involving any type of motive or intention (e.g., to communicate distress, to die). Rates of DSH estimated on general hospital presentations vary from country to country. In Europe there are particularly high rates of DSH in England, Ireland, France, and Finland (Schmidtke, Brahe, De Leo, Kerkhof, Bjerke, et al., 1996), where DSH is one of the most common reasons for hospital admission. Rates are generally higher in females than males, especially in teenagers (Hawton & Harriss, 2008), and younger people (Hawton, Bergen, Casey, Simkin, Palmer, et al., 2007). Rates also tend to be higher in areas of socio-economic deprivation and social fragmentation (i.e., characterized by poor social networks) (Gunnell, Peters, Kammerling, & Brooks, 1995; Hawton, Harriss, Hodder, Simkin, & Gunnell, 2001).

The majority of DSH episodes among individuals presenting to hospitals involve self-poisoning (Hawton et al., 2007; Schmidtke et al., 1996). In the community, however, self-injury, especially self-cutting and other forms of self-mutilation, are more common, particularly in young people (Madge, Hewitt, Hawton, de Wilde, Corcoran, et al., 2008).

DSH is often linked to interpersonal and social problems (e.g., break-up of relationships, social isolation). Many patients have psychiatric disorders, for example, depression and personality disorders, often complicated by alcohol or drug misuse (Haw, Hawton, Houston, & Townsend, 2001; Suominen, Henriksson, Suokas, Isometsä, Ostamo, et al., 1996). DSH has been linked to certain psychological characteristics, including deficiencies in problem-solving (Linehan, 1987; Pollock & Williams, 2004), low self-esteem and impulsivity (Mann, 2003), and a tendency to feel hopeless (MacLeod, Tata, Tyrer, Schmidt, Davidson, et al., 2005). One model for DSH incorporates the notions of a sense of failure, entrapment, and lack of escape potential (Williams, Crane, Barnhofer, & Duggan, 2005).

DSH is often repeated, with 20%–30% of individuals experiencing a repeat episode within 12 months (Owens, Horrocks, & House, 2002). This indicates extensive persistent or recurrent distress, which places considerable demands on general hospital and psychiatric services. The healthcare costs of DSH are therefore considerable (Sinclair, Gray, & Hawton, 2006).

There is a strong association between DSH and suicide, the risk of eventual suicide being highest in the year after an episode and increasing with age (Hawton, Zahl, & Weatherall, 2003; Owens *et al.*, 2002). The risk of suicide is also further increased in those who repeat DSH (Zahl & Hawton, 2004). DSH is also linked to physical disorders and, in the long term, greater risk of death from natural as well as unnatural causes (Hawton, Harriss, & Zahl, 2006).

Due to the strong link between DSH and suicide, all national suicide prevention strategies include a focus on DSH prevention (Department of Health, 2002; US Department of Health and Human Services, 2001; Health Service Executive, the National Suicide Review Group & Department of Health and Children, 2005; Ministry of Health New Zealand, 2006). Thus, in many countries considerable and increasing attention is being paid to improving clinical services for DSH patients and developing more effective means of aftercare. As a result, guidelines for service design and short-term management of DSH patients have been developed, such as those produced in the United Kingdom by the National Institute for Health and Clinical Excellence (NICE) (National Collaborating Centre for Mental Health, 2004).

In this chapter we consider how the care of DSH patients, especially those presenting to hospital, might be improved. We take an evidence-based approach by considering, where possible, the findings of systematic reviews of the existing research literature and original research. Specifically, we examine what can be learned, first, from studies of patients' attitudes to clinical services, second, from investigation of staff attitudes to patients, third, from clinical trials of different therapeutic approaches to aftercare, and, finally, from studies of services. We conclude the chapter with a summary of how this information can be used to design more effective services for DSH patients.

What can be Learned from Studies of Service Users' Attitudes Towards DSH Services?

The experiences of individuals presenting to hospital following an episode of DSH were examined in a systematic review of quantitative and qualitative studies (Taylor, Hawton, Fortune, & Kapur, 2009). Electronic databases were searched and experts in the field were contacted to identify any relevant studies of participants of either gender or any age who had contact with hospital services after engaging in self-poisoning or self injury. Thirty-one studies from nine countries met the inclusion criteria. These were assessed for quality and relevance using a combination of two quality appraisal tools (Critical Appraisal Skills Program, 2002; Social Care Institute for Excellence, 2006). The standard of the majority of studies (74%) was classified as strong or acceptable.

Over half of the studies ($n = 16$) examined patients' experiences of care in the United Kingdom. Other countries where studies had been conducted included North America ($n = 6$), Sweden ($n = 3$), New Zealand ($n = 2$), Australia ($n = 1$), Finland ($n = 1$), Ireland ($n = 1$), and the Netherlands ($n = 1$). Service users who had self-poisoned accounted for the majority of participants in 15 studies, reflecting the preponderance of self-poisoning in DSH patients who present to hospital services (Hawton *et al.*, 2007). Although the review included studies from several countries, many with different healthcare systems and clinical practices, the experiences reported by participants were very similar.

General perceptions of management

Service user involvement in treatment decisions was one of the most important aspects of care influencing satisfaction. Participants in the studies often reported being given little information about their care or being treated without explanation as to why the treatment was necessary and what the expected outcome was. Several participants described difficulty understanding the information provided to them (Horrocks, Hughes, Martin, House, & Owens, 2005; Wiklander, Samuelsson, & Asberg, 2003).

Although some service users in studies from the United Kingdom (Carrigan, 1994; National Collaborating Centre for Mental Health, 2004) and Sweden (Wolk-Wasserman, 1985) thought staff were *'awfully competent'* and *'well trained'*, they also felt staff often lacked knowledge about DSH, which participants perceived as contributing to their negative attitudes towards DSH patients. When patients felt staff did not know about or understand self-harm they were more likely to be perceived as operating on misconceptions about why people self-harm (Carrigan, 1994; National Collaborating Centre for Mental Health, 2004).

Accident and emergency department

Individuals presenting to hospital following a DSH episode often felt they were treated differently from other patients because they had self-harmed. One patient said: 'They wouldn't touch me ... they looked at me as if to say "I'm not touching you in case you flip on me" ... they didn't actually say it, it was their attitude' (Horrocks *et al.*, 2005, p. 12). Although one cannot be certain that this accurately reflected staff behaviour, this perception of such an attitude is important.

Some participants also complained that staff were unconcerned about their mental health and focused only on physical problems; for example:

> On the occasions I have been admitted to an A&E [Accident and Emergency] department they have concentrated on medically patching me up and getting me out. Never have I been asked any questions regarding whether this is the first time I have self-harmed or if I was to do it again or how I intend to deal with it. (Brophy, 2006, p. 50)

Participants also often reported that waiting times were too long and that they were left without information regarding their physical condition, making some service users anxious and frightened. Regular provision of updates on health status and checking those waiting for treatment were associated with positive experiences (Palmer, Strevens, & Blackwell, 2006): 'All they have to say is, we're here if you need us, don't think you're on your own' (Horrocks *et al.*, 2005, p. 9).

Physical treatment

Perceived inappropriate behaviour and a lack of empathy among hospital staff led to negative experiences of care. Inappropriate behaviour often took the form of threats or humiliating experiences: 'The last time I had a blood transfusion the consultant said that I was wasting blood that was meant for patients after they'd had operations or accident victims. He asked whether I was proud of what I'd done' (Brophy, 2006, p. 50).

Some service users reported that staff threatened to withhold treatment due to the nature of the injuries or in an attempt to coerce them into promising not to self-harm again. When staff were perceived as acknowledging and being considerate of participants' psychological state during physical treatment, service users were more satisfied with their care: 'He … took great pains to suture very neatly – when I commented on this he said "I don't want it to leave any scars" to which I replied that I am covered in them. He said "not on my watch"' (Palmer *et al.*, 2006, p. 18).

Psychosocial assessment

Although psychosocial assessment is a cornerstone of recommended care for those arriving at hospital following an episode of DSH, it is not routinely provided (Bennewith, Gunnell, Peters, Hawton, & House, 2004; Kapur, House, Creed, Feldman, Friedman, *et al.*, 1998). Positive experiences of the assessment were more likely when staff explained the reasons for, and goals of, the assessment and involved service users in treatment decisions. Clear, two-way communication and perceived empathy also contributed to satisfaction with care.

When participants could not understand the value of the assessment and felt it to be superficial and rushed, their satisfaction decreased (Hengeveld, Kerkhof, & van der Wal, 1988; Horrocks *et al.*, 2005). 'I got the impression that [the psychiatrist] wanted to get it over and done with as quickly as he could and get on with whatever it is he had to do next. There was nothing personal about it' (Horrocks *et al.*, 2005, p. 16).

Discharge and referral for aftercare

Many service users reported feeling ill-prepared to leave hospital for both physical and psychological reasons (Horrocks *et al.*, 2005). Many reported they were not given referrals for aftercare appointments (National Collaborating Centre for Mental Health, 2004). Some were given contact numbers for various mental health services; however, the majority felt uncomfortable initiating contact. Those that were referred for subsequent care often faced long waits for appointments (Hume & Platt, 2007; National Collaborating Centre for Mental Health, 2004). 'I had to wait 12 weeks. A lot can happen in 12 weeks. When the appointment came I was, like, I didn't really see the point' (Hume & Platt, 2007, p. 5).

The majority of participants were generally satisfied with care, although some said they would not return to hospital if they had another DSH episode.

Aftercare

The majority of service users indicated a willingness to engage in treatment to help minimize their self-harm. Often this treatment took the form of psychotherapy. The opportunity to talk about their problems and circumstances that led to their self-harm was important to many and was described as a positive result of their care (Crockwell & Burford, 1995):

> It has been very, very useful, because there are lots of things that I never really talked about that happened in my past that I'd never been able to face before, and we're actually in the process of starting to work through those things, which I never thought I'd be able to do. (Bywaters & Rolfe, 2002, p. 30)

The perceptions of staff behaviour played a major role in satisfaction with aftercare: participants were more satisfied if they felt that the therapist was genuinely concerned about them, respected them and did not try to belittle them (Bywaters & Rolfe, 2002).

Individuals who did not attend their aftercare appointments cited difficulty understanding referral instructions (Dower, Donald, Kelly, & Raphael, 2000), lack of optimism in their recovery (Hume & Platt, 2007), and anxiety over the stigma related to self-harm (Crockwell & Burford, 1995). Those unwilling to use aftercare were more likely to have a history of repeated DSH or feel they were beyond help (Hume & Platt, 2007).

Those that ended treatment early felt they had got all they could get out of it or that the sessions didn't help or cited difficulties with their therapist as the reason for termination (Bywaters & Rolfe, 2002; Dower *et al.*, 2000). One study found service users placed high responsibility on their clinician to 'fix' them (Crockwell & Burford, 1995). Although service users who completed aftercare said that the opportunity to talk to someone about their problems was a valuable aspect of care, many service users found opening up difficult which led to anxiety (Bywaters & Rolfe, 2002; Dower *et al.*, 2000): 'It felt like the counselling was making the self-harm worse, because they want to know every niggly detail to get a full picture. I don't want to go through that again' (Bywaters & Rolfe, 2002, p. 31).

Adolescents

Adolescent participants were generally more positive about their experience of aftercare. Most welcomed the opportunity to talk about the circumstances leading up to their self-harm (Bolger, O'Connor, Malone, & Fitzpatrick, 2004; Burgess, Hawton, & Loveday, 1998). Both parents and adolescents appreciated having a therapist to talk to as it made it easier to discuss difficult subjects. 'It is helpful because there's some stuff you can't really talk about or just having the psychologist there, like having someone else there, there's some stuff that I could talk to my mum about that I couldn't talk to her one on one' (Hood, 2006, p. 103).

However, the success of aftercare involving family participation was dependent on the relationship between the adolescent and his or her family members. Several service users explained that they felt stifled by their family's presence (Hood, 2006, p. 103): 'I just wouldn't be able to say that whole thing because I didn't want my parents to know.'

Family therapy also made some adolescents anxious when divorced or separated parents and family members were in attendance. These adolescents found it difficult to participate while worrying about family tensions, although these would often be common goals or material for therapy.

Clinical care implications

Increased and improved communication between service staff and those who self-harm   Satisfaction is increased by allowing service users to take responsibility for their care. This may be achieved by keeping them abreast of their physical and mental status, providing treatment options, and explaining procedures and the reasons for using them. These explanations about treatment should be provided in lay terms. Adolescent service users also suggested including service users in planning provision and service design.

Greater staff knowledge of self-harm and how to deal with patients after a DSH episode   Better information and specific training on how to deal with DSH patients might increase professionals' understanding and interactions with self-harm patients. Staff working with adolescent service users should receive specialized training specific to adolescent needs.

Increased empathy towards those who self-harm   Respondents' perceptions of staff were important to their engagement with and perception of care. Therefore, the relationship between client and clinician is an important measure of the quality of care. Positive experiences were associated with staff who participants felt were kind, respectful and non-judgemental.

Improved access to local services and aftercare   Respondents highlighted the need for more mental health professionals working in hospitals and local facilities to decrease waiting times. Many study participants were unaware of local services that provide support to individuals who self-harm. They often urged professionals to provide patients with more information about local formal support services and how to contact them (Brophy, 2006; Bywaters & Rolfe, 2002).

Participants felt that it was essential that services be as accessible as possible by being staffed 24 hours a day and providing walk-in services (Bywaters & Rolfe, 2002). It was also suggested that services offer alternatives to hospital, such as having nurses working in the community who can treat self-inflicted wounds (Brophy, 2006; Bywaters & Rolfe, 2002). Adolescents suggested locating facilities centrally and providing telephone services.

Provision of better information about self-harm for patients, carers, and the general public
Individuals who self-harm do not always understand what is happening to them or why they do it. Furthermore, because DSH is highly stigmatized, many people may feel they are alone. Many service users suggested that more information be provided to them about self-harm and its prevalence.

Support and information for carers was also suggested by DSH patients and their friends and families (Bywaters & Rolfe, 2002). Better information for the general public was also called for to help alleviate some of the stigmatization faced by individuals who self-harm (Bywaters & Rolfe, 2002).

What can be Learned from Studies of Staff Attitudes to DSH Patients?

There is a general impression that individuals who self-harm are unpopular with health service staff and are challenging to manage, especially in non-psychiatric settings (Holdsworth, Belshaw, & Murray, 2001). The attitudes held by clinical staff towards people who harm themselves, together with their knowledge about self-harm, are likely to influence their clinical practice and the experiences and outcomes of those they treat. The study of staff attitudes towards those who self-harm gained momentum in the early to mid-1970s, when it became apparent that generally negative attitudes characterized medical staff in A&E departments and elsewhere in hospitals, who were frequently the first point of contact for the patient on admission to hospital.

We have reviewed studies of staff attitudes towards those who self-harm in order to establish:

(i)   the nature and prevalence of staff attitudes to those who self-harm;
(ii) staff knowledge and understanding of self-harm;
(iii) the influence of staff characteristics, patient characteristics, and social and cultural contexts, on attitudes towards DSH patients and understanding of the behaviour; and
(iv) the impact of training on staff attitudes and knowledge.

General attitudes

The majority of studies described staff attitudes as negative. For example, Patel (1975) found that, in general, staff did not consider self-poisoning patients satisfying to treat or nurse, and that more hostility and less sympathy was felt towards these patients than those suffering from other physical illness. In general, participants in this study did not view self-harm as being related to mental illness. Several papers have reported derogatory and critical comments being expressed about those who self harm. 'Why does he never do it right and save us a lot of trouble?' (the majority of nurses in the study sample had heard this statement being expressed) (McLaughlin, 1997).

The perception of DSH as a self-inflicted problem may contribute to staff attitudes that DSH patients are less deserving than others, not least because they take away resources meant for those with physical illness.

> Staff often see self-harmers as time-wasters, and don't understand the feelings of despair, lone-
> liness, and guilt. I think resources are becoming tighter and tighter and maybe this affects the

way that staff act. Beds being used by people who deliberately self-harm are not available to 'real' patients. They think that self-harmers do not deserve to be there. (Hemmings, 1999)

DSH patients are also described as being manipulative and '*attention-seeking*', although there is some evidence that a distinction is drawn between patients perceived to have self-harmed for '*manipulative*' reasons, and those whose act genuinely represents despair ('depressive' motives), with more sympathy for the latter (Ramon, Bancroft, & Skrimshire, 1975).

Emotional reactions

Irritation and anger are the two emotions most commonly reported by staff when confronted by a DSH patient. 'You think that they're troublesome, time-consuming, and are on the ward unnecessarily, which is for physically sick people who really need the acute care' (Wolk-Wasserman, 1985).

Feelings of powerlessness, particularly in dealing with those who repeatedly self-harm, were common:

> I sometimes feel helpless when dealing with people who self-harm. What can I really do for them? I sometimes get frustrated and feel that they are wasting ambulance time when the same people are being brought to hospital again and again and nothing seems to be done for them. (Palmer *et al.*, 2006)

This can lead to a sense of frustration and lack of accomplishment, particularly by those who feel that they lack adequate skill in dealing with DSH patients (Herron, Ticehurst, Appleby, Perry, & Cordingley, 2001; Pallikkathayil & Morgan, 1988). A sense of fear and insecurity is frequently reported, particularly regarding future suicide risk. 'I'm frightened a lot about the thought that some time one of them will succeed in taking their own life' (Wilstrand, Lindgren, Gilje, & Olofsson, 2007, p. 74).

However, many studies also reveal that a proportion of staff do feel genuine sympathy for at least some DSH patients. This is particularly the case if the patient has a mental illness, obvious social problems, seeks help or if staff can identify with the patient, their family, or friends. 'I clearly see a human being before me ... who has been desperate and who cannot find anything better to do, who cannot solve his or her problems in any other way' (Wolk-Wasserman, 1985).

Knowledge and understanding of DSH

General understanding of DSH and the motivation of patients who self-harm varied widely between studies. In a large recent study of emergency medical and psychiatric personnel, 85% stated they felt they could understand why a patient might self-harm (Palmer *et al.*, 2006). In other studies, relieving tension, self-punishment, and seeking attention are cited as possible reasons (Friedman, Newton, Coggan, Hooley, Patel, *et al.*, 2006). As might be expected, psychiatrists have greater levels of knowledge than non-psychiatric doctors and nurses (Crawford, Geraghty, Street, & Simonoff, 2003). In a study using case vignettes of DSH patients, understanding of DSH in medical doctors and nurses was positively correlated with sympathy and readiness to help (Ramon *et al.*, 1975).

The risk of suicide following DSH is often underestimated. In one study, only half of staff agreed that patients who self-cut should be considered at risk of suicide (Friedman *et al.*, 2006). A common belief appeared to be that those who are serious about suicide rarely mention their intention to anyone, which may lead to those expressing suicidal thoughts and plans not being taken seriously (Sidley & Renton, 1996).

Variation in attitude by staff characteristics

Medical nurses generally express more sympathy towards and readiness to help DSH patients than physicians (Ramon *et al.*, 1975), and are more likely to view the DSH patients' actions as being appropriate to their situation (Platt & Salter, 1987). Medical doctors were found to express more hostility (Patel, 1975), higher levels of irritation, less personal optimism, and less willingness to help than medical nurses (Mackay & Barrowclough, 2005), although they were more likely than nurses to perceive that they have the necessary skills to care for DSH patients (Mackay & Barrowclough, 2005). Doctors tended to attribute 'manipulative' motives, whereas nurses assign depressive or escape motives to patients who self-harm (Ramon *et al.*, 1975).

Mental health clinicians appear to have a more positive attitude towards DSH patients than those working in emergency medicine (Commons Treloar & Lewis, 2008). Psychiatrists expressed more sympathetic attitudes towards this patient group than physicians (Hawton, Marsack, & Fagg, 1981), and were more likely to find DSH patients rewarding and challenging to care for and to impute suicidal motivation (Platt & Salter, 1987). Staff with psychiatric training were more likely to view some overdoses as being justified, to have an initial reaction which was sympathetic, and feel that more time should be spent talking to the DSH patient (O'Brien & Stoll, 1977). Medical nurses were more likely than psychiatrists to perceive DSH as attention-seeking behaviour (Platt & Salter, 1987).

The nature of the workplace also appears to be important, with the most negative attitudes prevailing in the emergency departments of general hospitals and more positive attitudes in intensive care units and psychiatric hospitals (de Rose & Page, 1985).

The association between personal characteristics such as religion, gender, or age and attitude towards those who self-harm is less clear; the findings of studies tend to be contradictory. Staff with greater experience feel more capable of caring for this patient group, although whether attitudes become more or less positive with increased experience is less clear (Samuelsson, Asberg, & Gustavsson, 1997).

Influence of patient characteristics on staff attitudes

The influence of the gender and age of a patient upon staff attitudes is unclear, although there is a suggestion that women who self-harm are seen as being less likely to complete suicide in the future (Bailey, 1994), and that suicide risk may be underestimated in the young (Lönqvist & Suokas-Muje, 1986).

A much more consistent finding was the strongly negative attitudes expressed towards patients who repeatedly self-harmed, with one study, for example, reporting that 59% of participants agreed that they were intolerant of DSH patients with multiple admissions (Palmer *et al.*, 2006). Two-thirds of general hospital staff stated that they felt more sympathetic to those patients presenting for the first time with DSH than repeaters (Bailey, 1994). Those who repeat were likely to be seen as being manipulative:

> I think the patients who self-harm repeatedly tend to cause a sense of frustration and failure in staff who care for them … it feels that we are just patching them up and not solving anything. (Samuelsson, Sunbring, Winell, & Asberg, 1997)

Conversely, patients who make a serious attempt on their life, judged by lethality of the method and circumstances of the act, are regarded with more sympathy: 'I find I deliver more sincere care to the individuals who appear to be genuine in an attempt to take their life' (Mackay & Barrowclough, 2005).

The degree to which patients are perceived as being responsible for their actions appears to influence the level of sympathy they elicit. Reduced responsibility was attributed to those who were clearly mentally ill (Crawford, Turnbull, & Wessely, 1998) and to those with problems seen as being out of their control (May, 2001).

Effect of training on staff attitudes

Education about DSH in general, and training in how to manage DSH patients, was consistently found to result in more positive attitudes, increased self-rated confidence in dealing with these patients, and improvements in knowledge and understanding leading to more accurate assessments (Pallikkathayil & Morgan, 1988; Samuelsson *et al.*, 1997). Studies which have examined persistence of these attitudes demonstrate that benefit was maintained over time (Smith, 2002).

Following training, more individuals reported feeling that they had the necessary skills to play their part in the assessment and treatment of DSH patients, and better equipped to handle patients at risk of suicide (Palmer *et al.*, 2006). The single study that failed to show improvement following training only made use of a notice board and information folder in the emergency department (May, 2001), suggesting a more formal and interactive approach is required for training to be successful in changing attitudes.

Improving staff attitudes

Several studies highlighted requests from staff for specific training in the management of DSH, and for emphasis to be placed on it in both medical and nursing undergraduate education (Palmer *et al.*, 2006). Requests for more available advice and support were also made: 'Services may be improved by having nurses who specialize in helping manage the frequent A&E attendees' (Creed & Pfeffer, 1981).

Improved support structures for staff who deal with DSH patients, including the opportunity for debriefing following specific events and clinical supervision, were highlighted as being of potential benefit.

Separation of DSH patients from other patients was a common theme, with specialist wards (or at least designated areas within a ward) proposed as a way of better meeting the needs of this patient group. A&E departments were widely recognized as being a non-ideal environment in which to hold and treat DSH patients, with particular concerns raised regarding privacy for assessments and lack of adequate time to spend talking to these patients in this busy environment. 'Staff are usually too busy to give much attention to this client group which surely can't be good if they are feeling suicidal', and 'The environment is not conducive to their needs, there is a lack of privacy' (Palmer *et al.*, 2006).

Few thought subsequent admission to general medical wards was helpful, suggesting instead the use of specialist wards with staff specifically trained in the management of DSH patients.

Implications

There is a clear need to improve professional attitudes towards individuals who self-harm, particularly towards those individuals who do so repeatedly, or with little suicidal intent. Access for general hospital staff to formal training about self-harm, better supervision, and more ready access to psychiatric support is likely to be the most effective way of achieving this.

What do we Know about Effectiveness of Psychosocial and Physical Treatments for DSH Patients?

People who have self-harmed face a range of problems. This means that it is unlikely that a single therapeutic approach will be appropriate for all patients. Those with severe mental illness will require intensive psychiatric care, which may need to begin in an in-patient psychiatric setting, especially for those at serious risk of suicide. Some patients will have major alcohol or drug misuse disorders necessitating referral to substance misuse services. A substantial proportion of patients do not come into these categories. Many of these will be facing major psychosocial problems. They are also likely to be experiencing high levels of distress and psychiatric symptoms, which in many cases will amount to psychiatric disorders according to accepted classification systems (Haw *et al.*, 2001). In this section we consider the evidence regarding the efficacy of treatments particularly focused on this group of patients.

Our current knowledge of the evidence is based on a recently completed systematic review conducted within the auspices of the Cochrane Collaboration (Hawton, Taylor, Arensman, Gunnell, Hazell, *et al.*, 2009). This review is an update of an earlier one, in which no convincing evidence was found regarding efficacy of any single treatment approach, although there were some indications that problem-solving therapy might be more effective than treatment as usual or control therapy (Hawton, Arensman, Townsend, Bremner, Feldman, *et al.*, 1998; Townsend, Hawton, Altman, Arensman, Gunnell, *et al.*, 2001).

In the present review, 41 relevant randomized controlled treatment studies (RCTs) were identified. Nearly half of the studies were conducted in the United Kingdom, 10 in the United States, and the remainder in other European countries. Most studies were focused on adults, few on adolescents, and none on older people. There was a large number of categories of treatment, most being psychosocial treatments. Only a few treatment modalities were evaluated in three or more RCTs. These were psychological therapies ($n = 12$), intensive intervention ($n = 3$), telephone contact ($n = 3$), and antidepressant therapy ($n = 3$).

Psychological therapy

Included in this category were studies in which a specific psychological therapy was usually compared with treatment as usual. The psychological treatments were mostly Cognitive Behaviour Therapy (CBT) or problem-solving therapy (which includes CBT principles). These studies were combined in a meta-analysis.

There was some evidence that psychological therapy is associated with greater attendance at treatment sessions. There was reasonably strong evidence that it reduces repetition of DSH. Thus, on the basis of data available from four trials, significantly fewer patients repeated DSH in the first six months after entering therapy; from the results of seven trials there was a near significant reduction in repetition between six and 12 months; combining data from three trials, it was found that significantly fewer patients repeated DSH in the period greater than 12 months after trial entry. Combining data from all 11 trials with information on repetition of DSH produced evidence that the repetition rate at the last point of follow-up was significantly reduced in patients entering psychological therapy. In addition, summing the total number of repeat episodes indicated a far lower mean number of episodes in patients who received psychological therapy (mean 0.9 per patient) compared with those in the control treatment groups (mean 3.18).

Data on suicides were reported for nine studies, with no suicides in five of them. In the other four trials there were fewer suicides in the psychological therapy patients (3/527 versus 8/527 patients), but the difference was not statistically significant. Depression scores were significantly lower in patients allocated to psychological therapy than in the control condition at six months (data from five trials) and 12 months (five trials) after entering the studies. Hopelessness scores and suicidal ideation showed a broadly similar pattern, although based on results of a small number of trials. There were also indications of benefits of psychological treatment for patients' problems and problem-solving skills, but again based on the results of few studies.

Intensive intervention

This category includes studies in which patients in the experimental group had greater access to therapists than those in standard care and where efforts were made to keep in contact with patients through some form of outreach. There were three studies in this group. In one study patients were initially briefly admitted to a psychiatric in-patient unit and then provided with out-patient care (van der Sande, van Rooijen, Buskens, Allart,

Hawton, *et al.*, 1997), in another they were offered appointments, including one at home, regular reminders, and a home visit in case of a missed appointments (Allard, Marshall, & Plante, 1992), and in a third patients were seen by a community health team worker immediately after discharge and a home visit arranged, followed by regular contact with a therapist (Welu, 1977). All comparisons were with usual care. A meta-analysis showed no differences in rates of repetition of DSH between the treatment groups.

Telephone contact

There were three trials in which telephone contact was provided in addition to usual care in order to increase motivation for treatment, provide support, aid management to each participant's care, and help patients identify and access suitable services (Cedereke, Monti, & Ojehagen, 2002; Clarke, Taylor, Watts, Williams, Feldman, *et al.*, 2002; Vaiva, Vaiva, Ducrocq, Meyer, Mathieu, *et al.*, 2006). There was no apparent effect on the proportions of patients repeating DSH.

Antidepressant therapy

The possible effect of treatment with antidepressants has been tested in DSH patients in three trials, none of them conducted very recently. One compared mianserine/normafensine versus placebo, another mianserine versus placebo, and the third paroxetine plus psycho-therapy versus psychotherapy alone (Verkes, van der Mast, Hengeveld, Tuyl, Zwinderman, *et al.*, 1998). There was no evidence of a significant impact of antidepressant therapy on repetition of DSH. In a *post hoc* analysis, patients who were repeaters of DSH but had a prior history of fewer than five episodes at trial entry repeated less often than similar patients who received placebo (Verkes *et al.*, 1998).

Other studies of interest

There have been some other single studies of specific treatment approaches which have produced results which may be of relevance to service and treatment provision.

In a Belgian study in which a nurse followed up at home DSH patients who had not attended an initial out-patient appointment and encouraged them to attend, there was an increased rate of attendance and a near significant lower rate of repetition compared with patients who were only offered out-patient appointments but did not receive a visit from the nurse if they did not attend (van Heeringen, Jennes, Buylaert, Henderick, De Bacquer, *et al.*, 1995). In a study from Germany, DSH patients who were offered aftercare with the same therapist who assessed them in hospital were significantly more likely to attend appoint-ments than those offered aftercare with a different therapist (Torhorst, Moller, Burk, Kurz, Wachtler, *et al.*, 1987). In Australia, a trial was conducted in which DSH patients were routinely sent postcards asking about their welfare, in addition to usual treatment (Carter, Lewin, Stoney, Whyte, & Bryant, 2005; Carter, Child, Page, Clover, & Taylor, 2007).

While this had no apparent benefit when compared with usual care alone in terms of the proportions of patients who repeated DSH, there was a reduced mean number of episodes in the postcards group – a result driven entirely by a difference in a small group of female multiple repeaters.

Providing patients with an emergency contact card giving 24-hour access to emergency telephone advice from a psychiatrist was evaluated in two studies, but did not appear to have greater benefit on repetition than usual care alone (Evans, Tyrer, Catalan, Schmidt, Davidson, *et al.*, 1999; Morgan, Jones, & Owen, 1993). Similarly, where general practition-ers sent DSH patients a letter following discharge from hospital offering an appointment and also received specific advice from hospital staff about aftercare, no advantage compared with routine care was evident (Bennewith, Stocks, Gunnell, Peters, Evans, *et al.*, 2002).

Summary of results of treatment studies

There is now robust evidence that short-term psychological therapy is of benefit for many DSH patients, including a reduction in the risk of repeated self-harm. This should there-fore be available in services. Continuity of care and having a home visit may improve patient attendance at aftercare appointments. It is unclear at present whether outreach using telephone or postcard contact over and above usual care conveys extra benefits.

What do we Know about Variations between Services for DSH Patients?

Clearly there are likely to be major differences between countries in the types of service that are available for DSH patients due to differences in healthcare systems and availability and orientation of mental health services. Differences are, however, also likely to be found within individual countries. Variations in services for DSH patients in England were recently investigated (Bennewith *et al.*, 2004; Bennewith, Peters, Hawton, House, & Gunnell, 2005). The study included 32 general hospitals with A&E departments, randomly selected within eight regions covering the whole country, based on four hospi-tals per region, stratified for self-harm admission rates. In each hospital a prospective eight-week audit of management of self-harm episodes in people aged 18 years and over was conducted and interviews were carried out with hospital staff.

A designated self-harm service was available at 23 of the 32 hospitals. However, at 11 hospitals, more than half the service structures recommended in a national guideline (Royal College of Psychiatrists, 1994) were not in place. Nearly all the hospitals had guide-lines for medical management of self-harm patients but only just over half had guidelines for psychosocial management. Less than half had a self-harm planning group. Routine contact with general practitioners within 24 hours of patients being discharged from emergency departments happened in only half the hospitals.

From the audit of DSH patients there was wide variation in the proportion of patients who received a psychosocial assessment (median 55%; range 36%–82%), were admitted to a medical bed in the hospital (median 42%; range 22%–83%), were admitted to psychiatric in-patient care (median 9.5%; range 2.5%–23.8%), and had mental health service follow-up (median 31%; range 35%–82%). At hospitals without a designated DSH service, assessments of patients were far more likely to be conducted only by junior trainee psychiatrists. Overall, 42% of patients were assessed by a liaison psychiatry/self-harm service nurse.

Factors associated with patients not receiving a psychosocial assessment were younger age, no previous self-harm, and not being admitted to a medical bed. Patients were also less likely to receive an assessment if they presented to hospital between 5 pm and 9 am, a period which includes the peak time for DSH presentations (Bergen & Hawton, 2007), or at weekends.

Summary

Across general hospitals in England, a country with well-developed mental health services and with generally positive policies with regard to service provision for DSH patients, there is a wide variation in the availability and staffing of services. In spite of national guidance that all DSH patients should receive a psychosocial assessment (National Collaborating Centre for Mental Health, 2004; Royal College of Psychiatrists, 1994), this does not happen in many cases. There is wide variation in the extent to which aftercare is provided. Better services are clearly needed in many hospitals. These should facilitate provision of psychosocial assessments and aftercare in a far higher proportion of patients than appears to happen in many hospitals. The situation in the United Kingdom is probably reflected in many other countries.

What Can One Conclude from the Current Evidence about the Most Effective Design and Activities of a Service for Deliberate Self-harm Patients?

The findings of the reviews and specific studies we have discussed and other evidence and guidance (e.g., National Collaborating Centre for Mental Health, 2004) suggest many features that should be included in the design of general hospital and aftercare services for DSH patients. Since the evidence from much of the research literature shows considerable consistency across several countries, our conclusions about service planning are likely to have international relevance.

General hospital services (Box 19.1)

All hospitals should have agreed guidelines for the management of individuals who self-harm, and these should parallel national guidelines in countries where these exist. Formal training should be made available to all hospital staff who regularly treat those who self-harm. Such training should address knowledge, understanding, attitudes, self-awareness, communication, and behaviour. It may also be useful to seek patient contributions to such teaching. Patients should be seen promptly and be invited to play a role in decisions

> **Box 19.1   General hospital services for DSH patients**
>
> Guidelines for acute care.
> Formal training for all staff who treat those who self-harm.
> Designated treatment areas.
> Prompt feedback to patients regarding physical well-being and treatments.
> Involvement of patients in clinical decision-making wherever possible.
> Support and supervision for staff.
> Self-harm planning group.

regarding their medical care. Treatment is likely to be easier in specifically designated areas of the general hospital (e.g., clinical decisions units) where staff can acquire greater experience and confidence in managing this patient group. Explanations about treatment should be provided in simple lay terms that patients can understand. Support and supervision should be available for A&E department and general medical staff to assist them in their management of DSH patients. A self-harm planning group should exist in every hospital and meet at regular intervals. The membership of such a group should involve all relevant parties, including representatives of A&E department staff, psychiatric services, social services, and local community agencies, both statutory (e.g., substance misuse) and non-statutory (e.g., Samaritans). Given the specific needs of under-18s and older adults, those involved in their care should have their own planning groups.

Psychiatric services in the general hospital (Box 19.2)

Psychiatric services should provide a specialist team that takes responsibility for the assessment and management of those who self-harm once they are medically fit to be assessed. The team should be multidisciplinary and all members should receive specific training in the assessment and aftercare of DSH patients. Assessments should take place in a timely manner in a designated room where confidentiality can be preserved. Carers should be involved in assessments, where appropriate, and their needs should also be assessed. The service provided should be as consistent as possible, ensuring that all patients, regardless of what time they present, receive the same standard of care. Regular support and clinical supervision should be made available to all staff in addition to ongoing training and education. Audit of the DSH services against national guidelines (where they exist) may assist ongoing improvement and development of the service.

Aftercare (Box 19.3)

Some form of aftercare should be planned for all patients following an episode of self-harm, regardless of whether specialist input is deemed necessary. Where indicated, psychological treatments in the form of CBT or problem-solving should be readily available.

Box 19.2   Psychiatric services for DSH patients in the general hospital

Specialist DSH services should be available in all major hospitals.
Psychosocial assessment in line with national guidelines.
Multidisciplinary staffing.
Specific training in assessment and aftercare following DSH.
Consistent service 24 hours per day.
All patients should receive a psychosocial assessment.
Minimize waiting times for assessment.
Private area for assessment.
Involvement of carers in assessment.
Regular support and supervision for all staff.
Regular audits.

Box 19.3   Aftercare of DSH patients

Available to all patients.
Emergency phone access.
Psychological treatment.
Continuity of care where possible.
Support and information for carers.
Involvement of service users in planning aftercare.
Timely follow-up.
Specific services for adolescents and for older adults.

There is some evidence that outreach via home visits, postal, or phone contact may be effective. Continuity of care is preferable, where feasible. As far as is possible patient input into treatment decisions should be sought and carers should be provided with support and information. Any aftercare provided should take place within a reasonable time period. Specific aftercare arrangements should be in place for adolescents, with particular focus on family support and involvement.

Conclusions

In many hospitals patients who present to general hospital following intentional self-poisoning or self-injury represent a relatively neglected patient group. Yet their needs are considerable and their risk of future suicidal behaviour is elevated. Fortunately, the development of national suicide prevention strategies in many countries has helped focus more attention on these patients. There is now considerable evidence on which to base planning of services and care for them. We have used evidence from reviews of studies of patients' attitudes, staff attitudes, and effectiveness of treatments, as well as specific individual research studies, to indicate some of the factors that should be considered in the development of services. Clearly there will be other specific needs determined by local conditions and resources, but the key points and principles that we have highlighted should be relevant in most circumstances.

References

Allard, R., Marshall, M., & Plante, M. C. (1992). Intensive follow-up does not decrease the risk of repeat suicide attempts. *Suicide and Life-Threatening Behavior, 22*, 303–314.

Bailey, S. (1994). Critical care nurses' and doctors' attitudes to parasuicide patients. *The Australian Journal of Advanced Nursing, 11*, 11–16.

Bennewith, O., Gunnell, D., Peters, T., Hawton, K., & House, A. (2004). Variations in the hospital management of self-harm in adults in England: observational study. *British Medical Journal, 328*, 1108–1109.

Bennewith, O., Peters, T. J., Hawton, K., House, A., & Gunnell, D. (2005). Factors associated with the non-assessment of self-harm patients attending an Accident and Emergency Department: Results of a national study. *Journal of Affective Disorders, 89*, 91–97.

Bennewith, O., Stocks, N., Gunnell, D., Peters, T. J., Evans, M. O., & Sharp, D. J. (2002). General practice based intervention to prevent repeat episodes of deliberate self-harm: Cluster randomised controlled trial. *British Medical Journal, 324*, 1254–1257.

Bergen, H. & Hawton, K. (2007). Variations in time of hospital presentation for deliberate self-harm and their implications for clinical services. *Journal of Affective Disorders, 98*, 227–237.

Bolger, S., O'Connor, P., Malone, K., & Fitzpatrick, C. (2004). Adolescents with suicidal behaviour: Attendance at A&E and six-month follow-up. *Irish Journal of Psychological Medicine, 21*, 78–84.

Brophy, M. (2006). *Truth Hurts: Report of the National Inquiry into Self-harm among Young People.* London: Mental Health Foundation.

Burgess, S., Hawton, K., & Loveday, G. (1998). Adolescents who take overdoses: Outcome in terms of changes in psychopathology and the adolescents' attitudes to care and to their overdose. *Journal of Adolescence, 21*, 209–218.

Bywaters, P. & Rolfe, A. (2002). *Look Beyond the Scars: Understanding and responding to self-injury and self-harm.* London: NCH.

Carrigan, J. T. (1994). The psychosocial needs of patients who have attempted suicide by overdose. *Journal of Advanced Nursing, 20*, 635–642.

Carter, G. L., Child, C., Page, A., Clover, K., & Taylor, R. (2007). Modifiable risk factors for attempted suicide in Australian clinical and community samples. *Suicide and Life-Threatening Behavior, 37*, 671–680.

Carter, G. L., Lewin, T. J., Stoney, C., Whyte, I. M., & Bryant, J. L. (2005). Clinical management for hospital-treated deliberate self-poisoning: comparisons between patients with major depression and borderline personality disorder. *Australian and New Zealand Journal of Mental Health Nursing, 39*, 266–273.

Cedereke, M., Monti, K., & Ojehagen, A. (2002). Telephone contact with patients in the year after a suicide attempt: does it affect treatment attendance and outcome? A randomised controlled study. *European Psychiatry, 17*, 82–91.

Clarke, T., Taylor, T., Watts, C. J., Williams, K., Feldman, R. A., & Sherr, L. (2002). Self-harm in adults: A randomised controlled trial of nurse-led case management versus routine care only. *Journal of Mental Health*, *11*, 167–176.

Commons Treloar, A. J., & Lewis, A. J. (2008). Professional attitudes towards deliberate self-harm in patients with borderline personality disorder. *Australian and New Zealand Journal of Mental Health Nursing*, *42*, 578–584.

Crawford, M. J., Turnbull, G., & Wessely, S. (1998). Deliberate self-harm assessment by accident and emergency staff – An intervention study. *Journal of Accident and Emergency Medicine*, *15*, 18–22.

Crawford, T., Geraghty, W., Street, K., & Simonoff, E. (2003). Staff knowledge and attitudes towards deliberate self-harm in adolescents. *Journal of Adolescence*, *26*, 623–633.

Creed, F. H. & Pfeffer, J. M. (1981). Attitudes of house-physicians towards self-poisoning patients. *Medical Education*, *15*, 340–345.

Critical Appraisal Skills Programme (2002). *10 Questions to Help You Make Sense of Qualitative Research*. Milton Keynes: Milton Keynes Primary Care Trust.

Crockwell, L. & Burford, G. (1995). What makes the difference? Adolescent females' stories about their suicide attempts. *Journal of Child and Youth Care*, *10*, 1–14.

Department of Health (2002). *National Suicide Prevention Strategy for England*. London: Department of Health.

de Rose, N. & Page, S. (1985). Attitudes of professional and community groups toward male and female suicide. *Canadian Journal of Community Mental Health*, *4*, 51–64.

Dower, J., Donald, M., Kelly, B., & Raphael, B. (2000). *Pathways to Care for Young People who Present for Non-fatal Deliberate Self-harm*. Queensland: School of Population Health, The University of Queensland.

Evans, K., Tyrer, P., Catalan, J., Schmidt, U., Davidson, K., Dent, J., Thornton, S., Barber, J., & Thompson, S. (1999). Manual-assisted cognitive-behaviour therapy (MACT): A randomized controlled trial of a brief intervention with bibliotherapy in the treatment of recurrent deliberate self-harm. *Psychological Medicine*, *29*, 19–25.

Friedman, T., Newton, C., Coggan, C., Hooley, S., Patel, R., Pickard, M., & Mitchell, A. J. (2006). Predictors of A&E staff attitudes to self-harm patients who use self-laceration: Influence of previous training and experience. *Journal of Psychosomatic Research*, *60*, 273.

Gunnell, D. J., Peters, T. J., Kammerling, R. M., & Brooks, J. (1995). Relation between parasuicide, suicide, psychiatric admissions, and socioeconomic deprivation 30. *British Medical Journal*, *311*, 226–230.

Haw, C., Hawton, K., Houston, K., & Townsend, E. (2001). Psychiatric and personality disorders in deliberate self-harm patients. *British Journal of Psychiatry*, *178*, 48–54.

Hawton, K., Arensman, E., Townsend, E., Bremner, S., Feldman, E., Goldney, R. Gunnell, D., Hazell, P., van Heeringen, K., House, A., Owens, D., Sakinofsky, I., & Träskman-Bendz, L. (1998). Deliberate self-harm: Systematic review of efficacy of psychosocial and pharmacological treatments in preventing repetition. *British Medical Journal*, *317*, 441–447.

Hawton, K., Bergen, H., Casey, D., Simkin, S., Palmer, B., Cooper, J., Kapur, N., Horrocks, J., House, A., Lilley, R., Noble, R., & Owens, D. (2007). Self-harm in England: A tale of three cities. Multicentre study of self-harm. *Social Psychiatry and Psychiatric Epidemiology*, *42*, 513–521.

Hawton, K. & Harriss, L. (2008). Deliberate self-harm by under-15-year-olds: Characteristics, trends and outcome. *Journal of Child Psychology and Psychiatry*, *49*, 441–448.

Hawton, K., Harriss, L., Hodder, K., Simkin, S., & Gunnell, D. (2001). The influence of the economic and social environment on deliberate self-harm and suicide: An ecological and person-based study 21. *Psychological Medicine*, *31*, 827–836.

Hawton, K., Harriss, L., & Zahl, D. (2006). Deaths from all causes in a long-term follow-up study of 11,583 deliberate self-harm patients. *Psychological Medicine*, *36*, 397–405.

Hawton, K., Marsack, P., & Fagg, J. (1981). The attitudes of psychiatrists to deliberate self-poisoning: Comparison with physician and nurses. *British Journal of Medical Psychology, 54,* 341–348.

Hawton, K., Taylor, T., Arensman, E., Gunnell, D., Hazell, P., Townsend, E., *et al.* (2009). Psychosocial and pharmacological treatments for deliberate self-harm. *Cochrane Database of Systematic Reviews* (Submitted).

Hawton, K., Zahl, D., & Weatherall, R. (2003). Suicide following deliberate self-harm: Long-term follow-up of patients who presented to a general hospital. *British Journal of Psychiatry, 182,* 537–542.

Health Service Executive, the National Suicide Review Group & Department of Health and Children (2005). *Reach Out: National strategy for action on suicide prevention 2005–2014.* Dublin: Health Service Executive.

Hemmings, A. (1999). Attitudes to deliberate self-harm among staff in an accident and emergency team. *Mental Health Care, 2,* 300–302.

Hengeveld, M. W., Kerkhof, A. J. F. M., & van der Wal, J. (1988). Evaluation of psychiatric consultations with suicide attempters. *Acta Psychiatrica Scandinavica, 77,* 283–289.

Herron, J., Ticehurst, H., Appleby, L., Perry, A., & Cordingley, L. (2001). Attitudes toward suicide prevention in front-line health staff. *Suicide and Life-Threatening Behavior, 31,* 342–347.

Holdsworth, N., Belshaw, D., & Murray, S. (2001). Developing A&E nursing responses to people who deliberately self-harm: The provision and evaluation of a series of reflective workshops. *Journal of Psychiatric and Mental Health Nursing, 8,* 449–458.

Hood, A. (2006). Improving outcomes for suicidal individuals. Ph.D. thesis, Department of Psychology, University of Auckland, Auckland.

Horrocks, J., Hughes, J., Martin, C., House, A., & Owens, D. (2005). *Patient Experiences of Hospital Care following Self-harm: A qualitative study.* Leeds: University of Leeds.

Hume, M. & Platt, S. (2007). Appropriate interventions for the prevention and management of self-harm: A qualitative exploration of service-users' views. *BMC Public Health, 7,* Art. 9.

Kapur, N., House, A., Creed, F., Feldman, E., Friedman, T., & Guthrie, E. (1998). Management of deliberate self-poisoning in adults in four teaching hospitals: Descriptive study. *British Medical Journal, 316,* 831–832.

Linehan, M. M. (1987). Dialectical behavior therapy for borderline personality disorder. Theory and method. *Bulletin of the Menninger Clinic, 51,* 261–276.

Lönqvist, J. & Suokas-Muje, J. (1986). Staff's attitudes toward patients who attempt suicide. *Crisis, 7,* 47–53.

Mackay, N. & Barrowclough, C. (2005). Accident and emergency staff's perceptions of deliberate self-harm: Attributions, emotions and willingness to help. *British Journal of Clinical Psychology, 44,* 255–267.

MacLeod, A. K., Tata, P., Tyrer, P., Schmidt, U., Davidson, K., & Thompson, S. (2005). Hopelessness and positive and negative future thinking in parasuicide. *British Journal of Clinical Psychology, 44,* 495–504.

Madge, N., Hewitt, A., Hawton, K., de Wilde, E. J., Corcoran, P., Fekete, S., van Heeringen, K., De Leo, D., & Ystgaard, M. (2008). Deliberate self-harm within an international community sample of young people: Comparative findings from the Child & Adolescent Self-harm in Europe (CASE) Study. *Journal of Child Psychology and Psychiatry, 49,* 667–677.

Mann, J. J. (2003). Neurobiology of suicidal behaviour. *Nature Reviews Neuroscience, 4,* 819–828.

May, V. (2001). Attitudes to patients who present with suicidal behaviour. *Emergency Nurse, 9,* 26–32.

McLaughlin, C. (1997). The effect of classroom theory and contact with patients on the attitudes of student nurses towards mentally ill people. *Journal of Advanced Nursing, 26,* 1221–1228.

Ministry of Health New Zealand (2006). *The New Zealand Suicide Prevention Strategy 2006–2016.* Wellington: Ministry of Health New Zealand.

Morgan, H. G., Jones, E. M., & Owen, J. H. (1993). Secondary prevention of non-fatal deliberate self-harm. The green card study. *British Journal of Psychiatry, 163,* 111–112.

National Collaborating Centre for Mental Health (2004). *Clinical Guideline 16. Self-harm: The short-term physical and psychological management and secondary prevention of self-harm in primary and secondary care.* London: National Institute for Clinical Excellence.

O'Brien, S. E. & Stoll, K. A. (1977). Attitudes of medical and nursing staff towards self-poisoning patients in a London hospital. *International Journal of Nursing Studies, 14,* 29–35.

Owens, D., Horrocks, J., & House, A. (2002). Fatal and non-fatal repetition of self-harm: Systematic review. *British Journal of Psychiatry, 181,* 193–199.

Pallikkathayil, L. & Morgan, S. (1988). Emergency department nurses' encounters with suicide attempters: A qualitative investigation. *Scholarly Inquiry for Nursing Practice, 2,* 237–253.

Palmer, L., Strevens, P., & Blackwell, H. (2006). *Better Services for People Who Self-harm: Data summary – Wave 1 baseline data.* London: Royal College of Psychiatrists.

Patel, A. R. (1975). Attitudes towards self-poisoning. *British Medical Journal, 2,* 426–430.

Platt, S. & Salter, D. (1987). A comparative investigation of health workers' attitudes towards parasuicide. *Social Psychiatry and Psychiatric Epidemiology, 22,* 202–208.

Pollock, L. R. & Williams, J. M. (2004). Problem-solving in suicide attempters. *Psychological Medicine, 34,* 163–167.

Ramon, S., Bancroft, J. H., & Skrimshire, A. M. (1975). Attitudes towards self-poisoning among physicians and nurses in a general hospital. *British Journal of Psychiatry, 127,* 257–264.

Royal College of Psychiatrists (1994). *The General Hospital Management of Adult Self-harm: A consensus statement on standards for service provision* (Council Report CR32). London: Royal College of Psychiatrists.

Samuelsson, M., Asberg, M., & Gustavsson, J. (1997). Attitudes of psychiatric nursing personnel towards patients who have attempted suicide. *Acta Psychiatrica Scandinavica, 95,* 222–230.

Samuelsson, M., Sunbring, Y., Winell, I., & Asberg, M. (1997). Nurses' attitudes to attempted suicide patients. *Scandinavian Journal of Caring Sciences, 11,* 232–237.

Schmidtke, A., Bille-Brahe, U., De Leo, D., Kerkhof, A., Bjerke, T., Crepet, P. Haring, C., Hawton, K., Lönqvist, J., Michel, K., Pommereau, X., Querejeta, I., Phillipe, I., Salander-Renberg, E., Temesváry, B., Wasserman, D., Fricke, S., Weinacker, B., & Sampaio-Faria, J. G. (1996). Attempted suicide in Europe: Rates, trends and sociodemographic characteristics of suicide attempters during the period 1989–1992. Results of the WHO/EURO Multicentre Study on Parasuicide. *Acta Psychiatrica Scandinavica, 93,* 327–338.

Sidley, G. & Renton, J. (1996). General nurses' attitudes to patients who self-harm. *Nursing Standard, 10,* 32–36.

Sinclair, J. M., Gray, A., & Hawton, K. (2006). Systematic review of resource utilization in the hospital management of deliberate self-harm. *Psychological Medicine, 36,* 1681–1693.

Smith, S. E. (2002). Perceptions of service provision for clients who self-injure in the absence of expressed suicidal intent. *Journal of Psychiatric and Mental Health Nursing, 9,* 595–601.

Social Care Institute for Excellence (2006). *Using Qualitative Research in Systematic Reviews: Older people's views of hospital discharge.* London: SCIE.

Suominen, K., Henriksson, M., Suokas, J., Isometsä, E., Ostamo, A., & Lönqvist, J. (1996). Mental disorders and comorbidity in attempted suicide. *Acta Psychiatrica Scandinavica, 94,* 234–240.

Taylor, T., Hawton, K., Fortune, S., & Kapur, N. (2009). Attitudes towards clinical services among people who self-harm: Systematic review. *British Journal of Psychiatry, 194,* 104–110.

Torhorst, A., Moller, H. J., Burk, F., Kurz, A., Wachtler, C., & Lauter, H. (1987). The psychiatric management of parasuicide patients: A controlled clinical study comparing different strategies of outpatient treatment. *Crisis, 8,* 53–61.

Townsend, E., Hawton, K., Altman, D. G., Arensman, E., Gunnell, D., Hazell, P. House, A., & van Heeringen, K. (2001). The efficacy of problem-solving treatments after deliberate self-harm: Meta-analysis of randomized controlled trials with respect to depression, hopelessness and improvement in problems. *Psychological Medicine, 31,* 979–988.

US Department of Health and Human Services (2001). *National Strategy for Suicide Prevention: Goals and objectives for action.* Rockville, Maryland: Public Health Service.

Vaiva, G., Vaiva, G., Ducrocq, F., Meyer, P., Mathieu, D., Philippe, A., Libersa, C., & Goudemand, M. (2006). Effect of telephone contact on further suicide attempts in patients discharged from an emergency department: Randomised controlled study. *British Medical Journal, 332,* 1241–1245.

van der Sande, R., van Rooijen, L., Buskens, E., Allart, E., Hawton, K., van der Graaf, Y., & van Engeland, H. (1997). Intensive in-patient and community intervention versus routine care after attempted suicide. A randomised controlled intervention study. *British Journal of Psychiatry, 171,* 35–41.

van Heeringen. C., Jannes, S., Buylaert, W., Henderick, H., De Bacquer. D., & Van Remoortel, J. (1995). The management of non-compliance with referral to out-patient after-care among attempted suicide patients: A controlled intervention study. *Psychological Medicine, 25,* 963–970.

Verkes, R. J., van der Mast, R. C., Hengeveld, M. W., Tuyl, J. P., Zwinderman, A. H., & van Kempen, G. M. (1998). Reduction by paroxetine of suicidal behavior in patients with repeated suicide attempts but not major depression. *American Journal of Psychiatry, 155,* 543–547.

Welu, T. C. (1977). A follow-up program for suicide attempters: Evaluation of effectiveness. *Suicide and Life-Threatening Behavior, 7,* 17–20.

Wiklander, M., Samuelsson, M., & Asberg, M. (2003). Shame reactions after suicide attempt. *Scandinavian Journal of Caring Sciences, 17,* 293–300.

Williams, J. M. G., Crane, C., Barnhofer, T., & Duggan, D. (2005). Psychology and suicidal behaviour: Elaborating the entrapment model. In K. Hawton (Ed.), *Prevention and Treatment of Suicidal Behaviour: From science to practice* (pp. 71–90). Oxford: Oxford University Press.

Wilstrand, C., Lindgren, B. M., Gilje, F., & Olofsson, B. (2007). Being burdened and balancing boundaries: A qualitative study of nurses' experiences caring for patients who self-harm. *Journal of Psychiatric and Mental Health Nursing, 14,* 72–78.

Wolk-Wasserman, D. (1985). The intensive care unit and the suicide attempt patient. *Acta Psychiatrica Scandinavica, 71,* 581–595.

Zahl, D. L. & Hawton, K. (2004). Repetition of deliberate self-harm and subsequent suicide risk: long-term follow-up study of 11,583 patients. *British Journal of Psychiatry, 185,* 70–75.

CHAPTER TWENTY

After the Suicide Attempt: The Need for Continuity and Quality of Care

Lars Mehlum and Erlend Mork

Abstract

Suicide attempters presenting at general hospitals are a high-risk patient population posing significant challenges to hospital staff and aftercare providers. However, due to lack of knowledge, high work stress, and lack of coordination, clinicians frequently provide insufficient psychosocial assessments and treatments. This is problematic since suicide attempters are well known for their high risk of repeat suicide attempts and completed suicide. Most experts in suicide prevention would regard them as a key target group for preventive interventions and there is room for substantial improvements in this field. Over the years, various treatment approaches to improve the continuity of care have been developed, but with mixed outcomes. Based on experiences from these studies we have formulated a set of recommendations for the clinical management and care of suicide attempters. We propose a set of requirements that seem to be important to ensure continuity of care in defined catchment areas over extended periods of time. We highlight results from some of our own recent studies of the Norwegian chain of care model and provide recommendations for policy and clinical practice.

Introduction

Attempted suicide is a major public health problem in most countries. Not all suicide attempters come to the attention of healthcare services. However, patients who are referred for general hospital treatment after a suicide attempt or non-suicidal self-injurious behaviour

International Handbook of Suicide Prevention: Research, Policy and Practice, First Edition.
Edited by Rory C. O'Connor, Stephen Platt, Jacki Gordon.
© 2011 John Wiley & Sons, Ltd. Published 2011 by John Wiley & Sons, Ltd.

are numerous enough (Doshi, Boudreaux, Wang, Pelletier, & Camargo, 2005; Platt, Bille-Brahe, Kerkhof, Schmidtke, Bjerke, *et al.*, 1992) to represent a significant clinical challenge to the hospitals and their staff who have a responsibility to provide adequate and effective treatment. Hospital services provided for suicide attempters may, however, vary greatly (Kapur, House, May, & Creed, 2003). An additional problem is poor communication between patients and staff, which has been frequently reported in studies examining the experiences of patients seeking help after suicidal behaviour (Taylor, Hawton, Fortune, & Kapur, 2009). Time constraints and work stress may exacerbate problems, facilitating negative staff attitudes towards the patients (Suokas & Lönqvist, 1989). Several studies have also indicated a lack of staff knowledge with regard to suicidal behaviour (Taylor *et al.*, 2009), which may lead to the discharge from hospital of many patients without adequate clinical assessments having been carried out (Bennewith, Peters, Hawton, House, & Gunnell, 2005; Bergen & Hawton, 2007). A British study by Kapur, House, Dodgson, May, and Creed (2002) reported that patients who had been admitted for self-poisoning and who had not received a psychosocial assessment were more likely to poison themselves again. There is reason to believe that, in the long run, these unfavourable conditions may create vicious circles, reducing suicide attempters' willingness to seek services from the healthcare system in the aftermath of a suicidal episode and thus increasing their vulnerability to making further suicide attempts.

Follow-up studies have, indeed, shown that suicide attempters run high risks of repeat suicide attempts and completed suicide during the first year following discharge (Angst, Stassen, Clayton, & Angst, 2002; Goldacre, Seagroatt, & Hawton, 1993; Haw, Bergen, Casey, & Hawton, 2007; Suominen, Isometsa, Suokas, Haukka, Achte, *et al.*, 2004). Improved care for suicide attempters after discharge from hospital has thus been highlighted as an area that should receive a high priority for its considerable suicide prevention potential (Mann, Apter, Bertolote, Beautrais, Currier, *et al.*, 2005). Discharge planning and post-discharge support in the form of integrated follow-up care, usually at home, has been increasingly and successfully used as a cost-effective approach in patient care in other major medical fields, such as treatment of heart failure (Phillips, Wright, Kern, Singa, Shepperd, *et al.*, 2004), care of the elderly (Naylor, Brooten, Campbell, Jacobsen, Mezey, *et al.*, 1999), high-risk pregnancies (Brooten, Roncoli, Finkler, Arnold, Cohen, *et al.*, 1994), and low birth-weight infants (Brooten, Kumar, Brown, Butts, Finkler, *et al.*, 1986). It has also been put into practice within mental health with good results (Glover, Arts, & Babu, 2006). However, it is well known that deficits in such care planning and follow-up support may adversely affect the continuity of general patient care (Kripalani, LeFevre, Phillips, Williams, Basaviah, *et al.*, 2007).

In the field of suicide prevention, the state of affairs is less favourable. Attempts have, indeed, been made to deliver integrated follow-up care programmes, but results have so far been mixed (Crawford, Thomas, Khan, & Kulinskaya, 2007; Hawton, 2005). The scope of this chapter is to provide an overview of the current state of treatments which have shown some efficacy in reducing repetition rates of suicidal behaviour. We will also present recommendations for the aftercare treatment of suicide attempters. We will focus closely on one of the aftercare programmes for which there is some evidence of a reduction in the rate of attempted suicide – a multidisciplinary chain of care system for patients hospitalized after a suicide attempt (Dieserud, Loeb, & Ekeberg, 2000) – and we will present some of our own experiences and studies with this type of follow-up programme. The term 'attempted suicide' is here defined broadly as an acute, non-fatal act of self-harm deliberately carried out with or without suicide intent. This corresponds well to common usage in contemporary clinical settings and to typical definitions of 'deliberate self-harm'.

The Magnitude of the Problem

Presentations to general hospitals after attempted suicide

Despite the fact that suicide attempters have been found to have a strongly increased risk of completed suicide (Owens, Horrocks, & House, 2002), epidemiological data on this group are insufficient (with regard to both quantity and quality) in many nations, settings, and population segments due to differences in definitions and the lack of compulsory registration of suicide attempts (Mittendorfer Rutz & Schmidtke, 2009). With the exception of Ireland, no country has managed to establish a national monitoring system for presentations to healthcare services for attempted suicide. The Irish National Registry of Deliberate Self-Harm, established in 2002, reported that 11,700 deliberate self-harm presentations involving 9,218 individuals were made to hospital emergency departments in Ireland in 2008 (Reulbach & Perry, 2009), representing a rate of 200 per 100,000, which was an increase of 6% from the previous year. There were more presentations among women (223 per 100,000) than among men (180 per 100,000), higher rates among younger people (with a peak rate for women in the 15–19 year age group), and higher rates in cities than in rural districts. Drug overdose was the most common method of self-harm (72%), followed by cutting (21%). Presentations peaked in the hours around midnight and alcohol consumption was very frequently (42%) reported among these patients (Reulbach & Perry, 2009). As will become evident from the following paragraphs the Irish data are consistent with most other hospital-treated self-harm studies.

Scandinavian countries have national patient registers containing information on hospital admissions for attempted suicide, although these registers have not been established specifically for the purpose of monitoring hospital presentations for this type of problem. Kopjar, Dieserud, and Wiik (2005) reported an annual incidence of 120 hospital admissions for intoxication with medical drugs and biological substances per 100,000 in Norway. The incidence was higher among women (144 per 100,000) than men (94 per 100,000) and peaked among women aged 20–24 years.

A number of high quality studies have been conducted in England and Wales, where several local and regional monitoring systems have been in place for extended periods of time. Based on data collected from 31 general hospitals over a study period of eight weeks, Gunnell, Bennewith, Peters, House, and Hawton (2005) were able to report characteristics of 4,033 episodes of self-harm. More episodes involved women (54.8%) than men (45.2%), but the median age (33 years) did not differ by gender. As in Ireland, overdose was by far the most common method of self-harm (79.4%), while cutting was the second most common (11.4%). Presentations for self-harm episodes peaked during the evening and at night.

Apart from these significant exceptions, data on the epidemiology of attempted suicide in different parts of the world have been produced by studies, centres, or clusters of centres with a special interest in this field. Reported incidence rates vary widely from site to site and over time. It is unclear whether these differences are valid or due to variability between studies in their case definitions, research methods, and sampling procedures. To overcome some of these obstacles, in 1989 a group of European centres initiated a multi-centre study of hospital presentations for attempted suicide (parasuicide) using a standardized method-ology. The 16 centres in 13 countries reported varying rates of attempted suicide for women (from 69/100,000 in Spain to 462/100,000 in France) and for men (from 45/100,000 in Spain to 314/100,000 in Finland) (Schmidtke, Bille-Brahe, De Leo, Kerkhof, Bjerke, *et al.*, 1996). Based on data from the Centers for Disease Control, Silverman (2009) reported the incidence of hospitalizations due to intentional self-harm in the United States as approxi-mately 135/100,000 (155/100,000 among women and 110/100,000 among men) in 2006. As in Europe, poisoning was the most frequent method of self-harm.

Based on the above, it is safe to say that presentations to general hospitals for attempted suicide are numerous in most countries, although incidence rates vary widely. Thus, except in small hospitals, hospital staff must be prepared to treat one or more of these patients daily. As we have seen, the patients are often young, have frequently used poisoning as the method of injury, and come to the hospital in the late hours of the evening or at night. Psychiatric disorder, often with a high level of comorbidity, is highly prevalent in suicide attempters presenting to general hospitals (Suominen, Henriksson, Suokas, Isometsa, Ostamo, *et al.*, 1996). Follow-up studies have shown that suicide attempters are at high risk of repeat suicide attempts (Bille-Brahe, Kerkhof, De Leo, Schmidtke, Crepet, *et al.*, 1997; De Leo, Padoani, Lönqvist, Kerkhof, Bille-Brahe, *et al.*, 2002; Hulten, Jiang, Wasserman, Hawton, Hjelmeland, *et al.*, 2001) and completed suicide (Angst *et al.*, 2002; Goldacre *et al.*, 1993; Haw *et al.*, 2007; Suominen *et al.*, 2004), especially during the first year after discharge; this is often linked to their high rate of drop-out from aftercare treat-ment (Haw *et al.*, 2007).

Follow-up Treatments for Suicide Attempters

Attempted suicide and suicidal ideation have, understandably, been included as important outcome variables in many clinical studies, some of which have targeted suicide attempters for treatment and some have not. Below we provide an overview of treatment studies, which include individuals who have had at least one previous suicide attempt. One rela-tively recent systematic review of randomized controlled trials (Crawford *et al.*, 2007) examined whether psychosocial interventions in addition to (or instead of) standard care could reduce subsequent completed suicide. Eighteen studies were found eligible for inclusion with a total population of 3,918 participants. No significant difference in the total rate of suicide was found between the active treatment conditions and among those receiving standard care. The authors concluded that the 'Results of this meta-analysis do not provide evidence that additional psychosocial interventions following self-harm have a marked effect on the likelihood of subsequent suicide' (Crawford *et al.*, 2007, p. 11). This disheartening conclusion should, however, be interpreted with caution. The systematic review consisted of interventions that varied greatly in type of intervention (intervention studies versus treatment studies), population under study, and in the intensity of the intervention. Since the follow-up periods were short and the numbers of suicide deaths in the studies were small, the confidence intervals around the pooled difference in suicide rates were wide. As a consequence, some of these interventions *might* be effective in reducing suicide deaths, and others not. At the current time, we do not know of any additional psychosocial interventions that have proved to be efficacious in reducing subsequent suicide to a larger extent than standard care.

Several systematic or narrative reviews (Crawford & Kumar, 2007; Hawton, 2005; Mann *et al.*, 2005) have examined the effectiveness of psychosocial interventions in reducing *repetition rates of suicide attempts*. Brief structured psychotherapies, more specifically Cognitive Behaviour Therapy (Brown, Ten Have, Henriques, Xie, Hollander, *et al.*, 2005), problem-solving therapy (Salkovskis, Atha, & Storer, 1990), and interpersonal psychotherapy (Guthrie, Kapur, Mackway-Jones, Chew-Graham, Moorey, *et al.*, 2001) have yielded reduced repetition rates of suicide attempts and increased patient adherence to active treatment compared with standard care. Furthermore, several treatments specifically developed for patients with borderline personality disorder with a pattern of repetitive suicide attempts, such as Dialectical Behaviour Therapy (Linehan, Heard, & Armstrong, 1993) and mentalization-based therapy (Bateman & Fonagy, 1999), have proved to be successful in reducing subsequent rates of suicide attempts. Rudd, Williams, and Trotter (2009) highlight some characteristics that appear to be common in treatments that are effective in reducing repetition of suicide attempts: the treatments specifically target suicidal behaviour; they have a system for dealing with poor compliance and motivation; and adopt a safety plan with easy access to treatment in case of crises. Most of the psychotherapeutic interventions described above were not specifically developed for patients presenting to general hospitals after attempted suicide, and they are still not accessible to the majority of suicide attempters. There is, however, reason to believe that several aspects or components of these treatments might be very useful in improving treatment compliance and reducing repetition rates in suicide attempters in the short to medium term (see also Chapter 19, this volume).

Recommended Standards of Care and Aftercare of Suicide Attempters

Since our empirical data on effective treatments are still inadequate in many aspects, uniform and authoritative quality standards of care have been lacking. Nevertheless, there have been many local efforts targeting improvement in the quality and continuity of care for suicide attempters presenting at general hospitals. In several countries these efforts increased in frequency from the early 1990s when suicide attempts treated in hospital were targeted as part of the first wave of national suicide prevention plans (National Research and Development Centre for Welfare and Health, 1993; Nationella rådet för självmordsprevention, 1995; Norwegian Board of Health, 1994; Sundhedsstyrelsen, 1998).

Detailed practice guidelines for the clinical management and aftercare of patients presenting to general hospitals or accident and emergency departments after a suicide attempt have since been issued in several countries (American Psychiatric Association, 2003; Boyce, Carter, Penrose-Wall, Wilhelm, & Goldney, 2003; Norwegian Board of Health, 2001; Royal College of Psychiatrists, 2004). Due to the lack of evidence from empirical studies to guide clinical practice in this field, these guidelines are expert consensus documents based on the challenges and risk factors associated with this patient population and experiences from clinical practice. There is substantial overlap between the different practice guidelines. Key elements include:

(a) *Planning*. All general hospitals or emergency medical centres should have a suicide attempt service planning group or coordinator. The group/coordinator should be responsible for ensuring that practice guidelines are implemented (including establishing the guidelines, training of staff in the contents of the guidelines, and ensuring effective collaboration between all local health organizations to develop properly integrated services) and evaluated.

(b) *Monitoring*. All general hospitals or emergency medical centres should have a monitoring system for suicide attempt-related hospital admissions and plan service provision accordingly.

(c) *Guidelines*. All general hospitals or emergency medical centres should establish written guidelines describing procedures and allocating responsibilities for the management and aftercare of suicide attempters.

(d) *Training*. All general hospitals or emergency medical centres should ensure proper training of all staff before they are allowed to conduct psychosocial assessments and should provide ongoing supervision to clinical staff with the responsibility for conducting these assessments.

(e) *Psychosocial assessment*. All general hospitals or emergency medical centres should ensure that all persons presenting after a suicide attempt are given a systematic psychosocial assessment of needs and risks, including an evidence-based suicide risk assessment.

(f) *Aftercare*. All general hospitals or emergency medical centres should implement an agreed management plan for patients while in hospital, if needed. This usually includes implementation of collaboration between the hospital and aftercare providers, ensuring that aftercare can be established within seven days of discharge.

Of course, even though practice guidelines and standards may have been issued by health authorities and formally adopted by the hospital, it is an empirical question whether these guidelines are really implemented and observed in clinical practice.

Adherence to Recommended Treatment Standards

There are many potential obstacles to efforts aimed at providing treatment in accordance with recommendations. Many patients leave hospital without receiving adequate psychosocial assessments (Bennewith *et al.*, 2005; Bergen & Hawton, 2007). This could be due, in part, to the fact that a substantial proportion of suicide-attempting patients present to general hospitals at night and during the weekend (Bergen & Hawton, 2007; Hickey, Hawton, Fagg, & Weitzel, 2001) when specialist services for suicide attempters often are unavailable. Comparing services delivered at six general hospitals in the United Kingdom, Kapur and colleagues (2003) found that hospital services provided for suicide attempters vary greatly, in terms of whether patients receive specialist psychosocial assessment and whether specific follow-up arrangements are made after the episode. As noted above, psychosocial assessment is an important issue since those not being psychosocially assessed are at greater risk of subsequent repetition of suicide attempts (Hickey *et al.*, 2001; Kapur *et al.*, 2003).

A few studies have aimed specifically at examining national practice guidelines and standards. Based on a postal survey of standards for deliberate self-harm services in National Health Service trusts in England, Slinn, King, and Evans (2001) identified substantial shortcomings. Forty per cent of trusts did not have a policy document covering services for suicide attempters presenting to the hospital and 58% had not established a suicide attempt planning group. Also training and supervision of staff was reported to be below standard. A Dutch study (Verwey, van Waarde, van Rooij, Gerritsen, & Zitman, 2006) found that local clinical guidelines for management of suicide attempt patients were available only at 39% of general hospitals in the Netherlands. When available, the content varied greatly and the quality was deemed unsatisfactory compared with international and national standards. Most of the local guidelines did not address issues of implementation and monitoring and less than half addressed regulations for aftercare.

The Norwegian Chain of Care Model

Targeted improvements in the quality and continuity of care for suicide attempt patients admitted to general hospitals were among the main objectives in the Norwegian National Strategy for Suicide Prevention (Norwegian Board of Health, 1994). At the time this strategy was launched, a chain of care model had been developed in close collaboration between general hospitals and local municipalities and had achieved some positive results, indicating possible relapse preventive effects (Dieserud *et al.*, 2000). This model was therefore recommended for widespread use by the health authorities (Norwegian Board of Health, 1996), and specific guidelines for the clinical management of suicide attempters presenting at general hospitals were issued (Norwegian Board of Health, 2001). Supported by time-limited governmental funding, about 30% of Norwegian general hospitals with an emergency department implemented chain of care programmes in the period 1995–1999 (Mork, Ekeid, Ystgaard, Mehlum, & Holte, 2001). The main components of this nationally recommended chain of care model are: close monitoring of suicide attempt-related hospital admissions; systematic psychosocial and suicide risk in-hospital assessment of suicide attempters; and structured collaboration between hospitals and aftercare providers to ensure that patients receive adequate follow-up treatment. Suicide attempt service teams or coordinators at the hospital and the local municipality level were made responsible for the smooth running of these functions.

Evaluating adherence to the model

After having conducted nationwide interview studies on hospitals' practices both in 1999 and 2006 (Mehlum *et al.*, 2010b; Mork *et al.*, 2001), we reported on quality indicators of the hospital services provided for patients admitted after a suicide attempt and the extent to which hospitals were able to work according to the standards of a chain of care model (Box 20.1).

In both 1999 and 2006 most hospitals had routines for suicide risk assessment of patients hospitalized after suicide attempts and for referral for aftercare treatment. However, only about half of the hospitals reported having a suicide attempt service team or coordinator responsible for the care and follow-up of suicide attempters. These results are only slightly more favourable than those reported in the previously mentioned Dutch and British studies (Slinn *et al.*, 2001; Verwey *et al.*, 2006). Written policy documents, including a quality assurance system (persons responsible for the adherence to guidelines

---

Box 20.1   Quality indicators of general hospital services provided for patients admitted a suicide attempt in Norway

- The hospital has a monitoring system for admissions due to suicide attempts and is able to provide data on last year's number of patients treated after a suicide attempt.
- The hospital has a team or a coordinator responsible for care and follow-up of suicide attempters.
- The hospital has written guidelines for the management and care of suicide attempters.
- The hospital provides regular training of staff in management and care of suicide attempters.
- The hospital provides systematic supervision of staff working with suicide attempters.
- The hospital has structured collaboration with aftercare providers.
- The hospital has a written procedure for clinical suicide risk assessment.
- The hospital staff routinely make suicide risk assessment of suicide attempters.
- The hospital has a specific procedure for training of new personnel in clinical suicide risk assessment.
- The hospital has specific guidelines for follow-up care of suicide attempters after discharge.
- The hospital has a specific procedure for follow-up of patients who have not been assessed for suicide risk.
- The hospital refers at least 90% of suicide attempters for follow-up care after discharge.
- The hospital establishes contact with the aftercare provider(s) no later than the first workday after discharge.

and conducting regular evaluations and revisions of the guidelines), were present in 27% of hospitals in 1999 and in 40% of hospitals in 2006. About half of the hospitals reported having provided training in management and care of suicide attempters within the last three years, but only one-third of hospitals provided systematic training in suicide risk assessment for new staff. A monitoring system for admissions following attempted suicide was present at about one-third of the hospitals.

On the basis of this analysis, it is reasonable to conclude that, despite the clear recommendations by national health authorities, there was still substantial variability in the quality of care indicators between hospitals, similar to what has been reported in other countries (Kapur *et al.*, 2003; Slinn *et al.*, 2001; Verwey *et al.*, 2006).

Sustainability of quality over time

In the search for possible explanations of the seemingly widespread difficulty of adhering to quality standards in the clinical management of suicide attempters presenting to general hospitals, many factors have been considered. After scrutinizing numerous reports from hospitals and chain of care projects throughout the country, we conclude that typical barriers are organizational change, downsizing, change of leadership, and loss of key personnel. These factors may, over time, negatively influence standards and routines for clinical management at hospitals and their emergency departments. We found some evidence for such an effect in a recent 10-year catchment area study where a significant increase in re-admission rates was observed following a major organizational change (Mehlum *et al.*, 2010a). This observed increase could not be explained by changes in socio-demographic or clinical patient characteristics.

To explore the issue of long-term sustainability of quality standards in the chain of care for suicide attempters, we used interview data from our nationwide study (Mehlum *et al.*, 2010b). These data, collected at two time points (1999 and 2006) for each hospital (87% of all general hospitals in Norway), allowed us to investigate which aspects of hospital quality of care standards were most robust against deterioration over time, and which characteristics of hospital practice predict a high quality level in the long run. We found that hospitals which had provided staff with training in management and care of suicide attempters *and* had established written guidelines for the clinical management of suicide attempters in 1999 were significantly more likely to have quality standards more in accordance with the national recommendations in 2006 than hospitals which had neither or only one of these quality indicators in 1999. Educating and updating staff in clinical management of suicide attempters and in assessment skills have been emphasized as important suicide preventive measures in several recent reviews (Links & Hoffman, 2005; Mann *et al.*, 2005). This is all the more important since standardized questionnaires and/or interviews developed for the purpose of evaluating suicide intent and suicide risk have so far not been able to predict suicide more effectively than clinical evaluations. The good clinical interview thus remains the gold standard in suicide risk assessment and it is very important that clinical staff are adequately trained in the use of the clinical interview on this subject.

In a second longitudinal interview-based study we collected data from community health services in a stratified sample (*n* = 47) of municipalities in Norway and found that a chain of care structure was present in only 32% (15 of 47) of municipalities (Mork, Mehlum, Fadum, & Rossow, 2009). This study highlighted several factors at the hospital level that could potentially contribute to a chain of care structure in the community health services in the hospital's catchment area: community health services with a chain of care structure were significantly more likely to be situated in the catchment area of a hospital that had implemented a chain of care programme in the 1990s than community health services that did not have such a structure (80% versus 31%). Furthermore, maintaining a structured collaboration with aftercare providers (both in 1999 and 2006) and having a team or a coordinator in the hospital (both in 1999 and 2006) were highly predictive of the presence or absence of a chain of care structure in the community health services in 2006 (Mork *et al.*, 2009). A significantly higher likelihood of having a chain of care structure was also observed for community health services collaborating with hospitals that had written guidelines with a quality assurance system, training and systematic supervision of staff, and routinely gave patients information about available aftercare providers/services during discharge in both 1999 and 2006.

Our studies of quality standards across hospitals and local communities have the advantage of being nationwide, multi-level, and longitudinal, using uniform measurements which facilitate comparison. A limitation to these studies is the lack of patient data. We rely instead on key informants among staff at local hospitals and their account of the quality of care delivered to patients. We do not know whether our findings would be similar or different if assessments had been patient-based.

Conclusions and Recommendations for Policy and Clinical Practice

The results of the studies we have reviewed suggest that interventions aimed at establishing written local policy guidelines and giving regular training of staff in the psychosocial assessment and management of patients admitted to general hospitals following a suicide attempt are important for maintaining a high level of quality of care over extended periods of time in the face of barriers (noted above). Several recent reviews have also emphasized the importance of educating and updating staff in the clinical management of suicide attempters and in assessment skills as important suicide preventive measures (Links & Hoffman, 2005; Mann *et al.*, 2005). Interventions such as these might appear to be inexpensive and easy to implement. However, they require awareness in managers and staff of the severity and magnitude of the problem and a will to maintain focus on the problem over extended periods of time. Our finding of an interaction effect between 'training of staff' and 'written guidelines, including a quality assurance system' indicates that it could be of relatively little benefit to train staff if there are no guidelines clarifying the responsibilities of different members of staff with respect to the clinical management and care of suicide attempters and ensuring that treatment is provided according to quality standards.

The maintenance of a system for monitoring patients presenting for suicide attempts at general hospitals is an important basis for making systematic evaluations of the quality of care by clinicians, hospital managers, planners, and the ongoing development of services (see Hawton, Bale, Casey, Shepherd, Simkin, *et al.*, 2006). Such a system might also be necessary for sustaining managers' and staff's awareness and motivation. Monitoring could also be useful for clinicians in order to follow trends in suicidal behaviours in their catchment area population. Nevertheless, the majority of hospitals appear to have difficulty in establishing and maintaining such a monitoring system by themselves. Hence, there may be a need for national or regional initiatives to coordinate this type of work. Such initiatives would do well to learn from the Irish example (Reulbach & Perry, 2009).

Maintaining good collaboration within the hospital and with providers of aftercare for suicide attempters seems to be important in order to maintain a successful chain of care over time, as indicated by our studies of community health services (Mork *et al.*, 2009). It is noteworthy that this particular element of the chain of care model seemed to be most closely associated with the observed rate reduction in attempted suicides in the catchment area under study by Dieserud and coworkers (2000). This is a relatively inexpensive type of intervention, estimated to cost community healthcare approximately one person-year (specialist nurse) per 100,000 inhabitants, taking into account all labour costs (Dieserud, Loeb, & Ekeberg, 2001). We are unaware of any cost-effectiveness studies on this type of intervention model. We would argue, however, that the potential savings in terms of reduced human suffering and use of in-patient treatments are substantial.

It seems that we are still only at the beginning of developing and evaluating effective treatments and ways of combining interventions and contributions from different specialists, clinical units, and providers of healthcare to create a cohesive chain of care for suicide attempters. We have highlighted the many clinical challenges and methodological problems in building our knowledge base. There is certainly a need for studies that can address the content and structure of treatment programmes and their theoretical underpinnings. More studies at both system and patient outcome levels are needed to improve our understanding of what works and for whom. In future studies, however, it will be important to select the specific outcomes with care. If some of our interventions aim to increase suicidal patients' access to emergency treatments when in crisis and help them to use health services more adequately, it may be necessary to reconsider the assumption that if more patients present for treatment, then this is a negative outcome. To seek treatment may be lifesaving and, for some patients, it might represent improvement rather than relapse.

References

American Psychiatric Association (2003). Practice guideline for the assessment and treatment of patients with suicidal behavior. *American Journal of Psychiatry*, 1–60.

Angst, F., Stassen, H. H., Clayton, P. J., & Angst, J. (2002). Mortality of patients with mood disorders: Follow-up over 34–38 years. *Journal of Affective Disorders*, 68, 167–181.

Bateman, A. & Fonagy, P. (1999). Effectiveness of partial hospitalization in the treatment of borderline personality disorder: A randomized controlled trial. *American Journal of Psychiatry*, 156, 1563–1569.

Bennewith, O., Peters, T. J., Hawton, K., House, A., & Gunnell, D. (2005). Factors associated with the non-assessment of self-harm patients attending an Accident and Emergency Department: Results of a national study. *Journal of Affective Disorders*, 89, 91–97.

Bergen, H. & Hawton, K. (2007). Variations in time of hospital presentation for deliberate self-harm and their implications for clinical services. *Journal of Affective Disorders, 98*, 227–237.

Bille-Brahe, U., Kerkhof, A., De, Leo. D., Schmidtke, A., Crepet, P., Lönqvist, J., Michel, K., Salander-Renberg, E., Stiles, T. C., Wasserman, D., Aagaard, B., Egebo, H., & Jensen, B. (1997). A repetition–prediction study of European parasuicide populations: A summary of the first report from part II of the WHO/EURO Multicentre Study on Parasuicide in co-operation with the EC concerted action on attempted suicide. *Acta Psychiatrica Scandinavica, 95*, 81–86.

Boyce, P., Carter, G., Penrose-Wall, J., Wilhelm, K., & Goldney, R. (2003). Summary Australian and New Zealand clinical practice guideline for the management of adult deliberate self-harm. *Australasian Psychiatry, 11*, 150–155.

Brooten, D., Kumar, S., Brown, L. P., Butts, P., Finkler, S. A., Bakewell-Sachs, S., Gibbons, A., & Delivoriapapadopoulos, M. (1986). A randomized clinical trial of early hospital discharge and home follow-up of very-low-birth-weight infants. *New England Journal of Medicine, 315*, 934–939.

Brooten, D., Roncoli, M., Finkler, S., Arnold, L., Cohen, A., & Mennuti, M. (1994). A randomized trial of early hospital discharge and home follow-up of women having caesarean birth. *Obstetrics & Gynecology, 84*, 832–838.

Brown, G. K., Ten Have, H. T., Henriques, G. R., Xie, S. X., Hollander, J. E., & Beck, A. T. (2005). Cognitive therapy for the prevention of suicide attempts: A randomized controlled trial. *Journal of the American Medical Association, 294*, 563–570.

Crawford, M. J. & Kumar, P. (2007). Intervention following deliberate self-harm: Enough evidence to act? *Evidence-Based Mental Health, 10*, 37–39.

Crawford, M. J., Thomas, O., Khan, N., & Kulinskaya, E. (2007). Psychosocial interventions following self-harm: Systematic review of their efficacy in preventing suicide. *The British Journal of Psychiatry, 190*, 11–17.

De, Leo. D., Padoani, W., Lönqvist, J., Kerkhof, A. J., Bille-Brahe, U., Michel, K., Salander-Renberg, E., Schmidtke, A., Wasserman, D., Caon, F., & Scocco, P. (2002). Repetition of suicidal behaviour in elderly Europeans: A prospective longitudinal study. *Journal of Affective Disorders, 72*, 291–295.

Dieserud, G., Loeb, M., & Ekeberg, O. (2000). Suicidal behavior in the municipality of Baerum, Norway: A 12-year prospective study of parasuicide and suicide. *Suicide and Life-Threatening Behavior, 30*, 61–73.

Dieserud, G., Loeb, M., & Ekeberg, O. (2001). Suicide and suicide attempts in Baerum 1984–95. *Tidsskrift For Den Norske Laegeforening, 121*, 1026–1031.

Doshi, A., Boudreaux, E. D., Wang, N., Pelletier, A. J., & Camargo, C. A. (2005). National study of US emergency department visits for attempted suicide and self-inflicted injury, 1997–2001. *Annals of Emergency Medicine, 46*, 369–375.

Glover, G., Arts, G., & Babu, K. S. (2006). Crisis resolution/home treatment teams and psychiatric admission rates in England. *The British Journal of Psychiatry, 189*, 441–445.

Goldacre, M., Seagroatt, V., & Hawton, K. (1993). Suicide after discharge from psychiatric inpatient care. *The Lancet, 342*, 283–286.

Gunnell, D., Bennewith, O., Peters, T. J., House, A., & Hawton, K. (2005). The epidemiology and management of self-harm amongst adults in England. *Journal of Public Health, 27*, 67–73.

Guthrie, E., Kapur, N., Mackway-Jones, K., Chew-Graham, C., Moorey, J., Mendel, E., Marino-Francis, F., Sanderson, S., Turpin, C., Boddy, G., & Tomenson, B. (2001). Randomised controlled trial of brief psychological intervention after deliberate self-poisoning. *British Medical Journal, 323*, 135–138.

Haw, C., Bergen, H., Casey, D., & Hawton, K. (2007). Repetition of deliberate self-harm: A study of the characteristics and subsequent deaths in patients presenting to a general hospital according to extent of repetition. *Suicide and Life-Threatening Behavior, 37*, 379–396.

Hawton, K., Townsend, E., Arensman, E., Gunnell, D., Hazell, P., House, A., *et al.* (2005). Psychosocial and pharmacological treatments for deliberate self-harm. *The Cochrane Library*, *3*.

Hawton, K., Bale, L., Casey, D., Shepherd, A., Simkin, S., & Harriss, L. (2006). Monitoring deliberate self-harm presentations to general hospitals. *Crisis*, *27*, 157–163.

Hickey, L., Hawton, K., Fagg, J., & Weitzel, H. (2001). Deliberate self-harm patients who leave the accident and emergency department without a psychiatric assessment: A neglected population at risk of suicide. *Journal of Psychosomatic Research*, *50*, 87–93.

Hulten, A., Jiang, G. X., Wasserman, D., Hawton, K., Hjelmeland, H., De, Leo. D., Ostamo, A., Salander-Renberg, E., & Schmidtke, A. (2001). Repetition of attempted suicide among teenagers in Europe: frequency, timing and risk factors. *European Child and Adolescent Psychiatry*, *10*, 161–169.

Kapur, N., House, A., Dodgson, K., May, C., & Creed, F. (2002). Effect of general hospital management on repeat episodes of deliberate self-poisoning: Cohort study. *British Medical Journal*, *325*, 866–867.

Kapur, N., House, A., May, C., & Creed, F. (2003). Service provision and outcome for deliberate self-poisoning in adults – Results from a six centre descriptive study. *Social Psychiatry and Psychiatric Epidemiology*, *38*, 390–395.

Kopjar, B., Dieserud, G., & Wiik, J. (2005). Deliberate self-poisonings treated in hospitals. *Tidsskrift for den Norske Laegeforening*, *125*, 1798–1800.

Kripalani, S., LeFevre, F., Phillips, C. O., Williams, M. V., Basaviah, P., & Baker, D. W. (2007). Deficits in communication and information transfer between hospital-based and primary care physicians: Implications for patient safety and continuity of care. *Journal of the American Medical Association*, *297*, 831–841.

Linehan, M. M., Heard, H. L., & Armstrong, H. E. (1993). Naturalistic follow-up of a behavioral treatment for chronically parasuicidal borderline patients. *Archives of General Psychiatry*, *50*, 971–974.

Links, P. S. & Hoffman, B. (2005). Preventing suicidal behaviour in a general hospital psychiatric service: priorities for programming. *Canadian Journal of Psychiatry*, *50*, 490–496.

Mann, J. J., Apter, A., Bertolote, J., Beautrais, A., Currier, D., Haas, A., Hegerl, U., Lönqvist, J., Malone, K., Marusic, A., Mehlum, L., Patton, G., Phillips, M., Rutz, W., Rihmer, Z., Schmidtke, A., Shaffer, D., Silverman, M., Takahashi, Y., Varnik, A., Wasserman, D., Yip, P., & Hendin, H. (2005). Suicide prevention strategies: A systematic review. *Journal of the American Medical Association*, *294*, 2064–2074.

Mehlum, L., Jørgensen, T., Diep, L. M., & Nrugham, L. (2010). Impact of reorganization on the continuity of care for patients admitted after suicide attempt to a general hospital: A naturalistic 10-year catchment area study. *Archives of Suicide Research*, *14*(2), 173–183.

Mehlum, L., Mork, E., Reinholdt, N. P., Fadum, E. A., & Rossow, I. (2010). Quality of psychosocial care of suicide attempters at general hospitals in Norway – A longitudinal nationwide study. *Archives of Suicide Research*; *14*(2), 148–159.

Mittendorfer Rutz, E. & Schmidtke, A. (2009). Suicide attempts in Europe. In D. Wasserman & C. Wasserman (Eds.), *Oxford Textbook of Suicidology and Suicide Prevention. A global perspective* (pp. 123–126). Oxford: Oxford University Press.

Mork, E., Ekeid, G., Ystgaard, M., Mehlum, L., & Holte, A. (2001). Psychosocial follow-up after parasuicide in Norwegian general hospitals. *Tidsskrift for den Norske Laegeforening*, *121*, 1038–1043.

Mork, E., Mehlum, L., Fadum, E. A., & Rossow, I. (2009). *Collaboration between General Hospitals and Community Health Services in the Care of Suicide Attempters in Norway – A longitudinal study*. Oslo: National Centre for Suicide Research and Prevention, University of Oslo.

National Research and Development Centre for Welfare and Health (1993). *Suicide can be Prevented: A target and action plan for suicide prevention*. Helsinki: Painatuskekus OY.

Nationella rådet för självmordsprevention (1995). *Stöd i självmordskriser: nationellt program för utveckling av självmordsprevention*. Stockholm: Socialstyrelsen.

Naylor, M. D., Brooten, D., Campbell, R., Jacobsen, B. S., Mezey, M. D., Pauly, M. V., & Schwartz, J. S. (1999). Comprehensive discharge planning and home follow-up of hospitalized elders: A randomized clinical trial. *Journal of the American Medical Association, 281*, 613–620.

Norwegian Board of Health (1994). *Norwegian National Plan for Suicide Prevention* (vols. Statens Helsetilsyns Skriftserie 1995–4). Oslo: Norwegian Board of Health.

Norwegian Board of Health (1996). *The Baerum Model* (vols. Statens Helsetilsyns Skriftserie 1996–1). Oslo: Norwegian Board of Health.

Norwegian Board of Health (2001). *Guidelines for Monitoring, Treatment and Aftercare of Parasuicide Patients Admitted to General Hospitals in Norway* (vols. Statens Helsetilsyns Utredningsserie 2001–3). Oslo: Norwegian Board of Health.

Owens, D., Horrocks, J., & House, A. (2002). Fatal and non-fatal repetition of self-harm: Systematic review. *British Journal of Psychiatry, 181*, 193–199.

Phillips, C. O., Wright, S. M., Kern, D. E., Singa, R. M., Shepperd, S., & Rubin, H. R. (2004). Comprehensive discharge planning with postdischarge support for older patients with congestive heart failure: A meta-analysis. *Journal of the American Medical Association, 291*, 1358–1367.

Platt, S., Bille-Brahe, U., Kerkhof, A., Schmidtke, A., Bjerke, T., Crepet, P., Deleo, D., Haring, C., Lönqvist, J., Michel, K., Philippe, A., Pommereau, X., Querejeta, I., Salander-Renberg, E., Temesvary, B., Wasserman, D., & Faria, J. S. (1992). Parasuicide in Europe: The WHO/EURO Multicentre Study on Parasuicide. I. Introduction and preliminary analysis for 1989. *Acta Psychiatrica Scandinavica, 85*, 97–104.

Reulbach, U. & Perry, I. J. (2009). *2008 Annual Report of the National Registry of Deliberate Self Harm*, http://www.nsrf.ie (on-line), available at http://www.nsrf.ie/reports/2008AnnualReport NRDSHExeSumm072009.pdf, accessed 1 August 2009.

Royal College of Psychiatrists (2004). *Assessment following Self-harm in Adults* (Report No. CR122). London: Royal College of Psychiatrists.

Rudd, M. D., Williams, B., & Trotter, D. R. M. (2009). The psychological and behavioural treatment of suicidal behaviour. In D. Wasserman & C. Wasserman (Eds.), *Oxford Textbook of Suicidology and Suicide Prevention. A global perspective* (pp. 427–437). Oxford: Oxford University Press.

Salkovskis, P. M., Atha, C., & Storer, D. (1990). Cognitive-behavioural problem solving in the treatment of patients who repeatedly attempt suicide: A controlled trial. *British Journal of Psychiatry, 157*, 871–876.

Schmidtke, A., Bille-Brahe, U., De Leo, D., Kerkhof, A., Bjerke, T., Crepet, P., Haring, C., Hawton, K., Lönqvist,J., Michel, K., Pommereau, X., Querejeta, I., Phillipe, I., Salander-Renberg, E., Temesvary, B., Wasserman, D., Fricke, S., Weinacker, B., & Sampaio Faria, J. G. (1996). Attempted suicide in Europe: Rates, trends and sociodemographic characteristics of suicide attempters during the period 1989–1992. Results of the WHO/EURO Multicentre Study on Parasuicide. *Acta Psychiatrica Scandinavica, 93*, 327–338.

Silverman, M. M. (2009). Suicide attempts in North America. In D. Wasserman & C. Wasserman (Eds), *Oxford Textbook of Suicidology and Suicide Prevention* (pp. 117–122). Oxford: Oxford University Press.

Slinn, R., King, A., & Evans, J. (2001). A national survey of the hospital services for the management of adult deliberate self-harm. *Psychiatric Bulletin, 25*, 53–55.

Sundhedsstyrelsen (1998). *Forslag til handlingsplan til forebyggelse af selvmordsforsøg og selvmord i Danmark*. Copenhagen: Sundhedsstyrelsen.

Suokas, J. & Lönqvist, J. (1989). Work stress has negative effects on the attitudes of emergency personnel towards patients who attempt suicide. *Acta Psychiatrica Scandinavica, 79*, 474–480.

Suominen, K., Isometsa, E., Suokas, J., Haukka, J., Achte, K., & Lönqvist, J. (2004). Completed suicide after a suicide attempt: A 37-year follow-up study. *American Journal of Psychiatry, 161*, 562–563.

Suominen, K. H., Henriksson, M. M., Suokas, J., Isometsa, E. T., Ostamo, A., & Lönqvist, J. (1996). Mental disorders and comorbidity in attempted suicide. *Acta Psychiatrica Scandinavica, 94*, 234–240.

Taylor, T. L., Hawton, K., Fortune, S., & Kapur, N. (2009). Attitudes towards clinical services among people who self-harm: A systematic review. *The British Journal of Psychiatry, 194*, 104–110.

Verwey, B., van Waarde, J. A., van Rooij, I. A. L. M., Gerritsen, G., & Zitman, F. G. (2006). Availability, content and quality of local guidelines for the assessment of suicide attempters in university and general hospitals in the Netherlands. *General Hospital Psychiatry, 28*, 336–342.

CHAPTER TWENTY-ONE

Treating the Suicidal Patient: Cognitive Therapy and Dialectical Behaviour Therapy

Nadine A. Chang, Barbara Stanley, Gregory K. Brown, and Amy Cunningham

Abstract

A wide variety of psychotherapeutic and psychopharmacological interventions has been used to prevent future suicide attempts. Cognitive Therapy (CT) and Dialectical Behaviour Therapy (DBT) have been indicated as commonly used and effective therapeutic techniques. CT is a short-term, structured treatment that focuses on modifying dysfunctional beliefs and behaviour to solve current problems. Cognitive case conceptualizations, developed by identifying negative automatic thoughts, situational precursors to these thoughts, emotional and behavioural consequences of the thoughts, and core beliefs are used to guide the specific cognitive and behavioural strategies used in treatment. Cognitive interventions, including cognitive restructuring, Socratic questioning, and risk assessment and safety planning, as well as behavioural techniques such as guided imagery, creating a Hope Kit, and activity scheduling, are reviewed. DBT is a psychotherapeutic intervention that blends the cognitive and behavioural strategies found in CT with acceptance-based techniques. It is a one-year treatment package incorporating both individual and group psychotherapy that focuses on identifying and changing the behaviours that cue and reinforce suicidal acts, teaching effective coping skills, and problem-solving. Skills groups teach mindfulness, emotion regulation, distress tolerance, and inter-personal effectiveness, while individual sessions provide patients the opportunity to practise thinking dialectically when assessing maladaptive behaviour. This chapter provides an overview of both CT and DBT, highlighting the theory and format of each treatment as well as efficacy for the prevention

International Handbook of Suicide Prevention: Research, Policy and Practice, First Edition.
Edited by Rory C. O'Connor, Stephen Platt, Jacki Gordon.
© 2011 John Wiley & Sons, Ltd. Published 2011 by John Wiley & Sons, Ltd.

of repeat suicide attempts. Key similarities between CT and DBT are outlined, and future directions for psychotherapeutic interventions for suicide are discussed.

Introduction

Approximately one million people worldwide die by suicide each year, making it one of the top three leading causes of death for individuals between the ages of 15 and 34 years (WHO, 2003). In addition, it is estimated that 10 to 20 times more people make non-fatal suicide attempts or engage in non-suicidal self-injury behaviours (WHO, 2003). Systematic reviews of evidence-based treatments for suicide prevention have included a variety of psychotherapeutic and psychopharmacological treatments (Fleischmann, Bertolote, Wasserman, De Leo, Bolhari, *et al.*, 2008; Gunnel & Frankel, 1994; Hawton, Townsend, Arensman, Gunnell, Hazell, *et al.*, 2000; Kapur, & Gask, 2009). Cognitive Therapy (CT) (Brown, Ten Have, Henriques, Xie, Hollander, *et al.*, 2005) and Dialectical Behaviour Therapy (DBT) (Linehan, 1993; Shearin & Linehan, 1994) are two of the most widely used psychotherapeutic approaches and have been found to be highly effective in preventing repeat suicide attempts. This chapter provides an overview of CT and DBT, a brief review of the efficacy of both treatments for preventing suicide attempts, a summary of theoretical models and format of treatment, and a review of each treatment strategy. Key similarities of CT and DBT are then presented and future directions for developing psychotherapeutic interventions for suicidal patients discussed.

Given the many different terms and definitions used in the literature, it is important to clarify that the terms used in this chapter follow those listed in Wenzel, Brown, and Beck's (2009) *Cognitive Therapy for Suicidal Patients: Scientific and Clinical Applications*:

- Suicide: death caused by self-inflicted injurious behaviour with any intent to die as a result of the behaviour.
- Suicide attempt: a non-fatal, self-inflicted, potentially injurious behaviour with any intent to die as a result of the behaviour. A suicide attempt may or may not result in injury.
- Suicidal act: a self-inflicted, potentially injurious behaviour with any intent to die as a result of the behaviour. A suicidal act may or may not result in death (suicide).
- Suicide ideation: any thoughts, images, beliefs, voices, or other cognitions reported by the individual about intentionally ending his or her own life.
- Deliberate self-harm (DSH): inflicting harm upon oneself without the intent to die as a result of the behaviour.

Cognitive Therapy

Cognitive therapy is a structured, short-term, present-oriented psychotherapeutic treatment directed towards modifying dysfunctional thinking *and* behaviour and solving current problems. The therapist formulates cognitive case conceptualizations that include the identification of negative automatic thoughts, situations that prompted these thoughts, and the emotional and behavioural reactions to these thoughts. In addition, the therapist identifies core and intermediate beliefs that are associated with these automatic thoughts. The cognitive case conceptualization, then, is used to guide the selection of specific cognitive and behavioural strategies that are used to treat the presenting disorder (Beck, 1995).

Theoretical model

The cognitive model of suicide conceptualizes the suicidal mode as an organized response resulting from the interaction of cognitive, affective, behavioural, and physiological processes (Rudd, 2004, 2006; Wenzel, Brown & Beck, 2009) and emphasizes the constructs of acute hopelessness and attentional fixation as major components of suicide risk. Hopelessness refers to the expectation that the future is bleak and that the patient might as well give up. Attentional fixation refers to the cognitive process that results in the conclusion that suicide is the only option available to resolve current problems. The suicidal mode may be activated during the interaction of predisposing vulnerabilities, such as psychiatric disturbances (e.g., depression) or core beliefs (e.g., unbearability), and proximal triggers, such as a recent loss (e.g., break-up of a relationship).

The cognitive model of suicidal acts, that is, self-inflicted, potentially injurious behaviour with any intent to die as a result of the behaviour, which may or may not result in death (Wenzel, Brown & Beck, 2009), incorporates dispositional vulnerability factors and cognitive processes associated with psychiatric disturbance and suicidal actions. Dispositional vulnerability factors include impulsivity, problem-solving deficits, and other dysfunctional attitudes (Wenzel & Beck, 2008). Although these constructs do not directly lead to suicidal acts, they are associated with suicidal acts by potentially activating negative schemas (cognitive frameworks that guide information processing) (Wenzel, Brown, & Beck, 2009), are stressful themselves, and influence cognitive processes during a suicidal crisis (suicide ideation and behaviour). For example, social problem-solving impairment and an over-generalized memory style (a pattern of summarizing a number of events instead of identifying a specific event) (Williams & Broadbent, 1986) may quickly exacerbate feelings of hopelessness and make it difficult for the individual to access specific information that would assist in effective problem-solving and identify more adaptive alternatives to suicide (Wenzel, Brown, & Beck, 2009).

Cognitive processes associated with psychiatric disturbances are particularly sensitive to internal and external experiences. During times of stress, negative schemas are activated; maladaptive thoughts and interpretations prompt maladaptive emotional, physiological, and behavioural reactions that further reinforce the negative schema. However, this does not always result in suicidal behaviour. In suicidal individuals, negative schemas become stronger or activate other negative schemas as a result of the interaction between dysfunctional cognitions and maladaptive reactions. As this occurs, feelings of hopelessness and/or helplessness gain strength, and there is a greater chance that a suicide schema will be activated. The activation of a suicide schema, in conjunction with life stress and feelings of hopelessness, increases the likelihood that the individual will have difficulty in disengaging from suicide-related cognitions and problem-solving effectively, exacerbate his or her sense of desperation, and increase suicide ideation. The suicide attempt occurs when this combination of factors passes a critical threshold unique to each individual. CT aims to prevent suicide behaviour by providing patients with coping skills to survive a crisis, such as problem-solving skills and social skills.

Description of treatment

Cognitive therapy was developed as a brief, individual psychotherapy treatment that occurs over approximately 10 weekly or bi-weekly sessions. These sessions can be augmented by telephone calls between sessions. Case management services, such as reaching out to patients who have disengaged from treatment or providing appropriate referrals for further treatment, are considered to be important for conducting the treatment. In addition, team meetings that include other therapists and case managers who provide treatment for suicidal patients are considered to be an indispensable part of the intervention. CT for suicidal patients consists of three phases: early, intermediate, and later. The early phase of treatment focuses on socializing the patient to CT, establishing rapport and engaging the patient in treatment, obtaining informed consent, conducting a psychological evaluation, assessing suicide risk, and, importantly, conveying a sense of hope (Wenzel, Brown, & Beck, 2009).

One of the initial goals of treatment is to obtain an accurate account of the events that occurred before, during, and after the recent suicidal crisis that brought the patient into treatment. During this phase of the intervention, patients have the opportunity to 'tell their story' about the events that led to the suicidal crisis. When addressing a suicidal crisis, a timeline of events leading up to the crisis, incorporating the activating event, cognitions, emotions, and behaviours, is constructed. Key automatic thoughts are identified, along with the resulting emotions. Timelines may contain a single or multiple activating events and many different cognitive, emotional, or behavioural reactions to those events. The consequences of the suicide behaviour are also examined to determine aspects that may be reinforcing the behaviour, and a list of adaptive alternatives is compiled. The timeline is instrumental in developing the cognitive case conceptualization of the suicidal crisis, elucidating times when interventions and/or coping strategies can be used to prevent a future crisis. This timeline is also a useful resource later in treatment when preparing for relapse prevention.

The cognitive case conceptualization is the basis of the cognitive therapy model for suicide. It provides the framework for understanding the patient, assessing his or her negative core beliefs and dysfunctional thinking, and selecting the appropriate interventions. The relationship between thoughts, feelings, and behaviours is a major concept that assists in the cognitive case conceptualization. A main focus of cognitive treatment is modifying the individual's dysfunctional thoughts and beliefs to more appropriate ones and introducing behavioural strategies, such as behavioural activation and coping strategies.

The safety plan should be conducted early in CT treatment. The clinician and patient collaboratively develop a list of hierarchically arranged coping strategies that the patient can use during a suicidal crisis. It is usually formatted like a cue card or flowchart that patients can quickly refer to for guidance. The safety plan consists of warning signs, coping strategies patients can use independently, people whom patients can contact for support or help with their crises, and contact information for mental health professionals, such as therapists, hospitals, or suicide hotlines. Safety planning has been thought to be so effective for lowering suicide risk that it has been further developed as a stand-alone crisis intervention strategy (Stanley, Brown, Brent, Wells, Poling, *et al.*, 2009; Stanley & Brown, 2010).

The intermediate phase of CT focuses on teaching patients effective cognitive and behavioural strategies (described in more detail below) to manage suicide ideation and lower the risk of suicidal acts. Techniques for coping with a suicidal crisis are evaluated in depth and then practised both in and out of session. In the later phase of treatment, the clinician and patient address relapse prevention using guided imagery to test adaptive coping strategies and, upon satisfactory completion of those exercises, they ultimately prepare for termination of therapy, usually involving referrals to other mental health professionals to maintain treatment continuity (Wenzel, Brown, & Beck, 2009).

A goal of CT is to modify an individual's core beliefs; in suicidal patients, core beliefs revolve around themes of helplessness, unlovability, and worthlessness. A major strategy for change in CT is cognitive restructuring, identifying negative automatic thoughts and replacing them with more adaptive ones (Beck, 1995). Using techniques such as Socratic questioning and guided discovery (asking questions to stimulate critical thinking and guide patients in evaluating the evidence supporting or refuting their automatic thoughts), and behavioural experiments (testing the validity of patients' cognitive distortions in real-life situations) (Wenzel, Brown, & Beck, 2009), the patient learns to recognize how cognitions, those active during a suicidal crisis, for example, mediate his or her affect and behaviour and to understand that alternative thoughts can result in different affect and behaviours. Perhaps one of the most informative exercises is examining automatic thoughts during a suicidal crisis. This is the best time to evaluate these thoughts, called 'hot cognitions', as they occur in real time and are at their clearest.

Several techniques are used in cognitive restructuring. The clinician and patient work collaboratively to identify cognitive distortions and examine the evidence that supports or disproves the thought or belief. Alternative hypotheses are then generated and tested. Imagery can also be used to address hopelessness; to counter a patient's report that the future looks empty, the patient is asked to imagine his or her life in the future. This exercise facilitates the implementation of another strategy, problem-solving, in order to determine the steps needed to get to that future point. Problem-solving consists of brainstorming solutions and assessing the advantages and disadvantages of each alternative. Problem-solving may focus on situations leading up to suicide ideation, with the goal of decreasing hopelessness. It is essential to gather information about the focus of the patient's hopeless feelings and devise an action plan to cope with those feelings.

Because suicidal patients are so focused on their various reasons for dying, compiling a list of reasons for living can be beneficial in preventing a suicidal crisis. This list can be written down for future reference, but during a crisis the Hope Kit may be more effective. The Hope Kit (Wenzel, Brown & Beck, 2009) is a visual memory aid that reminds patients of their reasons for living. It can be a box, scrapbook, or even a webpage consisting of a collection of meaningful items (photos, letters, inspirational passages, etc.) that is placed in an accessible location so that it may be reviewed during times of crisis. Constructing a Hope Kit has proved to be an enjoyable and meaningful experience for patients, who frequently find themselves identifying additional reasons for living during this process.

A more portable reminder system involves coping cards. Coping cards are concise reminders that use the patient's own words to facilitate adaptive thinking during a suicidal crisis; they contain strategies for dealing with distress, which for suicidal patients may prompt hopelessness and suicide ideation. Patients are encouraged to keep the cards in a wallet, purse, or other easily accessible location and use them during a crisis as well as outside of crisis in order to practise adaptive ways of thinking. Coping cards may consist of reminders to evaluate negative automatic thoughts and beliefs, lists of evidence that refute a negative core belief, lists of coping strategies to choose from during a suicidal crisis, statements that motivate the patient to work towards his or her goals or to practise adaptive coping skills, or even emergency numbers to use during a crisis.

Behavioural strategies are also used in CT, incorporating activity scheduling to foster a sense of mastery and pride, improving social networks and maintaining treatment compliance. With activity scheduling, the clinician and patient compile a list of activities that increase the patient's engagement with their environment, increase opportunities for positive reinforcement and improve motivation, which are entered into the patient's weekly activity schedule. The patient's social support network is also evaluated and improved by plans to enhance existing relationships or develop new ones. Social engagements are initiated and also entered into the activity schedule. Affect and cognitions are assessed prior to engaging in an activity and then again afterwards. Engaging in the behaviour is likely to be reinforcing because of the positive effect on the patient's mood, resulting in more positive cognitions, a greater sense of self-efficacy and diminished feelings of hopelessness. Because suicidal patients also frequently face other problems, such as substance abuse or psychiatric and physical problems, increasing their compliance with other treatment must be an integral part of therapy. Inter-agency collaboration is key to overall success for the suicidal patient in CT.

During the final phase of CT, a Relapse Prevention Task is conducted in which patients have an opportunity to actively demonstrate that they are able to implement the skills developed throughout the course of treatment. The relapse prevention task consists of three guided imagery exercises in which patients imagine suicidal crises and then systematically describe the manner in which they would cope with them. The primary aim of this task is to assist patients in 'over-learning' specific skills so that they remember to use them during a crisis. If patients have difficulty identifying or applying the skills learned during treatment, the clinician knows that more work needs to be done in therapy and termination is delayed. Additional issues that are addressed in the later phase of treatment include: anticipation of lapses, consolidation of learning, and maintenance of treatment goals.

Empirical support

Meta-analyses of randomized controlled trials (RCTs) have demonstrated the effectiveness of CT across a wide range of disorders, including depression, generalized anxiety disorder, panic disorder, social phobia, PTSD, eating disorders, and schizophrenia. CT has been found to be more effective in reducing symptoms than pharmacotherapy alone, and, when conducted in conjunction with pharmacotherapy, results are maintained beyond the end of treatment (Butler, Chapman, Forman, & Beck, 2006; Tarrier, Taylor, & Gooding, 2008).

CT for suicidal patients has been adapted from CT approaches for psychiatric disturbances such as depression. An early adaptation of cognitive behavioural interventions for suicidal individuals targeted deficits in problem-solving skills. When compared with treatment as usual (TAU), CT focusing on problem-solving was found to be more effective in reducing depression and hopelessness at the end of treatment and at one-year follow-up and in reducing repeat suicide attempts at six months post-treatment (Salkovskis, Atha, & Storer, 1990). Though both CT and problem-solving therapy (PST) identify stressors, emphasize goal-setting and aim to decrease hopelessness, the primary goal of PST is to teach alternative solutions to a stressor so that suicide no longer appears to be the only viable option, while CT focuses on changing the cognitive distortions and negative core beliefs that precipitate a suicidal crisis (Stewart, Quinn, Plever, & Emmerson, 2009).

Expanding the focus of previous interventions, Brown and colleagues (2005) developed a 10-session CT intervention based on Beck's theory of suicide, namely, that suicide is perceived as the only solution to the unbearability of an individual's core beliefs (Wenzel, Brown, & Beck, 2009). This intervention targeted identifying and modifying maladaptive thoughts and behaviours that occurred prior to suicidal crises, developing reasons for living, improving social functioning, and maintaining treatment compliance. An RCT was conducted on 120 patients who had recently attempted suicide and who were evaluated in an emergency department (Brown *et al.*, 2005). Patients were randomly assigned to receive or not receive the CT intervention. Participants in either treatment condition were allowed to receive usual care as practised in the community and participants were followed over an 18-month period. Results of this study indicated that 24% of suicide attempters in CT made another suicide attempt during active treatment compared with 42% of patients in the control condition. Importantly, individuals who were assigned to the CT intervention were approximately 50% less likely than those in the control condition to re-attempt during follow-up. At baseline, there were no group differences on other measures associated with suicidal risk, including depression and hopelessness, and results demonstrated that participants assigned to the CT intervention were less severely impaired than those in the control condition.

Dialectical Behaviour Therapy

Dialectical Behaviour Therapy (DBT) is a cognitive behavioural treatment developed by Marsha Linehan in 1993. It is a unique blend of the traditional change-focused work found in cognitive therapy with the acceptance-based work found in Eastern traditions. DBT was developed for individuals struggling with chronic suicidality and first validated for women with borderline personality disorder (BPD).

Theoretical model

DBT is a theory-driven treatment based on a biosocial model of psychopathology: the development and maintenance of the pervasive emotional dysregulation experienced by suicidal individuals with BPD is assumed to be both biologically and environmentally cued. Biologically, it is believed that these individuals are constitutionally different from healthy controls: they are highly sensitive to emotional stimuli, experience emotions more intensely, and have a slower return to baseline functioning after an emotional reaction. Environmental influences, which are believed to begin in childhood, range from abuse to a poor temperamental fit between the child and caregivers. Linehan (1993) refers to these factors as the invalidating environment. Thus, the child fails to learn to trust and value his or her internal experience. This invalidating environment continues throughout the individual's life, taking various forms, including peer rejection, difficult/abusive family relationships, and emotional invalidation.

A key aspect of the biosocial model is its transactional nature. Linehan (1993) describes the biological and environmental vulnerabilities as contributing to each other, increasing the person's distress. For example, a person with high emotional sensitivity (biological vulnerability) who is told by her parents that her emotions are not real (invalidating environment) becomes more sensitive to her emotional reactions (biological vulnerability).

The biological and environmental vulnerabilities lead to the pervasive emotion dysregulation commonly experienced by individuals with BPD. During an emotional response, individuals with BPD have significant difficulty diverting attention away from emotional stimuli or, when needed, increase their physiological response. These deficits lead to a host of cognitive and behavioural problems, including distorted information processing, mood-dependent behaviour, impulsivity, and dissociation.

DBT views suicidal acts as learned and reinforced coping strategies to decrease emotion dysregulation. Specifically, DBT views suicidal acts as problem-solving behaviour aimed to reduce distress caused by negative emotional arousal. From a DBT perspective, suicidal acts are a result of two interacting conditions: deficits in effective emotion regulation and distress tolerance skills; and personal and environmental influences that limit or inhibit the use of existing effective skills (Miller, Rathus, & Linehan, 2007).

Format of treatment

Given the emphasis in DBT on treating chronically suicidal individuals, the treatment was designed to address the specific problems listed above. The treatment teaches patients effective coping skills and is designed to motivate, reinforce, and generalize the use of these skills. The treatment also focuses on identifying and changing the learned behaviours that cue and reinforce suicidal acts. Standard DBT, as described by Linehan (1993), is a one-year treatment package that requires patients to attend weekly skills groups and individual psychotherapy sessions conducted by a DBT clinician. In addition, phone coaching is made available for patients to utilize when emotionally dysregulated to assist them with using these skills in everyday life. Lastly, in view of the difficulties inherent in providing effective treatment to chronically suicidal individuals, clinicians must attend weekly group consultation meetings.

Skills groups

Given the underlying assumption that suicidal individuals lack effective coping skills, DBT teaches patients how to cope effectively with negative emotions and stressful life events. There are four skills modules: mindfulness, emotion regulation, distress tolerance, and interpersonal effectiveness. Mindfulness is the core module and is repeated multiple times throughout the year. This module teaches the patient to make the conscious decision to be aware of and live in the present moment. The emotion regulation module is designed to provide psychoeducation on emotions, assist the patient in identifying and labelling emotions, and teach techniques for increasing or decreasing emotional responses. The distress tolerance module teaches the patient how to cope effectively with negative emotions and stressful life events without inflicting harm on him- or herself or making the situation worse. Finally, the interpersonal effectiveness module teaches the patient how to have his or her needs met in a relationship without pushing the other individual away.

Individual psychotherapy

While important skills are taught during the skills group, patients in DBT are also required to attend individual psychotherapy sessions, where the focus is on increasing the ability to think dialectically, or, in other words, looking at multiple aspects of every situation. In addition, problematic behaviour that was engaged in during the week is analysed by examining the details of the events leading up to the problematic behaviours. Increasing commitments to engage in effective coping are then obtained. Given the multiple problems and recurrent crises that are common in the lives of patients with BPD, DBT offers a hierarchical structure to guide the therapy session. All life-interfering behaviours, such as suicidal acts, DSH, or behaviours that are potentially life-threatening (such as extreme low weight from anorexia) are addressed first. In the absence of life-interfering behaviours, treatment-interfering behaviours, namely, things that get in the way of the therapist and patient effectively working together towards a common goal, whether patient- or therapist-generated, are addressed next.

In the absence of life- and therapy-interfering behaviours, the focus then shifts to quality of life-interfering behaviours, which can range from depression or anxiety to substance use disorders. It is likely that these are the problems with which the patient initially presents. Linehan (1993) sets these as lowest priority because, if life- or therapy-interfering behaviours are occurring, treatment focusing on quality of life-interfering behaviours cannot be effective.

Telephone coaching and consultation group

A unique intervention offered in DBT is telephone coaching, which is intended to help with the generalization of skills in the natural environment and at the moment that the patient is experiencing distress. Thus, patients are encouraged to contact the therapist for assistance between sessions when they are experiencing urges to engage in problematic behaviours and are having trouble choosing a coping strategy. In addition, patients are encouraged to contact the therapist if questions arise when they are attempting to use a new coping skill.

Given the inherent difficulties and stress that therapists experience when offering treatment to chronically suicidal patients, DBT requires that the therapist attends a weekly consultation meeting. Its purpose is to ensure that the therapist receives the support required to maintain the treatment. In addition, consultation groups often function as peer supervision where therapists can discuss problematic behaviours and receive feedback on effective ways to intervene.

DBT suicide prevention protocol

Because suicidal acts occur frequently in individuals with BPD, specific suicide prevention protocols were developed to guide therapists in responding effectively to suicidal behaviour. These protocols have been clearly defined (Linehan, 1993) and are summarized below. The therapeutic tasks in addressing suicidal acts include responding actively enough to stop the patient from inflicting serious harm or death *and* doing so in a way that will reduce the likelihood of future suicidal acts. The dialectical tension arises between choosing to intervene directly in the patient's life to ensure his or her safety and emphasizing autonomy by teaching the patient new skills to actively cope with overwhelming emotional distress (Linehan, 1993). From a DBT perspective, there are three rules to follow when addressing suicidal acts: first, these behaviours are always analysed in depth; second, patients cannot contact their therapist for 24 hours after engaging in a suicidal act in order to avoid reinforcing the behaviour; and, third, suicidal patients should not be given potentially lethal drugs.

The protocol for assessing previous suicidal behaviours in DBT is similar to that used with CT. On learning that a suicidal act has occurred, the primary therapist initially assesses the patient's current level of suicide ideation, intent, and plan, and the frequency, intensity, and severity of the behaviour. After this assessment, the therapist conducts a detailed chain analysis, which is a moment-to-moment examination of all of the events that led up to, and occurred after, the suicidal act. The therapist elicits sufficient detail to gain an understanding of the environmental, emotional, and cognitive responses and behavioural reactions that preceded the suicidal behaviour. In addition, consequences of the suicidal act are examined for any reinforcing properties. After this chain analysis is completed, a list of alternative solutions to suicidal acts is created collaboratively. When developing this list, the therapist and patient jointly consider the issue of tolerating the emotional distress versus acting on it. Next, the focus moves to a discussion of the negative intra- and interpersonal effects of suicidal behaviour on friends, family, and the therapeutic relationship.

Lastly, it is important to ensure that the patient is committed to utilizing the new behavioural options in the face of future urges. It is critical to offer ample validation of the emotional pain the patient is/was experiencing at the time the behaviour occurred. The dialectic of invalidating the behaviour and validating the emotional distress can be tricky to balance and therapists must remain aware of this at all times.

Protocol for responding to current suicidal urges

The protocol for responding to current suicidal urges is similar to that stated above. The first therapeutic task is to remove, or convince the patient to remove, any lethal objects from immediate reach. While doing this, the therapist is 'empathically instructing' the patient not to engage in self-destructive behaviour and maintaining that suicide/DSH is not an effective solution. The therapist also directly suggests or generates hopeful statements and solutions aimed at resolving the suicidal cue. It is vital that the therapist maintains contact with the patient until his or her safety is secured. Once that has been done, the protocol for addressing previous suicidal behaviour is initiated.

Empirical support

There have been nine published RCTs conducted across five research laboratories demonstrating the efficacy of DBT, with five specifically addressing suicidality and deliberate self-harm (DSH, inflicting harm upon oneself without the intent to die as a result of the behaviour) (Koons, Robins, Tweed, Lynch, Gonzalez, *et al.*, 2001; Linehan, Armstrong, Suarez, Allmon, & Heard, 1991; Linehan, Comtois, Murray, Brown, Gallop, *et al.*, 2006; van den Bosch, Koeter, Stijen, Verheul, & van den Brink, 2005; Verheul, van den Bosch, Koeter, de Riddler, Stijnen, *et al.*, 2003).

The original RCT demonstrating efficacy in reducing suicidal crises was conducted by Linehan and colleagues (1991). This study randomized 44 suicidal women with BPD to DBT or treatment as usual (TAU). Individuals treated with DBT experienced significant reductions in DSH and suicidal behaviours (including suicides, suicide attempts, and suicidal acts) through one year of treatment. Following this study, Koons *et al.* (2001) conducted a RCT comparing 28 women randomized to either DBT or TAU. They also found that individuals in DBT reported a significantly greater reduction in suicide ideation, hopelessness, depressive symptoms (as measured by the Beck Depression Inventory), and anger variables than those in the TAU condition after six months of treatment.

In 2003, Verheul and colleagues (2003) conducted an RCT to examine the impact of baseline severity of psychopathology on the efficacy of DBT over a 12-month follow-up period. Fifty-eight women were randomly assigned to either DBT or TAU, and those in DBT experienced a significant reduction in DSH. A follow-up study was conducted by van den Bosch *et al.* (2005) examining the sustained efficacy of DBT. This study demonstrated that the superior effects of DBT were maintained at six months post-treatment.

Lastly, Linehan *et al.* (2006) conducted an RCT designed to examine the unique effects of DBT. One hundred and one individuals with BPD were randomized to DBT or community treatment by experts. Results indicated that individuals in DBT were half as likely to make a suicide attempt, required less hospitalization for suicide ideation, and had lower medical risk across all suicide attempts and DSH than those in the control condition. While the empirical investigation of the efficacy of DBT continues, the existing studies demonstrate an evidence base for providing DBT to suicidal individuals with BPD.

Comparison of CT and DBT for Suicide

Both DBT and CT have demonstrated superior treatment effects in reducing suicidal crises over TAU. Therefore, it is important to consider the unique elements when selecting a treatment. Compared with CT for suicidal patients, DBT is more time- and labour-intensive.

Specifically, DBT, as conducted in the RCTs aimed at preventing suicide, is a one-year treatment that requires the patient to attend both individual psychotherapy sessions and skills groups weekly, along with the therapist providing out-of-hours phone coaching and attending a consultation group, whereas CT is a concise and often time-limited intervention. One reason for this significant difference relates to the goals of the treatments. While the primary goal of CT is to increase the patient's ability to cope with suicide ideation/urges more effectively, the end goal for DBT is to help the patient build an overall life worth living.

While both DBT and CT are applicable to suicide behaviour and developing skills for managing suicidal crises, DBT uses more behavioural strategies for managing suicidal behaviour while CT uses more cognitive ones. Another significant difference is the populations for which the treatments were designed. DBT is empirically validated in women with BPD who engage in suicidal behaviour, whereas CT has been tested and shown to be effective in trans-diagnostic populations. In addition, CT for suicidal adults uses cognitive conceptualizations to guide treatment, placing a heavy emphasis on the patient's maladaptive cognitive patterns. In contrast, DBT uses the biosocial model to understand pathology and places a more equal emphasis on maladaptive cognitive and behavioural patterns. This difference can be seen when examining a suicidal act. From a CT perspective, a cognitive or internal experience can serve as the cue for a suicidal act in the timeline, whereas from a DBT perspective the prompting event for suicidal behaviour is always an external or environmental cue.

Conclusions and Recommendations for Future Research

Cognitive Therapy decreases patients' risk for suicide by teaching them to recognize the warning signs of suicidal behaviour and to use cognitive and behavioural strategies to cope with thoughts of suicide. Similarly, Dialectical Behaviour Therapy focuses on coping effectively with emotion dysregulation and learning to tolerate life stressors that cannot be changed. Both interventions incorporate the management of maladaptive thoughts and behaviours to reduce symptoms and decrease the risk of future suicide attempts. The techniques described in the present chapter can be utilized in a variety of treatment contexts; they are not limited to CT- or DBT-trained clinicians. Because the specific treatment modality that decreases suicidal behaviour requires further investigation, additional RCTs are needed to compare therapeutic interventions and their effectiveness in reducing risk for suicide. A fundamental question when comparing the effectiveness of therapeutic approaches is determining which aspects of the treatment are shared and which are unique.

References

Beck, J. S. (1995). *Cognitive Therapy: Basics and beyond*. New York: Guilford Press.
Brown, G. K., Ten Have, T., Henriques, G. R., Xie, S. X., Hollander, J. E., & Beck, A. T. (2005). Cognitive therapy for the prevention of suicide attempts: A randomized controlled trial. *Journal of the American Medical Association, 294*, 563–570.

Butler, A., Chapman, J., Forman, E., & Beck, A. T. (2006). The empirical status of cognitive-behavioral therapy: A review of meta-analyses. *Clinical Psychology Review, 26*, 17–31.

Fleischmann, A., Bertolote, J. M., Wasserman, D., De Leo, D., Bolhari, J., Botega, N. J., De Silva, D., Phillips, M., Vijayakumar, L., Varnik, A., Schlebusch, L., & Thanh, H. T. T. (2008). Effectiveness of brief intervention and contact for suicide attempters: A randomized controlled trial in five countries. *Bulletin of the World Health Organization, 86*, 703–709.

Gunnell, D. & Frankel, S. (1994). Prevention of suicide: Aspirations and evidence. *British Medical Journal, 308*, 1227–1233.

Hawton, K., Townsend, E., Arensman, E., Gunnell, D., Hazell, P., House, A., & van Heeringen, K. (2000). Psychosocial versus pharmacological treatments for deliberate self harm. Cochrane database of systematic reviews (online: Update Software). 2, CD001764.

Kapur, N. & Gask, L. (2009). Introduction to suicide and self-harm. *Psychiatry, 8*, 233–236.

Koons, C. R., Robins, C. J., Tweed, J. L., Lynch, T. R., Gonzalez, A. M., Morse, J. Q., Bishop, G. K., & Butterfield, M. I. (2001). Efficacy of dialectical behavior therapy in women veterans with borderline personality disorder. *Behavior Therapy, 32*, 371–390.

Linehan, M. M. (1993). *Cognitive-Behavioral Treatment of Borderline Personality Disorder*. New York: Guilford Press.

Linehan, M. M., Armstrong, H. E., Suarez, A., Allmon, D., & Heard, H. L. (1991). Cognitive-behavioral treatment of chronically parasuicidal borderline patients. *Archives of General Psychiatry, 48*, 1060–1064.

Linehan, M. M., Comtois, K. A., Murray, A. M., Brown, M. Z., Gallop, R. J., Heard, H. L., Korslund, K. E., Tutek, D. A., Reynolds, S. K., & Lindenboim, N. (2006). Two-year randomized controlled trial and follow-up of dialectical behavior therapy vs. therapy by experts for suicidal behaviors and borderline personality disorder. *Archives of General Psychiatry, 63*, 757–766.

Miller, A. L., Rathus, J. H., & Linehan, M. M. (2007). *Dialectical Behavior Therapy with Suicidal Adolescents*. New York: Guilford Press.

Rudd, M. (2004). Cognitive therapy for suicidality: An integrative, comprehensive, and practical approach to conceptualization. *Journal of Contemporary Psychotherapy, 34*, 59–72.

Rudd, M. (2006). Suicidality in clinical practice: Anxieties and answers. *Journal of Clinical Psychology, 62*, 157–159.

Salkovskis, P., Atha, C., & Storer, D. (1990). Cognitive-behavioural problem solving in the treatment of patients who repeatedly attempt suicide. A controlled trial. *British Journal of Psychiatry, 157*, 871–876.

Shearin, E. N. & Linehan, M. M. (1994). Dialectical behaviour therapy for borderline personality disorder: Theoretical and empirical foundations. *Acta Psychiatrica Scandinavica, 89*, 61–68.

Stanley, B. & Brown, G. K. (2010). *Safety Planning: A brief intervention to mitigate suicide risk*. Manuscript submitted for publication.

Stanley, B., Brown, G., Brent, D., Wells, K., Poling, K., Curry, J., Kennard, B., Wagner, A., Cwik, M., Klomek, A., Goldstein, T., Vitiello, B., Barnett, S., Daniel, S., & Hughes, J. (2009). Cognitive-behavioral therapy for suicide prevention (CBT-SP): Treatment model, feasibility, and acceptability. *Journal of the American Academy of Child and Adolescent Psychiatry, 48*, 1005–1013.

Stewart, C. D., Quinn, A., Plever, S., & Emmerson, B. (2009). Comparing cognitive behavior therapy, problem solving therapy, and treatment as usual in a high risk population. *Suicide and Life-Threatening Behavior, 39*, 538–547.

Tarrier, N., Taylor, K., & Gooding, P. (2008). Cognitive-behavioral interventions to reduce suicide behaviour: A systematic review and meta-analysis. *Behavior Modification, 32*, 77–108.

van den Bosch, L. M. C., Koeter, M. W. J., Stijen, T., Verheul, R., & van den Brink, W. (2005). Sustained efficacy of dialectical behaviour therapy for borderline personality disorder. *Behaviour Research and Therapy, 43*, 1231–1241.

Verheul, R., van den Bosch, L. M. C., Koeter, M. W. J., de Ridder, M. A. J., Stijnen, T., & van den Brink, W. (2003). Dialectical behaviour therapy for women with borderline personality disorder: 12-month randomised clinical trial in the Netherlands. *British Journal of Psychiatry, 182*, 135–140.

Wenzel, A. & Beck, A. T. (2008). A cognitive model of suicidal behavior: Theory and treatment. *Applied and Preventive Psychology, 12*, 189–201.

Wenzel, A., Brown, G., & Beck, A. T. (2009). *Cognitive Therapy for Suicidal Patients: Scientific and clinical applications*. Washington, DC: American Psychological Association.

Williams, J. M. G. & Broadbent, K. (1986). Autobiographical memory in suicide attempters. *Journal of Abnormal Psychology, 95*, 144–149.

World Health Organization (WHO) (2003). *World Health Report 2003. Shaping the future*. WHO: Geneva.

CHAPTER TWENTY-TWO

Clinical Trial Feasibility Studies of the Collaborative Assessment and Management of Suicidality

David A. Jobes, Katherine Anne Comtois, Lisa A. Brenner, and Peter M. Gutierrez

Abstract

The Collaborative Assessment and Management of Suicidality (CAMS) is an evidence-based therapeutic framework that uses a multi-purpose clinical assessment, treatment planning, tracking, and outcome tool called the Suicide Status Form (SSF). In this chapter we describe two major aspects of CAMS: the overall philosophy of the CAMS approach; and specific CAMS clinical procedures that are guided by using the SSF as a therapeutic roadmap. CAMS care is fundamentally designed to enhance the therapeutic alliance and increase the patient's motivation to function as an active participant in their own clinical care. CAMS is an out-patient-oriented approach that endeavours to keep suicidal patients *out* of an in-patient hospital setting by the collaborative development of a 'Crisis Response Plan'. Moreover, CAMS care focuses clinical treatments on those issues that directly and indirectly make the patient suicidal (the so-called 'drivers' of suicidal thoughts and behaviours). A final aspect of CAMS care focuses on the development of reasons for living and a sense of purpose and meaning in life. While there are persuasive correlational data that support the use of the CAMS and the SSF, the authors are currently engaged in two feasibility clinical trial studies of the approach. The chapter concludes with lessons learned from these studies and next steps for this novel approach to suicidal risk.

International Handbook of Suicide Prevention: Research, Policy and Practice, First Edition.
Edited by Rory C. O'Connor, Stephen Platt, Jacki Gordon.
© 2011 John Wiley & Sons, Ltd. Published 2011 by John Wiley & Sons, Ltd.

Introduction

Based on recognized clinical need and shaped by ongoing clinical research and applications in various settings, the Collaborative Assessment and Management of Suicidality (otherwise known as CAMS) represents a novel, multifaceted approach to working with suicidal patients. CAMS is intended to assist clinicians with many issues which make caring for suicidal patients so challenging (Jobes, Rudd, Overholser, & Joiner, 2008). The CAMS approach, which includes use of the Suicide Status Form (SSF), has been developed over a 20-year period and is supported by clinical research published in peer-reviewed journals (e.g., Arkov, Rosenbaum, Christiansen, Jonsson, & Munchow, 2008; Conrad, Jacoby, Jones, Lineberry, Shea, *et al.*, 2009; Jobes, 1995, 2000; Jobes, Jacoby, Cimbolic, & Hustead, 1997; Jobes & Mann, 2000; Jobes & Drozd, 2004; Jobes, Wong, Conrad, Drozd, & Neal-Walden, 2005; Jobes, Kahn-Greene, Greene, & Goeke-Morey, 2009).

CAMS is best understood as a clinical framework that guides the intervention process. As such, it can be employed by clinicians from a wide range of orientations. The CAMS approach heavily emphasizes the assessment of risk using the SSF. Moreover, we believe that the collaborative assessment process used in CAMS is in itself therapeutic. When employed over multiple sessions, the CAMS clinical framework creates an extensive documentation trail, enhances risk management, potentially decreases the prospect of malpractice liability, and ultimately improves clinical care. To date, CAMS has been *out-patient*-oriented with an explicit goal of keeping suicidal patients *out* of the hospital. However, current CAMS research is underway to apply the framework to intensive *in-patient* work. Finally, CAMS has been used to organize individual clinical work, but other applications of CAMS are being considered to organize group treatment.

As the developers of CAMS, we acknowledge that the framework does not meet the needs of every suicidal patient in all clinical settings. Nevertheless, we have found the approach is remarkably flexible and adaptable to a range of clinical settings and mental health providers. It does also appear to be useful with a broad spectrum of suicidal patients. Critically, CAMS is very much an evolving clinical framework which is shaped, modified, and influenced by clinical practice and ongoing research.

In this chapter, we describe the established tenets of CAMS and lessons learned from two feasibility trials of CAMS by research teams at the Denver Veterans Affairs Mental Illness Research, Education, and Clinical Center (MIRECC) and at the University of Washington. We have found this clinical research to be extraordinarily enlightening, sometimes surprising, and always helpful in our continuing quest to establish evidence for use of CAMS and the SSF, and replicate findings previously shown in four correlational treatment-oriented studies (Arkov *et al.*, 2008; Jobes *et al.*, 1997; Jobes *et al.*, 2005; Jobes, Kahn-Greene, *et al.*, 2009). Our ultimate goal is to conduct rigorous, well-powered, randomized clinical trial research of CAMS to support and replicate its potential effectiveness in 'real-world' clinical settings in order to provide a fully evidenced-based approach to a major contemporary clinical challenge.

CAMS Therapeutic Philosophy

As described elsewhere (Jobes, 2006, 2009), CAMS is grounded in a specific therapeutic philosophy. This philosophy largely eschews traditional 'medical model' approaches to suicide risk wherein suicidal ideation or behaviours are relegated to symptom status under the larger umbrellas of mental disorders and psychopathology. The suicidology literature is replete with many examples citing psychopathology as the principal aetiological basis of suicide. In CAMS, while we never ignore psychopathology, we tend to focus our treatment on mental disorders and symptoms only when the patient reports that the mental disorder is contributing to their suicidality. In CAMS we do not assume that targeting and treating the mental disorder with psychotherapy and/or medications will necessarily have *any* impact on suicidal thinking or behaviours. This stance is also supported by the broader clinical literature (e.g., see recent review of suicide treatment research by Wenzel, Brown, & Beck, 2008). Not unlike Beck's approach to treating individuals who attempt suicide, we tend specifically to target suicidal thinking and behaviours as the focus of treatment, independent of psychiatric diagnosis (Brown, Steer, Henriques, & Beck, 2005; Wenzel, Brown, & Beck, 2008). Similar to Linehan's (1993) approach in Dialectical Behaviour Therapy (DBT), we share the view that suicidal behaviours have a 'functional' purpose within the coping repertoire of patients. In turn, CAMS utilizes many DBT-related concepts about the importance of skill-building and the development of better coping strategies, all of which work towards the overarching goal of developing a life worth living.

Another central philosophical point in CAMS is the basic clinical stance towards discussing the topic of suicide with any suicidal patient. Essentially our position is as follows. People are capable of ending their own lives. Suicides happen on a daily basis around the world. In CAMS we try very hard to avoid the common debate between clinician and patient as to *whether* suicide is an option for the patient. Our position is that suicide is always an option and that we as clinicians have limited ultimate control over patient actions. That said, we are clear and forthright about our suicide prevention bias and state that mental health acts create a legal duty to protect patients who are imminently a danger to themselves (or others). In turn, we acknowledge that voluntary or involuntary hospital stays are sometimes necessary to help keep patients as safe as possible (Jobes & O'Connor, 2009).

Empathy with the Suicidal Wish

It is our contention that a strong alliance with a suicidal person begins with how we respond to the topic of suicide when it first arises. Orbach (2001) has helpfully noted that any successful clinical engagement on the topic of suicide begins with an empathic understanding of the suicidal wish. In this sense it is absolutely critical for the clinician to fully hear, be open to, not judge or react negatively to any disclosures of suicidal thoughts or behaviours by the patient. We understand it is hard not to react negatively to suicidal communications: clinicians naturally feel a sense of anxiety and worry for the patient's well-being which is also mixed with fears about our responsibility to the patient and possible liability. Nevertheless, to be best positioned to help such patients, it is absolutely necessary that the clinician overrides their natural anxiety. Doing so requires being fully and empathically engaged with why and how the patient yearns for suicide. However, this does not include clinician endorsement of suicide as an option. Clinicians can be clear about our suicide prevention agenda and still be empathic of the patient's suicidal suffering. A therapeutic assessment can occur when a clinician is fully able to understand and appreciate a patient's suicidal struggle as a reflection of desperate psychological pain. In our experience, when such an assessment happens, it may help decrease the prospect of suicidal behaviour.

In acknowledging the focus on suicide prevention and empathizing with the suicidal wish, CAMS clinicians can disengage from the typical power struggles that often ensue in clinical care of the suicidal patient. In CAMS, we purposefully propose a sensible alternative: the patient has forever to be dead. We would therefore like them to consider fully engaging in a life-saving treatment that could help them learn to cope differently, have their needs met, and create the prospect of a life with purpose and meaning. In our view, the patient has everything to gain and really nothing to lose. This is in part related to the fact that they can obviously choose to engage in suicidal behaviour post-treatment. To this end, we routinely request a three-month commitment to a potentially life-saving course of care. We have found that this approach can also decrease contentious power struggles with patients (Jobes, 2006). Moreover, our experience suggests that suicidal patients view clinicians who utilize the CAMS approach as being empathic of their situation, which bodes well for a prospective healing alliance. What we have observed in clinical practice is that suicide often drives a wedge of different and competing agendas between patient and clinician. In CAMS, we endeavour to remove that wedge by joining with the patient in a mutual goal of having needs met and finding better ways of coping. This approach fundamentally relies on the development of a collaborative clinical alliance and a process that targets interventions on what makes the patient suicidal, what we refer to as the 'drivers' of the patient's suicidality. In terms of drivers of suicidality, we differentiate 'direct' drivers (e.g., suicidal hopelessness) from 'indirect' drivers (e.g., breakthrough symptoms of PTSD).

Maintaining a Suicide Focus

In the ideal course of CAMS care, the clinician and the patient should be as focused as possible on those thoughts, feelings, and behaviours that lead the patient to suicide as a means of coping and having their needs met. A CAMS clinician should therefore make no apologies for this singular preoccupation. Indeed, in supervision of the aspiring CAMS clinician in clinical trial research, we entreat them routinely to reassert that CAMS is expressly designed as a suicide-specific life-saving therapeutic framework conceptualized systematically to eliminate suicide as a coping option.

Over the years, one relatively common criticism of the CAMS framework is that it is *too* suicide-focused. For example, clinicians have asked: *what if my patient does not want to talk about suicide every time we meet?* Our response is to reassert the CAMS agenda, saying that talking about other non-suicide related topics is fine, but only *after* the patient is no longer at risk of relying on suicidal coping. We are thus unabashed about our goal of moving suicidal coping off the psychological radar screen. In our experience this potentially life-saving clinical goal simply may not happen if the dyad (i.e., patient–clinician) avoids talking about what actually makes the patient suicidal and addressing that issue (i.e., drivers) or those related problems (i.e., indirect drivers). The CAMS clinician needs to ensure that they do not lose the patient to suicide while addressing other non-suicide-related issues. In this sense, the CAMS framework embraces use of adjunctive treatments, as needed (e.g., use of medications or couples therapy). While some clinicians may feel uncomfortable with the persistent emphasis on suicide, we remind them that a patient's other issues are better addressed if they are alive. We feel this blunt stance helps clarify what suicide is. This kind of frank reality testing can thereby remove some of the patient's distorted or magical thinking related to suicide.

Collaboration

As demonstrated in many psychotherapy treatment studies, the quality of the clinical alliance is the single best predictor of optimal outcomes (Horvath & Symonds, 1991). Suicide can pose perhaps the most common direct challenge or threat to the clinical alliance by creating adversaries (patient versus clinician), often resulting in a preoccupation as to whether the patient can or should take their life. Therefore, it has always seemed critical to us to find a way of ensuring the best possible alliance with suicidal patients. The CAMS approach creates a structure, a framework, and platform for engaging the patient on the topic of suicide and forming a strong clinical alliance.

The notion that the clinician and patient would actually *join* each other through a shared, in-depth focus on the patient's suicidal suffering is central to the collaborative emphasis of CAMS. In this regard, we try not to over-emphasize suicide *per se*; we would rather shift the focus to the underlying issues that ultimately lead to patients desiring suicide (i.e., the thoughts, feelings, and behaviours that are wrapped up in most suicidal states). Thus, the emphasis of CAMS is collaboration, both literal and symbolic. For example, in the initial assessment phase, we seek permission to sit next to the patient to co-produce a thorough and thoughtful assessment (using the SSF) of what makes the patient suicidal. In the next phase of the approach, the patient is actually engaged as a 'co-author' of their own treatment plan, working side-by-side, literally and figuratively, in an effort to figure out how to cope differently should a future suicidal crisis occur and what can be done about the causes of their suicidality.

One of the readily observable behavioural manifestations of collaboration is that *both* parties have equal input within the initial and ongoing course of care. The equal sharing between patient and clinician is something that we expressly monitor when we are performing adherence ratings of CAMS clinicians in our clinical research. In other words, if either the clinician or the patient is dominating the bulk of the interactions in taped sessions we review within our research studies, we provide constructive feedback to the clinician to endeavour to find ways to ensure more balance within the clinical interactions.

The CAMS notion that the patient is a 'co-author' of their suicide-specific treatment plan is not mere rhetoric; we really want to see the clinician engage with the patient and seek the patient's input and ideas about what will work.

Clarifying the CAMS Agenda

From the preceding section, it follows that the collaborative emphasis of the CAMS approach is enhanced by efforts to clarify our central focus: *what makes you suicidal and how can we fix that?* In this sense, we pursue a therapeutic agenda that seeks to displace suicidal coping with adaptive alternatives and problem-solving skills. Moreover, we clearly and regularly remind the patient that this is a suicide-specific therapeutic framework; we thus intend to focus on those things that directly and indirectly lead to suicidal thoughts and behaviours. We also endeavour to remind the patient that, beyond the development of alternative coping strategies, we are highly invested in their pursuit of purpose and meaning.

As will be articulated in the next section, there is overt and continuous attention paid to a specific agenda within the more structured assessment and treatment planning phases of CAMS. However, within the less structured phases of each session the overarching agenda and philosophy can and should be re-invoked. We believe that collaboration with the patient is ultimately enhanced and strengthened by clearly emphasizing that we are working together to eliminate suicidal coping. When this is done correctly, the patient–clinician dyad becomes a clinical team, studying and learning from past suicidal episodes as means of handling things differently in the future. By working together to target incidences of suicidal thoughts, a shared endeavour can emerge to find meaningful alternatives to those destructive thoughts and behaviours while also trying to address the legitimate needs that underlie virtually every suicidal state.

CAMS Clinical Framework: Assessment of Suicidal Risk

Collaborative suicide risk assessment

Use of the CAMS framework begins with a thorough and collaborative suicide assessment. It is expressly acknowledged that both the patient and the therapist possess necessary expertise to identify direct and indirect 'drivers' of suicidality. In addition to clarifying the nature of the patient's suicidality, the assessment process provides both parties with the information necessary to engage in collaborative treatment planning directed towards mitigating factors contributing to suicidal ideation (Jobes *et al.*, 2005).

Identifying direct and indirect drivers of suicidality

With CAMS, suicide risk assessment is facilitated via use of the SSF, a multi-purpose risk assessment tool that includes both quantitative and qualitative items (Jobes, 2006; Jobes *et al.*, 1997; Jobes & Mann, 1999; Jobes, Nelson, *et al.*, 2004). Research has demonstrated that the measure has acceptable reliability and validity (Conrad *et al.*, 2009; Jobes *et al.*, 1997). The qualitative items on the SSF provide important context for interpreting quantitative ratings (Jobes, 2006) and allow the patient to use their own words to describe factors believed to increase risk for suicidal behaviour (Jobes, Kahn-Greene, *et al.*, 2009). Use of the patient's own words regarding their suicidality and psychological distress is a means of demonstrating the importance of the patient's worldview and the clinician's commitment to collaboration. In addition, patients who are able to are encouraged to write down their responses on the SSF. We believe that this type of participation in the therapeutic process facilitates an increased sense of shared ownership.

Using the SSF, the clinical dyad identifies direct (e.g., suicide-specific thoughts, feelings, and behaviours) and indirect (e.g., homelessness, depression, substance abuse, posttraumatic stress disorder, isolation) factors which lead to the patient's suicidality. Direct drivers are believed to increase the risk of future self-inflicted death. To aid in the assessment process, the following five theoretically-based factors are included in the SSF: psychological pain; stress; agitation; hopelessness; and self-hate. The first three were derived from Shneidman's (1993) theoretical 'cubic' model of suicide (Jobes, 2006). Shneidman (1993) suggested that individuals are at the highest risk of suicide when these three factors occur simultaneously. Stress, similar to the construct referred to by Shneidman (1993) as 'press', is the degree of life stressors that negatively impact upon psychological functioning. Agitation (perturbation) refers to intense emotional unrest and a sense that urgent action must be taken. The fourth factor, hopelessness, has been shown to predict future suicide risk (Beck, Brown, Berchick, Stewart, & Steer, 1990; Beck, Steer, Kovacs, & Garrison, 1985). Finally, Baumeister's (1990) escape theory of suicide suggests that suicidality is reflective of a fundamental attempt to escape from unacceptable perceptions – an unbearable experience – of the self.

Use of the SSF also allows the clinician to work with the patient to identify life circumstances which are further contributing to suicidality. These indirect drivers are often situational and psychosocial in nature (e.g., economic hardship, relationship or job losses). In completing the SSF, the patient is asked to rate themselves, qualitatively and quantitatively, on each of the five factors. For example, they are queried regarding their level of psychological pain, defined as hurt, anguish, or misery in your mind, from 1 (low pain) to 5 (high pain). The patient is then prompted to respond to the following question: '*What I find most painful is* …' This process allows the therapist and the patient to identify both factors underlying suicidality and circumstances contributing to these direct drivers. Identification and monitoring of suicide-specific thoughts, feelings, and behaviours and stressors are essential in the CAMS framework and help to shape treatment planning.

During the initial session, the clinician and the patient also work together to clarify current and historical factors that may contribute to suicide risk. For example, some of these variables include previous suicidal behaviour, substance abuse, health problems, and loss. This information helps determine the immediacy of suicidal risk, as well as guiding treatment planning. For example, identifying a history of substance misuse and then linking intoxication to increased suicidal ideation may prompt the dyad to include abstaining from alcohol use as a goal of treatment. This is an example of keeping the focus on suicide even when addressing other psychiatric issues.

Collaboratively deconstructing the relationship between direct and indirect drivers of suicide is focal in CAMS. It is in this process that the dyad can create a treatment plan aimed at decreasing thoughts, feelings, and behaviours (direct drivers) and psychosocial stressors (indirect drivers) fuelling potential suicidal ideation and behaviours. In other words, using assessment information obtained with the SSF enables the patient and clinician to function as co-authors of the suicide-specific treatment plan (Jobes, 2006).

CAMS Clinical Framework: Problem-Focused Interventions that Eliminate Suicidal Drivers

Crisis response planning

Once an initial assessment of the drivers of suicidality is completed using the SSF, the clinical dyad shift their attention to the development of crisis-oriented coping and the development of a suicide-specific treatment plan. A major focus of intervention in the first session is the *Crisis Response Plan* that helps to increase the patient's ability to cope with current and future crises, thereby averting or at least delaying suicidal behaviour during the course of CAMS organized care.

Originally adapted from the work of Rudd, Joiner, and Rajab (2001), crisis response planning in CAMS has much in common with commitment to treatment statements (Rudd, Mandrusiak, & Joiner, 2006) and safety plans (Lewis, 2007; Stanley, Brown, Karlin, Kemp, & von Bergen, 2008) developed by other suicidologists. It is emphatically *not* a 'no-suicide' or 'no-harm' contract, a widely used approach that has neither empirical support nor any protective value from a liability perspective. Within CAMS, our goal in crisis response planning is to address the direct and indirect drivers identified by the SSF. Crisis response planning is always the first step in the development of the larger treatment plan and is the principal focus within the initial session. Crisis response planning is revisited each week until the patient's suicidality resolves (i.e., three consecutive clinical contacts where there are no suicidal thoughts, feelings, or behaviours). Throughout CAMS-organized care, the treatment plan consistently targets the key drivers of suicidality gleaned from the SSF. This treatment planning process conveys the clinician's understanding of the primary aetiological issues of the patient's suicidality which may then instil some measure of hope that these issues can in fact be addressed.

In our experience, many suicidal patients have previously completed some version of a plan to control imminent suicidal behaviour. However, it is rare for clinicians working outside the CAMS framework to explain a larger understanding of the suicide drivers. When crisis response planning is done properly, the patient can better appreciate the treatment goal: to learn new ways of coping (while still appreciating that seemingly unbearable forces haunt the suicidal patient). Reality-based time limits in a first session may truncate the full exploration of all suicidal drivers. It is therefore useful to note that identified problems, beyond maintaining safety and eliminating suicide coping, will be further addressed in subsequent sessions or by referrals. This emphasis helps to give the patient a wider perspective on treatment, helping them appreciate that there are both short- and long-term goals within this suicide-specific approach.

Crisis response planning can be done in a variety of ways: a strength of CAMS is that clinicians are free to be creative with interventions. Engaging in problem-solving with the patient on how to reduce access to lethal means as much as possible is inherent to crisis response planning and another means by which to foster collaboration. It is particularly important to address access to firearms. For instance, a patient in one of our trials lived in a house that had an apartment over the adjacent garage. The renter who lived in the garage apartment had a loaded gun that he sometimes brought into and left in the main house, thereby providing the patient with repeated access to lethal means. With support of the CAMS clinician, the patient was able to ask the renter to refrain from bringing the gun into the house and to keep it locked in his apartment. The renter readily agreed to this plan, and the patient's immediate access to the gun was thus eliminated. For those means, such as jumping or drowning, which cannot be removed, efforts can similarly focus on reducing access. For example, another trial patient agreed to keep his car keys in his wife's purse by her side of the bed at night. Because she was a light sleeper, she would be aware of any attempt on his part to drive his car to a bridge where he had considered jumping. While not every patient is able completely to block access to lethal means, creating a buffer of some sort can help reduce the risk of impulsive attempts and demonstrates a good faith effort on the patient's part to take more responsibility for potential suicidal behaviour.

It is important to ensure that the patient has in place a specific plan in case suicidal ideation or urges arise. One way to accomplish this is through the use of a 'crisis card', which can be made from the clinician's business card. A business card is small enough to fit in a wallet or purse pocket so that the patient can have ready access to it at all times. In addition, a business card contains all relevant contact information for the clinician which can be used by the patient or anyone else who might be helping the patient in a crisis. Working collaboratively with the patient, the dyad outlines on the back of the card four to six steps the patient can take to avert suicidal behaviour if suicidal ideation or urges increase. The explicit goal is to develop steps to distract or re-direct the patient from suicidal thinking and behaviours. Options are as varied as the patients we treat, and may include reading a book, taking a walk or jog, going to the gym, watching TV, calling a friend, going to sleep, etc. As this work is done during the first session, these are coping strategies to be used to help the patient if they should find themselves feeling impulsive, lonely, and suicidal. All the initial crisis steps on the crisis card are thus designed to be actions that the patient can take without direct clinical support. Accordingly, the final step offered by the CAMS clinician involves directly accessing clinical support. In other words, the clinician explains that the main goal of the crisis card is to help the patient take specific coping actions to learn that there are ways of handling their darkest moments. However, in turn it should be made clear that, if the patient's coping efforts are insufficient, the clinician will be accessible to the patient as back-up crisis support. Part of this intervention further requires the acknowledgment that there are alternatives in a crisis should the clinician not be immediately available. In other words, the CAMS clinician helps the suicidal patient better understand what to do in case of an emergency. We therefore provide information about contacting a crisis line (should the CAMS clinician not be available) as an alternative to going to a hospital emergency department because a crisis line worker can provide immediate assistance and help mobilize the most appropriate resources, if an emergency response is indicated.

Once access to lethal means and crisis strategies are addressed, a next step is to consider possible barriers to attending treatment. As with any effective intervention, it is essential that the patient attends sessions regularly and does not dropout prematurely. Even with the best of intentions in the initial session, practical issues may interfere or patients may find themselves reluctant to talk repeatedly about suicide. Thus, it is important in the initial session to work with the patient to identify as many barriers to treatment as possible and problem-solve strategies to resolve them. For instance, with low-income patients, access to bus passes or other transportation may be needed. Alternatively, sessions may need to be scheduled when a patient with substance abuse problems is least likely to be intoxicated or a patient with insomnia is most likely to be alert. It is usually quite useful to talk about strategies the clinician can take to reduce the patient's discomfort.

Finally, we can work to establish existing interpersonal supports in the patient's life that the clinician can call if the patient fails to attend treatment or the clinician is worried about imminent risk. The clinician can ask the patient for names of supportive friends, family, clergy, etc. who might be able to play this role, write down their contact information, and obtain a release to disclose information in case it is necessary to call someone regarding imminent risk or to locate the patient. This process can also remind the patient of individuals who have or will provide support, assures their contact information is available, and, often, provides reasons for living by highlighting people who would be hurt if the patient died by suicide.

Within CAMS the initial SSF assessment and crisis response plan should be photocopied for the patient to take home. Each subsequent CAMS session would then involve routine checking of the utility of the patient's crisis card and larger crisis response plan to assess whether both are effective or in need of modification.

Targeting and treating suicidal drivers

As previously noted, suicidal drivers in CAMS are divided between direct and indirect influences. Both kinds of drivers must be addressed in treatment but are considered differently. Direct drivers are the focus of CAMS-organized sessions. The patient is thus oriented to this emphasis each week, as needed to assure that this emphasis remains a focus. Ideally, indirect drivers are addressed in session only to the extent that they elucidate the direct drivers. The indirect drivers are also discussed in terms of finding alternative resources to address them, such as case management or social services assistance, referral for psychiatric medications, a post-traumatic stress disorder (PTSD) treatment programme or vocational counselling. Focusing on indirect drivers (e.g., depression) in CAMS should therefore occur when the direct drivers have been sufficiently addressed and in situations where focusing on an indirect driver helps to clarify the role of, or decreases, a direct driver. For instance, the indirect driver of depression may properly become a focus in CAMS care as it may relate to a direct driver of the patient's hopeless thoughts about life or their sense of being a burden on others. The patient is always reminded throughout CAMS organized care that the first goal of the approach is explicitly to eliminate suicidal coping as a way of responding to the stresses of their lives and working on other ways to respond. Once suicidality is no longer present, focus can then be redirected to indirect drivers, either with the same clinician or by referral to an appropriate alternative form of care.

The CAMS framework does not prescribe a specific intervention for any particular direct or indirect driver. Instead, the clinician is encouraged to use the skills and strategies they already know, particularly evidence-based approaches. Thus, the CAMS framework is problem-focused and flexible rather than strategy-focused and rigid. The clinician does not then have to learn an entirely new repertoire of theory or interventions or stop using techniques in which they have expertise. It can be quite helpful for the clinician to have access to a consulting team of colleagues when certain clinical strategies are not working, or when a clinician does not know an effective strategy. One of the major lessons learned in our clinical research has been the importance of providing support in the form of consultation to our CAMS clinicians. This consultation team approach is common across other evidence-based treatments for suicide (e.g., Brown *et al.*, 2005; Linehan, 1993).

The development of purpose and meaning

While our feasibility trials have provided valuable concrete information about assessing and treating suicidal patients, we have also seen a need within the intervention for something more abstract, but definitely critical. This often elusive but essential treatment focus is to help a suicidal person find a way to live their life with *purpose* and *meaning*. The more existential aspects of treating suicidal patients have perhaps been somewhat overshadowed by leading approaches that place a heavy emphasis on the specific development of concrete coping skills, improved help-seeking, and better problem-solving (see, e.g., interventions described by Rudd *et al.*, 2001; Wenzel *et al.*, 2008). A notable exception is provided in Dialectical Behaviour Therapy, the well-validated cognitive-behavioural treatment developed by Linehan (1993). As previously noted, DBT emphasises the importance of a patient developing a life worth living.

With this consideration in mind, we have sought to include, as a final component of the CAMS framework, the explicit development of *plans, goals, and hope for the future*. These specific constructs emerged empirically from previous research comparing SSF-obtained 'Reasons for Living' (RFL) with suicidal treatment-seekers and non-suicidal control group samples (Jobes, 2006). In this line of study, we observed that non-suicidal individuals had *twice* as many RFLs focused on these largely aspirational constructs which help people get through the difficulties of life. Indeed, meaningful plans and obtainable goals to which people aspire naturally spawn a sense of hope. It is well known that the abject loss or absence of hope is pervasive in suicidal states (Beck *et al.*, 1985; Beck *et al.*, 1990). Thus, the idea of building hope within the patient, explicitly and directly, makes perfect sense and is emphasised in CAMS accordingly.

While the development of existential purpose and meaning has been a clear-cut goal in our current treatment studies, it has proved difficult thus far to weave this emphasis reliably into routine CAMS organized care. This may be due in part to the fact that so many of the suicidal patients in our current trials are extremely ill and struggle with extraordinarily challenging lives. Indeed, patients from our VA and Harborview samples often struggle with unemployment, homelessness, and/or substance abuse. It follows that presenting any higher-order aspirations to such patients can be experienced as an abject empathic failure, when eating, basic shelter, generating any income or finding transportation represents daily challenges. However, while lofty existential goal-setting may not be immediately appropriate for these particular samples, we have nevertheless seen a distinct need for instilling a sense of hope in these suicidal patients. Treatment of these patients therefore focuses in large measure on helping them to find jobs and housing and staying sober, while at the same time linking these indirect drivers of suicidality to direct drivers (e.g., hopelessness). When basic needs are addressed, the potential for considering the longer-term hope of meaning and purpose can be introduced. It is also important to acknowledge that meaning and purpose in life is individualistic, and possible for all humans. In previous studies with higher-functioning suicidal college students (Jobes *et al.*, 1997) and active duty military personnel (Jobes *et al.*, 2005), a direct focus on purpose and meaning has been more tenable.

Whatever the case, we know that hope is crucial for any suicidal patient. It is something that should be implicit and explicit in every CAMS organized session. Now that we have laid the foundations for understanding how the CAMS works, we will close with further examples of lessons learned from our continuing feasibility studies of CAMS in two distinctly different clinical settings.

Feasibility Study: Denver VA Mental Illness Research, Education, and Clinical Center

This project was our first effort to explore whether the CAMS framework could be implemented in a real-world setting and to assess whether use of CAMS would help patients resolve their suicidality more rapidly that those receiving treatment as usual. Suicidal patients being treated at the Denver VA Mental Illness Research, Education, and Clinical Center (MIRECC) receive individualized treatment based on their clinical needs. At this VA, in common with many others, a collaborative interdisciplinary team approach is utilized, and a full range of treatments and programmes (e.g., individual and group psychotherapy, psychoeducation, family treatment, supportive individual and group psychotherapy, employment assistance, pharmacotherapy, and acute emergency care) is offered. Veterans entering treatment are carefully screened for a range of issues, including potential danger to self or others, and, when indicated, in-patient psychiatric hospitalization is pursued. Specifically, a patient deemed to be at imminent risk for suicidal behaviour, who is unable to follow a safety plan developed with their primary mental health clinician, would likely be hospitalized in order to maintain safety.

Based upon empirical evidence in support of CAMS (Jobes *et al.*, 2005), members of the VISN 19 MIRECC research team were interested in whether this systematic targeted out-patient approach to care would decrease patients' suicidal ideation and/or negative psychiatric outcomes (Brenner *et al.*, 2006). The sample for the current project is being drawn from veterans seeking services from the Mental Health Clinic, and engages providers working in this setting. In our trial we originally intended to recruit only out-patients who were suicidal but found over time that we needed to recruit similarly from in-patient psychiatric care to generate sufficient samples. Individuals who consent to participate in the study are randomly allocated to enhanced treatment as usual (which includes close research monitoring of suicidality via outcome measures) or CAMS organized care. Conducting the project in this setting has allowed us to collect information regarding more traditional outcomes (e.g., suicidal ideation), as well as data regarding the feasibility of conducting CAMS in a busy VA medical center out-patient clinic.

We have learned that patients are generally receptive to receiving treatment that specifically focuses on their suicidality. However, many patients struggle with a range of indirect drivers for their suicidality. Although VA clinicians are skilled at providing or obtaining case management for their patients, they reported being challenged by shortage of session time to devote adequate attention to both direct and indirect drivers of suicidality. One recommendation made by CAMS clinicians is to increase the initial session time to 90 minutes. Several of the study clinicians are clinical nurse practitioners who provide medication management in addition to psychotherapy. Time-related challenges have also arisen within this context.

Challenges related to implementing a new treatment practice within an existing system have plainly occurred and provided opportunities to both clinicians and research team members to explore means of implementing new models of care. For example, over the course of the study we have explored several different strategies to facilitate entry of information obtained on the SSF into the VA electronic medical record. Support from medical center administration has been vital to explore creative ways to utilize elements of CAMS, and reinforced for us the importance of working *with* systems when trying to implement change (even for time-limited projects).

We have also found that relatively brief training was not sufficient to facilitate a change in practice. Our clinicians were very receptive to receiving training, but the nature of their schedules required breaking trainings into shorter sessions, meeting on weekends, and reading about CAMS outside of their normal work day. Such additional time demands may be too much for some systems, which has led us to think creatively about the most efficient way to provide clinician training. One solution was to adopt a model of consistent consultation. This is accomplished by CAMS consultants listening to clinician tapes, identifying strengths and weaknesses using a fidelity rating form, and providing feedback to the clinician in a timely manner. Another benefit of this approach is that we now have a standardized adherence scale for use in future research and clinician training efforts. Also of interest to the team has been our ability to document the chaotic nature of participants' lives. We recognize more clearly the wide range of challenges faced by VA patients who become suicidal, and the need for significant effort on the part of both clinician and patient to address the multitude of direct and indirect drivers. Barriers to individuals consistently participating in CAMS organized care have included patient hospitalization at outside facilities, incarceration, and lack of access to a telephone. We know that such challenges are not unique to our patient population, as evidenced by the second feasibility study which was initiated after the VA study was under way.

CAMS next-day appointment feasibility study at Harborview Medical Center

A small pilot study funded by the American Foundation for Suicide Prevention has examined the use of CAMS in a setting where it has not been used previously, namely an out-patient crisis intervention services clinic of a large urban medical center. So-called 'next day appointments' (or, more appropriately, next available appointments) are a treatment delivery strategy developed with emergency and in-patient departments to provide immediate follow-up for patients admitted post-suicide attempt or with significant suicidal ideation who do not have access to out-patient follow-up care. These appointments lead to brief treatments (two to three months) focusing on resolving the crisis and providing linkage to long-term services. Harborview Medical Center, a large county hospital in Seattle, Washington, has a psychiatric emergency room, consultation–liaison psychiatry services for the medical/surgical units, and three in-patient psychiatry units. Many of the patients seen in these services do not have health insurance or access to clinicians who can follow up on their suicide risk post-discharge. Similar to the VA trial, this study was designed to evaluate whether crisis intervention services organized by CAMS are feasible and acceptable to patients and clinicians and likely to show benefit compared with crisis intervention services as usual.

Participants for this study are recruited from the in-patient psychiatry and consultation–liaison psychiatry service and given a next available appointment with a CAMS or usual care clinician in the Crisis Intervention Service. CAMS-organized care is provided in accordance with clinic guidelines and long-term services are referred out rather than provided by the CAMS clinician. So far, four important issues have been learned in this feasibility study.

First, CAMS is an eminently trainable model. The majority of clinicians in our study (psychiatry, psychology, and social work, masters and doctoral level) were able to learn CAMS to adherence on their first case based on reading the treatment manual, one day of training, one to two months of weekly team supervision, and feedback from adherence coding of their session videotapes. The supervision/consultation component of this study is much more extensive than what was initially provided in the VA study and informed changes made in that study (described above). While achieving adherence was not difficult for most clinicians, it was somewhat more difficult for case management-focused clinicians who had less psychotherapy experience to draw upon. While they did an excellent job of finding resources to address indirect drivers, it was more difficult for them to address the direct drivers during the session. In future implementations of CAMS, we recommend training for case managers who will benefit from training in psychotherapeutic crisis interventions and treatment for the most typical direct drivers.

Second, CAMS is acceptable to most patients, with very few patients dropping out of care. It was rare in CAMS for a patient to leave while suicidality remained high; those who dropped out were more likely to do so as suicidality had been all or mostly resolved and further referrals were being established. Patients generally reported satisfaction with the treatment they received and would recommend it to others.

Third, it is clear that case management is critical for patients receiving next available appointments who are often homeless and without financial support. Having an external case manager who is not the CAMS clinician is more efficient, as it allows the CAMS clinician to remain focused on the direct drivers and not have most of session time taken with the case management of indirect drivers. The CAMS clinician can refer to the external case manager on an as-needed basis while maintaining clinical responsibility for the case and the case manager is not required to manage crises.

Finally, many of the individuals in our study were also abusing or dependent on drugs or alcohol. The majority of those with substance abuse problems appear to be amenable to CAMS and benefit in terms of resolved suicidality with the adjunct of substance-specific interventions, naltrexone or antabuse, or referral to intensive out-patient substance abuse treatment. The exception to this appears to be cases of substance dependence when highly lethal suicidal behaviour is consistently triggered by substance use. When patients cannot prevent themselves from using substances, they in turn may not be able to prevent suicidal behaviour. These cases are not amenable to brief psychotherapy and require an intensive out-patient or in-patient intervention. Lessons learned from these two ongoing feasibility studies have thus significantly informed our thinking about future research on CAMS, as will the final results, when available.

Next Steps for CAMS Clinical Trial Research

The next steps for CAMS are an elaboration and extension of the ideas and research described in this chapter. Based on our feasibility research, we hope to pursue larger, well-powered, randomized clinical trials of the approach. Having worked out a number of methodological, procedural, and pragmatic issues, we now feel well positioned to conduct the definitive randomized clinical trial research to investigate the causal impact of CAMS on suicidal patients. While we pursue funding for this type of research, still other CAMS-related feasibility projects are continuing.

For example, colleagues at the Menninger Clinic in Houston, Texas are currently conducting a feasibility trial of CAMS in an in-patient psychiatric setting. While CAMS was originally developed as a way to organize out-patient care, we are nevertheless interested in seeing whether an intensive in-patient treatment organized by the CAMS framework can meaningfully impact upon longer-term chronic suicidal patients over the course of a 50–60-day stay. Among other things, as part of this latter study we intend to make discharge contingent on the patient being able to demonstrate an acquired competency in coping differently (in contrast to their pre-hospitalization coping skill set).

In another study within the VA system, we are investigating a different version of CAMS training with implications for downstream clinical treatment process and outcomes. This study, which is being conducted at the Charleston, South Carolina VA Medical Center, will examine live CAMS training provided by the first author in contrast to 'e-learning' web-based training. One of the strengths of CAMS is the relative accessibility of the training, but the larger translational goal – making the training 'stick' and getting better adoption and adherence by clinicians – has been more of a challenge and is therefore a major goal of this particular line of research.

Other adaptations of CAMS to varied clinical settings are also under way. A short one-to-three session version of applying the CAMS framework to treating suicidal patients is now being studied in two out-patient clinics in Copenhagen, Denmark. Various other collaborators are looking at possible adaptations of CAMS for group treatment modalities for suicidal patients. Clinician collaborators in Australia are using a version of CAMS in a short-term primary care coordinated intervention. Finally, a recent grant with the Indian

Health Service will enable us to study the feasibility of using CAMS with high-risk suicidal Native Americans. Thus, there are a number of next steps in our ongoing efforts to apply CAMS to different populations, cultures, and clinical settings.

Conclusion

As research collaborators we have learned much from our efforts to make CAMS work in busy treatment settings. CAMS has never been an 'ivory tower' approach to assessing and treating suicidal risk; all the research done to date has been in 'real-world' clinical settings (Jobes, Bryan, & Neal-Walden, 2009). What has emerged in this work is that CAMS is first and foremost a philosophy of clinical care for the suicidal patient. CAMS is also a set of clinical procedures that uses the SSF as a framework to guide assessment, treatment planning, tracking, and outcomes of care. In our studies we have worked out many methodological and procedural issues in our efforts to create treatment adherence and fidelity. In so doing, we have further fleshed out key components of crisis response planning, as well as the importance of focusing on direct and indirect drivers of suicidality. In our research we have seen how collaborating with the suicidal patient to understand what makes them suicidal enables the dyad to bring a problem-focused approach to treatment that has the potential systematically to eliminate the need for suicidal coping. When whole new coping skills are created, buttressed by crisis response planning, then the clinical dyad is uniquely positioned to treat suicidal drivers. In turn, a crucial and potentially life-saving door can then be opened that enables the patient to pursue essential reasons for living replete with plans, goals, and hope for the future, such that they may actually one day realize a life with purpose and meaning.

References

Arkov, K., Rosenbaum, B., Christiansen, L., Jonsson, H., & Munchow, M. (2008). Treatment of suicidal patients: The collaborative assessment and management of suicidality. *Ugeskrift for Laeger, 170*, 149–153.

Baumeister, R. F. (1990). Suicide as escape from self. *Psychological Review, 97*, 90–113.

Beck, A. T., Brown, G., Berchick, R. J., Stewart, B. L., & Steer, R. A. (1990). Relationship between hopelessness and ultimate suicide: A replication with psychiatric outpatients. *American Journal of Psychiatry, 147*, 190–195.

Beck, A. T., Steer, R. A., Kovacs, M., & Garrison, B. (1985). Hopelessness and eventual suicide: A 10-year prospective study of patients hospitalized with suicidal ideation. *American Journal of Psychiatry, 142*, 559–563.

Brenner, L. A., Gutierrez, P. M., Homaifar, B. Y., Huggins, J., Devore, M. D., Kemp, J., & Nagamoto, H.T. (2006). Intensive Outpatient Treatment for Suicidal Veterans: A Randomized Clinical Trial and Feasibility Investigation: Unpublished research protocol (06-1058). Department of Veterans Affairs, VISN 19 MIRECC, Denver, CO.

Brown, G. K., Steer, R. A., Henriques, G. R., & Beck, A. T. (2005). The internal struggle between the wish to die and the wish to live: A risk factor for suicide. *American Journal of Psychiatry, 162*, 1977–1979.

Conrad, A. K., Jacoby, A. M., Jobes, D. A., Lineberry, T. W., Shea, C. E., Arnold Ewing, T. D., Schmid, P. J., Ellenbecker, S. M., Lee, J. L., Fritsche, K., Grenell, J. A., Gehin, J. M., & Kung, S. (2009). A psychometric investigation of the suicide status form with suicidal inpatients. *Suicide and Life-Threatening Behavior, 39,* 307–320.

Horvath, A. O. & Symonds, B. D. (1991). Relation between working alliance and outcome in psychotherapy: A meta-analysis. *Journal of Counseling Psychology, 38,* 139–149.

Jobes, D. A. (1995). The challenge and the promise of clinical suicidology. *Suicide and Life-Threatening Behavior, 25,* 437–449.

Jobes, D. A. (2000). Collaborating to prevent suicide: A clinical-research perspective. *Suicide and Life-Threatening Behavior, 30,* 8–17.

Jobes, D. A. (2006). *Managing Suicidal Risk: A collaborative approach.* New York: Guilford Press.

Jobes, D. A. (2009). The CAMS approach to suicide risk: Philosophy and clinical procedures. *Suicidology, 14,* 3–7.

Jobes, D. A., Bryan, C. J., & Neal-Walden, T. A. (2009). Conducting suicide research in naturalistic settings. *Journal of Clinical Psychology, 65,* 382–395.

Jobes, D. A. & Drozd, J. F. (2004). The CAMS approach to working with suicidal patients. *Journal of Contemporary Psychotherapy, 34,* 73–85.

Jobes, D. A., Jacoby, A. M., Cimbolic, P., & Hustead, L. A. T. (1997). The assessment and treatment of suicidal clients in a university counseling center. *Journal of Counseling Psychology, 44,* 368–377.

Jobes, D. A., Kahn-Greene, E., Greene, J., & Goeke-Morey, M. (2009). Clinical improvements of suicidal outpatients: Examining suicide status from responses as moderators. *Archives of Suicide Research, 13,* 147–159.

Jobes, D. A. & Mann, R. E. (1999). Reasons for living versus reasons for dying: Examining the internal debate of suicide. *Suicide and Life-Threatening Behavior, 29,* 97–104.

Jobes, D. A. & Mann, R. E. (2000). Reasons for living versus reasons for dying: Examining the internal debate of suicide: Reply. *Suicide and Life-Threatening Behavior, 30,* 182.

Jobes, D. A., Nelson, K. N., Peterson, E. M., Pentiuc, D., Downing, V., Francini, K., & Kiernan, A. (2004). Describing suicidality: An investigation of qualitative SSF responses. *Suicide and Life-Threatening Behavior, 34,* 99–112.

Jobes, D. A. & O'Connor, S. S. (2009). The duty to protect suicidal clients: Ethical, legal, and professional considerations. In J. L. Werth, E. R. Welfel, & G. A. H. Benjamin (Eds.), *The duty to protect: Ethical, legal, and professional considerations for mental health professionals* (pp. 163–180). Washington, DC: American Psychological Association.

Jobes, D. A., Rudd, M. D., Overholser, J. C., & Joiner, T. E., Jr. (2008). Ethical and competent care of suicidal patients: Contemporary challenges, new developments, and considerations for clinical practice. *Professional Psychology: Research and Practice, 39,* 405–413.

Jobes, D. A., Wong, S. A., Conrad, A., Drozd, J. F., & Neal-Walden, T. (2005). The collaborative assessment and management of suicidality vs. treatment as usual: A retrospective study with suicidal outpatients. *Suicide and Life-Threatening Behavior, 35,* 483–497.

Lewis, L. M. (2007). No-harm contracts: A review of what we know. *Suicide and Life-Threatening Behavior, 37,* 50–57.

Linehan, M. M. (1993). *Cognitive-behavioral treatment of Borderline Personality Disorder.* New York: Guilford Press.

Orbach, I. (2001). Therapeutic empathy with the suicidal wish: Principles of therapy with suicidal individuals. *American Journal of Psychotherapy, 55,* 166–184.

Rudd, M. D., Joiner, T., & Rajab, M. H. (2001). *Treating suicidal behavior: An effective, time-limited approach.* New York: Guilford Press.

Rudd, M. D., Mandrusiak, M., & Joiner, T. E., Jr. (2006). The case against no-suicide contracts: The commitment to treatment statement as a practice alternative. *Journal of Clinical Psychology*, *62*, 243–251.

Shneidman, E. S. (1993). Suicide as psychache. *The Journal of Nervous and Mental Disease, 181*, 145–147.

Stanley, B., Brown, G. K., Karlin, B., Kemp, J. E., & von Bergen, H. A. (2008). *Safety Plan Treatment Manual to Reduce Suicide Risk: Veteran version.* Unpublished manuscript.

Wenzel, A., Brown, G. K., & Beck, A. T. (2008). *Cognitive Therapy for Suicidal Patients: Scientific and clinical applications.* Washington, DC: American Psychological Association.

CHAPTER TWENTY-THREE

Modes of Mind and Suicidal Processes: The Potential Role of Mindfulness in Changing Minds

J. Mark G. Williams, Danielle S. Duggan, Catherine Crane, and Silvia Hepburn

Abstract

People differ markedly in their reactions to distressing events and feelings. Understanding these differences is critically important, as some, rather than being helpful, may create the conditions in which suicidal ideas persist and escalate. This is particularly likely if the reactions involve either trying to suppress suicidal feelings or ruminating about what it means to have them. In this chapter we suggest that people are doing the best they can to deal with their mental pain, but that problems arise when a 'discrepancy-based' ('doing') mode of mind is applied habitually and inflexibly to try to alleviate distressing problems or emotional states. Consistent with this theory, we present data showing that suicidal people tend to drift into unhelpful patterns of discrepancy-based processing when trying to solve hypothetical interpersonal problems, are more likely to rely on suppression and avoidance to deal with unwanted experiences, and report using suppression as a coping strategy to deal with suicidal thoughts. Mindfulness training, an approach that teaches people to recognize when the 'doing' mode of mind is being activated in unhelpful situations and to shift to a 'being' mode of mind, is associated with self-acceptance and flexibility of response, rather than with old habitual ways of responding. We present some preliminary evidence suggesting that such training may be beneficial to people at risk of suicidal ideation and behaviour, reducing their reliance on avoidance as a response style and providing some protection against increases in self-discrepancy, in part through letting go of inappropriate ideals for themselves.

International Handbook of Suicide Prevention: Research, Policy and Practice, First Edition.
Edited by Rory C. O'Connor, Stephen Platt, Jacki Gordon.
© 2011 John Wiley & Sons, Ltd. Published 2011 by John Wiley & Sons, Ltd.

Introduction

The aim of our research over many years has been to understand the psychological processes that combine with adverse social circumstances to make someone feel trapped and suicidal. In previous work (Williams, Crane, Barnhofer, & Duggan, 2005), we have described the conditions in which suicidal ideation or behaviour[1] first occurs: the co-occurrence of feelings of extreme pressure to get out or escape and the feeling that there is, in fact, no escape possible – 'arrested flight' (O'Connor, 2003; Williams, 2001). Situations of arrested flight (*defeat, no escape and no rescue*) are regarded as the initial 'setting conditions' for suicidal behaviour and may arise either from actual circumstances (such as bullying or sexual abuse) or from a person's *perception* of how things are (feeling defeated, a failure, no options).

In this chapter we explore the hypothesis that the way people *react* to distressing stimuli, including the presence of suicidal thoughts and behaviours, is critical in determining whether these problems become 'adhesive', perpetuating a sense of entrapment. In particular, we suggest that the greatest difficulties arise when: (a) the presence of distressing situations, thoughts, or feelings immediately and automatically trigger a sense of discrepancy; (b) a mode of mind which has developed to support discrepancy-reduction (the 'doing' mode) is adopted to solve the problem, but fails to do so; and (c) there is a tendency to resort automatically to increasingly maladaptive forms of discrepancy-based processing, such as rumination and experiential avoidance, which over time may become habitual responses to discrepancies of all types.

Background

We start by looking at the thought patterns described by our suicidal patients. These are generally highly negative, global, and self-referent, such as 'I'm a complete failure, a burden'. David Rudd has summarized the sorts of thoughts and feelings that we see all too often in our patients in his Suicide Cognitions Scale (Rudd, Joiner, & Rajab, 2004). Items (*and their related categories*) include: 'This world would be better off without me' (*Perceived Burdensomeness*); 'I can never be forgiven for the mistakes I have made' (*Unlovability*); 'No one can help solve my problems' (*Helplessness*); and 'I can't stand this pain anymore' (*Poor Distress Tolerance*).

The first three categories of thoughts and feelings of burdensomeness, unlovability, and helplessness show all the hallmarks of arrested flight (defeat, no opportunities for escape or rescue), which are so important in the initial activation of suicidal thoughts and planning. But notice the fourth category within this scale: it reflects how much we can *tolerate* such pain. Distress tolerance is a critical aspect of Linehan's Dialectical Behaviour Therapy (Linehan, 1993) and has been explored by Israel Orbach (Orbach, Mikulincer, Sirota, & Gilboa-Schechtman, 2003), who finds that it is not only the degree to which people experience mental pain that distinguishes suicidal from non-suicidal people, but how much they are able to tolerate such pain.

We suggest that many suicidal cognitions might pass by themselves were it not for the fact that the mind automatically reacts to such thoughts by activating its 'doing' mode, in which discrepancy-based processing is used to try to solve the problem.

A trivial example will illustrate how successful this mode can be for *external* problems in everyday life. If we want milk on our cornflakes, this 'doing' mode will monitor the amount of milk in the fridge, take note when there is only a little left, plan to go to a shop to buy milk and return home, and regularly assess how far we are from achieving our goal – in this case to have milk at home for our breakfast cereal. This mode is often activated automatically when there is a discrepancy between our current and desired states, and usefully draws on information from the past when similar problems have been experienced before, or to the future to imagine where we want to get to.

In many situations the discrepancy-based processing of the 'doing' mode is extremely functional, forming the basis of self-regulatory activity and the ability to attain goals (Carver & Scheier, 1998). However, when it is used inflexibly to deal with emotional difficulties or distressing thoughts it can tragically backfire. For example, when discrepancies occur in emotional states (e.g., feeling unloved and unforgivable when we want to feel loved and accepted), our 'doing' mode is automatically activated to focus on monitoring and reducing the discrepancy. However, often no immediate action can be taken to reduce the discrepancy and help us reach our desired end-point, so that concentrating on the discrepancy may only serve to increase it. In such circumstances there are essentially two options: either to shift to an alternative mode of processing (the 'being' mode – see later) or redouble efforts to solve the problem using the original mode. Where people persist in attempting to solve the problem using the 'doing' mode, the mind can be easily drawn into maladaptive forms of processing, for example, rumination and suppression.

Ruminating (repetitive, self-focused thinking) feels as though it should help, but actually makes mood worse and activates other depressive cognitive processes which impair the ability to solve problems effectively (Lyubomirsky, Tucker, Caldwell, & Berg, 1999; Watkins & Teasdale, 2001). In particular, the brooding aspect of rumination, or the relative balance of a person's tendency to brood versus reflect, may be particularly related to suicidality (Crane, Barnhofer, & Williams, 2007; Morrison & O'Connor, 2008). Suppressing unpleasant thoughts and feelings may work in the short term, but evidence suggests that this can lead to thoughts 'bouncing back' into the mind yet more strongly (for a review on thought suppression see Wenzlaff & Wegner, 2000), so that they eventually become difficult to avoid or suppress.

When people find their emotional problems unsolved despite their best efforts, they also often react to their own inner feelings as if they were external threats that have to be eliminated or dangers from which they have to escape. Activity of the 'doing' mode of mind involves keeping in mind mental representations related to things which have happened in the past or which the individual is worried might occur in the future. While the mind is busy with memories of the past and images of the future, what is actually occurring 'now', which might provide alternative perspectives or solutions, is often missed. These ideas are summarized in Box 23.1.

In the sections that follow we present the findings of several studies which, using convergent methodologies, examine elements of the 'mode of mind' hypothesis as it applies to suicidal people. First, we describe how suicidal patients completing a behavioural problem-solving test (the Means Ends Problem-Solving task (MEPS) (Platt & Spivack, 1975)) respond with poor solutions, which evidence maladaptive forms of discrepancy-based processing. Second, we show that suicidal people score differently from healthy

---

Box 23.1   Characteristics of the 'doing' mode of mind when used on inappropriate problems

- Once activated is difficult to inhibit.
- Finds no immediate behavioural solution.
- Continues to focus on discrepancy (encourages judgement and striving).
- Motivation to avoid or escape unpleasantness (leads to attempts at thought suppression).
- Motivation to understand and analyse discrepancy (leads to rumination, activates low mood and other depressive cognitive processes).
- Relives relevant past and pre-lives future (leading to discounting of the 'now').
- Discrepancy is increased (exacerbates the original problem and motivates further futile attempts at eliminating it through rumination and thought suppression).

---

controls on a self-report scale that assesses one maladaptive aspect of the 'doing' mode of mind, the tendency to engage in experiential avoidance. Third, we give details of a new questionnaire, based on the White Bear Suppression Inventory (Wegner & Zanakos, 1994), designed to assess people's *reactions* to the 'problem' of their own suicidal thoughts, in particular, the degree to which they report attempts to suppress suicidal thoughts when feeling low.

Finally, we discuss how a form of mental training called mindfulness meditation, which encourages people to recognize when the 'doing' mode of mind is being activated and to adopt an alternative 'being' mode, may help to protect people with a history of suicidal ideation from using this discrepancy-based/'doing' mode of mind in inappropriate circumstances. Preliminary evidence suggests that it may help people to reduce the extent to which they engage in experiential avoidance and to let go of inappropriate ideals for themselves, so that they are less prone to experience impossible discrepancies between how things are and how they want them to be (Crane, Barnhofer, Duggan, Hepburn, Fennell, *et al.*, 2008).

Study 1

Do suicidal patients show evidence of maladaptive forms of discrepancy-based processing characteristic of over-reliance on a 'doing' mode of mind?

It is well-known that suicidal patients are poorer at solving problems than other psychiatric patients (Pollock & Williams, 2001). We were interested to explore *why* this is the case and whether there is any evidence to suggest that this might be the result of maladaptive forms of discrepancy-based processing. The most commonly used method of assessing problem-solving deficits is the Means-End Problem-Solving (MEPS) test, which asks individuals to provide possible solutions to a number of hypothetical scenarios (Platt & Spivack, 1975). For each MEPS scenario, participants are told the beginning of a story in which a character has a problem, and the end of the story which states that the problem has been overcome. Participants are required to complete the middle section of the story, providing the way(s) in which they think the problem might be solved. There is evidence that this task correlates highly with the ability of patients to solve their own real-life problems (Rotheram-Borus, Troutman, Dopkins, & Shrout, 1990; Schotte & Clum, 1987). To examine evidence for over-reliance on 'doing' mode processes, we decided to examine the transcripts of patients' MEPS solutions to look at what patients report when they are asked to solve one of these problems.

Forty-nine patients who had recently attempted suicide[2] and had a history of previous suicidal behaviour were recruited from the Accident and Emergency department of the John Radcliffe Hospital in Oxford and were included in a longitudinal study (for further details of the study methodology, see Crane & Duggan, 2009). The participants had extensive histories of depression and suicidality. Over three-quarters (37 out of 49) met diagnostic criteria for a current episode of major depressive disorder at first assessment. Of the 12 who were not currently depressed, seven met criteria for past depression. Overall, they reported an average of 2.6 past episodes of depression, with their first onset episode occurring at an average age of 26 years. Hospital records confirmed that they had made an average of 5.6 suicide attempts, including the index attempt. However, this number rose to 10.6 when self-reported attempts, which were not confirmed by hospital records, were included.

Examination of participants' problem-solving transcripts indicated that, when faced with the task of resolving the discrepancy highlighted in the problem scenario, patients were often drawn off into ruminative cycles which had various effects (e.g., worsening their mood, distracting them with memories, increasing the discrepancies between the start and desired end-point), or gave responses that avoided or ignored the discrepancy, thereby failing to solve the problem altogether. Boxes 23.2, 23.3, and 23.4 give some examples of these types of responses.

Participant A avoids dealing with the discrepancy identified in the task, and hence fails to solve the problem at all. Participant B provides a solution eventually, but first veers off the task, telling a story that takes her away from the present moment.

Participant C provides one possibility (go round and introduce yourself), but discounts this as impossible and concludes that the problem cannot be solved. Participant D fails to provide any solutions, instead entering a story from the past, ruminating on this. This appears to increase the discrepancy between the start and desired end-point; the participant fails to use the information generated from the memory to solve the current ('present moment') problem.

Participants E and F are both drawn into ruminative cycles: participant E focuses on the reasons for the problem, and participant F on possible negative outcomes. Neither provides any possible solutions.

The above examples suggest that, for many participants, the difficulties shown in problem-solving are associated with use of maladaptive aspects of the 'doing' mode of mind, characterized by over-thinking, avoidance, and rumination. Participants' responses often

---

Box 23.2   Relationship problems

The story begins with a couple having an argument, and one of them leaving. Participants were asked to solve the problem with the outcome that everything ends up fine between the couple.

Participant A: 'She could leave him.'

Participant B: 'He went off stressing, she was laughing at him, and then she went and talked to her mum and her mum goes she has to calm down and an argument takes two people to argue not one and she must have been bitching at him as well as him bitching at her, go and speak to him, so they had a little chat and she said that she was sorry and he said that he was sorry and they kiss and make up and everything is fine between her and her boyfriend!'

Box 23.3   New neighbourhood

The story begins with a character moving to a new neighbourhood and wanting to meet people. Participants were asked to solve the problem with the outcome that the character makes friends in their neighbourhood.

C: 'I don't speak to anybody that's here anyway. I must admit that if I'm in the garden I might say hello. S'pose you could go round and introduce yourself but I wouldn't be able to do that. I did when they moved in over the road. I put my hand up just to acknowledge them, but I didn't speak to them.'

D: 'I've been there, I've been in the same situation. I used to live in a village, I loved my family, I was with my family, and friends. I moved, I went to another neighbourhood where I didn't know no one, we got our own property (me and my partner), we made friends, had plenty of friends but now that friendships ended and no way of mending it. The only alternative ways I know is going back over to the area I used to live, knocking on my friends' doors, saying sorry, telling them it's my fault, that everything has gone wrong, please don't be bitter with me, at the end of the day you were my friends, I'm here to apologize for everything I've done and please forgive me and hopefully let me back into your neighbourhood.'

---

show their avoidance in dealing with the issue directly or ruminating on the problem. Many participants related the problem only to themselves, and then generated habitual responses which were not always relevant, or which increased the discrepancy between the start and end-point, rather than reducing it.

This provides some preliminary evidence that suicidal patients show impaired problem-solving because of maladaptive responses indicative of an over-reliance on the 'doing'

Box 23.4   Work problems

The story begins with a person not getting on with their supervisor. Participants were asked to solve the problem with the outcome that the person is liked by the supervisor.

E: 'He doesn't like the way his supervisor tells him to get on with his job and work. He feels he's not getting paid enough money for the job he's doing and he wants more money for the same amount of hours worked.'

F: 'The only alternative is where you try to sort the situation out but the person you try to sort the situation out with is very stubborn, not understanding and they just don't want to listen, much as you tell them what you want and what you don't want and what can happen they just still carry on ignoring you and not listening, goes in one ear and out the other.'

---

mode of mind, including high levels of rumination, avoidance, and off-task thinking. In the next study, we wanted to see whether the same tendencies could be demonstrated in suicidal people using a self-report measure, which assesses use of these types of response as a habitual style.

Study 2

Self-report measure of maladaptive aspects of the 'doing' mode

In this study we explored whether suicidal people report increased dependence on the use of avoidance or suppression to deal with unwanted experiences relative to controls, as predicted by the mode of mind hypothesis.

This study used a sub-group of 29 of the 49 suicidal people who took part in Study 1. These 29 participants were representative of the original sample on demographic and clinical measures. Participants completed the Acceptance and Action Questionnaire (AAQ), a measure which assesses experiential avoidance (Hayes, Strosahl, Wilson, Bissett, Pistorello, *et al.*, 2004). Hayes and colleagues (2004) describe the concept of experiential avoidance as the inability to tolerate unpleasant internal experiences, such as negative sensations, thoughts, or feelings. The AAQ consists of nine items measuring the extent to which people are able to take action and respond to difficulties as well as the extent to which they engage in experiential avoidance (e.g., 'I am able to take action on a problem even if I am uncertain what is the right thing to do'; 'I'm not afraid of my feelings'; and 'When I evaluate something negatively, I usually recognize that this is just a reaction, not an objective fact').

Suicidal patients' scores were compared with those of a student sample, reported in the literature. As discussed above, we expected patients to score higher on this measure of

Table 23.1 Comparison of group scores on the Acceptance and Action Questionnaire (AAQ)

Sample	Mean AAQ total	Standard deviation	Sample size
Our study participants	43.22	6.59	29
Undergraduate sample	34.20	6.78	381

experiential avoidance than normal controls. To calculate the comparison norms the male and female undergraduate scores on the AAQ were pooled (see Hayes *et al.*, 2004).

Table 23.1 shows the means, standard deviations, and sample sizes for both our participants and an undergraduate comparison sample. As expected, AAQ scores were significantly higher for our sample than for the undergraduate comparison sample, indicating that the participants in our sample display styles of processing which are more frequently characterized by avoidance of unpleasant experiences and indecision in the face of uncertainty.[3]

The results from the questionnaire study above confirm that avoidance appears to be a common processing style for those who engage in suicidal behaviour, and these tendencies were also observable in the patients' solutions to the problem-solving items on the MEPS. However, these findings do not tell us whether patients utilize avoidance and suppression as a strategy to cope with the occurrence of suicidal thoughts in particular. It is to this issue that we turn in Study 3.

Study 3

Developing a measure of how people relate to suicidal thoughts

Although intrusive thoughts and images of suicide may be unpleasant, it is not inevitable that people will respond to them with avoidance. Many commonly used scales asking about suicidal ideation do not address the issue of how individuals relate to their suicidal thoughts, that is, whether they try to avoid them, dwell on them, or to what extent they find their thoughts distressing. For example, Beck's Scale for Suicidal Ideation (Beck, Kovacs, & Weissman, 1979; Beck, Brown, & Steer, 1997) consists primarily of statements regarding practical aspects of suicide (e.g., 'I have access or anticipate having access to the method that I would choose for killing myself and also have or shall have the opportunity to use it'; 'I have a specific plan for killing myself'; 'I have completed a suicide note'), and attitudes towards the idea of death and suicide (e.g., 'I accept the idea of killing myself'; 'I am not, or only a little, concerned about killing myself because of my family, friends, religion, possible injury from an unsuccessful attempt, etc.'), rather than the suicidal thoughts themselves. Only two questions refer to thoughts about suicide ('I have long periods of thinking about killing myself' and 'I continuously think about killing myself'), and these relate to the frequency and duration of thoughts, rather than how individuals feel about their suicidal ideation. Our interest here is to understand how people *relate* to their suicidal ideation. To this end, with the permission of Professor Daniel Wegner, we adapted the White Bear Suppression Inventory (Wegner & Zanakos, 1994) to refer to suicidal thoughts.

The White Bear Suppression Inventory for Suicidal Ideation   The White Bear Suppression Inventory (WBSI) (Wegner & Zanakos, 1994) is a self-report questionnaire designed to assess chronic tendencies to suppress negative thoughts. It consists of statements which directly relate to suppression of thoughts, such as 'I have thoughts I try to avoid', but also of statements relating to the frequency and perceived controllability of intrusive thoughts and images. Blumberg (2000) divided the items into three sub-scales: suppression (four items); self-distraction (three items); and unwanted intrusive thoughts (eight items). We adapted the 15-item WBSI to refer specifically to suicidal thoughts: the White Bear Suppression Inventory for Suicidal Ideation (WBSI-si).

The order of items was changed to make the questions easier and the questionnaire was approved by Daniel Wegner. The WBSI-si is intended to measure the tendency to suppress suicidal thoughts (see Box 23.5).

Study 3 used a sub-sample of participants who were originally recruited to take part in a clinical trial of mindfulness-based cognitive therapy (MBCT) for people who had previously experienced suicidal ideation or attempted suicide but were currently non-suicidal (Hepburn, Crane, Barnhofer, Duggan, Fennell, *et al.*, 2009, also see later). The 35 trial participants who were randomly allocated to receive treatment as usual were invited to take part in Study 3, and 26 accepted.[4] Eighteen participants had never attempted suicide, but reported instances of ideation which included a suicide plan or method. The other eight participants had made between one and three suicide attempts in their lives. At the time of Study 3, their depression scores were in the sub-clinical range on the Beck Depression Inventory (Beck, Steer & Brown, 1996). Their suicidal ideation at this time was low (average score 1.9 on the Beck Scale for Suicidal Ideation, Beck *et al.*, 1979).

The total WBSI-si and the individual sub-scales all had high levels of internal reliability (WBSI-si total $\alpha = 0.78$; suppression, $\alpha = 0.85$; distraction, $\alpha = 0.83$, intrusions, $\alpha = 0.77$). Table 23.2 shows the mean scores for the total WBSI-si and the three WBSI-si sub-scales. Higher numbers indicate more suppression of suicidal thoughts.

As Table 23.2 shows, items on the suppression sub-scale were the most strongly endorsed, with a mean rating of 3.89, corresponding to an 'agree' rating (items are scored from '1: strongly disagree' to '5: strongly agree'). The distraction and intrusions sub-scales were endorsed at the 'neither agree nor disagree' level. This suggests that people who have been suicidal in the past, but who are currently relatively well, report that they try to suppress suicidal thoughts that come to mind, but reports are inconclusive with regard to the use of distraction and the perceived intrusiveness of suicidal thoughts when they feel low.

Given the high internal consistency across the questionnaire as a whole, we used the total WBSI-si score in order to explore how suppression of suicidal thoughts might relate to severity of worst-ever suicide ideation. Worst ever suicide ideation was measured using a modified written version of the Beck Scale for Suicide Ideation (Beck & Steer, 1993) based on the clinician-rated Scale for Suicidal Ideation worst-point suicidality interview, which has been used in several studies (e.g., Joiner, Steer, Brown, Beck, Pettit, *et al.*, 2003). We found a significant correlation between the total score on the WBSI-si and worst-ever suicide ideation on the Scale for Suicide Ideation ($r = 0.78$; $p < 0.001$). It seems that the

Box 23.5   The White Bear Suppression Inventory for Suicidal Ideation (WBSI-si)

When they feel really bad, some people find that they experience suicidal thoughts. The statements below describe some ways that people have reacted to their own suicidal thoughts, but everybody is different. When thoughts about suicide come into your mind, how do you feel about them? Please read each statement carefully, circling a number to indicate how much you agree with it.

Strongly disagree	Disagree	Neutral	Agree	Strongly agree
1	2	3	4	5

When I feel very low and things get too much for me:

1.   My thoughts return frequently to the idea of suicide (Intrusion).
2.   I cannot erase images of suicide that come to my mind (Intrusion).
4.   Suicidal thoughts keep jumping into my head (Intrusion).
5.   I wonder why I have the suicidal thoughts I do (Intrusion).
6.   I wish I could stop thinking of suicide (Intrusion).
8.   I try not to tell anyone about the suicidal thoughts I have (Intrusion).
9.   I prefer not to think about suicide (Suppression).
10.   I try to avoid suicidal thoughts (Suppression).
12.   The suicidal thoughts sometimes come so fast I wish I could stop them (Intrusion).
13.   I sometimes stay really busy just to keep suicidal thoughts from intruding on my mind (Distraction).
14.   I have suicidal thoughts that I cannot stop (Intrusion).
16.   I try not to think about suicide (Suppression).
17.   I often do things to distract myself from my suicidal thoughts (Distraction).
18.   My suicidal thoughts sometimes make me really wish I could stop thinking altogether (Distraction).
20.   I always try to put suicidal thoughts out of mind (Suppression).

Note: The original adaptation of the WBSI scale also included five Comfort Items to be calculated as a separate measure 'The Comfort Scale'.

3.   Suicidal thoughts come into my mind but do not bother me.
7.   I take comfort from thoughts about suicide.
11.   Thinking about suicide makes me feel calm.
15.   Thinking about suicide makes me feel better.
19.   I think about suicide to help myself cope.

Table 23.2   Mean scale scores and item endorsement on the White Bear Suppression Inventory for suicide ideation (WBSI-si)

	WBSI-si Total (15 items)	WBSI-si Suppression (4 items)	WBSI-si Distraction (3 items)	WBSI-si Intrusions (8 items)
Scale mean (SD)	46.04 (10.59)	15.54 (4.57)	8.38 (3.40)	22.12 (7.28)
Mean per item	3.07	3.89	2.79	2.77

more severe a participant's suicide ideation has been in the past, the more likely they are to report that they try to suppress suicidal thoughts at times when they feel low.

It is perhaps unsurprising that people who have suffered greatly from suicidality in the past, and are fearful of potential relapse into a future episode of depression, should attempt to suppress suicidal thoughts that occur. However, if suicidal thoughts are immediately and automatically followed by attempts to suppress them, push them away, or elaborate upon them in a ruminative way, the result is likely to be further *enmeshment* in suicidal thinking. We have seen how such responses contribute to ineffective problem-solving in everyday scenarios and it is easy to envisage how much more toxic they are likely to be when applied to the problem of 'fixing' the broken self, or the mental pain associated with it.

Reducing Dependence on the 'Doing' Mode of Mind

If inappropriate and inflexible use of the 'doing' (discrepancy-based) mode is at the basis of both rumination and suppression, what alternative processing options do people have available to them?

Segal and colleagues (Segal, Williams, & Teasdale, 2002) argue that there is an alternative mode that can be consciously initiated: the 'being' mode of mind. In this mode of mind there is no immediate felt need to achieve particular goals, only to accept and allow things to be as they are in this moment. Resting in the 'being' mode allows people to remain in the present moment more fully. Segal and colleagues (2002) describe how the 'being' mode represents a step away from conceptual thought processes (where thoughts are taken to be accurate reflections of reality) towards sensory experience. This means that the discrepancies which may trigger automatic habits of mind in the 'doing' mode are seen from a de-centred perspective and may allow people to 'be with' things as they are, without getting caught up in ruminative cycles about how they *should* be or without trying to avoid things as they are. For a summary of the key aspects of the 'being' mode of mind see Box 23.6.

One potential way to teach people to utilize the 'being' mode of mind and simultaneously to reduce over-dependence on the 'doing' mode, and in particular its habitual and maladaptive aspects, is through training in mindfulness meditation. One form of therapy incorporating mindfulness meditation techniques is Mindfulness Based Cognitive

---

Box 23.6   The alternative ('being') mode that is cultivated in mindfulness practice

1.   Non-striving
'Being' mode focuses on letting go of striving towards or away from certain goals.
2.   Approach
'Being' mode encourages remaining open, 'turning towards' the difficult and the unpleasant.
3.   Thoughts as mental events
'Being' mode views thoughts as 'products' of the mind that arise, stay around for a while, and disperse.
4.   Living in the present moment
'Being' mode focuses on present-moment experience. Memories are recognized as memories that are arising now; past and future images are seen for what they are, images arising here and now.
5.   Direct (non-conceptual) experience
In the 'being' mode, the focus is on direct, sensory experience. It is non-conceptual, intuitive, and experiential.
6.   Intentional
'Being' mode involves *intentionally* paying attention to whatever is arising in the external and internal world.

Therapy (MBCT), which combines Buddhist meditation practices with cognitive therapy for depression. Patients are taught a variety of meditation practices over eight weeks. These practices are intended to cultivate the capacity to recognize situations in which the 'doing' mode of mind is activated habitually and to give people the option of switching into a 'being' mode of mind where this might be helpful (e.g., to interrupt cycles of rumination). MBCT also gives people space to reflect on and clarify their values, goals, and intentions, through both the personal insight gained through sustained meditation practice and the use of exercises which explicitly explore the experience of pleasant and unpleasant events.

MBCT has a rapidly increasing evidence base. Two randomized controlled trials have shown that it reduces relapse rates in patients with three or more episodes of depression by 40%–50% (Ma & Teasdale, 2004; Teasdale, Segal, Williams, Ridgeway, Soulsby, *et al.*, 2000), while a third has shown that it is comparable in efficacy with maintenance treatment with antidepressants (Kuyken, Byford, Taylor, Watkins, Holden, *et al.*, 2008). Research is also increasingly exploring the use of MBCT in groups with ongoing symptoms of depression, including in some studies those patients with current/recent suicide ideation (e.g., Barnhofer, Crane, Hargus, Amarasingh, Winder, *et al.*, 2009; Eisendrath, Delucchi, Bitner, Fenimore, Smit, *et al.*, 2008; Kenny & Williams, 2007; Kingston, Dooley, Bates, Lawlor, & Malone, 2007).

The Effects of Mindfulness on the Triggers for the 'Doing' Mode

In order to explore whether MBCT is able to reduce the extent to which patients at risk of suicide ideation or behaviour engage in maladaptive use of the 'doing' mode of mind, we examined data from a pilot randomized controlled trial comparing MBCT with a delayed treatment condition. Thirty-three participants in this trial were allocated to the immediate treatment group and 35 participants were allocated to the waitlist condition (these participants were invited to take part additionally in Study 3 described earlier in this chapter). Participants had a mean age of 42 years, an average of 5.6 previous episodes of depression, and 38% reported having made one or more suicide attempts in the past; they were at high risk of deterioration and relapse in the absence of treatment. In examining this group we explored two questions: first, whether MBCT had any impact on patients' actual perceptions of self-discrepancy (i.e., on the conditions which trigger the 'doing' mode in the first place); and, second, whether patients reported less use of avoidance as a habitual coping style after treatment with MBCT (see Crane *et al.*, 2008 for more details of methodology and self-discrepancy findings).

Self-discrepancy

Perceived discrepancies between the actual and ideal self (the self-characteristics that a person values, and wishes or hopes to possess) are closely linked to depression (e.g., Strauman, 1989). Whether discrepancies arise from negative perceptions of the actual self, ambitious or unattainable goals for the ideal self (e.g., reflecting perfectionism, a factor which has been linked to suicidality (e.g., O'Connor, 2007)), or a combination of these factors, once primed, self-discrepancies result in depressed affect (Strauman, 1989). The 'doing' mode of mind will also tend to be activated, resulting in rumination (Papadakis, Prince, Jones, & Strauman, 2006), avoidance, and often an increase (rather than the desired decrease) in the discrepancy itself.

Participants in the trial described above completed a Self-Description Questionnaire (Carver, Lawrence, & Scheier, 1999), listing characteristics that described their 'ideal' self-concept, and then rated their current similarity to each characteristic. They completed this questionnaire at baseline assessment and following treatment with MBCT (or the comparable waiting period). Self-discrepancy data were available for 19 participants allocated to MBCT and 23 allocated to the waitlist condition, after accounting for dropouts and missing data.

The results showed that, as predicted, by the end of the treatment period there were large and significant differences between the treatment and control groups in levels of ideal self-discrepancy, such that the MBCT group had a smaller discrepancy than the control group. This result was accounted for largely by increases in self-discrepancy over time in those allocated to the waitlist condition, which is likely to represent the reactivation of self-discrepancies in a high-risk group. However, it was also the case that, in the MBCT group, the more the participants had disengaged from unhelpful or unattainable self-guides (such as the goal to 'be physically attractive' or 'to always be in control') and

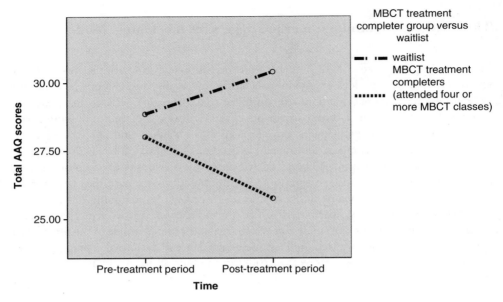

Figure 23.1   Changing scores on the Acceptance and Action Questionnaire (AAQ) measured before and after a course of Mindfulness-Based Cognitive Therapy (MBCT).

replaced these with more adaptive alternatives, the more they shifted towards having smaller discrepancies between their actual and ideal self at the end of treatment.

These results suggest that one way in which MBCT protects against relapse and recurrence in depression is by specifically targeting the discrepancies that initially trigger the 'doing' mode of mind. MBCT may help participants to recognize and let go of unhelpful self-related goals, as well as to develop more adaptive alternatives. Additionally, MBCT appears to limit the extent to which self-discrepancy increases over time, perhaps by modifying habitual responses to self-discrepancies. The second question we wished to address was therefore whether MBCT also reduced patients' tendency to respond to unwanted experiences with avoidance.

Effects of MBCT on experiential avoidance

Twenty-one patients allocated to MBCT and 24 allocated to the waitlist condition completed the Acceptance and Action Questionnaire (Hayes *et al.*, 2004) at both the pre- and post-treatment period assessments. Participants in the treatment group had significantly lower post-treatment avoidance scores on the AAQ than those in the waitlist condition, despite the absence of significant differences in their scores pre-treatment (see Figure 23.1).[5] This finding supports the idea that MBCT may help people to 'switch modes', so they are more able to take action when uncertain and be less avoidant of negative experience, potentially reducing the escalation in reactions to such experiences that might otherwise occur.

Conclusions

This chapter has investigated the hypothesis that, for suicidal patients, inappropriate or inflexible use of the 'doing' mode of mind in response to emotional problems and unpleasant internal stimuli may contribute to an escalation, rather than a resolution, of distress. Specifically, we suggest that when faced either directly with the experience of unpleasant emotional states or with problems which activate such states, focusing on discrepancies may serve only to increase them. Although an alternative mode of mind, the 'being' mode, is potentially available, people instead often use increasingly maladaptive forms of discrepancy-based processing to try to resolve their problems, in particular attempting to suppress or avoid difficulties, or dwelling on difficulties in a way that is ruminative and unproductive.

The data presented here demonstrate that suicidal patients use ineffective 'doing' mode processes when trying to solve hypothetical interpersonal problems and report elevated levels of experiential avoidance both on a general questionnaire measure, the Acceptance and Action Questionnaire, and on a questionnaire specifically designed to assess reactions to suicidal thoughts (the White Bear Suppression Inventory for Suicidal Ideation). Although inflexible use of the 'doing' mode in response to difficulties appears to be a characteristic of suicidal cognition, we also present evidence that this can be targeted in therapy. MBCT aims to help patients learn new ways of dealing with their thoughts and feelings so that they are able to react to them in more productive ways. Preliminary evidence suggests that, for people who have been depressed and suicidal, MBCT has positive effects on perceptions of self-discrepancy and also reduces reliance on experiential avoidance as a means of coping.

Recent research by O'Connor and colleagues (O'Connor, Fraser, Whyte, MacHale, & Masterton, 2009) indicates that the ability both to disengage from unattainable goals and to re-engage with alternatives is key to short-term outcome in suicide attempters. Cultivation of the 'being' mode through mindfulness training has the potential to assist people in recognizing situations when goal re-adjustment is necessary, in clarifying values, and in having the courage to move in new directions. There is nowhere where this is more challenging than in adopting a new relationship towards distressing thoughts, feelings, and memories. However, there is nowhere more rewarding to discover that there is an alternative path, of acceptance and engagement with life in the present moment than when having to cope with these distressing thoughts, feelings, and memories.

Notes

1   Suicidal behaviour is used here rather than 'parasuicide' or 'deliberate self-harm' in an attempt to stress the continuum between suicidal ideation, behaviour, and suicide.

2   Patients who had engaged in habitual self-cutting were excluded from this study. However, suicide intent scores were not used as a criterion for study inclusion.

3   There was a moderate to large significant difference for the mean total score obtained on the AAQ between our sample and the undergraduate sample ($t(408) = 6.92$, $p < 0.01$, $\eta^2 = 0.11$).

4   This sub-sample included 11 males and 15 females aged between 27 and 56 years ($m = 41.11$ years, SD = 9.33).
5   There was a significant time x treatment group interaction F $(1,46) = 6.07$, $p < 0.05$ in this analysis.

References

Barnhofer, T., Crane, C., Hargus, E., Amarasinghe, M., Winder, R., & Williams, J. M. G. (2009). Mindfulness-based cognitive therapy as a treatment for chronic depression: A preliminary study. *Behaviour Research and Therapy, 47*, 366–373.

Beck, A. T., Brown, G., & Steer, R. A. (1997). Psychometric characteristics of the scale for suicide ideation with psychiatric outpatients. *Behaviour Research and Therapy, 35*, 1039–1046.

Beck, A. T., Kovacs, M., & Weissman, A. (1979). Assessment of suicidal intention; The Scale for Suicide Ideation. *Journal of Consulting and Clinical Psychology, 47*, 343–352.

Beck, A. T. & Steer, R. A. (1993b). *Manual for the Beck Scale for Suicide Ideation.* San Antonio, TX: Psychological Corporation.

Beck, A. T., Steer, R. A., & Brown, G. (1996). *Beck Depression Inventory II Manual.* San Antonio, TX: Psychological Corporation, Harcourt Brace.

Blumberg, S. J. (2000). The White Bear Suppression Inventory: Revisiting its factor structure. *Personality and Individual Differences, 29*, 943–950.

Carver, C. S., Lawrence, J. W., & Scheier, M. F. (1999). Self-discrepancy and affect: Incorporating the role of feared selves. *Personality and Social Psychology Bulletin, 25*, 783–792.

Carver, C. S. & Scheier, M. F. (1998). *On the Self-Regulation of Behavior.* Cambridge: Cambridge University Press.

Crane, C., Barnhofer, T., Duggan, D. S., Hepburn, S. R., Fennell, M. J. V., & Williams, J. M. G. (2008). Mindfulness-Based Cognitive Therapy and self-discrepancy in recovered depressed patients with a history of suicidality. *Cognitive Therapy and Research, 32*, 775–787.

Crane, C., Barnhofer, T., & Williams, J. M. G. (2007). Reflection, brooding and suicidality: A preliminary study of different types of rumination in individuals with a history of major depression. *British Journal of Clinical Psychology, 46*, 497–504.

Crane, C. & Duggan, D. S. (2009). Overgeneral autobiographical memory and age of onset of childhood sexual abuse in patients with recurrent suicidal behavior. *British Journal of Clinical Psychology, 48*, 93–100.

Eisendrath, S. J., Delucchi, K., Bitner, R., Fenimore, P., Smit, M., & McLane, M. (2008). Mindfulness-Based Cognitive Therapy for treatment-resistant depression: A pilot study. *Psychotherapy and Psychosomatics, 77*, 319–320.

Hayes, S. C., Strosahl, K., Wilson, K. G., Bissett, R. T., Pistorello, J., Toarmino, D., Polusny, M. A., Dykstra, T. A., Batten, S. V., Bergan, J., Stewart, S. H., Zvolensky, M. J., Eifert, G. H., Bond, F. W., Forsyth, J. P., Karekla, M., & McCurry, S. M. (2004). Measuring experiential avoidance: A preliminary test of a working model. *Psychological Record, 54*, 553–578.

Hepburn, S. R., Crane, C., Barnhofer, T., Duggan, D. S., Fennell, M. J. V., & Williams, J. M. G. (2009). Mindfulness-Based Cognitive Therapy may reduce thought suppression in previously suicidal participants: Findings from a preliminary study. *British Journal of Clinical Psychology, 48*, 209–215.

Joiner, T. E., Steer, R. A., Brown, G., Beck, A. T., Pettit, J. W., & Rudd, M. D. (2003). Worst-point suicidal plans: A dimension of suicidality predictive of past suicide attempts and eventual death by suicide. *Behaviour Research and Therapy, 41*, 1469–1480.

Kenny, M. A. & Williams, J. M. G. (2007). Treatment-resistant depressed patients show a good response to mindfulness-based cognitive therapy. *Behaviour Research and Therapy, 45,* 617–625.

Kingston, T., Dooley, B., Bates, A., Lawlor, E., & Malone, K. (2007). Mindfulness-Based Cognitive Therapy for residual depressive symptoms. *Psychology and Psychotherapy-Theory Research and Practice, 80,* 193–203.

Kuyken, W., Byford, S., Taylor, R. S., Watkins, E., Holden, E., White, K., Barrett, B., Byng, R., Evans, A., Mullen, E., & Teasdale, J. D. (2008). Mindfulness-Based Cognitive Therapy to prevent relapse in recurrent depression, *Journal of Consulting and Clinical Psychology, 76,* 966–978.

Linehan, M. (1993). *Cognitive-Behavioral Treatment of Borderline Personality Disorder.* New York: Guilford Press.

Lyubomirsky, S., Tucker, K. L., Caldwell, N. D., & Berg, K. (1999). Why ruminators are poor problem solvers: Clues from the phenomenology of dysphoric rumination. *Journal of Personality and Social Psychology, 77,* 1041–1060.

Ma, S. H. & Teasdale, J. D. (2004). Mindfulness-Based Cognitive Therapy for depression: Replication and exploration of differential relapse prevention effects. *Journal of Consulting and Clinical Psychology, 72,* 31–40.

Morrison, R. & O'Connor, R. C. (2008). A systematic review of the relationship between rumination and suicidality. *Suicide and Life-Threatening Behavior, 38,* 523–538.

O'Connor, R. C. (2003). Suicidal behavior as a cry of pain: Test of a psychological model. *Archives of Suicide Research, 7,* 297–308.

O'Connor, R. C. (2007). The relations between perfectionism and suicidality: A systematic review. *Suicide and Life-Threatening Behavior, 37,* 698–714.

O'Connor, R. C., Fraser, L., Whyte, M. C., MacHale, S., & Masterton, G. (2009). Self-regulation of unattainable goals in suicide attempters: The relationship between goal disengagement, goal reengagement and suicidal ideation. *Behaviour Research and Therapy, 47,* 164–169.

Orbach, I., Mikulincer, M., Sirota, P., & Gilboa-Schechtman, E. (2003). Mental pain: A multidimensional operationalization and definition. *Suicide and Life-Threatening Behavior, 33,* 219–230.

Papadakis, A. A., Prince, R. P., Jones, N. P., & Strauman, T. (2006). Self-regulation, rumination and vulnerability to depression in adolescent girls. *Development and Psychopathology, 18,* 815–829.

Platt, J. J. & Spivack, G. (1975). *Manual for the Means-End-Problem-Solving (MEPS): A measure of inter-personal problem solving skill.* Philadelphia, PA: Hahnemann Medical College Hospital.

Pollock, L. R. & Williams, J. (2001). Effective problem solving in suicide attempters depends on specific autobiographical recall. *Suicide and Life-Threatening Behavior, 31,* 386–396.

Rotherham-Borus, M. J., Troutman, P. D., Dopkins, S. C., & Shrout, P. E. (1990). Cognitive style and pleasant activities among female adolescent suicide attempters. *Journal of Consulting and Clinical Psychology, 58,* 554–561.

Rudd, M. D., Joiner, T. E., & Rajab, M. H. (2004). *Treating Suicidal Behavior: An effective, time-limited approach.* New York: Guilford Press.

Schotte, D. E. & Clum, G. A. (1987). Problem-solving skills in suicidal psychiatric patients. *Journal of Consulting and Clinical Psychology, 55,* 49–54.

Segal, Z. V., Williams, J. M. G., & Teasdale, J. D. (2002). *Mindfulness-based Cognitive Therapy for Depression: A new approach to preventing relapse.* New York: Guilford Press.

Strauman, T. J. (1989). Self-discrepancies in clinical depression and social phobia: Cognitive structures that underlie affective disorders? *Journal of Abnormal Psychology, 98,* 14–22.

Teasdale, J. D., Segal, Z. V., Williams, J. M., Ridgeway, V. A., Soulsby, J. M., & Lau, M. A. (2000). Prevention of relapse/recurrence in major depression by mindfulness-based cognitive therapy. *Journal of Consulting and Clinical Psychology, 68,* 615–623.

Watkins, E. & Teasdale, J. D. (2001). Rumination and overgeneral memory in depression: Effects of self-focus and analytic thinking. *Journal of Abnormal Psychology, 110*, 353–357.

Wegner, D. M. & Zanakos, S. (1994). Chronic thought suppression. *Journal of Personality, 62*, 615–640.

Wenzlaff, R. M. & Wegner, D. M. (2000). Thought suppression. *Annual Review of Psychology, 51*, 59–91.

Williams, J. M. G. (2001). *Cry of Pain: Understanding suicide and attempted suicide.* London: Penguin.

Williams, J. M. G., Crane, C., Barnhofer, T., & Duggan, D. S. (2005). Psychology and suicidal behaviour: Elaborating the entrapment model. In K. Hawton (Ed.), *Prevention and Treatment of Suicidal Behaviour.* Oxford: Oxford University Press.

CHAPTER TWENTY-FOUR

The Role of the Therapist in the Treatment of the Suicidal Patient

Konrad Michel

Abstract

Health professionals who are called to see a patient who has attempted suicide are faced with a difficult task: on the one hand, as clinicians they have to conduct a diagnostic interview in order to detect psychiatric morbidity and to develop a treatment plan. On the other hand, they must be open to listen to the patient and to avoid a clinician-dominated interviewing style. Here it will be argued that in order to establish a therapeutic alliance with the suicidal patient, a patient-oriented clinical approach is essential. In the assessment of psychiatric pathology and the management of its treatment, the health professional is the expert. However, when the focus is on the patient's inner experience of pain, frustration, and self-hate, the patient is the expert of his or her story and the associated biographical context. Only patients 'know' what led them to the development of their suicidal behaviour. The quality of the therapeutic alliance largely depends on the interviewer's listening abilities and the patient's sense of being understood. Special attention should be placed on the patient's life-oriented goals, which in a suicidal crisis have been existentially threatened. In treating suicidal individuals the interviewer should focus on the patient's suicide-related narrative in order to achieve a shared understanding of the suicidality. Once a therapeutic alliance is established, it may become a basis for a long-term therapeutic attachment, which has the potential to be protective even with minimal contact. However, active maintenance of the therapeutic relationship appears to be important for a long-term preventive effect.

International Handbook of Suicide Prevention: Research, Policy and Practice, First Edition.
Edited by Rory C. O'Connor, Stephen Platt, Jacki Gordon.
© 2011 John Wiley & Sons, Ltd. Published 2011 by John Wiley & Sons, Ltd.

Introduction

Rather surprisingly, it has so far been difficult to demonstrate the effectiveness of treatments for suicide attempters, the group with the highest risk of suicide. From the handful of formalized treatments that have demonstrated a reduction of suicidal behaviour, most had a follow-up of only six or 12 months (Guthrie, Kapur, Mackway-Jones, Chew-Graham, Moorey, *et al.*, 2001; Salkovskis, Atha, & Storer, 1990; van Heeringen, Jannes, Buylaert, Hendrick, De Bacquer, *et al.*, 1995), although there are now some studies with longer follow-up periods (Brown, Ten Have, Henriques, Xie, Hollander, *et al.*, 2005; Fleischmann, Bertolote, Wasserman, De Leo, Bolhari, *et al.*, 2008; Linehan, Armstrong, Suarez, Allmon, & Heard, 1991; Linehan, Comtois, Murray, Brown, Gallop, *et al.*, 2006). The reasons are manifold (De Leo, 2002; Goldney, 2000). One of them, although well known to experienced clinicians, tends to get little attention: the fact that suicide and attempted suicide as human phenomena do not fit into the traditional illness model, but are forms of behaviour, which require of the therapist a different therapeutic approach from that used when treating 'common' psychiatric disorders. This chapter will focus on principles of the therapeutic relationship with suicidal patients based on clinical experience shared by an international working group of psychotherapists, as well as on research-based insights related to therapeutic alliance.

The Communication of Suicidal Intent

The encounter between the suicidal patient and the health professional is far from straightforward. Although suicidal individuals frequently visit health professionals before acting on their suicidal impulses, suicide is rarely addressed in consultation. In a psychological autopsy study of 571 suicides in Finland, in which a healthcare professional had been contacted prior to the suicide, Isometsä, Heikkinen, Marttunen, Henriksson, Aro, and colleagues (1995) found that at the last visit the issue of suicide had been discussed in only 22% of the cases (39% in psychiatric consultation, 11% in general practice, and 6% in another medical consultation). An increase in the frequency of visits to general practitioners prior to suicide and attempted suicide has been found (Appleby, Amos, Doyle, Tommenson, & Woodman, 1996; Michel, Runeson, Valach, & Wasserman, 1997), suggesting that the reasons for the visits to health professionals are related to the development of a suicidal crisis. Fifty per cent or more of individuals ending their lives by suicide have seen a general practitioner or a medical specialist within a month of their death (Michel, 1986; Pirkis & Burgess, 1998). It is not at all rare that patients see a health professional only a few hours before completing suicide. In the Finnish study, 18% of those who had contacted a physician had done so on the day of their suicide, yet even then the issue of suicide was discussed in only one fifth of these cases. So, undeniably, there is a serious communication problem between suicidal patients and health professionals. As a rule, suicidal persons, even if they are under medical care, rarely talk about their intentions, nor do they spontaneously mention past suicide attempts. For instance, in Bern, general practitioners had no knowledge of previous attempts in 67% of suicide attempters who were under their care (Michel, 1986).

It is surprising that suicidal people generally do not feel that suicidality has something to do with health problems. We asked suicide attempters one year after the attempt who they thought in retrospect could have helped in order to prevent their act of deliberate self-harm. Only 10% mentioned a health professional, 20% mentioned relatives or friends, while 52% said nobody (Michel, Valach, & Waeber, 1994). In the same study, 50% said they could not have accepted help at that particular time. Therefore, in the lead-up to suicide or attempted suicide many individuals consider suicide plans as something 'private' which they do not readily want to share with others, particularly health professionals.

There are several aspects that may make it difficult for an individual to disclose suicidal ideation:

- the fear of not being understood or taken seriously ('oh, well, we all have our ups and downs');
- the fear of getting useless advice ('you must think positively');
- the fear of being labelled mentally ill and admitted to a psychiatric hospital against one's own will ('you won't leave this room until the police arrive');
- the fear of giving away the – seemingly – only possibility of escape from a difficult situation ('I will have to inform your family').

Furthermore, patients, above all men, generally find it difficult to talk to their physician about emotional problems because they feel ashamed or they are reluctant for fear of stigmatization. Consequently, they may choose to stay on safe ground by presenting with physical problems only. It should also be taken into account that the suicidal person is in a world radically different from the busy life of the health professional, who will quite easily find meaning in life through his or her work. For suicidal individuals, the meaning of one's life is at stake; human existence is questioned. Suicidal persons feel a failure, they hate themselves for this; being vulnerable and fragile, they are devoid of any protective shield.

For health professionals a central issue is that their training equips them to detect pathology and to diagnose psychiatric disorders, but rarely to conceptualize behaviour. Suicidal behaviour challenges care providers because it falls outside the usual range of disorders admitted to emergency units. Suicide and attempted suicide are behaviours, not illnesses or accidents. The problem is not very different in the psychiatric wards where suicide attempters are referred from the general hospital. The following is a statement by a 36-year-old man after discharge from a crisis intervention unit:

> I got very angry when they kept asking me if I would do it again. They were not interested in my feelings. Life is not such a matter-of-fact thing and, if I was honest, I couldn't say if I would do it again or not. What was clear to me was that I could not have enough trust in any of these doctors to really talk openly about myself. (Michel, Dey, & Valach, 2001, p. 232)

In a UK study patients who had been hospitalized after attempting suicide said that they had found nurses and social workers more helpful than doctors (Treolar & Pinfold,

1993). Interestingly, the highest correlation between help received and staff attributes related to listening behaviour and sympathy towards the patients. This may not be so surprising, because medical health professionals, in seeing suicidal patients, have a dual role. As clinicians responsible for the patients they must recognize and diagnose psychiatric disorders, prescribe medication, and decide on the 'management' of the patient. As therapists they must be good and empathic listeners, working towards a shared understanding of the patient's very individual and subjective experience. These two roles are basically incompatible: in explaining suicidal development in a biographical context, the patient is the expert of his or her story; while in assessing psychopathology and deciding on treatment, the clinician is the expert.

The Aeschi Working Group (http://www.aeschiconference.unibe.ch), an international group of clinicians and therapists committed to patient-oriented treatment of suicidal individuals, has come to the conclusion that, in order to establish a therapeutic alliance, the clinician should first focus on the patient's personal suicidal experience, before switching to the more traditional clinician's role, actively exploring the patient's mental state. Experience shows that, if an interview starts with the traditional patient–clinician interaction, it will be very difficult to move away from it (see appendix, below, for guidelines for clinicians).

To make it clear: the Aeschi Working Group has no doubt that the adequate treatment of psychiatric disorder is a major factor in reducing the risk of suicide. However, treatment of depression is not equal to treatment of suicidality. Furthermore, in spite of 'fight depression' campaigns and an increase in antidepressant prescriptions, depression is still underdiagnosed, and when diagnosed, under-treated. In Sweden, antidepressants were found in the toxicological screening in less than 20% of 5,281 suicides (Isacsson, Holmgren, Wasserman, & Bergman, 1994), although depression has repeatedly been found to be present in 50% or more of completed suicides (Conwell, Duberstain, Cox, Herrmann, Forbes, *et al.*, 1996; Lönqvist, 2000). Physical complaints may cover psychiatric pathology, above all pain, autonomic symptoms, and gastrointestinal problems (Lin, von Korff, & Wagner, 1989). Rutz, Walinder, von Knorring, Rihmer, and Philgren (1997) pointed out that there may be a specific male depressive syndrome, with more acting-out and less obvious depressive mood or apathy.

Considering the recognized difficulties in communication between therapist and patient (e.g., Isometsä *et al.*, 1995), it is hardly surprising that adherence to follow-up appointments after a suicide attempt has been found to be low, often not more than 50% (Kurz, Möller, Bürk, Torhorst, Wächtler, *et al.*, 1988). In their study Brown *et al.* (2005) introduced case managers who actively maintained contact with patients, reminding them of their appointments, and making referrals to mental health and social services, with a view to keeping as many as possible in treatment.

Assessing Suicide Risk: Patient-Oriented versus Physician-Oriented Approach

Assessing suicide risk in a busy clinical setting usually means that the interviewer applies a structured style of assessment, examining the present mental state, particularly focusing on symptoms of affective disorder or psychosis, and, perhaps, asking about a history of past suicidal behaviour. Such interviews tend to move quickly from the surface-level story ('What did you do?') through an assessment of current risk ('Are you suicidal now?'), to decisions about the disposition of the patient (Rogers & Soyka, 2004). Patients often feel impersonally processed, with little opportunity to explore, from their own perspective, what actually lies behind the act of self-harm. Rogers and Soyka (2004) argued that a 'one-size-fits-all' approach actually serves to distance and marginalize suicidal patients and, paradoxically, contributes to a patient's suicidality. The medical intervention model, often in the form of crisis intervention, may well serve to keep the person alive in the short term, but it may not help the person to live in the long run. In the view of Rogers and Soyka (2004), the crisis model 'unambiguously creates a power imbalance placing the clinician in an expert, directing, and evaluative position' (p. 11), leaving the patient little room to re-establish his or her lost sense of self-reliance. Thus, the medical model can be perceived as meeting the needs of the clinician rather than those of the client. The emphasis is on facts in contrast to the context and meaning of the patient's suicidality, with the suicidal person's story largely a taboo subject.

Quite obviously, although psychiatric disorders are risk factors for suicide, it is the person who decides to act on suicidal impulses. What is needed is an approach to the suicidal person beyond psychopathology, that is, a patient-oriented approach.

For instance, Jobes' Suicide Status Form (SSF)(Jobes, 2006) is a structured interview focusing on the patient's inner experience of psychological pain, stress, agitation, hopelessness, and self-hate. It is the central clinical tool of the Collaborative Assessment and Management of Suicidality (CAMS) (see Jobes, Chapter 22, above). What makes it special is that the interview is performed collaboratively: interviewer and patient sit next to each other, the patient filling in the answers, with the active help of the interviewer. This clearly puts the patient in the expert's position, while the interviewer's stance is, 'I want to see it through your eyes'. The therapeutic alliance, as the essential therapeutic vehicle for life-saving clinical care, is the basic spirit behind CAMS, with the patient's view the absolute assessment 'gold standard'.

Therapeutic Alliance: Some Basics

Therapeutic alliance is a process in which a patient allows a therapist to enter his or her personal world in order to initiate a process of intra-psychic change. Trust within the patient–therapist dyad is the prerequisite for such an extraordinary thing to happen between two people. A therapist who can be trusted and a patient who is motivated to share his or her inner experience are the essential elements of a therapeutic interpersonal dynamic. Once a treatment alliance has been established, a bond between patient and therapist will ensue, which will often be lasting, continuing beyond the formal termination of treatment.

It is crucial to understand the collaborative aspect of therapeutic alliance as an interactive, recursive, and creative process, directed towards shared goals. This requires an interpersonal process in which the therapist is prepared to learn empathically from the patient in order to reach a shared view of the patient's problems and goals. Horvath, Gaston, and Luborsky (1993) distinguished three universal aspects of the therapeutic alliance: first, the patient's perception that the interventions offered are both relevant and potent; second, congruence between the patient's and therapist's expectations of the short- and medium-term goals of therapy; and, third, the patient's ability to forge a personal bond with the therapist and the therapist's ability to present as a caring, sensitive, and sympathetic helping figure. An early therapeutic alliance has consistently been found to have a significant influence on therapy outcome (Horvath & Symonds, 1991). For example, Saltzman, Luetgert, Roth, Craeser, and Howard (1976) found that alliance in the third session was most predictive of adherence to treatment. This was interpreted as meaning that, while the limited experience of therapist and client with each other at the end of the first session was generally not enough to predict the future course of events, in the third session the viability of the therapeutic relationship was evident, with the alliance having taken root. It also means that therapeutic alliance is established very early in treatment. In the Saltzman *et al.* (1976) study the positive therapist variables predictive of effective outcomes were respect, understanding, openness, involvement, and continuity.

Experienced clinicians recognize that the quality of the therapeutic relationship is also a moderator variable for outcomes in pharmacotherapy. For example, Krupnick, Sotsky, Elkin, Watkins, and Pilkonis (1996) analysed 619 recorded interviews with 225 patients who participated in the National Institute of Mental Health collaborative study of treatments for depression (Elkin, Shea, Watkins, Imber, Sotsky, *et al.*, 1989). In this study, depressed patients were randomly assigned to one of four conditions: cognitive-behavioural therapy; interpersonal psychotherapy; clinical management combined with the antidepressant imipramine; and clinical management combined with placebo. The quality of the therapeutic alliance was rated with the Vanderbilt Therapeutic Alliance Scale (VTAS) (Hartley & Strupp, 1983). Alliance scores were significantly associated with outcome, for both psychotherapies as well as for active and placebo pharmacotherapy. Furthermore, a significant association between the strength of the alliance and the probability of remission was found.

Therapeutic Alliance with the Suicidal Patient

> The therapeutic relationship is vital to effective treatment of suicidality. The best techniques applied without error at precisely the right time are of limited, if any, value when an adequate therapeutic relationship and treatment alliance does not exist. (Rudd, Joiner, & Rajab, 2001, p. 13)

Two established scales for measuring the therapeutic alliance, the Vanderbilt Therapeutic Alliance Scale (VTAS) and the Penn Helping Alliance Questionnaire (Morgan, Luborsky, Crits-Christoph, Curtis, & Solomon, 1982) may serve as a basis to consider practical aspects of therapeutic alliance building. Both scales share certain assumptions, which are relevant for the therapeutic relationship with the suicidal patient.

(1)   Acknowledgement of the patient's own thoughts and feelings. Understanding the experience of failure, self-hate, and mental pain from the patient's perspective and communicating one's awareness of understanding requires an empathic stance.

(2)   Recognition of the patient's goals and the patient's need for autonomy. Patients have their own conscious or unconscious beliefs and goals, which need to be respected and understood. While trying to reach empathic understanding of the patient's goal of death

by suicide, the therapist should carefully probe for the client's life-oriented goals and facilitate the client's movement towards them.

(3) *Working together in a joint effort.* A meaningful working alliance requires a shared model of understanding of the patient's vulnerabilities and the development towards suicide.

(4) *The therapist's engagement and competence.* The therapist conveys a non-judgemental attitude, providing a sense of safety and trust, and uses his or her professional skills in maintaining a meaningful therapeutic relationship. Patients in a suicidal crisis need someone who cares and who is not frightened by suicidal impulses.

A major challenge in psychotherapy with suicidal patients is the need for the therapist to be fully engaged in the treatment and affectively attuned to the patient's experience. One of the most difficult aspects is the therapist's ability to show empathy for the patient's suicidal wish and to refrain from trying to talk the patient out of it. Psychotherapy with suicidal patients may evoke in the therapist strong counter-transference reactions, including intense feelings of anger, helplessness, and the urge to withdraw. Yet the therapist's genuine effort to understand and accept the patient's subjective experience, without attempting to change it, is crucial to the patient's capacity to bear mental pain, which previously appeared to be unbearable.

Understanding and acceptance are essential for establishing a treatment alliance that gives the patient an opportunity to sustain hope in the face of unbearable anguish and hopelessness. The empathic therapist communicates verbally and non-verbally that the patient's affective experience, even his or her suicidality, is understandable, given his or her situation and internal experience. The therapist who validates the patient in a fundamental way demonstrates the belief that the patient has the capacity to bear these feelings and to uncover non-suicidal choices. The therapist sees and reflects the capacity that the patient cannot yet experience, and holds the hope when the patient feels hopeless about the possibility of change.

While the clinician may make use of specific therapeutic interventions to help the patient to postpone and ultimately revoke the suicidal plan, the therapeutic strategy should be based on an empathic understanding of the desire to die:

> Being empathic with the suicidal wish means assuming the suicidal person's perspective and 'seeing' how this person has reached a dead end without trying to interfere, stop, or correct the suicidal wishes. This means that the therapist attempts to empathize with the patient's pain experience to such a point that he/she can 'see' why suicide is the only alternative available to the patient ... Instead of working against the suicidal stream and trying to instantly increase the patient's motivation to live by persuasion or commitment to a contract, the therapist takes an empathic stance with the suicidal wish and brings it to full focus. (Orbach, 2001, p. 173)

In an out-patient setting, interventions such as between-session contact and telephone sessions may enable the patient to cope with affective intensity and strengthen the therapeutic alliance. It is generally accepted that reaching out to patients, especially with regard to attending treatment session, facilitates treatment engagement. At the same time, therapists have to be aware of the risk of defining the treatment frame too narrowly, and thereby missing an opportunity to help the patient cope with overwhelming affect and to strengthen the alliance.

Therapeutic alliance is specifically addressed in several formalized treatments for suicidality. For instance, in cognitive-behaviour therapy, the therapeutic relationship is characterized by 'collaborative empiricism' (Beck, Rush, Shaw, & Emery, 1979), in which the clinician and patient work together to examine the 'data' of the patient's thoughts, feelings, and behaviours, with the therapeutic goal of developing systematic (often homework-based) treatments that emphasize cognitive restructuring and working with certain schemas, modes, and automatic thoughts. Cognitive-behavioural (CB) approaches are usually rather directive and instructive, that is, markedly different from either psychodynamic or humanistic approaches. The CB approach emphasizes the therapist's role as an active and engaged expert, with a focus on three areas: symptom management (crisis resolution); skill building; and personality development (Rudd et al., 2001, p. 43). In the initial treatment phase the therapist obtains the patient's commitment to treatment, including the agreement to attend and participate in the sessions, work towards achieving the treatment goals, complete homework assignments, and actively participate in other aspects of treatment in order to better manage their suicidal crises. Rudd, Joiner, Trotter, Williams, and Cordero (2009) recently identified common elements of effective treatments, distilled from a review of available randomized clinical trials targeting suicidality. One such element was providing patients with simple and understandable models for their suicidality. These are assumed to facilitate hope, with likely positive implications for motivation, commitment, and overall treatment compliance.

In dialectical behavioural therapy (DBT) (Linehan, 1993a), alliance is largely achieved through the therapist's active engagement in the therapeutic relationship. A central element in DBT concerns the tension between accepting the client exactly as he or she is at that moment and simultaneously pushing the client towards changing maladaptive behavioural patterns. The DBT therapist regularly inquires about suicidal behaviour and urges, and conducts a risk assessment. Maintaining an attachment to the therapist is considered part of the attachment to life more broadly. For individuals suffering from borderline personality disorders (BPD) the relationship with the DBT therapist becomes the opportunity to learn to cope with interpersonal conflicts. The therapeutic relationship is further representative of the central dialectic of DBT, i.e., the ongoing expression of acceptance on the part of the therapist towards the client as well as a powerful agent for change. In DBT, validation strategies are crucial in reducing emotional arousal when a patient presents in a state of high distress, as is frequently the case with suicidal individuals with BPD (Linehan, 1997). Because emotional arousal interferes with cognitive processing and performance, the client should be sufficiently emotionally regulated to process new information in order that treatments may be maximally effective.

One of the difficulties encountered by therapists when treating suicidal patients is the feeling of being overwhelmed or even hopeless when patients have chronic or recurring episodes of suicide ideation or make repeated suicide attempts. Peer supervision or a 'consultation team' (Linehan, 1993b) for therapists is highly recommended, and in most treatment programmes, required as part of the therapeutic work.

Understanding Suicide as Goal-Directed Behaviour

In a developmental view of living organisms, biological, psychological, and social processes of adaptation to the environment are seen as basic conditions of life. These models imply that health in a biological as well as psychological sense is not a static condition, but a continuous process. We have proposed an approach to understanding suicidal behaviour based on action theory or the theory of goal-directed action (Michel & Valach, 1997). This represents a developmental systems theory that conceptualizes actions in terms of goals. According to Carver and Scheier (1998) goal involvement is critical to life. Without goals, behaviour loses form and people's lives fall apart. Actions, including suicide and attempted suicide, are not seen as caused by a single event but understood in the context in which they develop, and the associated goals.

In an action theoretical model suicide is seen as an alternative to original life-career goals. Life-career goals may relate to relationship goals (e.g., to maintain a stable partnership) or work-related goals (e.g., to achieve a secure income to support the family). In critical times, when a person's self-evaluation is negative ('I have failed, I am a failure'), suicide may appear as a possible solution to a subjectively unbearable state of mind, and may re-emerge throughout life as a possible goal in similar critical life situations. Suicide may thus become a (usually quite temporary) goal, a possible solution, when the realization of a person's long-term goals and projects are seriously threatened. The immediate goal of a suicidal action is to escape from an unbearable state of mind dominated by psychic pain, which may amount to a state of traumatic stress, dissociation, automatism, and analgesia, secondary to negative and often humiliating experience. After a suicide attempt, life-oriented goals may re-emerge as alternative priorities. It is not at all uncommon that, the morning after a suicide attempt, a patient wants to go to work or school.

With the conscious representation of goal-directed processes being an integral aspect of intention-building and goal-setting, in an action theoretical frame of understanding, individuals are capable of giving their accounts of these processes which precede suicidal behaviour, and which are relevant explanations of suicidal behaviour. Narratives represent the way people explain beliefs, desires, intentions, and choices that shape human actions. Regarding the therapist's role, an action theoretical approach asks for a patient-oriented attitude. When it comes to the patient's very individual story, the patient is the expert (of his or her biography), while the interviewer is the facilitator or co-author. The patient's own narrative is the main joint goal, and interviewing is a joint goal-directed action.

Where the Truth Lies: Narrative Interviewing

Based on a study of suicide notes, Leenaars (1988) concluded that suicide, although often appearing as a solution to a current interpersonal situation, is strongly related to certain aspects of the individual's biography. Autobiographical stories are symbolized accounts of actions of human beings that have a temporal dimension. Stories have a beginning, a middle, and an end. A listener enters into the temporal world the narrator constructs, helps in the telling, and thus narratives are jointly accomplished, according to shared knowledge and interaction rules. The discourse about projects and actions becomes a joint action in itself. The story is held together by recognizable patterns of events called plots. Central to the plot structure are human predicaments and attempted resolutions (Sarbin, 1986). A good narrative interview encompasses all the relevant facts, makes sense of the experience, is non-stigmatizing, permits the maximum allowable hope, and will be credible to both the clinician and the patient.

In a narrative, one's actions are related to those of others, and are thereby given a meaning. Thus, the narrative has a function in the development and maintenance of the unity of a "career" (i.e., in re-establishing the identity of a person). It includes the subjective interpretation of life events according to a person's own beliefs and goals. The clinical outcome of a narrative discourse is often a new story with a new ending.

The literature on attachment, mentalizing, and suicide intervention converges in recognizing the therapeutic value of narrative, that is, telling the story to an empathic listener (Holmes, 2001, p. 80–94). These approaches promote emotion regulation in part by providing an attachment relationship in which patients can achieve *narrative coherence* (Holmes, 2001) in relation to their suicidal state. Bateman and Fonagy (2006) articulated the patient's fundamental autonomy and the corresponding limits of the therapist's responsibility along similar lines: 'I can't stop you harming yourself or even killing yourself, but I might be able to help you understand what makes you try to do it and to find other ways of managing things' (p. 113).

The basic assumption is that, as much as the psychiatrist or psychotherapist possesses the techniques and skills to *conduct* a good interview, the patient has the skills to *contribute to* a good interview. The development towards suicide and attempted suicide is always very individual. According to the theory of goal-directed action, people explain their own actions and understand the actions of others through stories they tell ('Well, it's a long story…'). Only when the story behind an act of self-harm has been shared with another person can there be a common ground for a therapeutic relationship, whether in hospital or in an out-patient setting. 'When we are able to formulate the right story, and it is heard in the right way by the right listener, we are able to deal more effectively with the experience' (Adler, 1997, p. 28).

Although in the suicidal crisis the perception of the present situation and the self may be coloured by depressed mood and cognitions, individuals who survive usually have a good narrative competence, provided that the interviewer is prepared to assume an open, non-judgemental, and supportive attitude. Story-telling needs a sensitive listener. If we do not feel understood, we may prematurely end our story.

The therapist and the patient need to review the past together to learn how the patient's life and the perspectives for the future have become unendurable. Empathic understanding allows the therapist, along with the patient, to grasp how suicide came to be seen as the only available solution. Only then can a therapeutic process begin.

In a clinical study based on single interviews with suicide attempters we found that patients' ratings of the quality of the therapeutic relationship in the Penn Helping Alliance Questionnaire were significantly higher when the interview opening contained either of the words 'tell' or 'story' (Michel, Dey, Stadler, & Valach, 2004). Therapist interventions should thus include the demonstration of interest and respect, encouraging the patient to develop the narratives. Patients often ask: 'How far back do you want me to go?' or 'Where do you want me to start?' They usually start with a life project relevant for the suicidal action in question (e.g., retirement and increasing isolation). After the interviewer's opening question, patients usually embark on their self-narrative, which in its first part may last between five and 20 minutes. This phase should not be interrupted by the interviewer, except for clarifying questions.

In Bern, we use video-playback (Young, Valach, Dillabough, Dover, & Matthes, 1994) in a second session to re-expose the patient to the suicidal crisis. Patients are asked to interrupt the video at any time and comment or provide further information. The therapist, on the other hand, raises questions about possible alternative coping mechanisms. In these self-confrontation sessions, patients often are emotionally charged, but invariably find it useful to re-live the crisis in a secure environment. It has proved to be helpful for the therapist to make a written summary which is handed to the patient and discussed in a third session, providing a starting point for jointly developing individual coping skills for future critical situations.

The Provision of a Secure Base: Long-term Anchoring

In clinical experience, safety measures, such as telephone numbers and addresses of important others, are usually some of the first items on the list of behavioural strategies. On their first admission to the crisis intervention unit many suicide attempters say that they had not been aware of the crisis unit and the help they could have received there. It is to be hoped that, in the future, these people will turn to the crisis centre if it is associated with a positive memory. Ideally, a crisis unit or a practising therapist should provide a safe place for suicidal patients, or, in the words of John Bowlby, a secure base (Bowlby, 1988). According to attachment theory, in adult life attachment behaviour is activated in 'times of calamity', while it may not be observable when things go well.

This may be an explanation for the remarkable finding that sending standardized letters or postcards to suicide attempters over several years reduces the risk of suicide (Carter, Clover, Whyte, Dawson, & D'Este, 2005; Motto & Bostrom, 2001). A minimal offer of care may thus have a stabilizing effect. The results strongly suggest that, besides availability and continuity in providing a secure base, active maintenance of a therapeutic relationship, even if minimal, plays an important role in the long-term aftercare of individuals who have attempted suicide.

A similar effect can be expected from a long-term therapeutic relationship with a health professional. The following quote from a patient illustrates this:

> He [the general practitioner] was like a rock. He really was, he was genuinely concerned for me and I could tell he was. He was really worried and in a way he made me feel better, you know that someone cared and he, you know, he would see me every, maybe every month every two months just to see how everything was and till he retired really so he was a great help. (Sinclair & Green, 2005, p. 1114)

In many healthcare systems GPs play a crucial role because of their accessibility after hours in times of crisis. Similarly, accessibility and continuity of psychiatrists and psychotherapists seeing suicidal patients are important protective factors. When a clinician is not available, alternatives should be provided. Some authors clearly state that clinicians unwilling to provide such accessibility should not treat suicidal patients (McKeon, 2009, p. 46).

With a focus on long-term pharmacotherapy, the Angst, Angst, Gerber-Werder, and Gamma (2005) study, in which 406 patients were followed up over 40–44 years, provides indirect evidence for the protective effect of an ongoing therapeutic relationship with a health professional. Long-term pharmacotherapy, which included antidepressants, antipsychotics, and mood stabilizers, was associated with a significantly lower suicide rate compared with the non-medicated group. Although most of this effect could be explained by the effect of the medication, it can be argued that long-term pharmacotherapy requires a sound therapeutic alliance.

Conclusion

A positive therapeutic relationship is a basic condition for any therapy to be effective. From a therapist it requires empathy, engagement, listening ability, openness, and respect for others. In this chapter it has been argued that a narrative interviewing style and a non-judgemental, patient-oriented understanding of suicidality are core elements for establishing a therapeutic alliance with a suicidal individual. Clinical experience suggests that, in a short-term, as well as long-term, perspective, therapeutic alliance may often be the main – although largely unspecific – therapeutic element that keeps a suicidal person alive. While some patients will need intensive long-term therapy, others may benefit from only a minimal long-term offer of help by a reliable and trusted health professional.

References

Adler, H. M. (1997). The history of the present illness as treatment: Who is listening and why does it matter? *Journal of the American Board of Family Practice, 10*, 28–35.

Angst, J., Angst, F., Gerber-Werder, R., & Gamma, A. (2005). Suicide in 406 mood-disorder patients with and without long-term medication: A 40 to 44 years' follow-up. *Archives of Suicide Research, 9*, 279–300.

Appleby, L., Amos, T., Doyle, U., Tommenson, B., & Woodman, M. (1996). General practitioners and young suicides. *British Journal of Psychiatry, 168*, 330–333.

Bateman, A. & Fonagy, P. (2006). *Mentalization-based Treatment for Borderline Personality Disorder: A practical guide.* New York: Oxford University Press.

Beck, A. T., Rush, A. J., Shaw, B. F., & Emery, G. (1979). *Cognitive Therapy of Depression.* New York: Guilford Press.

Bowlby, J. (1988). *A Secure Base: Clinical applications of attachment theory.* London: Routledge.

Brown, G. K., Ten Have, T., Henriques, G. R., Xie, S. X., Hollander, J. E., & Beck, A. T. (2005). Cognitive therapy for the prevention of suicide attempts: A randomized controlled trial. *Journal of the American Medical Association, 294*, 563–570.

Carter, G. L., Clover, K., Whyte, I. M., Dawson, A. H., & D'Este, C. (2005). Postcards from the EDge project: Randomised controlled trial of an intervention using postcards to reduce repetition of hospital treated deliberate self poisoning. *British Medical Journal, 331*, 805–807.

Carver, C. S. & Scheier, M. F. (1998). *On the Self-regulation of Behaviour*. Cambridge: Cambridge University Press.

Conwell, Y., Duberstain, P. R., Cox, C., Herrmann, J. H., Forbes, N. T., & Caine, E. D. (1996). Relationship of age and Axis I diagnoses in victims of completed suicide: A psychological autopsy study. *American Journal of Psychiatry, 153*, 1001–1009.

De Leo, D. (2002). Why are we not getting any closer to preventing suicide? *British Journal of Psychiatry, 181*, 372–374.

Elkin. I., Shea, M. T., Watkins, J. T., Imber, S. D., Sotsky, S. M., Collins, J. F., Glass, D. R., Pilkonis, P. A., Leber, W. R., Docherty, J. P., Fiester, S. J., & Parloff, M. B. (1989). National Institute of Mental Health Treatment of Depression Collaborative Research Program. General effectiveness of treatments. *Archives of General Psychiatry, 46*, 971–982.

Fleischmann, A., Bertolote, J. M., Wasserman, D., De Leo, D., Bolhari, J., Botega, N. J., De Silva, D., Phillips, M., Vijayakumar, L., Varnik, A., Schlebusch, L., & Thanh, H. T. T. (2008). Effectiveness of brief intervention and contact for suicide attempters: A randomized controlled trial in 5 countries. *Bulletin of the World Health Organization, 86*, 703–709.

Goldney, R. D. (2000). Prediction of suicide and attempted suicide. In K. Hawton & K. van Heeringen (Eds.), *International Handbook of Suicide and Attempted Suicide* (pp. 107–146). Chichester: John Wiley & Sons, Ltd.

Guthrie, E., Kapur, N., Mackway-Jones, K., Chew-Graham, C., Moorey, J., Mendel, E., Marino-Francis, F., Sanderson, S., Turpin, C., Boddy, G., & Tomenson, B. (2001). Randomised controlled trial of brief psychological intervention after deliberate self poisoning. *British Medical Journal, 323*, 135–137.

Hartley, D. & Strupp, H. H. (1983). The therapeutic alliance: Its relationship to outcome in brief psychotherapy. In J. Masling & N. J. Hillsdale (Eds.), *Empirical Studies of Psychoanalytic Theories* (vol. 1, pp. 1–37). Hillsdale, NJ: Lawrence Erlbaum.

Henry, W. P. & Strupp, H. H. (1994). The therapeutic alliance as interpersonal process. In A. O. Horvath & L. S. Greenberg (Eds.), *The Working Alliance: Theory, research and practice* (p. 68). New York: John Wiley & Sons, Inc.

Holmes, J. (2001). *The Search for the Secure Base: Attachment theory and psychotherapy*. New York: Routledge.

Horvath, A. O., Gaston, L., & Luborsky, L. (1993). The therapeutic alliance and its measures. In N. Miller, L. Luborsky, J. P. Barber, & J. P. Docherty (Eds.), *Psychodynamic Treatment Research: A handbook for clinical practice* (pp. 247–273). New York: Basic Books.

Horvath, A. O. & Symonds, B. D. (1991). Relation between working alliance and outcome in psychotherapy: A meta-analysis. *Journal of Counseling Psychology, 38*, 139–149.

Isacsson, G., Holmgren, P., Wasserman, D., & Bergman, U. (1994). Use of antidepressants among people committing suicide in Sweden. *British Medical Journal, 308*, 506–509.

Isometsä, E. T., Heikkinen, M. E., Marttunen, M. J., Henriksson, M. M., Aro, H. M., & Lönqvist, J. K. (1995). The last appointment before suicide: Is suicide intent communicated? *American Journal of Psychiatry, 152*, 919–992.

Jobes, D. A. (2006). *Managing Suicidal Risk: A collaborative approach*. New York: Guilford Press.

Krupnick, J. L., Sotsky, S. M., Elkin, I., Watkins, J., & Pilkonis, P. A. (1996). The role of the therapeutic alliance in psychotherapy and pharmacotherapy outcome: Findings in the National Institute of Mental Health Treatment of Depression Collaborative Research Program. *Journal of Consulting and Clinical Psychology, 64*, 532–539.

Kurz, A., Möller, H. J., Bürk, F., Torhorst, A., Wächtler, C., & Lauter, H. (1988). Evaluation of two different aftercare strategies of an outpatient aftercare program for suicide attempters in a general hospital. In H. J. Möller, A. Schmidtke, & R. Welz (Eds.), *Current Issues in Suicidology* (pp. 414–418). Berlin: Springer.

Leenaars, A. (1988). *Suicide Notes.* New York: Human Sciences Press.

Lin, E. H. B., von Korff, M., & Wagner, E. H. (1989). Identifying suicide potential in primary care. *Journal of General and Internal Medicine, 4,* 1–6.

Linehan, M. M. (1993a). *Skills Training Manual for Treating Borderline Personality Disorder.* New York: Guilford Press.

Linehan, M. M. (1993b). *Cognitive-behavioral Treatment of Borderline Personality Disorder.* New York: Guilford Press.

Linehan, M. M. (1997). Validation and psychotherapy. In A. Bohart & L. Greenberg (Eds.), *Empathy Reconsideration: New directions in psychotherapy* (pp. 353–392). Washington, DC: American Psychological Association.

Linehan, M. M., Armstrong, H. E., Suarez, A., Allmon, D., & Heard, H. L. (1991). Cognitive-behavioral treatment of chronically parasuicidal borderline patients. *Archives of General Psychiatry, 48,* 1060–1064.

Linehan, M. M., Comtois, K. A., Murray, A. M., Brown, M. Z., Gallop, R. J., Heard, H. L., Korslund, K. E., Tutek, D. A., Reynolds, S. K., & Lindenboim, N. (2006). Two-year randomized controlled trial and follow-up of dialectical behavior therapy vs therapy by experts for suicidal behaviors and borderline personality disorder. *Archives of General Psychiatry, 63,* 757–766.

Lönqvist, J. K. (2000). Psychiatric aspects of suicidal behaviour: Depression. In K. Hawton & K. van Heeringen (Eds.), *International Handbook of Suicide and Attempted Suicide* (pp. 107–146). Chichester: John Wiley & Sons, Ltd.

McKeon, R. T. (2009). *Suicidal Behavior.* Cambridge, MA: Hogrefe & Huber.

Michel, K. (1986). Suizide und Suizidversuche: Könnte der Arzt mehr tun? (Suicide and attempted suicide: Could the physician do more?). *Schweizerische Medizinische Wochenschrift, 116,* 770–774.

Michel, K., Dey, P., Stadler, K., & Valach, L. (2004). Therapist sensitivity towards emotional life career issues and the working alliance with suicide attempters. *Archives of Suicide Research, 8,* 203–213.

Michel, K., Dey, P., & Valach, L. (2001). Suicide as goal-directed action. In K. van Heeringen (Ed.), *Understanding Suicidal Behaviour: The suicidal process approach to research and treatment* (pp. 230–254). Chichester: John Wiley & Sons, Ltd.

Michel, K., Maltsberger, J. T., Jobes, D. A., Leenaars, A. A., Orbach, I., Stadler, K., Dey, P., Young, R. A., & Valach, L. (2002). Discovering the truth in attempted suicide. *American Journal of Psychotherapy, 56,* 424–437.

Michel, K., Runeson, B., Valach, L., & Wasserman, D. (1997). Contacts of suicide attempters with GPs prior to the event; a comparison between Stockholm and Bern. *Acta Psychiatrica Scandinavica, 95,* 94–99.

Michel, K. & Valach, L. (1997). Suicide as goal-directed action. *Archives of Suicide Research, 3,* 213–221.

Michel, K., Valach, L., & Waeber, V. (1994). Understanding deliberate self-harm: The patients' views. *Crisis, 15,* 172–178.

Morgan, R., Luborsky, L., Crits-Christoph, P., Curtis, H., & Solomon, J. (1982). Predicting the outcomes of psychotherapy by the Penn Helping Alliance rating method. *Archives of General Psychiatry, 39,* 397–402.

Motto, J. A. & Bostrom, A. G. (2001). A randomized controlled trial of post-crisis suicide prevention. Psychiatric Services, *52,* 828–833.

Orbach, I. (2001). Therapeutic empathy with the suicidal wish: Principles of therapy with suicidal individuals. *American Journal of Psychotherapy, 55,* 166–184.

Pirkis, J. & Burgess, P. (1998). Suicide and recency of health care contacts. A systematic review. *British Journal of Psychiatry, 173,* 462–474.

Rogers, J. R. & Soyka, K. M. (2004). 'One Size Fits All': An existential-constructivist perspective on the crisis Intervention approach with suicidal individuals. *Journal of Contemporary Psychotherapy, 34,* 7–22.

Rudd, M. D., Joiner, T. E., & Rajab, H. (2001). *Treating Suicidal Behavior: An effective, time-limited approach.* New York: Guilford Press.

Rudd, M. D., Joiner, T. E., Trotter, D., Williams, B., & Cordero, L. (2009). The psychosocial treatment of suicidal behavior: A critique of what we know and don't know. In P. Kleespies (Ed.), *Behavioral Emergencies: An evidenced-based resource for evaluating and managing risk of suicide, violence, and victimization* (pp. 339–350). Washington, DC: American Psychological Association.

Rutz, W., Walinder, J., von Knorring, L., Rihmer, Z., & Philgren, H. (1997). Prevention of depression and suicide by education and medication: Impact on male suicidality. An update from the Gotland study. *International Journal of Psychiatry in Clinical Practice, 1,* 39–46.

Salkovskis, P. M., Atha, C., & Storer, D. (1990). Cognitive-behavioural problem solving in the treatment of patients who repeatedly attempt suicide. A controlled trial. *British Journal of Psychiatry, 157,* 871–876.

Saltzman, C., Luetgert, M. J., Roth, C. H., Craeser, J., & Howard, L. (1976). Formation of a therapeutic relationship: Experiences during the initial phase of psychotherapy as predictors of treatment duration and outcome. *Journal of Consulting and Clinical Psychology, 4,* 546–555.

Sarbin, T. R. (Ed.) (1986). *Narrative Psychology: The storied nature of human conduct.* New York: Praeger.

Sinclair, J. & Green, J. (2005). Understanding resolution of deliberate self harm: Qualitative interview study of patients' experiences. *British Medical Journal, 330,* 1112–1115.

Treolar, A. J. & Pinfold, T. J. (1993). Deliberate self-harm: An assessment of patients' attitudes to the care they receive. *Crisis, 14,* 83–89.

van Heeringen, C., Jannes, S., Buylaert, W., Henderick, H., De Bacquer, D., & van Remoortel, J. (1995). The management of non-compliance with referral to out-patient after-care among attempted suicide patients: A controlled intervention study. *Psychological Medicine, 25,* 963–970.

Young, R. A., Valach, L., Dillabough, J. A., Dover, C., & Matthes, G. (1994). Career research from an action perspective: The self-confrontation procedure. *Career Development Quarterly, 43,* 185–196.

Appendix

The Aeschi Guidelines for Clinicians (Michel, Maltsberger, Jobes, Leenaars, Orbach et al., 2002)

(1)   The goal for the clinician must be to reach, together with the patient, a shared understanding of the patient's suicidality. This goal stands in contrast to a traditional medical approach where the clinician is in the role of the expert in identifying the causes of a pathological behaviour and to make a diagnostic case-formulation. It must be made clear, however, that in the Aeschi working group's understanding a psychiatric diagnosis is an integral part of the assessment interview and must be adequately taken into consideration in the planning of further management of the patient. The active exploration of the mental state, however, should not be placed first in the interview, but follow a narrative approach.

(2)   The clinician should be aware that most suicidal patients suffer from a state of mental pain or anguish and a total loss of self-respect. Patients, therefore, are very vulnerable and have a tendency to withdraw. Experience suggests, however, that after a suicide attempt there is a 'window' in which patients can be reached. Patients at this moment are open to talk about their emotional and cognitive experiences related to the suicidal crisis, particularly if the clinician is prepared to explore the intra-subjective meaning of the act with the patient.

(3)   The interviewer's attitude should be non-judgemental and supportive. For this the clinician must be open to listen to the patient. Only the patient can be the expert of his or her own individual experiences. Furthermore, the first encounter with a mental health professional determines patient compliance to future therapy. An empathic approach is essential to help patients re-establish life-oriented goals.

(4)   A suicidal crisis is not just determined by the present, it has a history. Suicide and attempted suicide are inherently related to biographical or life career aspects, and the clinician should aim to understand them in this context. Therefore, the interview should encourage patients to deliver their self-narratives ('I should like you to tell me, in your own words, what is behind the suicide attempt …'). Explaining an action, and making another person understand what made the individual do it, puts a suicidal crisis into perspective and can be instrumental in re-establishing the individual's sense of mastery.

(5)   New models are needed to conceptualize suicidal behaviour that provide a frame for the patient and clinician to reach a shared understanding of the patient's suicidality. An approach that does not see patients as objects displaying pathology but as individuals that have their good reasons to perform an act of self-harm will help to strengthen the rapport. The most common motive is to escape from an unbearable state of mind (or the self). A theoretical model that understands suicide actions as goal directed and related to life-career aspects may prove to be particularly useful in clinical practice.

(6)   The ultimate goal should be to engage the patient in a therapeutic relationship, even in a first assessment interview. In a critical moment in a patient's life meaningful discourse with another person can be the turning point in that life-oriented goals are re-established. This requires the clinician's ability to empathize with the patient's inner experience and to understand the logic of the suicidal urge. An interview in which the patient and the interviewer jointly look at the meaning of the suicidal urge sets the scene for dealing with related life-career or identity themes. The plan of a therapy is, so to speak, laid out.

CHAPTER TWENTY-FIVE

Recognition of Suicide Risk, Crisis Helplines, and Psychosocial Interventions: A Selective Review

Rory C. O'Connor, Susan Rasmussen, and Annette Beautrais

Abstract

The overarching objective of this chapter is to review the current developments and effectiveness of a selection of activities, including recognition of risk, crisis helplines, and psychosocial interventions, which are integral to a growing number of national suicide prevention strategies. This chapter is divided into three sections. In Section I we review issues concerned with the recognition and assessment of risk in selected institutional contexts (namely prisons and emergency departments). Better recognition of suicide risk in prisons is paramount, given that the risk of suicidal behaviour is elevated in those who are incarcerated and on remand compared with the general population. As the numbers presenting to emergency departments (EDs) with suicidal behaviour and self-harm have increased in recent decades, identifying and treating individuals is an economic, as well as a personal and a social imperative. In Section II, we review what is known about the effectiveness of crisis helplines and consider some of the challenges inherent in undertaking research into their effectiveness. The final section describes and evaluates the effectiveness of some recently developed psychosocial interventions (i.e., crisis cards, postcards, social support, and network interventions) and multi-level approaches to suicide prevention. We end with general observations about the development and evaluation of interventions which, if implemented, should increase their quality and effectiveness.

International Handbook of Suicide Prevention: Research, Policy and Practice, First Edition.
Edited by Rory C. O'Connor, Stephen Platt, Jacki Gordon.
© 2011 John Wiley & Sons, Ltd. Published 2011 by John Wiley & Sons, Ltd.

Introduction

Psychosocial interventions should incorporate activities which aid in the identification and assessment of suicide risk. To be effective, they must be feasible to implement and acceptable to those at whom they are targeted, and they must meaningfully engage those who seek help. The purpose of this heterogeneous chapter is to review a selection of activities, including crisis helplines and psychosocial interventions, which are integral to a growing number of national suicide prevention strategies. There are three main aims: first, to review issues relating to the recognition and assessment of suicidal risk in prisons and emergency departments; second, to investigate whether crisis helplines are effective in reducing suicide risk; and, third, to provide a critical overview of new developments using brief, 'low-intensity', psychosocial interventions and multi-level approaches to suicide prevention which are not described in detail elsewhere in this Handbook. Psychological therapies are excluded here as they are described in other chapters (see Chapters 21–24). This chapter concludes with some discussion of the challenges to successful development and evaluation of psychosocial interventions as well as future directions.

The terms 'suicide attempt' and 'self-harm' are often used interchangeably in the suicidology literature. For the present purposes, we use the term 'suicide attempt'/'behaviour' to refer to self-injurious behaviour with evidence of suicidal intent. 'Self-harm' is used to describe all other self-harming behaviour where suicidal intent was not explicitly ascertained.

Section I Recognition and Assessment of Risk in Prisons and Emergency Departments

Prisons

In many prisons suicide is the most common cause of death. When suicides occur within prison they tend to attract institutional, public, and political attention. Prisons face censure for failing to protect the health and well-being of prisoners in their care, and they are obliged to conduct extensive inquiries about the events leading to the suicide. In the aftermath of a suicide, the roles and responsibilities of prison staff are examined, and the failures to recognize the distress and/or plans of the prisoner, and avert the suicide are explored in minute, legal, and coronial detail. While both the suicide and the subsequent inquiry are stressful for prison staff, they must, at the same time, address the distress of other inmates and institute efforts to minimize the possibility of a suicide cluster (Daigle, Daniel, Dear, Frottier, Hayes, *et al.*, 2007; Hayes, 1995).

The risk of suicidal behaviour in jails and prisons arises both because prisoners are a population with multiple and high risks for suicidal behaviour, and because legal charges and incarceration are stressful events. The risks of suicidal behaviour in prisoners have been compared with those of the general population in studies in different countries: all studies report higher rates of suicidal ideation and behaviour in prison populations. The risk of suicide in prisoners is estimated as three times higher than in the general population (Fazel, Grann, Kling, & Hawton, 2010). The risk of suicidal ideation and attempt was estimated, in a UK study, as 7.5 times higher in individuals detained for pre-trial reasons compared with the general population, while the risk of suicide attempt in prisoners was estimated at six times that of their general population peers (Jenkins, Bhugra, Meltzer, Singleton, Bebbington, *et al.*, 2005). While most studies of prisoners have focused on males, recent studies of female prisoners report similarly elevated risks of suicidal behaviour (Fazel *et al.*, 2010; Marzano, Fazel, Rivlin, & Hawton, 2010).

As noted above, prisoners' risk of suicide arises, in large part, because they come into prison with a burden of multiple, often chronic, risk factors for suicidal behaviour. These factors include psychiatric illness, drug and alcohol addiction, history of suicidal behaviour, poor family environment poor psychosocial support, and social isolation and alienation. A study from Austria identified five specific risk factors for suicide among inmates: prior suicide attempts or threats of suicide; psychiatric illness; psychotropic medication prescribed during imprisonment; a very violent offence precipitating arrest; and housing in a single cell (Fruehwald, Matschnig, Koenig, & Bauer, 2004). Other studies have recommended that, since almost all prisoners have psychiatric illnesses, suicide prevention within prisons must proceed with a focus on treating those illnesses (Jenkins *et al.*, 2005).

Once detained, already vulnerable individuals may then have to cope with drug withdrawal at the same time as they have to confront the shameful consequences of arrest and sentencing and the trauma, stresses, and fears of withdrawal of freedom and living in prison (Jenkins *et al.*, 2005; Konrad, Daigle, Daniel, Dear, Frottier, Hayes, *et al.*, 2007). Prison stresses may include violence, bullying, loneliness, withdrawal of psychosocial support, worries about family and future, and lack of meaningful activity. Prisoners are at highest risk for suicide during the first week of incarceration; risk also increases with length of stay, so that those with very long ('life') sentences are at particularly high risk. While the difficulty of identifying individuals at heightened risk of suicide from a population in which almost every individual is already at elevated risk of suicide is acknowledged, profiles of suicide at-risk prisoners have been developed. One profile is of a young male detained and awaiting trial for the first time for a minor, often substance-related crime, who is often intoxicated when arrested and who dies by suicide within hours of arrest. To prevent suicide at this time, jails and police custody cells need to focus on initial procedures, including reception, screening and provision of information, housing and care. A second high-risk period occurs around the time of a court appearance, especially if the detainee expects a guilty verdict and/or a long sentence. In contrast to these pre-trial inmates, the prisoner profile is of an older, violent offender who has been in prison for several years, and whose suicide is precipitated by events within prison or within his family, the latter often being a relationship break-up (Konrad *et al.*, 2007). While typical risk profiles might be useful, they are not invariant in time or person; the risk profile for an individual prisoner may change over time and with alterations to personal or family circumstances.

To address prisoners' higher suicide risk, many countries have implemented suicide prevention programmes within prisons and jails (Daigle *et al.*, 2007). These programmes typically include screening of incoming prisoners and detainees for suicide risk, gatekeeper education for staff, institutional suicide 'proofing' by minimizing ligature points, surveillance, housing at-risk prisoners in cells with another prisoner, attention to bullying, and provision of peer support programmes and access to mental health services.

A key component of prevention programmes is screening incoming detainees or prisoners for suicide risk. Given the risk of suicide shortly after admission, screening is done immediately on intake, and repeated each time an individual is transferred to another institution or when situations change. Screenings are typically conducted by prison officers as part of the intake procedure, using brief, structured checklists of known prison suicide risk factors. In the absence of a standard checklist, each institution usually develops its own. However, checklists commonly cover the same issues, including assessment of current intoxication; history of substance abuse; shame, guilt, and fear about the alleged offence; hopelessness, anxiety, or depression; history of diagnosis and treatment for psychiatric illness; observation of psychotic symptoms or bizarre behaviours; a plan for suicide; and extent of psychosocial support. In addition, observations of suicide risk may be sought from arresting officers and records of any prior incarcerations are checked for flagged suicide risk. Those individuals revealed to be at risk are then evaluated by mental health professionals, housed in prison hospital wards until risk is assessed as reduced, and/ or placed under surveillance. The screening checklist provides a basis for communicating risk to other staff and to other facilities, if a prisoner is transferred. Staff are advised, however, that assessments have limited utility and that risk is dynamic and may alter with changed circumstances (Daigle, Labelle, & Cote, 2006; Daigle *et al.*, 2007; Kerkhof & Bernasco, 1990; Konrad *et al.*, 2007).

Emergency departments

Emergency departments (EDs) are key sites for identifying and treating individuals with suicide ideation and suicide attempts. Presentations to EDs for suicidal behaviour have increased during the last two decades and show no sign of declining (Larkin, Smith, & Beautrais, 2008). Those who make suicide attempts are typically discharged after medical stabilization and psychosocial evaluation, but are at high risk of further suicide attempts and suicide (Gibb, Beautrais, & Fergusson, 2005; Larkin, Smith, & Beautrais, 2008; Owens, Horrocks, & House, 2002). Those who present with suicide ideation alone have heightened risks of returning to the ED with further ideation or with suicide attempts which are as high as those who present with attempts (Larkin, Beautrais, Gibb, & Laing, 2008). Furthermore, up to 12% of ED patients who attend for medical reasons only reveal suicide ideation if queried but are typically never assessed for this (Claassen & Larkin, 2005).

Suicidal ED patients with substance abuse, depression, conduct disorder, or impulsivity are at high risk of suicidal behaviour and death in the months and years after their ED discharge (Crandall, Fullerton-Gleason, Aguero, & LaValley, 2006; Gairin, House, & Owens, 2003; Owens *et al.*, 2002). Up to 25% of suicide attempters seen in the ED make another attempt, 5%–10% eventually die by suicide, and risks of homicide, accidents, disease, and premature death in general are increased (Beautrais, 2004; Cuijpers & Schoevers, 2004; Zahl & Hawton, 2004).While most suicidal ED patients are discharged to follow-up care, the majority fail to engage in post-ED treatment (Kurz & Moller, 1984;

Monti, Cedereke, & Öjehagen, 2003). For many, the ED may be their only source of healthcare (Miller & Taylor, 2005). Consequently, EDs have a responsibility to assess suicide risk, engage patients, and initiate treatment. However, effective ED-delivered treatments to achieve rapid improvement of depressive symptomatology and suicidal ideation are often lacking. Typically, ED interventions have focused on medical treatment, psychosocial assessment, advising on restricting access to the means of suicide, and developing plans for safe discharge of patients (Jacobs, 1999; Rudd, 2006; Shea, 2002).

Three distinct profiles of ED patients at significant risk of suicidal ideation and behaviour can be identified: first, presentation to the ED with transparent suicidal ideation or following a suicide attempt; second, presentation with mental health problems that are not suicide-related; and, third, presentation with physical problems but with hidden suicide ideation.

Patients who visit EDs for medical, surgical, and mental health reasons often present with well-recognized risk factors for suicidal behaviour. These factors include being male, antisocial, violent, aggressive, impulsive, homeless, psychiatrically ill, and/or engaged in substance abuse. Patients at risk for suicide may not present explicitly for suicidal ideation or behaviour, but they may attend for trauma, assault, domestic abuse, or substance problems. Other high-risk groups likely to present to EDs include young people who have dropped out of school or who are not affiliated with school, college, or workplace, those with conduct disorder, and those in foster and welfare care; patients with severe, chronic mental disorders, including those with depression, psychosis, and personality disorders; and older adults with physical health problems, persistent pain, disability, and/or depression. A comprehensive ED suicide screening programme should screen all non-trauma presentations for suicide risk.

Instruments which screen for suicide risk in the ED must be brief, easily understood by patients, culturally appropriate, readily administered in busy general hospital settings, capable of generating rapidly available responses for review by ED staff, and able to detect suicidal ideation, planning, and risk in the range of patient groups outlined above. Currently, no suicide screening tool is universally accepted and recommended. In contrast, a 20-year-long, multi-million dollar investment in developing ED-based screening instruments for hazardous alcohol use has resulted in a suite of well-established, widely used tools, such as AUDIT, ASSIST, and DAST (Academic ED SBIRT Research Collaborative, 2007; Babor, McRee, Kassebaum, Grimaldi, Ahmed, *et al.*, 2007). The successful use of these tools in EDs provides both a persuasive argument that ED staff have the time and willingness to conduct screening for mental health problems, and a model for the development of tools to screen for suicide risk.

There are several candidate suicide screening tools which could be used, abbreviated, and/or adapted for use with adolescent and adult populations (Asarnow, Baraff, Berk, Grob, Devich-Navarro, *et al.*, 2008; Brown, 2009; Cooper, Kapur, Dunning, Guthrie, Appleby, *et al.*, 2006; Copelan, Messer, & Ashley, 2006; Folse, Eich, Hall, & Ruppman, 2006; Healy, Barry, Blow, Welsh, & Milner, 2006; Horowitz, Wang, Koocher, Burr, Smith, *et al.*, 2001; Larzelere, Andersen, Ringle, & Jorgensen, 2004; Meneese & Yutrzenka, 1990; NSW Department of Health, 2004; Olfson, Weissman, Leon, Sheehan, & Farber, 1996; Patel, Harrison, & Bruce-Jones, 2009; Paykel, Myers, Lindenthal, & Tanner, 1974; Posner, Oquendo, Gould, Stanley, & Davies, 2007; Shedler, 2000; Shedler, Beck, & Bensen, 2000;

Skoog, Aevarsson, Beskow, Larsson, Palsson, *et al.*, 1996; Tishler, Reiss, & Rhodes, 2007). Alternatively, suicide screening questions could be embedded within broader assessments of mental health, high-risk behaviours, or events (e.g., Lowenstein, Koziol-McLain, Thompson, Bernstein, Greenberg, *et al.*, 1998; Rhodes, Lauderdale, He, Howes, & Levinson, 2001) or they could be asked independently (e.g., Folse *et al.*, 2006; Wintersteen, Diamond, & Fein, 2007).

Of particular relevance to developing a feasible ED suicide screening tool is the work conducted by Larkin and colleagues who embedded suicide screening questions in self-administered mental health screening conducted with over 5,000 patients, using a mini-computer platform. Of 1,590 screened patients in one study, 185 (11.6%) acknowledged suicidal ideation and 31 (2%) reported planning to kill themselves. Almost all of those with suicidal ideation (97%) acknowledged symptoms consistent with mood, anxiety, and/or substance-related disorders. Structured medical record review revealed that 25 of the 31 patients planning suicide were undetected during their index visit, and that four attempted suicide within 45 days of the visit (Claassen & Larkin, 2005; Larkin & Classen, 2007). This study has been replicated in different countries, and questions on the computerized QPD (Quick PsychoDiagnostics) panel have been translated into Spanish.

This research suggests that suicidal patients tend to be missed by trained emergency physicians (Larkin & Classen, 2007). Non-psychiatric adult ED patients were screened with and without providing clinical feedback to ED staff. Clinicians missed 94.6% of suicidal ideation patients and 80.6% of planners. When repeated in the same setting with computerized feedback on 768 patients, suicidal ideation was present in 52 (6.8%) and 13 (1.7%) had a suicide plan (SP), resulting in 38 (73.1%) and 13 (100%) referrals for suicidal ideation and suicide plan, respectively. Documentation of mental health diagnoses increased to 21.2% for ideation and 38.5% for planning patients, suggesting that computerized screening with provider feedback can significantly improve the rates of psychosocial referral for silently suicidal patients in the ED.

Larkin's substance abuse screening using the same computerized tool suggests that ED patients may be more willing to respond honestly to computerized than face-to-face screening, with the computerized questionnaire capturing the more positive endorsements for drugs, while physician interview captured more participants for alcohol (Hamann, Larkin, Brown, Schwann, & George, 2007). Research comparing personal versus computerized screening for suicidal ideation is warranted, particularly given the time and personnel advantages offered by computerized screening.

Research is needed to determine the type of screening tool which best captures suicidal ideation in a general ED setting, and can be readily administered by ED staff. There is an inherent tension between identifying those at genuine and imminent risk of suicide versus over-identification and further burdening an already challenged ED system (Britto, 2001; Institute of Medicine, 2002; Nawar, 2007). Despite the existence of several candidate tools, there is no generally agreed upon, widely accepted, practical, and psychometrically strong ED suicide screening tool, nor a realistic screening process. However, at present the Beck Hopelessness Scale has the best generic application for screening for suicide risk amongst adults, adolescents, in-patients, out-patients, and people seeking assistance from EDs (Ministry of Health and New Zealand Guidelines Group, 2003).

Section II Crisis Helplines

It is estimated that at least 10% of calls to crisis helplines include thoughts of suicide (Fakhoury, 2000). In the United Kingdom in 2008, Samaritans received 5,159,698 contacts (primarily by phone) with 19.1% (517,335) of the dialogue contacts including an expression of suicidal feelings at the time of contact (Samaritans, 2009). Although telephone hotlines have been part of suicide prevention activities and centres for several decades (Day, 1974; Shneidman & Farberow, 1957), empirical data to support their effectiveness has only recently been gathered (e.g., Gould, Kalafat, Harris Munfakh, & Kleinman, 2007). Indeed, in 2001, the American Academy of Child and Adolescent Psychiatry noted that the effectiveness of helplines was unknown and required further evaluation (AACAP, 2001). A number of early studies focused on distal outcome measures as indices of effectiveness. Such studies often compared the suicide rates in regions with and without helplines/crisis programmes, while others employed pre-post study designs (e.g., Dew, Bromet, Brent, & Greenhouse, 1987; Riehl, Marchner, & Moller, 1988). Taken as a whole, these studies yielded mixed support for helplines, with a recent meta-analysis concluding that although individual studies do not always yield an effect, overall they have a significant, albeit small and inconsistent, effect (Lester, 1997). In addition, a number of studies suggested that helplines are likely to attract females rather than males (e.g., Gould *et al.*, 2007). A US study found that young White females were significantly over-represented as callers to helplines (Miller, Coombs, Leeper, & Barton, 1984).

A key limitation of population-based analyses is that they employ crude indices of effectiveness (e.g., gross suicide rates) which are not specific to those who use the helpline, nor do they control for confounders, that is, other activities that may impact on regional suicide rates (Mishara & Daigle, 2000). Moreover, such analyses do not provide any insight into which components of a crisis call response are effective. Consequently, a number of research groups have endeavoured to evaluate the effectiveness of helplines by tracking proximal outcomes from the beginning to the end of crisis calls (Gould *et al.*, 2007; Kalafat, Gould, Harris Munfakh, & Kleinman, 2007; King, Nurcombe, Bickman, Hides, & Reid, 2003), or by silently monitoring crisis calls (Mishara, Chagnon, Daigle, Balan, Raymond, *et al.*, 2007a, 2007b). It is also important to understand the broader context of the helpline, including how they have been advertised/promoted, what level/expertise of staffing is required/available, opening hours, etc.

King and colleagues were among the first to investigate the immediate impact of telephone counselling on suicidal young people (King *et al.*, 2003). As part of the Australian National Youth Suicide Prevention Strategy, the Kids Help Line (KHL) was enhanced to deliver telephone counselling to callers under 18 years of age, 24 hours per day, seven days per week. King *et al.* (2003) conducted an independent evaluation of the effectiveness of this service for suicide prevention. In their naturalistic, uncontrolled evaluation, 101 callers who indicated either suicidal ideation or intent completed measures of mental state, suicidal ideation, and suicidal urgency at the beginning and end of their calls. The findings were promising, yielding statistically significant reductions in callers' mental state scores, suicidal ideation, and suicidal urgency from the beginning to the end of the call.

Building upon the work of King *et al.* (2003), Gould *et al.* (2007) extended the crisis helpline evidence base to include a follow-up assessment 2–4 weeks post-call to determine whether the telephone intervention had a longer-term impact on risk and behaviour. In Gould *et al.*'s study, adult callers were recruited from eight crisis services across the United States (*n* = 1,085). In addition to assessing suicidality at the start and end of the call, 35% (*n* = 350) of the callers were followed up within three weeks of their crisis call. This study yielded a number of notable findings. First, more than half of the callers had current self-harm/suicidal plans, with almost 60% having a history of suicide attempt. Second, intent to die, hopelessness, and psychological pain decreased significantly during the course of the call. Third, in the 2–4 weeks following the call, hopelessness, and psychological pain continued to decrease although intent to die did not. While King's and Gould's findings are encouraging, these authors urge caution: both studies were uncontrolled; therefore, it is difficult to determine what caused the reduction in suicidality, hopelessness, and psychological pain and whether these could be plausibly attributed to the crisis line. For example, it is plausible that seeking help via the helpline represented the peak of a caller's crisis and that their levels of suicidality would have subsided without intervention (King *et al.*, 2003). Moreover, the low follow-up participation rate potentially limits the generalizability of the findings, although this is a recognized challenge within suicidology more widely (e.g., Moller, 1989).

Active ingredients of telephone hotlines

As suggested above, it is important to understand why a telephone intervention may be effective. The work by Mishara and colleagues has led the way in this respect, elucidating the active and important ingredients of the telephone intervention (Mishara & Daigle, 1997, 2000; Mishara *et al.*, 2007a, 2007b). In one such study, Mishara and Daigle (1997) listened unobtrusively to 617 calls by suicidal individuals from two Canadian suicide prevention centres. Subsequent cluster analysis of the response profiles of the calls yielded two distinct styles of telephone intervention, labelled Rogerian and directive. Although the volunteers at the suicide prevention centre routinely evaluated suicide risk, and developed a contract with callers which inevitably involved directive questions, Mishara and Daigle (1997) found that, as the use of Rogerian techniques increased, the more likely it was that a contract was established with callers and levels of depression decreased. Rogerian techniques usually included empathy and warmth which are understood to facilitate the 'therapeutic' relationship (Rogers, 1951). In the study by Mishara and Daigle, the Rogerian style was characterized by active listening with higher use of acceptance, approval, and incomplete thought helper responses, whereas the directive style had higher frequencies of more directive responses, including orientation/investigation, information/suggestion/advice, reflection, information about helper, and rejection (Mishara & Daigle, 1997). Whereas the Rogerian versus directive style relationship held for chronic and non-chronic callers, reduced suicidal urgency was only associated with high levels of Rogerian techniques in the non-chronic callers.

More recently, Mishara *et al.* (2007b) investigated the extent to which helper behaviour and telephone intervention style were related to short-term outcomes. They silently monitored 1,413 crisis calls according to individual ratings as well as the following four factors based on previous research and interviews with suicide prevention centre directors: (1) supportive approach and good contact; (2) active listening; (3) collaborative problem-solving; and (4) negative style. Their analyses revealed that positive call outcomes (i.e., significant improvement from the start to the end of the call) were predicted by (i) helper empathy and respect, (ii) supportive approach and good contact, and (iii) collaborative problem-solving (Mishara *et al.*, 2007b). Collaborative problem-solving includes questions about the problem, alternative solutions, resource issues, suggesting a plan of action, possibly including a no-harm contract. Supportive approach and good contact is characterized by the provision of moral support, offering to telephone back, and reframing and talking about one's own experience.

There are many ethical and practical obstacles to undertaking research into the effectiveness of telephone helplines. Although the research reported here highlights the characteristics of telephone interventions which are associated with better outcome, these good practice 'principles' need to be further disseminated. Call centres should be routinely assessed for quality control purposes. However, more innovative research is required to determine the extent to which such crisis lines impact on subsequent suicide attempt and completed suicide rates over the medium and longer term. This is a challenging task as crisis lines are likely to be part of a complex range of interventions. So it may be more feasible to evaluate them in terms of reach, uptake, acceptability, and perhaps follow-up of a sample. At present, we have evidence that they are effective between two and four weeks following a crisis call. What about the months and years following a telephone intervention? Finally, it is worth exploring further the feasibility of delivering brief telephone psychotherapy. One recent study yielded evidence in a small RCT ($n = 55$) that telephone delivered therapy (Solution Focused Brief Therapy or Common Factors Therapy) improved pre-post therapy outcomes compared with waiting list controls (Rhee, Merbaum, Strube, & Self, 2005).

Section III Selected Psychosocial Interventions

Emergency or crisis cards

One of the major challenges with secondary prevention is that 25%–50% of self-harm patients fail to attend follow-up out-patient appointments (Moller, 1989). As a result, emergency, crisis, or 'green' card interventions have been developed in an attempt to tackle this non-adherence. Crisis cards were originally intended as advocacy devices (Sutherby, Szmukler, Halpern, Alexander, Thornicroft, *et al.*, 1999; Sutherby & Szmukler, 1998), but more recently they have been considered as potentially useful intervention tools. The crisis card usually takes the form of a token which guarantees 24-hour crisis consultation, often including re-admission to hospital (e.g., Cotgrove, Zirinsky, Black, & Weston, 1995). Although two of the earlier studies (Cotgrove *et al.*, 1995; Morgan, Jones, & Owen, 1993) offered promise (yielding non-significant (trends) reductions in repeat self-harm in treatment group versus control group), a more recent, large-scale ($n = 827$) intervention study found no significant effect on the overall self-harm repetition rate at six months (Evans, Morgan, Hayward, & Gunnell, 1999) or 12 months (Evans, Evans, Morgan, Hayward, & Gunnell, 2005) post-intervention. Moreover, there was some evidence that crisis cards were not beneficial for those with a past history of self-harm (Evans *et al.*, 1999, 2005). Consequently, subsequent studies may want to focus their attention on first-time self-harmers. Indeed, Evans *et al.* (2005) recommend that qualitative work is undertaken with first-timer self-harm patients in the refinement of any future crisis card interventions.

Postcard interventions

As noted above, one of the challenges in designing interventions for suicidal populations is that, no matter how effective the ingredients of the intervention, the intervention is unlikely to be beneficial if those for whom the intervention is targeted do not engage with it as intended/required. Therefore, to counter the recognized low rates of compliance in suicidal patients (e.g., Kurz & Moller, 1984; Moller, 1989), a range of strategies has been developed. For example, some clinicians have employed manual-assisted interventions, such that if the patient drops out of treatment, they still potentially have access to the treatment manual (e.g., Tyrer, Thompson, Schmidt, Jones, Knapp, *et al.*, 2003). Another approach which has received attention recently is 'postcard' intervention. Patients are sent postcards enquiring after their well-being at regular intervals following their discharge from hospital (Motto & Bostrom, 2001; Carter, Clover, Whyte, Dawson, & D'Este, 2005, 2007).

This latter, low-cost intervention was originally designed by Motto and Bostrom (2001) for high-risk persons who quickly discontinued out-patient contact (i.e., they refused continuing care). Their study had three hypotheses: (1) that regular contact from someone interested in the recipient's well-being would increase feelings of connectedness and reduce social isolation; (2) that, to be effective, the contact had to be initiated by the concerned individual; and (3) that this systematic approach would have suicide-protective effects. They randomly allocated those patients who had refused ongoing care ($n = 843$) into two groups: patients in the intervention group received a letter at least four times a year for five years (they received a total of 24 contacts over five years), whereas those in the control group received no further contact. All of the participants had been admitted to in-patient facilities because of a 'depressive or suicidal state' (p. 829). The letter was tailored to each recipient but its content was minimal. An example is: 'Dear —— It has been some time since you were here at the hospital, and we hope things are going well for you. If you wish to drop us a note we would be glad to hear from you' (Motto & Bostrom, 2001, p. 829).

The results were encouraging. There was a significant reduction in the rate of suicide in the contact versus the no contact group, and this reduction was significant for the two years following discharge from hospital.

This methodology has been subsequently modified and shown to be somewhat effective in the *Postcards from the Edge* project in Australia (Carter *et al.*, 2005, 2007). General hospital-treated, deliberate self-poisoning patients in the intervention group were sent eight postcards in the 12 months following their index self-poisoning episode (at 1, 2, 3, 4, 6, 8, 10, and 12 months), while the control group received treatment as usual. Groups were compared on two indices of repeat deliberate self-harm at 12 (Carter *et al.*, 2005) and 24 months (Carter *et al.*, 2007) following discharge. Although there was no significant reduction in the proportions of people self-poisoning in the intervention group at either follow-up, there was a significant reduction in the rate of repetition, that is, the total number of repetitions per group. The intervention also yielded a total of 110 bed days saved at 12-month follow-up (Carter *et al.*, 2005).

However, a recent postcard trial from New Zealand yielded a null effect with ED patients and also suggests that postcards may only work in specific sub-groups (Beautrais, Gibb, Faulkner, Fergusson, & Mulder, 2010). The intervention did not reduce the proportion of patients re-presenting with self-harm or the total number of self-harm re-presentations. The intervention in this RCT consisted of the mailing of six postcards during the 12 months following index ED attendance for self-harm (n = 153 in the post-card intervention + treatment as usual condition and n = 174 in the treatment as usual condition). This study highlighted a number of issues which are important to consider when conducting real-world trials. First, are all of the necessary data available (during the trial) to terminate a trial early and what is the knock-on effect on statistical power if an intervention appears to have yielded a significant effect before the *a priori* recruitment target is reached? In the present study, the trial was terminated early as interim data suggested a large and statistically significant reduction in self-harm re-presentations, but this interim analysis did not take account of history of self-harm which was not available until the trial ended.

Second, are the healthcare staff (or those who will be expected to administer the intervention) willing and able to participate in research, including recruitment of participants to the proposed study, as their reluctant attitudes and behaviour may contribute (as it did in this study) to the decision to terminate a trial? Third, is it worth adopting a stratified randomization procedure? As was the case in this study, despite randomization and masking procedures, there were pre-existing differences in prior history of self-harm ED presentations between the intervention and control groups. Beautrais *et al.* (2010) suggest that consideration should be given to stratifying recruitment according to numbers of participants in each trial arm with high versus low prior self-harm presentations.

Taken together, the Beautrais, Carter, and Motto studies suggest that these low-cost interventions may offer promise, but only in some sub-groups of suicidal populations. In addition to the design issues noted above, a number of questions warrant future investigation before we can definitively judge the effectiveness of postcard interventions. First, how generalizable is the postcard intervention? Is it equally effective for men and women as well as for other sub-groups (those who self-cut, patients with psychosis, young people versus older adults)? Indeed, *post hoc* analyses presented in the self-poisoning study suggest that the intervention is effective for women but not for men (Carter *et al.*, 2005). Related to the issue of effectiveness across different demographic groups, the Orygen Youth Health Research Centre in Melbourne, Australia has recently completed a three-year randomized trial of 15–24 year-olds with a history of self-harm (Robinson, Hetrick, Gook, Cosgrave, Pan Yuen, *et al.*, 2009), suicidal ideation, or suicide attempts who were not accepted into the Orygen Youth Health service (a specialist mental health service). Although the main outcome findings from the Orygen study are not yet published, 'participants liked receiving the postcards, they tended to keep them and they found the strategies promoted in them helpful' (Robinson, 2010). We await the publication of the outcome data to inform our understanding of the effectiveness of postcards in a young adult population.

A second question requiring investigation centres on how this intervention reduces repetition (in those populations in which it works): what is the mechanism of effect? Motto and Bostrom (2001) offer one possible explanation. They present some quotations from a sub-sample of their participants who wrote to them expressing their gratitude: 'Just knowing that someone cares means a lot'. Although these letters were supportive of a 'feeling connected' hypothesis (Motto & Bostrom, 2001), more systematic, qualitative analysis is required to improve understanding of the mechanism of effect. Indeed, we are currently investigating whether such postcards reduce feelings of entrapment. Third, do postcard interventions protect against completed suicide following deliberate self-poisoning? Apart from the Motto study, to our knowledge the effect of postcards on completed suicide has not been replicated. Fourth, what is the optimal intensity and duration of such an intervention? The Carter *et al.* (2007) study suggests that the postcard intervention maintained its effect 12 months following receipt of the final postcard, but this finding needs to be replicated.

Social support and social network interventions

The role of social factors is well established in the aetiology of suicidal behaviour, with social isolation being a consistent correlate of suicidality (Haw & Hawton, 2008; Mahadevan, Hawton, & Casey, 2010). Indeed social support acts as a moderator within the suicidal process, increasing risk when it is absent and protecting against suicide when present (e.g., King & Merchant, 2008; O'Connor, 2003; Perkins & Hartless, 2002). It is also central to numerous theories of suicide (Durkheim, 1897; O'Connor, Chapter 11, above; Ribeiro & Joiner, Chapter 10, above). However, social support can take many different forms; in some cases, what is important is the provision of emotional support (e.g., being there to listen during a crisis), yet in other cases instrumental support is imperative, for example, having someone available who can help solve a problem or challenge. It can also serve to provide a sense of identity or belongingness, with the absence of the latter (i.e., thwarted belongingness) being directly implicated in suicide risk (Joiner, 2005).

Consequently, there have been recent attempts (King, Kramer, Preuss, Kerr, Weisse, *et al.*, 2006; King, Klaus, Kramer, Venkataraman, Quinlan, *et al.*, 2009) to determine whether a social support-oriented intervention (the Youth-nominated Support Team, a psychosocial social network intervention) could be useful in managing suicide risk among suicidal adolescents. The aim of the Youth-nominated Support Team – Version 1 (YST-1; King, Kramer, & Preuss, 2000) was to enhance the standard care of adolescents following psychiatric hospitalization by providing psychoeducation for nominees (see below) from different domains of the young person's life and facilitating supportive contact between these nominees and the suicidal adolescent. In short, the YST aims to provide emotional and appraisal support which should help the young person reframe their mental health problems and informally help with problem-solving.

The rationale for the YST-1 intervention was three-fold. First, parental psychiatric morbidity is more common in families of suicidal adolescents (King, Segal, Naylor, & Evans,

1993); second, connectedness or having a sense of belonging with teachers and school can be protective; and, third, fostering supportive relationships with unrelated adults may buffer against negative environmental influences (Grossman & Rhodes, 2002). In addition to testing the utility of the intervention (compared with treatment as usual, TAU) in reducing suicidality and subjective distress, the authors also reasoned that gender may moderate any effect, with girls responding better to the intervention than boys.

In the YST-1 condition (which is TAU + YST-1; King *et al.*, 2006), adolescents were asked to nominate up to four support persons from their school, community, or family (including one peer-support person). Following consent/permission, the support persons completed psychoeducational sessions which lasted approximately 1½–2 hours. The sessions had the following aims:

- to help the person understand the adolescent's psychiatric disorder and treatment plan;
- to help the person understand suicide risk factors;
- to help the person understand effective communication strategies; and
- to ensure the person had emergency contact information.

Following the brief training, the support persons were asked to maintain weekly contact with the suicidal adolescent and to discuss concerns, activities, and the treatment plan (as they arose), and to be generally supportive. The support persons were in frequent contact with intervention specialists. At six-month follow-up, relative to TAU, there were no main effects for YST-1 on suicide ideation or attempts, internalizing symptoms or related functional impairment. However, as predicted, there were modest, gender-specific effects. Girls who received YST-1 reported significant decreases in suicidal ideation and mood-related functional impairment reported by their parents compared with girls who received TAU only. However, there were no statistically significant between-group differences in female suicide attempts at follow-up. A notable limitation of the study was that attrition was higher in the YST-1 versus TAU condition, thereby limiting the generalizability of these findings.

Given the promising findings from YST-1, King and colleagues modified the YST (YST-II) and recently published the outcome of a large-scale randomized controlled intervention trial (King *et al.*, 2009). They made two major changes to the protocol. First, the pool of support persons could only be drawn from (parent-approved) adults; the option of nominating a peer-support person was removed. Second, to improve protocol feasibility, they reduced the regular support contact time from six months to three months. In addition to considering gender as a moderator, suicide attempt history was also considered as a moderator in the YST-II trial.

Consistent with the YST-1 study, the findings from YST-II were modest and did not yield a consistent picture across outcome measures to recommend clinical application, at least in its current form (King *et al.*, 2009). The YST reduced suicidal ideation in the short term (at six-week follow-up) following hospitalization in those with multiple suicide attempt history. It also had some success in reducing adaptive impairment in adolescents without multiple suicide attempt history. The effects were small (which is not surprising as YST is a supplementary intervention) and, in contrast to the findings from YST-1

(King *et al.*, 2006), they were not moderated by gender. Moreover, the positive events were not robust across the other measures of psychological distress (including hopelessness and depression). The lack of robustness may reflect the complexity of an adolescent population, where further consideration of developmental stage is required. Although the findings for this social network intervention are somewhat disappointing, there is some evidence of potential beneficial effects which could be isolated, tailored and incorporated into other multi-faceted treatments/interventions (King *et al.*, 2009). In addition, harnessing other types of social support should be investigated as well as the feasibility of such interventions across different age and ethnic groups.

Multi-level approaches to suicide prevention

Multi-level approaches are included here as they usually contain a substantial psychosocial component. In recent years there has been a growth in multi-level approaches to the prevention of depression and suicide (Hegerl, Wittmann, Arensman, Van Audenhove, Bouleau, *et al.*, 2008; MacKenzie, Blamey, Halliday, Maxwell, McCollam, *et al.*, 2007). Such approaches tend to combine public health/awareness campaigns with better identification and treatment of those at risk of suicide, as well as reducing stigma and supporting recovery. The advantage of multi-level approaches, in contrast to the single-intervention approaches discussed elsewhere in this chapter, is that synergistic relationships may yield more powerful and detectable suicide prevention effects (Althaus & Hegerl, 2003). The Nuremberg Alliance Against Depression (NAAD)/European Alliance Against Depression (EAAD) and the ongoing Optimizing Suicide Prevention Programmes and their Implementation in Europe (OSPI-Europe) are noteworthy exemplars of community-based multi-level or multi-faceted suicide prevention programmes.

The NAAD, which forms the basis for EAAD and OSPI, was conducted in the German city of Nuremberg. Its effects were evaluated with respect to a one-year baseline and in comparison with a control region, Wuerzburg. The NAAD intervention comprised four levels of intervention (Hegerl *et al.*, 2006) and these were also employed in EAAD:

Level 1   cooperation with general practitioners (e.g., advanced training);
Level 2   public relations campaigns aimed at the general public (poster campaigns, leaflets, and public events);
Level 3   cooperation of community facilitators (e.g., priests, teachers, police); and
Level 4   high-risk groups and self-help.

Level 1 involved providing interactive workshops and training materials for GPs to improve the diagnosis and treatment of depression and a video to give to patients to help them/their family understand their disorder/treatment. A range of public relations campaigns, including large public billboards, brochures, and cinema spots, were developed to raise the profile of depression as part of Level 2. The aim of Level 3 was to target those people in the community to whom depressed or suicidal individuals may turn in times of distress or who may be instrumental in their decision to access care. The community facilitators (who included teachers, counsellors, priests, nurses, police, pharmacists, etc.) received specially prepared educational packages about how to recognize the signs of depression and the different treatment pathways.

Working with the media to improve their reporting practices, thereby reducing potential imitative suicides, was also a feature of Level 3. Finally, as part of Level 4, suicide attempters were offered an emergency card (consistent with Morgan *et al.*, 1993) guaranteeing direct access to a specialist in the event of a further crisis.

The findings from the evaluation were encouraging. Compared with the control region, there was a significant decrease in the frequency of suicidal acts (i.e., completed suicides and suicide attempts) and suicide attempts (secondary outcome criterion) in Nuremberg during the two-year intervention. This decrease was in the order of a 24% reduction in suicidal acts compared with baseline in Nuremberg (although this reduction is largely accounted for by suicidal attempts; there was no significant differences in completed suicide rates between the two regions). As the intervention and control populations are relatively small (480,000 and 270,000 inhabitants, respectively), and completed suicide has a relatively low base rate, the study was probably insufficiently powered to detect a significant change in completed suicide.

In the light of the positive results in Nuremberg, the European Alliance Against Depression (EAAD; http://www.eaad.net), including 18 international partners from 16 different countries, was established in 2004 (Hegerl *et al.*, 2008). EAAD also employs the four-level approach, but as yet there is no evidence to show that this is successful in different countries across Europe. Nonetheless, a number of lessons have been learned thus far, as highlighted by Hegerl, Wittenburg, Arensman, Audenhove, Coyne, *et al.* (2009). First, the multi-level approach appears to be readily implementable across different European countries. Second, development of the intervention should be bottom-up, starting at the local level, thereby fostering local alliances. Third, although the public health campaign focuses on depression, it is likely to have broader destigmatizing effects (generalizing to other mental health problems).

Based on EAAD, the European Commission has funded another multi-level suicide prevention project, Optimizing Suicide Prevention Programmes and their Implementation in Europe (OSPI-Europe). This four-year programme, scheduled to run until 2012, aims to provide European member states with 'an evidence based, efficient concept for suicide prevention along with the corresponding materials and instruments for the multi-faceted intervention and guidelines for the implementation process' (Hegerl, Wittenburg, Arensman, *et al.*, 2009). Distinct from EAAD, the OSPI intervention will be supplemented with other evidence-based interventions and implemented in intervention and control regions in four European countries (Germany, Hungary, Ireland, and Portugal). We await the outcome of this international collaboration.

General Observations about the Development and Evaluation of Interventions

Irrespective of type, more careful consideration should be given to the development and evaluation of all interventions (psychosocial, psychological, and pharmacological) to reduce suicidal behaviour. Too often we rush to pilot interventions which have little or no grounding in evidence, *and* the lessons learned are frequently missed as systematic and comprehensive evaluations are not yet standard components of suicide prevention interventions.

We believe that a better understanding of the *mechanisms* underpinning an intervention will lead to more positive outcomes. By better understanding we mean an explicit articulation not only that one expects an intervention to work but *how* or *why* it should work. What are the mechanisms by which the intervention will lead to a reduction in suicidal behaviour? There are no shortcuts to answering this question; detailed pilot/development work, which is iterative in nature, is required, together with a critical appraisal of the existing research evidence as well as an appreciation of previous experience and practice.

By way of illustration, there are several issues to consider when designing a public health intervention to increase help-seeking behaviour among young men. Obviously the measurement of help-seeking behaviour would be considered (including the accuracy of the method of measurement, and generic issues around reliability and validity). However, detailed consideration should also be given to understanding how the intervention may work (i.e., how it exerts its influence) and its acceptability to young people. For example, the intervention may be designed to target and change attitudes towards help-seeking behaviour; it is the change in attitudes which is hypothesized to impact on help-seeking behaviour (as there is an established literature on the attitude–behaviour relations and the specific beliefs/attitudes would be determined at the development phase of the intervention). Consequently, if attitudes are not measured as part of the trial, and the trial is not effective, our understanding of why the intervention did not work would be limited. Moreover, if the intervention has been effective, and attitude change has occurred and is shown to account for the change in help-seeking behaviour, we can be confident that it contributed to the intervention's effectiveness. In short, the successful delivery of complex interventions is an iterative process which requires substantial resources directed at development and piloting.

An insufficient focus on the early phase of piloting and development is not specific to suicidology itself; rather, it is a charge often levelled at complex interventions used across the health service, public health practice and social policy. As a consequence, in 2000 the Medical Research Council (UK) published a framework to aid researchers in the development and evaluation of complex interventions (Campbell, Fitzpatrick, Haines, Kinmonth, Sandercock, *et al.*, 2000). This guidance was updated in 2008 (Craig, Dieppe, Macintyre, Michie, Nazareth, *et al.*, 2008; www.mrc.ac.uk/complexinterventionsguidance). In addition to a call for greater attention directed at development, it emphasized a less linear model of evaluation, the integration of process and outcome evaluation and the recognition that interventions would likely benefit from being tailored to the local context.

Conclusions

In this chapter, we describe 'good practice' principles in the recognition and assessment of suicide risk in prisons and emergency departments. These principles underline the complexity of the suicidal process and emphasize that risk assessment protocols must be multifaceted, taking account of the individual, their circumstances, and their environment. There has also been some movement towards determining whether crisis helplines prevent suicide and, if so, how they may do so. However, much more research is required to evaluate their effectiveness systematically, and new, innovative study designs are required. It is also clear from the studies included herein that we are some way off recommending any of the low-intensity psychosocial interventions to reduce the repetition of self-harm or completed suicide. The evidence for their effectiveness is mixed and, furthermore, there are too many unanswered questions about *when*, *where*, and *how* they may exert their influence. There is some promising evidence for the effectiveness of multi-level approaches to suicide prevention (in Germany), but it is not yet clear what the active ingredients are or whether such approaches are effective internationally. Finally, suicidologists should devote more time and effort to the early phases of intervention development, taking care to understand the potential mechanisms of effect and considering the wider healthcare context before rushing to undertake a definitive explanatory trial.

References

Academic ED SBIRT Research Collaborative (2007). An evidence-based alcohol screening, brief intervention and referral to treatment (SBIRT) curriculum for emergency department (ED) providers improves skills and utilization. *Substance Abuse, 28*, 79–92.

Althaus, D. & Hegerl, U. (2003). The evaluation of suicide prevention activities: State of the art. *World Journal of Biological Psychiatry, 4*, 156–165.

American Academy of Child and Adolescent Psychiatry (2001). Practice parameter for the assessment and treatment of children and adolescents with suicidal behavior. *Journal of American Academy of Child and Adolescent Psychiatry, 40*, 24S–51S.

Asarnow, J. R., Baraff, L. J., Berk, M., Grob, C., Devich-Navarro, M., Suddath, R., Piacentini, J., & Tang, L., *et al.* (2008). Pediatric emergency department suicidal patients: Two-site evaluation of suicide ideators, single attempters, and repeat attempters. *Journal of American Academy of Child & Adolescent Psychiatry, 47*, 958–966.

Babor, T., McRee, B., Kassebaum, P., Grimaldi, P., Ahmed, K., & Bray, J. (2007). Screening, brief intervention and referral to treatment (SBIRT): Toward a public health approach to the management of substance abuse. *Substance Abuse, 28*, 7–30.

Beautrais, A. L. (2004). Further suicidal behavior among medically serious suicide attempters. *Suicide and Life Threatening Behavior, 34*, 1–11.

Beautrais, A. L., Gibb, S. J., Faulkner, A., Fergusson, D., & Mulder, R. T. (2010). Postcard intervention for repeat self-harm: randomized controlled trial. *British Journal of Psychiatry, 197*, 55–60.

Britto, M. T., Klostermann, B. K., Bonny, A. E., Altum, S. A., & Hornung, R. W. (2001). Impact of a school-based intervention on access to healthcare for underserved youth. *Journal of Adolescent Health, 29*, 116–124.

Brown, G. K. (2009). A review of suicide assessment measures for intervention research with adults and older adults, available at http://www.nih.gov/suicideresearch/adultsuicide.pdf, accessed 19 March 2010.

Campbell, M., Fitzpatrick, R., Haines, A., Kinmonth, A.L., Sandercock, P., Spiegelhalter, D., *et al.* (2000). Framework for the design and evaluation of complex interventions to improve health. *British Medical Journal, 321*, 694–696.

Carter, G. L., Clover, K., Whyte, I. M., Dawson, A. H., & D'Este, C. (2005). Postcards from the EDge: Randomised controlled trial of an intervention using postcards to reduce repetition of hospital treated deliberate self-poisoning. *British Medical Journal, 331*, 805–807.

Carter, G. L., Clover, K., Whyte, I. M., Dawson, A. H., & D'Este, C. (2007). Postcards from the EDge: 24-month outcomes of a randomised controlled trial for hospital-treated self-poisoning? *British Journal of Psychiatry, 191*, 548–553.

Classen, C. A. & Larkin, G. L. (2005). Occult suicidality in an emergency department population. *British Journal of Psychiatry, 186,* 352–353.

Cooper, J., Husain, N., Webb, R., Waheed, W., Kapur, N., Guthrie, E., & Appleby, L. (2006). Self-harm in the UK: Differences between South Asians and Whites in rates, characteristics, provision of services and repetition. *Social Psychiatry and Psychiatric Epidemiology, 41,* 782–788.

Cooper, J., Kapur, N., Dunning, J., Guthrie, E., Appleby, L., & Mackway-Jones, K. (2006). A clinical tool for assessing risk after self-harm. *Annals of Emergency Medicine, 48,* 459–466.

Copelan, R. I., Messer, M. A., & Ashley, D. J. (2006). Adolescent violence screening in the ED. *American Journal of Emergency Medicine, 24,* 582–594.

Cotgrove, A., Zirinsky, L., Black, D., & Weston, D. (1995). Secondary prevention of attempted suicide in adolescence. *Journal of Adolescence, 18,* 569–577.

Craig, P., Dieppe, P., Macintyre, S., Michie, S., Nazareth, I., & Petticrew, M. (2008). Developing and evaluating complex interventions: The new Medical Research Council guidance. *British Medical Journal, 337,* 979–983.

Crandall, C., Fullerton-Gleason, L., Aguero, R., & LaValley, J. (2006). Subsequent suicide mortality among emergency department patients seen for suicidal behavior. *Academy of Emergency Medicine, 13,* 435–442.

Cuijpers, P. & Schoevers, R. A. (2004). Increased mortality in depressive disorders: A review. *Current Psychiatry Reports, 6,* 430–437.

Daigle, M. S, Daniel, A. E., Dear, G. E., Frottier, P., Hayes, L. M., Kerhof, A., Konrad, N., Liebling, A., & Sarchiapone, M. (2007). Preventing suicide in prisons, part II: International comparisons of suicide prevention services in correctional facilities. *Crisis, 28,* 122–130.

Daigle, M. S., Labelle, R., & Cote, G. (2006). Further evidence of the validity of the Suicide Risk Assessment Scale for prisoners. *International Journal of Law & Psychiatry, 29,* 343–354.

Day, G. (1974). The Samaritan movement in Great Britain. *Perspectives in Biology and Medicine, 17,* 507–512.

Dew, A. J. M., Bromet, E. J., Brent, D., & Greenhouse, J. B. (1987). A quantitative literature review of the effectiveness of suicide prevention centers. *Journal of Consulting and Clinical Psychology, 55,* 239–244.

Durkheim, E. (1897). *Le suicide.* Paris: Alcan.

Evans, J., Evans, M., Morgan, H.G., Hayward, A., & Gunnell, D. (2005). Crisis card following self-harm: 12-month follow-up of a randomised controlled trial. *British Journal of Psychiatry, 187,* 186–187.

Evans, M. O., Morgan, H. G., Hayward, A., & Gunnell, D. (1999). Crisis telephone consultation for deliberate self-harm patients: effects on repetition. *British Journal of Psychiatry, 175,* 23–27.

Fakhoury, W. (2000). Suicide: A call sheet audit: Data from Saneline. *Psychiatric Bulletin, 24,* 98–101.

Fazel, S., Grann, M., Kling, B., & Hawton, K. (in press). Prison suicide in 12 countries: An ecological study of 861 suicides during 2003–2007. *Social Psychiatry & Psychiatric Epidemiology.*

Folse, V. N., Eich, K. N., Hall, A. M., & Ruppman, J. B. (2006). Detecting suicide risk in adolescents and adults in an emergency department: A pilot study. *Journal of Psychosocial Nursing and Mental Health Services, 44,* 22–29.

Fruehwald, S., Matschnig, T., Koenig, F., & Bauer, P. (2004). Suicide in custody: Case-control study. *British Journal of Psychiatry, 185,* 494–498.

Gairin, I., House, A., & Owens, D. (2003). Attendance at the accident and emergency department in the year before suicide: Retrospective study. *British Journal of Psychiatry, 183,* 28–33.

Gibb, S. J., Beautrais, A. L., & Fergusson, D. M. (2005). Mortality and further suicidal behaviour after an index suicide attempt: A 10-year study. *Australian and New Zealand Journal of Psychiatry, 39,* 95–100.

Gould, M. S., Kalafat, J., Harris Munfakh, J. L., & Kleinman, M. (2007). An evaluation of crisis hotline outcomes part 2: Suicidal callers. *Suicide and Life-Threatening Behavior, 37*, 338–351.

Grossman, J. B. & Rhodes, J. E. (2002). The test of time: Predictors and effects of duration in youth mentoring relationships. *American Journal of Community Psychology, 30*, 199–219.

Hamann, C., Larkin, G., Brown, B., Schwann, C., & George, V. (2007). Differences in computer prompted self-report and physician-elicited responses in screening of emergency department patients for substance use and abuse. *Annals of Emergency Medicine, 50*, S43.

Haw, C. & Hawton, K. (2008). Life problems and deliberate self-harm: Associations with gender, age, suicidal intent and psychiatric and personality disorder. *Journal of Affective Disorders, 109*, 139–148.

Hayes, L. M. (1995) *Prison Suicide: An overview and guide to prevention*. Washington, DC: US Department of Justice, National Institute of Corrections.

Healy, D. J., Barry, K., Blow, F., Welsh, D., & Milner, K. K. (2006). Routine use of the Beck Scale for Suicide Ideation in a psychiatric emergency department. *General Hospital Psychiatry, 28*, 323–329.

Hegerl, U., Althaus, D., Schmidtke, A., & Niklewski, G. (2006). The alliance against depression: 2-year evaluation of a community-based intervention to reduce suicidality. *Psychological Medicine, 36*, 1225–1233.

Hegerl, U., Wittenburg, L., and the European Alliance Against Depression Consortium. (2009). The European Alliance Against Depression: A multilevel approach to the prevention of suicidal behavior. *Psychiatric Services, 60*, 596–599.

Hegerl, U., Wittmann, M., Arensman, E., Van Audenhove, C., Bouleau, J.-H., *et al.* (2008). The 'European Alliance Against Depression (EAAD)': A multifaceted, community-based action-programme against depression and suicidality. *World Journal of Biological Psychiatry*, 51–58.

Hegerl, U., Wittenburg, L., Arensman, E., van Audenhove, C., Coyne, J. C., McDaid, D., *et al.* (2009). Optimising suicide prevention programs and their implementation in Europe (OSPI Europe): An evidence-based multi-level approach. *BMC Public Health, 9*, 428.

Horowitz, L. M., Wang, P. S., Koocher, G. P., Burr, B. H., Smith, M. F., Klavon, S., & Cleary, P. D. (2001). Detecting suicide risk in a pediatric emergency department: Development of a brief screening tool. *Pediatrics, 107*, 1133–1137.

Institute of Medicine (2002). *Reducing Suicide: A national imperative*. Washington, DC.

Jacobs, D. G. (1999). *Guide to Suicide Assessment and Intervention*. San Francisco, CA: HC Printing.

Jenkins, R., Bhugra, D., Meltzer, H., Singleton, N., Bebbington, P., Brugha, T., Coid, J., Farrell, M., Lewis, G., & Paton, J. (2005). Psychiatric and social aspects of suicidal behaviour in prisons. *Psychological Medicine, 35*, 257–269.

Joiner, T. (2005). *Why People Die by Suicide*. Cambridge, MA: Harvard University Press.

Kalafat, J., Gould, M. S., Harris Mufakh, J. L., & Kleinman, M. (2007). An evaluation of crisis hotline outcomes Part 1: Nonsuicidal crisis callers. *Suicide and Life-Threatening Behavior, 37*, 322–337.

Kerkhof, A. J. F. M. & Bernasco, W. (1990). Suicidal behavior in jails and prisons in the Netherlands: Incidence, characteristics, and prevention. *Suicide and Life-Threatening Behavior, 20*, 123–137.

King, C. A., Klaus, N., Kramer, A., Venkataraman, S., Quinlan, P., & Gillespie, B. (2009). The Youth-Nominated Support Team – Version II for suicidal adolescents: A randomized controlled intervention trial. *Journal of Consulting and Clinical Psychology, 77*, 880–893.

King, C. A., Kramer, A., & Preuss, L. (2000). *Youth-nominated Support Team Intervention Manual*. Ann Arbor, MI: University of Michigan, Department of Psychiatry.

King, C. A., Kramer, A., Preuss, L., Kerr, D. C. R., Weisse, L., & Venkataraman, S. (2006). Youth-nominated support team for suicidal adolescents (Version 1): A randomized controlled trial. *Journal of Consulting and Clinical Psychology, 74*, 199–206.

King, C. A. & Merchant, C. R. (2008). Social and interpersonal factors relating to adolescent suicidality: A review of the literature. *Archives of Suicide Research, 12*, 181–196.

King, C. A., Segal, H. G., Naylor, M., & Evans, T. (1993). Family functioning and suicidal behavior in adolescent in-patients with mood disorders. *Journal of American Academy of Child & Adolescent Psychiatry, 32*, 1198–1206.

King, R., Nurcombe, B., Bickman, L., Hides, L., & Reid, W. (2003). Telephone counselling for adolescent suicide prevention: Changes in suicidality and mental state from beginning to end of a counselling session. *Suicide and Life-Threatening Behavior, 33*, 400–411.

Konrad, N., Daigle, M. S., Daniel, A. E., Dear, G. E., Frottier, P., Hayes, L. M., *et al.* (2007). Preventing suicide in prisons, Part I. Recommendations from the International Association for Suicide Prevention Task Force on Suicide in Prisons. *Crisis, 28*, 113–131.

Kurz, A. & Moller, H. J. (1984). Help-seeking behavior and compliance of suicidal patients. *Psychiatrische Praxis, 11*, 6–13.

Larkin, G. L., Beautrais, A. L., Gibb, S., & Laing, N. (2008). The epidemiology of presentations for suicidal ideation to the emergency department. *Academic Emergency Medicine, 15*(5) (Suppl. 1), S208–S209.

Larkin, G. & Claassen, C. (2007). Trends in emergency department use of gastric lavage for poisoning events in the United States, 1993–2003. *Clinical Toxicology, 45*, 164–168.

Larkin, G. L., Smith, R. P., & Beautrais, A. L. (2008). Trends in US Emergency department visits for suicide attempts, 1992–2001. *Crisis, 29*, 73–80.

Larzelere, R. E., Andersen, J. J., Ringle, J. L., & Jorgensen, D. D. (2004). The child suicide risk assessment: A screening measure of suicide risk in pre-adolescents. *Death Studies, 28*, 809–827.

Lester, D. (1997). The effectiveness of suicide prevention centers: A review. *Suicide and Life-threatening Behavior, 27*, 304–310.

Litman, R. E., Farberow, N. L., Shneidman, E. S., Heilig, S. M., & Kramer, J. A. (1965). Suicide prevention telephone service. *Journal of the American Medical Association, 192*, 107–111.

Lowenstein, S. R., Koziol-McLain, J., Thompson, M., Bernstein, E., Greenberg, K., Gerson, L. W., Buczynsky, P., & Blanda, M. (1998). Behavioral risk factors in emergency department patients: A multisite survey. *Academic Emergency Medicine, 5*, 781–787.

Mackenzie, M., Blamey, A., Halliday, E., Maxwell, M., McCollam, A., McDaid, D., MacLean, J., Woodhouse, A., & Platt, S. (2007). Measuring the tail of the dog that doesn't bark in the night: The case of the national evaluation of Choose Life (the national strategy and action plan to prevent suicide in Scotland). *BMC Public Health, 7*, 146.

Mahadevan, S., Hawton, K., & Casey, D. (2010). Deliberate self-harm in Oxford University students, 1993–2005: A descriptive and case control study. *Social Psychiatry and Psychiatric Epidemiology, 45*, 211–219.

Marzano, L., Fazel, S., Rivlin, A., & Hawton, K. (2010). Psychiatric disorders in women prisoners who have engaged in near-lethal self-harm: Case-control study. *British Journal of Psychiatry, 197*, 219–226.

Meneese, W. B. & Yutrzenka, B. A. (1990). Correlates of suicidal ideation among rural adolescents. *Suicide and Life Threatening Behavior, 20*, 206–212.

Miller, H. L., Coombs, D. W., Leeper, J. D., & Barton, S. N. (1984). An analysis of the effects of suicide prevention facilities on suicide rates in the United States. *American Journal of Public Health, 74*, 340–343.

Miller, T. & Taylor, D. (2005). Adolescent suicidality: Who will ideate, who will act? *Suicide and Life-Threatening Behavior, 35*, 425–435.

Ministry of Health and New Zealand Guidelines Group (2003). *Best Practice Evidence-based Guideline. The assessment and management of people at risk of suicide for Emergency Departments and Mental Health Service Acute Assessment Settings*. Wellington.

Mishara, B. L., Chagnon, F., Daigle, M., Balan, B., Raymond, S., Marcoux, I., Bardon, C., Campbell, J. K., & Berman, A. (2007a). Comparing models of helper behavior to actual practice in telephone crisis intervention: A Silent Monitoring Study of Calls to the US 1-800-SUICIDE Network. *Suicide and Life-Threatening Behavior*, *37*, 291–307.

Mishara, B. L., Chagnon, F., Daigle, M., Balan, B., Raymond, S., Marcoux, I., Bardon, C., Campbell, J. K., & Berman, A. (2007b). Which helper behaviors and intervention styles are related to better short-term outcomes in telephone crisis intervention? Results from a Silent Monitoring Study of Calls to the US 1-800-SUICIDE Network. *Suicide and Life-Threatening Behavior*, *37*, 308–321.

Mishara, B. & Daigle, M. (1997). Effects of different telephone intervention styles with suicidal callers at two suicide prevention centers: An empirical investigation. *American Journal of Community Psychology*, *25*, 861–885.

Mishara, B. L. & Daigle, M. (2000). In D. Lester (Ed.), *Helplines and Crisis Intervention Services: Challenges for the future* (pp. 153–171). Philadelphia, PA: Brunner Routledge.

Moller, H. J. (1989). Efficacy of different strategies of after-care for patients who have attempted suicide. *Journal of the Royal Society of Medicine*, *82*, 643–647.

Morgan, H. G., Jones, E. M., & Owen, J. H. (1993). Secondary prevention of non-fatal deliberate self-harm. The Green Card Study. *British Journal of Psychiatry*, *163*, 111–112.

Monti, K., Cedereke, M., & Öjehagen, A. (2003). Treatment attendance and suicidal behavior 1 month and 3 months after a suicide attempt: A comparison between two samples. *Archives of Suicide Research*, *7*, 1543–6136.

Motto, J. A. & Bostrom, A. G. (2001). A randomized controlled trial of postcrisis suicide prevention. *Psychiatric Services*, *52*, 828–833.

Nawar, E. W., Niska, R. W., *et al.* (2007). National Hospital Ambulatory Medical Care Survey: 2005 emergency department summary. *Advance Data*, *386*, 1–32.

New South Wales Department of Health (2005). *Framework for Suicide Risk Assessment and Management for New South Wales Health Staff*, North Sydney.

O'Connor, R. C. (2003). Suicidal behaviour as a cry of pain: Test of a psychological model. *Archives of Suicide Research*, *7*, 297–308.

Olfson, M., Weissman, M. M., Leon, A. C., Sheehan, D. V., & Farber, L. (1996) Suicidal ideation in primary care. *Journal of General Internal Medicine*, *11*, 447–453.

Owens, D., Horrocks, J., & House, A. (2002). Fatal and non-fatal repetition of self-harm: Systematic review. *British Journal of Psychiatry*, *181*, 193–199.

Patel, A. S., Harrison, A., & Bruce-Jones, W. (2009). Evaluation of the risk assessment matrix: A mental health triage tool. *Emergency Medicine Journal*, *26*, 11–14.

Paykel, E. S., Myers, J. K., Lindenthal. J. J., & Tanner, L.(1974). Suicidal feelings in the general populations: a prevalence study. *British Journal of Psychiatry*, *124*, 460–469.

Perkins, D. F. & Hartless, G. (2002). An ecological risk-factor examination of suicide ideation and behavior of adolescents. *Journal of Adolescent Research*, *17*, 3–26.

Posner, K., Oquendo, M. A., Gould, M., Stanley, B., & Davies, M. (2007). Columbia Classification Algorithm of Suicide Assessment (C-CASA): Classification of suicidal events in the FDA's pediatric suicidal risk analysis of antidepressants. *American Journal of Psychiatry*, *164*, 1035–1043.

Rhee, W. K., Merbaum, M., Strube, M. J., & Self, S. M. (2005). Efficacy of brief telephone psychotherapy with callers to a suicide hotline. *Suicide and Life-Threatening Behavior*, *35*, 317–328.

Rhodes, K. V., Lauderdale, D. S., He, T., Howes, D. S., & Levinson, W. (2001). Better health while you wait: A controlled trial of a computer-based intervention for screening and health promotion in the emergency department. *Annals of Emergency Medicine*, *37*, 284–291.

Riehl, T., Marchner, E., & Moller, H. J. (1988). Influence of crisis intervention telephone services ('Crisis Hotlines') on the suicide rate in 25 German cities. In H. J. Moller, A. Schmidtke, & R. Welz (Eds.), *Current Issues in Suicidology* (pp. 431–436). Berlin: Springer-Verlag.

Robinson, J. (2010). Personal communication to Rory O'Connor, 13 April 2010.

Robinson, J., Hetrick, S., Gook, S., Cosgrave, E., Pan Yuen, H., McGorry, P., & Yung, A. (2009). Study protocol: The development of a randomised controlled trial testing a postcard intervention designed to reduce suicide risk among young help-seekers. *BMC Psychiatry*, *9*, 59.

Rogers, C. R. (1951). *Client-centred Therapy*. Boston, MA: Houghton Mifflin.

Rudd, M. D. (2006). Suicidality in clinical practice. *Journal of Clinical Psychology*, *62*, 157–160.

Samaritans (2009). *Information Resource Pack 2009*. Surrey: Samaritans.

Shea, S. (2002). *The Practical Art of Suicide Assessment: A guide for mental health professionals and substance abuse counselors*. New York: John Wiley & Sons, Inc.

Skoog, I., Aevarsson, O., Beskow, J., Larsson, L., Palsson, S., Waern, M., Landahl, S., & Ostling, S. (1996). Suicidal feelings in a population sample of nondemented 85-year-olds. *American Journal of Psychiatry*, *153*, 1015–1020.

Shedler, J. (Ed.) (2000). The Shedler Quick Diagnostics Panel (QPD Panel): A psychiatric 'lab test' for primary care. *Handbook of Psychological Assessment in Primary Care Settings*. Mahwah, NJ: Lawrence Erlbaum.

Shedler, J., Beck, A., & Bensen, S. (2000). Practical mental health assessment in primary care: Validity and utility of the Quick Diagnostics Panel. *The Journal of Family Practice*, *49*, 614–621.

Shneidman, E. S. & Farberow, N. L. (1957). *Clues to Suicide*. New York: Blakison.

Skoog, I., Aevarsson, O., *et al.* (1996). Suicidal feelings in a population sample of nondemented 85-year-olds. *American Journal of Psychiatry*, *153*, 1015–1020.

Sutherby, K. & Szmukler, G. (1998). Crisis cards and self-help crisis initiatives. *Psychiatric Bulletin*, *22*, 4–7.

Sutherby, K., Szmukler, G., Halpern, A., Alexander, M., Thornicroft, G., Johnson, C., & Wright, S. (1999). A study of 'crisis cards' in community psychiatric service. *Acta Psychiatrica Scandinavica*, *100*, 56–61.

Tishler, C. L., Reiss, N. S., & Rhodes, A. R. (2007). Suicidal behavior in children younger than twelve: A diagnostic challenge for emergency department personnel. *Academy of Emergency Medicine*, *14*, 810–818.

Tyrer, P., Thompson, S., Schmidt, U., Jones, V., Knapp, M., Davidson, K., *et al.* (2003). Randomized controlled trial of brief cognitive behaviour therapy versus treatment as usual in recurrent deliberate self-harm: the POPMACT study. *Psychological Medicine*, *33*, 969–976.

Wintersteen, M. B., Diamond, G. S., & Fein, J. A. (2007). Screening for suicide risk in the pediatric emergency and acute care setting. *Current Opinions in Pediatrics*, *19*, 398–404.

Zahl, D. L. & Hawton, K. (2004). Repetition of deliberate self-harm and subsequent suicide risk: long-term follow-up study of 11,583 patients. *British Journal of Psychiatry*, *185*, 70–75.

CHAPTER TWENTY-SIX

Antidepressants and Suicide Prevention

Robert D. Goldney

Abstract

In the last two decades there has been concern that antidepressant medications, particularly the newer selective serotonin re-uptake inhibitors (SSRIs), could precipitate suicide in vulnerable persons. Formidable methodological constraints imposed by the low base rate of suicide limit the feasibility of conventional randomized controlled trials (RCTs) to test this possibility. Early reassuring meta-analyses of RCTs have given way to a general consensus that young persons do have an increased risk of suicidality with SSRIs. However, there is increasing protection from suicidality with increasing age. Pharmaco-epidemiological studies have provided an added perspective, and the paucity of completed suicide associated with SSRIs among young people in whole of population data, or in series of consecutive suicides, is not consistent with a risk of suicide *per se*. Nevertheless, clinicians must be aware of the potential for the emergence of suicidality, whatever the explanation may be. Furthermore, on the basis of aggregate data, which it must be emphasized may not necessarily apply to an individual patient, it is now possible to calculate the risks of treatment. These need to be balanced not only against the potential benefits of carefully administered antidepressants, but also the risk of inadequate treatment of a condition with considerable morbidity and suicide risk in its own right.

International Handbook of Suicide Prevention: Research, Policy and Practice, First Edition.
Edited by Rory C. O'Connor, Stephen Platt, Jacki Gordon.
© 2011 John Wiley & Sons, Ltd. Published 2011 by John Wiley & Sons, Ltd.

Introduction

It has long been recognized that suicide is associated with depression. The logical corollary is that antidepressant measures will reduce the likelihood of suicide. However, in the last two decades there has been intense professional and media concern about the possibility that antidepressant medications, particularly the selective serotonin re-uptake inhibitors (SSRIs), could have the unwanted effect of precipitating suicide. This chapter addresses a number of aspects associated with this important public health issue.

Historical Perspective

In 1828 in England, Burrows wrote that suicide was 'a feature of melancholia' (Burrows, 1828, p. 413), while in 1877 in the United States, Eastman, the Secretary of the New England Psychological Society, noted in relation to a discussion on melancholia that, among members, there was 'a nearly unanimous feeling that the suicidal impulse was inherent in this form of illness and should be assumed in every case' (Eastman, 1877, p. 99). Furthermore, in England in 1892, Savage stated that 'all melancholic patients must be considered suicidal till they are fully known' (Savage, 1892, p. 1232); that even 'simple melancholia of very slight depth is a very common cause of suicide' (p. 1231); and that 'waves of depression occur in many neurotic but otherwise sane people, which often lead to suicide' (p. 1232).

Systematic research in the twentieth century confirmed these early clinical observations. Psychological autopsy studies indicated that approximately two-thirds of those who died by suicide had significant depressive conditions at the time of their death (Lönqvist, 2000), and Harris and Barraclough (1997) used meta-analysis to demonstrate that patients with dysthymia and major depression had 12 to 20 times, respectively, the standardized mortality ratio due to suicide of those without those mood disorders.

Notwithstanding this strong association, it has also long been recognized that caution is needed in the treatment of depression lest initial improvement should give the depressed individual the necessary impetus to end their life. Indeed, Savage (1892) noted that 'with the entry on convalescence suicidal attempts are common' (p. 1231), and in the mid-twentieth century, just before the advent of antidepressant medication, Mayer-Gross, Slater, and Roth (1955) wrote that 'with beginning convalescence, spontaneously or after convulsion treatment, the risk of suicide once more becomes serious as retardation fades' (p. 212).

Despite those cautionary clinical observations, it is probably fair to say that there was a generally uncritical acceptance that the treatment of depression, by whatever means, would be beneficial and result in an alleviation of suicide risk. However, in the last 20 years, as noted above, there has been additional professional and community concern about the possibility that SSRI medications could precipitate suicidal behaviours, particularly in young people. This arose from the initial clinical report of Teicher, Glod, and Cole (1990) of the emergence of suicidal behaviour in association with the antidepressant Fluoxetine.

Subsequently other reports (Healy, Langmaak, & Savage, 1999; Khan, Warner, & Brown, 2000; Healy & Whitaker, 2003) led authorities such as the UK Medicines and Healthcare products Regulatory Agency (MHRA) and the American Food and Drug Administration (FDA) to issue warnings about the use of SSRI antidepressants because of the risk of increasing the likelihood of suicide.

Since these initial concerns were raised there has been a plethora of research addressing this issue, often with sensational media accompaniment. It has also been the subject of vigorous academic debate (Healy, 2009a, 2009b; Brent, 2009a, 2009b), and as Barbui, Cipriani, and Geddes (2008) have noted perceptively, at times the same data 'have been interpreted as reinforcing and consolidating two opposing positions' (p. 34).

Sources of Information

There are specific constraints in establishing whether any interventions will reduce or promote suicide. Gunnell and Frankel (1994) noted that 'no single intervention has been shown in a well conducted randomized controlled trial to reduce suicide'. Such a comment is at first impression sobering, but there are formidable obstacles in demonstrating whether any measure can prevent or, indeed, promote suicide. For example, there is the ethical problem of including suicidal persons in the placebo arm of a randomized controlled trial (RCT). Perhaps even more daunting is the fact that, although suicide is dramatic and tends to remain in a clinician's or researcher's mind, the reality of the situation is that it has a low base rate; it is therefore impossible to select sufficient numbers of high risk persons to participate in a RCT. To illustrate this, it has been calculated that if one were to utilize the RCTs of antidepressants which have been published, then it would have been necessary to have recruited about 1.9 million subjects to detect a 20% decrease in suicide (Gunnell & Ashby, 2004).

This has led to the examination of suicidal ideation and behaviours (variously described as attempted suicide and self-harm, which, for convenience, are sometimes grouped together as suicidality), including meta-analyses of findings from RCTs in which the efficacy of antidepressants versus placebo has been assessed. After initial reassuring results, subsequent studies have demonstrated an increased risk of suicidality in younger persons. However, the implications of that finding are open to differing interpretations. Indeed, other studies using alternative research methods have provided an added perspective to this finding; they will also be addressed in this chapter.

Evidence from Randomized Controlled Trials

Several studies have demonstrated reduced suicidal ideation in drug versus placebo RCTs (e.g., Letizia, Kapik, & Flanders, 1996; Szanto, Mulsant, Houck, Dew, & Reynolds, 2003). In addition, initial meta-analytic studies from the Netherlands by Storosum, van Zwieten, van den Brink, Gersons, and Broekmans (2001), using research submitted to their Medicines Evaluation Board, and from the United States by Khan *et al.* (2000), using

FDA data, found no differences in suicidality between antidepressant and placebo. However, subsequent, more detailed meta-analyses have not only consistently demonstrated that there is an association, but that it is age-dependent.

One of the first meta-analyses to substantiate an association between antidepressants and suicidality was that of Fergusson, Doucette, Glass, Shapiro, Healy, *et al.* (2005), who analysed 702 RCTs of antidepressants involving 87,000 patients. Although there was no association between SSRIs and suicide, they reported a two-fold increase of suicide attempts in patients receiving SSRIs compared with placebo, but no difference between SSRIs and tricyclic antidepressants. They calculated the number needed to treat for harm and derived a figure of 684 persons.

A similar meta-analytic study of pharmaceutical company data presented to the United Kingdom MHRA was reported by Gunnell, Saperia, and Ashby (2005). In a review of over 40,000 patients in 477 randomized controlled trials they found no evidence of increased suicide, but added cautiously that 'important protective or hazardous effects cannot be excluded' (p. 385). With regard to self-harm, they described 'weak evidence of an increased risk' (p. 385) (odds ratio (OR) = 1.57; 95% CI = 0.99–2.55), but, in subsequent correspondence, Saperia, Ashby, and Gunnell (2006) noted that, following further analysis, the OR reduced to 1.21 (95% CI = 0.87–1.83). In their initial publication, Gunnell *et al.* (2005) calculated the number needed to treat for non-fatal self-harm and derived a figure of 759 patients. They extended their research to include a measure of the benefits of treatment and reported that the number of individuals needed to treat for a response defined as both self- and clinician report of much or very much improved was between four and seven patients.

A meta-analysis of RCTs concerning children and adolescents was conducted in the United States by Hammad, Laughren, and Racoosin (2006). Twenty-four RCTs involving 4,582 patients had been submitted to the FDA, 16 for major depression. They found an increased risk ratio of suicidality with SSRI medication compared with placebo of 1.95 (95% CI = 1.28–2.98) for all indications of depression, and of 1.66 (95% CI = 1.02–2.68) for major depression.

In the United Kingdom, a similar meta-analysis on RCTs for youths treated for depression was performed by Dubicka, Hadley, and Roberts (2006) on data submitted to the Committee on Safety of Medicines. There were 16 RCTs with 2,741 patients, and the results were similar to those of Hammad *et al.* (2006), with 'self-harm or suicide-related events' (p. 393) occurring more often in those youths treated with antidepressants (OR = 1.70; 95% CI = 1.1–2.54; *p* = 0.01). They explained their results clearly, noting that 'in a sample of 100 young people being treated with antidepressants, approximately 5 would demonstrate some form of self-harm or suicidality, as opposed to 3 on placebo' (p. 396). However, they also stated that although 'there was a trend for individual suicidal thoughts, attempts and self-harm to occur more often in youths taking antidepressants than in those given placebo ... none of these differences was statistically significant' (p. 393).

Probably the most comprehensive analysis so far, that of Stone, Laughren, Jones, Levensen, Holland, *et al.* (2009), which had been presented to the US FDA in December 2006, has been published recently, presumably in order to provide wider dissemination of the facts, even though the analyses have not been updated (Geddes, Barbui, & Cipriani, 2009). Stone *et al.* (2009) examined 372 placebo controlled antidepressant trials involving

99,000 patients and found a strongly age-dependent effect, with an increase in suicidal behaviour, including suicide, in adults under the age of 25. They reported an odds ratio for all suicidal behaviour and suicidal ideation of 1.62 (95% CI = 0.97–2.71), 0.79 (95% CI = 0.64–0.98) and 0.37 (95% CI = 0.18–0.76) for those aged less than 25 years, 25 to 64 years, and 65 years or older, respectively. When those with suicidal ideation alone were excluded, the odds ratios were 2.30 (95% CI = 1.04–5.09), 0.87 (95% CI = 0.58–1.29), and 0.06 (95% CI = 0.01–0.58) for the three age groups, respectively.

They noted that the risk of suicidality in young adults under the age of 25 years was comparable with that of children and adolescents. In further analysing the age-dependent nature of their findings, they calculated that the odds ratio for suicidal behaviour and suicidal ideation declined 2.6% per year of age, and for suicidal behaviour alone it declined 4.6% per year of age.

Other Research Methods

As informative as the above findings may be, the studies examined so far have their shortcomings, as in fact do all studies. Most individual studies examined were of short duration, and patients most at risk for suicide were likely to have been excluded. Furthermore, the overriding constraint, as noted before, is the low base rate of suicide and the prohibitive numbers needed to demonstrate either a significant beneficial or harmful effect. Indeed, Ludwig and Marcotte (2005) have stated that 'it is an open question whether any RCT could ever satisfactorily identify the effects of SSRIs on suicide' (p. 250). They also asserted that 'there are applications that cannot be answered through the use of RCTs', and that 'non-experimental methods may be the only source of guidance for health policy-makers' (p. 268). Indeed, it is of note that, following their comprehensive meta-analysis, Stone *et al.* (2009) stated that 'it would not be surprising if epidemiological studies (or long-term randomized trials) showed a different picture' (p. 7).

It is therefore pertinent to examine other research methods which can assist understanding of this complex and important clinical issue.

Follow-up of clinical intervention

There have been few very long-term studies of the treatment of mood disorders. Indeed, the reports of Angst, Stassen, Clayton, and Angst (2002) and Angst, Angst, Gerber-Werder, and Gamma (2004) stand alone, as they described up to 44-years follow-up of 406 patients with mood disorders, with and without long-term medication. They found the standardized mortality ratio (SMR) for suicide among patients with untreated unipolar depression to be 38.07 compared with the treated patients' SMR of 11.86, a highly significant difference ($p < 0.001$). They concluded that there was 'a significant suicide reducing effect of antidepressants' (Angst *et al.*, 2002, p. 175).

An early, broad, community-oriented approach was reported by Rutz, von Knorring, and Walinder (1992) in which a depression recognition and management programme for general practitioners and the community on the Swedish island of Gotland resulted in greater use of antidepressants and less use of other psychotropic medications, a reduction in admissions for depression, and fewer suicides. There has been debate as to whether the reduction in suicide was statistically significant (McDonald, 1995; Williams & Goldney, 1994), but Rihmer, Rutz, and Pihlgren (1995) demonstrated a statistically significant reduction in those who died by suicide who had had a depressive diagnosis.

Initial pharmaco-epidemiological studies

A pharmaco-epidemiological approach using data from antidepressant sales and national suicide statistics was employed by Isacsson (2000), who had predicted that there would be a 25% decrease in suicide with a five-fold increase in antidepressant prescribing. With the introduction of the SSRI antidepressants there was a marked increase in prescribing to the extent that antidepressant use in Sweden increased from 1% to 3.4% of the population between 1991 and 1996. This allowed a natural experiment to address Isacsson's hypothesis. He found that there was a 19% reduction in suicide between 1991 and 1996 and there were no groups (age, gender, county) where the rate decreased in the absence of increased antidepressants. He also analysed data for Finland, Denmark, and Norway and found similar results.

Following this initial series of analyses there were reports from a number of other countries which allowed Ludwig and Marcotte (2005) to examine SSRI use and suicide in 27 countries. They found a strong association between an increase in antidepressant prescribing and a reduction of suicide in those over the age of 15; the data were not conclusive for those aged 10–15 years. They noted that an increase of one pill per capita was associated with a 2.5% reduction in suicide rates, or, put another way, one suicide could be averted for every 300,000 SSRI antidepressant pills sold.

It should be noted that, more recently, Reseland, Bray, and Gunnell (2006) have suggested that there was only 'mixed evidence' (p. 354) to substantiate the conclusion that the reduction in suicide in Nordic countries could definitely be attributed to the increase in antidepressants. Furthermore, some other countries did not show the same effect. Thus, Castelpietra, Morsanutto, Pascolo-Fabrici, and Isacsson (2008) referred to early negative reports from Italy, Northern Ireland, Iceland, and Slovenia. However, in a further analysis of more up-to-date antidepressant use and suicide in the Friuli Venezia Giulia (FVG) region of Italy, they concluded that 'suicide rates in FVG have declined in agreement with the hypothesis that the use of antidepressants may prevent suicide' (p. 382). There have been other similar consistent reports since the comprehensive work of Ludwig and Marcotte (2005), including new data from Denmark (Søndergård, Kvist, Lopez, Andersen, & Kessing, 2006), Finland (Korkeila, Salminen, Hiekkanen, & Salokangas, 2007), and Norway (Bramness, Walby, & Tverdal, 2007).

It is important to acknowledge that, while these reports may be reassuring to clinicians, neither the clinical follow-up studies nor the pharmaco-epidemiological approach can exclude the possibility that an overall reduction in suicide in association with increased antidepressant prescribing may have obscured an increase in suicide in some susceptible persons.

This was addressed by Gunnell and Ashby (2004), who calculated that there may have been an additional 35 (out of approximately 4,500) suicides each year related to antidepressants. However, they noted that their assumptions were 'based on the worst case scenario that the findings in relation to non-fatal self-harm in paediatric trials are applicable to suicidal deaths in adults' (p. 36). It is pertinent that they acknowledged that 'there is no evidence that the findings from the paediatric trials can be extrapolated to adults, nor indeed that the strength of associations are the same for fatal and non-fatal self-harm' (p. 36). They also noted that the findings were based on trials generally less than 10 weeks in duration, and that any suicide risk early in treatment could be offset by longer-term improvement. These caveats are hardly trivial, but, even with such assumptions, the confidence levels of their results were such that there could have been a null or beneficial effect of the SSRIs. It is hardly unexpected that such hypothetical calculations fuelled the debate, and further more sophisticated pharmaco-epidemiological studies followed.

Further pharmaco-epidemiological studies

An influential study in this debate was that of Jick, Kaye, and Jick (2004), who analysed data from the United Kingdom General Practice Research Database (GPRD) which contains over 35 million patient years of information. Using a very rigorous research methodology, they delineated between 35,000 and 50,000 persons who had had antidepressant treatment initiated with one of either two tricyclic antidepressants, amitriptyline or dothiepin, or one of two SSRI antidepressants, fluoxetine or paroxetine. Jick *et al.* (2004) reported that there were similar risks of emerging suicidal behaviour after starting each of these antidepressants. They also found that those who had been on the antidepressant less than 10 days were more than four times as likely to have their first suicidal behaviour compared with those who had been on their antidepressant for more than 90 days before their suicidal behaviour; and the risk of suicide was even greater in that first 10 days, being 38 times more likely than among those who had been on their antidepressant for more than 90 days. They reported that there was no trend between the drugs and they also noted that the gradation of risk was consistent with antidepressants not being immediately effective, with an increased risk in those who were newly diagnosed and newly treated. It is fair to add that this is the pattern of morbidity and mortality for any potentially life-threatening condition: the risk is greater when the condition is most acute.

In an accompanying editorial, Wessely and Kerwin (2004) noted that 'the results confirm that antidepressant prescription is indeed associated with suicidal behaviour, and strongly so. This simply means that antidepressants are being prescribed for the right indication, and that they do not immediately eliminate suicide risk. That we knew' (p. 380). They also noted perceptively that such results would be unlikely to allay community concerns, particularly 'as society becomes increasingly obsessed with questions of risk and then blame' (p. 380).

It is important to note that Jick *et al.* (2004) extended their study to examine adolescent suicide. They found no suicides in persons aged 10–19 years who were receiving one or other of the study drugs. However, they did report that there were 15 persons in that age group on the GPRD who had died by suicide, and none had received an antidepressant drug.

That the Jick *et al.* (2004) data were not simply an artefact of British practice has been demonstrated by subsequent reports from other countries. Isacsson, Holmgren, and Ahlner (2005) in Sweden reported a toxicological study of over 14,000 suicides between 1992 and 2000 and compared them with control subjects. They found that SSRIs were under-represented compared with other antidepressants in those who died by suicide (OR = 0.83; 99% CI = 0.77–0.90). Addressing the issue of suicide in younger persons, they found that, in the 15–19-year age group, SSRIs had a lower relative risk (0.14; 95% CI = 0.05–0.43) for suicide compared with non-SSRI antidepressants; and in those under the age of 15 years, there were 52 suicides and no SSRIs were found by toxicological screening, although there were seven in whom other antidepressants were detected. In a Danish study, Søndergård, Kvist, Andersen, and Kessing (2006a) found that none of the 42 suicides aged 10–17 years between 1995 and 1999 had been treated with SSRIs in the two weeks prior to their deaths, and none of the 37 boys who died by suicide had ever been treated with antidepressants at any time during the study period.

There have been three similar toxicological studies from the United States. Leon, Marzuk, Tardiff, and Teres (2004) reported SSRIs in two of 54 consecutive suicides under the age of 18 years between 1993 and 1998; Moskos, Olson, Halbern, Keller, and Gray (2005) found none of 49 consecutive suicides aged 13–21 years had any antidepressant at autopsy; and Leon, Marzuk, Tardiff, Bucciarelli, Markham, *et al.* (2006) noted that only one of 36 consecutive suicides under the age of 18 between 1999 and 2002 had ingested an SSRI.

These six studies of either whole of population data or in series of consecutive suicides in young persons, from four different countries, have a total of 574 young suicides. However, only nine (1.6%) had had recent exposure to SSRIs. Bearing in mind the approximate 60% prevalence of mood disorders present in those young persons who die by suicide (Shaffer, Gould, Fisher, Trautman, Moreau, *et al.*, 1996), rather than implicating SSRI antidepressants as a precipitant or cause of suicide, it could be argued that very few of those young persons who died by suicide had had the potential benefit of such medication (Dudley, Goldney, & Hadzi-Pavlovic, 2009). Indeed, one might ask, perhaps provocatively, why the media have not picked up on these findings and criticized practitioners for not at least having a trial of antidepressants in those vulnerable young persons.

Additional studies

There have been at least two other large population-based studies of patients who had been hospitalized either for depression or a suicide attempt. Olfson, Marcus, and Shaffer (2006) examined US Medicaid beneficiaries who had received in-patient treatment for depression, and were able to match 784 suicide attempters with 3,635 controls and 94 suicides with 435 controls. Antidepressant drug treatment was associated with both attempted suicide and suicide among children and adolescents. They noted, however, that the suicide finding was based on only eight deaths and they could not exclude the possibility that more severely ill patients would have been treated with antidepressants.

Similar results emerged from the Finnish study of Tiihonen, Lönqvist, Wahlbeck, Klaukka, Tanskanen, *et al.* (2006), who examined those who had been hospitalized for a suicide attempt. They followed 15,390 patients for an average of 3.4 years and found current use of an antidepressant was 'associated with a markedly increased risk of attempted suicide and, at the same time, with a markedly decreased risk of completed suicide and death' (p. 1358). That pattern was similar for those aged 10–19 years. They concluded that 'our results suggest that antidepressant treatment may contribute to a substantial decrease in mortality among this patient population' (p. 1366).

Reports using data from managed healthcare organizations in the United States have provided an additional perspective. Valuck, Libby, Sills, Giese, and Allen (2004) examined the records of 24,119 adolescents between 12 and 18 years who were diagnosed with major depression. They found that treatment with an antidepressant for at least six months significantly reduced the occurrence of a suicide attempt compared with treatment for less than eight weeks, and that overall antidepressant use was not associated with the likelihood of suicide attempts.

Simon, Savarino, Operskalski, and Wang (2006) used data from a pre-paid health plan to identify 65,103 patients with 82,285 episodes of depression. They were able to examine suicidal behaviour documented before and after the prescription of antidepressants, and concluded that 'the risk of suicide attempt was highest in the month before starting antidepressant treatment and declined progressively after starting medication' (p. 41). They also estimated the risk of suicide in the acute phase of treatment as about one in 3,000 treatments, and for attempted suicide it was about one in 1,000 treatments, the latter figure being similar to the one in 684 of Fergusson *et al.* (2005) and the one in 759 of Gunnell *et al.* (2005).

An innovative use of data from Denmark has also provided reassuring results. Søndergård, Kvist, Andersen, and Kessing (2006b) used population registers to identify 438,625 patients who had purchased at least one prescription of an antidepressant. Those who had purchased SSRIs twice or more had a decreased rate of suicide (RR = 0.63; 95% CI = 0.56–0.71) compared with those who purchased SSRIs once only. The same group (Søndergård, Lopez, Andersen, & Kessing, 2007) did a similar analysis on 31,422 patients who had been diagnosed with a depressive disorder either as a hospital in- or out-patient. They noted that those patients had an increased rate of suicide, but that 'those who continued treatment with antidepressants had a decreased rate of suicide compared with those who purchased antidepressants once' (p. 163) (RR = 0.31; 95% CI = 0.26–0.36). Naturally, these two studies do not preclude the possibility that antidepressants could contribute to suicidality early in the course of treatment.

A review of observational studies of the treatment of patients with moderate or severe depression has recently been published by Barbui, Esposito, and Cipriani (2009). Based on eight studies including more than 200,000 patients, the authors calculated that exposure to SSRIs resulted in decreased suicide or attempted suicide among adults (OR = 0.57; 95% CI = 0.47–0.70), but for adolescents the risk was increased (OR = 1.92; 95% CI = 1.51–2.44). They acknowledged that this result could have been confounded by severity, with those adolescents who had received SSRIs being more severely depressed and suicidal than those who had not been so prescribed.

Differential effects of antidepressants

There is increasing evidence that not all antidepressants have the same potential for being associated with suicidality. For example, Barbui *et al.* (2009) found that paroxetine and venlafaxine increased risk more than other antidepressants. However, the increased risk associated with venlafaxine could be related to selective prescribing to patients with a 'higher burden of suicide risk factors' (p. 365) (Mines, Hill, Yu, & Novelli, 2005), although the increased risk associated with paroxetine was consistent with previous findings (Tiihonen *et al.*, 2009). A recent comprehensive review of efficacy and adverse effects of antidepressants by Cipriani, Furukawa, Salanti, Geddes, Higgins, *et al.* (2009) concluded that, although sertraline and escitalopram had the best tolerability and efficacy, sertraline was the least likely to be associated with suicidal behaviour (Geddes *et al.*, 2009).

Discussion

It would be possible to provide further information addressing this issue, and it is probable that the individual reader will be surprised or even disturbed that certain of their favoured studies have been omitted. However, there is a law of diminishing returns in terms of the utility of the information that it is feasible to obtain from even the most sophisticated of previous or potential future trials. Indeed, the most valuable data will probably emerge from well-conducted observational studies.

In interpreting this research, one is reminded of the title of a paper by Balon (2003): 'Selective serotonin reuptake inhibitors and suicide: Is the evidence, as with beauty, in the eye of the beholder?' (p. 293). It is also sobering to reflect on the words of the epidemiologist Bradford Hill (1962), who asked: 'When does a heap become a heap? The answer, I submit, is not to be found tidily tucked in the formulae of tests of significance, useful as they may be. In it there must always be an element of the subjective – the subjective judgement of the particular respondent, of you and me' (p. 188).

So what can one make of these data? As Hammad *et al.* (2006) stated, 'an overall interpretation of this finding and its implications for clinical practice are less clear' (p. 338). Is there an idiosyncratic response in some people to antidepressants? Is it possible that antidepressants, in contrast to placebo, give other adverse effects which draw attention to those persons, resulting in greater detection of suicidality? Could it be related to the unwanted effect of agitation or an akathisia-like syndrome (inner restlessness and need to continually move)? By contrast, could it be related to the allaying of anxiety by antidepressants resulting in a facilitation of the verbalization and communication of suicidality, as suggested by Hammad *et al.* (2006)? There is also the possibility that antidepressants may be precipitating bipolarity in previously undiagnosed bipolar patients, with resultant agitation and emergence of suicidality (Seemuller, Severus, Moller, & Riedel, 2009).

There may be other explanations for this apparent increase in suicidality in young persons. However, it is challenging to reconcile these apparently robust data with the paucity of completed suicide in young persons in those studies which have examined whole of population suicides, or series of consecutive suicides, as noted above. It is also pertinent to reflect on the finding of Bridge, Barbe, Birmaher, Kolko, and Brent (2005) that emergent suicidality in medication-free psychotherapeutic treatment of depression in adolescents of 12.5% was 'comparable to rates observed in antidepressant trials' (p. 2174).

Notwithstanding these caveats and the paradoxical nature of the finding, we are left with consistent evidence that suicidality is increased in young persons in association with antidepressants. Whereas the overall number needed to harm (NNH) for adults is about one in 700–1,000 (Fergusson *et al.*, 2005; Gunnell *et al.*, 2005; Simon *et al.*, 2006), the NNH for children and adolescents is less favourable, about one in 120–140 (Brent, 2009a; Bridge, Iyengar, Salary, Barbe, Birmaher, *et al.*, 2007).

While it is important to know the NNH, it is equally important to balance that with the number needed to treat (NNT) for significant improvement. For whole of population data this has been calculated at between one in four to seven (Gunnell *et al.*, 2005) and for children and adolescents, one in 10 (Brent, 2009a; Bridge *et al.*, 2007). What this means for young people is that 12 to 14 times as many would benefit from antidepressant treatment than would experience suicidality.

Whether these are considered to be acceptable risks will, naturally, depend on the interpretations of individual clinicians, their patients, and, in the case of many young people, their families. Furthermore, the risks of treatment need to be reconciled with the well-documented risks associated with no treatment. In fact, there has been concern that warnings about the potential risks of antidepressants have led to an under-utilization of antidepressants in young people (Libby, Orton & Valuck, 2009; Nemeroff, Kalali, Keller, Charney, Lenderts, *et al.*, 2009).

The possibility that this could have led to an unintended increase in suicide through under-treatment of depression has also been raised (Gibbons, Brown, Hur, Marcus, Bhaumik, *et al.*, 2007). While a comprehensive recent review by Wheeler, Metcalfe, Martin, and Gunnell (2009) noted that overall there appeared to be no evidence of increased suicide as a result of regulatory changes, they acknowledged that 'there was weak evidence of an increase in suicide amongst young women internationally' (p. 579). This is of concern and highlights the challenge confronting the individual clinician faced with the assessment and management of depression, particularly in young persons.

While it is not the purpose of this chapter to provide specific guidelines for the treatment of depression in either adults or children and adolescents, it is important to state that antidepressant measures are not necessarily the first line of treatment for depression in any age group. Indeed, particularly for children and adolescents, non-pharmacological approaches are advisable before the use of antidepressants (Dubicka & Wilkinson, 2007; March & Vitiello, 2009). However, what can be stated with confidence is that, as a result of these recent studies, when antidepressants are considered to be clinically appropriate, both the potential risks and benefits can now be more fully appreciated and compared.

Conclusion

It is unlikely that there will ever be RCTs to demonstrate a reduction of suicide with antidepressants because of the constraints of the low base rate and the enormous number of subjects needed for such a study. However, despite the methodological challenges involved in clarifying this important clinical issue, there are increasing amounts of data about the effectiveness of antidepressants in reducing suicide. Furthermore, there are now calculations available to compare the numbers needed to treat for the emergence of any suicidality as opposed to the numbers needed to treat for clinical improvement.

It is important to recognize that all treatments have potential risks and we need to consider all of the evidence, including the historical perspective, with full disclosure and discussion with patients and their relatives. This includes evaluating the risk of not treating, as well as balancing the potential risks and benefits of treatment. We are now better informed in this regard and clinical decisions can be made accordingly.

References

Angst, J., Angst, F., Gerber-Werder, R., & Gamma, A. (2005). Suicide in 406 mood-disorder patients with and without long-term medication: A 40 to 44 years' follow-up. *Archives of Suicide Research, 9*, 279–300.

Angst, F., Stassen, H. H., Clayton, P. J., & Angst, J. (2002). Mortality of patients with mood disorders: Follow-up over 34–38 years. *Journal of Affective Disorders, 68*, 167–181.

Balon, R. (2003). Selective serotonin reuptake inhibitors and suicide: Is the evidence, as with beauty, in the eye of the beholder? *Psychotherapy and Psychosomatics, 72*, 293–299.

Barbui, C., Cipriani, A., & Geddes, J. R. (2008). Antidepressants and suicide symptoms: Compelling new insights from the FDA's analysis of individual patient level data. *Evidence Based Mental Health, 11*, 34–36.

Barbui, C., Esposito, E., & Cipriani, A. (2009). Selective serotonin reuptake inhibitors and risk of suicide: A systematic review of observational studies. *Canadian Medical Association Journal, 180*, 291–297.

Bramness, J. G., Walby, F. A., & Tverdal, A. (2007). The sales of antidepressants and suicide rates in Norway and its counties 1980–2004. *Journal of Affective Disorders, 102*, 1–9.

Brent, D. A. (2009a). Selective serotonin reuptake inhibitors and suicidality: A guide for the perplexed. *Canadian Journal of Psychiatry, 54*, 72–74.

Brent, D. A. (2009b). Youth depression and suicide: Selective serotonin reuptake inhibitors treat the former and prevent the latter. *Canadian Journal of Psychiatry, 54*, 76–77.

Bridge, J. A., Barbe, R. P., Birmaher, B., Kolko, D. J., & Brent, D. A. (2005). Emergent suicidality in a clinical psychotherapy trial for adolescent depression. *American Journal of Psychiatry, 162*, 2173–2175.

Bridge, J. A., Iyengar, S., Salary, C. B., Barbe, R. P., Birmaher, B., Pincus, H. A., Ren, L., & Brent, D. A. (2007). Clinical response and risk for reported suicidal ideation and suicide attempts in pediatric antidepressant treatment. *Journal of the American Medical Association, 297*, 1683–1696.

Burrows, G. M. (1828). *Commentaries on the Causes, Forms, Symptoms, and Treatment, Moral and Medical, of Insanity*. London: Thomas and George Underwood.

Castelpietra, G., Morsanutto, A., Pascolo-Fabrici, E., & Isacsson, G. (2008). Antidepressant use and suicide prevention: A prescription database study in the region Friuli Venezia Giulia, Italy. *Acta Psychiatrica Scandinavica, 118*, 382–388.

Cipriani, A., Furukawa, T. A., Salanti, G., Geddes, J. R., Higgins, J. P., Churchill, R., Watanabe, N., Nakagawa, A., Omori, I. M., McGuire, H., Tansella, M., & Barbui, C. (2009). Comparative efficacy and acceptability of 12 new-generation antidepressants: A multiple-treatments meta-analysis. *The Lancet, 373*, 746–758.

Dubicka, B., Hadley, S., & Roberts, C. (2006). Suicidal behaviour in youths with depression treated with new-generation antidepressants. *British Journal of Psychiatry, 189*, 393–398.

Dubicka, B. & Wilkinson, P. (2007). Evidence-based treatment of adolescent major depression. *Evidence Based Mental Health, 10*, 100–102.

Dudley, M., Goldney, R., & Hadzi-Pavlovic, D. (2009). Adolescents dying by suicide are not taking SSRIs. *Canadian Medical Association Journal, Electronic letter,* available at http://www.cmaj.ca/cgi/eletters/180/3/291.

Eastman, B. D. (1877). Report of the proceedings of the New England Psychological Society. *American Journal of Insanity, 34*, 98–101.

Fergusson, D., Doucette, S., Glass, K. C., Shapiro, S., Healy, D., Herbert, P., & Hutton, B. (2005). Association between suicide attempts and selective serotonin reuptake inhibitors: Systematic review of randomised controlled trials. *British Medical Journal, 330*, 396–402.

Geddes, J. R., Barbui, C., & Cipriani, A. (2009). Risk of suicidal behaviour in adults taking antidepressants. *British Medical Journal, 339*, b3066.

Gibbons, R. D., Brown, C. H., Hur, K., Marcus, S. M., Bhaumik, D. K., Erkens, J. A., Herings, R. M., & Mann, J. J. (2007). Early evidence on the effects of regulators' suicidality warnings on SSRI prescriptions and suicide in children and adolescents. *American Journal of Psychiatry, 164*, 1356–1363.

Gunnell, D. & Ashby, D. (2004). Antidepressants and suicide: What is the balance of benefit and harm. *British Medical Journal, 329*, 34–38.

Gunnell, D. & Frankel, S. (1994). Prevention of suicide: Aspirations and evidence. *British Medical Journal, 308*, 1227–1233.

Gunnell, D., Saperia, J., & Ashby, D. (2005). Selective serotonin reuptake inhibitors (SSRIs) and suicide in adults: Meta-analysis of drug company data from placebo controlled, randomised controlled trials submitted to the MHRA's safety review. *British Medical Journal, 330*, 385–390.

Hammad, T. A., Laughren, T., & Racoosin, J. (2006). Suicidality in pediatric patients treated with antidepressant drugs. *Archives of General Psychiatry, 63*, 332–339.

Harris, E. C. & Barraclough, B. (1997). Suicide as an outcome for mental disorders – A meta-analysis. *British Journal of Psychiatry, 170*, 205–228.

Healy, D. (2009a). Are selective serotonin reuptake inhibitors a risk factor for adolescent suicide? *Canadian Journal of Psychiatry, 54*, 69–71.

Healy, D. (2009b). Perplexity is our product. *Canadian Journal of Psychiatry, 54*, 75.

Healy, D., Langmaak, C., & Savage, M. (1999). Suicide in the course of the treatment of depression. *Journal of Psychopharmacology, 13*, 94–99.

Healy, D. & Whitaker, C. (2003). Antidepressants and suicide: Risk–benefit conundrums. *Journal of Psychiatry and Neuroscience, 28*, 331–337.

Hill, A. B. (1962). The statistician in medicine. *Journal of the Institute of Actuaries, 88*, 178–191.

Isacsson, G. (2000). Suicide prevention – A medical breakthrough? *Acta Psychiatrica Scandinavica, 102*, 113–117.

Isacsson, G., Holmgren, P., & Ahlner, J. (2005). Selective serotonin reuptake inhibitor antidepressants and the risk of suicide: A controlled forensic database study of 14857 suicides. *Acta Psychiatrica Scandinavica, 111*, 286–290.

Jick, H., Kaye, J. A., & Jick, S. S. (2004). Antidepressants and the risk of suicidal behaviors. *Journal of the American Medical Association, 292*, 338–343.

Khan, A., Warner, H. A., & Brown, W. A. (2000). Symptom reduction and suicide risk in patients treated with placebo in antidepressant clinical trials: An analysis of the Food and Drug Administration database. *Archives of General Psychiatry, 57*, 311–317.

Korkeila, J., Salminen, J. K., Hiekkanen, H., & Salokangas, R. K. (2007). Use of antidepressants and suicide rate in Finland: An ecological study. *Journal of Clinical Psychiatry, 68*, 505–511.

Leon, A. C., Marzuk, P. M., Tardiff, K., Bucciarelli, A., Markham, P. T., & Galea, S. (2006). Antidepressants and youth suicide in New York City, 1999–2002. *Journal of the American Academy of Child and Adolescent Psychiatry*, 45, 1054–1058.

Leon, A. C., Marzuk, P. M., Tardiff, K., & Teres, J. J. (2004). Paroxetine, other antidepressants, and youth suicide in New York City: 1993 through 1998. *Journal of Clinical Psychiatry*, 65, 915–918.

Letizia, C., Kapik, B., & Flanders, W. D. (1966). Suicidal risk during controlled clinical investigations of Fluvoxamine. *Journal of Clinical Psychiatry*, 57, 415–421.

Libby, A. M., Orton, H. D., & Valuck, R. J. (2009). Persisting decline in depression treatment after FDA warnings. *Archives of General Psychiatry*, 66, 633–639.

Lönqvist, J. (2000). Psychiatric aspects of suicidal behaviour: Depression. In K. Hawton & K. van Heeringen (Eds), *The International Handbook of Suicide and Attempted Suicide* (pp. 107–120). Chichester: John Wiley & Sons, Ltd.

Ludwig, J. & Marcotte, D. E. (2005). Anti-depressants, suicide, and drug regulation. *Journal of Policy Analysis and Management*, 24, 249–272.

March, J. S. & Vitiello, B. (2009). Clinical messages from the Treatment for Adolescents with Depression Study (TADS). *American Journal of Psychiatry*, 166, 1118–1123.

Mayer-Gross, W., Slater, E., & Roth, M. (1955). *Clinical Psychiatry*. London: Cassell.

McDonald, A. J. D. (1955). Suicide prevention in Gotland. *British Journal of Psychiatry*, 166, 402.

Mines, D., Hill, D., Yu, H., & Novelli, L. (2005). Prevalence of risk factors for suicide in patients prescribed venlafaxine, fluoxetine, and citalopram. *Pharmacoepidemiology and Drug Safety*, 14, 365–366.

Moller, H-J., Baldwin, D. S., Goodwin, G., Kasper, S., Okasha, A., Stein, D. J., Tandon, R., Versiani, M., & the WPA Section on Pharmacopsychiatry (2008). Do SSRIs or antidepressants in general increase suicidality? *European Archives of Psychiatry and Clinical Neuroscience*, 258 (Suppl. 3), 3–23.

Moskos, M., Olson, L., Halbern, S., Keller, T., & Gray, D. (2005). Utah youth suicide study: Psychological autopsy. *Suicide and Life-Threatening Behavior*, 35, 536–546.

Nemeroff, C. B., Kalali, A., Keller, M. B., Charney, D. S., Lenderts, S. E., Cascade, E. F., Stephenson, H., & Schatzberg, A. F. (2007). Impact of publicity concerning pediatric suicidality data on physician practice patterns in the United States. *Archives of General Psychiatry*, 64, 466–472.

Olfson, M., Marcus, S. C., & Shaffer, D. (2006). Antidepressant drug therapy and suicide in severely depressed children and adults: A case control study. *Archives of General Psychiatry*, 63, 865–872.

Reseland, S., Bray, I., & Gunnell, D. (2007). Relationships between antidepressant sales and secular trends in suicide rates in the Nordic countries. *British Journal of Psychiatry*, 188, 354–358.

Rihmer, Z., Rutz, W., & Pihlgren, H. (1995). Depression and suicide on Gotland. An intensive study of all suicides before and after a depression-training program for general practitioners. *Journal of Affective Disorders*, 35, 147–152.

Rutz, W., von Knorring, L., & Walinder, J. (1992). Long-term effects of an educational program for general practitioners given by the Swedish Committee for the Prevention and Treatment of Depression. *Acta Psychiatrica Scandinavica*, 85, 83–88.

Saperia, J., Ashby, D., & Gunnell, D. (2006). Suicidal behaviour and SSRIs: Updated meta-analysis. *British Medical Journal*, 332, 1453.

Savage, G. (1892). Suicide and insanity. In D. H. Tuke (Ed.), *A Dictionary of Psychological Medicine* (pp. 1230–1232). London: J. & A. Churchill.

Seemüller, F., Severus, E., Möller, H-J., & Riedel, M. (2009). Antidepressants and suicidality in younger adults – Is bipolar illness the missing link? *Acta Psychiatrica Scandinavica*, 119, 166–167.

Shaffer, D., Gould, M. S., Fisher, P., Trautman, P., Moreau, D., Kleinman, M., & Flory, M. (1996). Psychiatric diagnosis in child and adolescent suicide. *Archives of General Psychiatry*, 53, 339–348.

Simon, G. E., Savarino, J., Operskalski, B., & Wang, P. S. (2006). Suicide risk during antidepressant treatment. *American Journal of Psychiatry, 163*, 41–47.

Søndergård, L., Kvist, K., Andersen, P. K., & Kessing, L. (2006a). Do antidepressants precipitate youth suicide? A nationwide pharmacoepidemiological study. *European Child and Adolescent Psychiatry, 15*, 232–240.

Søndergård, L., Kvist, K., Andersen, P. K., & Kessing, L. V. (2006b). Do antidepressants prevent suicide? *International Clinical Psychopharmacology, 21*, 211–218.

Søndergård, L., Kvist, K., Lopez, A. G., Andersen, P. K., & Kessing, L. V. (2006). Temporal changes in suicide rates for persons treated and not treated with antidepressants in Denmark during 1995–1999. *Acta Psychiatrica Scandinavica, 114*, 168–176.

Søndergård, L., Lopez, A. G., Andersen, P. K. & Kessing, L. V. (2007). Continued antidepressant treatment and suicide in patients with depressive disorder. *Archives of Suicide Research, 11*, 163–175.

Stone, M., Laughren, T., Jones, M. L., Levenson, M., Holland, P. C., Hughes, A., Hammad, T. A., Temple, R., & Rochester, G. (2009). Risk of suicidality in clinical trials of antidepressants in adults: Analysis of proprietary data submitted to US Food and Drug Administration. *British Medical Journal, 339*, b2880.

Storosum, J. G., van Zwieten, B. J., van den Brink, W., Gersow, B. P. R., & Broekmans, A. W. (2001). Suicide risk in placebo-controlled studies of major depression. *Archives of General Psychiatry, 158*, 1271–1275.

Szanto, K., Mulsant, B. H., Houck, P., Dew, M. A., & Reynolds, C. F. (2003). Occurrence and course of suicidality during short-term treatment of late-life depression. *Archives of General Psychiatry, 60*, 610–617.

Teicher, M. H., Glod, C., & Cole, J. O. (1990). Emergence of intense suicidal preoccupation during fluoxetine treatment. *American Journal of Psychiatry, 147*, 207–210.

Tiihonen, J., Lönqvist, J., Wahlbeck, K., Klaukka, T., Tanskanen, A., & Haukka, J. (2006). Antidepressants and the risk of suicide, attempted suicide, and overall mortality in a nationwide cohort. *Archives of General Psychiatry, 63*, 1358–1367.

Valuck, R. J., Libby, A. M., Sills, M. R., Giess, A. A., & Allen, R. R. (2004). Antidepressant treatment and risk of suicide attempt by adolescents with major depressive disorder: A propensity-adjusted retrospective cohort study. *Central Nervous System Drugs, 18*, 1119–1132.

Wessely, S., & Kerwin, R. (2004). Suicide risk and the SSRIs. *Journal of the American Medical Association, 292*, 379–381.

Wheeler, B. W., Metcalfe, C., Martin, R. M., & Gunnell, D. (2009). International impacts of regulatory action to limit antidepressant prescribing on rates of suicide in young people. *Pharmacoepidemiology and Drug Safety, 18*, 579–588.

Williams, J. M. G. & Goldney, R. D. (1994). Suicide prevention in Gotland. *British Journal of Psychiatry, 165*, 692.

PART III

Suicide Prevention: Bringing Together Evidence, Policy, and Practice

CHAPTER TWENTY-SEVEN

Suicide Prevention Strategies: Case Studies from across the Globe

Gergö Hadlaczky, Danuta Wasserman, Christina W. Hoven, Donald J. Mandell, and Camilla Wasserman

Abstract

In the light of the more than 1.5 million annual suicide deaths worldwide projected for 2020, suicide prevention is clearly a high priority. Moreover, the goal of suicide prevention is achievable (Wasserman, 2004). This chapter describes theoretical aspects such as the familiar primary, secondary, and tertiary model of suicide prevention, and compares it with the US Institute of Medicine model which adopts universal, selective, and indicated approaches. Suicide preventive efforts of inter-governmental bodies, such as the World Health Organisation (WHO) and European Union (EU), and area-specific programmes in Sweden, Uganda, Hong Kong, and Japan are also discussed as examples. Systematic inter-governmental collaboration, between policy planners, relevant decision-makers, clinicians, professional organizations, as well as researchers is a prerequisite in the successful prevention of suicides.

Introduction

In this chapter, we present two commonly used, evidence-based frameworks for classifying preventive strategies applied in public health: (a) the familiar 'primary, secondary, tertiary' prevention model; and (b) the US Institute of Medicine (IOM) model, which incorporates

International Handbook of Suicide Prevention: Research, Policy and Practice, First Edition.
Edited by Rory C. O'Connor, Stephen Platt, Jacki Gordon.
© 2011 John Wiley & Sons, Ltd. Published 2011 by John Wiley & Sons, Ltd.

universal, selective, and other indicated approaches. Examples of current applications of suicide prevention activities and programmes from across the globe are cited.

Model of Primary, Secondary, and Tertiary Prevention

In this section we describe suicide prevention by reference to three stages of prevention: primary, secondary, and tertiary. These respectively refer to activities before suicidal behaviours occur, as suicidal behaviours occur, and after suicidal behaviours occur.

Thus, *primary prevention* consists of activities intended to discourage or interfere with completion of suicides before the onset of suicidal behaviour is noted. Such activities can be divided into two categories. The first type are actions that afford protection against suicide by reducing, or, where possible, entirely eliminating, known risk factors. These actions are designed to restrict both behaviours and means of completing suicide, such as by limiting access to locations that are frequently used for suicide attempts (so-called 'suicide hot spots') and/or to guns, poisons, etc. Primary prevention also encompasses other activities that address distal factors, such as promoting awareness, recognition, empathy. and better understanding of mental illness and suicide. Tackling bullying in schools or combating alcohol consumption also constitute primary prevention. The second type of primary prevention activities involve promoting protective factors. Examples include promoting healthy lifestyles, enhancing school safety, increasing opportunities for readily available counselling, training gatekeepers (key persons, such as police officers, who in the course of their working lives come into contact with people suffering from emotional troubles), and by setting up telephone or Internet helplines. While these latter activities are aimed at reducing mental health problems and thereby addressing risk factors for suicide, they also have the potential to promote protective factors, for example, by equipping individuals with information on ways to look after themselves.

Secondary prevention seeks to identify illness in its earliest stages. In suicide prevention this may involve conducting screenings for particular populations considered to be at heightened risk, varying from complete urban or rural populations, to narrowly selected populations considered to be at heightened risk, such as institutionalized older adults, etc. Suicide screening makes use of: structured or semi-structured interview protocols; biological tests such as the dexamethasone suppression test (DST), which has demonstrated high accuracy in predicting suicide among depressed and schizophrenic in-patients (Jokinen, Nordström, & Nordström, 2008; Mann & Currier, 2007); and where available, valid and reliable psychometric scales. While many scales yield relatively low positive predictive values, sorely limiting their usefulness, examples of recommended scales include Paykel's Suicide Ladder (Paykel, Myers, Lindethall, & Tanner, 1974), the NO HOPE Scale (Bech & Awata, 2009), and the Columbia Classification Algorithm of Suicide Assessment (C-CASA) (Posner, Oquendo, Gould, Stanley, & Davies, 2007).

A major advantage of screening is that it can be relatively cheap. However, several aspects of screening need to be considered to ensure cost-effectiveness, such as the efficacy and validity of the screening method, the cultural compatibility (a method that effectively identifies suicidal individuals in one culture may be less effective in others), as well as the raw costs: paper versus online questionnaires are usually cheaper, but less effective than, for instance, interview-based screening methods.

Tertiary prevention generally consists of arresting the progression of ill-health and suffering after clinical manifestation and/or diagnosis of symptomatology. Examples may be psychological or pharmacological treatment of clinically diagnosed patients who exhibit signs of suicidality.

For further information on the primary, secondary, and tertiary prevention model, see Wasserman and Durkee (2009).

The Institute of Medicine (IOM) Model

The US Institute of Medicine (1994) proposed a new framework, known as the IOM model, based on Gordon's (1987) operationally defined classification of disease, which parses prevention into the '*universal*,' '*selective*', and '*indicated*' categories. For this reason, the model is also known as the USI.

Universal prevention strategies are those that address entire populations and are carried out with no prior screening for suicide risk. An example of a universal prevention strategy involves training programmes directed at doctors of medicine in general practice (GPs) to enhance recognition and treatment methods for people with depression and associated suicidal behaviour. Such training has been implemented in Gotland County, Sweden. Gotland County (*län*), by dint of it being essentially an island off the east coast of Sweden, is ideal for implementing such a programme: nearly every resident ($n = {\sim}57{,}000$) would most likely seek medical care from island practitioners, and nearly all of the GPs in Gotland County attended lectures covering descriptions of symptoms, aetiology, pathogenesis, the biological roots of depression, examples of depressive illness in older adults, and aspects of emergency and long-term treatment, including prevention of affective disorders (Rutz, von Knorring, & Wålinder, 1989; Rutz, Wålinder, Eberhard, Holmberg, von Knorring, *et al.*, 1989). Thus, this prevention strategy can be classified as 'universal', inasmuch as it aims to reduce suicide through improving the prospects of detection and treatment of suicidal individuals in the *entire population* of Gotland County. The rationale is that with the new knowledge held by GPs, suicide risk will be assessed in all patients, regardless of physical malady, even in those coming in for something as relatively innocuous as the common cold or hearing loss from impacted ear wax.

Selective prevention strategies target population sub-sets composed of individuals regarded as at risk for suicide solely by virtue of their belonging to these sub-sets. Sub-set selection is based on known biological, social, and/or environmental risk factors for suicide, such as unemployment, marital dissolution, at-risk age, low income or sexual abuse. Targeting at-risk population sub-sets is likely to enhance the impact of preventive efforts for two reasons. First, the proportion of potential suicide victims is higher in these groups (although, of course, not all their members are at risk). Second, more effective target-oriented efforts may eliminate or mitigate the specific risk factors on which sub-set selection is based. Examples of selective prevention strategies are: intervention programmes for children with clinically depressed parents or for victims of physical or sexual abuse (Yip, 2005); event-centred interventions focused on adverse life events, such as the loss of a loved one, physical injury, rape, etc. (Burns & Patton, 2000); and interventions focused on victims of war, displacement, famine or other modes of violence (Hoven, Duarte, Lucas, Wu, Mandell, *et al.*, 2005; National Institute of Mental Health, 2002; WHO, 2002).

The purpose of *indicated prevention* is to identify and treat individuals who exhibit early signs of suicidal behaviour or afflictions often associated with suicidality. Screening, treatment, and close follow-up of people with depression, bipolar disorder, anorexia, and alcohol abuse, and also follow-up of prior suicide attempters and individuals who exhibit self-harming behaviour are examples of groups for which such strategies are indicated (Bertolote, Fleischmann, De Leo, & Wasserman, 2004; Yip, 2005). Moreover, individuals may be referred to programmes of indicated prevention, not only as a result of targeted screening, but also by lay people in the general population attuned to signs of risk, including parents, teachers, clergy, and peers. The more that is known about these indicated prevention programmes, the more likely it is that at-risk individuals will be referred to them. It is vital, therefore, to take full advantage of the cumulative, and possibly synergistic, effects of pursuing universal strategies such as the dissemination of mental health information to the general public, while at the same time applying the selective and indicated prevention methods, like the intervention programmes for at-risk individuals and the indicated programmes for depression sufferers described above.

Positive effects from these synergistic efforts have been demonstrated in multi-level preventive efforts, such as those implemented by the European Alliance Against Depression (Hegerl, Althaus, Schmidke, & Niklewski, 2006). This universal prevention programme consists of a professional publicity campaign directed at health professionals, as well as at the general public. It was launched in order to enhance awareness of depression and its symptoms, and to destigmatize attitudes towards mental illness, as well as to increase sufferers' motivation to seek help. Lectures and events, including a short film, were organized. These explicated characteristics of depression and brochures, leaflets, and posters with key information were also distributed. Training sessions were also offered to influential facilitators from the community, such as police officers, teachers, and geriatric caregivers, with the aim of enhancing their capacity to detect individuals having affective disorders, and to apply their new knowledge and skill in order to assist them in finding and obtaining the requisite primary care. Primary care workers, in turn, received further training in the diagnosis and treatment of depression and other mental illnesses. At the same time several *indicated prevention* initiatives were launched, for example, several self-help groups were formed to assist people in the throes of suicidal crises, including suicide attempters and their families. The measured outcome of this panoply of preventive efforts was a significant reduction in the number of suicide attempts (as compared with a control region without exposure to such intervention). There was also a decline, albeit not statistically significant, in the total number of completed suicides (Hegerl *et al.*, 2006; Hegerl, Wittenberg, & European Alliance Against Depression Consortium, 2009).

Suicide Prevention Programmes and Actions across the Globe

WHO and EU

In recent years, mental health policies and actions in Europe have greatly benefited from key documents issued by the World Health Organization (WHO) and the European Commission. The Mental Health Declaration (WHO, 2005) reflected official recognition of the need to develop and implement measures to reduce preventable causes of mental illness and suicide. The health ministers of all 52 participating member states of the WHO European region signed the Declaration, accepting responsibility for achieving this goal. Means of combating the causes of mental illness and suicide were adapted by the signatory countries on the basis of identified needs, available resources, and constitutional processes. Implementation, monitoring, and evaluation of these preventive efforts are coordinated by the WHO/EURO Mental Health Programme, with the help of other leading WHO Collaborating Centres (Wasserman, Mårtensson, & Wasserman, 2009). One example of such a centre is the Swedish National Centre for Suicide Research and Prevention of Mental Ill-Health at Karolinska Institute (NASP) which serves to coordinate and promote mental health and suicide prevention in the WHO European region.

A further impetus for prevention of mental illness and suicide in Europe was an important publication issued by the European Commission in response to the WHO Mental Health Declaration. The purpose of this 'Green Paper' (European Commission, 2005) was to create a platform of communication among relevant decision-makers and experts from different member states in order to facilitate and stimulate discussion of prevention measures, public health policies, and healthcare reforms aimed at promoting mental health and reducing suicide rates.

The Mental Health Declaration and the Green Paper were followed by a high-level EU conference during which the 'European Pact for Mental Health and Well-being' was adopted by the 27 EU member states (European Commission and World Health Organization, 2008). The Pact officially acknowledges that mental well-being is a human right, such that mental illness and suicide are to be considered significant problems throughout Europe, requiring concerted efforts at the EU level to help bring about a reduction in these problems. The Pact calls for action in five priority areas to prevent depression and suicide:

- improving the training of health professionals and key stakeholders;
- restricting access to potential means of completing suicide;
- taking measures to raise awareness of mental health in the general public, as well as among health professionals and other relevant groups;
- taking measures to reduce risk factors for suicide, such as excessive alcohol consumption, drug abuse, bullying and social exclusion, depression, and stress; and
- providing support mechanisms, such as emotional support helplines, following suicide attempts and for people bereaved by suicide.

It was also agreed that the Pact should be followed up by monitoring trends and activities, as well as by recommending suitable activities in member states, and their stakeholders (European Commission and World Health Organization, 2008).

Examples of suicide prevention in different continents

Sweden   The National Centre for Suicide Research and Prevention (NASP) was created in Sweden in 1994 following a parliamentary resolution to meet the need for knowledge about suicide and suicide prevention. In cooperation with the National Board of Health and Welfare and the National Institute of Public Health, NASP set up a Swedish National Council for Suicide Prevention. The Council comprised representatives from various community organizations, such as the Federation of County Councils, the Armed Forces, the National Police Board, and Central Board of the Church of Sweden (Wasserman, Nordenskiöld, Ramberg, & Wasserman, 2009). In 1995, the first Swedish national programme for the development of suicide prevention was published (National Council for Suicide Prevention, 1995). However, the programme was never ratified by the Swedish Parliament, and this lack of legislative backing meant that suicide prevention continued to depend mainly on the goodwill of the stakeholders.

Nevertheless, after the WHO Mental Health Declaration (WHO, 2005) was issued, the Swedish Government called for a more comprehensive suicide prevention programme to be ratified by Parliament. The new programme, drawn up jointly by the National Board of Health and Welfare, the National Institute of Public Health, and NASP, with contributions from six regional networks and organizations was completed in 2006 (Swedish National Board of Health and Welfare and Swedish National Public Health Institute, 2006). The programme includes the following strategies:

- promoting better life opportunities for groups most in need;
- minimizing alcohol consumption in target and high-risk groups;
- reducing the availability of means for completing suicide;
- training gatekeepers in management of suicide risk;
- supporting health services in suicide prevention;
- disseminating knowledge of evidence-based methods for preventing suicide;
- raising the competence of health professionals;
- systematically analysing all suicides that occur in the healthcare system in the course of care and for 28 days after discharge (the 'Lex Maria' regulations contained in the Act on Professional Activity in Health and Medical Services); and
- supporting voluntary organizations.

This comprehensive programme was ratified by the Swedish Parliament in June 2008. Activities comprising the prevention programme are continuously evaluated, along with process-oriented and epidemiological measures. In Sweden, suicide rates are now steadily declining in all age groups except among young people aged 15–24 years, whose rates are stable (Wasserman, Nordenskiöld, *et al.*, 2009).

Uganda   The Adjumani district of northern Uganda has a population of approximately 200,000 inhabitants, with some 100 deaths by suicide in 2004 (Ovuga & Boardman, 2009). Alcohol abuse and depression are also frequent (Ovuga, 2005; Ovuga, Boardman, & Wasserman, 2007). A comprehensive suicide prevention plan, based on the notion that prevention is the collective responsibility of every member of society, was implemented in 2007.

A series of seminars on suicide, depression, and alcohol abuse have been held for representatives from various sectors of the community: political leaders; healthcare; and education, etc. Their purpose is to inform participants of the importance of removing stigma surrounding suicide and mental illness, enhancing knowledge about suicide and depression, and strengthening political support and commitment to combat suicide. Primary care workers and other community facilitators have been trained to act as gatekeepers, and partnerships with agencies abroad were established to secure technical support for psychosocial services in the district. Motivation for suicide prevention activities was boosted by the introduction of district-wide policies and regulations regarding mental health promotion and suicide reduction (Ovuga & Boardman, 2009).

The Adjumani programme has not yet been fully evaluated. However, positive effects have already been observed. The authors report observing an increase in and greater openness in public discussion about suicide and mental illness. The local judicial system has also stopped prosecuting suicide attempters, although attempted suicide is still considered a criminal offence in Uganda.

Japan　In a suicide intervention study, Japanese researchers conducted a government-financed, controlled community study over a four-year period in the Akita prefecture in northern Japan (described by Mandell, 2009). Compared with other parts of Japan, the Akita area records an alarmingly high annual rate of suicide, with nearly half of surveyed residents stating they had close friends or relatives who had ended their own lives. The lead researcher, Dr H. Sasaki, describes problems of isolation, especially during the winter months, as one of the major factors. After confirming the high rates of suicide, a community outreach programme was designed and implemented, focusing on bringing together all members of the community and expanding social ties beyond nearby friends and family. Group activities were held in designated community buildings, aimed at promoting social interaction, reducing isolation, and conducting programmes to increase mental health awareness. With a budget of over 16 million yen (approximately US$180,000), investigators led by Yutaka Motohashi (2007) followed six Akita towns where such outreach programmes were implemented between 2001 and 2004. They found that even with a relatively uncomplicated intervention, suicide rates in experimental towns decreased by 50% as compared with control towns which saw no reduction.

Hong Kong　In Hong Kong, suicide prevention activities are carried out by government bodies, independent organizations, and university-affiliated research centres. The government has, for example, created fast-track clinics for depressed and suicidal older adults and a 24-hour crisis centre for suicidal individuals. Independent organizations offer help to people with known risk factors for suicide, such as unemployment or financial difficulties. The university-affiliated centres play a key role in improving doctors' skills in detecting suicidal behaviour and carrying out community-based suicide prevention activities (Yip, 2009a). Prevention activities intended to restrict access to the means of suicide have also been implemented in Hong Kong. As 50% of suicide deaths are as result of jumping from high-rise buildings, numerous safety measures have been applied to such 'hotspots' (Chen & Yip, 2009). A recent study attempted to restrict access to the second most common method of suicide in Hong Kong, carbon monoxide (CO) inhalation via the oxygen-starved burning of charcoal in sealed areas: in response to its popularity, bags of charcoal were removed from open-access areas in supermarkets in one Hong Kong district. Preliminary results from implementing this strategy show a decrease in charcoal-burning suicides in the district where the strategy was implemented, as compared with numbers in a similar district without such restriction (Yip, 2009b).

Unfortunately, coordination of the suicide prevention activities among the various stakeholders in Hong Kong is lacking, resulting in overlapping preventative efforts in some areas and neglect in others (Yip, 2009a). To reduce inefficiencies, a clear governmental commitment to a public health approach would encourage coordinated implementation of suicide prevention activities.

Cross-cultural   In an international study (Armenia, Azerbaijan, Brazil, China, Egypt, Georgia, Israel, Russia, Uganda) spanning five continents, researchers looked at the role of public awareness in promoting mental health, including in suicide prevention (Hoven, Wasserman, Wasserman, & Mandell, 2009). The rationale for this study was that cultural differences concerning the discussion of death or psychopathology may limit the help-seeking behaviour of those in need of intervention. Adhering to an empirically designed approach and with the financial support of the World Psychiatric Association and World Health Organization, Hoven *et al.* (2009) implemented a standard mental health aware-ness programme in schools in the nine countries listed above. Participants were asked to rate how comfortable they felt discussing mental health issues, both before and after the intervention. Results showed a significant increase in willingness to be open about their problems, suggesting that raising awareness of mental ill-health including suicidality, may contribute significantly to the mental well-being of the target population, regardless of cultural or societal differences.

The examples of suicide prevention efforts in the above-mentioned countries under-score the importance of creating a socio-political platform for preventive activities. An ideal solution would involve the creation of suicide prevention centres, connected to universi-ties with strong research and educational records, which would generate dialogue and cooperation among relevant government bodies and independent organizations, as well as coordination of the work of researchers, clinicians, and policy-makers. Once such a net-work is established, implementation of various preventive efforts may become easier and more thorough, with the potential for improved coordination and evaluation. A suicide prevention network is important for reducing suicide and for sharing the knowledge and experiences from the specific suicide prevention activities and experiences. A far-reaching enthusiastic network often takes a long time to establish, indeed, longer than it takes to modify existing suicide prevention activities or to develop new ones.

Dilemma of Evidence-Based Suicide Prevention

Evidence-based medicine aims to apply the best possible evidence collected by rigorous scientific methods to inform health-oriented decision-making. The best evidence base comprises numerous studies utilizing controlled trials demonstrating superior treatment efficacy. However, since randomized controlled trials are frequently not feasible or practical for assessing or evaluating the effectiveness of suicide interventions, methods of lower 'evidence value', such as quasi-experimental and ecological designs, need to be used instead. The most robust statistical methods for analysing data collected by these methods (such as time-series analysis) often require information covering long periods of time, both before and after an intervention. Thus, the process of determining the evidence base for universal or selective prevention strategies often takes more time than simply evaluating the efficacy of drugs. Hence, few studies of suicide prevention strategies, such as those described above, are carried out, and those that have been conducted constitute a limited and possibly inferior evidence base, as compared with studies with randomized control designs.

The relatively scant resources allocated to suicide prevention efforts make it difficult to justify investing in anything but strategies with a strong evidence base. The decision-makers who wish to employ universal and selective prevention strategies may encounter the dilemma of practicality: should a strategy that is based on the social and ecological characteristics of suicides in a region with a relatively weak evidence base (such as training of GPs in a region where GPs lack formal training in suicide) be used, or should one with a strong evidence base, but aimed at less relevant suicide-related factors for the region (such as firearm restrictions in a region where only a moderate number of suicides involve firearms) be adopted? Applying 'unproven' preventive efforts may be seen as diverting resources from established efforts that have been shown to save lives. On the other hand, the prospective gains from a prevention strategy lacking a sufficient evidence base may be lost during the lengthy establishment period. Determining the right course of action in this kind of dilemma is difficult, but the problem highlights an important requirement for maximizing success in future suicide prevention: both those who implement and those who evaluate suicide prevention strategies must collaborate in order to establish the most contextually appropriate criteria for *every* suicide prevention strategy.

Conclusion

We have demonstrated that prevention of suicide is achievable, and given the deaths of more that one million persons worldwide per year (Wasserman, 2004), it is certainly a necessary goal to find ways to prevent these untimely deaths. Achieving this goal requires systematic inter-governmental collaboration between policy planners, relevant decision-makers, clinicians, and professional organizations, as well as researchers. To facilitate the requisite mutual learning, and in order to attain the universal goal of reducing suicide rates across the globe, such cooperation is indispensable.

References

Bech, P. & Awata, S. (2009). Measurement of suicidal behaviour with psychometric scales. In D. Wasserman & C. Wasserman (Eds.), *Oxford Textbook of Suicidology and Suicide Prevention: A global perspective* (pp. 305–312). Oxford: Oxford University Press.

Bertolote, J. M., Fleischmann, A., De Leo, D., & Wasserman, D. (2004). Psychiatric diagnoses and suicide: Revisiting the evidence. *Crisis, 25*, 147–155.

Burns, J. M. & Patton, G. C. (2000). Preventive interventions for youth suicide: A risk factor-based approach. *Australian and New Zealand Journal of Psychiatry, 34,* 388–407. Cited in D. Kimokeo (2006), *Research-Based Guidelines and Practices for School-Based Suicide.*

Chen, Y-Y. & Yip, P. (2009). Prevention of suicide by jumping: Experiences from Taipei City (Taiwan), Hong Kong and Singapore. In D. Wasserman & C. Wasserman (Eds.), *Oxford Textbook of Suicidology and Suicide Prevention: A global perspective* (pp. 369–371). Oxford: Oxford University Press.

European Commission (2005). *Green Paper. Improving the mental health of the population: Towards a strategy on mental health for the European Union.* Brussels: European Communities.

European Commission and World Health Organization (2008). European pact for mental health and well-being. *EU High-Level Conference: Together for Mental Health and Well-being.* Brussels: European Commission.

Gordon, R. (1987) An operational classification of disease prevention. In J. A. Steinberg & M. M. Silverman (Eds.), *Preventing Mental Disorders* (pp. 20–26). Rockville, MD: US Department of Health and Human Services.

Hegerl, U., Althaus, D., Schmidtke, A., & Niklewski, G. (2006). The alliance against depression: 2-year evaluation of a community-based intervention to reduce suicidality. *Psychological Medicine, 36,* 1225–1233.

Hegerl, U., Wittenberg, L. & European Alliance Against Depression Consortium (2009). Focus on mental health care reforms in Europe: The European alliance against depression: A multilevel approach to the prevention of suicidal behavior. *Psychiatric Services, 60,* 596–599.

Hoven, C., Duarte, C., Lucas, C., Wu, P., Mandell, D. J., Goodwin, R. D., Cohen, M., Balaban, V., Woodruff, B. A., Bin, F., Musa, G. J., Mei, L., Cantor, P. A., Aber, L., Cohen, P., & Susser, E. (2005). Psychopathology among New York City public school children 6 months after September 11. *Archives of General Psychiatry, 62,* 545–552.

Hoven, C., Wasserman, D., Wasserman, C., & Mandell D. J. (2009). Awareness in nine countries: A public health approach to suicide prevention. *Legal Medicine, 11,* S13–S17.

Institute of Medicine (1994). New directions in definitions. In P. J. Mrazek & R. J. Haggerty (Eds.), *Reducing Risks for Mental Disorders: Frontiers for preventive intervention research* (pp. 19–30). Washington, DC: National Academy Press.

Jokinen, J., Nordström, A., & Nordström, P. (2008). ROC analysis of dexamethasone suppression test threshold in suicide prediction after attempted suicide. *Journal of Affective Disorders, 106,* 145–152.

Mandell, D. J. (2009). Symposium report: General comments and discussion: Social issues of suicide. *Legal Medicine, 11,* S581–S583.

Mann, J. J. & Currier, D. (2007). A review of prospective studies of biologic predictors of suicidal behavior in mood disorders. *Archives of Suicide Research, 11,* 3–16.

Motohashi, Y., Kaneko, Y., Sasaki, H., & Yamaji, M. (2007). A decrease in suicide rates in Japanese rural towns after community-based intervention by the health promotion approach. *Suicide and Life-Threatening Behavior, 37,* 593–599.

National Council for Suicide Prevention (1995). *Support in Suicidal Crises. The Swedish National Programme to Develop Suicide Prevention.* Stockholm: Modin Tryck.

National Institute of Mental Health (2002). *Mental Health and Mass Violence: Evidence-based early psychological intervention for victims/survivors of mass violence.* A Workshop to Reach Consensus on Best Practices. NIH Publication No. 02-5138. Washington DC: US Government Printing Office.

Ovuga, E. (2005). *Depression and Suicidal Behaviors in Uganda. Validating the response inventory for stressful life events (RISLE).* Ph.D. thesis. Stockholm: Karolinska University Press.

Ovuga, E. & Boardman, J. (2009). Suicide prevention in Uganda. In D. Wasserman & C. Wasserman (Eds), *Oxford Textbook of Suicidology and Suicide Prevention: A global perspective* (pp. 759–761). Oxford: Oxford University Press.

Ovuga, E., Boardman, J., & Wasserman, D. (2005). The prevalence of depression in two districts of Uganda. *Social Psychiatry and Psychiatric Epidemiology, 40*, 439–445.

Paykel, E. S., Myers, J. K., Lindenthall, J. J., & Tanner, J. (1974). Suicidal feelings in the general population: A prevalence study. *British Journal of Psychiatry, 124*, 460–469.

Posner, K., Oquendo, M. A., Gould, M., Stanley, B., & Davies, M. (2007). Columbia Classification Algorithm of Suicide Assessment (C-CASA): Classification of suicidal events in the FDA's pediatric suicidal risk analysis of antidepressants. *American Journal of Psychiatry, 167*, 1035–1043.

Rutz, W., von Knorring, L., & Wålinder., J. (1989). Frequency of suicide on Gotland after systematic postgraduate education of general practitioners. *Acta Psychiatrica Scandinavica, 80*, 151–154.

Rutz, W., Wålinder, J., Eberhard, G., Holmberg, G., von Knorring, A. L., von Knorring, L., Wistedt, B., & Aberg-Wistedt, A. (1989). An educational programme on depressive disorders for general practitioners on Gotland: Background and evaluation. *Acta Psychiatrica Scandinavica, 79*, 19–26.

Swedish National Board of Health and Welfare and Swedish National Public Health Institute (2006). *Proposal for the National Programme for Suicide Prevention: Public health and individual-oriented strategies and actions.* Stockholm: National Board of Health and Welfare.

Wasserman, D. (2004). Evaluating suicide prevention: Various approaches needed. *World Psychiatry, 3*, 153–154.

Wasserman, D. & Durkee, T. (2009). Strategies in suicide prevention. In D. Wasserman & C. Wasserman (Eds.), *Oxford Textbook of Suicidology and Suicide Prevention: A global perspective* (pp. 381–388). Oxford: Oxford University Press.

Wasserman, D., Mårtensson, E., & Wasserman, C. (2009). World Health Organization and European Union policy action, responsibilities and solutions in preventing suicide. In D. Wasserman & C. Wasserman (Eds.), *Oxford Textbook of Suicidology and Suicide Prevention: A global perspective* (pp. 369–371). Oxford: Oxford University Press.

Wasserman, D., Nordenskiöld, A., Ramberg, I-L., & Wasserman, C. (2009). Suicide prevention in Sweden. In D. Wasserman & C. Wasserman (Eds.), *Oxford Textbook of Suicidology and Suicide Prevention: A global perspective* (pp. 817–819). Oxford: Oxford University Press.

WHO (2002). *World Report on Violence and Health.* Geneva: World Health Organization.

WHO (2005). *Mental Health Declaration for Europe: Facing the challenges, building solutions: Report from the WHO European Ministerial Conference.* Geneva: World Health Organization.

Yip, P. (2005). A public health approach to suicide prevention. *Hong Kong Journal of Psychiatry, 15*, 29–31.

Yip, P. (2009a). *Suicide Prevention in Hong Kong.* In D. Wasserman & C. Wasserman (Eds.), *Oxford Textbook of Suicidology and Suicide Prevention: A global perspective* (pp. 765–766). Oxford: Oxford University Press.

Yip, P. (2009b). Prevention of suicides due to charcoal burning. In D. Wasserman & C. Wasserman (Eds.), *Oxford Textbook of Suicidology and Suicide Prevention: A global perspective* (pp. 369–371). Oxford: Oxford University Press.

CHAPTER TWENTY-EIGHT

Suicide in Asia: Epidemiology, Risk Factors, and Prevention

Murad M. Khan and Ehsan Ullah Syed

Abstract

Asia is the world's largest continent, occupying approximately half the earth's land mass and containing half the world's population. Although ethnically, culturally, economically, and religiously diverse, there are a number of factors common to all Asian countries, as well as some important differences. It is estimated that suicides in Asia contribute 60% to the global one million suicides annually, with three Asian countries (viz. China, India, and Japan) accounting for more than 40% of this figure. Other Asian countries with high suicide rates include Kazakhstan, Sri Lanka, and South Korea. The majority of people dying by suicide in Asia are young, and pesticides are one of the most common methods used. In many Asian countries, the male to female ratio is much narrower and in China it is reversed. Given that there are 10–20 attempts for every completed suicide and at least six people are directly affected by a suicide or a serious attempt, there may be as many as 60 million people in Asia suffering from the consequences of a suicidal act every year, but postvention remains a neglected area in Asia. Due to a variety of legal, socio-cultural, and religious factors suicide rates in many Asian countries are grossly underestimated and there are huge research and knowledge gaps. A fifth of Asian countries either do not collect national mortality statistics on suicide or even if they do, they do not report them to the World Health Organization (WHO). To reduce the enormous burden of suicide in Asia, there is a need for more and better research to inform policy and establish culturally relevant suicide prevention programmes.

International Handbook of Suicide Prevention: Research, Policy and Practice, First Edition.
Edited by Rory C. O'Connor, Stephen Platt, Jacki Gordon.
© 2011 John Wiley & Sons, Ltd. Published 2011 by John Wiley & Sons, Ltd.

Introduction

Asia is the largest continent of the world spanning almost half of the earth's land mass with a total area of 44,479,000 km². It spans a vast region from Turkey in the west to Japan in the east and includes the archipelagos of Indonesia, Malaysia, and Philippines in the southeast.

It comprises regions as culturally diverse as: the Central Asian republics of the former Soviet Union (USSR); the Middle East, which is predominantly Muslim and Arabic-speaking; and the Far East, comprising Chinese, Malay, Japanese, and Korean people, speaking a medley of oriental languages and following a variety of religions ranging from Buddhism and Hinduism to Catholicism and Islam. The diversity and heterogeneity of Asian cultures and religions sometimes makes it very complex to understand as a single region.

Quite frequently, Asian cultures are lumped together under the heading 'Asia' or 'Asian', and while there are many commonalties there are also important differences among Asian people. Notwithstanding these differences, strong family ties and spiritual aspects of religious practices and beliefs are a common thread running through the heart of Asia. Although urbanization and industrial development have led to many changes in Asian societies (so-called 'Westernization'), this has had both positive and negative effects.

Asia is also home to over half of the world's inhabitants with a population of more than 3.8 billion. China and India alone contribute almost 2.6 billion of this population. At the other extreme, there are countries such as Saudi Arabia which have a large land mass but are sparsely populated.

There is a great variation in the average gross domestic product (GDP) of Asian countries with higher levels in East Asia up to US$8.1 trillion (in China) and the lowest level in the Pacific Islands region at US$4.4 billion. The healthy life expectancy (HALE) of Asia is also quite variable. Afghanistan, for example, has a HALE of 35 years for men, while countries such as Kuwait and Qatar have a HALE of 67 for both sexes.

Poverty is endemic in Asia, and large numbers of Asian people live on less than US$1 a day. In many regions of Asia the population lives in less than ideal conditions, with political instability, financial mismanagement, corruption, and poor human rights being commonplace. On-going armed conflicts in many regions in Asia and the consequent displacement of people exacerbates the problem. Poverty is often cited as the underlying cause of poor health in Asia. A number of national surveys show a clear relationship between poverty and poor health status, such as high mortality rates, high rates of childhood illness, and lower utilization of health services (Pappas, Akhtar, Gergen, Hadden, & Khan, 2001).

Mental health in Asia has been a focus of international interest due to disturbing reports coming out of Asian countries wherever such research is carried out. In particular, the data about suicide show that a few largely populated countries in Asia account for 60% of the world's suicides. Applying the estimate that for each suicide there are at least 10–20 attempted suicides and at least six people are directly affected by each suicide, up to 60 million people may be suffering from the consequences of a suicide in Asia every year

(Beautrais, 2006). This, in turn, may contribute to the high prevalence of common mental disorders observed in many Asian countries.

Contribution of Asian Suicides to Global Suicide Rates

According to the World Health Organization (WHO) there are approximately one million global suicides annually (representing an annual rate of 16/100,000) (World Health Organization, 2001). Global rates have shown a steady increase over the last 50 years. This figure is projected to increase to 1.53 million annually by the year 2020. This rise is in sharp contrast to significant advancements in recognition and treatment of mental disorders, development of effective and safer psychotropics, and improvement in mental health services in many countries.

A closer inspection of suicide mortality data from some Asian countries offers a possible explanation: decreases in suicide rates in developed countries like Finland (Wilson, 2004) and England (Department of Health, 2002) are offset by huge increases in suicides in many Asian countries. For example, in India annual suicides increased 175% from 40,000 in 1970 to 108,000 in 2000 (Girdhar, Dogra, & Leenaars, 2003). In China, rates of suicide have increased from about 17/100,000 in 1980s to 28/100,000 in 1990s with 287,000 annual suicides in 2000s (Phillips, Li, & Zhang, 2002). In Pakistan, the number of deaths by suicide has risen from a few hundred up until the 1980s to more than 3,000 in 2003 (Khan, 2007). In Bangladesh, the overall national rates have increased from 8/100,000 between 1972 and 1988 to 10/100,000 in 1992–1993, while in Thailand, the country recorded increasing rates from 1970 (4/100,000) to 1980 (8/100,000), with further rises in 1998 (8.3/100,000), and in 1999 (World Health Organization, 2005). Suicide rates in Sri Lanka increased from 6.5/100,000 in the 1950s to 39.5/100,000 in 1985 (Maracek, 1998). South Korea's suicide rate rose from 6.8/100,000 in 1982 to 23.8/100,000 in 2004, while in Hong Kong rates increased from 11.8/100,000 to 18.6/100,000 between 1995 and 2004 (Wei & Chua, 2008).

Suicide statistics in Asian countries

The Mortality Database of the WHO lists deaths registered in national vital registration systems of different countries, by underlying cause of death (World Health Organization, 2003). It is important to acknowledge that the scale of the problem may be underestimated in some countries, including countries in Asia: given the stigma associated with suicide and the classification systems used, there can be a tendency to classify deaths of undetermined intent as accidents rather than as possible suicides.

The WHO database shows that there is no information on suicide for at least 19 Asian countries comprising 20.7% of the population. These countries do not report their suicide mortality statistics to the WHO. Suicide occurs in all non-reporting countries as well, but due to religious, legal, and cultural factors, official data collection and reporting are largely neglected.

Data from non-reporting Asian countries underestimate the true extent of the problem due to outdated population estimates and unreliable civil registration systems. China is an example of this problem. The official suicide rate published by the National Surveillance of Disease System is based on the information gathered by 145 surveillance sites across the entire country, which are sample-based using cluster random sampling. The population covered by the surveillance sites is about 100 million people, or 10% of China's population, and statistics from these sites are used to calculate suicide rates for the country overall (Phillips, Li, *et al.*, 2002). According to the surveillance system, the projected rates for China for 1999 were 13.9/100,000 (16.8/100,000 for rural areas and 4.0/100,000 for urban areas). These rates are considered underestimates based on the inability of the surveillance system to adequately track suicides in rural China, where the majority of people reside and where studies confirm that suicide rates are three to four times higher than in urban areas. When population distribution was corrected, the recalculated rates ranged from 22 to 30 per 100,000 (Phillips, Li, *et al.*, 2002).

Many non-reporting countries include those with a majority Muslim population, including 'mega-countries' with populations in excess of 100 million such as Pakistan, Indonesia, and Bangladesh. Suicide is regarded as a criminal offence in many Islamic countries, and religious and social factors influence the classification and registration of suicides. For example, in Pakistan and Kuwait both suicide and attempted suicide are criminal offences and many families do not disclose the true nature of the act for fear of harassment by police and/or for social reasons. Instead, they claim the act to be either an accident or a homicide (Khan, 2005). A recent study of suicide and undetermined deaths in 17 Islamic countries showed that in many culturally unacceptable suicidal deaths may be hidden in the 'Other Violent Death (OVD)' category of death classification, thereby artificially lowering suicide rates in these countries (Pritchard & Amanullah, 2007).

This is further compounded by the stigma of mental illness and psychiatric help-seeking in Asian countries leading to under-reporting of suicides, which may be as high as 30%–100% (World Health Organization, 2003). In some Asian countries, increasing suicide rates are denied for political reasons: acknowledgement of high or increasing rates may be viewed as a failure of government policies.

For all of these reasons, both suicide and attempted suicide may be under-reported in some Asian countries, leading to difficulties in estimating accurate national suicide rates. The lack of accuracy and reliability of suicide data makes it difficult to interpret the apparently low suicide rates in some countries, to compare Asian and Western suicide rates, or, indeed, to compare suicide rates among Asian countries, and makes it difficult to study trends within countries over time (Beautrais, 2006).

Trends within Asia

Despite the limitations in the availability of data, huge variations are observed in reported rates in Asian countries (Table 28.1). Rates of above 15/100,000 are seen in countries such as Kazakhstan, Japan, South Korea, China, and Sri Lanka, rates of 10/100,000 are seen in India, Singapore, and Kyrgyzstan, while those with low rates include Kuwait, Armenia, and Azerbaijan.

Table 28.1 Suicide rates (per 100,000 population) in Asian countries by year and gender (most recent year available) as reported to the WHO, as at 2008

Country	Year	Males	Females	Total	WHO estimates (2002)[a]
Kazakhstan	2005	45.0	8.1	25.9	37.14
Japan	2006	34.8	13.2	23.7	24.62
South Korea	2006	29.6	14.1	21.9	18.17
Sri Lanka	1996	NA	NA	21.6	31.91
Hong Kong	2005	22.0	13.1	17.4	–
China (selected areas)	1999	13.0	14.8	13.9	20.94
India	1998	12.2	9.1	10.6	17.38
Singapore	2006	12.9	7.7	10.3	10.28
Kyrgyzstan	2005	15.3	3.2	9.2	14.80
Turkmenistan	1998	13.8	3.5	8.6	12.50
Thailand	2002	12.0	3.8	7.8	11.08
Israel	2003	10.4	2.1	6.2	4.78
Uzbekistan	2003	8.1	3.0	5.5	9.01
Bahrain	1988	4.9	0.5	3.1	4.37
Tajikistan	2001	2.9	2.3	2.6	5.10
Philippines	1993	2.5	1.7	2.1	1.68
Kuwait	2002	2.5	1.4	2.0	1.78
Armenia	2003	3.2	0.5	1.8	3.35
Azerbaijan	2002	1.8	0.5	1.1	4.42
Iran	1991	0.3	0.1	0.2	8.22
Syria	1985	0.2	0.0	0.1	0.56
Jordan	1979	0	0	0	17.17

[a] The World Health Organization has estimated total number and rates of suicides for 194 countries of the world (World Health Organization, 2002). Estimates were based on four different levels of evidence: **Level 1/2**: Death registration data, complete or incomplete, containing useable information on causes of death is available for the country, and used to adjust regional YLD (Years Lost due to Disability) distributions for causes with significant case fatality. Partial country-specific information on incidence or prevalence of non-fatal causes is available. **Level 3**: Other forms of information on child and adult mortality or causes of death (e.g., verbal autopsy) are available. Country-specific information on mortality for specific causes is available. Partial country-specific information on incidence or prevalence of non-fatal causes is also available. **Level 4**: Country information on level of adult mortality not available and it is predicted from child mortality level or cause of death information for most causes not available, and cause pattern predicted using cause-of-death models. Partial country specific information on incidence or prevalence of non-fatal causes is available. http://www.who.int/mental_health/prevention/suicide_rates/en/index.html. Reproduced by kind permission of WHO.

Over the last two decades there has been a steep rise in suicide rates in many Asian nations, particularly in those with highly developed economies such as Japan, South Korea, and Hong Kong. Economic growth, as well as downturn, have been cited as closely associated factors for suicide in all three countries: South Korea saw unprecedented economic progress with a concomitant breakdown of social structures and increases in drug use, crime, and divorce (Ben Park & Lester, 2006); Hong Kong suffered a major economic downturn following the end of British rule with unemployment rising to a historic high of 8.3% in 2003, and among those who completed suicide in the 25–59 year age group,

Table 28.2   Suicide rates reported in different studies of Asian countries (including WHO non-reporters)[a]

Country	City/district	Year(s)	Rates per 100,000/year	Reference
Bangladesh	Jessore	1983–2002	39.6	ICDDR (2003)
Bhutan	–	2001	8.2	Dema & Dema (2009)
Bahrain	–	1995–2004	3.0	Al Ansari *et al.* (2007)
Iran	Ilam	1995–2002	18.2	Janghorbani & Sharifrad (2005)
Indonesia	Jakarta	1995–2004	5.8	Diani (2009)
Jordan	–	1980–1985	2.1	Daradkeh (1989)
Mongolia	Huhhot	1986–1991	3.8	Wang *et al.* (1997)
Nepal	Lalitpur	1997–1999	3.7	Thapa & Carlough (2000)
Pakistan	Rawalpindi	2006	2.86	Khan *et al.* (2008b)
Saudi Arabia	Dammam	1986–1995	1.1	Elfawal (1999)
Turkey	Trabzon	1995	2.60	Bilici *et al.* (2002)
UAE	Dubai	1992–2000	6.2	Koronfel (2002)
Vietnam	–	2002	0.98	Thanh & Minh (2009)
Yemen	–	2006	1.19	Saleh (2006)

[a] These were either diagnosed as suicides or died as a result of intentional self-harm and were registered as such by the legal authorities in the respective countries.

48% were unemployed and thus vastly over-represented (Chan, Yip, Wong, & Chen, 2007); and Japan with its strong work ethic and over-emphasis on occupational performance has seen occupation-related suicides due to tough work hours and demands. In 2004, some 70% of all suicides in Japan were among middle-aged males – those most likely to suffer in an economic downturn – with many of those who died leaving suicide notes citing financial problems as reasons for their deaths (Takashi, Takeo, & Yoshitomo, 2005).

Israel is geographically located within the Arabic Middle East, but many of its social and health indicators are significantly better than its neighbouring countries. It spends 7.9% of its GDP on health, which is close to many countries in the developed world. Israel reports a relatively low suicide rate of 6.1/100,000, which is higher than other Middle Eastern countries but less than other industrialized nations in the West (Central Bureau of Statistics, 2008). Studies from Turkey (Altindag, Ozkam, & Oto, 2005; Bilici, Bekaroglu, Hocaoglu, Gürpinar, Soylu, *et al.*, 2002) and Iran (Janghorbani & Sharifrad, 2005; Zarghami & Khalilian, 2002) highlight the growing problem of suicide in different parts of the two countries, respectively.

For countries such as Cambodia, Myanmar, Bhutan, Syria, Laos, Afghanistan, and North Korea (amongst others) data are neither reported to WHO nor are there any published studies by individual researchers; reports in the lay press seem to indicate that suicides not only take place regularly but are on the increase. For example, Bhutan's main newspaper, *Kuensel*, quoting police records, stated that there were 22 suicides in just the first two months of 2009 in the country compared with annual figures of 58 in 2001 and 34 in 2006 (Dema & Dema, 2009). This would give a suicide rate of 8.2/100,000 in 2001 and approximately 7.1/100,000 in 2006 (Table 28.2 summarizes a range of studies which

Table 28.3   Psychological autopsy studies in Asian countries

Study		Country	n	Sample	Type of study
1	Apter *et al.* (1993)	Israel	43	Selected (young males 18–21 years)	Case series
2	Cheng (1995)	Taiwan	113	Selected (aboriginal)	Case-control
3	Arieli *et al.* (1996)	Israel	49	Selected (Ethiopian Jews)	Case series
4	Vijayakumar & Rajkumar (1999)	India	100	Unselected	Case-control
5	Phillips *et al.* (2002b)	China	519	Unselected	Case-control
6	Gururaj *et al.* (2004)	India	269	Unselected	Case-control
7	Zhang *et al.* (2004)	China	66	Selected (rural)	Case-control
8	Chiu *et al.* (2004)	Hong Kong	70	Selected (elderly)	Case-control
9	Altindag *et al.* (2005)	Turkey	26	Selected (females)	Case-control
10	Conner *et al.* (2005)	China	505	Unselected	Case series
11	Chen *et al.* (2006)	Hong Kong	150	Unselected	Case-control
12	Li *et al.* (2007)	China	114	Selected (15–24 years old)	Case-control
13	Abeyasinghe & Gunnell (2008)	Sri Lanka	372	Unselected	Case-control
14	Samaraweera *et al.* (2008)	Sri Lanka	31	Unselected	Case-control
15	Wong *et al.* (2008)	Hong Kong	85	Selected (adults 30–49 years)	Case-control
16	Khan *et al.* (2008a)	Pakistan	100	Unselected	Case-control
17	Chavan *et al.* (2008)	India	101	Unselected	Case series
18	Zhang & Zhou (2009)	China	66	Unselected	Case-control
19	Wong *et al.* (2009)	Hong Kong	17	Selected (gamblers)	Retrospective case series
20	Zhang *et al.* (2009a)	China	105	Selected (young 15–34 years, rural)	Case series
21	Zhang *et al.* (2009b)	China	392	Selected (young 15–34 years, rural)	Case-control

report suicide rates in Asian countries). Similarly, in Indonesia the *Jakarta Post* gave suicide rates as 5.8/100,000 for the years 1995–2004 in the capital Jakarta (Diani, 2009).

Risk Factors for Suicide in Asia

Information on risk factors for suicide in Asian countries derive from more than 20 psychological autopsy studies that have been completed (Table 28.3). The majority of these studies are from China and Hong Kong, with contributions from India, Sri Lanka, Taiwan, Pakistan, Israel, and Turkey. These studies (with some exceptions) provide evidence of strong links between depression, schizophrenia, alcohol abuse, and suicide (Cheng, Chen, Chen, & Jenkins, 2000; Khan, Mahmud, Karim, Zaman, & Prince, 2008; Phillips, Yang, Zhang,

Wang, Ji, *et al.*, 2002; Samaraweera, Sumathipala, Siribaddana, & Bhugra, 2008; Vijayakumar & Rajkumar, 1999). In China and India the association between depression and suicide is reported to be less strong than that found in Taiwan, Hong Kong, and Pakistan.

A psychological autopsy case-control study of 100 suicides in Chennai, India found mood disorder in only 25% of the sample (Vijayakumar & Rajkumar, 1999). When adjustment disorder with depressed mood was included, the figure rose to 35%. Phillips *et al.* found that only 40% of their 519 suicides in China were suffering from depression (Phillips, Yang, *et al.*, 2002). Similar results are obtained from two psychological autopsy studies in Sri Lanka with 48% and 37% of the suicide subjects, respectively, deemed to be suffering from depression (Abeyasinghe & Gunnell, 2008; Samaraweera *et al.*, 2008). However, psychological autopsy studies from Taiwan (Cheng *et al.*, 2000) and Pakistan (Khan *et al.*, 2008) showed depression to be present in 87% and 79% of the suicide subjects, respectively. Other studies from Hong Kong on older adult suicides and 30–49-year-olds revealed that 76% and 51%, respectively, were suffering from depression at the time of suicide (Chiu, Yip, Chi, Chan, Tsoh, *et al.*, 2004; Wong, Chan, Chen, Chan, Law, *et al.*, 2008).

A number of authors (Jacob, 2008; Vijayakumar, John, Pirkis, & Whiteford, 2005) have argued that the causal role of depression in suicide has limited validity, while acute life stress and events play a greater role in suicides in Asia. These stressful life events include marital, relationship, and family problems as well as financial stress, all of which are also common precipitants of suicide attempts in the West. However, as Beautrais (2006) highlights, 'there may be cultural, historical, and contextual features of suicidal behaviour in Asia which may mean that acute life stresses more often lead to suicide in Asia than in the West' (p. 56). For example, in a number of Asian countries such as India (Kumar, 2004), China (Li, Phillips, Zhang, Xu, & Yang, 2007), Pakistan (Khan *et al.*, 2008), Iran (Zarghami & Khalilian, 2002) and those of central Asian republics (Campbell & Guiao, 2004) life stresses that young women face put them at high risk of psychological distress and subsequently suicidal behaviour: these include early marriage and motherhood, low social status, domestic violence, economic dependence on husband, and lack of personal autonomy. Among Asian males, economic and financial stresses, pressure to work long hours, loss of a job, and gambling, coupled with the shame and humiliation surrounding these events, may be potent precipitants of suicide. An example is a recent spate of suicides in India by farmers, which was directly attributed to financial losses due to the failure of cotton crops (Mishra, 2006). Pressure to achieve in exams is also cited as a precipitant in adolescent suicide deaths in Japan and India, where population pressures lead to intense competition for admission to prestigious schools (Beautrais, 2006).

Other authors have cautioned against 'reductionist' interpretations that portray the suicide 'victim' in a developing country as an impulsive individual who over-reacts to personal setbacks and in the context of an emotionally charged situation ingests easily accessible pesticides (Khan, 2005). With poor medical facilities for resuscitation there is a high ingestion to fatality ratio. This is because pesticides contain organophosphate compounds that when ingested require urgent and specific medical management, often intensive care, in particular ventilation. Yet in many circumstances this is not possible as individuals have to travel long distances to seek medical help, losing vital time in the process.

By contrast, reductionist models hold the individual responsible for their actions, focusing on the immediate proximal factors (e.g., a row with a significant other), and failing to take account of important underpinning distal factors (e.g., depression that may be related to, and arise because of, adverse social factors) (Moscicki, 1995). However, life-events and stresses and depression are not mutually exclusive, though they may be located at different points along the suicidal pathway. Hence, a model that takes into account both distal and proximal factors would better explain the differences in Asian and Western studies on suicide.

Insights into risk factors can also be thwarted by measurement problems. In particular, the use of Western instruments to measure depression in Asian countries may under-estimate the true prevalence of depression. For example, Phillips, Shen, Liu, Pritzker, Streiner, *et al.* (2007) used expanded culture-sensitive probes for depression in their psychological autopsy study in China, thereby increasing the number of subjects found to be depressed from 26.4% (using a standard questionnaire) to 40.2% (Phillips *et al.*, 2007). As a result, Phillips *et al.* (2007) recommend using a 'dimensional' rather than a 'dichotomous' approach in diagnosing depression, otherwise many sub-threshold cases, who, nevertheless, have a high risk of suicide in Asian countries, are likely to be missed.

The high levels of distress experienced by people in Asia due to adverse social circumstances adds credence to this argument. This may mean that the threshold for compromised mental health is set at a higher level, thereby 'hiding' the depressed mood that many experience. In other words, even if an individual is feeling low and depressed, they are expected to remain functional and fulfil their responsibilities because they have no other alternative. For example, in many Asian countries where there is no safety net of state support or welfare for the unemployed, people are expected to go out and work even if they become depressed.

Alcohol abuse or dependence also features in Asian suicides, though there is a great variation between different countries For example, alcohol abuse has been reported to be present in 44%, 34%, and 7% of suicides in Taiwan (Cheng, 1995), India (Vijayakumar & Rajkumar, 1999), and China (Phillips, Yang, *et al.*, 2002), respectively.

Figures can mask sharp gender differences too: for example, one study of completed suicide from Sri Lanka showed that almost two-thirds (61.4%) of males, but only 2.5% of females, were problem drinkers or alcohol-dependent (Abeyasinghe & Gunnell, 2008). Alcohol drinking is forbidden in Islam and rates of alcohol abuse are generally low in Muslim suicides: in Pakistan there was only one case of alcoholism among 100 suicides (Khan *et al.*, 2008), though a higher rate (7/21, 33%) was seen in secular Turkey (Bilici *et al.*, 2002).

Suicide is an important cause of death among those with schizophrenia, and approximately 10%–15% of patients with schizophrenia eventually kill themselves. Psychological autopsy studies give varying rates of schizophrenia in Asian suicides: in two studies in Sri Lanka schizophrenia was diagnosed in 12% and 11% of suicide deaths, respectively (Abeyasinghe & Gunnell, 2008; Samaraweera *et al.*, 2008), while the corresponding figures in other studies were 2% in Pakistan (Khan *et al.*, 2008), 7% in China (Phillips, Yang *et al.*, 2002), 8% in India (Vijayakumar & Rajkumar, 1999), and 7% in Taiwan (Cheng, 1995).

Previous history of DSH: high rates of fatality in first-time attempters

Suicide studies from a number of Asian countries, such as India, China, Sri Lanka, and Pakistan, show high rates of fatality in first-time attempters and as a consequence, previous history of attempted suicide in completed suicides is not as high as in Western studies (Eddleston, Karalliedde, Buckley, Fernando, Hutchinson, *et al.*, 2002). It is postulated that the choice of method (high incidence of pesticides and insecticides) coupled with poor medical facilities may offer a partial explanation for this observation (Gunnell & Eddleston, 2003).

Religious and cultural factors

Worldwide suicide rates tend to be lower in countries in which the predominant religion has strong sanctions against suicide (Bertolote & Fleischmann, 2002). The Islamic religion strongly condemns suicide (as well as alcohol which is closely associated with suicide), declaring it to be a major sin with exponents denied entry into heaven. Simpson and Conklin (1989) compared suicide rates of Christian and Islamic countries using a 71-nation cross-national analysis and showed that Islam has an independent effect in lowering suicide rates within many different nations (Simpson & Conklin, 1989).

In Asia, there are at least 20 countries with a majority Muslim population and suicide rates tend to be low in these countries. However, as Beautrais (2006) points out, in other Asian countries, the issue of religion and suicide is more complex, 'with the legacies of cultural practices that sanctioned suicide still apparent in current suicide statistics'. Two examples highlight this view: in India, despite being declared illegal, *suttee* (self-immolation by widows on the funeral pyre of their dead husbands), and in Japan, *hari-kari*, a form of altruistic suicide in which men kill themselves to save their honour, continue to be practised.

Gender differences

Gender differences in Asian suicides present interesting findings as compared with the West. Globally, more men than women kill themselves: in Western countries the typical ratio is 3–4 male suicides for every female suicide. However, in many Asian countries this difference is much narrower (e.g., India and Bangladesh) (Ruzicka, 1998) and in some cases (e.g., China) it is reversed, with higher rates in women than men, especially in rural areas (Phillips, Li, *et al.*, 2002).

The relatively higher rates in Asian women reflect the high rates of psychiatric morbidity found in this group. Table 28.4 summarizes the suicide rates of women in cities and districts of selected Asian countries. Many Asian societies are strongly male-dominated and

Table 28.4 Suicide rates of women in city/districts of selected Asian countries

City/country	Rates/100,000	Year(s)	Reference
Ghizer, Pakistan	61.04[a]	2000–2004	Khan *et al.* (2009)
Khulna, Bangladesh	27.0[b]	1996–1997	Yusuf *et al.* (2000)
Batnam, Turkey	9.3	2000	Altindag *et al.* (2005)
Ilam, Iran	26.4	1995–2002	Janghorbani & Sharifrad (2005)
Vellore, India	148.0[c]	1992–2001	Aaron *et al.* (2004)
Rural areas, China	30.7	1995–1999	Phillips *et al.* (2002a)

[a] Age group 15–24 years.
[b] Age group 10–50 years.
[c] Age group 10–19 years.

women play a largely subordinate role. This, in turn, contributes to high levels of distress leading to high rates of psychiatric morbidity and subsequently suicidal behaviour.

Higher rates of suicidal behaviour are also observed in married as compared with single women in Asian societies, leading some authors to conclude that unlike the West, where marriage is protective against psychiatric morbidity and suicidal behaviour, in Asian societies marriage is a source of stress for women (Khan, 2005). Factors contributing to this include early age at marriage, lack of autonomy in choosing a male partner (arranged marriage), pressure to have children early in marriage (in many cases for a male offspring), economic dependence on husband, and the joint family system (living with in-laws, other married brothers and/or unmarried sisters of the husband). Domestic violence is also a serious problem in many Asian countries (Vizcarra, Hassan, Hunter, Munoz, Ramiro, *et al.*, 2004). Under these circumstances, the young married woman's position is severely compromised, making her vulnerable to psychiatric morbidity and suicidal behaviour. In some areas of Turkey suicide is one of the five leading causes of death among young women (Tezcan & Guciz Dogan, 1990).

Common Methods of Suicide in Asian Countries

The availability of certain methods of suicide in a particular setting has a strong bearing on suicide rates. In any given setting the ratio of completed to attempted suicide is approximately 1 to 10–20. However, when more lethal methods of intentional self-harm are used more commonly (e.g., organophosphate pesticides in some Asian countries), the case-fatality ratio becomes high and rates of completed suicide approach that of attempted suicide. Controlling common methods of suicide can reduce suicide rates (at least in the short term). In Asia, one of the most common methods of suicide is ingestion of pesticides, which as a result of their organophosphate content lead to high case-fatality ratio. For example, in China, pesticides account for approximately 60% of suicides and approximately 80% of non-fatal suicide attempts (Conner, Phillips, Meldrum, Knox, Zhang, *et al.*, 2005). Conner *et al.* (2005) suggest 'suicides that are impulsive and of low intent are likely to be carried out by women, younger people and those with more acute stress, who then use pesticides stored in the home to make a suicide attempt'. Hence, in Asia many impulsive acts with low suicidal intent result in death (and therefore become suicides) due to the lethality of the substances (pesticides) involved, along with delayed and poor medical treatment. By contrast, in the West an individual with similar suicidal intent would be more likely to survive because she or he would use a less toxic substance (e.g., benzodiazepines or paracetamol) and would be more likely to receive better and timely medical care.

While hanging remains one of the most common methods of suicide across Asia, there is evidence that the popularity of methods can vary across regions. For example, in the Far Eastern countries of Singapore and Hong Kong, jumping from tall buildings appears to be a common method of suicide (Loh, Tan, Sim, Lau, Mondry, *et al.*, 2007; Yip & Tan, 1998), while in the south Asian countries of India, Sri Lanka, and Pakistan, as well as China, ingestion of pesticides is common for both attempted as well as completed suicide (Eddleston *et al.*, 2002). In Middle Eastern countries, such as Iran and Turkey, self-immolation and use of firearms for suicide is relatively common (Bilici *et al.*, 2002; Janghorbani & Sharifrad, 2005). Campbell and Guiao (2004) draw attention to the neglected but growing problem of self-immolation among young Muslim women in parts of the Middle East and Central Asia, which increasingly is becoming a cause of death and disability (Campbell & Guiao, 2004). Similarly, charcoal-burning in Hong Kong (Yip & Lee, 2007), use of a 'wheat pill' (containing aluminium phosphide) in Pakistan (Aziz & Awan, 1999), and yellow oleander seeds in Sri Lanka (Eddleston *et al.*, 2002) are examples of country-specific suicide methods.

The Challenge of Suicide Prevention in Asia

In 1995, the WHO declared suicide to be a global public health problem and the United Nations called upon member countries to devise national suicide prevention programmes (United Nations, 1996). Few Asian countries have responded to this call.

In many Asian countries communicable diseases and maternal and child health take precedence over non-communicable diseases. Mental health has very low priority in these situations. Furthermore, health and social sectors receive only a small fraction of the national budget, and few Asian countries have a separate budget for mental health. As a consequence, the ratio of mental health professionals to population in many Asian countries is very wide. For example, in Pakistan the ratio is one psychiatrist to 0.5–1 million population, compared with one psychiatrist to approximately 25,000 of the population in the United Kingdom (Karim, Saeed, Rana, Mubbashar, & Jenkins, 2004). Under these circumstances suicide prevention tends to gets neglected.

Japan is one of the few countries in Asia which has a government-supported nationwide suicide prevention programme. The explicit aim of the programme, initiated in 2000, was to reduce the suicide rate in the country by 30% by 2010 by focusing on three critical areas: pre-intervention (assessment of risk factors for suicide); intervention (identification of high-risk groups); and post-intervention (psychological support for family and friends bereaved by suicide) (Nakao & Takeuchi, 2006).

Management of depression

The relative role of depression and psychosocial stressors in Asian suicides has been discussed above. However, as Xaio *et al.* (2008) argue, 'irrespective of whether their absolute level of risk is somewhat lower in Asian countries, people with depression and related disorders form a distinct group for whom suicide prevention efforts should be targeted' (Xiao, Khan, Nam, Phillips, Thomkangkoon, *et al.*, 2008, p. 78).

Suicide rarely happens in a vacuum and there is invariably an interval between onset of suicidal thoughts/ideation and the act of suicide, which may vary from hours to days and weeks. In Asian countries suicidality is often not addressed, partly because of lack of awareness, but also because families and subjects do not know where to seek help, may lack the resources (healthcare in many Asian countries is out-of-pocket expenditure), or lack of adequate mental health services where these issues could be addressed. For example in India only 24 of 269 suicide victims were in contact with a mental health professional or family physician or were in treatment before the suicide (Gururaj, Isaac, Subbakrishna, & Ranjani, 2004). Studies have shown the effectiveness (and cost-effectiveness) of both pharmacological and psychological therapies in treating depression in Asian countries such as India (Patel, Chislom, Rabe-Hesketh, Dias-Saxena, Andrew, *et al.*, 2003) and Pakistan (Ali, Rahbar, Naeem, Gul, Mubeen, *et al.*, 2003). Consistent with this, Xiao *et al.* (2008) recommend three avenues to address depression in Asia:

(1)   encourage people with depression to seek professional care;
(2)   educate primary care health professionals to recognize depression and related disorders; and
(3)   improve the quality of treatment of depression and other disorders that convey suicide risk.

Management of deliberate self-harm

The WHO estimates that for every suicide there are at least 10–20 acts of deliberate self-harm (DSH). If one extrapolates from this estimate, in China there would be between 2.8 million and 5.6 million DSH acts; in India 1–2 million; in Sri Lanka 50,000 to 100,000; in Pakistan between 30,000 and 60,000; and in Japan between 300,000 and 600,000 DSH acts annually.

Many suicides are completed by individuals who have previously engaged in DSH. While the medical management of DSH is important and needs attention, the underlying psychological issues are rarely addressed, thereby missing an excellent opportunity to engage with those at high risk of future suicide: in the WHO SUPRE-MISS study of characteristics of DSH patients seen in emergency care settings in eight developing countries (including five Asian countries viz. China, India, Vietnam, Iran, and Sri Lanka) it was observed that between 46.5% and 98.3% patients were not referred for follow-up of any type. This reflects the lack of adequate mental health facilities where these patients can be referred for follow-up. In a study from India, 13% of 269 suicides had made at least one previous attempt, but 82% of these had not received any follow-up care after their DSH attempt (Gururaj *et al.*, 2004).

We propose that there is a need for every DSH patient to undergo a psychiatric evaluation, no matter how innocuous the act may appear. Emergency room personnel in Asian countries need to be trained in both medical as well as psychiatric management of DSH cases.

Controlling access to methods of suicide

Controlling access to common methods has been found to affect suicide rates. As already discussed, in Asian countries self-poisoning with pesticides is one of the most common methods for completing suicide (especially in the rural areas), accounting for 60% of suicides in China (Phillips, Yang, *et al.*, 2002) and 71% in Sri Lanka (Somasundaram & Rajadurai, 1995).

Safer storage of pesticides may be one of the means of prevention. A study by Hawton, Ratnayeke, Simkin, Harriss, and Scott (2009) on the acceptability of lockable storage devices for pesticides in Sri Lanka has yielded promising results. At the end of the 18-month study period, the majority of the 400 study households targeted kept the pesticides locked in boxes provided to them (Hawton *et al.*, 2009).

Another example comes from Vijayakumar and Satheesh-Babu (2009), who studied suicide incidence in farmers in the Andhra Pradesh state in India. They compared four villages which had stopped using chemical pesticides (CP) in favour of non-pesticide management (NPM) with four villages that continued to use CP. The number of suicides in the NPM villages reduced by 78.6% compared with 47.7% in the CP villages. Although the differences were not statistically significant (due to small numbers), the authors concluded that there was a definite trend in the reduction of suicides in NPM villages (Vijayakumar & Satheesh-Babu, 2009).

Restricting other methods of suicide, such as charcoal-burning in Hong Kong (Yip & Lee, 2007), or by introducing automatic barriers on subway platforms in Japan and Singapore (McCurry, 2006) are culture-specific and have also been found to be effective in decreasing suicide rates.

The role of media in reporting suicides in Asia

There is good evidence that media portrayal of suicide can lead to suicide contagion (so-called 'copycat suicides'), particularly if the original suicide is given undue prominence, sensationalized, glorified, or explicitly described (Pirkis & Blood, 2001). Before 1998, charcoal-burning suicide was unheard of in Hong Kong. After the first publicized incident, there were a series of copycat suicides. Charcoal-burning, from being unknown, immediately rose to be the third most common means of suicide in Hong Kong by the end of 1998, and by 2004 it had become the second most common, after jumping from heights (Yip & Lee, 2007). The method has now been exported to other countries in the Asia–Pacific region via media reporting (Beautrais, 2006). In Asia, media reports of suicide can be much more graphic and dramatic than what is deemed acceptable in the West. This example suggests the need for media guidelines on reporting practices (Beautrais, 2006) to be adopted across Asia.

Social policies

Many low-income Asian countries have social policies that do little to alleviate the suffering of the masses. Poverty, unemployment, illiteracy, lack of civic facilities, poor access to health facilities, the absence of health insurance or welfare are factors that adversely impact the overall mental health status of the population. In Pakistan and India, almost 50% of people live around or below the poverty line, though both countries are nuclear powers.

Vijayakumar, Pirkis, and Whiteford (2005) argue for a social and public health response to suicide, which should complement a mental health response. This approach acknowledges that 'suicide is preventable, and promotes a framework for developing an integrated system of interventions across multiple levels within society including the individual, the family, the community, and the healthcare system'. Modifying attitudes towards suicide through educational programmes and legal avenues (e.g., decriminalizing suicide) are key components of this approach.

Some call for governments in Asian countries to strive to reduce the enormous disparities between the rich and poor and introduce social policies that are fair, just, and equitable and that would address the real problems of the people (Patel & Kleinman, 2003).

National suicide prevention strategies/programmes

The importance of national suicide prevention programmes is well acknowledged, yet despite this very few such programmes exist in Asian countries. There is an urgent need therefore to develop these, ensuring that they are culturally relevant. Furthermore, to be effective they 'should take a risk factor approach to suicide prevention and provide a framework for universal, selective and indicated interventions at a number of levels' (Vijayakumar, Pirkis, *et al.*, 2005). Thus, programmes should: focus on restricting access to pesticides; provide training in early detection and management of common mental disorders to all primary healthcare professionals; upscale mental health services at primary care level and make them accessible to people; promote responsible media reporting of suicide cases; raise awareness about suicide; and provide support to families bereaved by suicide. As already described, many Asian countries lag behind more Westernized countries on these measures.

Future Directions

Suicide in Asia is a major public health problem with current data providing a gross underestimation of the overall burden of such deaths. Yet resources and preventive programmes to address the problem are lacking and there are huge research and knowledge gaps that need to be filled, including a need for more and better information and research to inform policy and the development of effective programmes. This includes an outstanding need for data collection at district, provincial, and national levels in all countries in Asia. Such data would be useful for analytical epidemiological studies of the characteristics of high-risk groups and the changes in those characteristics that take place over time.

We conclude that more well-planned research on risk factors specific to Asian countries and the relative contribution of these factors is urgently needed. The findings of such research could be used to test interventions in Asian settings.

One way forward could be to establish regional centres for suicide monitoring/surveillance and research, given the many commonalities in culture, social, and economic conditions across different regions of Asia. Sharing and exchanging information and research findings among nations with similar findings could greatly enhance the quality of the individual programmes. Crucially, all Asian countries should be encouraged to report suicide mortality data to the WHO. This would improve the registration and classification of suicides in individual countries.

Conclusions

Asia is the largest continent in the world and contributes substantially to the global burden of suicide. Clearly, as Beautrais (2006) states 'if 60% of global suicides occur in Asia there is an urgent need to reduce suicide rates in Asia if we are to achieve significant reduction in world suicide rates'. Yet the problem is not receiving the attention it deserves. Mental health *per se* has low priority in most Asian countries and within that, suicide prevention even less so. With limited resources, poorly established primary and mental health services, and weak political processes, suicide prevention poses a formidable challenge in Asian countries. Hence, there is a need for public health approaches to address the problem of suicide in Asia. This will be possible only when governments, public and mental health professionals, non-governmental organizations in collaboration with international organizations such as the WHO and International Association for Suicide Prevention (IASP) work more closely together. Only then can the seemingly impossible task of reducing suicide rates in Asia be accomplished.

References

Abeyasinghe, R. & Gunnell, D. (2008). Psychological autopsy study of suicide in three rural and semi-rural districts of Sri Lanka. *Social Psychiatry and Psychiatric Epidemiology*, *43*, 280–285.

Al Ansari A., Hamadeh, R. R., Ali, M. K., & El Offi, A. (2007). Suicide in Bahrain in the last decade. *Crisis*, *28*(1), 11–15.

Ali, B. S., Rahbar, M. H., Naeem, S., Gul, A., Mubeen, S., & Iqbal, A. (2003). The effectiveness of counseling on anxiety and depression by minimally trained counselors: A randomized controlled trial. *American Journal of Psychotherapy*, *57*, 324–336.

Altindag, A., Ozkan, M., & Oto, R. (2005). Suicide in Batman, southeastern Turkey. *Suicide and Life-Threatening Behavior*, *35*, 478–482.

Apter, A., Bleich, A., King, R. A., Kron, S., Fluch, A., & Kotler, M. (1993). Death without warning? A clinical postmorten study of suicide in 43 Israeli adolescent males. *Archives of General Psychiatry, 50*, 138–142.

Arieli, A., Gilat, I., & Aycheh, S. (1996). Suicide among Ethiopian Jews: A survey conducted by means of a psychological autopsy. *Journal of Nervous and Mental Disease, 184*, 317–319.

Aziz, K. & Awan, N. R. (1999). Pattern of suicide and its relationship to socio-economic factors/ depressive illness in the city of Lahore. *Pakistan Journal of Medical Sciences 15*, 289–294.

Beautrais, A. (2006). Suicide in Asia. *Crisis, 27*, 55–57.

Ben Park, B. C. & Lester, D. (2006). Social integration and suicide in South Korea. *Crisis, 27*, 48–50.

Bertolote, J. M. & Fleischmann, A. (2002). A global perspective on the epidemiology of suicide. *Suicidologi, 7*, 6–8.

Bilici, M., Bekaroglu, M., Hocaoglu, C., Gürpinar, S., Soylu, C., & Uluutku, N. (2002). Incidence of completed and attempted suicide in Trabzon, Turkey. *Crisis, 23*, 3–10.

Campbell, E. A. & Guiao, I. Z. (2004). Muslim culture and female self-immolation: Implications for global women's health research and practice. *Health Care for Women International, 25*, 782–793.

Central Bureau of Statistics (2008). Israel, available at http://www1.cbs.gov.il/reader/cw_usr_view_ Folder? ID=141, accessed 8 July 2009.

Chan, W. S., Yip, P. S., Wong, P. W., & Chen, E. Y. (2007). Suicide and unemployment: What are the missing links? *Archives of Suicide Research, 11*, 327–335.

Chavan, B. S., Singh, G. P., Kaur, J., & Kochar, R. (2008). Psychological autopsy of 101 cases from northwest region of India. *Indian Journal of Psychiatry, 50*, 34–38.

Chen, E. Y., Chan, W. S., Wong, P. W., Chan, S. S., Chan, C. L., Law, Y. W., Beh, P. S., Chan, K. K., Cheng, J. W, Liu., K. Y., & Yip, P. S. (2006). Suicide in Hong Kong: A case-control psychological autopsy study. *Psychological Medicine, 36*, 815–825.

Cheng, A. T. (1995). Mental illness and suicide. A case-control study in east Taiwan. *Archives of General Psychiatry, 52*, 594–603.

Cheng, A. T., Chen, T. H., Chen, C. C., & Jenkins, R. (2000). Psychosocial and psychiatric risk factors for suicide. Case-control psychological autopsy study. *British Journal of Psychiatry, 177*, 360–365.

Chiu, H. F., Yip, P. S., Chi, I., Chan, S., Tsoh, J., Kwan, C. W., Li, S. F., Conwell, Y., & Caine, E. (2004). Elderly suicide in Hong Kong – A case-controlled psychological autopsy study. *Acta Psychiatrica Scandinavica, 109*, 299–305.

Conner, K. R., Phillips, M. R., Meldrum, S., Knox, K. L., Zhang, Y., & Yang, G. (2005). Low-planned suicides in China. *Psychological Medicine, 35*, 1197–1204.

Daradkeh, T. K. (1989). Suicide in Jordan 1980–1985. *Acta Psychiatrica Scandinavica, 79*(3), 241–244.

Dema, K. & Dema, T (2009). Suicide – A slap in the face of society. *Kuensel Newspaper, Bhutan, 26 June 2009*, available at http://www.kuenselonline.com/modules.php?name=News&file=articl e&sid=12850, accessed 31 August 2009.

Department of Health (2002). *National Suicide Prevention Strategy for England*, available at http:// www.dh.gov.uk/en/Publicationsandstatistics/Publications/PublicationsPolicyAndGuidance/ DH_4009474.

Diani, R. (2009). Rising suicides worry psychiatrists. *The Jakarta Post, 13 September 2009*.

Eddleston, M., Karalliedde, L., Buckley, N., Fernando, R., Hutchinson, G., Isbister, G., Konradsen, F., Murray, D., Piola, J. C., Senanayake, N., Sheriff, R., Singh, S., Siwach, S. B., & Smit, L. (2002). Pesticide poisoning in the developing world – A minimum pesticides list. *The Lancet, 360*, 1163–1167.

Elfawal, M. A. & Awad, O. A. (1997). Firearm fatalities in eastern Saudi Arabia: Impact of culture and legislation. *American Journal of Forensic Medicine and Pathology, 18*, 391–396.

Girdhar, S., Dogra, A. T., & Leenaars, A. (2003). Suicide in India, 1995–1999. *Archives of Suicide Research, 7*, 389–393.

Gunnell, D. & Eddleston, M. (2003). Suicide by intentional ingestion of pesticides: A continuing tragedy in developing countries. *International Journal of Epidemiology, 32*, 902–909.

Gururaj, G., Isaac, M. K., Subbakrishna, D. K., & Ranjani, R. (2004). Risk factors for completed suicides: A case-control study from Bangalore, India. *International Journal of Injury Control and Safety Promotion, 11*, 183–191.

Hawton, K., Ratnayeke, L., Simkin, S., Harriss L., & Scott, V. (2009). Evaluation of acceptability and use of lockable storage devices for pesticides in Sri Lanka that might assist in prevention of self-poisoning. *BMC Public Health, 9*, 69.

Jacob, K. S. (2008). The prevention of suicide in India and the developing world: The need for population-based strategies. *Crisis, 29*, 102–106.

Janghorbani, M. & Sharifrad, G. (2005). Completed and attempted suicide in Ilam, Iran (1995–2002): Incidence and associated factors. *Archives of Iranian Medicine, 8*, 119–126.

Karim, S., Saeed, K., Rana, M. H., Mubbashar, M. H., & Jenkins, R. (2004). Pakistan mental health country profile. *International Review of Psychiatry, 16*, 83–92.

Khan, M. M. (2005). Suicide prevention and developing countries. *Journal of the Royal Society of Medicine, 98*, 459–463.

Khan, M. M. (2007). Suicide prevention in Pakistan: An impossible challenge? *Journal of the Pakistan Medical Association, 57*, 478–480.

Khan, M. M., Mahmud S., Karim M. S., Zaman, M., & Prince, M. (2008). Case-control study of suicide in Karachi, Pakistan. *British Journal of Psychiatry, 193*, 402–405.

Koronfel, A. A. (2002). Suicide in Dubai, United Arab Emirates. *Journal of Clinical Forensic Medicine, 9*, 5–11.

Kumar, V. (2004). Poisoning deaths in married women. *Journal of Clinical Forensic Medicine, 11*, 2–5.

Li, X. Y., Phillips, M. R., Zhang, Y. P., Xu, D., & Yang, G. H. (2007). Risk factors for suicide in China's youth: A case-control study. *Psychological Medicine, 38*, 397–406.

Loh, M., Tan, C. H., Sim, K., Lau, G., Mondry, A., Leong, J. Y., & Tan, E. C. (2007). Epidemiology of completed suicides in Singapore for 2001 and 2002. *Crisis, 28*, 148–155.

Maracek, J. (1998). Culture, gender and suicidal behaviour in Sri Lanka. *Suicide and Life-Threatening Behaviour, 28*, 69–81.

McCurry, J. (2006). Japan promises to curb number of suicides. *The Lancet, 367*, 383.

Mishra, S. (2006). Farmers' suicide in Maharashtra. *Economic and Political Weekly, 41*, 1538–1545.

Moscicki, E. K. (1995). Epidemiology of suicidal behaviour. *Suicide and Life-Threatening Behavior, 25*, 22–35.

Nakao, M. & Takeuchi, T. (2006). The suicide epidemic in Japan and strategies of depression screening for its prevention. *Bulletin of the World Health Organization, 84*, 492–493.

Pappas, G., Akhtar, T., Gergen, P. J., Hadden, W. C., & Khan, A. Q. (2001). Health status of the Pakistani population: A health profile and comparison with the United States. *American Journal of Public Health, 91*, 93–98.

Patel, V., Chisholm, D., Rabe-Hesketh, S., Dias-Saxena, F., Andrew, G., & Mann, A. (2003). Efficacy and cost-effectiveness of drug and psychological treatments for common mental disorders in general health care in Goa, India: A randomised controlled trial. *The Lancet, 361*, 33–39.

Patel, V. & Kleinman, A. (2003). Poverty and common mental disorders in developing countries. *Bulletin of the World Health Organization, 81*, 609–615.

Phillips, M. R., Li, X., & Zhang, Y. (2002). Suicide rates in China, 1995–99. *The Lancet, 359*, 835–840.

Phillips, M. R., Shen, Q., Liu, X., Pritzker, S., Streiner, D., Conner, K., & Yang, G. (2007). Assessing depressive symptoms in persons who die of suicide in mainland China. *Journal of Affective Disorders, 98*, 73–82.

Phillips, M. R., Yang, G., Zhang, Y., Wang, L., Ji, H., & Zhou, M. (2002). Risk factors for suicide in China: A national case-control psychological autopsy study. *The Lancet, 360*, 1728–1736.

Pirkis, J. & Blood, R. W. (2001). Suicide and the media, Part I: Reportage in nonfictional media. *Crisis, 22*, 146–154.

Pritchard, C. & Amanullah, S. (2007). An analysis of suicide and undetermined deaths in 17 predominantly Islamic countries contrasted with the UK. *Psychological Medicine, 37*, 421–430.

Ruzicka, L. T. (1998). Suicide in countries and areas of the ESCAP region. *Asia-Pacific Population Journal, 13*, 55–74.

Saleh, M. A. B. Q. (2006). Mental Health in Yemen: Obstacles and challenges: Arizona State University, available at http://www.wfmh.org/TRANSC/Maan%20Bari%20Saleh.ppt, accessed 28 August 2009.

Samaraweera, S., Sumathipala, A., Siribaddana, S., & Bhugra, D. (2008). Completed suicide in Sinhalese in Sri Lanka: A psychological autopsy study. *Suicide and Life-Threatening Behavior, 38*, 221–228.

Simpson, M. E. & Conklin. G. H. (1989). Socio-economic development, suicide and religion: A test of Durkheim's theory of religion and suicide. *Social Forces, 67*, 945–964.

Somasundaram, D. J. & Rajadurai, S. (1995). War and suicide in northern Sri Lanka. *Acta Psychiatrica Scandinavica, 91*, 1–4.

Takashi, A., Takeo, N., & Yoshitomo, T. (2005). Karajisatsu in Japan: Characteristics of 22 cases of work-related suicide. *Journal of Occupational Health, 47*, 157–164.

Tezcan, S. & Guciz Dogan, B. (1990). The extent and causes of mortality among reproductive age women on three districts of Turkey. *Nufusbil Derg, 12*, 31–39.

Thanh, H. T. T. & Minh, D. P. (2009). Suicide prevention in Vietnam. In D. Wasserman & C. Wasserman (Eds.), *Oxford Textbook of Suicidology and Suicide Prevention: A global perspective* (pp. 779–782). Oxford: Oxford University Press.

Thapa, B. & Carlough, M. C. (2000). Suicide incidence in the Lalitpur district of Central Nepal. *Tropical Doctor, 30*(4), 200–203.

United Nations (1996). *Prevention of Suicide: Guidelines for the formulation and implementation of national strategies*. New York: United Nations (document ST/SEA/245).

Vijayakumar, L., John, S., Pirkis, J., & Whiteford, H. (2005). Suicide in developing countries (2): Risk factors. *Crisis, 26*, 112–119.

Vijayakumar, L., Pirkis, J., & Whiteford, H. (2005). Suicide in developing countries (3): Prevention efforts. *Crisis, 26*, 120–124.

Vijayakumar, L. & Rajkumar, S. (1999). Are risk factors for suicide universal? A case-control study in India. *Acta Psychiatrica Scandinavica, 99*, 407–411.

Vijayakumar, L. & Satheesh-Babu, R. (2009). Does 'no pesticide' reduce suicide? *International Journal of Social Psychiatry, 55*, 401–406.

Vizcarra, B., Hassan, F., Hunter, W. M., Munoz, S. R., Ramiro, L., & De Paula, C. S. (2004). Partner violence as a risk factor for mental health among women from communities in the Philippines, Egypt, Chile, and India. *International Journal of Injury Control and Safety Promotion, 11*, 125–129.

Wei, K. C. & Chua, H. C. (2008). Suicide in Asia. *International Review of Psychiatry*, *20*, 434–440.

Wilson, J. F. (2004). Finland pioneers international suicide prevention. *Annals of Internal Medicine*, *140*, 853–856.

Wong, P. W. C., Chan, W. S. C., Chen, E. Y. H., Chan, S. S. M., Law, Y. W., & Yip, P. S. F. (2008). Suicide among adults aged 30–49: A psychological autopsy study in Hong Kong. *BMC Public Health*, *8*, 1–9.

World Health Organization (2001). T*he World Health Report 2001. Mental Health: New understanding, new hope*. Geneva: World Health Organization.

World Health Organization (2003). *Mortality Database*. Geneva: World Health Organization.

World Health Organization (2005). *Suicide Prevention: Emerging from darkness*. Geneva: World Health Organization.

Xiao, S., Khan, M., Nam, Y., Phillips, M., Thomkangkoon, P., Pirkis, J., & Hendin, H. (2008). Improving treatment in Asia of depression and other disorders that convey suicide risk. In H. Hendin, M. Phillips, L. Vijayakumar, J. Pirkis, H. Wang, P. Yip, D. Wasserman, J. M. Bertolote & A. Fleischmann (Eds.), *Suicide and Suicide Prevention in Asia* (pp. 77–87). Geneva: World Health Organization.

Yip, P. S. F., & Lee, D. T. S. (2007). Charcoal-burning suicides and strategies for prevention. *Crisis*, *28* (Suppl. 1), 21–27.

Yip, P. S. F. & Tan, R. C. E. (1998). Suicides in Hong Kong and Singapore: A tale of two cities. *International Journal of Social Psychiatry*, *44*, 267–279.

Yusuf, H. R., Akhter, H. H., Rahman, M. H., Chowdhury, M. E., & Rochat, R. W. (2000). Injury-related deaths among women aged 10–50 years in Bangladesh, 1996–97. *The Lancet*, *355*(9211), 1220–1224.

Zarghami, M. & Khalilian, A. (2002). Deliberate self-burning in Mazandaran, Iran. *Burns*, *28*, 115–119.

CHAPTER TWENTY-NINE

School-based Strategies for Youth Suicide Prevention

Alison M. Lake and Madelyn S. Gould

Abstract

This chapter describes school-based suicide prevention strategies that have undergone evaluation and have demonstrated effects on factors related to teen suicide. Types of school-based suicide prevention strategies covered by this review are screening for at-risk youth, adult and peer gatekeeper training, skills training, and comprehensive or 'whole school' programmes. Wherever possible, the chapter includes more than one evaluated programme exemplifying each strategy. The goals and methods of each programme are described, and results of evaluation research are summarized. Although none of these programmes can be said conclusively to reduce rates of youth suicide, beneficial effects of several programmes have been demonstrated to date. School-based screening programmes have been shown successfully to identify at-risk youth and to link them to mental health services. One gatekeeper training programme has been shown to improve adult and youth knowledge and attitudes about suicide; another has demonstrated success in linking gatekeeper-identified youth with mental health treatment; and a peer gatekeeper training programme with a screening component has been shown to reduce self-reported youth suicide attempts. Three skills training programmes have produced decreases in suicidal ideation. An ecological intervention has demonstrated improvements in youth attitudes towards help-seeking. Finally, two comprehensive school programmes have been associated with declines in youth suicide rates, although it is not known whether this decline is a programme effect. Of all the programmes reviewed, only one skills training programme demonstrated a potential for adverse effects. Based on these results, each of these types of youth suicide prevention programmes merits continued trials.

International Handbook of Suicide Prevention: Research, Policy and Practice, First Edition.
Edited by Rory C. O'Connor, Stephen Platt, Jacki Gordon.
© 2011 John Wiley & Sons, Ltd. Published 2011 by John Wiley & Sons, Ltd.

Introduction

The school setting provides numerous opportunities for suicide prevention efforts target-ing adolescents. The classroom, where many adolescents spend much of their time, may be used as a site for mental health screening or for psychoeducational programming. Members of the school population – students and adults including administrators, teach-ers, counsellors, and other staff who come into regular contact with youth – may be enlisted as suicide prevention personnel. Finally, the school as a system or social environ-ment may be designed or redesigned with the aim of promoting health and providing support for at-risk students. To be feasible, each of these approaches must win the endorse-ment of school administration, and must not be perceived as an undue strain on limited school resources such as staff time and classroom time.

School-based suicide prevention programmes emerged on a widescale in the 1980s, in response to a dramatic rise in youth suicide rates from 1950 to 1980. The first wave of school-based suicide prevention programmes was composed primarily of classroom-based, psychoeducational (suicide 'awareness' or suicide 'de-stigmatization') curricula directed towards the student body as a whole (Garland, Shaffer, & Whittle, 1989; Garland & Zigler, 1993; Shaffer & Gould, 2000). These types of curricula are based on the premise that misconceptions about suicide abound, and that students may not recognize or respond constructively to signs of suicide risk in themselves or in their peers. Suicide awareness pro-grammes thus aim to improve students' knowledge about and attitudes towards suicide, as a means to increase the likelihood of peer referral or self-referral of suicidal youth for help.

Evaluation of suicide education curricula has yielded mixed results and has identified several potential drawbacks to this approach (Ciffone, 1993, 2007; Kalafat & Elias, 1994; Kalafat & Gagliano, 1996; Overholser, Hemstreet, Spirito, & Vyse, 1989; Ploeg, Ciliska, Dobbins, Hayward, Thomas, et al., 1996; Portzky & van Heeringen, 2006; Shaffer, Vieland, Garlandd, Rojas, Underwood, et al., 1990; Shaffer, Garland, Vieland, Underwood, & Busner, 1991; Silbert & Berry, 1991; Spirito, Overholser, Ashworth, Morgan, & Benedict-Drew, 1988; Vieland, Whittle, Garland, Hicks, & Shaffer, 1991; see also reviews in Guo & Harstall, 2002; Gould, Klomek, & Batejan, 2009). The most significant drawback is the possibility that these initiatives may have iatrogenic effects (i.e., adverse effects caused by the programme itself), especially on the minority of youth who are most at risk. Evaluation of three school-based psychoeducational programmes revealed that a minority of students who had not iden-tified suicide as a possible way to solve problems prior to attending a suicide awareness programme did so after attending the programme (Shaffer et al., 1991). Evaluation of another suicide awareness programme showed some increases in hopelessness and maladaptive coping strategies among male students following exposure to the curriculum (Overholser et al., 1989). Finally, there is evidence that exposure to a suicide awareness curriculum may cause distress in students with a history of suicide attempts (Shaffer et al., 1990).

A further limitation of general suicide awareness curricula is that the mechanism by which these programmes might prevent youth suicide is not well specified. Educating adolescents about suicide risk leaves the burden on the adolescents to reach out to inform adults of their own or a peer's vulnerability. However, the reluctance of teenagers to con-fide in adults regarding their own or a peer's vulnerability has been well demonstrated

(Cigularov, Chen, Thurber, & Stallones, 2008; Gould, Velting, Kleinman, Lucas, Thomas, *et al.*, 2004; Husky, McGuire, Flynn, & Olfson, 2009; Wyman, Brown, & Inman, 2008). This reluctance to confide in adults has been shown to persist despite improvements in knowledge and attitudes about suicide following school-based psychoeducation (Cigularov *et al.*, 2008; Wyman *et al.*, 2008). Importantly, adolescents with past suicide attempts or recent suicidal ideation are significantly less likely to request help or to endorse communicating with adults about their distress than are lower-risk adolescents (Carlton & Dean, 2000; Husky *et al.*, 2009; Rickwood *et al.*, 2007; Wyman *et al.*, 2008). Deficits in adolescent help-seeking behaviour pose a significant barrier to the effectiveness of suicide awareness programming, and to other adolescent suicide prevention strategies. Throughout this review, we will revisit the difficulties posed by this barrier and will make note of the ways each programme reviewed here attempts to address or circumvent it.

Subsequent to mixed evaluations, general suicide education programmes have fallen out of favour, and none of the evaluated programmes reviewed in this chapter relies on universal 'suicide awareness' education as its sole strategy. This chapter focuses instead on later-developed, school-based suicide prevention programmes which have been evaluated and shown to have beneficial effects. It should be noted that much research in this area is still preliminary. The programme evaluations cited here include small-scale efficacy and feasibility trials, whose findings have yet to be replicated or extended. In addition, evaluations often assess 'surrogate endpoints' such as improved knowledge and attitudes about suicide, risk factor reduction, enhancement of protective factors, linkage to treatment, and increases in helping or help-seeking behaviour, each of which may or may not ultimately translate into a change in suicide rates (Brown, Wyman, Brinales, & Gibbons, 2007). Positive findings warrant continued attention to the programmes this chapter describes. However, conclusions about programme effectiveness should be postponed pending further evaluation. Evaluated programmes were identified through web-based searches using PubMed, PsycINFO, and Google Scholar, and through review of the bibliographies of cited articles. Types of strategies employed in these programmes include screening for at-risk youth, gatekeeper training, skills training, and an ecological or 'whole school' approach. Although some programmes combine more than one of these suicide prevention strategies, each programme will be listed under the type of strategy it fits best. Although suicide postvention, lethal means restriction, and college- or university-based programming for young adults are also important, we will limit this review to suicide prevention programmes designed for implementation in secondary schools.

Screening for At-Risk Youth

The use of universal mental health screening as a suicide prevention strategy is based on the valid premises that psychiatric conditions such as affective and substance use disorders are significant risk factors for suicidal behaviour, and that these conditions are widely under-identified and under-treated in adolescents (Gould, Greenberg, Velting, & Shaffer, 2003; Gould, King, Greenwald, Fisher, Schwab-Stone, *et al.*, 1998; Shaffer, Gould, Fisher, Trautman, Moreau, *et al.*, 1996). Detecting the presence of psychiatric risk factors and securing mental health treatment for vulnerable youth thus has tremendous potential to mitigate these risk factors and to reduce the rates of youth suicide. The goal of school-based screening for suicide risk and other mental health problems is to identify youth who screen positive for psychiatric symptoms associated with suicide risk, and to link them to mental health services before a suicidal crisis arises.

A number of brief self-report instruments that screen for suicide risk factors such as suicidal ideation and attempt history, depression, anxiety, and substance use have been tested and found to be valid and reliable for use among adolescents and young adults (Joiner *et al.*, 2002; Reynolds, 1990, 1991; Shaffer & Craft, 1999; Thompson & Eggert, 1999). Because large numbers of students may be identified by the screening tool as potentially at-risk, school-based screening programmes should include arrangements for second-stage screening for screen-positive students, as well as provision of referrals for students confirmed as at risk (Reynolds, 1991). Evaluation of a screening programme in six New York State high schools demonstrated screening's effectiveness in securing mental health treatment for at-risk youth. Of 317 students who screened positive for psychiatric risk factors for suicide, 71.6% were not in treatment at the time (Gould, Marrocco, Hoagwood, Kleinman, Amakawa, *et al.*, 2009); follow-up two years later revealed that 69.2% of the untreated, at risk students had sought and obtained mental health treatment following the screen. Parents' perceptions of mental health problems proved an important factor in determining whether youth were linked to services, leading the study's authors to recommend psychoeducation for parents as a complement to a school-based screen.

In addition to effectively achieving its goals, school-based screening for suicide risk appears to be free of iatrogenic effects. A group-randomized, controlled trial in six high schools in New York State reported that students who were exposed to questions about suicidal ideation and attempt history at baseline were no more distressed or suicidal at follow-up than were controls (Gould, Marrocco, & Kleinman, 2005). Importantly, there was no evidence of a negative impact, and some evidence of a positive impact, of suicide-risk screening on high-risk students in particular. Among students identified at baseline as depressed, those in the experimental condition were slightly but significantly less distressed at follow-up than were controls. Among students with prior suicide attempts, those in the experimental condition demonstrated significantly less suicidal ideation at follow-up than did controls.

Example: TeenScreen

TeenScreen evolved from a stand-alone questionnaire (Shaffer & Craft, 1999) into a two-stage screening programme which can be implemented in secondary school classrooms to identify students at risk for suicide and other mental health problems (Scott, Wilcox, Schonfeld, Davies, Hicks, *et al.*, 2009; Shaffer, Scott, Wilcox, Maslow, Hicks, *et al.*, 2004). The TeenScreen National Center for Mental Health Checkups offers free evidence-based screening materials, protocols and technical assistance to school districts, communities, and primary care physicians interested in implementing the programme (http://www.teenscreen. org/). In the first stage of the programme, a brief self-report questionnaire is administered during class time to all students for whom parental consent and youth assent have been obtained

(Brown & Grumet, 2009; Shaffer *et al.*, 2004). Questionnaires currently offered for this purpose include the 14-item paper-and-pencil Columbia Health Screen (CHS) and the computerized 52-item Diagnostic Predictive Scales (DPS). The CHS screens for depression, anxiety, anger and irritability, substance use, suicidal ideation, and past suicide attempt; the DPS screens for the presence of any mental health disorder. In the second stage of the TeenScreen schools programme, students who screen positive for suicide risk on the self-report questionnaire then participate in a face-to-face, on-site clinical interview with a school-based mental health professional. Students identified as at risk at the second stage are referred to a case manager, who will communicate with the youth's family and assist in linking the youth to mental health services for further evaluation.

One measure of the effectiveness of school-based screening is its ability to identify at-risk students who had not previously been identified as at risk. When TeenScreen was administered to a convenience-based sample of 1,729 students from seven high schools in the New York City metropolitan area using the Columbia Suicide Screen (CSS) as the first-stage instrument, the screen identified 100% of students in the highest risk group (assessed through a diagnostic interview as having either recent suicidal ideation or a past suicide attempt, in combination with a current mood, anxiety, or substance use disorder), including 37% who had not been identified as at risk by school personnel (Scott *et al.*, 2009). A further measure of screening's effectiveness is whether youth identified as at risk can be successfully linked to mental health services. Following administration of TeenScreen in 13 middle and high schools in Washington, DC, 62% of screen-positive youth were successfully linked with mental health services (attending at least one appointment) by one month after the screen, and 70% by six months after the screen (Brown & Grumet, 2009). Notably, at six months after screening, 86% of youth referred to school-based mental health treatment had attended at least one session, compared with only 41% of youth referred to non-school-based, community providers. The significance and generalizability of these findings are limited, however, by a student participation rate of only 14%, partly a result of the study's requirement of active parental consent for participation in TeenScreen.

Limitations

There are a number of practical obstacles to the implementation of universal school-based screening for suicide risk. To be ready to provide referrals for students identified as at risk, schools need to have relationships with accessible mental health providers in place before any screening programme is implemented (Gutierrez, Watkins, & Collura, 2004; Hallfors, Brodish, Khatapoush, Sanchez, Cho, & Steckler, 2006); once referrals are made, school personnel may need to devote considerable effort to follow up to ensure the connection to services is completed. Despite the high rates of sensitivity and specificity achieved by screening questionnaires, screenings in general school populations tend to yield large numbers of false positives (students who screen positive for suicide risk but who are found not to be at risk upon further evaluation), placing a significant burden on schools and mental health providers. Perhaps partly for these reasons, school-wide student screening programmes have been rated by high school principals and other school personnel as significantly less acceptable than curriculum-based and staff training programmes (Eckert, Miller, DuPaul, & Riley-Tillman, 2003; Miller, Eckert, DuPaul, & White, 1999; Scherff, Eckert, & Miller, 2005). Moreover, some community members have also voiced opposition to screening efforts, describing these efforts as a violation of the family's right to privacy (Ashford, 2005) because of their misconception that the screening of their children is mandatory (Weist, Rubin, Moore, Adelsheim, & Wrobel, 2007). Because suicide risk 'waxes and wanes' over time, multiple screenings may be necessary to minimize 'false negatives' (at-risk students who screen negative for suicide risk at a particular point in time) (Berman & Jobes, 1995) and to identify all at-risk students. Finally, the ultimate success of this strategy is dependent on the effectiveness of the mental health services to which youth are referred.

Discussion

School-based mental health screening programmes have the demonstrated capacity to identify at-risk youth who may not otherwise have been identified, and to link at-risk youth to mental health services who might otherwise have gone untreated. Screening may therefore be expected to reduce rates of adolescent suicide by mitigating the risk factor of untreated psychopathology. However, whether screening in fact reduces rates of adolescent suicide has not been evaluated. Low student participation rates may reduce the reach of screening programmes, and low consumer acceptability ratings by school personnel may negatively impact the feasibility of implementing screening programmes in schools. Nonetheless, screening provides an effective way to identify and refer at-risk youth without relying on teenagers to initiate help-seeking for themselves or for their peers (Husky *et al.*, 2009).

Gatekeeper Training

Gatekeeper training is designed to give teens and adults in the school environment the knowledge and skills needed to identify at-risk youth and to take appropriate action (Garland & Zigler, 1993; Gould *et al.*, 2003; Kalafat & Elias, 1995). Like screening programmes, gatekeeper training programmes are geared towards early detection and intervention with youth at risk of suicide. In comparison with screening programmes, however, gatekeeper training programmes use different mechanisms of identification and different criteria for assessing risk. As previously noted, screening uses validated self-completion questionnaires and face-to-face clinical interviews to assess students for suicidal ideation and behaviours as well as for symptoms of underlying affective and substance use disorders, which are known long-term risk factors for suicidal behaviour (Brent, Perper, Moritz, Allman, Friend, *et al.*, 1993). Gatekeeper training instead relies on trained lay people in the students' day-to-day environment to recognize and respond to outwardly visible warning signs of imminent suicide risk (Rudd, Berman, Joiner, Nock, Silverman, *et al.*, 2006). Warning signs include verbalizations (e.g., talk about dying and/or suicide, saying goodbye) and behavioural changes (e.g., reckless behaviour, giving away possessions, sudden changes in mood) that can be read as possible 'cries for help' in the period immediately preceding a suicide attempt. In contrast to the one-time or periodic assessment that can be provided by screening programmes, training members of the school community as gatekeepers, when effective, should keep students under almost daily surveillance for the emergence of these warning signs.

Gatekeeper training programmes have been developed for both adults and teens. Gatekeeper training for school personnel is based on the premise that improving school adults' knowledge about and attitudes towards suicide will empower those adults to recognize warning signs of suicide risk in students, and to intervene with students identified as at risk. Training adults in the school environment to take the active step of reaching out to potentially at-risk youth presents a possible way around the barrier of adolescents' failure to seek help. Gatekeeper training for students is based on the premise that teenagers are more likely to confide in peers than in adults (Aseltine & DeMartino, 2004; Kalafat & Elias, 1994, 1995), and that unprepared students may fail to respond constructively to confidences from an at-risk peer. Like suicide awareness curricula, gatekeeper training programmes for students may be offered to all students during class time, but these programmes differ from general suicide awareness curricula in their emphasis on specific steps students can take in responding to or intervening with an at-risk peer – including encouraging that peer to confide in an adult. These programmes often use participatory role play to build students' skills and confidence in the gatekeeper role.

Example 1: Question, Persuade, and Refer (QPR)

QPR gatekeeper training is designed for all adults in regular contact with youth, including teachers, school administrators, school nurses and counsellors, and support staff. The training can be delivered onsite by a certified QPR instructor, or completed online in the span of one to two hours (http://qprinstitute.com). QPR stands for the three steps gatekeepers are taught to use when faced with a potentially suicidal student: Question, Persuade, and Refer (Quinnett, 1995, 2007). QPR-trained gatekeepers should be equipped to recognize the warning signs of suicide, to feel confident in approaching and questioning youth about suicide, and to refer the youth to treatment.

A randomized, controlled trial of QPR provided gatekeeper training for 166 school staff across 16 schools in the school district of Cobb County, Georgia (Wyman *et al.*, 2008). One hundred and seventy-six staff from 16 matched schools in the district served as controls, and participants were stratified by job role. Staff completed a suicide prevention survey before the training and at one-year follow-up. The evaluation demonstrated improvements in school staff members' knowledge of suicide warning signs, and in their self-perceived preparedness to perform a 'gatekeeper' role in their school. However, only a small proportion of staff (14%) reported an increase in actual communication with students about suicide. These staff tended to be those who reported communication with students about thoughts and feelings prior to the training. Similarly, the majority of referral behaviours occurred in those school staff already in close communication with students. This finding suggests that gatekeeper training should not, or need not, target all adults in a school, since only a sub-set of school staff may be predisposed or positioned to make effective use of the training. In this evaluation, these 'natural gatekeepers' were more likely to be found among staff in health and social services roles (i.e., school nurses and counsellors). The evaluation included no direct measures of staff members' interactions with students and did not assess programme effects on rates of identification and referral of suicidal students for treatment, on rates of mental health service use, or on rates of depression or suicidal behaviour.

Although a version of QPR has been developed for students, the QPR Institute suggests this training might be most appropriate for students already in 'peer helper' roles, and recommends that students be trained only after all school adults whom students might approach for help have already received QPR training (http://www.qprinstitute.com). QPR Institute also recommends that gatekeeper training be implemented not as a stand-alone intervention but as one piece of a 'systems approach' to youth suicide prevention.

Example 2: SOS – Signs of Suicide

SOS – Signs of Suicide is a two-day classroom-based intervention for students developed by the non-profit organization Screening for Mental Health, Inc., originator of National Depression Screening Day (http://www.mentalhealthscreening.org/). Although the SOS programme includes a screening component, its 'primary objectives are to educate teens that depression is a treatable illness and to equip them to respond to a potential suicide in a friend or family member using the SOS technique' (http://www.mentalhealthscreening.org/). SOS begins with an 'action-oriented' educational curriculum (implemented via video and group discussion) in which the students learn to ACT: Acknowledge the signs of depression or suicidal thoughts in a friend; let the friend know you Care and want to help; and Tell a responsible adult. The curriculum is followed by a brief self-screening for depression and other risk factors associated with suicide. Schools are given the option of conducting the screening anonymously, in which case the students evaluate their own level of risk and are provided with instructions about seeking treatment if needed. In the event that scores are kept anonymous, the school has no means of identifying or following up screen-positive youth in accordance with the goals of school-based screening; in this context, the screen functions as a self-education tool. For this reason, this chapter classifies SOS as a peer gatekeeper programme, rather than as a screening programme.

A survey evaluation of the implementation of SOS in 92 US high schools reported favourable ratings by school personnel, with higher ratings given to the educational than to the screening component (Aseltine, 2003). No adverse reactions to the programme were found. The evaluation also reported a 60% increase in student help-seeking behaviour in the 30 days following the programme, as compared with the monthly average in the previous year. Help-seeking was measured in terms of the number of students reporting to the school nurse or school counsellor for help with emotional problems. A smaller increase in students seeking help on behalf of friends did not reach statistical significance. Neither the risk status nor the clinical outcomes of the self-referring students are known, and the evaluation did not include a control group. A subsequent randomized controlled trial of the SOS programme in five urban high schools in Connecticut and Georgia reported modest improvements in students' knowledge and attitudes about suicide following the programme, but no effect on help-seeking behaviour or suicidal ideation as measured by student self-reports (Aseltine & DeMartino, 2004). Importantly, this evaluation showed a significant decrease in students' self-reported suicide attempts in the three months following implementation of the programme. Although the mechanism is unclear, the evaluators speculate that students' improved understanding of depression and suicide may be responsible for the reduced suicide attempt rate, independent of any change in help-seeking or suicidal thoughts. In the evaluation's second year, the programme was extended to four additional high schools in suburban western Massachusetts and reported comparable results (Aseltine, 2007).

Example 3: Many Helping Hearts

An evaluation of the Many Helping Hearts peer gatekeeper training programme was conducted by Stuart, Waalen, and Haelstromm (2003) in eight high schools in Vancouver, British Columbia. Two half-day 'skill-based training sessions' covered the following: '(a) active listening skills, (b) self-care and setting limits, (c) crisis theory, (d) signals of suicide, (e) suicide risk assessment, (f) role-play scenarios involving suicidal youth, and (g) community resources' (Stuart *et al.*, 2003, p. 324). A total of 65 adolescents participated in the evaluation, which employed a questionnaire administered before the training, immediately after the completion of training, and three months following training. The evaluation demonstrated significant self-reported improvements in knowledge, attitudes, and skills following training and at the end of three months. However, the study did not include a control group and did not evaluate actual helping or help-seeking behaviour before or after the training. Effects on suicidal thoughts and behaviours were also not evaluated.

Additional Gatekeeper Training Programmes of Note

Applied Suicide Intervention Skills Training (ASIST) (see http://www.livingworks.net/) is an adult gatekeeper training programme which can be implemented in communities, workplaces, or schools. ASIST training takes the form of two full days of instruction and role-play, and provides crisis intervention skills that are intended to prepare participants to respond competently to individuals at imminent risk of suicide. An evaluation of the fidelity and effectiveness of ASIST training for telephone crisis workers is underway (Gould, 2009). ASIST has not yet been evaluated in a secondary school setting.

The Yellow Ribbon Suicide Prevention Program (http://www.yellowribbon.org) is a community-based youth suicide prevention programme that provides training for adult and peer gatekeepers, seminars for parents, and guidelines for community action. An important tool of the programme is the 'It's OK to ask 4 help!' Yellow Ribbon card. Yellow Ribbon also has not been evaluated specifically for use in schools.

Limitations

Systematic evaluation of the effectiveness of school-based gatekeeper training programmes in preventing youth suicide presents a challenge that has not fully been met. Although these programmes effectively improve trainees' confidence in their abilities to recognize warning signs and to intervene with at-risk students (e.g., King & Smith, 2000), it is largely unknown to what extent self-reported knowledge and confidence translate into behaviour. Like school-based screening programmes, gatekeeper training programmes can also be evaluated in terms of their success in identifying at-risk youth and linking them to mental health services. An evaluation of service use by at-risk youth identified through a gatekeeper training programme in the Los Angeles Unified School District reported that 72% of youth referred to community or school-based mental health treatment had received treatment five months after contact with the programme, based on interviews with randomly selected parents (Kataoka, Stein, Nadeem, & Wong, 2007). For the most part, the services used were not the services to which the youth had been referred. As in the case of school-based screening, parents' perceptions of the need for mental healthcare were a determining factor in referral follow-through. This rate of linkage to services following gatekeeper intervention is comparable with the rates found for school-based screening programmes (e.g., Brown & Grumet, 2009; Gould *et al.*, 2009). However, there has been no parallel evaluation of the sensitivity or specificity of gatekeepers' identification of at-risk youth, and there has been some suggestion that gatekeepers may under-identify youth in need of intervention (Kataoka, 2003, 2007).

Discussion

Like school-based screening programmes, gatekeeper training programmes require that schools establish adequate referral networks or other treatment resources prior to implementation of the programme. There is some suggestion that gatekeeper training is most effective in the context of pre-existing channels of communication between students and school adults. In the event that gatekeeper training successfully facilitates communication between at-risk youth and a caring adult or peer, it is possible that this supportive interaction may have a protective effect independent of any treatment referral that is given; however, this possibility has not yet been evaluated.

Skills Training

In contrast to suicide awareness curricula, classroom-based skills training programmes may or may not focus explicitly on the issue of suicide. Instead, these programmes aim to prevent suicide through the enhancement of problem-solving, coping, and cognitive skills which have been found to be impaired in suicidal youth (e.g., Asarnow, Carlson, & Guthrie, 1987; Cole, 1989; Rotheram-Borus, Trautman, & Dopkins Schrout, 1990). They may also target communication and other social skills with the goal of increasing social connectedness, another area where suicidal youth have been shown to have deficits (Berman & Jobes, 1991; Borowsky, Ireland, & Resnick, 2001; Borowsky, Resnick, Ireland, & Blum, 1999; McKeown, Garrison, Cuffe, Waller, Jackson, *et al.*, 1998). It is hoped that developing these skills may 'immunize' students against suicidal feelings and behaviours, and may help to mitigate suicide risk factors such as depression, hopelessness, and drug abuse. Some skills training programmes (e.g., Klingman & Hochdorf, 1993) include a peer gatekeeper component, where students learn how to interact with peers in crisis, but a primary goal of these programmes is to endow students with protective skills before their distress reaches crisis levels. Skills training programmes may be presented universally or may be targeted at a specific population known to be at higher risk of suicide, for example, Native American youth (LaFromboise & Howard-Pitney, 1994, 1995; LaFromboise & Lewis, 2008), or potential high school dropouts (Eggert, Thompson, Herting, & Nicholas, 1994; Eggert, Thompson, Herting, & Randell, 2001). Often more intensive than either suicide awareness curricula or peer gatekeeper training programmes, these programmes may be delivered in one or more sessions per week over the course of a semester or a school year, rather than in a few hours or days.

Example 1: Zuni/American Indian Life Skills Development Curricula

The Zuni Life Skills Development Curriculum (ZLS) was developed specifically for the Zuni pueblo in New Mexico, in response to that community's concern about its rising rate of youth suicide (LaFromboise & Howard-Pitney, 1994, 1995). Zuni cultural values were taken into account in the design of the curriculum's content and protocols (LaFromboise & Howard-Pitney, 1994). ZLS is designed to be taught during a regular class period, three times a week, for 30 weeks in one school year. The course covers the following seven units: '(a) building self-esteem; (b) identifying emotions and stress; (c) increasing communication and problem-solving skills; (d) recognizing and eliminating self-destructive behavior, such as pessimistic thoughts or anger reactivity; (e) receiving suicide information; (f) receiving suicide intervention training; and (g) setting personal and community goals' (LaFromboise & Howard-Pitney, 1995).

A controlled evaluation of ZLS used pre- and post-intervention self-report surveys in combination with a behavioural evaluation of students' role plays at the end of the course. The evaluation found reductions in self-reported suicidal ideation and hopelessness in the intervention group, but no reduction in depression. There was no programme effect on students' self-efficacy. During role play, the intervention group demonstrated improvements in problem-solving skills and in suicide intervention skills, more notably in milder suicide scenarios (LaFromboise & Howard-Pitney, 1995). More recently, this programme has been expanded into the American Indian Life Skills Development Curriculum (AILS), which retains certain pan-Indian values, but can be further adapted for use in different tribal communities. The authors of the programme emphasize the importance of developing relationships with school administrators, community leaders, and parents, whose support and endorsement can be critical to the success and survival of the programme (LaFromboise & Lewis, 2008).

Example 2: Reconnecting Youth, CAST and CARE

Reconnecting Youth (RY) is a semester-long course for high school students at risk of dropout, which targets school performance, drug involvement, and suicide risk (Eggert, 2001; http://www.reconnectingyouth.com/ry/index.html). The course, scheduled to meet daily, aims to enhance protective factors and reduce risk factors for suicide using two mechanisms: life skills training and the mobilization of social support in the form of a positive peer network structure (Eggert, Thompson, Herting, & Nicholas, 1995). Evaluation of a 'Personal Growth Class' (which later became Reconnecting Youth) compared a one-semester course focused on interactions within the classroom (Group I), a two-semester course with a more expansive focus on interactions and activities outside the classroom (Group II), and an assessment-only group (Group III) (Eggert *et al.*, 1995; see also Thompson, Eggert, & Herting, 2000). The evaluation reported significant decreases in suicide risk behaviours (including suicide thoughts, threats, and attempts) and risk factors (including depression, hopelessness, and anger) in all three groups, with greater decreases in groups I and III. All three groups showed increases in self-esteem and social support, but only groups I and II (the intervention groups) showed a significant increase in personal control. An interesting implication of these findings is that exposure to the study's assessment tool, the Measure of Adolescent Potential for Suicide (MAPS), may itself have produced effects comparable with those of the semester-long course. The MAPS is a comprehensive, two-hour interview, which is followed by a personal introduction to a school 'case manager' and an information-sharing call to the youth's 'parent of choice' (Eggert *et al.*, 1995). The authors speculate that this activation of social support may be responsible for potential assessment effects on suicidal behaviour and suicide risk factors, and note that the assessment-only group showed no improvement in personal control.

Two shorter programmes developed by the Reconnecting Youth Prevention Research Program have also been evaluated. CAST (Coping and Support Training) shares the aims and strategies of Reconnecting Youth, but is designed to meet bi-weekly for six weeks. CARE (Care, Assess, Respond, Empower) (formerly C-CARE or Counsellors CARE) provides a two-hour assessment interview (the MAPS), followed by one brief, motivational counselling session and a 'social network connections intervention' involving a school-based case manager and/or teacher and a parent or guardian of the youth's choice (Thompson, Eggert, Randell, & Pike, 2001; see also Randall, Eggert, & Pike, 2001; Eggert, Thompson, Randell, & Pike, 2002). An evaluation comparing the effects of CAST, CARE, and treatment-as-usual reported significant decreases in depression, hopelessness, and suicidal ideation for both intervention groups as compared with treatment-as-usual, as well as significant increases in personal control and problem-solving skills for the CAST intervention group only (Thompson *et al.*, 2001). Significant decreases in anger and anxiety were reported for girls in the CARE and CAST intervention groups, but not for boys.

Despite these promising initial results, negative effects of Reconnecting Youth (RY) have also been reported (Cho, Hallfors, & Sanchez, 2005; Hallfors, Cho, Sanchez, Khatapoush, Kim, *et al.*, 2006; Sanchez, Steckler, Nitirat, Hallfors, Cho, *et al.*, 2007; Thaker, Steckler, Sanchez, Khatapoush, Rose, *et al.*, 2008). A large-scale randomized controlled effectiveness trial of RY in two urban school districts reported mixed results, including increased anger at programme completion and increased high-risk peer bonding at six-month follow-up in the intervention group as compared with controls (Cho *et al.*, 2005). Greater fidelity of implementation and greater exposure to the programme (i.e., higher attendance) were unexpectedly associated with worse outcomes, including increased anger, increased alcohol use, and increased high-risk behaviours (Sanchez *et al.*, 2007).

The evaluators warn of potential iatrogenic effects of clustering high-risk youth for intervention purposes. Noting the positive findings of preliminary efficacy trials of RY, the evaluators suggest that preliminary efficacy trials may provide insufficient evidence for determining any programme's effectiveness, and recommend these be followed up with independent, larger-scale effectiveness trials (Hallfors *et al.*, 2006; Sanchez *et al.*, 2007). Finally, evaluators described potential barriers to implementation of RY, including the challenges of securing classroom time, classroom space, and administrative support, identifying qualified teachers, and training teachers in new and unfamiliar tasks (Thaker *et al.*, 2008).

Example 3: Good Behavior Game

The Good Behavior Game (GBG) is a behaviour management technique designed for universal implementation in elementary school classrooms (for students aged six through 12 years). Students are divided into competitive teams, which lose points or privileges in the event of rule-breaking or disruptive behaviour by any team member (Barrish, Saunders, & Wolf, 1969). GBG can be played while other classroom activities proceed as usual. Short-term efficacy trials have demonstrated GBG's effects on reducing aggressive and disruptive behaviour, a potential risk factor for suicide (Ialongo, Werthamer, Kellam, Brown, Wang, *et al.*, 1999; Kellam, Rebok, Ialongo, & Mayer, 1994). More recently, the long-term effect of GBG on young adult suicide risk has been evaluated in an epidemiologically-based randomized trial involving 41 classrooms in 19 Baltimore schools (Wilcox, Kellam, Brown, Poduska, Ialongo, *et al.*, 2008). First-grade classrooms (students six years of age) were randomly assigned to GBG, to Mastery Learning (ML, a classroom based intervention designed to improve reading achievement, with the secondary effects of reduced depression and increased self-esteem), or to a control condition. Classrooms remained in their assigned condition for two years, and 83% of participating students were interviewed 15 years later. Participants in the GBG condition were half as likely to have experienced suicidal ideation by young adulthood as participants in the control conditions. An effect of GBG on suicide attempts did not reach statistical significance. No significant effects were reported for ML on suicidal ideation or suicide attempts by young adulthood. Results were similar for boys and for girls. Evaluators of the effects of GBG speculate that the game interrupts the development of antisocial behaviour by promoting affiliation with non-deviant peers and reducing peer rejection of disruptive youth (van Lier, Vuijk, & Crijnen, 2005).

Limitations

Skills training curricula are relatively intensive interventions which require greater commitments of students' and teachers' time than do school-based screening or peer gatekeeper training programmes. In cases where these interventions selectively target higher risk populations (such as students at risk of school dropout), there is some risk that the social affiliations fostered by the programmes may do more harm than good.

Discussion

Skills training curricula are designed to enhance protective factors and reduce risk factors for youth suicide through the development of cognitive and social skills. The small-group activities used to develop these skills also play a role in enhancing social affiliations and potentially social connectedness. Unlike screening and gatekeeper programmes, skills training programmes are not designed with the primary aim of connecting at-risk individuals to mental health services in or outside of school. Instead, skills training programmes are designed to deliver classroom-based help in the form of life skills and social support to all students enrolled in the programme. To the extent that the programmes are effective, they should be able to reach even students who would not have asked for help.

Ecological and Comprehensive Approaches

Comprehensive or 'whole school' approaches to school-based youth suicide prevention aim to create a competent school community in which members of all school populations are aware of options and resources for preventing youth suicide (Iscoe, 1974; Kalafat & Elias, 1995). Comprehensive programmes may include establishment of suicide prevention as a school priority endorsed by school administrators, development of administrative protocols for handling suicide-related events (including procedures for responding to a student seeking help), psychoeducational resources for parents, gatekeeper training for counsellors, teachers, and students, skills training either for all students or for students in higher-risk groups, and establishment of relationships between school personnel and community mental health providers (Kalafat, 2003; Kalafat & Elias, 1995; Kalafat & Ryerson, 1999; Prevention Division of the American Association of Suicidology, 1999; Wyn, Cahill, Holdsworth, Rowling, & Carlson, 2000; Zenere & Lazarus, 1997). Comprehensive programmes may include the explicit goal of transforming the culture, climate, or social ecology of the school, to ensure that the school environment is positive and health-promoting (Felner & Felner, 1989; Kalafat, 2003; Kalafat & Elias, 1995; Wyn *et al.*, 2000). It has been suggested that the World Health Organization's concept of the health promoting school (http://www.who.int/school_youth_health/gshi/hps/en/index.html) (Lee, 2009) has its greatest potential for impact in the area of mental health (Stewart-Brown, 2006; Whitman, Aldinger, Zhang, & Magner, 2008; Wong, Lee, Sun, Stewart, Chen, *et al.*, 2009). Premises for invoking this concept in the context of youth suicide prevention specifically are that a cohesive and supportive school environment may be protective against suicide risk and that fostering a school climate of open communication may facilitate help-seeking on the part of a student in crisis.

Example 1: MindMatters

A 'whole school' suicide prevention programme based on the WHO health promoting school model, MindMatters defines its three key dimensions as (a) promotion of a healthy school ethos or environment, (b) a student curriculum designed to enhance resilience and connectedness, and (c) the development of community partnerships and referral pathways. The MindMatters curriculum includes units on enhancing resilience, grief and loss, bullying and harassment, and understanding mental illness, which can be integrated into standard courses such as English, health, or drama. MindMatters was first piloted in 24 secondary schools in Australia (Wyn *et al.*, 2000). Since then, staff from 82% of Australia's secondary schools have participated in MindMatters professional development workshops (http://www.mindmatters.edu.au). Participants tend to perceive the programme as effective (Australian Council for Educational Research, 2006). Lack of time in the curriculum and teachers' prioritization of academic programming over mental health promotion have been identified as barriers to the successful implementation of the programme. Following a one-day informational workshop, school stakeholders in four US school districts rated MindMatters favourably in terms of its relevance and potential impact in their communities (Evans, Mullett, Weist, & Frantz, 2005). MindMatters has also been adapted for use in Germany (http://www.leuphana.de/mindmatters-schule). Evaluation of MindMatters has to date extended only to its feasibility and acceptability; the effectiveness of the programme in reducing youth suicide has not been evaluated.

Example 2: Dade County Public Schools Suicide Prevention and School Crisis Management Program (DCPS SPSCMP)

The Suicide Prevention and School Crisis Management Program implemented in the Dade County (Florida) Public School system includes development of formal policies and procedures for addressing students' suicidal behaviour, establishment of a 8–10 person 'crisis team' at each school, educational programming for parents and school staff, and several levels of skills training for students, extending from pre-kindergarten to twelfth grade (Zenere & Lazarus, 1997). The skills training curriculum focuses on communication, decision-making, stress management, and drug awareness, and explicitly introduces the topic of suicide in a semester-long tenth grade 'Life Management Skills' course. A longitudinal analysis of annual trends in students' suicidal behaviour as reported to the Youth in Crisis Hotline showed a 62.79% decrease in the average yearly number of completed student suicides in Dade County Public Schools in the five years following introduction of the programme. The evaluation also reported a significant decrease in rates of suicide attempts, but no change in rates of suicidal ideation (Zenere & Lazarus 1997). However, the evaluation was descriptive and did not include a comparison group.

Example 3: Maine Youth Suicide Prevention Program/Lifelines/ASAP

The Maine Youth Suicide Prevention Program (MYSPP) (http://www.maine.gov/suicide) is a comprehensive school programme that involves establishment of a school-based Crisis Intervention Team, written agreements between school administrators and community crisis response services, development of protocols and procedures to guide staff in identifying and referring suicidal students, gatekeeper training for school personnel, parents, and students, and support services for troubled students (including Reconnecting Youth courses) as needed. MYSPP is based on the Lifelines School-Based Suicide Response

Program, a comprehensive programme with adult and peer gatekeeper training at its core (Kalafat, 2003). The Lifelines student curriculum, which promotes help-seeking and prepares students to respond to suicidal peers, can be taught by regular classroom teachers in four sessions of a health class. A survey evaluation of this curriculum found programme participants were more likely to tell an adult about a suicidal friend and were more likely to tell the friend to call a hotline, according to student self-report (Kalafat & Elias, 1994). Student reactions to the curriculum were positive. Implementation of a related, gatekeeper-focused comprehensive programme, the Adolescent Suicide Awareness Program (ASAP), was followed by a countywide decline in youth suicide rates that was not matched at the state or national level (Kalafat & Ryerson, 1999). However, there is insufficient evidence to describe this decline as a programme effect. The Lifelines/ASAP curriculum can be implemented with fidelity by trained school personnel and sustained over a period of years (Kalafat & Ryerson, 1999; Kalafat, Haley, Lubell, & O'Halloran, 2007).

Example 4: Sources of Strength

Sources of Strength is designed to enhance social-ecological protective factors associated with reduced suicide risk across the school population by training 'peer leaders' to disseminate anti-suicide messages and to provide positive models of communication with trusted adults (Wyman, personal communication, 2009). The programme is based on the premise that the influence of peer leaders will be more effective at transforming general student attitudes than a curriculum-based programme. The developers describe the intervention as based on a 'communication model' in contrast to the 'surveillance' model underlying most gatekeeper training (Sources of Strength Newsletter 2009). They emphasize using the preventive power of positive relationships with adults and peers within the school environment as an adjunct to referral of troubled youth to mental health services, which may be hard to come by especially in more rural areas (Wyman, personal communication, 2009). Like other comprehensive programmes, Sources of Strength begins with the establishment of administrative support and basic administrative suicide prevention protocols, but the programme is unique in its targeted attempt to transform school climate using peer influence and positive messaging.

Sources of Strength was evaluated in a randomized controlled trial in 18 high schools in three US states (Wyman, personal communication, 2009). Designated peer leaders and a representative sample of other students were surveyed at baseline and at four-month follow-up. The evaluation reported significant increases in peer leaders' expectations of help from adults, norms for help-seeking from adults, rejection of 'codes of silence', and numbers of 'trusted adults' identified. Programme effects on connectedness were strongest for peer leaders with low connectedness at baseline, whereas programme effects on peer referrals for adult help were strongest in peer leaders already making referrals at baseline. Significant improvements in expectations of help from adults and in help-seeking norms were also reported at the school population level, with a significantly greater improvement in students with a history of suicidal ideation. Programme effects on suicidal ideation were not significant. All findings were based on self-report, with no behavioural measures included. The authors note that a larger sample and a longer time frame will be required before programme effects on suicidal behaviour can be evaluated.

Limitations

The more comprehensive the approach, the greater the commitment of time and other resources a programme will require on the part of the school community. It may be that only schools, districts, or states with higher than average exposure to youth suicide will be adequately motivated to adopt and sustain 'whole school' suicide prevention programmes. Grouping together multiple suicide prevention strategies presents a challenge for programme evaluation as well, as the discrete effects of each programme component are difficult to assess. Further evaluation of the effectiveness of these programmes is needed.

Discussion

Comprehensive approaches to school-based youth suicide make explicit what is often implied by more targeted approaches: the necessity of involving and gaining the support of members of all school populations, including school administrators and parents as well as teachers and counsellors, and the necessity of establishing links with mental health providers and resources outside the school. Within this framework, comprehensive approaches may make use of each of the other strategies discussed here, including gatekeeper training and skills training components. Although none of the 'whole school' programmes discussed here explicitly mentions school-based screening, it is to be expected that the periodic implementation of universal screening might place relatively little burden on schools already subject to the high degree of commitment and organization required by a comprehensive approach. To the extent that these programmes successfully transform the climate or culture of a school, improvements in adolescent help-seeking behaviour may be expected as a result.

Conclusion

School-based suicide prevention programmes reviewed here aim to prevent youth suicide by laying the groundwork for an efficient response to a suicidal crisis, by educating diverse members of the school community to respond constructively to a suicidal student, by enhancing known protective factors such as problem-solving skills and social connectedness, and/or by identifying youth at long-term or imminent risk of suicide and linking them to appropriate mental health services. To varying degrees depending on the strategy used, any school-based suicide prevention programme will need to overcome the challenges of winning support from school personnel, competing for time with academic programming, surmounting or mitigating deficits in adolescent help-seeking behaviour, and ensuring itself free of iatrogenic effects.

Beneficial effects of several programmes have been demonstrated to date. School-based screening programmes have been shown successfully to identify at-risk youth and to link them to mental health services. A gatekeeper training programme has been shown to improve adult and youth knowledge and attitudes about suicide and to increase self-reported referral behaviour in school staff already in close communication with students. Another gatekeeper training programme demonstrated success in linking gatekeeper-identified youth with mental health treatment. A peer gatekeeper training programme with an anonymous screening component (SOS) has reported a reduction in youth suicide attempts, although the mechanism for achieving this reduction is unclear. Three skills training programmes have demonstrated decreases in self-reported suicidal ideation. An ecological intervention has demonstrated improvements in youth attitudes towards help-seeking. Two comprehensive school programmes (DCPS SPSCMP and ASAP) have been associated with a decline in youth suicide rates, but it is unknown whether this decline was in fact a programme effect. Of all the programmes reviewed, only one skills training programme (RY) demonstrated any potential for adverse effects, possibly based on clustering youth with a high-risk profile. Based on these results, each of these types of programmes merits continued trials.

References

Ainley, J., Withers, G., Underwood, C., & Frigo, T. (2006). *National Survey of Health and Well-Being Promotion Policies and Practices in Secondary Schools: Report to the Australian Principals' Associations Professional Development Council.* Canberra: Australian Council for Educational Research.

Asarnow, J., Carlson, G., & Guthrie, D. (1987). Coping strategies, self-perceptions, hopelessness, and perceived family environments in depressed and suicidal children. *Journal of Consulting and Clinical Psychology, 55*, 361–366.

Aseltine, R. (2003). An evaluation of a school based suicide prevention program. *Adolescent and Family Health, 3*, 81–88.

Aseltine, R. H., Jr, James, A., Schilling, E. A., & Glanovsky, J. (2007). Evaluating the SOS suicide prevention program: A replication and extension. *BMC Public Health, 7*, 161.

Aseltine, R. H., Jr. & DeMartino, R. (2004). An outcome evaluation of the SOS Suicide Prevention Program. *American Journal of Public Health, 94*, 446–451.

Ashford, E. (2005). The fight over screening students to prevent suicide. *Education Digest: Essential readings condensed for quick review, 71*, 52–56, available at www.eddigest.com.

Barrish, H. H., Saunders, M., & Wolf, M. M. (1969). Good Behavior Game: Effects of individual contingencies for group consequences on disruptive behavior in a classroom. *Journal of Applied Behavior Analysis, 2*, 119–124.

Berman, A. L. & Jobes, D. A. (1991). *Adolescent Suicide: Assessment and intervention.* Washington, DC: American Psychological Association.

Berman, A. L. & Jobes, D. A. (1995). Suicide prevention in adolescents (age 12–18). *Suicide and Life Threatening Behavior, 25*, 143–154.

Borowsky, I. W., Ireland, M., & Resnick, M. D. (2001). Adolescent suicide attempts: Risks and protectors. *Pediatrics, 107*, 485–493.

Borowsky, I. W., Resnick, M. D., Ireland, M., & Blum, R. W. (1999). Suicide attempts among American Indian and Alaska Native youth: Risk and protective factors. *Archives of Pediatrics and Adolescent Medicine, 153*, 573–580.

Brent, D. A., Perper, J. A., Goldstein, C. E., Kolko, D. J., Allan, M. J., Allman, C. J., & Zelenak, J. P. (1988). Risk factors for adolescent suicide: A comparison of adolescent suicide victims with suicidal inpatients. *Archives of General Psychiatry*, 45, 581–588.

Brent, D. A., Perper, J. A., Moritz, G., Allman, C., Friend, A., Roth, C., Schweeers, J., Balach, L., & Baugher, M. (1993). Psychiatric risk factors for adolescent suicide: A case-control study. *Journal of the American Academy of Child and Adolescent Psychiatry*, 32, 521–529.

Brown, C. H., Wyman, P. A., Brinales, J. M., & Gibbons, R. D. (2007). The role of randomized trials in testing interventions for the prevention of youth suicide. *International Review of Psychiatry*, 19, 617–631.

Brown, M. M. & Grumet, J. G. (2009). School-based suicide prevention with African American youth in an urban setting. *Professional Psychology: Research and Practice*, 40, 111–117.

Carlton, P. A. & Deane, F. P. (2000). Impact of attitudes and suicidal ideation on adolescents' intentions to seek professional psychological help. *Journal of Adolescence*, 23, 35–45.

Cho, H., Hallfors, D. D., & Sanchez, V. (2005). Evaluation of a high school peer group intervention for at-risk youth. *Journal of Abnormal Child Psychology*, 33, 363–374.

Ciffone, J. (1993). Suicide prevention: A classroom presentation to adolescents. *Social Work*, 38, 197–203.

Ciffone, J. (2007). Suicide prevention: An analysis and replication of a curriculum-based high school program. *Social Work*, 52, 41–49.

Cigularov, K., Chen, P. Y., Thurber, B. W., & Stallones, L. (2008). What prevents adolescents from seeking help after a suicide education program? *Suicide and Life-Threatening Behavior*, 38, 74–86.

Cole, D. A. (1989). Psychopathology of adolescent suicide: hopelessness, coping beliefs, and depression. *Journal of Abnormal Psychology*, 98, 248–255.

Eckert, T. L., Miller, D. N., DuPaul, G. J., & Riley-Tillman, T. C. (2003). Adolescent suicide prevention: School psychologists' acceptability of school-based programs. *School Psychology Review*, 32, 57–76.

Eggert, L. L., Thompson, E. A., Herting, J. R., & Nicholas, L. J. (1994). Prevention research program: Reconnecting at-risk youth. *Issues in Mental Health and Nursing*, 15, 107–135.

Eggert, L. L., Thompson, E. A., Herting, J. R., & Nicholas, L. J. (1995). Reducing suicide potential among high-risk youth: Tests of a school-based prevention program. *Suicide and Life-Threatening Behavior*, 25, 276–296.

Eggert, L. L., Thompson, E. A., Herting, J. R., & Randell, B. P. (2001). Reconnecting youth to prevent drug abuse, school dropout and suicidal behaviors among high-risk youth. In E. F. Wagner & H. Waldron (Eds.), *Innovation in Adolescent Substance Abuse Interventions* (pp. 51–84). Oxford: Elsevier Science.

Eggert, L. L., Thompson, E. A., Randell, B. P., & Pike, K. C. (2002). Preliminary effects of brief school-based prevention approaches for reducing youth suicide – risk behaviors, depression, and drug involvement. *Journal of Child and Adolescent Psychiatric Nursing*, 15, 48–64.

Evans, S. W., Mullett, E., Weist, M. D., & Franz, K. (2005). Feasibility of the MindMatters School Health Promotion Program in American schools. *Journal of Youth and Adolescence*, 34, 51–58.

Felner, R. D. & Felner, T. Y. (1989). Primary prevention programs in the educational context: A transactional–ecological framework and analysis. In L. A. Bond & B. E. Compas (Eds.), *Primary Prevention and Promotion in the Schools* (pp. 13–49). Newbury Park, CA: Sage.

Garland, A., Shaffer, D., & Whittle, B. (1989). A national survey of school-based, adolescent suicide prevention programs. *Journal of the American Academy of Child and Adolescent Psychiatry*, 28, 931–934.

Garland, A. F. & Zigler, E. (1993). Adolescent suicide prevention: Current research and social policy implications. *American Psychologist*, 48, 169–182.

Gould, M. S. (2009). Effectiveness of Suicide Hotline Training. National Institute of Mental Health (NIMH) grant R01MH082537-01A1.

Gould, M. S., Greenberg, T., Velting, D., & Shaffer, D. (2003). Youth suicide risk and preventive interventions: A review of the past 10 years. *Journal of the American Academy of Child and Adolescent Psychiatry, 42*, 386–405.

Gould, M. S., King, R., Greenwald, S., Fisher, P., Schwab-Stone, M., Kramer, R., Flisher, A. J., Goodman, S., Canino, G., & Shaffer, D. (1998). Psychopathology associated with suicidal ideation and attempts among children and adolescents. *Journal of the American Academy of Child and Adolescent Psychiatry, 37*, 915–923.

Gould, M. S., Klomek, A. B., & Batejan, K. (2009). The role of schools, colleges and universities in suicide prevention. In D. Wasserman & C. Wasserman (Eds.), *Oxford Textbook of Suicidology and Suicide Prevention: A global perspective* (pp. 551–560). Oxford: Oxford University Press.

Gould, M. S., Marrocco, F. A., Hoagwood, K., Kleinman, M., Amakawa, L., & Altschuler, E. (2009). Service use by at-risk youths after school-based suicide screening. *Journal of the American Academy of Child and Adolescent Psychiatry, 48*, 1193–1201.

Gould, M. S., Marrocco, M. A., & Kleinman, M. (2005). Evaluating iatrogenic risk of youth suicide screening programs: a randomized controlled trial. *Journal of the American Medical Association, 293*, 1635–1643.

Gould, M. S., Velting, D., Kleinman, M., Lucas, C., Thomas, J. G., & Chung, M. (2004). Teenagers' attitudes about coping strategies and help-seeking behavior for suicidality. *Journal of the American Academy of Child and Adolescent Psychiatry, 43*, 1124–1133.

Guo, G. & Harstall, C. (2002). Efficacy of suicide prevention programs for children and youth. *HTA 26: Services A. Health Technology Assessment*. Alberta Heritage Foundation for Medical Research, Alberta, Canada.

Gutierrez, P. M., Watkins, R., & Collura, D. (2004). Suicide risk screening in an urban high school. *Suicide and Life-Threatening Behavior, 43*, 421–428.

Hallfors, D., Brodish, P. H., Khatapoush, S., Sanchez, V., Cho, H., & Steckler, A. (2006). Feasibility of screening adolescents for suicide risk in 'real-world' high school settings. *American Journal of Public Health, 96*, 282–287.

Hallfors, D., Cho, H., Sanchez, V., Khatapoush, S., Kim, H. M., & Bauer, D. (2006). Efficacy vs effectiveness trial results of an indicated 'model' substance abuse program: Implications for public health. *American Journal of Public Health, 96*, 2254–2259.

Husky, M. M., McGuire, L., Flynn, L., Chrostowski, C., & Olfson, M. (2009). Correlates of help-seeking behavior among at-risk adolescents. *Child Psychiatry and Human Development, 40*, 15–24.

Ialongo, N. S., Werthamer, L., Kellam, S. G., Brown, C. H., Wang, S., & Lin, Y. (1999). Proximal impact of two first-grade preventive interventions on the early risk behaviors for later substance abuse, depression, and antisocial behavior. *American Journal of Community Psychology, 27*, 599–641.

Iscoe, I. (1974). Community psychology and the competent community. *American Psychologist, 29*, 179–188.

Joiner, T. E., Pfaff, J. J., & Acres, J.G. (2002). A brief screening tool for suicidal symptoms in adolescents and young adults in general health settings: Reliability and validity data from the Australian National General Practice Youth Suicide Prevention Project. *Behaviour Research and Therapy, 40*, 471–481.

Kalafat, J. & Elias, M. (1994). An evaluation of a school-based suicide awareness intervention. *Suicide and Life Threatening Behavior, 24*, 224–233.

Kalafat, J. & Elias, M. (1995). Suicide prevention in an educational context: Broad and narrow foci. *Suicide and Life Threatening Behavior, 25*, 123–133.

Kalafat, J. & Gagliano, C. (1996). The use of simulations to assess the impact of an adolescent suicide response curriculum. *Suicide and Life Threatening Behavior, 26*, 359–364.

Kalafat, J. & Ryerson, D. A. (1999). The implementation and institutionalization of a school-based youth suicide prevention program. *Journal of Primary Prevention, 19,* 157–175.

Kalafat, J. (2003) School approaches of youth suicide prevention. *American Behavioral Scientist, 46,* 1211–1223.

Kalafat, J., Haley, D., Lubell, K., O'Halloran, S. O., & Madden, M. (2007). Evaluation of Lifelines Classes: A component of the school-community based Maine youth suicide prevention project. Draft Report Prepared for the National Registry of Evidenced Based Programs and Practices. Rutgers University Graduate School of Applied and Professional Psychology, Piscataway, NJ.

Kalafat, J., O'Halloran, S., & Underwood, M. (2003). Lifelines: A school-based youth suicide response program. Rutgers Graduate School of Applied and Professional Psychology, Piscataway, NJ.

Kataoka, S. H., Stein, B. D., Lieberman, R., & Wong, M. (2003). Suicide prevention in schools: Are we reaching minority youths? *Psychiatric Services, 54,* 1444.

Kataoka, S. H., Stein, B. D., Nadeem, E., & Wong, M. (2007). Who gets care? Mental health service use following a school-based suicide prevention program. *Journal of the American Academy of Child and Adolescent Psychiatry, 46,* 1341–1348.

Kellam, S. G., Rebok, G. W., Ialongo, N., & Mayer, L. S. (1994). The course and malleability of aggressive behavior from early first grade into middle school: Results of a developmental epidemiologically-based preventive trial. *Journal of Child Psychology and Psychiatry, 35,* 259–282.

King, K. A. & Smith, J. (2000). Project SOAR: a training program to increase school counselors' knowledge and confidence regarding suicide prevention and intervention. *Journal of School Health, 70,* 402–407.

Klingman, A. & Hochdorf, Z. (1993). Coping with distress and self-harm: The impact of a primary prevention program among adolescents. *Journal of Adolescent Psychiatry, 16,* 121–140.

LaFromboise, T. D. & Howard-Pitney, B. (1994). The Zuni life skills development curriculum: A collaborative approach to curriculum development. *American Indian and Alaska Native Mental Health Research: The Journal of the National Center, Monograph Series, 4,* 98–121.

LaFromboise, T. D. & Howard-Pitney, B. (1995). The Zuni life skills development curriculum: Description and evaluation of a suicide prevention program. *Journal of Counseling Psychology, 42,* 479–486.

LaFromboise, T. D. & Lewis, H. A. (2008). The Zuni life skills development program: A school/community-based suicide prevention intervention. *Suicide and Life-Threatening Behavior, 38,* 343–353.

Lee, A. (2009). Health-promoting schools: Evidence for a holistic approach to promoting health and improving health literacy. *Applied Health Economics & Health Policy, 7,* 11–17.

McKeown, R. E., Garrison, C. Z., Cuffe, S. P., Waller, J. L., Jackson, K. L., & Addy, C. L. (1998). Incidence and predictors of suicidal behaviors in a longitudinal sample of young adolescents. *Journal of the American Academy of Child and Adolescent Psychiatry, 37,* 612–619.

Miller, D. N., Eckert, T. L., DuPaul, G. J., & White, G. P. (1999). Adolescent suicide prevention: Acceptability of school-based programs among secondary school principals. *Suicide and Life Threatening Behavior, 29,* 72–85.

Overholser, J. C., Hemstreet, A., Spirito, A., & Vyse, S. (1989). Suicide awareness programs in the schools: Effect of gender and personal experience. *Journal of the American Academy of Child and Adolescent Psychiatry, 28,* 925–930.

Ploeg, J., Ciliska, D., Dobbins, M., Hayward, S., Thomas, H., & Underwood, J. (1996). A systematic overview of adolescent suicide prevention programs. *Canadian Journal of Public Health, 87,* 319–324.

Portzky, G. & van Heeringen, K. (2006). Suicide prevention in adolescents: A controlled study of the effectiveness of a school-based psycho-educational program. *Journal of Child Psychology and Psychiatry, 47,* 910–918.

Prevention Division of the American Association of Suicidology (1999). *Guidelines for School Based Suicide Prevention Programs.*

Quinnett, P. (1995). *QPR: Ask a Question, Save a Life.* The QPR Institute, Spokane, Washington, available at http://www.qprinstitute.com.

Quinnett, P. (2007). *QPR Gatekeeper Training for Suicide Prevention: The model, rationale and theory,* available at http://www.qprinstitute.com.

Randell, B. P., Eggert, L. L., & Pike, K. C. (2001). Immediate post intervention effects of two brief youth suicide prevention interventions. *Suicide and Life-Threatening Behavior, 31,* 41–61.

Reynolds, W. M. (1990). Development of a semi-structured clinical interview for suicidal behaviors in adolescents. *Psychological Assessment, 2,* 382–390.

Reynolds, W. M. (1991). A school-based procedure for the identification of adolescents at risk for suicidal behaviors. *Family Community Health, 14,* 64–75.

Rickwood, D. J., Deane, F. P., & Wilson, C. J. (2007). When and how do young people seek professional help for mental health problems? *Medical Journal of Australia, 187,* S35–S39.

Rotheram-Borus, M. J., Trautman, P. D., Dopkins, S. C., & Shrout, P. E. (1990). Cognitive style and pleasant activities among female adolescent suicide attempters. *Journal of Consulting and Clinical Psychology, 58,* 554–561.

Rudd, M. D., Berman, A. L., Joiner, T. E., Jr, Nock, M. K., Silverman, M. M., Mandrusiak, M., van Orden, K., & Witte, T. (2006). Warning signs for suicide: Theory, research, and clinical applications. *Suicide and Life-Threatening Behavior, 36,* 255–262.

Sanchez, V., Steckler, A., Nitirat, P., Hallfors, D., Cho, H., & Brodish, P. (2007). Fidelity of implementation in a treatment effectiveness trial of Reconnecting Youth. *Health Education Research, 22,* 95–107.

Scherff, A. R., Eckert, T. L., & Miller, D. N. (2005). Youth suicide prevention: A survey of public school superintendents' acceptability of school-based programs. *Suicide and Life-Threatening Behavior, 35,* 154–169.

School Mental Health Promotion Program in American Schools. *Journal of Youth and Adolescence, 34,* 51–58.

Scott, M. A., Wilcox, H. C., Schonfeld, I. S., Davies, M., Hicks, R. C., Turner, J. B., & Shaffer, D. (2009). School-based screening to identify at-risk students not already known to school professionals: The Columbia Suicide Screen. *American Journal of Public Health, 99,* 334–339.

Shaffer, D. & Craft, L. (1999). Methods of adolescent suicide prevention. *Journal of Clinical Psychiatry, 60,* 70–74.

Shaffer, D. & Gould, M. S. (2000). Suicide prevention in schools. In K. Hawton & K. van Heeringen (Eds.), *The International Handbook of Suicide and Attempted Suicide.* Chichester: John Wiley & Sons, Ltd.

Shaffer, D., Garland, A., Vieland, V., Underwood, M. M., & Busner, C. (1991). The impact of curriculum-based suicide prevention program for teenagers. *Journal of the American Academy of Child and Adolescent Psychiatry, 30,* 588–596.

Shaffer, D., Gould, M. S., Fisher, P., Trautman, P., Moreau, D., Kleinman, M., & Flory, M. (1996). Psychiatric diagnosis in child and adolescent suicide. *Archives of General Psychiatry, 53,* 339–348.

Shaffer, D., Scott, M., Wilcox, H., Maslow, C., Hicks, R., Lucas, C. P., Garfinkel, R., & Greenwald, S. (2004). The Columbia SuicideScreen: Validity and reliability of a screen for youth suicide and depression. *Journal of the American Academy of Child and Adolescent Psychiatry, 43,* 71–79.

Shaffer, D., Vieland, V., Garland, A., Rojas, M., Underwood, M. M., & Busner, C. (1990). Adolescent suicide attempters. Response to suicide-prevention programs. *Journal of the American Medical Association, 264,* 3151–3155.

Silbert, K. L. & Berry, G. L. (1991). Psychological effects of a suicide prevention unit on adolescents' levels of stress, anxiety and hopelessness: Implications for counselling psychologists. *Counselling Psychology Quarterly, 4*, 45–58.

Spirito, A., Overholser, J., Ashworth, S., Morgan, J., & Benedict-Drew, C. (1988). Evaluation of a suicide awareness curriculum for high school students. *Journal of the American Academy of Child and Adolescent Psychiatry, 27*, 705–711.

Stewart-Brown, S. (2006). *What is the Evidence on School Health Promotion in Improving Health or Preventing Disease and, Specifically, What is the Effectiveness of the Health Promoting Schools Approach?* Copenhagen: World Health Organization Regional Office for Europe.

Stuart, C., Waalen, J. K., & Haelstromm, E. (2003). Many helping hearts: An evaluation of peer gatekeeper training in suicide risk assessment. *Death Studies, 27*, 321–333.

Thaker, S., Steckler, A., Sanchez, V., Khatapoush, S., Rose, J., & Hallfors, D. D. (2008). Program characteristics and organizational factors affecting the implementation of a school-based indicated prevention program. *Health Education Research, 23*, 238–248.

Thompson, E. A. & Eggert, L. L. (1999). Using the suicide risk screen to identify suicidal adolescents among potential high school dropouts. *Journal of the American Academy of Child and Adolescent Psychiatry, 38*, 1506–1514.

Thompson, E. A., Eggert, L. L., & Herting, J. R. (2000). Mediating effects of an indicated prevention program for reducing youth depression and suicide risk behaviors. *Suicide and Life Threatening Behavior, 30*, 252–271.

Thompson, E. A., Eggert, L. L., Randell, B. P., & Pike, K. C. (2001). Evaluation of indicated suicide risk prevention approaches for potential high school dropouts. *American Journal of Public Health, 91*, 742–752.

van Lier, P. A. C., Vuijk, P., & Crijnen, A. A. M. (2005). Understanding mechanisms of change in the development of antisocial behavior: The impact of a universal intervention. *Journal of Abnormal Child Psychology, 33*, 521–535.

Vieland, V., Whittle, B., Garland, A., Hicks, R., & Shaffer, D. (1991). The impact of curriculum-based suicide prevention programs for teenagers: An 18-month follow-up. *Journal of the American Academy of Child and Adolescent Psychiatry, 30*, 811–815.

Weist, M., Rubin, M., Moore, E., Adelsheim, S., & Wrobel, G. (2007). Mental health screening in schools. *Journal of School Health, 77*, 53–58.

Whitman, C. V., Aldinger, C., Zhang, X., & Magner, E. (2008). Strategies to address mental health through schools with examples from China. *International Review of Psychiatry, 20*, 237–249.

Wilcox, H. C., Kellam, S. G., Brown, C. H., Poduska, J. M., Ialongo, N. S., Wang, W., & Anthony, J. C. (2008). The impact of two universal randomized first- and second-grade classroom interventions on young adult suicide ideation and attempts. *Drug & Alcohol Dependence, 95*, S60–73

Wong, M. C., Lee, A., Sun, J., Stewart, D., Cheng, F. F., Kan, W., & Ho, M. (2009). A comparative study on resilience level between WHO health promoting schools and other schools among a Chinese population. *Health Promotion International, 24*, 149–155.

Wyman, P. A., Brown, C. H., Inman, J., Cross, W., Schmeelk-Cone, K., Guo, J., & Pena, J. B. (2008). Randomized trial of a gatekeeper training program for suicide prevention: Impact on school staff after one year. *Journal of Consulting and Clinical Psychology, 76*, 104–115.

Wyn, J., Cahill, H., Holdsworth, R., Rowling, L., & Carson, S. (2000). MindMatters, a whole-school approach promoting mental health and wellbeing. *Australian and New Zealand Journal of Psychiatry, 34*, 594–601.

Zenere, F. J. & Lazarus, P. J. (1997). The decline of youth suicidal behavior in an urban, multicultural public school system following the introduction of a suicide prevention and intervention program. *Suicide and Life Threatening Behavior, 27*, 387–403.

CHAPTER THIRTY

Media Influences on Suicide and Attempted Suicide

Jane Pirkis and Merete Nordentoft

Abstract

This chapter examines the 'Werther effect' (the phenomenon where there is an increase in rates of completed or attempted suicide following the depiction of an individual's suicide in the media). There is strong evidence for the Werther effect operating in traditional news media (e.g., newspapers, television news), and there would also seem to be a significant risk of it operating in entertainment media (e.g., fictional television shows/series, fictional films, stage plays) and newer media (e.g., the Internet), although the findings from studies in these areas are somewhat more equivocal. Various interventions have been put in place to address the Werther effect across the three forms of media. Guidelines for journalists and editors appear to be effective in promoting responsible reporting in traditional news media, providing media professionals are engaged. Resources for stage and screen writers may also have potential in the entertainment media, although to date these have not been well evaluated. Several solutions have been proposed to address the issue of pro-suicide websites (e.g., the use of voluntary guidelines and the self-regulation of sites, the use of filtering software, collaboration between the mental health sector and the mass media, the development of alternative websites that promote help-seeking behaviour, and legal controls), but again these have not been subject to rigorous evaluation. Further work is required to fully understand the mechanisms by which the Werther effect might operate, but it is clear that addressing the Werther effect across the full gamut of different media has the potential to prevent suicide.

International Handbook of Suicide Prevention: Research, Policy and Practice, First Edition.
Edited by Rory C. O'Connor, Stephen Platt, Jacki Gordon.
© 2011 John Wiley & Sons, Ltd. Published 2011 by John Wiley & Sons, Ltd.

Introduction

This chapter examines the 'Werther effect', or the phenomenon where there is an increase in rates of completed or attempted suicide following the depiction of an individual's suicide in the media. The term, which is credited to American suicidologist Philips (1974), has its origins in a novel by Goethe, entitled *The Sorrows of Young Werther*, published in 1774 and inspired by a painful love affair in the writer's own life. The novel's plotline follows the fortunes of a young man called Werther who falls in love with a woman whom he cannot marry because she is above his social standing and already engaged. As a consequence, Werther takes his own life. Following publication of the book there was a series of suicides in Europe, and there was strong circumstantial evidence that the book had influenced a number of individuals in their final act. Some were dressed in a similar fashion to Werther, some used a pistol to take their own lives just as Werther had done, and some were found at the scene of their death with a copy of the book. Public concern led to the book being banned in a number of countries (Thorson & Oberg, 2003).

Evidence for the Werther effect remained largely anecdotal until the 1970s, when the first research studies on this topic commenced. Since then over 100 scientific studies examining the relationship between media reporting or portrayal of suicide and actual suicidal behaviour have been conducted. The effect has been demonstrated in a range of traditional media, from both news and entertainment genres. Concern is now being expressed about the potential for newer media to exert a similar influence. This chapter begins by clarifying some definitional issues. It then outlines the evidence for the Werther effect operating in traditional news media (e.g., newspapers, television news), traditional entertainment media (e.g., fictional television shows/series, fictional films, stage plays), and newer media (e.g. the Internet). It also describes potential interventions that may ameliorate the effect in different media, and provides detail of evaluations of these interventions. Finally, it provides a discussion of the theoretical mechanisms by which the Werther effect might operate.

Definitional Issues

Nomenclature is very important in suicidology, and has been discussed in detail by Silverman in Chapter 1, above. The term 'attempted suicide' is used in this chapter to refer to 'a self-inflicted, potentially injurious behaviour with a non-fatal outcome for which there is evidence (either explicit or implicit) of intent to die', and the term 'suicide' is used to refer to the situation where such a 'suicide attempt result[s] in death' (Silverman, Berman, Sanddal, O'Carroll, & Joiner, 2007, p. 273).

The term 'Werther effect' is used in the manner intended by Phillips (1974, p. 341) to refer to '[an increase in] the number of suicides ... after the story of a suicide is publicized in the [media]'. The terms 'suicide contagion', 'imitation suicide', 'copycat suicide' are often used interchangeably with the Werther effect, but although the terms are related, the latter is more specific. The Werther effect can be thought of as a form of suicide contagion, where the index suicide is described in the media (as opposed to occurring within a social network, where the index suicide is typically known to the imitator). The term contagion has its roots in the infectious diseases literature, and implies transmission of a health state. In the suicidality context, transmission requires the mechanism of imitation or copycat behaviour, and this in turn relies on elements drawn from social learning theory such as identification, modelling, and priming (Bandura, 1971; Berkowitz, 1984; Sacks & Eth, 1981; Schmidtke & Schaller, 2000; Stack, 1991; Taiminen, Salmenpera, & Lehtinen, 1992; Tousignant, Mishara, Caillaud, Fortin, & St Laurent, 2005).

The Werther Effect in Traditional News Media

Summary of the evidence

Scientific investigation into the Werther effect in the news media began in the 1970s when Phillips (1974) published his seminal study which retrospectively compared the number of suicides occurring in the months in which a front-page article on suicide appeared in the US press with the number occurring in the months in which no such article appeared. During the 20-year study period, there were 33 months in which a relevant front-page article was published, and there was a significant increase in the number of suicides in 26 of those months.

Numerous studies have followed Phillips' initial study. Collectively, these studies have strengthened the body of evidence in a number of ways. First, they have used improved methodologies. For example, Wasserman (1984) and Stack (1990b) both replicated the findings from Phillips' original study when they extended the observation period, used more complex time-series regression techniques, and considered rates rather than absolute numbers of suicides. Second, these studies have examined different media. For instance, Bollen and Phillips (1982) and Stack (1989) looked at the impact of suicide stories given national coverage on US television news and found that there were significant increases in suicide rates following such broadcasts. Finally, although most of the early studies were conducted in the United States and considered completed suicide only, later studies have broadened the scope to Asian and European countries and have included a focus on suicide attempts. For example, recent studies by Cheng and colleagues (Cheng, Hawton, Chen, Yen, Chen, *et al.*, 2007; Cheng, Hawton, Lee, & Chen, 2007) and Yip, Fu, Yang, Ip, Chan, *et al.* (2006) demonstrated increases in completed and attempted suicide rates following reportage of celebrity suicides in Taiwan and Hong Kong, respectively.

Systematic reviews of these studies have consistently drawn the same conclusion: that there is strong evidence for the Werther effect operating through traditional news media (Pirkis & Blood, 2001a; Stack, 2000, 2005). These reviews have also observed some common features of the Werther effect that are evident from the source studies. The impact is usually at its maximum within the first three days and then levels off within two weeks (Bollen & Phillips, 1982; Phillips & Carstensen, 1986), although sometimes it lasts longer (Fu & Yip, 2007). It is facilitated by prominent coverage and repetition of stories (Etzersdorfer, Voracek, & Sonneck, 2001, 2004; Hassan, 1995). It is accentuated when the person described in the story and the reader or viewer are similar in some way (Stack, 1990a), or when the person described in the story is a celebrity and is held in high regard by the reader or viewer (Cheng, Hawton, Lee, *et al.*, 2007; Stack, 1987, 1990b; Wasserman, 1984; Yip *et al.*, 2006). Particular sub-groups in the population (e.g., young people, people with depression) may be especially vulnerable to engaging in imitative suicidal behaviours (Cheng, Hawton, Chen, Yen, Chang, *et al.*, 2007; Phillips & Carstensen, 1986, 1988). Finally, and perhaps most importantly, overt description of suicide by a particular method may lead to increases in suicidal behaviour employing that method (Ashton & Donnan, 1979, 1981; Cheng, Hawton, Chen, Yen, Chang, *et al.*, 2007; Etzersdorfer, Voracek, & Sonneck, 2001, 2004; Phillips & Carstensen, 1986, 1988; Veysey, Kamanyire, & Volans, 1999).

Potential interventions

The primary intervention designed to address irresponsible reporting of suicide in the news media takes the form of media guidelines which target journalists and editors from print and broadcast media. The International Association for Suicide Prevention's Suicide and the Media Task Force recently identified over 30 such guidelines from around the world, and took the lead in jointly developing international guidelines with the World Health Organization for use in countries with no local guidelines (International Association for Suicide Prevention and World Health Organization, 2008). Some countries have begun to positively reinforce the content of their guidelines by offering awards to journalists for exemplary reporting (Dare, Andriessen, Nordentoft, & Pirkis, forthcoming).

The content of these guidelines is shaped by the empirical evidence of the Werther effect. They typically recommend that suicide should be reported in a manner that does not sensationalize or glamorize the behaviour, or give it undue prominence. They reinforce the message that modelled behaviour is particularly likely to occur in circumstances where the method or location of a given suicide is explicitly described, and/or when the suicide of a revered celebrity is reported. They suggest that the media can play a positive role by educating the public about suicide and by providing contact details for agencies which can help or support vulnerable readers or viewers. Most also urge media professionals to take particular care when interviewing people bereaved by suicide, who may be at particular risk themselves. Some note that journalists who report on suicide should be given debriefing opportunities (Pirkis, Blood, Beautrais, Burgess, & Skehan, 2006).

Relatively few evaluations of these media guidelines have been conducted. Process evaluations which have considered the reach of such guidelines have produced mixed results. On the one hand, an evaluation of a set of Australian guidelines and associated resources which followed a sample of journalists who had been actively exposed to them yielded positive findings. In total, 50% of those who had received a drop-in visit from the organization responsible for disseminating the materials were aware of them 12 months later, as were 67% of those who had received a more comprehensive briefing, and 50% of those who had received the materials by mail. Of those who were aware of the resources, 46% of the drop-in group had used them, as had 36% of the briefing group, and 17% of the mail-out group (Skehan, Greenhalgh, Hazell, & Pirkis, 2006).

On the other hand, Jamieson (2001) conducted interviews with 20 journalists from high-circulation newspapers in the United States who had written a story in 2000 about an individual's suicide, and found that none was familiar with any media guidelines on reporting suicide. Some did, however, express agreement with the sentiment of the guidelines, understanding the need for sensitive, respectful, and non-sensationalist reporting, and acknowledging the existence of the Werther effect. Tully and Elsaka (2004) reported similar findings to those of Jamieson (2001) when they conducted interviews with 11 media professionals about New Zealand's guidelines, although, unlike Jamieson, they did not select their respondents in any systematic way. Tully and Elsaka (2004) concluded that the guidelines were largely ignored by media professionals.

Impact and outcome evaluations have produced more consistent and generally positive findings with respect to the effectiveness of media guidelines. Michel, Frey, Wyss, and Valach (2000) demonstrated that the implementation of media guidelines in Switzerland led to less sensational and higher quality reporting. Pirkis, Dare, Blood, Rankin, Williamson, *et al.* (2009) reported similar findings when they evaluated the effectiveness of the Australian guidelines mentioned above. Etzersdorfer and colleagues went one step further in an Austrian study (Etzersdorfer & Sonneck, 1998; Etzersdorfer, Sonneck, & Nagel Kuess, 1992; Etzersdorfer *et al.*, 2001, 2004; Sonneck, Etzersdorfer, & Nagel Kuess, 1994). They demonstrated that the introduction of media guidelines regarding the reporting of suicides on the Viennese subway not only resulted in a reduction in the reporting of these suicides, but also led to a 75% decrease in the rate of subway suicides and a 20% decrease in the overall suicide rate. The impact of the Swiss guidelines dropped off as a function of time (Michel, Maillart, & Reisch, 2007), whereas the impact of the Austrian guidelines was largely maintained (Niederkrotenthaler & Sonneck, 2007). The longevity of the impact of the Australian guidelines has not yet been tested.

Given that the content of most media guidelines is strikingly similar, it is likely that the differences in the above evaluation findings may relate to the processes by which different guidelines are developed and implemented. In particular, close involvement of media professionals at all stages seems to be important (Pirkis *et al.*, 2006). The Australian guidelines were developed by the Department of Health and Ageing, which purposefully sought input from a reference group that included representatives from a range of media organizations. They have been actively disseminated by the Hunter Institute of Mental Health, which has conducted information sessions, offered advice, distributed electronic and printed copies of the guidelines and supporting materials, worked with media organizations (e.g., professional and regulatory bodies, individual media outlets) to incorporate aspects of the guidelines into codes of practice and editorial policies, and provided on-going follow-up and promotion (Pirkis *et al.*, 2006; Skehan *et al.*, 2006). By contrast, the New Zealand guidelines were developed by the Ministry of Health with only minimal input from journalists, who therefore did not feel committed to the process or the product. The dissemination process has also been more improvised than its Australian equivalent (Pirkis *et al.*, 2006). It is perhaps not surprising, therefore, that the Australian evaluation results are positive, whereas the results from New Zealand are less encouraging.

More direct evidence for the contention that media 'buy-in' underpins the success of guidelines comes from the above-mentioned work on the Austrian guidelines. Niederkrotenthaler and Sonneck (2007) found that the positive impacts associated with the guidelines were most pronounced in regions with strong media collaboration.

The Werther Effect in Traditional Entertainment Media

Summary of the evidence

A substantial number of studies have also been conducted to investigate the extent to which the Werther effect might operate in traditional entertainment media. As with the studies of traditional news media, these tend to employ ecological designs whereby rates of completed or attempted suicide in a given area are considered before and after the presentation of a particular media stimulus (usually a television show or film depicting a suicide). Reviews of these studies have found that they produce some strong evidence for the Werther effect operating via these media, but that overall the evidence is more equivocal than that for the traditional news media (Pirkis & Blood, 2001b).

An example of the equivocal nature of the evidence comes from a series of studies conducted in the United Kingdom which examined the impact of an episode of the popular soap opera *East Enders* on attempted suicides. In the episode of interest, Angie, a much-loved character in her mid- to late-30s, attempted suicide by overdose. Various authors looked at emergency department presentations and hospitalizations for suicide attempts in different geographical areas in the United Kingdom for various equivalent periods before and after the episode was aired. Some found significant increases in suicide attempts across the board (Ellis & Walsh, 1986; Fowler, 1986; Sandler, Connell, & Welsh, 1986), others found significant increases only in suicide attempts by similar methods and/or among groups sharing characteristics with Angie (Platt, 1987; Williams, Lawton, Ellis, Walsh, & Reed, 1987), and still others found no change (Daniels, 1986).

Several studies have used more sophisticated designs than the simple before-and-after approach to examine the Werther effect in traditional entertainment media. The best known of these is a study by Schmidtke and Hafner (1988) which examined suicide rates in Germany before and after a six-episode series depicting the railway suicide of a 19-year-old male student. The series was shown for the first time in 1981, and again in the following year. The authors reported a significant increase in railway suicides after the first series which attenuated by 70 days, and a similar (though less marked) increase after the second series which again dropped off after a similar period.

Other innovative studies have addressed one of the key criticisms of the ecological approach, which is that it is not possible to determine whether any increase in attempted or completed suicide following a media stimulus can be attributed to those individuals who actually viewed the media stimulus. Incorrectly making such an attribution is an example of the 'ecological fallacy' (Durkheim, 1951). Several studies have looked in more detail at the cases which comprise the group attempting suicide following a particular television show with suicide content and have questioned members of the group as to whether they saw the show and whether it influenced their decision to attempt suicide. Again, the findings are equivocal. For example, Hawton and colleagues found that there was no statistically significant increase in cases of deliberate self-poisoning or self-injury presenting to the general hospital in Oxford following an episode of the United Kingdom television drama *Casualty* aired in 1993 in which a 15-year-old girl ingested 50 paracetamol tablets, and that very few of those presenting after the programme had seen it and still fewer were influenced by it (Simkin, Hawton, Whitehead, Fagg, & Eagle, 1995). By contrast, the same group of investigators found that there was a significant increase in presentations to emergency departments and psychiatric services across the United Kingdom following an episode of *Casualty* broadcast in 1996 in which an RAF pilot attempted suicide, again by ingesting 50 paracetamol tablets. They surveyed as many as possible of those presenting in the week after the programme and found that 20% had seen it, of whom about a quarter (5% of the sample) had been influenced by it (Hawton *et al.*, 1996).

Potential interventions

Work on potential interventions to counteract the Werther effect in traditional entertainment media is not well advanced. Australia is one of the few countries to have taken a systematic approach to dealing with fictional depictions of suicide. The Hunter Institute of Mental Health, the organization responsible for disseminating Australia's guidelines for reporting of suicide in the news media, has been funded to assist scriptwriters and playwrights to portray suicide in a responsible manner. The Hunter Institute has developed printed and web-based resources, and has run a number of workshops with writers from a range of genres, including popular television series. It has collaborated closely with entertainment media professionals, mental health clinicians and people affected by suicide, in order to ensure accuracy and relevance. The processes, impacts and outcomes of this intervention have yet to be evaluated (Pirkis, 2009).

The Werther Effect in Newer Media

Summary of the evidence

A recent proliferation of pro-suicide websites has led to concerns that the Werther effect may operate in newer media like the Internet. These websites typically describe suicide methods (e.g., provide details of doses of medication that would be fatal in overdose), provide chat rooms for suicidal individuals and/or implicitly or explicitly encourage suicide pacts (Mehlum, 2000).

A recent study by Biddle, Donovan, Hawton, Kapur, & Gunnell (2008) demonstrated the ease with which it is possible to find such sites. These investigators searched the Internet by entering 12 suicide-related search terms into the four most popular UK search engines and analysing the first 10 sites that each search returned. This method identified 90 sites specifically devoted to the topic of suicide. Half of these sites were regarded by the investigators as 'encouraging, promoting or facilitating suicide'. These pro-suicide sites typically occurred in the first few 'hits' of each search, increasing their likelihood of being accessed over sites that might provide more beneficial information (e.g., where to seek help for mental health problems). 'Top ranked' sites frequently provided explicit information about different suicide methods, including their lethality and the degree of pain associated with them (Biddle *et al.*, 2008).

Three lines of evidence are cited in support of the claim that pro-suicide websites can lead to loss of lives. The first draws on the body of literature about the impact of more traditional news media (e.g., newspapers and television) on suicidal behaviour (cited above: Pirkis & Blood, 2001a; Stack, 2000, 2005). Concern has been expressed that the influence of the Internet might be greater than that of newspapers and television because of its broad reach, and because pro-suicide websites are more explicit and directive in nature than straight news reports.

The second line of evidence comes from a mounting number of descriptive case studies which link an individual's suicidal act to their contact with a specific website. With minimal effort, we identified 20 individual cases reported in the scientific literature, usually involving young people who sought web-based information about a particular suicide method (most commonly poisoning by drugs or toxic gas) (Alao, Sodenberg, Pohl, & Alao, 2006; Beatson, Hosty, & Smith, 2000; Becker, Mayer, Nagenborg, El-Faddagh, & Schmidt, 2004; Chodorowski & Sein, 2002; D'Hulster & van Heeringen, 2006; Forsthoff, Hummel, Moller, & Grunze, 2006; Gallagher, Smith, & Mellen, 2003; Mishara & Weisstub, 2007; Nordt, Kelly, Williams, & Clark, 1998; Prior, 2004; Wehner & Gawatz, 2003). Some of these individuals were found dead with, for example, a printout of relevant information from the given website. Others, some of whom subsequently died and some of whom survived, presented to the emergency department and told staff of their information source. We also identified a number of documented suicide pacts in which individuals attempted or completed suicide with chat room companions, either online or at a designated meeting spot (Mehlum, 2000; Mishara & Weisstub, 2007). Several of these pacts involved a dominant, older person and one or more younger, more vulnerable people.

The third line of evidence comes from analytical studies which have attempted to link Internet use to suicidality, at an individual or group level. In Korea, Ryu and colleagues demonstrated that high school students who qualified as being addicted to the Internet according to a standardized scale were significantly more likely to be suicidal and/or depressed than their non-addicted peers (Kim, Ryu, Chon, Yeun, Choi, *et al.*, 2006; Ryu, Choi, Seo, & Nam, 2004). In Australia, Byard, Simpson, and Gilbert (2006) found that suicides by plastic bag asphyxiation (a method commonly recommended on pro-suicide websites) increased over time as a function of Internet availability.

Potential interventions

Various solutions to the Internet issue have been proposed, including the use of voluntary guidelines and the self-regulation of sites (Becker *et al.*, 2004; Hitosugi, Nagai, & Tokudome, 2007; Mishara & Weisstub, 2007), the use of filtering software (Mishara & Weisstub, 2007), collaboration between the mental health sector and the mass media (Mehlum, 2000), and the development of alternative websites that promote help-seeking behaviour (Becker *et al.*, 2004; Mehlum, 2000; Mishara & Weisstub, 2007). There is a dearth of descriptive evidence in the scientific literature regarding instances in which these interventions have been put in place, and there is no evaluative information about their effectiveness.

Legal control of pro-suicide websites has generally been regarded as being too difficult to implement (Mehlum, 2000; Mishara & Weisstub, 2007), with the result that Australia is the only country to have introduced legislation that uses criminal sanctions to restrict the operation of such sites (Pirkis, Neal, Dare, Blood, & Studdert, 2009). The law makes it an offence to use the Internet or any other carriage service to disseminate material intended to counsel or incite suicide, and violators face substantial fines. The introduction of this legislation sparked much debate, with concerns expressed that the law is over-inclusive, interferes with the individual's right to die, and has no jurisdiction over off-shore websites. Its impact has not yet been rigorously evaluated, but it appears to have deterred Australian individuals and organizations who might otherwise have posted pro-suicide material on local websites, since none now appear to exist (Pirkis, Neal, *et al.*, 2009).

Theoretical Mechanisms Underpinning the Werther Effect

Various theoretical mechanisms have been put forward as candidate explanations of how the Werther effect might operate, most of which draw on Bandura's (1971, 1977) social learning theory. This theory asserts that behaviour can be shaped by an observer imitating a model with whom or she identifies in some way. Support for social learning theory as an explanation for the Werther effect comes from much of the evidence described above. For example, the fact that there is a consistent pattern of evidence for the Werther effect operating in the traditional news media, but more equivocal evidence for it operating in the traditional entertainment media makes sense in the light of social learning theory, since an observer might be more likely to identify with a real person than a fictional one. Similarly, the fact that the strength of the Werther effect is related to the amount and prominence of coverage is consistent with social learning theory, in that greater exposure to the model might be expected to maximize the influence on the observer. The fact that the Werther effect is apparently greater when the observer and model are similar or when the model is a celebrity and regarded highly by the observer is also in line with social learning theory, since both scenarios might promote strong identification with the model by the observer. The observed method-specific effects also make sense in the context of social learning theory, since the observer might copy the behaviour as closely as possible.

An additional mechanism may come into play in the case of pro-suicide Internet sites. As noted, these sites often contain detailed information about suicide methods. Sometimes they even provide direct avenues for obtaining them. Knowledge and availability of methods have been shown to be related to suicide risk in other areas of suicide prevention research (Hawton, Bergen, Simkin, Brock, Griffiths, *et al.*, 2009; Hawton, Simkin, Deeks, Cooper, Johnston, *et al.*, 2004; Nordentoft, 2007; Nordentoft, Qin, Helweg-Larsen, & Juel, 2007), and increasing access to means of suicide via the Internet may be equally hazardous.

Conclusions

There is strong and consistent evidence for the Werther effect operating in the traditional news media: statistically significant increases in completed and attempted suicide rates have been shown to consistently follow news reports of suicide. There is also evidence for the Werther effect operating in the traditional entertainment media, although the findings from studies in this area are more equivocal and more research is required to tease out the circumstances which may lead individuals to copy the behaviour of fictional models. It would also seem that there is a significant risk of the Werther effect operating through newer media, such as the Internet, although the phenomenon is much more difficult to examine in this context because these media are more volatile.

Guidelines to encourage responsible reporting of suicide have been developed to counter-act the Werther effect in traditional news media, and these seem to work provided that media professionals are involved in their development and dissemination. Interventions to address the Werther effect in traditional entertainment media and newer media are less well developed and require further evaluation. Interventions to address the Werther effect are relatively cheap, and even those which are not yet optimally evaluated are unlikely to cause harm.

Suicide is complex and has multiple causes. Addressing the Werther effect will go some way to preventing this major public health problem, although it clearly must be supported by a range of other preventive strategies.

References

Alao, A. O., Sodenberg, M., Pohl, E. L., & Alao, A. L. (2006). Cybersuicide: Review of the role of the internet on suicide. *Cyberpsychology and Behavior, 9*, 489–493.

Ashton, J. R. & Donnan, S. (1979). Suicide by burning: A current epidemic. *British Medical Journal, 2*, 769–770.

Ashton, J. R. & Donnan, S. (1981). Suicide by burning as an epidemic phenomenon: An analysis of 82 deaths and inquests in England and Wales in 1978–79. *Psychological Medicine, 11*, 735–739.

Bandura, A. (1971) *Psychological Modelling: Conflicting theories*. Englewood Cliffs, NJ: Prentice Hall.

Bandura, A. (1977). Self-efficacy: Towards a unifying theory of behavioural change. *Psychological Review, 84*, 191–215.

Beatson, S., Hosty, G. S., & Smith, S. (2000). Suicide and the internet. *Psychiatric Bulletin, 24*, 434.

Becker, K., Mayer, M., Nagenborg, M., El-Faddagh, M., & Schmidt, M. (2004). Parasuicide online: Can suicide websites trigger suicidal behaviour in predisposed adolescents? *Nordic Journal of Psychiatry, 58*, 111–114.

Berkowitz, L. (1984) Some effects of thoughts on anti- and pro-social influences of media effects. *Psychological Bulletin, 95*, 410–427.

Biddle, L., Donovan, J., Hawton, K., Kapur, N., & Gunnell, D. (2008). Suicide and the internet. *British Medical Journal, 336*(7648), 800–802.

Bollen, K. A. & Phillips, D. P. (1982). Imitative suicides: A national study of the effects of television news stories. *American Sociological Review, 47*, 802–809.

Byard, R. W., Simpson, E., & Gilbert, J. D. (2006). Temporal trends over the past two decades in asphyxial deaths in South Australia involving plastic bags or wrapping. *Journal of Clinical Forensic Medicine, 13*, 9–14.

Cheng, A. T. A., Hawton, K., Chen, T. H. H., Yen, A. M. F., Chang, J. C., Chong, M. Y., Liu, C. Y., Lee, Y., Teng, P. R., & Chen, L. C. (2007). The influence of media reporting of a celebrity suicide on suicidal behaviour in patients with a history of depressive disorder. *Journal of Affective Disorders, 103*, 69–75.

Cheng, A. T. A., Hawton, K., Chen, T. H. H., Yen, A. M. F., Chen, C. Y., Chen, L. C., & Teng, P. R. (2007). The influence of media coverage of a celebrity suicide on subsequent suicide attempts. *Journal of Clinical Psychiatry, 68*, 862–866.

Cheng, A. T. A., Hawton, K., Lee, C. T. C., & Chen, T. H. H. (2007). The influence of media reporting of the suicide of a celebrity on suicide rates: A population-based study. *International Journal of Epidemiology, 36*, 1229–1234.

Chodorowski, Z. & Sein, A. J. (2002). Internet as a means of persuading a patient to commit suicide. *Przegl Lek, 59*, 375–376.

D'Hulster, N. & van Heeringen, K. (2006). Cybersuicide: The role of the internet in suicidal behaviour: A case study. *Tijdschr Psychiatr, 48*, 803–807.

Daniels, R. G. (1986). Emotional crises imitating television. *The Lancet, 1*(8485), 856.

Dare, A., Andriessen, K., Nordentoft, M., & Pirkis, J. (forthcoming). Media awards for responsible reporting of suicide: The experience of three countries.

Durkheim, E. *Suicide*. New York: Free Press.

Ellis, S. J. & Walsh, S. (1986). Soap may seriously damage your health. *The Lancet, 1*(8482), 686.

Etzersdorfer, E. & Sonneck, G. (1998). Preventing suicide by influencing mass-media reporting: The Viennese experience 1980–1996. *Archives of Suicide Research, 4*, 64–74.

Etzersdorfer, E., Sonneck, G., & Nagel Kuess, S. (1992). Newspaper reports and suicide. *New England Journal of Medicine, 327*, 502–503.

Etzersdorfer, E., Voracek, M., & Sonneck, G. (2001). A dose–response relationship of imitational suicides with newspaper distribution. *Australian and New Zealand Journal of Psychiatry, 35*, 251.

Etzersdorfer, E., Voracek, M., & Sonneck, G. (2004). A dose–response relationship between imitational suicides and newspaper distribution. *Archives of Suicide Research, 8*, 137–145.

Forsthoff, A., Hummel, B., Moller, H. J., & Grunze, H. (2006). Suicidality and the internet: Danger from new media. *Nervenarzt, 77*, 343–345.

Fowler, B. P. (1986). Emotional crises imitating television. *The Lancet, 1*(8488), 1036–1037.

Fu, K. W. & Yip, P. S. F. (2007). Long-term impact of celebrity suicide on suicidal ideation: Results from a population-based study. *Journal of Epidemiology and Community Health, 61*, 540–546.

Gallagher, K. E., Smith, D. M., & Mellen, P. F. (2003). Suicide asphyxiation by using pure helium gas. *American Journal of Forensic Medicine and Pathology, 4*, 361–363.

Hassan, R. (1995). Effects of newspaper stories on the incidence of suicide in Australia: A research note. *Australian and New Zealand Journal of Psychiatry, 29*, 480–483.

Hawton, K., Bergen, H., Simkin, S., Brock, A., Griffiths, C., Romeri, E., Smith, K. L., Kapur, N., & Gunnell, D. (2009). Effect of withdrawal of co-proxamol on prescribing and deaths from drug poisoning in England and Wales: Time series analysis. *British Medical Journal, 338*, 2270.

Hawton, K., Simkin, S., Deeks, J., Cooper, J., Johnston, A., Waters, K., Arundel, M., Bernal, W., Gunson, B., Hudson, M., Suri, D., & Simpson, K. I. (2004). UK legislation on analgesic packs: before and after study of long term effect on poisonings. *British Medical Journal, 329*, 1076.

Hawton, K., Simkin, S., Deeks, J., O'Connor, S., Keen, A., Altman, D. G., Philo, G., & Bulstrode, C. (1996). Effects of a drug overdose in a television drama on presentations to hospital for self poisoning: Time series and questionnaire study. *British Medical Journal, 318*, 972–977.

Hitosugi, M., Nagai, T., & Tokudome, S. (2007). A voluntary effort to save the youth suicide via the internet. *International Journal of Nursing Studies, 44,* 157.

International Association for Suicide Prevention and World Health Organization (2008). *Preventing Suicide: A resource for media professionals.* Geneva: World Health Organization.

Jamieson, P. (2001). *Reporters' Knowledge of Guidelines and Contagion.* Philadelphia, PA: Annenberg Public Policy Center.

Kim, K., Ryu, E., Chon, M. Y., Yeun, E. J., Choi, S. Y., Seo, J. S., & Nam, B. W. (2006). Internet addiction in Korean adolescents and its relation to depression and suicidal ideation: A questionnaire survey. *International Journal of Nursing Studies, 43,* 185–192.

Mehlum, L. (2000). The internet, suicide, and suicide prevention. *Crisis, 21,* 186–188.

Michel, K., Frey, C., Wyss, K., & Valach, L. (2000). An exercise in improving suicide reporting in print media. *Crisis, 21,* 71–79.

Michel, K., Maillart, A., & Reisch, T. (2007). Monitoring of Suicide Reporting in Print Media 10 Years after the Publication of Media Guidelines: Did you expect anything else? Paper presented at the International Association for Suicide Prevention XXIV World Congress – Preventing Suicide Across the Lifespan: Dreams and Realities.

Mishara, B. L. & Weisstub, D. N. (2007). Ethical, legal, and practical issues in the control and regulation of suicide promotion and assistance over the internet. *Suicide and Life-Threatening Behavior, 37,* 58–65.

Niederkrotenthaler, T. & Sonneck, G. (2007). Assessing the impact of media guidelines for reporting on suicides in Austria: Interrupted time series analysis. *Australian and New Zealand Journal of Psychiatry, 41,* 419–428.

Nordentoft, M. (2007). Prevention of suicide and attempted suicide in Denmark. Epidemiological studies of suicide and intervention studies in selected risk groups. *Danish Medical Bulletin, 54,* 306–369.

Nordentoft, M., Qin, P., Helweg-Larsen, K., & Juel, K. (2007). Restrictions in means for suicide: An effective tool in preventing suicide: The Danish experience. *Suicide and Life-Threatening Behavior, 37,* 688–697.

Nordt, S. P., Kelly, K., Williams, S. R., & Clark, R. F. (1998). 'Black Plague' on the internet. *The Journal of Emergency Medicine, 16,* 223–225.

Phillips, D. P. (1974). The influence of suggestion on suicide: Substantive and theoretical implications of the Werther effect. *American Sociological Review, 39,* 340–354.

Phillips, D. P. & Carstensen, L. L. (1986). Clustering of teenage suicides after television news stories about suicide. *New England Journal of Medicine, 315,* 685–689.

Phillips, D. P. & Carstensen, L. L. (1988). The effect of suicide stories on various demographic groups, 1968–1985. *Suicide and Life Threatening Behavior, 18,* 100–114.

Pirkis, J. (2009). Suicide and the media. *Psychiatry, 8,* 269–271.

Pirkis, J. & Blood, R. W. (2001a). Suicide and the media: (1) Reportage in non-fictional media. *Crisis, 22,* 146–154.

Pirkis, J., & Blood, R. W. (2001b). Suicide and the media: (2) Portrayal in fictional media. *Crisis, 22*(4), 155–162.

Pirkis, J., Blood, R. W., Beautrais, A., Burgess, P., & Skehan, J. (2006). Media guidelines on the reporting of suicide. *Crisis, 27,* 82–87.

Pirkis, J., Dare, A., Blood, R. W., Rankin, B., Williamson, M., Burgess, P., & Jolley, D. (2009). Changes in media reporting of suicide in Australia between 2000/01 and 2006/07. *Crisis, 30,* 25–33.

Pirkis, J., Neal, L., Dare, A., Blood, R. W., & Studdert, D. (2009). Legal bans on pro-suicide websites: An early retrospective from Australia. *Suicide and Life-Threatening Behavior, 39,* 190–193.

Platt, S. (1987). The aftermath of Angie's overdose: Is soap (opera) damaging to your health? *British Medical Journal Clinical Research Edition, 294,* 954–957.

Prior, T. I. (2004). Suicide methods from the internet. *American Journal of Psychiatry, 161,* 1500–1501.

Ryu, E-J., Choi, K. S., Seo, J. S., & Nam, B. W. (2004). The relationship between internet addiction, depression, and suicidal ideation in adolescents. *Taehan Kanho Hakhoe Chi, 34,* 102–110.

Sandler, D. A., Connell, P. A., & Welsh, K. (1986). Emotional crises imitating television. *The Lancet, 1,* 856.

Sacks, M. & Eth, S. (1981) Pathological identification as a cause of suicide on an inpatient unit. *Hospital and Community Psychiatry, 32,* 36–40.

Schmidtke, A. & Hafner, H. (1988). The Werther effect after television films: New evidence for an old hypothesis. *Psychological Medicine, 18,* 665–676.

Schmidtke, A. & Schaller, H. (2000). The role of mass media in suicide prevention. In K. Hawton & K. van Heeringen (Eds.), *The International Handbook of Suicide and Attempted Suicide.* Chichester: John Wiley & Sons, Ltd.

Silverman, M. M., Berman, A. L., Sanddal, N. D., O'Carroll, P. W., & Joiner, T. E. (2007). Rebuilding the Tower of Babel: A revised nomenclature for the study of suicidal behaviors. Part 2: Suicide-related ideations, communications and behaviors. *Suicide and Life-Threatening Behavior, 37,* 264–277.

Simkin, S., Hawton, K., Whitehead, L., Fagg, J., & Eagle, M. (1995). Media influence on parasuicide: A study of the effects of a television drama portrayal of paracetamol self-poisoning. *British Journal of Psychiatry, 167,* 754–759.

Skehan, J., Greenhalgh, S., Hazell, T., & Pirkis, J. (2006). Reach, awareness and uptake of media guidelines for reporting suicide and mental illness: An Australian perspective. *International Journal of Mental Health Promotion, 8,* 28–34.

Sonneck, G., Etzersdorfer, E., & Nagel Kuess, S. (1994). Imitative suicide on the Viennese subway. *Social Science and Medicine, 38,* 453–457.

Stack, S. (1987). Celebrities and suicide: A taxonomy and analysis. *American Sociological Review, 52,* 401–412.

Stack, S. (1989). The effect of publicized mass murders and murder–suicides on lethal violence, 1968–1980: A research note. *Social Psychiatry and Psychiatric Epidemiology, 24,* 202–208.

Stack, S. (1990a). Audience receptiveness, the media, and aged suicide, 1968–1980. *Journal of Aging Studies, 4,* 195–209.

Stack, S. (1990b). A re-analysis of the impact of non-celebrity suicides: A research note. *Social Psychiatry and Psychiatric Epidemiology, 25,* 269–273.

Stack, S. (1991) Social correlates of suicide by age: Media impacts. In A. Leenaars (Ed.), *Lifespan Perspectives of Suicide: Timelines in the suicide process.* New York: Plenum Press.

Stack, S. (2000). Media impacts on suicide: A quantitative review of 293 findings. *Social Science Quarterly, 81,* 957–972.

Stack, S. (2005). Suicide in the media: A quantitative review of studies based on non-fictional stories. *Suicide and Life Threatening Behavior, 35,* 121–133.

Taiminen, T., Salmenpera, T., & Lehtinen, K. (1992). A suicide epidemic in a psychiatric hospital. *Suicide and Life-Threatening Behavior, 22,* 350–363.

Thorson, J., & Oberg, P.A. (2003). Was there a suicide epidemic after Goethe's Werther? *Archives of Suicide Research, 7,* 69–72.

Tousignant, M., Mishara, B., Caillaud, A., Fortin, V., & St Laurent, D. (2005). The impact of media coverage of the suicide of a well-known Quebec reporter: The case of Gaetan Girouard. *Social Science and Medicine, 60,* 1919–1926.

Tully, J. & Elsaka, N. (2004). *Suicide and the Media: A study of the media response to 'Suicide and the media: The reporting and portrayal of suicide in the media – A resource'*. Christchurch: School of Political Science and Communication, University of Canterbury.

Veysey, M. J., Kamanyire, R., & Volans, G. N. (1999). Antifreeze poisonings give more insight into copycat behaviour. *British Medical Journal, 319*, 1131.

Wasserman, I. M. (1984). Imitation and suicide: A re-examination of the Werther effect. *American Sociological Review, 49*, 427–436.

Wehner, F. & Gawatz, O. (2003). Suicidal yew poisoning – from Caesar to today – or suicide instructions on the internet. *Arch Kriminol, 211*, 19–26.

Williams, J. M. G., Lawton, C., Ellis, S. J., Walsh, S., & Reed, J. (1987). Copycat suicide attempts. *The Lancet, 2*, 102–103.

Yip, P., Fu, K., Yang, K., Ip, B., Chan, C., Chen, E., Lee, D. T. S., Law, F. Y. W., & Hawton, K. (2006). The effects of a celebrity suicide on suicide rates in Hong Kong. *Journal of Affective Disorders, 93*, 245–252.

CHAPTER THIRTY-ONE

Suicide Prevention through Restricting Access to Suicide Means and Hotspots

Ying-Yeh Chen, Kevin Chien-Chang Wu, and Paul S. F. Yip

Abstract

Restricting access to suicide means and locations is a component in prevention strategies of almost all prevention centres worldwide. In this review, we describe the rationale underpinning such approaches in general, as well as for specific methods of suicide. We review the age, sex, and country distribution of several common methods of suicide, including medication over-dose, pesticide poisoning, gas poisoning, jumping, firearms, and hanging. Current evidence supporting policies to restrict access to suicide means and hotspots is summarized. In the case of suicides involving self-poisoning and firearms, direct restrictions on selling/purchasing of these lethal or highly toxic means (e.g. guns, pesticides, pills) through regulatory controls is generally effective in reducing suicide. For suicide by self-poisoning, prevention approaches can also involve reducing the toxicity of substances used. Current evidence indicates the effec-tiveness of erecting barriers at jumping hotspots in reducing suicidal leaps. As ligature points and ligatures are universally available, restricting access to these suicide means is not a reason-able prevention strategy except in certain controlled environments such as psychiatric hospitals and prisons. Despite the limited opportunities in relation to hanging, restricting access to suicide means and hotspots are effective and feasible strategies in preventing suicide.

Introduction

In this review, the terms 'suicide' and 'suicide deaths' refer to self-harm behaviours that have resulted in fatal consequences and 'suicide attempt' refers to self-harm behaviours that did

International Handbook of Suicide Prevention: Research, Policy and Practice, First Edition.
Edited by Rory C. O'Connor, Stephen Platt, Jacki Gordon.
© 2011 John Wiley & Sons, Ltd. Published 2011 by John Wiley & Sons, Ltd.

not cause death. Suicide is a complex phenomenon arising from the interplay of multiple factors, such as psychiatric disorders, psychological characteristics, life events, and genetic/biological factors to name a few. When someone is hopeless and suicidal, access to specific methods of suicide is a vital issue; it serves as a crucial element in determining the likelihood of suicidal thoughts being translated into a suicide attempt or death (Hawton, 2007). In this chapter, we review the characteristics of individuals adopting different methods of suicide and explore the existing evidence on the effectiveness of prevention practices that restrict access to the means and sites of suicide. After reviewing the empirical evidence on suicide prevention through restriction to means and hotspots (popular locations where suicide events are clustered), we apply the concept of utility functions from economic theories/models to the formulation of individual choices in suicide (Cutler, Glaeser, & Norberg, 2001; Hamermesh & Soss, 1974; Marcotte, 2003). Essentially, the concept of utility is premised on the assumption that, all things being equal, an individual's behaviour is governed by their quest to maximize their satisfaction, that is, that (all things being equal) they will choose the option which is expected to bring benefits. If we apply this theory to suicide, we suggest that when individuals weigh up life-and-death choices, they will choose suicide if they view the expected utility or benefit of killing themselves to outweigh that of continuing to live. Within this theoretical model, access to suicide means and locales can directly influence life-and-death choices, and therefore is included as a variable in the utility function. Other contributory factors include individual preference for specific suicide means, as well as the socio-cultural and symbolic values of different methods. In this chapter, we suggest that restriction of access to the means of suicide might reduce the utility of death and thus render those at risk more willing to live through the moment of crisis.

Rationale and Evidence

Restricting access to suicide means and popular suicide locations is an important element of suicide prevention strategies in many countries (e.g., Centre for Suicide Research and Prevention, 2005; Lee & Liao, 2006; United Nations, 1996; US Department of Health and Human Services, 2001). Such activities reflect burgeoning evidence showing that restricting access to a wide variety of methods and sites of suicide is an effective and relatively simple approach to suicide prevention (Beautrais, 2007a). In fact, one recent large-scale meta-analysis has demonstrated that method restriction is one of the few effective suicide prevention strategies (Mann, Apter, Bertolote, Beautrais, Currier, *et al.*, 2005).

There are two key factors underpinning the effectiveness of these strategies. First, a suicide crisis is often short-lived, with impulsiveness and ambivalence being common features of the suicidal process (Daigle, 2005). The impulsive nature of many suicides implies that these individuals tend to use the method most easily accessible to them, and if a dangerous method is not available at the time of the crisis, we may be able to 'buy' some time, so that (in some cases at least) suicidal impulses will pass without fatal consequences (Gunnell, 2005). Making a lethal method less available can hence reduce (completed) suicides. Second, not all methods are equally favoured: individuals may have a particular preference for a certain method or may favour a particular place for their suicide

Table 31.1 Individual socio-demographic and country characteristics associated with choice of suicide method

Method of suicide	Characteristics
Poisoning	
Medication overdose	Females in Western countries, particularly in Canada, United Kingdom, and Nordic countries.
Pesticide	Young women with no pre-existing psychiatric history, common in developing countries, such as China, Sri Lanka, and Peru.
Motor vehicle exhaust gas	Well-planned suicide among middle-aged males in motorized countries, such as United Kingdom, Australia, and New Zealand.
Charcoal-burning	Economically active middle-aged males experiencing financial problems, common in Hong Kong and Taiwan.
Jumping	
From bridges	Young males comorbid with psychotic disorders, examples of iconic jumping bridges include Golden Gate Bridge in San Francisco, Jacques Cartier Bridge in Montreal, Westgate Bridge in Melbourne, Bosphorus Bridge in Istanbul, and Clifton Suspension Bridge in Bristol.
From buildings	Elderly or young individuals who reside in tall residential buildings, more frequently adopted by psychotic patients, common in Hong Kong, Singapore, Taipei City, and other populated cities.
Firearms	Common method in all socio-demographic groups in the United States and some South American countries (such as Argentina and Uruguay), more frequently used by males in some European countries such as Switzerland, Finland, and France. Legislative controls are particularly effective for youth firearm suicide.

(De Moore & Robertson, 1999). The desirability of a certain method or place of suicide is determined by multiple factors, including personal preferences (e.g., fear of disfigurement, certainty of death), media influences and socio-cultural acceptability, etc. (Clarke & Lester, 1989; Daigle, 2005; Marks, 1977). For individuals with specific preferences, the probability of turning to an alternative or less appealing method is less likely when the preferred suicide means/spots are restricted (Clarke & Lester, 1989). International variations in the common suicide methods being used and characteristics of individuals who tend to choose certain methods of suicide are summarized in Table 31.1.

Restricting Access to Suicidal Means and Hotspots in Suicide Prevention

Suicide by poisoning

1 Medication overdose   Increased frequency of suicide by drug overdose was observed in the period between the 1950s and 1980s in several Western countries (Bille-Brahe & Jessen, 1994; De Leo, Conforti, & Carollo, 1997; Gunnell, Middleton, & Frankel, 2000; Hawkins,

Edwards, & Dargan, 2007; Moens, Loysch, Honggokoesoemo, & van de Voorde, 1989; Whitlock, 1975). Agents commonly used for self-poisoning during this time period included barbiturates, dextropropoxyphene (an analgesic in the opioid category), and tricyclic antidepressants (Nordentoft, 2007). A declining trend in suicide by drug overdose occurred in the last decades of the twentieth century when safer medications were developed to replace medications with higher lethality, such as benzodiazepines for barbiturates and serotonergic agents for tricyclic antidepressants (McClure, 1987; Nordentoft, 2007). Numerous studies have shown that no marked substitution occurs when prescribing is reduced for those medicines with higher fatality (Clarke & Lester, 1989; Ohberg, Lönqvist, Sarna, Vuori, & Penttila, 1995; Schapira, Linsley, Linsley, Kelly, & Kay, 2001).

Medication overdose, however, is still a common method of suicide, particularly among women, in several Western countries, such as Canada, the Nordic countries, and the United Kingdom (Ajdacic-Gross, Weiss, Ring, Hepp, Bopp, *et al.*, 2008). In the United Kingdom, self-poisoning with analgesics, especially paracetamol or co-proxamol (dextropropoxyphene in combination with paracetamol), has raised considerable concern. Easy availability of these analgesics has been shown to be an important reason for the prevalence of the phenomenon (Gunnell, Hawton, Murray, Garnier, Bismuth, *et al.*, 1997; Hawton, Ware, Mistry, Hewitt, Kingsbury, *et al.*, 1995). This could be due to prescribing practices in particular, when there is a large interval between psychiatric patients' appointments, giving rise to the prescribing of large quantities of analgesics or other psychotropic drugs. Legislation to restrict sales of paracetamol as well as other analgesics (e.g., aspirin) was enacted in 1998 in the United Kingdom, initial and longer-term (three-year) benefits on mortality and morbidity risks associated with paracetamol overdose have been reported (Hawton, Townsend, Deeks, Appleby, Gunnell, *et al.*, 2001; Hawton, Simkin, Deeks, Cooper, Johnston, *et al.*, 2004). Only very limited evidence of substitution to other kinds of analgesic (e.g., ibuprofen, a relatively safer analgesics in overdose), has been found (Hawton *et al.*, 2004). In addition, the withdrawal of co-proxamol (a more toxic analgesic), from the market in 2005 in the United Kingdom has reduced poisoning mortality associated with painkillers (Hawton, Bergen, Simkin, Brock, Griffiths, *et al.*, 2009). Overall, then, there is reasonably encouraging evidence that legislative measures can reduce suicide deaths by analgesic overdose. Furthermore, a change of prescription practice, such as prescribing less toxic medication and smaller amounts of drugs per visit, should be considered for psychotropic drugs in order to prevent suicide by overdosing, for example, community nurses providing psychotropic drugs during home visits.

2 Pesticide poisoning   Self-poisoning with pesticide is the most common method of suicide in many developing countries (Eddleston, 2000; Eddleston & Phillips, 2004; World Health Organization, 2006). The easy access to, and the high toxicity of, pesticides are thought to contribute to the high suicide rates in rural areas of several Asian countries with dominant agricultural economies (such as rural China and Sri Lanka) (Gunnell & Eddleston, 2003). The fact that pesticide poisoning carries such a high fatality rate largely accounts for the higher female and young adult suicide death rates in China (Pearson, Phillips, He, & Ji, 2002; Phillips, Yang, Zhang, Wang, Ji, *et al.*, 2002). The age and sex profiles of suicide cases that are caused by pesticide poisoning mirror that of the group who most frequently engage in non-fatal self-harm in Western countries (Gunnell, 2005;

Mishara, 2007), suggesting that the accessibility of lethal suicide methods is a crucial element in determining the outcome of a suicide act.

Many Western studies conclude that suicide is completed by individuals who suffer from depressive illness or other psychiatric conditions (Cavanagh, Carson, Sharpe, & Lawrie, 2003; Mortensen, Agerbo, Eriksson, Qin, & Westergaard-Nielsen, 2000). In contrast, studies in China have shown that the majority of people who attempt or complete suicide by intentional ingestion of pesticide do not have a psychiatric disorder (Pearson *et al.*, 2002; Phillips *et al.*, 2002). Rather, such suicides are usually an impulsive act undertaken during family quarrels (Pearson *et al.*, 2002). Despite the fact that such suicidal acts are often not premeditated or well planned, ease of access to highly lethal pesticides stored at home results in high rates of completed suicides. The context of pesticide self-poisoning hence suggests the possibility of preventing suicide through restricting the access to these dangerous household chemicals.

In both Western Samoa and Jordan, research data have shown that restricting the use of toxic pesticides has been associated with a reduction in suicides by pesticide poisoning (Abu al-Ragheb & Salhab, 1989; Bowles, 1995). However, before the development of less toxic, effective, and economically acceptable alternatives for agricultural use, simply banning highly lethal, yet commonly used, pesticides was not an acceptable option in developing countries (Gunnell & Eddleston, 2003; Hawton, 2005). One other possibility to reduce the availability of toxic pesticides is to design a secure storage policy such that only the licensed owner can have access to the pesticides stored in the locked containers. An evaluation of the acceptability and use of a lockable pesticide storage device in Sri Lanka has indicated that it is a very acceptable measure in reducing suicides and accidental poisoning (Hawton, Ratnayeke, Simkin, Harriss, & Scott, 2009).

3.1 Gas poisoning: domestic gas poisoning   The 'coal gas story' is probably the most salient example of reducing overall suicide rates through restricting access to a lethal method of suicide (Kreitman, 1976). Prior to the 1960s in the United Kingdom, the most common method of suicide was self-poisoning by domestic coal gas, with this mode accounting for approximately half of suicide deaths at this time. Then, during the late 1950s through to the early 1970s, natural gas (i.e., gas supplies with a lower carbon monoxide (CO) content) was introduced on a region by region basis. Kreitman (1976) analysed suicide data throughout this period and found that the decrease in CO content of domestic gas was concomitant with a steady decrease in both male and female suicide rates in England and Wales. Similar findings were also reported in Australia (Burvill, 1990), Japan (Lester & Abe, 1989a), and the United States (Lester, 1990b), although partial substitution towards motor vehicle exhaust gas suicide (MVEGS) was found in Australia and the United States, particularly among males (Burvill, 1990; Lester, 1990b).

3.2 Gas poisoning: motor vehicle exhaust gas suicide   Motor vehicle exhaust gas suicide (MVEGS) is a common method of suicide in several motorized countries: it is more commonly adopted by middle-aged males (Brennan, Routley, & Ozanne-Smith, 2006; Routley, 2007; Routley & Ozanne-Smith, 1998). As this method involves some preparation, such suicides tend to be premeditated and well planned, rather than acts of impulsive self-harm enacted under transient crisis. MVEGS is particularly appealing to individuals who prefer to end their lives at places away from their homes, so that they can spare their family members from the trauma of discovering the body (De Leo, Evans, & Neulinger, 2002; Pirkola, Isometsa, & Lönqvist, 2003; Routley, 2007). The location and the age and sex distribution of individuals using this method again underscores the relationship between availability of suicide means and specific suicides. Counter-measures to prevent MVEGS include installing catalytic converters to decrease CO emission levels, development of CO detectors in vehicles, modification of exhaust pipes to be incompatible with hose attachments, and signs displaying a helpline at MVEGS hotspots (Routley, 2007). Several studies have demonstrated the effect of the installation of catalytic converters on reducing MVEGS (Amos, Appleby, & Kiernan, 2001; Lester, 1989; Lester & Abe, 1989b; Lester & Clarke, 1988; Mott, Wolfe, Alverson, MacDonald, Bailey, *et al.*, 2002; Shelef, 1994). For example, Mott has reported that in the United States, legislation to install catalytic converters in new vehicles was enacted in 1975 and the MVEGS rates declined 43% over the period 1968–1988 (Mott *et al.*, 2002). A comparison between the United States and the United Kingdom has revealed that the relatively late introduction of the legislation in the United Kingdom (in 1993) has reversed the MVEGS pattern in these two countries (Clarke & Lester, 1987): in the 1950s the MVEGS rate was five times higher in the United States compared with the United Kingdom, whereas in 1984 the MVEGS rate in the United Kingdom was twice that of the United States. While the legislation was originally introduced for environmental reasons (to decrease CO pollution) and not specifically intended as a suicide prevention measure, the associated benefit in decreasing suicide is nonetheless remarkable. A reduction of MVEGS has also been reported following helpline signage at MVEGS hotspots (King & Frost, 2005). The impact of other measures, such as the modification of exhaust pipes to be incompatible with hose attachments and the development of sensors to detect harmful carbon-monoxide levels in vehicles, on MVEGS is still in need of further evaluation.

3.3 Gas poisoning: charcoal-burning suicides   Burning barbecue charcoal in an enclosed space to create CO intoxication has become a popular method of suicide in both Taiwan and Hong Kong in the past 10 years (Kuo, Conwell, Yu, Chiu, Chen, *et al.*, 2008; Liu, Beautrais, Caine, Chan, Chao, *et al.*, 2007; Yip & Lee, 2007). Having been portrayed by the media as a calm, painless, non-violent, yet highly lethal way to end one's life, the novel method, first reported in Hong Kong, quickly spread to Taiwan and other nearby Asian countries (Kuo *et al.*, 2008; Lee, Chan, Lee, & Yip, 2002; Lin & Lu, 2008; Liu *et al.*, 2007; Yip & Lee, 2007). In both Hong Kong and Taiwan, the new method has outstripped several traditional suicide methods and has become the second most common method used (Kuo *et al.*, 2008; Lin & Lu, 2008; Yip & Lee, 2007). This increase in charcoal-burning suicide has not been accompanied with a compensatory reduction in other suicide means (Liu *et al.*, 2007). It has been hypothesized that the new method has drawn a new cohort of individuals who would not have considered suicide if death by charcoal-burning had not been publicized (Liu *et al.*, 2007). The hypothesis is further supported by the observation that the socio-demographic and clinical characteristics of individuals who completed suicide by charcoal-burning were distinct from those who completed suicide by other means: individuals who adopted the novel method were more likely to be economically active, middle-aged men under financial stress, who otherwise had no pre-existing psychiatric disorders (Chen, Liao, & Lee, 2009; Kuo *et al.*, 2008;

Liu *et al.*, 2007). The high desirability of the new method among specific sub-groups hints at the possibility of suicide prevention through controlling the easy accessibility to charcoal. Supporting evidence for this comes from a preliminary community intervention study in Hong Kong: this has revealed that removing charcoal from open shelves and making it necessary for the customer to ask a shop assistant to obtain charcoal for purchase has considerably reduced the number of local suicides (Yip, 2009; Yip, Law, Fu, Law, Wong, *et al.*, 2010). No obvious substitution has been observed (Yip, 2009; Yip *et al.*, 2010). The success further supports the feasibility of suicide prevention that make it difficult to obtain or access suicide means.

Suicide by jumping from a height

Suicide by jumping from a height is a prevalent method of suicide in populated cities or countries where high-rise buildings are widely available, such as Hong Kong, Singapore, and New York City (Beautrais, 2007b; Chen, Gunnell, & Lu, 2009; Gunnell & Nowers, 1997; Marzuk, Leon, Tardiff, Morgan, Stajic, *et al.*, 1992; Yip & Tan, 1998). In these places, most of the jumping suicides take place at residential buildings (Abrams, Marzuk, Tardiff, & Leon, 2005; Chen, Gunnell, & Lu, 2009; Yip & Tan, 1998). The method is particularly favoured by older citizens, as it is an easily accessible, assuredly lethal, and a technically simple way for physically fragile, older adults residing in tall buildings to end their lives (Abrams *et al.*, 2005; Chen, Gunnell, & Lu, 2009; Copeland, 1989; Yip & Tan, 1998). Jumping from residential buildings is also commonly adopted by youths whose suicides are impulsive, and ease of access to tall buildings increases the risk of fatality for these unplanned, impulsive suicide attempts (Yip, 1997; Yip & Tan, 1998). People with recognized psychiatric disorders have also been reported to be more likely to take their own lives by jumping from high-rise buildings (Chen, Lee, Chang, & Liao, 2009).

Restricting access to potential jumping sites requires much more effort in view of the large number of high-rise buildings in populated areas. For example, hotspots in public buildings such as department stores and hospitals have been identified (Chen, Gunnell, & Lu, 2009; Chen & Yip, 2009). Possible prevention measures might include installing simple padlocks on windows in residential households and raising awareness of the risk of jumping suicide in the community, in particular, among family members who share a home with someone who is considered to be vulnerable (Centre for Suicide Research and Prevention, 2005). The security guard in residential and commercial buildings could also be trained to look out for any potentially suicidal people and to intervene as necessary. For example, access to the roof and entry to the top of buildings could be closely monitored. Finally, enhancing building regulations to incorporate safety measures into the design of new buildings/structures may be potential prevention strategies themselves (Beautrais, 2007b).

Other types of locations, mostly bridges (Beautrais, 2007b; Gunnell & Nowers, 1997), can be the sites for many suicides. Such places, often called jumping 'hotspots', are frequently used because of their reputation, media attention, easy access, cultural significance, or the aesthetic appeal of the spot (Beautrais, 2007b; Reisch & Michel, 2005). Examples of these hotspots include Golden Gate Bridge in San Francisco (Lafave, LaPorta, Hutton, & Mallory,

1995), Jacques Cartier Bridge in Montreal (Prevost, Julien, & Brown, 1996), Westgate Bridge in Melbourne (Coman, Meyer, & Cameron, 2000), Bosphorus Bridge in Istanbul (Cetin, Gunay, Fincanci, & Ozdemir Kolusayin, 2001), Muenster Terrace in Bern (Reisch & Michel, 2005) and Clifton Suspension Bridge in Bristol (Bennewith, Nowers, & Gunnell, 2007). The characteristics of those who jump from these popular jumping spots differ from suicides in general; they tend to be younger, predominantly male, and more likely to have comorbid psychotic disorders (Beautrais, 2001; Cantor, Hill, & McLachlan, 1989; Coman, Meyer, & Cameron, 2000; Lindqvist, Jonsson, Eriksson, Hedelin, & Bjornstig, 2004). The appeal or mystique of these special places may serve as an important element of method choice, making replacement by other suicide means or places less likely. Erecting safety barriers has been shown to be effective in reducing suicides at jumping hotspots (Beautrais, 2001; Bennewith, Nowers, & Gunnell, 2007; O'Carroll & Silverman, 1994). Importantly, the introduction of such measures has not increased suicides at nearby jumping sites (Beautrais, 2001; Bennewith, Nowers, & Gunnell, 2007; O'Carroll & Silverman, 1994).

In Chapter 30, above, Jane Pirkis and Merete Nordentoft highlight the importance of minimizing sensationalist reporting by the media and present the evidence to support this. We, too, argue that attention should also be paid to restricting sensational reports of suicide in particular, to discourage reporting of the means used and/or references to identifiable suicide hotspots. For example, legislation curtailing media reporting of suicides in the subways of Vienna, Austria led to a marked reduction in such suicides (Etzersdorfer & Sonneck, 1998). Similarly, recent studies have shown that when fencing has been erected to reduce access to a popular jumping site, the consequent reduction in media reporting helped to 'de-mystique' the site and, hence, decrease suicidal jumps in the surrounding areas (Bennewith, Nowers, & Gunnell, 2007; Chen, Gunnell, & Lu, 2009; Reisch & Michel, 2005). Other possible strategies to reduce hotspot suicides may include restricting access to the site (e.g., restricting pedestrian access to popular suicide bridges), installation of on-site telephone helplines, introduction of surveillance and patrols, and improved rescue and response efforts (Beautrais, 2007a).

Firearms suicide

Suicide through firearm use is common in countries where guns and rifles can be obtained legally and therefore have higher rates of firearm ownership: this suicide method is extremely rare in countries with stringent gun control laws (Ajdacic-Gross *et al.*, 2008; Leenaars, 2007). The United States has the highest rate of firearm suicide among industrialized countries (Brent & Bridge, 2003), and studies there have consistently concluded that states with strict gun control legislation have lower suicide rates (Boor & Bair, 1990; Lester, 1990a; Lester & Murrell, 1980). Furthermore, there is evidence from quasi-experimental studies indicating that the implementation of firearm control laws is associated with decreasing suicide rates (Brent, 2001) in the United States (Loftin, McDowall, Wiersema, & Cottey, 1991), Canada (Caron, 2004; Lester & Leenaars, 1993), Australia (Cantor & Slater, 1995; Ozanne-Smith, Ashby, Newstead, Stathakis, & Clapperton, 2004), New Zealand (Beautrais, Fergusson, & Horwood, 2006), and Austria (Kapusta,

Etzersdorfer, Krall, & Sonneck, 2007). Such legislation has been found to be particularly effective in decreasing suicide rates among youths. Although there has been some evidence of method-switching (Klieve, Barnes, & De Leo, 2009; Rich, Young, Fowler, Wagner, & Black, 1990), the overall impact on the youth suicide rate has been largely favourable.

Studies directly evaluating the relationship between suicide and gun ownership also provide ample evidence on the association between firearm availability and suicide (Brent & Bridge, 2003; Brent, Perper, Goldstein, Kolko, Allan, *et al.*, 1988; Brent, Perper, Allman, Moritz, Wartella, *et al.*, 1991; Brent, Perper, Moritz, Baugher, Schweers, *et al.*, 1993; Shah, Hoffman, Wake, & Marine, 2000). This line of research uses a case-control design, comparing the prevalence of guns in the homes of those who have taken their own lives with that of controls. Most of these studies are from the United States, with the results consistently supporting a significant association between household gun ownership and suicide (Brent *et al.*, 1988; Brent *et al.*, 1991; Brent *et al.*, 1993; Shah *et al.*, 2000). These studies also indicate that having guns in the home brings an increased risk for young age groups in particular, and for people with no apparent psychopathology. As a household with a loaded gun dramatically increases the risk of impulsive suicide (Brent & Bridge, 2003), restricting the availability of firearms at home is particularly effective in preventing suicide in youths and those who have no pre-existing mental health problems.

Existing laws relating to gun controls in the United States, Canada, Australia, New Zealand, and the United Kingdom include mandatory firearm registration, requirement for owner licensing, setting/enforcing a minimum age for licensing, periodic examination and renewal of licences, requirements for a mandatory cooling-off period (a waiting period in which a certain amount of time must pass between gun purchase and gun possession), and interviewing/home visiting of new applicants/gun owners before licensing or renewing a licence (Ajdacic-Gross, Killias, Hepp, Gadola, Bopp, *et al.*, 2006). Other measures to prevent firearms suicide through method restriction can also include firearm safety counselling and safer firearm storage practices, especially in the homes of high-risk individuals. However, the effectiveness of these approaches requires further empirical examination (Brent & Bridge, 2003).

Suicide by hanging

Hanging is the most common method of suicide in many countries (Ajdacic-Gross *et al.*, 2008). Indeed, the prevalence of this highly lethal method has increased in recent decades in several Western countries, particularly among young men (Beautrais, 2000; Wilkinson & Gunnell, 2000). As ligature points and ligatures are universally available, preventing hanging suicide through method restriction is generally not possible. The exception may be institutional settings, such as psychiatric hospitals and prisons, where it may be possible to prevent hangings by the removal of ligature points. However, research in the United Kingdom focusing on patients in contact with mental health services found that only a small proportion of hangings actually took place in the controlled environments themselves; the majority (90%) of such deaths were in the community (Gunnell, Bennewith, Hawton, Simkin, & Kapur, 2005).

Concluding Comments and Future Opportunities

International suicide patterns reflect differences in method availability and acceptability according to differences in national policies/laws and socio-cultural influences (Ajdacic-Gross *et al.*, 2008; Farmer & Rohde, 1980; Stack & Wasserman, 2005). Ample evidence has indicated that restricting the access to suicide methods and hotspots is an effective strategy in preventing suicide. Restricting the accessibility of suicide means and hotspots is most effective for unplanned, impulsive suicides, and in those circumstances where a particular suicide means is favoured, for example, because it is thought to be painless or glamorous.

In economic analyses of suicide and current theories of suicide method restriction, time is an important issue. In economic models, it is often assumed that people tend to discount future values. For example, individuals would consider £100 in 10 years' time to be of lower value than £100 now. In this way, future values or utilities are *discounted*. Furthermore, the discount rates might vary among people and circumstances.

We suggest that the notion that future utilities or values are discounted can be usefully applied to suicidology insofar as those at risk of suicide might discount future utilities at too high a rate when in crisis due to their emotional state or some other abnormal psychological mechanisms. Such individuals tend to have a vision of a doomed future because, at their moment of crisis, they have discounted the value or utility of their life (as they see it) in the future. However, their utility function might indicate that if they are prevented from ending their life at a particular moment in time, they might subsequently choose to live because at this later time, their accumulated discounted utility of life is greater than that of death. Furthermore, if access to a suicide method is made more difficult, this may serve to attenuate the appeal or value of death. We therefore suggest that irrespective of whether a suicide is rational or irrational, impulsive or planned, factors associated with the utility functions of suicide choices could be the focus of effective interventions. In particular, suicide method restrictions might borrow time and space for potential suicide victims to reconsider or readjust their utilities of life as their mood or reasoning patterns shift. As shown in the above review of empirical evidence, restriction of access to suicide means and hotspots does have effects on preventing the suicides of those who are impulsive or have a more fixed preference for a certain suicide means.

The utilities model provides some insights and directions for future economic and psychological research into suicide prevention through restricting access to suicide means and hotspots. Furthermore, developments in neuro-economics (an approach that draws on neuroscience, economics, and psychology to study the process of decision-making) (Camerer, Loewenstein, & Prelec, 2004) might also offer a new way for us to 'see', through neuro-imaging and event-related potentials (a measure of the electric potentials on the scalp), how those at risk of suicide might respond to different factors in their utility functions of life or death choices. Combining suicide utility analysis and neuro-economics might thereby elucidate how much impact each means restriction intervention might have on individual suicide choice. In turn, this might lead to the identification of other acceptable and cost-effective ways to prevent suicide by the restriction of means.

Acknowledgements

The authors would like to thank the editors for their comments and Annette Beautrais for many useful discussions.

References

Abrams, R. C., Marzuk, P. M., Tardiff, K., & Leon, A. C. (2005). Preference for fall from height as a method of suicide by elderly residents of New York City. *American Journal of Public Health, 95,* 1000–1002.

Abu al-Ragheb, S. Y. & Salhab, A. S. (1989). Pesticide mortality. A Jordanian experience. *The American Journal of Forensic Medicine and Pathology, 10,* 221–225.

Ajdacic-Gross, V., Killias, M., Hepp, U., Gadola, E., Bopp, M., Lauber, C., Schnyder, U., Gutzwiller, F., & Rossler, W. (2006). Changing times: A longitudinal analysis of international firearm suicide data. *American Journal of Public Health, 96,* 1752–1755.

Ajdacic-Gross, V., Weiss, M. G., Ring, M., Hepp, U., Bopp, M., Gutzwiller, F., & Rossler, W. (2008). Methods of suicide: International suicide patterns derived from the WHO mortality database. *Bulletin of the World Health Organization, 86,* 726–732.

Amos, T., Appleby, L., & Kiernan, K. (2001). Changes in rates of suicide by car exhaust asphyxiation in England and Wales. *Psychological Medicine, 31,* 935–939.

Beautrais, A. L. (2000). Methods of youth suicide in New Zealand: Trends and implications for prevention. *The Australian and New Zealand Journal of Psychiatry, 34,* 413–419.

Beautrais, A. L. (2001). Effectiveness of barriers at suicide jumping sites: A case study. *The Australian and New Zealand Journal of Psychiatry, 35,* 557–562.

Beautrais, A. L. (2007a). Suicide by jumping. A review of research and prevention strategies. *Crisis, 28* (Suppl. 1), 58–63.

Beautrais, A. L. (2007b). The contribution to suicide prevention of restricting access to methods and sites. *Crisis, 28* (Suppl. 1), 1–3.

Beautrais, A. L., Fergusson, D. M., & Horwood, L. J. (2006). Firearms legislation and reductions in firearm-related suicide deaths in New Zealand. *The Australian and New Zealand Journal of Psychiatry, 40,* 253–259.

Bennewith, O., Nowers, M., & Gunnell, D. (2007). Effect of barriers on the Clifton suspension bridge, England, on local patterns of suicide: implications for prevention. *British Journal of Psychiatry, 190,* 266–267.

Bille-Brahe, U. & Jessen, G. (1994). Suicide in Denmark, 1922–1991: The choice of method. *Acta Psychiatrica Scandinavica, 90,* 91–96.

Boor, M. & Bair, J. H. (1990). Suicide rates, handgun control laws, and sociodemographic variables. *Psychological Reports, 66,* 923–930.

Bowles, J. R. (1995). Suicide in Western Samoa: An example of a suicide prevention program in a developing country. In R. Diekstra (Ed.), *Preventive Strategies on Suicide* (pp. 173–206). Leiden: Brill.

Brennan, C., Routley, V. & Ozanne-Smith, J. (2006). Motor vehicle exhaust gas suicide in Victoria, Australia 1998–2002. *Crisis, 27,* 119–124.

Brent, D. A. (2001). Firearms and suicide. *Annals of the New York Academy of Sciences, 932,* 225–239.

Brent, D. A. & Bridge, J. (2003). Firearms availability and suicide. Evidence, interventions, and future directions. *American Behavioral Scientist, 46,* 1192–1210.

Brent, D. A., Perper, J. A., Allman, C. J., Moritz, G. M., Wartella, M. E., & Zelenak, J. P. (1991). The presence and accessibility of firearms in the homes of adolescent suicides. A case-control study. *Journal of the American Medical Association, 266*, 2989–2995.

Brent, D. A., Perper, J. A., Goldstein, C. E., Kolko, D. J., Allan, M. J., Allman, C. J., & Zelenak, J. P. (1988). Risk factors for adolescent suicide. A comparison of adolescent suicide victims with suicidal inpatients. *Archives of General Psychiatry, 45*, 581–588.

Brent, D. A., Perper, J. A., Moritz, G., Baugher, M., Schweers, J., & Roth, C. (1993). Firearms and adolescent suicide. A community case-control study. *American Journal of Diseases of Children, 147*, 1066–1071.

Burvill, P. W. (1990). The changing pattern of suicide by gassing in Australia, 1910–1987: The role of natural gas and motor vehicles. *Acta Psychiatrica Scandinavica, 81*, 178–184.

Camerer, C. F., Loewenstein, G., & Prelec, D. (2004). Neuroeconomics: Why economics needs brains. *The Scandinavian Journal of Economics, 106*, 555–579.

Cantor, C. H., Hill, M. A., & McLachlan, E. K. (1989). Suicide and related behaviour from river bridges. A clinical perspective. *British Journal of Psychiatry, 155*, 829–835.

Cantor, C. H. & Slater, P. J. (1995). The impact of firearm control legislation on suicide in Queensland: Preliminary findings. *Medical Journal of Australia, 162*, 583–585.

Caron, J. (2004). Gun control and suicide: Possible impact of Canadian legislation to ensure safe storage of firearms. *Archives of Suicide Research, 8*, 361–374.

Cavanagh, J. T. O., Carson, A. J., Sharpe, M., & Lawrie, S. M. (2003). Psychological autopsy studies of suicide: A systematic review. *Psychological Medicine, 33*, 395–405.

Centre for Suicide Research and Prevention. (2005). *Research Findings into Suicide and its Prevention. Final report.* Hong Kong: The University of Hong Kong.

Cetin, G., Gunay, Y., Fincanci, S. K., & Ozdemir Kolusayin, R. (2001). Suicides by jumping from Bosphorus Bridge in Istanbul. *Forensic Science International, 116*, 157–162.

Chen, Y. Y., Lee, M. B., Chang, C. M., & Liao, S. C. (2009). Methods of suicide in different psychiatric diagnostic groups. *Journal of Affective Disorders, 118*, 196–200.

Chen, Y. Y., Liao, S. C., & Lee, M. B. (2009). Health care use by victims of charcoal-burning suicide in Taiwan. *Psychiatric Services, 60*, 126.

Chen, Y. Y., Gunnell, D., & Lu, T. H. (2009). Descriptive epidemiological study of sites of suicide jumps in Taipei, Taiwan. *Injury Prevention, 15*, 41–44.

Chen, Y. Y. & Yip, P. S. F. (2009). Prevention of suicide by jumping: experiences from Taipei City (Taiwan), Hong Kong and Singapore. In D. Wasserman (Ed.), *Oxford Textbook of Suicidology and Suicide Prevention* (pp. 569–572). Oxford: Oxford University Press.

Clarke, R. & Lester, D. (1987). Toxicity of car exhausts and opportunity for suicide: Comparison between Britain and the United States. *Journal of Epidemiology and Community Health, 41*, 114–120.

Clarke, R. & Lester, D. (1989). *Explaining Choice of Method. Suicide: Closing the exits.* New York: Springer Verlag.

Coman, M., Meyer, A. D., & Cameron, P. A. (2000). Jumping from the Westgate Bridge, Melbourne. *The Medical Journal of Australia, 172*, 67–69.

Copeland, A. R. (1989). Suicide by jumping from buildings. *American Journal of Forensic Medicine and Pathology, 10*, 295–298.

Cutler, D. M., Glaeser, E. L., & Norberg, K. E. (2001). Explaining the rise in youth suicide. In J. Gruber (Ed.), *Risky Behavior among Youths* (pp. 219–269). Chicago: The University of Chicago Press.

Daigle, M. S. (2005). Suicide prevention through means restriction: assessing the risk of substitution. A critical review and synthesis. *Accident, Analysis and Prevention, 37*, 625–632.

De Leo, D., Conforti, D., & Carollo, G. (1997). A century of suicide in Italy: a comparison between the old and the young. *Suicide and Life-Threatening Behavior, 27*, 239–249.

De Leo, D., Evans, R., & Neulinger, K. (2002). Hanging, firearm, and non-domestic gas suicides among males: a comparative study. *The Australian and New Zealand Journal of Psychiatry, 36*, 183–189.

De Moore, G. M. & Robertson, A. R. (1999). Suicide attempts by firearms and by leaping from heights: A comparative study of survivors. *American Journal of Psychiatry, 156*, 1425–1431.

Eddleston, M. (2000). Patterns and problems of deliberate self-poisoning in the developing world. *QJM: Monthly Journal of the Association of Physicians, 93*, 715–731.

Eddleston, M. & Phillips, M. R. (2004). Self poisoning with pesticides. *British Medical Journal, 328*, 42–44.

Etzersdorfer, E. & Sonneck, G. (1998). Preventing suicide by influencing mass media reporting: The Viennese experience 1980–1996. *Archives of Suicide Research, 4*, 67–74.

Farmer, R. & Rohde, J. (1980). Effect of availability and acceptability of lethal instruments on suicide mortality. An analysis of some international data. *Acta Psychiatrica Scandinavica, 62*, 436–446.

Gunnell, D. (2005). Time trends and geographic differences in suicide: implications for prevention. In K. Hawton (Ed.), *Prevention and Treatment of Suicidal Behaviour: From science to practice* (pp. 29–52). Oxford: Oxford University Press.

Gunnell, D., Bennewith, O., Hawton, K., Simkin, S., & Kapur, N. (2005). The epidemiology and prevention of suicide by hanging: a systematic review. *International Journal of Epidemiology, 34*, 433–442.

Gunnell, D. & Eddleston, M. (2003). Suicide by intentional ingestion of pesticides: A continuing tragedy in developing countries. *International Journal of Epidemiology, 32*, 902–909.

Gunnell, D., Hawton, K., Murray, V., Garnier, R., Bismuth, C., Fagg, J., & Simkin, S. (1997). Use of paracetamol for suicide and non-fatal poisoning in the UK and France: Are restrictions on availability justified? *Journal of Epidemiology and Community Health, 51*, 175–179.

Gunnell, D., Middleton, N., & Frankel, S. (2000). Method availability and the prevention of suicide – A re-analysis of secular trends in England and Wales 1950–1975. *Social Psychiatry and Psychiatric Epidemiology, 35*, 437–443.

Gunnell, D. & Nowers, M. (1997). Suicide by jumping. *Acta Psychiatrica Scandinavica, 96*, 1–6.

Hamermesh, D. S. & Soss, N. M. (1974). An economic theory of suicide. *Journal of Political Economy, 82*, 83–98.

Hawkins, L. C., Edwards, J. N., & Dargan, P. I. (2007). Impact of restricting paracetamol pack sizes on paracetamol poisoning in the United Kingdom: A review of the literature. *Drug Safety, 30*, 465–479.

Hawton, K. (2005). Restriction of access to methods of suicide as a means of suicide prevention. In K. Hawton (Ed.), *Prevention and Treatment of Suicidal Behaviour: From science to practice* (pp. 279–291). Oxford: Oxford University Press.

Hawton, K. (2007). Restricting access to methods of suicide. Rationale and evaluation of this approach to suicide prevention. *Crisis, 28* (Suppl. 1), 4–9.

Hawton, K., Bergen, H., Simkin, S., Brock, A., Griffiths, C., Romeri, E., Smith, K. L., Kapur, N., & Gunnell, D. (2009). Effect of withdrawal of co-proxamol on prescribing and deaths from drug poisoning in England and Wales: Time series analysis. *British Medical Journal, 338*, b2270.

Hawton, K., Ratnayeke, L., Simkin, S., Harriss, L., & Scott, V. (2009). Evaluation of acceptability and use of lockable storage devices for pesticides in Sri Lanka that might assist in prevention of self-poisoning. *BMC Public Health, 9*, 69.

Hawton, K., Simkin, S., Deeks, J., Cooper, J., Johnston, A., Waters, K., Arundel, M., Bernal, W., Gunson, B., Hudson, M., Suri, D., & Simpson, K. (2004). UK legislation on analgesic packs: Before and after study of long term effect on poisonings. *British Medical Journal, 329*, 1076.

Hawton, K., Townsend, E., Deeks, J., Appleby, L., Gunnell, D., Bennewith, O., & Cooper, J. (2001). Effects of legislation restricting pack sizes of paracetamol and salicylate on self-poisoning in the United Kingdom: before and after study. *British Medical Journal, 322*, 1203–1207.

Hawton, K., Ware, C., Mistry, H., Hewitt, J., Kingsbury, S., Roberts, D., & Weitzel, H. (1995). Why patients choose paracetamol for self poisoning and their knowledge of its dangers. *British Medical Journal, 310*, 164.

Kapusta, N. D., Etzersdorfer, E., Krall, C., & Sonneck, G. (2007). Firearm legislation reform in the European Union: impact on firearm availability, firearm suicide and homicide rates in Austria. *British Journal of Psychiatry, 191*, 253–257.

King, E. & Frost, N. (2005). The New Forest Suicide Prevention Initiative (NFSPI). *Crisis, 26*, 25–33.

Klieve, H., Barnes, M., & De Leo, D. (2009). Controlling firearms use in Australia: Has the 1996 gun law reform produced the decrease in rates of suicide with this method? *Social Psychiatry and Psychiatric Epidemiology, 44*, 285–292.

Kreitman, N. (1976). The coal gas story. United Kingdom suicide rates, 1960–71. *British Journal of Preventive and Social Medicine, 30*, 86–93.

Kuo, C. J., Conwell, Y., Yu, Q., Chiu, C. H., Chen, Y. Y., Tsai, S. Y., & Chen, C. C. (2008). Suicide by charcoal burning in Taiwan: Implications for means substitution by a case-linkage study. *Social Psychiatry and Psychiatric Epidemiology, 43*, 286–290.

Lafave, M., LaPorta, A. J., Hutton, J., & Mallory, P. L. (1995). History of high-velocity impact water trauma at Letterman Army Medical Center: A 54-year experience with the Golden Gate Bridge. *Military Medicine, 160*, 197–199.

Lee, D. T., Chan, K. P., Lee, S., & Yip, P. S. (2002). Burning charcoal: A novel and contagious method of suicide in Asia. *Archives of General Psychiatry, 59*, 293–294.

Lee, M. B. & Liao, S. C. (2006). Risk factors and prevention strategy of suicide. *Formosan Journal of Medicine, 10*, 366–373.

Leenaars, A. A. (2007). Gun-control legislation and the impact on suicide. *Crisis, 28* (Suppl. 1), 50–57.

Lester, D. (1989). Changing rates of suicide by car exhaust in men and women in the United States after car exhaust was detoxified. *Crisis, 10*, 164–168.

Lester, D. (1990a). Capital punishment, gun control, and personal violence (suicide and homicide). *Psychological Reports, 66*, 122.

Lester, D. (1990b). The effect of the detoxification of domestic gas in Switzerland on suicide in the United States. *American Journal of Public Health, 80*, 80–81.

Lester, D. & Abe, K. (1989a). Car availability, exhaust toxicity of car exhaust. *Annals of Clinical Psychiatry, 1*, 247–250.

Lester, D. & Abe, K. (1989b). The effect of restricting access to lethal methods for suicide: A study of suicide by domestic gas in Japan. *Acta Psychiatrica Scandinavica, 80*, 180–182.

Lester, D. & Clarke, R. V. (1988). Effects of reduced toxicity of car exhaust. *American Journal of Public Health, 78*, 594.

Lester, D. & Leenaars, A. (1993). Suicide rates in Canada before and after tightening firearm control laws. *Psychological Reports, 72*, 787–790.

Lester, D. & Murrell, M. E. (1980). The influence of gun control laws on suicidal behavior. *The American Journal of Psychiatry, 137*, 121–122.

Lin, J. J. & Lu, T. H. (2008). High-risk groups for charcoal-burning suicide in Taiwan, 2001–2005. *Journal of Clinical Psychiatry, 69*, 1499–1501.

Lindqvist, P., Jonsson, A., Eriksson, A., Hedelin, A., & Bjornstig, U. (2004). Are suicides by jumping off bridges preventable? An analysis of 50 cases from Sweden. *Accident, Analysis and Prevention, 36*, 691–694.

Liu, K. Y., Beautrais, A., Caine, E., Chan, K., Chao, A., Conwell, Y., Law, C., Lee, D., Li, P., & Yip, P. (2007). Charcoal burning suicides in Hong Kong and urban Taiwan: An illustration of the impact of a novel suicide method on overall regional rates. *Journal of Epidemiology and Community Health, 61*, 248–253.

Loftin, C., McDowall, D., Wiersema, B., & Cottey, T. J. (1991). Effects of restrictive licensing of handguns on homicide and suicide in the District of Columbia. *New England Journal of Medicine, 325*, 1615–1620.

Mann, J. J., Apter, A., Bertolote, J., Beautrais, A., Currier, D., Haas, A., Hegerl, U., Lönqvist, J., Malone, K., Marusic, A., Mehlum, L., Patton, G., Phillips, M., Rutz, W., Rihmer, Z., Schmidtke, A., Shaffer, D., Silverman, M., Takahashi, Y., Varnik, A., Wasserman, D., Yip, P., & Hendin, H. (2005). Suicide prevention strategies: A systematic review. *Journal of the American Medical Association, 294*, 2064–2074.

Marcotte, D. E. (2003). The economics of suicide, revisited. *Southern Economics Journal, 69*, 628–643.

Marks, A. (1977). Sex differences and their effect upon cultural evaluations of methods of self-destruction. *Omega, 8*, 65–70.

Marzuk, P. M., Leon, A. C., Tardiff, K., Morgan, E. B., Stajic, M., & Mann, J. J. (1992). The effect of access to lethal methods of injury on suicide rates. *Archives of General Psychiatry, 49*, 451–458.

McClure, G. M. (1987). Suicide in England and Wales, 1975–1984. *British Journal of Psychiatry, 150*, 309–314.

Mishara, B. L. (2007). Prevention of deaths from intentional pesticide poisoning. *Crisis, 28* (Suppl. 1), 10–20.

Moens, G. F., Loysch, M. J., Honggokoesoemo, S., & van de Voorde, H. (1989). Recent trends in methods of suicide. *Acta Psychiatrica Scandinavica, 79*, 207–215.

Mortensen, P. B., Agerbo, E., Erikson, T., Qin, P., & Westergaard-Nielsen, N. (2000). Psychiatric illness and risk factors for suicide in Denmark. *The Lancet, 355*, 9–12.

Mott, J. A., Wolfe, M. I., Alverson, C. J., MacDonald, S. C., Bailey, C. R., Ball, L. B., Moorman, J. E., Somers, J. H., Mannino, D. M., & Redd, S. C. (2002). National vehicle emissions policies and practices and declining US carbon monoxide-related mortality. *Journal of the American Medical Association, 288*, 988–995.

Nordentoft, M. (2007). Restrictions in availability of drugs used for suicide. *Crisis, 28* (Suppl. 1), 44–49.

O'Carroll, P. W. & Silverman, M. M. (1994). Community suicide prevention: The effectiveness of bridge barriers. *Suicide and Life-Threatening Behavior, 24*, 89–91.

Ohberg, A., Lönqvist, J., Sarna, S., Vuori, E., & Penttila, A. (1995). Trends and availability of suicide methods in Finland. Proposals for restrictive measures. *British Journal of Psychiatry, 166*, 35–43.

Ozanne-Smith, J., Ashby, K., Newstead, S., Stathakis, V. Z., & Clapperton, A. (2004). Firearm related deaths: The impact of regulatory reform. *Injury Prevention, 10*, 280–286.

Pearson, V., Phillips, M. R., He, F., & Ji, H. (2002). Attempted suicide among young rural women in the People's Republic of China: possibilities for prevention. *Suicide and Life-Threatening Behavior, 32*, 359–369.

Phillips, M. R., Yang, G., Zhang, Y., Wang, L., Ji, H., & Zhou, M. (2002). Risk factors for suicide in China: A national case-control psychological autopsy study. *The Lancet, 360*, 1728–1736.

Pirkola, S., Isometsa, E., & Lönqvist, J. (2003). Do means matter? Differences in characteristics of Finnish suicide completers using different methods. *Journal of Nervous and Mental Disease, 191*, 745–750.

Prevost, C., Julien, M., & Brown, B. P. (1996). Suicides associated with the Jacques Cartier Bridge, Montreal, Quebec 1988–1993: Descriptive analysis and intervention proposal. *Canadian Journal of Public Health*, *87*, 377–380.

Reisch, T. & Michel, K. (2005). Securing a suicide hot spot: Effects of a safety net at the Bern Muenster Terrace. *Suicide and Life-Threatening Behavior*, *35*, 460–467.

Rich, C. L., Young, J. G., Fowler, R. C., Wagner, J., & Black, N. A. (1990). Guns and suicide: Possible effects of some specific legislation. *American Journal of Psychiatry*, *147*, 342–346.

Routley, V. (2007). Motor vehicle exhaust gas suicide. Review of countermeasures. *Crisis*, *28* (Suppl. 1), 28–35.

Routley, V. H. & Ozanne-Smith, J. (1998). The impact of catalytic converters on motor vehicle exhaust gas suicides. *Medical Journal of Australia*, *168*, 65–67.

Schapira, K., Linsley, K. R., Linsley, A., Kelly, T. P., & Kay, D. W. (2001). Relationship of suicide rates to social factors and availability of lethal methods: Comparison of suicide in Newcastle upon Tyne 1961–1965 and 1985–1994. *British Journal of Psychiatry*, *178*, 458–464.

Shah, S., Hoffman, R. E., Wake, L., & Marine, W. M. (2000). Adolescent suicide and household access to firearms in Colorado: Results of a case-control study. *Journal of Adolescent Health*, *26*, 157–163.

Shelef, M. (1994). Unanticipated benefits of automotive emission control: Reduction in fatalities by motor vehicle exhaust gas. *The Science of the Total Environment*, *146–147*, 93–101.

Stack, S. & Wasserman, I. (2005). Race and method of suicide: Culture and opportunity. *Archives of Suicide Research*, *9*, 57–68.

United Nations (1996). *Prevention of Suicide Guidelines for the formulation and implementation of national strategies*. New York: United Nations.

US Department of Health and Human Services (2001). *National Strategy for Suicide Prevention: Goals and objectives for action*. Rockville, MD: US Department of Health and Human Services.

Whitlock, F. A. (1975). Suicide in Brisbane, 1956 to 1973: the drug-death epidemic. *Medical Journal of Australia*, *1*, 737–743.

Wilkinson, D. & Gunnell, D. (2000). Comparison of trends in method-specific suicide rates in Australia and England & Wales, 1968–97. *Australian and New Zealand Journal of Public Health*, *24*, 153–157.

World Health Organization (2006). *The Impact of Pesticides on Health: Preventing intentional and unintentional deaths from pesticide poisoning*. Geneva: WHO.

Yip, P. S. F. (1997). Suicides in Hong Kong, 1981–1994. *Social Psychiatry and Psychiatric Epidemiology*, *32*, 243–250.

Yip, P. S. F. (2009). Prevention of suicide due to charcoal burning. In D. Wasserman & C. Wasserman (Eds.), *Oxford Textbook of Suicidology and Suicide Prevention* (pp. 595–597). Oxford: Oxford University Press.

Yip, P. S. F., Law, C. K., Fu, K. W., Law, Y. W., Wong, P. W. C., & Xu, Y. (2010). Restricting the means of suicide by charcoal burning poisoning. *British Journal of Psychiatry*, *196*, 241–242.

Yip, P. S. F., & Lee, D. T. S. (2007). Charcoal-burning suicides and strategies for prevention. *Crisis*, *28* (Suppl. 1), 21–27.

Yip, P. S. F. & Tan, R. C. (1998). Suicides in Hong-Kong and Singapore: A tale of two cities. *International Journal of Social Psychiatry*, *44*, 267–279.

CHAPTER THIRTY-TWO

The Sequelae of Suicide: Survivors

Onja Grad

The sting of death is less sharp for the person who dies than it is for the bereaved survivor.
(Toynbee, in Shneidman, 1972)

Abstract

Experiencing the suicide of someone close is like experiencing an emotional tsunami that hits the individual, family, class at school, unit in the hospital, or the community. The emotions experienced and reactions encountered are various, ranging from sadness, despair, yearning, agitation, and disbelief to fear, anger, anxiety, and arguably most difficult of all, blame, guilt, shame, stigma, and social withdrawal. One's reaction to suicide death is very individual and depends on personal, socio-cultural, and situational factors. The process of mourning takes time and energy, and has an impact on the mourner's life. Some bereaved go through this rite of passage alone or in their families, some need the support of other suicide survivors in peer groups, and some need professional help or even treatment. The length of bereavement is variable and is dependent on the survivor's own, unique way of dealing with loss. It is important to identify when the so-called usual bereavement process transforms into prolonged, complicated, or bereavement-related major depression and the individual or the family need therapy. Besides family and friends affected by the suicide of somebody close to them, the impact on the professionals who dealt with the deceased (psychiatrists, therapists, nurses, teachers, etc.) is considerable and they also need support.

International Handbook of Suicide Prevention: Research, Policy and Practice, First Edition.
Edited by Rory C. O'Connor, Stephen Platt, Jacki Gordon.
© 2011 John Wiley & Sons, Ltd. Published 2011 by John Wiley & Sons, Ltd.

Introduction

Even though death by suicide has as long a history as mankind, its impact on those left behind, nowadays called survivors of suicide, has been overlooked, tabooed, neglected, and stigmatized. These individuals and 'these families have in the past been ignored or, even worse and more often, blamed for the tragedy of having a family member commit suicide' (McGoldrick, 1987, p. vi); or as Shneidman calls the tragedies that continue after the self-destructive act, 'the illegacy of suicide' (1972, p. xi). Contrary to past beliefs and actions, we now know that survivors of suicide have to work through a long and painful process of accepting, acknowledging, and expressing their numerous emotions and behaviours in order to be able to move on with their lives. For various reasons (biological, psychological, and environmental) the suicide bereaved are at increased risk of developing suicide behaviour themselves, either because of biological determinants or because of identification with someone close who had in the past completed suicide.

The Problem of Terminology

In the 1960s (Shneidman, 1969, pp. 1–30), when we became aware of the problems that suicide usually provokes in the micro- and macro-environment, there were many ambiguities about the words suicide survivor, grief, bereavement, and mourning. For example, there was no consensus on terminology nor was there recognition of the range of different problems that can arise as a result of suicide. The term postvention was created and introduced by Edwin Shneidman (1972, pp. ix–xi) for any type of activity which occurs after a suicide event, and 'aims at mollifying the inimical psychological sequelae in the survivor-victim'. The word suicide survivor has been used in the past for two groups: first, for those who have survived their own suicide attempt and, second, for those who were relatives or friends of someone who have completed suicide. After some time, however, the term suicide survivor was abandoned for the category of suicide attempters and is now exclusively applied to survivors of completed suicides. It refers to everyone who is significantly negatively affected by the suicide of someone in their social network (Jordan, 2008). More recently, the meaning of this term has been extended to include anyone who has witnessed (or participated in) the suicidal act (e.g., a train driver or an accidental witness of the suicidal act) (Andriessen, 2009). The new word postvention became the synonym for all sorts of activities aimed at helping suicide survivors in order to facilitate recovery after experiencing the suicide of someone close, to raise resilience and coping skills, and to prevent adverse outcomes including suicide attempts (Andriessen, 2009; Shneidman, 1993, pp. 161–179).

The words grief, bereavement, and mourning as applied to suicide survivors have been used interchangeably ever since Shneidman's introduction in the 1970s. They are defined as follows in Hornby's (2005, p. 77) dictionary. Bereavement is defined as 'the state of sorrow over the death or departure of a loved one'. Grief is 'deep mental anguish, as that arising from bereavement'. Mourning is defined as 'actions or expressions of one who has suffered a bereavement'. It is also worth noting that the definitions employed by researchers (e.g., Stroebe & Stroebe, 1987, pp. 7–25) and/or clinicians (Zisook & Shear, 2009, pp. 76–74) are similar as evidenced below:

(1) According to Stroebe and Stroebe (1987): bereavement is the objective situation of an individual who has recently experienced the loss of someone significant and is the cause of grief and mourning; grief is the emotional (affective) response to loss, which includes a number of psychological and somatic reactions; and mourning refers to the acts expressive of grief, which are shaped by the mourning practices of a given society or culture.
(2) According to Zisook and Shear (2009): bereavement is used to refer to the fact of the loss; grief describes emotional, cognitive, functional, and behavioural responses to the death or other kinds of loss; and mourning is the behavioural manifestation of grief, which is influenced by social and cultural rituals, such as funerals, visitations, etc.

In addition, some authors use the term 'grief work' (Rothaupt & Becker, 2007) to describe the mourning process and reflect the significant mental 'work' involved in coming to terms with loss through suicide.

The Number of Suicide Survivors

Another problem in this field is the difficulty in estimating the number of suicide survivors affected by every suicide. Although a figure of six people is often cited and accepted by suicidologists, this was an arbitrary estimate put forward by Shneidman (in McIntosh, 1987, p. 21) who, in his legendary and frequently cited foreword to the first book on suicide survivors (Shneidman in Cain, 1972, p. x), posited the ratio of '200,000 survivor-victims on 50,000 committed suicides'. Ironically, this means that his first estimation was not six but four survivors per suicide. But nevertheless, the ratio cited remained six and this number has been repeated ever since and has almost attained the status of a fact, even though some authors argue that a community-based longitudinal study to determine the real extent of impact of suicide has yet to be done (Jordan, 2008; McMenamy, Jordan, & Mitchell, 2008). An even more liberal number of 'six to ten' was suggested by Bland (1994), who found 28 different 'types' of suicide survivors following 214 suicide deaths, who sought help in the five years following the deaths (Knieper, 1999). Indeed, this number is likely to be an underestimate as it did not include some groups of survivors, such as different professionals who were potentially affected (e.g., teachers, physicians, nurses, social workers, therapists, jail personnel, etc.) (Grad, 2009, pp. 609–613).

The Trajectory of the Bereavement Process

When a person decides to take his or her own life, their story ends, but other, difficult and painful stories begin in the group of newly bereaved next of kin. This affected group usually consists of relatives of the deceased, their colleagues and friends, working partners, neighbours, teachers, general practitioner, therapist (if the deceased was in therapy or hospitalized at the time of the act), and other mental health workers. Each of them experiences their own, and at times very different, emotional reactions, depending on many factors: gender and age of the bereaved, the length and quality of the relationship with the deceased, the age of the deceased, the stage of life cycle of the bereaved and the whole family at the time of death, the time elapsed since suicide, exposure to the body immediately after death, method of suicide, anticipation of the act (related to previous threats, suicide attempts, or mental illness of the deceased), the available social support, and the personality of the bereaved survivor. These and many other factors determine the uniqueness of each individual's bereavement process.

After centuries of overlooking suicide survivors' diverse needs and painful experiences, the first wave of research that followed the 'disclosure' and acknowledgement of the group claimed that suicide survivors' bereavement is different and more difficult than the bereavement following other modes of death (Cleiren, 1993; Cleiren, Grad, Zavasnik, & Diekstra, 1996; Dunne, 1987; Farberow, Gallagher-Thomson, Gilewski, & Thompson, 1992; Grad & Zavasnik, 1996; Hauser, 1987; Hawton & Simkin, 2003). A number of recent studies suggest that survivors of suicide express higher levels of depression, more guilt, shame, and rejection and feel more social stigmatization (and thus receive less social support from the environment) than those bereaved by other modes of death (Dunne & Dunne-Maxim, 2009; Sakinofsky, 2007). Other studies, however, have concluded that the bereavement process for the survivors of suicide is actually quite similar to those bereaved by other means (Jordan, 2001; McDaid, Trowman, Golder, Hawton, & Sowden, 2008; McIntosh, 2003). Others still indicated that those suicide survivors who seek clinical help differ from those included in randomized trials (Grad & Zavasnik, 1999).

Even though the path of bereavement after suicide is as unique as the survivor's fingerprints (Clark, 1995, p. 12; Clark & Goldney, 2000, p. 470), there are some commonalities that need to be understood and accepted both by the bereaved in order to survive and to move forward, and by the caregivers to support and help them. Indeed, some of the components of bereavement are universal, such as sadness, crying, yearning after the deceased, denial of death, changes in eating, sleeping and social habits, fatigue, etc. The intensity and the duration of all emotional reactions are again quite unique for each bereaved, and it is important that their family and other lay and professional helpers tolerate, understand, and support this uniqueness. However, some processes and experiences are more typical of the bereavement following suicide.

Feeling guilty is one of the most common sequelae of suicide of someone close. The reasons for guilt may be different for each survivor (even in the same family) and include one or several of the following:

- feeling that they did not recognize the warning signs threatening suicidal behaviour or that they had not prevented the suicidal behaviour when in retrospect they think they could have done so;
- not being able to react in time to stop the suicide due to special circumstances, for example, due to not living close enough or not living together (e.g., parents of adult children);
- not paying enough attention to previous suicide attempts, depressed behaviour, the effects of long-lasting mental disorders or even illness;
- relief in the case where suicide has ended suffering of a chronic mental or physical illness (especially when members of the family or the caregiver became fed up and wished the suffering would stop);
- thoughts and fears of personally contributing to the individual's decision to end their life (e.g., because of separation, divorce, threat to leave, a quarrel before the suicidal act, etc.); and
- overestimating one's own responsibility and ability to stop the suicidal process and diminishing the power of mental illness.

The second very frequent theme of suicide bereavement is searching for reasons for the individual's decision to end his or her life. It is difficult to accept that someone close to you has not communicated their thoughts and problems, and has not asked for help or showed any recognizable signs of the risk. The bereaved meticulously investigate their own behaviour and that of the deceased before the suicide and they try to find internal (psychological and biological) and external reasons and explanations for the act. This investigation often results in blaming themselves and others, and consequent anger towards different people and circumstances. The most painful of all is guilt-fuelled self-blame. Besides blaming oneself, the survivors are inclined to blame others, asking why they did not prevent the suicide. This blaming can be directed at other members of the close and extended family, colleagues, friends, schoolmates, and very often at those professionals who took care of the suicidal person: doctors, therapists, nurses, sometimes teachers, and superiors at work.

Blame and anger can be directed at the deceased for letting the survivor down or leaving them alone with all of the problems. These feelings are very difficult and painful for the bereaved to admit to themselves and even more difficult to express openly (Grad & Zavasnik, 1997; Tekavčič Grad & Zavasnik, 1992). For the suicide survivor it is important to know whether the suicide was a personal, wilful decision or an act driven by particular problems, mental illness, or some other difficult circumstances. The so-called subjective reasons produce anger and feelings of unworthiness in the survivor of suicide (Jordan, 2008).

As noted above, some problems are specific to the bereavement following suicide compared with other modes of death. One such problem is lower self-esteem, embedded in the social stigma of suicide. In turn, such stigma brings additional and particular challenges to caregivers as they attempt to help suicide survivors (Cvinar, 2005; Dunne & Dunne-Maxim, 2004). Anecdotal evidence suggests that many survivors report changed behaviour within their social network: they feel that they are being looked down upon or overlooked by others and they interpret this as arising because of the taboo associated with suicide. What is the extent of their own projection onto others, based on guilt and shame and what is the more objective reaction from the environment has yet to be studied.

The self-stigmatizing process of the survivors often makes them unable to accept social support even though offered by the people around them (Jordan, 2008). Furthermore, suicide survivors report what has been termed 'social ineptitude' of the surrounding network (Dyregrov, 2003), that is, when people do not know how to react or talk to them and consequently prefer to ignore the fact completely or even withdraw from the survivor's circle (survivors often describe how people they know cross the street in order to avoid meeting them).

One of the frequent, but quite specific, problems of suicide survivors is that they start to worry that some other members of the family might become suicidal. As a consequence extra care and caution are directed towards those family members who want to retain the same lifestyle as prior to suicide, which for the other family members seems too dangerous (Dunne and Dunne-Maxim, 2009, p. 606; Jordan, 2001).

As summarized above, it is still unclear whether bereavement following suicide is any different from that following other modes of death. Some studies suggest that bereavement after all kinds of unexpected, sudden deaths (including suicides, traffic fatalities) show more similarities than differences (Callahan, 2000; Ellenbogen & Gratton, 2001; Harwood, Hawton, Hope, & Jacoby, 2002; Hawton & Simkin, 2003; McIntosh, 1992), whereas others claim that the term complicated grief (indefinitely prolonged grief with dysfunctional emotional regulations) is more common after unexpected and violent deaths such as suicide (Hawton, 2007). Furthermore, Jordan (2001, p. 91) reviewed the literature on bereavement following different modes of death and claimed that the 'grief process from suicide differs' from other types of bereavement in 'the thematic content of grief, social process surrounding the survivors and impact of suicide on family systems'.

Thus, we can say that there is equivocal evidence that bereavement after suicide is somewhat different from other types of bereavement, but most of all it is strongly determined with the very individual bio-psycho-social determinants of the person mourning the suicide of someone close.

The Course of Bereavement after Suicide Death

Each suicide is a puzzle comprising numerous pieces in the form of explanations, reasons, influencing or precipitating factors, not to mention the interplay between biological, psychological, and environmental factors, as well as the many stereotypes and prejudices. The same is true for the course of bereavement following the suicide of someone close. A number of theoretical models have been developed to understand this process. Indeed, Freud (1957) proposed one of the first models of bereavement (in 1917) in which he claimed that the bereaved should be able to work through their loss first and that the final outcome of this process should be a detachment from the deceased in order to start new relationships. Lindemann (Rothaupt & Becker, 2007) repeated Freud's notion that healthy resolution of grief 'involved confronting the reality of the loss and severing the emotional bonds with the deceased, allowing for the building of new relationships'. Following Freud and Lindemann, there was a considerable gap in subsequent developments until the late 1960s and beyond when the modern theories were established by Kübler-Ross (1969), Bowlby (1991), and Parkes (1993), who each proposed stage theories with different goals as the final result of bereavement. Kübler-Ross talks about mourners' acceptance of a death, while both Bowlby and Parkes claim that the bereaved should recover and re-organize to the pre-death functioning level. The authors of the end of twentieth century are more task-oriented (Davies, 2004; Walsh & McGoldrick, 2004; Worden, 1991), proposing that the aim of the mourning process is a relocation and memorializing of the deceased (meaning 'connection of the bereaved with the deceased in a new way'), adaptation to the loss, and finally reinvestment in other relationships and life pursuits. This new orientation allows ongoing relationships and emotional connections with the bereaved, supporting ongoing rituals, marking of special occasions, and recognizing the uniqueness in individuals' experiences of grief and mourning (Rothaupt & Becker, 2007).

We can, however, hardly squeeze all the bereaved into these theoretical models as each survivor has their own perspective, time schedule, experiences, social background, demands from their environment and socio-cultural traditions, religious and ethnic expectations, and, most of all, very personal, individual, and intimate needs. Suicide is a rare event and when it happens nobody is prepared, not even those families in which suicide has occurred in previous generations, or those where suicide was the final act of many threats or attempts before it actually happened. Because suicide is often a sudden, unpredictable, and at times violent death, it brings many expected and unexpected feelings, behaviours, as well as physical and social reactions in the bereaved relatives and others who are affected. In fact, suicide bereavement is a particularly painful experience for which a Western individual is definitely not prepared. It brings shock, sadness, anguish, anger, guilt, regret, anxiety, fear, loneliness, depression, depersonalization, intrusive images, the feeling of being overwhelmed, and agitation (Grad, 1996; Zisook & Shear, 2009). Suicide brings many additional problems to the bereavement process, some connected to the unexpected trauma and some connected to the real or projected unfavourable reactions of others.

Suicide survivors have had a long history of maltreatment by society, ranging from all sorts of punishment either of themselves or of the body of the deceased (Knieper, 1999), to experiencing the awkward silences and difficulties in communication as well as difficulties in offering and accepting social support. This history of maltreatment explains, in part, why survivors of suicide frequently report that support is not available, even though this is not entirely true any more, at least in some parts of the world (Andriessen & Farberow, 2002). However, even in the developed countries such as in Europe and the United States, only a minority of survivors (approximately one quarter) search for and receive help following suicide bereavement (Saarinen, Viinamaki, Hintikka, Lehtonen, & Lönqvist, 1999). There are numerous potential explanations for this low uptake including: survivors may deny and suppress any difficulties to avoid pain and keep emotional balance; they may try to avoid being pitied or blamed; they may fear that admitting problems would lower their self-esteem and make them even more insecure; they (particularly male survivors) may be reluctant to share their problems because they do not believe in help-seeking, in therapy or in therapists: some prefer other ways of venting their feelings (substance abuse, over-working, etc.); and some might fear public exposure through admitting the need for help and therapy (Grad, 2005). It is also true that the majority of survivors do not need any help outside their inner circle of family and friends, especially when their grief takes an uncomplicated path (Saarinen, Viinamaki, Lehtonen, & Lönqvist, 2000, Zisook, Shear, & Irwin, 2009).

The term complicated grief has recently been introduced to distinguish grief which can lead to adverse health outcomes from the usual (in cultural and societal terms), non-complicated, ordinary, or expected grief (Stroebe, Schut, & Stroebe, 2007). Complicated grief, referred to as traumatic or prolonged grief disorder, is a newly defined diagnostic category (proposed for the DSM-V; Hawton, 2007), in which acute grief is prolonged into a state of chronic mourning, and the bereaved person has persistent and disruptive yearning, pining, and longing for the deceased (Hawton, 2007; Shear & Mulhare, 2008). Within the context of grief being the response to loss by death, the proposed criteria for complicated grief are that at least four (intrusive and distressing) symptoms of trauma are experienced by the bereaved which should cause marked and persistent dysfunction and should last at least six months. These symptoms include: avoidance of reminders of the deceased; feelings of futility; and feeling stunned, dazed, or shocked; excessive anger or bitterness; feelings that life without the deceased is worthless, etc. (Mitchell, Kim, Prigerson, & Mortimer-Stephens, 2004; Stroebe & Stroebe, 2007).

Some report that spouses who are closer to the deceased appear to suffer the poorest health and show a higher level of complicated grief than the more conflicted and ambivalent ones (Mitchell *et al.*, 2004). However, the evidence is mixed, as Parkes and Weiss (1983) reported the opposite pattern of findings to Mitchell and colleagues. The former found that widowed individuals who had more ambivalent, conflicted marriages were more adversely affected by the loss than those with less conflicted relationships (Parkes & Weiss, 1983). Taken together, these two studies highlight the need for further research in this area. Nevertheless, it is extremely important to properly diagnose complicated grief as soon as possible to minimize the risk of mental (including suicidality) and physical health problems.

To continue with the focus on pathology, we should also mention bereavement-related major depression. Grief and depression are similar, both involving low mood, sadness, and social withdrawal. However, there are some clear differences between a grieving individual and an individual with grief-related major depression: the grieving individual experiences positive and negative emotions, while a depressed individual tends to be consistently in a stable negative mood with few or no positive feelings about themselves (Zisook & Shear, 2009). In clinical practice therapists are often faced with the difficult problem of chronic grief reactions. These are excessive in duration and never come to a satisfactory conclusion (Worden, 1991). They can last many years without decreasing in intensity. It is as if the bereaved wants to preserve the deceased in everyday life, to strengthen their bond or idealize something that was very important to the bereaved (whether or not it really existed). It is usually therapy-resistant, because the bereaved needs to preserve the intact image of the deceased to fill the void of the now absent and possibly complicated or ambivalent relationship.

Suicide Survivors' Needs and Help Offered

When suicide strikes a family and friends, it feels like an emotional tsunami (Jordan, 2008). The leading researchers in the field of bereavement have found that bereaved persons (after any kind of loss) are at excessive risk of suicidal ideation compared with non-bereaved controls, and they named this effect the 'broken heart' (Stroebe, Stroebe, & Abakoumkin, 2005). Suicide survivors, though, experience equivalent or even heightened risk (Stroebe, Stroebe, & Schut, 2003; Stroebe, Schut, & Stroebe, 2007).

The postvention literature describes numerous ways of helping survivors. These include individual, family, or group help. Such help can be offered by professional counsellors or therapists, but also by lay survivors of suicide who struggled through the same process and can serve as a model that recovery is possible. Despite the diversity in how postvention care is provided, all aim to ease the process of mourning and to help the survivors acknowledge, understand, accept, and express their own feelings and reactions. An important part of each survivor's healing is their own understanding of the general causes for suicide, which should be a part of the survivor's own explanations about their own particular case (Jordan, 2008). This understanding of the suicidal process, its psychopathological components, and the different psychosocial factors that can contribute to suicide, usually helps the survivor to accept and forgive the decision made by the deceased.

Both lay and professional help should use the following few principles that propose where to start, what to say, and how to proceed with the survivor through support or therapy.

The non-structured agenda of care for the survivors: content and process

When individual or group therapy starts, each survivor should have the time and a safe space to introduce themselves, explaining why they decided to ask for help. It is extremely important to observe the subtle undertones of emotions when survivors are talking for the first time: what they choose to tell, how they talk about the deceased, and how they describe the relationship with the deceased. It is important that the bereaved talks extensively about the details of suicide, how the body was found, and who found it, especially if it was a very violent mode of death and the person who found the body was traumatized by its sight, irrespective of whether seeing this was accidental or intentional. This may result in frequent and disturbing flashbacks of the transformed or mutilated body that can persist as inner intrusive pictures for a long time after the death. Focused, patient, and active listening by the caregiver helps the survivors to work through their own doubts, queries, and regrets of 'if only I had' and 'if only I had not'. When talking about their past life with the deceased and about present life without them, the survivor remembers the valuable scenes and memories that help to rebuild their new inner life without the deceased. It is important to know which activities are supportive or helpful, making the survivor's life more bearable. The process of mourning is tiring, emotionally draining and demanding, painful and confusing, unpleasant and energy-consuming, but it is absolutely essential for the survivor's healing. It represents the passage from denial of the death through to resisting the reality and considering the impact of the loss, towards the final transformation of the roles and ways of life and finally trying to resume living in a way similar to that before the suicide.

Rituals

Clinical practice teaches us how important it is that the survivor thinks and talks about the funeral, the grave, the meaning it has for them, where they picture the deceased, and that they find a place where they can have inner dialogue with the deceased. The survivor should talk about the plethora of questions which arise following a suicide and which have no definite answer but remain open, so they need to explore them and find their own, unique answers. Besides the neverending questions about the reasons behind the suicide, there are many practical questions: about everyday life; about the rituals and how much the rituals help them; how long they can leave the deceased's belongings as they are; and whether it is natural to cry or not in front of other family members, or hide the tears to protect them. They ask themselves and the therapist if they are going insane when they experience the presence of the deceased in the room, when they can smell them, or see them in a crowd. They want to know if and how they should tell their children about the mode of death and reasons for suicide, at what age, and if the children should attend the funeral, what to do about other rituals, and whom to involve, etc. The therapist's role is to accept and tolerate any kind of emotion or thought and to normalize almost everything but obvious pathology.

Individual needs

It is important to help the survivors accept that mourning of family members is unique, and that everyone does it differently in terms of timing, content, and behaviour. The grave may be a helpful place for one family member, but it may mean nothing to another. Often, for example, children and adolescents do not want to visit the grave and want to avoid talking about the deceased. In turn, this can be difficult for those who would like to talk about their deceased loved one all of the time. These differences are sometimes perceived wrongly by some family members as not feeling sadness at the loss or even forgetting the deceased too quickly (Dunne & Dunne-Maxim, 2004).

One of the helpful procedures in the bereavement process is remembering the positive and valuable bonds and different events that were shared over the years between the deceased and the bereaved. It helps to talk about these, as talking brings the virtual presence of the deceased back to reality. Photos and videos can be useful tools in this process as well, as is often proved in clinical practice.

Symbols and other Substitutes for Remembering the Deceased

Working through the loss can take different forms. Some of them are recognizable and very transparent (e.g., verbal expressions, overt behaviours) and others are more ambiguous and difficult to understand. These can be symbolic objects, places, symbolic activities, or new, unknown inner experiences such as dreams, letters written to the deceased, things, animals or individuals that function as symbolic replacements for the deceased with a special meaning for the survivor (Grad & Zavasnik, 2003).

Dreams

Freud described dreams as the royal road to the unconscious world of the dreamer (1950, pp. 8–33); Kübler-Ross (1975, in Garfield, 1996, p. 188), on the other hand, called dreams about the dead 'true contacts on the spiritual plane'. Although some suicide survivors do dream, many complain that they do not have dreams or that they do not have them often enough (Garfield, 1996). Dreams can represent the dreamer's wish to see, touch, or talk to the deceased once more; they can serve as the catalyst for preparation to resolve unfinished business; they can satisfy a need or needs that the bereaved has; and they can be comforting and helpful or problematic and painful. The survivor's dreams can also reflect where in the bereavement process the dreamer is (Garfield, 1996, pp. 186–211). Usually, at the beginning of mourning, dreams are rare, while later in the bereavement process dreams become more frequent (Zisook, Shear, & Irwin, 2009, p. 2405). This is connected to the usual disturbances of sleeping pattern at the beginning of mourning, when the bereaved individuals have many different problems with sleeping (they can hardly get any sleep at all). The content of the dreams can reflect suicide survivors' ambivalent feelings about the deceased, in which case they can take the form of nightmares. They can represent various real, memorized scenes from their past life together, sometimes with a negative outcome (e.g., trying to save the deceased unsuccessfully from realistic or imaginary situations, bitterly quarrelling with the deceased, being rudely rejected by them, or painfully seeing their dead body again), or they can include the chaotic thoughts and explanations of the reasons for suicide, which can be very upsetting for the bereaved.

The dreams may also reflect the conscious or unconscious fear of their own death, which could have started with the death of a close person or even before it (Yalom, 2008, p. 263). The comforting, positive, and reassuring dreams that come later in the grief process are soothing, as the underlying message (whether implicit or explicit) interpreted by the dreamer is often about the peacefulness of the deceased, their farewell to the bereaved, and the consolation of their pain and yearning (Grad & Zavasnik, 2003).

Symbolic replacements

A grave or a tombstone is the most symbolic place where the survivors usually find peace, reconciliation, and some sort of imaginary or spiritual connection with the deceased. They try to use the grave as a meeting place, where they talk to or with the deceased (Wertheimer, 1991, p. 8) or where family members can meet and be with the deceased. They arrange the grave or tombstone and in doing so, preserve the feeling that they can do something for the deceased. Indeed, some survivors jealously take care of the symbolic place, not letting anyone else touch it or change anything there. The grave or tombstone is a solid and permanent memory of the deceased, as many survivors worry that their memory and the inner picture of their loved one might disappear with time.

Some bereaved prefer another special place to be a symbolic place of reunion – it may be the ocean where the ashes were scattered, or it may be a special place where the deceased and the bereaved were together on a special occasion and the place had an important meaning for both parties. It may be just a place at home, especially assigned for this purpose (Conley, 1987, p. 171). Some people let themselves believe that some person, animal, or an object represents the dead loved one and even if they used to be very rational before the suicide, they let themselves be comforted by these imaginative explanations. The therapist's role is to accept, tolerate, and normalize these self-help processes.

The survivor may choose to write letters to the deceased, a farewell letter, or an angry letter or a forgiving letter. They each may have a therapeutic purpose in coming to terms with the loss of a loved one. Some bereaved need to do something that would symbolically represent the deceased and make their life (and death) meaningful (Imber-Black, 2004, p. 356; Yalom, 2008, p. 67). They start projects, raise funds, support research studies – all with the purpose of symbolically preserving the memory and/or the name of the deceased.

End of the Bereavement

It is almost impossible to generalize about when the mourning process is finished. Some authors, including Bowlby (1991, p. 101), say it never finishes: 'Mourning never ends. Only as time goes on, it erupts less frequently.' However, the potential ending of bereavement depends on many factors: how and when it started; how intense it was; what and how many obstacles were in the way; and how close and intertwined the lives of the deceased and the bereaved were. One of the signs of adaptation to a new situation is when the bereaved can think of the deceased without pain or when they can reinvest the emotions into a new life (Worden, 1991, p. 18). One of the possible signs of the improvement and healing is having a sense of gaining some new values, priorities, and wisdom.

Caregivers and other Professionals after the Suicide of Their Client

Relatives and friends in the closest circle are those first affected when suicide occurs, but there is also a wider circle of people who suffer many similar emotional reactions but who are often forgotten, for example, teachers and schoolmasters in different schools, general practitioners and their teams, mental health workers, nurses and social workers, etc. These people may work in different facilities, such as old people's homes, hospitals, rehabilitation centres and prisons. All these survivors may have invested a lot of professional and personal knowledge, energy, and responsibility and have developed a strong relationship with their client (or patient). In turn, they too feel shocked, sad, rejected, guilty, angry, disappointed, and frustrated (Grad & Michel, 2005; James, 2005). They can also feel embarrassed or ashamed, inadequate, or even incompetent as professionals and they may fear legal litigations (Grad, 1996). For those who work with highly suicidal individuals, experiencing one or more suicides is, sadly, an occupational hazard. Nevertheless, when a suicide death of a patient does happen, it is always very stressful if not debilitating, especially for an inexperienced, young therapist at the beginning of his or her career. They need to receive immediate debriefing, support, and supervision from someone who is not their superior or in any way connected to the hierarchy of the institution in which the therapist (or any other caregiver or a responsible person) works (Grad, 2009, p. 612). When a patient, a client, or a student completes suicide, it is important to help and support the surviving caregivers and other professionals who have been affected by the death. For those who are entering a profession with a high probability of suicide in their client group (e.g., mental health workers), their training should prepare them for this possibility. This tragic event can occur early in their formative years or any time later in their professional career, so they should know both how to detect and treat the suicidal patients at the time, and what support and supervision are available for themselves if they need it.

Conclusions

Any death causes turmoil in the lives of those left behind. If the death is sudden, violent, and self-inflicted such as in suicide, it is even worse and it can provoke an emotional tsunami (Jordan, 2008) in the relatives, friends, schoolmates, colleagues, therapists, and other professionals who worked with or knew the deceased. When suicide strikes, each survivor starts a long journey of working through their own, unique pattern of bereavement. Most of them (there are estimated to be at least six million new survivors worldwide) receive help within their own social network of family and friends, while a quarter of them seek help and find it in their wider environment, including specialist support. Those who need such specialist support are the ones developing prolonged or complicated grief reactions. The scarce research from 50 years ago is becoming more varied and adequate. However, in the research into the effects of suicide postvention, it is still difficult to produce a methodologically sound RCT (McDaid *et al.*, 2008), preferably combined with qualitative analysis of the bereavement process.

In some parts of the world, therapeutic support is already available and offered in different settings and with different content, while in other parts, even in some with a very high incidence of suicide, help is still non-existent and support networks ought to be developed as a matter of urgency. Suicide survivors can find help and support in peer groups and with volunteers or with highly specialist therapists, as individuals or as a family. Each form of help aims to achieve the same outcome: to find a way through the individual maze of different emotional, physical, behavioural, cognitive, social, and spiritual components of bereavement and to reach the stage where the grieving suicide survivor can accept their loss and continue living their life.

References

Andriessen, K. (2009). Can postvention be prevention? *Crisis, 30,* 43–47.
Andriessen, K. & Farberow, N. L. (2002). *European Directory of Suicide Survivors Services.* Le Barade: IASP.

Bland, D. (1994). *The Experiences of Suicide Survivors 1989–June 1994*. Baton Rouge, LA: Baton Rouge Crisis Intervention Center.

Bowlby, J. (1991). *Attachment and Loss: Sadness and depression* (pp. 81–112). London. Penguin.

Callahan, J. (2000). Predictors and correlates of bereavement in suicide support group participations. *Suicide and Life-Threatening Behavior, 30*, 104–124.

Clark, S. (1995). *After Suicide: Care for the bereaved* (pp. 3–104). Melbourne. Hill of Content.

Clark, S. E. & Goldney R. D. (2000). Impact of suicide on relatives and friends. In K. Hawton & K. van Heeringen (Eds.), *The International Handbook of Suicide and Attempted Suicide* (pp. 467–484). Chichester: John Wiley & Sons, Ltd.

Cleiren, M. P. H. D. (1993). *Bereavement and Adaptation. A comparative study of the aftermath of death* (pp. 115–201). Washington, DC: Hemisphere Publishing.

Cleiren, M. P. H. D., Grad, O, Zavasnik, A., & Diekstra R. F. W. (1996). Psycho-social impact of bereavement after suicide and fatal traffic accident: A comparative two-country study. *Acta Psychiatrica Scandinavica, 94*, 37–44.

Conley B. H. (1987). Funeral directors as first responders. In E. J. Dunne, J. L. McIntosh, & K. Dunne-Maxim (Eds.), *Suicide and its Aftermath: Understanding and counselling the survivors* (pp. 171–182). New York: W. W. Norton.

Cvinar, J. G. (2005). Do suicide survivors suffer social stigma: A review of the literature. *Perspectives in Psychiatric Care, 41*, 14–21.

Davies, R. (2004). New understandings of parental grief: Literature review. *Journal of Advanced Nursing, 46*, 506–512.

Dunne, E. J. (1987). Special needs of suicide survivors in therapy. In E. J. Dunne, J. L. McIntosh, & K. Dunne-Maxim (Eds.), *Suicide and its Aftermath: Understanding and counselling the survivors* (pp. 193–207). New York: W. W. Norton.

Dunne, E. J. & Dunne-Maxim, K. (2004). Working with families in the aftermath of suicide. In F. Walsh & M. McGoldrick (Eds.), *Living Beyond Loss: Death in the family* (pp. 272–284). New York: W. W. Norton.

Dunne, E. J. & Dunne-Maxim, K. (2009). Why suicide loss is different for the survivors. In D. Wasserman & C. Wasserman (Eds.), *Suicidology and Suicide Prevention. A global perspective* (pp. 605–608). Oxford: Oxford University Press.

Dyregrov, K. (2003). Micro-sociological analysis of social support following traumatic bereavement: Unhelpful and avoidant responses from the community. *Omega: Journal of Death and Dying, 48*, 23–44.

Ellenbogen, S. & Gratton, F. (2001) Do they suffer more? Reflections on research comparing suicide survivors to other survivors. *Suicide and Life Threatening Behavior, 31*, 83–90.

Farberow, N. L., Gallagher-Thomson, D., Gilewski, M., & Thompson, L. (1992). Changes in grief and mental health of bereaved spouses of older suicides. *Journal of Gerontology, 47*, 357–366.

Freud, S. (1950). *The Interpretation of Dreams*. New York: Random House.

Freud, S. (1957). Mourning and melancholia. In J. Strachey (Ed.), *The Standard Edition of the Complete Psychological Works of Sigmund Freud* (pp. 237–260). New York: Basic Books.

Garfield, P. (1996). Dreams in bereavement. In D. Barrett (Ed.), *Trauma and Death* (pp. 186–211). Cambridge, MA: Harvard University Press.

Grad, O. (1996). Suicide: How to survive as a survivor? *Crisis, 17*, 136–142.

Grad, O. (2005). Suicide survivorship: An unknown journey from loss to gain – From individual to global perspective. In K. Hawton (Ed.), *Prevention and Treatment of Suicidal Behaviour: From science to practice* (pp. 351–369). Oxford: Oxford University Press.

Grad, O. (2009). Therapists as survivors of suicide loss. In D. Wasserman & C. Wasserman (Eds.), *Suicidology and Suicide Prevention: A global perspective* (pp. 609–613). Oxford: Oxford University Press.

Grad, O. T. & Michel, K. (2005). In K. M. Weiner (Ed.), *Therapeutic and Legal Issues for Therapists Who Have Survived a Client Suicide* (pp. 71–81). New York: Haworth Press.

Grad, O. & Zavasnik, A. (1996). Similarities and differences in the process of bereavement after suicide and after traffic fatalities in Slovenia. *Omega, 33,* 243–251.

Grad, O. T. & Zavasnik, A. (1997). Shame: The unbearable legacy of suicide. In D. De Leo, A. Schmidtke, & R. F. W. Diekstra (Eds.), *Suicide Prevention: A holistic approach* (pp. 163–166). Boston, MA: Kluwer.

Grad, O. & Zavasnik, A. (1999). Phenomenology of bereavement process after suicide, traffic accident and terminal illness (in spouses). *Archives of Suicide Research, 5,* 157–172.

Grad, O. & Zavasnik, A. (2003) Symbolic expressions of loss in suicide survivors. XXII. World Congress of the IASP, *Abstract Book,* 103. Stockholm, Sweden.

Harwood, D., Hawton, K., Hope, T., & Jacoby, R. (2002). The grief experiences and needs of bereaved relatives and friends of older people dying through suicide: A descriptive and case-controlled study. *Journal of Affective Disorders, 72,* 185–194.

Hauser, M. J. (1987). Special aspects of grief after a suicide. In E. J. Dunne, J. L. McIntosh, & K. Dunne-Maxim (Eds.), *Suicide and its Aftermath: Understanding and counselling the survivors* (pp. 57–73). New York: W. W. Norton.

Hawton, K. (2007). Complicated grief after bereavement. *British Medical Journal, 334,* 962–963.

Hawton, K. & Simkin, S. (2003). Helping people bereaved by suicide. *British Medical Journal, 327,* 177–178.

Hornby, A. S. (2005). *Oxford Advanced Learner's Dictionary of Current English.* Oxford: Oxford University Press.

Imber-Black E. (2004). Rituals and the healing process. In F. Walsh & M. McGoldrick (Eds.), *Living Beyond Loss: Death in the family* (pp. 340–358). New York: W. W. Norton.

James, D. (2005). Surpassing the quota: Multiple suicides in a psychotherapy practice. In K. M. Weiner (Ed.), *Therapeutic and Legal Issues for Therapists Who Have Survived a Client Suicide* (pp. 9–24). New York: Haworth Press.

Jordan, J. R. (2001). Is suicide bereavement different? A reassessment of the literature. *Suicide and Life-Threatening Behavior, 31,* 91–102.

Jordan, J. R. (2008). Bereavement after suicide. *Psychiatric Annals, 38,* 679–685.

Knieper, A. J. (1999). The suicide survivor's grief and recovery. *Suicide and Life Threatening Behavior, 29,* 353–364.

Kübler-Ross, E. (1969). *On Death and Dying.* New York: Macmillan.

Kuramoto, S. J., Brent, D. A., & Wilcox, H. C. (2009). The impact of parental suicide on child and adolescent offspring. *Suicide and Life-Threatening Behavior, 39,* 137–151.

McDaid, C., Trowman, R, Golder, S., Hawton, K., & Sowden, A. (2008). Interventions for people bereaved through suicide: Systemic review. *The British Journal of Psychiatry, 193,* 438–443.

McGoldrick, M. (1987). Foreword. In E. J. Dunne, J. L. McIntosh, & K. Dunne-Maxim (Eds.), *Suicide and its Aftermath: Understanding and counselling the survivors* (pp. v–vi). New York: W. W. Norton.

McIntosh, J. L. (1987). Suicide as a mental health problem: epidemiological aspects. In E. J. Dunne, J. L. McIntosh, & K. Dunne-Maxim (Eds.), *Suicide and its Aftermath: Understanding and counselling the survivors* (pp. 19–30). New York: W. W. Norton.

McIntosh, J. L. (1992) Control group studies of suicide survivors: A review and critique. *Suicide and Life Threatening Behavior, 23,* 146–160.

McIntosh, J. L. (2003). Suicide survivors: The aftermath of suicide and suicidal behavior. In C. D. Bryant (Ed.), *Handbook of Death and Dying,* Vol. 1 (pp. 339–350). Thousand Oaks, CA: Sage.

McMenamy, J. M., Jordan, J. R., & Mitchell, A. M. (2008). What do suicide survivors tell us they need? Results of a pilot study. *Suicide and Life Threatening Behavior, 38,* 375–389.

Mitchell, A. M., Kim Y., Prigerson H. G., and Mortimer-Stephens M. (2004). Complicated grief in survivors of suicide. *Crisis*, 25, 12–18.

Parkes, C. M. (1993). Bereavement as a psychosocial transition: Process of adaptation to change. In M. Stroebe, W. Stroebe, & R. Hansson (Eds.), *Handbook of Bereavement* (pp. 91–101). New York: Cambridge University Press.

Parkes, C. M. & Weiss, R. S. (1983). *Recovery from Bereavement*. New York: Basic Books.

Rothaupt, J. W. & Becker, K. (2007). A literature review of Western bereavement theory: From decathecting to continuing bond. *The Family Journal*, 15, 6–15.

Sakinofsky, I. (2007). The aftermath of suicide: Managing survivors' bereavement. *Canadian Journal of Psychiatry*, 52, 129–136.

Saarinen, P. I., Viinamaki, H., Hintikka J., Lehtonen, J., & Lönqvist, J. (1999). Psychological symptoms of close relatives of suicide victims. *European Journal of Psychiatry*, 13, 33–39.

Saarinen P. I., Viinamaki, H., Lehtonen, J., & Lönqvist, J. (2000). Is it possible to adapt to the suicide of a close individual? Results of a 10-year prospective follow-up study. *International Journal of Social Psychiatry*, 46, 182–190.

Shear, M. K. & Mulhare, E. (2008). Complicated grief. *Psychiatric Annals*, 38, 662–670.

Shneidman, E. S. (1969). Prologue: Fifty-eight years. In E. S. Shneidman (Ed.), *On the Nature of Suicide* (pp. 1–30). San Francisco, CA: Jossey-Bass.

Shneidman, E. S. (1972). Foreword. In C. A. Cain (Ed.), *Survivors of Suicide* (pp. ix–xi). Springfield, IL: Charles C. Thomas.

Shneidman, E. S. (1993). *Suicide as Psychache* (pp. 161–179). Northvale, NJ: Jason Aronson.

Stroebe, W. & Stroebe, M. S. (1987). The symptomatology of grief. In W. Stroebe & M. S. Stroebe (Eds), *Bereavement and Health: The psychological and physical consequences of partner loss* (pp. 7–25). Cambridge: Cambridge University Press.

Stroebe, M., Stroebe, W., & Schut, H. (2003). Bereavement research: Methodological issues and ethical concerns. *Palliative Medicine*, 17, 235–240.

Stroebe, W., Stroebe, M. S., and Abakoumkin, G. (2005). The broken heart: Suicidal ideation in bereavement. *American Journal of Psychiatry*, 162, 2178–2180.

Stroebe, W., Schut, H., & Stroebe, M. S. (2007). Health outcomes of bereavement. *The Lancet*, 370(9603), 1960–1973.

Tekavčič Grad, O. & Zavasnik A. (1992) Aggression as a natural part of suicide bereavement. *Crisis*, 3(2), 65–69.

Walsh, F. & McGoldrick, M. (2004). Loss and the family: A systemic perspective. In F. Walsh & M. McGoldrick (Eds.), *Living Beyond Loss: Death in the family* (pp. 3–27). New York: W. W. Norton.

Wertheimer, A. (1991). *A Special Scar* (pp. 189–190). London: Routledge.

Worden, J. W. (1991). *Grief Counseling and Grief Therapy: A handbook for the mental health practitioner*. New York: Springer Verlag.

Yalom, I. D. (2008). *Staring at the Sun* (pp. 31–77). London: Piatkus Books.

Zisook, S. & Shear, K. (2009) Grief and bereavement: What psychiatrists need to know. *World Psychiatry*, 8, 67–74.

Zisook, S., Shear, K. M., & Irwin, S. (2009). Death, dying and bereavement. In B. J. Sadock, B. A. Sadock, & P. Ruiz (Eds.), *Kaplan and Sadock's Comprehensive Textbook of Psychiatry*, Vol. II. (pp. 2378–2407). Philadelphia, PA: Lippincott Williams & Wilkins.

CHAPTER THIRTY-THREE

Challenges in US Suicide Prevention Public Awareness Programmes

Jane L. Pearson[1]

Abstract

Awareness is considered the initial step in suicide prevention efforts in the United States and many nations around the world. Yet there is limited research to guide effective approaches to increasing awareness. A recent review by Dumesnil and Verger (2009) provides a helpful overview of international suicide prevention awareness efforts and called for expert consensus on approaches. An edited book by Hornik (2002) is another comprehensive summary of successful public health communication efforts across the world, with examples of efforts that were more or less successful. Using lessons learned from these reviews, this chapter considers some specific targeted campaign efforts in the United States. Included are efforts aimed at federal and state policy-makers; the news media and entertainment media; and two US demographic groups: high school youth and military veterans. It reviews the goals and intended outcomes for these awareness programmes and highlights opportunities for research for these particular target audiences. Safety issues unique to suicide prevention efforts are considered. With these conclusions in mind, the chapter considers some current research challenges: efficient means of assessing awareness needs in target groups; and how to work with cultural values within target groups, using an example that harnesses new media.

Introduction

Based on the recommendations of the United Nations/World Health Organization publication *Prevention of Suicide: Guidelines for the Formulation and Implementation of National*

International Handbook of Suicide Prevention: Research, Policy and Practice, First Edition.
Edited by Rory C. O'Connor, Stephen Platt, Jacki Gordon.
© 2011 John Wiley & Sons, Ltd. Published 2011 by John Wiley & Sons, Ltd.

Strategies (United Nations, 1996), most national suicide prevention strategies call for increased public awareness that suicides can be prevented. At a more local level, many suicide prevention advocacy groups develop their own ways of increasing awareness, including highway billboards and local television and radio spots. Borrowing from marketing ideas (e.g., brand recognition of a campaign) and social science theories of behaviour change, these efforts have assumed that for necessary behaviour change to take place, awareness, attitudes/beliefs, and intentions need to change before behaviours shift (see, e.g., *Theory of Reasoned Action* by Fishbein & Ajzen, 1975; also Aldrich & Cerel, 2009; Fishbein, 2008).

Dumesnil and Verger (2009) recently conducted a review of depression and suicide awareness campaigns which included efforts from many nations. Some of these were specifically focused on depression and/or suicide prevention, while others were aimed at increasing acceptance of those with mental disorders. The review included reports of campaigns published between 1987 and 2007. Campaign goals varied with regard to their focus, including awareness of the prevalence of a disorder, improving perceptions of the mentally ill, reducing discrimination against those with mental illness, improving help-seeking, and reducing suicide rates. Target audiences included the public, those with mental disorders, as well as health professionals. Some efforts were brief, while others were sustained; some efforts used television media only, while others used multiple media modes and training (e.g., television, billboards, websites, brochures, kits for professionals). The review provides useful tables that summarize several categories of campaigns: short media campaigns; gatekeeper training; long national programmes; and long local and community programmes. Due to the variation in these efforts, as well as the limitations in the designs of the evaluations, Dumesnil and Verger (2009) were not able to draw clear conclusions about what type of efforts were most successful in meeting the intended campaign goals. However, they did conclude that those efforts that were more focused and sustained, and employed several types of media, appeared to be more successful. While campaigns mounted at a national level may seem more efficient in that they can reach a wider audience, Dumesnil and Verger concluded that 'it appears necessary to organize programmes at a local level, to target relatively limited and homogenous populations, and to adapt messages to them' (p. 1211). This is consistent with social marketing principles that are aimed at segmented, targeted groups. To further improve effectiveness, they also recommended that organizations conduct a needs assessment of the target audience before a programme is designed, use a theoretical model appropriate for the campaign goal, and use reliable indicators for effects.

These recommendations are consistent with the growing field of public health communication. Following an Annenberg Public Policy Center supported meeting, Public Health Communication: Evidence for Behaviour Change, Hornik (2002) edited a book by the same title which provides a helpful overview of a variety of campaigns, their design challenges, and evaluation successes and failures. Efforts described range from AIDS prevention and substance use prevention, to increasing seat belt use, with examples from several countries. His epilogue provides a concise summary of the design and evaluation challenges in communication programmes. The review of various evaluation design approaches (e.g., pre-post, variations of time-series designs) is particularly valuable for organizations planning to implement and evaluate a campaign, and for the suicide prevention researchers who may provide technical advice, particularly for the evaluation.

In addition to the many challenges faced in public health campaigns, suicide awareness campaigns carry additional concerns of potential, untoward effects. To consider those concerns more carefully, several agencies in the US Department of Health and Human Services and the Annenberg Foundation Trust at Sunnylands, convened a workshop to consider both safe and effective messaging in suicide prevention (Chambers, Pearson, Lubell, Brandon, O'Brien, *et al.*, 2005). Among the challenges discussed were the potential actions that could inadvertently 'normalize' an undesired behaviour. Getting the public to accept the notion that suicide is a problem, such as 'suicide is a leading cause of death among young people', is clearly laudable. However, while this is factually accurate, the public doesn't know that this 'leading cause' is a very infrequent event, and certainly not a 'normal' event for young people, even for youth with mental disorders. This becomes a particular challenge where an aim of a campaign includes efforts to reduce stigma associated with mental disorders along with suicide prevention awareness. First, mental disorders are relatively prevalent compared with suicide behaviours, so pairing them can create confusion. Second, most advocacy groups would like to see individuals with mental disorders face less stigma. However, becoming more 'accepting' of suicidal thoughts and behaviour in a public campaign is a risky proposition. Trying to convey that we should be accepting of individuals but not their suicidal behaviour is a complex task. As noted by Cialdini (2003), 'Public service communicators should avoid the tendency to send the normatively muddled message that a targeted activity is socially disapproved but widespread' (p. 108). Thus, the potential to do harm in a campaign by contributing to ideas that suicide is widespread, and whether it is seen as an 'acceptable' or a discouraged behaviour is of significant concern.

Chambers and colleagues (2005) provide a theoretical example that highlights this concern for a radio campaign for a segmented audience: Some North American Indian nations have very high rates of suicide. A campaign, mounted through Indian radio stations which has a broad Indian audience and highlights the high prevalence of suicide, may send the message that such behaviour is inevitable and expected. Groups with the high rates may get the message that they have experienced an expected behaviour, and groups with the lower rates are 'lagging behind' the inevitable. Campaigns that are more targeted in terms of audience and message, such as informing individuals who are in a suicidal crisis to seek help from a hotline, may be more successful. Organizations interested in using public awareness campaigns were pointed to steps for planning and evaluating their campaigns, including the development of a logic model (a systematic way of visually depicting an organization's resources, activities, and anticipated outcomes). These included identifying the target population, the target problem, the theory used to address the problem, what aspects of the campaign needed to be tested (for both intended and unintended effects), having an implementation plan (specificity, duration, intensity, reach), and evaluation (the CDC Evaluation Workgroup has a useful website on developing a logic model and plans for evaluation).

As noted by Dumesnil and Verger (2009), expected outcomes of campaigns need to be realistic in view of the range and intensity of the efforts. If the focus of a campaign is on increasing awareness as the goal, realistic outcomes for that goal need to be considered. Seasoned health communication experts consistently find that advocates behind campaigns often expect too much with regard to behaviour changes (e.g., see Smith, 2002). Whether awareness about suicide can shift a broad range of behaviours (including providing support to those who have attempted, as well as support to family survivors) and then sustain them, is doubtful given how complex social interactions are. Expecting improvements in clinical care for individuals at risk for suicidal behaviour are probably even more distant, complex, and difficult outcomes to obtain from awareness programmes that do not include training of professionals. Dumesnil and Verger (2009) point to successful awareness campaigns that had specific target audiences which included gatekeeper training for professionals. Noting these 'lessons learned', efforts are made in this chapter to focus on the most likely successful proximal (short-term) outcomes.

This chapter considers awareness efforts focused on three target audiences: (1) federal and state policy-makers; (2) two aspects of media: newspaper and the entertainment media; and (3) two outreach efforts to sub-groups of the public: youth in schools and veterans of military service in the community. For each of these three areas, efforts to define a problem, a potential goal, and at least one outcome are made. The chapter conclusions list areas of agreement for what are considered the most effective approaches. A final summary of areas of needed research is offered.

Target Audience: Federal and State Policy-Makers

In the United States, suicide prevention advocates saw that suicide prevention was rarely identified as a priority for relevant federal service or research agencies, and if it was, it was not often sustained in any programmatic fashion. In this way, 'the problem' was defined as the low frequency with which relevant federal agencies consistently identified suicide prevention as 'mission relevant'. Similarly, recognizing that US resources for suicide prevention are often controlled at the state level, advocates examined state policies. The problem is defined as few states specifically addressing suicide as a public health problem. To address these problems, advocates identified legislators and state office officials as the target audience to develop state-level organizations or offices with strategies that, at a minimum, put suicide prevention 'on the map'. Communication with policy-makers may have been personal contacts with legislators; TV, newspaper, and radio advertisements; or billboards near a state capitol building. The content of these advocacy-instigated communications was varied, and the stories of personal family losses to suicide that advocates were willing to share were no doubt compelling. Indeed, some of the most active congressional efforts came from legislators who themselves had lost a family member to suicide, and shared their experiences with their peers. In this example, an awareness campaign is very focused on direct contacts with policy-makers and their staff. State-level suicide prevention advocates can monitor their progress in achieving awareness among current policy-makers through ongoing tracking of who has been contacted, and who has been made aware of the problem, possibly through public meeting records.

The next step after awareness is the expectation that policy-makers will take action. There are several compelling examples of evidence for meeting the goal of having policy-makers understand that 'suicide is preventable'. At the federal level, there are several examples prior to the establishment in 2001 of the US National Strategy for Suicide Prevention (NSSP) (US Department of Health and Human Services, 2001). In 1997 the US Senate passed Resolution 84 which recognized suicide as a national problem and declared suicide prevention to be a national priority. Two years later, Surgeon General Satcher released a *Call to Action to Prevent Suicide* from the US Public Health Service (1999). After the release of the NSSP, the US Department of Health and Human Services agencies began to more consistently coordinate suicide prevention efforts (DeMartino, Crosby, EchoHawk, Litts, Pearson, *et al.*, 2003). In 2004 the Garrett Lee Smith Memorial Act (P.L. 108–355) became the first US federal law to provide specific funding for youth suicide prevention programmes. These programmes were designed to complement efforts by state suicide prevention strategies. Forty-eight states and territories now have a suicide prevention plans (Suicide Prevention Resource Center, 2009). Key to much of this effort was Suicide Prevention Action Network's (SPAN USA) advocacy devoted to communicating directly with federal and state policy-makers. Policy-makers come and go, so communication and awareness for federal and state leaders is a perennial challenge, one recognized by advocates who continue to sustain their efforts.

While public health officials may be persuaded by well-informed advocates, they are probably further persuaded by evidence of public opinion and beliefs. In an effort to benchmark public experience with, and beliefs about, suicide, SPAN-USA was again instrumental in obtaining public opinions about suicide prevention through a partnership with Research!America, a not-for-profit public education and advocacy alliance. In a 2004 telephone survey of 800 representative adults, 38% affirmatively responded to the question, 'Has anyone ever told you they were contemplating suicide?' In a 2006 survey with the same methodology, nearly half of the respondents (48%) strongly agreed that 'many suicides and suicide attempts can be prevented'. The lack of belief that suicide was preventable did not appear to be linked to overt discrimination or stigma about mental health. In the same 2006 survey, a vast majority (89%) indicated that mental health was as important as physical health (Research!America, 2006). It remains to be seen whether a more recent survey will find a greater proportion of US adults believing that suicide is preventable. These survey efforts also establish useful baseline markers for future evaluation efforts.

Target Audience: News and Entertainment Media

One can argue that the content provided by the news and entertainment industry is a reflection of the audience it serves. It can offer a glimpse into whether suicide is seen as preventable, whether as part of news or entertainment. How the media depict suicide deaths has been of particular interest to suicide prevention advocates and researchers, due to evidence of modelling and clustering, particularly among youth (e.g., see reviews by Insel & Gould, 2008; Pirkis, Burgess, Francis, Blood, & Jolley, 2006; and Chapter 30 by Pirkis & Nordentoft, above). News media recommendations are considered relevant internationally (World Health Organization (WHO), 2008), as well as being included in nation-specific suicide prevention strategies for this reason. Most describe the most appropriate ways in which to report suicide, as well as approaches to reduce harm (i.e., what not to do). However, the degree to which such recommendations are known, accepted, and implemented are rarely assessed. That is, are the press and producers aware of recommendations for safe reporting on suicide? Do they see the recommendations as valid and do they modify their practice in light of the guidelines?

In the United States, the first media reporting recommendations were made publicly available in the mid-1990s. They were the result of a 1989 workshop that focused on reducing youth suicide contagion. The recommendations were developed and published by the Centers for Disease Control and Prevention (CDC) in 1994. The publication was in *Mortality and Morbidity Weekly Reports* (*MMWR*) which provides information on health and fatality trends among state and federal public health officials, and is not likely to be seen by many journalists (CDC, 1994). Indeed, prior to the 2001 release of media recommendations in the United States (e.g., National Institute of Mental Health, 2002) researchers at the Annenberg Public Policy Center at the University of Pennsylvania interviewed reporters who had written a story about suicide in the top 100 circulation US newspapers and found that virtually none was aware of any recommendations concerning the depiction of information about suicide (Jamieson, Jamieson, & Romer, 2003). While state and federal public health officials should be made aware of media guidelines, the MMWR publication did not aim directly at what should have been the target audience of journalists.

There are two encouraging examples that indicate that awareness among journalists can improve and that the depictions of suicide in news media can be changed for the better. Fu and Yip (2008) assessed styles (e.g., story placement, use of photos) of media reporting on suicides in Hong Kong before and after the release of the WHO media recommendations. After the Hong Kong Jockey Club Centre for Suicide Research and Prevention held a public seminar and press conference (attended by at least 10 newspapers) and distributed nearly 1,000 free manuals explaining both WHO media recommendations (what to do) and examples of copycat suicides (what not to do), changes in media practices were examined. Headlines and the use of pictorial content were more frequently in compliance with recommendations after the release. While the launch of the recommendations was supported by schools of journalism, and may have influenced journalists' and editors' awareness and behaviours, direct measurement of awareness among reporters and editors was not assessed.

Another effort by the Annenberg Public Policy Center serves as an example of how media reports about suicide patterns and statistics can be influenced and improved. In surveying newspaper coverage of suicide topics, the Annenberg Public Policy Center discovered a media-perpetuated myth that suicide risk increased over the winter holidays. Beginning in 2000, the Policy Center began issuing a press release highlighting the myth and providing accurate US vital statistics data which illustrated that, in fact, rates are higher in the spring and autumn, and lower in the winter months. While there is some risk in highlighting myths (people may remember the myth better than the fact), this effort did prove to be effective in creating more accurate reporting between 2000 and 2005 (Annenberg Public Policy Center, 2005). More relevant to the goal of improving awareness that suicide is preventable, journalists wishing to address patterns of suicide rates also had the opportunity to describe more accurately the risk and protective factors for suicide, as well as providing information on ways to seek help.

Improving awareness that suicide is preventable through the entertainment media has also been a focus for federal and advocacy organizations. The Entertainment Industries Council, Inc. (EIC) is a non-profit organization that provides information, awareness, and understanding of major health and social issues among the entertainment industries and to audiences at large. EIC aims to represent the best examples of accuracy in depicting health and social issues on screen in feature films, TV and music videos, music, and even comic books. The Substance Abuse and Mental Health Services Administration (SAMHSA) and the National Institute of Mental Health have provided assistance in helping EIC to reward examples of accuracy through the annual PRISM award. EIC makes available to the industry the publication *Depression and Bipolar Disorder*. This on-line document has a Section VII, on Depression and Suicide Prevention, which includes warning signs for suicide, as well as approaches to suicide prevention. The publication also includes information about the potential for imitation when reporting on celebrity suicide deaths, and ways to provide helpful depictions.

There has been no published research of the potential effect of EIC's efforts on industry awareness of their role in suicide prevention or whether the industry, overall, has improved its depictions of suicide. Evaluations of EIC's efforts are probably needed more than ever. Work by Patrick Jamieson at the Annenberg Public Policy Center has found an increase in suicide portrayals in the top selling US films since 1950 (personal communication, August 2009). In addition, youth are increasingly exposed to more TV and movies via their own computer downloads and DVD purchases (Nielsen, 2009). Research efforts that address youth perceptions of TV and film media depiction of suicide, and whether youth perceive it as preventable are critically needed.

The Annenberg Public Policy Center and SAMHSA recently convened the meeting Media Recommendations V2.0, which was intended to consider ways in which the media recommendations could be updated by new research, as well as consider the current modes of news communication, including blogs, reader comments, and the ease with which news stories and consumer comments can be shared via web widgets (e.g., 'Ways to share this story', such as Facebook, Twitter, etc.). Suicide prevention advocates now face the challenge of increasing awareness of suicide content among web administrators and consumers, particularly among those who produce and share stories through web-based media. With regard to research needs, the tracking of news stories through the web media would allow for a way of learning both about which suicide depictions are forwarded, as well as how broad (how many users) and saturated (how many users get the same, or even repeated, information from their network) social networks are with regard to this topic.

Specific Target Outreach Programmes

US high school students

Recent US efforts that have focused on school-based youth suicide prevention offer some insight into ways of increasing awareness among school-attending youth. The Signs of Suicide (SOS) programme targets high school youth and provides a multifaceted approach that includes both didactic presentations and self-assessments related to depression, alcohol use, and suicidal risk. It was developed by the creators of National Depression Screening Day (Screening for Mental Health, Inc.) and is now listed on the SAMHSA National Registry of Effective Programs (NREP). The didactic presentation includes a video presentation that illustrates several scenarios of high school youth who are experiencing depression, alcohol problems, and suicidal ideation. The video also shows how to appropriately help a peer by seeking assistance from a trusted adult using the mnemonic, ACT: Acknowledge, Care, and Tell. At the end of the screening procedure, youth can be referred to mental health providers. Two separate follow-up evaluations of this programme have indicated that youth exposed to the programmes, on average, have greater knowledge about suicide and depression, more adaptive attitudes about seeking help, and fewer self-reported suicide attempts (Aseltine & DeMartino, 2004; Aseltine, James, Schilling, & Glanovsky, 2007).

SOS is promising as a universal approach to increasing youth awareness. Its effects on the most at-risk youth, however, are not yet clear. Higher-risk youth who find themselves in limited resource schools may not find referral assistance readily available. In addition, self-selected clustering among youth at risk (Joiner, 2003), along with reports by distressed high school youth that they are reluctant to seek adult professionals for help (Carlton & Deane, 2000; Wyman, Brown, Inman, Cross, Schmeelk-Cone, *et al.*, 2008), and rather prefer to seeking help from peers (in person or via the web), and were reluctant to use a crisis line (Gould, Velting, Kleinman, Lucas, Thomas, *et al.*, 2004), suggests that increased efforts to influence peer norms for help-seeking may be needed. Particular media may also have differential influence on youth audiences. Klimes-Dougan, Yuan, Lee, and Houri (2009) recently reported that higher-risk high school students (those experiencing depressive symptoms and suicide ideation) exposed to a billboard simulation of a suicide prevention message, were less likely to endorse help-seeking attitudes, and endorsed more maladaptive coping than their peers exposed to a suicide prevention TV advert. Similar to troubled youth, adults already in distress appear to be little influenced by public campaigns. Goldney and Fisher (2008) found that individuals who already suffered from depression and suicide ideation did not find public education programmes designed to improve mental health literacy of any tangible benefit.

In sum, these youth awareness efforts may be most effective for youth with mild or moderate risk, as well as possibly being effective in encouraging low-risk youth to assist their peers in help-seeking. Additional efforts, however, are needed to assist the peer helpers who take on this significant responsibility, as well as efforts to better identify and help the most at-risk youth.

Recent military veterans

The US Veterans' Health Administration (VA) has faced a unique and urgent challenge in health messaging for suicide prevention. There are no previously established models for developing campaigns with the right balance between high-risk targeted efforts and a population-based approach for preventing suicide in such a demographically and geographically diverse group. Current veterans are diverse and include older adolescents (ages 18, 19), as well as National Guard and Reserve units which often are comprised of young to middle-aged adults who are temporarily leaving other careers to serve. Given the increasing suicide rate among veterans from the Iraq and Afghanistan wars (Kang & Bullman, 2008), and increasing rates of mental health problems among recently active duty veterans (Seal, Metzler, Gima, Bertenthal, Maguen, *et al.*, 2009), the VA saw that their messaging needed to address the highest risk group, as well as being appropriate to the majority of veterans who are at less risk.

In collaboration with SAMHSA, the VA added a 24-hour crisis line associated with the National Suicide Prevention Lifeline, 1-800-273-TALK, by providing a telephone menu option for veterans. The veteran calls are routed to a VA call centre where VA staff trained in crisis interventions are able to identify the caller's geographic location by their area code, identify local VA resources, and link to the VA medical record if the caller wishes. The individual can also be linked to a VHA suicide prevention coordinator familiar with resources in the veteran's location. For the effort to reach at-risk veterans and their families, advertising of the hotline had to be universal, with a message that would also be meaningful to those less at risk. The outreach message is, 'It takes the courage and strength of a warrior to ask for help'. Developers of this message intend to convey that the VA cares about the mental health of veterans and about preventing suicide (Knox & Bossarte, 2009). This provides a unique opportunity to examine how crisis-call outreach can facilitate behaviour change (convincing callers to follow-up on a referral) among high-risk individuals.

After a year of the VA suicide prevention hotline implementation, the VA selected the Washington, DC area to further advertise this service through displays in subway cars, subway stations, and on buses for three months (Department of Veterans Affairs press release, 2008). Preliminary analyses indicate that there was a significant increase in calls to the suicide prevention hotline from telephone numbers in the DC area during the awareness campaign (Knox & Bossarte, 2009). Analyses of the demographic characteristics of the callers are under way. The campaign's broader effect across veterans as a larger group is not known. The degree to which veterans who are not in crisis have viewed the outreach message, and see suicide as preventable, has not yet been researched.

A more recent expansion of VA suicide prevention efforts is the availability of a one-to-one chat service for veterans who prefer reaching out for assistance using the Internet. Called 'Veterans' Chat', the new service enables veterans, their families, and friends to go online where they can anonymously chat with a trained VA counsellor (Department of Veterans Affairs press release, 2009). If 'the chatter' is determined to be of a crisis nature, the counsellor can take immediate action to transfer the person to the VA suicide prevention hotline for further counselling and referral. This new effort has not yet been evaluated with regard to awareness or help-seeking content, nor with regard to the number of anonymous individuals who get referred to VA services related to suicidal crisis. However, the quality of counsellor interactions and likelihood of callers intending to seek referrals provided by the National Lifeline is currently being researched by Madelyn Gould and her associates (National Institute of Mental Health, 2009).

Conclusions and Research Needs

Conclusions

Of the publications and US programme efforts reviewed here, there are several areas of agreement consistent with Dumesnil and Verger's (2009) review of international suicide prevention awareness efforts. These can serve to inform advocacy groups, policy-makers, and practitioners preparing for awareness campaigns regarding the most effective approaches. These include the following areas of agreement: (1) short-term, broad campaigns are not likely to have a significant impact on any particular group. Given the low likelihood of a benefit, the risk of unintended consequences (e.g., normalization) may suggest more risk than benefit from the effort. (2) Within a target group, knowing the knowledge level, cultural values, and 'problem' to address makes the development of the message and its implementation more likely to succeed. (3) Sustained and multi-pronged efforts (professional education, local outreach to multiple settings) that complement public campaigns are likely to be more successful. (4) Consider various approaches for pilot testing (e.g., focus groups, checking Internet web visits), and overall evaluation efforts to determine the most safe and efficient messages and media investments for future plans.

Research needs

Regarding future research needs, much is yet to be learned about efficient ways of the following: assessing awareness needs in target groups; developing messages compatible with cultural values within target groups; and understanding how best to harness new media while addressing ethical concerns. This chapter concludes with some examples of research that highlight these challenges.

Assessing awareness and sources of information

One area ripe for US research on awareness is to ask individuals where they get information about suicide, and also how various groups of interest vary in their information sources and attitudes about suicide. A New Zealand study is an example of how researchers used an ongoing, longitudinal study to take advantage of a defined sampling frame and prior mental health histories of respondents when assessing a target group's knowledge and attitudes about suicide. Beautrais and her colleagues found that in 2002, over 80% of youth in a defined cohort aged 25 years reported information learned about suicide was from radio and television news (Beautrais, Horwood, & Fergusson, 2004). These youth, on average, also estimated the annual number of youth suicides in New Zealand to be 10 times more that the actual number. From their responses to items from the Suicide Opinion Questionnaire (Domino, Moore, Westlake, & Gibson, 1982), there seemed to be an interesting mix of optimism and 'appropriate stigma' against suicidal acts: 90%

agreed that no matter how bad things may seem, they were never bad enough for suicide. Interestingly, 73% indicated that there are some situations in which they could understand why people take their own lives, with significantly more frequent endorsement of understanding among those who had a personal history of attempting, as well as having family members who had attempted suicide. These findings illustrate a complex picture. Ideally, they suggest that separate outreach and targeting of messages that balances respect for the individual (who engaged in the suicide act), but also emphasizes more vigilance of warning signs and life-preserving attitudes may be needed for those at higher risk.

A second target group that US-based suicide researchers seem to have neglected are middle-aged adults outside of the Veterans system. An increase in the rate of middle-aged suicide deaths between 1999 and 2004 was noted by CDC (2007), but few programmatic efforts appear to have addressed this segment of the US population. Individuals aged 45–64 years who have a 2006 suicide rate of 16 per 100,000, have nearly double the annual number of suicides (12,009) compared with individuals aged 15–29 years (6,749) (CDC WISQARS). Unlike school settings, there are few workplace programmes available to assess employee understanding of suicide, or to conduct research to assess suicide risk and protective factors outside the US military. A Swedish study by Hedström and colleagues examined the potential risk of suicide death exposure of employee peers versus family members on later suicide deaths. They found an unexpected significant degree of peer worker exposure for men, particularly among worksites with fewer than 100 employees (Hedström, Liu, & Nordvik, 2008). The authors suggest an action theory-based model that accounts for increased suicide risk due to awareness of another's suicide death through multiple ways: seeing sympathy and glorification expressed for a suicide decedent; increased self-efficacy to carry out the suicide method ('if he can, I can'); less social contextual pressure dissuading suicide as an option; and the suicide act becomes less of a theoretical option to more of a real possibility.

This theory could be used to determine how sympathy for co-workers who died by suicide can be disentangled from attitudes about suicide that are associated with both exposure risk and resilience. Assessing attitudes in a postvention programme, in combination with data on the sources of information workers in these settings may have about suicide, could be used to develop effective and safe awareness programmes for employee-based efforts.

Working with cultural values of target groups and harnessing new media

Several examples in this chapter suggested that renewed efforts are needed to determine contemporary media sources of information about suicide (e.g., newspaper websites, blogs, social networking sites). Individuals who use these networks are often visiting these sites because they share cultural values and common experiences. Silenzio and his colleagues (Silenzio, Duberstein, Tang, Tu, & Homan, 2009) provide an example of reaching an at-risk and under-served group through such social media. Young adult lesbian, gay, and bisexual (LGB) individuals repeatedly report higher rates of suicide ideation and attempts (Suicide Prevention Resource Center, 2008). They also report that the Internet is an important resource for them to connect with LGB peers. Silenzio and colleagues determined the breadth (how many users) and density (how many links among users) of online social networks for self-identified LGB youth, and view this passive approach to tracking public information as a feasible way of conducting research with this hard-to-access group. However, even if feasible, Silenzio and colleagues wisely recommend further consideration of the ethical issues of using public social media sites for prevention efforts, particularly among youth who may not appreciate the potential consequences of this shared information. However, while this ethical issue may seem unique to this population and form of media, it has been argued that any public messaging effort potentially exposes a population to an assumed intervention without consent (Chambers *et al.*, 2005). Thus, for both safety and efficiency reasons, continued research on suicide prevention public awareness programmes, in particular to understand those that are effective for the most vulnerable individuals, is still needed within the broader suicide prevention strategies.

Note

1   The views presented here are those of the author, and do not necessarily represent the views of the National Institute of Mental Health, or the US Department of Health and Human Services.

References

Aldrich, R. S. & Cerel, J. (2009). Development of effective message content for suicide intervention: Theory of planned behavior. *Crisis, 30*, 174–179.

Annenberg Public Policy Center (2005), *Holiday Suicide Reporting Gets More Accurate*, available at http://www.annenbergpublicpolicycenter.org/NewsDetails.aspx?myId=177, accessed 1 September 2009.

Aseltine, R. H., Jr. & DeMartino, R. (2004). An outcome evaluation of the SOS suicide prevention program. *American Journal of Public Health, 94*, 446–451.

Aseltine, R. H., Jr., James, A., Schilling, E. A., & Glanovsky, J. (2007). Evaluating the SOS suicide prevention program: A replication and extension. *BioMed Central, 7*, 161.

Beautrais, A. L., Horwood, L. J., & Fergusson, D. M. (2004). Knowledge and attitudes about suicide in 25-year-olds. *Australian and New Zealand Journal of Psychiatry, 38*, 260–265.

Carlton, P. A. & Deane, F. P. (2000). Impact of attitudes and suicidal ideation on adolescents' intentions to seek professional psychological help. *Journal of Adolescence, 23*, 35–45.

CDC Web-based Injury Statistics Query and Reporting System (WISQARS), available at http://www.cdc.gov/injury/wisqars/index.html, accessed 1 September 2009.

CDC (1994). Suicide contagion and the reporting of suicide: Recommendations from a national workshop. *Morbidity and Mortality Weekly Report, 43*, 9–18.

CDC (2007). Increases in age-group-specific injury mortality – United States, 1999–2004. *Morbidity and Mortality Weekly Report, 56*, 1281–1284.

Chambers, D. A., Pearson, J. L., Lubell, K., Brandon, S., O'Brien, K., & Zinn, J. (2005). The science of public messages for suicide prevention: A workshop summary. *Suicide and Life-Threatening Behavior, 35*, 134–145.

Cialdini, R. B. (2003). Crafting normative messages to protect the environment. *Current Directions in Psychological Research, 12*, 105–109.

DeMartino, R. E., Crosby, A. E., EchoHawk, M., Litts, D. A., Pearson, J., Reed, G. A., & West, M. (2003). A call to collaboration: The federal commitment to suicide prevention. *Suicide and Life-Threatening Behavior, 33*, 101–110.

Department of Veterans Affairs Press Release (2008). *VA Rolling Out Suicide Hotline Ads in DC*, available at http://www1.va.gov/opa/pressrel/pressrelease.cfm?id=1538, accessed 25 May 2010.

Department of Veterans Affairs Press Release (2009). *VA Chat Service Added to Suicide Prevention*, available at http://www1.va.gov/opa/pressrel/pressrelease.cfm?id=1757, accessed 25 May 2010.

Domino, G., Moore, D., Westlake, L., & Gibson, L. (1982). Attitudes towards suicide: A factor analytic approach. *Journal of Clinical Psychology, 38*, 257–262.

Dumesnil, H. & Verger, P. (2009). Public awareness campaigns about depression and suicide: A review. *Psychiatric Services, 60*, 1203–1213.

Entertainment Industries Council (n.d.). *Depression and Bipolar Disorder*, available at http://eiconline.org/resources/publications/z_sdhs/Bipolar_FINALw%20linking.pdf, accessed 25 May 2010.

Fishbein, M. (2008). A reasoned action approach to health promotion. *Medical Decision Making, 28*, 834–844.

Fishbein, M. & Ajzen, I. (1975). *Belief, Attitude, Intention, and Behavior: An introduction to theory and research*. Reading, MA: Addison-Wesley.

Fu, K. W. & Yip, P. S. (2008). Changes in reporting of suicide news after the promotion of the WHO media recommendations. *Suicide and Life-Threatening Behavior, 38*, 631–636.

Garrett Lee Smith Memorial Act, CR 150. P.L. 108–355 (2004).

Goldney, R. D. & Fisher, L. J. (2008). Have broad-based community and professional education program influenced mental health literacy and treatment seeking of those with major depression and suicidal ideation? *Suicide and Life-Threatening Behavior, 38*, 129–142.

Gould, M. S., Velting, D., Kleinman, M., Lucas, C., Thomas, J. G., & Chung, M. (2004). Teenagers' attitudes about coping strategies and help-seeking behavior for suicidality. *Journal of the American Academy of Child and Adolescent Psychiatry, 43*, 1124–1133.

Hedström, P., Liu, K. Y., & Nordvik, M. K. (2008). Interaction domains and suicide: A population-based panel study of suicides in Stockholm, 1991–1999. *Social Forces, 87*, 713–740.

Hornik, R. C. (Ed.) (2002). *Public Health Communication: Evidence for behavior change*. Mahwah, NJ: Lawrence Erlbaum.

Insel, B. J. & Gould, M. S. (2008). Impact of modeling on adolescent suicidal behavior. *Psychiatric Clinics of North America, 31*, 293–316.

Jamieson, P., Jamieson, K. H., & Romer, D. (2003). The responsible reporting of suicide in print journalism. *American Behavioral Scientist, 46*, 1643–1660.

Joiner, T. E., Jr. (2003). Contagion of suicidal symptoms as a function of assortative relating and shared relationship stress in college roommates. *Journal of Adolescence, 26*, 495–504.

Kang, H. K. & Bullman, T. A. (2008). The risk of suicide among US veterans after returning from Iraq or Afghanistan war zones. *Journal of the American Medical Association, 300*, 652–653.

Klimes-Dougan, B., Yuan, C., Lee, S., & Houri, A. K. (2009). Suicide prevention with adolescents: Considering potential benefits and untoward effects of public service announcements. *Crisis, 30*, 128–135.

Knox, K. L. & Bossarte, R. M. (2009). *Suicide Prevention Research – Enabling activities funded through VA's Office of Mental Health*. Presentation at the 2009 Department of Defense/Veterans Administration Suicide Prevention Conference. San Antonio, TX.

National Institute of Mental Health (2002). *Reporting on Suicide: Recommendations for the media*, available at http://www.nimh.nih.gov/health/topics/suicide-prevention/reporting-on-suicide-recommendations-for-the-media.shtml, accessed 9 January 2009.

National Institute of Mental Health (2009). *Recovery Funds will Support of Evaluation of Suicide Prevention Training*, available at http://www.nimh.nih.gov/science-news/2009/recovery-funds-will-support-evaluation-of-suicide-prevention-training.shtml, accessed 25 May 2010.

Nielsen (2009). *How Teens Use Media*, available at http://blog.nielsen.com, accessed 9 January 2009.

Pirkis, J. E., Burgess, P. M., Francis, C., Blood, R. W., & Jolley, D. J. (2006). The relationship between media reporting of suicide and actual suicide in Australia. *Social Science Medicine*, *62*, 2874–2886.

Research!America (2006). *Mental Health Not Given Equal Importance, Americans Say*, available at http://www.researchamerica.org/release_06sept28_mentalhealthpoll; http://www.researchamerica.org/uploads/pollreport2004teensuicide.pdf; http://www.researchamerica.org/uploads/poll2006mentalhealth.pdf, accessed 9 January 2009.

S. Res. 84; 105th Congress, Cong. Rec 143 (1997) (enacted).

SAMHSA National Registry of Effective Programs, available at http://www.nrepp.samhsa.gov, accessed 05/25/10.

Screening for Mental Health, Inc., available at http://www.mentalhealthscreening.org, accessed 25 May 2010.

Seal, K. H., Metzler, T. J., Gima, S. K., Bertenthal, D., Maguen, S., & Marmar, C. R. (2009). Trends and risk factor for mental health diagnoses among Iraq and Afghanistan veterans using Department of Veteran Affairs Health Care, 2002–2008. *American Journal of Public Health*, *99*, 1651–1658.

Silenzio, V. M. B., Duberstein, P., Tang, W., Tu, X., & Homan, C. (2009). Connecting the invisible dots: Network-based methods to reach a hidden population at risk for suicide. *Social Science and Medicine*, *69*, 496–474.

Smith, W. (2002). From prevention vaccines to community care: New ways to look at program success. In R. C. Hornik (Ed.), *Public Health Communications: Evidence for behavior change* (pp. 327–356). Mahwah, NJ: Lawrence Erlbaum.

Suicide Prevention Resource Center, State information, available at http://www.sprc.org/stateinformation/plans.asp, accessed 9 January 2009.

Suicide Prevention Resource Center (2008). *Suicide Risk and Prevention for Lesbian, Gay, Bisexual, and Transgender Youth*. Newton, MA: Education Development Center, Inc., available at http://www.sprc.org/library/SPRC_LGBT_Youth.pdf, accessed 1 April 2010.

United Nations/World Health Organization (1996). *Prevention of Suicide: Guidelines for the formulation and implementation of national strategies* (ST/ESA/245). Geneva: World Health Organization.

US Department of Health and Human Services (2001). *National Strategy for Suicide Prevention. Goals and objectives for action*. Rockville, MD: US Department of Health and Human Services, Public Health Service.

US Public Health Service (1999). *The Surgeon General's Call to Action to Prevent Suicide*. Washington, DC: Public Health Service.

World Health Organization (2008). *Preventing Suicide: A resource for media professionals*. Geneva: WHO Press, available at www.who.int/entity/mental_health/prevention/suicide/resource_media.pdf, accessed 25 May 2010.

Wyman, P. A., Brown, C. H., Inman, J., Cross, W., Schmeelk-Cone, K., Guo, J., & Pena, J. B. (2008). Randomized trial of a gatekeeper program for suicide prevention: 1-year impact on secondary school staff. *Journal of Consulting and Clinical Psychology*, *76*, 104–115.

CHAPTER THIRTY-FOUR

What Kind of Research Do We Need in Suicidology Today?

Heidi Hjelmeland and Birthe Loa Knizek

Abstract

This chapter takes a critical look at current mainstream suicidological research. Drawing from the philosophy of science, it considers the extent to which research has been focused on *explaining* suicidality rather than *understanding* it, and argues that we need to do more research on the latter to advance the cause of suicide prevention. Currently, suicide research is broadly classified as (neuro)biological, epidemiological, or intervention-based. Each of these approaches mainly focuses on *explanations* of suicidality by employing quantitative methodology, with much of this research being repetitive and/or reductionist. We argue that an increased focus on *understanding* suicidal behaviour in different cultural contexts and extending the use of qualitative methodology are essential to the advancement of the discipline of suicidology. Irrespective of whether or not they are suicidal, human beings neither behave according to the rules of causal determinism nor are they disconnected from their context. Thus, our research needs to develop so that we take more account of the complexity of suicidality as a phenomenon and of human beings as individuals. This requires a stronger focus on cultural perspectives: studying suicidal behaviour in or from different cultural contexts will teach us more about how to understand this behaviour. Although much research would benefit from using a combination of qualitative and quantitative methodology, it seldom does. Consequently, there is a vast abundance of quantitative studies which needs to be re-balanced with a stronger focus on qualitative research. The huge amounts of data available from quantitative studies provide a solid foundation

International Handbook of Suicide Prevention: Research, Policy and Practice, First Edition.
Edited by Rory C. O'Connor, Stephen Platt, Jacki Gordon.
© 2011 John Wiley & Sons, Ltd. Published 2011 by John Wiley & Sons, Ltd.

for qualitative studies to investigate factors related to suicidal behaviour in more depth. On the one hand, qualitative research may complement quantitative research by answering 'how' and 'why' questions. On the other hand, findings from qualitative studies may inform the development of new quantitative studies.

Introduction

Based on a brief but critical discussion of the current mainstream suicidological research, this chapter outlines what kinds of research we need in order to move the field of suicidology forward. We begin by drawing the distinction between *explanation* and *understanding* as described by philosophers of science (e.g., von Wright, 2004 [1971]). Studies focusing on *explanations* most often use hypothetico-deductive or experimental methodologies, usually employing quantitative approaches. The main framework of such studies is the biomedical illness model (e.g., von Uexküll & Wesiack, 1988) and, although the concept of cause is not always explicitly stated, such studies mainly use the linear cause-and-effect framework in their search for underlying causes of suicidal behaviour based on the principles of the natural sciences (Hjelmeland & Knizek, 2010). This focus is probably underpinned by 'the assumption that "real science" is about cause and effect relations' (Harré & Moghaddam, 2003, p. 2). The consequence of this is, however, reductionism: 'the tendency to reduce explanations to the smallest units possible' (Harré & Moghaddam, 2003, p. 2), and in so doing we lose the whole person in their individual context.

Studies concerned with *understanding* focus on the meaning(s) suicidal behaviour has for the individual (e.g., Fleischer, 2000), normally using qualitative approaches. Such studies centre on how individuals interpret themselves, their actions, and their surroundings; consequently, hermeneutics, the theory of interpretation, is essential (Ricoeur, 1974).

Although the concepts of explanation and understanding are interrelated, they must be understood on their own terms. Below we suggest that most of today's mainstream suicidological research unilaterally focuses on explanations, very often in terms of linear cause-and-effect-type thinking, and is dominated by repetitive (risk factor) and reductionist (biological) studies. We argue that to move the field forward, we need to broaden the methodological scope and increase studies focusing on understanding suicidal behaviour in different cultural contexts.

A Critical Look at Mainstream Suicidological Research

In Hjelmeland and Knizek (2010) we discuss current mainstream suicidological research and part of that discussion is reviewed and elaborated on herein.

Current mainstream suicidological research can be crudely categorized into three main groups: (1) (neuro)biological research, including genetic studies, brain-imaging studies, and studies of the hormones and neurotransmitters involved in suicidal behaviour or related mental disorders; (2) epidemiological research, focusing on rates, trends, and risk factors in different groups in different parts of the world; and (3) intervention studies, for instance, randomized controlled trials (RCTs), usually considered to be the gold standard in intervention research. Although they are not yet particularly numerous in the suicidological field, RCTs are often highlighted as the kind of research we should now encourage.

The thinking behind each of the three approaches outlined above reflects a view that suicide can be largely described in terms of linear cause-and-effect relationships, and such studies all attempt to *explain* suicidal behaviour in terms of different risk (and protective) factors. Such studies, thus, make important contributions to our knowledge base. However, inevitably, they *all* have limitations insofar as they are unable to provide a comprehensive *understanding* of the phenomenon. As a result, they should never be the end-point of research.

Limitations of (neuro)biological studies

Biological research provides knowledge on, for instance, hormones and neurotransmitters involved in, or genetic predispositions to, suicidal behaviour or related mental disorders. Moreover, different neuro-imaging techniques can provide information from live subjects on both structures and functions of the central nervous system associated with suicidal behaviour. This type of research operates explicitly from the biomedical illness approach and has a strong reductionist focus on human beings isolated from their individual and social context. However, whether, for instance, a genetic predisposition will manifest itself as actual behaviour is dependent on whether other factors are activated or not: research in neuroplasticity has demonstrated that there seem to be few limits to what the brain can do and develop into with different environmental stimulations (e.g., Doidge, 2007), and that biological patterns in the brain can be both created and changed by experience (e.g., Mogensen, 2007).

One major challenge for (neuro)biological research is to demonstrate how the results can be utilized in suicide prevention. Mann (2005), for instance, has argued that brain imaging can be a useful tool to estimate suicide risk. However, this research raises a number of ethical questions in terms of how/when/if such results can/should be utilized: knowing that one has a genetic predisposition or a biological structure connected to suicidality is bound to influence a person's behaviour, as well as that of the people in their surroundings.

People are complicated, reflective beings and it is highly unlikely that we behave in a linear fashion whether we are suicidal or not. Because of 'its symbolic basis, the flow of human conscious experience ... is not reducible to any finite set of bio-physical causes' (Pickering & Skinner, 1990, p. 2). Still, researchers tend to deal with complexity by reducing or neutralizing aspects of it (Gilgen, 1995). In our view, it would be more valuable to focus on people's experiences rather than on biological structures (which may have developed *because of* some particular experiences). Moreover, in order to capture the complexity of suicidality, psychiatry and neurobiology must move away from the linear cause-and-effect thinking and instead adopt perspectives from modern physics; drawing on, for instance, catastrophe theory (Castrigiano & Hayes, 1993) or chaos theory (Masterpasqua & Perna, 1997; Toomela, 2007). Chaotic systems analysis and epistemology are important in both the biological and behavioural sciences (e.g., Krippner & Winkler, 1995) and therefore in suicidology too:

> The mind–brain system that supports human consciousness is … a uniquely complex mix of physical, biological and socio-cultural systems, integrated within an historical process. The flow of experience generated by the interplay of causes and effects within this process will be correspondingly complex. Describing this flow will require more than just a combination of terms from the natural sciences. (Pickering & Skinner, 1990, p. 2)

In other words, we need more than reductionist biological approaches.

The (neuro)biological research on psychiatric disorders associated with suicide has not been able to demonstrate *how* mental disorders are related to suicidal behaviour (with the possible exception of hearing voices that incite suicide during a psychotic episode). The vast majority of people suffering from mental disorders do not kill themselves (e.g., Blair-West, Mellsop, & Eyeson-Annan, 1997). Moreover, the relationship between mental disorders and suicidal behaviour varies across cultures (e.g., Vijayakumar, 2005). Thus, it is obvious that suicidality is about something else/more than mental disorders *per se* (Gustafsson & Jacobsson, 2000). Besides, 'Being told that one "has schizophrenia" or "suffers from depression" interpreted as biological illness seldom has any meaning when the people concerned know fully well that they have problems that need exploring, relationships that are at fault, and situations that upset them' (Fernando, 2003, pp. 177–178). We therefore need to look beyond mental disorders if we want to *understand* what suicidal behaviour is all about.

Limitations of epidemiological (risk factor) studies

Epidemiological research provides information on rates, trends, and risk factors in different groups and time periods in different parts of the world. Numerous epidemiological studies have been published over the last decades. However, we still know very little about *how* the common risk factors are related to suicidal behaviour, and *why* it is that the vast majority suffering from them *do not* kill themselves. Risk factor studies mainly use questionnaires or structured interviews with predetermined and standardized questions. However, it is rarely taken into account that many of the questions asked can be answered differently by the same person at the same time if the informants relate the questions to different contexts. In fact, we rarely know whether informants respond in an 'abstract' way or if they tie their answers to specific situations (Toomela, 2007). Importantly, responses are *interpretations* of the questions based on the context in which they appear (Baldurson & Pedersen, 1992). *Context* here refers to both the setting and/or particular circumstances in which individual respondents find themselves, and the structure, wording, and positioning of items within a questionnaire or interview guide. Further limitations of this approach are outlined under the heading 'Limitations of quantitative studies in general', below.

Limitations of RCT studies

In medical circles, RCT studies are usually considered the only valid (gold standard) approach to provide an evidence base for intervention, whereas other studies (e.g., observational studies) are often dismissed as inadequate to contribute to the evidence base (Chelmow, 2005). Such a view was, however, elegantly refuted by Smith and Pell (2003) when they humorously pointed out that if RCT studies are required to obtain a valid evidence base, we still have no evidence for the usefulness of parachutes when jumping out of airplanes since that has not yet been tested in an RCT study!

Even if the RCT design is the 'gold standard', it is nevertheless an imperfect research method which leaves a great deal of the variance unexplained. In order to make the groups as comparable as possible, RCT studies normally have to be stripped down to include only a few basic variables, and consequently the context of the patients is lost (Ekeland, 1999). By losing the context, one risks losing factors that may decrease/increase the risk of suicide. Also, RCTs find out what is effective in an average individual independent of their context; such patients do not exist in real life. Moreover, 'The nature of a relationship or a difference between groups cannot be understood unless all exceptions are understood' (Toomela, 2007, p. 13). Rather, exceptions to the 'rule' must be understood, analysed, and accounted for before we can get a complete understanding of the phenomenon under study (Toomela, 2007). If an RCT study yields a statistically significant difference between two different treatments, this result does not help us to understand *why* this intervention seems to be working very well in some of the individuals in the experimental group, fairly well in others, not at all in yet others, and maybe is harmful to others still, as can be the case in some drug trials (Noller & Bibace, 2005).

Limitations of quantitative research approaches in general

It is often assumed that if we use standardized questions, we get more objective results. However, with all its different definitions, 'objectivity' is in itself a rather subjective concept (Kvale, 1994). Moreover, different psychological mechanisms can underlie the same 'objective' score and '"Objective scores" … may actually cover rich individual differences that can never be discovered unless studies explicitly go beyond numbers and start to ask questions about whether there are different ways to reach the same "objective" score or not' (Toomela, 2007, p. 11). The same mean value can also result from very different distributions of data; therefore, it is necessary to look at individual scores in order to interpret the dataset. Facts isolated from the whole context or facts that describe the average group differences but not the exceptions are not sufficient to understand people's minds (Toomela, 2007).

The linear cause-and-effect thinking focusing only on a few variables is too simplistic; it does not take the whole individual and their particular context into consideration simultaneously, which is necessary if we want to understand why a particular person at a particular time in his or her life is contemplating, or has actually carried out, a suicidal act. A linear understanding of causality can contribute to a blurring of the relationships that are essential for the individual by fixating on an organic cause of the suffering, thereby failing to take account of the context that is making the person suffer (Fernando, 2003; Toomela, 2007).

The Kind of Research We Need Today

Based on the critical evaluation of current mainstream research above, our suggestions as to what kind of research we need in the field today are: (1) studies which take cultural/contextual perspectives into consideration; and (2) studies using different types of qualitative methodology. In other words, we need to change our focus from *explanation* to *understanding*.

Why cultural studies?

The short answer to this question is that by looking at a phenomenon in or from different cultural contexts, we can get a better understanding of the phenomenon itself. However, two important points require emphasis from the outset: culture should not be viewed as an explanatory variable and traditional cross-cultural studies may not be what we need now since they are plagued by many of the problems outlined above. We explain this further below, but first we elaborate on why we now need more studies taking cultural perspectives into consideration.

Geertz (1973) has pointed out that there 'is no such thing as a human nature independent of culture. We are ... incomplete or unfinished animals who complete or finish ourselves through culture – and not through culture in general but through highly particular forms of it' (p. 49). According to Canetto (2008), we cannot theorize 'about clinical phenomena as if they were culture-free, ahistorical boxes into which people can be placed' (p. 264). In other words, if we want to *understand* suicidal behaviour, it is absolutely essential to take the cultural context into consideration.

The well-recognized risk factors vary in size, shape, and kind from one cultural context to the next (e.g., Vijayakumar, John, Pirkis, & Whiteford, 2005). Even between different groups and individuals within the same cultural context, they depend on a complex interplay between internal and external factors. In other words, it may not be the individual risk factors (e.g., unemployment, mental disorders, sexual abuse) *per se* that are related to suicidal behaviour, but simply factors that make life difficult or unbearable for the individual. Take depression, for example, often quoted as the most important risk factor for suicide. The vast majority, around 95% or more, of people with a diagnosis of depression do *not* kill themselves (e.g., Blair-West, Mellsop, & Eyeson-Annan, 1997). Thus, the predictive power of depression is limited. Including the cultural perspective complicates matters further. First, many authors have pointed out that of all psychiatric diagnoses depression is the one that raises most questions concerning cross-cultural validity (Fernando, 2003; Jadhav & Littlewood, 1994; Kleinman & Good, 1985). Second, even if we were to accept cross-cultural validity, the association between depression and suicide has *not* been found to be strong in non-Western parts of the world (e.g., Chan, Hung, & Yip,

2001; Phillips, Yang, Zhang, Wang, Li, *et al.*, 2002; Yang, Phillips, Zhou, Wang, Zhang, *et al.*, 2005; Zhang, Conwell, Zhou, & Jiang, 2004). Thus, regardless of whether we accept that cross-cultural validity is lacking for a depression diagnosis, or the finding of a weak relationship between depression and suicide outside the West, it is problematic to focus on depression as a cross-cultural risk factor for suicidal behaviour.

The validity problem is, however, not limited to the diagnosis of depression. The trans-cultural meaning of *all* the traditional psychiatric diagnoses is very uncertain, since they are based on a unicultural, ethnocentric, Western psychiatry (Fernando, 2003). Moreover, it has been extensively documented that the cultural aspects have not been taken into consideration, to any large extent, in the development of DSM-IV. Indeed, study findings which questioned the universality of mental disorders were not incorporated in the final version of this manual (Hughes, 1998; Jenkins, 1998; Kirmayer, 1998; Lewis-Fernandez, 1998; Mezzich, Kirmayer, Kleinman, Fabrega, Parron, *et al.*, 1999). Still, the DSM-IV is widely used around the world, and, when identification and treatment of mental disorders simultaneously are highlighted as the most important suicide preventive efforts (e.g., Bertolote, Fleischman, De Leo, & Wasserman, 2003; Cavanagh, Carson, Sharpe, & Lawrie, 2003), this is problematic.

It might be more fruitful to focus on an array of symptoms rather than collating them to form specific diagnoses, since an understanding of symptoms helps us to select and tailor our therapeutic intervention better than diagnoses (Charlton, 2000). Moreover, to find out what the different symptoms *mean* to people, we need qualitative approaches. This is not only important in studies across cultures but also makes sense across individuals within the same cultural context, since individual differences may outweigh the differences between cultural groups in both extent and importance (Fernando, 2002). In this way, findings from studies in different cultural contexts may teach us something valuable about the relationship between the various symptoms related to depression and suicidal behaviour, not only in different cultures but also within our own.

What exactly are regarded as symptoms must be explored as individual experiences in the particular socio-cultural context in which they occur, because it is in that particular context that they have meaning and significance for the individual (Fernando, 2003). For instance, suicidality is related to hopelessness/helplessness (e.g., Shneidman, 1985). However, symptoms/factors leading to hopelessness/helplessness might differ across cultural contexts. For instance, in developing societies with little or no official social security systems and where elderly people therefore depend on their children in order to survive when they are no longer able to earn a living themselves, impotence/barrenness may have more devastating consequences than may be the case in societies with ample social security systems. We should therefore focus more on the meaning(s) of the individual symptoms and behaviours, and then we are back to where we started this chapter, namely, to the difference between explanation and understanding. Taking the cultural context into consideration, it makes more sense to focus on understanding rather than on explanation. The focus should include the meaning(s) people assign to suicidal behaviour in different cultures, both Western and non-Western. This is particularly important as most countries are multicultural.

When we look at suicidal behaviour from a cultural perspective as outlined above, it becomes clear that the biomedical illness model fails to provide the necessary theoretical framework for studying this phenomenon. The vast majority of people suffering from or struggling with the common risk factors, whether biological, psychiatric, psychological or social, do not kill themselves and we need to know *why* some of them engage in suicidal behaviour while others do not. One alternative is to study suicidal behaviour within the framework of communication theory, where suicidal acts are viewed as acts of communication (Knizek & Hjelmeland, 2007). This connects the individual with their context. For this reason, it is well suited to study suicide and suicidality in different cultural contexts, since communication, while universal, may have different aspects/meanings in different settings (Hjelmeland, Knizek, Kinyanda, Musisi, Nordvik, *et al.*, 2008). There are also other relevant frameworks, for instance, entrapment theory (Williams, 1997) or action theory (Michel & Valach, 2001). However, when working qualitatively, it is not *always* necessary to have a theoretical framework to start with, but rather build new theories through systematic and transparent analysis of the data, like, for instance, in Grounded Theory (Glaser & Strauss, 1967).

Regardless of the framework used, it is important to emphasize that culture should not be treated as a causal or explanatory variable. According to Valsiner (1988), culture remains largely undefined in many of the cross-cultural studies, and is often just taken to be equivalent to nations or regions. Often, culture is viewed as a static entity that in itself is rendered explanatory power (Berliner, 2001). However, culture is not a static entity; it is constantly developing, perhaps faster now than ever because of mass media communication, mass tourism, as well as voluntary and forced migration (the global village). Furthermore, culture is a *process* of interaction between the person and their surroundings; the dynamics that arise in the interaction between the person and their environment cannot be explained in a linear cause-and-effect relationship (Berliner, 2001; Valsiner, 2003).

Most studies with a cultural focus in suicidology have employed a quantitative cross-cultural approach. However, there are numerous methodological problems inherent in such studies. For instance, we do not always know what we are comparing. Using the same instruments in different cultures raises problems with reliability and validity. Furthermore, because culture is often treated as an explanatory variable in such studies, this makes it easy to overlook the real reasons for the differences found. According to Berliner (2001), culture as a substantial, or essentialist or causal concept will erase real social and/or political life conditions, and if instead of culture we talk about oppression, marginalization, racism, unemployment, and stigmatization we contextualize people's life situation. In fact, culture is not a measurable variable at all (Jenkins, 1994). But if culture is impossible to measure, how can we then study cultural perspectives?

One alternative might be to get rid of the 'cross' in 'cross-cultural' and conduct 'cultural' studies, where a phenomenon is studied in depth within one particular cultural context, be that Western or non-Western. This was eloquently expressed by the Zambian psychologist Robert Serpell (2005, personal communication): 'I used to be a cross-cultural psychologist, but now I'm not so cross anymore'. In view of the high number of studies from the Western parts of the world (see below), we now need more studies from the rest of the world, as well as studies from different ethnic minority/immigrant groups in Western countries. There are, however, a number of obstacles to such an endeavour. For instance, there are difficulties in getting funding for such studies, as well as a lack of resources and/ or competence in developing countries (Patel & Sumathipala, 2001). Even if such studies are conducted, some editors in Western-based scientific journals are reluctant to publish studies with a cultural perspective from non-Western parts of the world, particularly from developing countries. They are sometimes considered to be of little relevance to their readership, and at times submitted papers are of low quality due to difficulties that authors may have in writing in English (Patel & Sumathipala, 2001). Such attitudes not only impede the development of an evidence base to inform suicide prevention efforts in non-Western contexts, but they also hinder the advancement of suicidology itself. This is also an ethical issue insofar as editors through these biases may actually be contributing to the prevailing inequities in global research (Sumathipala, Siribaddana, & Patel, 2004). If research from developing countries cannot get published, this, in turn, affects the possibility of getting funding for such research. Editors have a moral duty to pay attention to the barriers researchers in developing countries are facing, and a moral obligation to publish studies from developing countries (Patel & Sumathipala, 2001). However, it is important to emphasize that this does not mean that the quality requirements for papers from developing countries should be lower than for Western papers. That 'would be at best patronizing and at worst discriminatory' (Patel & Sumathipala, 2001, p. 409). However, if, for instance, the main problems are with style and/or language, journals could perhaps consider collaborative editorial styles (Patel & Sumathipala, 2001; Vetter, 2003), rather than simply rejecting the papers. In view of the fact that most Western societies today are multicultural, it would seem that the failure to advance the evidence base through publication of such papers constitutes something of a missed opportunity. Cultural and cross-cultural approaches are, however, complementary. Both are important, but if we want to study the *meaning(s)* of suicidal behaviour, either within one or across different cultural contexts, we need studies using different types of qualitative methodologies.

Why qualitative methodology?

Qualitative studies develop 'understandings of the phenomena under study, based as much as possible on the perspective of those being studied' (Elliott, Fischer, & Rennie, 1999, p. 216). Suicidal behaviour is a conscious *act* which is the end result of a *process*, and this process is unique for each individual (Shneidman, 1985). A qualitative approach will allow us to look at relationships between important factors that we would not be able to investigate in quantitative studies using predetermined and standardized questions and thus contribute to insight in such processes (Flick, 2007; Malterud, 2002). Numbers alone cannot provide all the evidence needed for intervention, and qualitative studies can make a major contribution to bridging the gaps between theory and practice (Malterud, 2001). Besides, not everything can be operationalized and measured numerically, such as, for instance, culture as mentioned above (Jenkins, 1994). Thus, qualitative analysis can help to illuminate and thereby deepen the understanding of the ways in which culture, through processes such as norms, traditions and oppression may contribute to suicidality.

Within the paradigms of social sciences and humanities there is no such thing as *the* truth (Lyotard, 1979; Rorty, 1991), especially not when mental phenomena are involved (Foucault, 1971). Instead, these disciplines acknowledge that human beings are not mechanical machines that respond to stimuli in a linear fashion, but that we are able to reflect about the world and our own actions. Here, hermeneutics, the theory of interpretation, comes to the fore (Ricoeur, 1974). Hermeneutics can contribute to suicidology by a systematic and in-depth investigation of the individual's implicit intentions and feelings. However, here criticism often arises from the 'quantitative camp', since a systematic hermeneutic analysis might result in several different interpretations of an informant's story, which is not in keeping with the natural science paradigm where it is believed that there is one single truth to be found (Anderson, 1995). However, according to Hafting (2005) an individual's experience cannot be true or false, since it is genuine for the individual and cannot be tested or questioned by others. She also refers to Kvale, who says (our translation): 'A patient always tells the truth, and it is the doctor's or psychologist's task to find out what he is telling the truth about' (in Hafting, 2005, p. 3440). Thus, in the hermeneutics tradition, the role of the researcher is to substantiate his or her interpretations (Ricoeur, 1974), that is, to demonstrate that the particular interpretation he or she reaches is plausible, based on the available data.

It is important to acknowledge here that quantitative research is not free from interpretations either; standardized questions in quantitative research require *reading*, and thus responses to them are founded on individual *interpretations* based on each individual's as well as each question's context (Baldurson & Pedersen, 1992). As Kvale (1994) points out, 'even tables and correlation coefficients require a qualitative interpretation of their meaning' (p. 163). So, interpretation is present and highly relevant in both quantitative and qualitative research, although the level of consciousness about this may seem to be higher in qualitative research. Leder (1990) has even claimed that medical research is flawed because it often fails to acknowledge that research results are outcomes of interpretations. Illustratively it has, for instance, been demonstrated that something as 'objective' as an x-ray can be interpreted very differently by different doctors (Måseide, 2002). In good qualitative research the importance of interpretation is acknowledged and made explicit through a systematic and transparent analysis that makes it possible for readers to follow the process. Thus, instead of being a neglected factor, interpretation is a central methodological point that is addressed rigorously.

Criticisms of qualitative methods   Below, we will demonstrate that qualitative studies are 'few and far between' in the international suicidological journals, reflecting the fact that qualitative methodology does not have a central place in suicidological research at present. In 1994, Kvale listed 10 common standard objections to qualitative research, and although, at that time, he claimed that these objections were outdated, they are still often voiced by reviewers and editors in our field today. These 10 standard objections are that qualitative research:

(1)   is not scientific, but only reflects common sense;
(2)   is not objective, but subjective;
(3)   produces biased and unreliable results;
(4)   produces unreliable results because of leading questions;
(5)   produces results that are not inter-subjective, since different interpreters find different meanings;
(6)   is too person-dependent;

(7) is only exploratory and does not involve hypothesis testing;
(8) is not quantitative;
(9) produces results that are not generalizable; and
(10) is not valid, but rests on subjective impressions.

Kvale (1994) elegantly rebutted these objections, arguing that none of these common objections was valid if the qualitative research is conducted properly. Unfortunately, we do not have space here to elaborate on all of these, but we briefly mention one that is often encountered, namely, that it is not possible to draw generalizations from qualitative studies.

Of course, we cannot generalize statistically, but there are other types of generalization. One example is theoretical generalization, where we link the findings of our study with our own personal and professional experience as well as with what we find in the existing literature (Smith & Osborn, 2003). Another example is analytical generalization, where we look at to what degree a finding can be directive or instructive for what is going to happen in another situation (Kvale, 1997). This is similar to what is done in the legal system or in clinical work. By a systematic qualitative analysis the individual's intentions, feelings, perceived influences, etc. are illuminated and by that it is possible to describe the subjective meaning of the suicidal process. Such analyses can also provide detailed descriptions of the relationship and dynamics between the individual and their social context. Findings like these are important for the suicidology field, but can be transferred to other settings only if others recognize their relevance, in particular, how appropriate these are to a given situation or context. In analytical generalization, it is the *users* of the knowledge who are responsible for deciding whether (if at all) the results are applicable to their situation. The researcher's responsibility is thus to provide enough documentation to enable the users to generalize analytically, based on an appreciation of the similarities and differences between the research situation and the real-life situation in which he or she is interested. The validity of such generalization depends on how relevant the compared characteristics are, which again depends on detailed, compact, and rich descriptions of the case (Kvale, 1997). For a discussion of the rest of the standard objections to qualitative research, we refer the reader to Kvale (1994), which we suggest should be compulsory reading for all journal editors who have yet to embrace qualitative research.

Combining qualitative and quantitative methodology

Quantitative and qualitative methods are complementary; in quantitative studies we get relatively superficial information from many subjects, whereas in qualitative studies we get in-depth information from a few subjects. And the basic principles for quantitative and qualitative methodology are actually quite similar; in both we are dealing with a systematic and reflective development of new knowledge and the process is (or at least it should be), open for inspection and challenge (Malterud, 2002). Indeed, many of the objections to qualitative methodology actually apply to research in general (Kvale, 1994). If only quantitative methodology is accepted, as seems to be the case in some journals, this limits the range of research questions that can be asked. If you have only a hammer available, there is a limit to what type of carpentry you can do and if you want to build a house, you need the whole tool box, not just the hammer. In other words, methodological pluralism is what the field needs today.

In studies where both quantitative and qualitative methodological approaches are used/ integrated, we will get more knowledge: 'A scientist who wishes to maximize the empirical content of the views he holds and who wants to understand them as clearly as he possibly can must therefore introduce other views; that is, he must adopt a pluralistic methodology' (Feyerabend, 1995, p. 200) since 'all methodologies, even the most obvious ones, have their limits' (p. 203). Quantitative and qualitative methodologies can be used simultaneously to answer different scientific questions. Or qualitative studies can be used to generate hypotheses that are then tested in quantitative studies that are, again, followed up with qualitative studies in order to understand the findings from the quantitative studies further. Research is an iterative process.

There are three possible outcomes of studies which integrate quantitative and qualitative approaches: (1) the results are complementary and thus they provide a fuller picture of how things are related to each other and how they contribute to suicidal ideation and/ or behaviour; (2) the results are convergent and thus help to validate each other; or (3) the results are contradictory and thereby indicate areas in which more research is needed (Flick, 2007). With the current overwhelming dominance of quantitative studies in the field (see below), we maintain that there is considerable need to increase the proportion of good quality, qualitative research.

State of Affairs in Suicidological Journals

In the following section, we present the state of affairs with regard to the publication of cultural and qualitative studies in the three main international suicidological journals, namely, *Crisis*, *Suicide and Life-Threatening Behavior* (*SLTB*), and *Archives of Suicide Research* (*ASR*). In the four-year period 2005–2008, only 3% of the studies published in these journals employed a qualitative approach (this breaks down into 7% of studies published in *Crisis* and 2% in both *SLTB* and *ASR*). What is more, the qualitative element was often, but not always, a small appendix to a mainly quantitative study. The low proportion of qualitative studies published in these journals (which concurs with similar findings in psychological journals in general, Marchel & Owens, 2007) may say something about the position held by qualitative research in suicidology at present. Indeed, the editor of *SLTB* recently stated in a rejection letter (T. Joiner, July 2009) that even excellent qualitative studies cannot compete with experimental and longitudinal studies.

The paucity of qualitative studies within the discipline has been highlighted before. In 2002, *ASR* published a special issue on 'Qualitative versus quantitative studies in suicidology' and therein Goldney (2000) and Leenaars (2002a, 2002b) argued that both approaches were needed in the field. However, there has since been a change of editor of that journal and in her inaugural editorial, the new editor listed criteria for 'successful manuscripts' that in many ways seem to exclude qualitative studies; for instance, inclusion of testable hypotheses and statistical analyses (Stanley, 2007). Moreover, Stanley particularly encouraged submissions of neurobiological, epidemiological and clinical trial, and intervention studies which she described as 'under-represented'.

Of course, journal editors may not carry the *full* responsibility for the low publication rates of qualitative studies. Other possible explanations are low submission rates and/or low quality of the submitted manuscripts. However, editors may contribute to a low submission rate in at least two ways: (1) by their arguments for rejecting qualitative studies (see the example of Joiner above) they may discourage qualitative researchers from submitting their manuscripts to a particular journal; and (2) systemically: if it is made difficult to get qualitative studies published, this may in turn discourage researchers from conducting qualitative studies at all, since access to funding requires publication. Moreover, the first author's extensive experience as a reviewer, and thereby access to the reviews of fellow reviewers, has shown that not only is the quality of some of the submissions low, so is the quality of some of the reviews. Arguments such as low number of cases, inability to generalize results statistically, etc., are sometimes used for recommending rejection of qualitative studies. Thus, editorial boards need more reviewers with competence in qualitative methodology. Worth noting is that already in 1999, the National Institute of Mental Health Consortium of Editors on Development and Psychopathology (1999) published an Editorial Statement where they acknowledged their responsibility to also publish qualitative studies. Editors in 29 journals signed this commitment, including editors of highly prestigious psychiatric and psychological journals, such as *American Journal of Psychiatry*, *Archives of General Psychiatry*, and *Journal of Consulting and Clinical Psychology*. Perhaps it is time for editors of suicidological journals to adopt such an explicit responsibility too.

Nineteen per cent of all the publications (quantitative and qualitative) came from non-Western parts of the world (34% in *Crisis*, 16% in *ASR*, and 15% in *SLTB*). However, it is not as if culture is some 'thing' that is only found outside the West (although that seems to be a common perception in the West), and only 8% of the studies published mentioned culture in some form in the title and/or in the abstract and thus reflected a specific cultural focus (15% in *Crisis*, 12% in *ASR*, and only 4% in *SLTB*). The current editors of both *Crisis* (De Leo, 2008) and *ASR* (Stanley, 2007) emphasized the importance of (cross-) cultural studies in their inaugural editorials.

We also looked at how many of the articles published from the West actually had the name of the country or region where the study was conducted in the title, compared with articles from other parts of the world. This might, at least to some extent, show whether the authors are conscious of the fact that *all* studies are conducted within a specific cultural context and thus that there are potential limitations to generalizing the results to other contexts. Seventy-four per cent of the non-Western studies mentioned the region/country of the study in the title, compared with 22% of the studies from the West (75% versus 55% in *Crisis*, 76% versus 20% in *SLTB*, 74% versus 12% in *ASR*).

All in all, *Crisis* had the highest proportion of publications with a cultural focus and/or qualitative methodology, although 7% (*n* = 6) qualitative studies is not particularly impressive.

Conclusions

Suicidological research needs to move away from the present almost completely unilateral focus on *explanations* and towards a stronger focus on *understanding* suicidal behaviour in different cultural contexts. Whether suicidal or not, human beings do not behave in a linear fashion, nor are they disconnected from their context. Consequently, we need to take into account both the complexity of the phenomenon as well as that of human beings when planning our research studies. This is as relevant in intervention research as it is in other types of suicidological research. In short, we need quantitative *and* qualitative studies from *all* parts of the world. Quantitative suicidological research also needs to move away from the simplistic linear cause-and-effect thinking. Moreover, we should make better use of the extensive collection of quantitative studies to develop qualitative studies to facilitate a deeper understanding of the plethora of well-recognized suicide risk factors. In addition, when conducting suicidological research in parts of the world where little or no research has been conducted, we recommend starting with qualitative methodology rather than importing quantitative instruments developed elsewhere.

Our advocacy for qualitative research is supported by Fulford, Sallah, and Woodbridge (2007), who argue that qualitative methodology is important within the mental health services since: 'phenomenology and related disciplines, as rigorous approaches to analysing experience supported by detailed theoretical frameworks, provide tools for more effective and inclusive ways of understanding differences not only between individuals but also between cultures in the way they experience the world' (p. 39). There seem, however, to be some (mainly political?) obstacles to overcome in order to change the research focus in the field. Suicidological researchers in recent years have had some manuscripts rejected *because* they used qualitative methods or *because* they contained a cultural perspective (with such reasons explicitly stated in the letters from editors). Michell (2003a) has argued that a problem in psychological research is that choice of research methodology is based more on personal, political or economic interests than on scientific arguments. Moreover, regarding research on mental health in general, Fernando (2003) pointed out that 'Changing the culture of research so that it is bottom-up (i.e., starts with user views and needs identified by people who suffer mental health problems) is likely to threaten vested interests of the psychiatric establishment and so requires a political will to enforce' (p. 205). This might be relevant to the suicidological research in particular, and here the editors of our journals have an important responsibility if they want to further develop our research field. Michell (2003b) has claimed that 'the quantitative imperative is an egregious, potentially self-perpetuating form of methodological error' (p. 5), resulting in closed-system thinking where psychological attributes that are not measurable/quantifiable are excluded from being researched. It is important to note that 'No methodology can in itself warrant scientific quality – the crucial condition is how the process of knowledge aggregation and organization is handled and presented' (Malterud, 2001, p. 399). Thus, we now need pluralistic methodologies to develop new suicidological knowledge, and in this way, progress from simply explaining suicidal behaviour to understanding it.

References

Anderson, W. T. (1995). *The Truth about the Truth. De-confusing and re-constructing the postmodern world*. New York: G. P. Putnam.

Baldurson, E. B. & Pedersen, B. T. (1992). Interpretation and meaning. *Nordisk Psykologi, 44*, 147–164.

Berliner, P. (2001). Transcultural psychology. From cross-cultural psychology to community psychology. *Psyke & Logos, 22*, 91–112.

Bertolote, J. M., Fleischman, A., De Leo, D., & Wasserman, D. (2003). Suicide and mental disorders: Do we know enough? *British Journal of Psychiatry, 183*, 382–383.

Blair-West, G. W., Mellsop, G. W., & Eyeson-Annan, M. L. (1997). Down-rating lifetime suicide risk in major depression. *Acta Psychiatrica Scandinavica, 95*, 259–263.

Canetto, S. S. (2008). Women and suicidal behaviour: A cultural analysis. *American Journal of Orthopsychiatry, 78*, 259–266.

Castrigiano, D. P. L. & Hayes, S. A. (1993). *Catastrophe Theory*. Reading, MA: Addison-Wesley.

Cavanagh, J. T. O., Carson, A. J., Sharpe, M., & Lawrie, S. M. (2003). Psychological autopsy studies of suicide: A systematic review. *Psychological Medicine, 33*, 395–405.

Chan, K. P. M., Hung, S. F., & Yip, P. S. F. (2001). Suicide in response to changing societies. *Child and Adolescent Psychiatric Clinics of North America, 10*, 777–795.

Charlton, B. (2000). *Psychiatry and the Human Condition*. Abingdon: Radcliffe Medical Press.

Chelmow, D. (2005). Evidence-based medicine: Quantitatively moving from the universal to the particular. In R. Bibace, J. D. Laird, K. L. Noller, & J. Valsiner (Eds.), *Science and Medicine in Dialogue. Thinking through particulars and universals* (pp. 139–158). Westport, CT: Praeger.

De Leo, D. (2008). Editorial: Crisis – The road ahead. *Crisis, 29*, 171–172.

Doidge, N. (2007). *The Brain that Changes Itself*. Melbourne: Scribe.

Ekeland, T-J. (1999). Evidence-based treatment: Quality assurance or instrumental mistake. *Tidsskrift for Norsk Psykologforening, 36*, 1036–1047.

Elliott, R., Fischer, C. T., Rennie, & D. L. (1999). Evolving guidelines for publication of qualitative research studies in psychology and related fields. *British Journal of Clinical Psychology, 38*, 215–229.

Feyerabend, P. (1995). Anything goes. In W. T. Anderson (Ed.), *The Truth about the Truth* (pp. 199–203). New York: G. P. Putnam.

Fernando, S. (2002). *Mental Health, Race and Culture*. New York: Palgrave.

Fernando, S. (2003). *Cultural Diversity, Mental Health and Psychiatry. The struggle against racism*. New York: Brunner-Routledge.

Fleischer, E. (2000). *The Speaking Silence. Suicide and suicide attempt as speech-act*. Odense: Odense Universitetsforlag.

Flick, U. (2007). *Managing Quality in Qualitative Research*. London: Sage.

Foucault, M. (1971). *Madness and Psychology*. Copenhagen: Rhodos.

Fulford, K. W. M., Sallah, D., & Woodbridge, K. (2007). Philosophical tools for cultural psychiatry. In K. Bhui & D. Bhugra (Eds.), *Culture and Mental Health. A comprehensive textbook* (pp. 37–46). London: Edward Arnold.

Geertz, C. (1973). *The Interpretation of Cultures*. New York: Basic Books.

Gilgen, A. R. (1995). Prefatory comments. In F. D. Abraham & A. R. Gilgen (Eds.), *Chaos Theory in Psychology* (pp. xv–xvii). Westport, CT: Praeger.

Glaser, B. G. & Strauss, A. L. (1967). *The Discovery of Grounded Theory*. Chicago, IL: Aldine.

Goldney, R. D. (2002). Qualitative and quantitative approaches in suicidology: Commentary. *Archives of Suicide Research, 6*, 69–73.

Gustafsson, L. & Jacobsson, L. (2001). On mental disorder and somatic disease in suicide: A psychological autopsy study of 100 suicides in northern Sweden. *Nordic Journal of Psychiatry, 54*, 383–395.

Hafting, M. (2005). The individual stories and the professional conversation. *Tidsskrift for Den norske lægeforening, 125*, 3440–3441.

Harré, R. & Moghaddam, F. (2003). Introduction: The self and others in traditional psychology and in positioning theory. In R. Harré & F. Moghaddam (Eds.), *The Self and Others. Positioning individuals and groups in personal, political, and cultural contexts* (pp. 1–12). Westport, CT: Praeger.

Hjelmeland, H. & Knizek, B. L. (2010). Why we need qualitative research in suicidology. *Suicide and Life-Threatening Behavior, 4,* 74–80.

Hjelmeland, H., Knizek, B. L., Kinyanda, E., Musisi, S., Nordvik, H., & Svarva, K. (2008). Suicidal behaviour as communication in a cultural context. A comparative study between Norway and Uganda, *Crisis, 29,* 137–144.

Hughes, C. C. (1998). The glossary of 'culture-bound syndromes' in DSM-IV: A critique. *Transcultural Psychiatry, 35,* 413–421.

Jadhav, S. & Littlewood, R. (1994). Defeat depression campaign: Some medical anthropological queries. *Psychiatric Bulletin, 18,* 572–573.

Jenkins, J. H. (1994). Culture, emotion, and psychopathology. In S. Kitayama & H. R. Markus (Eds.), *Emotion and Culture* (pp. 307–335). Washington, DC: American Psychological Association.

Jenkins, J. H. (1998). Diagnostic criteria for schizophrenia and related psychotic disorders: Integration and suppression of cultural evidence in DSM-IV. *Transcultural Psychiatry, 35,* 357–376.

Kirmayer, L. J. (1998). The fate of culture in DSM-IV. *Transcultural Psychiatry, 35,* 339–342.

Kleinman, A. & Good, B. (Eds) (1985). *Culture and Depression: Studies in the anthropology and cross-cultural psychiatry of affect and disorder.* Berkeley, CA: University of California Press.

Knizek, B. L. & Hjelmeland, H. (2007). A theoretical model for interpreting suicidal behaviour as communication. *Theory and Psychology, 17,* 697–720.

Krippner, S. & Winkler, M. (1995). Studying consciousness in the postmodern age. In W. T. Anderson (Ed.), *The Truth about the Truth. De-confusing and re-constructing the postmodern world* (pp. 161–169). New York: G. P. Putnam.

Kvale, S. (1994). Ten standard objections to qualitative research interviews. *Journal of Phenomenological Psychology, 25,* 147–173.

Kvale, S. (1997). *InterViews. An introduction to qualitative research interviewing.* London: Sage.

Leder, D. (1990). Clinical interpretation: The hermeneutics of medicine. *Theoretical Medicine, 11,* 9–24.

Leenaars, A. A. (2002a). The quantitative and qualitative in suicidological science: An editorial. *Archives of Suicide Research, 6,* 1–3.

Leenaars, A. A. (2002b). In defence of the idiographic approach: Studies of suicide notes and personal documents. *Archives of Suicide Research, 6,* 19–30.

Lewis-Fernandez, R. (1998). A cultural critique of the DSM-IV dissociative disorders section. *Transcultural Psychiatry, 35,* 387–400.

Lyotard, J. F. (1979). *Knowledge and the Postmodern Society.* Århus: Sjakalen.

Malterud, K. (2001). The art and science of clinical knowledge: Evidence beyond measures and numbers. *The Lancet, 358,* 397–400.

Malterud, K. (2002). Qualitative methods in medical research – Presumptions, possibilities and limitations. *Tidsskrift for Den norske lægeforening, 112,* 2468–2472.

Mann, J. (2005). What does brain imaging tell us about the predisposition to suicidal behavior. *Crisis, 26,* 101–103.

Marchel, C. & Owens, S. (2007). Qualitative research in psychology: Could William James get a job? *History of Psychology, 10,* 301–324.

Måseide, P. (2002). The x-ray picture and the medical thinking – A sociological analysis. In K. T. Elvebakken & P. Solvang, P. (Eds.), *Health Images. Health and sickness in cultural perspective.* Bergen: Fagbokforlaget.

Masterpasqua, F., & Perna, P. A. (Eds) (1997). *The Psychological Meaning of Chaos. Translating theory into practice.* Washington, DC: American Psychological Association.

Mezzich, J. E., Kirmayer, L. J., Kleinman, A., Fabrega, H., Parron, D. L., Good, B. J., Lin, K.-M., & Manson, S. M. (1999). The place of culture in DSM-IV. *The Journal of Nervous and Mental Disease, 187,* 457–464.

Michel, K. & Valach, L. (2001). Suicide as goal-directed action. In K. van Heeringen (Ed.), *Understanding Suicidal Behaviour. The suicidal process approach to research, treatment and prevention* (pp. 230–254). Chichester: John Wiley & Sons, Ltd.

Michell, J. (2003a). Pragmatism, positivism and the quantitative imperative. *Theory and Psychology, 13,* 45–52.

Michell, J. (2003b). The quantitative imperative. Positivism, naïve realism and the place of qualitative methods in psychology. *Theory and Psychology, 13,* 5–31.

Mogensen, J. (2007). Plasticity of the Brain in Relation to Psychological Traumas and Their Recovery. Paper presented at the Traumatized Child International Conference. Symptoms, consequences and treatment in an international perspective, Copenhagen.

National Institute of Mental Health Consortium of Editors on development and Psychopathology (1999). Editorial statement. *Journal of Research on Adolescence, 9,* 489–490.

Noller, K. L. & Bibace, R. (2005). The centrality of the clinician: A view of medicine from the general to the particular. In R. Bibace, J. D. Laird, K. L. Noller, & J. Valsiner (Eds.), *Science and Medicine in Dialogue. Thinking through particulars and universals* (pp. 99–108). Westport, CT: Praeger.

Patel, V. & Sumathipala, A. (2001). International representation in psychiatric literature. *British Journal of Psychiatry, 178,* 406–409.

Phillips, M. R., Yang, G., Zhang, Y., Wang, L., Ji, H., & Zhou, M. (2002). Risk factors for suicide in China: A national case-control psychological autopsy study. *The Lancet, 360,* 1728–1736.

Pickering, J. & Skinner, M. (1990). Introduction. In J. Pickering & M. Skinner (Eds.), *From Sentience to Symbols. Readings on consciousness.* New York: Harvester Wheatsheaf.

Ricoeur, P. (1974). *The Interpretation. An attempt on Freud.* Frankfurt: Suhrkamp.

Rorty, R. (1991). *Objectivity, Relativism, and Truth.* Cambridge: Cambridge University Press.

Shneidman, E. (1985). *The Definition of Suicide.* Northvale, NJ: Jason Aronson.

Smith, J. A. & Osborn, M. (2003). Interpretative phenomenological analysis. In J. A. Smith (Ed.), *Qualitative Research Methods. A practical guide to research methods* (pp. 51–80). London: Sage.

Smith, G. C. S. & Pell, J. P. (2003). Parachute use to prevent death and major trauma related to gravitational challenge: Systematic review of randomised controlled trials. *British Medical Journal, 327,* 1459–1461.

Stanley, B. (2007). New directions for the Archives of Suicide Research. *Archives of Suicide Research, 11,* 1–2.

Sumathipala, A., Siribaddana, S., & Patel, V. (2004). Under-representation of developing countries in the research literature: Ethical issues arising from a survey of five leading medical journals. *BMC Medical Ethics, 5,* doi:10.1186/1472-6939-5-5.

Toomela, A. (2007). Culture of science: Strange history of the methodological thinking in psychology. *Integrative Psychological and Behavioral Science, 41,* 6–20.

Valsiner, J. (1988). Culture is not an independent variable: A lesson from cross-cultural research for 'mainstream' psychology. Paper presented at The Contributions of Cross-Cultural Psychology to Mainstream Psychological Theory symposium at the XXIV International Congress of Psychology, Sydney.

Valsiner, J. (2003). Culture and its transfer: Ways of creating general knowledge through the study of cultural particulars. In W. J. Lonner, D. L. Dinnel, S. A. Hayes, & D. N. Sattler (Eds.), *Online Readings in Psychology and Culture* (Unit 2, Chapter 12), available at http://www.wwu.edu/~culture.

Vetter, N. (2003). Editorial: Research publication in developing countries. *Journal of Public Health Medicine, 25,* 189.

Vijayakumar, L. (2005). Suicide and mental disorders in Asia. *International Review of Psychiatry,* 17, 109–114.

Vijayakumar, L., John, S., Pirkis, J., & Whiteford, H. (2005). Suicide in developing countries (2). Risk factors. *Crisis, 26,* 112–119.

von Uexküll, T. & Wesiack, W. (1988). *Theory of Human Medicine. Foundations of medical thinking and action.* Munich: Urban & Schwarzenberg.

von Wright, G. H. (1971/2004). *Explanation and Understanding.* Ithaca, NY: Cornell University Press.

Williams, M. (1997). *Cry of Pain. Understanding suicide and self-harm.* London: Penguin.

Yang, G-H., Phillips, M. R., Zhou, M. G., Wang, L.-J., Zhang, Y.-P., & Xu, D. (2005). Understanding the unique characteristics of suicide in China: National psychological autopsy study. *Biomedical and Environmental Sciences, 18,* 379–389.

Zhang, J., Conwell, Y., Zhou, L., & Jiang, C. (2004). Culture, risk factors and suicide in rural China: A psychological autopsy case control study. *Acta Psychiatrica Scandinavica, 110,* 430–437.

CHAPTER THIRTY-FIVE

Understanding the Relationship between Mental Illness and Suicide and the Implications for Suicide Prevention

Brian L. Mishara and François Chagnon

Abstract

Although the presence of a mental disorder is highly associated with suicide in developed countries, there is little research on the mechanisms that explain why people with a mental disorder are at greater risk of suicide. We describe alternative explanatory models of the relationship between mental disorders and suicide and their implications for prevention activities. For example, living with mental disorders leads to increased exposure to well-known and easily identified risk factors, suggesting the need for greater focus of prevention activities on improving the lives of persons with mental disorders. We challenge the simple conclusion that, because mental disorders and suicide may be highly associated, therefore treating mental disorders is the best suicide prevention strategy. We suggest that understanding *why* people with a mental disorder are at greater risk of suicide can help us to understand why only a minority of people with mental disorders complete suicide, as well as how to prevent suicide in persons with mental disorders.

Introduction

Evidence from numerous empirical studies, mostly using psychological autopsy methods, suggests that up to 90% of persons who die by suicide have a diagnosable mental disorder (Arsenault-Lapierre, Kim, & Turecki, 2004; Cavanagh, Carson, Sharpe, & Lawrie, 2003;

International Handbook of Suicide Prevention: Research, Policy and Practice, First Edition.
Edited by Rory C. O'Connor, Stephen Platt, Jacki Gordon.

Fleischman, Bertolote, Belfer, & Beautrais, 2005; Hawton & van Heeringen, 2009; Suominen, Henriksson, Suokas, Isometsä, Ostamo, *et al.*, 1996; Wasserman & Wasserman, 2009; Yoshimasu, Kiyohara, & Miyashita, 2008). These meta-analyses and reviews have shown that the most common diagnoses are affective disorders, substance abuse disorders, personality disorders, and schizophrenia. However, the proportion of persons who die by suicide who have a mental disorder has been found to be much less in some Asian studies using comparable methodologies (Phillips, Zhang, Shi, Song, Ding, *et al.*, 2009). Despite the strong association between suicide and mental disorder in Western countries, there are many hundreds of other factors that are associated with suicide risk (Mishara & Tousignant, 2004). These factors range from macro-level variables, such as unemployment, to individual demographic characteristics, such as gender, age, and marital status, and a wide range of social variables (e.g., social support) and psychological characteristics of the individual (e.g., personality traits and coping mechanisms). Certain environmental variables at the time of the suicide attempt are also associated with increased risk, such as the presence of, or easy access to, lethal means. Consequently, it is often said that suicide is multi-determined.

Given the strong association between suicide and mental disorders in developed countries, national strategies for suicide prevention have tended to focus on the treatment of mental illnesses as the most important preventative action. However, we need to note that the vast majority of people with a mental disorder will *not* complete suicide: a mental disorder is not a sufficient cause of suicide. It is the thesis of this chapter that an understanding of the mechanisms underlying the association between mental disorders and suicide can elucidate promising methods in suicide prevention. We describe alternative explanatory models of the relationship between mental disorders and suicide and their implications for prevention activities. We suggest that understanding *why* people with a mental disorder are at more risk of suicide can help us to understand why only a minority of people with mental disorder complete suicide and how to prevent suicide in persons with mental disorders. This understanding can also lead to the identification of numerous interventions to prevent suicide that go beyond simply treating mental disorders. It should be noted that in a minority of cases in developed countries, at least 10% according to psychological autopsy studies, suicides occur without the presence of a mental disorder. Furthermore, mental disorders are much less often associated with suicide in some Asian studies, and we do not have sufficient data to determine the extent of the association in most under-developed countries.

We suggest that the association between suicide and mental disorders can be understood according to a number of models, which may not be mutually exclusive. These are described below.

Explanatory Models of the Relationship between Mental Disorders and Suicide

Suicide and mental disorders have a common aetiology

The research literature demonstrates that there is a significant overlap between factors associated with suicide and factors associated with the development of a mental disorder. These factors include biogenetic vulnerability (Brent & Melhem, 2008; Brezo, Klempan, & Turecki,

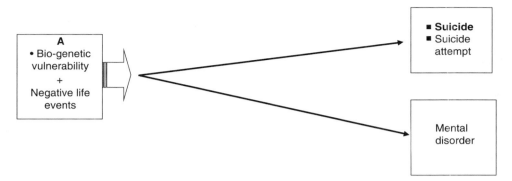

Figure 35.1   Model: suicide and mental disorders have a common aetiology.

2008; Currier & Mann, 2008; Ernst, Mechawar, & Turecki, 2009; Mann, Arango, Avenevoli, Brent, Champagne, *et al.*, 2009; Roy, Sarchiopone, & Carli, 2009; Voracek & Loibl, 2007) and early negative life events (Afifi, Boman, Fleisher, & Sareen, 2009; Andover, Zlotnick, & Miller, 2007; Ball & Links, 2009; Carballo, Akamnonu, & Oquendo, 2008; Christoffersen, Soothill, & Francis, 2007; Draper, Pfaff, Pirkis, Snowdon, Lautenschlanger, *et al.*, 2008; Makhija, 2007; McIntyre, Soezynska, Mancini, Lam, Woldeyohannes, *et al.*, 2008; Pagura, Cox, Sareen, & Enns, 2008).

Additionally, negative early life events, such as child abuse and neglect, are associated with adult suicidality, as well as increased risk of mental disorders (Afifi *et al.*, 2009; Andover *et al.*, 2007; Christoffersen *et al.*, 2007; Draper *et al.*, 2008; Makhiji, 2007; McIntyre *et al.*, 2008; Pagura *et al.*, 2008). According to this explanatory model, there is an association between suicide and mental disorders simply because the same factors that increase the risk of becoming suicidal and eventually completing suicide are also associated with developing a mental disorder. According to this model, there is no direct causal link between mental disorders and suicide; their association is simply due to the fact that they both have common determinants (see Figure 35.1).

Some mental disorders are alternatives to suicide

Freud (1955) felt that mental disorders can develop as means of controlling impulses for self-destruction. For example, in his analysis of the case of the 'Rat Man', he contended that obsessive compulsive disorders with their ritualistic practices can be interpreted as a means of focusing psychic energies in order to not feel compelled to act upon suicidal impulses. Similarly, alcohol or drug abuse disorders may develop out of an attempt at self-medication (Bolton, Cox, Clara, & Sareen, 2006; Bolton, Robinson, & Sareen, 2009). In this way, the abuse of substances may be a way of avoiding or trying to diminish suicidal impulses, and may thus be an alternative to suicide. Another possible explanation of the relationship with alcohol and drug abuse is that these may

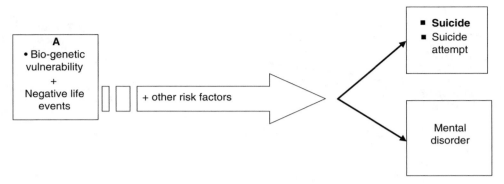

Figure 35.2   Model: some mental disorders are alternatives to suicide.

constitute indirect or 'slow' methods of ending one's life without engaging in a direct overt suicide attempt.

According to this model (see Figure 35.2) the various factors associated with greater suicide risk may lead to either suicidal behaviours or the development of a mental disorder (including substance abuse disorders).

Suicide is a direct consequence of mental disorders

This explanation is the most common lay understanding of why persons with mental disorders are at greater risk of suicide than those without such disorders. According to this model, the symptoms of the mental disorder are a key factor involved in the development of suicidal behaviours. Symptoms of mental disorders associated with suicide include: psychotic command hallucinations, where an individual may, for example, hear voices that tell him or her to kill him- or herself by jumping off of a building; and depressive delusions, when a person suffering from clinical depression perceives their current situation as being hopeless and interminable, and feels powerless to change the situation, despite the fact that the problems may be temporary and that help is available, resulting in the (mis)perception that suicide is the only way to stop their current suffering.

There are numerous other cognitive distortions associated with mental disorders. Also alcohol and many drugs diminish one's capacity to make rational decisions and to fully understand the consequences of one's behaviour. Alcohol and drugs may increase impulsivity and, consequently, the risk of suicidal behaviours (Dougherty, Marsh-Richard, Hatzis, Nouvion, & Mathias, 2008; Nagoshi, Wilson, & Rodriguez, 1991). In all these instances, by assuming that the suicidal person would not have killed him- or herself had she or he not had these symptoms of the mental illness, it can be concluded that the symptoms of the mental disorder are somehow an important causal factor in the suicide or suicide attempt (see Figure 35.3).

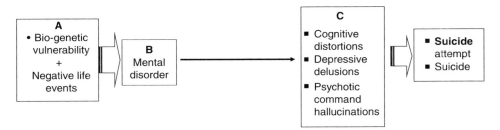

Figure 35.3 Model: suicide is a direct consequence of mental disorders.

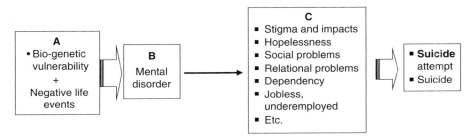

Figure 35.4 Model: suicide is the result of the consequences of living with a mental disorder.

Suicide is a result of the consequences of living with a mental disorder

People who live with a mental disorder in contemporary society are more likely to have a number of important risk factors that have been associated with suicide in empirical research. For example, social integration, being married, and having good social support are important protective factors against suicide attempts, and being single is an important risk factor (Afifi, Cox, & Enns, 2006; Agerbo, Byrne, Eaton, & Mortensen, 2004; Agerbo, Qin, & Mortensen, 2006; DeKlyen, Brooks-Gunn, McLanahan, & Knab, 2006). To take another example, the Quebec Health Survey (Légaré, Lebeau Richard, Boyer, & St-Laurent, 1995) showed that people who said that they had a confidant had half the probability of having attempted suicide in the past year than people who did not have a confidant. People who have a mental disorder are more likely to suffer from social exclusion, they are less likely to be married, have less support from their social network, and those who are married are more likely to become divorced (Afifi *et al.*, 2006; Morgan, Burns, Fitzpatrick, Pinfold, & Priebe, 2007).

Unemployment is also associated with suicide, and persons with mental disorders are much more likely to be unemployed or, if they do have a job, under-employed. Other factors, such as being stigmatized (Alonso, Buron, Rojas-Ferreras, de Graaf, Haro, *et al.*, 2009; Sudak, Maxim, & Carpenter, 2008), marginalized or dependent, which are often associated with mental disorders, can be considered risk factors for suicide. According to this model (see Figure 35.4), it is not the symptoms of the mental disorder in and of itself that result in an increased suicide risk, but rather the effects of living with a mental disorder. In addition to many of the problems already mentioned, the feeling of hopelessness experienced by many people with a chronic mental disorder is an important risk factor for suicide. People with chronic mental disorder may feel hopeless about ever living without the disorder.

Suicide results from treatment: it is 'iatrogentic' or related to inadequate, inappropriate or incomplete treatment

Although persons with mental disorders may be offered treatment with appropriate medication, therapy, and social support, a substantial number of persons with mental disorders may not take their medications, complete therapy, or participate in activities intended to increase their social support (Heilä, Isometä, Henriksson, Heikkinen, Marttunen, *et al.*, 1999; Isometä, Henriksson, Aro, Heikkinene, Kuoppasalmi, *et al.*, 1994; Keks, Hill, Sundram, Graham, Bellingham, *et al.*, 2009; Oquendo, Kramali, Ellis, Grunebaum, Malone, *et al.*, 2002; Suominen, Isometä, Henriksson, Ostamo, & Lönqvist, 1998; Suominen, Isometä, Henriksson, Ostamo, & Lönqvist, 1999; Taiminen & Kujari, 1994). Non-compliance with treatment and inadequate treatment may be important risk factors for suicide. In this case, it is not the mental disorder in and of itself that results in greater suicide risk, but rather inadequate, inappropriate, or incomplete treatment for the disorder. This lack of appropriate or continued treatment may be due to factors associated with the service providers (such as poor communication about the importance of adhering to treatment regimes, inadequate diagnostic skills, and providing inadequate treatment), characteristics of the patients (such as rebelliousness or a conscious or unconscious wish not to get better), or may be related to side-effects of some treatments (e.g., psychotropic medication).

There is another way in which treatment for mental disorders may increase suicide risk. The current controversial warning on SSRI (antidepressant) medications for young people (Hall & Lucke, 2006; Isacsson, Holmgren, & Ahlner, 2005; Hetrick, Merry, McKenzie, Sindahl, & Proctor, 2007), which indicates that SSRIs may result in a small number of cases of increased suicide risk, is an example of an iatrogenic effect (meaning that the negative consequence may be associated with the attempt at treatment). The treatment in and of itself may result in increased suicide risk. The explanation given to this effect may be two-fold. First, a person who is in the depths of despair and profoundly affected by a mental disorder may not have the energy or ability to organize a suicide attempt. As the treatment begins to have an effect, the person may have better organizational skills and be able to mobilize sufficient energy to attempt suicide before the full effects of the treatment are obtained and the major symptoms of the disorder significantly diminished. Second, the small improvement at the beginning of treatment may be enough to improve cognitive abilities for the person to realize that he or she is suffering from a distressing mental disorder, but again before there are decreases in symptoms, such as depressive rumination. In such a situation a person may feel hopeless about the current situation of living with a mental disorder and be at greater risk of suicide, since the full effects of the medication on depressive rumination have not yet occurred (see Figure 35.5).

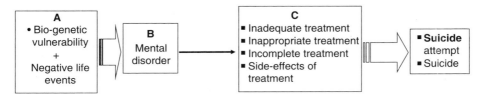

Figure 35.5   Suicide results from treatment, it is 'iatrogenic' or related to inadequate, inappropriate, or incomplete treatment.

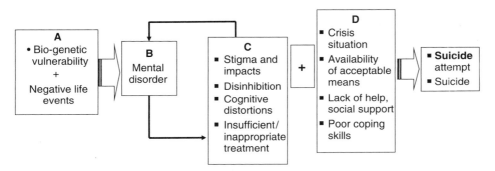

Figure 35.6   Model with the addition of the crisis situation.

Aspects of the crisis situation

Suicide attempts often occur in a crisis where the anxiety, psychic pain, and feelings of being overwhelmed, helpless, and hopeless in the situation increase the suicide risk (Mishara & Tousignant, 2004). Persons with a mental disorder may be more likely to experience crisis situations because of their fragile social supports and difficulties in coping with everyday problems (Figure 35.6). Additionally, a situation which may seem to be manageable to someone without a mental disorder may be perceived as an insurmountable crisis by someone whose coping skills, cognitive abilities, and general resilience have been compromised by the disorder.

In a crisis situation, several factors are associated with the outcome. If a means of suicide that is acceptable to the person is readily available, such as having a firearm in the home of someone who considers a firearm a 'good' method to complete suicide, the risk that a suicide death will occur in the home is between two- and nine-fold (Brent, Perper, Allman, & Moritz, 1991; Christoffel & Naureckas 1994; Klieve, Sveticic, & De Leo, 2009). Having good social support available, for example, by living with family members, can protect against suicide. However, having poor social support and no one available during a crisis, which (as we have seen) is more likely among persons with mental disorders, increases the risk of a suicide occurring (Taylor & Stanton, 2007). Having poor coping skills to deal with the crisis also increases suicide risk (Asarnow, Carlson, & Guthrie, 1987; Botsis, Soldatos, Liossi, Kokkevi, & Stefanis, 1999; Curry, Miller, Waugh, & Anderson, 1992; Gould, Velting, Kleinman, Lucas, Thomas, *et al.*, 2004; Josepho & Plutchik, 1994; Kotler, Finkelstein, Molcho, Botsis, Plutchik, *et al.*, 1993; Spirito, Francis, Overhosler, & Frank, 1996; Wilson, Stelzer, Bergman, Kral, Inayatullah, *et al.*, 1995). Persons with mental disorders may be considered at greater risk of having poor coping skills (Taylor & Stanton, 2007; Wu, Wu, Liao, Chang, & Tang, 2009).

Prevention Activities for People with Mental Disorders

There are opportunities for suicide prevention according to each explanation of the relationship between mental disorders and suicide and in terms of each of the factors potentially involved. In terms of biogenetic vulnerability, it is possible that future research will lead to the identification of vulnerable individuals who may benefit from early interventions to prevent their attempting suicide later in life. We have not yet identified reliable bio-markers or genetic indicators of individuals at risk of suicide. If reliable indicators are identified, this will pose a number of ethical dilemmas as well as practical concerns, including ethical concerns about who has the right to know about genetic and biological risk factors and the ethics of determining when diagnostic indicators are sufficiently reliable and associated with enough effective preventive interventions to be of practical use (Mishara & Weisstub, 2007, 2008). In particular, the identification of individuals at risk of low-incidence outcomes such as suicide attempts may become a 'self-fulfilling prophecy' due, for example, to changes in parental behaviours when they learn their child has a suicide risk; the identification in and of itself may cause problems to the individual. On the other hand, prevention of negative life events, such as child abuse and neglect, are possible today and can have the potential of reducing suicide later in life (see Figure 35.7).

It is obvious that treating mental disorders should have effects in suicide prevention (Figure 35.8). However, as indicated in Figure 35.8, activities to decrease the negative impact of mental disorders in society may be as important as, or perhaps even more important than, the effect of increasing treatment of mental disorders. Reducing stigma and negative impacts of mental disorders by providing better programmes and social support could have great potential (Taylor & Stanton, 2007). Furthermore, the education of caregivers and the general public and the creation of supportive environments also could have a major impact in preventing suicide (Morgan *et al.*, 2007).

In a crisis situation (see Figure 35.9), the availability of a crisis intervention, such as a telephone helpline, may decrease the risk of a suicide death (Mishara, Chagnon, Daigle, Balan, Raymond, *et al.*, 2007a, 2007b). Controlling access to means of suicide, such as firearms control, safe storage of pesticides, and barriers on bridges, will also decrease the risk of a suicide death (e.g., Christoffel & Naureckas, 1994; Hawton, 2007; Mishara, 2007). Anything that can be done to increase social support for persons with mental disorders would be beneficial, as would educational activities to teach effective coping skills. In addition, increased social support and improving coping skills can help people better

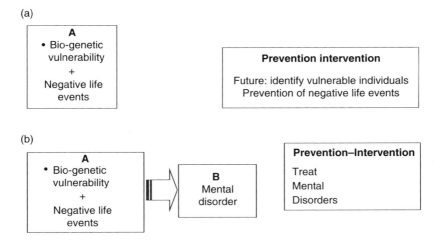

Figure 35.7 Implications of common aetiology and direct consequences models for prevention (a) Prevention according to the common aetiology model. (b) Implications of the direct consequences model.

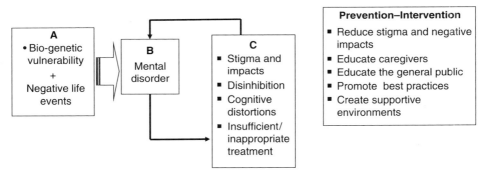

Figure 35.8 Implications of the model of suicide as the result of the consequences of living with a mental disorder for prevention.

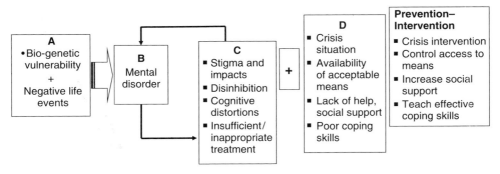

Figure 35.9 Implications for prevention of adding to the model the crisis situation.

deal with the impact of living with a mental disorder and can decrease the overall risk of suicidal behaviour.

Why the Risk for Different Mental Disorders Varies During the Course of the Disorder

When suicides are more likely to occur during the course of mental disorders varies depending upon the specific disorder. For example, in the case of affective disorders, it is more likely that suicide will occur early in the disorder. In the case of major depression, the greatest risk is in the first three months and during the first depressive episode (Bostwick & Pankratz, 2000; Mattisson, Bogren, Horstmann, Munk-Jörgensen, & Nettelbladt, 2007). This contrasts with schizophrenia, where the risk is greatest between the second and sixteenth year, and half of suicides occur during hospital admission (Pompili, Mancinelli, Ruberto, Kotzalidis, Girardi, *et al.*, 2005). In the case of Alzheimer's disease, the risk is greatest early on (Erlangsen, Zarit, & Conwell, 2008; Haw, Harwood, & Hawton, 2009), and in the case of alcohol abuse the suicide risk increases substantially after 10 years of abuse (Conner, Beautrais, & Conwell, 2003).

Why do some mental disorders have higher risk early and others much later? It is only possible to speculate, since there is little research on this question. One possible explanation is that suicide risk is highest in the period when symptom intensity is at its greatest. However, this is certainly not the case in some disorders, such as Alzheimer's disease, where symptoms increase over time, yet the greatest risk is early. Another explanation is that the consequences of living with the disorder are greater later on when social supports are lost and the disorder enters a chronic phase. In some disorders, the greater risk early on may be related to the stigma and shock of learning that one has a mental illness. In the case of alcoholism, the greater risk may be related to biochemical effects on the brain and the likelihood of having more illnesses associated with alcohol abuse (Vinod, Kassir, Hungund, Cooper, Mann, *et al.*, 2010). However, people who abuse alcohol may take many years before they lose their social support and are unable to continue at work, which would indicate that it is the social consequences of the disorder rather than the symptoms or more direct consequences of the disorder that result in increased suicide risk. In some instances, the severity of symptoms, for example, in advanced Alzheimer's disease or during a first acute psychotic episode, may protect against suicide by simply decreasing the ability to organize a suicidal act.

Conclusions

The association between mental illness and suicide is one of the most researched topics in suicidology. The association is found across the world. Despite indications that this association may be much lower in Asia, and the lack of data on the topic from Africa and other areas, in developed Western countries as many as 90% of persons who take their own lives have a diagnosable mental disorder. However, it is important to understand why people with mental disorders are at greater risk of suicide in order to develop appropriate prevention activities. Although the treatment of mental disorders would most certainly have an effect on reducing suicide rates, other factors may play important, or perhaps even more important, roles. Even where people with mental disorders have been successfully identified and offered appropriate treatments, substantial numbers do not adhere to treatment protocols, do not take sufficient medication or refuse medication totally, and do not complete therapy sessions or appear for appointments for follow-up contacts after a suicide attempt. Although most research on treatment compares people who adhere to treatment protocols with a control group with alternative treatment or no treatment, there is little focus on those who do not adhere to treatment, which may be more common in the case of suicide deaths. Furthermore, living with mental disorders leads to increased exposure to well-known and easily identified risk factors, suggesting the need to focus prevention activities on improving the lives of persons with mental disorders. Finally, help in crisis situations, which may occur more frequently with persons with mental disorders, is another important component in a global suicide prevention strategy.

Any global suicide prevention strategy should include a combination of complementary actions whose total effect may significantly reduce suicide incidence. It is necessary to challenge the simple conclusion that, because mental disorders and suicide may be highly associated, therefore treating mental disorders is the best suicide prevention strategy. In the absence of clear evidence about the relative effectiveness of different suicide prevention activities, effective suicide prevention strategies must include a diversity of activities. Priorities should be guided by considerations such as the possibility of implementing different activities in the specific cultural context, their ability to best reach high risk groups, and ethical considerations that the risk of harm is minimized. It is hoped that future research will increase understanding about *why* having a mental disorder results in greater risk of suicide. It is most certainly a combination of the models outlined herein that best explains this relationship. However, the relative role of each of the explanatory factors needs to be clarified better in future research.

References

Afifi, T. O., Boman, J., Fleisher, W., & Sareen, J. (2009). The relationship between child abuse, parental divorce, and lifetime mental disorders and suicidality in a nationally representative adult sample. *Child Abuse and Neglect, 33,* 139–147.

Afifi, T. O., Cox, B. J., & Enns, M. W. (2006). Mental health profiles among married, never-married, and separated/divorced mothers in a nationally representative sample. *Social Psychiatry and Psychiatric Epidemiology, 41,* 122–129.

Agerbo, E., Byrne, M., Eaton, W. W., & Mortensen, P. B. (2004). Marital and labor market status in the long run in schizophrenia. *Archives of General Psychiatry, 61,* 28–33.

Agerbo, E., Qin, P., & Mortensen, P. B. (2006). Psychiatric illness, socioeconomic status, and martial status in people committing suicide: A matched case-sibling-control study. *Journal of Epidemiology and Community Health, 60,* 776–781.

Alonso, J., Buron, A., Rojas-Ferreras, S., de Graaf, R., Haro, J., de Girolamo, G., Bruffaerts, R., Kovess, V., Matschinger, H., & Vilagut G. (2009). Perceived stigma among individuals with common mental disorders. *Journal of Affective Disorders, 118,* 180–186.

Andover, M. S., Zlotnick, C., & Miller, W. I. (2007). Childhood physical and sexual abuse in depressed patients with single and multiple suicide attempts. *Suicide and Life-Threatening Behavior, 37*, 467–474.

Arsenault-Lapierre, G., Kim, C., & Turecki, G. (2004). Psychiatric diagnoses in 3275 suicides: A meta-analysis. *BMC Psychiatry, 4*, 37.

Asarnow, J. R., Carlson, G. A., & Guthrie, D. (1987). Coping strategies, self-perceptions, hopelessness, and perceived family environments in depressed and suicidal children. *Journal of Consulting and Clinical Psychology, 55*, 361–366.

Ball, J. S. & Links, P. S. (2009). Borderline personality disorder and childhood trauma: Evidence for a causal relationship. *Current Psychiatry Reports, 11*, 63–68.

Bolton, J., Cox, B., Clara, I., & Sareen, J. (2006). Use of alcohol and drugs to self-medicate anxiety disorders in a nationally representative sample. *Journal of Nervous and Mental Disease, 194*, 818–825.

Bolton, J. M. Robinson, J., & Sareen, J. (2009). Self-medication of mood disorders with alcohol and drugs in the National Epidemiologic Survey on Alcohol and Related Conditions. *Journal of Affective Disorders, 115*, 367–375.

Bostwick, J. M. & Pankratz, V. S. (2000). Affective disorders and suicide risk: A reexamination. *American Journal of Psychiatry, 157*, 1925–1932.

Botsis, A. J., Soldatos, C. R., Liossi, A., Kokkevi, A., & Stefanis, C. N. (1994). Suicide and violence risk. I. Relationship to coping styles. *Acta Psychiatrica Scandinavica, 89*, 92–96.

Brent, D. A. & Melhem, N. (2008). Familial transmission of suicidal behavior. *Psychiatric Clinics of North America, 31*, 157–177.

Brent, D., Perper, J. A., Allman, C. J., & Moritz G. M. (1991). The presence and accessibility of firearms in the homes of adolescent suicides. A case-control study. *Journal of the American Medical Association, 266*, 2989–2995.

Brezo, J., Klempan, T., & Turecki, G. (2008). The genetics of suicide: A critical review of molecular studies. *Psychiatric Clinics of North America, 31*, 179–203.

Carballo, J. J., Akamnonu, C. P., & Oquendo, M. A. (2008). Neurobiology of suicidal behavior. An integration of biological and clinical findings. *Archives of Suicide Research, 12*, 93–110.

Cavanagh, J. T., Carson, A. J., Sharpe, M., & Lawrie, S. M. (2003). Psychological autopsy studies of suicide: A systematic review. *Psychological Medicine, 33*, 395–405.

Christoffel K. K. & Naureckas, S. M. (1994). Firearm injuries in children and adolescents: Epidemiology and preventive approaches. *Current Opinion in Pediatry, 6*, 519–524.

Christoffersen, M. N., Soothill, K., & Francis, B. (2007). Violent life events and social disadvantage: A systematic study of the social background of various kinds of lethal violence, other violent crime, suicide, and suicide attempts. *Journal of Scandinavian Studies in Criminology and Crime Prevention, 8*, 157–184.

Conner, K. R., Beautrais, A. L., & Conwell, Y. (2003). Moderators of the relationship between alcohol dependence and suicide and medically serious suicide attempts: Analyses of Canterbury Suicide Project data. *Alcoholism, Clinical and Experimental Research, 27*, 1156–1161.

Currier, D. & Mann, J. J. (2008). Stress, genes and the biology of suicidal behavior. *Psychiatric Clinics of North America, 31*, 247–269.

Curry, J. F., Miller, Y., Waugh, S., & Anderson, W. B. (1992). Coping responses in depressed, socially maladjusted, and suicidal adolescents. *Psychological Reports, 71*, 80–82.

DeKlyen, M., Brooks-Gunn, J., McLanahan, S., & Knab, J. (2006). The mental health of married, cohabiting, and non-coresident parents with infants. *American Journal of Public Health, 96*, 1836–1841.

Dougherty, D. M., Marsh-Richard, D. M., Hatzis, E. S., Nouvion, S. O., & Mathias, C. W. (2008). A test of alcohol dose effects on multiple behavioral measures of impulsivity. *Drug and Alcohol Dependence, 96*, 111–120.

Draper, B., Pfaff, J. J., Pirkis, J., Snowdon, J., Lautenschlager, N. T., Wilson, I., & Almeida, O. P. (2008). Long-term effects of childhood abuse on the quality of life and health of older people: Results from the Depression and Early Prevention of Suicide in General Practice project. *Journal of the American Geriatrics Society, 56*, 262–271.

Erlangsen, A., Zarit, S. H., & Conwell, Y. (2008). Hospital-diagnosed dementia and suicide: A longitudinal study using prospective, nationwide register data. *American Journal of Geriatric Psychiatry, 16*, 220–228.

Ernst, C., Mechawar, N., & Turecki, G. (2009). Suicide neurobiology. *Progress in Neurobiology, 89*, 315–333.

Fleischmann, A., Bertolote, J. M., Belfer, M., & Beautrais, A. (2005). Completed suicide and psychiatric diagnoses in young people: A critical examination of the evidence. *American Journal of Orthopsychiatry, 75*, 676–683.

Freud, S. (1955), L'Homme aux rats. Protocole original du cas (1909d). *Revue Française de Psychanalyse, 35*, 475–526.

Gould, M. S., Velting, D., Kleinman, M., Lucas, C., Thomas, J. G., & Chung, M. (2004). Teenagers' attitudes about coping strategies and help-seeking behavior for suicidality. *Journal of the American Academy of Child and Adolescent Psychiatry, 43*, 1124–1133.

Hall, W. D. & Lucke, J. (2006). How have the selective serotonin reuptake inhibitor antidepressants affected suicide mortality? *Australian and New Zealand Journal of Psychiatry, 40*, 941–950.

Haw, C., Harwood, D., & Hawton, K. (2009). Dementia and suicidal behavior: A review of the literature. *International Psychogeriatrics, 21*, 440–453.

Hawton, K. (2007). Restricting access to methods of suicide. Rationale and evaluation of this approach to suicide prevention. *Crisis, 28* (Suppl. 1), 4–9.

Hawton, K. & van Heeringen, K. (2009). Suicide. *The Lancet, 373*, 1372–1381.

Heilä, H., Isometsä, E. T., Henriksson, M. M., Heikkinen, M. E., Marttunen, M. J., & Lönqvist, J. K. (1999). Suicide victims with schizophrenia in different treatment phases and adequacy of antipsychotic medication. *Journal of Clinical Psychiatry, 60*, 200–208.

Hetrick, S., Merry, S., McKenzie, J., Sindahl, P., & Proctor, M. (2007). Selective serotonin reuptake inhibitors (SSRIs) for depressive disorders in children and adolescents. *Cochrane Database Systematic Review, 3*, Article CD004851.

Isacsson, G., Holmgren, P., & Ahlner, J. (2005). Selective serotonin reuptake inhibitor antidepressants and the risk of suicide: A controlled forensic database study of 14 857 suicides. *Acta Psychiatrica Scandinavica, 111*, 286–290.

Isometsä, E. T., Henriksson, M. M., Aro, H. M., Heikkinene, M. E., Kuoppasalmi, K. I., & Lönqvist, J. K. (1994). Suicide in major depression. *American Journal of Psychiatry, 151*, 530–536.

Josepho, S. A. & Plutchik, R. (1994). Stress, coping, and suicide risk in psychiatric inpatients. *Suicide and Life-Threatening Behavior, 24*, 48–57.

Keks, N. A., Hill, C., Sundram, S., Graham, A., Bellingham, K., Dean, B., Opeskin, K., Dorissa, A., & Copolov, D. L. (2009). Evaluation of treatment in 35 cases of bipolar suicide. *Australian and New Zealand Journal of Psychiatry, 43*, 503–508.

Klieve H., Sveticic J., & De Leo, D. (2009). Who uses firearms as a means of suicide? A population study exploring firearm accessibility and method choice. *BMC Medicine, 7*, 52.

Kotler, M., Finkelstein, G., Molcho, A., Botsis, A. J., Plutchik, R., Brown, S. L., & van Praag, H. M. (1993). Correlates of suicide and violence risk in an inpatient population: Coping styles and social support. *Psychiatry Research, 47*, 281–290.

Légaré, G., Lebeau Richard, A., Boyer, R. & St-Laurent, D. (1995). Santé mentale. Détresse psychologique. Idées suicidaires et parasuicides. In C. Bellerose, C. Lavallée, L. Chénard, & M. Levasseur (Eds.), *Santé Québec. Et la santé, ça va en 1992–1993? Rapport de l'Enquête sociale et de santé 1992–1993*. Vol. I (pp. 217–246). Québec: Santé Québec, Ministère de la Santé et des Services sociaux, Gouvernement du Québec.

Makhija, N. J. (2007). Childhood abuse and adolescent suicidality: A direct link and an indirect link through alcohol and substance misuse. *International Journal of Adolescent Medicine and Health, 19*, 45–51.

Mann, J. J., Arango, V. A., Avenevoli, S., Brent, D. A., Champagne, F. A., Clayton, P., Currier, D., Dougherty, D. M., Haghighi, F., Hodge, S. E., Kleinman, J., Lehner, T., McMahon, F., Moscicki, E. K., Oquendo, M. A., Pandey, G. N., Pearson, J., Stanley, B., Terwilliger, J., & Wenzel, A. (2009). Candidate endophenotypes for genetic studies of suicidal behavior. *Biological Psychiatry, 65*, 556–563.

Mattisson, C., Bogren, M., Horstmann, V., Munk-Jörgensen, P., & Nettelbladt, P. (2007). The long-term course of depressive disorders in the Lundby Study. *Psychological Medicine, 37*, 883–91.

McIntyre, R. S., Soczynska, J. K., Mancini, D., Lam, C., Woldeyohannes, H. O., Moon, S., Konarski, J. Z., & Kennedy, S. H. (2008). The relationship between childhood abuse and suicidality in adult bipolar disorder. *Violence and Victims, 23*, 361–372.

Mishara, B. L. (2007). Prevention of deaths from intentional pesticide poisoning. *Crisis, 28* (Suppl. 1), 10–20.

Mishara, B. L., Chagnon, F., Daigle, M., Balan, B., Raymond, S., Marcoux, I., Bardon, C., Campbell, J. K., & Berman, A. (2007a). Comparing models of helper behavior to actual practice in telephone crisis intervention: A silent monitoring study of calls to the US 1-800-SUICIDE network. *Suicide and Life-Threatening Behavior, 37*, 293–309.

Mishara, B. L., Chagnon, F., Daigle, M., Balan, B., Raymond, S., Marcoux, I., Bardon, C., Campbell, J. K., & Berman, A. (2007b). Which helper behaviors and intervention styles are related to better short-term outcomes in telephone Crisis intervention? Results from a silent monitoring study of calls to the US 1-800-SUICIDE network. *Suicide and Life-Threatening Behavior, 37*, 310–323.

Mishara, B. L. & Tousignant, M. (2004). *Comprendre le suicide*. Montréal: Presses de l'Université de Montréal.

Mishara, B. L. & Weisstub, D. N. (2007). Ethical, legal, and practical issues in the control and regulation of suicide promotion and assistance over the internet. *Suicide and Life-Threatening Behavior, 37*, 58–65.

Mishara, B. L. & Weisstub, D. N. (2008). The rights to die and the duty to save: A reflection on ethical presuppositions in suicide research. In D. N. Weisstub & G. D. Pintos (Eds.), *Human Rights and Health Care* (pp. 353–374). New York: Springer.

Morgan, C., Burns, T., Fitzpatrick, R., Pinfold, V., & Priebe, S. (2007). Social exclusion and mental health: Conceptual and methodological review. *British Journal of Psychiatry, 191*, 477–483.

Nagoshi, C., Wilson, J., & Rodriguez, L. (1991). Impulsivity, sensation seeking, and behavioral and emotional responses to alcohol. *Alcoholism: Clinical and Experimental Research, 15*, 661–667.

Oquendo, M. A., Kramali, M., Ellis, S. P., Grunebaum, M. F., Malone, K. M., Brodsky, B. S., Sackeim, H. A., & Mann, J. J. (2002). Adequacy of antidepressant treatment after discharge and the occurrence of suicidal acts in major depression: A prospective study. *American Journal of Psychiatry, 159*, 1746–1751.

Pagura, J., Cox, B. J., Sareen, J., & Enns, M. W. (2008). Factors associated with multiple versus single episode suicide attempts in the 1990–1992 and 2001–2003 United States National Comorbidity Surveys. *Journal of Nervous and Mental Disease, 196*, 806–813.

Phillips, M. R., Zhang, J., Shi, Q., Song, Z., Ding, Z., Pang, S., Li, X., Zhang, Y., & Wang, Z. (2009). Prevalence, treatment, and associated disability of mental disorders in four provinces in China during 2001–05: An epidemiological survey. *The Lancet, 373*, 2041–2053.

Pompili, M., Mancinelli, I., Ruberto, A., Kotzalidis, G. D., Girardi, P., & Tatarelli, R. (2005). Where schizophrenic patients commit suicide: A review of suicide among inpatients and former inpatients. *International Journal of Psychiatry and Medicine*, *35*, 171–190.

Roy, A., Sarchiopone, M., & Carli, V. (2009). Gene–environment interaction and suicidal behavior. *Journal of Psychiatric Practice*, *15*, 282–288.

Spirito, A., Francis, G., Overhosler, J. C., & Frank, N. (1996). Coping, depression, and adolescent suicide attempts. *Journal of Clinical Child Psychology*, *25*, 147–155.

Sudak, H., Maxim, K., & Carpenter, M. (2008). Suicide and stigma: A review of the literature and personal reflections. *Academic Psychiatry*, *32*, 13.

Suominen, K. H., Henriksson, M., Suokas, J., Isometsä, E. T., Ostamo, A., & Lönqvist, J. K. (1996). Mental disorders and comorbidity in attempted suicide. *Acta Psychiatrica Scandinavica*, *94*, 234–240.

Suominen, K. H., Isometsä, E. T., Henriksson, M. M., Ostamo, A. I., & Lönqvist, J. K. (1998). Inadequate treatment for major depression both before and after attempted suicide. *American Journal of Psychiatry*, *155*, 1778–1780.

Suominen, K. H., Isometsä, E. T., Henriksson, M. M., Ostamo, A. I., & Lönqvist, J. K. (1999). Treatment received by alcohol-dependent suicide attempters. *Acta Psychiatrica Scandinavica*, *99*, 214–219.

Taiminen, T. J. & Kujari, H. (1994). Antipsychotic medication and suicide risk among schizophrenic and paranoid inpatients. A controlled retrospective study. *Acta Psychiatrica Scandinavica*, *90*, 247–251.

Taylor, S. E. & Stanton, A. L. (2007). Coping resources, coping processes, and mental health. *Annual Review of Clinical Psychology*, *3*, 377–401.

Vinod, K. Y., Kassir, S. A., Hungund, B. L., Cooper, T. B., Mann, J. J., & Arango, V. (2010). Selective alterations of the CB1 receptors and the fatty acid amide hydrolase in the ventral striatum of alcoholics and suicides. *Journal of Psychiatric Research*, *44*, 591–597.

Voracek, M. & Loibl, L. M. (2007). Genetics of suicide: A systematic review of twin studies. *Wiener Klinische Wochenschrift*, *119*, 463–475.

Wasserman, D. & Wasserman, C. (2009). *Oxford Textbook of Suicidology and Suicide Prevention: A global perspective*. New York: Oxford University Press.

Wilson, K. G., Stelzer, J., Bergman, J. N., Kral, M. J., Inayatullah, M., & Elliott, C. A. (1995). Problem solving, stress, and coping in adolescent suicide attempts. *Suicide and Life-Threatening Behavior*, *25*, 241–252.

Wu, H. C., Wu, C. K., Liao, J. W., Chang, L. H., & Tang, I. C. (2009). Coping strategies of hospitalized people with psychiatric disabilities in Taiwan. *Psychiatric Quarterly*, *81*, 23–34.

Yoshimasu, K., Kiyohara, C., & Miyashita, K. (2008). Suicidal risk factors and completed suicide: Meta-analyses based on psychological autopsy studies. *Environmental Health and Preventive Medicine*, *13*, 243–256.

CHAPTER THIRTY-SIX

Achievements and Challenges in Suicidology: Conclusions and Future Directions

Rory C. O'Connor, Stephen Platt, and Jacki Gordon

Abstract

The purpose of this chapter is to take stock and reflect on 'where are we now?' in our understanding of suicide and its prevention, and to consider 'where do we need to go next?' To do this, we asked the Handbook contributors to nominate the key achievements of recent years and to outline the key challenges for the future. We then classified these achievements and challenges according to whether they referred to research, policy, or practice. The majority of achievements cited were within the research domain. These included advances in our understanding of the biological, psychological, and social factors implicated in the suicidal process. Although fewer contributors cited policy achievements, the impact of such policies is believed to be extensive. Within the practice domain, there was recurrent focus on evidence-based practice, with the importance of developing and implementing clinical and psychosocial interventions highlighted. Whereas practice elements were largely under-represented as achievements, they were the most commonly reported domain in response to the future challenges question. The difficulties around developing and evaluating interventions were reported frequently. Research challenges included obtaining universal agreement on definitions of suicidality, improving our understanding of typologies of those at risk, and obtaining a clearer understanding of the genetic bases of suicide risk. The sustainability of suicide prevention initiatives was cited as a key policy challenge, together with a range of issues related to international suicide prevention policy and action. By bringing together insights from research, policy, and practice, and

International Handbook of Suicide Prevention: Research, Policy and Practice, First Edition.
Edited by Rory C. O'Connor, Stephen Platt, Jacki Gordon.
© 2011 John Wiley & Sons, Ltd. Published 2011 by John Wiley & Sons, Ltd.

by learning from our challenges as well as achievements, we should be better placed to translate suicidological science and policy into saving lives.

Introduction

The impetus for this Handbook grew out of the 12th European Symposium on Suicide and Suicidal Behaviour (ESSSB12), which provided a platform to share the latest international suicidological research. When compiling this volume we built upon the overarching theme of ESSSB12, 'Working Together to Prevent Suicide: Research, Policy and Practice', with a view to targeting anyone with an interest in understanding the suicidal process, from prevention to postvention and from wide-scale policy to individual crisis intervention. From Part I of this Handbook, it is evident that the antecedents of suicidal behaviour are complex and various, distal as well as proximal. This book brings together this evidence and highlights that suicide prevention efforts need to embrace this complexity. However, in refining our efforts to understand and tackle suicidal behaviours, we need to move beyond reductionist explanations of suicidality, integrating evidence and practice from across disciplines, cultures, and methods.

The purpose of this chapter is to take stock and reflect on 'where are we now?' in our understanding and to consider 'where do we need to go next?' Therefore, in formulating this chapter we thought that it would be fruitful to harness the expertise of those intimately involved in suicide research, policy, and practice. To this end, we asked the Handbook contributors to nominate key achievements of recent years and to outline the key challenges for the future. Specifically, we asked them to identify the following:

- The three most significant achievements in suicidology over the past 25 years or so.
- The three most significant challenges/difficulties that the discipline faces as we move forward into the next 25 years.

We are extremely grateful to our authors' insightful contributions which form the backbone of this chapter and are summarized in Tables 36.1–36.3. For ease of exposition, we have classified the achievements and challenges according to whether they refer (predominantly) to research, policy, or practice. Although research also pervades the policy and practice domains, for present purposes the research domain is characterized as basic scientific research which informs our understanding of the suicidal process. Many of these suggestions (across all domains) could have been classified into more than one of the categories, but we have limited each suggestion to a single category. As we have combined different suggestions into single entries in some cases, we have also interpreted these within a broader context (i.e., we have combined entries according to themes). As a result, we offer a disclaimer. The interpretation of the contributors' achievements and challenges was ours; therefore, the views reported herein reflect our views rather than those of any individual contributor. As noted in the Introduction, suicide attempt and self-harm are often used interchangeably in the literature; in this chapter, when we use the term 'suicide attempt'/'behaviour', we refer to self-injurious behaviour with evidence of suicide intent. 'Self-harm' is used to describe all other self-harming behaviours where suicidal intent is not explicitly ascertained.

Suicidology's Achievements in the Past 25 Years

We begin by summarizing contributors' views regarding key achievements. From a cursory inspection of Table 36.1, it is evident that the majority of those identified are from within the research domain. This is not surprising and reflects the growth in suicidology's research evidence base (and arguably, too, that the contributors to this Handbook are mainly researchers). As a discipline, we have reasonable evidence about suicide risk factors, some limited evidence of the effectiveness of treatments, and scant evidence for the effectiveness of policy-driven suicide prevention strategies. We have made considerable progress towards a consensus on how suicidal behaviour and completed suicide are defined. Historically, suicidology has been bedevilled by confusion and inconsistency over definitions; thanks to the work of O'Carroll, Berman, Maris, Moscicki, Tanney, *et al.* (1996) and Silverman, Berman, Sanddal, O'Carroll, and Joiner (2007a, 2007b), among others, there is greater appreciation of such definitional/operationalization difficulties. Although progress has been made, the task is not complete, however; there is much work still to be done because there is, as yet, no universally agreed definition of suicidal behaviour.

Contributors nominated many advances in suicide research across different domains as significant achievements. These included enhancing our understanding of biological (e.g., serotonergic system), social (e.g., environment), and psychological factors (e.g., personality and cognition) in suicidality. Indeed, we now have considerable insight into what leads to the ineffable psychological pain that precedes a suicide attempt. Our contributors also emphasized the importance of theoretical perspectives and the development and testing of theoretical models. As illustrated in several chapters (e.g., Chapters 8–11), the last 25 years have witnessed a marked growth in the range of idiographic (focusing on the individual) and nomothetic (focusing on groups) models of suicidal behaviour. The challenge now is to continue to test and refine these models, most of which are heuristic rather than descriptive. It is also important that we do not throw out the baby with the bathwater every time we develop a new model: we should build on the successes of existing models, modifying and refining them as appropriate.

Suicidology has also benefited from major technological advances, in particular in the fields of genetics, neuroimaging and neurobiology. For example, we now have a much clearer appreciation of the role of the serotonergic/noradrenergic systems and hypothalamic–pituitary–adrenal axis in suicidal behaviour (see Chapter 8). There is also growing recognition that we need to move beyond the psychiatric models of suicidal behaviour, with an acceptance that suicide is more than a by-product of mental disorder; rather, it is better conceptualized as a phenomenon in its own right.

We also have a much better appreciation of the scale, incidence, and prevalence of self-harm and suicide. There has been a welcome growth in large-scale, international epidemiological research, which allows us to identify more confidently high-risk groups and factors beyond the traditional risk groups/factors. In recent years, we have learned more about the range of high-risk groups and precipitating and protective factors, including some that were previously under-acknowledged.

Several countries have established monitoring systems for hospital-treated self-harm, which not only provide detailed clinical and socio-demographic profiling of those who

Table 36.1 Summary of suicidology's achievements in the past 25 years, nominated by suicidology experts

Research

Move towards a consensus on definitions of suicidal behaviour/completed suicide.

International advances in suicide research across domains (psychological, psychiatric, biological, social, and epidemiological).

Universal acceptance of the interplay of biology, psychology, environment, and cultural influences in the understanding of the phenomenon of suicide.

Discovery that the serotogenergic system plays a fundamental role in impulse/aggression control and suicidal behaviour.

Development of biological suicidology (neurobiology, genetics, neuroimaging).

Development and testing models of suicidal behaviour.

Recognition that current mental disorder is often a necessary, but not sufficient, condition for suicidal behaviour; personality and psychosocial factors play an important role.

Development and validation of controlled, postmortem research methods.

Establishment of common monitoring systems of self-harm across different countries.

Improved insight into extent of 'hidden cases' of suicide and self-harm.

Adoption of Columbia Classification Algorithm of Suicide Assessment (C-CASA) by US Food and Drug Administration.

Large-scale epidemiological research in the general population and among high-risk groups; identification of risk factors.

Increased attention, research, and knowledge in the field of bereavement after suicide.

Policy

International recognition of suicide and suicidal behaviour as major public health problems.

Development of national suicide prevention strategies in many countries across the globe.

Development of suicide prevention efforts in large parts of Asia.

Influence on national and international policy (advocacy).

Increased awareness that there is the potential to prevent suicide.

Policy initiatives to reduce stigma associated with mental ill-health and suicidal behaviour (mainly in Western countries).

Restrictions on access to the means of suicide.

Increased influence of survivors' and survivors' organizations on policy.

Strengthened national and international suicide prevention organizations.

Practice

Implementation of evidence-based, multifaceted, suicide prevention programmes.

Development of new psychosocial treatments for suicidality.

Application of evidence-based approaches to treatment and prevention.

Beginnings of population-level prevention trials.

The role of survivors in suicide prevention efforts.

Destigmatization of mental illness and suicide.

Discovery of the specific anti-suicidal effect of lithium.

Acceptance that suicide is a behaviour *sui generis*, not simply a 'by-product' or symptom of mental disorder.

Development and validation of some psychosocial treatments.

Development of crisis helplines.

self-harm, but which, in the fullness of time, will further advance our understanding of those factors which predict repeat self-harm and completed suicide. Community-based studies (e.g., Child and Adolescent Self-harm in Europe, CASE; Hawton, Rodham, & Evans, 2006), combined with increased destigmatization of mental health problems, have also contributed to our awareness of the extent of 'hidden' cases of suicide and self-harm (O'Connor, Rasmussen, Miles, & Hawton, 2009). Indeed, it is now well recognized that, for example, the actual scale of adolescent self-harm is much greater than originally assumed when estimates of prevalence were extrapolated from hospital-treated self-harm studies. Suicidology has also expanded beyond the phenomenology of suicide and self-harm to include bereavement following suicide and postvention more generally (see Chapter 32). Indeed, survivors of suicide make up large constituencies of all the major international suicide prevention organizations and their contribution to understanding the suicidal process is invaluable.

Although fewer contributors cited policy achievements in comparison with research achievements, the impact of such policies is believed to be extensive. The most commonly reported policy achievement was the widespread recognition of suicide as a major public health problems which in turn has led to national suicide prevention strategies being developed in many countries throughout the world. More generally, national governments, often working in partnership with third sector organizations, have recognized not only the need to reduce the overall prevalence of mental health problems/conditions but also to destigmatize mental health more broadly. It is also noteworthy that suicide prevention efforts have extended beyond Western countries, and are now developing in large parts of Asia and elsewhere. Arguably, policy initiatives which have restricted access to suicide means with high lethality have been among the most important policy achievements to date. For example, the detoxification of domestic gas in the United Kingdom led to a marked decline in the suicide rates in the 1960s (Kreitman, 1976) and, more recently, the introduction of legislation (in 1998) limiting the pack sizes of analgesics sold over the counter has been associated with a reduction in suicide deaths from paracetamol and salicylates in the year following the change in legislation (Hawton, Simkin, Deeks, Cooper, Johnston, *et al.*, 2004). The restriction of access to lethal means of suicide is cited as one of two types of prevention activities (the other being physician education in the recognition and treatment of suicide) for which there is extensive and convincing evidence of effectiveness in reducing suicide (Mann, Apter, Bertolote, Beautrais, Currier, *et al.*, 2005) thereby pointing to the importance of their inclusion in national strategies.

In respect of identified practice achievements, there is some overlap with the research and policy domains. This is to be expected as research should inform both policy and practice. A recurrent theme of the practice achievements was the emphasis on *evidence-based* practice. Time and again, our experts highlighted the importance of developing and implementing clinical and psychosocial interventions which are evidence-based (see also Challenges sections below). Such interventions tend to be targeted at clinical or sub-clinical populations which are at elevated risk of suicide. Another range of promising interventions have been developed in response to the now well-accepted evidence for the Werther effect, including guidelines for journalists and editors on responsible reporting. Furthermore, the importance of involving those working in the media industry in the process of developing these guidelines testifies to the importance of bringing together researchers with those who understand and/or actually work in the field.

Another achievement is the growth in crisis helplines which receive calls from those who are distressed or suicidal. A key advantage of such initiatives is ease of access: a vulnerable caller can speak to someone who will listen and, in some cases, signpost or refer the caller to appropriate services. Although the availability of such services is welcome, it is unclear how effective they are in terms of preventing suicide; and, if effective, by what mechanism they protect against suicide and self-harm (see Chapter 25 for a discussion). This is not a criticism of helplines; rather, it highlights the difficulties inherent in evaluating such interventions. In summary, as a discipline we have moved forward in terms of developing a range of interventions in recent decades, but we have yet to determine the extent to which they are efficacious, effective, and generalizable across different populations and contexts (see Challenges sections below).

At the general population level, there have been some tentative efforts at trialling population-based prevention programmes (e.g., European Alliance Against Depression (EAAD); Optimizing suicide prevention programs and their implementation in Europe (OSPI Europe); Hegerl, Althaus, Schmidtke, & Niklewski, 2006; Hegerl, Wittenburg, Arensman, van Audenhove, Coyne, *et al.*, 2009), but much more work is required to determine their effectiveness (including the factors that shape this) and their longer-term sustainability.

There have also been considerable advances in the pharmacological treatment of depression using antidepressants (see Chapters 3 and 26). Although the effectiveness of psychopharmacology across different populations in suicide prevention specifically is unclear, there is growing evidence that lithium may reduce suicide risk, in particular among patients with bipolar disorder, though the mechanism of effect is not clearly understood (Saunders & Hawton, 2009; Tondo & Baldessarini, 2009). Another major achievement, as noted above, is the recognition that suicidal behaviour is not simply a by-product or symptom of mental disorder. This has likely contributed to a change in Western society's attitude to suicide and self-harm, as well as how it is treated clinically.

Suicidology's Challenges in the Forthcoming 25 Years

Practice challenges

Table 36.2 illustrates the range of challenges in implementing evidence-based practice in suicidology, as perceived by our experts. Whereas practice elements were largely under-represented as achievements, they were the most commonly reported domain in response to the question about future challenges. Again, this is consistent with the state of the science; at a macro-level, the overarching challenge facing suicidology is how best to translate suicidological science and policy into saving lives. This is a recurrent theme in the practice domain, which is succinctly summarized by the first entry in Table 36.2: 'Improve knowledge of what works and what does not work in suicide prevention'. We need to move beyond describing the phenomena of suicide and self-harm to translating our knowledge into action. This is consistent with the philosophy of science approach outlined in Chapter 34, which posits that suicidology has disproportionately focused on *explaining* suicide rather than *understanding* it. We need to better understand the particular

Table 36.2 Summary of suicidology's practice challenges in the forthcoming 25 years, nominated by suicidology experts

Improve knowledge of what works and what does not work in suicide prevention.

Standardize suicide risk assessment protocol.

Improve prediction of suicide risk: who will engage in suicidal behaviour and when?

Develop evidence-based practices for treating those at risk.

Translate knowledge of predispositional characteristics of suicide risk into effective treatment and prevention.

Improve awareness of how best to evaluate effects of therapy for suicidal people.

Demonstrate the efficacy, effectiveness, and cost-effectiveness of interventions.

Ensure the implementation of effective interventions.

Develop intervention strategies that will increase the likelihood that suicidal individuals will adhere to treatment programmes.

Improve help for suicidal people who will not seek treatment in conventional sense.

Implement uniform procedures for the aftercare of self-harm patients nationally and internationally.

Improve continuity of care for self-harm and suicidal patients.

Develop more and innovative brief interventions which can be delivered in emergency departments.

Match different treatments to different types of suicidal people (better differentiation between different kinds of patients).

Develop more accurate and therapeutically useful models of suicide.

Improve understanding of the relationship between psychotropic and non-psychotropic medications to suicidal behaviour.

Develop medication (other than lithium) that clearly and convincingly reduces the risk of suicide.

Distinguish between suicidal iatrogenic effects of medication treatments from events associated with illness, life stress, and tailor medication regimens accordingly.

Enhance the relationship between predominantly voluntary work conducted on helplines (and by third sector organizations, more generally) with 'professional' treatments.

---

circumstances associated with better outcomes (to look inside the black box as it were). Things seldom work or do not work but work better under some circumstances, and so a more fruitful approach is understanding what works for whom and under what circumstances (Pawson & Tilley, 1997).

Many contributors cited the standardization and utility of suicide risk assessment protocols (and variants thereof) as a major challenge. Within the practice domain, this is, perhaps, one of the fundamental issues. Is it possible to reliably assess risk of suicide or suicidal behaviour with an acceptable degree of sensitivity (i.e., correct identification of those who will subsequently engage in suicidal behaviour) and specificity (i.e., correct identification of those who will not go on to engage in suicidal behaviour)? The short answer is 'no'. Indeed, it is well recognized that the prediction of future suicidal behaviour is notoriously difficult, limited by the low specificity of the established risk factors (e.g., NHS Centre for Reviews and Dissemination, 1998; US Preventive Services Task Force, 2004). Consider, for example, the recommendation by the UK's National Institute for Clinical and Health Excellence (NICE, 2004):

> All people who have self-harmed should be assessed for risk; this assessment should include identification of the main clinical and demographic features known to be associated with risk of further self-harm and/or suicide, and identification of the key psychological characteristics associated with risk, in particular depression, hopelessness and continuing suicidal intent.

Although it is good clinical practice to conduct a comprehensive risk and/or psychosocial assessment following a self-harm episode, there is not yet sufficient evidence that such risk assessments are sensitive/specific to the prediction of repeat self-harm and suicide. Part of the complexity, historically, relates to the lack of a standard protocol, together with the fact that, although those who have attempted suicide are indeed at heightened risk of further suicidal behaviours, most do not repeat self-harm or die by suicide in the future. Nonetheless, in recent years there have been a number of noteworthy attempts to address this dearth of evidence in the literature (e.g., Cooper, Kapur, Dunning, Guthrie, Appleby, et al., 2006). Cooper et al. (2006) developed a risk-stratification model for use in accident and emergency departments which prioritizes sensitivity over specificity. Their aim was to identify those who were at low risk of attempting suicide in the six months following an index self-harm episode. Although their model, the Manchester Self-Harm rule (MASH; no history of self-harm, no history of psychiatric treatment, did not use benzodiazepines in current attempt), identified all 22 suicide deaths and 94% of those who self-harmed again within six months, specificity was low (approximately 26%). While in this case, focusing on high sensitivity rather than specificity is reasonable as it is in an acute setting, this study highlights a major difficulty in suicidology: the low positive predictive value of screening tools. Indeed, the scale of the 'prediction' challenge can be summarized as follows: not only do we, as suicidologists, have to predict *who* will attempt suicide, but we also have to predict *when* someone will attempt suicide. At present, this is a challenge we have yet to overcome.

In respect of prediction, the benefits of national linkage databases and cohort studies, which link psychosocial and clinical history with attempted and completed suicide, are enormous. They allow us to quantify the relative risk of suicide/attempted suicide associated with particular risk and protective factors. However, a future challenge is to determine which study design is most beneficial in such studies: there are advantages and disadvantages of employing case-control studies, nested case-control studies, panel studies, suicide registers, and so on. Although there are several countries (e.g., Denmark) where such studies are commonplace, a key challenge in our pursuit of better prediction will be to extend these methods internationally.

Suicidology brings with it unique challenges. To know what works we need to gather reliable and valid evidence that delivering intervention X brings about change Y (and the circumstances under which such outcomes are effected). Deciding on X should be reasonably straightforward, as it should be derived from the growing research evidence. This basic suicidological science should highlight candidate interventions which are likely to be effective and for whom. However, agreeing on Y, an appropriate outcome measure, is somewhat more problematic. As we are interested in the prevention of suicide, we should examine the change in the rates of suicide following the delivery of any given intervention. Yet, as suicide is a statistically rare event (combined with the usually relatively small estimated effect size for any given intervention), the sample sizes required to reliably investigate the efficacy or effectiveness of any intervention are usually prohibitive, with the result that it is difficult to conclude whether or not an intervention has saved lives. For this reason, we usually employ proxy outcome measures relating to behaviour which occurs more frequently (e.g., suicide attempts) or which can be operationalized in terms of clinically significant change scores before and after an intervention (e.g., suicidal ideation, suicidal intent or hopelessness). The disadvantage of employing proxy measures is that the generalizability of the findings is potentially circumscribed to outcomes which do not include suicide itself. Nonetheless, given that suicidal ideation and behaviour are key predictors of completed suicide, such findings are invaluable components of the suicide prevention evidence base. The use of samples of patients who have engaged in 'serious' self-harm resulting in hospital admission has been proposed as a promising approach to overcoming (some of) the limitations arising from the absence of an agential perspective in psychological autopsy studies.

More generally, we need to think of much more innovative ways of evaluating interventions in order that we develop a more sophisticated understanding of not only what works, but also why and how. Moving beyond studies of efficacy and clinical effectiveness, the cost-effectiveness of any given intervention should also be considered as an important outcome measure in order that we can better understand whether (and how and for whom) it is feasible to implement these. The value of cost-effectiveness analyses is highlighted in the POPMACT trial with self-harm patients: the clinical outcomes between the treatment and control arms were non-significant, but there was some evidence that the intervention may be more cost-effective than treatment as usual (Byford, Knapp, Greenshields, Ukoumune, Jones, *et al.*, 2003).

Issues concerning interventions were cited many times by our contributors. These issues are not unique to suicidology; rather, they represent generic challenges in the development and evaluation of complex interventions (see Chapter 25 for discussion). For the present purposes these challenges are broadly defined as encompassing the following domains: (1) development; (2) implementation; (3) evaluation; (4) adherence; and (5) consistency and quality of aftercare. In respect of development, there is a considerable onus on the research and clinical communities to translate the increasing knowledge of the suicidal process (i.e., the complex interplay between biology, psychology, social and cultural factors) into more effective psychosocial and pharmacological interventions. As noted above, this is not without its difficulties, and there are no shortcuts: it will take time to determine how best to translate knowledge into practice. Not only do clinical or psychosocial interventions have to be efficacious, but they also have to be pragmatic, effective, and, crucially, implementable. This latter point is included to highlight the centrality of political and policy drivers. Over the past 50 years, suicidologists and others have raised the profile of suicide prevention. We need to maintain, if not increase, the momentum to ensure that policy planners provide the resources to implement these evidence-based interventions. A pivotal part of the implementation process is evaluation; as highlighted earlier, it is imperative that we refocus our emphasis on effectiveness. Although it is important to demonstrate the efficacy of an intervention, the litmus test of the intervention is whether it is life-saving and can be rolled out within the healthcare system for which it was designed.

Any good evaluation should also include consideration of the extent to which the target population engages with the intervention (e.g., does the nature of the intervention engage with those it intends to reach in sufficient number, in particular, does it reach those who are most likely to benefit from it?). This is particularly challenging in the present context, as suicidal patients are often difficult to engage/maintain in treatment. Consequently, we need to understand which factors engender engagement and develop strategies which increase adherence to treatment/intervention programmes. In addition, we should recognize that some suicidal people will not seek treatment in the conventional sense but we can still help them. Finally, we need to enhance the quality and consistency of aftercare of those patients who present to hospital following an episode of self-harm. The issue of aftercare is addressed in a number of chapters in this Handbook. For example, Hawton and colleagues (Chapter 19) define the essential ingredients of appropriate and effective services and the clinical management of self-harm patients (including recommendations on treatment and staff training). Moreover, they also reinforce the notion that the aftercare of self-harm patients should be a key component of national suicide prevention strategies (see also Chapter 20). The longer-term management of self-harm is also being considered by the UK National Institute for Health and Clinical Excellence, with the publication of clinical guidelines scheduled for late 2011 (http://guidance.nice.org.uk/CG/WaveR/82).

There is also growing recognition that there is not a 'one size fits all' treatment intervention for suicidal individuals/preventing suicide. This raises a major challenge, not only in implementation terms, but also in establishing the effectiveness evidence base, as it is very difficult to evaluate an intervention in which we match different treatments to different types of suicidal people. This is not an insurmountable problem, however. For example, there is evidence from recent postcard (e.g., Carter, Clover, Whyte, Dawson, & D'Este, 2005) and social network (King, Kramer, Preuss, Kerr, Weisse, & Wenkataraman, 2006) interventions that the effectiveness of interventions is often population- and context-specific (see Chapter 25). The reality that one size does not fit all is further highlighted by another recent postcard intervention study in New Zealand, which yielded no evidence of an effect on repeat self-harm of administering six postcards during the 12 months following hospital-treated self-harm (Beautrais, Gibb, Faulkner, Fergusson, & Mulder, 2010). We need to build an evidence base that explicates the factors associated with success/effectiveness. Only through understanding such factors can we translate the evidence base into effective practice.

Whereas model development within suicidology has generated countless research questions and hypotheses in the recent past, extending this knowledge and expertise to the development of therapeutically useful models of suicide is especially welcome. Work to this end is underway (for examples, see Part II of this Handbook). Jobes' Collaborative Assessment and Management of Suicidality (CAMS) is a new evidence-based therapeutic framework which is using such models to guide clinical management (Chapter 22). Williams and colleagues' use of mindfulness to address suicidality is another novel therapeutic approach (Chapter 23). In addition, Chapter 24 reviews the role of the therapist in the treatment of the suicidal patient.

The role of medication in suicide prevention was also highlighted by our contributors. This is unsurprising since untreated depression is probably the most important clinical predictor of completed suicide (together with a previous suicide attempt). Although the development and judicious use of antidepressants in the treatment of depression is well established, there are several challenges relating to suicide prevention. First, apart from lithium and the growing evidence for clozapine, other medicines which clearly and convincingly reduce the risk of suicide need to be developed. In addition, the relationship between psychotropic and non-psychotropic medication and how this interplay relates to suicidal behaviour needs to be more clearly established. Another major challenge to those involved in the treatment of suicidal patients is to develop a more sophisticated appreciation of the potential risks versus benefits of selective serotonin re-uptake inhibitors (SSRIs). This is a particularly timely challenge in the light of the recent debate about the suggested iatrogenic effects of SSRIs when administered to young people, balanced against the evidence that they provide protection from suicidality with increasing age (see Chapter 26). Indeed, when considering emergent suicidality following an intervention (psychosocial or pharmacological), it is important to distinguish the suicidal iatrogenic effects from events associated with illness and life events more generally. In addition, pharmacogenetics and pharmacogenomics should improve psychiatry's ability to predict antidepressant drug responses and also lead to the development of personalized medical treatments (Moller & Rujescu, 2010).

The final practice suggestion highlighted the need to enhance the relationship between the (largely) voluntary work conducted on mental health/suicide prevention helplines with 'professional' treatments. This emphasizes a broader challenge: how can we engender/ strengthen links between statutory and voluntary organizations to ensure and sustain collaborative gain? Key issues here include ensuring that there are clear signposting and referral pathways and that the unique and invaluable role of the third sector is not lost. Moreover, it would be fruitful to further develop the role of the third sector as a strong voice for the service user and survivor.

Research challenges

Some of the achievements cited earlier in this chapter also feature within the challenges sections (see Table 36.3). The first entry, standardization of a nomenclature/classification system for suicidology, was noted earlier, and its entry under achievements reflects the distance we have moved forward in appreciating the complexities and nuances of operationalization. Nevertheless, we have yet to agree an international classification system. A major challenge will be not only to agree a universal nomenclature but also to ensure that it is implemented and that the agreed terminology enters everyday (as well as professional) discourse. It is 50 years since suicide was decriminalized in the United Kingdom (1961) but '*to commit* suicide' is still in common parlance, repeatedly appearing in the mainstream national media outlets despite being contrary to editorial and journalistic guidance (e.g., British Broadcasting Corporation editorial guidelines, 2010). Indeed, we took a decision to avoid the use of the term 'commit' suicide in this Handbook.

Given that a past history of self-harm/suicide attempt is the best predictor of completed suicide, but most people who self-harm/attempt suicide do not take their own lives, a more comprehensive understanding of the relationship between all types of self-harm/ attempted suicide and suicide should be prioritized. Such an understanding may help us further identify sub-types of those who are at more risk of repeat self-harm/suicide attempts and completed suicide. A concerted focus on linking self-harm/suicide attempt data with suicide mortality statistics at a national level would help to answer the self-harm/suicide attempt–completed suicide relationship question. It would also go some way to addressing

Table 36.3   Summary of suicidology's research and policy challenges in the forthcoming 25 years, nominated by suicidology experts

---

Research

Standardize nomenclature/classification system for suicidology.

Link self-harm data to suicide mortality data at a national level.

Develop innovative study designs which take account of the low base rate of suicide (which makes prospective studies of proximal risk very difficult).

Foster cross-disciplinary and cross-national research.

Advance biological suicidology, including genetics.

Advance genetics, neurobiology, and neuroimaging to understand the 'suicidal brain' both during and outside suicidal states.

Develop and refine endophenotypes and consider that there may not be one single neurobiology of suicide. Integrate this refinement with gene x environment interactions.

Elucidate the role of epigenetic phenomena in suicide and self-harm.

Establish typologies of different types of suicidal people.

Improve understanding of suicide in low and middle income countries and other cultures.

Reach consensus on ethical dilemmas in conducting basic and applied suicide prevention research.

Challenge the trend towards greater reductionism in suicidology research.

Employ a broader range of methods to generate new knowledge.

Policy

Achieve a significant reduction in suicide across the world.

Mobilize political influence such that governments prioritize suicide prevention.

Achieve sustainability of effective evidence-based suicide prevention programmes.

Integrate suicide prevention policy across other risk domains (substance use, social care, financial strain, deprivation, abuse, etc.).

Develop a 'gold standard(s)' for the evaluation of suicide prevention strategies/programmes.

Develop policy and action to prevent suicide in the developing world.

Implement policy initiatives to reduce pesticide deaths worldwide.

Obtain up-to-date regional and national suicide statistics in a timely fashion.

Fund suicide research throughout the world.

---

the issue of low base rates (as sample sizes would inevitably be larger at a national level) and help to identify any socio-demographic differences across and within countries. In addition, a better understanding of suicide risk and protective factors would follow from more cross-national and cross-disciplinary working. As noted throughout this Handbook (see also Introduction), suicide prevention will succeed only through mutual learning across disciplines and countries.

Advancing biological and genetic suicidology emerged as a key challenge for the next 25 years. This has four, albeit related, entries under research. Beyond the general statement of improving and refining the methods and techniques specific to biological and genetic suicidology, it is important to understand the defining characteristics of the suicidal mind both during and outside of suicidal states. Indeed, from the clinical and neuropsychological literature, we know that a suicidal patient who has recovered is often difficult to distinguish from someone who has never been suicidal. Consequently, it would be clinically and theoretically useful to explore, via neurobiology and neuroimaging, the nature or extent to which suicidality changes brain architecture, chemistry or circuitry and whether this is evident in someone who has recovered but who remains vulnerable. New technologies, including those to examine gene expression differences, single nucleotide polymorphism, and DNA methylation arrays, should help elucidate the genetic and epigenetic mechanisms (Fiori & Turecki, 2010). Advances in neuroimaging could also provide more evidence in support of theoretical models of suicidality, for example, the differential activation model and the integrated motivational–volitional model of suicidal behaviour (see Chapters 11 and 23).

Further development and refinement of endophenotyping is another future challenge. We need to gather clearer evidence of the relationship between behavioural symptoms of suicide and their genetic bases. There is growing evidence that disadvantageous decision-making may be a potential endophenotype for suicidal vulnerability (Courtet, Guillaume, Malafosse, & Jollant, 2010). The refinement of the endophenotype is further complicated by the growing acceptance that the aetiology and course of suicide risk are determined, in part, by gene x environment interactions. We need a more detailed understanding of those environmental/social stressors which are especially suicidogenic (and why), as well as a closer appreciation of the critical times in a person's life when the experience of such stressors is particularly pathogenic (and why). Another challenge is to illuminate the role of epigenetic phenomena in suicide and self-harm.

Although we have reasonable evidence about many of the major risk factors for suicide (e.g., depression, childhood adversity), as described in the practice section, we need to establish better typologies of different types of suicidal people who engage in suicidal behaviour. We also need to better understand protective factors, as these too inform strategies/practices to reduce suicide. These are not new suggestions; indeed, there have been many attempts to identify more fine-grained profiles of those who attempt suicide (Arensman & Kerkhof, 1996; O'Connor, Sheehy, & O'Connor, 1999 for reviews). The inherent difficulty is that we need to move beyond *descriptive* profiles to developing profiles which have predictive and discriminant validity. Related to the issue of typologies is our habitual application of Western models to understanding suicide in different cultures, including low/middle income countries, without giving due consideration to the characteristics of these different socio-cultural and socio-economic contexts. Although it is important to determine the extent to which Western models are useful across cultures, greater recognition of cultural and economic differences is long overdue. As an example, psychological autopsy studies suggest that the rate of mood disorders among those who have died by suicide is markedly lower in India (e.g., Vijayakumar & Rajkumar, 1999) and China (e.g., Phillips, Yang, Zhang, Wang, Ji, *et al.*, 2002) than it is in Western countries (e.g., Foster, Gillespie, & McClelland, 1997). Consequently, policy and practice should reflect these different profiles and greater recognition of these differences should stimulate more research to improve understanding of the suicidal process in non-Western countries, and importantly, the implications for suicide prevention activities.

The final three research challenges are methodological in nature. The first relates to the ethical dilemmas of working in this field, of which there are many. To this end, a recent study which solicited views of ethics committee members on the risks, benefits, and ethical problems in suicide research is helpful (Lakeman & Fitzgerald, 2009). This study identified several key ethical issues, including: justification for research; access to the population; potential harm to participants; potential harm to the researcher; participant competency and consent; researcher competency; responsibilities of the researcher to participants; maintaining confidentiality; and dealing with families. It is clear from this study and elsewhere (e.g., Mishara & Weisstub, 2005) that there are differing views on the ethics of suicide research and that there is no international consensus; rather, decisions about what is ethically acceptable can vary as a function of the ethics committee members' moral views on suicide and their toleration of risk. To this end, a major pragmatic challenge for the future is how to balance the potential risk that a suicidal participant may take their own life during a study with the potential advance in knowledge and/or practice. Needless to say, all research ought to be conducted in an ethically sound manner.

The second challenge asks whether, as a discipline, we have become too reductionistic in our pursuit of identifying the genes, the brain chemistry, the traits, and the cognitions associated with suicide risk. Every tragic death is the end-product of a complex interplay between biology, psychology, and social, economic, and cultural factors; the privileging of one set of determinants over another is unhelpful, both theoretically and in terms of learning lessons for implementation. A related third challenge is the need to recognize the value of the widest possible range of research methods to generate new knowledge. The use of qualitative and mixed/multiple methods has increased in recent years, but the frequency of published quantitative studies swamps qualitative studies. However, it is important to note that the future of research in suicidology should not be dictated by the qualitative versus quantitative debate; rather, it should be driven by the research question. The use of mixed/multiple methods is likely to become standard practice in the future, allowing us not only to quantify the prevalence of suicidal behaviours but also to understand their phenomenology. We should not only employ new methods and novel combinations of methods (as appropriate), but we should also look to other disciplines for new insights and perspectives.

Policy challenges

The title of this volume is the *International Handbook of Suicide **Prevention***, and suicide *prevention* is both an appropriate and achievable goal of public policy. (The *elimination* of suicide, on the other hand, should be recognized as an impossible goal.) However, this leads to the obvious question: what is a feasible reduction in the suicide rate for any given country? As such, what might be considered achievable will be constrained or dictated to some extent at least by a number of factors. These include: what's known (both about the patterning of suicides in a given country and about effective interventions); available resources (financial and otherwise, including the infrastructure to support suicide prevention endeavours); decisions to invest in interventions to address proximal versus distal factors (the effects of which may not be evident for many years); and timescales.

In most countries where a reduction in the suicide rate is specified as a policy target, it is as part of a national suicide prevention strategy and the setting of that target has emerged from a mixture of political and policy drivers which have been informed by expert opinion. The setting of targets has advantages and disadvantages. On the one hand, a target can serve to mobilize political influence such that governments prioritize suicide prevention. On the other hand, targets can be demotivating: failure to meet them may be interpreted as failure of the strategy, with negative implications for resources/funding. Questions under active consideration within policy communities include: should there be more proximal targets, such as rates of hospital-treated self-harm? How reliable are the data on which targets are judged? How can national targets take into account the impact of national or international events on the achievement of suicide prevention targets? The recent international recession, characterized by economic turbulence and increased unemployment, is a good example of how international events can potentially impact on national suicide rates (see Gunnell, Platt, & Hawton, 2009).

The sustainability of suicide prevention programmes is also a major challenge. Although each country employs different implementation models, many countries (e.g., Scotland) provide substantial, pump-primed funding for a specified period of time, with the intention that, over time, the suicide prevention activities become mainstreamed, that is, funded through other sources. As we are in the midst of a period of financial and economic austerity across the globe, the pressure on suicide prevention budgets is likely to grow more acute. Consequently, a major challenge will be to think of sustainable means of delivering effective, evidence-based suicide prevention programmes that, for example, can be mainstreamed within existing services and which are not exclusively reliant upon government support. An unexpected by-product of economic austerity, however, may be a renewed drive to integrate suicide prevention policy with policies in other risk domains (e.g., the substance use and social care sectors). On balance, this integration should be a positive development, but it gives rise to a new challenge: namely, ensuring that the focus on suicide prevention is not diluted to an unacceptable degree. Another related issue is concerned with the evaluation of suicide prevention programmes. In terms of those public health interventions which are known to be effective in saving lives, we have a limited evidence base from which to select in the first instance, and it is likely that evaluation budgets will be further constricted. This may yield short-term savings, but incur longer-term costs (including in terms of lives lost), since it will not be possible to differentiate between effective and ineffective interventions.

As noted above, suicide is becoming a major public health concern in developing countries where, despite growing awareness of the scale of the problem, more needs to be done to develop suicide prevention policy and action. In particular, international policy initiatives should target deaths by pesticides, specifically in Asia, where this method accounts for 60% of suicides in China (Phillips *et al.*, 2002) and 71% in Sri Lanka (Somasundaram & Rajadurai, 1995). Possible approaches to restricting access to means (e.g., via promoting safer storage of pesticides) may represent one initiative to reduce death by pesticide (Hawton, Ratnayeke, Simkin, Hariss, & Scott, 2009). There is a more detailed discussion of such prevention strategies and ways forward in Chapters 27, 28, and 31.

The final two challenges are research-oriented, but have been included in the policy domain because they will not be achieved without the support and drive of policy planners. The provision of reliable and up-to-date national and regional statistics should be straightforward for most countries. Nonetheless, in some countries there is a lag of at least 12–24 months (often more) before the publication of national suicide rates. In cases where suicide rates rise unexpectedly, such publication lags will impinge on a country's ability to respond effectively and in a timely fashion to changes in the scale or nature of the challenge. We urge governmental or other national agencies to publish up-to-date statistics promptly, as accurate prevalence data are essential to the effective monitoring and prevention of suicide. Needless to say, in countries/regions where suicides are relatively small in number, modest fluctuations need to be interpreted with care; hence, the convention in some countries to use rolling averages across years to investigate trends. Finally, it is increasingly difficult to obtain funding for large-scale research into suicide prevention. Suicidologists face a major challenge to provide compelling evidence to convince government, research councils, and other funding agencies to prioritize suicide prevention research. Indeed, as well as drawing on the best available evidence, targeted programmes of research should be integral to all national suicide prevention strategies. If the discipline is to prosper in the next 25 years, better quality and larger-scale basic and applied suicidological science and practice needs to be funded. To achieve this goal, as a discipline we need to consider new partnerships, new methods of funding, and appropriate research designs and protocols which will maximize our learning, knowledge, and understanding.

Conclusions

One thing is clear: suicide is a complex phenomenon. The fact that suicidology is based on insights from many sources, and, indeed, different perspectives, is therefore an undoubted strength. This Handbook has pulled together these insights and provides something of a kaleidoscope as we view suicide through different prisms. Suicide is not just a phenomenon: it is a tragic and human issue, one that is at last achieving some recognition internationally as an important public health issue too. In response, policy planners and practitioners are likely to turn to suicidology and suicidologists for help, including answers to the questions 'what do we know about suicide?' and 'how can we reduce the numbers of people attempting or completing suicide?' The answers to these questions are unlikely to come from one source, nor should they.

As we have seen from this Handbook, suicidology although developing, currently provides a fragmented picture. This points to a need for ongoing dialogue and genuine collaboration to 'join up' the best available research evidence with intelligence about what works (or is likely to work) in given circumstances and for whom. Ultimately, however, suicide prevention may best be considered an art as well as a science. By bringing together insights from research, policy, and practice, we hope that this book takes us one step further in the science and art of the possible.

References

Arensman, E. & Kerkhof, A. J. (1996). Classification of attempted suicide: A review of empirical studies 1963–1993. *Suicide and Life-Threatening Behavior, 26*, 46–67.

BBC Editorial Guidelines (2010). Available at http://www.bbc.co.uk/guidelines/editorialguidelines/page/guidelines-harm-suicide/, accessed 12 July 2010.

Beautrais, A. L., Gibb, S. J., Faulkner, A., Fergusson, D., & Mulder, R. T. (2010). Postcard intervention for repeat self-harm: randomized controlled trial. *British Journal of Psychiatry, 197*, 55–60.

Byford, S., Knapp, M., Greenshields, J., Ukoumunne, O. C., Jones, V., Thompson, S., Tyrer, P., Schmidt, U., & Davidson, K. (2003). Cost-effectiveness of brief cognitive behaviour therapy versus treatment as usual in recurrent deliberate self-harm: A decision-making approach. *Psychological Medicine, 33*, 977–986.

Carter, G. L., Clover, K., Whyte, I. M., Dawson, A. H., & D'Este, C. (2005). Postcards from the Edge: randomized controlled trial of an intervention using postcards to reduce repetition of hospital treated deliberate self-poisoning. *British Medical Journal, 331*, 805–807.

Cooper, J., Kapur, N., Dunning, J., Guthrie, E., Appleby, L., & Mackway-Jones, K. (2006). A clinical tool for assessing risk after self-harm. *Annals of Emergency Medicine, 48*, 459–466.

Courtet, P., Guillaume, S., Malafosse, A., & Jollant, F. (2010). Genes, suicide and decisions. *European Psychiatry, 25*, 294–296.

Fiori, L. M. & Turecki, G. (2010). Gene expression profiling of suicide completers. *European Psychiatry, 25*, 287–290.

Foster, T., Gillespie, K., & McClelland, R. (1997). Mental disorders and suicide in Northern Ireland. *British Journal of Psychiatry, 170*, 447–452.

Gunnell, D., Platt, S., & Hawton, K. (2009). The economic crisis and suicide. *British Medical Journal*, 2009; 338:b1891.

Hawton, K., Ratnayeke, L., Simkin, S., Hariss, L., & Scott, V. (2009). Evaluation of acceptability and use of lockable storage devices for pesticides in Sri Lanka that might assist in prevention of self-poisoning. *BMC Public Health, 9*, 69.

Hawton, K., Rodham, K., & Evans, E. (2006). *By Their Own Hand. Deliberate self-harm and suicidal ideas in adolescents*. London: Jessica Kingsley.

Hawton, K., Simkin, S., Deeks, J., Cooper, J., Johnston, A., Waters, K., Arundel, M., Bernal, W., Gunson, B., Hudson, M., Suri, D., & Simpson, K. (2004). UK legislation on analgesic packs: Before and after study of long-term effect on poisonings. *British Medical Journal*, doi:10.1136/bmj.38253.572581.7c.

Hegerl, U., Althaus, D., Schmidtke, A., & Niklewski, G. (2006). The alliance against depression: 2-year evaluation of a community-based intervention to reduce suicidality. *Psychological Medicine, 36*, 1225–1233.

Hegerl, U., Wittenburg, L., Arensman, E., van Audenhove, C., Coyne, J. C., McDaid, D., van der Feltz-Cornelis, C. M., Gusmão, R., Kopp, M., Maxwell, M., Meise, U., Roskar, S., Sarchiapone, M., Schmidtke, A., Värnik, A., & Bramesfeld, A. (2009). Optimizing suicide prevention programs and their implementation in Europe (OSPI Europe): An evidence-based multi-level approach. *BMC Public Health, 9*, 428.

King, C. A., Kramer, A., Preuss, L., Kerr, D. C. R., Weisse, L., & Wenkataraman, S. (2006). Youth-nominated support team for suicidal adolescents (Version 1): A randomized controlled trial. *Journal of Consulting and Clinical Psychology, 74*, 199–206.

Kreitman N. (1976). The coal gas story. United Kingdom suicide rates, 1960–71. *British Journal of Preventive and Social Medicine, 30*, 86–93.

Lakeman, R. & Fitzgerald, M. (2009). The ethics of suicide research. The view of ethics committee members. *Crisis, 30*, 13–19.

Mann, J. J., Apter, A., Bertolote, J., *et al.* (2005). Suicide prevention strategies: A systematic review. *Journal of the American Medical Association, 294*, 2064–2074.

Mishara, B. L. & Weisstub, D. N. (2005). Ethical and legal issues in suicide research. *International Journal of Law and Psychiatry, 28*, 23–41.

Moller, H. J. & Rujescu, D. (2010). Pharmacogenetics – Genomics and personalised psychiatry. *European Psychiatry, 25*, 291–293.

National Institute for Health and Clinical Excellence (2004). *Self-harm: The short-term physical and psychological management and secondary prevention of self-harm in primary and secondary care.* Clinical Guideline CG16. London: British Psychological Society and Royal College of Psychiatrists.

NHS Centre for Reviews and Dissemination. Deliberate self-harm. (1998). *Effective Health Care Bulletins, v*, 1–12.

O'Carroll, P. W., Berman, A. L., Maris, R., Moscicki, E., Tanney, B., & Silverman, M. (1996). Beyond the Tower of Babel: A nomenclature for suicidology. *Suicide and Life-Threatening Behavior, 26*, 237–252.

O'Connor, R. C., Rasmussen, S., Miles, J., & Hawton, K. (2009). Self-harm in adolescents: Self-report survey in schools in Scotland. *British Journal of Psychiatry, 194*, 68–72.

O'Connor, R. C., Sheehy, N. P., & O'Connor, D. B. (1999). The classification of completed suicide into subtypes. *Journal of Mental Health, 8*, 629–637.

Pawson, R. & Tilley, N. (1997). *Realistic Evaluation.* London: Sage.

Phillips, M. R., Yang, G., Zhang, Y., Wang, L., Ji, H., & Zhou, M. (2002). Risk factors for suicide in China: A national case-control psychological autopsy study. *The Lancet, 360*, 1728–1736.

Saunders, K. & Hawton, K. (2009). The role of psychopharmacology in suicide prevention. *Epidemiologia e Psichiatrica Sociale, 18*, 172–178.

Silverman, M. M., Berman, A. L., Sanddal, N. D., O'Carroll, P. W., & Joiner, T. E. (2007a). Rebuilding the Tower of Babel: A revised nomenclature for the study of suicide and suicidal behaviors. Part 1: Background, rationale, and methodology. *Suicide and Life-Threatening Behavior, 37*, 248–263.

Silverman, M. M., Berman, A. L., Sanddal, N. D., O'Carroll, P. W., & Joiner, T. E. (2007b). Rebuilding the Tower of Babel: A revised nomenclature for the study of suicide and suicidal behaviors. Part 2: Suicide-related ideations, communications and behaviors. *Suicide and Life-Threatening Behavior, 37*, 264–277.

Somasundaram, D. J. & Rajadurai, S. (1995). War and suicide in northern Sri Lanka. *Acta Psychiatrica Scandinavica, 91*, 1–4.

Tondo, L., & Baldessarini, R. J. (2009). Long-term lithium treatment in the prevention of suicidal behavior in bipolar patients. *Epidemiologia e Psichiatrica Sociale, 18*, 179–183.

US Preventive Services Task Force (2004). Screening for suicide risk: Recommendation and rationale. *Annals of Internal Medicine, 140*, 820–821.

Vijayakumar, L. & Raikumar, S. (1999). Are risk factors for suicide universal? A case-control study in India. *Acta Psychiatrica Scandinavica, 99*, 407–411.

Name Index

Aaron, R. 255
Abe, K. 549, 550
Abed, R. 65
Abeyasinghe, R. 255–6, 493, 494, 495
Abrams, R. C. 551
Abu al-Ragheb, S. Y. 549
Academic ED SBIRT Research
   Collaborative 439
Accortt, E. E. 317
Adler, H. M. 428
Afifi, T. O. 101, 102, 611, 613
Agerbo, E. 79, 218, 228, 613
Agnew, N. 29
Agnew, R. 244
Agren, H. 136
Ahrens, B. 204
Ajdacic-Gross, V. 33, 34, 38, 39, 548, 552–4
Ajzen, I. 185, 186, 578
Akers, R. 243
Akiskal, H. 62–4, 68, 113
Al Ansari A. 492
Alao, A. O. 538
Alaraisanen, A. 78, 79
Alcántara, C. 36, 256
Aldrich, R. S. 578

Alexopoulos, G. 316, 318
Ali, B. S. 499
Allan, S. 187
Allard, R. 342
Allard, Y. E. 256
Allebeck, P. 37
Alonso, J. 613
Althaus, D. 448
Altindag, A. 492, 493, 497
Amador, X. 81, 296
Amanullah, S. 490
American Academy of Child and Adolescent
   Psychiatry 441
American Psychiatric Association (APA) 19,
   76, 109, 358
Amos, T. 550
Anderson, M. 297
Anderson, W. T. 600
Andover, M. S. 611
Andriessen, K. 29, 562, 567
Anglin, D. M. 242
Angst, F. 354, 356, 461
Angst, J. 60–65, 67, 430, 461
Anguelova, M. 140
Annenberg Public Policy Center 582

International Handbook of Suicide Prevention: Research, Policy and Practice, First Edition.
Edited by Rory C. O'Connor, Stephen Platt, Jacki Gordon.
© 2011 John Wiley & Sons, Ltd. Published 2011 by John Wiley & Sons, Ltd.

Antypa, N. 204
Appleby, L. 29, 35, 41, 42, 44, 48, 420
Apter, A. 292, 302, 318, 493
Arango, V. 134–6, 140
Arato, M. 137
Arborelius, L. 138
Arean, P. A. 316
Arensman, E. 120–122, 126, 637
Arie, M. 155, 157, 162
Arieli, A. 493
Arkov, K. 384
Arsenault-Lapierre, G. 83, 609
Asarnow, J. 439, 516, 616
Aseltine, R. H., Jr. 295, 298, 513–15, 584
Ashby, D. 459, 463
Ashford, E. 512
Ashton, J. R. 534
Asnes, D. P. 280
Associate Minister of Health
   (New Zealand) 212
Aston-Jones, G. 137
Atlantis, E. 277
Audenaert, K. 156
Australasian College for Emergency
   Medicine 127
Avishai-Eliner, S. 139
Awad, O. A. 492
Awan, N. R. 498
Awata, S. 476
Aziz, K. 498
Azmitia, E. C. 140
Azorin, J-M. 64

Babor, T. 439
Baca-Garcia, E. 84
Bah, J. 140
Baier, C. 241
Bailey, S. 338, 339
Bainbridge, W. S. 239
Bair, J. H. 552
Baker, M. 277
Baker, W. 242
Balarajan, R. 37
Balázs, J. 60, 62, 63
Baldessarini, R. 40, 63, 65, 67, 86, 140, 630
Baldurson, E. B. 594, 600
Ball, J. S. 611
Ball, S. A. 96

Balon, R. 466
Bandura, A. 186, 263, 533, 539
Bankston, W. B. 236
Baracia, S. 190
Barbui, C. 459, 465, 466
Bar-Joseph, H. 298
Barker, D. J. P. 276, 277, 279
Barnhofer, T. 412
Barr, C. S. 141
Barr, W. 126
Barraclough, B. 40, 61, 64, 283, 458
Barrish, H. H. 519
Barrow, J. C. 187
Barrowclough, C. 338, 339
Bartfai, A. 155
Bateman, A. 112, 357, 428
Baumeister, R. 175, 182, 192, 389
Beatson, S. 538
Beautrais, A. L. 14, 83, 101, 110, 313, 438,
   445, 489, 490, 494, 496, 500–502, 548,
   551–3, 586, 634
Bech, P. 476
Beck, A. T. 16, 18, 40, 161, 162, 174, 182,
   191, 205, 371, 372, 389, 393, 408,
   409, 426
Beck, J. S. 371, 373
Becker, E. S. 153
Becker, K. 538, 539, 563, 566–7
Beevers, C. G. 203
Bell, M. D. 79, 82, 88
Bellivier, F. 140
Benazzi, F. 63
Bennett, A. J. 141
Bennewith, O. 48, 126, 333, 343, 354,
   358, 552
Ben Park, B. C. 491
Ben-Shlomo, Y. 276
Berenbaum, H. 87
Bergen, H. 344, 354, 358, 359
Berk, M. 37
Berkowitz, L. 533
Berliner, P. 598
Berman, A. L. 10, 17, 512, 516
Bernal, G. 36
Bernasco, W. 438
Berry, G. L. 508
Bertolote, J. M. 35, 43, 239, 247, 317, 478,
   496, 597

Betts, V. T. 262
Bhagwagar, Z. 135
Bhansali, P. 138
Bhui, K. S. 47
Bibace, R. 595
Bibby, P. 254
Biddle, L. 35, 292, 294, 297, 537, 538
Bilici, M. 492, 495, 498
Bille-Brahe, U. 11, 42, 44, 354, 356, 547
Binks, C.A. 112, 113
Bishop, S. 240
Bjerkeset, O. 276, 278, 281, 282
Blaine, B. 277
Blair-West, G. W. 594, 596
Bland, D. 563
Blankenship, V. 202
Blazer, D. G. 312
Blood, R. W. 500, 533, 536, 538
Blow, F. C. 313, 320
Blumberg, S. J. 409
Boardman, J. 480, 481
Bolger, S. 334
Bollen, K. A. 533, 534
Bolton, J. M. 611
Boor, M. 552
Borkovec, T. D. 200, 206
Borowsky, I. W. 516
Bose, A. 254
Bossarte, R. M. 585
Bostrom, A. G. 429, 444, 446
Bostwick, J. M. 618
Botsis, A. J. 616
Botzung, A. 162
Bourgeois, M. 81
Bowlby, J. 429, 567, 572
Bowles, J. R. 549
Boyce, P. 358
Boyle, P. 218, 228
Bradley, R. G. 141
Bramness, J. G. 462
Branas, C. C. 266
Brannick, T. 236
Breault, K. 236, 239
Brennan, C. 549
Brenner, L. A. 394
Brent, D. A. 85, 135, 139, 140, 292, 294,
    295, 459, 467, 512, 552, 553, 610, 615
Brezo, J. 97, 140, 182, 610

Bridge, J. A. 68, 467, 552, 553
Bridges, F. S. 281
Britto, M. T. 440
Broadbent, K. 153, 154, 371
Brodsky, A. 114
Brodsky, B. S. 137
Brooten, D. 354
Brophy, M. 332, 333, 335
Brown, A. S. 277
Brown, B. 263
Brown, C. H. 509
Brown, G. K. 16, 164, 172, 300, 301, 357,
    370, 373, 375, 385, 393, 420, 422, 439
Brown, J. L. 175
Brown, M. M. 511, 516
Brown, M. Z. 110
Brown, R. P. 137
Brown, S. 78
Brown, S. M. 140
Bruce, M. L. 319
Brunner, H. G. 140
Brunner, J. 137
Brunson, K. L. 139
Brunstein Klomek, A. 295, 300, 301
Bryk, A. S. 244
Buchanan, R. W. 76, 77
Buka, S. L. 217, 218, 227, 228
Bulik, C. M. 296
Bullman, T. A. 585
Bunting, J. 215, 216
Burchard, E. M. L. 276
Burford, G. 334
Burgess, P. 420
Burgess, S. 334
Burns, C. 257
Burns, J. M. 478
Burr, W. 239
Burrows, G. M. 458
Bursztein, C. 292, 302
Burvill, P. W. 37, 549
Butler, A. 374
Byard, R. W. 538
Byford, S. 633
Bywaters, P. 334–6

Caldwell, C. B. 78
Caldwell, T. M. 257, 260
Callahan, J. 566

Camerer, C. F. 554
Camidge, D. R. 45
Campbell, E. A. 494, 498
Campbell, M. 450
Canetto, S. S. 314, 315, 318, 596
Canli, T. 135
Cannon, M. 277
Cantor, C. H. 552
Caplan, R. D. 230
Capurso, A. 310, 312
Carballo, J. J. 135, 611
Carley, S. 39
Carlough, M. C. 492
Carlson, H. E. 283
Carlton, P. A. 509, 584
Caron, J. 52, 266
Carpenter, W. T. 76
Carrigan, J. T. 332
Cartensen, L. L. 534
Carter, G. L. 301, 342, 429, 444–6, 634
Carver, C. S. 192, 403, 413, 427
Caspi, A. 141
Cassidy, C. 40
Castelpietra, G. 462
Castrigiano, D. P. L. 594
Cattell, H. 316
Cavanagh, J. T. O. 40–41, 94, 99, 549,
    597, 609
CDC 582, 587
Cedereke, M. 120, 342
Central Bureau of Statistics 503
Centre for Suicide Research and
    Prevention 546, 551
Cerel, J. 578
Cetin, G. 552
Chambers, D. A. 579, 588
Chan, J. 124, 311
Chan, K. P. M. 596
Chan, S. 204
Chan, W. S. 492
Chandler, M. J. 269
Chapman, A. L. 16, 174
Charlton, B. 597
Charlton, J. 216
Chavan, B. S. 493
Chelmow, D. 595
Chen, E. Y. 493
Chen, V. C. 123

Chen, Y. W. 62
Chen, Y. Y. 481, 550–552
Cheng, A. T. 94, 98, 493–5, 533, 534
Chew, K. S. Y. 39
Chitsabesan, P. 123
Chiu, H. F. 124, 316, 493
Cho, H. 298, 518
Chodorowski, Z. 538
Christoffel K. K. 615, 616
Christoffersen, M. N. 611
Chua, H. C. 489
Cialdini, R. B. 579
Ciarrochi, J. W. 96
Ciffone, J. 508
Cigularov, K. 509
Cipriani, A. 302, 466
Claassen, C. A. 438, 440
Clark, S. 564
Clarke, R. 547, 548, 550
Clarke, T. 342
Clarkin, J. F. 112
Cleary, A. 236
Cleiren, M. P. H. D. 564
Clum, G. A. 182, 186, 405
Cochran, S. V. 318
Cohen, L. S. 317
Coid, J. 111
Cole, D. A. 102, 516
Colucci, E. 236, 237, 239
Coman, M. 552
Commission for Rural Communities
    262
Commons Treloar, A. J. 338
Commonwealth Department of Health and
    Aged Care 322
Comstock, G. W. 237, 240
Conaghan, S. 156
Congdon, E. 135
Conklin, G. 237, 238, 496
Conley B. H. 572
Conner, K. R. 14, 95–100, 172, 293, 493,
    497–8, 618
Connolly, J. F. 261
Conrad, A. K. 384, 389
Conwell, Y. 17, 310–316, 318, 321, 422
Cook, P. J. 317, 321
Cooper, J. 34, 42, 46, 125, 127, 439, 632
Cooper, L. M. 96

Cooper, S. J. 134, 136
Copelan, R. I. 439
Copeland, A. R. 551
Corcoran, P. 28, 127
Cornelius, J. R. 98, 99
Correll, C. U. 283
Coryell, W. 78, 136
Costa Jr., P. T. 97
Cote, G. 19
Cotgrove, A. 301, 443
Courtet, P. 637
Covin, R. 201
Craft, L. 510
Craig, P. 450
Crandall, C. 438
Crane, C. 40, 403–5, 413
Crawford, M. J. 339, 354, 356, 357
Crawford, P. 263
Crawford, T. 337
Creed, F. H. 339
Crisp, A. 277
Critical Appraisal Skills Programme 331
Crockwell, L. 334
Cross Government Obesity Unit 276
Crowell, S. E. 112
Cuijpers, P. 438
Cullen, A. 261
Currier, D. 133, 137, 141, 294, 476, 611
Curry, J. F. 616
Cutcliffe, J. 256
Cutler, D. M. 546
Cutright, P. 236, 237, 239, 240, 242
Cvinar, J. G. 565

Daigle, M. 19, 437, 438, 441, 442, 546, 547
Daniels, R. G. 536
Daniels, W. M. 139
Danigelis, N. 236
Danto, B. 237, 239
Danto, J. M. 237, 239
Daradkeh, T. K. 492
Dare, A. 534
Darke, S. 95–7, 99
Davidson, K. M. 112, 156
Davidson, R. M. 254
Davis, K. L. 112
Day, G. 441
De, T. 312

Deane, F. P. 509, 584
Degenhardt, L. 95
DeKlyen, M. 613
De Leo, D. 11, 17, 19, 29, 33, 44, 124, 125, 200, 310, 311, 313–17, 319–22, 356, 420, 547, 550, 603
Dema, K. 492
Dema, T. 492
DeMartino, R. 298, 513, 514, 581, 584
De Moore, G. M. 547
Department of Veterans Affairs Press Release 585
Dernovsek, M. Z. 242
de Rose, N. 338
Dervic, K. 65, 236, 239, 242
Dew, A. J. M. 441
DeWall, N. 175
De Wilde, E. J. 242
D'Hulster, N. 538
Diani, R. 492, 493
Dick, D. M. 95
Diefenbach, G. J. 325
Diekstra, R. F. W. 310, 311, 315
Dieserud, G. 354, 363
Diez-Roux A. V. 218
Dilsaver, S. C. 62
Dixon-Gordon, K. L. 16
Doey, T. 35
Doidge, N. 593
Dombrovski, A. Y. 154, 158, 316
Domino, G. 586
Donnan, S. 534
Doshi, A. 354
Dougherty, D. M. 98, 612
Dower, J. 334
Drake, R. E. 82
Draper, B. 311, 315, 316, 322, 611
Drever, F. 215
Dritschel, B. H. 154
Driver, K. 65
Drozd, J. F. 384
Du, L. 140, 141
Duarté-Vélez, Y. M. 36
Duberstein, P. R. 17, 99, 313, 314, 317
Dubicka, B. 460, 467
Dudley, M. 261, 464
Duffy, D. F. 45
Dugas, M. J. 202, 203, 206

Duggan, D. S. 405
Dumais, A. 39
Dumesnil, H. 577–80, 586
Dunn, A. J. 137
Dunne, E. J. 564–6, 570
Dunne-Maxim, K. 564–6, 570
Dunner, D. L. 60
Durkee, T. 297, 299, 477
Durkheim E. 35, 38, 238, 239, 243, 247,
     315, 322, 446, 536

Eastman, B. D. 458
Ebrahim, S. 283
Eckert, T. L. 512
Eddleston, M. 33, 35, 45, 255, 265, 493, 496,
     498, 548, 549
Eggert, L. L. 510, 517, 518
Eisendrath, S. J. 412
Eisenhandler, S. A. 311
Ekeberg, Ø. 28
Ekeland, T-J. 595
Eklund, M. B. 138
Elfawal, M. A. 492
Elias, M. 508, 512, 513, 520, 522
Elkin. I. 424
Ellenbogen, S. 566
Elliott, R. 599
Ellis, S. J. 536
Ellis, T. E. 40, 182
Ellison, C. G. 239
Elmquist, J. K. 283
Elovainio, M. 281
Elsaka, N. 535
Else, I. R. N. 36
Engelberg, H. 283
Engstrom, G. 136
Entertainment Industries Council 583
Enticott, P. G. 39
Erikson, E. H. 309, 323
Erlangsen, A. 618
Ernst, C. 611
Eshun, S. 242
Eskin, M. 242
Eth, S. 533
Etzersdorfer, E. 534, 535, 552, 553
European Commission 479
Evans, J. 154, 190, 444
Evans, K. 343

Evans, M. O. 444
Evans, S. W. 521
Exeter, D. 218, 220, 228

Fagg, J. 15
Fakhoury, W. 441
Fan, J. 141
Farberow, N. L. 441, 564, 567
Farmer, R. 554
Favazza, A. R. 174
Fawcett, J. 313, 320
Fazel, S. 437
Felner, R. D. 520
Felner, T. Y. 520
Fenton, W. S. 77
Fergusson, D. 460, 465, 467
Fernando, S. 594, 596, 597, 604
Fernquist, R. 236, 239, 240, 242
Ferrada-Noli, M. 37
Feyerabend, P. 602
Fiori, L. M. 637
Fishbein, M. 578
Fisher, L. J. 584
Fiske, A. 310, 315, 318
Fitzgerald, M. 638
Fleischer, E. 592
Fleischmann, A. 35, 69, 239, 247, 317, 370,
     420, 496, 610
Flesher, S. 88
Flett, G. L. 188, 189
Flick, U. 599, 602
Fliege, H. 48
Florio, E. R. 321
Folse, V. N. 439
Fonagy, P. 112, 357, 428
Forsthoff, A. 538
Foster, J. 127
Foster, T. 94, 98, 637
Foucault, M. 599
Fountoulakis, K. N. 68
Fowler, B. P. 536
Fox, A. J. 214
Francis, L. J. 240
Frankel, S. 370, 459
Freedland, K. E. 39
Fresco, D. M. 202
Freud, S. 566, 571, 611
Fridell, M. 99

Friedman, R. A. 299
Friedman, T. 337, 338
Friedmann, H. 101
Frost, N. 550
Fruehwald, S. 437
Fu, K. W. 534, 582
Fulford, K. W. M. 604
Furmark, T. 140
Furnham, A. 260

Gagliano, C. 508, 522
Gairin, I. 438
Gajalakshmi, V. 254
Galdas, P. M. 318
Galfalvy, H. 136
Gallagher, K. E. 538
Gannon, P. J. 140
Garfield, P. 571
Garland, A. F. 508, 512
Garrison, C. Z. 17
Garroutte, E. M. 257
Gartside, S. E. 138
Gask, L. 44–6, 370
Gasse, C. 280
Gatz, M. 318
Gawatz, O. 538
Gayle, S. 228
Geddes, J. R. 460, 466
Geertz, C. 596
Georgiana, S. 236, 238, 240, 241, 247
Gibb, B. E. 141
Gibb, S. J. 14, 438
Gibbons, R. D. 68, 293, 467
Gibbs, L. M. 153, 157, 162
Giesen-Bloo, J. 112
Gilat, I. 294
Gilbert, P. 187
Gilbody, S. 120
Gilgen, A. R. 593
Girard, C. 239
Girdhar, S. 489
Glaser, B. G. 598
Glashouwer, K. A. 205
Glicksohn, J. 39
Glover, G. 354
Goldacre, M. 354, 356
Goldberg, J. 63
Goldblatt, P. O. 214

Goldney, R. D. 229, 258, 260, 420, 462, 564, 584, 602
Goldsmith, S. K. 264
Goldstein, R.B. 113
Goldston, D. B. 123, 256, 257
Gollwitzer, P. M. 193
Gomberg, E. S. L. 95
Gone, J. P. 36, 256
Good, B. 596
Goodwin, F. K. 60–65
Gordon, R. 477
Gottesman, II. 78
Gould, M. S. 35, 40, 296–9, 441, 442, 508–10, 512, 515, 516, 581, 584, 616
Grad, O. 563–5, 567, 568, 571, 572
Graham, H. 212, 226
Gratton, F. 566
Gray, J. 256
Green, J. 429
Greening, L. 240
Greenland, S. 217
Greig, T. C. 88
Grek, A. 314, 319
Grøholt, B. 28, 123
Gross, C. 138
Grossman, D. C. 266
Grossman, J. B. 447
Grytten, J. 254
Guciz Dogan, B. 497
Guiao, I. Z. 494, 498
Gunderson, J. G. 111
Gunnell, D. 47, 120, 255–6, 265, 277, 293, 297, 317, 321, 330, 355, 370, 459, 460, 463, 465, 467, 493, 495, 496, 546–9, 551, 553, 639
Guo, G. 508
Gupta, A. 255
Gururaj, G. 493, 499, 500
Gustafsson, L. 594
Gut-Fayand, A. 84
Gutheil, T. G. 114
Guthrie, E. 357, 420
Gutierrez, P. M. 511
Guzzetta, F. 63, 65, 67

Hafner, H. 536
Hafting, M. 600
Hakko, H. 39

Halbwachs, M. 238
Hall, W. D. 614
Hallfors, D. 511, 518, 519
Hallstrom, T. 277
Hamann, C. 440
Hamermesh, D. S. 546
Hamilton, M. 39
Hammad, T. A. 292, 460, 466
Han, T. S. 277
Hardy, D. J. 162
Hariri, A. R. 140
Harkavy-Friedman, J. M. 154, 156
Harned, M. S. 103
Harré, R. 592
Harrington, J. 202
Harrington, R. 301
Harris, E. C. 40, 60, 61, 64, 283, 458
Harriss, L. 311, 317, 330
Harrow, M. 81
Harstall, C. 508
Hartless, G. 446
Hartley, D. 424
Harwood, D. M. J. 313–16, 566
Hasin, D. 95
Hassan, R. 534
Hauser, M. J. 564
Haw, C. 100, 313, 330, 354, 446, 618
Hawgood, J. 313
Hawkins, L. C. 547–8
Hawton, K. 1, 15, 16, 28, 37, 42–6, 60–65,
    78–85, 110, 120, 121, 123, 125, 163, 190,
    200, 213–15, 258, 259, 262, 266, 295, 311,
    317, 330, 331, 338, 340, 342, 344, 354,
    357–9, 362, 370, 438, 446, 500, 537, 539,
    546, 548, 549, 564, 566, 568, 610, 616,
    629, 630, 634
Hayes, L. M. 436
Hayes, S. C. 407, 408, 414
Hayes, S. A. 594
Haynes, R. 228
Hazell, P. L. 301
Health Service Executive 331
Healy, D. 439, 459
Hedström, P. 587
Heeren, A. 163
Hegerl, U. 67, 297, 448, 449, 478, 630
Heikkinen, M. E. 35, 99, 100
Heilä, H. 77, 80, 614

Heim, C. 139
Heller, T. 44, 310
Hellerstein, D. 81
Hemenway, D. 102
Hemmings, A. 337
Hempstead, K. 256
Hengeveld, M. W. 333
Henn, F. A. 136
Hennen, J. 40, 86, 140
Henriksson, M. M. 77, 83, 98
Henriksson, S. 67
Hepburn, S. R. 161, 409
Hepple, J. 125
Herron, J. 337
Herva, A. 277
Hesselbrock, M. 95
Hetrick, S. 614
Hetzel B. S. 317
Hewitt, M. 254
Hewitt, P. L. 188, 189
Hickey, L. 127, 359
Higley, J. D. 138
Hill, A. B. 162, 163, 466
Hill, D. L. 257
Hintikka, J. 261
Hirsch, J. K. 254, 256, 261, 262
Hirschi, T. 244
Hitosugi, M. 538
Hjelmeland, H. 16, 200, 592, 598
Hjern, A. 37
Hochdorf, Z. 516
Hodgkinson, C. A. 140
Hoffman, B. 362
Hogarty, G. E. 87, 88
Holdsworth, N. 336
Holmes, J. 428
Hood, A. 334, 335
Horn, A. 266
Hornby, A. S. 562
Hornik, R. C. 577, 579
Horowitz, L. M. 439
Horrocks, J. 332, 333
Horvath, A. O. 387, 423, 424
Hoven, C. 478, 482
Howard-Pitney, B. 263, 517
Høyer, G. 36
Hsiao, W. C. 254
Hu, W. H. 80

Huang, Y. Y. 141
Huey, S. J. 301
Hughes, C. C. 597
Hull, J.W. 111
Hultén, A. 123, 125, 356
Hume, M. 333, 334
Hunt, I.M. 110
Hunter, E. C. 156, 191
Husky, M. M. 509, 512

Ialongo, N. S. 519
Ichise, M. 138
Ilgen, M. A. 95–8, 103
Imber-Black, E. 572
Inglehart, R. 242
Ingram, R. E. 205
Insel, B. J. 581
Inskip, H. M. 78
Institute of Medicine 440, 477
International Association for Suicide
   Prevention 534
Irving, H. W. 254
Isacsson, G. 67, 422, 462, 464, 614
Iscoe, I. 520
Isometsä, E. 65, 260, 420, 422, 614

Jacob, K. 494
Jacobs, D. G. 439
Jacobsson, L. 594
Jacoby, R. 313, 314
Jadhav, S. 596
James, A. 123, 295
James, D. 572
Jamieson, P. 535, 582, 583
Jamison, K. R. 60–65
Janal, M. N. 94, 95, 99
Janghorbani, M. 492, 497, 498
Jenkins, J. H. 597–9
Jenkins, R. 11, 297, 437
Jensen, B.F. 39
Jessen, G. 39, 47, 547
Jick, H. 463, 464
Jo, K.H. 321
Jobes, D. A. 10, 11, 193, 384–6, 388–90,
   393, 394, 398, 423, 512, 516
Joe, S. 236, 237, 242
Johnson, J. 163
Johnsson, E. 99

Johnston, A. 126
Joiner, T. E., Jr. 11, 19, 40, 100, 102, 165,
   170–173, 175–7, 193, 409, 446, 510, 584
Jokinen, J. 476
Jollant, F. 158
Jones, J. S. 134
Jordan, J. R. 562–6, 569, 573
Josepho, S. A. 616
Judd, F. 257, 260, 262
Judge, K. 212

Kalafat, J. 441, 508, 512, 513, 520, 522
Kanbur, R. 254
Kang, H. K. 585
Kaplan, K. J. 81
Kaplan, M. S. 281, 284, 314
Kapur, N. 29, 35, 41, 42, 44–6, 48, 120, 127,
   333, 354, 359, 361, 370
Kapusta, N. D. 68, 257, 552–3
Karch, D. L. 95
Karim, S. 498
Karvonen, K. 83
Kaslow, N. J. 236
Kataoka, S. H. 516
Katz, L. Y. 68, 293, 300
Kaufman, J. 138
Kaviani, H. 155, 157, 162
Kay, W. K. 240
Ke, L. 140
Keilp, J. G. 153, 154, 156, 159–63
Keks, N. A. 614
Kellam, S. G. 519
Kellermann, A. L. 261
Kelly, S. 216
Kemperman, I. 16
Kendler, K. S. 96
Kennedy, G. J. 323
Kenny, M. A. 412
Kerkhof, A. J. F. M. 200, 205, 206, 438
Kerkhof, A.J. 120, 637
Kerwin, R. 463
Kessler, R. C. 10, 15, 21, 62, 94, 182
Khalilian, A. 492, 494
Khan, A. 86, 459
Khan, F. 34
Khan, M. M. 254, 489, 490, 492–5, 497
Khantzian, E. J. 96
Khouzam, H. R. 318

Kim, C. 65, 83
Kim, K. 538
Kim, Y. K. 321
King, C. A. 301, 446–8, 634
King, D. A. 153
King, E. 550
King, K. A. 516
King, R. 441, 442
King, S. R. 242
Kingree, J. B. 100
Kingston, T. 412
Kirkpatrick, B. 76, 85
Kirmayer, L. J. 597
Kishi, T. 283
Klausner, E. J. 318
Kleinman, A. 501, 596
Klieve H. 553, 615
Klimes-Dougan, B. 584
Klingman, A. 516
Klomek, A. B. 294
Klonsky, E. D. 45, 174
Kloos, A. L. 293
Knieper, A. J. 563, 567
Knizek, B. L. 16, 592, 598
Knox, K. L. 585
Kochman, F. J. 64
Kocmur, M. 242
Koenig, H. G. 236, 239
Koerner, N. 202, 203
Kohn, R. 101
Koller, G. 97
Kolves, K. 94, 313
Konrad, N. 437, 438
Konradsen, F. 255, 256
Koons, C. R. 379
Kopjar, B. 355
Korkeila, J. 462
Koronfel, A. A. 492
Kotler, M. 616
Kowalski, G. S. 238
Kposowa, A. J. 236, 241–4
Kraemer, G. W. 138
Kranitz, L. 239
Krasser, G. 16
Krause, N. 322
Kreitman, N. 15, 19, 33, 127, 214–16,
    549, 629
Kripalani, S. 354

Krippner, S. 594
Kronengold, H. 296
Kruger, G. 256
Krupnick, J. L. 424
Krysinska, K. 313
Kübler-Ross, E. 567, 571
Kubrin, C. E. 37
Kuh, D. 276
Kujari, H. 614
Kumar, P. 357
Kumar, V. 494
Kuo, C. J. 83–5, 550
Kupfer, D. J. 312, 318, 319
Kurz, A. 422, 438, 444
Kuyken, W. 412
Kvale, S. 595, 600–601

Lafave, M. 551
LaFromboise, T. D. 263, 517
Lakeman, R. 638
Lalonde, C. E. 269
Landheim, A. S. 96
Largey, M. 33
Larkin, G. L. 438, 440
Larzelere, R. E. 439
Lau, M. A. 203
Lau, T. 262
Lawlor, D. 278
Lazarus, P. J. 520, 521
Leder, D. 600
Lee, A. 520
Lee, D. T. S. 498, 500, 550
Lee, M. B. 546
Leenaars, A. 215, 427, 552, 602
Légaré, G. 613
Leibetseder, M. M. 155, 159
Leitner, M. 213
Lenzenweger, M. F. 111
Leon, A. C. 67, 464
Leong, F. T. L. 36
Lesage, A. D. 77, 79, 83, 94, 98, 110, 111
Lesch, K. P. 140
Leshem, R. 39
Lester, D. 28, 29, 38, 136, 215, 236–8, 441,
    491, 547–50, 552
Letizia, C. 459
Leverich, G. S. 63–5
Levin, K. A. 266

Lewine, R. R. 82
Lewinsohn, P. M. 123, 203
Lewis, A. J. 338
Lewis, G. 214
Lewis, H. A. 263, 517
Lewis, L. M. 390
Lewis, S. 87
Lewis-Fernandez, R. 597
Leyland, A. H. 266
Leyton, M. 135
Li, X. Y. 293, 494
Liao, S. C. 546
Libby, A. M. 293, 467
Lieb, K. 113
Lilley, R. 45, 120, 122
Lin, E. H. B. 422
Lin, J. J. 550
Lin, S. P. 277
Linden, M. 204
Lindqvist, P. 52
Linehan, M. 11, 16, 21, 110–112, 114, 174,
    300, 320, 330, 357, 370, 376–9, 385, 393,
    402, 420, 426
Links, P. S. 110–112, 362, 611
Litman, R. E. 10
Littlewood, R. 596
Liu, D. 138, 139, 142
Liu, K. Y. 29, 31, 33, 317, 550–551
Liu, Y. 254
Living is For Everyone Framework 322
LivingWorks 265
Loebel, J. P. 315
Loftin, C. 552
Loh, M. 498
Loibl, L. 40, 139, 611
Lönqvist, J. 338, 354, 422, 458
Lopez, A. D. 259
Lopez, J. F. 137, 140
Lorant, V. 37, 216
Low, L. 322
Lowenstein, S. R. 440
Lu, T. H. 550
Lu, X. Y. 283
Lu, Y. 37
Lucke, J. 614
Ludwig, J. 68, 317, 321, 461, 462
Lund, E. 36
Luoma, J. B. 10, 41

Lyotard, J. F. 599
Lyubomirsky, S. 403

Ma, S. H. 412
Mackay, N. 338, 339
Mackenbach, J. 212
Mackenzie, M. 448
MacKinnon, D. F. 64, 65
MacLeod, A. K. 155, 191, 330
Madge, N. 43–7, 122, 330
Maestripieri, D. 138
Magnusson, P. 280, 282–4
Mahadevan, S. 446
Makhija, N. J. 611
Malloy-Diniz, L. F. 154, 158
Malmberg, A. 258, 262
Malone, K. M. 10, 134
Maloney, E. 96
Malterud, K. 599, 601, 604
Maltsberger, J. T. 114
Mandell, D. J. 481
Mann, J. 10, 33, 40, 41, 62, 64, 65, 123,
    133–7, 139–41, 152, 163, 187, 212, 283,
    294, 295, 321, 330, 354, 357, 361, 362,
    476, 546, 593, 611, 618, 629
Mann, R. E. 384, 388
Maracek, J. 489
March, J. S. 300, 467
Marchel, C. 602
Marcotte, D. E. 461, 462, 546
Maris, R. 1, 11, 17, 28, 42, 110, 236,
    239, 240
Marks, A. 547
Markus, K. 266
Marshall, J. R. 38
Martin, G. 236, 237, 239
Martin R. L. 110
Marttunen, M. J. 83
Marzano, L. 437
Marzuk, P. M. 65, 154, 156, 551
Måseide, P. 600
Master, S. 175
Masterpasqua, F. 594
Masters, K. J. 302
Matthews, K. 138
Mattisson, C. 618
Maxwell, S. E. 102
May, P. A. 267

May, V. 339
Mayer-Gross, W. 458
McAuliffe, C. 124
McCleary, R. 39
McClelland, L. E. 175
McClure, G. M. 548
McCormick, R. A. 96
McCubbin, J. A. 175
McCullough, J. P. 175
McCurry, J. 500
McDaid, C. 564, 573
McDonald, A. J. D. 462
McGirr, A. 62, 65, 78–81, 83–5, 111
McGlashan, T. H. 110
McGoldrick, M. 562, 567
McGowan, P. O. 139
McGue, M. 96
McGuffin, P. 141
McGuiness, B. 277
McIntosh, J. L. 170, 310, 311, 314, 315, 563, 564, 566
McIntyre, R. S. 611
McKenzie, K. 36
McKeon, R. T. 430
McKeown, R. E. 317, 516
McLaughlin, C. 336
McMain, S. F. 112
McMenamy, J. M. 563
McNicoll, P. 256
Meaney, M. J. 139
Meehan, P. J. 21
Mehlum, L. 360, 361, 537–9
Meijer, O. C. 137
Melhem, N. 139, 140, 294, 610
Melle, I. 85
Meltzer, H. Y. 78, 85, 86, 137
Mendes, W. B. 157
Meneese, W. B. 439
Meneghel, G. 310
Merchant, C. R. 446
Meyer, J. H. 135
Meyer-Lindenberg, A. 141
Mezzich, J. E. 587
Michalak, E. E. 68
Michel, K. 185–6, 420, 421, 427, 428, 535, 551, 552, 572, 598, 604
Michell, J. 604
Middlebrook, D. L. 267, 268

Middleton, G. D. 237, 239
Middleton, N. 37
Miles, C. P. 78
Miller, A. L. 300, 376
Miller, D. N. 512
Miller, H. L. 136, 138, 441
Miller, J. W. 295, 300
Miller, K. 257
Miller, M. 102, 282
Miller, T. 439
Mines, D. 466
Minh, D. P. 492
Ministry of Health and New Zealand Guidelines Group 440
Ministry of Health New Zealand 331
Miranda, R. 204, 293
Mishara, B. 265, 441–3, 538, 539, 549, 610, 615, 616, 638
Mishra, S. 494
Mitchell, A. M. 568
Mittendorfer Rutz, E. 278, 355
Modestin, J. 86
Moens, G. F. 548
Mogensen, J. 593
Moghaddam, F. 592
Mohanty, S. 35
Moller, H. J. 438, 441–4
Molnar, B. E. 294
Molock, S. D. 237
Montano, C. B. 312, 314, 316
Monti, K. 439
Moore, C. A. 187
Morgan, C. 613, 616
Morgan, H. G. 343, 443, 444, 449
Morgan, R. 424
Morgan, S. 337, 339
Morgenstern, H. 217
Mork, E. 359, 360, 362, 363
Morrison, K. 111
Morrison, R. 40, 190, 201, 204, 403
Morrow, J. 201
Morselli, H. 236, 238
Mortensen, P. B. 549
Mościcki, E. K. 33, 495
Moskos, M. 464
Motohashi, Y. 266, 481
Mott, J. A. 550
Motto, J. A. 429, 444, 446

Muehlenkamp, J. J. 45, 268
Mueser, K. T. 87
Mukamal, K. J. 281, 282, 284
Mulhare, E. 568
Muller, D. J. 83
Munoz, S. R. 261
Murphy, G. E. 98, 99, 102, 316
Murray, C. J. L. 259
Murrell, M. E. 552

Nada-Raja, S. 41
Nagoshi, C. 612
Nakao, M. 498
National Center for Injury Prevention and
    Control 102
National Collaborating Centre for Mental
    Health 48, 331–4, 344
National Council for Suicide Prevention 480
National Institute for Clinical Excellence
    (NICE) 113, 126, 127
National Institute of Clinical and Health
    Excellence 631
National Institute of Mental Health 478, 582,
    585
National Institute of Mental Health
    Consortium of Editors on Development and
    Psychopathology 603
National Research and Development Centre
    for Welfare and Health 357
National Rural Health Alliance 258
National Strategy for Suicide Prevention 322
National Suicide Prevention Strategy 322
National Suicide Research Foundation
    (NSRF) 120–122, 125
Nationella rådet för självmordsprevention 357
Naureckas, S. M. 615, 616
Nawar, E. W. 440
Naylor, M. D. 354
Neeleman, J. 236, 241–2
Nemeroff, C. B. 136–9, 467
Neulinger, K. 313
New South Wales Department of Health 439
NHS Centre for Reviews and
    Dissemination 631
Niederkrotenthaler, T. 294, 297, 535, 536
Nielsen 583
Niklasson, F. 136
Nissen, S. E. 284

Nock, M. K. 10, 15, 21, 29, 35, 42–4, 47, 48,
    103, 157, 173, 177*n.1*, 295
Nolen-Hoeksema, S. 201, 204
Noller, K. L. 595
Noppa, H. 277
Nordentoft, M. 15, 539, 548
Nordström, P. 134, 136
Nordt, S. P. 538
Norwegian Board of Health 357–9
Nowers, M. 551
Noyce, R. 191, 204

O'Brien, M. 263
O'Brien, S. E. 338
O'Carroll, P. W. 2, 11, 19–21, 552, 627
O'Carroll, W. 41–2
O'Connor, D. B. 188, 204
O'Connor, R. C. 39, 40, 44, 120, 123, 155,
    156, 182, 186–93, 201, 204, 402, 403, 413,
    415, 446, 629, 637
O'Connor, S. S. 385
O'Leary, C. C. 292
O'Leary, D. 67
O'Reilly, D. 35
Oberg, P. A. 532
Ogden, C. A. 284
Ogloff, J. R. P. 39
Ohberg, A. 548
Ohgami, H. 67
Ohmann, S. 154, 156
Ojehagen, A. 120
Okayli, G. 85
Oldershaw, A. 157, 295
Oldham, J. M. 111, 113
Olfson, M. 48, 292, 439, 464
Oliver R. G. 317
Olivier, B. 138
Olson, L. M. 256
Onyike, C. 278
Oquendo, M. A. 62, 64, 134, 135, 611, 614
Orbach, I. 298, 385, 402, 425
Orbell, S. 193
Ordway, G. A. 136
Ormel, J. 96
Osborn, M. 601
Osgood, N. J. 311
Osler, M. 281, 282
Overholser, J. C. 508

Ovuga, E. 480, 481
Owens, D. 15, 42, 46, 120, 330, 331, 355, 438
Owens, M. J. 137
Owens, S. 602
Oyama, H. 267, 317, 321
Ozanne-Smith, J. 549, 552

Paffenbarger, R. S. 280
Page, A. 38,
Page, S. 338
Pagura, J. 611
Palinkas, L. 277
Pallikkathayil, L. 337, 339
Palmer, B. A. 77–9
Palmer, L. 332, 333, 337, 339, 340
Pandey, G. N. 134, 135
Pankratz, V. S. 618
Papadakis, A. A. 413
Papageorgiou, C. 202
Papakostas, G. I. 277
Pappas, G. 488
Parent, A. 140
Paris, J. 110–114
Parkes, C. M. 567, 568
Parsey, R. V. 135, 140
Partridge, K. B. 237, 240
Passamonti, L. 141
Patel, A. R. 336, 338
Patel, A. S. 439
Patel, V. 499, 500, 598, 599
Patton, G. C. 478
Pawson, R. 631
Paykel, E. 260, 439, 476
Pearce, J. 257
Pearl, M. 219
Pearson, V. 548, 549
Pedersen, B. T. 594, 600
Pell, J. P. 595
Penick, E. C. 95
Penn, D. L. 261, 264
Perkins, D. F. 446
Perna, P. A. 594
Perry, I. J. 122, 125, 355, 363
Pescosolido, B. 236–8, 240, 241, 247
Peto, R. 254
Pfeffer, J. M.
Phillips, C. O. 354

Phillips, D. P. 532–4
Phillips, M. R. 33, 35, 41, 94, 259, 489, 490, 493–7, 500, 548, 549, 597, 610, 637, 639
Pickering, J. 593, 594
Pickett, K. E. 219
Piedmont, R. L. 96
Pine, D. S. 138
Pinfold, T. J. 421
Pinquart, M. 318, 323
Pirkis, J. 294, 297, 420, 500, 533–9, 581
Pirkola, S. 68, 550
Platt, J. J. 403, 405
Platt, S. 37, 120, 124, 213–16, 219–22, 231n.2, 333, 334, 338, 354, 536
Ploeg, J. 508
Plotsky, P. M. 138–9
Plutchik, R. 616
Pokorny, A. D. 113
Pollock, L. 152, 157, 159, 161, 162, 182, 190, 330, 404
Pompili, M. 64, 83, 84, 161, 296, 618
Pope, W. 236
Portzky, G. 44, 123, 508
Posner, K. 11, 20, 296, 439, 476
Prescott, K. 45
Preuss, U. W. 95, 97, 99
Prevention Division of the American Association of Suicidology 520
Prevost, C. 552
Prior, T. I. 538
Pritchard, C. 490
Prochazka, H. 136
Prospective Studies Collaboration 276
Proudfoot, J. 230

Qin, P. 36, 79
Quan, H. 314
Quinnett, P. 268, 513
Quinton C. 125

Rabheru, K. 310, 318
Rabinowitz, F. E. 318
Raes, F. 163, 201
Raikumar, S. 638
Rajadurai, S. 500, 639
Rajkumar, S. 493–5
Ramon, S. 337, 338
Randell, B. P. 518

Rasmussen, S. 155, 187, 188, 191
Rathus, J. H. 300
Raudenbush, S. W. 244
Raust, A. 154, 158
Recupero, P. R. 294
Rehkopf, D. H. 217, 218, 227, 228
Reinecke, M. A. 40
Reisch, T. 551, 552
Reiss, N. S. 41
Renton, J. 338
Research!America 581
Reseland, S. 462
Restifo, K. 82
Reulbach, U. 355, 363
Reuter, M. 140
Reutfors, J. 38, 85
Reynolds III, C. F. 312, 318, 319
Reynolds, W. M. 510
Rhee, W. K. 443
Rhodes, J. E. 447
Rhodes, K. V. 440, 447
Rich, C. L. 99, 553
Rickwood, D. J. 509
Ricoeur, P. 592, 600
Riehl, T. 441
Rihmer, A. 60, 64
Rihmer, Z. 60–65, 67, 68, 462
Rinfrette, E. S. 320
Rinne, T. 138
Riordan, D. V. 278, 279, 284
Rippere, V. 190
Roberts, R. 278
Robertson, A. R. 547
Robichaud, M. 206
Robins, L. 110
Robinson, J. 445, 446
Robinson, W. S. 217
Roche, A. M. 292, 295
Rodgers, P. L. 296–7
Rodham, K. 45
Rogers, C. R. 442
Rogers, J. R. 423
Rohde, J. 554
Rohde, P. 300
Rolfe, A. 334–6
Rorty, R. 599
Rosen, A. 229
Rosenberg, M. L. 16, 18

Ross, C. 277
Ross, R. K. 314
Rossow, I. 94
Rothaupt, J. W. 563, 566–7
Rotheram-Borus, M. J. 301, 405, 516
Rounsaville, B. J. 317, 318
Routley, V. 549, 550
Roy, A. 40, 85, 94–6, 99, 141, 611
Royal College of Psychiatrists 343, 344, 358
Rubenowitz, E. 314
Rucci, P. 68
Rudd, M. 11, 19, 83, 102, 200, 357, 371,
    390, 393, 402, 424, 426, 439, 512
Rudnick, A. 81
Rujescu, D. 140
Rural Alive and Well 265
Rüsch, N. 154
Russell, J. J. 112
Rutherford, B. 40, 182
Rutz, W. 67, 422, 461, 477
Ruzicka, L. T. 496
Ryding, E. 135
Ryerson, D. A. 520
Ryu, E-J. 538

Saarinen, P. I. 567, 568
Sacks, M. 533
Sadikot, A. F. 140
Sadowski, L. S. 261
Sakamoto, S. 316
Sakinofsky, I. 564
Saleh, M. A. B. Q. 492
Salhab, A. S. 549
Salib, E. 29
Salkovskis, P. 357, 375, 420
Salter, D. 338
Saltzman, C. 424
Samaraweera, S. 493–5
Samaritans 441
Samuelsson, M. 338, 339
Sanchez, V. 518, 519
Sánchez-Gistau, V. 62–3, 65
Sandler, D. A. 536
Saperia, J. 460
Sarbin, T. R. 428
Sarchiapone, M. 64
SAS Institute 244
Satheesh-Babu, R. 500

Sato, T. 63
Saunders, K. 630
Savage, G. 458
Schaffer, M. 295
Schaller, H. 533
Schapira, K. 548
Scheier, M. F. 192, 403, 427
Scherff, A. R. 512
Schilling, E. A. 295
Schlesser, M. 136
Schmidtke, A. 15, 19, 28, 42, 120, 121, 330,
    355, 356, 533, 536
Schneider, B. 98, 313
Schoevers, R. A. 438
Schotte, D. E. 182, 186, 405
Schottenfeld, R. S. 96
Schulsinger, F. 139–40
Schwartz, D. A. 114
Schwartz-Stav, O. 296
Scocco P. 311, 320
Scogin, F. 318–19
Scoliers, G. 46
Scott, A. 124
Scott, M. A. 299, 510, 511
Scottish Executive 212
Screening for Mental Health, Inc. 584
Seal, K. H. 585
Seemüller, F. 466
Segal, Z. V. 411
Segerstrom, S. C. 202
Sein, A. J. 538
Selakovic-Bursic, S. 38
Sequeira, A. 140
Serna, P. 267
Shaffer, D. 124, 464, 508, 510, 511
Shah, A. 35, 311, 312
Shah, S. 553
Shahar, G. 294
Shahid, M. 45, 48
Sharifrad, G. 492, 497, 498
Sharma, B. R. 35
Shaw, J. M. 260
Shea, S. 439
Shear, K. 563, 567, 568
Shear, M. K. 568
Shearin, E. N. 320, 370
Shedler, J. 339–40
Sheehy, N. 182

Sheeran, P. 193
Sheikh, S. 260
Shelef, M. 550
Shenassa, E. D. 266
Shepherd, J. 254
Sher, L. 63, 97, 136
Shneidman, E. S. 10, 11, 182, 389, 441, 562,
    563, 597, 599
Siahpush, M. 256
Sidley, G. L. 154–5, 338
Siever, L. J. 112
Silbert, K. L. 508
Silenzio, V. M. B. 587–8
Silverman, M. M. 2, 11–14, 16, 17, 20, 21,
    177*n.1*, 356, 532, 552, 627
Silverton, L. 82
Silviken, A. 257
Silvonen, J. 230
Simkin, S. 537, 564, 566
Simon, G. 60, 63, 64, 278, 465, 467
Simon, N. M. 201
Simpson, M. 237, 238, 496
Sinclair, J. 83, 124, 155, 159, 161, 330, 429,
Singer, J. D. 244
Singh, B. 11
Singh, G. K. 256
Sinha, R. 317, 318
Siwach, S. B. 255
Skala, J. A. 39
Skegg, K. 42, 120
Skehan, J. 535
Skinner, M. 593, 594
Skoog, I. 440
Slater, P. J. 552
Slinn, R. 359–61
Sloggett, A. 214
Smith, G. C. S. 595
Smith, G. D. 283
Smith, H. R. 140
Smith, J. 516
Smith, J. A. 601
Smith, J. M. 190
Smith, S. E. 339
Smith, W. 580
Social Care Institute for Excellence 331
Soerensen, S. 318, 323
Sokero, P. 62, 67
Soloff, P. H. 110, 113

Solomon, R. L. 171
Somasundaram, D. J. 500, 639
Søndergård, L. 67, 462, 464, 465
Soni Raleigh, V. 37
Sonneck, G. 294, 297, 535, 536, 552
Soss, N. M. 546
Sourander, A. 295
Southern Midlands Council 265
Soyka, K. M. 423
Spathonis, K. 311, 315
Speckens, A. 190, 295
Spirito, A. 508, 616
Spivack, G. 124, 403, 405
Stack, S. 36–8, 236–40, 242–4, 247, 533, 534, 538, 554
Stanley, B. 137, 295, 300, 301, 373, 390, 602, 603
Stanley, M. 135, 137, 142
Stanton, A. L. 615, 616
Stark, C. 35, 216, 258, 261, 262, 266
Stark, R. 239, 241
Statewide Suicide Prevention Council 256
Statham, D. J. 85
Steele, M. M. 35
Steer, R. A. 409
Stein, D. 242
Stein, M. B. 139
Stellrecht, N. E. 176
Stewart, C. D. 375
Stewart-Brown, S. 520
Stoff, D. M. 137
Stoll, K. A. 338
Stone, M. 110, 111, 460, 461
Stoppelbein, L. 240
Storosum, J. G. 459
Strauman, T. J. 413
Strauss, A. L. 598
Stroebe, M. S. 563, 568, 569
Stroebe, W. 563, 568, 569
Strupp, H. H. 424
Stuart, C. 515
Stuckler, D. 37
Substance Abuse and Mental Health Services Administration 170
Sudak, D. M. 294
Sudak, H. 294, 613
Suicide Prevention Australia 263, 265
Suicide Prevention Resource Center 581, 587

Sumathipala, A. 598, 599
Sundhedsstyrelsen 357
Sunnqvist, C. 136, 139
Suokas-Muje, J. 338
Suokas, J. 354
Suominen, K. 330, 354, 356, 610, 614
Surrence, K. 204
Surtees, P. G. 96
Susser, E. S. 277
Sutherby, K. 443
Swann, A. C. 64
Swedish National Board of Health and Welfare 480
Swedish National Public Health Institute 480
Symonds, B. D. 387, 424
Szádóczky, E. 62
Szántó, K. 67, 316, 319, 459
Szmukler, G. 443

Taiminen, T. 533, 614
Takashi, A. 492
Takeuchi, T. 498
Tan, R. C. 498, 551
Tarrier, N. 87, 374
Tatz, C. 258, 260, 265
Taylor, D. 439
Taylor, P. J. 194
Taylor, R. 258
Taylor, S. E. 615, 616
Taylor, T. 331, 354
Teasdale, J. D. 403, 412
Teicher, M. H. 458
Tek, C. 76, 85
Tekavčič Grad, O. 565
Tester, F. J. 256
Tezcan, S. 497
Thaker, S. 518, 519
Thanh, H. T. T. 492
Thapa, B. 492
Thompson, C. 276
Thompson, E. A. 510, 518
Thomson, C. 311, 312, 315, 316, 318, 321
Thomson, H. 227, 228, 231*n*.3
Thornicroft, G. 262
Thorslund, J. 257
Thorson, J. 532
Tidemalm, D. 110, 126
Tiet, Q. Q. 97

Tiihonen, J. 135, 465, 466
Tilley, N. 631
Tishler, C. L. 41, 440
Tondo, L. 60–65, 67, 630
Toomela, A. 594–6
Tops, M. 163
Torhorst, A. 342
Tousignant, M. 533, 610, 615
Townsend, E. 340
Tran, X. V. 281
Traskman-Bendz, L. 136
Treolar, A. J. 421
Treynor, W. 190, 201
Trovato, F. 236
Trull, T. J. 96
Tsuang, M. T. 78
Tully, J. 535
Turecki, G. 79, 83, 84, 97, 140, 637
Turvey, C. 37, 314
Tyrer, P. 444
Tyrka, A. R. 141

Uher, R. 141
Ultee, W. 38
Uncapher, H. 316
United Nations 498, 546, 578
Unützer, J. 314, 319
Uren, Z. 215
US Department of Health and Human
    Services 331, 546, 581
US Preventive Services Task Force 631
US Public Health Service 581
Utsey, S. O. 36

Vaiva, G. 342
Valach, L. 185–6, 427
Valack, L. 598
Valenstein, M. 63, 64
Valsiner, J. 598
Valtonen, H. 62–4
Valuck, R. J. 465
van Beek, W. 163
van den Bosch, L. M. C. 379
van der Hoek, W. 255, 256
van der Sande, R. 341
van Heeringen, C. 163, 342, 420
van Heeringen, K. 1, 28, 123, 135, 137, 182,
    508, 538, 610

van Lier, P. A. C. 519
van Luyn, J. B. 206
van Orden, K. A. 171, 172, 193
van Spijker, B. A. J. 206
van Tubergen, F. 38, 236, 241
Värnik, A. 35
Verger, P. 577–80, 586
Verheul, R. 379
Verkes, R. J. 342
Verwey, B. 205, 359–61
Vetter, N. 599
Veysey, M. J. 534
Vieland, V. 508
Vijayakumar, L. 41, 493–5, 500, 501, 594,
    596, 638
Vinod, K. Y. 618
Vinokur, A. D. 230
Virkkunen de Jong, M. 136
Vitiello, B. 301, 467
Vizcarra, B. 497
Vohs, K. D. 192
Vollmayr, B. 136
von Uexküll, T. 592
Voracek, M. 40, 139, 611
Vörös, V. 317, 318
Vuori, J. 230

Wadsworth, T. 37
Waern, M. 314, 316
Wahab, S. 256
Waheed, W. 34
Wahlbeck, K. 277
Wainwright, N. W. 96
Walker, R. 240
Walsh, F. 567
Walsh, S. 536
Wasserman, C. 610
Wasserman, D. 1, 29, 141, 297, 299, 475,
    477, 479, 480, 483, 610
Wasserman, I. 241, 247, 533, 534, 554
Watkins, E. 190, 199–202, 403
Weaver, I. C. 142
Webster, D. W. 266
Wegner, D. M. 403, 404, 408–9
Wehner, F. 538
Wei, K. C. 489
Weinstock, L. M. 62
Weinstock, M. 163

Weishaar, M. E. 182
Weiss, G. K. 139
Weiss, R. S. 568
Weissman, M. M. 43, 315
Weisstub, D. N. 538, 539, 616, 638
Weist, M. 512
Wekstein, L. 10
Welch, S. S. 42
Wells, A. 201
Welu, T. C. 342
Wender, P. H. 85, 139
Wenzel, A. 161, 162, 182, 370–373, 375, 385, 393
Wenzlaff, R. M. 403
Wertheimer, A. 571
Wesiack, W. 592
Wessely, S. 463
Westefeld, J. S. 11
Westen, D. 111
Western Interstate Commission for Higher Education 265
Westheide, J. 154, 158
Westman, J. 37
Wexler, L. M. 256–7, 264
Wheeler, B. W. 293, 467
Whitaker, C. 459
Whitlock, F. A. 548
Whitman, C. V. 520
Whittington, C. J. 68
Widiger, T. A. 96, 97
Wiklander, M. 332
Wilcox, H. C. 94, 95, 519
Wiles, N. J. 276
Wilkinson, D. 553
Wilkinson, P. 467
Williams, J. 40, 371, 404
Williams, J. M. G. 152–4, 157, 159, 161–4, 182, 186–8, 190, 191, 193, 203, 330, 402, 404, 412, 462, 536
Williams, M. 598
Wilson, J. F. 489
Wilson, K. G. 616
Wilstrand, C. 337
Windfuhr, K. 28–9
Windle, M. 97
Wines, J. D. 95–7, 99
Winkler, M. 594
Wintersteen, M. B. 440

Wojnar, M. 94, 98
Wolk-Wasserman, D. 332, 337
Wong, M. C. 520
Wong, P. W. C. 492–4
Wood, A. 301
Worden, J. W. 567, 568, 572
World Health Organisation (WHO) 1, 35, 169–70, 370, 479, 489–91, 534, 548, 582
Wright, B. R. E. 241
Wrosch, C. 192
Wu, H. C. 616
Wyder, M. 35, 36
Wyman, P. A. 298, 299, 509, 513, 522, 584
Wyn, J. 520, 521

Xiao, S. 499

Yalom, I. D. 571, 572
Yang, G-H. 597
Yeh, J. Y. 36
Yerevanian, B. I. 67
Yip, P. 259, 315, 478, 481, 482, 498, 500, 533, 534, 550, 551, 582
Yoshimasu, K. 610
Young, E. A. 78
Young, R. A. 429
Ystgaard, M. 137
Yusuf, H. R. 497
Yutrzenka, B. A. 439

Zahl, D. L. 42, 120, 125, 331, 438
Zalsman, G. 64
Zanakos, S. 404, 409
Zanarini, M. C. 78, 110, 111, 113
Zarghami, M. 492, 494
Zavasnik, A. 564, 565, 571
Zenere, F. J. 520, 521
Zhang, J. 597
Zhang, X. 254, 259
Zhou, L. 94
Zhou, Z. 140
Zigler, E. 508, 512
Zill, P. 140
Zimmerman, M. 109, 111
Zimmermann, G. 87
Zisook, S. 81, 563, 567, 568, 671
Zouk, H. 39
Zweig-Frank, H. 110, 111

Subject Index

AAQ *see* Acceptance and Action Questionnaire
Aboriginal people 258, 260
Acceptance and Action Questionnaire
    (AAQ) 407–8, 414
acquired capability 171, 172, 174–7, 193
ACROSSnet 264
action theory 427, 428, 587, 598
ADHD *see* attention-deficit hyperactivity
    disorder
adolescents 291–302
    assessment of suicidality in 296
    crisis helplines for 441
    and depression 277, 300–301
    gatekeeper training 512–16
    and obesity 277
    school-based prevention
        programmes 507–24
    screening 297–9, 509–12
    and self-harm 43–4, 123–4, 334
    social support-oriented interventions
        446–8
    suicide epidemiology 292–3
    suicide prevention programmes 296–302
    suicide risk factors 293–6

treatment with antidepressants 68, 292–3,
    460, 463–5
see also young people
adoption studies 40, 85, 139
Aeschi Working Group 422
    guidelines for clinicians 433–4
affective instability (AI) 112
    see also emotion dysregulation (ED)
African Americans 36
age
    and attitudes to suicide 244
    and self-harm 123–5
    and suicide 35
    see also adolescents; children; old age;
        young people
aggression 84, 97–8
agitated depression 63
AI *see* affective instability
AILS *see* American Indian Life Skills
        Development Curriculum
alcohol use disorders (AUDs) 618
    alcohol abuse/dependence distinction 98
    as alternative to suicide 611
    distal risk factors 95–8

International Handbook of Suicide Prevention: Research, Policy and Practice, First Edition.
Edited by Rory C. O'Connor, Stephen Platt, Jacki Gordon.
© 2011 John Wiley & Sons, Ltd. Published 2011 by John Wiley & Sons, Ltd.

alcohol use disorders (AUDs) (*cont'd*)
  and increased risk of suicide 94
  proximal risk factors 98–100
  and suicide in Asian countries 495–6
  and suicide in depression 63
  and suicide in older people 313, 320
  and suicide in psychotic disorders 85
  and suicide in rural areas 255–6
  and suicide in youth 295 *see also* substance
    use disorders (SUDs)
aloneness 99–100
Alzheimer's disease 618
American Indian Life Skills Development
    Curriculum (AILS) 517
American Indians 267–8, 517
  see also indigenous people
amphetamine 95
analgesics 548, 629
anorexia nervosa 283
  see also eating disorders
anticipatory stress 201
antidepressants
  differential effects 466
  follow-up clinical interventions 461–2
  and increased risk of suicide 63, 68,
    457–68, 614
  pharmaco-epidemiological studies 462–5
  placebo-controlled trials 459–61
  treatment of deliberate self-harm 342
  treatment of depressive disorders 67–8
  use in adolescents and children 68, 292–3,
    460, 463–7
anxiety 60, 63
  in older people 312–13, 319–20
  see also rumination; worrying
Applied Suicide Intervention Skills Training
    (ASIST) 265, 298, 515
Archives of Suicide Research (*ASR*) 602–3
area-based initiatives 227–8
  see also geographical areas
arrested flight model 186–8, 402
Asian countries 487–502
  deliberate self-harm in 496, 499–500
  depression in 493–4, 499
  gender differences in suicide 496–7
  methods of suicide 33, 497–8
  suicide prevention 498–501
  suicide rates 489–92

suicide risk factors 492–7
suicide trends 490–492
youth suicide 293
see also charcoal burning
ASIST *see* Applied Suicide Intervention
    Skills Training
ASR see Archives of Suicide Research
attention 152–4, 158–9
attention-deficit hyperactivity disorder
    (ADHD) 295
Auditory Verbal Learning Test (AVLT) 154
AUDs *see* alcohol use disorders
Australia, indigenous people 258, 260, 265
  suicide in rural areas 257–8
autobiographical memory 40, 155, 159,
    161, 163, 190
autobiographical stories 427
  see also narratives
automatic self-associations 205
AVLT *see* Auditory Verbal Learning Test
avoidance 407–8, 414
awareness campaigns 577–88
  aimed at media 581–3
  aimed at military veterans 584–5
  aimed at policy-makers 580–581
  and cultural values of target groups 587–8
  ethical issues 588
  potential negative effects 579
  school-based 583–4
Axis I mental disorders 48, 60, 314

Beck Hopelessness Scale 191, 440
Beck Suicidal Ideation Scale 408, 409
behaviour, social cognitive model of 185–6
  see also suicidal behaviour
behavioural enaction 193
belongingness
  promoting feelings of 176
  thwarted 171–5
benzodiazepine 96
bereavement 564–8
  defined 562–3
  and depression 568
  end of 572
  theoretical models of 566–7
  see also grief
binge drinking 295
bipolar disorders 60–63, 67

birth weight
  and mental illness 276–7
  and suicide 278–9
BMI *see* body mass index
body mass index (BMI)
  calculating 276
  and depression 277–8, 281
  low 277, 280, 283–5
  and suicide 280–284
body weight 275–85
  in adolescence 277
  in adulthood 277–8
  birth weight 276–9
  in childhood 277
  and mental health 275
  see also body mass index (BMI)
borderline personality disorder (BPD) 84, 97,
    110–114
  and childhood abuse history 138
  and dialectical behaviour therapy 375–6
  management of suicidality in 111–13
  and self-harm 110
  and suicidal behaviour 110–111
  and therapeutic relationship 426
brain
  damage 161
  imaging 134–5, 140, 152, 593
  neuroplasticity 593
  post-mortem studies 134, 135, 140, 152
brooding 190, 201–2, 204, 403
Buddhism 246
bullying 294, 297
burdensomeness 40, 171–5

CAMS *see* Collaborative Assessment
    and Management of Suicidality
CAPS-14 *see* Child and Adolescent
    Perfectionism Scale
carbon monoxide poisoning 33, 481,
    549, 550
  see also charcoal burning; gas poisoning; motor
    vehicle exhaust gas suicide (MVEGS)
CARE (Care, Assess, Respond, Empower) 518
CASE *see* Child and Adolescent Self-Harm in
    Europe
CAST *see* Coping and Support Training
catastrophe theory 594
Catholicism 238–9

CBASP *see* Cognitive-Behavioural System of
    Psychotherapy
CBT *see* cognitive behavioural therapy
C-CASA *see* Columbia Classification
    Algorithm for Suicide Assessment
CET *see* cognitive enhancement therapy
chaos theory 594
charcoal burning 33, 481–2, 550–551
Child and Adolescent Perfectionism Scale
    (CAPS-14) 189
Child and Adolescent Self-Harm in Europe
    (CASE) 43–4, 47, 122
childhood abuse 137–9, 294, 611, 616
  see also childhood sexual abuse
childhood adversity 137–9
  see also childhood abuse; childhood
    sexual abuse
childhood sexual abuse 102, 123, 124,
    137, 139
  see also childhood abuse
children 291–302
  body weight 277
  and parental risk of suicide 36
  suicide epidemiology 292–3
  suicide prevention programmes 296–302
  suicide risk factors 293–6
  treatment with antidepressants 68, 292–3,
    460, 463–4
  see also adolescents
China
  gender differences in suicide 259
  prevalence of suicide 489, 490
  suicide in rural areas 259
cholesterol levels 283
'Choose Life' strategy 212, 231*n*.2
CHS *see* Columbia Health Screen
clozapine 85–6
coal gas 549
cocaine 95, 96, 98
Cognitive-Behavioural System of
    Psychotherapy (CBASP) 176
cognitive behaviour therapy (CBT)
  therapeutic relationship in 426
  treatment of adolescent depression
    300, 301
  treatment of deliberate self-harm 341
  treatment of schizophrenia 87
  treatment of suicide attempters 357

cognitive distortions 373, 375, 612
cognitive enhancement therapy (CET) 88
cognitive processing 201
cognitive reactivity 203
cognitive restructuring 373
cognitive rigidity 40, 162, 313
cognitive therapy (CT) 369–75
 compared to dialectical behaviour
  therapy 379–80
 empirical support 374–5
 mindfulness-based 163
 relapse prevention task 374
 theoretical model 371–2
 treatment of borderline personality
  disorder 112
 treatment strategies 372–4
cognitive variables 40
Collaborative Assessment and Management
 of Suicidality (CAMS) 383–98, 423
 clarifying the CAMS agenda 388
 collaboration 387–8
 crisis response planning 390–392
 development of purpose and
  meaning 393–4
 drivers of suicidality 386, 388–90, 394–5
 empathy with suicidal wish 385–6
 feasibility studies 394–5
 suicide focus 386–7
 suicide risk assessment 388–90
 therapeutic philosophy 385
Columbia Classification Algorithm for Suicide
 Assessment (C-CASA) 296, 476
Columbia Health Screen (CHS) 511
Columbia Suicide Screen (CSS) 124, 511
Columbia-Suicide Severity Rating Scale
 (C-SSRS) 296
Columbia University suicidality
 classification 20
communication theory 598
community-based programmes 321, 448
community healthcare 361–2
connectedness 176
conservative governments 38
Continuous Performance Test (CPT) 153, 158
Coping and Support Training (CAST) 518
coping cards 374
co-proxamol 548
copycat suicides 500, 532–3

 see also Werther effect
CPT see Continuous Performance Test
'cries for help' 512
 see also gatekeeper training; warning signs
crisis cards 391, 443–4
crisis helplines 441–3, 630
 for military veterans 585
 for young people 441
crisis response planning 390–392
crisis situations 615–16
Crisis, Journal of Crisis Intervention
 and Suicide Prevention 602–3
cross-cultural prevention strategies 482
CSS *see* Columbia Suicide Screen 124
C-SSRS *see* Columbia-Suicide Severity
 Rating Scale
cultural continuity 257
culturally-sensitive approaches 264, 265, 268
 see also indigenous people
cultural studies 596–9, 603
culture 35–7
curriculum-based programmes 508–9
 see also school-based prevention programmes

d2 task 154
DBT *see* dialectical behaviour therapy
decision making skills 158, 160–162
 and self-harm in adolescents 295
defeat 185, 187–90, 194
deliberate self-harm (DSH) 12, 15–16,
 119–28, 330–331, 355
 and age 123–5
 in Asian countries 495, 499–500
 association with suicide 331
 clinical care of patients 329–47
 definition 120
 and ethnicity 125–6
 and gender 121, 125
 incidence of 121–3, 330, 355
 Irish registry of 355
 patient aftercare 333–4, 345–6
 patient attitudes 331–6
 prediction of repeated 123–8
 repetition of 122–3, 330–331
 service planning 344–5
 staff attitudes to patients 332–4, 336–40
 treatment approaches 340–343
 trends 121

variations in service provision 343–4
see also non-suicidal self-injury (NSSI);
  self-harm; suicide attempt
delusions 80
dementia 313
Dementia Rating Scale 154
depressive disorders 59–69
  in adolescents 277, 300–301
  in Asian countries 494–5, 499
  association with suicide 61–2, 458, 618
  bereavement-related 568
  and childhood abuse 138
  comorbid with schizophrenia 83–4
  comorbid with substance use disorders 98–9
  cross-cultural validity of diagnosis 596–7
  differential activation hypothesis 203
  and negative affectivity 96–7
  and obesity 277–8
  and old age 310, 312, 318–19
  repetitive thinking in 202
  suicide prevention strategies 67–9
  suicide protective factors 65–7
  suicide risk factors 62–5
  treatment of 66–8, 297, 310, 314,
    318–19, 422, 458–9
  under-treatment of 422, 467
  worrying and rumination in 201, 205
  see also antidepressants
deprivation 217–18, 222–30
  see also socio-economic inequalities
dexamethasone suppression test (DST) 476
Diagnostic Predictive Scales (DPS) 511
dialectical behaviour therapy (DBT) 112,
    369–70, 375–9
  compared to cognitive therapy 379–80
  efficacy of 379
  suicide prevention protocols 378–9
  theoretical model 375–6
  therapeutic relationship in 426
  treatment of adolescent depression 300–301
  treatment of suicide attempters 357
  treatment strategies 376–8
diathesis–stress model 182, 186–7
differential activation hypothesis 187,
    189, 203
discrepancy-based processing 401–6, 411
diu mianzi 259
DNA methylation 142, 637

domestic gas poisoning 33, 549
DPS *see* Diagnostic Predictive Scales
dreams 571
drug use disorders (DUDs) 93–6, 99, 101
  and psychotic disorders 83, 84
DSH *see* deliberate self-harm
DSM-IV 109, 597
DST *see* dexamethasone suppression test
DUDs *see* drug use disorders

EAAD *see* European Alliance against
    Depression
early-life environment 137–9, 141–2
eating disorders 296
  see also anorexia nervosa
ecological approaches 520–523, 536, 538
economic recession 37–8
ED *see* emotion dysregulation
Edinburgh Risk of Repetition Scale 127
education 79, 82, 216–17
EIC *see* Entertainment Industries Council, Inc.
emergency departments
  suicide risk assessment in 438–40
  treatment of deliberate self-harm
    patients 332, 340
emotion dysregulation (ED) 112, 174,
    376, 380
emotional pain 175
emotional processing 201
empathy 385–6, 425
employment 213–15
  see also unemployment
endophenotyping 637
Entertainment Industries Council, Inc.
    (EIC) 583
entrapment 158, 185, 187–92, 194
environmental adversity 137–8, 376, 611
  and genes 141–2
epidemiological studies 594
epigenetics 142, 637
escape theory 389
escitalopram 466
ethical issues 588, 616, 638
ethnicity 36–7, 47, 125–6
European Alliance against Depression
    (EAAD) 297, 448–9
European Pact for Mental Health and
    Well-being 479

evidence-based prevention 482–3, 629, 633
experiential avoidance 407–8, 414

family history 65, 84–5, 294
farming 257–9
films 583
firearms 33
   availability of 262
   restricting access to 266, 552–3
   as suicide method in rural areas 257, 258,
     261, 266
fluency 152, 155–6, 159
fluoxetine 458, 463
food intake 284
Freud, Sigmund 182
   on bereavement 566
   on dreams 571
   on mental disorders 611
FTT *see* Future Thinking Task
future thinking 191–2
Future Thinking Task (FTT) 156, 191

Garrett Lee Smith Memorial Act 581
gas poisoning 33, 549–51
gatekeeper training 297–9
   community-based programmes 321
   'natural gatekeepers' 513–14
   school-based programmes 512–16
GBG *see* Good Behavior Game
gender differences 35, 64
   attitudes to suicide 244
   deliberate self-harm 121, 125
   methods of suicide 33, 34
   older people suicide 310, 317–18
   suicides in Asia 496–7
genes 139–42
   and early-life adversity 141–2
   epigenetic effects 142, 637
   serotonergic system 140–141
   stress-response related 141
geographical areas
   area-based initiatives 227–8
   compositional effects 217–18
   contextual effects 217–18
   socio-economic characteristics 217–18
Glasgow 218, 228
Goal Adjustment Scale 192
goal-directed action theory 427, 428

goals
   adjustment of 192
   re-engagement 191
Goethe, Johann Wolfgang 532
Good Behavior Game (GBG) 519
Gotland County 477
GPs 66–7, 429–30, 477
grief
   complicated 566, 568
   defined 563
   see also bereavement
grief work 563
guided discovery 373

Haddon matrix 265
hallucinations 80, 81, 611
hanging 33, 53, 255, 257
hari-kari 496
healthcare workers 65–7
   see also GPs
health inequality 212, 226–7
health-promoting schools 520–521
health psychology 193
healthy migrant hypothesis 37
help-seeking behaviour 261, 450, 509, 514
hermeneutics 600
Hong Kong 481–2, 489, 491–2, 551
hope 393–4
Hope Kit 373
hopelessness 40, 64, 174, 191–2, 205
   and cultural context 597
   and neuropsychological impairments 152,
     161, 162, 164
   in older people 320
'hot cognitions' 373
hotlines *see* crisis helplines
housing tenure 216–17
HPA axis *see* hypothalamic–pituitary–adrenal
   axis
humiliation 185, 187–91, 194
hypothalamic–pituitary–adrenal axis
   (HPA axis) 136–7, 139

iatrogenic effects 508, 519
IGT *see* Iowa Gambling Task
imitation suicide 532–3
   see also Werther effect
IMPACT trial 319

implementation intentions 193
impulse dyscontrol disorders 48, 83, 84
impulsive aggression 84, 97
impulsivity 39, 97–8
   and borderline personality disorder 112–13
   and suicide in adolescents 295
IMV *see* Integrated Motivational–Volitional
    Model
India 254–5, 496
indicated prevention 478
indigeneous people 36
   Australia 258, 260, 265
   New Zealand 260–261
   North America 256–7, 262, 264, 517
inequalities *see* socio-economic inequalities.
insight 81–2, 296
insomnia 320
Integrated Motivational–Volitional Model
    (IMV) 182–94
intent 16, 18–19
Internet
   addiction to 538
   in rising suicide awareness 585, 587–8
   suicide prevention sites 294
   suicide-promoting sites 294, 537–9
   web-based self-help interventions 206
interpersonal–psychological theory 169–77
interpersonal psychotherapy 357
interpersonal stress 99–101
Inuit people 257, 264
Inupiat people 256–7, 264
invalidating environment 376
IOM model 477–8
Iowa Gambling Task (IGT) 158, 162
Islam 28, 238–9, 246, 247, 490, 496
Israel 492

Japan 266–7, 481, 492, 498
jumping suicides 551–2

labour market 211, 213, 220
   see also employment; unemployment
leptin 283
lesbian, gay and bisexual (LGB)
    individuals 587–8
liberalism 244, 246
life events 64–5, 99
life satisfaction 244

lithium 67, 302, 630
'Living is for Everyone' 322
loneliness 99–100
   in older people 314

macro-economic indices 37
Manchester Self-Harm (MASH) rule 127, 632
manner of death 10–11
manual-assisted interventions 444
Many Helping Hearts 515
Maori people 260–261
MAPS *see* Measure of Adolescent Potential
    for Suicide
marital status 35–6, 79, 244, 246, 315
MASH *see* Manchester Self-Harm rule
MBCT *see* mindfulness-based cognitive
    therapy
Means-Ends Problem-Solving test
    (MEPS) 157, 405–7
Measure of Adolescent Potential for Suicide
    (MAPS) 518
media
   in Asia 500–501
   awareness campaigns directed at 581–3
   entertainment 536–7, 583
   guidelines 294, 534–6, 582
   news 533–6, 581–2
   web-based 537–9, 583, 587–9
   Werther effect 531–40
   and youth suicide 294
   see also Internet
medical illnesses 63
medication overdose 547–8
melancholia 458
memory 152, 154–5, 159
   autobiographical 40, 155, 159,
    161, 163, 190
memory-specificity training (MEST) 163
Mendelian randomization 283
mental disorders
   in adolescents 295
   and crisis situations 615–16
   negative effects of treatment 613–15
   in older people 312–13
   relationship with suicidal behaviour 594,
    609–18
   and suicide prevention 616–18
mental flexibility 156, 159–60

mental health awareness programmes 482
Mental Health Declaration 479, 480
mental health services 41
mental illness 40–41
   awareness of 263–6
   and low birth weight 276–7
   in rural areas 260–261
   and self-harm 48
   stigma of 263
mentalization-based therapy 112, 357
MEPS *see* Means-Ends Problem-Solving test
MEST *see* memory-specificity training
mianserine 342
migration 37, 40
military veterans 584–5
mind *see* modes of mind hypothesis
mindfulness 411–12
mindfulness-based cognitive therapy
   (MBCT) 163, 411–15
MindMatters 520–521
mind wandering 201
modes of mind hypothesis 401–15
   being mode 401, 411–12
   discrepancy-based processing 401–6, 411
   doing mode 401–8, 411
   mindfulness training 411–15
mood disorders 48, 60, 61
mood stabilizers 67, 68, 113
moral community hypothesis 241–2, 247
motivation 185–7
motor vehicle exhaust gas suicide
   (MVEGS) 549–50
mourning 563
multi-level approaches 448–9
MVEGS *see* motor vehicle exhaust
   gas suicide

NAAD *see* Nuremberg Alliance against
   Depression
narratives 427–9
NASP *see* National Centre for Suicide
   Research and Prevention
National Centre for Suicide Research and
   Prevention (NASP) 479, 480
National Confidential Inquiry (NCI) 41
national crises 176
National Registry of Deliberate Self-harm
   (NRDSH) 120–122, 125, 126, 355

National Strategy for Suicide Prevention
   (NSSP) 581
national suicide prevention strategies 212–13,
   226–31, 322, 639–40
   in Asian countries 498, 501
national tragedies 176
NCI *see* National Confidential Inquiry 41
negative affectivity 96–7
Network for International Collaboration on
   Evidence in Suicide Prevention
   (NICE-SP) 121, 122
(neuro)biological studies 593–4
neuro-economics 554
neuroplasticity 593
neuropsychological studies 151–64
   attention 152–4, 158–9
   decision making 158, 160–162
   fluency 152, 155–6, 159
   memory 154–5, 159
   mental flexibility 156, 159–60
   problem-solving 157, 160–162
neuroticism 96, 201
neurotransmitter systems
   noradrenergic 136, 137
   serotonergic 134–5, 137
newspapers 535, 538, 582
New Zealand
   indigenous people 260–261
   suicide in rural areas 257
next-day appointments 395–7
NICE-SP *see* Network for International
   Collaboration on Evidence in Suicide
   Prevention
NO HOPE scale 476
non-suicidal self-injury (NSSI) 12, 15–16,
   173, 295
   see also deliberate self-harm (DSH);
   self-harm
noradrenergic system 136, 137
normalensine 342
North America
   indigenous people 256–7, 263, 264, 517
   suicide in rural areas 256–7
Norway 359–62
NRDSH *see* National Registry of Deliberate
   Self-harm
NSSP *see* National Strategy for Suicide
   Prevention

NSSI *see* non-suicidal self-injury
Nuremberg Alliance against Depression
    (NAAD) 448
nursing homes 315

obesity 276–8
    see also body mass index (BMI);
        body weight
occupations 215–16, 258, 262
OCDS *see* Operational Classification for
    Determination of Suicide
olanzapine 86
old age 309–23
    and depression 310, 312, 318–19
    gender differences in suicide 310, 317–18
    general suicide prevention principles
        320–322
    national suicide prevention strategies 322
    protective factors 315
    in rural areas 266–7
    social attitudes to suicide in 311
    suicide characteristics 309–23
    suicide rates 310–311
    suicide risk assessment 316–17
    suicide risk factors 312–15
    treatment of mental disorders in 318–20
    under-reporting of suicide 311–12
Operational Classification for Determination
    of Suicide (OCDS) 18–19
opiates 95–7
opponent–process theory 171
Optimizing Suicide Prevention Programmes
    and their Implementation in Europe
    (OSPI-Europe) 448–9
Optional Thinking Test 124
OSPI-Europe *see* Optimizing Suicide
    Prevention Programmes and their
    Implementation in Europe

pain
    emotional 175
    tolerance to 175
painkillers 548, 629
paracetamol 548, 629
parasuicide 15, 16, 19
paroxetine 342, 463, 466
Paykel's Suicide Ladder 476
PDs *see* personality disorders

Penn Helping Alliance Questionnaire
    424, 428
Penn State Worry Questionnaire
    (PSWQ) 205
perception 153–4, 158–9
perfectionism 39, 187
    socially prescribed 188–90
perseverating cognition 201
personality disorders (PDs) 60, 63, 109–14
    comorbid with psychotic disorders 84
    in older people 313
    see also borderline personality disorder
        (BPD)
personality traits 39, 64
    in borderline personality disorder 112–13
pessimism 64
pesticide poisoning 25–6, 33, 255, 265–6,
    293, 497–8
    restricting access to 265–6, 500, 548–9
pharmacotherapy
    for adolescents 301–2
    and therapeutic relationship 424, 430
    treatment of borderline personality
        disorder 113
    treatment of depressive disorders 65, 67–8
    treatment of psychotic disorders 85–8
    see also antidepressants
physical illness 313–14
political liberalism 244
political regime 38
population-based prevention
    programmes 630
population-based studies 44, 441
postcard interventions 429, 444–6, 634
Postcards from the Edge project 444–5
postvention 299–300, 562, 569
primary prevention 297, 476
    in schools 297–9
prisons 436–8
problem-solving 40, 157, 160–162, 190
    tests 157, 405–7
problem-solving therapy (PST) 340, 341,
    357, 373, 375
PROSPECT trial 319
Protestantism 238–9
PST *see* problem-solving therapy
PSWQ *see* Penn State Worry Questionnaire
psychiatric in-patients 41

psychological approaches 181–2, 193
  see also arrested flight model; Integrated
     Motivational–Volitional Model (IMV);
     interpersonal–psychological theory
psychosocial interventions 68–9, 300–301,
     356–7, 436, 443–9
psychosocial stressors 65, 314–15
psychotherapy
  telephone-delivered 443
  transference-focused 112
  treatment of borderline personality
     disorder 112–13
  treatment of depressive disorders 68
  treatment of suicide attempters 357
psychotic decompensation 76, 81, 87, 88
psychotic disorders 75–7
  brief psychotic episodes 77, 79
  and comorbid psychopathology 83–4
  effect of treatment on suicide risk 85–8
  and family history of suicide 84–5
  and suicide 77–81
  suicide risk factors 79–81
  see also schizophrenia
public health communication 578–9
public holidays 38–9, 47

QPR *see* Question Persuade and Refer
Question Persuade and Refer (QPR) 268,
     298–9, 513–14

randomized controlled trials (RCTs) 593, 595
RAW *see* Rural Alive and Well (RAW)
RCTs *see* randomized controlled trials
Reasons for Living (RFL) 393
Reconnecting Youth (RY) 517–19
reductionism 592–4, 638
reflection 201, 204
religion 36–7, 235–48, 315, 496
  Buddhism 246
  Catholicism 238–9
  exposure to religious beliefs 240, 243,
     246, 247
  Islam 238–9, 246, 247, 496
  moral communities 241–2, 247
  Protestantism 238–9
  religious commitment 239–40, 243,
     246, 247
  religious integration 238–9, 243, 246

religious networks 240–241, 243,
     246, 247
religious orthodoxy 239, 240, 243, 246
World Values Survey 242–7
repetitive thinking 199, 201, 202
  see also rumination; worrying
retirement 315
RFL *see* Reasons for Living
rimonabant 284
Rogerian techniques 442
Rolls task 158
rumination 40, 190–191, 199–206, 403
  defined 200–201
  treatment of 205–6
Ruminative Response Scale 201
Rural Alive and Well (RAW) 265
rural areas 253–68
  in Australia 257–8
  in China 259
  help-seeking behaviours 261
  in India 254–5
  in North America 256–7
  occupational risks 258, 262
  prevalence of mental illness 260–261
  service access 262–4
  in Sri Lanka 255–6
  suicide method availability 261
  suicide prevention strategies 262–8
  in United Kingdom 258–9
RY *see* Reconnecting Youth

Samaritans 441
scar hypothesis 203
schema therapy 112
schizoaffective disorder 77, 78
schizophrenia 60, 75–81
  in Asian countries 495
  and birth weight 277
  comorbid with depressive disorders 83–4
  demoralization syndrome 82
  effect of treatment on suicide risk 85–8
  negative symptoms 76, 80
  positive symptoms 76, 80, 81, 87
  psychotic decompensation 76, 81,
     87, 88
  and suicide 77–81, 85–8, 618
  types of 76
  see also psychotic disorders

school-based prevention programmes 297–9, 482, 507–24, 583–4
  comprehensive approaches 520–523
  ecological approaches 520–523
  gatekeeper training 512–16
  iatrogenic effects 508, 519
  screening 509–12
  skills training 516–20
Scotland 219–26
screening 476–7
  adolescents 297–9, 509–12
  for substance abuse 440
  tools 297–9, 439–40
seasonality 38–9
secondary prevention 297, 476
  in schools 297–9
selective prevention 477–8
selective serotonin re-uptake inhibitors (SSRIs) 457–65, 614
  see also antidepressants
self-directed violence surveillance system 20
self-discrepancy 401, 413–14
self-focused attention 205
self-harm 2, 41–8, 627–9
  in adolescents 43–4
  and arrested flight model 188
  and borderline personality disorder 110
  clinical features 48
  cultural features 47
  definitions 41–2
  determining intent to die 16
  and future thinking 192
  management of 48, 634
  methods 45–6
  outcomes 46–7
  prevalence 42–4
  relationship with suicide 42, 46
  risk assessment 631–2
  socio-demographic features 47
  temporal features 47
  trends 44
  and socially-prescribed perfectionism 189–90
  and stress 189
  see also deliberate self-harm (DSH); non-suicidal self-injury (NSSI)
self-immolation 34, 496, 498
self-injury 45–6

self-poisoning 33, 45
  see also charcoal-burning; domestic gas poisoning; medication overdose; motor vehicle exhaust gas suicide (MVEGS); pesticide poisoning
serotonergic system 40, 134–5
  and genes 140–141
serotonin 40, 283
  see also serotonergic system
sertraline 466
'set-shifting' 156
sexual abuse 64
  in childhood 102, 123, 124, 137, 139
Signs of Suicide (SOS) 298, 514–15, 583–4
situational analysis 176
skills training 298, 516–20
SLBT see Crisis, Suicide and Life-Threatening Behavior
social class 82, 215–16, 221–6, 229, 244
social control theory 244, 246
social exclusion 175
social integration 37, 38
social integration theory 38
social learning theory 243–4, 246, 263
  and Werther effect 539
social network interventions 446–8, 634
Social Problem-Solving Inventory 157
Social Problem-Solving Skills Test (SPST) 157
social support
  and older people 315, 321–2
  and pain tolerance 175
social support-oriented interventions 446–8
socio-economic inequalities 213–18
  national policy response 226–31
  study from Scotland 219–26
socio-economic status 82, 88, 219, 226, 229–30
Socratic questioning 373
Sorrows of Young Werther, The 532
SOS *see* Signs of Suicide
Sources of Strength 522
SPAN *see* Suicide Prevention Action Network
sporting events 171, 176
SPST *see* Social Problem-Solving Skills Test
Sri Lanka 25–6, 255–6, 265–6
SSF *see* Suicide Status Form
SSRIs *see* selective serotonin re-uptake inhibitors

stagnating deliberation 201
statistics 640
stigma
   of mental illness 263
   of suicide 565–6
stress 163, 186–7
   anticipatory 201
   interpersonal 99–101
stress–diathesis model 64, 135–6
stress-response system 135–7
   and genes 141
Stroop task 153–4, 158–9, 163
substance use disorders (SUDs) 60, 63,
   93–103
   comorbid with psychotic disorders
      83, 84
   model of suicidal behaviour 100–103
   in older people 31, 320
   relationship with suicide 94–5, 100–103,
      611–12
   screening for 440
   suicide risk factors 94–102
SUDs *see* substance use disorders
suicidal behaviour
   epidemiology 42–3
   measurement of 20
   models of 182–3
   nomenclatures/classification systems 11–14,
      17–21
   prevalence of 42–3
suicidal capability 171, 172, 174–7, 193
suicidal desire 169–71, 175
suicidal ideation 12–14
   interpersonal–psychological theory
      170–172, 174
   measurement of 20
   prevalence of 43
   reactions to 408–11
suicidal intention 185–6, 192–3
suicidality 12, 14–15
suicidal plan 172, 193
suicidal thinking 199
   see also rumination; worrying
suicide
   acceptability of 241–8
   aetiology of 35–41
   and biological factors 40
   case ascertainment 28–9

classification systems/nomenclature 11–14,
   17–22, 635–8
   and cultural factors 35–6
   definitions 11–12, 14–16, 18, 28, 627
   and demographic factors 35
   epidemiology 27–34
   gender differences 34, 35, 64, 259, 310,
      317–18, 496–7
   as goal-directed behaviour 427
   illegal 28, 255, 496
   models of 182–3, 371–2
   prevalence of 1, 61–2, 29–33, 292
   relationship with self-harm 42, 46
   and socio-economic factors 35–8
   and temporal factors 38–9
   trends 29, 169–70
   under-reporting 10–11, 311–12
   see also suicide methods; suicide
      prevention strategies; suicide
      protective factors; suicide risk
      assessment; suicide risk factors;
      suicide survivors
Suicide and Life-Threatening Behavior
   (SLTB) 602–603
suicide attempt 1, 2, 11
   epidemiology 43, 355–6
   repetition of 14–15, 357
   as risk factor for completed suicide 60, 61,
      172, 293
   see also suicide attempters
suicide attempters 353–63
   effectiveness of treatment 420
   follow-up treatment 356–7
   monitoring hospital presentations 355,
      362–3
   Norwegian chain of care model
      359–62
   presentations to general hospitals 355–6
   psychosocial assessment 354, 358–9
   quality of care 359–61
   standards of care 357–9, 360–362
   see also suicide attempt
suicide clusters 218
   see also geographical areas
Suicide Cognitions Scale 402
suicide contagion 532–3
   see also Werther effect
suicide gesture 15

suicide hotspots 546
  for jumping suicide 551–2
  for motor vehicle exhaust gas suicide 550
suicide methods 33–4
  accessibility of 546–7, 549, 554
  in Asian countries 497–8
  charcoal-burning 33, 481–2, 550–551
  choice of 546–7
  firearms 33, 257, 258, 261, 262, 266,
    552–3
  gas poisoning 33, 549–51
  hanging 33, 255, 257, 553
  Internet as source of information
    about 537–9
  jumping from a height 551–2
  medication overdose 547–8
  motor vehicle exhaust gas suicide
    (MVEGS) 549–50
  pesticide poisoning 25–6, 33, 255–6,
    265–6, 293, 497–8, 500, 548–9
  restricting access to 265–6, 481–2, 500,
    545–54, 629
  in rural areas 262
  substitution of 548, 549, 551
  utilities model 546, 554
suicide pacts 538
Suicide Prevention Action Network (SPAN) 581
suicide prevention strategies 475–83, 639–40
  cross-cultural 482
  evidence-based 482–3, 629, 633
  indicated 478
  inter-governmental 479
  IOM model 477–8
  national 212–13, 226–31, 322,
    480–482, 498, 501
  primary 297, 476
  secondary 297, 476
  selective 477–8
  tertiary 299–300, 477
  universal 477
Suicide Prevention Strategy for England 229
suicide protective factors 613
  for adolescents 516–17, 523
  in depressive disorders 65–7
  for indigenous people 257
  for older people 315
  religion as 235–6
  see also secondary prevention

suicide risk assessment
  in adolescents 296
  CAMS framework 388–90
  in emergency departments 438–40
  in older people 316–17
  in prisons 436–8
  in therapeutic relationship 422–3
suicide risk factors 610
  in Asian countries 492–7
  for children and adolescents 293–6
  in depressive disorders 62–5
  in psychotic disorders 79–81
  in substance use disorders 94–102
  see also primary prevention
Suicide Status Form (SST) 383, 384,
    388–90, 423
suicide survivors
  attitudes towards 565–6
  caregivers/professionals as 572–3
  characteristics of bereavement process
    in 564–7
  and dreams 571
  and feelings of guilt 564–6
  individual needs 570
  number of 563
  and risk of suicide 569
  and rituals 570
  support for 569–70
  the term 562
  and therapy 569–70
  use of symbols and substitutes 570–572
suicide threat 13
suicidological journals 602–3
suicidology 1, 2, 9–10, 21, 591–2
  achievements 628–30
  biological and genetic 636–7
  challenges 630–640
  epidemiological studies 594
  ethical issues 616, 638
  evaluating effectiveness of
    interventions 632–4
  and generalization 601
  integrating qualitative and quantitative
    methods 601–2
  and interpretation 600
  journals 602–3
  (neuro)biological studies 593–4
  qualitative approaches 591–2, 599–604

suicidology (*cont'd*)
  quantitative approaches 591–2, 595–6,
      601–2, 604
  randomized controlled trials (RCTs)
      593, 594
  and reductionism 592–4, 638
  research 591–604
suppression 403–4, 408–11
suttee see self-immolation
Sweden 480
symbols 571–2

TASA *see* Treatment of Adolescent Suicide
      Attempters
Tasmania 265
taxonomy 12
TeenScreen programme 299, 510–511
Tele-Help/Tele-Check programme 321
telephone coaching 377
telephone psychotherapy 443
television 532, 533, 536–7
tertiary prevention 299–300, 477
Theory of Planned Behaviour (TPB) 185
theory of social integration 38
therapeutic alliance 423–6
therapeutic relationship 419–30
  assessing suicide risk 422–3
  disclosure of suicidal intent 420–422
  effect on pharmacotherapy outcomes
      424, 430
  narrative interviewing 427–9
  patient-oriented approach 422–3
  providing secure base 429–30
  see also therapeutic alliance
TMT *see* Trail-Making Test
'Tower of Babel' nomenclature 19
TPB *see* Theory of Planned Behaviour
TPH *see* tryptophan hydroxylase
Trail-Making Test (TMT) 156
Treatment of Adolescent Suicide Attempters
      (TASA) 301
tryptophan hydroxylase (TPH) 40
twin studies 40, 85, 139

Uganda 480–481
uncertainty, intolerance of 202–3

unemployment 37–8, 213–14, 230
  and suicide in psychotic disorders 79, 82
United Kingdom
  suicide in rural areas 258–9
  see also Scotland
United States
  firearms suicides 33, 352–3
  public awareness programmes
      580–588
  suicide terminology 15
  see also North America
universal prevention 477
urban policy 227

Vanderbilt Therapeutic Alliance Scale
      (VTAS) 424
venlafaxine 466
Verbal Fluency Test 156
volition 185–7
VTAS *see* Vanderbilt Therapeutic
      Alliance Scale
vulnerability 186–7

war 38
warning signs 512–13
  see also gatekeeper training
WBSI *see* White Bear Suppression
      Inventory
WBSI-si *see* White Bear Suppression Inventory
      for Suicidal Ideation
WCST *see* Wisconsin Card Sorting Test
Wechsler Memory Scale (WMS) 153, 154
weight *see* body weight
Werther effect 531–40
  in newer media 537–9
  the term 532
  theoretical mechanisms of 539
  in traditional entertainment media 536–7
  in traditional news media 533–6
White Bear Suppression Inventory
      (WBSI) 409
White Bear Suppression Inventory for Suicidal
      Ideation (WBSI-si) 409–11
Wisconsin Card Sorting Test (WCST) 156,
      159–60
WMS *see* Wechsler Memory Scale

World Values Survey 242–7
worrying 199–206
   defined 200
   psychological components 202–3
   treatment of 205–6

Yellow Ribbon Suicide Prevention
      Program 515
young people 579
   from indigenous cultures 257, 263
   prevalence of suicide in 44, 45
   and self-harm 47, 122–4
   and SSRIs treatment 457–8, 460,
      467, 614
   telephone counselling for 441

Youth-nominated Support Team–Version I
      (YST–I) 446–7
Youth-nominated Support Team–Version II
      (YST–II) 447
   see also adolescents
YST–I *see* Youth-nominated Support
      Team–Version I
YST–II *see* Youth-nominated Support
      Team–Version II

ZLS *see* Zuni Life Skills Development
      Curriculum
Zuni Life Skills Development Curriculum
      (ZLS) 517
Zuni People 263, 517